Selected Letters of
William Michael Rossetti

SELECTED LETTERS OF WILLIAM MICHAEL ROSSETTI

Edited by Roger W. Peattie

The Pennsylvania State University Press
University Park and London

Library of Congress Cataloging-in-Publication Data

Rossetti, William Michael, 1829-1919.
   [Correspondence. Selections]
   Selected letters of William Michael Rossetti / edited by Roger W. Peattie.
       p.   cm.
   Includes index.
   ISBN 0-271-00678-1
   1. Rossetti, William Michael, 1829-1919 — Correspondence.
2. Poets, English — 19th century — Correspondence. 3. Critics — Great
Britain — Correspondence. I. Peattie, Roger W. II. Title.
PR5249.R2Z48 1990
820.9 — dc19
[B]

                                                    90-3838

For Marlene, Thomas, and Matthew,
who were always interested
and helpful

Acknowledgments

My first debt is to the late Helen Rossetti Angeli, who before her death in 1969 gave permission for this edition and extended to me much kindness. Her daughter Imogene Dennis has continued likewise generous and understanding. Along with them I must name Professor William E. Fredeman, whose knowledge and support I have often called upon.

For promptly supplying information and for other kindnesses, I have to thank the following: Robert F. Atkins, Director, Sheffield City Libraries; Elaine Baird, Brighton Central Reference Library; Mary Bennett, Keeper of British Art, Walker Art Gallery, Liverpool; Professor G. E. Bentley, University of Toronto; Professor Thomas G. Bergin; George Brandak, Curator of Manuscripts, University of British Columbia Library; David Burnett, University Library, University of Durham; Professor R. H. Carnie, University of Calgary; Janice H. Chadbourne, Curator of Fine Arts, Boston Public Library; L. Channer, Custodian of Hogarth House, London; Professor C. L. Cline; the late Richard Curle; Margaret De Motte, Manchester Central Library; Alistair Elliot, University Library, Newcastle Upon Tyne; Ruth A. Evans, Schaffer Library, Union College; Charles E. Feinberg; Professor K. J. Fielding, University of Edinburgh; Doucet D. Fischer, Carl H. Pforzheimer Library; J. A. Fisher, Local Studies Librarian, Mitchell Library, Glasgow; the late Lilian Haddakin; Mihai H. Handrea, Carl H. Pforzheimer Library; Frank Herrmann; Mark Samuels Lasner; Professor Allan Life, University of North Carolina; Jack Lindsay; C. J. Lloyd, Local Studies Librarian, Stratford Reference Library, London; Alice Lock, Local Studies Librarian, Stalybridge Library, Stalybridge, Cheshire; Richard M. Ludwig, Princeton University Library; Jeremy Maas; Lady Mander, Wightwick Manor, Wolverhampton; John S. Mayfield; Professor Jerome J. McGann, California Institute of Technology; Professor J. K. McSweeney, Queen's University, Kingston, Ontario; Professor Edwin H. Miller; Mrs. Lucy O'Conor; J. Romero, Art and Architecture Division, New York Public Library; William St. Clair; Kenneth E. Smith, University Archivist, University of Sydney, N.S.W.; Dr. Vera Smith, Dacre, Penrith, Cumbria; Suzanne Spain, Bryn Mawr College; Professor Allen Staley, Columbia University; Mrs. Virginia Surtees; Professor R. H. Tener, University of Calgary; Raleigh Trevelyan; Mrs. Lorna Watson, University of Calgary; Sally Williams, Whitechapel Art Gallery; Kai Kin Yung, Registrar, National Portrait Gallery, London.

The librarians and keepers of the libraries listed in the "Manuscript Sources," especially of those institutions I visited personally, deserve more than the blanket thanks I offer them here for their efficient attention. I must also acknowledge their permission to publish, and quote from, manuscript material in their possession. I should like to thank several private owners of manuscripts. Virginia Surtees showed me the Rossetti letters in her possession, and allowed me to include a letter to Sydney Cockerell and Mrs. Angeli's letter to Cockerell announcing Rossetti's death. Rossetti's granddaughter, Mrs. Lucy O'Conor, placed her family letters at my disposal. Charles E. Feinberg and Dr. Gilbert Leathart allowed me to make copies of Rossetti's letters in their collections some years before these passed into public institutions. Mark Lasner and Terry Meyers sent me copies of the Rossetti letters in their collections.

Several grants-in-aid have been made by the Social Sciences and Humanities Research Council of Canada and the University of Calgary Research Grants Committee, which I am pleased to acknowledge. A Fellowship from the Humanities Institute of the University of Calgary in 1979-1980, when I was able to complete a large part of the annotation, deserves particular thanks. Publication has been made possible, in part, by a grant from the Endowment Fund of the University of Calgary, and by funds made available by the Offices of the Vice-President (Research), the Faculty of Humanities, and the Department of English of the University of Calgary. For this generous support from the University I am extremely grateful. I must thank also Mrs. Freda Adams, Mrs. Joyce Kee, and Mrs. Vi Lake for their alert secretarial help.

My greatest debt is to my wife, Marlene, who with kindly persistence urged me to complete this edition, and could always be depended on for support.

Contents

Abbreviations

AN
Autobiographical Notes of the Life of William Bell Scott, ed. W. Minto, 2 vols., 1892.

Baum
Dante Gabriel Rossetti's Letters to Fanny Cornforth, ed. P. F. Baum, 1940.

Bennett 1964
Ford Madox Brown (exhibition catalogue by Mary Bennett), Walker Art Gallery, Liverpool, 1964.

Bennett 1967
Millais (exhibition catalogue by Mary Bennett), Walker Art Gallery, Liverpool, and Royal Academy, London, 1967.

Bennett 1969
William Holman Hunt (exhibition catalogue by Mary Bennett), Walker Art Gallery, Liverpool, 1969.

Bentley
G. E. Bentley, Jr., *Blake Books, Annotated Catalogues of William Blake's Writings* (1977).

Blake
R. W. Peattie, "William Michael Rossetti's Aldine Edition of Blake," *Blake, An Illustrated Quarterly*, 12 (Summer 1978), 4-9.

Blodgett
Walt Whitman, *Leaves of Grass*, ed. Harold W. Blodgett and Sculley Bradley, 1965.

Bornand
The Diary of W. M. Rossetti, 1870-1873, ed. Odette Bornand, 1977.

Boyce
The Diaries of George Price Boyce, ed. Virginia Surtees, 1980.

CAH
H. R. Angeli, *Pre-Raphaelite Twilight, The Story of Charles Augustus Howell* (1954).

C & W
The Works of John Ruskin (Library Edition), ed. E. T. Cook and Alexander Wedderburn, 39 vols., 1903-12.

"Checklist"
R. W. Peattie, "William Michael Rossetti's Art Notices in the Periodicals, 1850-1878: An Annotated Checklist," *Victorian Periodicals Newsletter*, 8 (June 1975), 79-92.

Christina Rossetti
Mackenzie Bell, *Christina Rossetti, A Biographical and Critical Study* (1898).

Cline	*The Owl and the Rossettis, Letters of Charles A. Howell and Dante Gabriel, Christina, and William Michael Rossetti*, ed. C. L. Cline, 1978.
CWW	*Walt Whitman, The Correspondence*, ed. Edwin Haviland Miller, 5 vols., 1961-69.
DGRDW	W. M. Rossetti, *Dante Gabriel Rossetti as Designer and Writer* (1889).
DNB	*The Dictionary of National Biography.*
DW	*Letters of Dante Gabriel Rossetti*, ed. Oswald Doughty and John Robert Wahl, 4 vols., 1965-67.
FACC	W. M. Rossetti, *Fine Art, Chiefly Contemporary* (1867).
FLCR	*Family Letters of Christina Rossetti*, ed. W. M. Rossetti, 1908.
FLM	*Dante Gabriel Rossetti, His Family Letters, With a Memoir by William Michael Rossetti*, 2 vols., 1895.
Fredeman	William E. Fredeman, *Pre-Raphaelitism, A Bibliocritical Study* (1965).
Germ 1, 2, 3, 4	*The Germ* (No. 1, January 1850; No. 2, February 1850; No. 3, March 1850; No. 4, May 1850).
Gohdes, Baum	*Letters of William Michael Rossetti Concerning Whitman, Blake, and Shelley to Anne and Herbert Gilchrist*, ed. Clarence Gohdes and P. F. Baum, 1934.
Graves	Algernon Graves, *The Royal Academy of Arts, A Complete Dictionary of Contributors*, 8 vols., 1905-6.
Gunnis	Rupert Gunnis, *Dictionary of British Sculptors, 1660-1851* (rev. ed., [1968]).
HLB	R. W. Peattie, "William Michael Rossetti and the Defense of Swinburne's *Poems and Ballads*," *Harvard Library Bulletin*, 19 (October 1971), 356-65.
HLQ	R. W. Peattie, "Swinburne and his Publishers," *Huntington Library Quarterly*, 36 (November 1972), 45-54.
LPI	William E. Fredeman, *The Letters of Pictor Ignotus: William Bell Scott's Correspondence with Alice Boyd* (1976; reprinted from the *Bulletin of the John Rylands University Library of Manchester*, 58, Autumn 1975 and Spring 1976).
MS. Diary	W. M. Rossetti's unpublished diaries, 1862-1913, 18 vols., in AP.

NCBEL	*New Cambridge Bibliography of English Literature.*
Notebook	*Notebook of the Shelley Society, Part I* (1888).
PDL	*Praeraphaelite Diaries and Letters*, ed. W. M. Rossetti, 1900.
PLD	William E. Fredeman, *Prelude to the Last Decade: Dante Gabriel Rossetti in the Summer of 1872* (1971; reprinted from the *Bulletin of the John Rylands Library*, 53, Autumn 1970 and Spring 1971).
POLD	*Post Office London Directory.*
PR & PRB	W. Holman Hunt, *Pre-Raphaelitism and the Pre-Raphaelite Brotherhood*, 2 vols., 2d ed., 1913.
PRBJ	*The P.R.B. Journal, William Michael Rossetti's Diary of the Pre-Raphaelite Brotherhood*, ed. William E. Fredeman, 1975.
PWS	*The Poetical Works of Shelley, with a Memoir*, ed. W. M. Rossetti, 2 vols., 1870.
PWS 1878	*The Complete Poetical Works of Shelley, with a Memoir*, ed. W. M. Rossetti, 3 vols., 1878.
PWW	*Poems by Walt Whitman*, ed. W. M. Rossetti, 1868.
RP	*Rossetti Papers, 1862 to 1872*, ed. W. M. Rossetti, 1903.
RRP	*Ruskin, Rossetti, Pre-Raphaelitism, Papers 1854 to 1862*, ed. W. M. Rossetti, 1899.
SL	*The Swinburne Letters*, ed. Cecil Y. Lang, 6 vols., 1959-62.
SR	*Some Reminiscences of William Michael Rossetti*, 2 vols., 1906.
Surtees	Virginia Surtees, *The Paintings and Drawings of Dante Gabriel Rossetti, A Catalogue Raisonné*, 2 vols., 1971.
Swinburne Library	T. J. Wise, *A Swinburne Library* (1925).
Troxell	*Three Rossettis: Unpublished Letters to and from Dante Gabriel, Christina, William*, ed. Janet Camp Troxell, 1937.
TW	Amy Woolner, *Thomas Woolner, His Life in Letters* (1917).
Wellesley	*The Wellesley Index to Victorian Periodicals*, ed. Walter E. Houghton, 3 vols., 1966-79.
Wood	Christopher Wood, *Dictionary of Victorian Painters* (2d ed., 1978).

Works	*Works of Dante Gabriel Rossetti*, ed. W. M. Rossetti, 1911.
Worth	George J. Worth, *James Hannay, His Life and Works* (1964).
WWC	Horace L. Traubel, *With Walt Whitman in Camden*, 4 vols., 1906-53.

The following abbreviations are also used:

FMB	Ford Madox Brown
CGR	Christina Georgina Rossetti
DGR	Dante Gabriel Rossetti
WMR	William Michael Rossetti
WBS	William Bell Scott

Manuscript Sources

AP	Angeli-Dennis Papers, University of British Columbia Library
Arizona	Arizona State University Library
Berg	Berg Collection, New York Public Library
Berkeley	Bancroft Library, University of California
BL	British Library
Bodleian	Bodleian Library, Oxford
Boston	Boston Public Library
Bristol	University of Bristol Library
Bucknell	Bucknell University Library
Columbia	Columbia University Library
Cornell	Cornell University Library
Delaware Art Museum	
Duke	Duke University Library
Durham	University Library, Durham
Exeter	University of Exeter Library
Fitzwilliam	Fitzwilliam Museum, Cambridge
Folger	Folger Shakespeare Library
Glasgow	University of Glasgow Library
Harvard	Houghton Library, Harvard University
Hogarth House	Hogarth House, London
Huntington	The Huntington Library
Illinois	University of Illinois Library
Indiana	Indiana University Library

Indianapolis	Indianapolis-Marion County Public Library
Iowa	University of Iowa Library
Kansas	University of Kansas Library
LC	Library of Congress
Leeds	Brotherton Library, University of Leeds
Liverpool	Brown, Picton and Hornby Libraries, Liverpool
National Library of Scotland	
Newcastle	University Library, Newcastle Upon Tyne
NPG	National Portrait Gallery, London
NYP	New York Public Library
Ohio	Beeghly Library, Ohio Wesleyan University
Pennsylvania	Pennsylvania State University Library
PM	Pierpont Morgan Library
Princeton	Princeton University Library
Reading	University of Reading Library
Rutgers	Archibald Stevens Alexander Library, Rutgers State University
Rylands	John Rylands University Library of Manchester
St. John's Seminary	Edward Laurence Doheny Library, St. John's Seminary, Camarillo, California
Syracuse	Syracuse University Library
Texas	Harry Ransom Humanities Research Center, University of Texas, Austin
Trinity College, Cambridge	Trinity College Library, Cambridge
Trinity College, Dublin	Trinity College Library, Dublin
UBC	University of British Columbia Library (Penkill Papers)
UCLA	University of California at Los Angeles Library
V&A	Victoria and Albert Museum Library
V. Surtees	Mrs. Virginia Surtees, London

Wellesley   Wellesley College Library
Yale   Yale University Library

Introduction

I

William Michael Rossetti (1829-1919) always thought of himself as the third Rossetti: a civil servant who devoted his spare hours to periodical criticism and editorial work. Occasionally he published poems and, in the early days of the Pre-Raphaelite Brotherhood, produced drawings, but these he regarded as amateur efforts not to be compared with the work of his brother, Dante Gabriel (a year older than himself), and sister, Christina (a year younger). His modesty has encouraged writers on the Pre-Raphaelites to undervalue his achievement as a man of letters, and to overlook the complexity of his character, the range and quality of his friendships, and the broadness of his sympathies.

In 1845 at the age of fifteen he entered the Excise Office through the intervention of Sir Isaac Goldsmid, in whose house the now nearly blind Gabriele Rossetti had taught Italian, and became the financial stay of his impoverished family. By this time his brother was a student at Sass's Art Academy, and would soon proceed to the Royal Academy Antique School. At first Rossetti chafed under the harshness of his situation, but he was saved from consuming resentment by his willingness to assess circumstances realistically and to tolerate the necessity of sacrifice. What were later to be popularized as his abiding defects, his dullness of character and his obtuseness in dealing with the posthumous reputations of his brother and sister, need to be reinterpreted from the perspective of his early life. His dullness masked an undemonstrative pessimism which at times exacted from him a heavy emotional toll; what appeared to be obtuseness might be called more accurately a fondness for bald, factual statement.

II

William Rossetti's career as a man of letters began in 1848 with the formation of the Pre-Raphaelite Brotherhood, of which he was secretary and keeper of "The P.R.B. Journal." In the following year he undertook the editing of the *Germ*, in which he published his first critical prose. For freshness of judgment and sensitivity to new works, his reviews of Arnold's *The Strayed Reveller and Other Poems* and Clough's *The Bothie of Toper-na-fuosich* deserve to stand beside the contribution of Dante Gabriel and Christina to the magazine. In what was one of the earliest reviews of Arnold's first volume, Rossetti neatly defined the essence of Arnold's work: "a well-poised and serious mind shows itself in every page" (*Germ* 2).

Clough's *Bothie*, a neglected poem when Rossetti wrote about it, he entered into with relish, praising its novel fusion of unsophisticated life with the speech and manners of an Oxford reading party, and judging the stately hexameters intrinsically appropriate: "The metre ... harmonizes with the spirit of primitive simplicity in which the poem is conceived" (*Germ* 1). It was these reviews which launched him as a writer on art and literature in the periodical press, first in the *Critic* (1850-56) and then in the *Spectator* (1850-58), the New York *Crayon* (1855-56), and the *Saturday Review* (1858). From 1860 to 1878 he was a regular contributor to *Fraser's Magazine* (1861-65), the *Reader* (1863-64), the *Pall Mall Gazette* (1865), the *Academy* (1869-78), and to more than half a dozen lesser papers. From 1878 to 1895 he published some sixty reviews in the *Athenaeum*, mostly on Shelley, about whom he had already written extensively in the *Academy*, and Italian literature. As undoubtedly the best-informed Shelleyite of his day, Rossetti's Shelley reviews are historically important, but it is the art notices (comprising about sixty percent of his seven hundred periodical articles) which are his most distinguished contribution to Victorian periodical criticism.

From the beginning Rossetti was not "the ordinary newspaper ignoramus" that the painter Edward J. Poynter considered the average art reviewer.[1] In 1855 Ruskin told him that he was "one of the few who understand the real rank of a critic."[2] George Du Maurier echoed this judgment in 1863 after reading Rossetti's review in *Fraser's* of the Royal Academy exhibition of that year: "I think he's the *only* critic who's not a hack and whose opinions are genuine & felt."[3] Of greatest interest are his reviews of the Pre-Raphaelites, which treat with detailed sharpness and objectivity the aims of the Brotherhood, its influence on the Victorian art scene, and the later careers of Hunt and Millais: he was never a mere promoter of the P.R.B. These reviews constitute the most significant and substantial body of contemporary commentary on Pre-Raphaelitism by one who was *au fait* with the principal artists. He also wrote notable reviews of Alma-Tadema, Dyce, Frith, Herkomer, William Henry Hunt, Landseer, Leighton, Legros, J. F. Lewis, Albert Moore, Henry Wallis, G. F. Watts, and Whistler, to whose novel technique Rossetti was keenly responsive.[4]

Rossetti's periodical writing prepared the way for the publication, beginning in the mid-1860s, of his major literary works: *Swinburne's Poems and Ballads, A Criticism* (1866), *Poems by Walt Whitman* (1868), and *The Poetical Works of Shelley* (1870). The study of *Poems and Ballads* began as a review for the *North American Review*, but American nervousness over Swinburne's poetry led to its appearance instead under the imprint of John Camden Hotten, who had succeeded Moxon as Swinburne's publisher following the withdrawal of *Poems and Ballads*. Like his reviews of the Pre-Raphaelites, the book eschews partisan criticism, and offers a trenchant analysis of the defects as well as the merits of Swinburne's work. Swinburne is "passionately sensuous" in his poetry, Rossetti argues, "chiefly because the passionate and sensuous are two ultimate and indestructible elements of poetry; ... he over-enforces them in expression chiefly because a mighty intoxication of poetic diction mounts to his head, and pours in an unruly torrent through his lips, and he forgets the often still nobler office of self-mastery and reticence." As for those who stop their ears at his "unseemlinesses," they do him an injustice by refusing to hear, "distinct and predominant above them, the flood of noble and divine music which these only mar with casual and separable though perverse discords" (p. 20). The argument, conducted throughout with rigor and disarming candor, had the desired effect of encouraging readers to reconsider *Poems and Ballads* and to question their restrictive beliefs about literature. The *Saturday Review*, which three months earlier had virulently attacked the book, commented: "For good or for evil, the poems of Mr. Swinburne are a fact in English literature. And no hysterics or vapours will avail to send them out of it. As an able and well-weighed effort to assist and hasten the calm judgement of the future, we think Mr. Rossetti's criticism deserves praise" (17 November 1866, p. 600).

A critic who could elicit this response from the *Saturday Review* was the right man to introduce Whitman to Victorian England. Writing on 6 July 1867 in the recently founded liberal-Catholic weekly, the *Chronicle*, Rossetti proclaimed Whitman as "beyond all comparison *the* poet of the epoch," but he conceded that the commonest complaint against him was well founded: "He not unfrequently alludes to gross things, and in gross words — the clearest, the bluntest, and nearly the least civilly repeatable words which can come uppermost to the lips." Without openly averring that genius was its own law, Rossetti staked his claim for Whitman on his "entire originality" before which "we must decline to restrict ourselves to any standard which would exclude him from court." *Leaves of Grass* was "intensely modern and intensely American; something which, without any exaggerated wildness of speculation or foolish worship of the untried, may be expected to stand in a relation to future poetic efforts hardly less typical and monumental than the Homeric poems towards Grecian and epic work, or those of Shakespeare towards English and dramatic.... His book is incomparably the *largest* poetic work of our period" (pp. 352-53). Rossetti's openness to new ideas and achievements, and his confident judgment of them, has nowhere been more impressively vindicated than in the case of Whitman.

A few months after the appearance of the *Chronicle* article, J. C. Hotten again displayed his initiative by asking Rossetti to edit a selection of Whitman's poems. Although Rossetti may have had qualms about associating the "immoral" Whitman with the publisher who had reissued *Poems and Ballads*, he seems not to have hesitated; he delivered the manuscript to Hotten on 2 October 1867. Again his strategy was first to acknowledge what could be considered offensive in Whitman's poems, though this time he began by chiding "a mealy-mouthed British nineteenth century," "this peculiarly nervous age" (pp. 20-21), for its narrow-mindedness and prudery. But to meet its objections he decided to expurgate not parts of poems (which he considered would be mutilation) but the whole of every poem to which exception might be taken. "I have been rigid in exclusion, because it appears to me highly desirable that a fair verdict on Whitman should now be pronounced in England on poetic grounds alone; and because it was clearly impossible that the book, with its audacities of topic and of expression included, should run the same chance of justice, and of circulation through refined minds and hands, which may possibly be accorded to it after the rejection of all such peccant poems'' (p. 22). The volume which resulted did not please Whitman, and proved an embarrassment to Rossetti; for it was a bowdlerized edition, however well founded his justification that it was the only form in which *Leaves of Grass* could be published in mid-Victorian England. About its importance in laying the foundation of Whitman's fame outside the United States during the rest of the century, there can, however, be no doubt.

To no poet, past or present, was Rossetti more devoted than to Shelley, and on no poet (unless it was his brother) did he lavish so much scholarly attention. The most substantial of his Shelley books is the two-volume *Poetical Works with Notes and a Memoir* (1870), which the poet's publisher, Moxon, commissioned after seeing Rossetti's articles on ''Notes and Emendations on Shelley'' in *Notes and Queries* (April 1868).

Rossetti pursued the editing of the text of Shelley and the writing of the Memoir with a passionate concern for detail and a fierce determination to work independently of those who urged caution or (in the case of the Shelley family) demanded a less than candid portrait of the poet. Nevertheless, he managed to tap several new sources, including Shelley's letters to Elizabeth Hitchener and a manuscript notebook containing unpublished portions of *Charles I*. He also secured the cooperation and goodwill of Shelley's chief surviving friend, Trelawny. As an editor Rossetti was a close and sensitive reader of the poems, but he emended the text with a freedom which quickly dated his edition, successor though it was to Mrs. Shelley's *Poetical Works* of 1839. His accomplishment as a biographer was more impressive. To guide him in writing he prepared a tabular compendium of the known facts of Shelley's life, in which he noted the conflicting treatment of the facts in Mrs. Shelley's edition, Medwin's *Life of Shelley* (1847), Hogg's *Life of Shelley* (1858), Trelawny's *Recollections of the Last Days of Shelley and Byron* (1858), and elsewhere. It was a method which allowed him to guard against the biases of his sources and to bring the truth into sharper focus. On the opening page of the Memoir, as a statement of his own intention, he quoted Browning's plea (from his Introduction to the spurious *Letters of Shelley* of 1852) for ''a biography composed in harmony with the present general disposition to have faith in him, yet not shrinking from a candid statement of all ambiguous passages.'' The Memoir was readily recognized as, in the words of Mathilde Blind, ''the first methodical narrative of the entire life of the poet.''[5] It was not supplanted until Edward Dowden's fuller *Life of Shelley* (1886).

In the years before the death of his brother in 1882, when a shift occurred in Rossetti's activities as a man of letters, his other scholarly undertakings included: ''Annotated Lists of Blake's Paintings and Drawings'' in Gilchrist's *Life of Blake* (1863; revised for the second edition, 1880); a translation of Dante's *Inferno* (1865); contributions to Early English Text Society volumes (1866, 1869); a series of Moxon's Popular Poets in twenty-one volumes; a parallel text of *Chaucer's Troylus and Cryseyde compared with Boccaccio's Filostrato* (1873, 1883) for the Chaucer Society; and the *Poetical Works of Blake, with a Memoir* (1874). Although Blake did not engage the intense devotion that Swinburne and Shelley inspired in him, his Blake work was undertaken with enthusiasm and served Blake's reputation well. The "Annotated Lists" continued into this century as the only catalogue of Blake's designs; while for thirty years, until John Sampson's *Poetical Works of Blake* (1905), Rossetti's volume was the most accessible edition of Blake's poems. The 104-page Memoir remained the only significant supplement to Gilchrist until Mona Wilson's *Life of Blake* (1927).

With the exception of an unsympathetic life of Keats (1887) and an edition of Shelley's *Adonais* (1891), Rossetti devoted his energies after 1882 almost exclusively to writing about his family. It was a job for which he had served a long apprenticeship. As editor and biographer of Shelley and Blake he had shown a particular bent for the assiduous accumulation and sorting of facts; as family historian, beginning in 1884 with "Notes on Rossetti and his Works" in the *Art Journal*, and ending in 1911 with editions of the *Works of Dante Gabriel Rossetti, Revised and Enlarged* and the *Diary* of his maternal uncle John William Polidori, his work was of a similar kind. At first he published at well-spaced intervals, principally the *Collected Works of Dante Gabriel Rossetti* (1886) and *Dante Gabriel Rossetti as Designer and Writer* (1889), but following the deaths of Ford Madox Brown in 1893, and his wife Lucy (Brown's daughter) and Christina Rossetti in 1894, he inherited vast quantities of family papers on which he worked for the rest of his life. Biographies, editions, bibliographies, articles, and collections of documents followed at almost yearly intervals. A substantial portion of the papers that he edited remained unpublished, and have since been dispersed and disordered, but what he did publish forms a monumental collection of factual detail concerning events, people, and dates, some of which scholarly research might never have recovered. All later Rossetti and Pre-Raphaelite studies have been heavily indebted to him.

Paradoxically, however, this achievement also lowered his reputation with those of his contemporaries who objected to his belief that all documents concerned with individuals and movements important in their own time were worthy of publication. Usually the same people objected even more strongly to his practice as a biographer of not consistently avoiding the warts of his subject, though he accepted that it was impossible to tell everything during the lifetime of the participants in the events of a life. The reviewer of Mackenzie Bell's *Christina Rossetti* in *Literature* (see Letter 537, where Edmund Gosse is suggested as the writer), who wrote of Rossetti "grinding his family annals to dust in the dark," and Robertson Nicoll, who complained that Rossetti was the "chief offender" among those who told too much about his brother's errors and sorrows (see Letter 536, Note 2) were prominent spokesmen for the contrary view. More recently, more tenable objections have been raised to his editing of the *Poetical Works of Christina Rossetti* (1904).[6]

III

Of major interest in this edition of Rossetti's letters is the rich context it provides for his varied activities as a man of letters during half a century. (Rossetti's diaries and incoming correspondence which have been extensively used in the annotation significantly enlarges this context.) The earlier letters show him excitedly caught up in the artistic and literary manifestations and enthusiasms of the Pre-Raphaelite Brotherhood, and amply document his own distinctive contribution as editor, critic, and even as poet in the mundanely realistic *Mrs. Holmes Grey*. The letters through to the end of the 1860s also offer a wealth of detail about the wider art scene, including the American Exhibition of British Art (New York, Philadelphia, Boston, 1857-58) for which he was secretary; the Hogarth Club; the Thomas Seddon, John Cross, and George Cruikshank subscription funds, and the amateur exhibition for Lancashire relief — projects which enlisted his services as the leading art critic of the day; the American art journal the *Crayon*, and the lesser-known periodicals for which he wrote art notices: *Weldon's Register*, the *London Review*, the *Chronicle*, the *Fine Arts Quarterly Review*, and the *Edinburgh Weekly Review*.

During the 1860s Rossetti began corresponding with Swinburne and Whitman, and when his letters to them are supplemented by those to Hotten and C. E. Norton, and to Whitman's friends Moncure Conway and W. D. O'Connor, we can follow from close quarters the vicissitudes of Swinburne's early career, and the uncertainties and pleasures which attended Rossetti's editing of Whitman. Swinburne and Rossetti were from the beginning the closest of friends, and in their letters of this period every matter of mutual concern was discussed and argued — Blake, the political events in France and Italy, which helped shape Swinburne's *Songs before Sunrise*, and the life and poetry of Shelley. Shelley is also the almost exclusive subject of his letters to William Allingham in the period 1868-1870, when he was formulating the editorial and biographical principles which guided his Shelley work. Shelley matters are seldom absent for long from the correspondence, but with the founding of the Shelley Society in 1885, they become particularly prominent. The large correspondence with Frederick J. Furnivall, the founder of the Society, and T. J. Wise, its secretary from 1887, constitutes the most comprehensive history of the Society that we have, and portrays Rossetti as the moderating influence among a body of fanatics and self-seekers.

Because the information which they provide is so extensive, the letters dealing with the posthumous fame of Dante Gabriel and Christina are of exceptional interest. Those to Watts-Dunton, Macmillan & Co., W. M. Colles of the Authors' Syndicate, Mackenzie Bell, and Lucy Rossetti offer a full account of Rossetti's scholarly bolstering of the reputations of his brother and sister. Equally fascinating is the insight the letters give into Rossetti's activities as Gabriel's and Christina's executor: his sale by auction of the contents of their houses in Cheyne Walk and Torrington Square; his bestowal of mementoes on their friends; his gifts of manuscripts and portraits to public institutions following Christina's death; his attempts to control what others wrote about them; his piecemeal sale to T. J. Wise, Fairfax Murray, Sydney Cockerell, and others of paintings, drawings, books, and manuscripts; and his archival instinct which led him to annotate or label every object of family significance which had found a resting place in his last London residence, 3 St. Edmund's Terrace, Primrose Hill.

IV

From these letters there emerges also an absorbing and sharply defined portrait of Rossetti the man, which renders inadequate the standard accounts. From Morris's "fool for a brother" (in retort to Dante Gabriel), through Edmund Gosse's 1928 attack on his integrity (see Letter 259, Note 4), to Jerome Thale's extraordinary judgment that he was "a failure as a human being,"[7] Rossetti has received strangely hostile treatment. A few friends of his later years—William Rothenstein, Sydney Cockerell, and Richard Curle — wrote sympathetically about him,[8] as more recently have W. E. Fredeman in his edition of *The P.R.B. Journal* (1975) and Georgina Battiscombe in her *Times Literary Supplement* review of Odette Bornand's edition of the *Diary of W. M. Rossetti, 1870-1873* (9 June 1978, p. 644). But a judgment based on the range of evidence provided by this edition has not been made.

About the nature of Rossetti's family relationships, the letters offer a necessary corrective to much that has been surmised by writers on Dante Gabriel and Christina. Edith Sitwell's claim that his "whole life was given to his family, to providing for their needs and bearing their worries" contains a large measure of truth, but the corollary that he "scarcely allowed himself the right to individual happiness"[9] is little more than a caricature. Although he confided to Catherine Hueffer in 1889 that his employment in the Excise Office in 1845 was a matter of "hard necessity, and was felt as such" (Letter 445), he did not in fact for long regard himself as the family drudge. Outside the family circle and within it he quietly asserted his independence. At the Excise Office he had the satisfaction of rising quickly through the ranks; while among Gabriel's Pre-Raphaelite friends he established himself as someone to whom they willingly deferred: as the assiduous secretary of the P.R.B., as the informed and tireless editor of the *Germ*, and from 1850 as an influential interpreter of Pre-Raphaelite art in the periodical press. With several of the original Pre-Raphaelite circle — Holman Hunt, F. G. Stephens, W. B. Scott, and J. L. Tupper — he remained firm friends until their deaths.

It is indisputable that his brother imposed on his good nature, borrowing money which he never repaid, taking for granted William's payment of his art school fees, and generally riding roughshod over his convenience. But then Gabriel treated other people in much the same way. William's refusal to complain, which is supposed to demonstrate his weakness of character, was rather a combination of loyalty to the family's belief in Gabriel's genius, and an acknowledgment that he owed his introduction into the Pre-Raphaelite circle to his brother. As for the rest of the family, they accepted William's support with dignity. Mrs. Rossetti's and Christina's attempt to found a school at Frome in 1853 was undertaken not so much because they anticipated success, but as a delicate demonstration that they would not unfeelingly continue to burden him. When in September 1853 Rossetti was promoted at the Inland Revenue (which the Excise Office had been renamed in 1849), "placing ... [him] on the class of £250, rising by £10 per annum to £300," it was with love and pride that he promptly suggested to his mother that the family could now be reunited in London as "the more economical as well as agreeable, and consequently the more rational" arrangement (Letter 31). It is possible that his protracted relationship from 1851 to 1860 with Henrietta Rintoul, the daughter of the proprietor and editor of the *Spectator*, might have resulted in their marriage, had his family's needs been less pressing — it is likely that the Frome experiment was related to Rossetti's growing attachment to Henrietta — but given R. S. Rintoul's opposition and Henrietta's own strong family allegiance, it was always an unpromising match.

Throughout the 1860s, as he became increasingly prominent as a critic and editor, Rossetti formed new and lasting friendships which either owed nothing to Gabriel (as in the case of Whitman, Moncure Conway, Richard Garnett, and Trelawny) or developed independently of Gabriel's friendship with them (as in the case of Swinburne, Whistler, and Anne Gilchrist).[10] More important, in 1869 he was promoted to Assistant Secretary of the Inland Revenue, "the first time," he boasted to his mother, "a Clerk in the Secretary's Office has been made Excise Secretary or Assistant Secretary." The salary of £800, combined with the £100 he earned annually from his literary work, brought him financial security for the first time. The pleasure this gave him is evident in his unusually lighthearted prose as he told his mother: "Dear Old Thing, / You and I are richer by £200 a year than when we parted yesterday.... I know the old Dear will be glad her goose passes muster as a sort of swan elsewhere than in the maternal bosom, and lose no time in telling her accordingly." It would allow him not only (he implied) to keep her and his sisters more comfortably, but he could now "set apart a definite portion of income annually for charitable purposes — perhaps £100 a year: the necessary proportion from each half-quarterly payment could easily be set apart, and the Old One could fork it out as almoner when occasion arises" (Letter 160). A few years later he would again think about marrying, though a letter he wrote to his mother at the time of his engagement suggests that he did not regard the advent of a wife as in any way lessening his responsibility to his family (see Letter 237, Note 2).

It is against this background of hard-won financial independence that the often discussed matter of Rossetti's behavior during the family crisis of 1872 needs to be assessed. W. B. Scott is the principal authority for the claim that Gabriel's breakdown and attempted suicide in June 1872 reduced William to a condition of depression and nervous exhaustion. Scott's statements in his *Autobiographical Notes* that William "was made seriously ill by his brother's state," and that he was "so prostrated by anxiety ... that F. M. Brown took all business matters out of his hands," were contested by Rossetti in a letter to the *Academy* (No. 481), which pointed out that, on the contrary, he managed his brother's financial affairs (and other matters as well) until Gabriel returned from Scotland to live at Kelmscott in September 1872. Letters 213-233, to Thomas and George Hake, C. A. Howell, Philip Webb, Murray Marks, Madox Brown, Frances Rossetti, and Scott himself, which are eminently composed and rational, confirm the essential truth of Rossetti's rejoinder, but they do not tell the whole story. W. E. Fredeman's *Prelude to the Last Decade*[11] presents overwhelming evidence of the severe toll on William's spirits throughout 1872. From as early as 5 June, when he quoted in his diary Swinburne's line "An end, an end, an end of all" as the likely outcome of the crisis, Rossetti periodically gave way to extreme melancholy, verging at times on hysteria. In the correspondence quoted by Fredeman, Scott twice relates this reaction to Rossetti's fears about Gabriel's debts (see his letter of 12 June to Alice Boyd quoted in Letter 214, Note 2). Scott is almost certainly correct about this; and one can further suggest, without detracting from the genuineness of William's distress over Gabriel's condition, that the prospect of his brother dead or incapacitated, and himself solely responsible for his debts, filled him with horror. (Perhaps Gabriel sensed this, for from this date their relationship became strained and they saw less of each other.) In a muted form, this foreboding plagued Rossetti again in 1882 during Gabriel's last illness and death, when he was uncertain about the claims that would be made against the estate; and in 1889, following the death of Francis Hueffer, as he contemplated Madox Brown's precipitate refusal of aid for Hueffer's family. Rossetti saw himself, in the event of the daily-anticipated collapse of Brown's own health, as the supporter of a much enlarged family. That Rossetti became so profoundly insecure at such times is a poignant commentary on the depth of his sacrifice and suffering during the early decades of his life.

As important as all this is, however, for understanding Rossetti's family relationships, it needs to be kept in perspective. In the case of his religious and political views, which were much less easily kept separate than his carefully managed life as a civil servant and man of letters, he remained admirably detached from his family's beliefs and prejudices. Mrs. Rossetti's and her daughters' fervent Anglo-Catholicism, and their (and Gabriel's) apparent conservatism in politics would have made William's agnosticism and radical liberalism anathema to the women, and his radicalism at the very least irritating to Gabriel, whose ironic comments about his brother's politics are noted by Fredeman.[12] On the one occasion when he and Gabriel openly clashed, over the proposed publication of William's *Democratic Sonnets*, Mrs. Rossetti and Christina sided with Gabriel in urging caution, though Gabriel's alarm seems to have been more for the presumed threat to William's job as a government official than over the views themselves. William's reply to his brother's plea (Letter 317) is a forthright assertion of his long-standing commitment to the ideas expressed in the sonnets.

Rossetti's religious views, with which Gabriel (it is usually assumed) would have been in general agreement, proved more troublesome, and led in 1876 to a painful rupture in family arrangements. With his tolerant and level-headed mother he seems never to have openly argued his agnosticism; she evidently respected her son's right to his views, and kept sadly quiet. Christina and Maria, on the other hand, were more insistent, the latter especially so during the final days of her life, when she confessed to William that "one principal motive of hers in entering the [All Saints] Sisterhood was to obtain from God the grace of conversion" for her brothers.[13] Christina could be strident in her proselytizing, and William soon discovered that silence was "the only course conducive to our mutual comfort" (Letter 568). After William's marriage to Lucy Brown in 1874, however, the differences became impossible to contain; for Lucy, whose thinking on religion closely paralleled Rossetti's own, not only found Christina's pietism almost repulsive, but would energetically defend her own and William's opinions. In a fine example of his literal, truthful prose, Rossetti recalled in *Some Reminiscences* that "the harmony in the household was not unflawed, and was sometimes rather jarringly interrupted" (2:422). The separation which resulted, with Mrs. Rossetti and Christina setting up house with Eliza and Charlotte Polidori, not only removed Rossetti for the first time from daily involvement in his family's affairs, but released him from financial obligation as well. "My mother," he recorded, "with her constant superiority to self-interest, declined an offer that I made to contribute to her support after her removal; and in fact she, with Christina in her wake, and joining resources with her sisters, had sufficient means for living in comfort on the quiet scale they affected."

Although strenuous efforts were made to smooth over the differences between Lucy and Christina, with affectionate letters being frequently exchanged between them, they always regarded each other with suspicion. Following Mrs. Rossetti's death in 1886, Rossetti was compelled to reiterate the unacceptability of Christina's religion to Lucy as the stumbling block to their again living under the same roof. At the same time, William's loyalty to Christina continued unabated. During her illness and recuperation in 1892, his absorption in her suffering was of an intensity that the overly sensitive Lucy must have thought was due to her alone. (This no doubt partly explains the rift between William and his wife discussed in the next section.) After Lucy died in Italy in April 1894, Rossetti immediately resumed his daily involvement in Christina's life, which continued until her own death eight months later.

V

Christina's death on 29 December 1894 left Rossetti and his children as the only surviving Rossettis. It also marked the close of an epoch, for in the same month he retired from the Inland Revenue. As his letters and diaries show, his job there had never been a sinecure, yet for forty-five years he had managed to combine it with demanding and fruitful literary work. W. E. Fredeman's description of him in the *P.R.B. Journal* as a "man of action" among the original Pre-Raphaelites justly sums up his whole career. Throughout this time he also maintained a wide and distinguished circle of friends, who valued him for that exemplary command of diplomacy, firmness, and scrupulous fairness, combined in equal measure with tolerance, generosity, and compassion, which his letters so constantly demonstrate.

At the same time, his life in the years after his marriage in 1874 had not been uniformly happy, though only Christina and Bell Scott seem to have penetrated his natural reserve to understand this. Gabriele Rossetti had been fond of calling him "saggio Guglielmo" in contrast to "ingegnoso Gabriele" and "vivace Christina"; or, with Maria, one of the "calms" set against Gabriel and Christina as the "storms." In two lines omitted by William from his translation of *Gabriele Rossetti, A Versified Autobiography* (1901), his father wrote of him: "Already, speaking of you, more than one / Entitle you the young philosopher."[14] One is reminded of William Rothenstein's judgment some ninety years later: "William Rossetti never said a cruel thing, nor ever an unwise one."[15] But the evidence of these letters is that this oversimplifies his character. For Rossetti was a deeply emotional man who rigorously disciplined himself to bear sorrow and calamity without complaint. The Book of Job, he told Lucy on 28 January 1889, commending her for reading it to their children, was "one of the great books of the world."[16] A remark he made to her a few days earlier about the response of the Hueffer children to their father's death reflected his own attitude: "I will confess that the stoical demeanour of the three children surprises me: if the highest ideal of life is to accept everything exactly as it comes, without emotion and without comment, they might teach a lesson to all of us" (Letter 442). The year 1872 appears to have been the only occasion when he could no longer hold emotion and discipline in balance, and then his reaction had been to withdraw into himself. Christina confided to Bell Scott in October 1873 "how very much alarmed they had been for William ever since Gabriel's illness.... For weeks ... he never uttered a word to any of them."[17] "Too long a sacrifice / Can make a stone of the heart" (Yeats, *Easter 1916*) seemed for a time to be true of William. Not until his engagement to Lucy in July 1873 did "the spell that seemed to hold him" (Scott's words) begin to break. Christina had continued her account to Scott by observing that he now talked of "'when Lucy is here'."

Rossetti's marriage, however, proved less felicitous than he had reason to expect. Although it promised well that Lucy's religious and political views, which she acquired from Madox Brown, were close to his own, she also inherited from her father his thorniness, impetuosity, and stubbornness. For some years Lucy's liveliness and sociability (she was fourteen years younger than William) saved him from premature staidness, and he enjoyed dining out and "at homes," and the enlarged social circle that came with them. Their five children, born between 1875 and 1881, gave him the chance to exhibit his tolerance and fairness in a new context, and to develop a quality that did not often show itself elsewhere: his humor. He encouraged the children to call him "Fofus" — "funny, fussy old fogey,"[18] wrote them lighthearted letters, and would entertain them on the piano with a cacophonous composition entitled "Fantasia Fofetica." Nor was he other than sympathetic when the two older girls later became involved in anarchist activities; he especially enjoyed their hanging out a red flag to mark his retirement from the Inland Revenue.

Lucy's health had never been strong, and by 1885 she began to show marked symptoms of consumption, from which her mother (Madox Brown's first wife) had died in 1846. As her condition worsened her personality became more taxing and unmanageable, until finally she fixed her suspicion on William himself. Two entries in his diary during the second half of 1893 reflect with characteristic frankness on the turmoil of his feelings:

> 25 July: I grieve to say that, for some cause or other, if not for *no* cause (and I affirm positively that none was given on my part) she [Lucy] has, ever since the early days of last November, been much less cordial in her demeanour towards me: this has become a matter of fixed continuance — I fear of permanency. I do, with little effect, my best to keep the matter under control. Since Lucy's illness developed in April, Olive (no longer myself) is her companion at night. Of course every allowance should be — and is — made for Lucy's tension of feeling, lowness of spirits, etc., consequent on her long and wearing illness.... This change in my relations of affection and home-life is about the most painful thing that could have occurred to me: deeply do I feel it, but must bear it as I may.

> 23 August: For the last 10 months or so I have almost entirely lost a certain brightness and elasticity of feeling and demeanour which (spite of my native reserve and retirement of character) had maintained and developed itself in family-life. The constant and depressing ill-health of some members of the family (Lucy, Christina, Brown) is one factor in this change of feeling: the other and more potent one is referred to under 25 July. As one lives on one enters upon new conditions of life, and one has to adapt oneself, with more or less reluctance and chafing, to the medium: it must be so with me, and perhaps I shall succeed, not less well than another.

Lucy left England in early October 1893 for Italy, never to return. William saw her again only for a few days before her death on 12 April 1894, though his frequent letters to her remained kindly and temperate. He returned to London on 16 April, following Lucy's burial at San Remo, and wrote at once to Christina (Letter 493), dwelling first on his consternation over the terms of Lucy's will, and only then recounting her death.

VI

Rossetti survived until the close of the First World War, suffering physically only in his last few years. Even before Christina's death he had regained something of that composure which had led Alice Boyd to exclaim in 1860: "one can't talk nonsense before such a grave man."[19] His old Pre-Raphaelite friend Arthur Hughes describes meeting him on 23 October 1894 at the New Gallery, when they discussed Christina's illness: "I asked him if she was very ill, he said 'Oh, yes, she is dying!' Poor fellow, he looked so beautiful I thought, his crisp white beard so neatly clipped and a beautiful sort of loose black overcoat, and all black general neatness, but better dressed or more carefully than of old, he struck one as so refined and really beautiful with a refining I could not help feeling came from many sorrows, and that look of uncomplaining acceptance that was always about him more or less.''[20] Hughes discerned what the letters confirm: that in his last years Rossetti felt at peace with himself and with the world. He had just begun his Memoir of Gabriel and was spending long hours with Christina checking her memories of their early life against his own. For the rest of his life he comforted himself in this way, dwelling on the past, not mournfully or regretfully, but actively (in keeping with his character) as family historian and archivist. Callers at 3 St. Edmund's Terrace were always as impressed as Hughes had been by his serenity and graciousness. Richard Curle wrote that to enter his house was to be carried back in time:

> It was a strange feeling to be thus transported at a step, but you had no sooner entered Mr. Rossetti's study, a little book-lined room at the back, and seen him sitting so serenely in his accustomed armchair by the fire, smoking his accustomed pipe, than the secret was revealed. It was he himself, this tranquil old man, with the grave, kindly eyes, who was the magician. By grouping around him the memorials of his distinguished relations and friends and the works of art he valued particularly, he had endowed them through the strength of his simple, upright, rare personality, with a twilight existence which ... kept the outer world at bay.[21]

Curle's attractive portrait, however, conveys little of the energy and alertness to the world around him which remained so marked a characteristic of the man. Into all his dealings with those who could further his family's fame he entered with gusto, whether he was negotiating with Macmillan over new editions of Christina's poems, or demanding that Waldorf Astor pay handsomely for unpublished works by his brother in the *Pall Mall Magazine*, or persuading the National Portrait Gallery to waive the rule which prevented them from accepting portraits of Christina and Madox Brown soon after their deaths. Some people and controversies of these later years wearied him, as had earlier Swinburne's prolonged feud with Hotten, and Watts-Dunton's wavering resolve to write a biography of Gabriel, but he managed them no less deftly or fairly. Two such matters figure prominently in the letters: the trial of handling the self-appointed biographer of Christina, Mackenzie Bell; and his attempt to moderate F. G. Stephens's response to Holman Hunt's *Pre-Raphaelitism and the Pre-Raphaelite Brotherhood* (1905) in which Stephens was unfairly and inaccurately treated. What is most impressive in the later letters is the consistency of Rossetti's character and opinions: his self-effacement in refusing an Italian honor (Letter 600); his continuing openness to new ideas and to literary and artistic experiments (he was the only one of the Pre-Raphaelites, William Rothenstein wrote, ''who was sympathetic towards the work of the younger writers and painters''); his faithfulness to the political radicalism of his youth; his constant kindness and compassion, movingly displayed in the letters to Ford (and Elsie) Madox Hueffer. To the end, Rothenstein remembered, ''his outlook on life was broad and humane.''[22]

VII

With the exception of a notable article on the political significance of his *Democratic Sonnets*,[23] Rossetti's religious and political views have been so little commented upon that it is necessary to provide a summary context for the substantial discussion of them in the letters.[24]

Although the Rossetti parents agreed that Frances Rossetti should bring up the children as Anglicans, neither brother was confirmed, and William claimed that by the age of fourteen "the Christian faith, as a scheme of mysteries and miracles — and ... any and every form of faith involving a supernatural mythology — became inoperative upon my mind; and so it has always remained." This rejection had little directly to do with the developments in scientific and theological thinking which troubled so many Victorians, but rather with the diversity of religious opinion within the Rossetti and Polidori families. Both his grandfather Gaetano Polidori and Gabriele Rossetti, though nominally Roman Catholic, professed no dogmatic faith. William soon discovered that his grandfather was little interested in religious questions, whereas his father vehemently dissented from "Catholic or ecclesiastical dogmas, and from the supernatural or legendary elements in the Christian tradition." Gabriele carefully abstained from directly instructing his children in what they should believe, though William was impressed when "on one exceptional occasion he made a vigorous *sortie*, commenting upon the scriptural narrative of Abraham ordered by Jehovah to sacrifice Isaac, and saying that he himself, under the like conditions, would have responded, *Tu non sei Dio, sei il diavolo!*"[25] But it was the coexistence within the family of warmly held Christian beliefs with no less warmly proclaimed unbelief which affected him most profoundly, and developed in him a skepticism toward any claim to have found final answers to speculative questions. (One is reminded of Leslie Stephen's observation in defense of his agnosticism that "there is not a single proof of natural theology of which the negative has not been maintained as vigorously as the affirmative."[26]) When the word agnosticism was coined in the 1860s, Rossetti "found it to be the clearest and the simplest definition of my mental position in relation to the supernatural — a position which amounts to this; that a number of things are affirmed by many people concerning matters beyond their observation, and beyond mine; and that, as I know nothing about those things, and am not conscious that anything can be known about them, I likewise *profess* to know nothing."

Rossetti's unbelief, then as later, brought him none of the agony or despair which he would have read about in a work of one of his favorite authors, Carlyle's *Sartor Resartus* (1838). There appear to have been two reasons for this: what he called the "bias in relation to political or national problems" implanted in him by his father, and his enthusiastic response to the poetry and ideas of Shelley and to the history of the French Revolution. Rossetti is another example of John Bicknell's observation in his essay on "The Unbelievers" that among the Victorians unbelief and radical politics were indistinguishable.[27] Gabriele Rossetti was, William tells us, "an earnest advocate of free nationalities, free institutions, independence of thought. He had suffered in the cause of constitutional liberty, and he longed, and indeed worked, for the emancipation of Italy from Austrian and dynastic thraldom." By 1848, the year of revolutions across Europe,

Rossetti had fully assimilated his father's views with the concepts of liberty and brotherhood he found in the works of Shelley — like a number of the freethinkers discussed by Susan Budd in *Varieties of Unbelief* (1977), Rossetti especially mentions the influence on him of *Queen Mab* — and with the constitutional and national ideals of the French Revolution. From this time, as the subjects and treatment in *Democratic Sonnets* show, Rossetti sympathized with all libertarian and revolutionary movements across Europe, and despised all contrivances for personal and national oppression. As a civil servant he could not be an activist (see Letter 446), but he never hid his views or apologized for them. That he considered himself an outsider from the prejudices and complacency of Victorian middle-class respectability (a point referred to often in the letters) made it easier for him to hold to his views unflinchingly. He seems not to have minded that he was often in the situation he describes in his article on "English Opinion on the American War," of openly proclaiming an unpopular point of view: "Almost up to the very fall of Richmond, to express a decisive adherence to the Northern cause was often to be singular and solitary in a roomful of company; the timorous adherent would be minded to keep silence, and the outspoken one would be prepared for a stare and an embarrassed pause to ensue upon his avowal."[28]

Bicknell includes in his essay a list of the touchstone issues on which Victorian Unbelievers held broadly similar positions: "Irish Home Rule, the Boer War, woman suffrage, the Franco-Prussian War, the Paris Commune, and the major episodes in England's advancing imperialism."[29] When the list is expanded to include the Crimean War, the Governor Eyre controversy, the American Civil War, the struggle for Italian unification, republicanism, and the Eastern Question, one has the full spectrum of nineteenth-century social and political issues which engaged Rossetti's sympathies. In every case he vigorously espoused the minority point of view, even when his closest friends (Swinburne in particular during his days of apostasy) held the contrary position.

Rossetti discovered, then, in the social democratic movements and the antidogmatic and antitraditional forces of his time a focus for his thinking about man and society. On a more personal level, as we have seen, he adopted an attitude which mingled fortitude with a sad but never sour pessimism. He came closest to explaining this attitude in his Taylorian lecture on Leopardi of 1891, and in his Shelley Society lecture on "Shelley and Leopardi" of 1892. In the Taylorian lecture he identified Leopardi's "strenuous internal self-assertion, which urged him to rise superior to whatever, in natural conditions, or in the stress of society or of the affections, seemed to threaten to bend or break his will."[30] In contrasting Leopardi's position with that of Shelley's, he remarked that Shelley was saved from "the sorrows of pessimism ... and from the hoodwinking of optimism ... by the maintainable — though I must admit, to my mind the very disputable — theory that man has the remedy within himself, and can, by a due exertion of reason and of will, improve himself and all his environment in a great, indeed an immense and immeasurable degree — so that advancement will go on by stage after stage until the hypothesis of Perfectability shall merge into the fact of Perfection.''[31] Throughout his life Rossetti reflected on both of these responses to existence, and tried always to measure the integrity of his own judgments and actions against them.

VIII

From the several thousand known Rossetti letters this edition prints less than a sixth. Only one scholarly edition of his letters has previously appeared, Clarence Gohdes's and P. F. Baum's *Letters of W. M. Rossetti to Anne Gilchrist* (1934). Twenty-six of his letters to Alexander Macmillan are included in Lona Mosk Packer's *The Rossetti-Macmillan Letters* (1963), and six to Charles and Kate Howell in C. L. Cline's *The Owl and the Rossettis* (1978). A small number of his letters have also been printed complete or nearly complete in W. E. Fredeman's *The P.R.B. Journal* (1975) and *Prelude to the Last Decade* (1971). Several letters from Fredeman's publications are republished here. Three other appearances of his letters need a word. Fourteen of his twenty-four letters to Whitman are printed in Horace Traubel's *With Walt Whitman in Camden* (1906-14); sixteen letters to Richard Garnett in *Letters About Shelley*, ed. Robert S. Garnett, 1917; and nine letters to Dante Gabriel Rossetti and William Allingham in his own *Rossetti Papers* (1903). The letters to Whitman are not annotated, while those in *Letters About Shelley* and *Rossetti Papers* are only casually annotated. Also the letters in the two latter volumes are printed with omissions, major ones in the case of the letters to Dante Gabriel and Allingham. Except for those to Garnett, the originals of which could not be traced, these letters have been included here. A very few of the other letters included have appeared in whole or in significant part in various books and articles. Previous publication of letters (except for brief extracts) is noted throughout.

A substantial number of Rossetti's letters to his family and to his closest friends have survived — Frances Rossetti (120), Lucy Rossetti (745), Madox Brown (43), Swinburne (103), Watts-Dunton (47), W. B. Scott (69), F. G. Stephens (153), and J. L. Tupper (90); as have important groups of letters to William Allingham (26), Macmillan & Co. (90), W. M. Colles and the Authors' Syndicate (161), T. J. Wise (127), F. J. Furnivall (24), Sydney Cockerell (31), Mackenzie Bell (123), and Fairfax Murray (34). But there are the inevitable lacunae. The paucity of letters (considering the number he would have written, as can be judged by the large number of their letters to him in the Angeli-Dennis Papers and elsewhere) to Christina (4) and Gabriel (36), both of whom periodically destroyed their incoming correspondence, to James Thomson, 'B.V.' (3), Trelawny (3), Edward Dowden (3), Frederic Shields (2), Thomas Woolner (3), Buxton Forman (5), and H. S. Salt (1), is to be lamented. Equally unfortunate is the total absence of letters to F. S. Ellis and Ellis & Co., Millais, Justin McCarthy, and Henrietta Rintoul. Henrietta, it must be assumed, returned his letters following the breaking of their engagement and Rossetti destroyed them.

In choosing the letters to print I have been guided by two considerations: their documentary value, and the extent to which they enlarge our understanding of Rossetti's outlook and character. Since the letters will be used most often by those seeking information about the poets, artists, and events with which Rossetti was associated, I have aimed above all at readability. Although Rossetti sometimes wrote unduly complex or ponderous sentences, omitted the article, or used a colon in place of a period or semicolon, his writing is seldom obscure. I have refrained therefore from burdening the text with *sic*. He consistently abbreviated relative pronouns and proper names at their second appearance in a letter. These (and the ampersand) have been silently expanded, except in the case of Fanny Cornforth, whose name rarely appears as other than F. in either the letters or diaries. His frequent hyphenating of words and phrases has been retained, except for words like today and seaside, but the dash at the end of a sentence when it accompanies a period has been eliminated. Variant spellings of Pre-Raphaelite, Siddal, and Francis Hueffer have been left, but words like Fraser for *Fraser's Magazine* have been normalized. When the title of a book, poem, or painting is referred to accurately by its full or short title, it has been italicized. The address, date, and closing of the letters have been regularized.

Finally, because of the documentary value of the letters, I have annotated them fully. In doing this I have had the great privilege of using Rossetti's own papers, now known as the Angeli-Dennis Papers, and the richness of the annotation owes much to this source.

1. *Ten Lectures on Art* (1879), p. 217.
2. *RRP*, p. 53.
3. *The Young George Du Maurier, A Selection of His Letters, 1860-1867*, ed. D. Du Maurier, 1951, p. 207.
4. See "Checklist."
5. *A Selection from the Poems of Shelley*, ed. M. Blind, Leipzig, 1872, p. v.
6. David Kent, "Sequence and Meaning in Christina Rossetti's *Verses* (1893)," *Victorian Poetry*, 17 (1979), 259-64.
7. "The Third Rossetti," *Western Humanities Review*, 10 (Summer 1956), 284.
8. For Rothenstein and Curle, see below; for Cockerell, see *The Best of Friends, Further Letters to S. C. Cockerell*, ed. Viola Meynell, 1956, p. 30.
9. "Christina Rossetti," in *English Women* (1942), p. 42.
10. For a discussion of his friendship with these individuals, see the first footnote on each.
11. *PLD*.
12. Leonid M. Arinshtein and W. E. Fredeman, "William Michael Rossetti's 'Democratic Sonnets'," *Victorian Studies*, 14 (March 1971), 247, Note 11.
13. "A Shadow of Dante: Rossetti in the Final Years (Extracts from W. M. Rossetti's Unpublished Diaries, 1876-1882)," ed. William E. Fredeman, *Victorian Poetry*, 20 (1982), 218.
14. R. D. Waller, *The Rossetti Family, 1824-1854* (1932), pp. 128, 152-53.
15. *Men and Memories, Recollections of William Rothenstein* (1932), 2:138.
16. Letter in AP.
17. *PLD*, p. 55.
18. Olivia Rossetti Agresti, "The Anecdotage of an Interpreter, Memories of a Dying Epoch," unpublished autobiography in the possession of Mrs. Imogene Dennis.
19. As reported by WBS in a letter to WMR, 26 December 1860; Durham.
20. W. E. Fredeman, "A Pre-Raphaelite Gazette: The Penkill Letters of Arthur Hughes to W. B. Scott and Alice Boyd," *Bulletin of the John Rylands Library*, 50 (Autumn 1967), 55.

21. "Victorian Portrait: William Rossetti and His Home," *The Listener*, 10 February 1944, p. 161.

22. *Men and Memories* (1931), 1:230.

23. See Note 12.

24. Unless otherwise indicated, quotations in this section are from *SR*, 1:118-29.

25. "Thou art not God, thou art the devil!" (WMR's translation). Cf. William's reaction as a boy to hearing the clergyman of St. Katharine's Chapel, Regent's Park, read 2 Kings 10, "which relates how King Jehu treacherously convened and slaughtered the worshipers of Baal, and obtained the express commendation of Jehovah for the act." He remembered "thinking to myself: 'Surely that was rather a 'fishy transaction' to be thus commended; is this what our religion consists of?'''

26. *An Agnostic's Apology* (1893), p. 13.

27. In *Victorian Prose, A Guide to Research*, ed. David J. DeLaura, 1973, pp. 478-80.

28. *Atlantic Monthly*, 17 (February 1866), 130.

29. *Victorian Prose*, p. 484.

30. *Studies in European Literature, being the Taylorian Lectures 1889-1899* (1900), p. 75.

31. MS. lecture in AP, f. 31.

1. TO FRANCES ROSSETTI[1]

Dear Mamma,

In her last letter Maria[2] told you that I had been invited to a musical soirée by Mrs. Moscheles,[3] and that she reserved an account of my proceedings on that occasion since she considered it probable that I might wish to do so myself. I now confirm her belief; and will inform you of all the particulars of that delightful conversazione. Arriving there before anyone else, I was ushered into the drawing-room, where I amused myself for I suppose at least half an hour in looking over the annuals, etc. etc., which lay on the table. Not long after this in came a cousin of young Moscheles,[4] who asked me about Papa's[5] health with great apparent *empressement*; and she was soon followed by Mrs. and Miss Moscheles[6] who reiterated the question. By degrees the room began to fill; and after a short period during which tea was carried round, a French boy, apparently of about my own age, sat down at the Piano; Mr. Moscheles watched his every movement with the eye of a connoisseur, beating time meanwhile, and seemed much pleased with his performance, which appeared to me really surprising for one of his age. Among the company was a German gentleman of the name, I believe, of Herst,[7] a rival in playing the violin of Sivori[8] the second Paganini, who favoured the ladies and gentlemen assembled with two or three airs on that instrument, which were universally, and to my poor judgement, most justly applauded. Miss Adelaide Kemble[9] sang some Italian airs very beautifully, which excited almost or quite as much admiration as the instrumental music of Mr. Herst. At a little before twelve o'clock I took leave, having spent a far more pleasant evening than I had anticipated, my expectations having been none of the most favourable.

Yesterday Mr. Sebag[10] called here when no one was at home except Gabriel[11] and myself: he asked very particularly about Papa, how he was getting on, where he was, who was with him, and many other questions of that sort, and at last ended with these somewhat singular words; "I did not come about the lessons, but to ask after Mr. Rossetti's health." Uncharitable as it is, I could not help in my mind placing the order of the sentence vice versa. Not long after his departure entered Dr. Heimann,[12] with his intended, an exceedingly pretty young lady, opinions being divided about her name, which I decide to be Barrett. She examined the "Illustrated Scrap-book," the first number of which she had already seen, and was delighted with Gabriel's designs, which she called exquisite. Dr. Heimann said that one of these days he would invite us to spend an evening with the lady and himself, but did not signify at whose house. Maria and Christina[13] wish to know if you consent that they should do so, in which case they would be happy to accept the Doctor's kind proposal, who says that he will drop a line when he has settled the day. Hoping that Papa's recovery is getting on at rapid stages, and with the best love of us all.

> I remain,
> Your affectionate son,
> W. Rossetti

P.S. Please to answer my enquiry about Doctor Heimann in your next letter.

MS: AP.

1. (1800-1886), WMR's half-English, half-Italian mother, to whom he was devoted, though less demonstratively so than DGR was to her. He explicitly rejected her devout Christian beliefs, but his account of her "clear perception and sound sense," her retirement, and her "life-long practice of moderating self-control" (*FLM*, 1:21-22) equally describes himself.

2. WMR's elder sister (1827-76). Letter 238, which he wrote to her when she joined the Sisters of All Saints, Margaret Street, and his description of her intellectual qualities in Letter 274 suggest that WMR held her in scarcely less reverence than he did DGR and CGR.

3. Charlotte Moscheles, wife of the Bohemian pianist Ignaz Moscheles (1794-1870) whose biography she wrote. After their marriage in 1826 they settled in London until 1846, when at Mendelssohn's invitation Moscheles became head of the piano department at the recently founded Leipzig Conservatory.

4. Felix Stone Moscheles (1833-1917), remembered for his friendship with George du Maurier in whose cartoons he often appeared. MS. Diary, 3 December 1880: "We spent the evening at the Hancocks [sister and brother-in-law of Mathilde Blind]: here I met Felix Moscheles, now a painter of no particular mark, who used as a schoolboy to accompany me to King's College School about 1843-4: I had hardly, or not at all, seen him since that remote date." 17 February 1890: "Called at the studio of Felix Moscheles ... at his invitation, to see the portrait of Browning which he painted in 1884. It is in some respects good, but I think the nose too long, and this gives a rather Jewish look. The picture is of a nymph in a sea-shell etc. [*The Isle's Enchantress*], for which Browning with over-facile goodnature wrote a few lines of verse printed in the R.A. catalogue 2 or 3 years ago, is a silly affair." The picture is not in Graves; see William Clyde DeVane, *A Browning Handbook* (1955), p. 574, for the newspaper publication of Browning's lines.

5. Gabriele Rossetti (1783-1854), Italian patriotic poet, commentator on Dante; professor of Italian at King's College London, 1831-47. WMR's lifelong love of Italy and his passion for minute textual and biographical studies were nurtured by his father's example.

6. Clara Moscheles, who married Antonin Roche, a teacher of French in London from about 1834. Roche was a friend of Maria Rossetti (*SR*, 1:27).

7. Almost certainly Heinrich Wilhelm Ernst (1814-65), who modelled his playing on Paganini. One of his London concerts was praised in the *Athenaeum*, 22 July 1843, p. 676.

8. Ernesto Camillo Sivori (1815-94), popular Italian violinist, played in London in the previous month (*Athenaeum*, 3 June 1843, p. 534).

9. (1814-79), daughter of Charles Kemble of the theatrical family. An opera singer, she made her first London appearance in Bellini's *Norma* in 1841.

10. Joseph Sebag-Montefiore (1822-1903), nephew of Sir Moses Montefiore, the stockbroker and Jewish spokesman, "whose surname he used by Royal Licence" (*Who Was Who*, 1:502). He was knighted in 1896, and in the same year appointed Italian Consul-General in London. During the early 1840s, when Gabriele Rossetti's health began to decline, he was one of his few pupils.

11. DGR (1828-82), who both used and relied on his brother. After his death WMR's efforts to secure his fame were unceasing.

12. Adolf Heimann (1809-74), whose doctorate was from Berlin, 1833, for a dissertation on the Orations of Thucydides. A teacher of German at University College School and from 1848 professor of German at University College, he instructed the Rossetti children in German in exchange for Italian lessons from Gabriele Rossetti. In 1843 he married Amelia Barnard, "a very pretty pleasant young English Jewess" (*FLM*, 1:110). WMR called him "one of the kindest and most encouraging friends of all our early youth" (*RRP*, p. 284). Following CGR's death WMR wrote to Mrs. Heimann as one of his sister's "oldest and best friends" (Letter 505).

13. CGR (1830-94). Her numerous letters to WMR lack the spontaneity of those she wrote to DGR. Only four WMR letters to her have been found.

2. TO FRANCES ROSSETTI

[10 April 1848],[1]

½ past 4

Dear Mamma,

There has not been the slightest disturbance all day: On arriving at the Office, I found that some of us had been requested to attend earlier than usual, and were

2

posted at the Exchange and elsewhere. They have now just returned, stating that the patriots quietly dispersed, as I told you they would, on being summoned so to do.

I with, I believe, nineteen others, remain here for the night, but there is not any prospect whatever of our constabular order finding the whereon to exercise itself. I understand that I shall not come home before the close of business tomorrow i.e. about 5 o'clock. Don't think, (but I am sure you will not) on any account of sitting up.

W. M. Rossetti

MS: AP.

1. Date of the abortive Chartist demonstration on Kennington Common. WMR, a clerk in the Excise Office in Old Broad Street, was one of the many special constables sworn in as part of the precautions to preserve law and order taken by the home secretary, the Duke of Wellington.

3. TO FRANCES ROSSETTI

Friday,
11 August [1848]

Dear Mamma,

I have settled to leave on Sunday at ½ past 10, by doing which, according to the table, I shall reach Brighton[1] at 1 o'clock. The only reason for not leaving tomorrow, is that I remember that is to be the first day of meeting for our poetical club,[2] and it would hardly do to fail being at my post on that momentous occasion.

Have you heard the wretched news from Italy?[3] Milan surrendered to the Austrians, who have now, as far as I can judge, recovered all they had lost. The only remaining prospect of success — with the exception of a sudden turn of fortune scarcely to be anticipated — is in the French intervention. It appears that France and England have settled the bases of a pacific mediation: but, should either party be dissatisfied with their terms, it seems decided that the French, at least, will not shrink from trying the chances of war.

I'm very glad to hear that I can have a room in the same house with you: I only trust that the company of the miniature Pistrucci[4] is not a fixture: if so, I'm sure the rent should be abated on the ground of nuisance in the immediate vicinity.

The old-established love from all to all and most particularly from

W. M. Rossetti

MS: AP.

1. Mrs. Rossetti was in Brighton with her father, Gaetano Polidori, and CGR.
2. The formation of the PRB was later in the fall of 1848. A number of art clubs and this proposed literary club preceded it (*PRBJ*, p. 108).
3. During the Five Days of March 1848 the Austrians were driven from Milan and Venice, but by the end of the first week of August Milan had surrendered, and an armistice was agreed upon which restored to Austria all her original possessions with the exception of Venice. Venice fell to Austria on 24 August, neither France nor England being prepared to go to war on her behalf, despite an impassioned appeal to the British foreign secretary, Lord Palmerston.
4. Luigi Pistrucci, son of one of Gabriele Rossetti's most constant friends, Filippo Pistrucci. Rossetti disapproved when Luigi succeeded him as professor of Italian at King's College in 1847 (*SR*, 1:36).

3

4. TO FREDERIC GEORGE STEPHENS[1]

Dear Stephens,

Many thanks for your letter, verses included, which enlivened me tremendously. I have copied them out that I may be able to read them henceforward without my eyes falling out. But I don't understand the 1st verse of stanza 4, which I decipher

> For this dreadful dense desiring: —

And why the inscrutable blank at the end of stanza 7?

Is it a fact that my cubes are erroneous in construction? I was not without vague misgivings at the time. Or are they merely slovenly in handling?

Have you seen Hunt's[2] verses? If not, it must be by a kind of second-sight intuition that you know them to be "Sombre, grand, like plumes on hearses"; for I did not tell you so, and indeed am not very clear as to their subject or mode of treatment.

I intended in my note to say that we should be with you for perspective purposes on the then Friday week; i.e. the Friday that is now to be next. But, in consequence of what you say, we'll come on Saturday, in all probability, or possibly on Thursday, since I might want to see you relative to going on the river, for which I feel inclined. But shall not I, in addition to 3 Tuppers,[3] be too much? I'll talk it over with Hunt.

> It is now past the hour of 12;
>   Gabriel's dozing in his chair.
> And so this letter I will shelve,
>   As soon, as may be, dear Brother.
>
> Not that I mean to go to bed
>   Quite yet. I have the P.R.B.
> Diary to write up instead:
>   Tho' there is nothing verily.
>
> I yesterday bought Woolner[4] Keats'
>   Letters & Life[5] for seven & six:
> You will agree this somewhat beats
>   Giving 14 for it — (or licks,
>
> As Schoolboys say): by this last rhyme,
>   You'll see how most hard up I am:
> Indeed this writing against time,
>   If not i' the vein, is a mere sham.
>
> Cordiality can speak in prose,
>   And say good morning & good bye
> For Ave & Adieu. Suppose
>   That I to do so now should try.

4

And yet, dear brother, I confess
Your full-leafed letter would deserve
A better answer. Nevertheless
Take this. And think it but a curve

Of the broad circle wherewith I
Encircle you in P.R.B.-
hood. And so, truly now, Good bye.
Yours, I to you as you to me,

W. M. Rossetti

Frederic George Stephens, P.R.B.

MS: Bodleian. Extracts in *PRBJ*, pp. 128-29, 197.

1. (1828-1907), member of the PRB and art critic. Although WMR commented after Stephens's death that "one need not overstate his intellectual or other merits" (Letter 591), and though he was often exasperated by Stephens's stubbornness, in particular over the quarrel with Holman Hunt, WMR corresponded with him for almost sixty years, a longer period than with anyone else.
2. William Holman Hunt (1827-1910). WMR's fondness for Hunt is obvious in his letters. Although after the 1860s there were long periods when they neither saw one another nor corresponded, something of the old intimacy was revived during the last decade of Hunt's life.
3. The brothers George J. F. (d. 1891), Alexander (partners in their father's firm, which printed the *Germ*), and John Lucas Tupper (see Letter 16, Note 1). In his obituary of John Lucas, WMR observed that George had "a special reputation as a facsimilist" (*Daily News*, 3 October 1879, p. 2).
4. Thomas Woolner (1825-92), "sculptor-poet" (Fredeman, p. 149) and member of the PRB. For many years he and WMR were "like affectionate brothers" (Letter 480), but WMR's earliest surviving letter to him (No. 88) was written on the occasion of Woolner's engagement in 1864, after which date they drifted apart.
5. *Life, Letters, and Literary Remains of John Keats*, ed. R. M. Milnes, 1848.

5. TO FREDERIC GEORGE STEPHENS

At Mr. Newnham, Builders,
High Street,
Ventnor,[1]
Thursday,
27 September 1849

Dear Stephens,

I have just received a message from Gabriel that several of us are thinking of calling our Magazine[2] "The P.R.B. Journal," and requesting me to give you my opinion at once. I guess that you, Hunt, and if he is returned, Millais[3] are the originators of the idea.

I will give you an unbiased and uncomplimentary opinion. I think it would be most injudicious. A man passing through the street sees a pamphlet lettered "The P.R.B. Journal": it may be the transactions of a scientific society for anything he knows to the contrary. But it may be said that, for one who sees the mere wrapper, twenty will see the etching and the first page; also that the majority will come prepared beforehand, either by advertisements or hearsay, for the real character of the book. Granted; but I verily believe there is a not inconsiderable section of the public who don't like walking into a shop and asking for a book by a title with the meaning of which they are totally unacquainted, — so far even as

5

not to know whether it be really expressed in letters or whether the purport of these be matter of general certainty. Thus far for the public and the magazine merely: now for the effects that would ensue to ourselves internally. The thing is *not*, strictly speaking, a P.R.B. Journal: we have two, I presume, active proprietors, Deverell[4] and Hancock,[5] who are not such. Deverell may probably become so at no very distant period, but Hancock, I conceive, works on principles of Art that must render himself unwilling, if he knows what the letters mean, ever to add them to his name. If this name be adopted, be sure that difficulties will arise. The public will be at once entitled to regard these two as P.R.B.s; they will themselves almost have a right to do so by implication and by the force of the *fait accompli*. Such Artists and critics as have begun to recognize you as a body tending towards definite aims in art will not know what to think of it: you will lose the distinctive character you possess, — your real character. You will observe that, being myself unaffected personally by these considerations, I speak solely from an outward point of view, as an observer. Again. In a letter Gabriel wrote me recently, he says that we have now 9 proprietors *including Herbert*.[6] Probably what Herbert said on the subject will never produce any actual result: but, if it is to do so, I am satisfied that he would most strongly object to become in any manner publicly connected with any section in art, more especially a section which, proceeding on somewhat the same sympathies as himself, seeks to out-Herbert Herbert. Nor is this all. Unless the magazine realizes a success greater, I admit, than I anticipate for it, at least at the opening of its career, we must do our best to look out for more proprietors, — concerning whom the same remarks as I have offered in the case of Hancock and Deverell will most certainly apply, — and probably with much greater force, even to the extent either of inducing them to decline joining us in the publication, or of literally precluding you, with any regard to the bearing of P.R.B. upon your position as Artists, from requesting their co-operation.

It appears to me that there is a very easy way of compromising the matter, obviating all these difficulties, and, at the same time, meeting our own desire (and no one is more anxious, or can be so, on the point than myself) to connect the "P.R.B." with our names in every possible way, artistic and literary; viz.: to have "P.R.B." printed on the cover, not as the title of the work, but by itself, as a kind of device or designation:[7] thus for instance

December

No. 1.	P.R.B.	Price 1/-

this will lead to an inference. When the public see the names of certain of us it will remind them that these are the painters of certain works in a certain style: and, at the same time, it will not affect those who either are not artists or are not recognized as P.R.B.s in art. This proposal was made long ago, and has never that I know of, been abandoned, though it has been suffered to be in abeyance: and it seems to me that now, when a step is thought of being taken in the same direction, a step that would jump over much more ground than P.R.B. actually covers, is the moment for finally adopting or relinquishing it.

Did you see a letter I wrote Woolner on the subject of my name being published as Editor? I hope, if the thing is to be, you are all united in the intention.[8]

Is your article on early Art[9] finished? I hear that it's "in a highly chaotic state," but am not certain whether that may not imply merely that it requires arrangement. I dare say you're aware what I'm writing — a blank verse narrative poem.[10] There are 584 lines done. I began it in the idea the whole would fall short of that; but it lengthens out as I advance: 700 is the very extremist amount of compression it will endure, I am certain: and it will not surprise me if it exceeds 800. I only hope I shall not find it growing too long for insertion. I would nurse my egotism by dilating on the intention and character of it, but that I calculate on your having seen my other letters, where the matter is fully treated.

This is a splendid place; — but perhaps you know it, so my eloquence is gagged.

What is doing with the Tuppers? John, (I can speak to him only), would be a most valuable acquisition to our magazine:[11] but I fear the chance, for the present, at least, is but small. The title, before the idea was started of calling it "The P.R.B. Journal," was, as sent to me, "Thoughts Towards Nature." Here the consonants are rather clogging: perhaps *toward* might be an improvement.[12] This is a very minor matter: yet the alteration, if advisable, might as well be made too.

My contribution to the 1st No. is, as you may probably know, to be a review of the *Bothie of Toper-na-fuosich*, by Clough, a hexametral poem, and *Sir Reginald Mohun*, Canto 1, by Cayley,[13] in what is usually called the Don Juan style, though even the metre is by no means identical. The former is most first rate; the latter exceedingly clever, neither, I believe, yet noticed. They will make a most interesting article, if properly treated: but I have not yet turned my thoughts to them at all, having touched nothing literally (or literarily) except my poem.

I shall be back on Tuesday, and long to see you all again. There's plenty to talk about and plenty, in all conscience, for me to do on my return. This magazine business has carved out work enough for me.

Should you feel inclined to answer this, pray don't baulk yourself: I shall be here to Sunday inclusive, on which day letters are delivered at this place and letters reach me the day after they are written. On Monday I shall be journeying homewards.

If anything definite is now known about it, write me, in case you reply, all particulars of what No. 1 will really cost, items and all. The mere postage of sending about prospectuses will be something; the advertising far more. The expense is rather frightening for P.R.B.s. If the thing succeeds, it is my greatest present desire; if it fails, a severe disappointment, to me, at least; for I know it deserves to encounter support.

W. M. Rossetti

Frederic George Stephens (not Manning)[14] P.R.B.

P.S. One word more about the magazine. The adoption of the title "The P.R.B. Journal" appears to me to be, as regards ourselves, a virtual exclusion of Hancock and Deverell and any others who might join us in a similar position from their proprietorship; as regards the public, a virtual recognition of their P.R.B.hood. If they do not combat the project, considering the former point of view, it can only be because they look to its results in the latter. An admission of this, I cannot but think, is an utter and unanswerable rejection of the idea, which carries in it injustice to them and a false position to ourselves.

If our original wish (of course far the most desirable, but, under present circumstances, impossible) to confine the proprietors to the P.R.B.s could have been followed out, I should still think "The P.R.B. Journal" an objectionable title as concerns the public: as it is, I conceive the advantages to be most problematic, not to say unexistent; the obstacles altogether overwhelming.

It strikes me now that even Woolner will be out of London, and that, unless Millais is back, you are the only representative of the brotherhood now in town: unless the rest have delegated to you their responsibility in this matter, it will take some time in deciding.

MS: Bodleian. Extract in *PRBJ*, pp. 204-5.

1. WMR was on holiday in the Isle of Wight with James Collinson.
2. *The Germ*; the first of four numbers appeared in January 1850.
3. John Everett Millais (1829-96). After early PRB days Millais and WMR seldom met or corresponded. None of WMR's letters to him has been found, and the dozen Millais letters to WMR in AP are not very revealing.
4. Walter Howell Deverell (1827-54) was influenced by the work of the PRB, but never became a member. He contributed four poems and an etching to the *Germ*. In an obituary WMR described him as "an artist from whose independent thought and keen sense of beauty we had felt warranted in anticipating results of unusual excellence" (*Spectator*, 11 February 1854, p. 159).
5. John Hancock (1825-69), sculptor, exhibited at the R.A. in 1843, at the Westminster Hall competition in 1844 (a statue of Chaucer considered "not in good taste" by the *Art Journal*), and at the Great Exhibition in 1851 (a highly praised statue of Beatrice, which was shown again in Paris in 1855) (Gunnis). Against WMR's claim that Hancock contributed nothing to the *Germ* "either in work or in money," Fredeman points out that "he was closely involved in the planning stages and ... voted on the title" (*PRBJ*, p. 189).
6. John Rogers Herbert (1810-90), who after his conversion to Catholicism about 1840 painted mostly biblical subjects in an early Christian style reminiscent of William Dyce and the Nazarenes (Wood).
7. The initials PRB were not used in the *Germ*.
8. His name did not appear.
9. Published in *Germ* 2 as "The Purpose and Tendency of Early Italian Art."
10. *Mrs. Holmes Grey*, which was not published until 1868 in the *Broadway*, pp. 449-59.
11. J. L. Tupper contributed poems and essays, and there were minor contributions by George and Alexander (*PRBJ*, p. 67).
12. Towards was used.
13. George John Cayley, *Some Account of the Life and Adventures of Sir Reginald Mohun* (1849); reviewed by WMR in *Germ* 3.

6. TO FRANCES ROSSETTI

Ventnor,
28 September 1849

Dear Mamma,

I am most pained to hear Papa has a return of bronchitis: I know you will not let him neglect it.

I wish I had something to inform you of; but, on reflection, find I can only muster some little gossip on the topics raised by your letter.

The only indication I have perceived of cholera hereabouts is the sticking up of a few bills stating the promptest remedies. I've not heard anyone talk of it except a person with whom I fell into conversation at Carisbrooke Castle, and he was a visitor from Lancashire and London: so that I suspect my box of pills will die of mere inanition.

I'm glad you like my sonnet for the wrapper of the "Thoughts."[1] It was a point of some delicacy to bring out the general intention and aim which are to actuate all of us, without entering too much into details and individual preferences. We had intended originally to write a sonnet each, and to choose from all these the one that might appear most suitable. But mine is the only one done yet, and the others have not thought it necessary to disturb it from its "bad eminence."[2] Did you hear that so great a man as Coventry Patmore[3] has given us a poem for insertion?

Stephens has, as you say, a most pensive and, I think, very prepossessing head. Millais is painting him for Ferdinand listening to Ariel.[4]

It is my intention to set off on Monday, and I calculate on being at home before dinner-time on Tuesday.

W. M. Rossetti

MS: AP. Extract in *PRBJ*, p. 199, misdated 23 September.

1. "When whoso merely hath a little thought" appeared on the cover of each number of the *Germ*.
2. Satan was "by merit rais'd / To that bad eminence" (*Paradise Lost*, 2:5-6).
3. (1823-96), "the first distinguished poet whom I knew." Having read his first volume, *Poems* (1844), WMR and DGR "came to Patmore fully primed to believe in and admire him" (*SR*, 1:83). He contributed a sonnet to each of *Germ* 1 and 2, and an essay on *Macbeth* to *Germ* 3.
4. *Ferdinand Lured by Ariel*, R.A., 1850 (Bennett 1967, No. 22).

7. TO FREDERIC GEORGE STEPHENS

3 October 1849

Dear Stephens,

Mr. Haynes'[1] estimate is for 3000 £2.7.6, for 4000 £2.18.6. I have ordered 4000.

I must confess I begin to feel nervous at voting away my colleagues' money; but I hope all will give me credit for good intentions, and will perceive that I find it out of my power to consult them in every emergency. The estimate, you will see is, for double the number, less than the price previously named to you. He says that the 3000 are already in hand.

In case you should want Woolner's address, here it is for you.

> "At Mr. Hobbs'
> George and Dragon,
> Near the Suspension Bridge,
> Great Marlow,
> Bucks.''

No sign of Gabriel's letter to me, as yet.

W. M. Rossetti

Frederic George Stephens, P.R.B.

I find that the volume of poems I reviewed[2] figures in last week's *Athenaeum* among the "Poetry of the Million." They do not cut it up, however.

MS: Bodleian. Extract in *PRBJ*, p. 203.

1. The printer of a prospectus for the *Germ*.
2. Arnold's *The Strayed Reveller, and other Poems*, *Germ* 2; *Athenaeum*, 29 September 1849, p. 982.

8. TO FREDERIC GEORGE STEPHENS

Wednesday Night,
16 January 1850

Dear Stephens,

Thank you for your list of Subscribers.[1] You are the only one that has carried out the decree of Thursday last. As I was not present when it was voted, I'm not certain what precise object was contemplated thereby; but it's always well to know whom we have. As to what you mean, however, about Belfast, St. Pancras, and the Isle of Man, I am in total darkness. What connexion has the subscriber at the one place with him at the other? Don't trouble yourself to answer this, though, as it certainly is not I who am to distribute their copies. I'll do what best I can to supply you with 2 more.

Now to an important point.

What you say about printing not so many as 700 of No. 2 is valuable, and I must confess that perhaps, but for you, the question would not have suggested itself to me. But I think 400 will not be too many.[2] Again, you assume there will be but few to give away, and that Collinson's[3] poem will be less attractive than Woolner's.[4] On the first point, there certainly will be fewer: but, as regards the latter, I fancy you're mistaken. Woolner's poem was a rather attractive *poem*, but not specially saleable in any one class, and no poetry, merely as such, is *really* attractive. Collinson's, on the contrary, is likely to get very much about in a certain circle, among the Catholics and the Puseyites, that is; and he has, besides, the means personally of introducing it to some rather influential men of the former. It will be very greatly admired by some, and altogether overlooked or

10

absolutely scouted by others: this is, I think, a more promising condition than the negatively fair one in which Woolner's was placed.

Last night we had two poems from W. B. Scott, a sonnet, and a blank-verse piece.[5] The latter, which will fill about 3½ pages, is very glorious, and must come into No. 2. What do you think of "The Purpose attempted in Early Italian Art" as a title for your Essay? It is the best we have been able to concoct. We think of having some posters — 100 or so — printed, showing some of the principal points in No. 1. They would cost not more than 12/- or 13/- and could be stuck up in one day, Tupper thinks, at an expense of 1/-.

I'm very sorry we shall miss you at Collinson's; but I know you would not fail at a P.R.B. meeting without adequate cause.

W. M. Rossetti

It's not quite certain but what we may print our names in the new No. If so, I presume we may publish yours.[6] Don't be too much frightened, however, as most probably we shall not.

MS: Bodleian. Extract in *PRBJ*, p. 222.

1. To the *Germ*.
2. Stephens suggested 300, George Tupper advised 500 and WMR agreed (*PRBJ*, pp. 43-44).
3. James Collinson (1825-81), member of the PRB, from which he resigned on Whit Monday 1850. Shortly after the date of this letter he proposed unsuccessfully to CGR, who was however briefly engaged to him later in the year. Collinson is usually dismissed both as a man and a painter, but throughout the 1850s WMR found much to praise in his pictures. For an account of his reviews, see R. W. Peattie, "W. M. Rossetti's Reviews of James Collinson," *Journal of Pre-Raphaelite Studies*, 5 (May 1985), 100-4.
4. *Germ* 2 opened with Collinson's *The Child Jesus*; *Germ* 1 with Woolner's *My Beautiful Lady*.
5. See Letter 9.
6. After *Germ* 1 most contributors were identified, but Stephens's article on "Early Italian Art" appeared with a pseudonym.

9. TO WILLIAM BELL SCOTT[1]

Wednesday,
16 January 1850

Dear Sir,

I scarcely know whether to express to you more thanks for your two poems, or more pleasure at reading them. When I say that the *Morning Sleep* appears to me not less fine than the *Dream of Love*,[2] I say all that I can or feel permitted to. It[3] will enrich the pages of *our* second No., which is to appear on the last of the present month. This will contain also a short poem of Patmore's, and an article by him on *Macbeth*.

My brother thinks you would not feel offended at my taking the liberty of showing you the enclosed verse-narrative of mine[4] (which may probably be published in our fourth No.) and asking you to inform me of any alterations that might be beneficial to it. I almost fear, however, this may be giving you too much trouble. I cannot but anticipate that you will find it very bald in matter and unelevated in tone and character; but it was written rather as a experiment in principle — an extreme one, perhaps — than anything else. I wanted to attempt, in a subject of commonplace life, a more systematically commonplace treatment than I remember to have met with in any poet.

Again thanking you for your kindness in our cause, I remain, dear Sir,

Most faithfully yours,
Wm. M. Rossetti

MS: Arizona.

1. (1811-90), poet, painter, writer on art, to whom WMR wrote some of his most affectionate letters. WBS's wide knowledge, skepticism in religion, and democratic sympathies helped to bridge the gap of almost twenty years between them, but WMR must have been drawn to him as well by exceptional personal qualities. As late as 1881 WMR was still addressing him as "Dearly beloved Scotus" (letter of 7 May [1881]; Arizona).
2. Published in the *Monthly Repository*, January 1838, pp. 46-49.
3. *Morning Sleep*. WBS's sonnet *Early Aspirations* appeared in *Germ* 3.
4. *Mrs. Holmes Grey*.

10. TO WILLIAM BELL SCOTT

50 Charlotte Street,[1]
Tuesday,
5 February 1850

Dear Sir,

Having been very much engaged recently with the bringing out of the 2nd No. of the *Germ* and nuisances consequent thereon, I have put off answering your letter from day to day, till at last I feel almost as much ashamed of doing it as of leaving it undone. I hope you will accept this, not as an excuse, but an apology.

Your very indulgent remarks on my poem[2] have served to put before me in a clearer light than ever the defects — at least the defects of principle — which I have no doubt are inherent in it. I feel that the characters of the husband and wife and the chief incident *are* exceptional. Even while writing it, I had my fears for the result in this respect; and now feel convinced that it is almost too ambitious, before a somewhat extended experience of real life, to attempt the embodiment of what is likely to strike as a metaphysical paradox.

The prospect of bringing out a 3rd *Germ* is, we all fear, not very distinct. I regret this, but cannot say I am disappointed. Certain it is that the sale of the 1st No. was very limited; and it would demand a sufficiently sanguine temper to anticipate better success for this. However it may turn out, we all have to thank you for enabling us to say without fear of disproof that the experiment has not been altogether undeserving of support.

I am, Dear Sir,
Most truly yours,
W. M. Rossetti

MS: Arizona.

1. The Rossettis lived at 38 Charlotte Street until Christmas 1835, when they moved to No. 50, remaining there until the beginning of 1851.
2. *Mrs. Holmes Grey*.

11. TO FREDERIC GEORGE STEPHENS

Saturday,
16 February 1850

Dear Stephens,

George Tupper has just called on me, saying that he and his brothers, being unwilling that the *Germ* should die, if avertable, have been thinking over the possibility of carrying it on at their own proper risk. Singularly generous, is it not? and this before they have received one farthing of our debt. I told him I should have great hesitation in accepting.

He will be at Gabriel's study tonight:[1] and wishes to meet as many of us as can be got together. I've written to Hunt, Collinson, Deverell, Woolner, and Hancock, and shall see Millais. You'll come, I know.

W. M. Rossetti

MS: Bodleian. Extract in *PRBJ*, p. 222.

1. See *PRBJ*, pp. 54-55.

12. TO WALTER HOWELL DEVERELL

Saturday,
16 February 1850

Dear Deverell,

We know the *Germ* can't continue on its present footing: but I had certainly no idea Tupper would think of taking it up himself. This, however, he proposes some idea of doing. I hope you'll be able to come to Gabriel's study to meet him tonight. I've written to all the other proprietors, and expect most, at least, of them.

Yours,
W. M. Rossetti

MS: Huntington.

13. TO FREDERIC GEORGE STEPHENS

Monday,
20 May 1850

Dear Stephens,

The long expected (query desired?) moment arrived on Saturday, and Tupper presented me the bill for Nos. 1 and 2. It stands thus:

No. 1 — £19. 1.6
No. 2 — £15.15.6
Total   £34.17.0

He wishes — (though he spoke, as always, in the most friendly manner) to be paid before the end of the month.

Reckoning on £5 from the Publishers, the amount for each of us will be

8)29.17
3.14.6

13

as far as my arithmetic allows me to compute fractions.

Will you let me know the state of the case in your own regard, *soon*, for you know the month runs but a few days longer.

There is another point — (about the No. of subscribers each of us can muster) on which I understand he will confer with you personally.

W. M. Rossetti

Frederic George Stephens, P.R.B.

MS: Bodleian. Published, omitting the final paragraph, in *PRBJ*, p. 229.

14. TO FREDERIC GEORGE STEPHENS

Monday,
10 June 1850

Dear Stephens,

As far as the accounts to which I have access show, you have received 76 copies of No. 1 and 12 of No. 2. Of 3 and 4 I know nothing.

I am not quite certain whether I understand you correctly as meaning that you want to fork out the amount paid to you by your subscribers. If so, you would be entering into a labyrinth of arithmetic at which my calculations never arrived; inasmuch as, if you do so for your part, each of us 8 ought also to do so for his. What I have done is to take Tupper's bill

£33.17. -

Deduct therefrom, what I have
received from the Publisher   <u>5. 8. 6</u>

<u>£28. 8. 6</u>

This I have divided among the eight of us,[1] which, making some allowance for Hunt's having paid the etchers' bill, gives about £3.14.6 each. Beyond this I have not elaborated our account so as to meet the case of each of us precisely.

Perhaps you are not aware that I have paid Tupper — (this was on May 27) — £14.17.6 — being for Gabriel and me, £2 of Deverell's, and the Publisher's money. Millais had his money ready: but, as he is out of town, I don't know whether I shall be able to get hold of it.

I did not know that there was an engagement to you for tomorrow; but shall come in all probability.

W. M. Rossetti

F. G. Stephens, P.R.B.

MS: Bodleian. Published, omitting the final paragraph, in *PRBJ*, pp. 229-30.

1. Collinson and Hancock in addition to those named, but both defaulted (*The Germ*, Introd. by WMR, 1901, p. 9).

15. TO DANTE GABRIEL ROSSETTI

429 Lawn Market,
Edinburgh,[1]
Saturday,
31 August 1850

Dear Gabriel,

You are aware, I think, that I wrote to W.B., asking him to tell me where his brother's[2] pictures may be seen. I have now just received his answer, in which he tells me of three.[3] He says: "you must leave yourself time to stay with me a day or two; and, when you arrive, come direct to my house" — i.e. 3 St. Thomas Street. He promises to show me a collection of David's sketches, which will surprise me.

I write this chiefly to give you a sort of an opportunity for answering. We can settle about meeting at Newcastle when I shall have fixed all my plans for leaving here.

Edinburgh is a splendid place — invaluable to a sketcher of the picturesque in matters of old gateways, old winding staircases (which issue into the street in the most dingy manner from all sorts of dirty houses) etc. The people generally seem in a state of squalor according to English notions.[4]

Here is what I saw written by an "Ecce Homo" beggar yesterday. He says it's his own. You should know that the Queen was here on Thursday and the guns have just boomed her departure:

> "The Queen she is but clay:
> The beggar is the same:
> They both may die upon one day;
> And both in dust remain
> Until that great and awful view
> When the last trump shall sound.
> No man can tell which of the two
> On that day shall be crowned."

Not bad, is it? But not his in all probability.

Now for a sample of Scotch religiousness: "Vivat Regina! The Bible! The Queen!! and the Prince!!! Just published a new and peculiarly thin edition of the holy scriptures in commemoration of the Queen's visit to Holyrood, to be had only at the Bible Warehouse" etc. etc.

I have done absolutely nought.

W. M. Rossetti

MS: AP.

1. WMR was on holiday in Edinburgh, followed by a visit to WBS in Newcastle. DGR did not join him in Newcastle.
2. David Scott (1806-49), historical painter of a romantic and mystical bent (Wood). WBS published a *Memoir* of him in 1850.
3. "As to the accessible pictures by my brother, there are the [*Vasco da*] *Gama* at the Trinity House at Leith; *Discord*, in Bonnar and Carfrae's Gallery, Castle Street; and the altarpiece in St. Patrick's Chapel, Lothian Street near the University" (letter of 30 August 1850; Durham).
4. WMR to Frances Rossetti, 28 August 1850: "Here I am in the heart of the old town. It is certainly a most splendid place for the student of the picturesque — all full of old houses, and

unaccountable dim passages or Closes in all possible odd corners of the streets. The houses have an antique falling to pieces air of which we have no idea in London: and you see the advertisement of 'Lodgings' hanging out from tenements you would suppose abandoned years ago to the rats. The great charm of the place consists in the unexpected combinations of mountains, sea, and houses, that meet you at every turn, ever varying and delightful. I am in (I think) the 5th story of a seven-storyed house: but there are many higher'' (AP).

16. TO JOHN LUCAS TUPPER[1]

50 Charlotte Street,
16 October 1850

Dear Tupper,

Woolner has not left town, it having eventually appeared that Aubrey de Vere[2] would not remain long enough in the North to sit for his portrait. I have fixed for you, George, George's friend (who is heartily welcome) and self, to call on him Friday this week. If this suits you, so much the better. I will look in on the afternoon appointed, at Barge Yard.

Hunt and Stephens are at Sevenoaks,[3] as, I suppose, you know. Gabriel is to join them in a day or two: Woolner thinks of accompanying him, and perhaps I may make a third in the goodly fellowship, as Dante says.[4] We had a jolly walk to Epping Forest, Woolner and I, on Sunday.

Any further news on Friday.

Yours,
W. M. Rossetti

MS: Leeds.

1. (1826-79), sculptor of medallions and of the statue of Linnaeus at the Oxford Museum; poet, a selection of whose poems WMR edited; anatomical draftsman at Guy's Hospital, 1849-63; drawing master at Rugby School from 1865. WMR described him as "learned in his department of art" (*FLM*, 1:151), "tenacious of the truth as he discerned it … [and] a steadfast and affectionate friend" (*Poems by J. L. Tupper* [1897], p. ix). Their large correspondence does not, however, suggest a lively friendship, and is occasionally marked by kindly irritation on WMR's part.
2. (1814-1902), poet and writer on Ireland. The list of Woolner's works in *TW* does not include a portrait of De Vere.
3. Hunt and DGR (and presumably Stephens) shared lodgings at Sevenoaks, DGR arriving on 23 October (DW, 1:93). Hunt and DGR painted background landscapes at nearby Knole Park, the seat of the Sackville family, Hunt for *Valentine Rescuing Sylvia from Proteus* (Bennett 1969, No. 19), DGR on a canvas later used for *The Bower Meadow* (Surtees 229). Neither Woolner nor WMR visited them.
4. Perhaps "sì ch'io fui sesto tra cotanto senno" (*Inferno*, 4:102), which John Ciardi (1977) translates: "making me sixth in that high company."

17. TO WILLIAM ALLINGHAM[1]

50 Charlotte Street,
Tuesday,
22 October 1850

Dear Allingham,

I send you the *Critic* containing my review of your poems;[2] and beg you to believe that the delay is not chargeable entirely on me. I have tried to embody — though not so fully as I could have wished — what you wrote me of the feeling in which you had conceived the *Music Master*. It appears to me that you have succeeded in the complete and adequate expression of that feeling.

I understand that Patmore's *Palladium* review[3] is in print; but have not seen it. Woolner gives me to understand, however, that there is not any sly poke at "your doxy," as you anticipated there would be.

Let me call your attention to an extract, in the *Critic*, from a translation of Dante,[4] of which I procured the insertion. It is remarkably literal, — surprisingly so considering that that most difficult of meters — the original *terza rima* — is retained. The author has some wish to get the complete work, if possible, into some magazine: and I spoke to Patmore about it with a view to the *Palladium*. He was greatly delighted with the translation, and will see what is to be done: nevertheless I suppose neither this nor any long work in poetry has any chance with a magazine. Separate publication would not, I fancy, offer insurmountable difficulties.

Will you excuse me for troubling you in a matter personal to myself. I had promised Mrs. Orme[5] to lend her our Blake MS.[6] and *Songs of Innocence* etc. On looking for them, they could not be found: and Gabriel is under the impression that you have them with you. If so, and if you find a *safe* way of sending them, may I ask their return *when you have no further occasion for them* as Mrs. Orme seems to take a great interest in the matter.

Most truly yours,
W. M. Rossetti

All here desire to be remembered to you.

MS: PM.

1. (1824-89), Irish poet and customs official; sub-editor of *Fraser's Magazine*, 1870-74, and editor until 1879. WMR corresponded with him throughout the 1850s and 1860s, but afterwards only occasionally. Allingham's break with DGR and Lucy Rossetti's dislike of him were probably wholly responsible for their drifting apart. The letters reveal that Allingham's intimacy with DGR also extended to WMR. Four of WMR's letters to Allingham predate by a couple of years the earliest DGR letters to him in DW.

2. *Poems* (1850); *Critic*, 15 October 1850, pp. 496-98. Woolner wrote to Allingham on 8 November 1850: "I am glad to hear from W. Rossetti that you liked his review on your poems; he bids fair to be one of our best in the review line — he takes more pains to discover the author's intention and less to display his own learning than most journalists" (*TW*, p. 9).

3. November 1850, pp. 385-91. Patmore's generally favorable review began dauntingly: "There are three hundred pages in this volume; and there are not more than thirty of them which ... ought to have been printed in their present condition."

4. By Charles Bagot Cayley (1823-83), long-suffering admirer of CGR. Three extracts from the *Inferno* appeared, 14 September, 1 and 15 October 1850, pp. 458, 481, 505-6. His translation of the complete *Commedia* was published in 4 vols. by Longman, 1851-55.

5. Eliza Orme, elder sister of Coventry Patmore's first wife, Emily Andrews. Her husband Charles, a prosperous distiller, was "not at all literary; his wife however, a lady ... of rich physique, with luminous dark eyes, had a refined taste and a great liking for the society of writers and artists" (*SR*, 1:89). WMR to Lucy Rossetti, 1 May 1892: "Yesterday I saw in the *Daily News* with real sorrow that my kind good old friend Mrs. Orme died on 28 April. Her age may have been I fancy towards 73: her surviving husband must be at least 10 years older. I must have first known Mrs. Orme, I think, in 1850, or even 1849; and for some 5 or 6 years ensuing no one did more than she to make me feel at my ease and give me some self-confidence on my entrance into life" (AP).

6. The Rossetti MS. of Blake, purchased by the brothers in 1847.

18. TO FREDERIC GEORGE STEPHENS

Thursday,
12 December [1850]

Dear Stephens,

Much to my regret, I have not the faintest idea or vague foreshadowing of any accessible Haymarket or other theatre order. I never by any chance get one myself; and am not certain I know any one having such at his command. Certainly they make no sign. Nor is Gabriel better off that I fancy.

He saw Millais' painting and design[1] the same day as you did, and came home down in the mouth. As he said, they — the design chiefly — "made him feel giddy." I must get sight of them with all speed.

Perhaps I may come tomorrow. Thank you for your promise for Saturday.

W. M. Rossetti

You were a defaulter to Hunt on Tuesday,[2] and I had Reynolds[3] and the Mad[4] all to myself — Millais and Collins[5] failing as well.

MS: Bodleian.

1. *The Woodman's Daughter* and *The Eve of the Deluge* respectively, Bennett 1967, Nos. 30 and 257 (see *PRBJ*, p. 241).
2. "I spent the evening with Hunt, being the only one of two or three engaged that did so" (*PRBJ*, 10 December, p. 86).
3. Possibly G. W. M. Reynolds (1814-79), novelist, journalist, Chartist, who incurred FMB's wrath ("the infamous scoundrel Reynolds") for publishing a woodcut of *Wycliffe* in *Reynolds's Miscellany* (*PDL*, pp. 145-46).
4. Hunt was nicknamed "the Maniac" (*PDL*, p. 19).
5. Charles Allston Collins (1828-73), painter of *Convent Thoughts* and other pictures inspired by the early work of the PRB. Around 1858 he gave up painting to become a writer (Wood).

19. TO WILLIAM ALLINGHAM

38 Arlington Street,[1]
14 January 1851

Dear Allingham,

I forwarded your books some while ago to the addresses you gave me; of which I should have apprised you long ago but for various interruptions, including, as you may observe, a change of residence. I am still so much occupied that I cannot do more just at present than answer your long unanswered last, reserving any news of my own, if any there be.

I can fully enter into your feelings on finding your volume[2] coupled with Kenealy's,[3] having myself been silly enough to trust to other people's reports as to the latter, and buy it.

I take William Allingham to be the author of *Wayconnell Tower*,[4] which my brother and self had admired before I heard from you. It does not strike me as more like Tennyson than is incident and, I fancy, unavoidably so, to all descriptive poetry of the present school.

The new edition of Mrs. Browning[5] (have you seen it?) contains but little new matter, — and, so far as I have seen, scarcely any alterations in the old. There is a *new* translation of the *Prometheus Bound*. I *am* a regular contributor to the *Critic*,[6] — the editor sending me a batch of (chiefly nonsense-) verse to review every now and then. I don't suppose he has received Mrs. Browning: but any notice of it I might send (which I should be inclined to do if I had time) would certainly be inserted.

As you do me the honour to ask my opinion about "artfulness" in poetry, I must say that I entirely agree with you as to its baneful influence, if made a substantial part of poetry, itself, instead of being confined to the best attainable expression of idea. Exceptional cases, such as *Kubla Khan*, may be admirable; but these are examples of this one quality, which cannot therefore, of course, interfere with any higher. I should say that *Where Claribel low lieth*[7] is an instance of its excess. I fancy, however, that the really great poets seldom fall into the mistake; for that where the "art" is most salient, it applies to the subtlest sense of the requirements of the fact.

As to the P.R.B. pictures preparing for next year, Millais will have 2, if not 3;[8] Hunt, it is hoped, 2, (the subjects from *Measure for Measure* and the *Two Gentlemen*);[9] Gabriel 1,[10] a small *genre* cabinet picture, whose point will be general combination rather than individual expression or meaning; Deverell 1 from *Hamlet*,[11] where the King dispatches him to England; Stephens 1 probably from *Griselda*.[12] Hunt's and Millais's will be greatly their best.

The Blake books have not arrived: and perhaps it might be worth while, in case they still remain at Liverpool, to notify my change of address, or Gabriel's, which is to "17 Red Lion Square."

Woolner is in Devonshire, where he had spent Christmas.

In haste,

Yours truly,
W. M. Rossetti

Do you mean to write often for Leigh Hunt. It is to be hoped — (and expected, I think) that his critique will have some effect.[13]

MS: PM.

1. The Rossettis moved to this address early in 1851.
2. *Poems* (1850).
3. Edward Vaughan Hyde Kenealy (1819-80), barrister and M.P. He published translations and verse, including in 1850 a second edition of *Goethe; a New Pantomine*, presumably the volume referred to.
4. Published in *Household Words*, 16 November 1850, p. 181.
5. *Poems* (1850). For a review in the *Critic* see Letter 21, Note 8.
6. Shortly after the appearance of *Germ* 2 on 31 January 1850, Edward William Cox (1809-79) invited WMR to review art exhibitions for the *Critic* of which he was editor. (Subsequently Cox wrote twice in the *Critic* on the *Germ*; *PRBJ*, p. 220.) Although Cox was unable to pay contributors, WMR willingly agreed, noting in *PRBJ*, p. 51, the advantages to the PRB: "it would enable us to review the exhibitions in our own feeling, and might besides lead to some other literary employment." WMR's first art notice appeared on 15 February 1850, and was followed during the next six months by at least a dozen others (see "Checklist"), after which he resigned to become art critic of the *Spectator*. F. G. Stephens succeeded him, but by [21 January 1851] Cox was complaining of him to WMR. (See also Cox to WMR [14 March 1851], quoted in *PRBJ*, p. 245.) On 3 October 1851, Cox offered WMR seven shillings a column if he would resume writing the art notices. WMR declined, suggesting Deverell instead (Cox to WMR, 15 December 1851), but there is no evidence that Deverell wrote for the *Critic* (AP).

As early as 1 April 1850, and regularly through 1851, WMR also contributed literary reviews. Although R. N. Dunbar's *The Nuptials of Barcelona; a Tale of Priestly Frailty and Spanish Tyranny* (2d ed., 1851) was representative of the books sent for review, he reviewed as well P. J. Bailey's *The Angel World*, T. L. Beddoes's *Death's Jest-Book*, and Meredith's *Poems* (1851).

7. By Tennyson.

8. *Mariana* (Bennett 1967, No. 30), *The Return of the Dove to the Ark* (Bennett 1967, No. 32), and *The Woodman's Daughter* were exhibited at the R.A., 1851.

9. *Valentine Rescuing Sylvia from Proteus*, from *The Two Gentlemen of Verona*, was exhibited at the R.A., 1851; but *Claudio and Isabella* (Bennett 1969, No. 17), from *Measure for Measure* not until 1853.

10. Probably the *Borgia* watercolor (Surtees 48), which was not exhibited until 1883.

11. *The Banishment of Hamlet*, National Institution, 1851.

12. Mentioned several times in *PRBJ*, but not otherwise identified by Fredeman.

13. Allingham's *Poems* (1850) was dedicated to Hunt. In an introductory note to "New Books Speaking for Themselves," *Leigh Hunt's Journal*, 7 December 1850, pp. 7-8, Hunt wrote of Allingham that "a more genuine young poet, or one more certain of fame, has not appeared even in these poetical days." He reprinted *Frost in the Holidays*, p. 9. In subsequent numbers Allingham published several poems: *Lonely Ruin* (14 December 1850, p. 22); *The Magic Cup* (21 December 1850, p. 38); *Evey* and *The Cottagers* (25 January 1851, pp. 119-20); and a story, "The Wedding Ring," 18 January 1851, pp. 105-8.

20. TO FREDERIC GEORGE STEPHENS

38 Arlington Street,
Tuesday,
[18 January 1851]

Dear Stephens,

To so punctilious a P.R.B. as yourself I need scarcely write on such an occasion. But, to keep my secretarial character unspotted from the world, I remind you that St. Agnes' Eve, Friday, is a P.R.B. night at your house. To the rest I have written, according to the vows.

I may as well take this opportunity of informing you — if you have not already become aware of the fact — that the *Spectator*, among other papers, has discontinued its admission-tickets, in the wake of the rather foolish and uncalled for hubbub that hurtles among the editorial and managerial interests. This is my excuse for being so unlucky as to have failed in fulfilling my promise as to the Wellington diorama.[1]

W. M. Rossetti

MS: Bodleian.

1. "Campaign of the Duke of Wellington," Gallery of Illustration, Regent Street.

21. TO WILLIAM ALLINGHAM

38 Arlington Street,
21 March 1851

Dear Allingham,

I am sending you the *Fable for Critics*[1] and a volume [con][2]taining two of Darley's[3] Tragedies. [The fo]rmer belongs to Hunt, but, as there's [noth]ing like appropriation, will [you] return it to me: the latter [m]y brother has read, and thinks very [hi]ghly of. His *Sylvia* I have myself [w]aded through — if one can talk [of] wading through the very essence of shallowness: and I know it to be

20

without exception the most foolish and petty futility that ever stagnated into rhyme. I believe I can borrow it for you: but will wait your verdict on the tragedies. For the other books you ask for: — the *Bigl[ow] Papers* I have missed for some whi[le.] Poe's works and the *Fool's Tragedy*[4] a[re] out, but you shall have the version: Beddoes's *Brides' [Tragedy]* — (to my great regret since rea[ding] the *Fool's*, although, when I read *it*, [I] thought it very poor) — we appe[ar] to have lost: the others we ha[ve] never had. Who is C. R. Kenne[dy?][5] The Blakes etc. came quite safe[ly].

I cannot remember any London review of Kenealy's book — your original verdict whereon was "the spluttering of conceited rascality." The other night, I heard Oxenford, the *Times* theatrical and musical critic, and general playwright,[6] a very lively and clever man, express high admiration of it: in my response to [whi]ch I cannot claim to have [r]ivalled your emphatic "trash."

The *Literary Gazette* has not [ye]t come across me: but I have [lo]ng purposed investing in the No. [for] February 8, observing that it delivers [i]tself concerning you.[7] Your experience of the *Critic* will not, I suspect, be very favouring. There was a pitiful review of Mrs. Browning a month or so ago,[8] the last master touch to whose "despicableness" is given by its being by a slavish prig from the *Spectator.*

Have you seen Ruskin's new book?[9] It is admirably outspoken, and ought to be practically useful — more than his previous wor[ks.] A pamphlet nominally "on the Construction of Sheepfolds" accompa[nies] it:[10] — a searching denunciation [of] priestism. I suppose the first wi[ll] occupy Patmore for some time t[o] come. He is by no means incli[ned] to acquiesce in Ruskin's theories without debate.

A few artistic news-scraps may be strung together to finish with, — as dry as beaded eggs: nor am I certain whether others may not have possessed you of them already. Gabriel will not [e]xhibit. Woolner has a monument to do for Wordsworth's tomb — satis[fac]tory enough; and, equally so, has [j]ust had sittings from Carlyle, and proposes to send his medallion [fro]m him to the exhibition.[11] Hunt's picture[12] is amazing in colour: it will take the shine in a double sense out of such as may have the misfortune to hang near it; and out of his critics too, I should hope. Millais will be ready with three pictures;[13] Deverell with one from *Hamlet* — his rustication after the death of Polonius; Stephens, I suspect, with none. My occupation, as you may have seen perhaps by the *Critic*, consists partly in grinning or sickening over volumes of jingle, and giving a helping hand to the smash which their own inh[e]re[nt] properties necessitate.

My seal — after which you so solicitously enquire — I take to represen[t] (to a vivid imagination, that is), a rock and an anchor: but one enjoys the pleasure of spatiating over organic and inorganic nature before formin[g] an opinion. Perhaps the anchor refers to m[y] hope of succeeding at last.

Truly yours,
W. M. Rossetti

MS: Illinois.

1. By James Russell Lowell, published in 1848, the same year as his *Biglow Papers*, 1st ser., mentioned below.

21

2. MS. damaged. I have restored in square brackets parts of words, and in a few cases entire words.

3. George Darley (1795-1846), Irish poet, whose pastoral drama *Sylvia* was published in 1827.

4. *Death's Jest-Book or the Fool's Tragedy* by Thomas Lovell Beddoes, published posthumously in 1850. His *Brides' Tragedy* appeared in 1822.

5. Charles Rann Kennedy (1808-67), lawyer, classical scholar, versifier.

6. John Oxenford (1812-77) also translated Spanish and German literature, and popularized in England the philosophy of Schopenhauer.

7. To the effect that Allingham could do better things if he would first "deal rigorously with himself" (pp. 111-12).

8. 1 February 1851, pp. 60-62, signed E. W. C. The reviewer prefaced his unfavorable assessment of Mrs. Browning by proclaiming himself one of those "who fill the important office of guiding and informing the public taste."

9. *Stones of Venice*, 1, published 3 March 1851.

10. Published 6 March.

11. The Wordsworth monument was a *Memorial Tablet with Medallion Portrait* for Grasmere Church, R.A., 1852. Woolner was dissatisfied with the Carlyle medallion and did not exhibit it in 1851. He modeled others, the first of which was exhibited at the R.A. in 1852 (*TW*, pp. 336-37; Graves).

12. *Valentine Rescuing Sylvia from Proteus*.

13. See Letter 19, Note 8.

22. TO JOHN LUCAS TUPPER

Tuesday,
3 June [1851]

Dear Tupper,

You were not far out in your conjecture as to my where and whatabouts on Saturday. I spent that and next day at Hammersmith, with a row to Richmond; so that your note did not reach me till dusk on Sunday.

This need not of course have prevented me from meeting you yesterday at the R.A.: but I had to be out in the evening with Gabriel (at the lady's whom you may have heard him designate as "the domestic Glyn,"[1] or "the godlike stunner") — and could not make it convenient to leave office earlier than usual.

Have you seen Ruskin's second letter?[2] A Clencher, isn't it?

Yours,

W. M. Rossetti

MS: Leeds.

1. DGR greatly admired the actress Isabella Dallas Glyn (1823-89). "Miss Glyn is godlike," he wrote to WMR after seeing her in Leigh Hunt's *Legend of Florence* in 1850 (DW, 1:92). "The domestic Glyn" was probably his future wife, Elizabeth Eleanor Siddal (1829-62).

2. On the Pre-Raphaelites in the *Times*, 30 May 1851.

23. TO WILLIAM BELL SCOTT

38 Arlington Street,
4 December [1851]

Dear Scott,

I have delayed too long answering your letter; and, now that I do so at last, am still at fault regarding what should have been the most important item of communication. You ask how I am to send the books I promised. The means, doubtless, might be compassed: but to my shame I confess that I have utterly forgotten *what* the books were, and no effort hitherto has brought me any nearer to the recollection. As to your returning *Sordello*,[1] I only hope you will reconcile yourself to keeping it a little longer, and determine to lose — or, as I think, gain — some leisure hours in mastering it. If you can make up your mind to beginning it over again, I fancy that the delight you would find in the earlier portions, now that the bristling asperity of the first reading has subsided, would *impulse* you triumphantly to a conclusion. You and Browning have the common vantage ground of unintelligibility to the *Athenaeum*,[2] which, I suspect, is halfway to a mutual intelligibility. Talking of Browning, I remember that Allingham tells me, in a letter I had from him recently, that Browning wrote him "a very kind note" about his volume.[3]

Have you seen this month's *Fraser's*? There is a cleverly written article on the poems of the year, in which a tragedy named *Violenzia*[4] is well spoken of, after having been very summarily dismissed by the general critic-pen at the time of its appearance, in terms, however, which raised a suspicion that there must be good in it. I shall shortly send you a No. of the *Critic*, in which "a new Glasgow poet" is discovered: — one Alexander Smith,[5] who, it seems, has sent some poems in MS. to the editor. There is some unquestionable ability and power of language in the extracts: but the whole had a *faux air* of Bailey's *Festus*, with frequent traces of other influences as well. I suppose, however, you are not yet quite recovered from the *Lily and the Bee*:[6] so that it may be prudent to delay the aspirant Smith till the lapse of time shall have relieved you from being "dark with excessive light."[7]

Dr. Samuel Brown[8] I met, one night only, at Patmore's, and found him very amiable and informing, with considerable range of mind and power of conversation. We "homologated" — to use his favourite term — at least, on my side, if that be not a bull. Hannay,[9] Hunt, and Millais, met him the same evening as myself.

Of the Ronges[10] I have not seen anything since my return to town; and of the Eppses[11] only on the evening when I acquitted me of Mrs. Scott's[12] commission. Will you tell Mrs. Scott, by the by, that my sisters find Mrs. Epps a "most fascinating" (unconsciously fascinating) woman: which verdict, I suspect, will occasion some amusement, mingled with sympathetic pleasure. But, indeed, I think Mrs. Epps *is* delightfully amiable.

Is Mrs. Scott again "in communion" with the Church Catholic Apostolic Roman? Or has she pardoned my heresies concerning "atrocious humbug"? The Countess Hahn-Hahn,[13] she may have observed, since the transit "from Babylon to Jerusalem," is said "to squeak and gibber in the Berlin streets" in sackcloth and hideousness. There are some strong things about Rome in Kingsley's *Yeast*[14] — which I have just read. Carlyle's thunderous utterances on religion in general, in the *Life of Sterling*, I suppose you have read.

As regards the beetle-prescription, for which Mrs. Norquoy[15] has a right to take out a writ against me, I find it to be of absurdly simple, and, I believe, familiar construction: — namely, a modicum of porter placed in some vessel whence escape is impracticable to the scarabee that has once been tempted in.

Our servant did really clear the kitchen at Charlotte Street by this means; and she has been similarly successful here. We have also tried it in the parlour, whither the black horrors have made incursion — and "with results"; whether final I know not yet.

What say you of the "Prince President"?[16] — "Oh! for a reign of terror!" seems at whiles to be the humanest aspiration just now.

Will you remember me at home, and to Mr. Budden[17] or anyone else who may possibly bear my name in mind; and pray, when you write again, enable me to clear my conscience as to the promised books. All here desire their kindest remembrances to Mrs. Scott and yourself.

Most truly yours,
W. M. Rossetti

MS: Arizona.

1. "Browning's noble (though sometimes desultory) poem of *Sordello*, so fascinating to the days of my youth" (*SR*, 2:481). WBS to WMR, 1 November 1851: "One becomes savage, even to cursing and swearing, on meeting with a work of power and penetration nullified in its effect, — at the same time that its demands on the attention are exorbitant, — by external artistic peculiarity. Browning's peculiarities are however not merely external. Tortuous writhing has become the natural motion of his soul. I wonder what he does or says when he wants more sugar to his tea" (Durham).

2. An unfavorable review of WBS's *Memoir of David Scott* appeared in the *Athenaeum*, 30 March 1850, pp. 339-41. A review of Browning's *Christmas Eve and Easter Day* on 6 April 1850, pp. 370-71, dismissed it as doggerel.

3. *Poems* (1850).

4. By William Caldwell Roscoe. "This Year's Song Crop," *Fraser's Magazine*, 44 (December 1851), 618-34, reviewed by Charles Kingsley (*Wellesley*, 2:414).

5. "A New Poet in Glasgow," 1 December 1851, pp. 567-68, by George Gilfillan, who is identified as the reviewer in *Poetical Works of Alexander Smith*, ed. William Sinclair, 1909, p. xii. Smith's *A Life Drama* appeared in the *Critic*, 1 March-1 December 1852.

6. Samuel Warren, *The Lily and the Bee. An Apologue of the Crystal Palace* (1851).

7. "Dark with excessive bright" (*Paradise Lost*, 3:380).

8. (1817-56), chemical researcher, who, after his failure to obtain the chair of Chemistry at Edinburgh in 1843, devoted himself to "realizing experimentally his doctrine of the atomic constitution of bodies" (*DNB*).

9. James Hannay (1827-73), novelist and journalist (see the bibliography in Worth). Although WMR is mildly disparaging about Hannay's character in *SR*, 1:163-64, there are no signs of disapproval in his letters. WMR gave Hannay's novel, *Singleton Fontenoy, RN*, a generous review in the *Critic*, 15 November 1850, pp. 554-55.

10. Johannes and Bertha Ronge, of whom WMR gives this account in *SR*: "Ronge, a native of Silesia, was a Catholic priest who towards 1849, getting disgusted with some ecclesiastical impostures regarding a renowned relic, 'the Holy Coat of Treves,' went about denouncing this chicanery, and for a while was talked of as almost a new Luther. He was excommunicated and disfrocked, or possibly he abjured Catholicism of his own accord. He came to England, having in his company Mrs. Ronge, a German lady, who ... had left or been divorced by her original husband, and had joined lots with the iconoclastic reformer. Mr. and Mrs. Ronge were at one time in Newcastle; and Mrs. Scott, with her passion for sidelights upon the faith, would not be contented without making their acquaintance" (1:134).

11. John Epps (1805-69), homeopathic physician, writer and lecturer on homeopathy; friend of Mazzini. WBS introduced Epps and his wife Ellen (d. 1876) to the Rossettis, Mrs. Scott having been a school friend of Mrs. Epps (*SR*, 1:133).

12. Letitia Margery Scott (1813-98), "a sprightly little woman, constantly talking in a pattering sort of way.... She had a knack at pirouetting round religious subjects, and she tried her luck in every doctrinal camp, from secularism to Roman Catholicism" (*SR*, 1:132).

13. Ida, Countess Hahn-Hahn gave an account of her conversion to the Church of Rome in *From Babylon to Jerusalem* (1851) and *From Jerusalem* (1852). In a preface to the latter, the translator of

both volumes, Elizabeth Atcherley, denied "the story that has recently run the course of the English newspapers, of her wandering about the most public streets of Berlin, covered with sackcloth and ashes" (p. vi).

14. Published anonymously in 1851.

15. Mrs. Scott's mother, "a rather formal but affable dame of the old school, whose prosaic utterances and outlook upon life formed an amusing interlude" to those of WBS (*SR*, 1:132).

16. Napoleon III, Charles Louis Napoleon Bonaparte (1808-73), whose *coup d'état* of 2 December 1851 dissolved the French Assembly. On 20 December he was elected President for a ten-year term.

17. W. H. Budden was employed in the Newcastle locomotive works of Robert Stephenson & Co. WMR describes him as "a man of some literary taste and aptitude" (*RRP*, p. 159).

24. TO WILLIAM BELL SCOTT

38 Arlington Street,
8 February 1852

Dear Scott,

Your *Bede*[1] (which I return) is an exceedingly impressive poem. I admire it highly — both in the general scope, the conduct, and the means of presentment. Of the first I have nothing but perfect acquiescence to express: on the last, as you ask my opinion, I shall hold myself absolved of impudence in saying what occurs to me.

The opening is very striking. Awful it should of course be — as you have made it: but I think one or two lines are almost too near the horrible. I remember two lines in Browning's *Christmas Eve* — something about "the last drops of blood — at the desiccated brain's white roots"[2] — about which Woolner has often expressed to me a feeling of real physical pain and horror. I don't by any means go the full length he does in that instance, nor in the present or similar instances: but I think the lines

> Scraping the mud out, and pouring in brain —

and

> And, conjured from far parts, I feel,
> Working hither like screws of steel,
> Fragments of hands and toes, —

will be generally found too powerful.[3] As regards the first, too, I have another doubt. As the resuscitation of consciousness takes place through physical means — Bede, when reawakened, being a recomposed man, and not a disembodied spirit — I doubt if he ought to be *aware* of the "pouring in brain," the repossession whereof must constitute his means of perception.

The descriptive passage beginning on p. 4[4] is glorious: so indeed is the whole of that page with its old human allusion; as again the reference to "Alfin" — and other touches elsewhere of the like kind. Greatly do I feel the vivid truth and terseness of the feet

> that so oft have left their prints
> Sea-filled on sands.

The "antiphone"[5] that follows stands out finely and appropriately as the most flowing and sounding passage of versification in the poem.

I am not quite certain about the lines where Bede speaks of not having realized his beliefs in heaven or purgatory. They come in finely as poetry, and strike the imagination: but I think they will be understood — and must perhaps logically be taken — to express, as a result of actual experience, that his beliefs were ill-founded. This question, I conceive, you have no intention to raise *quoad* Bede, whose status quo is rejected for us, but not for him as he had lived.

Either through one of those obstinate fits of stupidity which come over one at times, and which, when removed, seem unaccountable, — or through real obscurity of expression — I don't understand the lines about the "ravishing music from the pavement-stone."[6] I ought not to have confessed this to you till I had consulted Gabriel or Woolner — who could probably have cleared matters up: but, not having had the poem long, I have not done this yet. Shortly after, I observe the rhyme "lights" and "bright":[7] and further on, there are "foul" and "spoil,"[8] to which Budden has suggested an improvement which does "the syntax spoil."

On p. 15 — "As if struck down by an iron flail" is, I suspect, introduced for rhyme's sake.[9] The last line but 2 in the poem I should prefer in the same length as the rest of the passage;[10] and I notice that in one or two places, as in the lines

> Bishop and Master! — There he stands
> With rosy gills unchastened and large hands —

you make the change of meter occur in the middle of a couplet, whereas to my ear it would come better with the new rhyme.[11] But these are points of *taste* the statement of which to you from me is perhaps somewhat out of place.

Gabriel and I went yesterday to the private view of the British Institution — (to give you a word or two about which I have delayed sending your poem): and we were both delighted with your picture.[12] Do you agree with us in thinking it the best work of art you have produced? I scarcely suppose you will be glad to hear that it is so much the best thing in the place as to be the only good one — (among subject pictures). Notwithstanding this, it is not on the line: but it is *immediately* above so that I need not say it is much better hung than your last year's works were either at B.I. or R.A.[13] What can I tell you of the Exhibition beyond what your experience in past times informs you of already? In walking through it yesterday, we agreed that it was poorer than ever: but on reflection I don't suppose it was. To say that it was much the same as ever is condemnation enough. I need not dilate further on so empty a topic, as you will see in the next *Spectator* all I can spin out of it.

North's[14] acquaintance with Dennys[15] has resulted in the following blowing of trumpets. I should premise, if you are not aware of the fact, that North is bringing out a *North's Monthly Magazine*, price 2d.: in No. 2 whereof appears "The Confessions of a Pin," with exordium as follows: "We extract the foregoing sketch from a book of the highest literary merit and philosophical import, bearing the significant title of the *Alpha*, or first principle etc. Meanwhile, we warn the reader not to mistake a furtive philosopher for a mere philosophizing humanist. The Author of the *Alpha* is a man of strong and original genius, and we cordially recommend his book to our more thoughtful readers."

You may guess from the above that North is obliged to you for giving him occasion to know Dennys. In this 2nd No. of the Magazine,[16] by the by, appear Woolner's *From Thaw to Frost*, and a blow up of the Admiralty by Hannay — the names of both authors — to their horror, as I have reason to conjecture — being attached in full.

Turning to your Christmas letter — to see if any questions remain to be answered — I find one about the Ruskin article in the *Spectator*.[17] You are quite right in supposing it not mine: — but your surmise must have been dictated by considerable critical acumen — for I had looked the article over, and Gabriel, though he knew it was not to be mine, fancied on reading it that it must be. I got an architectural friend, as being more competent, to indite the article.

The "gifted Gilfillan" has been delivering himself concerning Tennyson in the *Critic*,[18] and treats him with the natural superiority of so great a soul over "a minor poet." Whom do you think he puts forward as Tennyson's superior? Thomas Aird!![19] He has also a hit against "a writer whom we have detected in various periodicals by the train of misty nonsense and persevering flattery with which he pursues the path of Tennyson," and who "has written an infinite deal of nothing on his versification." Is not this Patmore? What ineffable feelings would not his be towards the Bard of the Bible if he saw these lines.

Budden wrote me a third letter not long ago, telling me the subject of your new picture.[20] I hope to see it at the Academy. Please remember me to him if you have the opportunity.

I have not much P.R.B. news to tell you. Gabriel's picture[21] progresses: but I never see it, as he hates anyone to see or enquire after what he does while he is doing it. Hunt and Millais will come out in strength,[22] I assure you. Did you hear that the latter gained the prize (£50) at the Liverpool Academy for his last year's picture — which he has sold to boot?[23] And that two of the Directors of said Academy resigned in consequence, indignant at the shame done to art and artists by the award? Is not this good? And better still through the fact that Ansdell[24] was one of the protestors, — a man who had hitherto behaved in rather a friendly manner towards Hunt. But it seems he was an exhibitor.

Of course you know (better than I do) — what I see announced in the *Athenaeum*[25] — that a special department is being organized in the Board of Trade for the supervision of the Schools of Design? Is this for better or worse?

There is to be a conversazione on Wednesday of the Society of Friends of Italy[26] — which I purpose attending. Mazzini is to lecture.

I believe I have cleared off my rather long arrear of news: so with my best remembrances to Mrs. Scott and Mrs. Norquoy, believe me

Yours,
W. M. Rossetti

MS: Arizona.

1. *Bede in the Nineteenth Century*, "Being a Monologue of that industrious scholar, resuscitated at the call of Cardinal Wiseman, in his Discourse on the opening of Hartlepool Church, August 1851"; published in *Poems* (1854).

2. "With the lurking drop of blood that lies / In the desiccated brain's white roots" (*Christmas Eve and Easter Day*, 18:6-7).

3. The single line was revised; the poem begins:

> Ah, holy Christ! who calls me now,
> Straining the skin back over this brow —
> Drawing and cording together the bones
> With strings of nerve among sand and stones?

The three line passage was retained.

4. Beginning of Scene 2.

5. Beginning of Scene 3.

6. Retained.

7. Revised to read: "cells made bright / By magic flames withouten candles, white."

8. Retained. "Now no transcriber's fingers foul / The sheepskin or the Latin spoil!"

9. Revised to read: "As if under the wind of an iron flail."

10. "Drowning my new brave Life: I'm cast" (1854).

11. Revised to read: "Cardinal, master! there he stands, / With rosy face and large red hands."

12. *Boccaccio's Visit to Dante's Daughter.* WMR praised it in the *Spectator* as "the only intellectual treatment in the rooms.... The accessories of the picture — the costumes and antique furniture, the sunny background, and the painted and curtained arches of the chamber — have been studied with evident accuracy, and contribute sensibly to the unstrained and natural aspect of the whole" (28 February 1852, p. 206).

13. *The Fatal Sisters Selecting the Doomed in Battle* (British Institution); *The Trial of Sir William Wallace in Westminster Hall* (R.A.).

14. William North (1824-54), novelist, poet, editor, was introduced to WMR by James Hannay. He was "involved in the early planning stages of the *Germ*" (*PRBJ*, p. 196).

15. Edward Nichols Dennys published *The Alpha, or first principles of the human mind* in 1851.

16. No copy of *North's Monthly Magazine* has been located (see *PRBJ*, p. 226).

17. A review of *Stones of Venice*, 1; and *Examples of the Architecture of Venice* (*Spectator*, 20 December 1851, Supplement, p. 5). The reviewer was probably John Pollard Seddon (1827-1906), whose *Progress in Art and Architecture* was published in 1852. WMR reviewed volumes 2 and 3, *Spectator*, 23 July 1853, Supplement, pp. 5-6; 8 October 1853, pp. 974-75.

18. A review of *In Memoriam*, signed Apollodorus, 2 February 1852, p. 172.

19. Thomas Aird (1802-76), Scottish poet and newspaper editor.

20. *The Haunted House on Allhallows Eve*, R.A., 1852, praised by WMR in the *Spectator* as a "well-felt fairy treatment" (15 May 1852, p. 472).

21. *Giotto Painting the Portrait of Dante* (Surtees 54).

22. At the R.A., 1852, Hunt exhibited *The Hireling Shepherd* (Bennett 1969, No. 22). Millais exhibited *Ophelia, A Huguenot, on St. Bartholomew's Day*, and *Mrs. Coventry Patmore* (Bennett 1967, Nos. 34, 35, 37).

23. Hunt, not Millais, was awarded the £50 prize at the Liverpool Academy in 1851 for *Valentine Rescuing Sylvia from Proteus*. The picture was bought by Francis McCracken, the Belfast shipper, who was one of the earliest patrons of the Pre-Raphaelites. WMR reported the prize in the *Spectator* as "one of the most 'advanced' signs of the times [which] shoots meteorlike from the provinces across the London fog which encrusts Trafalgar Square," the latter a reference to the recent election of Frank Stone as R.A. Of the four elections that year WMR calls Stone's "the most objectionable" (15 November 1851, p. 1098).

24. Richard Ansdell (1815-85), Liverpool sporting and animal painter; president of the Liverpool Academy, 1845-46 (Wood).

25. 7 February 1852, p. 172.

26. "Its object was, by public meetings, lectures, the press, and especially by promoting the publication of works on the history of the Italian national movement, to foster a correct appreciation of the Italian question in England" (H. W. Rudman, *Italian Nationalism and English Letters* [1940], p. 97). The council of the Society included J. A. Froude, Leigh Hunt, W. S. Landor, G. H. Lewes, and W. J. Linton.

25. TO WILLIAM BELL SCOTT

38 Arlington Street,
Thursday,
25 March [1852]

Dear Scott,

The enclosed is "Woolner's last." He told me the other night that he had had a letter from you, and I advised him to send you the poem[1] with his answer. Finding him too lazy, and being confident that you will like to see it, and like it, when seen, I offered to supply his place. It appears to me a really most remarkable thing, full of the man's strong antagonistic honesty and personality, and bristling with vigorous expression. He showed it to Mrs. Carlyle — not daring to let Thomas himself know that he commits poetry — and she was considerably struck with it. By the by, at the one meeting of the Society of Friends of Italy which I have attended — when Mazzini lectured — I saw Mrs. Carlyle; who struck me as being something like Mrs. Scott, though on a larger scale, and with something too of her vivacity of manner. Of Woolner I may add — as I suppose the accustomed Woolnerian interval will elapse before you hear from him — that he will have as many as six works in the next R.A.,[2] including his Westminster Abbey competition monument to Wordsworth, and the medallion-head of Carlyle. It is to be hoped this appearance of his will bring him some of that publicity he has so long made art a claim, intellectually, to achieve.

Gabriel showed me, only the other day, a letter of yours in which you had enclosed some prospectus (if I remember rightly) of democratic tendency, for my behoof. Of course, Gabriel could not lay his hands upon it. I divined the *Linton*[3] *foot*. Was I correct? I should be rather glad to see the document, if you have another to spare.

Did you see in the *Athenaeum* of a few weeks ago a tardy notice of *Prince Legion*?[4] Its importance was not such as the delay might have justified: but, from some critics, the less they say the better compliment and the more satisfactory review.

Of course you are aware that Herbert's secession from the School of Design is traceable to the Cole[5] installation. Some highly unparliamentary expressions of the former in reference to the latter, immediately preceding his resignation, have been repeated to me: but I forget them. Deverell Senr.[6] also gets on arduously under the new regime: and the junior Deverell, who has resigned his morning mastership for an anticipated evening class, which does not seem in a hurry to make its appearance, tells me that, as Cole has really no functions to discharge, his appointment is equivalent to a *carte blanche* to meddle, intrude, and make mischief. In short, I suppose he will turn out an omnipresent Poynter[7] — a "native overbrooding" humbug, as well as a "foreign interloping" mediocrity.

Of what sort are the prospects of your Newcastle exhibition? I suppose you count on receiving many pictures from this year's London exhibitions. The Suffolk Street Gallery will (I think) have its private view on Saturday. Anthony[8] will be in great strength: and he has a picture for the R.A. — a view from Windsor forest — one of the most extraordinary pieces of nature possible. He is in some trepidation as to its hanging — especially as Creswick[9] is said to be on the committee (with, as I understand, Leslie and Redgrave[10]).

But the P.R.B. pictures will be the thing. Millais's are an immense advance: indeed, the only expression I can give to my belief of them is that they are perfect, and of the noblest order of perfection. The death of Ophelia (his chief work) is the idealism of loveliness — in the P.R. sense of idealism: and the head of Ophelia beautiful enough, I hope and incline to believe, to satisfy even the swinish critic-mind. The other picture is an incident of St. Bartholomew's Day: A Huguenot gentleman resisting the entreaties of his mistress, a Catholic lady, who urges him to wear the white scarf, the badge of Catholicism. This is no less wonderful: indeed, of the two, Gabriel likes it the better. He will send also, at Patmore's desire, a small portrait of Mrs. Patmore. Hunt's picture is quite as excellent as either of Millais's. It is an illustration of the Fool's catch in *King Lear*,

> Sleepest or wakest thou, jolly shepherd?
> Thy sheep be in the corn — etc.

and has a manful feeling of nature in it truly refreshing. He has another work in hand — a Christian symbolic one[11] — but there is some doubt whether it will be ready.

Is all this a twice-told tale? Perhaps so.

Millais's Carpenter's Shop[12] and *Mariana* are now in Edinburgh — as probably you know. I saw a notice (in the Scottish Press, I think) of moderate good sense and qualified admiration: and Gabriel tells me there is one, very well-written and appreciative, in the *Scotsman*.[13] Have you any knowledge of the authorship?

I am very anxious to see your elvish picture[14] — of which Budden gave me an expectation-raising description. I suppose we are safe to see it in the Academy.

I have just read Mrs. Crowe's[15] *Night Side of Nature* — excessively interesting and entertaining. Never having myself been a *dis*believer in ghosts, it has not added much to my receptivity on the subject: but it contains many most extraordinary things which it would tax the subtlest to explain on any physical theory. Unfortunately, the book is almost wholly unauthenticated. Names of persons known to the authoress are not given, and even the books she quotes from — and which she often affirms to be of indubitable authority — not often cited in any satisfactory manner. The reader may be quite willing to believe that Mrs. Crowe is right in claiming credibility for the sources of her narratives: but, in such a matter, it was surely incumbent on her to place the reader in a position, as far as possible, to verify her assertions.

My eye was caught the other day by some statement in the paper as to the restoration of fine old Hexham Abbey church. But there was some ominous proposal in connexion with it to pull down the Lady Chapel.[16] What does that imply? Is the chapel part of the old building? and have they stuck fast in restoration at a point which compels them not only to desist but to destroy? That would be pitiful indeed.

I have talked long enough now, I suppose: and it is dangerous to talk solo without the corrective of the *visible* satiety of the hearer, in case such exists. With my most cordial remembrances, therefore, to Mrs. Scott and Mrs. Norquoy, believe me

Yours,

W. M. Rossetti

In talking of the P.R.B. pictures, I should not have forgotten Brown's[17] Christ washing the Apostles' feet[18] — in intellectual respects chiefly admirable, and the best specimen as yet of his pictorial resources. He will also have one — if not two — more.

MS: Arizona.

1. WBS to WMR, 28 March [1852]: "I got your letter and the *Street Music* of Woolner's Regent's Park reverie, yesterday" (Durham).

2. Reviewed by WMR in the *Spectator*, 19 June 1852, p. 593: *Sketch for a Monument to William Wordsworth* ("the most intellectual work of the collection, and its art is equal to its idea"); two designs for medals, *England Rewards Agriculture* and *Competition of the Lever*, and medallion portraits of Wordsworth, a Lady, and Carlyle ("a speaking likeness of the man — not taken from the features outward only, but from the soul inwards; stern, impetuous, gigantically strong, and sad as only a great human soul can be").

3. William James Linton (1812-97), engraver, poet, radical, was a friend of WBS who introduced him to the Rossettis. "My brother appreciated his professional skill without concerning himself in his politics, which were more in my line" (*SR*, 2:327).

4. *Chorea Sancti Viti, or Steps in the Journey of Prince Legion*, Twelve Designs by W. B. Scott; *Athenaeum*, 28 February 1852, p. 257. WMR reviewed it in the *Spectator*, 5 July 1851, p. 644.

5. Henry Cole (1808-82), "a great public servant" (C. R. Fay, *Palace of Industry, 1851* [1951], p. 4), conceived and organized with Prince Albert the Great Exhibition. He was first director of the Victoria and Albert Museum, and as Felix Summerly was active as an "Art-Manufacturer" and promoter of children's books. In 1849 he suggested to the Select Committee inquiring into the government Schools of Design that they should be placed under the control of a newly created department of the Board of Trade. This reorganization was carried out early in 1852 with Cole as head (Q. Bell, *The Schools of Design* [1963], pp. 248-49). WBS to WMR, 19 February 1852: "As to Cole's appointment, I wait information. There is rebellion in the camp, and some say the Government Schools of Design are disgraced and all the functionaries with them by the appointment of Felix Summerly. The best of it is the very day before the announcement of his elevation in the *Times* he was holding a meeting at Bradford, whereat he denounced the Government Schools as 'so called' — and stigmatized them as 'begging institutions' — 'Institutions living on taxation' — etc.: cut vulgar jokes on the Venuses and Germanicuses that for his part he had never seen to have anything to do with designing. This display it has been supposed was an access of bile under the impression that all his agitation had failed to make a berth for himself in the School of Design" (Durham).

6. Walter Ruding Deverell (1801-53), father of W. H. Deverell, was secretary to the School of Design, Somerset House.

7. Ambrose Poynter (1796-1886), architect and art official, was a member of the Council of the Schools of Design and inspector of the branch schools. WBS to WMR, 28 March [1852]: "And the good Ambrose Poynter! never more shall we see him wagging his head at our honoured board! Never more shall the honest old Captain our chairman, express the heretical doubt 'Whether these visits of Mr. Poynter are *really* of much use!' The good Ambrose has made precipitate way for Felix. Verily the latter state of that office may be worse than the first" (Durham).

8. Henry Mark Anthony (1817-86), landscape painter and friend of FMB, studied under the Barbizon painters Corot and Dupré, 1834-40 (Wood). Of his lavish praise of Anthony's landscapes in the *Critic* and *Spectator*, WMR later wrote: "I may have rated them rather too high, in comparison with some other examples of landscape art; but the works which Anthony produced between some such dates as 1847 and 1857, were certainly very remarkable, and stood out saliently from the throng" (*SR*, 1:140-41). In 1852 Anthony exhibited five works at the Society of British Artists, Suffolk Street: *The Village Bridal*; *The Glen at Eve*; *The Ferry, Twilight*; *The Rocky Lane*; *Thoughtful*

Hours; and *Beech Trees and Fern* at the R.A. WMR reviewed them in the *Spectator*, 3 April 1852, p. 327; and 19 June 1852, p. 592.

9. Thomas Creswick (1811-69), landscape painter.

10. Charles Robert Leslie (1794-1859), historical genre painter; Richard Redgrave (1804-88), landscape and genre painter.

11. *The Light of the World* (Bennett 1969, No. 24), R.A., 1854.

12. *Christ in the House of His Parents* (Bennett 1967, No. 26).

13. 3 January 1852. The reviewer was Pauline, Lady Trevelyan (see "The Exhibition of the Royal Scottish Academy, 1852," reprinted in *Selections from the Literary and Artistic Remains of Pauline Jermyn Trevelyan*, ed. David Wooster, 1879, pp. 133-58).

14. *The Haunted House on Allhallows Eve.*

15. Catherine Crowe (1800?-76), novelist and writer on the supernatural. *Night Side of Nature* was published in 1848.

16. The east end of Hexham Abbey was extensively remodeled in the 1850s. Of the Lady Chapel or Chapel of Five Altars, which was demolished, WBS wrote to WMR on 28 March [1852]: "Perhaps you recollect a portion in a very infirm state looking towards the market place? That is the Lady Chapel, situated as usual eastward of the chancel. It is very much later than the cathedral itself, being *perpendicular*, and is cut-off from the interior by a blank wall behind the present altar" (Durham).

17. FMB's (1821-93) name occurs almost as frequently in WMR's letters as DGR's. After WMR's marriage to Lucy Brown the friendship was occasionally strained, but FMB seems to have been as fond of WMR as WMR was of him.

18. *Jesus Washing Peter's Feet* (Bennett 1964, No. 23), R.A., 1852. FMB also exhibited *The Pretty Baa-Lambs* (Bennett 1964, No. 21).

26. TO WILLIAM BELL SCOTT

38 Arlington Street,
Wednesday,
[Early October 1852]

My dear friend,

Truly am I concerned to hear you are not well: but, while I was at Newcastle, we had all noticed the fact, and I scarcely find it in my heart to regret that you are unwell *enough* to compel you to leave smoky atmosphere and "practical art"[1] for indolent recreation and Tynemouth or other country-place — the better (so runs a mental reservation of mine) the nearer London. You will now, I doubt not, be getting daily better, instead of daily worse.

I should — and would — have made response to your letter at once. But the fact is I received it one morning at breakfast just as I was about to start for the city, and, glancing over it, observed the fact of your being at Tynemouth, but not the wherefore. I then stuffed it into my pocketbook, whence I did not take it out for reperusal till this evening.

Gross mists of laziness have gathered round me since my return to London. I have actually not yet delivered the *Pilgrim's Progress*[2] to Mrs. Epps (*proh pudor!*) nor called on the Ronges. Worse still, I have never written to poor old Woolner[3] whose honest and friendly soul will not know what to make of me when, landing in Australia, he shall find the promised letter not awaiting him. This I must see right for mere shame; and will do likewise with my commission to Mrs. Epps with all convenient speed.

News I have little or none. Such items as occur to me I will run over briefly.

Patmore, whom I met this morning in an omnibus, has been back from Edinburgh only a few days: therefore, if you have not seen him already, you need not expect a call from him in the North. Mrs. Patmore is still in the modern Athens, but returns by next week. Hannay too is in a position to say, when he looks out of window, "This is my own, my native land":[4] but of his precise whereabouts I am ignorant, as he left London some fortnight or so ago without our having met for some days.

Gabriel is in a state of (one may say) compulsory inactivity: for he has been this long while looking out for a house without having yet settled on one. He has in his eye, however, very eligible rooms in Hampstead, close to where Brown is staying, and will, I think, very probably take them;[5] on doing which, it is to be calculated upon that he will set to with a will at finishing his picture for next year.

Hunt still sojourns at Hastings; Millais at Hayes, in Kent, where I saw him shortly after my return from Newcastle. He means to get ready two pictures[6] of about the size of the Huguenot — both subjects of his own. I saw the (of course wonderful) wooded background of the one he has begun, which belongs to the time of Charles II. Of the subject I form a conjecture, but have no certain knowledge. His brother[7] has painted a capitally faithful landscape from the same neighbourhood.

Is there any news of the missing Hamlet of Deverell (of whom I have known nought this long while)? and has my Gateshead notice[8] got you into any more hot water?

I observe from your note that Mrs. Scott's kind intentions as to writing to my sisters continue. Will you remember them and myself to her most kindly. Maria is about to migrate, with father and mother, in a day or two, to Brighton — there to remain probably some fortnight or more. We are in hopes that the change and sea-air may do some good to my father's shattered health.

I was to send you, I believe, more books than one, but can only remember one — the poems of Read,[9] the American. I find our copy of the new and collected edition has disappeared; but, unless we get one in decent time, will send you his *Lays and Ballads*, containing many of his principal things. One work that I promised was, I recollect, the poem of Homo,[10] over the advertisement of which we two misanthropes — (that is, *if* I am one, for that you are is a settled point) — laughed so preposterously one day after dinner: but the promise was contingent on the procuring of the book, and that I have, strange to say, pretermitted.

Do not fail to get well as soon as possible, and, when you are well, to be careful of remaining so.

Yours,

W. M. Rossetti

I address to Newcastle, being uncertain whether the mere address of "Tynemouth" would find you easily.

Have you yet read the universal Uncle Tom?[11] It is not stupid, as I expected, but really a talented and remarkable thing.

MS: Arizona.

1. At the Government School of Design, Newcastle.
2. Probably the *Pilgrim's Progress*, With Forty Illustrations by David Scott, engraved by W. B. Scott; reviewed by WMR in the *Spectator*, 1 March 1851, pp. 210-11.
3. Woolner sailed for Australia on 24 July 1852.
4. Hannay was a native of Dumfries.
5. See Letter 28.
6. *The Proscribed Royalist, 1651*, the background of which was painted "in a little wood near Hayes" (J. G. Millais, *Life and Letters of J. E. Millais* [1899], 1:165); and *The Order of Release* (Bennett 1967, No. 38). Both were exhibited at the R.A., 1853.
7. William Henry Millais (1829-99). *Hayes Common*, 1852-53 (Plate 83a in Allen Staley, *The Pre-Raphaelite Landscape*, 1973).
8. "Exhibition of Pictures by Living Artists," *Gateshead Observer*, 28 August 1852, p. 6. The exhibition, arranged by the North of England Society for the Promotion of the Fine Arts, contained "some rubbish and much triviality; but the interspersion of a modicum of good works renders the gallery well worthy of a visit." WMR gave highest praise to FMB's *The Pretty Baa-Lambs*; Deverell's *The Pet Parrot: A Sketch* and *The Morning Salute: A Sketch*; and WBS's six pictures: *Fair Rosamond Alone in the Bower, The Haunted House on Hallowmass [Allhallows] Eve, The Daughters of Odin, A Gleaner, Portrait of Johannes Ronge*, and *Portrait of the Secretary of the Government School of Design in Newcastle*.
9. Thomas Buchanan Read (1822-72), "some of whose pieces were much admired" by DGR (*FLM*, 2:90). *Lays and Ballads* (Philadelphia, 1849) and *Poems* (London, 1852) appear to be the editions referred to.
10. Not identified.
11. Harriet Beecher Stowe's *Uncle Tom's Cabin* was published in London in April 1852.

27. TO FREDERIC GEORGE STEPHENS

38 Arlington Street,
Thursday,
[11 November 1852]

Dear Stephens,

I hereby summon you to Hunt's on Friday the 26th of the present month, when the first revival of our long-forgotten P.R.B. meeting is to take place. He talks of being back in a fortnight.

You have heard of the election of Goodall.[1] The fact roused Millais to reopen the often vexed question of setting up a P.R.B. exhibition, and this was the first cause for the intended meeting. He has been somewhat calmed, however, by Leslie's assurance that his age alone caused his claims to be overlooked.[2]

W. M. Rossetti

I have left Broad Street, and so escaped the irruptions of G. Tupper. I am now at Somerset House.[3]

The penalties enacted against defaulters on P.R.B. nights are to be strictly enforced in the present case.

MS: Bodleian.

1. Frederick Goodall (1822-1904), landscape and genre painter, was elected A.R.A. in 1852 and R.A. in 1863 (Wood). WMR to WBS, 7 November 1852: "Have you heard that the genius Goodall is the elect associate of the R.A.s? Millais, Hunt, and Brown, being candidates. Of these 3, Millais was the only one balloted for. Goodall obtained 7 votes, Millais 5, that pitiful ass young [Henry Hall] Pickersgill, who did a *Romeo and Juliet* in last exhibition, 5, and another (if I remember aright) 3. However, the Academicians, on referring to their books, ascertained the fact that Millais is not yet of

the required age, 24, and decided that he could not be elected. Whether this was done before or after the ballot closed — so that he might otherwise have distanced the mighty Goodall — I know not: but Leslie speaks as if the case were so. Fools are rampant now to a hideous degree among the R.A.s and A.R.A.s, and promise soon to bear down in their 'mud-deluge' all hope of better things'' (Arizona).

2. Hunt to WMR, 3 November 1852: "This alters the affair somewhat, nevertheless, it does not do away with my desire for a meeting — nor, perhaps, altogether the expediency of considering the question above — since they have no excuse for neglecting Brown — and since Goodall will occupy the line which we want for our pictures, and which he must have been driven from, had his election not protected him: besides a body of men who can elect such men as [Frank] Stone, [William] Boxall, Scroggins, Snooks and Goodall shamelessly, must be guarded against, and can scarcely be joined, seeing that the aforesaid muffs will always be in the way of any good we might desire to do when amongst them — so pray send round summonses stating that each member's attendance is required for the consideration of important business — and still send to Brown — for he is virtually a PRB, and a meeting without him, now that Woolner has left us, would be melancholy indeed, (while you were asleep)'' (AP).

3. In 1849 the Excise Board was merged with Stamps and Taxes in a new Board of Inland Revenue, and the staffs were eventually moved from Old Broad Street to Somerset House. George Tupper's printing shop was in Barge Yard, Bucklersbury.

28. TO WILLIAM HOLMAN HUNT

38 Arlington Street,
15 November [1852]

Dear Hunt,

For some days I did not consider it worthwhile to answer your letter, having nothing particular to say: but, having seen the other day the base imbecility in which you indulge in writing to Millais — on the subject of the cat Cadmium — and reflecting that it will be impossible for me at any rate to sink lower than that, I sit down to let you know I still exist.

The subject on which you have convened a P.R.B. meeting is an important and interesting one,[1] and I have engaged Millais and Stephens to come. Brown seems somewhat reluctant to Pre-raphaelize himself, but may probably join after all.

Gabriel's pilgrimages after a studio have at length closed — in Blackfriars. He has found a second floor, in Chatham Place, the last house before Blackfriars Bridge, overlooking the river; one room with a balcony in which he can paint, if necessary. The other has two different aspects: and there is a bedroom as well. The rent is rather high — upwards of £60 with attendance: but the bargain is settled, and we shall move in, I suppose, in a day or two.

Stephens was with us yesterday. He is still doing the discobolus in the blessed antique school.

We shall be most glad to see you again, old fellow; not the less so that we have made up our minds you will not leave for Syria till after the opening of next exhibition at any rate.

W. M. Rossetti

Particular remembrances to Lear,[2] and to Gurney Patmore,[3] when you see him.

MS: Iowa.

1. See Letter 27.

2. Edward Lear (1812-88), topographical watercolorist and humorist, was a lifelong friend of Hunt. In August 1852 WMR joined Hunt and Lear at Fairlight, near Hastings, where they had gone to paint. Lear to WMR, 20 January 1853: "I had a few proofs of my Calabrian Lithographs of which I was going to beg your acceptance, lest you should think I had forgotten how good-naturedly you corrected my proofsheets [of *Journals of a Landscape Painter in Southern Calabria* (1852)] in the autumn" (AP).

3. Brother of Coventry Patmore.

29. TO WILLIAM BELL SCOTT

38 Arlington Street,
10 March [1853]

My dear friend,

I had got just into that state of reprobation regarding correspondence "to you-wards" at which one puts a good face on it, and, determining that one has really not had anything to say, resolves to wait for an occasion, — when your letter comes to show that the day of grace is not yet past. Here goes then for a clearance of the thick underwood of news — or no news — which has had time to grow between us since our last communing.

I have referred back to your former letter (dated, by Jove! the 9th November!!), in which you argue against me the question of printing the *Year of the World*[1] in your forthcoming (?) volume. What you say is convincing, though disappointingly so, and I believe your negative resolve is quite right and prudent. Your amply detailed elucidations of my difficulties in that poem[2] were very welcome, and should have called forth my thanks earlier. You do not now say anything of the new edition: I suppose your etchings[3] have distracted you from the subject of late. Are these yet published? I saw some notice of, or allusion to, them not long ago — I think, in a Scotch paper, but cannot accurately call to mind.

The *Plaint of Liberty*[4] will be a godsend. I have seen quite enough of it in reviews to know that it has real stuff, of admirable quality, in it — although the *Dispatch*[5] calls it the triumph of mediocrity, and *Tait*[6] treats the author as if he were some little schoolboy. I had been pondering the arcanum of its authorship, — and could not divest my mind of some suggestions concerning Tennyson and his rumoured war-paeans,[7] although rationally convinced at bottom that it could not be his. The name of Linton had never occurred to me. He has, I am confident, realized a permanent position by the book, if he choose to acknowledge it. Why should he not do so? He has attached his name already to principles quite as extreme, expressed in a manner yet more aggressive.

Of Woolner we are still without news. Weeks ago we saw in the *Times* that his vessel had arrived on the 25th October; and the Howitts[8] here find by letters from their emigrant relatives (who, you may remember, preceded Woolner's party, but were to have been joined by them) that they (emigrant Howitts) had started from Melbourne for the diggings only a day or two before the arrival of Woolner's ship. Not only have we not heard from Woolner, but no one, as far as we can discover, has heard from anyone of his party — which includes Bateman,[9] the "betrothed" of Annie Howitt.[10] We begin to think it — not indeed alarming, but odd.

There is some good news of Gabriel. One McCracken, of Belfast, who bought Hunt's *Valentine*, has become the purchaser of Gabriel's *Annunciation* picture,[11] simply on the reports he had heard of it from Hunt and others; has given him a £150 commission for a St. John and the Virgin domesticated together after the crucifixion;[12] and has set him in the (as he says) certain way of getting good commissions from Miller[13] of Liverpool. The *Annunciation* was greatly improved before its dispatch for Belfast: the other subject is still *in petto*. Gabriel — perhaps you know — has sent three water-colour designs to an "Exhibition of Drawings and Sketches" in Pall Mall, now in its third year of existence: Giotto painting Dante's portrait, a subject from the *Vita Nuova*, and another — two of them sold, the other Brown's property.[14] He is now redesigning the first for another water-colour,[15] which he is quite certain of selling to McCracken if to no one else. He had thought of getting it ready for the R.A., but there seems little chance of that: and as little of his exhibiting anything else. In fact — whether from a desire, on intelligible personal grounds, to "make the worse appear the better reason,"[16] or from sincere conviction so far as himself is concerned — he now declares that the notion of exhibiting in galleries is altogether a mistake, and that he won't, under any foreseeable circumstances, give in to it. He talks of exhibiting in a kind of private way — as at Colnaghi's,[17] for instance. However this may be — with his present commissions, and the prospect they open of others, his future seems now in his own hands, if he will only use it. He is full of projects of severe study, going to Florence, bringing out the *Vita Nuova* with elaborate etchings, subjects for pictures, etc. Have you heard of the house at Blackfriars Bridge, overlooking the river, where he and I have taken chambers? A jolly place, with capital lights and views, where we shall hope to see something of you in the June evenings.

P.R.B. intelligence of this year is as good as confined to Hunt and Millais; for Gabriel, as you see, will not exhibit; Collins has failed to get ready a large picture from the life of some female saint,[18] and will only, I understand, send a small head; Brown is similarly behindhand with two large modern subjects,[19] and is reduced to a little fireside picture — very nice, however; and Stephens has but a small portrait of his father.[20] (I don't think you know Stephens, by the by, either personally or by reputation — but he *is* one of the P.R.B.) Hunt is to appear with four pictures;[21] possibly one or two others, of a slight character, but I believe not. The chief is illustrative of a symbolic passage in the Apocalypse, — where Christ says that he will enter into the house of such as will admit him, and sup with them. He is seen knocking at the door in the moonlight. This is the picture Hunt is now engaged on, and he does not show it now: consequently I can tell you little positive about it, though confident it will come very fine and impressive. Next is the subject, which I think you have seen, of *Claudio and Isabella*, from *Measure for Measure*, painted for the greater part a year or two ago. Third is the sheep-picture he painted at Hastings — wonderful! wonderful! I assure you, not for truth only, but for poetry, beauty, sentiment, and interest. I incline, and so do we all, to like it the best of all he has done yet. Fourth is a portrait of an Oxford clergyman.

Millais has two pictures,[22] each of about the *Huguenot* dimensions, but rather larger — a *Proscribed Royalist*, of the Commonwealth times, concealed in a hollow tree, and receiving food from the hands of a love-sympathizing Puritan damsel, — and The Ransom of a Gordon, in the '45 troubles, by his wife, from the warden of some English keep. They are both splendidly painted — the second with some flesh perhaps the best I ever saw, and the first with a lovely background. I think, however, there is rather a want of strong purpose and intellectuality in them: they are somewhat too *domestic* perhaps, too much like subjects of the ordinary run painted by the ordinary men. The second will depend altogether on the expression, though, which I know he has conceived excellently; and it may not be quite fair to judge it in its present state with the heads undone. Both subjects are somewhat of the *Huguenot* class, but I think not so high of that class: and I suspect Millais will have to guard against choosing incidents the interest of which centres in one man and one woman sentimentally occupied — and which tend to an *ad captandum* tone. On the whole, I think Hunt will legitimately carry off the higher honours this year. At the same time, his works are not so entirely beyond the snarls of the little critics who don't understand their business as Millais's — who will really, I think, be unassailable on the grounds of "quaintness, unselect nature," and the many other *gags* those gentlemen deal in.

Do you care for a little general R.A. gossip? — for which, by the by, I hope and suppose your pictures are to furnish an item. Leslie has a *Rape of the Lock*,[23] in which Millais is the principal figure: Frith sends a small picture as his diploma-picture — an artist painting an orange-girl:[24] Egg[25] has nothing: Ward,[26] as you may have seen in the *Athenaeum*, will exhibit his Execution of Montrose, destined for the Parliament-house. On the whole, those who swear by the geniuses of this rather small fry seem likely to get what they will call a poor exhibition. Possibly it may be none the worse for that.

Hannay is married[27] — and laid up (or was so a few days ago) with rheumatism, which had assaulted him for a week or two before the happy day: but this latter could not be deferred on account of any such minor considerations, seeing that the bride's family were emigrating *en masse* to Australia, whither they have now started. His edition of Edgar Poe's poems, dedicated to Gabriel,[28] and with a capital prefatory notice, is out. Have you seen it? Patmore is in labour of a new volume[29] — the old poems greatly recast, the *Storm*, and some others — which is to appear within a month or so. I will not answer for his *nose*, not having seen him for some weeks. Masson,[30] that pleasant fine-minded Scotchman, has got elected Professor of English Literature at University College, with flaming testimonials from Carlyle and others. The *Purgatory* of Cayley's Dante-translation is on the eve of publication; and the "new poet," Alexander Smith's volume,[31] is out.

You make no mention of your health: — a grave omission, I should say, were it not that it rather induces me to suppose there is little to say on the subject, and little or no news is good news. We are all well enough: Christina, who goes on ploddingly enough with her drawing studies, not so continuously well as she had been for some while following her return from the country, but still, I am glad to say, far better than she was before.

I had borrowed Collier's[32] Shakespeare emendations, and think them on the whole most valuable: but I cannot say I sympathize with the two you instance. Dogberry's "losses" have just that blundering kind of aptness, I think, which makes that the right word: and the "blanket of the dark" appears to me quite justifiable enough to need no twisting or turning. In some cases the alteration evidences want of poetic feeling: as where, in the song *Who is Sylvia?* — he would change "fair is she" (a repeated rhyme) into "fair as free" — which is worthy of the *Hermit of Warkworth* school.[33] And I think the book is about five or six times its natural size, on the bookmaking principle, I presume. The repetition of "the corrected folio 1632" and such phrases becomes positively annoying: by far the greater part of the suggestions might have been printed in the mere tabular form of an errata, without a word from Mr. Collier. The emendations have been adopted, I may mention, in *Macbeth* as now travestied at the Princess's — firstrate getting-up and degraded acting.[34]

Have you seen Dyce's pamphlet on the National Gallery?[35] It was sent to the *Spectator* with a private note from Cole: which confirms me in interpreting it as a hint of things to come — especially as it comes in so pat to Uwins's[36] resignation of the Keepership. It looks very like a bidding for the post on Dyce's part — and it is to be hoped he may succeed, being probably the most competent man available.

I don't quite understand about Taylor's *Michael Angelo*.[37] Where have you "given him a notice"? I should like to see it.

Will you remember me most kindly to Mrs. Scott and Mrs. Norquoy — also to Miss Glyn,[38] if convenient; and accept our affectionate greetings for yourself and Mrs. Scott.

Yours,

W. M. Rossetti

I find I was not quite right about Woolner's party: as the Howitts have received a letter from Dr. Godfrey Howitt, on whom the intending diggers were to call at Melbourne, saying that Bateman had been there the night before to tea. But there is no mention of anyone else. However, there cannot be a doubt, I should say, that all is well. Being on the subject of that true fellow Woolner, let me subjoin you a sonnet Gabriel wrote in remembrance of him the other day, on the first fall of snow.

Woolner, tonight it snows for the first time.
Our feet knew well the path where, in this snow,
Mine leave one track. How all the ways we know
Are heavy in the long-unwonted rime!

Grey as their ghosts which now, in your new clime,
  Must haunt you, while those singing spirits reap
  All night the fields of hospitable sleep, —
Whose song, past all the sea, finds counterchime.
Can the year change, and I not think of thee,
  With whom so many changes of the year
So many years were watched — our love's degree
Alone the same? Ah! still for thee and me,
  Winter or summer, Woolner, here or there,
One grief, one joy, one loss, one victory.

This leads me to another point — of which, nevertheless, trust me, I had not thought when I introduced the sonnet affair. There was no diplomacy in the matter. The sonnet has been copied into the album of Miss Orme[39] — a sweet young girl, daughter of Patmore's sister-in-law, to whom you were to have been introduced. If you have any scrap you would not mind sending me for the same receptacle, I know it would be accepted as a very kind favour.

And so good-bye; and recover as your constitution will allow you from this huge snowball of gossip launched at you — with a stone too hidden unhandsomely in the middle — as is the custom with our little scamps.

MS: Arizona.

1. *The Year of the World: A Philosophical Poem on "Redemption from the Fall"* (1846). WBS to WMR, 9 November 1852: "Many small poets and critics have really a pique against a man for writing such a poem, and resent it as an insult. A volume of small pieces meets comparatively with favour or at least with a fair field" (Durham).
   2. WMR outlined his problems with the poem in a letter of 7 November 1852 (Arizona).
   3. For the Glasgow Art Union (WBS to WMR, 7 March 1853; Durham).
   4. Published anonymously in 1852. F. B. Smith, *Radical Artisan, William James Linton* (1973), does not claim the book for Linton.
   5. *Weekly Dispatch*, 27 February 1853, p. 134, declared the volume a "splendid specimen of paper, typography, and 'getting up,' in every way, and highly creditable to the printer," G. B. Richardson of Newcastle, but found the poetry "cold, didactic ... a triumphant platitude."
   6. *Tait's Edinburgh Magazine*, March 1853, pp. 186-87.
   7. Most of Tennyson's political poems of early 1852 were published anonymously or pseudonymously (see F.B. Pinion, *A Tennyson Companion* [1984], pp. 155-56).
   8. During the 1850s WMR was friendly with the literary couple Mary (1799-1888) and William (1792-1879) Howitt. Howitt, accompanied by his two sons, sailed for Australia in June 1852, with the triple purpose of visiting his brother Godfrey ("who was successfully established with his family in Melbourne"), joining in a gold dig, and seeking employment for his sons. He returned to England with one of his sons in December 1854 (Mary Howitt, *An Autobiography* [1899], 2:86, 111).
   9. Edward La Trobe Bateman (1816-97) sailed to Australia with Woolner.
   10. Anna Mary Howitt (1824-84), daughter of Mary and William Howitt. In the company of Barbara Leigh-Smith (Bodichon) she studied painting under Kaulbach in Munich, and gave a lively account of her experiences in *An Art Student in Munich* (1854). In the same year she exhibited at the National Institution a subject from Goethe's *Faust* — *Margaret returns home tortured by self-accusation*, which WMR reviewed enthusiastically: "There is none of that ultra-Germanism in the picture which one might have been disposed to predict from Miss Howitt's German studies and enthusiasms, but, on the contrary, an unmistakable adherence to the English Praeraphaelite practice, evidenced in the unconventional simplicity of the figure, the rendering of broad out-door sunshine, and the affectionate care bestowed upon the accessories.... It would be difficult to recall a first picture of more assured promise" (*Spectator*, 18 March 1854, pp. 302-3). Shortly afterwards Miss

Howitt developed an "extreme addiction" to spiritualism and "dropped painting in any form other than 'spirit-drawings'" (*SR*, 1:93, 171). In 1859 she married Alaric Alfred Watts, a colleague of WMR at the Inland Revenue, and for a time they were neighbors of DGR at 19 Cheyne Walk. WMR wrote her obituary in the *Athenaeum*, 2 August 1884, p. 145.

11. *Ecce Ancilla Domini!*

12. No picture with this subject is listed in Surtees.

13. John Miller (1796-1876), "the most open-handed of merchants, and the most lovable of Scotchmen and picture-collectors" (*SR*,1:226). WMR to Frances Rossetti, 16 October 1876, reporting his death: "He was a most delightful old man, and it does one good to think of him" (AP).

14. *Giotto Painting the Portrait of Dante*, bought by Thomas Seddon; *Beatrice Meeting Dante at a Marriage Feast, Denies Him Her Salutation* (Surtees 50), bought by Henry T. Wells, the portrait painter and miniaturist; *Rossovestita* (Surtees 45), which DGR gave to FMB.

15. Unfinished (Surtees 54 R. 1).

16. *Paradise Lost*, 2:113-14.

17. Paul and Dominic Colnaghi, fine-art publishing firm and print-seller.

18. *A Thought of Bethlehem. Part of the life of Madame de Chantal*, R.A., 1854. WMR judged it "by many degrees the most important and the best work which the painter has exhibited" (*Spectator*, 20 May 1854, p. 543). Collins's R.A. picture in 1853 was *Thou who hast given me eyes to see.*

19. *Work* and *The Last of England* (Bennett 1964, Nos. 25, 29) were in preparation at this date. FMB's picture at the 1853 R.A. was *Waiting* (Bennett 1964, No. 24), which WMR thought "the least imposing but one of the most finished and charming of the works he has exhibited at the Academy" (*Spectator*, 21 May 1853, p. 495).

20. Exhibited at the R.A., 1854.

21. Hunt exhibited three pictures at the R.A., 1853: *Claudio and Isabella, Our English Coasts* ("the sheep-picture"), and *New College Cloisters* (a portrait of Rev. John D. Jenkins; Bennett 1969, No. 21). The first picture described is *The Light of the World*.

22. See Letter 26, Note 6.

23. *Sir Plume demands the restoration of the Lock* was not exhibited until 1854.

24. William Powell Frith (1819-1909), *The Sleeping Model*. WMR's early reviews of Frith are sharply dismissive: *Sancho Tells a Tale to the Duke and Duchess* was "a clever piece of studio making-up, uninformed by any high apprehension of the subject" (*Critic*, 15 July 1850, p. 359); *The Village Pastor* did not go beyond "a very careless compilation of commonplace" (*Spectator*, 23 November 1850, p. 1122); *Hogarth Brought Before the Governor of Calais as a Spy* "offers nothing remarkable beyond his usual cleverness in its usual amount and expressed in his usual style. His admirers will think it a very excellent work, on account of the variety of its personations: we hold it to be a very meretricious one, by reason of their hacknied conventionality" (*Spectator*, 14 June 1851, p. 570). Of Frith's election as R.A., WMR commented archly that he was "an artist than whom none fitter can well be conceived, if popularity and the talents which ensure it are the test" (*Spectator*, 19 February 1853, p. 182). The reviews of *Ramsgate Sands*, *Derby Day*, and *The Railway Station* (see "Checklist") are more favorable, but continue the charge of shallowness and cleverness.

25. Augustus Leopold Egg (1816-63), appreciatively reviewed by WMR, 1850-58 (see "Checklist"). In an obituary WMR wrote: "He was an able painter of incident, character, and manners, from the picturesque point of view, embracing equally well romantic narrative and historic anecdote; and will remain in memory as (along with Mr. [J. C.] Hook) the most truly talented and distinguished amid the knot of painters of this class who were in the ascendant for six or seven years before the pre-Raphaelite movement began" (*Weldon's Register*, May 1863, p. 420).

26. Edward Matthew Ward (1816-79) specialized in scenes from English and French history. WMR often grudgingly praised him (see "Checklist"), but his review of *The Executioner tying Wishart's book around the neck of Montrose* was unfavorable (*Spectator*, 14 May 1853, p. 471).

27. 24 February 1853 (Worth, p. 114). His wife was Margaret Thompson, remembered by WMR as "a beautiful and most estimable lady" (*SR*, 1:165). She sat to DGR for Beatrice in the watercolor of *Dante's Dream at the Time of the Death of Beatrice* (Surtees 81). Two months before her marriage DGR drew her portrait (Surtees 322). A son, the first of five children, was born on Christmas Day, 1853.

28. "With the highest admiration and with brotherly regard."

29. *Tamerton Church-Tower and Other Poems* (1853).

30. David Masson (1822-1907), biographer and editor, remembered for his *Life of Milton* (1859-80). He remained at University College London until 1865. Masson married Emily Rosaline Orme, and WMR knew him through this connection.

31. *Poems*, of which there were two editions in 1853.

32. John Payne Collier (1789-1883), whose *Notes and Emendations to the Text of Shakespeare's Plays* (1853) reported the emendations he had forged in a copy of the Second Folio. He changed Dogberry's "A fellow that hath had *losses*" (*Much Ado About Nothing*, IV. ii. 88) to "leases"; and "Nor heaven peep through the *blanket* of the dark" (*Macbeth*, I. v. 52) to "blankness."

33. Thomas Percy, *The Hermit of Warkworth, a Northumbrian Ballad* (1771).

34. *Athenaeum*, 19 February 1853, pp. 234-35, approved the "expensive accessories and novel effects," and the acting of Charles and Ellen Kean as Macbeth and Lady Macbeth.

35. William Dyce, *The National Gallery, its formation and management, considered in a letter to Prince Albert* (1853).

36. Thomas Uwins (1782-1857), watercolorist and genre painter, became keeper of the National Gallery in 1847. Ralph Wornum succeeded him in 1855.

37. John Edward Taylor, *Michael Angelo, considered as a Philosophical Poet* (1840; 2d ed. 1852). WBS reviewed it in the *Gateshead Observer*, 15 January 1853, p. 6.

38. She was in Newcastle "playing Cleopatra, Portia and other Shakespearean characters" (WBS to WMR, 7 March 1853; Durham).

39. Helen Orme, who died in 1857 (WMR to William Allingham, 9 July [1857]; Illinois).

30. TO FRANCES ROSSETTI

Arlington Street,
10 April [1853]

Dearest Mamma,

Maria and I were sorry to find from your letter that you have not come upon a very cheering prospect on your arrival at Frome[1] — especially as matters seem to be in such a state that we might just as well have had you and Christina here a week longer. However, Maria is of opinion that the uncertainties regarding pupils which you seem to consider as *fresh* discouragements are only what you had been led to anticipate before your departure. Is it so?

You will sympathize with me — not, I am pleased to think, for my sake alone — in hearing that yesterday we got a letter from the antipodal Woolner, addressed to Gabriel. It was begun shortly before touching land, but goes on to the 1st November, a week or so later. There is a great deal of, to us, interesting detail; but the chief point for repeating to you is that he feels himself greatly invigorated by the climate, — stronger and more alert than for years. Miss Howitt, who forwarded the letter, has news of a somewhat more recent date. She tells Gabriel that Woolner had been first to the Ovens diggings — about 200 miles, if I remember aright, from Melbourne. Here, in 3 weeks' labour, each of the party made £20; not a fabulous sum certainly, yet not dispiriting either. They have now gone on to diggings some 60 miles further. We keep the letter for the present; as several of us are to meet, in Woolner's house on Tuesday, when the letter will be a pleasure to all, and to make sketches of each other or something else, at an appointed moment at which he is to be doing likewise. When the letter is disengaged, I will send it you, if you like.

Gabriel was here today — looking, I think, far from well. When he left, he was thinking of calling on Hannay, who is about again, he hears, at last. He desired his love through whoever might write, and said he would do so himself shortly.

Papa is tolerably cheerful, and seems somewhat less "tormentato" than usual.

42

Dutiful to your motherly monition to tell you "how my boil gets on," I have to report the almost total exhaustion of the first. I am still in a state of poultice for the second, but it has begun to discharge freely. Symptoms appear of one or two other minor ones, but I don't think they will give me much trouble. Maggie is unwearied in the dilution and application of linseed, and makes *almost* as kind a nurse as you, the incomparably kind. Let me not omit an item of news that will gratify you: I took my third dose of the green atrocity this morning. As for the fourth …? You will understand that I go to Somerset House as usual, and have done so since Thursday inclusive.

I have just been attempting two successive portraits of Christina to send you: but they came such shameful Guys that they found their legitimate home in the fire instead. Will you tell her that I have not forgotten her so utterly as my portraits, had she seen them, might have led her to suppose; and that I shall favour her soon with a missive. I can fancy her rather dreary and particularly objectless, in a state of extreme politeness, and some awe, towards the inn people.

In your favour, dearest Mamma, I depart from my pet little bit of pedantry — of which I know your abhorrence, and sign myself, as you know me to remain,

Your affectionate son,
W. M. Rossetti

MS: AP.

1. She and CGR had gone there to open a school in an effort to bolster the family's finances.

31. TO FRANCES ROSSETTI

Arlington Street,
12 September [1853]

Dear Mamma,

The Office affair is settled,[1] placing me on the class of £250 rising by 10 per annum to £300. The class consists of 9, and I am last upon it, of which I certainly cannot complain, being promoted over the heads of one or two in the succeeding class. Besides, it seems that the distinction between Excise men and Stamps men will still be preserved as regards future promotions — i.e. a vacancy occuring in a higher class by the death or retirement of an Excise man will be filled by the promotion of the Excise man next on the rotation, however many Stamps men there might be between; and vice versa. So it does not by any means follow, because there are 8 men before me, that I shall have to wait 8 vacancies. However, it is somewhat premature to begin looking out for another lift just now.

I wish, dear Mamma, you'd turn over matters in your mind in a "business-like way"; consider what your prospects and your expenses at Frome actually are, and what they would be if we were all to live together again in London;[2] and see whether this latter course would really not be the more economical as well as agreeable, and consequently the more rational. I should add that my increased salary will commence from 15th August, the date of the Treasury warrant for the new staff.

Will you thank Papa for the letter I have this evening received from him, and tell him I shall attend punctually to his directions about the *Arpa*.[3] I have been intending to take one round to Grandpapa[4] every evening since the receipt of the case, and shall do so positively in a day or two.

Somerset House,
15 September

Last night I performed the above adventure. Grandpapa appeared very well — also my aunts. He was evidently delighted to have the *Arpa*, and spoke of it in the highest terms. I suppose you will be aware that Aunt Charlotte[5] is to be in town shortly for a fortnight or upwards, whilst Lady Bath is in Scotland.

Do you know that the cholera is raging in Newcastle? As yet it seems to be confined — or chiefly so — to the riverside, and I hope it may not reach Scott's part of the town. The first case in London (Southwark) was reported yesterday.

I am about to take lessons at a riding-school (Knightsbridge Barracks) with Hunt, — beginning this afternoon. Gabriel is still at that water-colour he is doing for McCracken, for which I frequently sit to him in pose with Williams.[6] Hunt proposes going to Syria as soon as he shall have finished a small picture[7] he is engaged upon, which he expects to be about the beginning of November. He goes, that is, provided the affairs of the East, which now look warlike, should turn to the side of peace; if otherwise, he talks of taking a brief trip to Italy. Of Woolner we had the barest skeleton of news the other day: Miss Howitt having written to Gabriel that she had heard that such persons as Bateman, Woolner, and Smith,[8] were in being three or four months preceding — i.e. about April or May.

At length I send Christina brushes — so much out of date that I must ask her to pardon, instead of thanking, me. I hope they will at least be found good.

Some minor items of news which I may once have had have slipped my memory, I dare say, and lost their interest as well by lapse of time. I now look over your and Christina's outstanding missives, to see whether any queries remained unanswered.

You ask whether "Teodorico[9] does, in his sober senses, lay claim to the discovery of the perpetual motion." I refer you to Maria for the reply, if she has not already given it. I have seen him, by the by, only once since Maria left; for I scarcely ever dine at home. Indeed, I am not certain whether he comes on the appointed day, Saturday, or not. I always forget to ask.

I have done what I was doing in the German translation,[10] and nothing remains but to get the tin. This will not be more than a couple of pounds or so, as my share in the affair was but small.

Please give my love to Papa, Maria, and Christina; and tell the former that I have begun reading the *Arpa* through with much pleasure. Also, when you write, tell me how *you* and the rest are.

Your affectionate son,
W. M. Rossetti

MS: AP.

1. WMR to Frances Rossetti, 20 July [1853]: "You will remember that I have spoken sometimes of the amalgamation of my office with the Stamps and Taxes. The arrangements are now under discussion. I was told yesterday ... by one of the Secretaries that it is contemplated to promote me to a salary of (probably) £250 rising by annual progression to £300. From such a quarter the information is of course perfectly authentic. This is not bad: for, as you know, I am at present in a class rising only to £200; the last of 5 on the rotation of that class; and only looking forward in the natural course of things, and after the probable chance of many years' lapse, to getting into a class of from £200 to £250 or £300, I forget which. / That something in the way of promotion awaits me may be counted upon. But whether it may be to the precise amount stated, or how soon it may come, I cannot say. Most probably some months will elapse, for the official wheels move slowly. It is on this account I withhold the intelligence from Papa: he would be restless, constantly expecting the matter to be immediately settled, and unable to reconcile himself to any possible diminution of the advantage when it does come. I tell you and Christina of it not only to gladden your affectionate hearts, but with the view of most earnestly urging you not inconsiderately to undertake that burdensome and most distasteful charge of boarders. I believe in, perceive, and rely upon, a Providence not less than you do. Pray, dear Mamma, think of this, and let me hear from you on the subject" (AP).

2. The family was reunited in London by late March 1854 at 45 Upper Albany Street, later renumbered 166 Albany Street. Gabriele Rossetti died there on 16 April 1854.

3. Gabriele Rossetti's *L'Arpa Evangelica* (Genova, 1852).

4. Gaetano Polidori (1764-1853), Pisan-born father of Frances Rossetti. He taught Italian in London, c. 1790-1836, and published prose, verse, and translations. WMR remembered him as kind and tolerant, more bookish than Gabriele Rossetti, and with little taste for politics (*FLM*, 1:25-28).

5. Charlotte Polidori (1803-90), the second youngest sister of Frances Rossetti, was governess in the family of, and later companion to, the Dowager Marchioness of Bath.

6. *The First Anniversary of the Death of Beatrice* (Surtees 58). Williams, "a jobbing man, employed in our family" (*FLM*, 2:116), sat for the elderly man; WMR for the head of Dante.

7. Cf. Letter 32.

8. Bernhard Smith (1820-85) accompanied Woolner and Bateman to Australia where he settled permanently, becoming a police magistrate. For the claim that Smith was a member of the PRB, see Letter 413.

9. Teodorico Pietrocola-Rossetti (1826-83), WMR's cousin. See the summary of his life in Bornand, p. 74.

10. Not identified.

32. TO WILLIAM BELL SCOTT

38 Arlington Street,
23 October [1853]

My dear Friend,

What a disgraceful time since I wrote to you! But I will not apologize, for — shame to say — it would be repeating myself.

At last — after a delay which made some of his friends almost uneasy — we have news of Woolner and his party. Letters have arrived — not, I believe, from him individually, but from his companion Bernhard Smith to the latter's brother, who has sent notice thereof to Gabriel, asking him round to see them on Tuesday. At present, therefore, we are unacquainted with details; but we are informed in a general way that Woolner and Smith dug for seven months unsuccessfully; so unsuccessfully that the former was on his way back to Melbourne, purposing to try something in the way of art, — still, however, undaunted in spirit; and the latter was seeking or getting employment in the sheep-farming way. Of the rest of the party — Howitt etc. — I have not heard. Bad news this: but I don't think Woolner is the man to let himself be beaten by Fortune.

Gabriel has, I believe, been rather a better correspondent than myself of late: so perhaps you will have heard some of the news of friends I may have to impart.

He himself is engaged on an elaborate water-colour of a subject from the *Vita Nuova*,[1] an ancient treatment of which you may perhaps remember having seen at Millais's — Dante — on the first anniversary of Beatrice's death — designing, in memory of her, a figure of an angel, and roused from his abstraction by the entrance of visitors; of whom, in the present treatment, two are his future wife and father-in-law. I think this likely to be the best work Gabriel has yet brought to a completion. He is also doing a portrait of one of our aunts.[2]

My father, mother, and Christina, are still at Frome. The first had a bad attack of diarrhoea about a fortnight ago, from which, in his feeble state, serious consequences were apprehended; but he is now, apparently, as well as before. Christina, who was to have addicted herself to art with some zeal, has not done anything in that way for some time past.

Millais has [been] for a considerable while touring with Ruskin in Scotland, and the time of his return is still unsettled. Some days ago he was — perhaps still is — at Callander. He is doing a portrait of Ruskin[3] — a commission from the latter's father; and legendary rumours reach me, through Hunt through a third party, of his having invented a new style of architecture![4] It is, I understand, a fact, that he has been making some architectural designs or diagrams for Ruskin's use. Whether (as seems quite probable) he has introduced into these something inventive, and to what extent, whether merely decorative or really constituting the elements of a new style, I can only surmise at present; scarcely, I should think, to the last-mentioned extent. Ruskin, you may have seen in the *Athenaeum*, is to deliver two lectures to (I think) the Philosophical Society at Edinburgh[5] — one on architecture, chiefly domestic, one on art and its modern aspects. Have you read the *Stones of Venice*? I think it an admirable book on the whole. In the last volume are many allusions to the P.R.B., and one to Gabriel by name. He says that the only man he knows who has shown the power of designing in colour on a large scale is Watts;[6] but that he is sure Rossetti has the same power, and thinks Millais has.

Hunt has all but finished his sacred symbolic picture, *The Light of the World*. Did you see it? If not, I may say that it is the best modern work of its class I know, and Hunt's greatest. He is also advanced with a modern subject[7] to which he means to give a motto from the Book of Proverbs (I am not certain of the precise words) — "As he that taketh away a garment, so is he that singeth songs to a heavy heart": the sentiment to be embodied in a young swell singing to his mistress a song which moves her to compunctious sadness. I am not certain whether Hunt means this subject to be reported for the present save among friends. When he has done these two works, he is to start on his travels. His intended *compagnon de voyage*, Thomas Seddon,[8] (do you know him? a very good and talented fellow) has started already, and Hunt is engaged to meet him in Paris on the 1st November; but his being exact to time is more than doubtful. Even after they meet, it will be a question what they are to do. A visit to the East

— Syria, Egypt, etc. — and to Italy, is contemplated to be included in their tour. Hunt, however, is in great doubts as to the first part of this, looking to the present aspect of Eastern affairs, and the impediments they would probably throw in the way of artists. He is inclined to winter in Italy, and see what turns up, — altogether abandoning for the present, if necessary, the Eastern half of the plan; whereas Seddon wants to push on for Cairo at once. I suspect Hunt will limit himself after all to Italy, and be back in the spring. Have you heard that he has got the Liverpool £50 prize for his *Claudio and Isabella*? He has some expectation also of one of the Birmingham prizes for his sheep-picture.[9]

Masson is married to the pretty and engaging young girl you met as Miss Orme. Patmore, utterly extinguished, on the appearance of his new volume,[10] by the avalanche of Alexander Smith, is beginning, I believe, to emerge from under it to a limited extent by dint of rather hard advertising, and has sold a few copies of his book. This is too bad. I really think there is as much poetical stuff in him as in Smith, or more, though not of so obvious and besieging a kind. Hannay, I hear, "expects an addition to his family." He is to redeliver his lectures[11] this winter; and *Singleton Fontenoy* is to appear in one of the cheap shilling libraries. This, coupled with the recent republication of his minor naval tales under the name of *Sketches in Ultra-Marine*, will, it is to be hoped, extend his now tolerably established but restricted reputation.

We have received copies of Munro's[12] medallions of you and Millais. Yours is certainly like; but, I think, dubiously drawn and quaint. It is characteristic, but the character not enough concentrated and *permanent*, the features, mental and physical, not sufficiently combined. There is somehow a twist about the thing which would make me fancy the original — in person, by far, — and also in mind, more of an eccentric, as distinguished from an uncommon, person than you are. What is your own opinion?

I hope the choleratic atmosphere in which you have been living has not affected you to *any* extent. How does your health go on? and what are you doing? At the remote date of your last letter to me, you were at Hexham, doing a picture with a parsonage-garden in it.[13] How about your poems?

You asked me to give you "some of my foreign experiences." They are confined to Paris, and to only six days in Paris, and are by this time become so obsolete that I can scarcely venture to expatiate on them generally. In art, they are decidedly favourable in their impression. The exhibition of this year contained works from but few of the eminent men: but the average of attainment, the evidence of artistic training, capacity, and knowledge, the mastery of material and sureness of method, — in a word, the amount of style — were really refreshing after the straggling meaningless general result of an English exhibition. I remember (among others) some little bits of things by Meissonier[14] most exquisite in grace, ease, and light; a classic domestic scene, or, as the artists there call it, "Idylle," by Hamon,[15] with just enough of French piquancy in its refined naturalness to be charming; a magnificent portrait (single female head) by Ricard[16] — power, beauty, subtlety, and nobly peculiar painting, combined; and some historic cartoons by Chenavard,[17] in a large manly style. I don't say that I saw anything so fine or right as I believe Hunt, for instance, is capable of doing. But the impression I received was that France has a definite and recognized standing in art — has a body of artists who *are* artists and *a body*, and who, as a body, can and will turn you out a good workmanlike article of such kind as you may demand; while England, only having some clever men scattered among a multitude of imbeciles, possesses nothing that can be called a school or a standard.

Have you read Haydon's Memoirs?[18] An absorbingly interesting work. That, and that glorious work, Carlyle's Letters and Speeches of Cromwell, which I am now engaged upon, are with the *Stones of Venice*, the three good things I have come across of late.

Maria's love to Mrs. Scott; and my most particular remembrances to her, and to Mrs. Norquoy.

Yours,

W. M. Rossetti

MS: Arizona.

1. *The First Anniversary of the Death of Beatrice.*
2. Charlotte Polidori (Surtees 407).
3. Bennett 1967, No. 42. WMR to Allingham, 27 November [1853]: "Millais is back, having painted the background of his portrait of Ruskin — a mountain and torrent scene — by far the best, he says, of anything he has yet done" (Illinois).
4. Millais told Hunt that he and Ruskin "were deep in the designing of novel architecture." To C. A. Collins he explained that "Ruskin has discovered that I can design Architectural ornamentation more perfectly than any living or dead *party*. So delighted is he that in the evenings I have promised to design doors, arches, and windows for Churches etc., etc." (Mary Lutyens, *Millais and the Ruskins* [1967], pp. 80-81).
5. He delivered four lectures to the Philosophical Institution in November 1853, which were published as *Lectures on Architecture and Painting* (1854).
6. George Frederic Watts (1817-1904) exhibited two sizeable compositions in the 1840s: *Alfred meeting the Saxons to resist the Landing of the Danes*, in the House of Lords Competition of 1847; and *Caractacus led in triumph through the streets of Rome*, in the Westminster Hall competition of 1848 (Wood). Ruskin also knew the thirty-foot-long *Story from Boccaccio* painted in Italy in 1844 (see John Gage, *G. F. Watts, A Nineteenth Century Phenomenon*, Whitechapel Art Gallery, 1974, No. 7).
7. *The Awakening Conscience* (Bennett 1969, No. 27).
8. See Letter 45, Note 9.
9. *Strayed Sheep — Our English Coasts*, 1852. In reporting the Birmingham award in the *Spectator* WMR commented: "What makes the intention of this decision the more marked, is the fact that the first prize at Birmingham had hitherto ... been reserved for subjects of historic or dramatic interest. But the directors seem to think, and reasonably, that supreme merit, in whatever class, is the paramount consideration" (5 November 1853, p. 1070).
10. *Tamerton Church-Tower.*
11. The six lectures published in 1854 as *Satire and Satirists*. Delivered first in the summer of 1853, the last two were repeated at the Westminster Literary Institution in December 1853, and the full series at the Marylebone Literary Institution in January 1854 (Worth, p. 98).
12. Alexander Munro (1825-71), sculptor and member of the Pre-Raphaelite circle. He exhibited at the R.A., 1849-70 and at the British Institution, 1850-63 (Gunnis). WMR wrote that he "pushes sculpture to its extreme limit of pictorial effect" (*Spectator*, 11 June 1853, p. 568). Considering the many works that Munro exhibited, WMR's reviews of him are infrequent and seldom wholly approving (see "Checklist").
13. See Letter 33, Note 12.
14. Jean Louis Ernest Meissonier (1815-91) exhibited three works: *A l'ombre des bosquets chante un jeune poète*; *Un jeune homme lit*; and *Paysage*.

15. Louis Hamon (1821-74), *Idylle — ma soeur n'y est pas.*

16. Gustave Ricard (1823-73), *Portrait de Mlle Clauss.*

17. Paul Chenavard (1807-95), *Auguste Ferme Les Portes du Temple de Janus; Attila; Commencement de la Réforme.*

18. *The Life of Benjamin Robert Haydon from his Autobiography and Journals,* ed. Tom Taylor, 1853.

33. TO WILLIAM BELL SCOTT

45 Upper Albany Street,
30 [May 1854]

Dear Scott,

I have done you the "favour of a very particular kind" whereof you besought me, without finding it so *very* particular after all. Pray return me the passport when you have signed it. I will endeavour to have the viséing over before you come to London: if I should happen not to have found it feasible by the time you arrive, I will trust to your forgiving me, and return you the passport. I enclose with it a few instructions, though they are of little or no use, and very probably you have them already.

Are you aware that your picture[1] is not hung at the R.A.? I need not say how indignantly I write it. I have not yet seen the work; for the day when I and Gabriel called at Eckford's[2] for the purpose happened to be the day after the sending-in. Is it with him now? A noble picture by Anthony[3] was also rejected. Munro's medallion of you is hung. You will like both Hunt's works,[4] — the modern subject, as well as the sacred one. I don't remember another thing in the Academy exhibiting a grain of intellect save Poole's,[5] and, for landscape, the one of Anthony's which has been accepted.[6] Did you see Ruskin's letters in the *Times,*[7] one upon each of Hunt's pictures? As for what you mention — his praise of Gabriel, — the case is this. The long-pending water-colour[8] which the latter painted for McCracken, being at last finished, was sent by the purchaser to Ruskin, in whose oracles he believes. Ruskin hereupon wrote to Gabriel to say that it was "a thoroughly glorious work" — "the most wonderful piece of Italy he had ever seen, and not only of Italy, but of splendid landscape-painting"; hoped that Gabriel would suffer nothing to interfere with the development of his "noble thoughts"; and signed himself "yours respectfully." Shortly afterwards he called; saw at another man's house a coloured sketch by Gabriel of Dante meeting Beatrice in Paradise,[9] which he pronounced "celestial"; got Gabriel to inspect his Turners; and has bestowed upon him the series of his writings, although, as he expressed it, there was nothing in them which the recipient did not know better already. He gives them, "as Diomed gave his brazen arms for Glaucus's golden,"[10] in anticipation of a design Gabriel had promised him;[11] and he has commissioned a second design in water-colours. I think he is really enthusiastic; and that he will, as he certainly can, do Gabriel some practical service.

I have before me, with your last two, a letter of yours dated 10 March; wherein you say your *Vicarage Garden*[12] and selections from David's designs were to be at the Glasgow Art-Union show.[13] I had been there before receipt of that intimation; but your picture was not hung then. I understood that it and others remained for the time being on Edinburgh gallery-walls. Nor did I see the designs. There was a *rather* noticeable work by a Scotch artist Lees or Lies[14] — do you know him? Another, very clever in the French manner, by one Stevens.[15] It had been in the Paris exhibition when I was there last year. Of vile trash *ad libitum*.

The news of poor Agatha Traun's[16] death had first reached me in a letter from Mrs. Scott to Maria. The sweet comely little simple-hearted girl! The scene of which you suggest to me a misty outline, when Traun was with the Ronges must have been a curious one indeed, "significant of many things," as Carlyle says.[17] I have not seen aught of the family for a long while.

Your programme of the coming tour struck me very temptingly, and, in the first moments, I had half resolved to fix my company, you willing, upon you therein. Munich and Nuremberg, not to speak of intermediate matters, sound wooingly to my ear. I have not yet quite settled that the trip *shall* not be; though I think most likely it *will* not. Can you give me an idea of the expense? I mean on the assumption that I should take the shortest mode of joining you when you have started from Paris. As I saw that last year, and there are no pictures exhibited this year, I should find little to do there. A walking-trip in Cornwall with a friend is an alternative to which I had half committed myself, but not so entirely as to be a faith-breaker if I do not perform it. Why do you want to return by Ostend? No living soul within my experience has, whether in words or in print, anything but billingsgate to say of it.

Did you see something I wrote in the *Spectator* of the present Marlborough House exhibition?[18] In the preceding week I had called Redgrave's sham of a sacred picture "an inane vanity,"[19] with other prettinesses of the kind; and I was in some trepidation at the notion of his doing the polite to us (we went before the general private view at Cole's special invitation) in the hyena style. He was all graciousness, however. In the course of the inspection I said something of "Scott of Newcastle," when the great man in question observed that said Scott was "a dreamy sort of man and too much of a poet." He seemed to acquiesce, nevertheless, in the eulogiums which I vouchsafed to your knowledge and efficiency. So you see you are discovered, you "dreamy man." Redgrave, whom nature, if I am a physiognomist, commissioned to take the measure of your breeches, takes the measure of your brain.

Perhaps you have been wondering what has become of "the Folio."[20] I can scarcely tell you. The rules were enacted, the paraphernalia bought; but things have come to a deadlock in the hands of Millais. He kept the folio I know not how long, and now is gone to Scotland; possibly he has passed it on to Gabriel, who is not yet back from Hastings, or to someone else.

There is some expectation of Woolner's returning before the year is out. Hunt has left Cairo, we infer, and may now be at Jerusalem or Damascus. Hannay has packed up bag and baggage, wife and baby, and gone down to his father's place near Barnet — for some months, I suppose. Allingham (I think you have met him) gave up his Customs appointment and came to London intent on literature two or three months ago; literature has given him up, and he has resumed his Customs appointment, — to return to Ireland very shortly.

Receive your affectionate greetings for yourself and household.

Yours,

W. M. Rossetti

I see by the paper that Newcastle has had a shindy between its soldiers and its "peelers." Did you see anything of it?

MS: Arizona.

1. Possibly *Fair Rosamond alone in her Bower*, Royal Scottish Academy, 1854.
2. "Carver and Gilder, 8 Rose Court, Greek Street, Soho up a breakneck stair" (WBS to WMR, 23 March 1853; Durham).
3. Not identified.
4. *The Awakening Conscience* and *The Light of the World*.
5. Paul Falconer Poole (1807-79), *The Song of the Troubadours*, of which WMR wrote: "Poole is one of the very few men capable of really conceiving such a subject; and, whether with a good picture or with a bad picture, he forces you to feel it" (*Spectator*, 20 May 1854, p. 543).
6. *Nature's Mirror*.
7. 5, 25 May (C & W, 12:328-35).
8. *The First Anniversary of the Death of Beatrice*.
9. *Dante and Beatrice*, No. 44 in *DGRDW*, p. 272. It belonged to G. P. Boyce.
10. *Iliad*, 6:234-36.
11. For the DGR drawings and watercolors acquired by Ruskin in 1854, see *DGRDW*, pp. 23-25.
12. WBS to WMR, [17 August 1853]: "The picture I am doing is a Parsonage about a mile across the bridge through a great shade of beeches. This Parsonage of St. John's Lee is worthy a better painter and has a garden perfect in its way, which is the most part of my subject. There will be a girl tying up the flowers and a young fellow looking at her from the wicket" (Durham). The Art Union of Glasgow (see Note 13) purchased the picture for £30.
13. The 1853-54 exhibition of the Art Union of Glasgow was held in the Dilettanti Rooms, 151 Buchanan Street, Glasgow. No catalogue of the exhibition has been found, but on 19 January 1854 the Union issued a "List of Prizes, Paintings, etc. Purchased for Distribution, up to this date." WMR is probably referring to a showing of some of the pictures in London (in 1855 the Art Union purchases were shown at 121 Pall Mall; *Spectator*, 10 March 1855, p. 272).
14. The "List of Prizes" includes *A Winter Morning* by Charles Lees (1800-1880), portrait, landscape, and genre painter (Wood); and *The Point of View* by Joseph Lies, who may be the J. Lies listed in Graves.
15. John Stevens (1793-1868), genre and portrait painter. He lived mostly in Italy, but exhibited regularly in London (Wood). No picture by him is included in the "List of Prizes."
16. Daughter of Bertha Ronge by a former husband, whose presence in Newcastle with the Ronges, produced "a certain *mise en scène* very interesting to those who laudably hunger and thirst after gossip" (WBS to WMR, 25 March 1854; Durham).
17. Cf. "emblematic of much," *Life of John Sterling* (1851), Chap. 3.
18. "Models by the Italian Masters," 1 April 1854, p. 370.
19. No mention of Redgrave has been found in WMR's reviews of the previous weeks.
20. Folio Sketching Club, started by Millais on the pattern of the Cyclographic Society (*PRBJ*, p. 108).

34. TO WILLIAM BELL SCOTT

45 Upper Albany Street,
15 November [1854]

Dear Scott,

I ought to have acknowledged your book[1] and the great pleasure it gave me sooner.

It will afford me *real* satisfaction to do a review for the *Illustrated*. One always likes to express a decided opinion on a work which deserves to excite one, especially if one belongs to a select few in entertaining that opinion. You say the suggestion for a review comes from Munro at Oxford. If this is my Alexander Munro, the sculptor, I am surprised at his not having spoken to me already on the matter, as I saw him both yesterday and today: however, we shall meet again on Friday, and, as soon as I have a few definite hints to work from, I shall lose no time in setting to. I hope they will give me decent elbow room.

I had had thoughts of giving you my opinions upon each of the poems seriatim and in detail, as leisure should serve. Perhaps, however, that would, to you, be destitute of any amusement it might possess for myself: and, if I succeed in getting into print, the project will probably sleep.

Have you heard the how and the why of the note Carlyle wrote you on the subject? Probably Woolner may have told you: if not, you will learn through me what Tommaso in person told him. He (Carlyle) saw under your frontispiece — as he read it — "Poems by a Printer"; and, without reading the book to be called reading — most likely without looking into it — and not remembering your identity at the moment — forthwith indites a letter to the nascent genius intended to make him stick to his types for the printing of other men's books only. Carlyle was dismayed when in conversation with Woolner, he discovered the real state of affairs, — said that you had appeared to him a man something like himself, and one for whom he had a regard; but that the thing was done, and could not be mended.

Your penultimate letter spoke of Allingham's late pamphlet-volume[2] in terms of disparagement which I regretted to find coming from you. Really I cannot agree that the poems were not worth publishing. They appear to me to have clearness and even vigour and penetration of thought, and to be, in point of art, quite remarkable. I think Allingham a true, though not a great, poet and one who marks his vocation by doing nothing in a slovenly or slipshod style. He is now, I hear, engaged on a translation of Homer[3] — in Spenserian or octave stanzas, if I recollect aright. My good opinion of him does not save me from thinking that he has miscalculated his power here. To begin with, he knows little or nothing of Greek, if I am not greatly mistaken: and even that is not the most important consideration.

Your eyes or ears may have come across *The Angel in the House*[4] — a new poem. It is Patmore's, but *this is a secret*. The name is withheld because of the late onslaught in the *Times* upon a book by Patmore's father,[5] and the apparently prevalent notion that the two writers are identical. Hence Coventry anticipated prejudice and abortion should his name have appeared to the volume.

Gabriel is now staying with Brown at Finchley, to paint a white calf into a picture[6] he has begun. Hunt talks of leaving Jerusalem about March, and coming back through Constantinople, Italy, etc. Woolner is sturdier in body, and no less sturdy in mind, than ever. He will have written you since his return, I suppose. Indeed, now, I recollect for certain that he has.

A somewhat recent, but intimate and approved, friend of mine and others of us is just about to leave London to study for the Scotch bar in Edinburgh — his name James (or John) Ferguson McLennan[7] — a very lively, friendly, and thinking man. Should you at any time or by any chance come across him, I think you will not regret to have received this reminder of his name. His being acquainted with us may assure you that he knows yours.

Have you heard of the Working Men's College started in Red Lion Square by Maurice[8] and others? Ruskin is teaching drawing there, and I am not altogether certain but what I may enrol myself among his pupils. He is also lecturing on Decorative Matters at the Architectural Museum[9] near Westminster Bridge. I must manage to hear him.

Remembrances from all.

Yours,

W. M. Rossetti

Don't you find the war[10] an ever-recurring and supreme bore? What says your friend Linton to it? At least, we are not about to

Back desperately from street to street[11]

quite yet before the Cossacks. But I have my suspicion that the real thing to do, after all, would have been to act upon Nicholas's suggestion that Turkism in Turkey was dying out, and must be replaced by some mutual understanding of superior races; and thereupon to kick out effete Turks at the earliest opportunity, instead of bolstering them up. On the question of rights, there is a vast deal of sense in that of Carlyle's — "The Rights of Man are precisely as much as he can get."[12]

MS: Arizona.

1. *Poems* (1854). WMR recalled reviewing it for the *Illustrated London News* (*RRP*, p. 26), but a review has not been found.

2. *Day and Night Songs* was published as a 6d. pamphlet in 1853 and as a volume in 1854.

3. Never published.

4. *The Angel in the House: the Betrothal* (1854). For subsequent parts of the poem see Letter 41, Note 24.

5. Peter George Patmore (1786-1855), whose *My Friends and Acquaintances* was reviewed on 19 August 1854, p. 4.

6. *Found* (Surtees 64).

7. (1827-81) was called to the Scottish bar in 1857. *DNB* calls him a sociologist, remembered for *Primitive Marriage* (1865). WMR was introduced to him by Alexander Munro, whom McLennan knew at Cambridge. "His mind was rapid in its processes and full of acuteness; his speech had discernment and point. He was among the men whose society I should have best liked to cultivate; but his removal to Scotland interfered, and after that I only saw him two or three times" (*SR*, 1:170).

8. Frederick Denison Maurice (1805-72) was principal of the College until his death.

9. Three "Addresses on Decorative Colour" delivered in November and December 1854 (C & W, 12:474ff.).

10. Crimean War, 1854-56.

11. From W. J. Linton's (?) *To the Memory of Milton* (*The Plaint of Liberty*).

12. "I never thought the 'rights of Negroes' worth much discussing, nor the rights of men in any form; the grand point ... is the *mights* of men, — what portion of their 'rights' they have a chance of getting sorted out, and realized, in this confused world" (*Occasional Discourse on the Nigger Question, Fraser's Magazine*, 1849; separately 1853).

35. TO WILLIAM JAMES STILLMAN[1]

45 Upper Albany Street,
23 March 1855

Dear Sir,

Your letter of the 5th reached me on the 19th. I had fancied I might hear from you earlier; and, this not happening, I had already begun the enclosed article.[2] I am in hopes the line of treatment adopted will be in accordance with your views; you will see that I had begun writing on the topic upon which I feel most warmly, Preraphaelitism.

The copy of the *Crayon*[3] with which your letter indicates that you intended to oblige me has not come to hand. I had, however, seen the copy which you sent to Mr. Ruskin, and, if I recollect aright, am not "out of order" in appending my name to my contribution. I feel desirous that it should appear; not only from an abstract preference, but also because, having to speak so continually of Preraphaelites and others, my personal friends or acquaintances, I desire that no one may be able to accuse me of underhand favouritism. So far from feeling fettered by publicly showing that I am in a manner connected with those I write of, I shall express my opinions all the more freely. May I beg you to believe that the opinions I shall express are, in all cases, conscientiously mine, set down without exaggeration, and in no sort matter of favour or affection.

It would give me great pleasure to receive the *Crayon* regularly. Indeed, as a matter of business, I feel it would be of assistance to me in showing what topics I may most conveniently treat for the immediate purpose of the paper. As I am not acquainted with any American agent, perhaps you will be kind enough to have me supplied with the paper, deducting my subscription and the cost of transmission from payments falling due.

I have written the enclosed in uncertainty as to the length of article which you may actually expect or require. Generally speaking, I suppose the monthly letter will have materials sufficient for about the same length; but, if not, I shall feel it unnecessary to dilute such real matter as there may be for it by washy commonplaces or gossip. If I find occasion for *casual* letters, which I do not anticipate frequently, I can do them on the terms you mention. "Personal news artistic and of artistic men" would require deliberation and delicate handling from me. I will think over the proposal that I should write a kind of historic sketch of the P.R.B.[4]

Would you kindly inform me through what channel I am to receive payment, and at what times you contemplate making it — whether at stated intervals or at *any* period according to the work done intermediately. Also whether there is any particular method I should adopt for transmitting my contributions.

Believe me, Dear Sir,
Very truly yours,
W. M. Rossetti

MS: NYP.

1. (1828-1901), American painter, photographer, journalist. With John Durand he founded the art magazine the *Crayon* (New York, 1855-61), and enlisted WMR as London correspondent. During the 1860s he was American consul in Rome and Crete. His correspondence to the *Times* on the uprising in Herzegovina in 1875 began an "on and off" (WMR to Lucy Rossetti, 22 August 1885; AP) association with the paper which lasted until his appointment as Rome correspondent, 1886-97. MS. Diary, 13 August 1878: "Stillman called on me at Somerset House.... Gladstone asked him to call not long ago: he did so, and found Gladstone very frank, solid, and unassuming: at parting, Gladstone said that the country owes Stillman much for his outspoken correspondence in the *Times* from a comparatively early stage of the Herzegovinian Insurrection." 27 May 1886: "Fairfax Murray ... says that Stillman is now definitely appointed *Times* Correspondent in Rome, with off-excursions to Greece — salary £600, which Murray regards as equal to £800 in London. This is excellent news." Although Stillman wrote that with WMR "my relations were constant and cordial, and he was for many years my most valued English friend" (*Autobiography of a Journalist* [1901], 1:252); and WMR described Stillman as an acquaintance of DGR, but a "friend more especially of my own" (*FLM*, 1:286), there are no WMR letters to Stillman in the Stillman Collection at Union College, and only a handful of Stillman letters to WMR in AP. The only WMR letters to Stillman that have been found are business letters relating to the *Crayon* in the Durand Papers.

2. "Art News from London," *Crayon*, 25 April 1855, pp. 263-65. Over the next twenty months WMR contributed nineteen signed articles under this title (excepting December 1855). See "Checklist."

3. Throughout 1855-56 Stillman's and Durand's names appear as editors and proprietors, but for the first year or more Stillman seems to have done most of the work, until ill health forced him to relinquish the editing to Durand. Two letters from Durand to WMR concern Stillman's departure. 18 June 1856: "My partner's health does not warrant close business application, the duties and cares therefore as well as responsibility devolve upon myself. His abdication of the editorial department is a real loss but it cannot be helped." 11 December 1856: "I have now the sole direction and responsibility in name as well as in fact, (having had both for the past eight months)" (AP). In January 1857 Durand's name appears on the masthead alone.

John Brown Durand (1822-1908) is a shadowy figure, son of Asher Durand, whose biography he wrote. He is listed in the *National Academy of Design Exhibition Records* (1943) as an Honorary Member (Amateur), 1855-60 (1:140). A brief obituary in the *New York Times* describes him as a well-known member of the American community in Paris, and mentions his translations of Taine's essays on art, 1870, 1889 (20 October 1908, p. 9).

4. WMR did not publish such an article until "Pre-Raphaelitism. Its Starting Point and its Sequel," *Art Monthly Review*, August 1876, pp. 102-5.

36. TO JOHN LUCAS TUPPER

45 Upper Albany Street,
[Early May, 1855[1]]

Dear Tupper,

My handwriting must be a wondrous apparition to you now. Its motive cause is this.

I am writing summaries of British art-news for an American art-paper named the *Crayon*, published at 237 Broadway, New York, — the engagement coming to me through Ruskin.[2] The editor, an artist named W. J. Stillman, has now written to me, saying:

"Is it not possible that we may get some artistic contributions from some of them (the Preraphaelites).[3] We have endeavoured to make a point of communications from artists." Poems also are published in the paper.

I hear you have left Guy's, and have set up as a sculptor. *Possibly* you might care to do some literary art-work (I understand the "artistic contributions" spoken of to be *literary* ones): for that chance I write to you.[4]

My engagement is for 1 guinea for any "minor special letter" beyond the regular monthly one, and 7/- a column for *articles* (3 columns going to a page of *Athenaeum* size). Beyond my own engagement, however, I know nothing of the terms of payment.[5]

Yours truly, with my kind remembrances to your family,

W. M. Rossetti

The *Crayon* is not a bad paper — much better than anything of the kind here.

MS: Leeds.

1. Tupper's reply is dated 5 May 1855 (AP).
2. William Smith Williams to WMR, 3 February 1855: "The enclosed letter addressed to Mr. Ruskin by the Editor of the *Crayon* ... will explain to you the wish of Mr. Stillman to obtain the services of an English correpondent for this Journal, and the terms which he offers. It only remains for me to say that, Mr. Ruskin Senior having asked me if I knew of any writer on art who would be likely to accept an engagement of the kind, and whose view would accord with those of the Editor and whose ability [would] do credit to (his son's) Mr. Ruskin's recommendation, I mentioned your name and the fact of your connexion with the *Spectator*, as also your being the brother of an artist whom Mr. Ruskin knew and esteemed. / It is very gratifying to me to be requested by Mr. Ruskin to communicate with you in this matter, and to ask you if you feel disposed to accept the terms offered.... Your brother seemed to think that you would not be unwilling to do so" (AP).
3. WMR to Stillman, 27 May 1855: "The three principal Praeraphaelites are Hunt, my brother, and Millais. The first is at present in Jerusalem; and both he and my brother studiously avoid all public written representation of their views. Millais has no abstract reluctance of the kind, but he also never writes on the subject; indeed, if he felt inclined, he has no time" (NYP). He suggested instead Stephens, Tupper, Anna Howitt, C. B. Cayley, and WBS, each of whom contributed something. WMR ended up acting as Stillman's agent, requesting and transmitting contributions, and distributing payment.
4. Tupper's first contribution was a poem on Hunt's *Light of the World* (8 August 1855, p. 87). Between December 1855 and August 1856 he published a ten-part series, "Extracts from the Diary of an Artist."
5. The spotty records of payment in AP suggest that other contributors were paid 6/- a column for articles. Poetry was paid at a different rate; WMR proposed £2.2 for Tupper's thirty-one-line *Light of the World* (letter to Stillman, 29 September [1855]; NYP).

37. TO WILLIAM ALLINGHAM

45 Upper Albany Street,
[4 June 1855]

Dear Allingham,

Your poem[1] will I have no doubt, be most welcome to the Yankee editor, to whom, though I dispatched my monthly letter a day or two ago, I will send it at once without waiting for my next packet.

I shall not only be willing, but glad, to review your book[2] in the *Critic* — though, if it reaches me immediately, you must not chafe at some little delay. If you write to Cox, as you suggest, it will be all the more pleasant to me, as I have already, within a very brief space, had to volunteer two notices,[3] one of which is still pending.

Hughes's designs for your book are very delicate and sweet. They have lost not a little, certainly in the cutting, yet will not look otherwise than well to those who have not seen the original. Gabriel's or any others I have not beheld.

Is your Trinity College building the work of Woodward?[4] I have made his acquaintance lately through meeting him at Ruskin's. He is a supremely quiet man, evidently with something in him.

The *Spectator* notice of the R.A. goes through about 6 Nos.,[5] and is not finished yet. The papers pass from here to my mother, now at Hastings, thence to Newcastle, and thence to a third person; but, if I can lay my hands upon such part as has yet appeared, I will send it you.

You ask for some news. I am become the dullest and most niggardly of beings at letter-writing; but here goes.

Millais is immediately about to marry Mrs. Ruskin. The fact is no secret, yet I tell it you (if you don't know it) as a matter the less said about which the better. Hunt still at, or just out of, Jerusalem. Miss Siddall, who, you may be aware, is under an engagement to paint regularly for Ruskin when her health allows, at Oxford, where his friends pay her all kinds of attention. Of poor Barbara Smith,[6] fine-hearted admirable woman, I hear bad accounts. A letter from her arrived the other day at the Howitts, when I was there, — written from Naples, and showing that her health is still very precarious. Hannay's new novel[7] is out — and has had a most handsome notice in the *Athenaeum*, (where, by the by, he writes). Gabriel, having laid aside the *Found*, paints (I believe) water-colours, but I see them not. Gerald Massey,[8] thanks to the exquisiteness of public appreciation, is in his 5th (or subsequent) edition. Miss Howitt, who has been very unwell, apparently well again; the Ormes by me unseen for some while now. W. B. Scott, according to his last letter, dismal (I think you knew him?). For me, I do (or do not) "my duty in that state of life to which it hath pleased God to call me,"[9] and that is about as much as can be said.

This is a stony banquet of news, truly, whereto I have done nothing to garnish it, or make it look savoury. You will have to bolt it like an ostrich.

Yours,

W. M. Rossetti

You will not be going to Paris, I suppose? Probably I shall be there within a month or so — and Scott expects to go.

MS: Illinois.

1. *Aeolian Harp*, published in the *Crayon*, 11 July 1855, p. 23; and in *The Music Master*. WMR to Stillman, 4 June 1855: "I may add that he has already published two volumes, which have received respectful recognition from the public, and most cordial welcome from many of our best men — Tennyson, Landor, and others" (NYP). For W. S. Landor's praise of Allingham's poems, see *Letters to William Allingham*, ed. H. Allingham and E. B. Williams, 1911, pp. 218-19.

2. *The Music Master* (1855), illustrated by DGR, Millais, and Arthur Hughes (1832-1915), who did the majority of the illustrations. WMR reviewed it in the *Critic*, 1 April 1857, pp. 150-51.

3. Of Thomas Keightley's *An Account of the Life, Opinions, and Writings of John Milton*, *Critic*, 15 February 1856, pp. 92-93. The other notice is not identified.

4. Benjamin Woodward (1815-61), architect of the Trinity College Museum, Dublin, and of the Oxford Museum begun under Ruskin's supervision in 1855. WMR compared him to C. B. Cayley as "the most modest, retiring, and shyly taciturn man of noticeable talent whom it has ever been my fortune to meet" (*FLM*, 1:196).

5. Seven including a preliminary notice, 5 May-30 June 1855 (see "Checklist").

6. Barbara Leigh-Smith Bodichon (1827-91), amateur painter and one of the founders of Girton College, Cambridge, met the Rossettis through the Howitts. She is remembered in Pre-Raphaelite annals for lending DGR her Sussex home, Scalands, during his depression in 1870. MS. Diary, 12 June 1891: "Another of my old friends gone — Mrs. Bodichon: about the most capable and energetic woman I ever knew, and the one who has done the most solid and substantial work."

7. *Eustace Conyers* (1855); reviewed in the *Athenaeum*, 26 May 1855, pp. 612-13.

8. (1828-1907). *The Ballad of Babe Christabel, with other Lyrical Poems* (1854; 4th ed. enlarged, 1854; 1855).

9. *The Catechism.*

38. TO WILLIAM BELL SCOTT

Somerset House,
18 June [1855]

Dear Scott,

Your last note "blew me up" as I merited for the aridity of mine preceding, but I am not certain that you will discern any reformation in this. I am become the most sullen and incapable of human animals at letter-writing.

My main object in taking up the pen Newcastle-wards is to ask when you will be going to Paris. I shall undoubtedly go, and, in all probability, somewhere about the beginning of next month. I go partly for pleasure, partly for the purpose of giving some account of the place to the *Spectator*,[1] whose editor is, I can perceive, rather desirous that the expedition should not be delayed beyond whatever earliest date I may be able to get away from here. I do hope nevertheless that, if you are as willing to join me[2] as I am anxious to join you, we may manage not to miss each other: and I will endeavour to make any reasonable postponement in my power, if necessary for that object. Will you let me hear from you on the matter.

When I sent my last monthly letter to the American paper I told you of, the *Crayon*, I said to the editors I would like to send some extracts from your published volume. Their reply has not yet arrived: but, to be ready for my next dispatch about the 23rd of this month, I have copied out seven: *Love's Calendar*, *Midnight*, *A Study from Life*, and the sonnets to the P.R.B., on the Wind, about H. Van Eyck, and from Raffaelle.[3] As you will guess, brevity in the pieces selected has necessarily been looked to; in addition to which, as you are an artist and the paper is artistic, I considered that pieces having a bearing on art were entitled to a preference.

The account you gave me of your health, though it appears to be coloured by spleen and grotesque, made us uncomfortable. I hope body and mind are more elastic now.

What you say of Owen Meredith[4] is exactly my impression of that luminary: however, I have only seen extracts in the papers from his book. Have you heard, what seems to be an universally accepted fact, that he is the son of Bulwer, — Meredith being a pseudonym? Allingham's little volume is just out, with woodcuts by Millais, Hughes, and Gabriel. I am probably in for reviewing it in the *Critic*, which I shall be willing enough to do. Another review which I shall be more than willing to do, has, after seeming lapsed, turned up again, — that, namely, of your volume.[5] Mackay[6] had been away (I think, abroad); but, having now returned, and being reminded of the matter by Munro, he apologizes for oversight, and allows me half a column, — in which I shall, with all due speed, kick about to the extent of my contracted tether.

You ask me about Woolner's statue.[7] I fancied you would have been already aware that that matter is now among the "were to be." Poor old sturdy Woolner is done again. The subscribers of the money for the statue, who had promised to write on his behalf to Wentworth, did nothing after all; and Wentworth, after shillyshallying a deuce of a while, decides at length that he won't have a statue at all, but give the subscription-money to founding some scholarship in Australia. There seems little doubt that this decision will be carried out; although the ultimate determination of the subscribers is not yet received that I know of. Woolner, who left for this will-o'-the-wisp affair, which he was carrying on swimmingly in Australia, thinks of returning thither one of these days — when, quite unsettled — staying a year or two, and then back finally to England.

I do not understand your rune about "a good thick volume of poetry by the latest of all the new poets[8] — one I have no chance of seeing otherwise" — which Budden was to have brought me from you, and forgot. Thanks for the intended gift anyhow. If your mystic garment of words veils some book of your own, so much the better.

Millais, are you aware? is now at Perth, whither he started last Monday, to be married (tomorrow, I think,) to Miss Gray — erst Mrs. Ruskin. Such is the last act, for the present, of that curious and mournful tragicomedy.[9] Ruskin himself, for whom almost exclusively Gabriel is now engaged in working, has been very unwell of late, and staying at Tunbridge, but he will be back here on Thursday. I have met him, and know few men I like better.

Hunt, when he wrote last, was still at Jerusalem; but he was to have left that place shortly, and to be at Constantinople before now. I have a long-pending engagement to meet him at some point of the Continent on his return home; but, through combined want of money and want of time, I see little prospect of fulfilling it — highly desirous as I am to do so; — unless, indeed, which seems improbable, some arrangement could be hit on to suit the time when I shall be in Paris. Hunt has not had any picture ready to send over from the East to the R.A.; and a life-sized crayon head of his father[10] — admirably done — which was sent was rejected. Those toads the Academicians seem to get more iniquitous, supercilious, reckless, and infatuated, every year. I could tell many another story of their misdeeds this year. Have you one to tell of your own? I am not aware.

What a curious story (story, I suppose, in both senses) that is which you sent me about North's ghost![11] As Gabriel says, there is something awful in the man's pertinacity who, having failed, while alive, to force the Infinite Rep. upon the public, turns up again after death to do so. It is characteristic to the last degree, and, though I have a kindly corner in my memory for poor North, I cannot but laugh at the affair. I don't know what you think of the spirit-rappings. For myself, I have never been *convinced* that they are a mere tissue of imposture

59

(although this particular instance looks suspicious): but then I am scarcely ever convinced of anything either way.

Christina has been very ill this year, and is with my mother at Hastings. They have been there a month or so, and may probably remain as much longer. Maria salutes you and Mrs. Scott. So do I, and am

Your friend,

W. M. Rossetti

If you are to be in London this year, and will put up with Maria's and my humdrum style, I wish you would domiciliate with us — especially now that Mamma's absence gives us such ample room and verge in the way of spare beds etc.

MS: Princeton. Several sentences in *AN*, 2:31.

1. "The Paris Exhibition," 8 September 1855, pp. 935-36; and "Fine Art Section of the Paris Exhibition," 22, 29 September, pp. 983-84, 1017-18; 13, 20 October, pp. 1062-63, 1097-98.

2. WMR went to Paris in August. WBS traveled there earlier, staying on the way with WMR and Maria at Upper Albany Street. WMR to Frances Rossetti, 24 July 1855: "Scott made himself comfortable with us in his dreary way, and we with him.... He looks a good deal better, and even younger, than when I saw him last, and has grown a *retroussé* moustache" (AP).

3. They appeared between 12 September and 10 October 1855. All had been published in *Poems* (1854).

4. Edward Robert Bulwer Lytton (1831-91), son of the novelist Edward Bulwer-Lytton, published *Clytemnestra, the Earl's Return, the Artist and other Poems* in 1855.

5. *Poems* (1854).

6. Charles Mackay (1814-89), editor of the *Illustrated London News*, 1848-58(?) (*NCBEL*).

7. Woolner wrote to his father from Australia on 24 January 1854 about his hope of obtaining the lucrative commission for a statue of William Charles Wentworth (1793-1872), the advocate of colonial self-government. By the middle of 1854 he was confident enough to return to England to make plans for its execution, and told Mrs. Tennyson on 23 October that he had "solid grounds for hoping it will be given to me or I should not have left Australia for another year, as my works in Sydney were very much liked." Almost three years later he had not given up hope, but the commission was finally given to the Italian Pietro Tenerani (1789-1869), whose statue was erected in 1862 at the University of Sydney, which Wentworth had founded (*TW*, pp. 64, 104, 134-35; G. L. Fischer, "Notes on the statue of W. C. Wentworth in the Great Hall, the University of Sydney," typescript in the University of Sydney Archives). Woolner exhibited a medallion portrait of Wentworth at the R.A., 1856.

8. Not identified.

9. WBS to WMR, 21 June 1855: "Millais' marriage is not a pleasant event. What do you think of it? A lady whose complaint against her husband is that reported of Mrs. Ruskin is not an actress who will set much store by either good taste or the affections, and one may fear notoriety has got the better of the man who shares her role. However other men may see the matter in quite another light." Writing on 5 July 1855 from Wallington, where he was visiting the Trevelyans, he commented that Lady Trevelyan ("the most charming woman within my experiences") "takes a true view of the marriage affair. Women judge women best and have cool wits to decide on each other" (Durham).

10. Probably the portrait of William Hunt reproduced in *PR & PRB*, 1:264.

11. WBS's letter has not been found, but he wrote further on 21 June 1855: "... is not that about poor North most excellent. He and Dennys the author of *Alpha* were as jealous as old stays contending for entire and independent originality, and here is an American ghost-seer declaring that somebody else dictated to North as a mere medium!" (Durham).

39. TO WILLIAM JAMES STILLMAN

45 Upper Albany Street,
28 October [1855]

Dear Mr. Stillman,

It was with true regret that I saw in a recent *Crayon* an announcement portending its cessation at the end of the year;[1] and I can only say I hope that result may be averted. I have no desire to "do the magnanimous," nor any, in the abstract, to forego what I can fairly get; but I hope you will consider me as among the friends of the *Crayon*, who would be much better pleased to render their personal claims compatible with the interests of the work than to press those claims to its detriment. If any mode occurs to you in which I can serve the cause, I shall be happy to hear it.

Very truly yours,
W. M. Rossetti

MS: NYP.

1. "We must have more subscribers, or we shall close with the present year" (26 September 1855, p. 200). A weekly until 26 December 1855, it was published monthly from January 1856 to July 1861 when it ceased publication.

40. TO WILLIAM JAMES STILLMAN

45 Upper Albany Street,
17 December [1855]

Dear Mr. Stillman,

In your last received note you ask whether it would be practicable to get a photographic negative of some Praeraphaelite work, to be sent over and printed from in America.

The principal Praeraphaelites are three — Hunt, my brother, and Millais. There is also Ford Madox Brown, whom, although not so technically a Praeraphaelite, I count in reference to this matter, as he paints excellent pictures, embodying the same ruling principles.

Hunt is in Asia; and my brother thinks his things would not exhibit the Praeraphaelite characteristics in a form sufficiently tangible for your purpose.

Brown being on the spot, I spoke to him first. He and I both think that his most eligible work would be the Emigrants[1] — of which I spoke in one of my printed letters; but the purchaser of this, who holds the copyright, will not allow a photograph to be taken. Among the other works, the most suitable appears to us to be one from *King Lear.*[2] Millais, who is in Scotland, is also hampered by not having the control of the copyrights; but he writes me to take what steps I choose. The *Ophelia* seems the most *likely* to be obtainable; and nothing, I conceive, could answer more fully.

The reason why I write *at once* is this. Of course, I understand that the whole project is a mere suggestion — an idea which may or may not be realized. In that light I represented it to Brown and Millais. I said, however, that I *inferred* the photographs, if used, would be viewed as paid contributions; but the *Crayon* of December 5 contains a paragraph[3] which makes me somewhat doubt whether they would be wished for on that understanding. Millais, I imagine, would be tolerably indifferent on this point; but Brown might like to understand it clearly before he does anything in the matter. If therefore you would oblige me with a few words to state what is intended, and whether you would wish me to take further steps, I would thank you. You will excuse my particularity in entering upon these details; which I do merely with the view that no one may be committed to anything he does not contemplate.

My own view of the general question is that, if otherwise feasible, the printing of photographs from pictures would form a very interesting and desirable feature — far better than any form of engraving other than the artist's own etching.

I regret the contretemps which you mention regarding the subjects of Miss Howitt's and Tupper's papers. I have not heard from her since I wrote you last.

The poems of W. B. Scott were copied by me, with his concurrence, from a published volume. There was not the slightest occasion for any verbal or other acknowledgement of their receipt.

You allude to the rodomontading hubbub in the newspapers as to the relations of America and England. When England finds herself cheated by any government into a *real* row with America, it will be time for her to clap her governors into the asylum for idiots, or to take up her own quarters there. In the present instance, as far as I have heard of the merits, the Americans were quite right in putting down any interference of ours with their national laws and rights; and the blatant leader in our *Times*[4] was the first meddling attempt to make any serious mischief out of the affair.

My monthly letter will follow this pretty closely.

Believe me,
Very truly yours,
W. M. Rossetti

MS: NYP.

1. *The Last of England*; bought in September 1855 by the dealer David Thomas White, who sold it to B. G. Windus (Bennett 1964, p. 21).
2. *Lear and Cordelia* (Bennett 1964, No. 20).
3. On the expense of quality illustration, which was beyond what the *Crayon* could afford (pp. 360-61).
4. In the previous months the *Times* had frequently commented on the American reaction to Britain's attempt to enlist in the United States for its army in the Crimea. On 2 August 1855 it declared that the United States was legally right in its objections but morally wrong: "their sympathy is their own to give or to withhold, and we have no right to quarrel with our Transatlantic neighbours *if*, in the midst of democracy, they stretch out their hands to despotism, and look coldly on the cause of freedom" (p. 8).

41. TO WILLIAM BELL SCOTT

Somerset House,
14 April [1856]

Dear Scott,

It is certainly a brutal shame that I should never have written to you, especially after receiving more than one admonitory message. I think I have told you before that I have sunk into a condition of crass idleness as regards correspondence of any kind; and, having no excuse to offer, I can only repeat the fact. At last, however, here goes for the most recent news of the men about me.

You insinuate a sarcasm against Gabriel's indolence.[1] It is undeserved. Since Ruskin, now about 2 years ago, began commissioning and buying his water-colours, he has been doing works of that class[2] with really exemplary perseverance, and not without tangible result, though he still abstains from exhibiting. I think Ruskin must possess something like a score of his things by this time — some of which I have myself not seen. Those which I have seen include *Paolo and Francesca* in 3 compartments — the kissing business on one side, the tormented souls on the other, and midway Dante and Virgil; Queen Guenevere refusing her lover Launcelot a kiss when they meet over the grave of Arthur; Beatrice refusing Dante her salute at a marriage feast (a duplicate of one done some years ago, but carried a good deal further); one of the Kings and one of the shepherds led together by an angel to worship at the Nativity; a medieval woman, holding a man's arm, and singing (which Ruskin likes about the best of all). He has on hand the subject, long since projected, of a *Passover in the Holy Family*; a Monk Illuminating (which Ruskin, to our surprise, says is not in *his* line); and, for a Miss Heaton,[3] of Leeds, Dante led by Love in a vision to gaze on the corpse of Beatrice, over whom two ladies are lowering a sheet strewn with flowers. This is one of the largest, and, I incline to think, the best, thing he has done. He did talk of doing it in oil as soon as it is finished in water-colour; but now he seems minded to revert to the subject, already begun in oil, of an unfortunate girl in London streets recognized in dawnlight by her early sweetheart. There is also a portrait in water-colour of the archangel Browning, done when he was here last autumn, and as like him as can be. Gabriel and I saw him and his wife rather frequently at that time;[4] and at his house Tennyson, who read us *Maud* right through, and who, though he talked of scarcely anything except the abuse of *Maud*, is the most impressive man, both in person and otherwise, that I think I ever met. Browning too is a most glorious fellow; natural, simple, kind, vivid, witty, interested in everything worth being interested in, and seeming to possess a knowledge, often profound, always seemingly sufficient, of everything worth knowing. Why don't you say something in your letter about his two splendid new volumes?[5] or have you not read them? If not, procure them at once somehow or other, and fasten upon *Childe Roland, Bishop Blougram's Apology, Fra Lippo Lippi, Karshish the Arab Physician, A Toccata of Galuppi's* and the closing dedication of the book to his wife. Of course there are no end of others tremendously fine, but these occur to me in chief. Mrs. Browning, an interesting little woman, very diminutive but not particularly plain, the very embodiment of fragile sensitiveness, talking sensibly, but not saying anything very remarkable (except the remarkable atrocity that she adores Correggio) is writing a long poem,[6] whereof I know not the subject. Gabriel saw them again in Paris very frequently, having gone there in the autumn, and they are to be in London not long hence, prior to returning to Florence. The gain of Gabriel's Paris stay, I may add, was an intense admiration of Delacroix, at whom almost alone he seems to have looked in the Exhibition.

Hunt came back from Jerusalem with the addition of a cosmetic beard, and looking better settled in health, but otherwise little altered. He has taken a house in Claverton Terrace, Pimlico (not far from Thames Bank), a large house of handsome aspect, but in a dreary half-built neighbourhood, and, I think, not over healthy. Joined with him there are Halliday[7] and Martineau,[8] whom you may have heard of, or possibly seen; the latter an artist, the former something between artist and amateur. Both go in for Praeraphaelitism, and both look up to Hunt with a genuine reverence and affection. I think they may get on comfortably together. The only oil-picture which Hunt has sent to the R.A. is the *Scapegoat*;[9] to which are added three very elaborately made out water-colours[10] — a Jerusalem view by Moonlight, the Great Sphinx, and the plains of the Dead Sea. The *Scapegoat* is a very remarkable picture. Ruskin, with all his thick and thin upholding of Hunt, says it is only fit to be the sign of the Goat and Compasses; Woolner vows it is altogether ahead of anything Hunt had done before. I have only seen it twice; once by a wretched candlelight, once by the last waning of daylight. The first time I was rather disappointed with it than otherwise, though it never appeared to me other than a fine thing; the second I liked it so much better that, though I don't suppose I shall ever agree with Woolner, I believe lengthened acquaintance with it will make me rate it very high. With the public I fear it will be all but a failure, and certainly a theme for no little ridicule; but Horace's feeling about the *profanum vulgus*[11] is, I suppose, the only right one in art-matters. As to Hunt's other works besides several water-colour views, studies, etc. (though perhaps not so many nor quite so conspicuous as you might expect) there are three oil-pictures.[12] The first he had quite reckoned on sending to the R.A., but a few points remained to be finished, which he did not like to scamp. It is a small street-scene in Cairo: a young lantern-maker seated on his shop-board, in conversation with the girl he is plighted to, pressing his hand against her features through the black veil, to find out what she is like — being forbidden to look at her face till the marriage-day. Hunt witnessed such an incident on the spot. It is a capital little picture, but rather disappointing to me in not rendering the *beauty* of the incident in proportion to the character of it. The second is a half-figure (I think lifesized) of an Egyptian girl — most grand in character, colour, and design. Of this by far the better part is done. The third is Christ with the Doctors in the Temple, found by Joseph and Mary. This is the largest work Hunt has yet undertaken, and is to my judgement sure of being quite the best; indeed, I think it exceeds all other art that I know for combination of national peculiarity, individual character, and the right tone for such a subject. However, as yet neither Christ nor his mother is begun. Joseph's head is done — very fine, but I think scarcely Joseph; and what else he has yet painted is the heads and parts of the figures and costumes of some eight or nine Doctors, with a little of the background. He has got good employment for the ensuing year in finishing the picture.

Millais sends 5 pictures to the R.A.[13] The largest is named *Peace Concluded*: an Officer back from the Crimea, with his wife (Mrs. Ruskin-Millais) on the sofa, reading the *Times* news of the peace, and his two little girls, one of whom, playing with a Noah's Ark, has produced the lion, Russian bear, cock, and turkey, and finally brings out the dove with the olive-branch. "Rather puerile," I can fancy you saying. The picture is painted with great vigour and effect, less elaborately than aforetime, but still not giving much ground for dissatisfaction on that score. It is sold for £900 (!) exclusive of copyright: so you see Millais has not lost the art of success. The second picture is vastly above this. It has no subject — simply four girls (children) burning a heap of autumn-leaves, and is also not of the more elaborate order: but it is a tremendous piece of colour, mastery, and that kind of poetic feeling which, without exactly knowing wherein it resides, one recognizes in works of Titian or Giorgione. The third is (at least in the background) the most P.R.B. of his works this year, and otherwise very pathetic and beautiful: a blind girl, with her sister, seated on a roadside, after a shower, with sunlight shimmering again over the fields and a double rainbow in the sky. The fourth (of which I fancy I told you something before) represents a scene which may be imagined to take place in the first French Revolution. Some soldiers are defending an old church; a little girl has got wounded in the scuffle; and she has been laid down to sleep upon the Gothic effigy of a Knight. The girl is very nice, the stonework very delicate, if not very solid; the background figures meagre and unmeaning: altogether it is a pretty little work, hardly worthy of Millais. The fifth is quite a small thing — a little boy looking over Leech's book of designs from *Punch*. On the whole, it is undoubtedly true that Millais is confirming himself in the tendency to paint with greater breadth, and more for distant effect; but, if he keeps up to the standard of the *Autumn Leaves*, I conceive this to be still Praeraphaelitism, and perfectly legitimate. It is to be hoped he will not lose himself in obvious, popular, or frivolous subjects; but I think the want of Hunt's companionship may be felt on this point, unless he soon settles in London. He has been here just now, and returns to Perth tomorrow, to be back again in a fortnight or so. His wife, I believe, is on the eve of a confinement.[14] To me he looks rather gaunt and overworked; certainly he has been painting hard. He means now to do a spring picture[15] with all the trees in pink bloom, as a pendant to the *Autumn Leaves*; and a cliff and sea-shore picture[16] by night, with the rather absurd incident of a somnambulist girl followed by her father with a lantern. Doubtless he will make something strange and impressive out of it; but *meaning* is not apparent.

Collins, it seems, has after all failed to get anything ready in time. Hughes sends a pretty subject and very pretty picture named *April Love*, together with a work in 3 compartments from the *Eve of St. Agnes*, which most people seem to think his best thing, and which certainly has exquisite merits, though I think wanting in matter. Gabriel, though of course he sends nothing of his own, forwards a very bad portrait of Browning which has been lying with him for some while, done by a Yankee Titian named Page.[17] Woolner has his very beautiful and finished figure *Love* (a girl putting a lily in her hair) and two or three medallions.[18] Munro had a hurried Woman and Guardian Angel;[19] Inchbold[20] 3 very good landscapes. Brown does not send. Then there is Leighton's[21] Orpheus recovering Eurydice from Hell by playing to Pluto (a great subject) and Ward's Marie Antoinette taking leave of her family,[22] which Millais speaks very well of. Of these two I have not seen either. Miss Howitt sends a Boadicea meditating Vengeance[23] — conscientiously intended, but not, I think, happily achieved. You don't say whether you have forwarded anything.

Woolner has lately been down with Tennyson in the Isle of Wight, and has brought up, in plaster, the bust which he did of him there. It is a perfect likeness, and a capital work. Millais was so delighted with it that he has commissioned Woolner to do one of himself, and probably another of his wife. Woolner is looking out also for Ruskin; and it would not be a bad advertisement for other customers if he could show the three men together next year.

Patmore's poem[24] I had expected to see out a month ago; but it is still *in prospectu*; and the author, I hear, laid up with a carbuncle. He had contemplated 5 parts like the one already published; but seems now, and surely with reason, to lean to doing only one more, and that of a more lyrical character.

Your letter gives me hopes that you may probably at a not very distant date settle again in London. That would be one of the best things for me I can think of. Your name is often heard in our house, and none the less since the return of Maria, who never tires of your virtues and fascinations and Mrs. Scott's kindness, and looks upon everything connected with dingy Newcastle in rose-light. She and all of us were sorry to hear of the death of Mrs. Norquoy.

I did write the Ruskin review in the *Spectator*.[25] If it does not enforce the very admiring deference which I entertain for Ruskin and whatever he writes, I regret it. However, when one reviews book after book of the same man, it is difficult to say for each what one says for the whole body of them; and some extracts which I had inserted were cut out. The 4th volume is now all but out, I suppose. Besides this, Ruskin is editing a book of Turner's prints (*The Harbours of England*, I think) and, as I am told from a source which ought not to be doubtful, is writing a kind of Handbook for Young Painters.[26] He is a most indefatigable man.

In telling you news of Gabriel, I should not have omitted to mention two projects in which he is affected. First there is a reredos in the Llandaff Cathedral[27] which the promoters of the restorations now in progress there want to get painted, and they have applied to Gabriel. The funds are deficient, but subscriptions are promised; and, if £400 is raised, Gabriel will paint them a work in 3 compartments, or perhaps something less elaborate according to the terms. He proposed the Nativity for the middle, with David and Paul in the two wings; but the people seem to think there is some popish savour in these subjects, so the question is still to be settled. The second project is still more important. There is a millionaire in Manchester[28] (indeed he is said to be worth 14 millions, but that seems to me preposterous) who intends to ease himself of a little superfluous gold by giving a public park at Stalybridge, near Manchester, to the people, with museums, and what not, including a chapel. Millionaire knows Woodward, the architect of the Oxford University Museum, and Woodward knows Gabriel. Woodward is to have the building of the chapel, and the object is to get *carte blanche* into his hands, when he would get Gabriel to plaster his chapel from top to bottom and end to end with frescoes. That would be something worth setting one's hands to. Ruskin is in the project; and, though it looks perhaps rather chimerical as I write it, there appears to be serious chances of its coming to some positive result. However, for the present, all is thickly confidential.

The little book on Health,[29] of which Mrs. Epps sent me two copies, was duly transferred to the editor of the *Spectator*, with an intimation from me that it was sent for review. No notice, however, has yet appeared; possibly because (if I am not mistaken) the book is not of very recent date, possibly because it is looked upon as a *pamphlet*, and pamphlets are scarcely ever more than put down in the list of Books Received. I am sorry if Mrs. Epps has experienced any disappointment in the matter. There is a spiteful paragraph of notice of the book in the last *Athenaeum*: they seem to assume that it is by a practicing homoeopathist, and abuse it as a matter of course.

You see there is a new National Gallery row getting up, and the salary of your old crony Wornum[30] seems to be somewhat imperilled. There is an article on the question in the last *Spectator* with which I don't sympathize, for I think Eastlake and his assistants have not yet committed any so flagrant blunder as to call for fulmination. The Veronese, which you will see on coming to town, is assuredly an inferior picture; but I never saw ground for doubting its authenticity, and Ruskin swears that that is beyond question. If they kick out Eastlake, I don't suppose they will catch a better man, though there is such a thing to be found.

What pictures have you been painting, or what books reading? You tell me nothing on these scores. Maria was loud in her enthusiasm as to a corn-field of yours.[31] The last new book I read was Lewes's *Goethe*[32] — an able and interesting book written with ample preparation and calm impartiality, though I have no penchant for Lewes. Then there is a volume of poems under the name *Pinocchi* (a foolish affectation) done by a son of Mrs. Norton,[33] and which, I fancy from extracts, has at least cleverness and knack in it.

Do you know anything of Dallas,[34] an Edinburgh man who wrote a book called *Poetics*, and who lately married Miss Glyn? He is a man of talent and a pleasant man to know, albeit he sold himself to the devil by writing the *Times* review of *Maud* (which poem you abused too much in your last letter) and by telling Ruskin that Wilson[35] had created Wordsworth's fame, whereupon Ruskin told him he would rather take the opinion of a clown at the Surrey upon Wordsworth than Wilson's. Dallas is doing the art-notices for the *Times*.

Remember us to Mrs. Scott most kindly.

Yours,
W. M. Rossetti

MS: Arizona.

1. WBS to WMR, 6 April 1856: "To ask you to write is like asking me to teach — or Gabriel to

relax his industry and snatch a little idleness'' (Durham).

2. The following works are mentioned: *Paolo and Francesca da Rimini* (Surtees 75); *Arthur's Tomb* (Surtees 73); *Beatrice Meeting Dante at a Marriage Feast, Denies Him Her Salutation* (Surtees 50 R. 1); *The Nativity* (Surtees 71); *La Belle Dame Sans Merci* (''a medieval woman''; Surtees 76); *The Passover in the Holy Family: Gathering Bitter Herbs* (see Surtees 78, 78A, 78B); *Fra Pace* (''a Monk Illuminating''; Surtees 80); *Dante's Dream at the Time of the Death of Beatrice* (the oil replica [Surtees 81 R. 1] dates from 1871); *Found* (''an unfortunate girl''); *Browning* (Surtees 275).

3. Ellen Heaton whom Ruskin encouraged to buy paintings by Rossetti and Turner (C & W, 5:1).

4. WMR met Browning c. 1853, and remained friendly with him, despite the virulent suspicion that DGR developed towards him.

5. *Men and Women*, 2 vols., 1855. For WBS's reply see *RRP*, p. 134.

6. *Aurora Leigh* (1857).

7. Michael Frederick Halliday (1822-69), a parliamentary clerk in the House of Lords from 1839. He exhibited at the R.A., 1853-66, attracting attention with *Measure for the Wedding Ring* (1856), of which WMR wrote: ''The painting is in parts too thin, and the general treatment has a matter-of-fact tendency; but the study and resolute truth-telling which it displays are the sure discipline for a young painter'' (*Spectator*, 31 May 1856, p. 591).

8. Robert Braithwaite Martineau (1826-69) worked in Hunt's studio as a pupil c. 1851-52 (Wood). In his review of Martineau's first R.A. picture, *Kit's Writing Lesson* (1852), WMR praised the painter's diligence, but objected that ''some of the background objects are too prominent; their multiplicity and minuteness easily leading to this error'' (*Spectator*, 5 June 1852, p. 543).

9. Bennett 1969, No. 33.

10. *Jerusalem, by Moonlight; The Sphinx, Gizeh, looking towards the Pyramids of Sakhara* (Bennett 1969, No. 133); *View from the Mount of Offence*.

11. ''Odi profanum vulgus et arceo,'' *Odes*, III, i. 1.

12. *A Street Scene in Cairo: The Lantern Maker's Courtship* (Liverpool Academy, 1861); *The Afterglow in Egypt* (16 Hanover Street, 1864); *The Finding of the Saviour in the Temple* (German Gallery, 1860-62): Bennett 1969, Nos. 28, 29, 31.

13. *Peace Concluded*, 1856 (bought by John Miller). *Autumn Leaves; The Blind Girl; L'Enfant du Régiment; Portrait of a Gentleman* (''H. G. Chetwynd-Stapylton as a child''): Bennett 1967, Nos. 53, 51, 52, 50.

14. A son Everett (1856-97) was born on 30 May.

15. *Apple Blossoms* (Spring), R.A., 1859 (Bennett 1967, No. 58).

16. Probably *The Kingfisher's Haunt* (J. G. Millais, *Life and Letters of John Everett Millais* [1899], 2:468).

17. William Page (1811-85), portrait painter, lived in Italy, 1849-60, where he was friendly with the Brownings. The portrait of Browning was not hung.

18. Woolner exhibited four medallion portraits: W. C. Wentworth, G. W. Cole, Charles Ernest Howitt, and Carlyle.

19. Munro exhibited six works, but not the one described.

20. John William Inchbold (1830-88). In 1852, three years before Ruskin praised Inchbold in *Academy Notes*, WMR cited his R.A. picture, *A Study*, as evidence that ''In landscape art ... Pre-Raphaelitism is visibly making its way'' (*Spectator*, 19 June 1852, p. 593). Although WMR's final judgement was that Inchbold was ''harassed by ill success into losing or frittering away his finer powers'' (*SR*, 1:229), as late as 1878 he called *At Home: from High Wickham to Beachy Head* (R.A.) a ''choice work'' (*Academy*, 8 June 1878, p. 516). At the R.A., 1856 Inchbold exhibited only two works, *Mid Spring* and *The Burn, November*.

21. Frederic Leighton (1830-96). His picture, *The Triumph of Music*, was reviewed unfavorably by WMR. Comparing it with *Cimabue's Madonna Carried Through the Streets of Florence*, ''which gained him so rapid a reputation last year,'' he observed that it was ''as destitute as it could well be of executive beauty or charm, and of everything which made that picture valuable, — the colour coarse and hard, the composition null, the draperies thoroughly common in arrangement and design.... The only way to keep patience with it is to consider the temper of mind in which the work is conceived'' (*Spectator*, 24 May 1856, p. 571).

22. *The Last Parting of Marie Antoinette and her Son*.

23. Not hung.

24. *The Espousals* (1856), Bk. 2 of *The Angel in the House*. *Faithful for Ever* followed in 1860, and *The Victories of Love* in *Macmillan's Magazine* in 1861, both of which were reissued in 1863 as Part 2, Bks. 1 and 2, of *The Angel in the House*. A third part, ''of which some of the poems in *The*

Unknown Eros, and other Odes [1877-78] are almost certainly fragments'' (*Poems of Coventry Patmore*, ed. Frederick Page, 1949, p. viii), was interrupted by Emily Patmore's death in July 1862.

25. *Modern Painters* 3; 2 February 1856, pp. 145-46. WMR reviewed vol. 4 in the *Spectator*, 17 May 1856, pp. 535-36.

26. *The Elements of Drawing* (1857).

27. *The Seed of David* (Surtees 105). The centerpiece represents the Nativity; the two wings portray David, in one as shepherd, in the other as king.

28. Probably Robert Platt (1802-82), described in an obituary as "one of the largest cotton spinners in the world"; art patron and major contributor to the restoration fund of Chester Cathedral (*Stalybridge Reporter*, 17 June 1882, p. 3). According to Samuel Hill, *Bygone Stalybridge* (1907), he intended to give a park: "Plans were prepared by a local surveyor and designs submitted, but through some unexplained cause the idea was abandoned" (p. 232). His obituary noted that "At one time he intended building a church near his mills at the south end of the town, but the idea never matured."

29. Ellen Epps, *Practical Observations on Health and Long Life* [1855]; reviewed in the *Athenaeum*, 12 April 1856, p. 460.

30. Ralph Nicholson Wornum (1812-77) was associated with the Schools of Design from 1848 to 1854, when he was appointed keeper of the National Gallery and secretary to the trustees, a position he held until his death. On 12 April 1856 the *Spectator* criticized the director of the National Gallery, Charles Lock Eastlake (1793-1865), for his purchasing and cleaning policies, and referred to Veronese's *Adoration of the Kings* (purchased 1855) as a fraud (pp. 398-99). *The National Gallery Illustrated General Catalogue* (1973) notes that "some studio assistance is evident" in the picture (p. 781).

31. Not identified.

32. *The Life and Works of Goethe* (1855) by George Henry Lewes (1817-78), journalist and common-law husband of George Eliot.

33. Thomas Brinsley Norton (1831-77), second son of Caroline Elizabeth Norton (1808-77), who was known as "the Byron of poetesses." *Pinocchi*, published anonymously in 1856, was called by the *Athenaeum* "a Pre-Raphaelite book" (17 May 1856, p. 613).

34. Eneas Sweetland Dallas (1828-79) studied philosophy at Edinburgh under Sir William Hamilton. He published *Poetics*, a work of psychological aesthetics, in 1852; and wrote extensively for the *Times*, *Daily News*, *Saturday Review*, and *Pall Mall Gazette*. His marriage to Isabella Glyn was dissolved in 1874.

35. John Wilson (1785-1854), professor of Moral Philosophy at Edinburgh and major contributor to *Blackwood's Magazine*. He was the author of the largest number of the *Noctes Ambrosianae* papers (*Blackwood's*, 1822-35), in which he appears as "Christopher North."

42. TO WILLIAM JAMES STILLMAN

45 Upper Albany Street,
23 April [1856]

Dear Mr. Stillman,

I am glad to see by the last *Crayon* that the MS. of Stephens,[1] which, it was feared, might have miscarried in the "Pacific," arrived safe.

With my monthly letter, I submit a tale (merely inventive) by a sister of mine.[2] That she is a person of capacity I know, and she has a correct feeling for art: but I naturally feel reluctant to do anything that might look like *palming off* the work of relatives or immediate friends, and so I beg you, if the tale is not to your liking, to decline it frankly. On the other hand, if it *is* deemed suitable, my sister would of course be gratified.

I regretted to learn from one of the late letters from your office, that your health has been somewhat unsettled. I hope you may be fully set up again now, and am

Very truly yours,
W. M. Rossetti

MS: NYP.

1. Probably the first of four articles with the title "Some Remarks Upon the Life of B. R. Haydon," published between February and June 1856. The *Life* was by Tom Taylor.

2. CGR. The tale, "The Lost Titian," appeared in July 1856, pp. 200-202, signed with her initials (rptd. *Commonplace and Other Short Stories*, 1870). For it she was paid £1.16.0 (Durand to WMR, 11 December 1856; AP).

43. TO JOHN BROWN DURAND

45 Upper Albany Street,
22 June 1856

Dear Sir,

I received your letter of the 23rd ultimo, enclosing draft for £29.10, which I have distributed in the proper proportions, except Miss Howitt's[1] share, which awaits her directions, as she is out of town. You say in a note "A mistake has been made in drawing the draft: will rectify it the next remittance." I suppose this mistake is the having substituted 10/- for 12/-; which I mention, as I am not aware of any other mistake.

I am sorry to hear of the critical financial position of the *Crayon*.[2] As regards your intimation that you would wish to pay my monthly letters at £1.1 each, instead of £2.2, I shall answer with the same frankness which I appreciate in your letter. I shall continue for the present — and probably till the end of the year — writing for £1.1, being sincerely pleased to do the utmost in my power for the *Crayon*: but, as I can scarcely look upon this rate of payment as remunerative, I am not prepared to say that I should continue writing for it, in case the *Crayon* should go on after the end of the year. I leave it to you to pay my *last* monthly letter, written before the receipt of yours, either at £1.1 or £2.2, as may be most convenient.

The enclosed letter from Stephens will show you his view of the payment question. He does not there state distinctly — but I gathered from him in conversation — that, if you do not use, with payment, the articles on Praeraphaelitism,[3] he would anticipate either to receive back the tale[4] unused, or to be paid for it. Tupper I have not had an opportunity of seeing; but I *believe* he intends to continue writing.

With my best wishes I remain,

Very truly yours,
W. M. Rossetti

MS: NYP.

1. She contributed two articles entitled "Unpainted Pictures" (January, March 1856), for which she was paid £3.9.0 (Durand to WMR, 23 May 1856; AP).

2. Durand to WMR, 23 May 1856: "We have now reached a period in the year where we can calculate the prospects of the *Crayon* so far as the present year is concerned. From this time forth we shall be carrying it on at a loss, and so great a loss that, unless very favourable circumstances occur, it will be discontinued at the end of this year. We might stop it now, but we take pride in doing all we said we would at the beginning of the year and it will go on accordingly to the 1st January of 1857. In order however to make the loss as light as possible, we must discontinue payment for further contributions, except your own letters, which we should be sorry to lose. In regard to these, we say frankly, we should prefer to pay at the rate of one guinea each, instead of *two*, if you are willing,

under the circumstances, to make the reduction. / The circulation of the *Crayon* has increased this year over that of last year very considerably — and the writer does not doubt but in the course of two years, it would be large enough to sustain the magazine. But the capital being nearly exhausted — (what we had to command) — is a circumstance of itself acting unfavourably upon it, if it should be known to the public or even friends. And as to incurring obligations upon credit we are not willing to do it'' (AP).

3. Four articles entitled "The Two Pre-Raphaelitisms" were published in August, October, November, December 1856. For his payment, see Letter 46.

4. "The Reflection in Van Eyck's Mirror," *Crayon*, October 1856. For his payment, see Letter 46.

44. TO JOHN BROWN DURAND

45 Upper Albany Street,
21 November 1856

Dear Sir,

I have received your letter of the 21st October intimating that the question of continuing the *Crayon* is not yet decided, but would probably be so before my commencing the letter of the present month. You ask me at the same time to continue writing, unless you advise me to the contrary.

I should much regret if my failing to do this entailed any inconvenience or disappointment on you; but, upon the whole, I have felt disinclined to indite a letter which there may possibly be no opportunity of publishing.

My reasons, independently of that uncertainty, are these. In the first place, I am now writing at the reduced rate of £1.1 a letter which I willingly consented to accept till the end of the year, but which would not pay me for a continuance. Then, I have recently entered into an engagement with an Edinburgh journal[1] for art-contributions, including a weekly summary of news; which would make it somewhat tedious to do at the end of the month pretty nearly what I have been doing by instalments week by week, while of course, I could not think of sending you a mere transcript of my Scotch summaries. If the *Crayon* continues and you revert to the £2.2 rate I should like, however, with your permission to consider the matter further. In case, through one reason or another, my letters should cease while the *Crayon* continues, I may perhaps mention that Stephens, in a conversation I had with him, expressed his readiness to undertake the monthly letters[2] — though not at so low a rate as £1.1. Or, if you should at all like such an arrangement, I would gladly send you the Scotch paper containing my weekly summaries for any use you might be able to make of it[3] — of course, not expecting any remuneration.

If *possibly*, in the absence of my letter for the present month, you should care to avail yourself of an article which I wrote in the *Spectator* on an interesting event — the display of a first instalment of the Turner Bequest — I enclose the extract.

Believe me,
Very truly yours,
W. M. Rossetti

P.S. I had *begun* my monthly letter, with some particulars that might make the

71

Turner subject clearer to American readers: this also I enclose in case you should care to incorporate with the article any details from the letter.[4]

MS: NYP.

1. *Edinburgh Weekly Review*. During its brief existence from 28 February to 31 October 1857, WMR contributed three articles, "The Abstract and Naturalism in Art" (28 February, pp. 3-6), "Pre-Raphaelitism" (7 March, pp. 22-24), "The Externals of Sacred Art" (28 March, pp. 67-69); and ten summaries of art news, weekly from 28 February to 2 May.
2. London letters continued to appear in the *Crayon*, several of which may be by Stephens.
3. Extracts from the summaries were reprinted in May 1857, pp. 153-54; "The Abstract and Naturalism in Art" in March 1859, pp. 65-68, the latter with WMR's name.
4. WMR wrote four articles on the Turner Bequest for the *Spectator*, 1, 15, 29 November, 20 December 1856, pp. 1159-60, 1219, 1266, 1366. The second of these was reprinted in the *Crayon*, January 1857, pp. 23-24, with the introductory remarks referred to here.

45. TO WILLIAM BELL SCOTT

45 Upper Albany Street,
25 December [1856]

Dear Scott,

Many thanks for the *Leaves of Grass*,[1] which I have not yet received from Woolner, but shall be eager to read as soon as I get it. Woolner and others denounce the book in the savagest of terms; but I suspect I shall find a great deal to like, a great deal to be surprised and amused at, and not a little to approve — all mingled of course with a lot of worse than worthless eccentricity.

You sent me the other day also a Northern paper with a leader which I was glad to read upon your *St. Cuthbert*.[2] "The magnificent picture" is a phrase which, whether used by a man of insight or a humbug, portends celebrity, if not appreciation. Your Wallington work[3] will make you the greatest figure in North of England art safe enough, and will attract, I should think, visitors and renown from far and wide.

4 January [1857]

A happy new year to you and Mrs. Scott. I was interrupted in writing this on Christmas day, and have actually not had a spare half-hour since to sit down in to finish it.

The *Leaves of Grass* has come to hand. My best expectations are more than confirmed by what little I have read as yet; and Gabriel, who has had nothing but abuse for it hitherto, tends even towards enthusiasm. You could not have given me anything I should better like to receive.

What is Woolner's "centre sculpture for the Hall" at Wallington[4] to be, do you know? I asked *him* about it just after receiving your note, and he did not seem to have any distinct idea of either the subject or the extent of the commission. I hope it will be a good one, and that he will make a good thing of it; for really it is beginning to be high time he should take up his proper position.

Of Lady Trevelyan[5] I saw but very little the single time I met her (at Mrs. Loudon's[6]), but that little was all of the right sort. She seems particularly frank, unaffected, and good-humouredly willing to be pleased — as the eminent Sparkler (do you read *Little Dorrit?*) phrases it, a woman "with no nonsense about her, egad."[7] I had *rather* more conversation with Sir Walter,[8] whom I should judge to be a fine-minded man of both natural and acquired dignity. He would do very well for Don Quixote — not the Don of the caricaturist, however. Both spoke most lovingly of you.

Aurora Leigh was sent to Gabriel (as also to Woolner) by Mrs. Browning herself; and both of them are unboundedly enthusiastic about it. I have read as yet something less than 2 books of it, stuffed and loaded with poetic beauty and passionate sympathy and insight. It is certainly better than only a succession of fine things; though, even to take the book from that point of view, it would be quite a wonderful thing of its kind. I confess, however, I stand somewhat taken aback at the prospect of the 14,000 (I think) lines of blank verse, introspection, and humanitarian romance, and I would not venture to name any early day for coming to the end of it, even could I take it up at once for good. Splendid or indifferent, I am satisfied no blank-verse poem ought to be 14,000 lines long.

My trip this last summer was among the pleasantest I have to remember. I went first to the Isle of Wight, hoping to see, and perhaps be asked to spend a day or two with, Tennyson; but, on calling at his place, which is quite a handsome mansion in squirearchic grounds, I found he was in Wales with all his family. After going all round the West coast of the Island (Freshwater, the Needles, etc.) I crossed over, and got through Hampshire to Salisbury; wishing to look deeper into its glorious cathedral than a half-hour a year or two ago had enabled me, and also to see Stonehenge. Thence back to Southampton, and over to Havre, Rouen, Caen, Bayeux, Coutances, and Granville; a day at that marvellously picturesque castle-rock, Mont-St-Michel — (it was the first trip of any steamer thereto, and the quaint peasant-people flocked in from all sides to wonder at it); and two days in Jersey, where I met poor Tom Seddon,[9] now dead at Cairo, who was going to Brittany for a couple of months there with his wife before proceeding to the East. Rouen, spite of all I have heard tell of its modernization, is still the most medieval fine old place I know; Caen, besides other chuches, has the Abbaye aux Hommes containing William the Conqueror's bones; at Bayeux a most glorious cathedral, and the admirable tapestry — (I was told in the library where this is kept that they have no knowledge of Collingwood Bruce's book:[10] can this be right?); at Coutances another cathedral noble among the noblest. I am not certain but what the Norman Gothic — pointed-arched, I mean, or with combination of round and pointed arches — is the most dignified, great, and impressive, of all architecture — above even such magnificent efflorescent Gothic as that of Rouen. Of Jersey I saw but little; but the sea is deliciously blue-green, the rocks specially fantastic in form, and wonderful in colour — orange lichen of the most startling brilliancy especially common.

I have alluded to Thomas Seddon's death: you had probably met him among our set in London, though I am not certain. He was doing good service in the application of the Praeraphaelite principle to landscape of historic interest, such as Jerusalem, Egypt, etc., and in a year or two more would have made a very decided position. His sudden death (from dysentery out at Cairo at the age of 35) is very melancholy both for his own family, and for the wife whom he had only married some year and a half ago, and whom he leaves with a child. Hunt, like the fine fellow he is, was the first to suggest whether some public recognition and substantial fruit of his exertions might not be attained by exhibition of the works he has left, purchase of one by subscription for some public place, or something of the kind; and just now I shall be setting off to Brown's, where 4 or 5 of us are going to talk the matter over.

Now for a rapid dash at our news. Hunt is painting at his Christ and the Doctors,[11] having established himself for the present in the Crystal Palace for some use that he can turn the Alhambra Court to for the background. Gabriel has done four of his Tennyson designs,[12] and is preparing with some seriousness to paint the rood-screen for Llandaff Cathedral — subject the Nativity. Millais still at Perth. Woolner well on with his Tennyson bust in marble. Arthur Hughes with sufficiency of commissions, and a baby.[13] Hannay with a third do. (girl), and writing for the *Quarterly* etc. Patmore just now troubled with a carbuncle, — the second: that is bad. The Brownings back in Florence (no doubt): their presence in London most delightful to me and all of our set who know them. Brown, who has not yet set to work at *Work*, has done, *inter alia*, a small oil portrait of me,[14] capital in painting and likeness, which he has presented to my mother. I am to write the art of the *Edinburgh Weekly Review*: only that seems to hang fire.

With affectionate remembrances from all of us,

Your friend,

W. M. Rossetti

The "N.W." of my address should be used henceforward for postal convenience.

MS: Princeton. Extract in *AN*, 2:32-35.

1. The first edition of 1855. For WBS's account of acquiring copies of the book from Thomas Dixon, see *AN*, 2:32-33, 267-69. WBS called WMR's attention to the book on 22 May 1856, and sent him a copy as a Christmas gift on 22 December (*RRP*, pp. 134, 147). In 1868 WMR dedicated his edition of Whitman to WBS. Woolner to WBS, 29 December 1856: "I gave the book of dubious pretensions to W.M.R." (quoted in J. F. Cox's dissertation, "An Annotated Edition of Selected Letters of Thomas Woolner," Arizona State University, 1973, p. 76).
2. WBS to WMR, 28 September 1856: "I am more than half through with the first of my pictures, St. Cuthbert persuaded to leave his island and be made bishop" (Durham). The Northern paper is not identified.
3. Wallington was the Northumberland home of Sir Walter Trevelyan and his wife Pauline. WBS to WMR, 22 May 1856: "Have you heard of the splendid commission that has fallen to my lot? It is not likely you have, yet possible, through Munro. I am to paint the Hall at Wallington. There are 8 panels to be filled by canvas pictures, rather more than 6 feet square besides all the decoration, to be done partly on the stone and partly put into the wall on canvas, all of which will be partly done by myself partly by workmen and some part by Lady Trevelyan. The pictures are to illustrate the history and worthies of Northumberland. Is it not capital?" (Durham). See also the National Trust booklet, *Scenes from Northumbrian History by W. B. Scott* (1972).
4. *Mother and Child*, lifesize marble. Raleigh Trevelyan gives 1857 as the date when it was commissioned, November 1866 for its completion, and 2 July 1868 for its dispatch to Wallington ("Thomas Woolner and Pauline Trevelyan," *Pre-Raphaelite Review*, 2 [May 1979], 1, 26).
5. Pauline, Lady Trevelyan (1816-66), friend and patron of the Pre-Raphaelites. WMR visited Wallington with WBS in 1857 (see Note 8).

6. Jane Loudon (1807-58), horticultural writer, widow of the landscape gardener and writer on horticulture, John Claudius Loudon.

7. Edmund Sparkler remarked "of every successive young lady to whom he tendered a matrimonial proposal that she was 'a doosed fine gal — well educated too — with no biggodd nonsense about her'" (Bk. 1, Chap. 21).

8. Sir Walter Calverley Trevelyan (1797-1879). WMR recalls how on his visit to Wallington he became aware of Sir Walter's botanical interests: "he ate funguses which no one else would touch, and gave me a dish of them which I remember with a modified degree of pleasure" (*SR*, 1:262).

9. Thomas Seddon (1821-56). For a biographical sketch see WMR's circular on the Seddon subscription fund (Letter 48). From Seddon's first appearance at the R.A. in 1852 WMR praised him generously in the *Spectator* and later in the *Crayon* (see "Checklist"). He also wrote the *Spectator* obituary, 27 December 1856, pp. 1386-87, and acted as secretary to the subscription to purchase *Jerusalem with the Valley of Jehoshaphat* for the National Gallery.

10. John Collingwood Bruce (1805-92), antiquary and proprietor of Percy Street Academy, Newcastle, published *The Bayeux Tapestry Elucidated* in 1856. As a writer on Northern antiquities he was undoubtedly known to WBS.

11. *The Finding of the Saviour in the Temple.*

12. For the *Poems of Tennyson* (1857), illustrated by DGR, Hunt, Millais, and five artists of the previous generation. Of DGR's five illustrations, no drawing for *Sir Galahad* is recorded in Surtees. She gives 1856-57 as the dates of the designs for the remaining four illustrations (*St. Cecilia, King Arthur and the Weeping Queens, The Lady of Shalott, Mariana in the South*, Nos. 83-86).

13. Hughes married Tryphena Foord in 1855; their first son was named Arthur Foord (W. E. Fredeman, "A Pre-Raphaelite Gazette: the Penkill Letters of Arthur Hughes to W. B. Scott and Alice Boyd," *Bulletin of the John Rylands Library*, 49 [Spring 1967], 325).

14. Bennett 1964, No. 35.

46. TO FREDERIC GEORGE STEPHENS

45 Upper Albany Street,
29 December [1856]

Dear Stephens,

Some more *Crayon* tin (or rather a draft) is to hand, your share being set forth thus:

			£.	s.	d.
June 2	Haydon	14 colums @ 6/-	4.	4.	0.
Aug. 6	2 PRms.	9————————	2.	14.	0.
	Van Eyck	9————————	2.	14.	0.
Oct. 6	2 PRms.	11½————————	3.	9.	0.
Nov. 14	————————	12————————	3.	12.	0.
Dec. 9	————————	9————————	2.	14.	0.
			19.	7.	0.
Nov. 18	Less this amount remitted		10.	0.	0.
			9.	7.	0.

But "there's many a slip." The draft is only payable at 60 days after sight: so you must wait for the present, and I too.

The *Crayon* continues,[1] but my correspondence ceases — at any rate for the present. Durand, however, finishes up our connexion in the handsomest manner by paying me, entirely unasked and without obligation, the full rate of £2.2 to the end of the year, instead of £1.1.

About you he says: "Should it be in my power to resume English correspondence, I should be most happy to do so with yourself or with Mr. Stephens, as you or he might determine…. Please say to Mr. Stephens his articles have been appreciated, and that an occasional article similarly treated on any subject-matter that interests him — i.e., the elements of description so adhered to as to make text intelligible and entertaining — will be welcome and duly compensated as heretofore."

W. M. Rossetti

MS: Bodleian.

1. Durand to WMR, 11 December 1856: "It will be continued as usual with some modifications, the principal one being change of type, together with some economical changes imperative by the nature of things. Among the latter I am compelled reluctantly to discontinue the feature of a paid correspondence — at all events until an increased circulation will *positively* warrant it" (AP).

47. TO WILLIAM BELL SCOTT

Inland Revenue Office,
17 February [1857]

Dear Scott,

When Budden spent an evening with me just lately, and fascinated my Mamma, I told him to tell you to write me a long looked-for letter at once, and I would answer immediately. I am not quite certain whether this injunction and your letter are cause and effect, but at any rate I, much to your surprise, shall keep my promise, so here goes in answer to your sardonic missive. Indeed, I have for some weeks past adopted a systematic course of work — everything at its time — and should probably have written (and, if I have constancy enough, should continue to correspond) promptly, without any express promise.

Patmore, I believe, is now about well again: but his wife has had a very bad attack of illness — I have forgotten, or did not gather, the precise nature of it, — and is, I fear, still laid up. You may have seen that the *Angel in the House*, originally destined to "winnow the silver air"[1] through 7 books, is now advertised as complete in 2.

The *Leaves of Grass*, which I finished some weeks ago, delighted me immensely. I find a great deal very difficult to get at the core of, but far less to censure or scout, and far more to hail with some genuine enthusiasm, than I had expected. I am not even certain about "obliterating utterly with the blackest ink half a dozen lines and half a dozen words." There is nothing, I think, prepensely vicious in the book, but only an universality of sympathy (in fact, an anarchic and annihilating indiscriminateness), and an utter recklessness of conventional glozes of expression: and I should much hesitate to deny a strong man the privilege of putting his strong meat into the first words that come. You speak of the book as having a kind of biblical analogy. This is very much what I felt in reading it: in fact, it struck me as very much a 19th century Book of Job (so far as Job is an expression of feelings and experiences), with the same strenuous love of everything in nature under an immensely increased horizon, and the sense and awe of a personal God evaporated into something which might be equally called blind faith or utter atheism. One must not read the book in scraps: after sitting down to it for an hour or so, one gets into the swing of it, and it rolls one along with a power.

Aurora Leigh I am still reading. It is a most wonderful thing. One scarcely knows at what point to stop one's enthusiasm, the wealth of poetic thought and sympathy is so magnificent, and yet one feels that there is a certain excess in it. Ruskin calls it the most splendid thing in the English language.

I cannot only understand but heartily join in seconding your impulse to do something more in poetry. Still, I think you are right for the present in concentrating your energies upon art. I am quite anxious to see your *St. Cuthbert*, and delight that so brave a field, though late, lies open before you at last. I called at Chatham Place to see your photograph of the picture soon after I heard of its arrival; but Gabriel was out, and I could not light upon it. He speaks very warmly indeed of the picture, and Brown, who is a slow praiser, quite equally so.

Woolner's Tennyson advances splendidly: indeed it is now pretty nearly finished, and will be a noble thing. Bacon[2] also very fine. Dickinson,[3] of Bond Street, is intending to get up an exhibition of photographs of living celebrities, and has asked Woolner whether he would send the Tennyson there for the same time; and Woolner is debating whether to do this, or send to Colnaghi's. He is disinclined for the R.A. He seems to be now in working trim, and has just refused a definite offer to go out to Australia again, and undertake a £1000 sculptural job upon a bank.[4] In reference to his Tennyson I have a dim project which may possibly lead to something, and very probably to nothing. It is to get 100 people to subscribe a guinea each, buy the bust, and present it to some public institution. The thing, once firmly resolved upon, were certainly quite easy of accomplishment: 10 men might start together, speak each to 10 more, and the thing could be done in a week. I started the idea the other day in a vague casual manner, but Stephens, to whom I was speaking, grew red-hot for its execution, and I have since spoken to Brown, who seems also to think it feasible. *The whole affair is to be kept quite close at present*, as it may never come to a head,[5] and must not reach Woolner's ears in an immature state.

Munro I have seen only once or twice lately. His Newton, for the Oxford Museum series, appeared to me better than I had anticipated from its commencement, and better than the Galileo. He is now doing Hippocrates — an intensely uninteresting individual.

Thank you for your offer regarding the Seddon subscription.[6] I enclose you a list of the subscriptions hitherto definitely promised, and you must tell me what to put you down for. I think the list a prosperous one, considering. The meeting held at Hunt's on the 2nd went off excellently, Ruskin making a first-rate speech. He has also written something about Seddon for our new circular, which shall be sent to you as soon as out. The Society of Arts will hold the exhibition of Seddon's works in May, and the picture, when purchased, is to be offered to the National Gallery. You must have met Seddon, I think. He was socially a very pleasant fellow on the surface, and thoroughly a man of honour and a good friend. His pictures too are not by any means common things. I enclose also our first circular, in case you have not seen it. If any names of likely subscribers in your parts occur to you, let me know them, and I will tackle them without asking you to take any further trouble in the matter. If you want to write to Ruskin, you might take the opportunity of the subscription, as he is our treasurer.

There is an idea, which may not or may come to something, of getting up an art-journal in our set:[7] we shall speak to Ruskin about it the first opportunity. You are one of the men whose co-operation we should most hope for, and I wish you would let me know whether there would be any chance of our getting it.

This morning I made a venture of some interest to me by sending off to Macmillan[8] the Cambridge publisher some cantos of my translation of Dante's *Inferno*, asking whether he will undertake the expense of publication. I don't much suppose he will: I would try Smith & Elder after him, and the Oxford Parkers next, but, not being sanguine, shall not be disappointed at ill-success. I think I may have told you before that I have done the whole *Inferno* in the most literal blank verse, — all ready now with notes and introductions. I have also begun the *Purgatorio*, and shall probably finish the *Commedia*, even if I cannot enlist a publisher. The *Edinburgh Weekly Review*, of which the 1st No. is to come out on the 28th, has got my services for art-writing. My first paper is on "The Abstract and Naturalism in Art," and I have just begun one on "Praera-phaelitism." I shall like to do some theoretic writing of this kind, and only regret that the space is restricted.

Of Gabriel, Hunt, and Brown, I have little to tell you: the first being still, I think, at the last of his Tennyson designs, the third setting seriously to work on *Work*, and the second harnessed to his Christ in the Temple, which is a noble thing. It will most assuredly not be ready for the R.A.; probably indeed Hunt won't exhibit there at all this year.

Maria has been far from well some days past, but is getting better. This is her 30th birthday, and it is but yesterday we were children together kicking about.

Remember me most kindly to Mrs. Scott.

Always your friend,
W. M. Rossetti

MS: Arizona.

1. Possibly a misquotation of "Winnows the buxom Air" (*Paradise Lost*, 5:270).
2. For the Oxford Museum.
3. Dickinson Bros., "old-established print-sellers and photographic agents" (*SR*, 1:139).
4. Not mentioned in *TW*.
5. No other reference to the proposal has been found.
6. As secretary of the subscription fund WMR did much of the work. He remembered "having looked right through the *Court Guide*, name by name, so as not to miss thinking of any persons who might be addressed" (*SR*, 1:143). Ruskin served as treasurer, and addressed the Society of Arts on 6 May at the opening of its Seddon exhibition, his speech being reported in the Society's journal on 8 May (rptd. C & W, 14:464-70). Ruskin to WMR, [25 April 1857]: "Please let me know if Mrs. Seddon wishes to be present, as there are some things I would not lay stress upon if she will be. I would rather she were not as it will cramp me a little." [28 April 1857]: "I am in a violent state at the exclusion of the ladies, and am only going to wait for a day to make up my mind whether I *will* give that address at all: it was chiefly to the women I wanted to talk, and I think I shall simply refuse this, saying I find I'm too busy (which I am) to say what I had got to say, and then give a separate lecture

on the pictures somewhere else for the widow's benefit. / If you can get the women let in, of course I won't do this, but if you can't, I'll tell you tomorrow what I shall do.'' [29 April 1857]: "Dante has written me in strong terms of objurgation: so I must do as he wishes, and I will be true to the 6th if I don't catch cold meantime'' (Bodleian; copies made for C & W, but not included).

WMR reviewed the exhibition in the *Spectator*, observing that Seddon's pictures "display art of no common stamp, united with accuracy so consummate as to entitle them to be considered the first fruits of the new principle of undeviating fidelity applied to high historic landscape; to which it may be added, that the energy and spirit of a painter who exhibited his first work in 1852 and died in 1856, could hardly be better attested than by the fact that the line of his productions goes round three sides of the council-room of the Society of Arts'' (9 May 1857, p. 503). See Letter 50 for WMR's further effort on behalf of the family. He also reviewed J. P. Seddon's *Memoir* of his brother in the *Spectator*, 31 July 1858, p. 811.

7. Undoubtedly inspired by the *Crayon*, but it was not undertaken.

8. Alexander Macmillan (1818-96), to whom WMR was introduced in 1854 by J. F. McLennan. He refused the Dante translation in 1857, but published it at WMR's expense in 1865. WMR translated nineteen cantos of the *Purgatorio*, which he tried unsuccessfully to publish in 1900-1901 through the Authors' Syndicate.

48. TO WILLIAM ALLINGHAM

Seddon Subscription Fund

45 Upper Albany Street,
16 March 1857

Dear Allingham,

May I be allowed to solicit your attention to the case referred to in the accompanying copy of Resolutions.[1]

It is proposed, as you will perceive, to raise a subscription for the purchase of an oil-picture of Jerusalem painted by the late Mr. Thomas Seddon, and now remaining the property of his widow, and to offer the picture to the National Gallery. The sum of 400 guineas has been agreed upon as the price to be given for this work. The purchase will be so far beneficial to Mrs. Seddon; but it is the anxious desire of the Committee that the subscription may not be limited to this amount,[2] but that they may have in hand some further funds of which, after paying all contingent expenses, they shall be able to request Mrs. Seddon's acceptance.

The object of the Committee therefore is twofold: — To commemorate the exertions of an able artist by placing his principal work — a work invested, if only by its subject, with the highest and widest interest — where it may be studied by thousands; and to minister to the interests of his widow, and of the infant daughter whom he leaves behind.

As conducive to the purpose of the subscription, an exhibition of Mr. Seddon's pictures and sketches[3] is to be held during the month of May in the Council-room of the Society of Arts, who, with the most considerate promptitude, have acceded to the request of the Committee in this respect.

The Committee feel that they are not without a case which justifies them in coming before the public. They rely not so much upon the fact that Mr. Seddon was an artist of ability and high promise, or upon a natural sympathy for his widow and orphan, as upon his exertions in two important fields, — the art-education of the working-classes,[4] and the illustration, with the utmost fidelity of which art is capable, of the sacred and storied scenes of the East; a pursuit to which he devoted his later years, and which cost him his life.

As the son of a large Furniture-Manufacturer, Mr. Seddon sacrificed to family-claims his own natural inclination from early years to become a professional painter, and was engaged, till the age of about 30, in the design of furniture. His proficiency in this pursuit earned the silver medal of the Society of Arts in 1848.

He became at the same time intimately acquainted with the needs of the art-workman; and it was to his strenuous efforts, seconded at first by a single friend, and afterwards by several artists, that the North London School of Drawing and Modelling, founded in 1850, owed its origin; a school which was for some years the medium of sound art-instruction to throngs of working men, and which, until Mr. Seddon's first departure to the East, remained in a flourishing condition. The exertions which he underwent in this cause produced an illness which permanently affected his health.

On the spirit in which Mr. Seddon next entered upon the treatment of historic landscape in the East Mr. Ruskin has drawn up a brief memorandum, which is appended.[5] It may therefore be sufficient to notice here that, in 1853, he preceded Mr. Holman Hunt, by pre-arrangement, to the East, and was joined by him in Egypt; that he returned to England in 1854; and that, having married in the interval, he started again for Egypt in October 1856, but had scarcely reached Cairo when an attack of dysentery terminated his life at the early age of 35. It needs no professional acquaintance with art to appreciate to a certain extent the dangers and difficulties which a painter must have encountered who sat down on the spot, day by day for months together until his work was finished, to depict the landscape of Egypt and Palestine, undeterred by trying vicissitudes of climate, or the lawlessness of the inhabitants.

The picture of Jerusalem, which it is proposed to purchase and offer to the National Gallery, and which, with others, was visited by many persons at the artist's studio in 1855 and 1856,[6] includes some of the most remarkable sites of the Holy City: the Valley of Jehoshaphat, the Pool of Siloam, the Brook Kidron, Mount Moriah, once the site of the temple, now of the Mosque of El-Aksa, the Mount of Offence, the Tombs of David and of Absalom, the Mount of Olives. The accuracy of the rendering is attested in the following terms by the Rev. Canon Stanley[7] the author of *Sinai and Palestine*; "I have been much struck by the fidelity of this picture. Both in colour and in forms, it appears to me a most exact representation of the neighbourhood of Jerusalem. — A. P. Stanley." I address you in the hope that we may be favoured with your co-operation in this subscription: and am

Very truly yours,
W. M. Rossetti,
Honorary Secretary

MS: Illinois.

1. Passed at meetings on 4 January 1857 at the house of FMB, and on 2 February 1857 at the house of Holman Hunt (printed copy in the Trevelyan Papers, Newcastle). Hunt suggested the subscription to WMR on [22 December 1856] (AP).

2. The subscription realized £600 (*Memoir of Thomas Seddon*, p. 172).

3. "Which shall be open to sale" ("Resolutions").

4. Lowes Dickinson to WMR, 3 February 1857: "I don't know whether Mr. Maurice suggested to you as he did to me, the advisability of embodying in any circular you may be preparing regarding poor Seddon — of those particulars of his earlier life relating to the establishment of schools of art for working men" (AP).

5. Most of the opening paragraph of the memorandum is quoted in *Memoir of Thomas Seddon*, p. 171 (rptd. C & W, 16:465). A copy of the memorandum in WMR's hand in the Trevelyan Papers includes a second paragraph: "The accomplishment of such a purpose in the Holy Land involves both labour and danger such as the profession of an artist has never until now incurred: and it is hoped that the Committee will not be thought to have overrated either the claim on public gratitude which is involved in the sacrifice of the life of a man of genius to the serviceable veracity of his art, or the claim on public sympathy which that sacrifice confers upon his widow and orphan child" (Newcastle).

6. In 1855 Seddon displayed a number of pictures at a "semi-public exhibition at his studio, No. 14 Berners Street" (WMR in the *Spectator*, 14 April 1855, p. 392). WMR specifies eight works, five of them Egyptian subjects. In the following year Seddon sent three works to the R.A., and exhibited at his studio, now in Conduit Street, a number of new works, along with all or some of the works displayed in 1855. WMR reviewed this exhibition in the *Spectator*, 24 May 1856, p. 571; and in the *Crayon*, July 1856, pp. 210-11, where he commented that the practice of artists exhibiting in their studios possessed "various advantages over that of sending to a public exhibition (especially where the space is so limited, and the treatment generally so arbitrary, as in our Royal Academy), and one which seems not unlikely to rise in favour among us."

7. Arthur Penrhyn Stanley (1815-81), dean of Westminster from 1864. At this date he was canon of Canterbury. During 1852-53 he traveled in Egypt and Palestine, and published *Sinai and Palestine* in 1856. He was a member of the subscription committee.

49. TO WILLIAM BELL SCOTT

45 Upper Albany Street,
8 April [1857]

Dear Scott,

The Seddon Subscription *does* go on very well — quite beyond what any of us anticipated at starting: it really does not seem, after all, to be so very hopeless an enterprise to get people's hands into their pockets and out again. Mrs. Seddon, as you have understood, happily "does not need to come before the public for help." Still, her case is one, even in the money point of view, well deserving the sympathy of friends. She has nothing at all of her own, I believe, save £600 insured by her husband and some little money from his pictures; while her father is only a half-pay naval Captain, with heavy family-demands upon him, and only his half-pay (I believe) to meet them. However, we have always kept the mere charity view of the case in the background, when going beyond our own circle. The fund must now, I think, be up to £500, or close upon it.

Mr. Leathart[1] seems to have taken heart under your catechizing, for, in a second letter he wrote me on the Seddon affair, he asked after his chance of a thing from Gabriel.[2] If he is anxious after it, he will have a fine opportunity of displaying his patience, I expect.

Your view of the *Edinburgh Weekly Review* is very much my own (waiving the personal question):[3] still there was something right, though too thick and thin, in the Spasmodic articles,[4] as far as I looked into them. I don't know who wrote that series. The editor is J. W. Finlay, who, I know, dabbles a little with art, and may have written the Edinburgh art-notices. I brought in the (or one of the) political writer — Watts,[5] editor of the *Yorkshireman*, a fine fellow whom Woolner came across in Australia. The poorish article on *Aurora Leigh*[6] was also my introduction (though only as a matter of obligation to a mutual friend). The writer is a Capt. Aidé, who has written a volume of poems. These are, I think, the only writers I know.

I have not read Masson's book,[7] but have a very good opinion of it from observation, casual sight, and hearsay. He is a man I like also — equal, honest, and able.

I share your feeling about altering poems[8] — or other works of art. The changes are frequently injurious in themselves, and always destructive of keeping and genuineness. Let what you have done answer for its sins, and represent what you were when you did it; and do better another time — would be my principle. I don't quite gather from what you say whether you have seen or not some of Morris's tales.[9] I am not very familiar with them, but they are very strange fine things in their way — vague poeticism coruscating with meanings.

Yesterday I saw Millais's pictures for the R.A.[10] — both of the rapid and forcible order of painting. He has done, to my judgement, much better than either, yet each has *something very* fine. No. 1 is the largest picture he has produced, *A Dream of the Past*: an old knight coming back in gilded armour from the tournament carrying 2 children over a stream on his horse (a huge big carriage-horse unfortunately). There is a great deal, I think, of the right fine stuff and true spirit of chivalry in the notion, though scarcely carried far enough in subject: the knight is an elderly one, with a keen characteristic head — very right and good, though he might have been splendider. Glorious Scotch twilight background (same kind of thing as the *Autumn Leaves*). No. 2 is called the Escape of the Heretic: rather a melodramatic absurd subject, but with extraordinary power of dramatic crisis in its embodiment, if one seizes it aright (which many will not). It is a Protestant girl, who has been condemned to an *auto-da-fé*, and is in the yellow dress painted with devils. Enter two monks. No. 1 gags and binds No. 2, and turns out to be the girl's lover, come to rescue her. There is the old priest in the corner, gagged with his rosary, glaring and foaming. The girl is about to scream in astonishment, while she throws herself into her lover's arms: he rushes to catch her, dagger in hand, and with his lips out like this   , saying "hush" with a terrible amount of energy. Colour mostly brown and grey, execution decidedly hurried. This picture, which I take to be rather smaller than the Fireman,[11] has brought £1000 (!) from Agnew of Manchester:[12] the other, two or three times the size, is offered for the same sum (why I cannot perceive), but has not yet found a purchaser. Hunt does not exhibit.

What say you to the following project? A Mr. Ruxton[13] (once or still in the army, and a man of society) has the idea of importing British pictures into New York, so as to found a sort of permanent gallery there — one relay coming in as the previous one sells off. A Yankee millionaire, Russell[14] (I understand one of the first men in the States) will be down with capital, and it is said that the Upper Ten and the Lower Twenty[15] of New York are rife for a new lounge and fine art combined. Mr. Ruxton, of whom Woolner knows something, called upon him the other day to ventilate the project, and to ask whether that ass and beast, George Scharf Jun.,[16] was the right man for Secretary. Woolner of course scrunched Scharf (or thinks he did) — and said I was the man to consult. I went round therefore to Mr. Ruxton's on Sunday, and mean to give him a list of all the men I can think of to whom he ought to apply — of course the *right sort* to the exclusion of humbugs (unless a few of the potentates whose names may dazzle the Yankees). Mr. Ruxton seems leadable, and I think the project by no means unpromising. Would you like me to give your name? If matters prosper, the first lot of pictures might probably be exhibited towards October.

Does your wife know that Mrs. Epps has written a new novel, "Work,"[17] in which the fine arts play a conspicuous part? She asked me to give her my opinion on the MS., which I read and in many respects liked. It is mild, certainly, but sensible and uncommonly natural.

I am not without hopes of seeing you this year. Probably I shall be going to Manchester, whence the way will be both easy and attractive to Newcastle. Your Wallington pictures, as well as yourself, are things I want much to see.

Yours affectionately,
W. M. Rossetti

MS: Arizona.

1. James Leathart (1820-95), Newcastle industrialist. Under WBS's influence he formed a major collection of Pre-Raphaelite and other modern pictures. After Leathart's death WMR described the collection in the *Art Journal*, May 1896, pp. 129-34; and, when the collection was offered for sale at the Goupil Gallery in June and July 1896, wrote an introduction to the catalogue. The exhibition *Paintings and Drawings from the Leathart Collection*, Laing Art Gallery, Newcastle, 1968, reassembled part of the collection.

2. Leathart's first DGR purchase was *A Christmas Carol* (Surtees 98) in August 1859. WBS to WMR, 5 September 1858: "Leathart tells me he has had to refuse a picture from Gabriel — the *Christmas Carol* — from the fact of his funds being at present in a state of collapse, as he has got married, furnished splendidly and been to Switzerland with his young wife who is I think a nice sensible pretty girl" (Durham).

3. WBS to WMR, 5 April 1857, praised WMR's articles as "the best things in it. I subscribed on the faith of your name, and on the whole find it rather heavy and didactic like all Scotch local writings — when the Scotchman emigrates to London his dialetics give him a superiority, but they hold him too tightly in his native air. There's a sententiousness about the *E.W.R.* and at times an inefficiency. The writers don't see the horizon all round, one would say they see no part of the horizon at all" (Durham).

4. Three articles on "Spasmodic Poetry," 7, 14, 21 March 1857, pp. 17-19, 38-40, 51-53. In the first article the reviewer declared that "the spasmodic, though we do not consider it the highest, is yet a legitimate class of poetry."

5. Henry Edward Watts (1826-1904), journalist, translator of *Don Quixote*, biographer of Cervantes. In 1859 Woolner described him as "one of the cleverest political writers we have" (*TW*, p. 166).

6. 28 February 1857, pp. 7-9, by Charles Hamilton Aidé (1826-1906), composer, amateur artist, author of novels and verse, including *Eleanore; and other Poems* (1856). The mutual friend of WMR and Aidé is not identified. In November 1862 both men were guests, along with Swinburne and Laurence Oliphant, of Monckton Milnes at Fryston (James Pope-Hennesy, *Monckton Milnes, The Flight of Youth* [1951], p. 141).

7. *Essays Biographical and Critical* (1856).

8. WBS to WMR, 5 April 1857, objected to DGR's revision of *The Blessed Damozel* in the *Oxford and Cambridge Magazine*, November 1856 (Durham).

9. WBS to WMR, 5 April 1857: "Are not these tales by Morris [in the *Oxford and Cambridge Magazine*] very remarkable?" (Durham).

10. *A Dream of the Past; Sir Isumbras at the Ford* (Bennett 1967, No. 55); *The Escape of a Heretic*.

11. *The Rescue*, R.A., 1855.

12. Thomas Agnew (1794-1871), the art dealer, took his sons William and Thomas into the business as partners in 1850. They set up a branch in London late in 1860.

13. Augustus A. Ruxton (d. 1890). "Captain Ruxton had no sort of connexion with fine art ... but he felt a liking for pictures." His scheme for selling British art in the United States, with WMR as secretary, ran into difficulty from Ernest Gambart (1814-1902), "then the most prominent and resourceful picture-dealer in London," who had American plans of his own (*SR*, 1:264-65). Ruxton's and Gambart's cooperation, the former supplying the oils, the latter most of the watercolors, which followed Gambart's near abusive letters to WMR, is treated in Jeremy Maas, *Gambart, Prince of the Victorian Art World* (1975), pp. 94-97. The venture, which had only limited success because of the American financial crisis in the fall of 1857, brought WMR heavy work and some embarrassment.

14. Probably William Hepburn Russell (1812-72), described in the *Dictionary of American Biography* as a "freighter and founder of the Pony Express," whose business greatly expanded in 1857.

15. The term the "Upper Ten" was first used by the American journalist and writer Nathaniel Parker Willis. The *Athenaeum* referred to "the lower 'ten thousand'" in a review of *The Upper Ten Thousand: Sketches of American Society*, by a New Yorker (28 February 1852, p. 253).

16. George Scharf (1820-95), son of the lithographer of the same name, was the organizer of the Art Treasures Exhibition, Manchester, 1857. In the same year he was appointed first secretary of the National Portrait Gallery, becoming director in 1882.

17. Never published.

50. TO RICHARD BENTLEY[1]

45 Upper Albany Street,
8 May 1857

Sir,

Among the works left by the late Mr. Thomas Seddon, and now on view at the Society of Arts, as shown in the enclosed list, those numbered from 45 to 56 might, it is thought, be found of use to a publisher, being oriental sketches done on the spot, and very accurately studied in outline. Many of the sketches in the sketch-books are also of the same class. I beg leave therefore to invite your attention to these designs, which remain for disposal.

I am, Sir,
Your obedient humble Servant,
W. M. Rossetti

MS: Kansas.

1. (1794-1871), publisher of *Bentley's Miscellany* and the "Standard Novels" series.

51. TO WILLIAM HEPWORTH DIXON[1]

45 Upper Albany Street,
17 June [1857]

My dear Mr. Dixon,

The enclosed circular,[2] which I beg leave to submit to you, broaches a project, for which I am Secretary, for an exhibition of British art in New York. I have sent it round already to a certain number of artists, and shortly shall to others.

Millais, Hunt, E. M. Ward, Inchbold, and others, have already promised to do anything they can for the project, and I hope, and am naturally very anxious, to get up a creditable collection. Of course, the more publicity we obtain, the better.

If the *Athenaeum* would take any notice of the project,[3] in whatever light it might be viewed, that would be a great obligation. The American artists, and some capitalists and other public men in the States, I am glad to understand, receive the idea warmly.

> Very truly yours,
> W. M. Rossetti

MS: Boston.

1. (1821-79), historian, editor of the *Athenaeum*, 1853-69.

2. On 15 November 1858 George Tupper reminded Ruxton of an unpaid bill of £2.10.0 for "Lithographic Circulars" for the exhibition (AP). No printed circular has been found, but it was presumably identical to the circular in WMR's hand that he sent to C. E. Norton on 15 July 1867 (Letter 53). Passages quoted in the *Athenaeum* correspond to the latter.

3. The *Athenaeum* quoted at length from the circular on 20 June 1857, p. 796.

52. TO JOHN BROWN DURAND

45 Upper Albany Street,
17 June [1857]

Dear Mr. Durand,

I now beg to forward to you the enclosed copy of the circular broaching the exhibition project which I recently mentioned to you. A letter which I received the other day from Mr. Ruxton apprizes me that he has made your acquaintance, and has cause to be obliged to you for some kindness; and also, which I am very glad to hear, that the project seems to meet with favour rather than mistrust among American artists.[1]

> Believe me,
> Very truly yours,
> W. M. Rossetti

MS: NYP.

1. WMR to J. B. Durand, 22 May [1857]: "There is one point on which I entertain some misgivings — viz.: whether American artists will regard the project jealously, as an encroachment upon their proper ground. I can only, and most truly, say that the scheme is not conceived in any unfriendly or aggressive spirit, but quite the contrary; as we hope that, if the exhibition achieves any success, it will foster the love and seeking of art in America for the permanent advantage of American artists, as well as the benefit of Britishers by opening to them a second field of action" (NYP). Ruxton to WMR, 20 May 1857 (from New York): "The President and the Academy [see Letter 54, Note 1] are to meet this evening to discuss a plan for renting the only available rooms jointly with me. If they come to an agreement, the rooms will be placed at our disposal at a much lower rent, than if we had to hire them independently. It will be also much to our advantage to be associated in such a friendly manner with the native artists.... The feeling is so strongly in favour of our exhibition that no exertion will be spared on the part of the artists to bring it about. We may safely 'go ahead' with all our energies" (AP).

53. TO CHARLES ELIOT NORTON[1]

45 Upper Albany Street,
15 July [1857]

Dear Sir,

I regret to have been precluded from availing myself of the invitation you were so kind as to convey to me through my brother: but, as I did not receive his note till 12 o'clock last night, it was my ill-luck, and not neglect.

May I be allowed to send you the enclosed circular relative to the proposed American exhibition, in which I understand you feel an interest. From America we have received every encouragement, and I trust we shall be able to justify it.

My brother's note informed me that you leave for America today: so I am in some fear this note also may come too late.

Very faithfully yours,
W. M. Rossetti

New York Exhibition of British Art

It is in contemplation to organize in New York an annual exhibition of the works of living British artists — painters and sculptors.

There is good reason for believing that such an exhibition would be welcomed by the Americans. The wealthy classes in New York are well known to be lavishly sumptuous in the arrangement and decoration of their dwellings, and it is confidently anticipated that they would be glad not only to call in the aid of fine art for this purpose, but to have its productions brought home to them for that constant contemplation and study which exhibitions and museums of a similar order receive from the cultivated classes — indeed, from all classes — throughout Europe. The taste for art is growing in America, as it inevitably must grow with advancing wealth, population, and resources: Americans are already, in Europe, keen competitors at any sale of objects of virtu, or of antiquarian interest. The success which appears to have attended the exhibition of paintings of the Düsseldorf School[2] now for some years established in New York may also be deemed an encouraging precedent: it is difficult to imagine that, if the works of this alien school excite the interest of Americans, those of a race to which they are so closely allied in blood, character, and tradition, will be otherwise than successful with them.

Should the experiment prosper, it is hard to say where its results will stop. It would promise to be, in fact, the creation of a second public for British art, only inferior in importance to the public at home. The influence also of the exhibition upon the native art of America would probably be early and decisive; and a mutual action and reaction would be established, beneficial to both.

Active measures are already in progress for making the projected exhibition a fact. Mr. Augustus Ruxton, the original projector, left London for New York at the beginning of May, with the view of communicating with some of the leading men in the States, and of obtaining a gallery. Mr. Ford Madox Brown, the historical painter, has consented to accompany to America the works that may be offered, and to superintend the hanging and all other such preliminaries.[3] Contributors

86

may therefore rely upon it that justice will be done to their works. An unexceptionable guarantee-fund will be obtained before the works are removed for exhibition, including ample insurance — to the extent probably of not less than £50,000. An eligible offer has already been made for this purpose; and one main object of Mr. Ruxton's visit to America is to prosecute further enquiries on the matter. Exhibitors would be relieved from all expenses of transport; but a moderate percentage, to be fixed before final arrangements are made, would be charged upon the sale-price of any works disposed of out of the exhibition.

The first exhibition will, it is hoped, be opened in New York in October next, and remain open for some months,[4] and it would be for the contributing artists to determine whether any of their works which might remain unsold at the close of the term should be returned to them (transport-free), or should be left to reappear in the exhibition of the succeeding year.[5]

Much yet remains to be settled in connexion with the project, and I address you at some disadvantage, as the necessity of early arrangements with artists compels communication concurrently with the steps which are being taken in America. I trust, however, that due weight will be given to the merits of the project in the broader sense, and that you will accept for the present my assurance that nothing final will be done without ample guarantee. I may add that some personal communication with artists has already taken place in the matter, and the scheme has been so far very cordially and encouragingly greeted. Nor is the interest expressed confined to artists alone, or of a merely professional nature: among others who might be named, I am authorized to mention Mr. Ruskin particularly as one who entirely sympathizes in our object.

We court the offer, not only of works for sale, but of works of excellence already sold. I need not enlarge upon the importance of starting such a scheme with a strong exhibition.

I trust that we may be favoured with the contribution of some works from your hand. The entire collection should be in full readiness by the end of August for the transit to New York; and an answer at your earliest convenience, with particulars of any works which you might be disposed to send, would therefore be esteemed an obligation.

I am
W. M. Rossetti,
Secretary

MS: Harvard.

1. (1827-1908), American editor, translator, writer on literature and art; teacher at Harvard University, 1873-97. A friend of Ruskin, Carlyle, the Brownings, and DGR, he corresponded with WMR mostly about contributions to the *North American Review*, which he edited with J. R. Lowell.

2. Düsseldorf was a major artistic centre, 1830-70. Nazarene idealists and "liberal-revolutionary Realists" vied to dominate the School, but "after 1848 the briefly full-blooded Realist trend was diluted to suit the taste of a newly prosperous middle-class clientele" (Geraldine Norman, *Nineteenth-Century Painters and Painting: A Dictionary* [1977], pp. 77-78).

3. Brown complained in his diary on 17 January 1858: "I was to have gone over to hang the pictures. However, the scoundrel *Gambart* put a stop to all that, and all I had was the trouble to select the daubs" (quoted by J. Maas, *Gambart*, p. 95). Gambart evidently insisted on involving instead a

Mr. Frodsham, who was in charge of the French exhibition that Gambart was showing in New York at the same time. Between Ruxton and Frodsham friction quickly developed. Ruxton to WMR, 29 September 1857: "The *near relationship* of the French Exhibition gives me rather a difficult card to play.... Now and then in a delicate way, I have to defend the independent position of our Exhibition. Mr. Frodsham tried at first to drop the plural, and talk of our (Gambart's) French and English exhibition. He also wanted the cards of invitation to the private views to be sent in the same envelope.... If we gained confidence in England by the addition of Gambart's and Frodsham's names, we do not gain position here, for it is strange, in a city of traders, how much any enterprise gains in public estimation, if free from trade purposes." 10 October 1857: "Mr. Frodsham never came near me, to help in hanging the pictures except for one afternoon, when his object seemed to be to secure line places for Gambart's water-colours. I make no complaint against Mr. Frodsham, because he has his hands full with the French Exhibition, but it is rather hard to pay heavily for services which are not rendered." 20 October 1857: "Mr. Frodsham ... last night when the company were all assembled ... told me that he could not undertake to attend at the gallery to see to the sales of the pictures" (AP).

4. The exhibition opened on 19 October 1857 (see *RRP*, p. 185). Ruxton to WMR, 20 October 1857: "I was congratulated by everyone upon the successful start. 68 dollars were taken by the sale of catalogues at 15 cents each." 28 October 1857: "The English Exhibition has taken during the six days it has been open 500 dollars, about three times or certainly twice as much as the French. Two days out of the six were bitterly cold, and the three last days have been an unceasing pour of rain. Under the circumstances and considering the hard times, we are thought to have done remarkably well. The theatres are not paying current expenses. The artists of New York have all had their commissions withdrawn and I am afraid we must not expect many if any sales beyond two or three." 30 January 1858 (from Philadelphia): "Three thousand dollars were taken at New York."

Ruxton's plan to move the exhibition to Philadelphia and Boston was opposed by Gambart, who, Ruxton reported to WMR on 28 October 1857, "writes in strong terms giving Mr. Frodsham instructions to close the English Exhibition by the 1st of December, and telling him to assume authority over the Exhibition, the pictures having been consigned to him. Nothing being known of 'Ruxton,' so large an amount of property cannot be entrusted to him.... No man in his senses would lay out the sum of money I have expended in this enterprise, with the control of it entirely taken out of his hands. It amounts to this that Mr. Gambart is using my money for an Exhibition the credit and effect of which is to be given to him." Ruxton no doubt wrote equally firmly to Gambart, for the exhibition opened in Philadelphia early in February 1858. Ruxton to WMR, 18 January [1858]: "The Academy of Philadelphia has offered to pay the expenses of the Exhibition to that city — to set aside one thousand dollars to meet the freight and insurance of the pictures home to England, — and to apply the profits of the Exhibition during the months of February and March to the purchase of pictures from the collection for the public gallery. The Academy of Boston makes the same offer for the Exhibition during April and May. I have thought it right to accept such liberal proposals." By 22 March, when Ruxton began moving the pictures from Philadelphia to the Boston Athenaeum, sales numbered "56 or thereabouts," including Hunt's *Light of the World* (see Letter 60); John Brett's *A bank whereon the Wild Thyme grows* (£40); E. H. Wehnert's *The First Ragged-School* (£15.9.0); William Henry Hunt's *Stone Jugs* (£10); FMB's *Looking Towards Hampstead: from the Artist's Window* (£30); Joseph Wolf's *Wood Pigeon* (£40); R. B. Martineau's *Spelling Lesson* (£80); Leighton's *Reconciliation of the Montagues and Capulets over the dead bodies of Romeo and Juliet* (£400) (Ruxton to WMR, 11 February, 22 March 1858).

The Boston Exhibition was supplemented by pictures sent over by WMR. Ruxton to WMR, 13 April [1858]: "The new pictures will add quite an attraction to the Exhibition which is already received with favour in Boston. Boston moves slowly, but the week's receipts have averaged 50 dollars a day." 20 April [1858]: "Money seems plentiful again, but people are afraid to be liberal — Longfellow has bought the first picture, that by Miss F[anny] Steers, *The Rocks, Killarney* for £20.... I have been writing at least 20 letters today about Woolner's bronzes [medallions of Tennyson, Browning, and Carlyle] and some of the new pictures — and I hope I shall be able to bring up the sales before I have done to some 100 pictures.... Longfellow is thinking of Brown's [*English*] *Autumn Afternoon* [not in the catalogue; Bennett 1964, No. 28], the Athenaeum of the King Lear [*Lear and Cordelia*] — I want to fix that before I leave. Professor Agassiz gives unqualified praise to Brett's two pictures of the glacier and the two horns [*Glacier of Rosenlaui* (R.A., 1857); *Wetterhorn, Wellhorn, and Giger, Canton of Berne*]. His authority here is absolute, and praise from him will I hope secure the sale of the pictures. Mr. Norton is so much pleased with the *Twilight* by [William J.] Webbe that he says it must not be allowed to go home. Some ladies are talking of clubbing together to buy it. There are many converts to P.R.B.ism in Boston, Longfellow and Agassiz leading the way.

88

Such battles have been fought over King Lear and Hughes' baby in the flannel dressing gown [*Two-and-half Years Old*].'' (Ruxton's letters are in AP.)

5. Ruxton did not organize another exhibition, though he informed WMR on 19 August [1858] that ''Gambart has made very liberal propositions to me regarding an Exhibition in America this autumn — promising a collection of European pictures of a high class.'' Not only was Ruxton dispirited by wrangling with the artists whose pictures had been water damaged in Boston (see Letter 64, Note 2), he also little relished further dealings with Gambart. He would have been aware of Gambart's part in the rumor that Holman Hunt reported to WMR on [26 May 1858]: ''Anthony has written to you I suppose and expressed some anxiety in relation to his pictures. He had heard something said of a kind calculated to shake his shaky confidence — which made him speak to Gambart on the subject — who fell in with the absurd suspicion against Ruxton's solvency saying that he had opposed the movement from the first with a notion that Ruxton was not a man to repose confidence in — and that he repudiated all responsibility in the matter — making it, or letting it appear that the painters who had sold pictures would never get their tin and that others would not get their pictures'' (AP). Writing on 15 April 1859 to WMR, who had also been approached by Gambart about a future American exhibition, Ruxton advised: ''My own feeling on the subject is, that unless one were prepared to enter regularly into the picture dealing trade, it would be unpleasant to be connected with any enterprise entirely controlled by Gambart. I have seen enough of how matters are pushed and worked *in the trade*, to learn that half measures will not do — either a dealer, or — I was going to say, a gentleman.'' WMR recorded his judgment of Gambart in MS. Diary, 14 April 1902, on hearing of his death: ''He was a knowing and in his way an agreeable man.''

54. TO JOHN BROWN DURAND

45 Upper Albany Street,
1 September [1857]

Dear Mr. Durand,

I received yesterday your letter of the 18th ultimo. You will undoubtedly be by this time in possession of a letter of mine sending a provisional list of pictures: and perhaps Mr. Durand Sen.[1] has got my letter accepting on the part of our Committee the sub-tenancy of the rooms between Tenth Street and Fourth Avenue.[2] I do not therefore here enter into details: but in a day or two I expect to post you a printed catalogue of the pictures,[3] nearly (though not quite) final. The reluctance of owners to lend pictures — enhanced by their concessions to the Paris and Manchester exhibitions[4] — has been deplorably against us, especially in the case of some leading men, who are of course the least likely to have unsold pictures on hand: still, I think we can fairly call our exhibition a good one, and hope that opinion will be ratified by the American public.[5]

Mr. Ruxton is just now at Manchester. On Saturday he starts by the Persia for New York, taking with him a large section (perhaps the majority) of the exhibition: the remainder will follow as soon as possible afterwards.

That preliminary notice in the *Crayon*[6] was very gratifying to all of us — written just in the cordial, but independent, spirit we could have wished.

Pray accept Mr. Ruxton's and my thanks for a great deal of kindness you have shown in the matter, and trouble you have taken, and believe me

Very truly yours,
W. M. Rossetti

MS: NYP.

1. Asher Brown Durand (1796-1886), American engraver and landscape painter, was president of the National Academy of Design, 1845-61. The *Dictionary of American Biography* notes that he

89

lived in New York for "fifty-four years, where he was closely identified with every organized movement to foster the arts."

2. "The new gallery of the National Academy of Design" (*Crayon*, October 1857, p. 315). Ruxton to WMR, 22 September [1857]: "The Academy give me their rooms at $125 a month, and therefore if my returns do not prove so great as Broadway might command, the risk is proportionately less" (AP).

3. Ruxton to WMR, 16 December [1858]: "Two or three [pictures] named in your catalogue never came to America.... The New York catalogue was reprinted from yours, and the absence of the pictures was not found out till later" (AP).

4. *Exposition Universelle*, Paris, 1855; Art Treasures Exhibition, Manchester, 1857.

5. W. J. Stillman criticized the exhibition in a letter to WMR, 15 November 1857; extracts in *RRP*, pp. 187-89, but omitting the following passages: "Firstly your committee have sent us an immense amount of rubbish which has had the double effect of increasing Ruxton's burdens, and giving the collection a bad first impression.... The picture by [John] Cross [*The Burial of the Princes in the Tower of London, 1483*], the two [Francis] Danbys [only one picture in the catalogue, *The Advent of Spring*] and Frank Stone's whole contribution [five oils], with many minor ones, have added to the expense of transportation and absolutely diminished the receipts.... A poor English picture will not sell so well here as in England and costs as much to get here as a good one." Stillman gave Ruxton much of the credit for what success the exhibition enjoyed: "His arrangement of the pictures with regard to hanging etc. has been the admiration of Artists and connoisseurs and is indeed most just and impartial. There is no artist whose works are hung who has any reason to find fault. Mr. Frodsham has written home to the contrary but Mr. Frodsham's conduct in all respects as connected with the Exhibition may only be characterized as nefarious, mendacious and such as to make him as universal an object of dislike and contempt here as Ruxton's manliness, dignity and good sense have made him popular and indeed beloved" (AP).

6. August 1857, p. 251. Notices also appeared in September, October, November 1857, pp. 280, 314-15, 343-44.

55. TO JOHN BROWN DURAND

45 Upper Albany Street,
13 September [1857]

Dear Mr. Durand,

I posted you the other day a copy of our catalogue,[1] which no doubt you will have received before this: Ruxton too is already on his way to New York, and you and he will be in frequent communication.

There has been some correspondence between you and Stephens as to a notice of the pictures, which he thinks it would be well for me to do. I don't exactly know what kind of thing you expect, but I should fear, were I to write a regular notice, to incur some imputation of puffing my own affair, and also of favouring some exhibitors at the expense of others: besides, I conceive the Americans ought to judge for themselves, and speak their opinion for themselves. What I conceive I can quite legitimately submit to you, for any use you can turn it to as material to be worked up, is a thing in the nature of the enclosed — being memoranda as to the reputation which the several painters bear over here, and other matters of fact, useful to be known, if not already in the possession of whoever writes about the affair.[2]

Very truly yours,
W. M. Rossetti

Of course, the numbers in the enclosed correspond with those in the catalogue.

MS: NYP.

1. See Letter 54, Note 3.
2. The five-page memorandum is now at Yale, catalogued as "Brief Critiques of British Artists" by DGR.

56. TO WILLIAM BELL SCOTT

45 Upper Albany Street,
5 December [1857]

Dear Scott,

Thanks for the enclosed pleasant and communicative letter[1] (which I ought to have returned before). They have all discontinued work at Oxford this fortnight or so, what between cold and other causes: but I think one or two are now about resuming. Maybe I shall meet you there at Christmas: I wish to see the things greatly.

The great majority of artists have consented to leave their pictures in America the further time proposed: so possibly (I think not by any means certainly) yours[2] and others will remain. I gather that, even without this, the exhibition will just about comfortably pay its expenses: it goes on well (all except sales), and redounds altogether to the honour of P.R.B.ism[3] and defeat of slosh.

You remember our questioning about what the Evangelists Matthew and John say of their own knowledge. I read their gospels (and indeed the whole New Testament) through, marking all the passages bearing upon these points. I find that a great number of the miracles etc. are reported to have taken place in the presence of "the apostles" or some such phrase, which may *probably* imply the presence of the narrator himself. The cases in which that presence is definitely averred are but few: even these include, however, miracles, or clear professions on the part of Christ of miraculous power etc.; so that the enquiry does not greatly affect the general bearings of the matter.

I have been reading also, with great delight and wonder, Swedenborg's *Heaven and Hell*,[4] which I am sure is full of profoundest spiritual truths, — perhaps real bona fide "revelation." That his statements are to be accepted I do not doubt: the question how far and how they are to be accepted depends rather on the inner sense, correspondence, etc., whereon he dwells so much than on any doubts of the sceptical kind. I shall try to read his other books with convenient speed.

Good-bye now to you and Mrs. Scott, for I have other letters to attend to.

Yours always,
W. M. Rossetti

MS: Arizona.

1. Pauline Trevelyan's letter of 12 November 1857 to WBS describing the Oxford Union murals (quoted in R. Trevelyan, *A Pre-Raphaelite Circle*, p. 136). DGR, Burne-Jones, Morris, Arthur Hughes, J. H. Pollen, Val Prinsep, Spencer Stanhope, and Holman Hunt began the frescoes in 1857, and worked on them on and off for three years.
2. *The Burgher's Watch on the City Wall*; *The Old English Market Town, Hexham*. Both were shown at Philadelphia and Boston.
3. For favorable comment on the Pre-Raphaelites see *RRP*, pp. 182, 185, 188-89, 196; and the *Crayon* reviews (Letter 54, Note 6). Cf. Ruxton to WMR, 28 October 1857: "Many of the artists as

you may imagine cry out against the P.R.B.s, but most people return to them again and again, not understanding, but still being attracted towards them. I think myself that it would be safe to venture upon a distinct P.R.B. Exhibition if you can include such men as [John Wright] Oakes [Liverpool landscape painter] and Anthony and some others'' (AP).

4. Published in Latin in 1758, it was translated into English in 1778.

57. TO WILLIAM ALLINGHAM

Inland Revenue Office,
18 January [1858]

Dear Allingham,

The sum total of my *personal* acquaintance with publishers is just this: — I have met Macmillan, and subsequently wrote asking whether he would publish my Dante at his own risk, which he declined. I know with some intimacy Williams,[1] the reader to Smith & Elder, and asked him the same, which he declined recommending. I have a speaking acquaintance with young Parker,[2] but understand he rather fights shy of me.

Now whatever I can do in your service I shall be *truly glad* to undertake: but I thought it better in the first instance to explain to you that I have not much interest with publishers, and leave it to you either to put the matter into more influential hands (which you could assuredly do) or to tell me what you think fittest for me to attempt first.

As to America — In the early days of my dealings with the *Crayon*, the editors asked me whether I could get *them* early copies of English poems. Of course, that's not the thing: nor do I know anything of Ticknor and Fields[3] individually: but having the *Crayon* Editors and my friend Ruxton now in America to correspond with, I think I may learn something tangible, and will attend to it, and about Emerson.

As to the Christmas-book[4] — yours would undoubtedly be far better than others, and need not that I see be less popular. Do you mean an illustrated book? If so, I fancy you'd better first consult artists, and then go to a publisher with their names ready, or the publisher will find you a lot of his own muffs. If not illustrated, I can only leave the matter over with the other publishing question. Routledge's[5] books (illustrated) are the best of this kind to my thinking.

Gabriel *was* at Oxford 3 or 4 months — then went (with Miss Siddal for her health) to Matlock, and has been in London these few days. Today probably he returns to Matlock, and thence will have to revisit Oxford for a good while. The things there are very new, curious, and with a ruddy bloom of health and pluck about them — Gabriel's[6] very beautiful both in expression and colour: Jones's[7] next, and to some extent *more* exactly the right kind of thing. Val Prinsep[8] — a most loveable fellow — is the son of *the* Prinseps, and this his first work promises real power.

The *Crayon is* going on. I receive it monthly: it has much lost its character as an *art*-paper, but still pays some considerable degree of attention to art.

Millais is settled in London — 16 York Terrace, Regent's Park. He has been here several weeks but I have not yet seen him.

The Brownings, I hear, are to be in London this spring or summer, and elsewhere in England — I think Devonshire. The boy[9] got ill, and was almost given over, but is about well again now. I very much agree with (what I gather to be) your opinion of *Aurora Leigh*: there is a certain splendour and flood of expression about it which are quite overwhelming: but, after you have been overwhelmed, you get into a temper of resistance, and declare that it is all in excess — you would rather have the "one touch of nature"[10] than Mrs. Browning's one and a half. Still, it is a wonderful thing. I don't object to the *incident* of Marian's child but it is very much over finicalized in the writing.

Brown is all right — working at intervals on his large picture:[11] just now finishing a water-colour duplicate of the Christ and Peter.[12]

So here are all your questions answered by one who confesses himself to be as bad a correspondent as you proclaim *yourself* — and is also

Truly yours,

W. M. Rossetti

MS: Illinois.

1. William Smith Williams (1800-1875) was known to the Rossettis as the brother-in-law of Charles Jeremiah Wells (1800-1879), the author of *Joseph and his Brethren*, whom DGR and Swinburne lavishly overpraised; and as father-in-law of Lowes Dickinson. On Williams's recommendation WMR succeeded him as art critic of the *Spectator*.

2. John William Parker (1820-60), son of the publisher of the same name, entered his father's business in 1843.

3. Founded by William Davis Ticknor (1810-64) in 1832; known as Ticknor and Fields from 1854. Ticknor was the friend and publisher of Longfellow, Lowell, Emerson, and Hawthorne.

4. Not published.

5. George Routledge (1812-88), London publisher from 1843. Beginning with Allingham's *Music Master*, he issued numerous volumes distinguished in the history of Victorian wood engraving.

6. *Sir Launcelot's Vision of the Sanc Grael* (Oxford Union; Surtees 93).

7. Edward Burne-Jones (1833-98), who painted *Merlin and Nimue*.

8. Valentine Cameron Prinsep (1838-1904), whose subject was *Sir Pelleas and the Lady Ettarde*. He did not exhibit at the R.A. until 1862. His father was Henry Thoby Prinsep (1793-1878), Indian civil servant.

9. Robert Barrett Browning (1846-1912) studied painting in Antwerp and Paris, and exhibited at the R.A., 1878-84. MS. Diary, 27 March 1878: "Called by invitation on Browning, to see the picture just sent over from Antwerp by his son for the R.A. — an Antwerp brazier chasing a dish, lifesize. As a first work, it is really remarkable for solidity and strength of work, with a large amount of able object-painting. Saw also a dozen or so of his earlier studies, all more or less efficient — one very agreeable of an old Flemish chateau, now much neglected. Browning was very cordial, speaking warmly of Madox Brown, and of Nolly [Brown] — he referred particularly to the ship on fire in *Gabriel Denver*." WMR wrote briefly in the *Athenaeum* about four pictures sent from Belgium in 1880, three of which were exhibited at the R.A. (3 April 1880, p. 448). MS. Diary, 26 March 1881: "Went to see R. B. Browning's pictures: his father and Aunt [Sarianna Browning] there.... The principal work ... is a Franciscan notifying to a prisoner of the Antwerp Inquisition, lying naked on his prison-floor, that the time for putting an end to him has come: a well painted sensible picture, with a very difficult and on the whole skilfully treated foreshortening, but I think it by this time pretty clear that Browning is not a painter of *genius*, and will not ever in point of execution, advance very greatly beyond the highly creditable point of strength, firmness, and efficiency, without peculiar gift or charm, which he has now for 2 or 3 years past occupied."

10. *Troilus and Cressida*, III. iii. 175.

11. *Work*, on which he was engaged 1852-65.

12. See Bennett 1964, No. 23.

58. TO JOHN BRETT[1]

45 Upper Albany Street,
31 January [1858]

Dear Brett,

I shall write to Ruxton by this post (and ought to have done so before) telling him that you will sell the Violets for £21, or £20 if the extra £1 be a Yankee difficulty, and asking him to settle with you about transmission etc. His address is "A. A. Ruxton Esq., Chalvey Park, Slough."

You were asking after lodgings the other day. Passing on Friday through Gower Street, I noticed an "Apartments" card in the window of Millais's old house, No. 83, — a substantial, rather gloomy house, with a detached studio where Millais used to work. I know nothing of the details; but, if you are still houseless, it might perhaps be worth your while to look at the house. I hear also that the pleasant old-fashioned house once Hogarth's at Chiswick[2] — large garden etc. — is to be let very low — £25 a year or thereabouts. Gabriel had some thoughts of it once, and looked over and liked it; and, if I remember right, he thought it would be quite available for an artist with a few alterations.

Will you remember my mother and sisters (as well as myself) kindly to your sister and brother, whom they were very happy to see on their call the other day.

Yours truly,
W. M. Rossetti

MS: Hogarth House.

1. (1830-1902), painted landscapes and coastal scenes in a Pre-Raphaelite manner. About 1852 he "appeared to be somewhat smitten" with CGR (*FLCR*, p. 54). WMR wrote of the *Stonebreaker*, R.A., 1858: "Pre-Raphaelite pictures of much higher aim and standard have been painted, but none of more finished achievement within its limits" (*Saturday Review*, 15 May 1858, p. 504). Although, as Wood points out, Brett went on to paint "highly detailed, geological coast scenes of a rather repetitive formula," WMR continued to praise him. Of *The Cornish Lions*, R.A., 1878, he wrote: "This large and elaborate work shows Brett in full possession of his uncommon mastery over facts and appearances, the fruit of unremitting scrutiny and strenuous practice" (*Academy*, 8 June 1878, p. 516). No picture entitled "Violets" is listed in the New York, Philadelphia, or Boston catalogues of the American Exhibition of British Art.

2. Hogarth's country house from 1749. For an account of the house (now open to the public) to the end of the nineteenth century, see Austin Dobson, *William Hogarth* (new ed., 1907), pp. 143-44.

59. TO JOHN LUCAS TUPPER

Somerset House,
1 February [1858]

Dear Jack,

Curiously enough, the day after I saw you I *did* meet Woodward, who called on Ruskin at the National Gallery while I was there. *The* Hope is the Rev. Frederick William Hope,[1] 37 Upper Seymour Street, Portman Square. Among the Turner relics Ruskin showed me was a little Itinerary pocket-book,[2] full of sketches, and containing a MS. poem of some length: I am going to undertake its decipherment. This will be rather jolly.

Yours,
W. M. Rossetti

MS: Leeds.

1. (1797-1862), entomologist, who gave his collection of insects to Oxford in 1849, founding at the same time a professorship of Zoology.
2. The Greenwich Sketch Book (No. CII in A. J. Finberg, *A Complete Inventory of the Drawings of the Turner Bequest* [1909], 1:266-70), which contains the poem beginning "O Gold thou parent of Ambition's ardent blush." The poem is published in *The Sunset Ship, the Poems of J. M. W. Turner*, ed. Jack Lindsay, 1966, pp. 100-102.

60. TO WILLIAM HOLMAN HUNT

Somerset House,
23 February [1858]

Dear Hunt,

Ruxton has "accepted an offer, conditionally upon your approval, [of][1] £300 for the *Light of the World*.[2] It is from a gentleman, a Mr. Wolfe,[3] who has the finest collection of pictures in New York, and who apologizes for making an offer below the sum named, but pleads the pressure of the times, and inability to pay more just now. As far as the times go, it is a very good offer, and Ruxton hopes you will be inclined to accept it, for your picture will go into good company, and your name will become known in America." So says Ruxton, and — as far as I can judge on a matter which it is entirely for you to decide — the offer is not unreasonable.[4]

The sales have taken quite a brisk start now, offering very good prospects for the future, unaffected as we may hope it to be by commercial smash. It is said that the prospects for the exhibition intended at Boston in April and May are still better than at Philadelphia, but the present rate of sale threatens to leave little good to take there. I am working therefore to get new pictures from the artists who have sold (and a few others if possible). Is there anything you could send? Oriental water-colours, that oil landscape with the glittering sea at Hastings[5] (I believe it is in a finished state), or anything else? I should really be glad if it suited you to send, but of course could not bore you if you think unfit. The earliest convenient answer would oblige

Your
W. M. Rossetti

MS: Iowa.

1. MS. damaged.
2. Bennett 1969, No. 25: the original sketch for the Keble College picture.
3. John Wolfe, whose collection is described in the *Crayon*: "The English, French, Flemish, and Düsseldorf schools are represented with uncommonly judicious selections." Mention is made of pictures by H. J. Boddington, Samuel Prout, Clarkson Stanfield, J. D. Harding, C. R. Leslie, Meissonier, and Delacroix (January 1856, pp. 28-29). Wolfe was the cousin of the philanthropist and art patron Catharine Lorillard Wolfe, who about 1873 commissioned him to collect pictures for her Madison Avenue house.
4. Hunt to WMR, 24 February 1858: "I really cannot remember at this moment what my calculations were as to the time spent on the sketch of the *Light of the World* — And so can't tell what price I put upon it — to save time however — which looking further for the note that will not turn up at this moment might take — I write conditionally. I object very much to reducing the price of a picture — in fact never do it, as you know, yet am inclined for the sake of having a picture in a good collection in America to make sacrifice of my principle to some extent. If the price fixed was more than 300

guineas I must, however, refuse the offer of £300, but if this was the sum named — which you may know, I shall be obliged by your telling Ruxton that I shall be happy to accept Mr. Wolfe's offer — of course on the understanding that I reserve the copyright for engraving from the larger picture." 29 May 1858: "I send you an acknowledgement of the receipt of the cheque from Ruxton for £315 — the price, minus the ten per cent, paid by Mr. Wolfe" (AP).

5. *Fairlight Downs — Sunlight on the Sea*. Begun in 1852 and perhaps completed during a return visit to Fairlight in 1858, it was exhibited later that year at 120 Pall Mall (A. Staley, *The Pre-Raphaelite Landscape*, p. 65).

61. TO ALFRED WILLIAM HUNT[1]

New York Exhibition of British Art[2]

45 Upper Albany Street,
28 February [1858]

Dear Sir,

You may probably recollect my having been in communication with you last summer relative to this exhibition; and I have not forgotten that you would have been willing to contribute something, had opportunity served.

The pictures forming the exhibition are now at Philadelphia, and are to be at Boston in April and May: but at the former place — the panic which went so much against us at first having subsided — sales are beginning so briskly that it is doubtful whether enough pictures will remain for the exhibition in the latter. We are therefore desirous of obtaining a few additional pictures; and it occurs to me to address you, to ascertain whether it would now meet your convenience to contribute, which I should be delighted to find the case. I may add that the current of public appreciation in America has gone altogether with the "Prae-raffaelite" pictures.

An early answer would be an obligation, the time being necessarily limited (for receiving pictures) to the 12th March or thereabouts. Any works might be sent to Green's[3] (14 Charles Street, Middlesex Hospital) addressed to me; and it is suggested by the Director in America that any remaining unsold might, if the contributors choose, remain over for the ensuing (autumn) exhibition in New York.

Believe me, Dear Sir,
Very faithfully yours,
W. M. Rossetti

MS: Cornell.

1. (1830-96), Liverpool landscape painter and watercolorist, first exhibited at the R.A. in 1854. Nothing by him appears in the Boston catalogue.
2. Embossed heading.
3. Joseph Green. Ruxton to WMR, 10 October 1857: "Nothing could be more perfect than Green's packing" (AP).

62. TO WILLIAM BELL SCOTT

45 Upper Albany Street,
1 March 1858

Dear Scott,

Some half dozen of our friends, with myself, are contemplating the formation of a club,[1] consisting of members chiefly artistic, with a non-artistic minority, for the purpose of social intercourse; a primary object also being to have a room where any works of art by the members can be seen, as opportunity and convenience may dictate.

We propose to limit the number of members to about 50; the names of 43 have already been definitely proposed, including yours; and we are writing to them to ascertain what practical prospect exists of carrying the idea into execution.

Of these 43, 36 would be artistic, and 7 non-artistic members.

The latter class would pay about half the subscription of the former.

Supposing an annual expense of about £150, the artistic members would pay an annual subscription of about £3.10, the non-artistic of about £2.

Would you oblige me at your earliest convenience with an intimation whether you are disposed to join the club — as our further movements will be dependent upon the support which the first starting of the project receives.

The name of Hogarth Club has been suggested for the Society.

Always yours,
W. M. Rossetti

This semi-official concoction[2] must stand in lieu just now of better greeting or letter, for a good deal of work, (revived by much improving sales in America[3]) is on my hands. What say you to the above? Non-resident members like you would, it is proposed, be on the level of non-artistic members.

MS: Princeton.

1. Hogarth Club, a Pre-Raphaelite social and exhibition society. Its fortunes "were anything but brilliant ... and the club was dissolved in the spring of 1861" (*SR*). WMR's letters supplement the accounts of the Club in *SR*, 1:223-25; and Fredeman, p. 243.
2. The body of the letter is in another hand, perhaps CGR's.
3. American Exhibition of British Art.

63. TO JOHN BROWN DURAND

45 Upper Albany Street,
31 March [1858]

Dear Mr. Durand,

I have long been silent, and am now asking a favour. Not however on my own account, but a friend's, and I hope you will kindly excuse me.

I recollect the *Crayon* noticed some considerable while ago the poems of William Allingham,[1] and fancy they are probably as well known in America as they are here. In England Allingham has a choice reputation — cordially praised and well known by all the best men — Tennyson, Browning, Carlyle, Patmore, Landor, Leigh Hunt, etc. etc., as well as by all the artistic set with which I am connected. His poems, first published in (I think) 1850, took a *safe* position at once: afterwards a smaller set appeared,[2] and a couple of years or so ago the cream of the two was published in an edition illustrated by Millais etc. He is now thinking of a new volume, and also of a revised edition of these poems, already in their 3rd edition; and he wishes to ascertain whether there would be any advantageous prospect for him in an American edition, simultaneous with the English one. Ticknor and Fields is the firm he has more especially in his eye.[3] He has asked me to enquire about it to the best of my ability, and, as I know no such other reasonable chance of getting the question efficiently disposed of, I write to enquire whether you could — and would — without any particular trouble, obtain some notion of the chance existing. I must again apologize for bothering you in such a matter, and of course do not beg you to do anything in it unless it comes in your way.

I have had good accounts of the success of our Exhibition in Philadelphia, and hope the same will hold good of Boston, to which I have just been dispatching a reinforcement of some 40 works.

With kind regards,

Very truly yours,
W. M. Rossetti

MS: Iowa.

1. "A New English Poet," a review of *The Music Master*, April 1856, pp. 127-28.
2. *Day and Night Songs.*
3. Allingham reissued *The Music Master* in 1860 with the title *Day and Night Songs; and the Music Master*, but did not publish his next volumes of poems until *Laurence Bloomfield in Ireland* (1864) and *Fifty Modern Poems* (1865). In 1861 Ticknor and Fields published *Poems*, which contained "everything in the 1855 volume plus twenty other poems not published in England until 1865" (Fredeman, p. 187). Durand replied to WMR on 11 May 1858 that there was no prospect for Allingham's volume in New York: "the commercial hurricane though past is still apparent in a very cloudy dark dull aftersky nobody having a spark of enterprise beyond the scope of necessity and of old engagements. I think the publishers are worse off than any other class of *traders*. I have written to Messrs. Ticknor and Fields.... They are the most likely to undertake the publication of your friend's works — at the same time I doubt if they allow compensation in any shape, that expression of liberality being confined to such names, so popular ... as not to falsify the risk of being generous. I consider it generous for an American publisher to compensate a foreign author when he has the opportunity of stealing as it were in the shape of a reprint — a practice esteemed honest because authors are not on a level with goods that are worth legislating about.... It occurs to me to say that if the edition of Allingham is to be nicely illustrated there is a better chance of disposing of a considerable number of copies here than if not illustrated. Americans will sometimes contract with English publishers for a given number of copies of works of this class stipulating for a local title-page. Most of the Birket Foster books have been purchased in this way by D. Appleton & Co. of this city" (Illinois).

64. TO FRANCES ROSSETTI

Freshwater Gate,
1 September [1858]

Dearest Mamma,

Thanks for your little note received this morning. I am sorry you have to endure the bore of visits from D'Egville[1] etc., but am not without fear that, either just before or just after my return to town, such visits will be pretty frequent, as a lot of pictures are now about returning, some of which, as Ruxton learned a little while ago, have been severely damaged by a rainstorm while *en route* to the

98

vessel.[2] If any such visits *are* inflicted upon you, of course you can refer the visitor either to me by address or to Ruxton personally, and all I can beg of you is to subject yourself to as little annoyance in the matter as you can.

Will you tell Christina, in answer to a precedent note, that I *did*, shortly after leaving town, think of her *Common Objects of the Seashore*[3] with regret at not having brought it, but that some days ago, finding the book at a shop hereabouts, I purchased a copy for myself. It is sufficiently to the purpose. Also that little Solomon's[4] visit must have been paid under a misapprehension of something I said to him 2 or 3 months ago, as I had nothing of Gabriel's at home to show him, but may rather have offered to take him to Blackfriars. He is an unsightly little Israelite: but a youth of extraordinary genius in art — and perhaps otherwise.

Here we[5] are still, and here, spite of occasional gleams of projected removal to some other spot in the Island, we are likely in my opinion to remain, at least until Sunday week next, which will be my last holiday day: on Monday I ought to be back at Somerset House, and the position of colleagues there as regards leave will not admit of my outstaying my time. Tennyson[6] has been back since Friday, and took the trouble of looking me up on Saturday — but bent his steps through some mistake to Alum Bay — some six times too far off — where of course he could learn nothing of me. I spent Monday very pleasantly at his very commodious house (not half a mile from here), and shall return as often as I can spare myself from here. He found the Norway travelling very laborious. He and his wife (a most lovely human creature) like Gabriel's Arthur watched by weeping queens as well as, or better than, any other illustration in the edition.

Our sea-anemones — strawberry, red, brown and olive-yellow, and longer-feelered grey and greens, — mingled with an occasional crab or shell-fish, were beginning to get rather a nuisance: we have reduced their number to 9, which have been most flourishing these 3 days.

Your
W.M.R.

I shall post with, or soon after, this one or two *Athenaeums*. One No. never came; and the next following that not till the week after, or you should have had them in due course.

MS: AP. Extract in *RRP*, p. 208.

1. James T. Hervé D'Egville (c. 1806-80; Wood), landscape painter, seven of whose watercolors appear in the Boston catalogue of the American Exhibition of British Art.
2. Ruxton's letters to WMR, August 1858-November 1861, chiefly concern the damaged pictures. 19 August [1858]: "I went to see the King Lear [*Lear and Cordelia*] at M. Brown's, and I believe he does not think the damage so serious as he imagined. [FMB complained to WMR on [17 August 1858] that it had come back "with part of the stretcher torn away and a great bump in the centre of the canvas" (AP).] The canvas has been strained at the top of the picture — the roof of the tent — but the surface is *not in any way injured*. It is to be stretched on a new frame, and I hope all trace of the accident will be removed." [17 September 1858]: "It is more than probable I suppose, that every picture with a spot or stain will be considered ruined by its owner. I could not pay the full price for all these, but so far as my means will allow, I should wish to offer such sums as might be agreed upon, for the damaged pictures, as some measure of compensation for the loss sustained by their owners." 2 September 1861: "I have done as much as I could well do in that American business, and I think

that I have been treated with extreme want of courtesy and consideration by many of the artists. I have paid at least £1200 in compensation and losses. / Those responsibilities which I undertook without the shadow of legal claim, I have discharged, in some cases, with the utmost reluctance, in consequence of the tone assumed towards me by those I was wishing to treat with respect and consideration. / I have had no thanks for the exertions I made but only abuse, while writs and threatening letters have poured in upon me without stint. / I always shall remember with the greatest satisfaction, the kindness, zeal and disinterestedness you showed from first to last. I have regretted much more on your account than my own, that things turned out, as they did'' (AP).

3. By Rev. J. G. Wood, with plates printed in colors by Edmund Evans, 1857.

4. Simeon Solomon (1840-1905). In common with DGR, Swinburne, and Burne-Jones, WMR lavished praise on Solomon's early work. In reviewing his drawings, *The Waters of Babylon* and *The Shadow of Death*, exhibited at 120, Pall Mall in 1858, WMR called him ''that singular young genius ... an artist of endless invention and fantasy, from whose original and teeming brain all who have had an opportunity of in any way estimating its resources hope great things indeed'' (*Spectator*, 6 November 1858, p. 1172). After Solomon's arrest in 1871 for homosexual offences, WMR joined with Solomon's family and the Pre-Raphaelite circle in wishing never to hear his name again. For WMR's late reiteration of his rejection, see Letter 563.

5. WMR spent much of his time on the Isle of Wight in the company of Henrietta Rintoul and her mother, the daughter and widow of R. S. Rintoul, the founder and editor of the *Spectator*, who had died in April 1858. For some years WMR was engaged to Henrietta, who died a spinster in 1904.

6. For WMR's infrequent contacts with Tennyson, whom he met at Patmore's in 1848, see *SR*, 1:247-59, which contains a fuller account of the visit described here.

65. TO WILLIAM BELL SCOTT

45 Upper Albany Street,
14 November [1858]

Dear Scott,

I was glad to receive your note of a little while ago, announcing that you will have a reasonable tale of contributions[1] to the Hogarth. If you hear nothing further, please send them up (with Woolner's) at the time appointed. But I am not *very* certain that the assemblage will be got together: the members' responses come in rather scantily as yet. J. F. Lewis,[2] Brown, Brett, Morten,[3] Prinsep, Alfred Hunt of Liverpool, and yourself, are all that I recollect as having distinctly promised. I believe, however, we may pretty well depend also upon Holman Hunt, Gabriel, and Windus's[4] new picture, and that it *will* be done.

Your seconding and my proposing of McCallum[5] proved of no avail: Gabriel & Co. blackballed him (this of course *entre nous*). I should have liked to get him in; as, besides a personal liking not very much beyond the neutral, I am satisfied, from what he has — and still more what he has *not* — exhibited, that he has high capabilities as a landscape-painter: though I can see too the truth of your remark upon ''bad style of execution, and perhaps of motive.'' Munro also was most conclusively blackballed — not by Woolner, let me add, nor yet by me (twice over, as some doubt arose as to the mechanical operation of the balloting in his and the other cases); and, out of the whole list before you, only 4 — all non-artists — got in: Gillum,[6] Gaisford,[7] Hodgson,[8] and Marshall.[9] All present were (or seemed) surprised at such a fund of hostility. Inchbold, just back, has joined.

I must say that I agree with you about the ''beer and pipes'' system — though myself one of the most decided offenders. However, I have made a point of personally substituting coffee for beer since you wrote: we have now got two card-tables also, which contributes to giving the room a rather more social tone. I am looking out for an opportunity of speaking privately to Brown about the beer etc.: beyond doing which I feel a reluctance in putting myself forward. But Brown's adhesion to the same view — should he give it, which I doubt — would go a great way.

So you dined with fine old Miller of Liverpool lately. Brown is with him now (or just leaving): and I think of managing a visit myself from Saturday to Monday next.

Besides the other business at the Hogarth on the 5th, we elected 2 Honorary Members — Danby[10] (against my views) and Delacroix. I am very glad of the latter, though I fear the whole affair will be Greek to him, and the upshot uncertain.

Read, if you have not already read, Carlyle's *Friedrich*[11] — a very noble thing. With affectionate remembrances to Mrs. Scott,

Yours, My dear Friend,
W. M. Rossetti

MS: Arizona.

1. Nine watercolors (WBS to WMR, 24 October 1858; Durham).

2. John Frederick Lewis (1805-76). WMR set the tone of his many reviews of Lewis when he wrote of *The Arab Scribe — Cairo* (Old Water-Colour Society, 1852) that it was "a marvel of finish, delicacy, and completeness" (*Spectator*, 1 May 1852, p. 423).

3. Thomas Morten (1836-66); see Allan Life's "'That Unfortunate Young Man Morten'," *Bulletin of the John Rylands Library*, 55 (1972-73), 369-402 — the title is from Letter 107 — which gives an account of WMR's efforts, following Morten's suicide, to assist his widow. Although Morten exhibited at the R.A. in 1855, WMR did not review him until 1858 when he showed two works at the R.A. and three at the National Institution. Among the young painters at the National he was "the brightest spirit": "He has less clearness of artistic method and punctilio, but his is the seeing eye for character and expression. *Painting from Nature Out-of-doors*, where a young artist is beset by every form of distraction in the population of a fishing-village, is quite admirable in this respect…. The manner is exceedingly simple and unforced, the colour sparkling, and every detail easy and to the purpose" (*Spectator*, 20 March 1858, p. 320).

4. William Lindsay Windus (1822-1907) painted several Pre-Raphaelite pictures. (See Mary Bennett, "William Windus and the Pre-Raphaelite Brotherhood in Liverpool," *Liverpool Bulletin*, 7, no. 3 [1958-59], 19-31.) He exhibited twice at the R.A., *Burd Helen* in 1856 and *Too Late* in 1859 (presumably the picture referred to). WMR called *Burd Helen* "one of the most remarkable and noble works upon the walls," declaring that "the reality and dramatic pathos of the work, and its disciplined artistic refinement, rank it among the highest developments of the new school" (*Spectator*, 24 May 1856, pp. 570-71). Wood cites Ruskin's censure of *Too Late* (C & W, 14:233-34) as the reason for the painter's small output after 1850. More than a decade after Ruskin's review WMR lamented the departure of Windus from the art scene, and pointedly praised *Too Late* as "like *Burd Helen* … painted with singular delicacy of eye and hand; and with even higher attainment in items of realization, though the general effect was again filmy and retiring…. I would fain hope that it is not yet 'too late' for him to make up his mind that he is by nature and function a painter, and bound to resume and complete his course" (*Portfolio*, August 1870, p. 116).

5. Andrew McCallum (1821-1902) exhibited at the R.A., 1850-86. WMR had recently met him through J. C. Addyes Scott, who succeeded R. S. Rintoul as editor and proprietor of the *Spectator*. WBS to WMR, 24 October 1858: "Thanks for putting me in as seconding McCallum, who is really an ingenious fine fellow, and who just wants some kind and discriminating hand to help him out of a dreadfully bad style of execution and perhaps of motive in his art matters. Besides he has a delightful little handsome rich wife whom I should decidedly cultivate if I lived near enough" (Durham). Mrs. McCallum is remembered in a Pre-Raphaelite anecdote as the enquirer at the Pitti Palace after Chiaro dell' Erma's picture described in DGR's *Hand and Soul*.

6. William Gillum (1827-1910), army officer during the Crimean War, benefactor of Boys' Homes, Pre-Raphaelite patron, amateur artist who studied under FMB. (See Nikolaus Pevsner, "Colonel Gillum and the Pre-Raphaelites," *Burlington Magazine*, 95 [March 1953], 78 and 81.)

7. Thomas Gaisford (d. 1898), "a Sussex squire with a rather romantic aspect, owner of a fine library" (*SR*, 1:207). His library was sold in an eight-day sale at Sotheby's beginning on 23 April 1890 for £9236.15.6.

8. Probably J. Stewart Hodgson, who purchased DGR's watercolor version of *Dr. Johnson at the Mitre* (Surtees 119 R. 1) at the Plint sale in 1862.

9. John Marshall (1818-91), DGR's and FMB's doctor, was president of the Royal College of Surgeons, professor of Anatomy at the R.A., and author of numerous medical texts and papers, and *Anatomy for Artists* (1878).

10. Francis Danby (1793-1861), landscape and mythological painter, exhibited at the R.A., 1821-60. He was an A.R.A., but to his great disappointment was never elected R.A. (Wood). WMR consistently praised his landscapes, observing in a review of the R.A. in the year of Turner's final illness and death: "In the absence of Mr. Turner, Mr. Danby takes the lead in poetic landscape based on idea and invention" (*Spectator*, 28 June 1851, p. 619). With Danby's later mythological pictures WMR had little sympathy, dismissing him in 1858 as follows: "Mr. Danby is bad in *Ulysses at the Court of Alcinous*, and abominable in the *Death of Abel*" (*Saturday Review*, 15 May 1858, p. 504).

11. Published in six volumes, 1858-65, the first two volumes in 1858.

66. TO THE EDITOR OF THE *CRAYON*

London,
19 December 1858

The *Crayon* for November last makes mention of a picture by an English artist, Mr. Windus, now in the possession of Mr. Harrison, of Philadelphia,[1] and speaks of it as an illustration of Mrs. Browning's poem, *The Romaunt of the Page*. Will you allow me, on behalf of the artist,[2] to explain through the pages of the *Crayon*, that this is a mistake; and a mistake the more worthy of correcting, as it has enough plausibility to mislead even those who have seen the picture. *The Romaunt of the Page* is a story of a new-married bride, who being (under peculiar circumstances) unrecognizable by her bridegroom, follows him, a crusader, in Palestine, in the disguise of a page; and, seeking by indirect questions to discover whether he would approve her conduct, is cast into despair on learning that he would not. The picture is in reality an illustration of the old English ballad *Burd Helen*, and known under that title only, which it bore in the Royal Academy Exhibition and the Manchester Art-Treasures Gallery, to the English public. The story of *Burd Helen* is that of a girl who has been seduced by a young lord, and who, as the time approaches when her shame can no longer be concealed, haunts his steps a whole day long, dressed as a boy. He tries her love and endurance by various cruel tests, such as making her wade through the water, which his horse crosses (the moment represented in the picture); and, after she has proved herself unconquerable by all these he marries her. Of this story the picture will be found an exact and beautiful rendering — both in incident, in expression, and in suggestive accessories; whereas it would only be a loose and inefficient rendering of *The Romaunt of the Page*.

Your obedient servant,
W. M. Rossetti

Text: *Crayon*, February 1859, p. 59.

1. "Among the late additions to Mr. Harrison's gallery is a remarkable work by Windus" (p. 324).
2. WMR to Durand, 19 December 1858: "I called the artist's attention to the passage, and he would be glad if it could be set right" (NYP). Windus to WMR, 9 December 1858: "I have read nothing of Mrs. Browning's except *Aurora Leigh* but from your outline of the plot of the *Romaunt of the Page* it bears just sufficient resemblance to *Burd Helen* to make my picture pass for a bad illustration of it" (AP).

67. TO THOMAS DIXON[1]

45 Upper Albany Street,
[Early January 1859]

Dear Mr. Dixon,

I am very much obliged for your kindness in sending me the enclosed. The portrait of Chatterton[2] (indeed, *any* portrait of him) is new to me, and most interesting; showing a very remarkable head indeed, full of fire and strangeness: and, as it happens, we were all here wishing to see a head of him, having lately been reading Masson's narrative of his life.[3] The bridge at Sunderland[4] will evidently be an *engineering* and practical improvement; but, as regards appearance, I prefer even the awkward-shaped old bridge, or any that exhibits an upper curve and a little unexpectedness, in lieu of the dead-level, literal and typical, of the straight road-line. The notice of Scott's new picture[5] is the first intimation I had of its completion, and makes me anxious to see the photograph, and in due time the original. I like the subject hugely, and can see, through the indifferent criticism, that he has treated it with his usual thoughtful and sympathetic insight. The Christmas essay[6] reads to me like the production of a man with a natural gift, and some practice in clever writing, but not of a good school such as would bring out his real capabilities. There seems rather too much *determination* to be genial and spirited, which threatens commonplace in the very effort to avoid it. To *think* vividly and characteristically is the main thing: if a man does that, he cannot do better, I fancy, in point of *expression* than write with the most entire simplicity. The combination of the two is more really original than point and sparkle.

The 4 Nos. of the *Germ* which I sent you are all that appeared. It can be obtained at the publishers, Messrs. Tupper & Sons, 4 Barge Yard, Bucklersbury, London, E.C. — and I believe at the original price. At any rate, if anyone wanting to get it were to mention my name, I think no more would be charged, though I heard some rumours of a rise in price.

I should be delighted to further you in reading and appreciating Browning, whom I regard as quite *the* best of living poets. I know nothing in print that would be of much use; but here are a few rapid and formless hints which I write down as they occur to me. (I am intending to write a lengthy exposition of his great poem *Sordello*: but doubt whether it will ever find a publisher).

1. The great quality which raises Browning above all his contemporaries is his intense and unrestricted human sympathy — his power of entering into all kinds of character and emotion, and his dramatic depth in realizing them: something of the Shakespearean quality, very rare nowadays. He is thoroughly *a man*.

2. He is never afraid or unable to say what enters his head; but pours everything out richly and profusely — often rather by hints than detailed statement, which is the secret of his obscurity (so far as he really *is* obscure). He is utterly free both from prurience and from squeamishness — daring and high-minded.

3. He knows a most enormous variety of things in all departments of thought and enquiry: being, for instance, about the only poet who really understands fine art, and is to be relied upon in his judgements of it.

4. These qualities combined require his reader to keep his attention and thought well awake. He cannot be read as a mere pastime; but, with a fair exercise of thought, becomes exceedingly captivating, and ever new.

If you have not yet read him to any extent, and can get hold of his two volumes of collected *Poems*,[7] I think the best way to begin him is by reading the *Dramatic Lyrics* — short pieces full of energy and character, embodying the mind and purpose of different periods and types of mankind. Several are quite clear, others more puzzling or abstruse, and these might be laid aside until you get more into his tone of thought and expression. Next you might read his best stage-play *A Blot in the 'Scutcheon* — full of poetry and emotion, and plain sailing enough. Next *Pippa Passes* — the noblest (I think) along with *Sordello*, of all his longer works. This may seem at first sight rather scattered and unconnected: each scene introducing a new set of personages and interests. But, if you catch hold of the central thought, the difficulty is conquered. This thought is that our most trivial actions may be controlled to some great purpose by God. Pippa goes out on a holiday singing careless snatches of songs: and each of these snatches, unknown to her, exercises a strong and ennobling influence upon the persons who chance to hear it. A murderer and adulteress are overwhelmed with remorse: an artist who has been got to marry a female model by a practical joke is awakened to the power for good thus put into his hands: a patriot hesitating whether to deliver his country from oppression is roused to action: and so on: and at last a foul plot against Pippa herself is relinquished. Of the other dramas I should not much recommend an early perusal: some are dry and most of them require a certain mastery of the subject at starting. The early dramatic poem of *Paracelsus* is very grand, but abstruse. His last volume of short poems, *Men and Women*, contains many which offer no particular difficulty, and might be read from the first along with the *Dramatic Lyrics*: but it is not easy to know beforehand which to choose.

I think the long narrative poem *Sordello* about the noblest thing he has done. But it is by far the most difficult of all — exceedingly tangled and confusing, and only to be taken up at leisure, and after getting into Browning's manner. Another long poem, *Christmas Eve and Easter Day*, is in a familiar strain so far as the narrative part goes; but there is much abstract religious thought and argument in it, not always quite tangible: and it repels rather than attracts most readers.

I hope this is not disagreeably long. I love Browning so much, both as a writer and personally, and know so well how delightful he is to those who once fairly enter into him, that I am always anxious to get him read.

104

Have you extra copies of the Chatterton photograph, which it would be *no kind of inconvenience* to you to part with? I like it so much that, if you have, I would almost like to beg a copy — but by no manner of means otherwise.

Yours truly,

W. M. Rossetti

MS: Texas.

1. (1831-80), Ruskin's "Working Man of Sunderland," to whom he addressed the letters published as *Time and Tide by Weare and Tyne* (1867). By trade a corkcutter, Dixon's principal business was supplying corks to public houses, but he was happiest when reading and corresponding with writers and artists. A man of prodigious energy, he worked unceasingly for the establishment in Sunderland of educational and cultural bodies. He collected books indiscriminately, many of which he sent unsolicited to his correspondents, an activity which led WMR to describe him as a "sometimes inconvenient man" (*RP*, p. 179). Cook and Wedderburn write sympathetically about him (17:lxxviii-xxix), but the best account is by WBS (*AN*, 2:264-72), who was moved by Dixon's devotion to art and ideas.

2. No authentic portrait of Chatterton is known. See John H. Ingram, *The True Chatterton* (1910), pp. 335-38, for portraits said to be of him.

3. In *Essays Biographical and Critical*.

4. The cast-iron bridge which crosses the river Wear with a single span of 236 feet. Opened in 1796, it was widened in 1858-59 under the direction of Robert Stephenson.

5. *Bernard Gilpin* for Wallington. WBS to WMR, [21 August 1859]: "Tomorrow I exhibit for a week my new picture *Bernard Gilpin* before taking it down to Wallington" (Durham). All eight Wallington pictures were exhibited at intervals in the rooms of the Newcastle Literary Society.

6. Not identified.

7. *Poems: a New Edition* (1849).

68. TO THOMAS DIXON

45 Upper Albany Street,
7 June [1859]

Dear Mr. Dixon,

I have much pleasure in sending you the accompanying portrait of Browning — at least, my pleasure would be great if the portrait were a good one, which it unfortunately is not. It came out in a book published towards 1844 — Horne's *New Spirit of the Age* — and of course represents Browning as a much younger man than he now is. His hair remains much the same in quantity, but is grizzled, especially in a thick bush which he grows under the chin, not exactly amounting to a beard. The features in the print look rather too small and pinched; and a peculiar hawklike keenness of look is quite missed. It is the only published portrait I know: Woolner did an excellent medallion,[1] and my brother a small water-colour portrait, not less like perhaps, and still more satisfactory in a sympathetic sense. I send you also an envelope written in Browning's hand (which please keep if you care, as well as the portrait) and one of his recent letters to me, which please return at your convenience.

It relates, as you will gather, to a photograph portrait of Mrs. Browning, which they entrusted to me to get engraved for the new edition of *Aurora Leigh*; so you may soon see a portrait much less useless than that in the *National Magazine*,[2] which in all likelihood was utter rubbish. The new engraving has ultimately come such as to satisfy Browning fairly enough, though there were fears at first.[3] Perhaps the likeness will not yet quite correspond with your preconception: Mrs. Browning is an extremely small woman, the reverse of handsome, with fine dark hair and eyes, and an expression of exceeding sensitiveness in the face, and still more the voice.

Yours truly,
W. M. Rossetti

MS: Texas.

1. 1856; exhibited at the R.A., 1857.
2. 1857, p. 313. Engraved by Henry Linton after a medallion by Marshall Wood.
3. For three letters by Browning about the portrait, see *RRP*, pp. 208-13, 217-20. Arabel Barrett wrote to WMR on [4 April 1859] that she was "most anxious to know what has been done with respect to the portrait.... Unless great alterations were made, it would be painful to all related to my sister, that such a *caricature* of her (for it was really nothing less) should be published — and to her husband, I am sure it would be extremely distressing" (AP).

69. TO WILLIAM ALLINGHAM

Somerset House,
19 March [1860]

Dear Allingham,

Thanks probably to your troubling yourself once more about the matter, the *Nightingale Valleys*[1] for Christina and myself arrived the other night at Albany Street, along with copies for Hunt and Millais. Are these the identical copies originally set apart for the 4 of us, or are they fresh copies sent in substitution for old ones not duly received? I ask this because I don't feel quite clear about what I ought to do with the Hunt and Millais copies — my impression being rather strong that Hunt at any rate had previously received his. I shall keep them by me a little while in case you have anything further to explain about them.

Another strong impression of mine is that I saw somewhere (but where I cannot at all fix) a notice saying it is far the best collection extant of its kind: also that the *Athenaeum* included it, without comment, in one of the lists they frequently give of miscellaneous publications reaching them. So, if I am right on the latter point, you are not likely to see any notice of it *there*. Christina was much pleased and thankful to you for her copy, and, looking into it as soon as it came, found it to agree very much with her own notions of what ought to have been selected.

I have *not* done anything about the commentary on *Sordello*, which I am the more ashamed to confess as I had written to Browning himself mentioning the idea, and he expressed approval. Utter indisposition to writing has, I must admit, taken possession of me since my secession from the *Spectator*[2] and dropping from the *Saturday Review*[3] freed me from doing it as a routine matter of business. Yet I would really like, in a certain sense, to do the commentary: one serious objection is that there seems very little likelihood of getting it published in any form other than that of a separate pamphlet, which would cost something, and probably not sell a copy. I fear I shall never do the thing after all. Talking of *Sordello*, I have by me a letter from John Tupper telling me that "a great Cambridge Don, Professor Grote,[4] has not only read *Sordello*, but has set himself and a mutual friend to write out a prose version of some of the most knotty passages, in order to see how the two interpretations look side by side. But Grote is not yet sufficiently confident that he takes in *Sordello* in its total perfection, and is determined to give, at his first opportunity, an entire week to its serious perusal. One of the outcomes of his present conviction is that *Sordello*, on the score of difficulty, is much to be preferred to the *Agamemnon* of Aeschylus — his own words.'' This is curious news, and good.

I *do* agree in disliking "latest intelligence turned into poetry," and dare say I shall be scarcely half pleased with *Poems before Congress*,[5] which I have not yet seen. I also exactly agree with what you say about Louis Napoleon. I believe him to be a bad man — his motives selfish and vulgar; at the same time, I consider his whole course since he came into power *compatible* with his being a very great man, the spirit and motive being the whole quest[ion. He][6] has [cer]tainly, by hook or by crook, done a vast good to Italy, and I am not at all prepared to say that he is much out in his management of France. His person is assuredly repulsive: I saw himself in Paris — very like a clammy pork-butcher. Scores of photographs are to be had of him for small sums. I shall send you one (either in this letter or afterwards, as may prove more convenient): there was a most admirable one I saw months ago in a particular shop, showing him seated (very small size) in his cabinet with an expression of triumphant swindlerism which was the very thing. It was done just before he started for the Italian campaign. I shall get that if I can — if not, ano[ther].

The E. Burne Jones of the *Athenaeum is* our Jones: the notice[7] being done by a friend of mine and acquaintance (at least) of yours who has a prospect of permanent engagement for the art of the *Athenaeum*. I am not at liberty to name him. I read *In Weimar*[8] more hurriedly than I should have wished, and received a very pleasing impression of it: it is a great admiration of my mother and Christina, who, on the receipt of *Nightingale Valley*, were expressing regret that this poem does not represent you, *inter alia*, in that collection. I'm glad to hear of your Irish poem[9] — it is already too long since you intermitted systematic writing.

Ruskin makes indeed the most unconsciona[ble ?blund]erings every now and then in his poetic apprehension: his painful propensity for Longfellow is no new thing to me — he has coupled him with Browning in print ere now.[10] What he says about the *Psalm of Life* doing immense good,[11] though it outrages one's feelings, may perhaps have a kind of truth, keeping the literary side of the question aside. As to Lowell I have not a notion of what he means — is it the *Biglow Papers* or the sentimentalisms he refers to? The article (by Ruskin) in the last *Cornhill Magazine* on Holbein and Reynolds[12] seems to me the poorest piece of writing that ever came from his hand.

As to Petrarch's Letters.[13] I have a kind of notion (very indistinct) that you wrote to me some while ago about this book, and that I found it to be in my possession, and that I either did send it to you, or offered to do so; at [any rate I] will look for it again, and, if I find it, send it on, with your stockings through Reeves & Turner.[14]

News scanty, or not occurring to me at the moment. Hunt's Temple picture[15] is at last quite on the eve of completion: Gabriel lately, and very rapidly, at work on the Adoration of Kings and Shepherds, forming the centre of his Llandaff triptych: Woolner just now at Cambridge — looking, I suppose, after a bust of Sedgwick[16] which was on the cards. Boyce[17] asked me after you the other day, seeming a little surprised at not having heard from you in reply to more than one letter of his.

Yours always,
W. M. Rossetti

[How are] Customs in these times of decimation? Improved or retarded? or I have been thinking sometimes whether it would put you in the way of quitting altogether under some advantageous arrangement.

MS: Illinois.

1. Allingham's *Nightingale Valley, a Collection, including a great number of the Choicest Lyrics and Short Poems in the English Language*, published a year before Palgrave's *Golden Treasury* (1861).

2. When Thornton Hunt became editor of the *Spectator* towards the end of 1858 WMR was "somewhat reluctant to act" under him (*SR*, 2:298). Hunt to WMR, 28 December 1858: "I am obliged to you for so promptly informing me of your preference not to continue with the *Spectator*. It must be, of course, with regret that I see our pages lose a writer whose contributions would be an advantage and ornament to any journal" (AP).

3. Only one review by WMR in the *Saturday Review* has been identified, "The Fine Art of 1858 — Oil Pictures" (15 May 1858, pp. 500-506). In *SR* he explains that "the proprietor ... Beresford Hope, was decidedly adverse to Pre-Raphaelitism, while I had been championing its cause" (2:299).

4. John Grote (1813-66), Knightbridge Professor of Moral Philosophy at Cambridge, 1855-66; younger brother of George Grote (1794-1871), the historian of Greece.

5. By Mrs. Browning, 1860.

6. MS. damaged.

7. 3 March 1860, p. 309; a review by F. G. Stephens of Burne-Jones's St. Frideswide window for the Latin Chapel, Christ Church Cathedral, Oxford (A. Charles Sewter, *The Stained Glass of William Morris and his Circle — A Catalogue* [1975], p. 2).

8. Published in the *Athenaeum*, 10 March 1860, p. 340; and in *Fifty Modern Poems*.

9. *Laurence Bloomfield in Ireland*.

10. *Modern Painters*, 4; and in *The Elements of Drawing*, Appendix 2, "Things to be Studied." *Modern Painters*, 3, quotes "the exquisite lines of Longfellow on the sunset in *The Golden Legend*" (C & W, 6:446-47; 15:227; 5:229).

11. In a letter to Allingham, [February 1860]: "I believe the *Psalm of Life* to have had more beneficial influence on this generation of English than any other modern composition whatever, except Hood's *Song of the Shirt*." The letter continues: "From Lowell I have myself received more help than from any other writer whatsoever. I have not learned so much — but I have got help and heart from single lines, at critical times" (C & W, 38:330a).

12. "Sir Joshua and Holbein," C & W, 19:3-15.

13. WMR to Allingham, 15 April [1860]: "The Epistles (edition by a brother of my father's [Domenico Rossetti (1774-1842), bibliographer and editor of Petrarch]) seem to be wholly or chiefly in Latin verse, with Italian translations. I very much fear they are of the unreadable class" (PM).

14. Should be Reeves and Lovell.

15. *The Finding of the Saviour in the Temple*.

16. For Trinity College, Cambridge (*TW*, p. 338).

17. George Price Boyce (1826-97), landscape painter and watercolorist, exhibited mainly at the Old Water-Colour Society (Wood). He was a member of the Pre-Raphaelite circle, being especially intimate with DGR, from whom he purchased numerous works. WMR's reviews of Boyce, 1852-77 (see "Checklist"), are epitomized by a remark in his notice of the 1867 exhibition of the Old Water-Colour Society: "The name of Boyce is synonymous with truth, purity, and pleasureableness

of perception of nature; with bright, warm, cheering colour; and with a real artistic gift of the most genuine kind, though always unobtrusive and modestly used" (*Chronicle*, 4 May 1867, p. 135).

70. TO ELIZABETH BARRETT BROWNING

45 Upper Albany Street,
27 March [1860]

My dear Mrs. Browning,

Allow me to thank you very warmly for the copy of *Poems before Congress* which was sent to me the other day as "from the Author." There has surely been a great work done for Italy;[1] and, without being myself one of them, I sympathize with those who believe that the doer of the work has been of a truth actuated by great and glorious motives. I wholly respect also and sympathize with the courage which insists upon asserting this belief in the teeth of a public opinion as blatant and intolerant as that at home here; and, even had one not so strong motives for honouring the little book, the genius of it must transfigure questioning into reverence, or exasperate dissent into rancour. It appears to me to contain some of your very noblest writing and thought — perhaps more than any other work, in proportion to its bulk. I must gratify myself by instancing from my own particular admiration *Napoleon III in Italy*, *The Dance*, *A Court Lady*, and *A Curse for a Nation*.

I am a little ashamed of mentioning *Sordello* now, as I happened, in writing to Mr. Browning sometime ago, to name a notion of mine of writing a detailed exposition of it, which to my shame I have never done. But perhaps he might be pleased, or at least amused, to hear the following, which produced the same effect on me. A friend of mine[2] (himself frantically "Sordellivorous," as he phrases it) tells me that Professor Grote, of Cambridge (a brother, I understand, of the historian) has set himself and another person to "write out a prose version of some of the most knotty passages, in order to see how the two interpretations look side by side." In order also to master *Sordello* in its "total perfection," the Professor means, "at the earliest opportunity, to give an entire week to its serious perusal," having already arrived at the conviction, to use his own words, that, "on the score of difficulty, *Sordello* is much to be preferred to the *Agamemnon* of Aeschylus."

Please to excuse this gossiping interruption of perhaps some serious occupation, and to remember me with affectionate respect to Mr. Browning.

Very truly yours,
W. M. Rossetti

MS: Wellesley.

1. *Poems Before Congress* glorified Napoleon III's policy towards Italy and castigated England's.
2. J. L. Tupper.

71. TO WILLIAM BELL SCOTT

Somerset House,
14 May 1860

Dear Scotus,

I now apply myself with due deliberation to your letter.

As to *Sordello*, I must give you up,[1] hoping only that the pains of heresy don't await you round the corner of something or other. Only let me hint that he did not belong to "the *15th* century," but to the earlier half of the 13th. The particulars of him given (you would say *not* given) by Browning are nearer the truth too than most people would suppose — or at least nearer some versions and hints of the truth, for his life is involved in great obscurity. I have read the notice of him in Nostredame's Lives of the Provençal Poets,[2] and find an extended account of him in Tiraboschi's Italian Literature,[3] which I shall look carefully into one day.

I see you are going in for the British lion, having maybe learned to appreciate the noble brute while studying for the Una.[4] But you probably agree with me that one cannot judge any work involving even a moderate amount of intellect and originality by newspaper extracts, especially when culled for a hostile purpose. The *Poems before Congress* (which you really should read) are disfigured by Mrs. Browning's weaknesses and disagreeablenesses, but there is much fine element in them too. I don't remember that there is much about "grovelling England" etc., as you put it: and, if there was, I am by no means sure, considering our sublime national self-complacency, that such one-sided batteries are not as well directed against us as they could be against anything. The poem of *The Curse*, which was supposed to be aimed at England, turns out to be launched at the United States. For *Aurora Leigh*, I believe I agree with you: at least, I know that, after reading it through with a feeling of admiration that palled upon me, I laid it down with a bad taste in my mouth, and doubt very much whether I shall ever attack it again.

The circular about Hunt[5] was sent to you less with any idea that you could act upon it than as to a member of the Club, entitled to know what was going on. But the affair is shelved now, at Hunt's own desire: he seems to feel that it would clog rather than speed his progress to greater things, and that it is too bad to some of the members to invite them to incur any expense in such a cause. I think on the whole this may be the best finale to the affair, which was not wholly without its difficult side: the Club has done its part in *proposing* the recognition of Hunt's claims, the same as if the proposal had taken effect. The sale of the picture is now settled (if the arrangement of which Hunt told me yesterday week came to pass, as I cannot doubt). Gambart buys picture, copyright, and all, for £5,500, of which 3000 were to be paid last Wednesday in notes or coin, and the remainder by bills at 18 months' date. This certainly *is* a miraculous draught of loaves and fishes — though I have very little doubt that Gambart, being a wideawake man, can pay himself splendidly for the outlay by exhibition and engraving, and then finally resale of a picture which will be accumulating a huge reputation meanwhile at compound interest. A little while ago the receipts at the door were £30 a day, and a very easy sum in arithmetic will show what this would come to throughout

a year. I concur as to the poorness of what has been written about the picture —
though the *Athenaeum* article[6] is by a very good friend of mine. The one in
Fraser's[7] ought to be above the average: I have not seen it yet. It is by a son of Sir
F. Palgrave — a man of high cultivation in art and other matters, writer of an
essay on engraving at the close of Murray's Kugler, and also of an anonymous
book called *The Passionate Pilgrims*, which evokes the enthusiasm of Patmore
and some others.

Let me tell you, in as few words as I can manage (and speaking merely from
memory) the few pictures by which (of course next to *Una and the Lion*) the
R.A. of 1860 will dwell some little while in the mind. Millais's *Black Brunswicker*[8]
— very excellent, but not very interesting. Dyce — an English sea-cliff piece,[9]
and a landscape with Christ, called the *Man of Sorrows*. Little Solomon —
Moses's mother as nurse to the child,[10] very good and reasonable. A Yankee
named Whistler — a rough but magnificent piece of Reynoldsish-French colour,
a Lady at a Piano, — and some etchings.[11] Young Leslie — Dante's Matilda in
Eden,[12] very graceful and sweet, an unmistakable painter. Landseer's big Scotch
Flood[13] — disfigured by the poor soppy colour. Wells's miniatures,[14] really
noticeable (the miniatures are now reduced to 2 small stands in the middle of the
room — the wall-space which they used to occupy being appropriated to the
architecture). Hook's fisher-pictures,[15] very delightful, but increasing in unfinish
of execution. Large landscape by Anthony, with a bullock-drawn cart.[16] Elmore's
M. Antoinette exposed to the mob in the Tuileries[17] is a remarkable success in its
kind. There must be a few others worth mentioning, but only a few, and I cannot
hit upon them now. Hughes, Halliday, Inchbold (1 out of 2), Davis[18] (an admirable
picture of Ploughing now at the Hogarth), Campbell,[19] Boyce, are among the
rejected of my acquaintance. Also Marshall,[20] son-in-law to Miller of Liverpool,
who has exhibited before under the name of Peter Paul: he sent 3 pictures, one
being George Stephenson at the pit's mouth pondering a railway-engine model
— a little rude in manner, but essentially excellent — now at the Hogarth also. If
any Christian or early-Christian friend tells you that Herbert's Virgin going to the
Hill-Country[21] is "so sweet," please bear in mind that it is a perfect beast. At the
Old Water-colour, there are the most *marvellous* things by old Hunt[22] — especially
a couple of dried pilchards as a study of gold-colour for Ruskin, mentioned in the
Athenaeum.

It *must* be jolly certainly in your studio: and how gladly would I defy therein
the Trevelyans[23] and the Anti-tobacco Journals! But how about your influenza? I
hope there is nothing in it to make one uneasy, or you very comfortless. I have
always been curious to see what you would make of Grace Darling,[24] and trust it
would be in my power, as a conscientious and eminent critic, to pat your
foam-breakers on the back.

Do you know that Gabriel is about to marry,[25] or perhaps now married to,
Miss Siddall — whom you have heard about, and possibly seen? We were a little
taken by surprise at receiving from him at Hastings, about a month ago, the
definite announcement of the forthcoming event, to be enacted as soon as possible;

and still later he told us that it might probably be on this last Saturday, his 32nd birthday. She is a beautiful creature, with fine powers and sweet character: if only her health should become firmer after marriage, I think it will be a happy match. At all events, I am very glad that Gabriel is settled upon it. He leaves Blackfriars, but I think has not yet managed to suit himself elsewhere.

Love from home.

Yours always,

W. M. Rossetti

MS: Princeton. Extract in *AN*, 2:57-58.

1. WBS to WMR, 5 May 1860: "I have looked into *Sordello* with your exposition [letter of 5 February [1860]; AP] in my hand, and begin to think that with time and health, one could, by reading the book and nothing else, gradually lose the enjoyment of active distinct tangible things, and luxuriate in it. But having neither of these requisites I must content myself" (Durham).

2. Jean de Nostredame, *Les Vies des plus célèbres et anciens Poëtes Provensaux* (1575).

3. Girolamo Tiraboschi, *Storia della Letteratura Italiana* (1772-95).

4. WBS's picture of *Una and the Lion*, R.A., 1860.

5. A letter from J. H. Pollen to WMR, 4 May 1860, discussed plans for the Hogarth Club to give Hunt a dinner to mark the completion of *The Finding of the Saviour in the Temple*, which Gambart was showing at the German Gallery, and to start a subscription to buy one of his pictures (AP).

6. 21 April 1860, pp. 549-50, by F. G. Stephens.

7. 61 (May 1860), 643-47, by Francis Turner Palgrave (1824-97), son of the medieval historian Sir Francis Palgrave. As a student at Oxford he moved in the circle of Matthew Arnold, A. H. Clough, and J. C. Shairp, and later became a lifelong friend of Tennyson. Like WMR he was a civil servant and man of letters. His essay on Italian engraving appeared in the third edition of F. T. Kugler's *Handbook of Painting* (1855); *The Passionate Pilgrims* was published in 1858.

8. Bennett 1967, No. 59.

9. *Pegwell Bay, Kent*.

10. Simeon Solomon, *Moses*.

11. Whistler exhibited *At the Piano*; three etchings: *Thames — Black Lion Wharf*; *W. Jones, lime-burner*; *The Thames, from the Tunnel Pier*; and two drypoints: *Monsieur Astruc*, and *Portrait*. WMR was to become one of Whistler's staunchest champions, but he had not yet met him or reviewed him. DGR (and presumably WMR) made his acquaintance c. October 1862, several months after WMR praised *The 25 December, 1860, the Thames* (R.A., 1862) in the *London Review*: "The notable first appearance made by Mr. Whistler in the Academy Exhibition of 1860 bespeaks attention to this work. It is a study of broken ice and dingy white sky, broad and characteristic; of detail it has doubtless very little, and any which may exist could not well be traced in the position which the picture occupies" (10 May 1862, p. 439). WMR took Whistler's part in the Burlington Club fracas, and in 1878 appeared on his behalf at the Whistler v. Ruskin trial. In *SR* he observed that "For companionable pleasantry I have known no man superior to Whistler; and with people whom he liked he could be in every sense most agreeable" (2:318).

12. George Dunlop Leslie (1835-1921), landscape and genre painter who for a brief period painted in a Pre-Raphaelite style (Wood); son of C. R. Leslie. His picture was entitled *Matilda* and cited the *Purgatorio*, Can. 28.

13. Edwin Henry Landseer (1802-73); *Flood in the Highlands*.

14. Henry Tanworth Wells (1828-1903) exhibited eight miniatures.

15. James Clarke Hook (1819-1907) exhibited four pictures, at least two of which had fishermen as their subject.

16. *The huge Oak that o'ershadows the Mill*.

17. Alfred W. Elmore (1815-81), historical genre painter; *The Tuileries, June 20, 1792*.

18. William Davis (1812-73), Liverpool landscape painter and friend of the Pre-Raphaelites, described by WMR in an obituary in the *Academy* as "a painter, though but slightly known to London exhibition-goers, of genuine and rare qualities, especially as a landscape colourist" (2 June 1873, p. 205).

19. James Campbell (c. 1825/28-93), Liverpool genre and landscape painter, whose early pictures were influenced by the Pre-Raphaelites (Wood). Although he exhibited at the Pre-Raphaelite Exhibition,

Russell Place, 1857, and was a member of the Hogarth Club, next to nothing is known about his personal relationship with the Pre-Raphaelites. He exhibited at the R.A. in 1863, but is not mentioned in WMR's review of the exhibition in *Fraser's*.

20. Peter Paul Marshall (1830-1900), described by WMR as "an engineer by profession, and an amateur painter by liking" (*SR*, 1:222).

21. *And Mary, rising up*.

22. William Henry Hunt (1790-1864). For a list of the eleven pictures he exhibited, see *Old Water-Colour Society's Club, Twelfth Annual Volume, 1934-1935* (1935), pp. 48-49.

23. Sir Walter Trevelyan was an ardent campaigner for total abstinence, but his wife insisted that wine should be provided for guests (R. Trevelyan, *Pre-Raphaelite Circle*, p. 20).

24. One of WBS's pictures for Wallington.

25. He was married on 23 May.

72. TO FORD MADOX BROWN

Albany Street,
12 March [1861]

Dear Brown,

There was a meeting about Cross[1] at Foley's[2] (17 Osnaburgh Street, Regent's Park) on Thursday last, and resolutions passed for buying one or more pictures for some public place, to be hereafter determined, and for getting a committee,[3] of whom you should be one. Another meeting fixed for same place Thursday 21st, at 8 p.m., after which we shall print etc. Pray attend if you can, or otherwise write me anything you have to say. Subscription list[4] added, showing all the men present the other night. E. B. Stephens[5] Secretary and Armitage Treasurer.[6]

Your
W. M. Rossetti

Foley	£10.10	E. Foley	£5.0
Armitage	5.0	Thornycroft	5.0
Teniswood	3.3	Chamberlain	5.0
Watkin Jones	5.0	Placee	5.0
Fred. Hill	5.0	Edwards	5.0
Barker	5.0	Haydon	5.0
W.M.R.	10.0	Robertson	3.3
Stephens	5.0		

MS: AP.

1. John Cross (1819-61), historical painter, whose *Richard Coeur-de-Lion forgiving Bertrand de Gourdon* was awarded a £300 premium in the 1847 Westminster Hall oil-painting competition. WMR briefly noticed his death and announced a subscription fund in *Weldon's Register*, April 1861, p. 207. He published an obituary in the same journal, July 1861, pp. 8-10, when he was able to report that "the fund has now reached nearly £1000, and it may be hoped that at least two of the pictures [exhibited at the Society of Arts from early May 1861] will be purchased, and worthily bestowed. One of them ought ... to go to the National British Gallery: a picture of this class is absolutely needed there to show that we are not incapable of historical painting." *The Assassination of Thomas à Becket* was placed in Canterbury Cathedral, and *The Burial of the Young Princes in the Tower* in the Albert Museum, Exeter (*DNB*). WMR's considered opinion of Cross was that his later work did not live up to the promise of *Richard Coeur-de-Lion* (*SR*, 1:140).

2. John Henry Foley (1818-74) was during the 1840s "in the front rank of British contemporary sculptors" (Gunnis).

3. It included Holman Hunt, Millais, Woolner, G. F. Watts, Frith; and Daniel Maclise, the painter of four historical scenes for the House of Lords.

4. Chamberlain and Placee are not identified. Watkin D. Jones (fl. 1846-61), Edward Arlington Foley (1814-74; elder brother of J. H. Foley), Thomas Thornycroft (1815-85), Joseph Edwards (1814-83), and Samuel James Bouverie Haydon (1815-91) were sculptors. G. F. Teniswood was a pupil of J. H. Foley, who after Foley's death completed the seated figure of Prince Albert for the Albert Memorial (Gunnis). Barker is most likely the historical and battle painter, Thomas Jones Barker (1815-82). Robertson may be either Henry Robert Robertson or Charles Robertson, both landscape painters and engravers. Richard Ormond lists an F. Hill whose copy of J. R. Herbert's 1845 portrait of A. W. N. Pugin is in the Royal Institute of British Architects (*Early Victorian Portraits* [1973], 1:387).

5. Edward Bowring Stephens (1815-82), sculptor, exhibited at the R.A., 1838-83; and at the Westminster Hall competitions, 1844-45. In 1845-46 he was employed in the decoration of the Summer Pavilion at Buckingham Palace (Gunnis).

6. Edward Armitage (1817-96), historical and biblical painter, who won several prizes in the Westminster Hall competitions.

73. TO WILLIAM BELL SCOTT

Albany Street,
28 April [1861]

Dear Scotus,

Thanks for telling me your friendly opinion of my paper in *Fraser's*:[1] it is an encouragement. You have not, I think, "changed my point of view in considering Greek sculpture," for, even in the rabidest days of Praeraphaelitism, I could only have expressed much the same opinion when it came to writing it down for the public: within the last 2 or 3 years however I have certainly felt more *sympathy* for the antique in art, literature, and tone of character, than I used to. As for the Woolner passage, I quite feel that it puts the article somewhat out of scale, though what I say about him is not more than true according to my belief, and I hope to the fact. I was bound to say something about him, not only because I wanted to do so, but because Froude[2] wished it too: and I thought it best on the whole to get *all* about him into the one passage at the end.

About turbans I don't know, but I expect the majority of oriental costume etc. is really from time out of mind: parts may be modern, but I don't see how any can be Mohammedan. Indeed there is no such thing as Mohammedanism apart from Judaism and Christianity: it was merely an enlarging and reforming movement, analogous to Luther's, and still more to George Fox's or Joe Smith's.

I *did* attend the Hogarth meeting. Your letter[3] was read before (I think) any of the other business was broached. No one opposed it, and none seemed hostile to it (though of course several would not have supported it); but also no one came forward to champion it, and I think it clear that the matter will drop unless renewed. You will be aware that there were two conflicting parties mustered that evening,[4] both agreed that the Club cannot subsist on its then footing; the first wishing to make it a regular London Club for artists — the second, to make it a paying exhibition, comparatively indifferent whether the Club character is retained or not. The latter party won; but the question *how* it is to become a paying exhibiting body remains to be worked out, and there is no reason why your scheme should not yet receive its due share of attention. The present position of the Club is certainly most shaky. Some members have resigned; others undoubtedly will do so; others, even if they do not resign, will not exhibit. The non-artistic members, I should say, are almost sure to drop off, as the Club, become a paying exhibiting body, will clearly be little or nothing of a Club. I much doubt whether there will be strength in number of artists or in subscriptions for opening the paying campaign. The present notion does not extend beyond holding the exhibition in the present Club-room, but your idea might be entertained without at all affecting the resolution adopted at the meeting. If you really wish to press it, your right course is to put down a motion for the next general meeting — not a letter, which does not enable the meeting to take any *action* upon the question, only to gossip over it at best. You understand the paying exhibition is only to be *next* year, so Stephens has some plea for saying there is yet time for consideration.

I scarcely know whether I would have seconded your proposal at the meeting, or could do so on its being brought forward again. There are 2 great questions. — 1. Will the persons concerned have funds to carry on a paying exhibition at all: 2. Will it be better for them to exhibit their own works only, resulting in a small exhibition, or their own and other people's, resulting in a large one, and all the more expensive. On both points I feel very unsettled — though indeed I suspect there will *not* be funds for either project. Ruskin would not probably have been or be available for negotiating with the British Institution, as he has cut the Hogarth.[5]

I have not seen Cave Thomas's[6] pamphlet, except by extracts in the papers. It seems to be a fussy idea fussily expounded.

The Morris & Marshall firm have come out stronger than the issue of a circular — they have sent in a requisition for 900 superficial feet of space at the Great Exhibition!! Of course a 20th of the space will satisfy them. They think also of manufacturing their own painted glass throughout. I am looking out for a smash unless they are content with very moderate operations at starting.[7]

Here is the Cross circular I mentioned to you. The pictures, like Seddon's, are now at the Society of Arts.

Do you see that the *Literary Gazette*, in reviewing your Lectures,[8] terms you "a poet, if publishing poems entitles a writer to be so called"? Cutting that! I have seen notices also in the *Critic*[9] and *Art Journal:*[10] — all 3 so so, *Critic* best — and I think not elsewhere. I don't understand the delay in the *Athenaeum*.[11]

Our love to Mrs. Scott and you.

Your
W. M. Rossetti

How about your summer trip? I shall leave early this year — towards beginning of June; and am to go over with my mother and Christina to Coutances — excursions in prospect to Bayeux, Mont-St-Michel, Paris, etc.: then after a fortnight or less I expect to desert the ladies, and start off somewhither on my own hook (not *very* far) returning by Coutances, and bringing them home. I have some suspicions however that, when it comes to the point, my mother, and

Christina as a consequence, will prefer not going.[12] If so, I shall still start about the same time, but have no clear notion as to the destination.

I am reading your Shelley,[13] and the old enthusiasm for that wondrous man makes a bit of a blaze still. *Prometheus Unbound* is one of the most stupendous embodiments that human imagination has assumed in any form whatever.

MS: Arizona.

1. "British Sculpture; its Condition and Prospects," 63 (April 1861), 493-505. (Rptd. *FACC*, pp. 335-62.)

2. James Anthony Froude (1818-94), historian, friend and biographer of Carlyle; editor of *Fraser's Magazine*, 1860-74. Woolner's friendship with Froude dated from 1857. In 1875 he executed a bas-relief monument to Mrs. Froude (*TW*, p. 341).

3. WBS suggested in a letter to WMR on 2 March 1861 that the Hogarth Club should constitute itself an exhibiting body and negotiate the management of the ailing British Institution (*RRP*, pp. 260-62). WMR to WBS, 16 March [1861]: "Your notion of the British Institution seems really worth consideration, though I scarcely suppose it will become a *fait accompli*. I have mentioned it to one or two men, and they seem taken aback by it, but not hostile. I think much the best way of bringing it on (and it ought to be brought on) would be for you to address a letter to the Secretary or Committee, explaining your notion, and enclosing a motion on the subject (amounting to whatever you like) to be discussed at the next General Meeting. If it is left to be merely gossiped over, nothing is done. I think everybody who considers the subject has come to your conclusion that 'the Club must come out an associated body for exhibition purposes, or cease to be a body exerting any influence.' If the members were sensible, they would have agreed to Gabriel's motion last year that the Hogarth exhibitions should be paying-exhibitions, supported by all the strength of the Club: then the expectant Academician members would have resigned, and the others would have girt up their loins. I incline to think that would have been the best course of all; the exhibition being confined to our own members, all on their mettle, and any clever new men of the same class throwing in their lot with us, without our having the nuisance of becoming a hanging body for the whole mob of men who choose to send, and incurring the odium of rejections and preferences. That it would have paid and succeeded I feel entirely assured. The motion was rejected because several leading men want to keep on terms with the Academy. The same difficulty would affect the British Institution scheme, though possibly in a rather minor degree: i.e. expectant Academicians would not send, or would only send second-best. I suppose the most feasible way of doing the thing would be for the Hogarth to rent the British Institution from the landlord, or from the Directors if they renew their tenancy, and for us to assume the whole practical management, appointing our own hanging-committee etc. (the Directors appear to have been so indifferent on this point of late that perhaps even if they renew tenancy, they would not insist upon having a voice in the matter). Were I the daemon of the possible Hanging-committee, I would have it take very high ground indeed. I would proclaim by advertisement and otherwise that we mean to have no lame ducks, and will leave our walls half-covered rather. That every man whatever, and every style and class of art, shall have fair treatment by a committee (names to be annually advertised) who will make by majority of open votes 3 sections of the pictures as they come in — good, second-rate, and bad; reject the 3rd lot at once, and hang all the first in the best places before any of the 2nd. That the committee will listen to no extraneous influences or suggestions whatever, and, having made this profession of their course of action, will answer no questions as to motives of rejection etc.'' (Arizona).

4. G. P. Boyce recorded in his diary on 5 April 1861: "General meeting at the Hogarth. Stanhope's motion that there be a paying exhibition next year was carried by only one vote and that the Chairman's (F. M. Brown). Fripp's motion that the Club be made into a general artists' club quashed" (Boyce, p. 32). The proposers were John Roddam Spencer Stanhope (1829-1908), who painted *Sir Gawain and the Three Damozels at the Fountain* at the Oxford Union; and the landscape and genre painter, Alfred Downing Fripp (1822-95).

5. At the same meeting Boyce "Voted that in reply to Ruskin's letter of resignation in which he talks about 'boys playing at billiards' that his resignation should be accepted with a regret on the part of the Club that he should have couched his letter in terms offensive to the same" (Boyce, pp. 32-33).

6. William Cave Thomas (1820-1906), painter of historical, genre, and religious subjects of an "abstruse turn which has interfered with popular appreciation" of his work (WMR, *Spectator*, 26 May 1855, p. 555). Thomas was associated with the PRB and suggested the name for the *Germ*, but his friendship was more particularly with FMB. WMR gave considerable space to Thomas in his reviews during the 1850s, usually taking exception to the hardness and coldness of his compositions, which he attributed to his early association with the Nazarenes, but praising his drawing. In his notices of *The Protest* (R.A., 1854) and *The Heir cast out of the Vineyard* (R.A., 1856), WMR defined the strengths and faults of Thomas's work. *The Protest*, an allegory of "the vanity of ceremonial religion when powerless over the heart," is "moral in thought, cramped in invention, painted with science and mastery, but some hardness, eminent for fine design in the individual figures" (*Spectator*, 20 May 1854, pp. 543-44). *The Heir* is "remarkable for the intellectual aim controlling the treatment of the symbolic subject throughout. The parable being a type of Christ's mission and rejection, various incidents of the passion are used in its embodiment.... Mr. Thomas's eminence as one of the first draughtsmen in the country is visible in this picture, which, though it may not gain sympathy from many, ought to command the respect of all" (*Spectator*, 31 May 1856, p. 591). The appeal of Thomas's pamphlet was similarly limited: *Pre-Raphaelitism Tested by the Principles of Christianity: an Introduction to Christian Idealism* (1860).

7. The International Exhibition of 1862 was the firm's first public show, at which they were awarded two gold medals and attracted favorable press comment. Barbara Morris points out that "Commissions for stained glass and church furnishings followed on the firm's success" (*Morris and Company, 1861-1940*, Arts Council Exhibition, 1961, p. 7). WMR noted in his review of "The Fine Art of the International Exhibition" that the firm's "furniture and other decorative work in the Medieval Court ... stand far apart from most of the specimens in their vicinity" (*Fraser's Magazine*, 66 [August 1862], 199).

8. *Half-Hour Lectures on the History and Practice of the Fine and Ornamental Arts* (1861); 20 April 1861, pp. 364-65.

9. 30 March 1861, pp. 404-5.

10. n.s. 7 (April 1861), 128. "As a history for popular reading, this is one of the best books we know."

11. A review (probably by F. G. Stephens) appeared on 10 August 1861, pp. 192-93.

12. WMR, his mother, and CGR were in Paris, Normandy, and Jersey, 10 June-13 July.

13. *Poetical Works of Shelley*, ed. Mary Shelley, 1 vol. ed., 1853. Over the next few years WMR copiously annotated the volume, and in 1868 the notes formed the basis of his *Notes and Queries* articles on the text of Shelley.

74. TO WILLIAM BELL SCOTT

Somerset House,
8 May 1861

Dear Scott,

Your picture[1] is in the West Room, north wall, on accommodated line — the line passing towards the lower part of the picture: not a bad place by any means. It keeps its own well. I see you have altered it considerably since I was at Newcastle, making the widow younger; good policy, I presume, and right pictorial point of view, but I doubt (from a single not prolonged look at the picture) whether you have bettered the *expression*.

My present impression (and I believe it will be confirmed on examination) is that the exhibition is about the most favourable for the character of our school yet held. Praeraphaelitism seems to have done its work in making people study more fully and accurately and *paint* better; and now the second stage is rapidly coming on — of more masterliness, stronger style, more painterlike conception and energy. Wells (in oils), Hook (though too slovenly), Leighton, Ward, Faed[2] (in comparison with his former self), Watts, W. Linnell,[3] Mrs. Wells, come out strong: Hunt's little Cairo picture[4] looks to me, who never much sympathized with it, very powerful and vivid here.

My object in expounding my holiday-plans was by no means to hint an interference with your accompanying Mrs. Scott in Belgium, but rather to see whether the chance offered for my catching you up at any point of the trip. It is pretty well settled now that my mother, Christina, and I, do go to Coutances, I not remaining with them the whole time; and that we start first Monday or so in June. Jones[5] is not going to Venice, and speaks of not going anywhere.

Did you hear or see in the paper that Gabriel has had a child stillborn?[6] An infernal bore that, I should say.

Be not crusty, revered Scotus, if I repeat[7] that Mohammedanism is nothing but Judaism and Christianity re-proclaimed as by divine inspiration — in this sense: that the *Koran* insists upon the divine authority of everything in the ungarbled Old and New Testaments, and Mohammed announces himself as only one in a long line of prophets sent to enforce and re-enforce the same set of truths. The "ceremonial in relation to eating and washing etc." which you cite appears little if at all (to my recollection) in the *Koran*, and at any rate would turn out to be very much the same as in Judaism. The turban on the gravestone *is*, I believe, the sign of a Mohammedan: but it does not follow that the turban came in only with Mohammed. It might be equally conceivable that, after the mass of turban-wearing nations had adopted Mohammedanism, *retaining* the turban, the dissentients dropped it. But, as a matter of fact, I believe they have not all dropped it: surely many Eastern Jews wear it — the distinction, if I remember aright, being in the *colour*, not form, of this head-dress.

But enough of this, for I don't know enough about it to make my argufying worth attending to, and moreover believe with you that people may probably be going much too far in assuming that Eastern dress is *quite* the same as in Biblical times. Also I don't much like Woolner's Paul,[8] though what I object to is not the turban, but the face. Remember however that I did not say in *Fraser's* it was a well-conceived Paul, but an *individually* conceived one — which is most assuredly true.

But surely you are quite wrong in saying that Paul was a Roman, as if that settled the question of costume. Paul was a Jew born in Asia Minor: he was a *Roman citizen* only in the sense that he was legally entitled to some or all of the privileges of a Roman citizen — just as a Jew, Greek, Indian etc. etc. of the present day may hold the freedom of the city of London, or as the Indian Parsee merchant Sir Jamsetjee Jeejeebhoy[9] was an English Baronet.

You will have cursed me before you get to this point: so I will wedge in a goodby between your teeth in process of grinding.

Your
W. M. Rossetti

MS: Arizona.

1. *The Border Widow*, R.A., 1861.

2. Thomas Faed (1826-1900) painted "mainly sentimental scenes of Scottish peasant life" (Wood). In 1861 he exhibited *From Dawn to Sunset*, an illustration of Tennyson's line "So runs the round of life from hour to hour" (*Circumstance*, 1. 9).

3. William Linnell (1826-1906), landscape and genre painter; eldest son of John Linnell.

4. *A Street Scene in Cairo: the Lantern Maker's Courtship*.

5. Presumably Burne-Jones.

6. A girl, on 2 May.

7. See Letter 73.

8. In 1858 Woolner executed models of Moses, David, St. John, and St. Paul for the pulpit of Llandaff Cathedral (*TW*, p. 337).

9. (1783-1859), wealthy Indian merchant, whose philanthropy to the poor of India brought him a knighthood in 1842 and a baronetcy in 1858. "These were the very first distinctions of their kind conferred by Queen Victoria upon a British subject in India" (*Encyclopaedia Britannica*, eleventh edition).

75. TO FREDERIC GEORGE STEPHENS   [11 February 1862]

Dear Stephens,

I shan't be able to come till further notice. Poor Lizzie is dead:[1] you will see about it in the paper unfortunately — laudanum.

Your
W.M.R.

MS: Bodleian. Published: Basil Taylor, "F. G. Stephens and the P.R.B.," *Architectural Review*, 104 (October 1948), 173.

1. DGR's wife died in the early morning of 11 February.

76. TO FREDERIC GEORGE STEPHENS   Albany Street,
15 February [1862]

Dear Stephens,

Thank you for your friendly note. You will pardon my having been so abrupt in what I wrote on Tuesday.[1] The poor thing had been in the habit of taking laudanum for 2 or 3 years past in considerable doses, and on Monday she must have taken more than her system could bear. Gabriel, on returning late at night from the Working Men's College, found her in a hopeless state, and all the efforts of 4 doctors for 7 hours or more availed nothing.

If I could command your friendly offices in any way, be sure I should not hesitate to do so, being sure that it would be a satisfaction to you as well as us. But there is really nothing I know of.

The funeral is to be on Monday, after which I doubt whether Gabriel will ever reinhabit Chatham Place. He can for the present propose to himself nothing else than living with us,[2] and painting at Brown's. I write from Albany Street, having had to come up for a particular purpose, but pass all the day and night till after the funeral at Chatham Place.

Your
W. M. Rossetti

I am certain it would gratify Gabriel to see you whenever you might be at Albany Street after the funeral.

MS: Bodleian. Published: Basil Taylor, p. 173.

1. Letter 75.
2. See Letter 77, Note 4. WMR to Thomas Dixon, 4 May [1862]: "I have also to thank you for the true sympathy you express with my brother in his calamity. It is one of those blows which one has to bear when they come: and I am thankful to say he has borne it better than I could have anticipated from my knowledge of him" (Texas).

77. TO WILLIAM BELL SCOTT

Somerset House,
17 March [1862]

Dearly beloved Scotus,

I should indeed extremely like to see your picture.[1] I asked Leathart about it, and understood the Christian had been painted from Miss Hutchinson — I infer of Shields:[2] a very judicious choice I think for she has a really beautiful face expressive of everything good. I am rather sorry to hear you have added on a lump to the jaw and chin for religion's sake. It must damage the beauty of the face, and a Christian is not *bound* to be either old or ugly. Whether the picture is "really the thing" I cannot of course surmise: but I think, even assuming it to be partially defective, you are quite wrong in proposing in such case "to give up painting history or figure pictures altogether": the fact being that the qualities of art which you especially possess are the very ones needed for history, insomuch that you do historic art, *so far as it is historic*, better than any other Briton alive. The mighty Elmore himself can't rival you at that, though he can in manoeuvring a brush, and in painting a face which suits the ideal of beauty of a retired publican married to his ex show-barmaid.

All right about Italy,[3] I hope to Providence. But I don't think £50 will do it; it will, I fear, be pretty considerably dearer than my other Italian visit and that cost £45. You call it "our *autumn* excursion": is that a slip of the pen? I fancied it was reckoned to ensue upon your visit to London closing towards the beginning of July. I feel a little confident of *managing* the trip now, though it may be somewhat contrary to family unselfishness; because the removal,[4] and expenses consequent thereon, are not to take place till towards the end of October. That question is now as good as settled. You must know Cheyne Walk, Chelsea, and may perhaps be aware that it is a place which Gabriel — and indeed Praeraffaelism generally — has always had a special itch for. One house in particular, Tudor House, the remains of a mansion built by Queen Catherine Parr, has always allured him. After some negotiation, the landlord has agreed to sell the lease (19 years, I think) and fixtures for £225, with an annual ground rent of £100: but we cannot get in till October, because meanwhile some people connected with the Great Exhibition mean to take the house at (I believe) £100 a month. Gabriel is inveterately bent upon having this house, and its extreme desirableness in many respects is obvious to us all: so that there is now an almost certainty of our taking it.

There is a huge garden, covering, some say (though others tell me that is out of the question) more than 2 acres; stabling for 22 horses, let off at £20 a year, and perhaps eventually of great value to Gabriel for studios; a drawing-room with 7 windows' frontage, and a large room on the ground floor, either of which would make a fine studio: the latter will probably be fixed on to start with. The rest of the house, with this, would just about well accommodate the lot of us, admitting Swinburne, but leaving with one of my other Aunts the elderly Aunt[5] who now lives with us in Albany Street. We are sorry to do this, as the poor old dame is extremely frail, but it seems the only suitable arrangement. My mother will come. As regards Maria, there seems some difficulty because of her pupils' being at a distance, but some reasonable settlement will turn this obstacle. The distance from Somerset House is a good deal more than I would choose from preference; but omnibuses and boats make it of less weight, and I shall in many respects really enjoy the place. For river-view, character of house, etc., there is scarcely anything in London so capital.

You are right in supposing that Swinburne has nothing to do with the preparations: the project entirely meets his own liking, but no one could possibly behave with more freedom from self-obtrusion in such a case than he has done. Of course he will live to himself (in 2 rooms) and quite independently of the family. As for my being "chained up,"[6] beloved Scotus, there is a grain of truth in that, but it is more surface-truth than substance-truth, as I have absolute liberty and suiting of my own taste in points I care a trifle about, and, in matters like the present, it is *my own temper* rather to accommodate myself to the preferences of the other persons concerned than to set up and battle for a standard of my own. You are too hard upon poor Christina in attributing "predetermined notions" to her, for she effaces herself very much in all these things, and her only notion in questions involving expense is to abstain from it.

Your Turner-unburdening was read by me with extreme gusto. You think rather *more* of the *cleverness* of Thornbury's[7] book than I do, and not a bit more of its ingrained vulgarity of tone. About Turner, while I see the force of what you say, I cannot assent to the general state of feeling and opinion in which it results to you. *The* thing in a painter is that he should paint. Turner painted landscape with an insight, amplitude, and beauty unexampled (which I suppose you allow, though you rate him lower than I do): and, though it may be true that he dropped his hs, and had a mind and a character in many respects unenlarged and meagre, yet that deficiency can't cancel, nor much affect, the other gift: no more than Dante suffers as a poet because he was not a modern philanthrope, or Shakespeare because he was not an astronomer, or Newton as a mathematician because he was not a poet, or Stephenson as an engineer because he was not an artist, or Carlyle as a prose author because he is not a poet. There was a particular faculty of a great kind in great measure in the man, and the rest must take its chance.

I don't know, nor care, what *Blackwood's* says:[8] and indeed the typical *Blackwood's* of Christopher North[9] appears to me in roaring nonsense, and self-cockering conceit on account of one's own prejudices and stupidities, very much a parallel to the objectionable side of the Turner and other social artist-life. About eavesdropping, I don't think (if my memory serves me) that I expressed *disbelief* in it, but hesitation and wish to disbelieve. I will look up your brother's anecdote,[10] which has escaped my recollection.

I fancy (though we have never yet ascertained) that Gabriel's book[11] must be making a good business, as well as literary, position, from the way they advertise it etc. Christina's[12] might now come out any time the publisher chooses.

Love to Mrs. Scott.

Your

W. M. Rossetti

MS: Arizona.

1. *A Messenger of the New Faith: Rome, A.D. 100* (Royal Scottish Academy, 1868). WBS to WMR, 23 November 1862: "I have completely repainted my picture of the Household Gods and Christian cousin" (Durham). Miss Hutchinson is not identified.

2. Frederic James Shields (1833-1911), Manchester painter and illustrator, was deeply impressed by the Pre-Raphaelite pictures in the Manchester Art Treasures Exhibition of 1857, but he did not meet DGR and FMB, the two Pre-Raphaelites with whom he became most intimate, until May 1864 (E. Mills, *Life and Letters of Shields* [1912], pp. 82-83). When WMR met Shields is uncertain, but he undoubtedly heard of him while staying at the house of John Miller of Liverpool in 1857, "as a convenient station wherefrom to visit the great Art-treasures Exhibition" (*SR*, 1:226). WMR's reviews of Shields's contributions to the Old Water-Colour Society (see "Checklist") stress their "absolute and extreme literalism" (of *Crimea, Sounding a Retreat; Chronicle*, 4 May 1867, p. 135), and their superiority as designs. Of *By faith Abel offered unto God a more excellent sacrifice than Cain*, he wrote: "Abel, a naked figure save for a hide that hangs loosely about him, has been slain beside his altar as he knelt. Still on his knees, he has drooped backward; the *pose* has evidently been very carefully worked out in the artist's mind so as to express the three things needed — worship, the collapse of sudden death, and the protest to Heaven of the righteous blood crying from the ground" (*Academy*, 16 December 1876, p. 592). *Love and Time* he judged "the finest design" in the 1877 exhibition: "Love ... has snatched from Time his hour-glass, and holds it behind his back with the left hand; with the right he repels ... the left arm of Time, weaponed with his fatal scythe, as he advances and with his right reaches round to repossess himself of the hour-glass. Remarkably compact as a design, this is equally condensed as an intellectual symbol of the insidious inroads of time retarded and mitigated by affection" (*Academy*, 8 December 1877, p. 537).

3. WBS accompanied WMR to Rome and Venice, 2 July-12 August 1862.

4. After his wife's death DGR left Chatham Place, and lived briefly with his family at 45 Upper Albany Street, then at 59 Lincoln's Inn Fields, and from October 1862 at Tudor House, 16 Cheyne Walk. N. Pevsner gives 1717 as the date of the house, and prefers the name Queens House, which preserves the tradition of a connection with Henry VIII's sixth queen (*London* [1952], 2:95). Only Swinburne, Meredith, and WMR shared the house with DGR.

5. Maria Margaret Polidori (d. 1867), the eldest of Frances Rossetti's three unmarried sisters. The other aunt was the youngest of the sisters, Eliza (1810-93), who accompanied Florence Nightingale to the Crimea in 1854.

6. WBS to WMR, 8 March [1862]: "Gabriel's unsystematic expenditure and perhaps Christina's predetermined notions of things will soon chaw up Italy. I speak to you rather freely, do I? The fact is, my own luck in my family was always to be chained up, so I fear it in your case" (Durham).

7. George Walter Thornbury (1828-76), art critic of the *Athenaeum* until F. G. Stephens succeeded him in 1861. His leaving the *Athenaeum* was undoubtedly the result of the attacks of incompetence on the book referred to here, his *Life of Turner* published in November 1861 (see A. J. Finberg, *Life of Turner*, 2d ed., 1961, pp. 1-5). WMR reviewed the book in *Weldon's Register*, January 1862, pp. 7-13. Rptd. *FACC*, pp. 291-315, with additions from his obituary of Turner (*Spectator*, 27 December 1851, p. 1242), his review of John Burnet, *Turner and his Works* (1852) (*Spectator*, 5 June 1852, p. 544), and "Turner's Will" (*Weldon's Register*, September 1861, pp. 132-34).

8. Margaret Oliphant attacked Turner's character in her review of Thornbury in *Blackwood's Magazine*, 91 (January 1862), 17-34.

9. John Wilson.

10. David Scott recorded in his diary that during a visit to Turner's studio on 2 June 1822 he was twice reprimanded for making a memorandum of one of his pictures: "I was somewhat surprised, as no one had been in the room, and the door shut.... He must have a peep-hole, and yet he is really a great painter" (*Memoir of David Scott*, p. 42).

11. *The Early Italian Poets (Together with Dante's Vita Nuova)* (1861).

12. *Goblin Market and Other Poems* (1862).

78. TO FREDERIC GEORGE STEPHENS

Somerset House,
26 August [1862]

Dear Steph,

Thanks to you for so sedulously avoiding any clash between your interests and mine. The facts are briefly these.

Weldon's Register[1] under Weldon as *proprietor* became as good as bankrupt about April last, when I discontinued my contributions. It has since been sold to Archdeacon Jermyn,[2] with Weldon as *editor*.

Just after I left London Weldon wrote asking me to resume the monthly summaries, and to undertake other art-writing, saying that the Archdeacon (a brother of Lady Trevelyan) was anxious for my consent. Being more willing than otherwise to accommodate him, and make the small extra sum thence accruing, I have consented, since my return home, to resume the monthly summaries, on the understanding that the payment (£1.1 a page) is to be made punctually month by month. I intimated that, having to do art-matter elsewhere,[3] I would not undertake for Weldon anything except the summaries, unless something happened from time to time to be specifically proposed to me, and to suit my convenience. For the next No. however, at urgent request, I have done an article on the Campana Museum in Paris.[4]

So you see that, if you don't mind relinquishing the idea of the monthly summaries, there is no sort of clashing between us.

Would you like to resume French reading? if so what do you say to Friday? I to come to you the first Friday (say *next* week) and you to me the ensuing one. This of course as suits you.

Your
W. M. Rossetti

I gave Scott a note of yours forwarded to me. He seemed to think there was nothing for him to take action upon.

I see on coming to the address that my French proposal is probably premature.

MS: Bodleian.

1. *Weldon's Register of Facts and Occurrences relating to Literature, the Sciences and the Arts* was published monthly, August 1860-February 1864. Between December 1860 and February 1864 WMR contributed thirty-two articles under the title "Art Notes of the Month," and seven additional articles on general art matters (see "Checklist"). Walter Weldon (1832-85), a chemist by profession, spent a decade in journalism. After the demise of the *Register* he turned his attention to technological chemistry in which he achieved eminence, becoming in 1883 president of the Society of Chemical Industry.

2. Hugh Willoughby Jermyn (1820-1903) was at this date Rural Dean of Dunster in Somerset. In 1875 he became Bishop of Brechin, and in 1886 Primus of Scotland. WMR to Stephens, 16 March [1864]: "Weldon *is* done up; and the loss falls heavy, I am sorry to find, upon Archdeacon Jermyn" (Bodleian).
   3. WMR was art reviewer of the *London Review* for eleven months, beginning with an article on Maclise's Waterloo picture for the House of Lords (5 April 1862, pp. 323-24).
   4. "The Musée Napoléon Trois," September 1862, pp. 88-90. The museum housed the bulk of the collection formed in Rome by the Marquis de Cavelli Campana.

79. TO WILLIAM BELL SCOTT

Albany Street,
31 August [1862]

Dear Scott,

I take up the pen to answer your note, more through the resolution to be prompt and orderly than because I have anything to say.

Your sympathy with my suffering from atmospheric causes is appreciated: though we have not been *very* badly off here — not since Tuesday week, that is, when my mother left for Eastbourne. Today hints of approaching September, and perhaps I may have to console myself with a fire before bed-time.

I too got a letter from Inchbold about the same time that you did. It showed distinctly that he was out of health as well as spirits, though he seemed to be hoping better things from a diminution which had occurred in the heat. I answered him a week ago.

Leathart and his wife called here one day that I was out. I have not met him as yet, and could not answer for it that he is still in town. He called also on Gabriel, who dined with them, and seems to count upon Leathart's making some purchase.[1] The two water-colours he has just been about — the *Paolo and Francesca* triptych, and the Mariana from Tennyson[2] — are among his successes.

Will you tell Maria (though she probably has heard it direct) that Christina is getting sensibly stronger and better, as notified a day or two ago to our Aunt here.

I have seen most of my lot since returning to town: Hunt, who seems stranded; Woolner, well off for commissions, and swindled out of £1220 by his architect instead of the stipulated £400;[3] Jones, looking more settled in health; Allingham, in hopes of getting permanently transferred to London; Morris, the recipient of two Exhibition medals for the firm; Swinburne, who after introducing into his *Spectator* reviews imaginary quotations from phantasmal French poets of the dishevelled class, has now actually taken to writing entire reviews of these nonentities,[4] much to his present chuckling, and, I should fear, future confusion.

Ruskin proposed to take a room in our Chelsea house: the result remains to be seen.

Love to Mrs. Scott and Maria, as well as yourself from

Your
W. M. Rossetti

MS: Arizona.

1. Leathart bought *Paolo and Francesca* mentioned below. It is an enlarged replica of the watercolor of 1855 (Surtees 75 R. 1, where it is said to have been commissioned by Leathart). DGR's portrait of Leathart's wife (Surtees 343) is dated Christmas 1862.

2. A replica in color, with accessories added, of the pen and ink design *Mariana in the South* (Surtees 86 R. 1, where it is given two titles, *The Heart of the Night* and *Mariana in the Moated Grange*).

3. Not identified.

4. Swinburne wrote three reviews of Hugo's *Les Misérables* in the *Spectator*, June-August 1862, in which he cited Félicien Cossu and Ernest Clouet (R. H. Tener, "Swinburne as Reviewer," *Times Literary Supplement*, 25 December 1959, p. 755). For his articles on them, which did not appear, see *SL*, 1:72.

80. TO CHARLOTTE POLIDORI

45 Upper Albany Street,
22 September 1862

Dear Aunt Charlotte,

Your truly kind and welcome aid has now to be solicited. The day hitherto fixed for our going into the Chelsea House was 20 October, but the landlord now offers entrance on Michaelmas day; and we shall probably find it convenient to go, though not quite then, at an early day in October. We paid some months ago the first instalment of £25, and Gabriel and I expect to make up £100 in ready money between us for the entrance-day, so that your offered £100 in addition will settle the whole affair, and we shall have the great satisfaction of owing nothing to anybody except you.

My Aunt Margaret, I am glad to say is very tolerable: she appeared to me to be looking better than usual.

With our love.

Your affectionate and obliged
W. M. Rossetti

We are thinking what we shall have to do about servants: perhaps a middle-aged man and his wife would answer best. Do you happen to know anything available?

MS: AP.

81. TO ALGERNON CHARLES SWINBURNE[1]

45 Upper Albany Street,
2 November [1862]

Dear Swinburne,

I have undertaken to do for Mrs. Gilchrist[2] a descriptive catalogue (as far as I can manage it) of Blake's designs (not engravings), and want our MS. book to include. Could you let me have it, or tell me where it is? I suspect at Chelsea, in one of the boxes I saw there the other day, and not attainable just now. There is no special hurry, as I have plenty of other designs and owners of designs to attend to.

Among others Milnes[3] — whose collection I really *must* make an effort to see now. Could you give me any inkling of how it is to be managed? I am sorry to trouble you now after you have so often volunteered aforetime, but you know it has not been any of our faults that the inspection did not come off long ago.

Do you know of any other Blakes not likely to be within Mrs. Gilchrist's ken? She is still very anxious to get the book out by Christmas, so my time for compilation, though not vexatiously short, is only moderate.

I have given up the idea of writing about the book in *Fraser's*, after discussing with Froude the possible awkwardness of doing so in connexion with my suggestions for the book itself upon proofs etc.

Yours,
W. M. Rossetti

MS: Trinity College, Cambridge.

1. (1837-1909). WMR met Swinburne towards the close of 1860, three years after DGR first encountered him in Oxford. 1865-72 was the period of their greatest intimacy, but it was changed circumstances rather than waning regard that led to their seeing less of each other after 1872. They corresponded regularly until Swinburne's death. How two men of such diverse temperaments managed to remain friends for so long is less of a puzzle than it appears. WMR was not only a man of forthright judgment, whose steadying influence Swinburne often sought and accepted, but also a man of culture and wide sympathies whom Swinburne readily respected. Despite their disagreements over the American Civil War, the Eastern Question, Home Rule, the Boer War, and how to respond to WBS's *AN*, these differences "never made the smallest breach in our mutual good understanding." Without a doubt WMR felt the honor of a close friendship with a great and learned poet and critic, but this never blinded him to Swinburne's defects of character or art. The latter he acknowledged in *Swinburne's Poems and Ballads, A Criticism* (1866); the former he wrote about with an engaging and affectionate frankness in *SR*, 1:218-21.

2. Anne Burrows Gilchrist (1828-85), the widow of Alexander Gilchrist, who died in 1861 leaving his *Life of William Blake* (1863) unfinished. She completed the *Life* with the help of the Rossetti brothers, WMR contributing a catalogue and commentaries on a number of poems and designs. Although WMR corresponded with her frequently, Whitman in time taking the place of Blake as their common interest, they did not see much of one another. Their letters are almost without exception reserved and business-like.

3. Richard Monckton Milnes (1809-85), M.P., poet, friend of politicians and writers, is remembered chiefly for his biography of Keats, and for introducing Swinburne to the works of the Marquis de Sade. Swinburne arranged for WMR to examine Milnes's collection at Fryston Hall, Yorkshire, in early December (*SL*, 1:62-63), when WMR found himself in the company described in Letter 49, Note 6.

82. TO FREDERIC GEORGE STEPHENS

Somerset House,
20 November [1862]

Dear Steph,

Please allow me this time to call off our engagement for tomorrow, as Ruskin has just written asking Gabriel and me to dinner, and I have not seen him ever so long.

I am henceforward (if all holds good) to be at Tudor House every Monday, Wednesday, and Friday evening. Which will you appoint as the next day? Or, being nearer, you might look in for the chance as often as you like, and the oftener the welcomer.

Your
W. M. Rossetti

MS: Bodleian.

83. TO PAULINE, LADY TREVELYAN

45 Upper Albany Street,
7 December [1862]

My dear Lady Trevelyan,

The boon sought from you for the Lancashire project[1] — of which I enclose a new circular — is twofold. 1. That you should allow your name to appear as a Patroness — Sir Walter's name as a Patron would of course be similarly welcome; and I assume that, if it happened to suit, your names upon the Committee list would be no less acceptable: 2. That you should contribute any of your own artistic works, of whatever kind. I learn from the secretary that direct contributions of money for the relief of the distress do not come within the scope of the undertaking. I will inform him that you allow me to "put your name as one ready to assist," which I dare say he will consider sufficient authority for printing you as a Patroness henceforward, unless he hears to the contrary.

I am sorry to hear Sir Walter has been suffering, and trust the improvement will be lasting. Would you please to remember me to him: my sister also desires her remembrances.

Have you heard lately from Algernon Swinburne? He and I came up on Tuesday night from Mr. Monckton Milnes's, to whom he was about to return in a day or two, and then to go on to Wallington — I almost think tomorrow. However, having heard on Wednesday of your being in town from Mr. J. S. Purcell,[2] I wrote to inform Swinburne (who was just about to attend his grandmother's funeral at Ashburnham[3]) and presume you have probably seen or heard from him by this time. I believe I told him *16* Hanover Street by mistake.

Scotus will have the benefit of Gabriel's company for a fortnight or so from tomorrow — so at least it has been settled, if not unsettled again.

Believe me,
Very faithfully yours,
W. M. Rossetti

MS: Newcastle.

1. In 1862 the cotton famine resulting from the American Civil War brought the cotton industry of Lancashire nearly to a standstill. WMR reported in *Weldon's Register*, monthly from December 1862 to March 1863, on the progress of two exhibitions organized for the relief of the distress. The first was held in December by the combined Old and New Water-Colour Societies, and included works by FMB, Burne-Jones, and G. P. Boyce (*Weldon's Register*, February 1863, p. 300). The second exhibition, the one referred to here, was "got up chiefly by amateurs," and included "among the chief professional contributors, Messrs. Mulready, Millais, Stanfield, Roberts, and Boyce, and among the amateurs, Mr. Ruskin, Mrs. Bodichon, the Honourable Mrs. Richard Boyle, and Dr. Haden. Its money-success has been great; about £2000 having been realized by admissions and sales before the close of its first month. The Water-Colour Painters' Exhibition for the same purpose has also succeeded. The committee had sent £1000 to the Relief Fund by the end of January; and the estimated worth of the pictures, for which a lottery will be held, is £4725" (*Weldon's Register*, March 1863, p. 344). See also WMR's "Lancashire Fund Exhibitions," *London Review*, 17 January 1863, pp. 74-75, which briefly mentions the volume issued in connection with the amateur exhibition, *Poems, an Offering to Lancashire* (1863), to which DGR, CGR, and WBS contributed. The list of amateur exhibitors in the *London Review* does not include Lady Trevelyan.

2. John Samuel Purcell (1839-1924) entered the Inland Revenue Office at the age of seventeen. He became a principal clerk in 1867 and controller of Stamps in 1883.

3. The Countess of Ashburnham died on 26 November 1862 (*SL*, 1:64).

84. TO WILLIAM BELL SCOTT

Somerset House,
24 February [1863]

Dearly beloved Scotus,

The gap in our communications was beginning to appear something curious to myself, your co-sinner, when your note received this morning came to stir its depth.

I am glad to hear that the portrait of Mrs. Leathart[1] takes, though I rather infer from your phrase that it is voted rather a good picture than a good likeness. It is, I think, good in both respects, though not *unusually* so in likeness. Since Gabriel's return to town he has been engaged chiefly upon three things.[2] 1. The head of Joan of Arc with the sword, which I suppose you saw in London last year, but which he has worked on a vast deal these 6 weeks, and made exceedingly fine, almost his leading work. 2. A head of Grecian Helen, being a portrait of Annie Miller[3] begun some while ago, and sold now to Gambart. 3. A subject suggested to him by Browning a month or so ago, and for which he was all agog at the time — Helen dedicating in the Temple of Venus a goblet in the form of her own bosom (there is some old story to this effect). He chalked out the design forthwith, and declared he would at once paint it lifesize; but has done nothing further towards that end as yet, and speaks now of doing first only the bust of Helen and goblet lifesize, and the picture at some future time. The former would come as a companion to the Joan of Arc, being bought by the same man (Rose).[4] There is also a project for a third lifesize head — Fortune Shuffling Cards.

I *have* seen a little, but only a little of the *Reader*.[5] The Ludlow, Hughes, Kingsley, etc., set go quite against the grain with me; but I suppose the paper is a reasonably good one at least, and likely enough to succeed. I quite agree with you in anti-anonymity, and always practise it to the utmost of my chance. The *London Review* is no great pet of mine either, nor I apparently of it. Besides 2 papers of mine written within the last fortnight, they have had 3 others within the last 3 months, which seem likely never to get published: I am taking measures for getting this sort of thing set upon a right footing, or retiring from the post.[6] There has just lately been a change of Editors[7] — the present one, a Mr. Cunningham, being also an old *Saturday Review* man.

I hope you are right in thinking Stephens has come out strong in the *Register*. It had not struck me particularly, nor have I made myself familiar with what he has been writing. I know however that he has a considerable stock of information on subjects of decorative art such as he has been writing about in the Loan Collection.[8] It seems there has just appeared an anti-*Athenaeum* pamphlet,[9] quoting for reprobation various pungencies of his upon art, and of other men upon literature. Probably it will produce no more effect than other similar retaliations from the Belaboured Class.

Inchbold has been writing to me also, towards the 10th of this month — a letter with a pertinacious stitch in its side. As to his last landlady, it seems, as he put it — "The fact was, she lied": which seems to have greatly disquieted him. He is not well either; and Venice, on the day he wrote, was "quite misty, and cold, and dreary.'' I am pleased to gather from your note that he will not publish his appropriation of your subject till yours is out.[10]

About my prospects for a holiday this summer.[11] I don't think we proposed anything like a foreign trip together this time: my impression being that I expressed (what I still entertain) the belief that I shall not have tin enough this year (Chelsea expenses etc.) to go abroad with prudence, and that, when I suggested to you something of the sort for a subsequent year, your visits to the Farmacia, and long hiatus of tea, and general used-up-edness regarding those impostures, Italian nature and art, prompted you to the assertion that your foreigneering was now finally over. But mind, mine is not, nor my approbation of you as the prince of travelling companions: so, whenever after the present year, you're my man. I am yours, in all likelihood. In this state of things, I had had serious thoughts of quartering myself upon you (failing a kick in the breech) for the present year's holiday, and could find various points of interest for myself in the British Association,[12] if convenient in point of time. I would certainly be disposed to come, could I only be left wholly to your tender mercies, and not to those of evening and dinner partyizers whose goodnature, in the course of a month or five weeks, would I foresee, be something slightly formidable to my weaker nerves. Perhaps I might come to you for 10 days or so, flit into Scotland for another 10 days, and return to you for the third — *unintentionally*, so that I may not, to use the sublime words of Turner,[13] have to (beyond limits)

> ... fear the demon that in grim repose
> Expects his evening prey.

What say you? and could you give me your company and expletives into the cherished land of your birth?

You did not, I suppose, after all send the A.D. 100 picture to the British Institution.[14] That little picture lying at Chelsea of the old garden[15] (which I had not seen before) pleases me mightly in matter and feeling, and is, I think, one of the best pieces of your artistic handling. What are you about now?

Probably you have heard that I have been busily enough engaged upon a descriptive catalogue, for Gilchrist's book, of all Blake's pictures and designs. It was in hand from the end of October to the middle of January, and occupies some 50 pages of print. I am very well pleased to have had the doing of the job — also to have it done.

Did you see Christina's poem in last *Macmillan's*?[16] and did you hear of the overboiling kettle of enthusiasm which Dora Greenwell[17] sent her some 2 or 3 months ago? A vexatious amount of fizz, but really entering more into the special tone of the poems than anything I have seen in print.

Love to Mrs. Scott, and responses to the kindness of any enquiring friends, and a dig in the ribs to Olaf.[18]

Your
W. M. Rossetti

MS: Arizona.

1. By DGR. WBS to WMR, 22 February 1863: "The portrait as a picture is a great success. The other day Leathart had a grand dinner party, about 20, rather more than his room can hold, when the picture made the round of the table" (Durham).

2. DGR spent Christmas at Newcastle with WBS. The first work mentioned is *Joan of Arc* (Surtees 162). The second is *Helen of Troy* (Surtees 163), about which Boyce wrote in his diary: "[DGR] Is going on with Annie Miller's head, which he has converted into Helen of Troy — ships burning in the background" (Boyce, p. 37). WMR records the buyer as W. Blackmore (*DGRDW*, p. 41). The design referred to in 3 does not correspond in date to the chalk drawing *Troy Town*, c. 1870 (Surtees 219). Neither Surtees nor Marillier, whom she follows in assigning the date, explains their dating, though Surtees observes, in reference to a Browning letter which confirms what WMR says about the poet having suggested the subject, that "Possibly Rossetti made an earlier design of which there is no knowledge." DGR did not execute either of his proposed pictures based on the design, nor did he undertake "Fortune Shuffling Cards," a subject from his 1849 poem *The Card Dealer*.

3. A model to whom many of the Pre-Raphaelites were attracted. FMB recorded on 6 July 1856 that WMR took her boating, "forgetful it seems of Miss R[intoul].... They all seem mad about Annie" (*Diary of Ford Madox Brown*, ed. V. Surtees, 1981, p. 181). She sat to DGR, but it was Holman Hunt who attempted unsuccessfully to monopolize her, with the intention of first educating her and then marrying her.

4. James Anderson Rose (1819-90), solicitor and collector. In addition to *Joan of Arc* he owned several DGR drawings. WMR had "personal and business relations with him till almost the close of his life" (*SR*, 2:341), chiefly about Whistler (whose lawyer he was) and the will of Warington Taylor, for which WMR was a trustee. WMR to Lucy Rossetti, 26 February 1886: "I looked up Rose yesterday.... Rose talked to me a goodish deal about his books. It seems he has a library of some 10,000 volumes, and has just had them catalogued at a cost of £100 or so.... Rose says he is solicitor to the *Globe* and *Morning Post*, as well as the *Standard* (of which last I knew), and has even had something to do for the *Daily News* lately: he must I think have well-filled pockets" (AP).

5. The first number appeared on 3 January 1863. Its first editor was John Malcolm Forbes Ludlow (1821-1911), one of the founders, with F. D. Maurice and Charles Kingsley (1819-75), of the Christian Socialist movement. Thomas Hughes (1822-96) of *Tom Brown's School Days* was associated with them in the movement, and with Maurice and Ludlow in running the Working Men's College, where WMR would have known them. According to *NCBEL* David Masson succeeded Ludlow as editor sometime in 1863, but it is not known how long he remained. WMR contributed a dozen reviews of art books and exhibitions between 4 April 1863 and 15 October 1864 (see "Checklist").

6. Only two further papers by WMR appeared: "The British Institution," 28 February 1863, pp. 230-31; and a review of P. G. Hamerton's *A Painter's Camp in the Highlands*, and *Thoughts About Art*, 7 March 1863, p. 256.

7. *NCBEL* lists only Charles Mackay, 1860, and William Black (without dates). The editor mentioned here is probably Peter Cunningham (1816-69), who published editions of Goldsmith, Horace Walpole, and Dr. Johnson. WMR to J. L. Tupper, 11 October 1862 (Leeds), mentions discussions with a Mr. Little, presumably William Little, named in the journal as the proprietor.

8. "The Loan Collection at South Kensington," *Weldon's Register*, December 1862, pp. 213-20. Stephens also wrote on George Cruikshank, January 1863, pp. 257-59; and "Irish Art at South Kensington," February 1863, pp. 298-300.

9. *The Athenaeum Exposed* (1863).

10. WBS to WMR, 23 November 1862, reported that Inchbold "had painted exactly the same point I had done of the Horses of St. Mark, a piece of impertinence that rather puts me out, as I had begun to paint it on a larger scale, and had got no end of pigeons for it. He is a mis-stitched pair of leather breeches" (Durham). Inchbold exhibited *The Green Horses of St. Mark's* at the R.A. in 1873.

11. From 3-10 September 1863 WMR visited Belgium with DGR, the only occasion on which he accompanied him abroad.

12. Commencing on 26 August 1863 the British Association for the Advancement of Science met in Newcastle.

13. From the *Fallacies of Hope*, quoted in the R.A. catalogue, 1843, with reference to *The Sun of Venice going to Sea*. The line begins "Nor heeds the demon."

14. See Letter 77, Note 1.

15. Probably the *Gloaming — a Manse Garden in Berwickshire* of 1862, reproduced in Christopher Wood, *The Pre-Raphaelites* (1981), p. 88.

16. *Up-Hill.*

17. (1821-82), poet, essayist, biographer, known to the Rossettis "through Scott's introduction" (*SR*, 1:264).

18. WBS's dog.

85. TO FREDERIC GEORGE STEPHENS

Somerset House,
24 March [1863]

Dear Stephens,

I had engaged to convey to you on Thursday last a message from Whistler, to the effect that he wishes you could look up, at a forthcoming meeting of the Artists' and Amateurs' Society, Willis's Rooms, his White Woman, which he will send thereto along with some etchings: of course the object is that you should write something about it or them.[1] This message I forgot entirely till he reminded me of it yesterday. If you can attend to it, and don't understand all the details of time etc., I must refer you to him.

How do you get information for the *Athenaeum* relative to such matters as the purchasers and prices of works of art sold at auctions etc. etc.? Does the Auctioneer send a priced catalogue to your Office? I ask because the *Fine Arts Quarterly* has asked me to do this sort of summary for them,[2] and none of the papers *I* have been connected with ever seem to receive information of the kind referred to — it is left to me to pick up as I can.

Yours,
W. M. Rossetti

Saturday at Albany Street, you remember.

MS: Bodleian.

1. *Symphony in White, No. 1: The White Girl* was shown in London, Berners Street, in 1862, and reviewed in the *Athenaeum* (almost certainly by Stephens) as "a striking but incomplete picture" (28 June 1862, p. 859). Of the six etchings and dry-points exhibited at the R.A. in 1863 some or all were probably shown on 27 March at the Artists' and Amateurs' Conversazione. Stephens praised them in his *Athenaeum* review of the R.A. (23 May 1863, p. 688), and on 18 July 1863 commended the Dutch for awarding the artist a gold medal for them at the Exhibition of the Fine Arts at The Hague (p. 88). WMR reviewed the etchings shown at Willis's Rooms (and mentioned *The White Girl*) in the *Reader*, 4 April 1863, p. 342.

2. Between May 1863 and June 1867 WMR contributed seven summaries with the title "Fine Art Record," three reviews of London exhibitions, and a review of F. T. Palgrave's *Essays on Art* (see "Checklist"). WMR to J. L. Tupper, 20 May [1863]: "The paper intends to keep outside of anything like partizanship, and therefore has next to no *principles*. It is more for the purpose of information and connoisseurship" (Leeds).

86. TO ALEXANDER MACMILLAN

45 Upper Albany Street,
26 May 1863

My dear Sir,

With this note I leave two drawings by Blake[1] belonging to Mr. W. B. Scott, 14 St. Thomas's Crescent, Newcastle on Tyne. I borrowed them on Mrs. Gilchrist's account: and she told me some days back that, if I would place them in your hands before Thursday last, you would see whether anything could be done with them for the book.

I am ashamed to have missed the day, the matter having wholly slipped my memory meanwhile, but hope the opportunity may not be lost. Both the designs appear to me (and I may add to my brother) extremely fine. If one and not both could be used, I scarcely know which appears to me the more desirable: the decision might depend upon which style is the less represented in the selections already made, and upon the mode of engraving adopted. If neither can be used, perhaps you could make it convenient to return the designs to me within a month or so, by which time Mr. Scott will be in London.

Believe me, Dear Sir,
Very faithfully yours,
W. M. Rossetti

MS: Berg.

1. *A Human-limbed Elephant, dandling a similar Infant Elephant on his foot*, and *A Space of Sea, with a Rainbow*, Nos. 127 and 128 in WMR's catalogue in Gilchrist, where the owner is given as Mrs. W. B. Scott. Neither were included in Gilchrist, but both were engraved by WBS as Plates 2 and 3 of his *William Blake, Etchings from his Works* (1878).

87. TO THE EDITOR OF THE *READER*

16 Cheyne Walk,
31 October 1863

Sir,

I observe, in the *Reader* for today, the statement that the *Life of William Blake* by the late Alexander Gilchrist is "edited, as a preface, signed by the widow of the author, informs us, by Mr. Dante Rossetti and Mr. William Rossetti." Allow me to rectify this statement, which does not accurately represent the one made by Mrs. Gilchrist, and to give everybody his due. Mr. Gilchrist left the *Life* substantially finished. Mrs. Gilchrist has edited it, and (if I may be permitted to say so) very efficiently. My brother, Dante Rossetti, has edited the selections, contained in volume 2 of the book, from Blake's own writings; he has also supplied, in the *Life*, volume 1, some passages chiefly descriptive of works of art produced by Blake, and of the place he holds in the art. I have written an annotated catalogue of Blake's designs and pictures, and have also supplied two or three short passages in the *Life* volume, amounting altogether to a mere trifle.

W. M. Rossetti

Text: *Reader*, 7 November 1863, p. 544.

88. TO THOMAS WOOLNER

Albany Street,
7 June [1864]

My dearest old Friend,

Many and many congratulations[1] — most sincere and also most hearty — and from the rest of us as well. My mother especially wants me to say on her part how truly glad she feels, and how much she values you, and appreciates the good feeling you have always shown her, and in this instance in especial.

How absurd my previous letter will have seemed to you, and how dead will have been to your ears the sound even of Venice and Ravenna. Of course I had not then got your note, having slept last night at Chelsea. Yet yours was not the first notice I received of your coming happiness, my dear old boy, as I had met Stephens at the British Institution, and he had told me, with his invariable frank satisfaction in the good fortune of a friend. He told me also (was it you who told *him*?) of another coming marriage — Patmore, now a member of the only true church (!) to an Italian lady with a fortune of some £1000 a year.[2] I suppose Rome has set him up in health and spirit, and that he is likely to remain there.

I need not tell you that I am always the loyal servant of your wife, and always, as I am proud hitherto to have been

> Your affectionate friend
> W. M. Rossetti

When is it to be? Soon, I hope. Don't answer my last.

MS: Bodleian.

1. On 1 June Woolner became engaged to Alice Gertrude Waugh, whom he married on 6 September 1864 (*TW*, pp. 248, 253). Holman Hunt later married her sisters, Fanny (d. 1866) in 1865 and Edith in 1873.
2. Patmore's second wife, Marianne Byles, was not Italian but English. She was rich, however, and had become a Catholic eleven years before Patmore's conversion in 1864 (D. Patmore, *Life and Times of Coventry Patmore* [1949], pp. 132-33).

89. TO HORACE ELISHA SCUDDER[1]

45 Upper Albany Street,
27 November 1864

My dear Sir,

I have to thank you very sincerely for your note, and the accompanying review of Blake from the *North American Review*.[2] However I had already read the article; having seen it advertised, and strongly suspecting — from my knowledge of what has taken place on former occasions where a little openness to new impressions was needed, and a little boldness of opinion — that the book would be better estimated in America than in England. I found my anticipation more than confirmed, and derived much pleasure from a perusal of the article. It is (if I may say so to you without impertinence) far the best I have seen; and I am sorry to say that it is not *necessarily* so much a compliment as I mean it to be, for the English notices, with one or two exceptions amounting to tolerable, have been silly, poor stuff which an Englishman winces and blushes at — or ought to do so, at least.[3] My brother, who saw your article here yesterday, joins me in rating that very differently — as being positively not less than comparatively a worthy tribute to that very wonderful genius, the "mad man" of his discerning countrymen, Blake.

Your impression "that there is a vast heap of Blake's MSS." must, I fear, be based upon a misconception of something or other said in the *Life*. None of us who were concerned in issuing the *Life* know of a heap of MSS. — only some half dozen of letters, and a few scraps of poetry etc. — with one exception. That exception is a moderate-sized MS. volume belonging to my brother and myself, which contains a number of poems and beginnings of poems, pages of prose matter which we pieced together into the *Last Judgment* and an artistic essay in volume 2, sketches, personal jottings, etc. The book is not by me here; but I will look it up pretty soon, and, if I can find a convenient little bit to snip out,[4] I shall have great pleasure in sending it to you, just as a specimen of writing. The current handwriting varies considerably from the semi-print of the engraved books: it is small and somewhat cramped, often so as to be uneasy reading: otherwise precise and clear enough in itself.

If it would be in your way to pick up any designs or sketches of Blake (as well as engravings, which you refer to) I may perhaps inform you that Mr. Harvey,[5] Bookseller of 30 Cockspur Street, London, S.W., had — and I doubt not still has — some, varying from important water-colours to slight scraps: one of his tolerably recent catalogues specifies 33 of the latter sort, to be had in a lump for £1.16. You might possibly like to communicate with him at the address above given.

Dear Sir,
Very truly yours,
W. M. Rossetti

MS: Harvard.

1. (1838-1902), biographer, children's writer; editor of the *Atlantic Monthly*, 1890-98. In 1864 he began a lifelong association with the publishing firm of Henry O. Houghton, which became Houghton, Mifflin & Co. in 1880.
2. 99 (October 1864), 465-82, by Scudder.
3. Cf. Suzanne R. Hoover's account of several favorable reviews in British periodicals up to this date ("The Public Reception of Gilchrist's *Life of Blake*," *Blake Newsletter*, 8 [1974], 26-31).
4. David V. Erdman thinks that WMR may have sent Scudder the segment measuring 7.5 x 11.8 cm. which has been cut from the leaf (pp. 71-72) containing some of Blake's notes on a *Vision of the Last Judgment* (*The Notebook of William Blake*, rev. ed., 1977, p. 3).
5. Francis Harvey. A fragment of one of his catalogues (c. 1864) is listed in Bentley, No. 568.

90. TO FREDERIC GEORGE STEPHENS

166 Albany Street,
5 May [1865]

Dear Stephens,

Our good old friend the enthusiastic Mrs. Cameron[1] has been writing to me on other matters, and refers to some of her photographs now at 9 Conduit Street, which she would like me to write about. I shall be compelled to tell her the simple fact that I have no publication wherein to write about them (unless the *Fine Arts Quarterly Review*). Perhaps you will considerately regard the task as delegated to you:[2] no doubt you know her photographs and their exceptional artistic value. (Indeed I forget whether it was in the *Athenaeum* or *Reader* that a laudation of them has already appeared.[3]) She also tells me that a photograph she has just taken of Tennyson, and which she speaks of as a triumph, is gone to

Colnaghi's for me, and I dare say other copies are or will be there, which perhaps you would see no harm in looking up.

For myself I expect to be off to Italy almost as soon as I have out of hand my review of the R.A. for *Fraser's*:[4] probably on the 22nd, with my mother and Christina.

Your
W. M. Rossetti

Mrs. Cameron is for the present at Little Holland House.

MS: Bodleian.

1. Julia Margaret Cameron (1815-79), the photographer, was one of the seven Pattle sisters, another of whom was Mrs. H. T. Prinsep of Little Holland House. Comparing her to her sisters, Mary (Mrs. G. F.) Watts wrote: "If they were enthusiastic, she was so twice over; if they were persuasive, she was invincible" (*George Frederic Watts* [1912], 1:205). In *SR* WMR records that she "honoured me with a large share of her goodwill" (1:204).
2. Stephens wrote briefly about the photographs in "Fine Art Gossip," *Athenaeum*, 20 May 1865, p. 690.
3. *Reader*, 18 March 1865, pp. 320-21.
4. 71 (June 1865), 736-53.

91. TO WILLIAM BELL SCOTT
Somerset House,
14 August 1865

Dear Scotus,

You don't say when you are to be back in London, and I forget what precisely I was told about it before: we are to see Letitia tomorrow, and I shall enquire. I suppose your hour is pretty nearly come, and shall enjoy a confab when you do make your appearance.

It will be too bad if your subscribers[1] don't come punctually down with the dust or drop in faint recognition of the treasures of intellect and art which you have been lavishing upon them. But, from my own experience, I suspect that in such affairs there are very generally two or three (not more) defaulters at the finale — and among them some who are least excusable for defaulting.

There was never, I surmise, much chance of your getting Gabriel down to Penkill. He did however talk positively a fortnight or more ago of going out of town for some few days somewhither; but I don't suppose he has yet gone, or perhaps will go after all. I have not seen him for several days past, as I keep Christina company in Albany Street. Gabriel was thinking of the country about Arundel, or perhaps the art-collection at Alton Towers, but was of course undetermined. I am glad I did not see you after the "two nights of toothache and nightmare": you must have been a fearful object after such wrestlings of the spirit. Still more particularly do I hope you have had no more of the like incentives to blasphemy.

I have seen nothing of the *Fortnightly* since its first No., which did not seem to me so superior as it ought to have been. A review of *Atalanta*[2] was miserable, and Swinburne, after reading it, declared that he had at last discovered *the* typical

British fool. But I suppose the paper goes on more than reasonably well: Lewes and Atheism certainly get a much fairer field now than in the *Leader*[3] days: indeed I (and I dare say you) am often surprised at the liberty of speech on religious matters which our once Christian and cowering brethren of the Press allow themselves in these *Essays and Reviews* and Colenso days;[4] 3 or 4 years seem to have done what appeared cut out for 50 or 60. I have not seen Palgrave's art critique[5] to which you refer; generally speaking, I think him decidedly better worth hearing than Tom Taylor, but no doubt his pen-flourishes are not always reducible into any great amount of substantial significance.

I am glad Swinburne was right about the beechnuts.[6] I always had an inkling it might turn out as you say it does, but did not venture to say so, conscious that it would be put down as mere thick and thin partisanship. Did I tell you that Browning called at Albany Street three weeks or so ago to make Christina's acquaintance? He sat talking well and amusingly for an hour or so, and has since expressed himself to me as much gratified with what he saw of Christina. He wants to make his son a diplomatist — having, as he says, seen more than once how much power for good such persons have. He is engaged on a long poem concerning a Roman *cause célèbre* about 1690 of an elopement of a suffering angel of a wife with an apostolic priest, and the machinations and murder enacted by the husband.[7] The mazes and conflicting appearances of right and wrong in the case, and the difficulty of finding out who deserved to be hung — the husband was so, and rightly, as Browning finally concluded — took possession of his sympathies. I have been reading for the first time the *Dramatis Personae*,[8] and not on the whole with much satisfaction; I am sorry not to feel more. *Caliban* is very good; *Sludge* able and amusing, but I don't know that there is any pretext for writing it in verse; of the others most do not appear to me right — partly because they are hard to grasp satisfactorily, and chiefly because the prevailing mental tone of them is rather of ingenious and many-sided (but still very one-charactered) keenness than anything more accurately poetical. No doubt however, like Browning's other poems, one enjoys them more as one gets more familiar with them.

Kindest regards to Miss Boyd[9] from

Your
W. M. Rossetti

MS: Arizona.

1. When WBS resigned as headmaster of the Newcastle School of Design in 1863, subscribers commissioned from him a picture for the rooms of the Literary and Philosophical Society (see *LPI*, p. 8).

2. *Fortnightly Review*, 1 (15 May 1865), 75-80; by J. Leicester Warren.

3. G. H. Lewes assisted Thornton Hunt in editing the *Leader*, 1850-54, and was editor of the *Fortnightly* during its first two years, 1865-66. Lewes continued in the *Leader* the vigorous advocacy of Positivism that marked his *Biographical History of Philosophy* (1845-46).

4. Opposition to the liberal theology of *Essays and Reviews* (1860) led to the book being synodically condemned in 1864. John William Colenso's (1814-83) *Commentary on the Epistle to the Romans* (1861), and *The Pentateuch and the Book of Joshua Critically Examined*, Part 1 (1862), which questioned the historical accuracy of the books, resulted in his being deposed as Bishop of Natal.

136

Colenso appealed to the Judicial Committee of the Privy Council, which ruled in his favor on 20 March 1865.

5. "English Pictures in 1865," 1 (1 August 1865), 661-74.

6. WBS to WMR, [6 August 1865]: "You remember Browning's criticism on Swinburne's beechnuts in spring. After all Browning is wrong, the old beechnuts are seen in spring and summer, they do not *fall* in autumn, they are last year's nuts invariably we see lying under the trees. When one thinks over Browning's irregular, involved, and mannered method of poetizing as one may say, he himself is the last who should demand local colour" (Durham).

7. *The Ring and the Book* (1868-69).

8. Published in 1864.

9. Alice Boyd (1825-97), WBS's constant companion, who on the death of her brother in February 1865 became the incumbent of Penkill Castle.

92. TO FREDERIC GEORGE STEPHENS

Somerset House,
11 September [1865]

Dear Steph,

I have found your book[1] interesting, very readable, full of particulars that one likes to know and remember, and with some fine touches of criticism (though by the way I am not of your party in preferring Memling to Van Eyck). Therefore I should take it as a compliment if the dedication of such a book were offered to me by *any* one, and a very genuine satisfaction to receive it from so old, true, and valued a friend as you are. Very many thanks.

Your previous note shows me that, though you may be in harness still, your surroundings are refreshing, so I hope you may come back braced up pretty nearly as well as if you had had more of a leisured holiday.

I did know of Hunt's marriage[2] — *December* (not November) as Woolner told me a fortnight ago. *You* probably know that Woolner has a daughter about a month old now. I am glad about Hunt, presuming that he will be more at ease within himself, and I trust indeed genuinely happy.

Christina is reasonably well thank you — *somewhat* better decidedly, I should say, since her return from abroad, but I fear there is no fundamental change such as might save her from getting very unwell again at any time especially in the chills and damps now approaching (though by the by these past 9 days have been the most splendid summer weather of the year). The rest of us are well enough, including

Yours affectionately,
W. M. Rossetti

MS: Bodleian.

1. *Flemish Relics; Architectural, Legendary and Pictorial* (1866) was dedicated to WMR "in acknowledgement of tried affection and abundant kindness."

2. His forthcoming marriage to Fanny Waugh on 28 December 1865, at which WMR was a witness.

93. TO CHARLES ELIOT NORTON

166 Albany Street,
8 October [1865]

Dear Mr. Norton,

Let me first thank you for the beautiful and interesting book on the portraits of Dante:[1] the juxtaposition of the youthful and elderly heads was a happy thought, and the best evidence to the genuineness of both. One knows a master of his subject by his power of reticence: accordingly I see that you confine yourself to saying what there really is to say on this subject without spinning verbosities out of it. The book will be a choice item in the library of every Dantesco privileged, like myself by your kindness, to possess it. Gabriel also thanks you: I fear he may not have written to say so, but he does thank you sincerely. He is now engaged upon three oil-pictures[2] of such importance as is implied by their consisting of life-sized half-figures — 1. Venus naked in a bower of roses and honeysuckles; 2. the Bride of the Canticles, attended by her women, unvesting before (unseen) Solomon; 3. a lady playing on a stringed instrument, named the *Blue Bower*. This last he considers his best piece of painting work as yet.

I enclose the article on English Opinion upon the American War.[3] If this way of sending it, done up as a letter and not prepaid, is in any way unfitting, please let me know, and it shall be set right in future, when I send the Literary Summaries.[4] As you ask me to "let you have the first by the middle or end of November," I infer that, if I *post* it here by 15 November, that will be fairly good time, and so on to 15 February, May, etc. Any earlier time however, if more convenient to you, will be equally so to me. If it is the practice to bestow copies of the Review upon contributors, will you kindly give orders for me to be so supplied: if it is not the practice, I will get it for myself.

I suppose proofs are not to be thought of: if they were, I should much prefer getting them, as practice teaches one what to expect otherwise, even with the most careful printers.

Your last letter does not notice one point I had raised — that of publishing my name to what I write. I prefer this plan, and eschew the anonymous, and have signed my name to the enclosed — not without suspecting however that its appearing may be contrary to your system. If the name is omitted, perhaps you would consider some slight modifications in the form of the article necessary — as the change of "I" into "we": but I have endeavoured to avoid the need of any changes of importance. Perhaps, without my name, the title had better stand "An Englishman's Testimony as to English Opinion on the American War," or something to that effect.

Trusting the "slight illness" your letter mentions is quite gone, and with thanks for the attention you have been kindly giving to my Dante translation, I am

Very truly yours,
W. M. Rossetti

I ought to have used this thin foreign paper for my article, which I did not think of at the proper time.

MS: Harvard.

1. *On the Original Paintings of Dante* (1865). Norton to WMR, 9 May 1865, described it as his "contribution ... to the Dante Festival of this month in Florence" (AP).

2. *Venus Verticordia, The Beloved, The Blue Bower* (Surtees 173, 182, 178).

3. "English Opinion on the American War" appeared in the *Atlantic Monthly*, 17 (February 1866), 129-49, with WMR's name. Norton acknowledged the article on 1 December 1865: "It is, I think, the most candid statement and the ablest presentation of the subject which has been made, and I regret that its form prevents its publication in the *North American Review*. All the papers in the *Review* are impersonal in their form.... This being the case, I have thought best to offer your paper for publication to the Editor of *The Atlantic Monthly*.... The *Atlantic* has so large a circulation that your article will be read much more widely than if it were published in the *North American*" (*RP*, p. 162).

4. WMR sent one summary, "British Literary Review for the Quarter to 31 October 1865" (MS. in Folger Library), but Norton did not publish it.

94. TO ALGERNON CHARLES SWINBURNE

Somerset House,
2 January [1866]

Dear Swinburne,

I heard it rumoured lately that you are to be the Editor of a forthcoming "Moxon's Magazine."[1] If this is the fact, I should like to bring to your notice a MS. tale[2] lately sent over to me by a man you must have heard us mention more than once — Stillman, Yankee landscape-painter, and Consul lately in Rome, now Crete. I consider it a readable and creditable piece of work which even a magazine under your editorship might be prompt to accept. It embodies, and Stillman assures me without exaggeration, his knowledge of facts and experience of priests during 4 years' residence in Rome (I should add that his hatred of *Papalini* is not of the *Protestant* complexion); and embodies some very ugly facts. Froude, to whom I offered it, thought it a capital piece of work, but so damaging an exposé that it ought not to take the form of a mere story, but, if anything, of an authenticated narrative, and he has even asked Stillman to write such a narrative for *Fraser's*. This invitation might complicate the question of publishing the *story*; but, as I cannot wait all the time that would be needful for settling that point with a man domiciled in Crete, could you let me know what chance the story would stand from you, and *when*, in a general way; thereafter I could if needful send you the MS. at once, with full details of what Stillman says about it. He wants the money for it, so I am anxious to fasten it upon *some* editor, and you must not resent its getting into bad hands, if your good ones don't close upon it.

I have been reading deliberately through, and finished the other night, your Blake MS.[3] It is a splendid piece of the high-critical order of work, and an admirable model of such prose as only the fewest are capable of even attempting. I should consider its publication the greatest service at present possible to Blake, and hardly inferior to a full critical edition of his writings. Now that your position as a poet is so high above cavil, I think some tolerable number of people would read the essay on your account, and some, rather fewer, on Blake's. I don't know whether you can coerce Moxon into its publication — I wish you could: coercion

139

would infallibly be needed, on account of the wild shuffling of cards to which the names and ideas of Jehovah, Jesus, etc., are subjected — not to speak of the otherwise abstruse and crepuscular subject. Among the select few, I think the essay, if published, would produce an impression only inferior to that of your poems. I take it the only feasible form of publication would be that of a volume by itself.

These few items occur to me in detail as I write. I think a few of the shorter poems might advantageously be reprinted in, or as an appendix to, the essay; also a brief summary *list* of the meanings of Blake's mythical personages — as Los for Time, Enitharmon for space, etc. Various references to, and implications of, the Gilchrist book would have to be modified. The *Crystal Cabinet* I have always regarded (perhaps I may have mentioned this to you) as symbolizing a child in the womb: at the same time I must admit that I never attempted to follow out this idea into the details, and possibly it would break down under such an attempt. Your view of the *Mental Traveller* I think certainly better than mine[4] (though what I said was not really intended to exclude *some such sort* of view, as one out of many applications of my leading notion): yours is much more Blakeian, and admits of being worked out in a more Blakeian spirit than mine, which soon involves one in a doctrinaire atmosphere most antagonistic to Blake.

What shall I do with the MS? I understand you are out of town, or would call and leave it at once.

I need hardly tell you I read long ago the *Chastelard*[5] you favoured me with, or how many and how vivid pleasures the reading of it revived.

Yours,
W. M. Rossetti

MS: BL.

1. J. B. Payne of Moxon planned the magazine, but it never appeared.
2. Not listed in the bibliography of Stillman's periodical publications in Frances Miller, *Catalogue of the Stillman Collection*, Union College Library, 1974.
3. *William Blake, a Critical Essay* (1868), dedicated to WMR.
4. WMR's account appeared in Gilchrist's *Life of Blake*, 2:98.
5. Published in 1865.

95. TO ALGERNON CHARLES SWINBURNE

166 Albany Street,
7 January [1866]

Dear Swinburne,

Many thanks for the full details in your letter. It was only from Gabriel (in tête-à-tête) that I heard you were to edit Moxon's Magazine: so I have no reason for assuming that Payne[1] or others go about spreading inaccurate reports on that subject. Probably Gabriel spoke in loose terms, from what he had heard you say, thinking that I also knew the exact facts in the same degree he himself did. Thanks too for your hint that I might contribute to the Magazine, which I certainly will from time to time, so long as you may be connected with it.

As you propose it, I should feel obliged for your writing to Payne at your convenience about Stillman's story. I do not send it to you now, as that might be only a needless shifting it from place to place. It will be producible to you, Payne, or anyone else, whenever wanted. Perhaps meanwhile you would send Payne the enclosed slip copied from Stillman's letter to me, and which explains the *raison d'être* of the story.

About the Byron,[2] the money-question would no doubt depend in some degree upon how much you have done by way of preface — notes I presume there are none. Assuming there are from 10 to 15 pages of preface, or more, I should not see anything extravagant in your asking — considering that it is *you* — £50. The proposed £10 for the Keats seems to suggest however that Moxon has laid out a different scale of payment for these editorial performances; but the very least I can imagine your consistently asking, even if your prefatory work is short, is £25 for the Byron. I confess to a peculiar abhorrence of Buchanan,[3] and satisfaction that his Caledonian faeces are not to bedaub the corpse of Keats. About the Blake book I feel totally unable to say what you ought to ask for a first edition of 1000. Nor do I clearly discern whether you ought to ask in each case of publication a lump sum per edition, or close with the simple proportional and floating-account system which Moxon proposes. This latter proposal however appears to me by no means an unhandsome one: and, were it *my* luck to be you, and to have such an offer at command, I believe I should close with it, as being simple, and prima facie equitable. Your proper adviser on such a point, rather than myself, would no doubt be someone who can command his own price in the literary market, and who would know by experience whether purchase of MS., or profit on sale, turns out best. I fancy, if you closed with the profit on sale proposal, you might tag to it this demand — that, for the *first* edition of each book, you should be paid (*besides* the payment for copies sold) a certain proportional sum, say ⅓ or not less than ¼ of and according to the cost of printing, publication, etc. In some cases, as *Chastelard*, this sum would be a trifle; but would still just serve to mark the advent of a new book, and as a "bounty" on your sticking to Moxon. In other cases, as the Blake, the sum would be less insignificant, and would so far indemnify you against the possible fatuousness of a non-purchasing public.

I sent on to Gabriel yesterday that extract from the *John Bull:*[4] it is certainly delicious. On Tuesday I shall be at Chelsea, and, if Gabriel has not already passed the Byron on to Moxon, shall have much pleasure in looking into it.

Your offer to dedicate the Blake essay to me is most gratifying to the three phrenological bumps described as adhesiveness (or friendship), self-esteem, and love of approbation. Nothing could be a more pleasurable honour to me than to receive the dedication of *any* book of yours, and of this, from its associations, most especially. I will see whether I can mark in your MS. the passages about Gilchrist's book which seem to call for modification in the form of publication the MS. would now take. I doubt however whether I can do much in this way: the passages I was referring to are often no more than a word or two, scattered up and down, which presuppose such a knowledge of and starting-point from Gilchrist's book as would have been supplied by quoting its name at the head of a review article — nothing more: and these could be corrected easily enough even in the proofs. As to the reproduction in your essay of certain poems by Blake, my notion was merely this: that, in the half-dozen or so of instances in which you speak in some detail of short poems not actually before the reader — say the Broken Love[5] etc. — the value of what you say is scarcely to be seized without having the poems under one's eye, and that *these few* poems might therefore be either introduced into the text, or put in an appendix — the whole not occupying, I suppose, more than a dozen pages. Thus much, I conceive, could not be demurred to as trenching upon the most sensitive respect for Gilchrist's rights.

I reserve the 8000 Bs[6] for Tuesday, when I see Gabriel.

Yours always,
W. M. Rossetti

Gisli the Outlaw[7] has not yet come under my hand. What you say of it will make me bear it in mind.

I should have said above, concerning Stillman's story, that (as mentioned in my previous note) the proposal made by Froude to Stillman that he should embody the facts in an authenticated narrative for *Fraser's* may *possibly* be accepted, and that might *possibly* induce him to withdraw the *story* altogether from publication. Therefore it is offered subject to this contingency, which however I think a most unlikely one. May I trouble you to explain this to Payne so far as may be needful for perfect good faith towards Payne, but without suggesting to a timid mind any obstruction to the publishing of the story. As Stillman's agent in the matter, I authorize its publication unconditionally, short of future withdrawal by his express order.

MS: BL.

1. James Bertrand Payne (1833-98), manager from 1864 and shortly afterwards part owner of Edward Moxon & Co.; genealogist.
2. On 4 January Swinburne sought WMR's advice about the payment he should ask for his Byron selection in the ''Miniature Poets'' (1866), and reported that Payne wanted him to re-do the Keats volume which had been undertaken by Robert Buchanan (*SL*, 1:145-46). Keats did not appear in the series.
3. Robert Williams Buchanan (1841-1901), poet, novelist, author of ''The Fleshly School of Poetry.''
4. Probably the review of *Chastelard* which appeared on 23 December 1865: ''It is an unpleasant book, and one by all means to be kept out of the hands of the young and pure-minded, for the licentiousness of many of the images and profanity of not a few of the sentiments are such as happily are not often found in English poets'' (p. 836).
5. ''My Spectre around me night & day.''
6. It was stated at a Fenian trial that 8,000 Fenian brothers could be met with just outside Dublin (*SL*, 1:147).
7. By G. W. Dasent, Norse scholar and translator.

96. TO ALGERNON CHARLES SWINBURNE

166 Albany Street,
14 January [1866]

Dear Swinburne,

Along with this I shall be sending off the Blake MS. to Moxon by Parcels

Delivery. Wishing not to delay its dispatch, and finding (for the reasons previously stated) that I could not without some minuteness of research do anything effectual in the way of marking the alterable passages concerning Gilchrist's book, I have not attempted those markings, and trust to your friendly indulgence *pour ne pas m'en vouloir.*

I remember one detail which I meant to mention in my previous note about the MS., and then forgot. It is that, in several of the extracts you give from Blake's rhapsodic unrhymed verse (as in much else thereof unquoted) I am always offended by the unrhythmical divisions of lines which he allows to pass — I presume through mere reckless inattention — when, in many cases, a different division would preserve the true, and I suppose the undoubtedly felt by Blake himself, rhythmical flow. Had I been transcribing these passages, I should without the least hesitation have righted their rhythmical division. As you have not done so, I perceive there must be something to plead in favour of that literal adherence to the originals, and it is with diffidence that I still think the alteration ought to be made. The Abel[1] is a conspicuous instance.

Yours always,
W. M. Rossetti

MS: BL. Paragraph one is published in T. J. Wise, *A Bibliography of Swinburne* (1920), 2:393; paragraph two (except the opening sentence) in *Swinburne Library*, p. 44.

1. *The Ghost of Abel.*

97. TO CHARLES AUGUSTUS HOWELL[1]

Somerset House,
21 February 1866

Dear Howell,

It is with much satisfaction that I receive and accept your invitation to join a Committee for a Cruikshank testimonial. If the distinguished services of a whole lifetime deserve a testimonial, Cruikshank seems to have claims to one such as few could match. Temperance men, the bookselling and publishing interests, all classes who have got personal pleasure and exhilaration out of his works for so many years, down to children in the nursery — might reasonably testimonialize. Our proposed testimonial I understand to be more expressly aimed to express the deep respect and admiration of his singular artistic genius, and the affectionate personal respect, which the artistic and literary classes of the present generation, as of one or two generations preceding, entertain for Cruikshank: to be numbered among those who combine for such a purpose ought to be gratifying to anybody, and is very much so to me.

Yours truly,
W. M. Rossetti

MS: Texas.

1. (1840-90), half-English, half-Portuguese intimate of the Pre-Raphaelite circle, known to WMR since 1857. He was secretary to Ruskin and agent for DGR, Whistler, Burne-Jones, and G. F. Watts, all of whom parted from him with rancor. For a man who was principally a salesman, however

cultured and charming, he has received an extraordinary amount of attention, notably in *CAH* and Cline. WMR's friendship with Howell did not survive DGR's rejection of him (c. 1876), but after his brother's death WMR resumed business contacts, and wrote kindly of him in *FLM*. Howell was secretary of the Cruikshank Testimonial. For details of the subscription, see Letter 99.

98. TO THOMAS DIXON

166 Albany Street,
4 March [1866]

Dear Mr. Dixon,

In pursuance of the arrangement you propose I have asked a bookselling firm I often do business with (Messrs. Bickers & Son, Leicester Square) to send you the *Goblin Market* volume and the *Early Italian Poets*. I forget the exact price of these volumes, but think the two come to something like the sum I had named, 11/-: any difference may lie over for future adjustment. My *Inferno* must not be brought into present count, as I offered it to you as a gift in return for many gifts you had previously sent me; and it is rather I who remain your debtor *after* that *Inferno* than you my debtor on account of it.

The carte portrait of you is exceedingly well taken and an agreeable likeness: both my sister Christina and I made the remark that it looks something like Tennyson — which I hope you will put down among the prettiest compliments you ever received.

The particulars you give about some etchings and an old Bible seem to indicate that these are items worth looking after; but I am not prepared at present to name anyone for whom I could bespeak them.

I am very glad that you and others in your parts sympathize in the views I expressed and have always bluntly professed concerning the American struggle. I cannot hope however that anything I could at any time have said would have modified the feeling of resentment which Americans naturally — not to say justly — entertain against us English collectively. The fact that many writers of many times my importance have been on the side of the North has been known and proved all along. Not the less does it remain true that the English as a nation dislike the Americans as a nation (such at least is my persuasion), that the English governmental action was frigid if not actually hostile to the North, and that the loudest and most accepted voices on this side of the water howled in chorus for the South.[1] However the only reason why my opinions *appear in print* in an American Magazine at so late a date is that it is only lately that negotiations were opened with me on behalf of one American publication, a quarterly, for which I wrote that article, though it got eventually transferred to a monthly. I have seen a speech by Stephens[2] on secession — very well worth remembering by pro-Southerners as a conclusive avowal that slavery was the real cause of the war. From Emerson's Oration on Lincoln[3] I have only seen casual scraps quoted: it must be worth reading. Of F. Newman's[4] and Cairnes's[5] I never read anything on the subject.

Now will you allow me to introduce a matter in which my brother is interested: though I am by no means confident that it would be in your way to attend to it in any degree, and if not I must simply beg you to say so and leave it alone. My brother was lately told that in the Angel Inn, Corbridge, near Hexham, is a fine old table and a curious sconce (or candlestick apparatus to hang against a wall) of which his informant gave him sketches that will go to you herewith by bookpost. My brother, being an ardent collector of such things, wants to see whether they could be bought at a reasonable price, and thought that possibly the negotiation could be managed through your kindly intervention (though I must repeat that neither he nor I is at all *confident* you can attend to it, nor minded to trespass unfairly upon your good nature). He is not prepared at present to name any price, but would like to find out whether the things are to be had at all, and on what sort of terms. Whatever the upshot, will you let me have back the drawings at your convenience.

Very truly yours,
W. M. Rossetti

MS: Texas.

1. During the Civil War the British government was officially neutral, but its proclamation of neutrality on 13 May 1861 recognized the right of belligerency by the South. J. S. Mill, John Bright, and Goldwin Smith were prominent spokesmen for the North. Among WMR's immediate acquaintances, Browning and Burne-Jones were Northern sympathizers.

2. Alexander Hamilton Stephens (1812-83) had been Vice-President of the Confederacy.

3. Delivered at a memorial service for Lincoln held in Concord, New Hampshire, on 19 April 1865.

4. Francis William Newman (1805-97), scholar, writer on religious, social, and political questions; brother of John Henry Newman.

5. John Elliot Cairnes (1823-75), economist. In 1862 he published *The Slave Power*, a defense of the Northern cause.

99. TO GEORGE HEMING MASON[1]

Somerset House,
19 March [1866]

Dear Sir,

On the faith of the pleasure I had in meeting you last summer at the Prinseps, I take the liberty of addressing you on the following subject.

A project has been started (not by me, let me add) for getting up a subscription in honour and behalf of George Cruikshank. Ruskin is President — Sir Walter Trevelyan Vice-President — Huth[2] Treasurer — and C. A. Howell (3 York Villas, Brixton) Secretary: the provisional committee includes my brother, Burne-Jones, Swinburne, Simeon Solomon, Burton,[3] etc. The idea at first was to present Cruikshank with some token, simply as such, of the great regard wherein his abilities and character are held by the artistic classes at the close of his career (he is now 76,[4] though no one would think so to look at him). It has transpired however that he is in circumstances such as must render a compliment far less valuable to him than a substantial addition to his means — especially in view of the position his widow (several years younger than himself) would be left in by his death. It is therefore now proposed to give the project a far more extensive scope, and raise a really handsome sum of money — say £2000 or so[5] — which from Cruikshank's universal popularity, the Temperance organization, etc., seems quite feasible. The first step now agreed upon is to get a strong *artistic* nucleus for the Committee — all artists of position are to be addressed, without sectional preferences. May we have the advantage of your name on the Committee? After a few such personal letters as this, we shall next send circulars to the general artistic body, and then to other classes.[6]

I should explain that Cruikshank himself has not yet been consulted, so that the affair is for the present quite confidential: also that, whether in the Committee or otherwise, subscribers will be equally thanked for moderate as for larger donations.

I trust you may have been in the enjoyment of fair health since that evening we met, and that you will at all events excuse my addressing you upon the present matter.

Believe me, Dear Sir,
Very faithfully yours,
W. M. Rossetti

MS: Princeton.

1. (1818-72), landscape painter of English and Italian scenes. On 15 April 1866 WMR sent a circular about the Cruikshank Testimonial to C. E. Norton, explaining that "Without being 'hard up,' he is the contrary of well off, and some friends of his are desirous of making his mind easy in this his old age, with the prospect of leaving unprovided for a widow several years younger than himself. If it suited you, we should much like to add to the Committee list so acceptable an American name as yours.... Ruskin is President, and with his usual signal munificence, produces £100. Holman Hunt, Swinburne, Woolner, my brother, etc. etc., on the Committee. There seems no reason why, even in England alone, we should not raise a very handsome sum — without being all Ruskins even in the centesimal degree of openhandedness'' (Harvard).
2. Louis Huth (1821-1905), a member of the firm of merchant bankers founded by his father Frederick Huth; brother of Henry Huth the bibliophile; collector of blue china (to which DGR is said to have introduced him) and English pictures (*Times*, 15 February 1905, p. 11).
3. Frederic William Burton (1816-1900), landscape painter; director of the National Gallery, 1874-94.
4. Should be 73.
5. It is not known what the final sum was. By December 1866 more than £1000 had been subscribed (Letter 116), but several DGR-Howell letters in Cline (Nos. 232, 240, 242) suggest that the response was disappointing. About the only information on the administration of the subscription is given in two entries in WMR's diary. 4 December 1866: "Howell ... has given Cruikshank altogether about £600 since the subscription-plan was started" (*RP*, p. 198). MS. Diary, 5 March 1867: "Howell says that Cruikshank's money difficulties continue, causing the funds obtained by the subscription to be drawn upon by anticipation from time to time. [Henry Hugh] Armstead, who belongs to Cruikshank's volunteer corps, told Howell that the accounts, which are in Cruikshank's hands, are muddled or in arrears, and no distinct information obtainable about them: not that any suspicion of unfair dealing is hinted at." On 19 March 1867 WMR and DGR signed an application for a Civil List pension for the artist. MS. Diary, 23 May 1867: "Howell says that Cruikshank seems reasonably well satisfied with the pension of £95 ... but Mrs. Cruikshank not satisfied."
6. A circular signed by Howell and dated April 1866 appealed for Committee members (copy in the Norton Papers; Harvard).

100. TO THOMAS DIXON

Somerset House,
20 March [1866]

Dear Mr. Dixon,

Your two boxes of books were returned from my house yesterday through

146

Mann's Parcel Agency. Another parcel which you announced on the 15th, including the Derwentwater furniture drawings,[1] has not yet made its appearance; but, instead of that, the roll of chiefly caricature engravings, which do not comprise anything I should wish to appropriate. Thank you for them all the same: they will be returned shortly.

I sympathize generally in what you say about America, being myself a thorough democrat and political and social extremist. I think all men are born to the same natural rights, and should be bred to the exercise of them. In a society where all are not so bred, no doubt a great difference between the personal qualities of classes results: but even so I would take every man apart from his adventitious surroundings, and where it happens that the man of less advantages is nevertheless the better man of the two I would prefer him to the inferior man who had had the greater advantages. This is what I understand by democracy — *not* a preference of the poor and uneducated *because* they are poor and uneducated, to the well-off and refined — (though by the by I think the Christianity preached by Christ goes very much even to that extent). Carlyle in his *Nigger Question*[2] did undoubtedly foreshadow much of what has since come to pass: I was reading it afresh the other night. He does not justify slavery in its most brutal forms by any means: but I can't help thinking that, in his anxiety to lay out a practical arrangement upon a true and philosophical basis, he too much disregards the iniquitous conditions inherent in slavery itself, and its positive matter-of-fact inconveniences as well. I suspect the most satisfactory course, when the passions of the slaveholders prevented gradual and conciliatory abolition was (as Carlyle elsewhere says) "to sweep it with some celerity into the dust-bin"[3] — even as the Northern armies and government have now done.

Yours truly,
W. M. Rossetti

MS: Texas.

1. Probably a response to the enquiry on behalf of DGR in Letter 98.
2. *Occasional Discourse on the Nigger Question.*
3. Not identified.

101. TO CHARLES AUGUSTUS HOWELL

Somerset House,
16 April [1866]

Dear Howell,

Answer from Murray[1] enclosed. I have replied that, unless he answers to the contrary, we will enrol him as a Committee-man as well as subscriber.

Brett and Froude, finding the circumstances of the moment dissuasive of subscription, decline.

I have now written to Kirkup[2] and Norton.

You will observe by Murray's letter that he has sent me volume 3 of Crowe and Cavalcaselle:[3] so that is quite at your service whenever you like.

Just look at these newspaper cuttings — from *Pall Mall Gazette*[4] and *Star*. Is the information they contain correct?

Edmund Yates,[5] General Post Office, is the writer of the *Star* slip. You see we ought now to get out of dark corners with all possible speed, or a considerable slur will beset our operations, besides irritating crossfires of queries. Depend upon it it was a great mistake to order so few circulars, and not to print therein the office-bearers. We ought to have sown them broadcast, and especially in the press — not necessarily as invitations in all cases to join the Committee, but as announcements: each of the more stirring committee-men should have taken and diffused some 10 to 20 circulars at least. I would strongly recommend you (if you feel sufficiently empowered) to stop Yates's mouth at once by sending him the circular, as a bona fide invitation to join the Committee. He is not a man liked in our set, but quite a suitable man in the public eye. What has been done *by you* as to sending round the circulars? You see Gabriel, I, etc., offered to send them to a few personal acquaintances whose names occurred to us, but beyond that a vast deal remained to be done by you as the nominal organ of the Committee, but in fact on your own responsibility, which one must exercise in these cases somewhat autocratically, or nothing is done rightly or in time. I know you have — with the most heroic self-devotion and diligence — written the names of Ruskin etc. some scores of times, and sent to Lord Shaftesbury[6] etc., including, I *presume*, all the R.A.s and other members of leading artistic societies: but I don't yet know whether any systematic attempt was ever made to get at *all* the persons who ought to be asked to join the Committee, and thereafter to send them the invitation. Of course the time for doing all that was now when the Committee-circular is in (too scanty) circulation. A copy of it ought to be sent to *every* London newspaper of the least importance.

Also I would strongly advise you to draw up at once a new circular inviting subscriptions (not Committee-men), and get it printed at once — and afterwards, as soon as the Committee list is reasonably filled, get that printed on a separate half-sheet, and then directly send both together about all over the country. I should think 2000 copies only just sufficient to make a start with, and more might be needed afterwards. The compilation of a list of the persons to be invited to subscribe ought to be begun without delay. The labour would be too much for you to undertake fairly singlehanded, so, if you will tell me two letters of the alphabet for me to undertake (and others ought to undertake in like manner) I will set about it. I know no complete way of managing this job except by reading through a Directory — say Webster's, and extracting the names, with addresses, which seem feasible.

I fear I have been assuming a somewhat dogmatic, pragmatic, or dictatorial tone in this letter. You will know how to ascribe it to laconism more than Podsnappery,[7] and excuse it along with the many other *bévues* of

Your
W. M. Rossetti

Also advertising ought to begin *forthwith*.

MS: Texas.

1. Charles Fairfax Murray (1849-1919) became known to the Rossettis "towards 1867" (*SR*, 2:325). He was an accomplished painter in the style of DGR and Burne-Jones. Ruskin regarded him as "the most skilful ... beyond comparison" of the artists he employed in Italy to copy pictures and record frescoes and buildings (C & W, 30:72). Murray was pre-eminently a collector of paintings, drawings, fine books, and manuscripts. His special interest in the Pre-Raphaelites ensured regular contacts with WMR in the decades following the deaths of DGR and CGR.

2. Seymour Stocker Kirkup (1788-1880), painter, book collector, authority on Dante; "a leading and deservedly popular personage among the foreign residents in Florence," where he settled in 1824 (WMR, Obituary of Kirkup, *Athenaeum*, 29 May 1880, p. 696). A believer in Gabriele Rossetti's Dantesque theories, he corresponded with him, and later with WMR, who several times visited him in Florence.

3. Joseph A. Crowe and Giovanni B. Cavalcaselle, *A New History of Painting in Italy*, 3 vols., 1864-66.

4. The subscription was mentioned briefly on 24 March 1866, p. 4.

5. (1831-94), journalist, editor of *Temple Bar, Tinsley's Magazine*, and the *World*; employed by the Post Office, 1847-72. In his weekly column in the *Morning Star* on 2 April 1866 he wrote that he was "in receipt of communications from several correspondents, some asking for the names of the Cruikshank Testimonial Committee, others wanting to know where subscriptions can be sent. I am not in a position to answer either querists. If it be true that the well-worn Bis dat, etc., proverb is peculiarly applicable in this case, it would be expedient that the committee should make some sign" (p. 4).

6. (1801-85), social reformer and Evangelical churchman.

7. Mr. Podsnap in Dickens's *Our Mutual Friend*.

102. TO CHARLES ELIOT NORTON

166 Albany Street,
12 August [1866]

Dear Mr. Norton,

Founding — should I say presuming? — upon the general invitation in recent letters of yours for me to write upon such subject as might attract me for the *North American Review*, I am about to take up the subject of Swinburne's last *Poems and Ballads*.[1] I have not forgotten that, on my offering to write upon Swinburne's preceding works, you informed me that Mr. Lowell intended to treat that subject himself:[2] but, in my ignorance of whether he has actually done so or not, and surmising that, even if he has, a further article on the new volume may be admissible, I shall probably have begun or completed my review before your answer to this note could reach me. I perceive that I can't be in time for your next number (assuming it to appear early in October), so that I may be writing leisurely: and at any rate, while really desirous that my article should appear, I feel that your editorial discretion in the matter must, under the particular circumstances, be paramount, so that you must not regard me as attempting to *circumvent* your acceptance of the article, if seriously inconvenient. You have probably seen the book. It has got ferociously assaulted here[3] on moral etc. grounds, and not unreasonably: that I shall admit in my article, but shall not dwell very prominently on the point. It is my sense of the glorious poetic qualities of the book and the writer, my personal friendship for him, and my redoubled wish to stand up for him in my small way now that he is on his defence against fairly and unfairly aimed attacks, that determine me to write the article. I know you may say it would be more fittingly published *here* — and indeed I would prefer that, but have no vehicle for the publication that I can command — so it would be a great satisfaction to me if your convenience as editor and mine as contributor happen to coincide this time. From past experience I know that I must write with the editorial *we*. I trust to avoid doing anything compromising to that personal pronoun: but at any rate I should wish the article to appear in all substantial respects as I write it or not at all.

 With kind regards,

Yours very truly,
W. M. Rossetti

MS: Harvard. Extract in *HLB*, pp. 361-62.

 1. By this date J. B. Payne of Moxon's had withdrawn *Poems and Ballads*, which was soon reissued by John Camden Hotten (1832-73). Hotten also published WMR's defense of the volume, *Swinburne's Poems and Ballads, A Criticism*.

 2. Lowell published a disparaging review of *Chastelard* and *Atalanta in Calydon*, *North American Review*, 102 (April 1866), 544-55.

 3. Three attacks appeared simultaneously on 4 August: in the *Saturday Review*, the *Athenaeum*, and the *London Review* (see C. K. Hyder, *Swinburne's Literary Career and Fame* [1933], pp. 37-42).

103. TO THOMAS DIXON

166 Albany Street,
2 September [1866]

Dear Dixon,

 I have your two letters, August 26 and 29, to answer.

 I do possess a copy of Swinburne's *Poems and Ballads*, given me by the author, the most glorious perhaps of living English poets. At present I am not able to lend it to you or anyone, as I have undertaken to write a notice of it for the *North American Review*, and require to keep the volume by me during the process — and, before that is finished, it will in all probability be reissued by a different publisher, Hotten. As to giving you my opinion of the book, that is not to be knocked off in a sentence. I will try however at a few fragments and shreds of opinion.

 Swinburne's superiority over his contemporary poets, with the sole *possible* exception of Tennyson, appears to me to lie in his mastery of all the *literary or artistic* resources of poetry — versification, language, harmony, vividness of expression, etc.: there are *other* qualities in which Tennyson and Browning, at any rate, may be preferred. The denouncers of his book attack its blasphemy and indecency. As to blasphemy, Swinburne is certainly a pronounced antichristian, and something very closely resembling an atheist: I consider that he is right in entertaining these or any other speculative opinions which commend themselves to his own mind, and in expressing them as freely as Christians, Mohammedans, etc., express *their* speculative or traditional opinions. As to indecency, Swinburne is not in his own conduct even up to the average of immorality, nor do I think his writings are likely to do any practical harm to anybody fitted by taste and training to admire them. He certainly is however too destitute of the sense of modesty or propriety in thought, speech, or writing: and, as his intellectual sympathies carry him back very much to the state of Grecian or Roman society, abhorrent in many aspects of morals to the Christian and modern mind, and he expresses these sympathies and notions with the most unchastened fervour of words, there are several poems in his book which necessarily and rightly outrage ordinary readers. I think he acted very foolishly and recklessly in publishing such things at all, certain as they were to be abominated and damn the book: though I myself see no profound reason why grown men of tolerably enlarged mind should not write and read of such matters if they happen to feel inclined. It will be understood that the volume contains many poems which have no tincture of either blasphemy or indecency: and that there is *no* indecency in the way of foul gross words, obscene jokes or insinuations, or the like. It is all in the subject matter, the fervour of expression, and the indifference or even hostility of mind to what other people regard as morals and propriety.

5 September

I return the list of songs, among which, as far as I can judge from the titles, there are not any I should be anxious to obtain.

As to the MS. catalogue of Juvenile Books, which you now seem to imply was intended more especially for Swinburne, I can only recur to what I have suggested on some previous occasions — that any matters lying between you and him had much better be transacted between *you and him direct*, without my being in any way mixed up in them. The only effect of mixing me up in them is to cause certain delay, and to impose upon me an agency which possibly I am not anxious to undertake, and probably not likely to fulfil conveniently — for instance it is often weeks or even months that I don't happen to meet Swinburne, though at other times I may see him 2 or 3 times in as many days. I may add that from what I observed of the catalogue, I don't think it would prove to contain anything that Swinburne would want to order; it seems to be all of *modern* versions of the stories, *prettified* in tone and getting-up. And I may also repeat that I would advise you not to send Swinburne anything whatever without first obtaining his sanction for your so doing — otherwise there is no knowing whether he would not rather be without seeing the things at all, and being compelled to return them.

At the moment of my leaving Albany Street yesterday for Somerset House, a packing case came which I suppose to contain your picture.[1] I have not since then been back to Albany Street, but shall be there this afternoon, and will see and write to you about the matter in due course.

Yours truly,
W. M. Rossetti

MS: Texas.

1. See Letter 107, Note 1.

104. TO ALGERNON CHARLES SWINBURNE

16 Cheyne Walk,
25 September [1866]

Dear Swinburne,

I am delighted to find from the *Examiner*[1] that foes and friends were alike deluded in you, and that your morality more nearly resembles that of Lot when he fled from the Cities of the Plain than when he was domesticated with his daughters in a cavern. The article more especially pleases me in that I hope it may be enough to lessen considerably the risk that Hotten would otherwise have run in publishing the book. The wipe at Payne[2] is most deserved and satisfactory.

I hope you are getting on with your vindication,[3] or perhaps you have got it wholly out of hand by now. You saw what the *Athenaeum* said,[4] expecting it apparently to be in verse. I don't know how the fact reached the minor periodical — not through me assuredly. I am going well ahead with my review, having done more than as much again as what I read you. I think it will reach 100 pp. of MS., 30 to 35 of print.

A letter from good old Kirkup received the other day says this: "Tell Algernon Swinburne that he promised me his volume of poems. I should value it *the more* if the world has pecked at it. I have just read a very pretty Greek Commedy (sic — "Commedia") or rather an Italian *rifacimento* of Menander, which is lost, founded on the description by Donatus. It is beautiful Italian, and the author Dall' Ongaro[5] has given it more identity of character than Goldoni or Alfieri ever attempted. It is therefore more Shakespearian. But I am no critic, only grateful for a pleasure; very likely he will not find it so good." The Barone does our joint heart good by responding to an expression of mine with "Mazzini is a great man, the greatest statesman in Europe."

Will you pardon me for pulling a longer face before I close, and imploring you, on the ground of my last and some[6]

[Incomplete]

MS: BL. First two sentences published in *HLB*, p. 357.

1. A review of *Chastelard* and *Poems and Ballads* appeared on 22 September 1866, pp. 597-99. The reviewer was the editor Henry Morley, who had recently succeeded David Masson in the chair of English at University College London. Morley declared that Swinburne "sings of Lust as Sin, its portion Pain and its end Death. He paints its fruits as Sodom apples, very fair without, ashes and dust within." Hence the reference to Lot's escape with his two daughters from the destruction of Sodom and Gomorrah to a cave in the mountains and their subsequent incest (Genesis, 19).

2. "The withdrawal of that volume is an act of weakness of which any publisher who does not give himself up to the keeping of a milk-walk for the use of babes has reason to be heartily ashamed."

3. *Notes on Poems and Reviews*, issued by Hotten in October.

4. "If Mr. Swinburne's reply be in good metrical form, void of the offences, the general censure of which elicits the alleged forthcoming answer, the public may be congratulated" (22 September 1866, p. 371).

5. Francesco Dall' Ongaro (1808-73); his *Fasma* (1863) was based on the fragments of Menander's *Phasma*.

6. In his reply Swinburne referred to "your screed of friendly counsel concerning Bacchus" (*SL*, 1:187).

166 Albany Street,
30 September [1866]

Dear Mr. Norton,

Thanks for your letter of 12 September, with its friendly and candid statements as to my review of Swinburne.[1] I need only refer to my last letter to show that I am not unconscious that it is for you Editors, in the last resort, to say whether or not the review shall appear in your Quarterly. At the same time I don't think you will consider I am pressing a point unhandsomely when I express a conviction that you would only on the very strongest grounds see fit to decline a review which I have been writing on the faith of the following invitations in previous letters of yours:

9 January. "If you will do what you propose — take up from time to time, quarterly or at longer intervals as you choose, some subject with which you are sufficiently acquainted to write upon it with satisfaction to yourself — I shall regard it as a great favour. I will only beg you to take up any matter of art or literature on which you may like to express yourself, with confidence that what you write will be more than acceptable."

12 March. "Let me once more ask you to send me before long something for the Review from yourself. I leave the subject wholly to your choice, sure that it will be good."

In this latter letter, by the way, you were kind enough to say you would take care I should receive the next No. of the *North American Review*, "in which I would find something to interest me." This probably was an allusion to the review of Swinburne in the April No.: but that No. has not to this day reached me, and it is only yesterday that I for the first time heard from a friend that the notice is written in a tone not likely to be harmonized with by mine. (I ordered through a bookseller a copy of the No., as soon as I learned which No. it was, but have not yet received it.)

The notice which I am writing is now in an advanced state, and will make a longish article altogether. I think I must have done ⅔ of the whole, and may finish it within 3 weeks at furthest. That it expresses my candid (not personally biased) opinion I need not tell you: and I know several highly competent judges, including my brother and (more or less nearly) Ruskin, who rate Swinburne's poetic powers as high as I or anyone can. If you see the *Examiner* (No. for 22 September) you will find that one paper of high standing has even gone so far as to declare Swinburne essentially a moral writer — which is beyond what I do. Indeed I am satisfied that a candid reader — and I know I shall find such in you — will not pronounce my notice a one-sided one, though on certain points, and indeed in the main, an enthusiastic one, which I intend it to be, or it would be far indeed from expressing my opinions. The MS. is before me at the moment, and I would beg to refer you to pp. 2, 18, 22, and 62 to 74, (besides other passages) in proof that I by no means slur over what (to the best of my judgement) there really is to say against Swinburne.

As I said in my last, I should wish the review to appear without any alteration of consequence, or else not at all. If you decline it, and can readily succeed in what you so kindly offer to do — "try to get it published in some other reputable journal" — so much the better for me, and sincere thanks to you. If any difficulty attends such endeavours, please not to incur further trouble, but to let me have the MS. back at once.

Thanks also for what you say of forthcoming Cruikshank subscriptions.[2] You do not allude further to the money to my credit on account of my article in the *Atlantic Monthly*. I infer that it remains with you until the sum actually receivable by me shall reach $100.

I perceive you cannot yet have received the *Germ*, which disappoints me much. I had it posted to you towards the middle, or even beginning, of July — addressed (I should now suppose) to Ashfield, as that was the address on your then last letter. If it is still in default, will you let me know, and I will send another copy. I speak with certainty as to the dispatching of the former one.

The pictures which my brother has at present in hand are these:[3]

1. The *Lady Lilith*. This is a life-sized ¾ figure of a woman at her toilet combing out her golden hair. There are among the accessories, roses, fox-gloves, a looking-glass reflecting sunlit trees, and (probably to be introduced) a white kitten on the white dishabille of the lady. I have from the first considered it, on the whole, the very completest piece of harmonious executive art Gabriel has produced: and he himself with some others are of much the same opinion. The name comes (as you may remember) from an allusion to "Lilith the first wife of Adam" and her splendid hair, in the Brocken scene of *Faust*. Picture ⅘ done.

2. Venus. I think I must have named this before. Life-sized naked half-figure amid roses and honeysuckles, holding arrow and apple. Nimbus round the head, birds, butterflies, etc. ⅔ done.

3. A Sibyl. Life-sized ¾ figure, with a background of white and other marbles. I believe he means to call it a Sibyl, but his chief idea

[Incomplete]

MS: Harvard. Extract in *HLB*, pp. 362-64.

1. "I fear that your regard for the author and admiration of his powers may lead you, in the warmth of championship, to go farther in his defence or in assertion of his merits than the severe critical judgment of a Transatlantic Editor (the impersonation of posterity!) will allow him to accompany you.... I have not seen Swinburne's new volume — but only a few poems taken from it. / I confess to an invincible repugnance to sensuality in poetry. Whatever of power, imagination, melody or beauty there may be in the sensualistic school is of the same nature with the charm of the Siren's songs. It is not good art; — I am puritan enough to believe that good art cannot exist without good morals, — but, to be sure, my idea of good morals is not the puritan idea" (*RP*, p. 206; the passage following the oblique line is from the MS. letter in AP).

2. Norton to WMR, 28 May 1866: "I have some eight or ten pounds already, — Longfellow and Lowell heading the list of subscribers" (AP).

3. *Lady Lilith* (Surtees 205); *Venus Verticordia*; *Sibylla Palmifera* (Surtees 193).

106. TO ALGERNON CHARLES SWINBURNE

166 Albany Street,
30 September [1866]

Dear Swinburne,

You will have received the extracts from the *Examiner* and *Athenaeum*,[1] posted yesterday as soon as I received your letter.

It strikes me that the most *evident* sort of title for your pamphlet would be the best — and that this might do very well:

"Swinburne's Poems and Ballads."
A Reply to his Critics
by the Author,
Algernon Charles Swinburne.

If Hotten has sent you a *North American Review* containing the notice of *Atalanta* etc., he might, one would think, have sent to me also the copy which I ordered. This however has not been done yet, so I know of the notice only what you tell me. I must obtain it with all convenient speed; but what you say seems to show that it would be no use trying to modify my own review so as not to clash in detail with theirs — they will either have to publish mine, and thereby disavow their own previous outspurting, or else to decline mine. The latter seems the likelier alternative.

Does Payne claim half the profits of your American editions *prospectively*, or only up to the date of withdrawing *Poems and Ballads*?[2] Either demand would have to be tested by the *precise terms* of the agreement between you, him, and the American publisher: in default of knowing these exactly, I can only *surmise*, as a matter of abstract probability, that Payne is Jewing you more or less.

Many thanks for that poem from Dr. Neale's book:[3] there is an admirable ring in it. Some lines of it seem to be known to me aforetime, but I can't say where, nor whether in quite the same version of the hymn as a whole. Thanks also for another section of your letter,[4] of which I shall say no more.

Palgrave wrote to me on 26 September (from Thornes House, Wakefield), saying that he hears Gabriel mistakenly ascribes to him some share in producing the withdrawal of your book; and he proceeds: "I only learned of the suppression, like the rest of the world, after it had taken place. I had not then read the book, which I had got just in time. When I had read it, I thought two attacks upon its morale which I saw in the *Saturday* and *Athenaeum* unfair, and the suppression a thing to be regretted. Being then in the country, I began a paper saying this, and offered it to 3 or 4 Editors of periodicals, but was refused by each on different grounds."[5] He asks me to mention these facts to you, and I have no doubt you will be as perfectly convinced as I am that his statement is the strict truth. I should add that his letter is totally free from acerbity of any kind or towards any person.

Yours always,
W. M. Rossetti

I was forgetting to add that Woolner also most positively denies having had anything to do with the withdrawal of the book, or having so much as seen Payne

155

for some long while before that event: and Payne (which will not *add* strength to the assertion in your eyes) confirms Woolner in writing. It is through Scott that this reaches me.[6] Woolner's assertion is to me conclusive on the precise point — by which of course I don't mean to say that he has never expressed to anyone an opinion of any of your poems less enthusiastic — i.e. less appreciative — than my own.

Scotus turned up within an hour or so of my writing this. The old boy is flourishing, and we have been taking sweet counsel together — very mainly about *you* and your belongings. I showed him (I hope blamelessly) the pamphlet, which he pronounces to be very capital, and, *if one didn't know you*, very convincing. I have been advising him to reissue his own poems in a combined and carefully revised form,[7] and show the discerning public that even the colossal fame of a Buchanan is not absolutely the only poetic glory of contemporary Caledonia. I really think he should do this, and hope you will support the same cause on any fitting opportunity. His Lectures on Art[8] are exhausted, and a new edition wanted immediately by Longmans.

MS: BL.

1. See Letter 104, Notes 1 and 4.
2. See *SL*, 1:187.
3. Two verses from *Jerusalem, my happy home*, a sixteenth century hymn adapted from a poem in St. Augustine's (ascribed) *Liber Meditationum*, as printed in John Mason Neale's *Hymns, Chiefly Mediaeval, on the Joys and Glories of Paradise* (1865) (see *SL*, 1:188).
4. See Letter 104, Note 6.
5. The letter continues: "I daresay my estimate of the general value of the book may not agree with yours, but on the above point I am, I suppose, in harmony with you and your brother. At any rate these are the facts." Palgrave wrote again on 10 October: "I am much obliged to you for your kindness in clearing up my character with your brother and Swinburne.... There seems to be a kind of disinclination in the papers etc. which have not reviewed the book hitherto to say anything about it" (AP).
6. For WBS's letter see *RP*, p. 207. Woolner wrote further on the subject in three letters to WMR: 19 October, "I have just heard that Swinburne is writing a reply to the criticisms on his last book, and that he purposed attacking me as having instigated the critics to do so. / I not only did not do so, but I do not know a single critic who has attacked him, and it was only last evening that I even learned the name of one, and he is a person I have no knowledge of whatever. / If you chance to see Swinburne I should be obliged if you would tell him this, as I should like him to know the truth, and have no wonder his being angry if he believes in anything so absurd." 25 October, "From all I have heard on the matter it seems to me your opinion of Payne is severe: it appears he did it on compulsion: for there was a strong party of Exeter Hall sneaks meant to prosecute him with the 'utmost rigour of the law,' and he had high legal advice that he would not be able to stand against it. If this be a correct version it would have been more than heroism to fight under such conditions, and heroism is more than we have a right to expect in such circumstances. But I can quite understand the other side and that any amount of indignation would not only be quite possible but natural. / I am glad that was — so far as you knew — a false report of Swinburne believing I had urged the critics to write against him; — persons do tell horrid lies — for he has had hard lines meted out to him of late, and been fired at from so many sides that I should have regretted if he thought I had anything to do with his public treatment. At the same time from certain things I have seen I must say he exposed himself to his enemies, and I think it a pity he published some of them." 29 October, referring to WMR's defense: "I shall be interested in seeing your pamphlet as I dare say you will make out a better standpoint for him than he can for himself" (AP).
7. WBS did not do this until *Poems* (1875).
8. *Half-hour Lectures on the Fine and Ornamental Arts* (2d ed. rev., 1867).

107. TO FREDERIC GEORGE STEPHENS

2 October [1866]

Dear Stephens,

Scharf has now seen the portrait, and inclines to believe it *is* Sir K. Digby.[1] It has been sent round to the National Portrait Gallery, to be looked at as occasion may offer: any positive decision upon it cannot, it seems, be arrived at till near the end of the year.

I see (if you will pardon my saying so) that you don't know enough of what Swinburne has actually done, and probably don't feel sufficient curiosity about it, to form a complete opinion.[2] That poem on Cleopatra[3] was a comparative trifle written *in order* to accompany his friend Sandys's design. Neither he nor anyone would lay stress on that particular sample of his work: still I think you by no means do justice to its literary value.

I am very sorry to learn what you say of Tupper: it is new to me. The last time I saw him — about April, I suppose — he seemed to me looking much better than for years before, or perhaps at any time within my knowledge of him. What is supposed to be his malady?

Your

W. M. Rossetti

Do you see that that unfortunate young man Morten, who used to be a thorn in the side of the Hogarth Club, has committed suicide by hanging? It is a pity, for he had plenty of talent, and it seems could not (or *should* not) have been absolutely hard up, as Dickinson[4] was paying him a good annual allowance for some work done. I suppose it was worry at petty plagues, and exasperation at never having produced himself as he felt conscious of being qualified to do.

MS: Bodleian.

1. Sir Kenelm Digby (1603-65), naval commander and author. WMR was acting on behalf of Thomas Dixon, who wished to sell the portrait. The National Portrait Gallery did not acquire it.
2. WMR to Stephens, 15 September [1866]: "I hope you feel reflected rays of virtue upon you since the *Athenaeum* review of Swinburne" (Bodleian). For the review, see Letter 108, Note 11.
3. Published, along with the design that inspired it by the Pre-Raphaelite painter and illustrator Frederick Sandys (1829-1904), in the *Cornhill Magazine*, 14 (September 1866), 331-33.
4. Either Lowes Cato Dickinson (1819-1908), portrait painter and member of the family of photographic and print publishers (Dickinson & Co.) mentioned in Letter 47, Note 3, or the firm itself. Dickinson belonged to an Artists' Society with an address at Langham Chambers, Portland Place (*POLD*). Morten died at 18 Langham Street, Portland Place (A. Life, "'That Unfortunate Young Man Morten'," pp. 384-87).

108. TO ALGERNON CHARLES SWINBURNE

166 Albany Street,
7 October [1866]

Dear Swinburne,

Hotten — expressing the opinion that you would sanction or even prefer it — sent me on Friday morning the proof here enclosed of your pamphlet,[1] and requested me to call round upon him yesterday for some speech concerning it, which I did. After interchange of our views regarding the matter, I offered to write you about it, which he gladly accepted.

I think the pamphlet very excellent, and certain to raise your position in the eyes of those who, without knowing you personally, are capable of putting a candid and liberal construction on the facts. Indeed it appears to me pretty certain that the tide will now rapidly turn, and you and the book take even a higher standing than if all this blustering malignity and stupidity had not been vented forth. I like the latter portion of the pamphlet, beyond what you had read to me, even better than that first part: and, without being prepared to recede from the opinion I then expressed to you that so total a repudiation of anything immoral in the book were better avoided as being only partially candid or politic, I certainly admit that you have made out a better case for *Dolores* etc. than even I had anticipated, and, with the *Examiner* to back you, I think it *conceivable* or even probable that that version of the facts may prove swallowable by the public.

Now to details. Hotten tells me that "he has had an earnest talk with his solicitor, who strongly advises that all mention of the stupid threat of a prosecution should be omitted — also direct allusions to the firm Moxon & Co. Should anything take place, the solicitor says these might be used as evidence against your side."[2] I find in fact that Hotten would be relieved if the whole of paragraph 1 were omitted.[3] This of course is a matter for *your* decision only. For my own part, I would certainly defer to the solicitor's opinion as to alluding to the threatened prosecution (the *mode* in which he thinks that perilous to you is that your allusion might be adduced to show that you were perfectly aware of the objections professed against the book, and had nevertheless persisted in reissuing it after warning): I also would omit from page 1 the passage "Others, not I" to "furtive audacity" — presuming it to be legally a libel, and very likely to be caught hold of as such, to your manifest vexation even though you might possibly obtain a verdict upon the evidence.

Page 6. "Fight with beasts at Ephesus." This biblical quotation would by many be voted profane: I think, as your object is not to alienate neutrals but repel enemies, I would omit it.[4]

Page 6. "These somewhat vague terms," etc. to end of sentence. If I remember right, this was a passage I expressed dissent from when you read me the MS. I still think it would be futile to object to the non-definition of terms so obvious as Indecent and Blasphemous; and that the critics have quoted passages from your book sufficient to justify those terms in the eyes of the readers for whom they write. I should omit this sentence.[5]

Page 7. "In no passages of my writings" etc. This repudiation, though well founded in the main, appears to me too absolute. I consider that at any rate *Félise* may in all fairness be regarded — and *must* be regarded — as expressing your deliberate opinion on immortality, accessibility of God to man, etc.

Page 9. "I for one cannot conceive." This, and one or two of the stronger expressions in connexion with it, I would also omit. It certainly does appear to me that, if you so strongly aver that you cannot conceive anything "assailable or objectionable" in passionate writing about the sexual passion of one woman for another, the critics will have a very easy retort: "Then we were quite right in

158

saying that your mental constitution leads you to gloat over whatsoever is unnatural and proscribed in lust.''

Page 12, Note. ''Moxon & Company.'' It seems Hotten includes this in the allusions which he would omit to that eminent firm. I presume you will agree with him as little as I do.

Page 13 etc. *Dolores, Garden of Proserpine*, and *Hesperia*. I think what you say on this subject is so thoroughly well calculated to lighten the odium which has weighed upon *Dolores* singly that I would advocate some material indication, in the volume itself, of the connexion of the 3 poems when opportunity offers: as to entitle them (suppose) A Trilogy (or perhaps ''The Passionate Trilogy'' or ''A Trilogy of Desire'') —

1. *Dolores*
2. *Garden of Proserpine*
3. *Hesperia*.

I must say that, for my own part, though I was *conscious* of a certain relation between *Dolores* and *Hesperia*, I was only vaguely conscious of it in comparison to what I am now after reading your exposition; and of course the great majority of readers would have less advantages than I towards realizing the full scope of the three poems.

Page 16. *Spectator*. Did you see in the *Spectator* of 15 (or perhaps 8) September, a contemptible rhymed attack upon you[6] by some verse-emitter whom I should suppose to be probably either Pennell[7] or Locker?[8] I should not permit myself to allude to such vomit in writing to you, but that I think you may perhaps not have seen it, and might prefer to see it before finally committing to press what you have to say of the *Spectator*. It is not (as you may guess) *penes me*.

Page 22. ''Those whom all men scorn.'' I fear ''ought to scorn'' would be more accurate: or perhaps an italicizing of ''men'' might bring out the full meaning.[9]

You will, I know, understand that I would not have obtruded these scraps of remark upon you, but that I found Hotten was evidently anxious that the points which *he* thinks of essential importance should be brought under your notice, which he felt somewhat nervous as to doing otherwise than through me or other of your known friends.[10] I need not add that I don't make any allusion to a legion of bad printer's errors.

Hotten tells me the book will be on sale again tomorrow (Monday): that the article in the *Athenaeum*[11] was written by one Lush, son of a Q.C., — in the *Saturday* by John Morley,[12] and in the *Examiner* by Henry Morley: who, in yesterday's *Examiner*, has a long and laudatory notice of Christina,[13] again referring to you, and identifying the gist of *Dolores* with that of *Goblin Market*! A letter from the same *Examiner*[14] is enclosed herewith (I can't send the longer article, as it has to go to Christina, now in Gloucester). I see the more recondite-minded of the British public have made up their minds that you *shall* be an austere moralist, an unprotected male, a flagellant of a backsliding century; and it appears to me that version of the facts is destined to prevail over the short-sighted remonstrances of a timid but unconverted press.

Thanks for the *North American Review*,[15] which is indeed of the seediest. I wrote in resolute terms last Sunday to Norton, and *incline* to think that, out of mere regard for me, they will print my review substantially as it stands — perhaps with a reference to their own previous delivery, and intimation that they do not commit themselves to all the opinions I express.[16] It happens that yesterday I said something to Hotten about the affair, and he, entirely of his own accord, said he would like to print the article as a pamphlet. I made no definite response: but am not quite sure whether it might not be best, without further American shilly-shallying, to take up with Hotten's proposal. On reflection I think I could well avoid any appearance (which I mentioned to you before as a dissuasive) of having written the thing on his suggestion, by simply stating the real fact in a prefatory note. Would you at your convenience let me know which *you* would prefer — publication through Hotten or through the *North American*.[17] I cannot promise that your preference would *determine* me, but it would certainly be a very weighty element in determining. Hotten also told me by the by that Mill, M.P. is a great maintainer of your book, and might even, under fitting conditions, be likely to express himself in print.[18] I enclose further an extract from a Yankee paper.[19]

I shall soon be writing to Palgrave, and will tell him what you say[20] — much to his gratification, I am certain. This letter is already so long I cannot prolong it to say much — and indeed I know next to nothing — of our friends. Gabriel however talks of leaving tomorrow with Sandys for a fortnight or so at Winchelsea and neighbourhood. Scotus not yet back that I know of.

Yours always,

W. M. Rossetti

I believed myself justified in showing your pamphlet last night to Gabriel (alone). He shares my opinion of it, and even thinks it might be well to print it (besides the separate form) at the end of *Poems and Ballads*. I incline to the same opinion.

MS: BL. Extracts in *HLB*, pp. 358-60.

1. *Notes on Poems and Reviews*. For an account of the changes suggested by WMR, see *HLB*.
2. Quoted, but not always accurately, from Hotten's letter to WMR, 4 October 1866; AP. For example, Hotten wrote "against us," not "against your side."
3. In the proof (now at Harvard) the first two paragraphs of the published version were combined. Swinburne omitted the reference to a threatened prosecution against Hotten for reissuing *Poems and Ballads*, and also several abusive sentences (including the "Others, not I" passage) on Moxon's "unworthiness of trust." A subsequent reference to Moxon as Shelley's publisher remained (see "Page 12, Note"). Cancelled passages are printed in *Swinburne Replies*, ed. C. K. Hyder, 1966, pp. 127-28.
4. The quotation, from 1 Corinthians, 15:32, remained.
5. Swinburne readily excised the sentence, and also the passages objected to on "Page 7" and "Page 9," but he firmly resisted the suggested grouping of *Dolores*, *Garden of Proserpine*, and *Hesperia* (see *SL*, 1:197).
6. "The Session of the Poets" (15 September 1866, p. 1028), by Robert Buchanan.
7. Henry Cholmondeley Pennell (1837-1915), poet and writer on angling, published *Puck on Pegasus* (1861) and *Crescent, and other Lyrics* (1864).

8. Frederick Locker-Lampson (1821-95; Lampson was appended in 1885), poet of *London Lyrics* (1857 and many subsequent editions), anthologist, collector of the Rowfant Library. When WMR was editing Shelley he found Locker "most liberal and courteous" in lending his manuscripts and early editions of the poet (*SR*, 2:387).

9. Swinburne printed "all men should scorn."

10. In his reply Swinburne approved Hotten's "way of doing it. For of course a suggestion from you is a very different thing from a suggestion from him" (*SL*, 1:193).

11. 4 August 1866, pp. 137-38. Robert Lush (1807-81), who was appointed Lord Justice in 1880. C. K. Hyder points out that Robert Buchanan admitted he wrote the review (*Swinburne's Literary Career and Fame*, p. 275).

12. (1838-1923), statesman and man of letters.

13. A review of *Goblin Market and Other Poems* and *The Prince's Progress and Other Poems*; 6 October 1866, pp. 629-30.

14. A letter in defense of Swinburne by R. Monckton-Milnes, p. 627 (*SL*, 1:195).

15. See Letter 102, Note 2.

16. Norton to WMR, 18 October 1866: "I have no question that your paper on Swinburne will be written in an entirely candid spirit, and that it will be of critical value and genuine interest. Anything that you write comes commended to me not only by its intrinsic merit but by my cordial regard for yourself; — and you may be sure that I shall gladly publish your paper in the Review, unless the necessity of preserving a general consistency of tone on its critical judgements should be violated by so doing" (AP).

17. "I should infinitely prefer, I should regard as much the higher compliment, the appearance in London of a pamphlet of yours than the issue of an article in an American review" (*SL*, 1:194).

18. No comment by John Stuart Mill on *Poems and Ballads* (or on Swinburne) has been found.

19. Not identified.

20. See Letter 106, Note 5.

109. TO JOHN CAMDEN HOTTEN

74 & 75 Piccadilly,[1]
Friday,
[11 October 1866]

My dear Sir,

Here is the proof, received by me this morning, and a note (which I prepared beforehand for the chance of not seeing you) of the points raised in Swinburne's accompanying letter.[2] You will find that he has very mainly acquiesced in what you asked him to do. Swinburne's letter of course is fuller on some points than the within note, but I think you will understand herefrom all that needs doing.

Yours faithfully,
W. M. Rossetti

MS: Huntington.

1. Address of Hotten's premises; the letter is written on Hotten's embossed stationery.
2. *SL*, 1:199-200.

110. TO JOHN CAMDEN HOTTEN

Somerset House,
15 October [1866]

My dear Sir,

Another note from Swinburne reached me this morning. He wants

1. A passage on page 11 about Sappho seeing "her female favourite in the embrace of a man" to be altered thus: "at sight of her favourite by the side of a man."

161

2. No motto to the pamphlet.[1]

3. Page 6 — a certain quotation contains the word "effect" — should be "affect."

I finished my review of Swinburne yesterday. It is just about 100 pages of my MS., and would, I expect, make full 35 of the *North American Review*. To the best of my knowledge and belief they would print it, and would pay me £1.1 a page, making £36.15 or (I suspect) something nearer £40. I could not voluntarily forego the whole of this sum. But, if you are disposed to print the review as a pamphlet, I would, (considering the great preference which I find Swinburne would have for that form of publication, and the degree of uncertainty and unpleasantness attending the American plan) hand it over to you if it suits you (and of course I don't wish you to do anything which would not suit your own interest) to pay me £15 for the MS. on delivery, to take all the expenses of publication, and, after reimbursing yourself the total, to halve with me any possible profits.[2] I can't much suppose there would be any.

I would put my name to the pamphlet, and leave it almost exactly as it stands, with a prefatory note to explain the circumstances under which it was written. The only difference I should make in the review would be to soften a few expressions criticizing or censuring Swinburne. Of course those expressions, as they stand, are consistent with my real opinion, but they were introduced rather to meet the general tone which a quarterly is expected to assume — and other rather milder expressions would also be *consistent* with my opinion, and would be preferred by me for the pamphlet form. I need hardly add that the review, as a whole, expresses most hearty and even enthusiastic admiration for Swinburne's work. Would you give me your answer on this matter as soon as convenient — as, if the review is to go to America, I would like to send it without much delay.

Yours truly,

W. M. Rossetti

MS: Huntington. Extract in *HLB*, p. 364.

1. But see Letter 111.
2. Hotten to WMR, 17 October 1866: "Many thanks for your kind offer of your article. I will take it on the terms you name. Please let me have it at once" (AP).

111. TO JOHN CAMDEN HOTTEN

166 Albany Street,
19 October [1866]

My dear Sir,

It appears to me that the best reference to put to Swinburne's first quotation is simply

"Frédéric le Grand,"[1]

corresponding to his

"Carlyle."

Something might however be said in favour of

(without volume and page, which I certainly think Swinburne did not intend to print). To save time, I write to him by this post, to reply to you saying which he prefers: if even thus much delay, however, is objectionable, I think you would be quite justified in at once adopting

"Frédéric le Grand."

Yours truly,
W. M. Rossetti

MS: Huntington.

1. Printed thus.

112. TO CHARLES ELIOT NORTON

166 Albany Street,
21 October [1866]

Dear Mr. Norton,

You will not, I believe, complain of any breach of faith on my part when I say that my review of Swinburne will not after all be submitted to you. I found Swinburne's present publisher willing and pleased to issue it as a separate pamphlet; and, as I fully believed you would be rather obliged to me than otherwise for saving you any deliberation upon it with a view to its insertion or otherwise in the *North American*, I handed it over to this publisher the other day (*not* to my greater pecuniary advantage, be it understood), and it is in his printer's hands, and to be out, I hope, in a fortnight or less. I shall do myself the pleasure of sending you a copy when it reaches me. Since I wrote you last I have seen the *North American* containing the review of *Atalanta* etc., which I certainly think by no means an adequate recognition of Swinburne's genius and performances — also a review, for which no doubt I am indebted to you, of Dante translations including my own.[1] I found it an excellent article, and am much gratified at the kind and degree of commendation you find it consistent to bestow on my production.

Very truly yours,
W. M. Rossetti

MS: Harvard.

1. "Dante and his Latest English Translators," 102 (April 1866), 509-29. "He has preserved the substance, and in good measure the spirit, of his original.... But it also shows defects ... in a certain tendency toward the use of expressions more quaint than exact ... and a certain want of rhythmic grace and harmony in the structure of the verse."

113. TO HORACE ELISHA SCUDDER

166 Albany Street,
28 October 1866

Dear Mr. Scudder,

I ought to have expressed before now my thanks for the receipt of the *Drum-Taps*, and of Mr. O'Connor's[1] pamphlet upon Whitman: I regret much that my absence at the time in Italy prevented my having the pleasure of making Mr. Hubbard's[2] acquaintance, and it seems he did not, as I had suggested, call on my brother in my absence.

I have not even yet found a comfortable opportunity for giving the *Drum-Taps* that full and deliberate reading which I want to have of them. Among other interruptions, the book has been twice borrowed. I have read some of the poems however: especially the long one on Lincoln's funeral,[3] and the one you specially mention *O Captain, my Captain*: both most glorious. Whitman is a wonderful genius to me, and no less than a *great* poet: I am not at all sure but that one day he will stand out as the greatest English-writing poet of this period.

Mr. O'Connor's pamphlet I read the other day, and with very great pleasure. It gives an interesting and most gratifying insight into the personality of Whitman, and is, I think, a remarkably fine piece of energetic criticism and writing — somewhat over-pitched and flaring no doubt, but still very masterly and powerful. I must try to get hold of *Harrington*. I hope Whitman is aware that he has some most deep and even enthusiastic admirers in this country also: among them none more fervent or carrying more weight than Swinburne.

Of your Blake project[4] I have heard nothing since your letter of 24 April: I hope it may be progressing to your satisfaction. Swinburne's study on Blake is all printed now; and, unless something unexpected intervenes, ought to be out within a month or so. Phillips's[5] portrait of Blake is now in our National Portrait Gallery — after a hard tussle with recalcitrant Trustees, the Secretary tells me.

Believe me always
Very truly yours,
W. M. Rossetti

MS: Harvard. Brief extract in R. W. Peattie, "Postscript to Charles Kent on Whitman," *Walt Whitman Review*, 15 (June 1969), 109.

1. William Douglas O'Connor (1832-89), civil servant, journalist, author of an abolitionist novel, *Harrington* (1860); friend and champion of Whitman. "When the poet came to Washington, penniless and friendless, in December 1862, it was O'Connor who came to his assistance, gave him shelter, and found him employment. Of all his services to Whitman, the most famous was the publication of *The Good Gray Poet* (1866), an eloquent philippic against James Harlan, who, as secretary of the interior, had dismissed the poet from his clerkship" (*Dictionary of American Biography*).
2. Probably Richard William Hubbard (1816-88), American landscape painter.
3. *When Lilacs Last in the Dooryard Bloom'd*.
4. WMR to Scudder, 16 May 1866: "I remember that, after your first mentioning to me the views you then entertained as to a work founded upon Gilchrist's, I, as agreed on between us, wrote to Mrs. Gilchrist, asking what view she took of that project. She replied expressing some degree of reluctance to it in its then shape" (Harvard). Scudder did not produce a book on Blake.
5. Thomas Phillips (1770-1845), portrait painter, whose portrait of Blake was exhibited at the R.A. in 1807.

114. TO ALGERNON CHARLES SWINBURNE　　　　　19 November [1866]

Les Prospérités du - - -! Such is Urizen!

The name Laus Veneris must evidently be used by the writer as an ingenious designation of the complete *Poems and Ballads*.

This same *Star* very abusive to me:[1] *Saturday Review* complimentary to me[2] (quite contrary to my expectation), and with some degree of returning reason, still mingled with much vituperation, towards you.

I expect to see Hotten tomorrow.

Your
W. M. Rossetti

MS: BL.

1. His Swinburne pamphlet was called an "ill-advised defence ... a long-winded puff." The reviewer took exception to Buchanan being "sneered at, in a quite gratuitous way, as a poor and pretentious poetaster. What has Mr. Buchanan to do with the question of Mr. Swinburne's genius or his alleged nastiness?" (*Morning Star*, 19 November 1866, p. 3).

2. "An accomplished and gifted critic has undertaken the defence of one of the most wayward *enfants terribles* who have ever disturbed the serenity of the decencies and respectabilities of their time. A more difficult thing has seldom been better done. Mr. Rossetti writes with a soft melodious persuasiveness which conciliates when it fails to convince" (17 November 1866, pp. 600-601).

115. TO FREDERIC GEORGE STEPHENS 7 December [1866]

Dear Steph,

There is a point I particularly intended to mention to you on Wednesday, and forgot after all.

The French painter Legros,[1] whose works you have remarked, lives at 1 Victoria Grove Villas, Bayswater: it is a turning out of the main Bayswater Road, to your left hand as you go from Hammersmith, and, if I remember right, the *next before* Orme Square, in which Leighton used to live. I was there about a fortnight ago, and found he had at home 5 pictures (oil) all well advanced — 2, if I remember right, finished. 1, a Refectory with 2 monks doing penance;[2] 2, a Church in the Pyrenees District, with scattered congregation; 3, the Sower; 4, 5, landscapes. I think them all very fine works, and of a distinguished class. Had I any paper wherein to write, it would have been a great satisfaction to me to say something of them; but this is lacking, and I thought you might perhaps be willing or pleased to look up the works, and use them for "Gossip" or so.[3] I started the idea to Legros, who liked it, and would value a call from you: any little service in this sort of way might be a real help to him, and he happens to need such as times go. I understand you have met him: he is a man of quite exceptional capacity in various ways, and I value his character as well as performances. He can barely speak or understand English: but you might muster up French enough for him, and his wife[4] speaks both languages perfectly (an English-woman).

Marcliffe[5] shall come in due course: I am just about writing to Hotten as to the Swinburne critique.

Your
W. M. Rossetti

We missed the train on Wednesday!

MS: Bodleian.

1. Alphonse Legros (1837-1911), painter, etcher, professor of Fine Art at the Slade School from 1876, came to England to escape poverty and neglect in France. Whistler introduced him to the Rossettis. WMR reviewed him generously (see "Checklist"), hailing him in 1863 as "a painter upon whom the eyes of the discerning are already fixed, and who is almost certain to take one of the very highest seats in his profession" (*Reader*, 1 August, p. 119). In 1864 Legros painted WMR's portrait. Writing to Joseph Pennell on 13 December 1911 about Legros's death, WMR noted that he and DGR "were very intimate with Legros, until the unfortunate squabble between him and Whistler ensued, perhaps 1867. After that, we, although still very well-affected to Legros, lost sight of him: my brother had meanwhile aided him a good deal in finding purchasers for his works" (LC).

2. *The Refectory* (R.A., 1868).

3. Stephens wrote about *The Refectory* in the *Athenaeum*, 29 December 1866, p. 884, and briefly mentioned "a small, roughly-executed, but very effective landscape — a French village on a hill, at twilight."

4. Frances Rosetta, whom he married in 1864.

5. Not identified.

116. TO CHARLES ELIOT NORTON

166 Albany Street,
9 December [1866]

Dear Mr. Norton,

I have your two letters, of 18 October and 23 November.

I am practically certain that I did not send to Trübner & Co. the copy of the *Germ* intended for you. I shall now at once obtain from the publisher fresh copies of Nos. 3 and 4, and send these, with 1 and 2 already in my possession, to Trübner's.

On first receiving the earlier of your two letters, I asked my brother as to the point you raise — whether you could obtain from him one of his Tennyson drawings. I am ashamed to say that the lapse of time since then renders me a little uncertain as to the precise terms of the reply he gave me, but it amounted substantially to this: That he would not wish to break up the set, nor indeed to sell all or any item of it at a price which would be likely to be offered. He regrets therefore that he cannot fall in with your wishes in this instance. He asked me to add that he spoke to Burne Jones about some question which you asked long ago as to obtaining some work by Jones; and that the latter said he would write to you about it. My brother seems to be under the impression that Jones did not after all do this, and that you have never yet received any definite answer to your proposal. Jones's address, I may add, is 41 Kensington Square, London, W. Holman Hunt (from whom you express a wish also to obtain a drawing) is at present in Florence, and I am far from certain whether he is more likely to return thence to London within 2 or 3 months, or to go on to Jerusalem for as many years.

You ought by this time to have received my *Criticism* on Swinburne, of which I ordered you a copy to go through Trübner's. It will explain better than anything I could here say my attitude towards his work in its moral aspects: and moreover I think no one will get a clear notion of what these aspects themselves are except by reading the Poems through. I think the ordinary reviews may have a very misleading influence on that point. However I neither profess nor intend to be his "advocate" (as my very civil reviewers agree to term me) whether in moral or even in poetic respects, but his critic, and this very mainly in the poetic respects, not the moral — which latter I certainly consider of secondary importance, of the two.

Many thanks to you and all the other subscribers (to whom please to express these thanks whenever opportunity may offer) for the £9.13.1 for the Cruikshank Fund: I will, as you propose, make it even to £10. The subscription goes on very fairly here, standing (I suppose) already beyond £1000: it is proposed to keep it open till next summer, and then hand it over to Cruikshank.

Always truly yours,
W. M. Rossetti

MS: Harvard.

117. TO ALGERNON CHARLES SWINBURNE

166 Albany Street,
22 December [1866]

Dear Swinburne,

Here is a little series of incidents which demand your careful attention — and, I should suppose, consequent action. It looks as if you were not to have long to wait for enacting that *rôle* of Hugo towards *his* publisher.[1]

Some little while ago a Yankee millionaire, Mr. Graham,[2] called at Moxon's, and asked for a *Poems and Ballads*: they professed to have nothing to say to any such publication. On 15 December he returned, to look after a Tennyson bust, and again asked for a *Poems and Ballads*. Mr. J. Bertrand Payne was personally consulted in his presence, with the result that he was offered a copy if he cared to pay £1.1, which he did. Another American gentleman, Mr. Huntington,[3] witnessed the whole transaction (or else this following transaction). On 21 December Mr. Graham returned, again asked for another *Poems and Ballads*, and again received it for another £1.1. One copy has the clipped title-page with Moxon's name — the other, unclipped with same name: I have seen them at Hotten's — also *letters* from Messrs. Graham and Huntington attesting the aforenamed facts.

Hotten says he has made some personal enquiry, and is assured that the *Athenaeum* would admit a letter stating these facts.[4] He means, I believe, to offer some written matter on the subject to you — the value of which, I conceive, would consist in the authenticity of its *facts*, greater than my opportunities allow. If you write to the *Athenaeum*, he thinks your letter should be in London, if practicable, by Tuesday night: it appears to me that (if you feel no objection) it might be all the better he should see it before it goes to the *Athenaeum* office, so that there may be no chance of any mis-statement on any point of detail.

It appears to me tolerably obvious that you have also this further pull upon Mr. J. Bertrand Payne — that you are entitled to your proportional profit on the copies sold: and that a lawyer's letter applying to him to hand over such profit would produce a denial which could be pretty conclusively disposed of, or else a compliance which would tell its own tale.

Excuse summariness. I *suppose* you are out of town, from what Hotten said. Have you seen your American edition,[5] with blue (!!) edges?

Your
W. M. Rossetti

MS: BL. Extracts in *Swinburne Library*, pp. 27-28; and *HLQ*, pp. 45-46.

1. Perhaps a reference to Hugo's attacks on Louis Napoleon, *Napoléon le Petit* (1852) and *Les Châtiments* (1853), which were "sold under the counter to the profit of no one but the middlemen" (André Maurois, *Victor Hugo* [1956], p. 326).
2. James Lorimer Graham (1835-76), collector with a special interest in numismatics; American consul in Florence, where he lived from c. 1866. Swinburne became his friend and commemorated him in *Epicede* (*Poems and Ballads*, 2d ser., 1878).
3. William Henry Huntington (1820-85), correspondent in Paris of the *New-York Tribune*, 1858-78; friend of French radical politicians.
4. Swinburne replied that Hotten "should be the first mover" (*SL*, 1:216), but nothing seems to have been done.
5. *Laus Veneris and other Poems and Ballads*, New York: G. W. Carleton, 1866.

118. TO FREDERIC GEORGE STEPHENS

166 Albany Street,
23 December [1866]

Dear Stephens,

Thank you for being the first to inform me. I am indeed grieved for such a calamity to our dear old Hunt,[1] independently of the loss of so finely gifted and natured a woman as she herself always appeared to me.

I have followed your example — telling Mrs. Orme that, if it is anything approaching a party, I cannot come. I have also written to Hunt, offering, if any use or satisfaction to him, to go over to Florence.

Our best regards to your wife. I again spoke yesterday to Hotten about sending you my pamphlet.[2]

Your
W. M. Rossetti

MS: Bodleian.

1. Death of Fanny Hunt.
2. *Swinburne, A Criticism.*

119. TO ALGERNON CHARLES SWINBURNE

Somerset House,
27 December [1866]

Dear Swinburne,

I should really like to get a day or so at Holmwood:[1] but the particular circumstances of the moment are so adverse that I must give up the idea as thus:
1. I am absolutely bound to remain daily at Somerset House to end of year, having 2½ businesses to perform.
2. You may have heard that Holman Hunt had the misfortune of losing his wife at Florence on the 20th, leaving him with a baby. I feel deeply for his misfortune, and, not knowing what degree of embarrassment may be besetting his movements,

whether towards Jerusalem or home, I offered him by letter the other day to come over (if of any use or satisfaction to him) any day after 1 January — not with any view to my own enjoyment, as you may imagine under the circumstances. His answer has not yet come, but may come any day and require me to make off in a hurry.

3. Meanwhile I am getting on as I can with a job I am now undertaking — selection of old articles of mine to be published by Macmillan[2] — and which, with this possible serious interruption before me, I must make way with while I may — as for instance next Sunday, the only day I could otherwise have managed a day out of town.

As you convey so cordial a message from your father and mother, would you in thanking them from me bore them also with however much of the foregoing may be needed to make them perceive that I am not pleading excuses — which I assure you, with ordinary leisure, I should be quite on the opposite tack from pleading.

I think your view of the Payne affair quite correct.[3]

Many and very real thanks for the Robespierre,[4] which I heartily enjoy possessing. In haste which claims induglence.

Your
W. M. Rossetti

MS: BL.

1. The country house in Shiplake, Oxfordshire, purchased by Swinburne's father in 1865. WMR visited the Swinburnes there from 12-14 January 1867, when he found the poet "showing his ordinary peculiarities without bringing into play such as would distress his family.... Lady Jane Swinburne says that, when Algernon was quite a child, he already showed that habit of nervous movements or twitchings of fingers etc., and that they endeavoured to correct him of them, but had to give it up under the advice of a doctor who said that the attempt would do harm" (MS. Diary, 12, 14 January). For the remainder of his diary entries on the visit, see *RP*, pp. 220-21.

2. *FACC*. MS. Diary, 20 December 1866: "Macmillan says he finds my pamphlet on Swinburne (from which he wholly dissents) very much talked about, and thinks the Selection ought to succeed reasonably."

3. See Letter 117, Note 4.

4. Jérôme Pétion and Maximilien Robespierre, *Observations sur la nécessité de la réunion des hommes de bonne foi contre les intrigans, proposées à tous les Français* (1792).

120. TO JOHN LUCAS TUPPER

166 Albany Street,
18 February [1867]

Dear Tupper,

Thanks for your friendly expression of opinion about my Swinburne brochure. In the event (not perhaps so likely as you seem to think) of a second edition, I would certainly think over what you say about Browning, though I cannot answer for acting upon it. I see you look upon the matter from a considerably different point of view from what I do. I do not regard the fact mentioned concerning Browning's eyes[1] to amount to a "visual *deficiency*," but only peculiarity: and, as for "tearing his heart before the crowd," I cannot think that expression, even in its widest purview, applies to the case. You may be quite sure I would not do anything consciously to hurt or even irritate Browning's feelings. I know him personally, and do not perceive him to be a man — such as Tennyson is — likely to mind an illustrative reference to any such bodily individualism; and, if a man *is* free from these excessive susceptibilities, I think it much better and more convenient for all parties that he should be *treated* as free. Browning called on me the other day — weeks and weeks after the appearance of the book, which I should suppose him likely to have heard of, so far at any rate as his own share in it is concerned, meanwhile: and I could not perceive the very smallest trace in him of any uncomfortable feeling.

As to alliteration, I did not mean to be "hard upon" it — but on the contrary to affirm that it is a natural, legitimate, and effective expedient of a master of his writing-tools for showing that he *is* a master of them. But I said, and cannot but stick to it, that Swinburne alliterates too often.

With all greetings,

Yours very truly,
W. M. Rossetti

MS: Leeds.

1. "Browning is a double-sighted man — long-sighted with one eye, and short-sighted with the other: that is the exact analogue of his mental vision." WMR thought this "a heavy drawback to his freedom, consistency, and greatness, as a poet" (*Swinburne, A Criticism*, pp. 48-49). Tupper objected, invoking the Litany: "I grant there is a physio-psychologic interest in it: but the more apposite the parallel, the more awful it seems. To tear his heart before the crowd were enough surely in the case of a dead lion: but such 'demonstration' (I am a Guy's man still) on the living heart — Spare us, Good Lord!" (15 February 1867; AP).

121. TO CHARLES AUGUSTUS HOWELL

Somerset House,
21 February [1867]

Dear Howell,

Swinburne (still at Holmwood) says: "Perhaps, if you or if Howell (as he has seen the things about, and knows my chaos) could do it, it might save me a journey — to look over the scattered proofs of the Blake in my rooms (none are locked up or put away, I know), and see if slips (not *sheets*) H, I, K, are to be found corrected. Hotten says they are missing: and, whether found or not, tell him to get the book complete in sheets as soon as possible."

Please let me know whether you will undertake this job: if not, I will[1] — but at present know nothing likely to guide me to a successful result.

We were rather expecting you at Chelsea on Tuesday, and I can see that Fanny[2] has relented, and will only chaff — not billingsgate — you henceforward. Wornum asked us the same evening at the Burlington whether you ought not to be put down for membership: Gabriel explained that you thought of joining, but preferred postponing it awhile. If you join in or after July, you will only have to pay £2.12.6 subscription, instead of £5.5.

Love to Kate.

Your
W. M. Rossetti

As you speak of winding up the Cruikshank affair, and as I like to be business-like, let me add that 7/2 is due to me for postage. This has nothing to do with the sum I paid on account of the Yankee subscribers, and which will be reimbursed to me through Norton.

MS: Texas.

1. See Letter 122, Note 4.

2. Fanny Cornforth (1824-1906), whose name is usually abbreviated to F. in WMR's letters and diaries. She became Mrs. Timothy Hughes about a year after she met DGR, and Mrs. John B. Schott in 1879 (see Baum, pp. 8-9). As DGR's model, housekeeper, and mistress, she was more prominent in WMR's life than his cautious references to her in *FLM* would suggest. That he could enjoy her robust personality is clear from this letter. Increasingly, however, her belligerence affronted him, and after DGR's death he firmly rejected her, and relentlessly, though not always successfully, tried to obstruct the attempts of the Schotts to trade on DGR's name.

122. TO ALGERNON CHARLES SWINBURNE

Somerset House,
25 February [1867]

Dear Swinburne,

Thanks about Bendyshe.[1] Just as I wrote you last, he answered my original letter — of course consenting.

I enclose part of the page of *Pall Mall* (which was already by me) containing the Cambridge paragraph:[2] you see there are no particulars beyond what I reported. As to the No. containing the *Vittoria*[3] review, I may perhaps be able to trace it out next time I am at the Burlington Club — if so, will see further to it.

Hotten wrote me on 21 February[4] that he was anxious to get the Blake proofs settled, being plagued meanwhile by Moxon's people. I had already written (as already mentioned to you), to Howell, and have not yet any reply from him: if he does not reply by tomorrow, I must see what is to be done. Did Hotten send you the slip (reprinted from Cullen Bryant's[5] paper, New York *Evening Post*) concerning sale of your suppressed book by Moxon — or the laudatory but rather colourless notice (German) in the *Beilage Zur Zukunft?*[6]

I will look up the Blake facsimiles[7] as convenience shall serve — and would of course (I forgot to say this in replying to your previous letter) co-operate in any way you like in revising your Blake proofs.

Yours always,
W. M. Rossetti

MS: BL.

1. Thomas Bendyshe (1827-86), proprietor and editor from August 1865 of the recently defunct *Reader*. WMR wished to reprint in *FACC* several of the papers he had contributed to the journal.

2. Reporting a motion at the Cambridge Union "to exclude Swinburne's poems from books recommended for purchase. After some discussion, carried by a large majority that the book should remain on the list" (*Pall Mall Gazette*, 18 February 1867, p. 7).

3. By Meredith; reviewed 25 January 1867, pp. 10-11.

4. "I have written twice asking Mr. Swinburne to kindly let me have proofs back corrected. The fact is the Moxons are putting some pressure upon me through printers, and my only plan to rid myself of the nuisance is to complete printing and take the sheets from Bradbury & Evans" (AP). Diary, 22 February: "Called on Hotten relative to the proofs of Swinburne's *Blake*, which are in some muddle" (*RP*, p. 224).

5. William Cullen Bryant (1794-1878), American poet, was editor of the *Evening Post*, 1829-78.

6. 14 February 1867.

7. Illustrations for *William Blake*. Hotten to WMR, 21 February 1867: "We are working away at the facsimiles of Blake, and we shall please all admirers of the poet-artist. Out of the 15 or 16 you jotted down we propose to give five — as many as I can afford" (AP). Eight facsimiles were included, plus a decorated title-page which incorporated details from several of the illuminated books.

123. TO ALGERNON CHARLES SWINBURNE

Somerset House,
29 April [1867]

Dear Swinburne,

I have to thank you (days ago by rights) for the copy sent me of the *Song of Italy*: how highly I rate it I need not repeat. Even before receiving it I had asked the Editor of the *Chronicle*[1] (the one paper I am now writing in) whether he would accept a review of it from me — adding that I much agreed with you in the Mazzinian and anti-papal opinions expressed (the *Chronicle* being to some extent the organ of liberal *Catholicism*). The Editor replied that he would take a moderate-sized review, on the understanding that the poem would be treated from its literary side, not its political: *moderate-sized*, because he had already accepted from someone else a review of your poems generally[2] (not yet published). I agreed to these terms, and wrote the article a few days ago. If you see it, you will find that though I have not absolutely avoided all *allusion* to politics, I have declined expressing any *opinion*. The way all this is managed might seem strange to you but for my present explanation: with that, I trust you will see that the review is consistent with what else you know of me.

Old Kirkup wrote me on 23 March: "Remember me with affection to Swinburne. Tell him that I have written to Browning (!) to get the papers of Landor from Forster,[3] and send them to him — about 50 Latin odes, English poems, dialogues, letters, essays, etc. I have not got his Cleopatra and Augustus:[4] Swinburne should see it [I think you have it?] — one of his best. Tell him that, when Blake died, the Princess Sophia sent Mrs. Blake £100, which she returned gratefully, saying there were those more distressed than she was: and she went as a servant to some painter to prepare his colours. So the story came to Florence, and very likely true."[5]

All this should have reached you before, but for the chance of our not having come across each other.

Your affectionate
W. M. Rossetti

MS: St. John's Seminary.

1. Thomas Frederick Wetherell (1831-1908), a member of the Liberal Catholic circle of Lord Acton (see Guy Ryan, "The Acton Circle and the *Chronicle*," *Victorian Periodicals Newsletter*, 7

[June 1974], 10-24). During the existence of the *Chronicle*, 23 March 1867-15 February 1868, WMR contributed twenty-six reviews of literature and art, including a notice of *A Song of Italy*, 18 May 1867, pp. 189-90.

2. See Letter 128, Note 10.

3. John Forster (1812-76), biographer and historian, whose *Landor, a Biography* appeared in 1869. For Swinburne's discomfort at Kirkup's action, see *SL*, 2:10-11, 15-16.

4. Presumably *Antony and Octavius* (1856).

5. Swinburne repeated the story in *William Blake*, p. 81. For a discussion of the story, see G. E. Bentley, Jr., *Blake Records* (1969), p. 345.

124. TO THOMAS DIXON

166 Albany Street,
9 June [1867]

Dear Dixon,

Your last received note says that you "would rather like me to leave the portrait[1] at Pearson's."[2] I understand — that you would prefer my so leaving it to Pearson's fetching it himself from the Portrait Gallery. This I would very willingly have attended to, were it not that, 2 or 3 days before your note reached me, I had (after calling 2 successive days at Pearson's, and failing to find him in) written him a letter enclosing the document which has to be presented at the Gallery in order to obtain the picture back. I told him at the same time that, if he did not care to fetch the picture, he could return me the document, and I would fetch it: but, as he has not done this, I presume he has attended or will attend to the matter himself.

I would gladly see the printed matter you refer to, consequent upon Ruskin's letters,[3] whenever, and whichever form of transmission, may be quite convenient to you. Don't trouble yourself about it otherwise.

Ruskin, writing to me about the other matter,[4] told me that he would cut out of the reprint what he had said about Carlyle,[5] who, he said, was "furious" on the subject. This is all I know of it direct. The fact, I take it, is that Carlyle really did say to Ruskin something very like what Ruskin printed: but that Carlyle never intended it to be published at all, and that Ruskin somewhat overcharged the tenor of it — while on the other hand Carlyle now uses somewhat undue latitude of denial in repudiating the whole affair. It is a pity Ruskin could not or would not perceive that the statement, whatever it may have been, was not the sort of thing to publish in those downright terms.

Yours truly,
W. M. Rossetti

MS: Texas.

1. See Letter 107, Note 1.

2. Presumably a carrier.

3. Addressed to Dixon and published in various newspapers during 1867; in the same year collected as *Time and Tide by Weare and Tyne, Twenty-Five Letters to a Working Man of Sunderland*.

4. In Letter 22 (*Leeds Mercury*, 27 April) Ruskin wrote disparagingly of WMR as a political commentator in "English Opinion on the American War"; and added that "his brother and I taught him whatever he knows about art" (C & W, 17:478). MS. Diary, 27 May 1867: "One of the statements made by Ruskin (the only one to which I see any objection) being that whatever I know in art has been taught me by him and my brother, I wrote to Ruskin expressing my opinion that this

statement is both irrelevant, and beyond what he can have any positive knowledge of; that I should consider some modification of it in the forthcoming reprint proper; but that, if he makes no alteration, I shall still have the same regard for him as before." 29 May: "Ruskin replied to my letter [agreeing to excise the passages, see *RP*, 263-64] in friendly but perhaps somewhat overbearing terms." Dixon, who was embarrassed by Ruskin's dismissal, explained to WMR on 21 May: "Why you came to be mentioned was through friend Hills and a Manchester friend of his that are deeply interested in American politics and who felt rather riled with Mr. Ruskin's tremendous slashing into their doings of late in these Letters, so they addressed a note to me, which I at once sent to Mr. Ruskin deeming only fair that he should know what other folks thought of the Americans, especially what they felt respecting his utterances in these Letters. In one paragraph your name was given with that of J. S. Mill, Goldwin Smith, and others who had written on American History, whose conclusions they considered Mr. Ruskin ought to look at before uttering his views on American Politics — your article in the *Atlantic Monthly* being regarded by us all as most conclusive evidence of the justices of the Northern Cause: and gave you they considered a fair claim to be considered an Authority so you were quoted. They thought after these references had been made, Mr. Ruskin would have gone into the question more thoroughly and have come to a different conclusion. However they were quite disappointed. The reply however was just what I anticipated and so that I felt grieved that I had been so very simple as to send the note" (AP).

5. Ruskin reported Carlyle's statement to him that "he now cannot walk without being insulted, chiefly because he is a grey, old man; and also because he is cleanly dressed — these two conditions of him being wholly hostile, as the mob of the street feel, to their own instincts." Carlyle published a strong denial in the *Pall Mall Gazette* (C & W, 17:481).

125. TO WILLIAM BELL SCOTT

Somerset House,
19 June [1867]

Dear Scotus,

Letter forwarded to *Notes and Queries*,[1] *Wellington Street, W.C.*

The longer I last the more I perceive that tolerance is understood to mean tolerance of such opinions as one does like or doesn't much dislike — and justice to mean such treatment of other people as one wishes them to meet with. Otherwise I don't see how it is that you "don't agree at all with my view of the matter"[2] — i.e. that the Club do not hold the balance even between Whistler and Haden in asking Whistler to resign on pain of expulsion simply because Haden has complained of him, without ever knowing the rights and wrongs of the question otherwise, or asking what Whistler might have to say about it. This is just the Eyre-Gordon plan[3] on a miniature scale. Hang up Gordon out of the way because he is an inconvenience to Eyre and his set — not because he is proved to have done anything to which the law awards the punishment of hanging. Let it be your turn to be complained of behind your back at the Burlington, and required to resign on pain of expulsion without explanation, and you would possibly see a possibility of justice in some different directions as well as this one.

Gabriel as usual is made the scapegoat. It is "curiously the reverse of the fact" (as Carlyle says of Ruskin[4]) to say that "Swinburne found Whistler in this circle of Cheyne Walk": the fact to my personal knowledge being that, weeks or months before Gabriel (or I) had ever seen Whistler, Swinburne delighted in him, and used to urge Gabriel to get acquainted with him. And I remember most clearly Swinburne's expressing his satisfaction at having eventually brought Gabriel and Whistler together, and remarking that he had known "Whistler would be exactly the man Gabriel would like" — to which Gabriel replied that he could not say that was precisely the fact, although he was pleased to know him.

I didn't till now know you had any decided feeling against Whistler. Far be it from me to contest your right to take any view of him which seems to you the correct one — and equally far to deny that Whistler has in more than one instance put himself gravely in the wrong. I have told him so to his face before a roomful of people,[5] and Gabriel has done the like by letter in terms barely consistent with friendliness. But I am far, very far indeed, from thinking him a bad fellow or one to be summarily condemned and discarded on all counts taken together.

As regards the present Club affair, I happened to meet Wornum[6] on Saturday, and learned that, after calling on Whistler to resign and the remonstrances consequent thereon, the Club had asked for any explanation he liked to offer. Half an hour's conversation availed to show Wornum that calling upon a man to resign first and explain afterwards might possibly be not quite so satisfactory as calling upon him to explain first and (if needful) resign afterwards. I informed Wornum of my intention to leave the Club if Whistler is expelled — adding that I should do nothing by way of cabal or agitation or schemes of opposition now or at all, but simply consult my own personal preference in the matter of remaining in the Club or not.

You will understand the perfect placidity of mind towards yourself, dearly beloved Scotus, which coexists with all the preceding outpourings, and that I am as always

Most affectionately yours,
W. M. Rossetti

MS: Arizona.

1. "Early German Prints of Jason and Medea," signed P.C.A., Penkill Castle; 29 June 1867, p. 518.
2. MS. Diary, 14 June 1867: "Wrote to Scott, telling him about the Burlington-Whistler affair"; the letter has not been found. Whistler recently assaulted Seymour Haden (1818-1910), the surgeon and etcher, who was the husband of the painter's half-sister Deborah. Haden's threat to resign from the Burlington Club unless Whistler was expelled led to a motion for his expulsion being passed on 13 December. Both Rossetti brothers, who had lobbied on Whistler's behalf, resigned in protest. Many years later, in notes written for Whistler's biographer Joseph Pennell, WMR explained: "My opinion in that matter was not that Whistler had been blameless ... but that the club had no claim to interfere in an affair which had not occurred in the club premises, nor even in the United Kingdom" (E. R. and J. Pennell, *Life of Whistler* [1908], 1:143). For the relevant portions of WBS's letter of 17 June, and his reply of 25 June to this letter, see *LPI*, pp. 35-36. WMR to WBS, 4 July [1867]: "You will be dejected to hear that the prospect of Whistler's expulsion is not quite so certain and bright as before. Strange to say, among a body of a dozen English gentlemen (to go in for the *Saturday Review* style), a dim idea does, after what Whistler and others have had to say on the subject, present itself that to require a man to resign on pain of expulsion without explanation, on the complaint made to the Committee by one of its own members, is a little like a *faux pas*, getting the summoners into quite as much of a mess as the man summoned. There is some suggestion that the Committee will both withdraw their summons, and apologize for it into the bargain; and I think there is a fair chance of Whistler's complete triumph over Haden, if only he (Whistler) will be content with mild and unexasperating measures — which I urge him to be. However after all it may be quite as likely that your, Wornum's, and Haden's ideal of justice will prevail, and Whistler be expelled in default of resigning, which he clearly will not do" (Arizona).
3. Believing that George William Gordon was responsible for the Negro disturbances in Jamaica in

October 1865, the British governor, Edward John Eyre, ordered his trial by martial law and approved his hanging.

4. In his letter to the *Pall Mall Gazette* (see Letter 124, Note 5).

5. On the occasion of Whistler's story about his attack on the black "Marquis of Marmalade": "I expressed to himself, in company at our dinner-table, a very decided opinion adverse to ... [his] performance.... I was rather surprised that ... [he] took my protest in good part, without retort at the moment, or after-abatement of cordiality" (*SR*, 2:318). Moncure Conway recalled that WMR said: "'I must say, Whistler, that your conduct was scandalous.' (Stillman and myself were silent)" (*Autobiography, Memories and Experiences* [1904], 2:112).

6. Ralph Wornum, secretary of the Club.

126. TO MONCURE CONWAY[1]

Somerset House,
17 September [1867]

Dear Conway,

Much obliged to you for forwarding me the very gratifying letter from Mr. Burroughs.[2] If any good result ensues from my article on Whitman, it is all owing to you originally;[3] and among other points this — that Hotten has just lately asked me to make and edit a Selection from Whitman's poems, to be published here.[4] It is a thing I am extremely pleased to do; have already made and arranged the Selection, and shall in due course produce a prefatory notice. Would you kindly tell me what articles of yours concerning Whitman are accessible in London, as I should like to consult them, more especially for any personal particulars. There was one, I know, in the *Fortnightly*[5] — any in *Fraser's*?

As to the photograph of my brother's Magdalene,[6] I am not sure whether he still has any of the moderate number of copies he once possessed. He is at present (I believe) out of town; but I will endeavour to ascertain about the photographs at a convenient opportunity, and see what can be done.

I hope you found my most kind friend Mrs. Cameron in the best of health — as for *energies* I need not ask after them for they are inexhaustible.

I *do* write pretty regularly in the *Chronicle* — and when the free option is left me with initials appended, but sometimes also without.

Might I trouble you for a word or two of information on the points enclosed — points culled from Whitman's poems, and on which I should like to give a line of explanatory note in my Selection. Also is it correct that Emerson has reversed his admiring verdict on Whitman?[7] I have heard this affirmed more than once — and especially in a late letter from Stillman, who says that at last no one dared so much as mention Whitman's name in Emerson's hearing at his Club.

Yours always,
W. M. Rossetti

MS: Columbia.

1. (1832-1907), American clergyman and writer, was pastor of South Place Chapel in London, 1864-84. WMR met him in 1863 when he visited England to lecture on behalf of the Northern cause in the Civil War. He was a friend of Whitman, and was of considerable help to WMR during the preparation of *PWW*.

2. John Burroughs (1837-1921), American nature writer, was a friend of Whitman and author of *Notes on Walt Whitman as Poet and Person* (1867). Earlier in the year WMR obtained from Conway

a proof copy of Burroughs's pamphlet, which he cited in his *Chronicle* article on "Walt Whitman's Poems," 6 July 1867, pp. 352-54. Conway sent the article to Burroughs, who replied that it was "a grand and lofty piece of criticism" (*RP*, p. 270).

3. See Letter 127.

4. 9 September 1867: "Wrote to Hotten proposing to do the Whitman Selection for £25, and twelve copies of the book" (Diary, *RP*, p. 240).

5. "Walt Whitman," *Fortnightly Review*, 6 (15 October 1866), 538-48.

6. Either *Mary Magdalene Leaving the House of Feasting* (Surtees 88), or *Mary Magdalene at the Door of Simon the Pharisee* (Surtees 109).

7. 22 September 1867: "Conway ... denies that Emerson has ever turned against Whitman, but on the contrary admires him quite as much as he ever expressed in writing." On 18 March 1869 C. E. Norton told WMR that Whitman's indifference to social conventions "made intercourse with him by cultivated people difficult, even including ... Emerson" (Diary, *RP*, pp. 240, 386). Emerson's famous letter acknowledging the poet's gift of *Leaves of Grass* ("I greet you at the beginning of a great career") was dated 21 July 1855. Whitman allowed it to be printed in the *New York Tribune* on 10 October 1855.

127. TO ALGERNON CHARLES SWINBURNE

56 Euston Square,[1]
22 September [1867]

Dear Swinburne,

Your familiar handwriting, and *too* familiar allusions to personages and subjects which raise a blush on the cheek of *le coquin le plus éhonté*,[2] greet me (today only) after a long interval; during which I have been moving into this house, away to Penkill and Paris, and on my return sorry to hear troublous accounts of your health,[3] which however your letter seems to show fairly re-established for the present. Pray be regardful of it, for the sake of your and our poetical future, and of all who love a dear friend.

Thanks for Burroughs's book. But I already possess a copy given me by Conway, and before that had read the book in a proof copy also confided to me by that friendly Yankee. Scott has already also seen the book through me, therefore I shall be returning it to you at early convenience.

I see you are not aware that I have already said "a short and (let us hope) seasonable word on Whitman in the British ear." Somewhere towards May last Conway told me that he had just received some copies of Whitman's new (complete) edition,[4] which he knew Whitman would be pleased to get into hands whence criticisms could ensue; and he asked me whether I should be in the way of meeting this requirement. I at once, with great internal satisfaction, asked and obtained the sanction of the *Chronicle* for an article, which was published on 6 July, and which I know has had a certain *retentissement* in America, and possibly here as well: see enclosed a letter to Conway from that same Burroughs — *would you please return it to me at your convenience.* And as for England Hotten asked me a fortnight or so ago whether I would edit for him a Selection from Whitman with preface etc., which I am now working on — have arranged the Selection, and have just begun the preface, which, all things going well, ought to be finished within 2 or 3 weeks, or less. I have thought it absolutely necessary (*mânes de l'auteur de Justine, ne m'en voulez pas*) to exclude everything decidedly offensive according to the notions of the correct public — i.e. to exclude the

177

whole of whatever poems contain anything of this kind, for I could not condescend to use the literary gelding knife, and excise the peccant *passages* only. I am in considerable (perhaps too presuming) hopes that the book as I compile it may give Whitman a fair chance and start with the beloved British public such as he has never had yet, and may possibly even lead to an early demand for the complete works — which, Conway told me the other day, have just been sent over to him by Whitman, prepared, even to punctuation, exactly as he would want them to appear in England.[5]

My first intention was to ask your sanction for dedicating to you my Whitman Selection, in a brief letter in which I should be careful to notify, for the benefit of all enlightenable and unenlightenable readers, that the author of *Atalanta* recognizes an illustrious brother poet in the author of the *Leaves of Grass*. But on reflection — considering your dedication of the Blake to me, and to save fools the pleasure of clucking "Claw me claw thee" — I now project dedicating the book to Scotus, who gave me the original *Leaves of Grass*, and saying in my letter *to him* what needs to be said about you. Have I your approval for this?

Now for other points in your letter. Calling at Hotten's about this Whitman affair something like a fortnight ago, I asked about your Blake, and was told (to the best of my recollection) that it was going on all right, but necessarily deferred for the facsimiles. He showed me certain *other* Blake facsimiles, for a Blake reproduction he is contemplating.[6] They are certainly skilful, but I could not decide to my own satisfaction *exactly how far* skilful unless I had the originals to compare them with at the moment. I will speak — or if more ready to hand — write to Hotten about the Blake, and your friend's[7] copy of the *Poems and Ballads*, at an early opportunity. Will also see to Teulet,[8] Knox,[9] your father's book,[10] and the Percy Ballads[11] — as to which the only thing to do is to be on the subscriber's list, as certain "Humorous and Loose Songs" are sold to none others.

I had not reflected — nor probably known — about your fresh issue of *Poems and Ballads* not being marked 2nd Edition. It seems quite obvious it ought to be so on all possible grounds, and I think you would be well warranted in *requiring* it. It is very seldom I have so much as seen Hotten this 8 or 10 months past: but, whenever the subject has casually turned up, he has seemed to me fully satisfied with the sale of *Poems and Ballads*: the *Song of Italy*, he told me the other day, has been a disappointment as regards sale. Glad to hear of the *Siena* poem.[12]

Whistler I saw last 3 weeks or so ago. He considers that his campaign with the Burlington Club has been fruitful of triumphs to himself, and of nothing but confessed humiliations to his adversaries — and indeed I think he *has* managed extremely well, though at last with needless pertinacity of retaliation. I think at one time, if he had left the matter as it stood, he had conquered: now, short of casualties, I expect he *must* get expelled — unless indeed (which seems to me of some moment) the members as yet uncommitted against him should, after this great lapse of time, resent raking up the *scabreux* affair, and decline to hear anything about it.

This is a devil of a long letter, but then it is a devil of a time since I wrote you at all. Pray remember me warmly and gratefully to your family, and believe me always

Affectionately yours,

W. M. Rossetti

Howell probably back, but not yet seen by me: Gabriel back since Friday from a short stay with Allingham at Lymington — likely to go down again (at least he *says* so) by the end of this week.

I am getting towards the end of Ernest Hamel's Life of Robespierre, lately completed in 3 volumes,[13] and bought by me in Paris: *ce grand homme* comes out of it with increased *éclat*, and really cleared, I consider, of various charges, though something still remains behind. Hamel mentions the pamphlet you gave me[14] as *une rareté bibliographique*.

Admirable that letter of Mazzini's[15] on the "Peace peace where there is no peace" Congress.

I see I have omitted to express (what indeed *va sans dire*) how pleased I should be if you *do* write anything about Whitman,[16] apropos of Burroughs or otherwise.

MS: BL.

1. "A much larger and better-looking house" than 166 Albany Street, to which WMR, his mother, sisters, and Aunt Eliza moved in June 1867 (*SR*, 1:292; *RP*, p. 236).
2. See *SL*, 1:263-65.
3. WMR was in Paris 5-10 August. MS. Diary, 12 August 1867: "Poor Swinburne, it seems, lately, while breakfasting at Lord Houghton's, had an attack of insensibility, more perhaps in the nature of a fit than a faint. He remained insensible some long while: the Doctor called in absolutely prohibited his continuing to use any brandy or the like stimulant, but considered it necessary to allow him Champagne. He then went down with his father to Holmwood, and may probably be there still."
4. *Leaves of Grass* 1867.
5. MS. Diary, 19 September 1867: "Conway looked me up at Somerset House in consequence of a note I had sent him asking certain questions concerning Whitman. He says that Whitman has just sent over a set of his books containing the punctuation etc. etc. exactly as he would wish it to stand in an English edition. I recommended Conway to write to Hotten about it, saying that, if Hotten is willing to undertake a complete edition, I will willingly abandon my Selection. Conway however would still wish me to write a preface. I think that after all the Selection would give Whitman a better chance of making his way with English readers."
6. Hotten published a color facsimile of *The Marriage of Heaven and Hell* in 1868. MS. Diary, 20 November 1866, records that Hotten "has a project of printing Blake's rarer books for subscribers, 100, in facsimile at £5 a copy." *Jerusalem* is mentioned on 3 June 1867 (*RP*, p. 234), and *America* on 6 September, but neither was issued. Morton Paley suggests that the project was abandoned after the death in 1868 of Hotten's expert facsimilist, Henry Bellars ("John Camden Hotten, A. C. Swinburne, and the Blake Facsimiles of 1868," *Bulletin of the New York Public Library*, 79 [Spring 1976], 284-85).
7. J. L. Graham, who had ordered a *Poems and Ballads* from Hotten.
8. Jean Teulet, *Lettres de Marie Stuart* (1859).
9. John Knox, *History of the Reformation of Religioun within the Realme of Scotland* (1587).
10. Laurens Andrewe, *The Noble Lyfe & Natures of Man* (c. 1521), which F. J. Furnivall had borrowed for use in his *Babees Book*, Early English Text Society, 1868 (*SL*, 1:153-54).
11. *Bishop Percy's Folio MS.*, 4 vols. (*Ballads and Romances*, 3 vols., 1867-68; *Loose and Humorous Songs*, 1867), ed. J. W. Hales and F. J. Furnivall.
12. Published in *Lippincott's Magazine*, June 1868, pp. 622-29. According to T. J. Wise, the poem was previously issued (1868) as a pamphlet by Hotten "in order to secure the English copyright" (*A Bibliography of the Writings of Swinburne* [1919], 1:177).

13. *Histoire de Robespierre* (1865-67).
14. See Letter 119, Note 4.
15. See Letter 128, Note 7.
16. *To Walt Whitman in America* (*Songs before Sunrise*, 1871) was Swinburne's major tribute to Whitman, but he also discussed him in *William Blake* and *Under the Microscope* (1872).

128. TO ALGERNON CHARLES SWINBURNE

56 Euston Square,
10 October [1867]

Dear Swinburne,

Our last letters evidently crossed. Since that I have received this memorandum from Hotten, which will I hope meet your enquiries on those points.

What you say about Whitman's "bluster"[1] seems to me correct, and not to be omitted critically. I have taken it upon me to transfer the passage bodily to my preface, — not bringing your name into question, but ascribing the remarks to "a friend highly entitled to express an opinion, and an ardent admirer of Whitman." The only alterations I have made are to change *frothy and blatant ebullience* into *blatant ebullience*, and *very feeble* into *feeble* — to avoid any extra harshness. I so hope you don't object: if you do, of course I must cut the passage out of the preface again.

I read the Harvest poem[2] in a hurry, and thought it not quite up to his mark — so much so that I have not since then looked it up again to consider as to including it in the Selection. Your opinion satisfies me I was right. The poem got into the *Temple Bar* by a muddle: it ought (through Hotten's hands) to have gone into the *Fortnightly*.

The Selection, it seems, will not be out till after Christmas, but I suppose *soon* after. I *have* felt constrained to omit the whole poem about Night and Sleepers[3] — reluctantly, as you may be sure. Voices out of the Sea[4] and Lilacs[5] of course are in — and *Camps of Green*,[6] which is a most singular favourite of mine, but (to my surprise) not noticed by others to whom I have named it erewhile.

After finishing this letter I will see whether by possibility Mazzini's letter[7] is to be fished up here: if so, will enclose it — if not, you will understand that it is not to be found. It appeared — in the *Morning Star*, so far as my seeing of it is concerned — some few days before the date of my writing to you, — I should say between 16 and 20 September or very near thereabouts.

Your Garibaldi and other national poems[8] are good news, not to be further tampered with in this hasty note, so much is there to be said on such a question of inspiration and of art. About the results of the pseudo-Italian government's move,[9] it appears to me that it is *just a chance* whether a thorough crash ensues from it, or practically nothing ensues. May it prove the former.

The *Chronicle* on you[10] was a sufficiently lengthy *réchauffé* of the old commonplaces of abuse stopping short of the outrageous: but you will have seen it by now — a thoroughly ordinary piece of mediocrity.

Your essay on Arnold interested me much. There is a good deal in it which I can form little opinion about, not having read the poems under discussion: but much remains which I both apprehend, value, and greatly like — that about Wordsworth very fine. As for Christina, the praise is really *too* great, as you know she would be the first to say and feel; not the less acceptable on all grounds to us. Scotus also very apt.[11]

My complete edition of Whitman has had to be ruthlessly cut up for the Selection, as I found the alterations from previous editions swarming as far as I went with these. I have ordered through Hotten another copy from America. The *whole* preface to *Leaves of Grass* is to be reproduced — a sentence or two only omitted[12] unless Whitman raises an objection — for I think this excusable when only *prose* is in question.

Your affectionate
W. M. Rossetti

MS: BL.

1. In his letter of 6 October 1867 (*SL*, 1:267). Swinburne approved the revisions (*SL*, 1:270), and the passage was quoted in *PWW*.

2. *A Carol of Harvest for 1867*; first published in the *Galaxy* (New York), September 1867, and reprinted in *Tinsley's Magazine* in October. Since *Leaves of Grass* 1881 it has been entitled *The Return of the Heroes* (Blodgett, p. 358).

3. *Night Poem* (*Leaves of Grass* 1856); named *Sleep-Chasings* in the editions of 1860 and 1867, and *The Sleepers* since 1871 (Blodgett, p. 424).

4. In *Leaves of Grass* 1860 and 1867 the title was *A Word Out of the Sea*; entitled *Out of the Cradle Endlessly Rocking* since 1871. Since 1881 it has been the opening poem of the *Sea-Drift* group (Blodgett, p. 246).

5. *When Lilacs Last in the Dooryard Bloom'd*; since 1881 grouped with three short poems under the title *Memories of President Lincoln* (Blodgett, p. 328).

6. Since 1881 one of the *Songs of Parting*.

7. Addressed to the Geneva Peace Conference. A report of it appeared in the *Morning Star*, 18 September 1867, p. 4, and on the following day it was quoted in a leading article, p. 4.

8. *Songs before Sunrise*.

9. On 23 September 1867 the prime minister Urbano Rattazzi ordered the arrest of Garibaldi, who was openly preparing an attack on Rome. Rattazzi acted to appease the French whose garrison protected the Pope. Although Garibaldi escaped on 20 October, his advance on Rome was abortive, and he was re-arrested in early November. Not until 1870, during the French defeat at the hands of Prussia, did Napoleon III withdraw his troops from Rome. Victor Emanuel took possession of the city as the capital of Italy on 2 July 1871.

10. "Mr. Swinburne's Poetry," 28 September 1867, pp. 641-44, signed "H.N.O." Swinburne's "moral and intellectual nature is ... deeply tainted by the false conceptions which underlie the whole of his poetry."

11. In "Mr. Arnold's New Poems" (*Fortnightly Review*, 8 [October 1867], 414-45) Swinburne called CGR's *Passing Away* "the noblest of sacred poems in the language," and WBS's *Year of the World* "that wise and noble poem."

12. Nine phrases were omitted (see Morton Paley, "John Camden Hotten and the First British Editions of Walt Whitman," *Publishing History*, 6 [1979], 23-24, where they are listed).

129. TO ALGERNON CHARLES SWINBURNE

Somerset House,
29 October [1867]

Dear Swinburne,

That most grovelling of publications the *Broadway*[1] wrote to me some fortnight ago, asking me to contribute. I declined, instancing their prospectus as of itself enough to warn off any human writer. The Editor (Routledge) now tells me that the character of the Magazine is being altered,[2] and that various mighty writers ranging in calibre between Algernon Swinburne and Tom Taylor or Gerald Massey, are being invited. May I ask how this matter stands with you? *If* the Magazine becomes the converse of its heretofore self, and *if* you or other right men write in it, I of course should have no objection. But these are considerable *Ifs*, and without them I might probably decline again.

If I do send anything, I am thinking of beginning with that old Coroner's Inquest affair[3] — though indeed it is a chance whether they would take it, as what they *ask* me for is of course different sort of work. I am looking it through, finding (as I knew I should) that any 2 lines out of 3 need some amount of modification — especially for rhythm. I would not put my name to it (unless opportunity were given for fully explaining about date etc. etc.): but would probably give my initials.

I read Buchanan on Whitman:[4] not adequate, but calculated to do more good than harm. My Selection will progress to publication in due course.

Of course you are thinking more now about Garibaldi and Mazzini than anything else: so am I. There are stupendous possibilities half tangible in the air — downfall of Pope, Napoleon, and Italian Monarchy, and Republics in Italy and France.[5] But

> The Gods very subtly fashion
> Sadness with madness upon earth[6] —

and one can only hope, scarcely even guess. The equally glorious alternative that I suppose most of his friends now wish Garibaldi is either to proclaim with Mazzini a Republic in Rome, or to be killed: and I could almost find it in my heart to wish that the manner of his death were military execution by the soldiers of Victor Emanuel, so sublime and appalling would that martyrdom be, and its probable consequences so fulminating. But no doubt this is so unlikely as to be practically impossible.

Yours always,
W. M. Rossetti

MS: BL.

1. A monthly journal which began publication in September 1867 under the editorship of George Routledge's son, Edmund, who had become a partner in his father's firm in 1865. MS. Diary, 14 December 1867: "The regular price, for prose articles of any length, is £1. a page.... [Routledge] says the *Broadway* is commercially a great success — 40,000 per month circulation."

2. MS. Diary, 21 October 1867: "The Editor of the *Broadway* writes to me a second time (I declined the first) asking me to contribute. He says he is dropping the extra light character of the Magazine, and has invited Swinburne, Ruskin, Meredith, etc., to join."

3. *Mrs. Holmes Grey*, which appeared signed, dated 1849, and with a note explaining its origin in the early days of the PRB. WMR also contributed "Ruskin as a Writer on Art," March 1868, pp. 48-59.

4. *Broadway*, November 1867, pp. 188-95, a review of *Leaves of Grass* 1867.

5. See Letter 128, Note 9.

6. *Atalanta in Calydon*, ll. 1055-56. Swinburne wrote "Madness with sadness."

130. TO ALEXANDER ("ALECCO") IONIDES[1]

56 Euston Square,
17 November [1867]

Dear Mr. Ionides,

It happens unfortunately that a Neapolitan friend[2] of ours, who asked my sister when he could conveniently call, has been (*before* your note reached me) asked for Tuesday, so that it will not be practicable for me to absent myself. I should have much liked to meet again all of your family, as well as Sir Peter Braila,[3] to whom would you kindly present my respects and remembrances.

God be praised, Crete[4] seems going on with a degree of hopeful prospect proportioned to her heroism. Where is now the glorious news of total subjection of the Islanders with which a magnanimous British press regaled the ears of the Sultan as he quitted our shores? When I think of Crete, I am but too sadly compelled to blush for Italy — chiefly for her recreant government, and partly for herself as well.

With best regards to all,

Yours very truly,
W. M. Rossetti

MS: Harvard.

1. (1840-98), third son of Alexander Constantine Ionides, is the "tall young Greek" in George du Maurier's *Trilby* (1894).
2. Not identified.
3. 14 March 1867: "Alecco Ionides having invited me to be introduced to the new Greek Minister, Sir Peter Braila, I called on the latter" (Diary, *RP*, p. 226).
4. The Cretan insurrection against Turkish rule lasted from 1866 to 1868, during which the Sultan of Turkey, Abdul Aziz, visited England in July 1867. After the suppression of the insurrection Turkey granted the island limited autonomy.

131. TO WALT WHITMAN[1]

56 Euston Square,
15 November [1867]

My dear Sir,

Allow me with the deepest reverence and true affection to thank you for the copy of your complete poems[2] I have just received from you through our excellent friend Mr. Conway — and still more for the accompanying letter to him, in which you authorize me to make, in the forthcoming London issue of your poems, such verbal changes as may appear to me indispensable to meet the requirements of publicity in this country and time.[3]

I feel greatly honoured by your tolerance extended to me in this respect, and assure you that, if such a permission can in the nature of things be used rightly, it shall not be abused by me.

My Selection was settled more than a month ago, and is now going through the press. The only writing of yours from which I thought it at all admissible (with your consent applied for through Mr. Conway) to cut anything out was the prose preface to the first *Leaves of Grass*. As for the *poems*, I felt bound not to tamper with their integrity in any the slightest degree, and therefore any of them which appeared to contain matter startling to the length of British ears have been entirely excluded. But now, after your letter, it seems to me that all or most of these poems, with some minimum of verbal modification or excision, may very properly be included: and indeed that there is nothing to prevent a reprint of the revised copy of your complete poems (which you sent to Mr. Conway) coming out at once, *instead* of the mere Selection — subject only to modification or excision here and there as above named. Of course I would explain in print that the responsibility of this shabby job belongs to me — fortified only by your abstaining from prohibiting it; for such a prohibition would be sacred to me.

I have just written in this sense to the publisher Mr. Hotten.[4] I cannot clearly anticipate whether or not he will be disposed thus to sacrifice his outlay hitherto on the Selection, and embark at once on the complete edition.[5] If he does, it will please me all the better. I shall always hold it one of the truest and most prized distinctions of my writing career to be associated, in however modest a capacity, with the works of so great a poet and noble-hearted a man as you. The time is fast coming, here as elsewhere, when to be one of your enthusiastic admirers will only be to be one of the many: I shall remember, with a degree of self-congratulation, that in 1855 I was one of the few.

Dear Sir, believe me,
Most respectfully and truly yours
W. M. Rossetti

MS: LC. Published: *WWC*, 3:299-301.

1. Of WMR's twenty-four known letters to Whitman most are business-like discussions of *PWW*, or the subscriptions that he organized for the poet in 1876 and 1885. At all times he addressed Whitman with the deference due to the great poet of democratic and republican ideals. Although he admired Whitman from a distance, given his abiding tolerance of Swinburne or Trelawny or Joaquin Miller, there is no reason to think that closer contact would have diminished his regard. On the other hand, his patience with Whitmania was limited. On 14 December 1897 he wrote to Grace Gilchrist: "The name and fame of Whitman seem to be blazoning themselves forth more and more — as they ought to: but somehow I scarcely ever see anything written about him in what appears to me a right tone. Frothy and flaring laudation abounds: but to express in reasonable terms the reasonable, solid, and lofty homage to which his writings are entitled seems a very rare accomplishment" (LC).

2. See Letter 127, Note 4.

3. Whitman's countenancing of omissions from the preface to *Leaves of Grass* 1855 (*CWW*, 1:347) was stated loosely enough to allow WMR to interpret it as permission to alter the poems. But see Letter 133, Note 1.

4. He also offered "to forgo any remuneration to myself on the Selection" (MS. Diary, 17 November 1867).

5. Hotten to WMR, 18 November 1867: "If the *complete* poems did not make so bulky a book, I would gladly drop the 'selection' and do 'Walt Whitman's Works,' but I have now announced in many quarters the volume undertaken by you, and I think we had better let it appear with a prominent notice on flyleaf (as at first suggested) that the Complete Works will be given if a sufficient demand is apparent" (AP). WMR declared in a postscript to the volume that "a complete English edition ought to be an early demand of English poetic readers, and would be the right and crowning result of the present Selection" (p. 403).

132. TO WALT WHITMAN

56 Euston Square,
8 December [1867]

My dear Sir,

Your letter of 22 November reached me the other day through Mr. Conway.

You no doubt will by this time have received the one I addressed to you 2 or 3 weeks ago; but perhaps it may occur to me to repeat here some things said in that letter. I think the most convenient course may be for me first to state the facts about my Selection.

Some while back — I suppose before the middle of September — Mr. Hotten the publisher told me that he projected bringing out a Selection from your poems, and (in consequence of my review in the *Chronicle*) he asked whether I would undertake to make the Selection, and write any such prefatory matter as I might think desirable. Proud to associate myself in any way with your writings, or to subserve their diffusion and appreciation here, I gladly consented.

I at once reread through your last complete edition, and made the Selection. In doing this I was guided by two rules — 1, to omit *entirely* every poem which contains passages or words which modern squeamishness can raise an objection to — and 2, to include, from among the remaining poems, those which I most entirely and intensely admire. The bulk of poems thus selected is rather less than half the bulk of your complete edition; and, before my Selection went to the printer's hands, I had the advantage of revising it by the corrected copy you sent some while ago to Mr. Conway. I also added the prose Preface to *Leaves of Grass* — obtaining through Mr. Conway your permission to alter (or rather, as I have done, simply to *omit*) 2 or 3 phrases in *that Preface* (only). Thus my Selection is a verbatim reproduction of a good number of your poems, unaccompanied by the remainder. There is no curtailment or alteration whatever — and no modification at all except in these 3 particulars —

1. I have given a note here and there.
2. I have thought it better, considering the difference of a Selection from the sum total, to redistribute the poems into 5 classes, which I have termed — Chants Democratic, Drum Taps, Walt Whitman, Leaves of Grass, Songs of Parting.
3. I have given *titles* to many poems which in your editions are merely headed with the words of the opening line.

The Selection being thus made, I wrote a Prefatory Notice and Dedicatory Letter; and then consigned the whole affair to the publisher and printer, somewhere in the earlier days of October. My prefatory matter, and something like a third (I suppose) of the poems, were in print before your letter of 1 November, addressed to Mr. Conway, reached me; and now the Preface to *Leaves of Grass* is also in print, and I fancy the whole thing ought to be completed and out by Christmas, or very soon after.[1]

The letter which I wrote you on receipt of yours of 1 November said that I was about to consult the publisher as to dropping the mere Selection, and substituting a complete edition, only with slight verbal modifications. This however, the publisher proved unwilling to do, the Selection being so far advanced, advertised, etc. Therefore the Selection will come out exactly as first put together; and on reflection this pleases me decidedly better.

I now proceed to reply to the details of your letter of 22 November.

If any blockhead chooses to call my Selection "an expurgated edition," that lie shall be on his own head, not mine. My Prefatory Notice explains my principle of selection to exactly the same effect as given in this present letter; and contains moreover a longish passage affirming that, if such freedom of speech as you adopt were denied to others, all the great literature of the whole world would be castrated or condemned.

The form of title-page which you propose[2] would of course be adopted by me with thanks and without a moment's debate, were it not that my own title-page was previously in print: I enclose a copy. I trust you may see nothing in it to disapprove — as indeed in essentials it comes to much the same as your own model. However, I have already written to the publisher, suggesting that he should decide, according to the conveniences of the printing arrangements, which of the two shall eventually appear.

In making my Selection, I preserved all (I believe all) "the larger figures dividing the pieces into separate passages or sections," but did not preserve the numbers of the stanzas, — the *separation* of stanzas, however, continuing as in your edition. I am sorry now that I did not meet your preference in this respect, and that the printing has already proceeded too far for me to revert to the small numbers now. My wish was to get rid of anything of a merely external kind which ordinary readers would call peculiar or eccentric. Parrot-like repetitions of that charge have been too numerous already.

I need scarcely assure you that that most glorious poem on Lincoln *is* included in my Selection. It shall appear with your title "President Lincoln's Funeral Hymn." I had previously given it a title of my own, "Nocturn for the Death of Lincoln"; and in my Prefatory Notice it is alluded to under that title. A note of explanation shall be given.

I await with impatience the receipt of your paper on Democracy.[3] It will find in me no reluctant hearer, as I have always been a democratic republican, and hope to live and die faithful to the meanings of that glorious creed. The other printed matter you have so kindly sent me I received two evenings back from Mr. Conway. The newspaper articles are new to me: with the publications of Mr. O'Connor and Mr. Burroughs I was already familiar, and I entertain a real respect for those publications and their writers.

Believe me, I am grateful to you for your kindness in these matters, and for the indulgent eye with which you look upon a project which perhaps, after all, you would rather had never been entered upon. I am in some hopes that your indulgence will not be diminished when you see what the Selection itself actually looks like. In consequence of the correspondence which has passed since the Selection was made, I may possibly find occasion to add a brief P.S.:[4] it shall contain nothing you could object to. If the Selection aids the general body of English poetical readers to understand that there really is a great poet across the Atlantic, and to demand a complete and unmutilated edition, my desires connected with the Selection will be accomplished.

> Believe me, dear Sir,
> With the deepest respect,
> Yours,
> W. M. Rossetti

MS: LC. Published: *WWC*, 3:303-6.

1. 4 February 1868: "Hotten tells me that the Whitman Selection is to be out tomorrow" (Diary, *RP*, p. 297). But see Letter 138.
2. *CWW*, 1:351; it was not used.
3. "Democracy," published in the *Galaxy*, December 1867. In 1871 Whitman combined it with another essay to form the pamphlet *Democratic Vistas*.
4. In his postscript WMR absolved Whitman of any responsibility for "either prompting, guiding, or even ratifying" the volume (p. 402). MS. Diary, 19 November 1867: "I sent to Conway, for his consideration, a P.S. I propose adding to my Prefatory Notice."

133. TO WALT WHITMAN

56 Euston Square,
16 December [1867]

Dear Mr. Whitman,

The receipt of your letter of 3 December this morning would have made me feel miserable[1] were it not that before then the matter had already been set right, and my letter notifying that fact very nearly (no doubt) in your hands by this time. My first letter to you was written too much from the impulse of the moment; and, finding soon after from the publisher's statement that the original plan of the Selection *could* not be altered, I felt that it was also much better it *should* not be altered. I congratulate myself therefore on being quite at one with you concerning that point. Not one syllable of any one of your poems, as presented in my Selection, will be altered or omitted: that is the first intention and the final result.

Pray believe me however that, while I understood the latitude your first letter honoured me with in its widest sense, I still meant to take all proper precautions before acting upon it. I wrote at once to Mr. Conway enquiring whether he put the same interpretation upon it; and his letter in reply (18 November, now before me) replies — "I agree with you that Whitman's letter gives you all the liberty you could desire." I am now perfectly satisfied that it would have been most undesirable for you to give or for me (even if given) to act upon such liberty.

To be honoured by your friendship is as great a satisfaction and distinction as my life has presented or ever can present. I respond to it with all warmth and reverence, and the Atlantic seemed a very small space between us while I read and reread your letter.

I read your paper on Democracy (received a few days ago) with great pleasure and interest. I have always felt — and did so markedly while our own recent Reform discussions were going on — one main truth involved in your paper: That, after one has said that such and such people or classes are not exactly fitted to make the best use of political enfranchisement, one has said only a small part of the truth, the further point remaining that to induct these people or classes into the combined national life, and to constitute that life out of them along with all other classes, is an enormous gain. The consequence is that, with the intensest respect and admiration for Carlyle, I find constantly that to acquiesce in the express views he takes of late years of particular questions would be simply to abnegate my own identity.

The Selection goes on smoothly though not fast — the proofs now approaching their close. I suppose the volume will not fall much if at all short of 400 pages. You may possibly have seen the advertisement of it repeated several times in publications here, as enclosed (slip cut from the *Athenaeum*). The ''Portrait'' is a re-engraving (head and shoulders only, I believe), of the one, in the first *Leaves of Grass*, which was a capital piece of art-work. I have not yet seen the reproduction, but trust to find it adequately done.

Always yours,
W. M. Rossetti

MS: LC. Published: *WWC*, 3:306-8.

1. See Letter 131, Note 3. Whitman wrote: ''I will be candid with you, & say I had not the slightest idea of applying my authorization to a reprint of the full volume of my poems'' (*CWW*, 1:352).

134. TO JAMES MCNEILL WHISTLER

56 Euston Square,
16 December [1867]

Dear Whistler,

I'll come in the course of tomorrow (Tuesday) evening.[1] At the first blush I think the course you propose a very right and handsome one — such as must evoke any latent sparks of chivalrous or generous consideration towards you in the Committee. It will moreover make your attitude at the meeting foursquare and impregnable: that you *had* a presentable answer to the charges, but declined to give it because you repudiated all Club jurisdiction.

More tomorrow.

Yours more than ever,
W. M. Rossetti

It was understood on Saturday between Gabriel and me that I *could* not be at Chelsea yesterday: too much to do.

MS: Glasgow.

1. MS. Diary, 16 December 1867: ''Whistler asks me to come to him tomorrow, as he is thinking of drawing up a statement of his case, to be handed to his proposers [Louis] Huth and [William] Boxall, and by them to the Committee.'' 20 December: ''Whistler set to with Gabriel's co-operation, and drew up a statement ... which Gabriel tells me carries considerable effect with it.'' See also Letters 136-37.

135. TO ALGERNON CHARLES SWINBURNE

56 Euston Square,
26 December [1867]

Dear Swinburne,

Your note to Routledge[1] appears to me the only answer you could return in substance, and the right one in expression. I have of course posted it. Indeed I think you would have been warranted in saying something severer, for if he objected at all to the stipulation in your letter of 19 November he was bound to say so at once.

For myself I await his reply to my letter posted by you. I suppose in all probability that reply will close our connexion: if not, there is still scarcely any likelihood of my continuing to write there, as my only and expressed inducement for writing was the improvement the magazine would receive from one or two new men, especially you.

Thanks about Mazzini:[2] the confidence is sacred to me, and I withheld *your* letter to me even from Gabriel, though showing him the one to Routledge, and Routledge's own, as he was here at the moment of my opening the packet.

I *shall* be at Chelsea on Saturday, and rejoice to see you. The Blake reached me at last on Tuesday evening. I read at it till 2 a.m. Wednesday, and again that day aloud to Gabriel all the time he was painting — with (to both of us) a renewed and always increasing sense of its singular excellence, and (to qualified readers) very powerful interest. My mother was delighted at the Dedication.

Your affectionate
W. M. Rossetti

No reply as yet from the *Chronicle.*

MS: BL.

1. About WMR's proposal to review Swinburne's *Blake* in the *Broadway.* MS. Diary, 18 December 1867: "Routledge says he will accept ... an article about Blake, if not more than 7 pp. long. This is an inconveniently short space, and I am not much inclined to accept: but, before deciding, wrote to ask Swinburne's preference." 21 December: "Swinburne leaves it to me as to writing about his *Blake* ... and intimates some dissatisfaction with Routledge's proceedings, which I cannot but agree in. I dare say neither of us will get on long with the *Broadway.*" 30 December: "Received a further communication from Routledge about the Blake affair, and wrote finally discontinuing my connexion with the *Broadway,* except that, if he likes, I am willing to finish the Ruskin article — to be printed as sent in." Routledge to WMR, 2 January 1868: "The book will certainly be reviewed in the *Broadway* before long, and I regret that yours is not the pen that will write it" (AP); it was reviewed in June 1868, pp. 723-35.
2. "Mazzini is so much better as to write in a 'healthy' handwriting and say — in confidence to his adopted daughter — that if alive he *will* be here in a few days" (*SL,* 1:282).

136. TO JAMES MCNEILL WHISTLER

56 Euston Square,
7 January [1868]

Dear Whistler,

Here is the note[1] I proposed last night: whether its insertion in the appendix would be *reasonable or advisable* I am by no means prepared to affirm.

One of the points I was thinking of yesterday, but which slipped my memory at every right moment, is the one put into words in the fly-leaf.[2] I incline to think that something on that point — and probably not more full or elaborate than the enclosed — would be apposite.

Yours always,
W. M. Rossetti

It may and no doubt will be said that, after all that can be stated and proved on my part, I *have* committed certain assaults, and that that mere fact condemns me. Now to this my rejoinder is a simple one — namely, that I have repelled any taint or suggestion of dishonour as involved in certain assaults, but have not repelled nor wanted to repel the bare fact of the assaults. [Fortunately[3]] The world is understood to contain some gentlemen besides English gentlemen; some codes of social honour besides the English; and some communities in which practices such as that of duelling, or the summary castigation of any form of personal insolence, are not yet obsolete. This may or may not be unfortunate or censurable, but a fact it is: and it is also a fact that I happen to be a Virginian, a cadet of the Military Academy of West Point, and for many years a resident in France.

MS: Glasgow. Extract in Rosalie Glynn Grylls, *Portrait of Rossetti* (1964), p. 228.

1. Letter 137. See also Letter 134.
2. The paragraph following the signature.
3. Deleted.

137. TO JAMES MCNEILL WHISTLER

56 Euston Square,
7 January 1868[1]

Dear Whistler,

I heard the other day with astonishment and a measure of indignation that it has been alleged or insinuated by some person or persons that you were the reverse of sober during the meeting of the Burlington Club of the 13th December. From direct personal knowledge of the facts, I hereby affirm that statement to be a calumny, and one for which there is neither the shadow of a foundation nor the fragment of an excuse.

Always truly yours,
W. M. Rossetti

MS: Glasgow.

1. See Letter 136, Note 1.

138. TO WILLIAM DOUGLAS O'CONNOR

56 Euston Square,
12 February [1868]

My dear Sir,

I am much obliged for your letter of 20 January,[1] and especially for the intimation it contains that Mr. Whitman expresses himself satisfied with the state of things concerning the Selection: to have done anything seriously *displeasing* to him in that matter would have been to me a perpetual regret. The book *ought* to have been out these 8 or 10 days at least, but as far as I know it is not out even yet. I expect it daily. All this, of course, is the publisher's or printer's look-out.

Saturday Reviews, Athenaeums, etc., etc., make it a great refreshment (to such a critic as myself, who regard criticism as a humble function indeed in comparison with any true development of poetic invention) to come into contact with so enthusiastic, unconventional, and penetrating a critical mind and temper as yours. I assure you that no admirer of genius can be too admiring for my taste; and, though perhaps you would go more systematically than I on the principle of expounding beauties without detailing faults, still I too should very much have failed to express my real meaning if ever I appeared to dwell on the faults to the extent of making them in the least a sort of set-off against the beauties — a debtor and creditor account — in the case of so aboriginal and transcendent a genius as Whitman, or even in the case of many a writer much less exalted than he is. Though I might state both sides of the question plainly, I should always hope to make it apparent that there is about as much difference in their relative importance as between the front and back of a pack of cards.

I gave Swinburne your message,[2] and have his thanks and very cordial greetings to reconvey to you.

> Believe me always
> Very truly yours,
> W. M. Rossetti

MS: LC.

1. Printed with omissions in *RP*, pp. 342-43. "And I" in the third paragraph continues: "entirely sympathize with the inspiration which determines the manner and method of the critical service you aim to render Mr. Whitman's work, acknowledging its probable superiority to any that can move to efforts so imperfect and inferior as mine have been" (AP).

2. "I pray you to convey my thanks to Mr. Swinburne for his gracious message. I never for a moment expected him to reply to my letter, which I would have felt it an impertinence to send him if I had not just read his pamphlet [*Notes on Poems and Reviews*], and remembering that he was then beset by 'the assassins of the great Reviews,' and the little ones as well, thought that perhaps some line in mine [*The Good Gray Poet*] might comfort him, and express my sympathy, and so ventured to send it with a note" (AP).

139. TO JOHN LUCAS TUPPER

56 Euston Square,
8 March [1868]

Dear Tupper,

Of course the Whitman is a presentation copy which you are to oblige me by accepting: you may have forgotten that, the day you were here, I told you I should send it.

I also consider that much fair exception may be taken to the semi-metrical form of writing adopted by Whitman — indeed I have always had an objection even to such comparatively formed rhymeless metres as those of *Queen Mab* or *Thalaba*:[1] still, I allow for all this, take the man as he stands, accustom myself to the semi-metre and find it by no means wanting in mastery on its own showing — and on the whole admire Whitman greatly.

I have seen Hunt twice lately, and shall again tomorrow. He still contemplates going abroad, but it may I fancy hang over a longish while.[2] I am sorry to say he is ill, and looks extremely so. His doctor (Gull[3]) *had* told him it was asthma and indigestion, but now he seems to incline rather to connecting the illness with Hunt's old aguish attacks. His looks are really enough to make his friends feel concerned and anxious; and they can't be ascribed to mere general depression of spirits and system — as he was looking better when he came first to London, and *much* better within a month or so thereafter. His *Isabella*[4] picture is very fine.

I did not know that Stanhope[5] was back in Florence — he was in London lately: but probably you have good grounds for knowing. There is one man who *might*, I think, be disposed to think of the Rugby project: he is not an "affluent individual," but always hard up and of sufficiently expensive habits. But he has a fancy and turn for mural or monumental work, and in default of commissions, might perhaps be willing to do the thing for Art's and fame's sake. His name is George R. Chapman[6] — mainly a portrait-painter, but a man of ideas and aptitude in designing: he has before now done some work of somewhat the same kind (this I have not seen). He is the extreme reverse of anything Praeraphaelite in execution — indeed as an executant he is never quite right from *any* point of view of style. With all this he is emphatically an artist, and adapted for carrying out a *project* of design. Age about 33 to 35. I have not consulted him about the matter, thinking it best to reply to you first; but would communicate with him if wished. A letter addressed to the Arts Club, Hanover Square, would find him.

Yours always,
W. M. Rossetti

MS: Leeds.

1. Southey's *Thalaba the Destroyer* (1801).
2. WMR noted in his diary on 2 August that "Hunt has been gone for about a month back, and is now in Florence" (*RP*, p. 321).
3. William Withey Gull (1816-90), physician and lecturer at Guy's Hospital.
4. *Isabella and the Pot of Basil* (Bennett 1969, No. 41).
5. After the death of Fanny Hunt, Spencer Stanhope and his wife looked after Hunt's son Cyril (*PR & PRB*, 2:202).
6. Chapman ("died towards 1880," *FLM*, 2:173) was often in the company of the Rossettis during the 1860s. His *Three Sisters Sang of Love Together* of 1866 was painted from CGR's sonnet *A Triad* (*Paintings and Drawings from the Leathart Collection*, No. 32). He exhibited four portraits at the R.A., 1863-74, the first of which WMR praised for "its sense of a high class of beauty, a quality in which it stands perhaps unrivalled in the portrait art of the exhibition" (*Fraser's Magazine*, 67 [June 1863], 792-93). For WMR's visit to Chapman's studio in 1872, see Bornand, pp. 209-10.

140. TO JOHN LUCAS TUPPER

56 Euston Square,
15 March [1868]

Dear Tupper,

What you say about the Chapman suggestion is no doubt well weighed. I incline to think that, were he to be invited and to accept (which latter is as yet of course as dubious as the former), some embarrassment would ensue to me. His work is certainly not the sort of work you *advocate*, and perhaps not what you would even approve or like. I may however add to what I said before that Gabriel says Chapman is, as a draughtsman of the figure, decidedly capable — vastly superior, for instance, to Stanhope.

I saw Hunt again last Monday, and was immediately struck with his looking less unwell than the two preceding times. He feels also some improvement. His doctor makes him take tonics 7 times a day.

Thanks for your present of Barraclough's book[1] (yet to reach me). So far as I can anticipate its character, I would certainly not venture to review it (indeed, am not writing *anywhere* at present — the *Chronicle*, which I wrote in, being defunct): I should probably be wrong about its deservings, and certainly ignorant of its relation to other work of the same class. If the opportunity of recommending someone else to review the book occurs — which I can't answer for — I will bear in mind what you say.

Now about Swinburne and "the adorable Menken."[2] As you query "Menken," you seem not to know who this adorable is. It is Miss Adah Isaacs Menken, an actress from America, who made a great noise in London 3 or 4 years ago as Mazeppa, and since in other characters. Swinburne has a liaison with her. I am told by A, who has it from B, who has it from C, who has it from Swinburne's landlady, that, Miss Menken having one evening visited Swinburne at his lodgings, he besought her to stay into or through the night; and that, she declining this favour, he seized her, pulled her to the ground, and was throttling her, and a policeman had to be called in. A small *gentillesse* of excited and thwarted affection: Miss Menken was verily obliged to run for it. About "sucking her real blood" and so on I know absolutely nothing — nor do I know nor particularly surmise aught of your informant. Family fairly well.

Yours always,
W. M. Rossetti

MS: Leeds.

1. Not identified.
2. For Adah Isaacs Menken's (?1835-68) liaison with Swinburne, see *SL*, 1:276-77. WBS to WMR, 5 April [1868]: "[F. W.] Burton tells me Woolner has been entertaining his friends with an account of a quarrel between Swinburne and the Menken" (AP).

141. TO MONCURE CONWAY

56 Euston Square,
5 April [1868]

Dear Conway,

Thank you for informing me of the articles in the *London Review* and *Express*.[1] I have ordered but not yet seen them. There was also one, very eulogistic, in the *Sunday Times* of 28 March. The one in the *Academia* was, I hear, written by a Mr. Robertson with whom I have some acquaintance.

That statement of Hinton's[2] about your "mythical" anecdotes startled me: indeed I could scarcely persuade myself but that it must have been some *other* article in the *Fortnightly* that he referred to. I hope Walt had no hand in the stupid denial of what every rational person must perceive to be perfectly genuine and correct — and what moreover reflects no sort of discredit on him. But nothing saps character so much as the commonplaces of respectability.

Yours always,
W. M. Rossetti

MS: Columbia.

1. Reviews of *PWW* in *London Review*, 21 March 1868, pp. 288-89; and *Express*, 26 March 1868, p. 1. The other reviews mentioned were in *Sunday Times*, 29 March 1868, p. 7; and *Academia*, 21 March 1868, pp. 277-79. For the *Sunday Times* and *Academia* reviewers, see Letter 142, Notes 1 and 2.

2. Richard J. Hinton (1830-1901) emigrated to the United States from England in 1851, and served in the Union Army, 1861-65. His article on Whitman in the Rochester *Evening Express*, 7 March 1868, contained (in Whitman's words in a letter to his mother) "some pretty sharp cuts about his [Conway's] ridiculous anecdotes of me & you too" (*CWW*, 2:30). Conway to WMR, 30 March 1868: "There is a curious remark about my article in the *Fortnightly* which indicates to me that W.W. is now so related to Washington Society, that the accounts of him when he was 'one of the roughs' are not so pleasant. My anecdotes are not 'mythical'" (AP).

142. TO WALT WHITMAN

56 Euston Square,
12 April [1868]

Dear Mr. Whitman,

I received with thanks, and read with much interest, the article by Mr. Hinton which you sent me. Besides Mr. Hinton's own share in the article, I was particularly glad to see in full Emerson's letter written on the first appearance of *Leaves of Grass*. Of this I had hitherto only seen an expression or two extracted.

Will you allow me to respond by sending two English notices of the Selection. The one in the *Academia* I find is written by a Mr. Robertson[1] whom I have met occasionally — a Scotchman of acute intellectual sympathies. The alterations noted in ink in his article are reproduced by me from the copy which he himself sent me: I infer that they are in conformity with the original MS., but cut out by a less ardent Editor. The *Sunday Times* is edited by a Mr. Knight,[2] of whom also I have some slight personal knowledge: I think the review in that paper is very likely done by Mr. Knight himself. The *Academia* is a recently-started paper, chiefly scholastic, and I suppose of restricted circulation.[3] The *Sunday Times* has no doubt a very large circulation, and a good standing among weekly newspapers — not being however a specially *literary* organ.

You will, I think, have seen through Mr. Conway the notice, also eulogistic, in the *London Review*. I am told of a hostile one in the *Express*[4] (evening edition of *Daily News*), but have not seen it: the *Morning Star*[5] (the paper most closely connected with John Bright[6]) had a very handsome notice about a week ago — but, like all literary reviews in that paper, a brief one. These are all the notices I know of at present. Perhaps I ought to apologize for saying so much to you about a matter which I know plays but the smallest part in your thoughts and interests as a poet.

As to the sale of the book I really know nothing as yet — not having once seen the publisher since the volume was issued.

A glance at the *Sunday Times* notice recalls to my attention a sentence therein which I should perhaps refer to — about your having given express sanction etc. Where the writer gets this from I know not — certainly not from me: indeed the P.S. to the Selection asserts the exact contrary, and I have not so much as seen Mr. Knight for (I dare say) a couple of years.

With warmest regard and friendship,

Yours,

W. M. Rossetti

MS: LC. Published: *WWC*, 2:123-24.

1. John Forbes-Robertson, art critic, journalist, father of the actor Johnson Forbes-Robertson.
2. Joseph Knight (1829-1907), drama critic, editor of *Notes and Queries*, friend of Swinburne and DGR. When J. C. Francis was writing his memoir of Knight, WMR recalled for him Knight's visits to Cheyne Walk in the mid-1860s: "he was then a remarkably handsome, prepossessing-looking man, free from any sort of affectation, open and amusing in talk, without being bitter or unkind" (*Notes by the Way* [1909], p. xxvi).
3. Published from 1 January to 6 June 1868, it was directed at the "large class of ladies and gentlemen ... engaged in ... educating the young, [who] have no special representation in the newspaper press" (1 January, p. 5).
4. "We protest not only in the name of poetry but in the name of common sense against these wild barbarities of an unrestrained imagination."
5. 6 April 1868, p. 3.
6. (1811-89), M.P. and orator.

143. TO CHARLES KENT[1]

56 Euston Square,
23 April [1868]

Dear Sir,

A perusal yesterday of the notice in the *Sun* of the *Poems of Walt Whitman* which I selected has given me so much genuine pleasure that I am tempted to express a little of it to you. If my Selection had failed in all other quarters (which however I find is far from being the case) in exciting that sort and degree of sympathy with Whitman's work which I would fain evoke, it had at least succeeded most signally with your reviewer — and the gratification arising from even one such entire success would of itself be sufficient moral compensation for any pains I may have bestowed on the edition.

May I add that I think, if your reviewer saw the complete works of Whitman, he would find that the "indecencies or improprieties" are not so truly blameworthy as he probably supposes at present.[2] The review very discerningly points out that, as regards poetic or artistic execution, the thing which a reader needs to give Whitman is not pardon for the thing done, but *concession* as to the scheme of work undertaken. I think very nearly as much may be said with respect to the indecencies etc. Once concede that certain subjects which old books speak of may still be spoken of in new books, and (in some instances) in the directest terms, and I don't think there is much further to be charged against Whitman. No doubt however this is a large concession for readers of the present day to make, and I have aimed in my Introduction not to over or under state the matter on either side.

Yours truly and obliged,
W. M. Rossetti

MS: Yale. Published: R. W. Peattie, "Postscript to Charles Kent on Whitman," *Walt Whitman Review*, 15 (June 1969), 110-11.

    1. (1823-1902), man of letters, editor, and from 1850 proprietor of the *Sun*. Writing of his friendship with Dickens, Edmund Yates remarked his capacity for "warm-hearted hero-worship" (*Edmund Yates: his Recollections and Experiences* [1894], 2:93). Kent's review of *PWW* in the *Sun*, 17 April 1868, [p. 2], further demonstrates this capacity.

    2. "Whitman has written things that his own most ardent admirers would willingly let die.... the Collective Writings of Walt Whitman must indubitably be tainted, flawed, polluted — and that, too, with a taint, a flaw, a pollution in no conceivable way to be extenuated."

144. TO WILLIAM DOUGLAS O'CONNOR

Somerset House,
4 June [1868]

My dear Mr. O'Connor,

I really don't know whether Carlyle has used that expression about Whitman[1] or not: I don't recollect ever hearing of it until I saw it in the *Tribune* paragraph. There are two things, the first of which appears to me exceedingly unlikely, and the second likely enough. The first is that Carlyle has ever made himself adequately acquainted with Whitman's writings. The second is that, seeing passages of them here and there, or having such passages retailed to him by word of mouth, he has jumped to the conclusion that the poems are grotesque eccentricities, and has expressed that opinion in some offhand way — possibly the words set down in the *Tribune*. I suppose no one alleges that he has ever *published* this opinion — only expressed it in conversation. If however you are correct in saying that "years ago Carlyle's opinion of *Leaves of Grass* was very high" (a point of which I know nothing either way), it is difficult to suppose that he has ever *spoken* in such derogatory terms. I should perhaps add that I don't know Carlyle personally — only by sight, and through the report of friends.

Besides the *Athenaeum* and the *Saturday Review*,[2] which you mention, there is one other paper of leading literary importance which has reviewed the Whitman Selection — the *Examiner*:[3] it spoke to much the same purport as the *Athenaeum*. There have also been several (most of them laudatory) reviews in papers of reasonable standing, but not having the same sort of weight in literary matters. One of these was most fervently enthusiastic — the *Sun*, of 17 April. Have you seen it? The notice begins: "Opening this book has been to us a revelation. Reading it has yielded us exquisite pleasure. The remembrance of it sweetens life." The writer of this notice (not personally known to me, nor having any knowledge of Whitman except through the Selection) is the Editor of the paper, Mr. Charles Kent.

The publisher of the Selection seems fairly well satisfied with its sale (I know not the details) — except that, as he says, *all* publishing business has been in a very drooping state these late months.

With my most cordial and respectful regards to Whitman, if you have the opportunity of conveying them, believe me

Always truly yours,
W. M. Rossetti

MS: LC.

1. On 9 May in his "From Great Britain" column in the *New-York Tribune*, George Washburn Smalley (1833-1916), whose firsthand dispatches on the American Civil War had brought him fame, deplored the favorable review of *PWW* in the *Athenaeum* (25 April 1868, pp. 585-86), and reported that Carlyle had likened Whitman to "a buffalo, useful in fertilizing the soil, but mistaken in supposing that his contributions of that sort are matters which the world desires to contemplate closely" (*CWW*, 2:30). O'Connor's letter of 20 May enclosing the column is printed in *RP*, pp. 355-56, omitting the following passage: "I can believe anything of Mr. Smalley, whose venom and mendacity are sufficiently established by the assertions of his paragraph, outside of this particular one" (AP).
2. 2 May 1868, pp. 589-90. Although hostile to Whitman, the reviewer noted that WMR "has on many occasions done good service as a critic to literature and art, but we cannot look upon his present enterprise as one in any way beneficial to either."
3. 18 April 1868, pp. 245-46.

145. TO ALGERNON CHARLES SWINBURNE

Sunday,
[12 July 1868]

Dear Swinburne,

Very glad to learn the accident[1] got up by the British penny-a-liner had less to do with you than with him.

I leave you my notes made when Hotten wrote to Howell.[2] They are mixed up with my own comments in an embarrassing way, but show that Hotten's proposals (which my memory testifies were accepted as they stood) included these points:
1. That Hotten should pay you 9d. for each *Atalanta*, and 1/- for each *Chastelard*, received by him as the then stock on hand of Moxon.
2. That, on books of yours published by Hotten, he should pay you ¼ of the published price of said books.
3. This ¼ to be applicable "after the editions now [then] in contemplation are sold out," and to apply to "all copies *printed*" (whether *sold* or not).
4. That Hotten would pay you 2/- per copy of *Queen Mother* then in stock.
5. That Hotten would pay you (as far as he could then calculate) £50 to £100 on an edition of Blake consisting of 1000 copies.

Your
W. M. Rossetti

MS: BL. Extract in *HLQ*, p. 47.

1. His fainting or fit (according to Philip Henderson, *Swinburne, the Portrait of a Poet* [1974], p. 142) in the British Museum Library. See *RP*, pp. 318-19.
2. At the time of the transfer of Swinburne's books to Hotten in 1866. The notes are presumably those referred to in WMR's diary, 4 February 1873: "Howell tells me that Swinburne ... has at last

found the notes I took on the occasion of the conclusive interview between Swinburne and Hotten, when the business arrangements were first made; which notes I returned some years ago to Swinburne at his request, and which he forthwith proceeded to mislay. With them, I believe the rights and wrongs of the whole affair will become much more apparent'' (Bornand, p. 236). MS. Diary, 7 November 1867: "Met Swinburne at Hotten's, to talk over the business relations between them — Swinburne having as yet received from Hotten only the stipulated £200 for 1000 *Poems and Ballads*, and £50 on account. Hotten will now send in a statement of sales etc.''

146. TO WILLIAM ALLINGHAM

56 Euston Square,
29 November [1868]

Dear Allingham,

You are probably not aware yet of a Shelley affair in which I am engaged.[1] Knowing you will sympathize in it, and possibly do something towards promoting its efficient performance, I am tempted to write to you.

In March and April last I wrote in *Notes and Queries* — solely moved thereto by Shelleian zeal — certain Notes and Emendations on Shelley.[2] As you may not have seen them, I will order copies of the Nos. to be sent you. Payne (Moxon) thereupon asked me whether I would revise a Shelley prior to a reissue: also whether I would write something by way of a Life of him, for which he thought I might be able to obtain from the family certain unpublished materials. The thing — of course I at once clutched at the offer to unloose in any form the shoelatchet of that most divine man — hung over a long while: but within the last month is coming to a practical issue.

As regards the Life, it seems on enquiry that not only is the conclusion of Hogg's book[3] extant (though withheld), but that Garnett,[4] getting some while ago into communication with the Shelley family, has been put in possession of sundry materials, and adheres (though Payne believes he will never actually *do* it) to the project of writing a full Life. I must therefore set aside any notion of doing that, and limit myself to a Life of moderate length and without special new materials — say some 100 pages — prefatory to the poems. For this I am already reading up. As regards the poems themselves, I have set to with a will, and already gone through *Queen Mab*, *Alastor*, and about half the *Revolt of Islam* — finding (as no doubt you will feel) lots of small things to set right. (I work on the one volume edition,[5] which, as well as the other two editions, is stereotyped: but I must do my best to get Payne to sacrifice one set at least of his stereotype plates, if the reissue is to be any real credit to anyone.) The early part of *Mab* I have considerably revolutionized by aid of the only form of the poem which Shelley himself ever *published* — viz.: the so-called *Daemon of the World*, in the *Alastor* volume. The original *Alastor* (belonging to Swinburne) has set a thing or two right: and in likewise the original *Islam* (*Laon and Cythna* — also Swinburne's). Besides mere alterations in the text, I write such revisory notes as appear to me really needed — whether for justifying the alterations themselves or otherwise.

Now I know that you have always been a genuine Shelley scholar, and fancy you may very likely have by you some notes or suggestions of which if I can get the benefit, I ought by no means to despoil myself. Would you let me know whenever convenient how you stand provided herein and affected hereto — "*pro majore Shelleii gloria.*" I need not say that I should be proud to acknowledge in the edition whatever advantages I may derive from you.

Is it not a glorious chance this Shelley editing and biographizing? Willingly would I, not only be doing it for pay, but do it for nothing, or pay to do it.

How goes the world with you? Shall we perhaps be seeing you about Christmas?

Yours always,
W. M. Rossetti

MS: Illinois.

1. *PWS.*
2. 21 March, pp. 301-2; 11, 18, 25 April, pp. 333-36, 357-60, 384-87.
3. Thomas Jefferson Hogg, *Life of Shelley*, 2 vols., 1858. Displeased by the book, the Shelley family prohibited his further use of their papers, and the projected two concluding volumes were probably never written.
4. Richard Garnett (1835-1906), biographer and critic. He entered the British Museum Library in 1857, and was Keeper of Printed Books, 1890-99. WMR met him through Patmore "towards 1855" (*SR*, 1:86-87), but they did not see much of each other until WMR began editing Shelley. Garnett, who published *Relics of Shelley* in 1862 under the auspices of Sir Percy and Lady Shelley, was inclined to instruct WMR in the official view of the poet, but their friendship survived this. After WMR's marriage the two families became intimate.
5. *Poetical Works*, ed. Mary Shelley, 1840. According to Letter 200 the two other editions "now current" were *Poetical Works*, 3 vols., 1847; and *Works* (Poetry and Prose) in 1 vol., 1847.

147. TO WILLIAM BELL SCOTT

Somerset House,
1 December [1868]

Dear Scotus,

Many thanks for loan of Shelley MS.[1] I am sure it is his hand: and (assuming you don't object) think of getting it into my re-edition in facsimile.

Couldn't leave Percy Bysshe Shelley for Alf. Wm. Hunt.[2]

You will find my notes etc. don't fly off into *meaningless* raptures about the divine Shelley — extreme as my enthusiasm for him is and always shall be. For instance the utmost eulogium I have yet bestowed on *Queen Mab* is that it is "not *unmitigated* rubbish." It would give me the greatest pleasure to show you everything any evening after Friday you will come up to Euston Square, and dine. Fix one if convenient to yourself: with or without Letitia and Miss Boyd (is she back?) as you may find most appropriate. This by the by is a very offhand style of hospitality: but you will understand it.

I have always forgotten to tell you there are at Euston Square certain Bewicks and things sent up for your inspection by Dixon — perhaps 2 months ago.

I was much gratified to find Gabriel looking up his poetry: knew nothing of it before that evening. Gabriel, being an artist and a rational creature would, if he loses his eyesight for painting (which heaven forbid, and I by no means reckon for) quietly dispose of himself by a dose of prussic acid, were it not for some extraneous considerations: and, great as would be my sorrow in that event, I could not and never do dissuade him, for I quite agree in the point of view. But, considering all that militates against that solution, his right resource is most manifestly poetry, and I have frequently urged it upon him.[3]

Yours always,
W. M. Rossetti

If you are anything of a Shelleyite, you know a most glorious stanza in *Revolt of Islam*, beginning "Peace in the desert fields and villages" — Canto 9 or 10. I wish you would look it up, and ponder the words

> lest some tongue
> Be faithless to the fear yet unbetrayed:

and tell me what you think of them at your convenience. I have a theory about them — at least a surmise.[4]

MS: Princeton.

1. Two pages of the *Revolt of Islam*, with WBS's inscription "Given me by G. H. Lewes" (see Sotheby's catalogue, 25-28 March 1929, item 524); reproduced as a frontispiece in *PWS*, 2. WBS presented it to WMR on 2 December [1868] (Durham).
2. WBS was "to dine at Alfred Hunt's with old Miller, P. Marshall and Donald Currie. You are to be there I hope to save one from the Scottish trinity" (letter to WMR, 30 November 1868; Durham).
3. See WBS's letters of 30 November and 2 December in *RP*, pp. 372-73.
4. In *PWS* WMR suggested that "fear" (Can. 10, St. 12) was a misprint for "few," but he did not adopt it as an emendation (1:485).

148. TO WILLIAM ALLINGHAM

56 Euston Square,
6 December [1868]

Dear Allingham,

Thanks for your response. I have (from Swinburne) *Laon and Cythna*, along with the *Alastor* volume and *Posthumous Poems*: also, strange to say Peg Nicholson,[1] of which he has just picked up a facsimile reprint: but it would certainly be a convenience to me to see an original *Adonais*, *Cenci*, and *Queen Mab*, and if your copies can be made available for my benefit in any way agreeable to yourself, I should be grateful.

Has Sir P. Shelley[2] abandoned Field Place?[3] Who are the *two* sisters of Shelley still alive?[4] The impression on my memory from reading Hogg was that only He*ll*en (thus the name is always given) was living. Where do they live? Do you know anything about the firstborn of *all* Shelley's children, Ianthe Eliza?[5] Hogg records that she survived at the date of his book, and was suitably married. I have a chance of seeing Mrs. Hogg — the Mrs. Williams of Shelley's day.[6]

I do *not* expect to find the sense of everything Shelley wrote reducible into a dry prose form: but I trust you do not dissent from me in thinking that, when one comes across a very tangled passage, one should try how far it bears unravelling — and, when across a passage that seems simply void of congruous sense, one should consider whether or not it stands correctly printed.

I have not much news of friends to communicate. Gabriel (you will probably know) has of late been the reverse of brilliant both in health and in eyesight. The former much brushed up by a trip to Ayrshire; the latter weighs of late much less on his spirits, and he has just resumed work. I am very much in hopes the mischief will yield to the general improvement in health. He has just been paying some attention to some of his old poems — which would be a good thing. Morris translating something from the Icelandic[7] (which language he had been getting up for the purpose). Scott doing a translation of, or book based on, Albert Dürer's diary.[8] Hunt at Pisa, returning now to Florence: when on to Jerusalem heaven knows: some works of his now at Gambart's[9] — just sent over. I only heard the fact yesterday, and have not seen them yet. We here at this house fairly well. Christina has had for these 3 months or so an unusual spell of soundish health: rather less good just at present.

Browning's poem[10] I have not yet seen. Must get it tomorrow. But I grudge every moment diverted from Shelley. I *am* to write a life prefatory to the poems — some 100 pages or so, which will contain a good share of what needs saying.

Your

W. M. Rossetti

You know Mr. Macdonald[11] died lately, rather suddenly? Georgie Jones has been down to his funeral.

I agreed (my own proposal altogether) with Payne to do all *editing* of Shelley for £30. I have no doubt this is moderate, and so he seemed to think. I at same time proposed to leave all question about payment for the *Life* over till that project should be more defined. It now is so, and I mean to ask £100. I fancy he may raise no objection, but can't say.

MS: Illinois.

1. *Posthumous Fragments of Margaret Nicholson* (1810).

2. Percy Florence Shelley (1819-89), the poet's son, inherited the family title and estates in 1844 upon the death of his grandfather Sir Timothy Shelley. In 1848 he married Jane St. John, and was ruled by her zealous devotion to the protection of Shelley's name. WMR did not consult them over his Memoir, knowing that they did not "view with much favour any attempts in Shelleian biography which went resolutely on the line of outspokenness" (*SR*, 2:362). Through Garnett he was given access to "some miscellaneous scraps gleaned by himself," and to a notebook containing unpublished portions of *Charles I*.

3. The seat of the Shelleys in Horsham, Sussex, where the poet was born. Sometime before Mary Shelley's death in 1851, Sir Percy and his wife moved to Boscombe Manor near Bournemouth. Allingham reported on 18 December that "Field Place is ... now let to a Gas-Engineer" (*RP*, p. 375).

4. Hellen (1799-1885?) and Margaret (1801-87). In later years they often visited Boscombe, where on 29 October 1864 Allingham "sat between them at dinner" (Sylva Norman, *Flight of the Skylark* [1954], p. 106; *William Allingham, A Diary*, p. 107). MS. Diary, 25 January 1877: "Shields, being lately at Brighton, has met there the two surviving Misses Shelley ... very slim and upright, and youthful in figure. They seem to look on Percy with some horror, mingled with early affection; appear to know little or nothing about his poems; don't court conversation about him, but will nevertheless reply freely enough to enquiries coming naturally."

5. (1813-76), daughter of Shelley and Harriet, married Edward Jeffries Esdaile in 1837. She visited Sir Percy and Lady Shelley for the first time in 1858, and occasionally thereafter (Newman Ivey White, *Shelley* [1947], 1:726).

6. (1798-1884), common-law wife of Edward Williams who drowned with Shelley in 1822. She lived with T. J. Hogg from 1827, surviving him by twenty-two years. WMR expected to meet her at G. H. Lewes's on 7 February 1869, but she did not appear: "Mrs. Lewes says she does come

sometimes, but not often'' (*RP*, p. 382). When he finally encountered her at Trelawny's on 13 March 1872, she "entered readily and kindly into talk with me on any Shelleyan subject I started, though she did not continue of her own accord to dilate on any such matter" (Bornand, p. 177).

7. With Eiríkr Magnússon, Morris published translations of the *Grettis Saga* (1869) and the *Völsunga Saga* (1870).

8. *Albert Dürer: his Life and Works* (1869).

9. Not identified.

10. *The Ring and the Book*, 1 and 2, 1868.

11. Rev. George Browne Macdonald (1805-68), Georgiana Burne-Jones's father.

149. TO WILLIAM ALLINGHAM

56 Euston Square,
14 December [1868]

Dear Allingham,

Would you kindly give me your advice on a Shelley question of some importance: With a view to which I post you a *Cenci* — *not* the copy I am fully revising. Would you let me have it back at your convenience.

Shelley, like almost everyone else mixes up *you* and *thou* higgledy-piggledy in dialogue. I don't know whether our family, through being used to the practical plying of both these pronouns together in their proper places in Italian, are more sensitive to the misuse thereof than ordinary English people: but certain it is that I regard the blunder as a very tiresome one. I *could* not often commit it — at least could hardly at all pass it in print — in anything I might have to write myself.

You will see marked in the *Cenci all* the instances (I think all) where *thou* is used: the residue is *you*. My own theoretic preference would be to make all uniform — and more probably by the use of *you* throughout, save in addresses to God, or in abstract invocations, as to Death etc. But perhaps this is presumption: it is sure to be so called by many readers. A medium course which I also think feasible is to stick to *you* as the standard, and keep up uniformity in immediate sequences — as in the same sentence or speech:[1] but without going the whole hog throughout the drama: especially leaving *thou* in some of the most solemn or poetic passages (though Shelley does not seem to do *that* at all on system). Would you tell me what you think best. It would have much weight with me — though I don't engage to abide by it if self-will drags me the other way.

I suppose one needn't pay much — or any — attention to what the personages, as Italians, would really have said in Italian. Were that the test, all the speeches addressed to superiors or strangers (as Beatrice to Camillo etc.) must be *you*: and all the family and intimate speeches and those to decided inferiors, *thou*. Beatrice to Cenci *you*: Cenci to Beatrice *thou*. His being savage with her would make no difference.

Always yours,
W. M. Rossetti

MS: Illinois.

1. "This I have done in a few cases — such only as are peculiarly flagrant" (*PWS*, 1:502).

150. TO WILLIAM ALLINGHAM

56 Euston Square,
20 December [1868]

Dear Allingham,

The *Cenci* etc. volume would find me perfectly ready if you and it are ready.

I also am opposed to conjectural emendations, save under very strict control of critical judgement, and with scrupulous respect for existing texts at all plausible. Into the text I admit very few, and point them out in notes, along with others which are not admitted into the text at all.

About Shelley and his sister, I think you must have rather misapprehended my point of view. I never proposed to be other than "reticent of surmises, especially painful ones," or to indulge in "guesses in the dark."[1] What I said (if I remember the phrase in my former note) was that, if I acquired the *certainty* or *conviction* (of course based on evidence) that so-and-so was true, I should think the proper office of a biographer would be to say as much. Neither did I say or mean that Shelley's passion for his sister (if it existed at all) was lust without sentiment. Thus much to clear away any misapprehension: but perhaps we still differ somewhat about the essentials. For myself I think that to give the world a *correct* idea of the character of so great a man as Shelley is — if the two things clash — an object of greater moment than the feelings of worthy living persons: and Shelley, who scarcely wrote a page which would not, or which was not intended to, ruffle some worthy living persons would, I apprehend, be the last man to uphold a contrary view.

As for Swinburne I shall certainly show him my text and notes when occasion offers: opining that nobody is better qualified to keep me in the right on these points. If my deliberate opinion differs from his on any point, I shall stick to my own. About the Life it may or may not happen that he sees it before publication — and will make no difference either way.

Much obliged for your advice about *Cenci Thou and You*. Gabriel said: "Make everything uniform": but I have not the remotest idea of doing that. I think however that if I find (say) one Thou among 11 *Yous* in one same speech, I must alter that: explaining of course in my notes. My impression is that characteristic negligence had much more to do with Shelley's practice in that matter than Elizabethan precedent: and indeed that the Elizabethan precedent is itself mere carelessness — When it is a case of jumble, not of *significant* variation.

I have been re-reading *Zastrozzi* and *St. Irvyne*. What incredible performances! With all thanks and greetings,

Yours always,
W. M. Rossetti

MS: AP. Extract in *RP*, pp. 376-77.

1. Allingham's letter of 18 December (to which this is a reply) is printed in *RP*, pp. 374-75, but the omissions mask that the subject being discussed was Shelley's passion for his sister Elizabeth. In one passage Allingham urged: "Let your memoir ... be mainly narrative, illustrated of course from the letters etc." (AP).

151. TO JAMES JACKSON JARVES[1]

56 Euston Square,
15 February [1869]

My dear Sir,

I have not got by me the Blake book to refer to, nor does your letter say whether the Christ of which you speak is a *half*-figure. Assuming that it is so, I think I quite understand what picture this is[2] — a life-sized head-and-shoulders representation of Christ, with an interwoven vesture (of olive-trees and signature I have no recollection). The picture which I have in my mind's eye, and which I first saw (to the best of my recollection) at Mr. Strange's,[3] is an indubitable Blake, but, so far as my own taste goes, one of the very last I should wish to possess. I saw it last 2 or 3 years ago in the hands of Mr. Harvey, bookseller and print-dealer of St. James's Street.

I fear I can't give you much valid advice how to offer this picture. My impression is that the small knot of Blake collectors already know the picture much better than they like it. Lord Houghton is the only Blake collector whom I know of: rightly to be so called: Mr. Linnell[4] and Captain Butts[5] having their collections formed through long-standing circumstances, and not adding to them now that I know of, and Mr. Strange of course not wanting the picture back — indeed, I fancy he has ceased to be a Blake collector in any sense. As to price, I fancy there would be a difficulty in obtaining so much as £15 to £20 from a Blake *collector.* if one came across a Blake *enthusiast* having little or no knowledge of what is admirable and what defective in Blake's works, he might perhaps, seeing so salient and important a specimen (for it is unusual in scale), regard it as a prize, and pay accordingly.

The above, I fear, is not very satisfactory, but it is at least sincere: if there is any other point I can answer, I would gladly do so.

I have to thank you for the kind expressions in your letter regarding myself: if it has been my good fortune ever to please you by any critique of mine on matters of art, that is a pleasure which you have reciprocated to me.

Would you remember me affectionately to Hunt, if you see him, and to my cousin. From the latter I received a letter some month and a half ago; and ought to have answered it before now, but have been peculiarly busy over a revision of Shelley's poems. I believe I shall now be replying within a day or two. It is just possible that I might spend a day or two in Florence in April, and might perhaps have the pleasure in that case of making your personal acquaintance: but it is very dubious.

Yours very faithfully,
W. M. Rossetti

MS: Yale.

1. (1818-88), American collector and writer on art. In the early 1850s he settled in Florence, where he formed a collection of early Italian painting (now at Yale and the Cleveland Museum of Art) and a collection of Venetian glass (now in the Metropolitan Museum). WMR met him through T. Pietrocola-Rossetti in Florence in April 1869 (*RP*, p. 389).
2. *Christ Blessing* (Fogg Museum, Harvard).
3. J. E. Strange, owner of a large number of the designs listed in WMR's catalogue in Gilchrist.

4. John Linnell (1792-1882), landscape painter, had been Blake's friend and patron.
5. Captain Frederick Butts, son of Blake's friend and patron, Thomas Butts.

152. TO JOHN LUCAS TUPPER

22 February [1869]

Dear Tupper,

I fancy the best thing will be that we should start for Italy as soon as you can do that — March 25; and that the 2 days I can manage for medallion should precede that. I propose therefore to come down to you on March 23.

Guido[1] makes an effective defence: the question is whether it is a true one — whether his alleged motives of honour etc. were his real motives. How about forged letters, domestic tyranny, etc. etc.? As I understand it, Browning considers that Guido's motives were the worst possible: but, in making Guido speak up for himself, he necessarily substitutes other and comparatively good motives.

Your

W. M. Rossetti

MS: Leeds.

1. The husband in *The Ring and the Book*.

153. TO WILLIAM ALLINGHAM

Somerset House,
12 March [1869]

Dear Allingham,

I will very gladly secure for myself the *Cenci* etc. at the enclosed price of £2. I would not like to give less, as I incline to think that, by offering the book to others, I could decidedly exceed your estimate of £1.

Post Office order — William Michael Rossetti, 56 Euston Square, to William Allingham, Lymington.

I am in an advanced stage of the Shelley process — and will indulge myself in a few details.

The edition will present the following arrangement —
Prefatory Matter (Mrs. Shelley's and my own) —
Long Poems, arranged according to dates (including *Julian and Maddalo*, *Epipsychidion*, and various others hitherto mixed up with short ones) —
Miscellaneous Poems, according to years —
Fragments, according to dates (includes *all* fragments, even to so important a work as *Triumph of Life*) —
Translations, according to authors —
Appendix, according to dates (Juvenile poems, variations, etc.: I omit nothing I can discover however rubbishy) —
My own Notes.

I have now done, broadly speaking, the whole of the above, and have begun giving the volume its final reading. A few extras however are coming in at the close — some scraps extracted by Garnett, and as yet unpublished, and (in my own hands, received from him) one of Shelley's MS. books which contains, I find, a considerable bulk of *Charles the First* as yet unprinted, and which I am deciphering — no easy job. Some notes and verifications are still needed; and the whole memoir has to be written. For this however I have made notes from almost all the books needing to be consulted, and have also recopied the notes in a tabulated form (a heavy task), so as to see what the various authorities say on the same particular points. The memoir is to exceed 80 printed pages.[1] Allowing for the interval of a month in Rome (whereto I start about 25 March), I am in hopes of getting the whole thing finished by about the end of June. I have now been sticking to it — I may say incessantly — since the middle of November; and I know the time has been fully occupied, though possibly the results may seem meagre.

I did speak to Browning about the work one evening in January that he was at our house. He responded cordially, but did not enter into the subject in the way of suggesting or discussing any special point of treatment. I have by me his introduction to the spurious letters.[2]

You know something of the Irish language, I fancy? and perhaps can settle this small point for me. In *Swellfoot the Tyrant* one character (known to be meant for Castlereagh) is named Purganax. This should be Pyrganax, I discern — i.e. πυργος *castle*, and αναξ, king, *rey*. Now I should like to know whether the *reagh* in Castle*reagh* really means *king*, with which Shelley thus identifies it:[3] I surmise probably not.

There is also *Peter Bell the Third*, about which possibly your memory for literary items might assist me. The facts — as far as I have a vague apprehension of them — are these. It had got about in the literary world that Wordsworth was about to publish a poem named *Peter Bell*. Before that appeared, Hamilton Reynolds[4] wrote and published a poem named *Peter Bell* by way of burlesque: after that, out came Wordsworth's *Peter Bell*, and some amount of confusion ensued as to which was the genuine work, and which the parody. Thus we have *Peter Bell* 1 and 2. Shelley treats Reynolds's *Peter Bell* as 1, and writes *Peter Bell* 3 as a sort of continuation of Reynolds's story, not of Wordsworth's (with which it really has no sequency), although he had by that time also read Wordsworth's. Do you know any other or more accurate details? Reynolds's *Peter Bell* is not easily found, I understand: I have as yet failed to trace it in the British Museum catalogue, and know of no one who ever set eyes on it.

Did you ever hear of a Miss Rumley[5] in connexion with Shelley? Swinburne (who hears of it through the family of Karl Blind[6]) tells me that a lady of some such name (Garnett says she lives in Plymouth) has a quantity of Shelley writings and items bequeathed to her by her stepmother (?) Mrs. Gisborne — among them the bowl mentioned in the poetic letter to Mrs. Gisborne; that Miss Rumley has already destroyed(!!) two other boxfuls of Shelley relics; that what remains are to go, at Miss Rumley's death, to Henry Reveley, the engineer[7] (son of Mrs. Gisborne) whom Shelley knew; that Reveley is on his deathbed; and that, failing him, the relics would come to someone else[8] who has promised to entrust them to Mathilde Blind.[9] It is not suggested that the MSS. include unpublished poems, but they *might* prove to be useful even in that direction. I have hazarded a letter to Miss Rumley, but have no idea what, or whether any, response is likely to ensue.

Yours,

W. M. Rossetti

I should have said that Garnett assured me the Shelley family give full permission for my making what I can of the MS. book now in my hands.

MS: AP. Extract in *RP*, pp. 429-30.

1. It is 150 pages.
2. *Letters of Shelley* (1852). Browning was asked to write the introduction by Moxon, who had bought the letters at Sotheby's. Their authenticity was questioned within weeks of their publication, and they were eventually traced to the forger George Gordon de Luna Byron, who claimed to be Byron's natural son.
3. "I am informed that it may *possibly* mean that, but more probably 'Grey Castle'" (*PWS*, 2:547).
4. John Hamilton Reynolds (1796-1852), poet and friend of Keats. Reynolds's and Wordsworth's *Peter Bell* were published in 1819; Shelley's not until 1839 in Mrs. Shelley's one-volume edition.
5. Actually Elizabeth Rumble, whom Mathilde Blind believed to be "a natural daughter" of John Gisborne (*Letters About Shelley*, ed. R. S. Garnett, 1917, p. 29). Gisborne's wife Maria had been intimate with Mary Wollstonecraft and William Godwin, and in 1818 the Gisbornes became friendly with Shelley and Mary. Despite Garnett's intervention, WMR did not see the papers. Along with a number of Miss Rumble's books they were auctioned at Puttick & Simpson in London on 28 May 1878 (see W. R. Thurman, *Letters About Shelley from the Richard Garnett Papers*, Ph.D. Dissertation, University of Texas at Austin, 1972, pp. 368-71). She bequeathed the bowl mentioned in Shelley's *Letter to Maria Gisborne* (11. 57-75) to the British Museum (*RP*, pp. 431-33).
6. (1826-1907), German political refugee and writer, came to England following the Baden insurrection of 1848-49.
7. (1788-1875), son of Maria Gisborne by her first husband, the architect Willey Reveley. With financial aid from Shelley he designed a steamboat for use on the Mediterranean, but eventually abandoned the project.
8. Probably Mathilde Blind's Plymouth friend, T. W. Freckelton, whose letter to Garnett about Miss Rumble's papers is quoted in *RP*, pp. 432-33.
9. (1841-96), the step-daughter of Karl Blind; poet, biographer, Shelley enthusiast, and promoter of higher education for women. WMR to Frances Rossetti, [10 July 1870]: "She ... is sister of the young man [Ferdinand Cohen] who tried to assassinate Bismarck just before the war of 1866" (AP). For long periods she lived with the Madox Browns, and after Emma Brown's death it was rumored that FMB wished to marry her (Helen Rossetti Angeli, *Dante Gabriel Rossetti: his Friends and Enemies* [1949], pp. 49-50). In *SR* WMR wrote of her "fine, animated, speaking countenance, and ... ample stock of interesting and pointed conversation" (2:388).

154. TO ALGERNON CHARLES SWINBURNE

56 Euston Square,
14 March [1869]

Dear Swinburne,

Thanks for your sending on my note to Miss Rumble through Miss Blind: I have as yet no further news concerning it. I mentioned to Garnett the other day what you had told me about Miss Rumble. He knew nothing of the details, but was aware of the existence of a lady bearing this or a like name, related to Mrs. Gisborne, and living (he informs me) at Plymouth.

Pending your reply about "Audisne haec Amphiarae"[1] I had consulted Cayley also thereanent, and he tells me it is a line quoted by Cicero (*Tusculanae Disputationes* 2, 60) from the *Epigoni* of an unknown author. My ideas about "Seneca the tragedian" are a trifle vague, but I fancy he could not be quoted by Cicero. Unless anything more conclusive turns up, I have given in a note Cayley's fact, saying nothing about Seneca.

By the by Garnett tells me — as a fact known to him by ocular inspection — that it is simply "the impious name of *King*" in the *Ode to Liberty*: a disappointment to an expectant antitheist.[2]

Garnett has entrusted to me a MS. book of Shelley, containing a considerable quantity as yet unprinted of *Charles the First* — I fancy nearly twice as much as the printed portion. I have deciphered the major part of it, and it will be an important addition to the book. The deciphering process (no joke in this instance) does not leave one's mind well open to critical impressions: but as yet I incline to think the poetry of this addition is not of remarkable calibre for Shelley: there is a very good speech however of a Puritan condemned to lose his ears etc., addressed to Laud and the other Judges. Also it is interesting to find Shelley meant to intersperse some speeches in prose — those of Archy the Fool: and one gains much more insight into the general treatment proposed. It had always appeared to me — from the references to *Charles the First* scattered in Shelley's letters etc. — singular that his total product on that tragedy should be so small as the portion yet printed. *Why* Mrs. Shelley gave what she did and not the residue I can't conceive: one part is as finished and decipherable, and as vice versa, as the other part. Garnett has also given me some miscellaneous scraps gleaned by himself. Here is a musical snatch — which I feel warranted in putting among the complete poems:[3]

> If I walk in Autumn's even
>   While the dead leaves pass,
> If I look on Spring's soft heaven, —
> Something is not there which was.
> Winter's wondrous frost and snow,
> Summer's clouds, where are they now?

Arrivederci,
W. M. Rossetti

What an astonishing power of perfect melody in very imperfect rhymes Shelley had — *teste* the lines concluding this letter.

MS: BL.

1. Shelley's epigraph for *Prometheus Unbound*, "Audisne haec amphiarae, sub terram abdite?"
2. Until WMR printed "king" (St. 15) the word was represented by four asterisks. Swinburne preferred "Christ" (*SL*, 2:7-8).
3. *PWS*, 2:273.

155. TO ALGERNON CHARLES SWINBURNE

Somerset House,
18 March [1869]

Dear Swinburne,

Though I have no more *inclination* than you to accept "the impious name of King,"[1] I do think you go too far in saying that the passage thus becomes "positive and absolute nonsense" etc. The passage about "the axes and the rods" (I speak without having the actual words of the text under my eye) seems to bear the following sense — which I think is clearly not nonsense, though it may be rather a truism or platitude: "The name of King, strictly regarded, has no more potency than that of President, Governor, or what not: yet a government regulated by a man named King, with the traditions of personal loyalty, divine right, etc. etc., becomes far more powerful for dominating and coercive purposes than another government otherwise regulated." Then as to the fact of 6 asterisks (or I rather think they were 5) that I should regard as of no importance. The book was printed without Shelley's ever seeing the proofs (even supposing, which I do not suppose, that he would ever have considered how many asterisks there were): and I think the asterisks, few or many, merely represent the printer's reluctance to print the *word* which he found in the MS. sent to him. That such an omission was even exceptionally pusillanimous I think true: but those days of Hunt's 2 years in prison[2] etc. etc. were very different from our days: *Swellfoot*, which is surely not *vicious*, was just about the same time suppressed by the Vice Society.[3] On the whole I can't satisfy my own mind that *King* is other than Shelley's genuine word: and at any rate as it is in his MS. I feel bound to give it. I do *not* myself (even apart from the *King* business) suppose the word to be Christ, but God: for the context seems to cover an area of time and place more extensive than that of the Christian religion.

Miss Blind yesterday sent me back my letter to Miss Rumble, undelivered to that "blot upon the page of fame."[4] Miss Blind's reason is that she had already started the subject with Garnett (and of course I think she acts as she should act under the circumstances). I happened to see Garnett yesterday. It seems probable that he could take some practical steps as to the Rumble relics earlier than I could: so for the present I withdraw from the field — writing today to Miss Blind to explain the precise state of the case.

I wrote some little while ago to old Kirkup with a view to Trelawny.[5] He has responded, but omits — what I most wanted — Trelawny's address. His letter refers to you and Landor, and letters or papers — some 50 — in the possession of Forster, but which Kirkup had asked Browning to get from Forster for your benefit.[6] "There are scraps in Latin and English, not published except in newspapers, that it would be difficult if not impossible to meet with. I could tell Swinburne much about Landor's affairs, and his treatment by his family, and by parsons and parsons' wives in England etc."

This may probably be my last missive before I leave for Rome: but, if I have done with it before going, I will post you the rough decipherment of *Charles the*

209

First — i.e. on the assumption that meanwhile I find time for duly transcribing it in its proper places of insertion.

Your
W. M. Rossetti

I dreamed of you last night. You and I had an appointment to meet at a Bookseller's in Holywell Street: but, on going to pick you up there I found you had donned the clerical garb, and announced your conversion to the utmost strictnesses of the Christian faith and discipline. This is not chaff, but a fact.

You (among others) warned me not to be done by Payne. As yet my business relation to him is satisfactory: for he volunteered — and has done it — to pay me at once ⅔ of the 110 total for Shelley: though he has never seen a line of my work, and only knows from my own assertion that I have done anything. Did I tell you he projects a cheap series of poets[7] — Byron, Scott, Thomson, etc., complete — which I am going to edit in a rather cursory way? There are to be a few illustrations, and old Brown will do those for Byron.

MS: BL.

1. See Letter 154, Note 2.
2. In 1813 Leigh Hunt and his brother John were found guilty of libelling the Prince Regent in an article in the *Examiner*.
3. This was either late in 1820 or early in 1821. *Oedipus Tyrannus, or Swellfoot the Tyrant* was Shelley's contribution to the extensive satiric comment on the trial for infidelity of George IV's Queen Caroline.
4. *Ode to Liberty*, 15, 3.
5. Edward John Trelawny (1792-1881), whom WMR visited on 8 June, Kirkup having written on his behalf. Trelawny welcomed him as the son of Gabriele Rossetti, whom he had known; but it was WMR's vigorous enthusiasm for Shelley and his willingness to adjust to Trelawny's "peremptory and dictatorial" ways (*SR*, 2:371) that was his chief recommendation. Over the next decade Trelawny lavished on him reminiscences, the loan of manuscripts and books, and gifts, including the Shelley sofa of Letter 294. WMR flattered him with the dedication of *PWS*, and willingly served him by carrying messages to Claire Clairmont in Florence or Gérôme in Paris, by preparing for the printer the second edition of his *Recollections of Shelley and Byron*, and by translating his correspondence with the custodian of the Protestant Cemetery in Rome, where Trelawny was to be buried.
6. See Letter 123, Note 3.
7. "Moxon's Popular Poets," twenty-one volumes, each with an introduction by WMR. The earliest volumes are dated 1870; they continued to appear in various formats and bindings into this century. FMB's illustrations to the Byron were supplemented by two by his son Oliver. Gustave Doré illustrated the Hood, but for the other volumes Payne chose uniformly undistinguished artists.

156. TO FREDERICK JAMES FURNIVALL[1]

56 Euston Square,
23 May [1869]

Dear Furnivall,

Very many thanks for the copy of your father's bill:[2] to see the original, after a copy made out by you, would be a work of supererogation. Was your father a surgeon or a Doctor?

Some days ago I copied out on the enclosed slip a few particulars concerning Shelley which I had jotted down from time to time as they came to me viva voce. Would you kindly read what is recorded as on your authority, and return me the slip, correcting any looseness or inaccuracy you may observe. If you notice the distressing statements set down concerning Harriet Shelley, I may as well say that no *authority* worth speaking of is known to me for those statements.

I should really enjoy a day with your friendly hospitality at Egham, but know I shan't make one out, so I had better not palter with the subject. I am writing at the Memoir of Shelley now, and it will give me close work for a while — and after that there are lots of other things to do.

I received with thanks the other day the Chaucer volumes:[3] they show lots of hard work on your part, and I often admire your powers and *appetite* in that line. My Chaucer work will turn up again one of these days, but Shelley and a little else must be got out of the way first.

Best regards to your wife.

Very truly yours,
W. M. Rossetti

Your father's bill gives "Iter ad Londinium" May 1819, and then some nipple-shields etc., and "sent to Rome." Shelley and his wife were never in London (nor England) after the spring of 1818: so what was "sent to Rome" was probably the nipple-shields etc. (not merely the *bill*) procured by your father in London at Shelley's request for a confinement of Mrs. Shelley taking place in Italy — the present Baronet. Your father must have been a long-suffering man to attend to this if his bill of 1817 had never been paid. But I suppose you are *certain* of that fact: I am quite certain of the facts *I* state.

MS: Huntington.

1. (1825-1910), scholar and founder of literary societies. WMR's association with him dated from c. 1855, when he began contributing quotations for use in the English dictionary planned by the Philological Society, of which Furnivall was secretary. In the 1860s WMR annotated *The Stacyons of Rome* and wrote an essay on "Italian Courtesy-books" for Early English Text Society volumes edited by Furnivall. Between 1868 and 1872 he prepared for the Chaucer Society a text of *Chaucer's Troylus and Cryseyde, compared with Boccaccio's Filostrato* (1873-83). But it was not until the founding of the Shelley Society in 1886 that they corresponded regularly, or that WMR had much experience of Furnivall's notorious lack of "tact or discretion in almost every relation of life" (*DNB*). As their Shelley Society correspondence shows, however, WMR wrote accurately in *SR* that "he always got on extremely well with Dr. Furnivall" (2:389).
2. George Frederick Furnivall, a prosperous surgeon at Egham, Surrey, attended Shelley and his family during their residence at Bishopsgate and Marlow, 1815-18. Shelley found him congenial and they exchanged social calls.
3. Beginning in 1868 Furnivall issued reprints of the Cambridge, Corpus, Ellesmere, Hengwrt, Lansdowne, and Petworth MSS. of *The Canterbury Tales* (Chaucer Society Publications). In the same year he also prepared for the Society *A One-Text Print of Chaucer's Minor Poems.*

157. TO ALGERNON CHARLES SWINBURNE

Somerset House,
25 May [1869]

Dear Swinburne,

Thanks for your note about Forster: I have not yet seen the book.[1] I understand you to say that he gives *no* particulars (such as I should be bound to look up) concerning Shelley and Harriet, but simply asserts that he could give such if he liked.

It is, I assure you, my full intention to state plainly everything I can find: he who comes to me for biographic reticence is (as old Shelley said concerning *Epipsychidion*[2]) like a man going to a gin-shop for a leg of mutton. Indeed, with a view to preserving perfect independence and freedom from pressure on all such matters, I have foregone the great advantage it would have been to me on other grounds to know the Shelley family. Through Garnett or Allingham I could no doubt have easily got into communication with them; but have avoided it, lest Lady Shelley should say (for instance) "Pray say nothing painful about Harriet: consider poor Mrs. Esdaile's feelings." Now I do consider Mrs. Esdaile's feelings: but I consider still more the right which rational creatures have to understand such a specimen of the race as Shelley.

Did you see in last *Notes and Queries* an objection raised to your remarks on "the impious name of xxxx"?[3] It is no particular consequence to you, but I am tempted by the allurement of the subject to say a few words. I speak from memory, but believe you advance one or two statements of detail which cannot be maintained.

1. There are *not* 5 or 6 asterisks, but only 4 (this is positive): therefore nothing to suggest Christ, but rather King so far as this goes.

2. The Reviewer (*Quarterly* article on *Prometheus*,[4] 1820 or 1821) does not in any distinct way suggest that the asterisks represent the word Christ. He gives the whole passage (including "the pale name of Priest") and pounds away at it as an attack on religion, but does not come to closer quarters with the details.

3. Peacock (*Fraser's*, 1860[5]) gives Shelley's Letter sending over to him the MS. of the *Ode to Liberty*, and referring to a passage (no doubt this one) which might perhaps be found alarming by the printer, and he leaves it to the printer's discretion to leave a blank or what not. Therefore whatever was done, prudent or absurdly cowardly, was the printer's doing; and one cannot argue, from *Shelley's* audacity in other passages, that this passage, being emasculated, must have been something singularly audacious.

Did you ever read Thornton Hunt on Shelley — in the *Atlantic Monthly* for February 1863?[6] It is well worth looking at. Did you ever see a poem named The Calm attributed to Shelley (as coming through Trelawny) in an early volume of *Notes and Queries*?[7] I gave it a hurried reading the other day, and think it an imposture, but must reread it.

Your
W. M. Rossetti

In one of your translated passages from the *Cyclops*[8] there is a line beginning "Sleek with love-locks." I am not sure, from comment and punctuation, whether this applies to the *man* or the *woman*. Would you let me know at any time that serves.

The French elections[9] seem to be going right — at any rate Paris.

MS: BL.

1. Forster's *Landor, a Biography*.

2. In a letter of 22 October 1821 to John Gisborne: " ... you might as well go to a ginshop for a leg of mutton, as expect anything human or earthly from me" (*Letters of Shelley*, ed. F. L. Jones, 1964, 2:363).

3. 22 May 1869, pp. 475-76, by C. G. Prowett. "Swinburne has been beguiled by an over-eagerness to call Shelley an ally in a little fit of fanaticism against Christianity."

4. *Quarterly Review*, 26 (October 1821), 168-80.

5. Thomas Love Peacock, "Unpublished Letters of Shelley. From Italy — 1812 to 1822," *Fraser's Magazine*, 61 (March 1860), 301-19.

6. "Shelley. By One Who Knew Him," 11, pp. 184-204.

7. 23 July 1853, pp. 71-72.

8. In "Notes on the Text of Shelley" (*Fortnightly Review*, May 1869) Swinburne corrects several passages in Shelley's translation of Euripides' play. WMR quotes Swinburne's translations in *PWS*, 2:591-92.

9. Paris and all the large cities voted overwhelmingly against the government and its "vice-emperor," Eugène Rouher, who eventually resigned.

158. TO ROBERT BROWNING

56 Euston Square,
30 June [1869]

Dear Browning,

Swinburne informed me, soon after seeing you a week or two ago, that you had seen the documents concerning Shelley referred to in Forster's Life of Landor, and that your account of them amounts to this: — That Shelley did, strictly and literally, desert Harriet then pregnant and the child Ianthe, leaving them with 14/- as all funds; that you have seen a letter from Harriet proving this, written in very moving terms; that Shelley was at the time really insane from the use of laudanum; and that Lord Eldon had viva voce assigned, as the motive for his judgment concerning the children, the fact that Shelley had left them to starve, and the grandfather had supported them.

I have now written my Memoir of Shelley, and wish to deliver it to the publisher within a few days. I have aimed to be perfectly aboveboard in it, stating *every*thing of importance, good or bad. I love Shelley intensely, and openly proclaim as much: but have no wish to distort or suppress a single fact. As yet I have treated the separation as (substantially) carried out by Shelley for his own and not Harriet's convenience, but without unfeeling abruptness. The information now reaching me through Swinburne would require me to make again a careful collation of all evidence *pro* and *contra*, and to set forth the result — necessarily modified to some extent.

Would you kindly inform me whether the account of your statements, conveyed to me by Swinburne, is correct; whether I may be allowed to use it at all; and if so whether I may cite you as the source of the information, founded on the documents referred to by Forster.[1] The object of citing you, if done at all, would of course be to show that the statement is unimpugnable, and coming from no hostile source. If you would like me to call and get your answer by word of mouth, I will of course do so: save tomorrow (Thursday) and Saturday, any afternoon not earlier than 4½ would, I believe, be available as far as I am concerned.

I have cited, as motto to my Memoir, a certain sentence out of your essay on Shelley (in the forged Letters volume) saying that his biography ought to be done at once and candidly: also, in the body of the Memoir, a passage of some length in which you express the quality of Shelley as a poet. I say nothing about the book whence the extracts come, but simply that you are the writer. I very much hope you will not countermand either of these citations:[2] for, when *you* have said something about Shelley, it would be an impertinence to replace it by the opinion of anybody else — more especially of the Memoir-writer himself.

Yours most truly,
W. M. Rossetti

Would you remember me kindly to Miss Browning.[3]

MS: Wellesley.

1. 4 July 1869: "Browning called to talk over the Harriet Shelley affair. Swinburne had mistaken him in supposing that he had seen the documents named in Forster's *Life of Landor*.... What he has seen is a set of letters from Harriet, then in the hands of Hookham the publisher, and some or all addressed to him.... He quite confirms the drift of the correspondence as stated by Swinburne; authorizes me to use the information, but would not wish his name mentioned" (Diary, *RP*, p. 401). See *PWS*, 1:lxxiv-xxv, xcix.
2. The motto remained.
3. Sarianna Browning (1814-1903), the poet's sister. After their father's death in 1866 she became Browning's constant companion.

159. TO WILLIAM DOUGLAS O'CONNOR

56 Euston Square,
13 July [1869]

My dear Sir,

An English lady,[1] a valued friend of mine, lately became acquainted with the Selection from Whitman, and I then lent her the complete poems. Her enthusiasm is so intense, and so clear-sighted as well, and is to me so very interesting a phenomenon, that I am tempted to send you a transcript of the chief relevant passages in her letters. I send it to you rather than to the great poet himself, because I should feel that any Brown was guilty of a kind of impertinence in telling him that some Jones or Robinson admires him — he is far out of the low sphere of such complimentary messages. But, if you see fit to show him the enclosed, I have no objection, but quite the reverse.

The writer is a lady of earlyish middle age, and more than common literary cultivation. She is a person of remarkably strong sense, firm perception, solidity of judgement, with a rather strong scientific turn. My impression is that hitherto she has cared very little about *poetry* — no doubt accepting and highly prizing the few supereminent men, Shakespeare, Milton, etc., but not being at all drawn by sympathy towards verse as a form of expression, nor familiarizing herself with the ordinarily good level of verse-work of our times. If I had been asked how this lady would receive Whitman's poems, I should have replied — "She will glance into them, set them aside in her own mind as eccentric unavailable sort of work, and never touch the book again." And see how utterly I should have been mistaken! The result fairly astonishes me.

I don't mention the lady's name, and would rather not be pressed about it: in fact I have not told her that I communicate her letters to anyone, with a possible

214

chance of their reaching Whitman. Were I to consult her, perhaps she would withhold her assent: although, unconsulted, she would (I have little doubt) not like me much the worse for what I am doing.

If you see Whitman, would you recall me reverentially and affectionately to his remembrance. Whitmanic matters seem to have been quiescent enough in England of late: but such an incident as that of this lady shows that the dry fuel may take fire any day. Conway I have not seen for some while past (having myself been in Italy in the spring): I saw it stated in print the other day that he was gone or going to Russia. I hope we shall see him back here some day, for I like him greatly.

Believe me, Dear Sir,
Very faithfully yours,
W. M. Rossetti

I hope this letter will reach you: the address I give is the last known to me, but of an oldish date now.

MS: LC.

1. Anne Gilchrist.

160. TO FRANCES ROSSETTI

Euston Square,
30 July [1869]

Dear Old Thing,

You and I are richer by £200 a year than when we parted yesterday: today I am promoted at Somerset House to be Assistant Secretary, £800 a year, with virtually certain prospect of being Secretary at £1200 one day.[1] This however would not probably happen for some 10 years or so to come. I rather think also, but am not certain, that my present position entitles me to 2 months (instead of 6 weeks) of annual leave. The matter has been in prospect or rather suspense for somewhile back: but the actual vacancy (by retirement of the Secretary) only arose last Saturday, and the result was dubious till today, so I held my tongue about it in my usual inexpansive style. This is the first time a Clerk in the Secretary's Office has been made Excise Secretary or Assistant Secretary, and there was much conflict of interests and views, but my scale preponderates finally. I have made no *solicitation* direct or indirect, so the result pleases me the more. I know the old Dear will be glad her goose passes muster as a sort of swan elsewhere than in the maternal bosom, and lose no time in telling her accordingly.

I really think I must begin now to set apart a definite portion of income annually for charitable purposes — perhaps £100 a year: the necessary proportion from each half-quarterly payment could easily be set apart, and the Old One could fork it out as almoner when occasion arises.

I bought this afternoon (7/6) a fish like the one Gabriel had gilt, but a good bit larger: am not quite clear where to hang it up, but some place will be found. It is a fine specimen.

Goodbye to the Old Dear, and love to Maggie. Hope you are comfortable — indeed Maggie's note received this morning is an earnest of your being so.

Your

W. M. R.

MS: AP.

1. WBS to WMR, 8 August [1869]: "I open this note again to congratulate you on your appointment to the Under-Secretaryship. My dear W., the right thing happens sometimes, thank God. In your advanced life you will not have to fight against the feeling that your brother died with his heel against the world, and that you had to sacrifice the 20 best years of your life in provincial obscurity" (Durham).

161. TO DANTE GABRIEL ROSSETTI

56 Euston Square,
23 August [1869]

Dear Gabriel,

I have been reading your poems[1] all the evening with intense pleasure: they are (as I know from of old) most splendid, and ought to be published without any not seriously motived delay. Some of the old ones, like *Staff and Scrip*, to which my memory was entirely faithful but rather blurred, are even better than I would have affirmed.

I have been interrupted in reading the poems, and will finish the evening by writing down a few points as far as I have got, rather than complete the mere reading. I have made various, but not *many*, press corrections, not needing any notification. I think (spite of any theoretic objection) that "once wert" is an improvement, and have introduced it.[2]

Page 4. I incline to prefer the line if it stood (cancelling "and")

We will step down as to a stream.[3]

Page 6. I would put a comma —

only to be,
As then awhile, for ever now.[4]

Page 14.

till an English word
Broke silence first at Nineveh.[5]

One may confine one's view for the moment to the excavations which brought to light this particular bull, and so justify *English*. But in fact certain French excavations (conducted I think by an Italian whose name I know thoroughly but it eludes me now) had preceded Layard's.[6] If you think this point of consequence, perhaps *Frankish*, or (if you reject that) *Modern*, would do instead of *English*.

Page 16. Egyptian mummies —

Even to some
Of these thou wert antiquity.[7]

This statement, literally accepted, is no doubt true: but you know Egyptian civilization and art are far *older* than Ninevite, and I think the *impression* from your passage runs counter to this fact.

Page 18.

> Eldest grown of earthly queens.[8]

The same consideration arises, and more unevadeably.

Page 21. *Ave.* I would retain this, and consider your note a most ample saving clause.[9]

Page 25. I think I should prefer the last line as simply

> Mary Virgin full of grace.[10]

Page 30. I would punctuate:

> "Fight, Sir," she said: "my prayers etc.[11]

Page 63. Here are lines of unequal length:

> Hast felt thy soul prolong the tone
> And deemed its speech mine own

and so on. I would indicate it by difference of marginal setting as above:[12] but have not as yet altered it, being uncertain of your preference.

Page 65. It may be a prejudice, but Luna (though clearly the right word) has a rather rococo sound to me. Hecate is less correct, but I think I would substitute it. Dian and Cynthia (perhaps you think the latter *more* rococo) might also be considered of.[13]

Page 65. I doubt whether the effect of the *long* lines in this poem is quite satisfactory to the ear — as

> So my maiden, so my modest may.[14]

They have the great value of specializing the lyrical rhythm — and, if you advisedly like them, you are probably right.

Page 81. Heart, soul, and voice.[15]

It strikes me that *soul* here weakens the climax of the last line.

Page 85. *Mary in Summer.*[16] I could not *recommend* its omission, but can't exactly dissuade. It is very pretty.

Page 91. I am sorry to perceive, on reading this Italian Poem[17] with a strict technical view, that several lines are decidedly un-Italian in metre. Your knowledge of the fact will confirm mine — that one can't in Italian go on the merely accentual plan of *Christabel* etc. etc.: every foot (barring elision of vowels) must be 2 syllables and no more. All these lines are peccant ones:

[a] E piangendo disse
[b] Dello stanco sole
[c] Le sia domandata

[d] Nè ci prendo gioja (possibly admissible in virtue of the emphasis of Nè, but I don't think so)

[e] E le braccia bianche

Page 92.

[f] E disse ridendo

[g] La state talora (I believe La might be omitted without linguistic untruth)

[h] Che dicesti (Disti might do)

[i] Io debbo insegnargli (omit Io which can only count as a monosyllable).

Page 91. The following are *grammatical* slips.

Le sia domandat*a*.[18]

It is not you see (structurally) Be she asked, but Be *it* asked of her. Now the impersonal *it* can't be feminine. I am quite satisfied of this, but Maria would be the right person to *decide*.

Page 92.

Lung' or.[18]

The adverb ora = now is abbreviable into or: but the substantive ora = hour (and this, I suppose, can only be the substantive) is, like all feminine substantives, not so.

Page 100.

He hath it still complete.[19]

Another question of marginal setting.

Page 119.

Thou knowest that in these twain I have confess'd.[20]

I would print know'st: perhaps you dissent.

Page 129. Rosebower (instead of ivory) gate.[21] I fancy you might still find something better than either epithet.

Page 147. *The Choice.*[22] I incline to the admission of these sonnets.

Page 147.

Care, gold, and care.[23]

Is this rightly printed? I think the *drift* of the sonnet might gain if you could make the speaker jeer against thought — any serious purpose in life — as well as money-making. As long as he prefers pleasure to that, he seems to be about right — and I don't suppose you mean he should so seem altogether.

Put in *Placatâ Venere*[24] by all means — at any rate, so long as the collection remains private. I must re-read the poem before expressing a distinct opinion as to publication.

I was going to send you *Tinsley's*,[25] but learned today Dunn[26] is doing it.

Warm remembrances to Miss Boyd, and love to Scotus. We had no idea till this morning that you were gone. I am heartily glad you are.

Your

W. M. R.

Mamma and Maria find Folkestone so favourable to health that they will remain there another week — till about Thursday week. *Rather* better account of Henrietta Polydore[27] this morning.

P.S. Page 16. I also rather doubt the phrase "a pilgrim"[28] as applied to these Egyptians. I understand it to mean what we should call "an art-pilgrim" — a tourist with an archaeological object. I suspect these mummies were innocent of such purposes — or at the extreme utmost would have "done" Egypt. Nineveh is very distant and alien too. If it is a *religious* pilgrim — as a consulter of the Oracle at Delphi for instance — I believe it is equally or more untenable.

MS: AP. Extract in *RP*, pp. 453-55.

1. DGR had sent his brother the "Penkill" proofs, the first of the six complete and two partial sets of proofs and trial books which preceded the publication of *Poems* 1870 (see Robert N. Keane, "D. G. Rossetti's *Poems*, 1870: A Study in Craftsmanship," *Princeton University Library Chronicle*, 33 [Spring 1972], 193-209).

2. *Ave*, St. 1. "Thou once wert sister sisterlike!" (*Poems* 1870).

3. *The Blessed Damozel*, St. 13. Thus in *Poems* 1870.

4. *Ibid.*, St. 22. Thus in *Poems* 1870.

5. *The Burden of Nineveh*, St. 3. Thus in *Poems* 1870.

6. Austen Henry Layard (1817-94) located the city of Nineveh during excavations, 1845-51. Paul Émile Botta, son of the Italian historian Carlo Botta, carried out excavations on the site in 1842-43.

7. *The Burden of Nineveh*, St. 11. "Nay, but were not some / Of these thine own 'antiquity'?" (*Poems* 1870).

8. The line does not appear in *Poems* 1870.

9. DGR wrote that he "hesitated much to print *Ave*, because of the subject.... Do you think the foot-note is sufficient as a protest?" (DW, 2:714, where the footnote, which was omitted from *Poems* 1870, is quoted).

10. *Ave*, St. 7. "O Mary Virgin, full of grace!" (*Poems* 1870).

11. *The Staff and Scrip*, St. 15. Thus in *Poems* 1870.

12. *A Little While*. Three different marginal settings are used in *Poems* 1870.

13. *Plighted Promise*. "Have you seen Aurora fly" (*Poems* 1870).

14. *Ibid.* "So my maiden, so my plighted may" (*Poems* 1870).

15. *Love-Lily*. "Mind" replaced "soul" in *Poems* 1870. The last line reads: "Nor Love her body from her soul."

16. Not published until *Works*.

17. Beginning "La bella donna," which DGR later used in *A Last Confession*. Lower-case letters have been added in square brackets in front of the lines that WMR objected to. DGR omitted "E" from (a); retained (b), (d), (e), (g), (h), and (i); and revised (f) to read "E riprese ridendo" (*Poems* 1870). For (c), see Note 18.

18. This does not appear in *Poems* 1870.

19. *My Father's Close*.

20. *The Love-moon* (*The House of Life*). Thus in *Poems* 1870.

21. *Secret Parting* (*The House of Life*). "Her kisses faltered at their ivory gate" was revised: "Her tremulous kisses faltered at love's gate" (*Poems* 1870).

22. Three sonnets of *The House of Life* included in *Poems* 1870.

23. *The Choice*, Sonnet 1. "Vain gold, vain lore" in *Poems* 1870. No other revisions were made.

24. Entitled *Nuptial Sleep* (*The House of Life*) in *Poems* 1870.

25. An article on CGR by H. Buxton Forman appeared in *Tinsley's Magazine*, 5 (August 1869), 59-67. Forman's articles on DGR and WMR followed in September and October.

26. Henry Treffry Dunn (1838-99), DGR's studio assistant, was most often employed in attempting to organize Cheyne Walk. After DGR's death WMR found him both helpful and provoking in the complex task of settling DGR's estate. Dunn's alcoholism is noted in MS. Diary, 26 August 1885, after which WMR seldom mentions him. Towards the end of Dunn's life he was cared for by Theodore Watts-Dunton (see Gale Pedrick, *Life with Rossetti* [1964], pp. 227-28).

27. Daughter (d. 1874) of Frances Rossetti's brother, Henry Polydore.

28. *The Burden of Nineveh*, St. 11. "An alien" was substituted in *Poems* 1870.

162. TO DANTE GABRIEL ROSSETTI

56 Euston Square,
[24 August 1869]

Dear Gabriel,

I have just finished the proofs.

Page 157. I don't quite like

Many years, many months, and many days.[1]

If I remember right, there used to be a particular number given; which I think better in effect, though perhaps too mannered. I'm not sure but that I should prefer

For certain years and certain months and days.

Page 167. *Difficult* rhymes with *occult*.[2] It is a *class* of looseness I dislike: but I don't at all boggle at the effect here, and only mention the point in case you should never have noticed it before.

Page 169.

Life touching lips with Immortality.[3]

A very fine line: but I almost think I like the old original one best, as related to the picture. This new one seems to trench a little too much on the Ideal — which is not to me at all the effect of the picture, but only poetry by way of intensity, or one might say *saturation* — and the old line realized that.

Page 174. "May'st" occurred here.[4] I have changed this and cognate words — for instance "might'st" — into mayst and mightst: but, having got so far in the proofs, I find your spelling so systematically adopted that I infer you may like it best possibly. I decidedly prefer mine, and consider it strictly (not by any licence) right, and perhaps the *more* right of the two. In *Hand and Soul* I observe my method generally prevails in this matter: but once there is "mayest," which I think very dubiously permissible. I have made it *mayst* (p. 213).

Page 175.

Unto God's will she brought devout respect.[5]

There is something prosaic in this line, I think. I am certain it has tribulated you much, and probably you are not yourself satisfied with it.

Page 177. Venus Verticordia.[6] I think this title has been discussed with you before. Lemprière makes a very startling statement. "Venus was also surnamed ... Verticordia, because she could turn the hearts of women to cultivate chastity."

220

If this is at all correct, it is clear that the Verticordian Venus is, technically, just the contrary sort of Venus from the one you contemplate — she must be a phase of Venus Urania.

Page 185. The Bullfinch.[7] I would put it in: it is good, and relieves the *tension* of the collection. I don't however quite like the phrases "Brave head and kind," and "I felt made strong."

Placatâ Venere — should go in, even in a published form. For that, I think you might *perhaps* reconsider the title — which appears to me a nearer approach to indecorum than anything in the sonnet itself.

Page 199.[8] "Their crucifixes and *addolorate*.[9] I will not answer for it, but this sounds to me rather anachronistic. I am not sure that you would find *any* addolorata at these early dates, and am pretty confident such a treatment is not *characteristic* of the time. The Virgin with 7 swords stuck through her heart, and all that sort of thing, I think, is late: it smacks to me of Jesuitism, St. Theresa, etc.

Page 200. "The gallery at Florence." Better say "the *Pitti* Gallery"[10] (as further on). The Uffizi is fully as famous a gallery: the one most thronged with archaisms is the Accademia — but the collection is *comparatively* small. There would be very few archaisms in the Pitti, but I suppose some — am not very sure. Several in Uffizi.

Page 201. "Shown into the study of the famous artist."[11] This also has rather a modern sound to me: perhaps arbitrarily so.

Pages 202 and 207. "Church of San Rocco."[12] *Must* be changed: this Saint was not yet born — died in 1322.

Page 203. Frescoes.[13] Scotus (if I remember right) maintains there are *no* frescoes of this early period — only distempers. You might consult with him.

Page 206. Chiaro's model. Perhaps these early men did sometimes paint from bespoken models: it does not sound to me *characteristic*.[14]

Page 209. A sentence begins "Am I not," and has no ? The place to put the ? is not very evident, yet I think it should come somewhere.[15]

Page 216 (note). "The year just over"[16] should perhaps now be more clearly defined.

This finishes my budget. You will thank me for one or two corrections of misprints — especially a second r to *ir*retrievable in the Sibylla sonnet — and mirrored instead of mirro*w*ed on page 215 — etc.

Mamma sent Christina your letter about Miss Losh's architectural works etc.:[17] they must be very interesting, and ought to be properly recorded in print by some expert.

Love at Penkill from

Your

W. M. Rossetti

Today is delightfully hot again here, and I trust you are getting the benefit of it.

MS: AP. Extract in *RP*, pp. 455-57.

1. *Retro Me, Sathana* (*The House of Life*). "For certain years, for certain months and days" in *Poems* 1870.

2. *For Our Lady of the Rocks, by Leonardo.* Thus in *Poems* 1870.

3. *For a Venetian Pastoral, by Giorgione.* Thus in *Poems* 1870.

4. *For Ruggiero and Angelica, by Ingres.* "Mayst" in *Poems* 1870.

5. *Mary's Girlhood (For a Picture).* Thus in *Poems* 1870.

6. *Venus (For a Picture)* in *Poems* 1870.

7. Published with the title *Beauty and the Bird* in *Poems* 1870. The two phrases were revised.

8. The rest of the letter concerns *Hand and Soul*, which was not included in *Poems* 1870. The readings queried by WMR correspond to those in *Germ* 1, with the exception of "Page 201. Shown" (possibly a misreading by WMR) which is "shewn" in the *Germ*. When WMR published the tale in *Collected Works* (1886), he followed a copy which incorporated most of his suggestions.

9. "Their labours" in *Collected Works*.

10. Thus in *Collected Works*.

11. "Stood among the works of the famous artist" (*Collected Works*).

12. "Church of San Petronio" (*Collected Works*).

13. "Paintings in fresco" changed to "wall-paintings"; "portions of a fresco" to "portions of a picture" (*Collected Works*).

14. Thus in *Collected Works*.

15. "Am I not as a cloth drawn before the light, that the looker may not be blinded? but which sheweth thereby the grain of its own coarseness ... " (*Collected Works*).

16. "The catalogue of the year just over" was changed to "the latest catalogues" (*Collected Works*).

17. DW, 2:715-17. On his way to Penkill DGR had stayed with Alice Boyd's cousin Miss Losh (d. 1872) near Carlisle. The architectural works, principally the church of St. Mary, Wreay, were by Sara Losh (1785-1853), described by DGR as "the head of the family about the year 1830."

163. TO DANTE GABRIEL ROSSETTI

Euston Square,
28 August [1869]

Dear Gabriel,

A few words in reply to yours of Thursday.

I had a suspicion, but not distinct idea, that your Italian versification might be based on some analogy of very old poems. Have now looked (very slightly as yet, but will continue, and write further about it) into some old Italian poems. As yet I find no confirmation of your view in any save *very* old poems: in some of these apparent — but I think only *apparent* — confirmation. For instance, Odo delle Colonne,[1] 1245:

> Distretto core e amoroso
> Gioioso mi fa cantare
> E certo s'io son pensoso
> Non è da maravigliare.

My own belief is however that these irregularities are not of the *accentual-equivalent* class of yours, but reducible to 2 heads — non-elision of vowels, and rapid transition from iambic to trochaic structure. I scan thus:

> Distrét/to cór e á/moró/so
> Gióio/só mi/ fá can/táre
> E cér/to s'í/o són/ pensó/so
> Nón è/ dá ma/rávi/gliáre.

No doubt the trochees of 2 and 4 (particularly 2) are *arbitrary* trochees, not conformable to at any rate modern accentuation: still, I understand them to be theoretic trochees. One might say the same of your line

$$\text{É dis/sé ri/déndo}^2$$

but I don't think it could be *justified* at the present day.

It has struck me that *both* the objections I stated to

$$\text{Le sia domandata}^3$$

would be got over if you think fit to write

$$\text{Le ho domandata:}$$

this might be rather extra naive, yet I think not unpleasingly so. I am *all but* certain that domandat*a*, being now personal to the woman speaker, would be right.

Teodorico's address is 67 South Street, St. Andrews. I also had thought of him. He is not likely now to be long there — nor even in Great Britain, as he finds the climate inimical.

Page 23. You yourself had cancelled the full stop in my copy.[4]

Song and Music[5] I would retain.

Trip*t*ych is right: I had made the correction — and elsewhere S*i*ren (not S*y*ren).

Stratton Water. I don't think more explanation is *needed*: the passage as it stands conforms to the rapid transitions of the old ballads.[6]

Staff and Scrip. Neither do I think anything needed here: yet, if you like to put it in, quite apposite, so as to emphasize this point which gives the title to the poem.[7]

I agree with Scotus about *Sister Helen*:[8] have always considered it an exercise to one's ingenuity of comprehension, but not an unfair exercise. I really can't say there is anything else in particular I think in need of making-out — though I think it true various of the poems demand a poetical apprehension to seize them in their fullness. I fancy most readers will be abroad at the opening of *Nocturn*,[9] but will gradually as they proceed guess what the informing idea is. I wouldn't be disposed to elucidate.

Refusal of Aid[10] etc. I should be inclined to prefer the present title. That is, adopting your *general* view: My own general view is to the contrary effect — viz.: that the best thing would be to relegate this sonnet to its own real occasion and date by retaining the original title — and to give *throughout* the dates of composition as far as you can fix them, and unless major motives intervene.

My Sister's Sleep is, to my thinking, fully good enough to go in, after revision — and your present reason for putting it in conclusive. Christina is sending you a transcript, and will no doubt read the proofs of the poems as you suggest.

Tinsley's[11] purpose of putting me into a third article is I think clearly traceable: my *anticipation* however had been that you and I together would form No. 2.

Perhaps you have heard the great loss — the death of Leys.[12] Age only 54, cause of death not as yet notified, that I see. When will there be a successor to him?

All greetings at Penkill. Immensely and delightfully hot here still, but this *evening* may perhaps foreshow a change.

Your

W. M. Rossetti

Your question about *Violet or the Danseuse* is at last in *Notes and Queries*.[13] They can give no explanation: only that there is no evidence in favour of Miss Brougham nor (I should think not) of Lytton, who it seems had also been started.

Lucas Ionides married Miss Bird[14] yesterday, I believe.

MS: AP. Extract in *RP*, pp. 461-62.

1. A poet of the Siculo-Provençal school.
2. See Letter 161, Note 17 (f).
3. See Letter 161, Note 18.
4. *Ave*, 1. 45, has a cancelled full stop in the "Penkill" proofs at Princeton.
5. Not published until *Ballads and Sonnets*.
6. Sts. 10-12 were added in *Poems* 1870 (see DW, 2:721).
7. In an earlier version of the poem "there was something added where the damsel gives her the relics [St. 15] to develop this incident" (DW, ii. 721), but it was not included in *Poems* 1870.
8. At WBS's suggestion DGR added St. 1, *Poems* 1870 (DW, 2:721).
9. *Love's Nocturn*.
10. Published as *On the Refusal of Aid Between Nations*. DGR had considered "On the Refusal of Aid to Hungary 1849, to Poland 1861, to Crete 1867" (DW, 2:721).
11. See Letter 161, Note 25.
12. Hendrik Leys (1815-69), Belgian history painter. WMR described his visit to "La Maison Leys" in the *Academy*, 10 July 1875, pp. 47-48.
13. 28 August 1869, p. 176. DGR enquired about the rumor that the novel was by Julia Brougham (d. 1839), daughter of Henry Peter, Baron Brougham.
14. Elfreda Elizabeth Bird (1848-1929).

164. TO DANTE GABRIEL ROSSETTI

Euston Square,
30 August [1869]

Dear Gabriel,

In consequence of your letter of Friday, received this morning, Christina has now sent back your proofs. This will interfere with my replying at full, but I will answer as far as I can.

Page 16. I like much "thine own antiquity,"[1] and believe you can't do better than insert it. "A traveller" would do, but I agree with you in not entirely liking it — as too everyday in association. Would you prefer "an alien"?[2] which leaves untouched any point save only that of diversity of race etc.

Page 25. It used, I think, to be "St. Mary *the* Virgin." That is a little peculiar, but I think I like it on the whole the best. "St. Mary Virgin" better than "O Mary Virgin."[3]

Page 21. Capital Hs[4] — So far as I can speak without the immediate guidance of the proofs, I should be inclined to put them in on system in the *Ave*, as that poem starts from that point of view. Elsewhere sparingly, but would not hesitate wherever perspicuity is served.

Page 5. "Circlewise" I should not be minded to alter. Nor certainly "lying down her back."[5]

Page 147 etc. Coincidences with Browning.[6] This might be an incentive to putting dates to these poems (and to others, in *my* view). "Auspicious soul"[7] used to sound to me rather *précieuse*, but I am used to it now, and like it very well. So far as *meaning* goes, limpid, diaphanous, transparent, transpicuous, seems to come to much the same as "pellucid."

Page 157. "Many years" etc.[8] I am not insensible to the value of this line as it stands. The non-satisfying element of it to me is twofold — 1, that "Many" is a little like saying "a considerable number," or other such rather commonplace expression of numerousness, whereas I fancy an austere sort of reticence as to their being *numerous*, only suggesting something abstract which the reader fills out for himself, might be the more effective — or else a symbolic *precision*, as by saying "an hundred," "seventy-and-seven," or so on. 2, in the words "and many days," the word "many" appears to me to want stress of sound — the "quantity" of classical prosody: it is a word which passes off the tongue very rapidly. But all this may be wiredrawing.

Page 169. I *entirely* agree in your objection to "solemn poetry."[9] Only I don't myself feel the objection to be fatal without appeal to a line which on the whole pleases me, as expressing the picture.

Page 202. Substitute for San Rocco.[10] There are so many admissible ones that it is difficult to fix. Sant'Eustorgio or San Petronio sounds well to me: S. Michele, S. Grisostomo, S. Agnese, S. Prassede, S. Maria in Via Crucis (I don't know whether this name exists anywhere in fact). I presume you don't want, but the reverse, any name of church actually in Pisa.

I am tempted to add here what my notion was about "Miching Mallecho":[11] it may enliven a few minutes of discussion to you and Scotus. I might have sent it before to *Notes and Queries*, but am waiting for a spare hour to look into what has been heretofore suggested on the subject. The only explanation I have yet seen is in Keightley's *Expositor*[12] — Spanish Mucho Mallecho, very ill-done. Now this seems to me *unidiomatic* though quite appropriate. Suppose it were put in Italian — "Marry, this is molto malfatto (or French, "fort mal fait"): it means mischief." It seems a tame literal statement, without flavour or verbal point. Now in *Hiawatha* (the last book one would turn up in such a quest) I find the American Good Spirit is Gitche Manito, and the bad spirit

> Mitche Manito the Mighty,
> He the dreadful spirit of Evil.

Mitche Manito is a very close sound-likeness to Miching Mallecho; and the sense seems good too — "Marry, this is Apollyon (for instance — or "this is the very devil"): it means mischief." No doubt one is startled to think of Shakespeare using the name of a North-American demon: but I presume such a name *might* be

225

current in England then — might possibly be just lately spread abroad when *Hamlet* was written, and a kind of catchword to a theatrical audience. Does the coincidence seem to you plausible, or merely an incongruous chance?

Your

W. M. Rossetti

MS: AP.

1. See Letter 161, Note 7.
2. *The Burden of Nineveh*, St. 11. Thus in *Poems* 1870.
3. See Letter 161, Note 10.
4. Pronouns referring to God and Christ are consistently capitalized in *Ave*.
5. *The Blessed Damozel*. In *Poems* 1870 "circlewise" (St. 19) was retained; "lying down her back" (St. 2) became "Her hair that lay along her back."
6. DGR worried about the similarity between "They die not, — never having lived" (*The Choice*, Sonnet 1), and Browning's lines "The Three, I do not scorn / To death, because they never lived" (*In a Gondola*). "I know that I had never then read that poem, and that on first reading it this annoying fact struck me at once, but then this is not known to the world" (DW, 2:726).
7. *Love's Nocturn*, St. 6. Thus in *Poems* 1870, but changed to "translucent soul" in *Poems* 1881. DGR preferred "pellucid soul," but hesitated because Browning had used the phrase of Caponsacchi in *The Ring and the Book*.
8. See Letter 162, Note 1.
9. See Letter 162, Note 3.
10. See Letter 162, Note 12.
11. *Hamlet*, III. ii. 131. Encouraged by DGR (DW, 2:734-35) WMR explained his idea in *Notes and Queries*, 30 October 1869, pp. 367-68, where the spelling differs from that used here.
12. *The Shakespeare-Expositor* (1867).

165. TO DANTE GABRIEL ROSSETTI

56 Euston Square,
12 September [1869]

Dear Gabriel,

Your revised proofs[1] reached me the other day, and I have now looked them through so far (only) as to answer the points hitherto left aside in your letters.

Page 24.

The sea
Sighed further off etc.[2]

The present lines very good, and I assume better than the old ones, though I don't remember these last-named with entire clearness. But unfortunately there is a very serious objection which I had not reflected about before. Nazareth is *quite inland*, about equidistant from the Mediterranean and the Lake of Tiberias: the sea could no more be heard there than in London or Birmingham. I know one may care too much for objections of this sort, yet I think the local mendacity is too glaring.

Page 24. The 5 lines beginning "Then gloried thy deep eyes."[3] I like the last 2 lines — the first 3 not particularly. If you find anything better to be done — especially if preserving the impression of the last 2 lines — I would do it.

Page 23.

Thou wast a sister sisterlike.[4]

I think this the best form of the line.

Page 27.

> The cherubim, arrayed, conjoint.[5]

I presume "arrayed" means "ranged in order" rather than "robed." I can't think of any Latinized form of word in particular to meet either meaning: "encinct" might do pretty tolerably for the latter, but not well, and my own impression is that a *non*-Latinized word comes better in the place (as sounding less artificial) under *any* circumstances. "Deflect" might do for the mere purpose of Latinization: but I don't fancy you would approve it, nor do I much.

Page 5.

> Was she not stepping to my side
> Down all the trembling stair.[6]

I prefer trembling to tremulous — and think the objection, as connected with "stepping," infinitesimal. It would be another matter if the two words occupied like *positions* in the verse.

Page 6.

> With angels in strong level *flight*.[7]

I suppose this should on the whole be preferred to *lapse*. Yet I like the *visual impression* created by the latter word a good deal the better: it looks like sailing through the air without any *motion* of the wings (as one often sees birds), and gives more the idea of serial succession.

Page 10. I don't see anything awkwardly interpolated or too vague in the last stanza.[8]

Page 8. You say last line of stanza 3 sounds shortish. I don't perceive it at all as regards that line,

> Wherein Love descries his goal:

rather in regards

> And the funeral goes by[9] —

but would not on any account alter this last.

Page 93. Alteration of soul into mind[10] seems to me befitting.

Page 16. Stanzas 2 and 3[11] on this page are now, I think, very satisfactory. I don't see any serious objection either to the lines, which you have not restored, about the "leaguered citadels" etc. — though I suspect there is something in Brown's idea that there were no such things to be heard.

Page 23. Note.[12] I do think "all faiths" more unambiguous — having indeed myself understood the Christian as included in "classic" faiths, which I think it might be without any grave laxity of language.

Page 93.[13] Of the two, I think "Ah let not *hope*" superior. "Whose speech *Truth* knows not" a decided improvement.

Page 7. I think *Nocturn* is perceptibly clearer with the restored stanza 2,[14] which contains besides some very fine lines.

Page 12. These 3 stanzas[14] very apposite and effective. I think however the intonation of

Its old share[15]

is a little awkward: and more decisively so that of

Strive with love *and be love's foe*.[15]

Page 50. These stanzas also a gain.[16]

Page 39. *Sister Helen* is far clearer with the new opening stanza: and the one further on is a fine one.[17]

Tell Scotus I now have his proofs U and X,[18] and retain them unexamined till I hear further from him.

What do you and he think of the Byron affair[19] — if indeed you have had an opportunity of following its phases? The question is a practical one to me, as I must make *some* modification in the notice of Byron I wrote lately. At first I assumed that the story would scarcely bear being called in question: but the controversy inclines me to regard it as yet open to a good deal of doubt. The great point to determine would be about the child born of the incest, and kept by Lady Byron for somewhile, as affirmed by Mrs. Stowe: but nobody elucidates that. The first thing I did was to look up Byron's poems addressed to his half-sister, and I certainly consider that they tell *very strongly* against the story. One might explain them away as calculated deception, but I should hesitate to adopt that view. I dare say you remember a *different* legend which Swinburne used to diffuse as the cause of the separation: did he ever raise this incest suggestion also?

Your

W. M. Rossetti

By the way, I don't at all agree in the obloquy lavished on Mrs. Stowe.

Do you remember whether it is said that Byron was very *like* his half-sister? If so (someone of no authority told me the other day that so it was) the suggestion that there was really no blood-relationship between the two vanishes. Otherwise this suggestion, which someone made in the *Times*, deserves *some* consideration. The first Mrs. Byron was a divorced Lady Carmarthen, and notorious woman of pleasure. She was the mother of Augusta; and, if she played her husband Byron false, and bore Augusta to another man, there *could be* no "incest" — as the mothers of the poet and Augusta were two different women.

MS: AP. Extract in *RP*, pp. 465-67.

1. The second or "A Proofs."
2. *Ave*, St. 2. Thus in *Poems* 1870.
3. *Ave*, St. 2. "Then gloried thy deep eyes, and deep / Within thine heart the song waxed loud: / It was to thee as though the cloud / Which shuts the inner shrine from view / Were molten, and thy God burned through:" became "Then suddenly the awe grew deep, / As of a day to which all days / Were footsteps in God's secret ways:" (*Poems* 1870).

228

4. See Letter 161, Note 2.

5. *Ave*, St. 7. Thus in *Poems* 1870.

6. *The Blessed Damozel*, St. 11. "Strove not her steps to reach my side / Down all the echoing stair?" (*Poems* 1870).

7. *Ibid.*, St. 23. Thus in *Poems* 1870.

8. *Love's Nocturn*, St. 14, which appeared in *Poems* 1870 with "sleep" in "Wheresoe'er my sleep befall" changed to "dreams."

9. *Love's Nocturn*, Sts. 6 and 7. Thus in *Poems* 1870.

10. See Letter 161, Note 15.

11. *The Burden of Nineveh*, Sts. 4 and 5. For the earlier form of the stanzas and the rejected lines, see DW, 2:725-26.

12. See Letter 161, Note 9. The note reads in part: "Art still identifies herself with all faiths."

13. *Love-Lily*. In *Poems* 1870 the poem concludes:

> Ah! let not hope be still distraught
> But find in her its gracious goal,
> Whose speech Truth knows not from her thought
> Nor Love her body from her soul.

14. For WMR's objection to *Love's Nocturn*, see Letter 163, Note 9. DGR replied: "What you said of the foggy opening of *Nocturn* induced me to restore a second stanza which I had cut out in printing it, in case this might make things any clearer. I have also added three new stanzas towards the close of this poem to develop the sudden flight of the bogy on finding another bogy by the girl's bed" (DW, 2:734, where the new stanzas are identified as "probably" 17-19 in *Poems* 1870). See also DW, 2:738-39.

15. St. 18. Thus in *Poems* 1870.

16. See Letter 163, Note 6.

17. For "the new opening stanza," see Letter 163, Note 8. The "further" stanza is 17 (*Poems* 1870).

18. Of *Albert Dürer: His Life and Works*, which WMR was reading.

19. In "The True Story of Lady Byron's Married Life," *Macmillan's Magazine*, September 1869, Harriet Beecher Stowe (1811-96) claimed that the cause of Byron's separation from his wife was her discovery of his incestuous relationship with his half-sister Augusta Leigh. Mrs. Stowe's *Lady Byron Vindicated* followed in 1870. WMR concluded in his preface to Byron ("Moxon's Popular Poets," [1870]) that "For the present ... I feel it right to eliminate this gross and ghastly story from the materials of Byron's life: not to reject it, for it may yet prove to be true, but to exclude it as hitherto unverified" (p. xv).

166. TO DANTE GABRIEL ROSSETTI

Euston Square,
16 September [1869]

Dear Gabriel,

I did not yet know with any clearness that the Morrises were back.[1] Will call early — probably tomorrow, and send you word. Glad so far to hear what you say of Janie.

A deliberate reading of your revised proofs is still in prospect, so as to acquaint me with the various emendations and additions you have introduced. Meanwhile, on receipt of your letter of Tuesday, I have looked up the several points there named.

Page 12. *Nocturn.*

So when some lost legion etc.

I don't think this form of the stanza was open to *serious* objection, but the new form *is* an improvement.[2]

Page 7. Ditto. Stanzas 1 and 2 as now altered by you[3] are decidedly perspicuous, and I don't think more needs doing. I exactly agree with you as to the pros and cons of "Dreamland" — pros prevailing. I think it *considerably* better that the poem should be made to express an actual love, rather than an ideal amatory proclivity; and I think also, with you, that there is next to nothing in the poem to force the latter conception on the reader's notice.

Page 9. Stanza "As since man" etc.[4] The whole image, and especially (as verses) lines 2 and 3, are so good that I think you should make an effort to *adapt* rather than reject this stanza. I would not mind the repetition of rhymes to which you advert. I fancy that the only line which brings very saliently to the reader's notice the conception which you wish to exclude is the least good one of the stanza,

Thus within the world's wide girth.

If you were to alter this, and perhaps also make some verbal modification in the final line, I think the stanza as a whole would not conflict, to any extent worth noticing, with your improved general conception.

Page 8.

Thence are youth's warm fancies etc.[5]

I rather prefer the new version, but like the old one much also; and think on the whole the most important consideration is the getting rid of "whisperings" rhyming with "rings" — so that I would advocate the old form.

Nuptial Sleep. I like best of the two the alteration now in type. "Chirped" I personally have always had a certain antipathy to — though I never felt called upon to raise so mere a point of taste: I regard it as Leigh-Huntish — or perhaps more rightly Browningish. At the same time I think the *meaning* perfectly clear, and the term "graphic" — only a shade too much so. My impression is you will not do better than "Kissed at each other."[6] "Moaned" I think too strong, and might be misunderstood as meaning that they really began definite sentimental outpourings. "Crooned" might avoid this objection: but I suspect "Kissed" is best.

Penumbra. I have always enjoyed "rasp the sands,"[7] but must admit it can be called "violent and inexact" — which "chafe" remedies (or would you like "ridge"?). "Rasp" would be very true of shingles, but not of sands.

Dark Day. "Sowed hunger *once*"[8] seems to be the better.

Mary's Girlhood.

This is that blessed Mary.[9]

I do think the repetition of phrase in the Sibylla sonnet a sound — not a *very* grave — objection. "'Tis of that" seems to me too peculiar — too much of the P.R.B. twang. "Lo you the blessed Mary" might perhaps serve, unless you consider it too pretentious and magniloquent.

Venus. "She hath the apple"[10] never struck my ear disagreeably. If you think of anything escaping even the ghost of an objection, I would substitute it, but not bother over it to any extent.

Parted Love (a very fine sonnet). I myself feel no objection at all to the last line.[11] I like it rather better than your proposed substitute, but that also is quite satisfactory.

Card-Dealer very good indeed now.

Autumn Idleness, and *A Match with the Moon*. Both very good. The latter has a playful quaintness, but nothing exceptionable.

I am glad to hear you are writing so much, and to so good a result — and interested to hear of your "prose synopsis" plan:[12] I remember Alfieri[13] gives some curious details about the structural system of composition he adopted, and, if I can find the passage, and think it would amuse you, will send some particulars one day.

The wombat, whom I saw yesterday, is the greatest lark you can imagine: possibly the best of wombats I have seen. She (for I believe it is a she) is but little past babyhood, and of a less wiry surface than the adult wombat: very familiar, following one's footsteps about the room, and trotting after one if one quickens pace — and fond of nestling up into any hollow of arms or legs, and nibbling one's trousers etc. Wombat can by exertion and rigour be made to sit up like a man, but resists to the utmost of her force, which is indeed considerable. I am glad to perceive that Emma[14] is very fond of her. Wombat scares the cat, but fraternizes with the rabbits. Sighs from time to time, but emits no other sound that I heard.

I found F[anny] very well and in good spirits.

Now for the Italian poem.[15] I took it up with some hopes of rapidly pitching upon reconciling middle terms between your diction and Theodoric's, but find little occurs to me in that way. I have pencilled a few points on his MS: the [] are intended to mark points which I — and I am sure you — regard as inadmissible.

Theodoric and his wife had called on me at Somerset House on Monday: by this time they are *probably* out of England, and not to be back for months. He spoke to me (as he put it in his letter) of your "senarii": it did not happen to us to pursue the subject very systematically, but I understood him to imply that an Italian would regard the exceptional feet in your verses — not as simply laxities of dissyllabic metre, but as unauthorized interpolations of trisyllabic metre — and that this, though not wholly unexampled in old authors, was unallowable now. This really is not very different from your own view, only that you elect to use the thing as allowable. I understood Theodoric to regard such lines as these

E disse ridendo
La state talora

as consisting simply of two trisyllables apiece — just like the confessedly and *unalteringly* trisyllabic metre of Papa's *Salterio*[16] — senarii, as his own preface terms them —

231

Qual' alba tranquilla
Che lieto orizzonte,
Già dietro a quel monte etc.

Love to Scotus, and particular remembrances from all of us to Miss Boyd.

Your

W. M. Rossetti

MS: AP. Extract in *RP*, pp. 467-69.

1. From the spa at Bad-Ems in Hesse-Nassau, where Morris had taken his ailing wife.
2. For the revised stanza of *Love's Nocturn*, see DW, 2:738, but neither form of the stanza appears in *Poems* 1870.
3. The opening stanzas of the poem as they appear in *Poems* 1870.
4. Omitted from *Poems* 1870. William Sharp quotes the stanza in *Dante Gabriel Rossetti, A Record and a Study* (1882), p. 344.
5. St. 4 originally began "Youth's warm fancies all are there" (DW, 2:739). In *Poems* 1870 it begins "Poets' fancies all are there," and "rings" rhymes with "springs."
6. "Fawned on each other" (*Poems* 1870).
7. The phrase was omitted from *Poems* 1870.
8. Thus in *Poems* 1870.
9. Thus in *Poems* 1870. "This is that Lady Beauty" (*Sibylla Palmifera, Poems* 1870).
10. Thus in *Poems* 1870.
11. *The House of Life.* "And thy heart rends thee, and thy body endures" (*Poems* 1870). To answer WBS's objection that the line was "too violent" DGR thought of changing it to "And thy feet stir not, and thy body endures" (DW, 2:740).
12. DGR reported that he had begun *The Orchard Pit*, "but I have not yet got much beyond a careful synopsis in prose which I consider a very good plan of action" (DW, 2:740). The poem was first published by WMR in *Collected Works*.
13. Vittorio Alfieri (1749-1803), Italian dramatist. Before Gaetano Polidori came to England he had been Alfieri's secretary.
14. A servant at Cheyne Walk.
15. See Letter 161, Note 17.
16. *Iddio E L'Uomo, Salterio* (1833).

167. TO ALGERNON CHARLES SWINBURNE

Somerset House,
28 September [1869]
(interrupted — resumed
1 October)

Dear Swinburne,

Your letter about *Mrs. Holmes Grey*[1] will be henceforward for ever a satisfaction for me to reflect upon — and *would be* a far more than compensation for any letting-down I may have received at the hands of *Tinsley's*,[2] were it not that I really have been from first to last entirely equanimous on that matter. I have (as you know) a great respect for your critical opinion; but still believe you must over-estimate *Mrs. Holmes Grey* — for this reason if no other, that I was barely (or maybe *not* quite) 20 when I wrote the thing, and I don't see how a youth of that age *can* well have written the best piece of domestic tragedy since Balzac, allowing for Flaubert. However, so be it — Amen and Amen.

The possible turning of the poem into French by you would assuredly be about the greatest gratification to my self-esteem — not to speak of a deeper satisfaction of friendship — that could "in the scheme of providence" occur to me. The matter lies with you to do or not do as you may eventually find most manageable.

Much delighted also to find how highly you enjoyed Gabriel's new poems — which are indeed splendid: but *this* was not matter of much uncertainty.

Shelley proofs — now in *Prometheus* — take up a deal of my time. That poem will, I expect, fully complete volume 1, allowing for the Life, and the relevant portion of my notes, to get into the same volume — indeed I should rather have expected *Prometheus* to be *de trop* for volume 1: so presumably the proofs of said Life and Notes will be soon current.

Please to remember me particularly to your family.

Your affectionate
W. M. Rossetti

MS: BL.

1. *SL*, 2:28-29.
2. Forman, in his article on WMR (*Tinsley's Magazine*, October 1869, pp. 276-81), regretted that he had published the poem.

168. TO ALGERNON CHARLES SWINBURNE

56 Euston Square,
13 October [1869]

Dear Swinburne,

I thank you heartily for raising the subject of Ricciardi's Congress, and would most gladly join in an expression of adhesion.[1] I have not been able to set to at the thing these few days past, but have now just sat down to it, and enclose a suggested letter. I dare say you can improve it greatly, and leave it for your handling. It is in *fact* a mere first draft, and perhaps may read as such.

Michelet's[2] letter is very fine. I will return the *Rappel* to you by bookpost along with this.

I suppose our letter would do in English: but should be disposed to enclose it in a personal communication in Italian to Ricciardi — who (as I must have told you) is a very old friend of my father, and who, on my seeing him this year in Florence, invited me to appear at the Congress. But I explained to him that I should not be in the way of so doing.

No doubt you have done the Louis Bonaparte sonnets[3] *con amore* — i.e. *con odio*. He and his are in a bad way, I take it. The time had to come, and seems rapidly coming.

Yours with love
W. M. Rossetti

Your missive to the "minor periodical"[4] is very neat.

MS: BL.

1. Giuseppe Napoleone Ricciardi (1808-82), Italian patriot and republican, first visited England in 1833. He sought out Gabriele Rossetti and undertook to smuggle his books into Italy. His Anti-Council met briefly in Naples in December 1869, at the same time as the Oecumenical Council which Pius IX had called in Rome to proclaim papal infallibility and to oppose liberal ideas. For Swinburne's and WMR's joint letter, see *SL*, 2:53-54.

2. Jules Michelet (1798-1874), French liberal historian, whose letter of support to the Anti-Council was published in *Le Rappel*, 7 October 1869, p. 1.

3. *Intercession*, published in the *Fortnightly Review*, November 1869, and reprinted as Section 12 of *Dirae*, *Songs of Two Nations* (1875).

4. *Athenaeum*, to which Swinburne wrote disclaiming authorship of a note on Derwent Coleridge in *Christabel and the Lyrical and Imaginative Poems of S. T. Coleridge* (1869), which he had selected and introduced (*SL*, 2:30).

169. TO DANTE GABRIEL ROSSETTI

Somerset House,
14 October [1869]

Dear Gabriel,

What you write me[1] is not entirely new to me. Scott, writing on 11 October, and supposing no doubt that I was *au fait*, mentioned the fact: then, finding reason to doubt me privity, he wrote again to say so and impose silence.[2] But I shall and should be silent anyhow.

My frank opinion is that you have acted right on *both* occasions. Under the pressure of a great sorrow, you performed an act of self-sacrifice: it did you honour, but was clearly a work of supererogation. You have not retracted the self-sacrifice, for it has taken actual effect in your being bereaved of due poetic fame these 7½ years past: but you now think — and I quite agree with you — that there is no reason why the self-sacrifice should have no term.

There was no reason at all why you should mention the matter to me beforehand: you and I know each other of old, and shall continue so to do till (or perhaps after) one of us is a bogey.

Did Tebbs, when you consulted him on the legal complication, tell you that he had already of late been starting the subject to me? He did so one day that he called here while you were at Penkill: urging that the book ought to be recovered, and that he could obtain you a "faculty" without your personal intervention from first to last: and I promised him that, if a proper opening offered, I would represent it to you.

Howell has a very blabbing tongue: it is to be hoped rather than believed that he is a more faithful depositary of certain other confidences you wot of. Not that I mean to — or *can* — *assert* anything on this point.

Your
W. M. R.

How Tebbs had heard of the matter I can't say: but indeed everybody had heard of it. For myself I had never broached the subject to living soul.

My absence from Brown's yesterday does not imply that I am much amiss. I am not so, but still needed to put on a second mustard poultice yesterday. Today very fair.

MS: AP. Extract in *RP*, p. 473.

1. About the exhumation of his poems in the presence of Howell, the solicitor Henry Virtue Tebbs, and a Dr. Williams (DW, 2:751-52).

2. For WBS's letters see *LPI*, p. 41, and *RP*, p. 472.

170. TO ALGERNON CHARLES SWINBURNE

56 Euston Square,
18 October [1869]

Dear Swinburne,

These sonnets[1] are splendid work, equal to their occasion — *creepy* sort of stuff that one wouldn't even like to hear rumoured as being written of one, and left unseen in some man's desk. If you are as "Tenderhearted, meek and pitiful"[2] as Count Cenci, you will not let them get abroad.

As to the revisions — in No. 1 I prefer "Be rottenness,"[3] save only that it is somewhat forestalled by what precedes. In 4, "doomsday drink"[3] *probably*: "with eyeless sight"[3] certainly: "the secrets of seen things"[4] I like best as an expression, but fancy "the soul (rather than *sense*) of unseen things" will be more evident for most readers.

I noticed the other day a splendid motto for *Les Malheurs de la Vertu*[5] in the congenial pages of *Prometheus Unbound*.

> I felt thy torture, son [girl], with such mixed joy
> As pain and virtue give.

I write in a hurry, and without time to determine or express an opinion about the Ricciardi letter. Will turn it over, and write you again soon.

Your
W. M. Rossetti

MS: BL.

1. *Intercession* (see Letter 168, Note 3).
2. *The Cenci*, I. iii. 13.
3. Thus in *Fortnightly Review*.
4. "The soul of unseen things," *Fortnightly Review*.
5. De Sade's *Justine*.

171. TO ALGERNON CHARLES SWINBURNE

56 Euston Square,
24 October [1869]

Dear Swinburne,

I have been a long while in answering your letter: not through any very prolonged need of deliberation, but because leisure was scanty. Having now fully considered the matter,[1] I find myself quite ready to adopt your eloquent manifesto in a modified form, but not *without* some modification. I never have professed myself, and never have been nor am, an atheist. The utmost I can truthfully say about that is that theism appears to me an unfathomable mystery, and atheism another quite equally unfathomable. I can therefore, in many moods and for many purposes of discussion or speculation, stop short of theism, as an alien hypothesis, but cannot affirm atheism. Also, even if I could do this as a matter of opinion, I should be indisposed to do it with any glare of publicity, considering especially the pain it would cause to my mother (who however, I need hardly tell you, knows me for an antichristian).[2]

If the enclosed draft of mine suits you as a joint expression of feeling for yourself and me, I am prepared to abide by it: if not (and I need not say that I would wish you to consult solely your own preference in the matter), perhaps you would still be willing to sign the *joint* letter substantially according to my first draft (I have tried to improve an expression here and there), and to use your own unaltered draft for your own purposes. I must apologize for the seeming cheek of tampering with it, but know you are ready to understand all these things as they are meant. "Flame"[3] (instead of "salt") "of his spirit" seems to me needed for the exigencies of *translation*.

I now proceed to some of the details in your letter. I think the word *English* kings[4] reads less advantageously, and suspect besides that the same law may have prevailed in other feudal countries: therefore suggest another phrase as neither too limited nor too wide.

It would be quite clear to a dispassionate third person that your signature ought to precede mine — yours being (most properly) a *famous* name, and mine one of only few and faintish reverberations (apart from family associations). But, as you insist upon it, I waive my sense of the befitting, and sign first.

Your Te Hominem Laudamus[5] is indeed a splendid theme; and theme and treatment together might be such as to excite Shelley to envy for a pretermitted opportunity.

I rather fear my Italianizing of the letter will be unsatisfactory to Italian ears: still I agree with you that it ought to go in Italian *as well as* English. Of the two however I think the English the more essential: doubtless there will be many letters in non-Italian languages, each suitable to the audience more especially concerned. My own inclination would be to send the letter as an actual communication to Ricciardi and the Congress, and leave it to its chance of being thereafter published as such: and on this ground if no other I agree with you in thinking the English version most desirable. I have hardly made up my mind as to the publication in the *Rappel* as proposed by you. Certainly *you* ought to consult your own liking as to publishing it there: so all I will ask is that, if you decide upon so doing, you will give me notice beforehand, and I will then *forthwith* reply whether my name also is to appear.

I did see the *Temple Bar* on Whitman. Gabriel understands that series of articles is by Alfred Austin.[6] The one on Whitman is clearly — from *any* point of view of criticism — poor stuff: one in June on Browning seemed to me acute, though far too resolute in resisting his claims as a poet. You perhaps would be not far from agreeing in its main positions.

Yours always,
W. M. Rossetti

If you sign the English letter, I will then Italianize it; write a covering letter to Ricciardi; and send all again through your hands prior to actual transmission to Italy. Must I recopy the English letter because of an erasure? If yes, yes be it.

MS: BL.

1. See Letter 168, Note 1.
2. Cf. MS. Diary, 19 November 1866: "Swinburne ... speaks with great satisfaction of my

pamphlet — which however he has not ventured to make known to his mother, as it acknowledges his practical atheism etc., which matters, it seems, he never troubles her with."

3. Thus in *SL*.

4. "Some kings of our past" (*SL*).

5. *Hymn of Man* (*Songs before Sunrise*).

6. (1835-1913), poet, critic, political journalist; succeeded Tennyson as Poet Laureate in 1896. He wrote about Whitman in "The Poetry of the Future," *Temple Bar*, 27 (October 1869), 314-27; and about Browning, 26 (June 1869), 316-33.

172. TO ALGERNON CHARLES SWINBURNE

Somerset House,
29 October [1869]

Dear Swinburne,

I am extremely pleased that we can coalesce on the Ricciardi letter: have put in "eviration": I tampered with your original "castration," thinking the word somewhat ugly. I also quite agree in what your note says about atheism (unless it be as to the illogicality of believing in theism without believing in revelation, as to which I have not sufficiently reflected). My own mental attitude on the subject is pretty nearly this: — "I know very little about the phenomena of things, and still less about their principles. I (or others for me) can follow out the phenomena up to a certain point. To insist on following them out beyond that point is to indulge in guesswork: and the results of guesswork must not be rammed down our throats as either physical or metaphysical truths of unspeakable importance — especially considering that this result does not get over a difficulty, but merely steps beyond a difficulty about which there is no doubt, into a different difficulty about which there is no certainty." To my mind and temperament this view of the matter has hitherto sufficed: but it cannot be denied that multitudes of men, by an apparently irresistible craving of their nature, gravitate to a different view; and I am certainly not prepared to say that my view is *as much as* the finest human nature requires, while theirs is something *more than* it requires. Of the two, the fact seems to be rather the contrary — that I have too little, and they only enough. Robespierre was surely not much out, as a question of fact, in saying that theism was of the people, and atheism of the oligarchy: though possibly he had better not have tried to redress the balance by any authoritative or vicarious process.

I have not yet seen your *Telegraph* letter:[1] must send round for it.

Your motto to the Intercessions[2] is surprisingly good. Certainly I shall in a kind of way enjoy seeing them in print — the tiger-cat within me will enjoy it: but I sincerely deprecate the publication, and consider that Mrs. Grundy and M. Prudhomme will be nearest the right. They will only be speaking with the heart and lips of Shelley. "*Let* Buonaparte crawl a worm untrod."[3] That distich is consummate, and has shaken me with solitary laughter time after time. But I know all this is out of the *practical* region: the poems will be coming out all the same, and encountering such destiny as awaits them.

I admire *Hertha* exceedingly — and have little doubt it will prove one of your finest, as it certainly is of your loftiest poems. That tremendous metre repeated from *Atalanta* seems admirably applied: it has a kind of roll and shock of sound like some great exultant process of nature — volcano or the like. Your proposed stanza seems to me very fine and effective: though I incline to think the two lines

I am polestar and pole
To the seafarer, man

are not quite *aboriginal* enough for this opening stanza,[4] in which (maybe) every conception should come out of "the original gulf of things." Further on the image would be highly effective. The succeeding stanza

Before ever land was etc.

is singularly beautiful.

As soon as I find time, which is rather fragmentary with me at present, I will see to the Italianization etc. of the Ricciardi letter.

Your affectionate
W. M. Rossetti

I had occasion to enquire the other day about a Shelley autograph — a short letter of no particular importance: was pleased to find its market-value more than I had fancied, £1.5: a good important letter would be £12 or £14. I keep for you a photograph taken direct from Miss Curran's life-sized oil-portrait of Shelley:[5] comes much better to my eyes than any engraving. I possess a duplicate, so there can be no hesitation in your accepting: indeed *anyone* can get them for the ordering.

MS: BL.

1. *SL*, 2:39-42.
2. See Note 168, Note 3; "Ave Caesar Imperator, moriturum te saluto."
3. *A Counsel* (Section 10 of *Dirae*). The line was revised to read "But let the worm Napoleon crawl untrod."
4. In *Songs before Sunrise* the poem begins:

I am that which began;
Out of me the years roll;
Out of me God and man;
I am equal and whole.

5. Amelia Curran's portrait of 1819 (National Portrait Gallery).

173. TO JOHN CAMDEN HOTTEN

15 November [1869]

My dear Sir,

It is quite impossible for me to reply *per return* to the question you put:[1] I really don't recollect one way or the other. I noted down the points at the time in writing, and as soon as I reasonably can (but have much business of my own to attend to) will search for the memorandum at home. I am not confident however of finding it: for it is now a longish while ago since Swinburne referred to me on the subject, and I gave him the substance of all I knew — and I have a suspicion

238

that I also gave him the memorandum itself, asking him to return it, which he never did. But this remains to be tested.

Yours truly,
W. M. Rossetti

MS: Huntington.

1. 13 November 1869: "I wish to be quite accurate as to the percentage, or royalty, I agreed to allow Mr. Swinburne upon the books I publish for him. Was it not *one fourth* of the published price? There is no dispute as to this, but I should prefer my recollection of the precise percentage to be in harmony with your own" (AP). See Letter 145, Note 2.

174. TO JOHN CAMDEN HOTTEN

56 Euston Square,
18 November [1869]

My dear Sir,

I have now looked with some minuteness through my memoranda, and find no trace of the note I made concerning your arrangements with Swinburne:[1] I am therefore confident that I did some while back hand it over to him, and that he has not returned it to me. In the absence of the note, I cannot from memory say anything as to the percentage that was agreed upon.

Yours very truly,
W. M. Rossetti

MS: Huntington. Extract in *HLQ*, p. 47.

1. See Letter 173.

175. TO WILLIAM DOUGLAS O'CONNOR

56 Euston Square,
20 November [1869]

Dear Mr. O'Connor,

Your letter of 28 August has lain by me long, but not unheeded. From the first I have felt exceedingly desirous that something of what was written about Whitman by the lady I referred to should appear in some printed form.[1] Her enthusiasm has been equal to the position and occasion, and she has enlarged her remarks into the form herewith enclosed, which she offers for American publication in such form as you or Mr. Whitman himself may judge expedient. You will see that I have added a few introductory words of my own. As you and I are at one as to the value of what this lady said in the first instance, and as I have no doubt you will consider its value much enhanced in the form the writing has now taken, I shall spare any length of words here. Of course it *may* happen that you don't see your way clear to publication — though I am sanguine of a contrary result: but, should the former be the case, I would ask you to let me know in due course exactly how the matter stands, and then the lady will give final instructions as to the MS. — whether to return it to me or what else.

Will you again present as occasion shall serve my homage of love and admiration to Whitman. I think his works are filtering here, not very observably but surely.

In the *Academy* (the new literary review published by Murray,[2] and contributed to by many of our most cultivated writers) — No. 1 — there was an article on the French poet Baudelaire by Mr. Simcox,[3] himself a poet who has established a position of his own (I confess I have not yet read any work of his), and he there referred to Whitman in terms of general but decided recognition — as if all persons worth addressing on the subject were pretty well aware of and agreed upon his name and exalted claims. This would not have been the case in England a couple of years ago. Then the name — even if left uncoupled with some ribald rubbish — would have received some tag of explanation or vindication. I was sorry to see, by a newspaper Mr. Whitman sent me some little while back, that he had had a relapse of his old illness: the newspaper added however that he was then again well, and I heartily trust that satisfactory state of things continues.

Your letter falls foul of Mrs. Stowe — an old affair now. I confess I think she was justified in writing what she did — though, after all the counter-statements that have appeared, I now think (provisionally and pending any further elucidations) that the charge against Byron has come to nought. But Mrs. Stowe, having received it from her sincerely admired friend Lady Byron, naturally believed it, and, believing it, had, in my view, a right to publish it. I consider the character of a great genius the property of the world. Be the character good or bad, the intellect was great: and one ought to lose no opportunity of understanding what are the real relations (not merely those which the pupils of a Sunday School consent to be conscious of) of human personality in its two phases — intellect and character.

Conway is back from Russia, and was here with his wife a fortnight ago. Another very valued American friend of mine — Stillman, late Consul in Crete — was here at the same time. He left for New York on Wednesday, 17 November, but expects to be again for awhile in London before the winter is out. Do you know him? I hope your steel-making process[4] realizes your utmost anticipations.

Yours very truly,
W. M. Rossetti

It had occurred to the lady that Emerson might perhaps be ready to say a few words to pass on her remarks to American readers, and thus serve the cause materially. She is not on the whole *much* disposed to think this either likely or opportune; but I have thought it best just to mention it for your consideration. I was forgetting to explain (though indeed it is probably needless) that I have simply *transcribed* the lady's MS.: the composition is as wholly and solely hers as if the handwriting were hers also: — (still less needful to specify) that no payment from any publisher of the MS. is in question.

MS: Berg.

1. Anne Gilchrist's "A Woman's Estimate of Walt Whitman (From Late Letters by an English Lady to W. M. Rossetti)," *Radical*, 7 (May 1870), 345-59. Extracts from O'Connor's letter of 28 August appear in *RP*, pp. 459-60.

2. John Murray (1808-92), son of the founder and publisher of the *Quarterly Review*, published the first twelve numbers of the *Academy*, 9 October 1869-10 September 1870 (D. Roll-Hansen, *The Academy, 1869-1879* [1957], pp. 114-15).

3. George Augustus Simcox (1841-1905), poet, critic, classical scholar, published *Prometheus Unbound: a Tragedy* (1867) and *Poems and Romances* (1869). In his review of Baudelaire's *Oeuvres Complètes* (1868-69) he identified the poet's subject as "the ideal aspects of the life of Paris, just as Whitman's subject is the ideal aspects of American democracy. Baudelaire is the laureate of a corrupt and stationary society — Whitman of a fresh and growing society" (9 October 1869, pp. 4-5).
4. See *RP*, p. 459.

176. TO ALGERNON CHARLES SWINBURNE

56 Euston Square,
28 November [1869]

Dear Swinburne,

I have pencilled the illegible words in Ricciardi's note.[1] Scotus told me the other day that you had mentioned our letter for Ricciardi to Scott himself, Nettleship,[2] and Gabriel, and that they all 3 thought of signing it. Of this I had not the faintest idea, or I would have taken care to put the thing before them in practical shape at the right time. For myself, everyone *may*, as far as I care, know all about the affair: but the only person to whom I happen to have actually mentioned it is Brown — and that *after* the letter was dispatched. Gabriel I always regarded as a hopeless case. I have told Scotus he ought to send a separate letter of his own.

I have not seen Barbès'[3] letter, but that noble old man has always been one of my heroes since first I knew his name in 48. There was a most thrilling letter of Hugo's to him published some 7 or 8 years perhaps ago:[4] probably you saw it at the time. Your note contains good news of Flaubert[5] etc. — and especially *Before a Crucifix*. I mean to look up "Islam."[6]

Have the Republicans really revived the 93 calendar?[7] I was not aware of it: the lark of the thing is highly enjoyable, but one must confess inconvenient.

Yours always,
W. M. Rossetti

MS: BL.

1. His acknowledgment of WMR's and Swinburne's joint letter (extracts in *RP*, p. 483).
2. John Trivett Nettleship (1841-1902), animal painter and illustrator, was introduced to the Rossettis by Arthur O'Shaughnessy, whose *Epic of Women* (1870) he illustrated with Blake-like designs. WMR's diaries record many visits to his studio. In the *Academy*, 6 November 1875, WMR praised *On the Trail* for "the same forcible apprehension of the terrible leonine or tigrine nature which Mr. Nettleship has developed in many previous examples" (p. 487).
3. Armand Barbès (1809-70) was one of the leaders of the attempted overthrow of the National Assembly in May 1848, for which he was imprisoned until 1855. Swinburne marked his death with two sonnets published in *Songs before Sunrise*.
4. *Victor Hugo Oeuvres Complètes*, ed. Jean Massin, 1968-70, contains no letter to Barbès earlier than 1869. In 1839 Hugo saved Barbès from the guillotine by sending a plea in verse to Louis-Philippe.
5. Swinburne recommended *L'Éducation Sentimentale* (1870 [1869]).
6. An article by Emmanuel Deutsch in the *Quarterly Review*, October 1869.
7. Swinburne's letters to WMR occasionally followed the 1793 republican calendar, which dated the year 1 from 22 September 1792.

177. TO ALGERNON CHARLES SWINBURNE

56 Euston Square,
12 December [1869]

Dear Swinburne,

I dare say *Arethusa*[1] is right. At any rate I make neither alteration nor comment to it. I *had* put in Parode from your list, and still harken after it a little: but, from what you now say, have restored the blundered Epode.[2] In other respects I have followed *your* list in preference to Fleay's.[3]

Have not yet seen *Miss Kilmansegg*,[4] but expect I soon shall. The only man of our lot that I have heard speak of it is Scotus — with very middling sort of praise — but I expect it is at least clever. Gabriel in one of his "Book of Nonsense" epigrams has lately rhymed to Scotus

A pictor most justly ignotus —

which may console you under non-receipt of his Dürer book.

Gabriel is not partial to "Songs of the Republic": thinks well of *Songs before Sunrise* or other the like title.

Morley wouldn't stand my Shelley sonnet.[5] Professes to think it "very perfect" in execution, but "terribly physical" in idea. I confess this objection, which had not presented itself to me spontaneously at all, does not particularly impress me even now that it is enforced. Failing the *Fortnightly*, I don't know where else to send the sonnet to, so it lies with me not likely to be published for awhile. Having touched up sonnet since you saw it, I enclose it to be returned at convenience.

Thanks about *Hymn to Mercury*.[6] I will see what can be done when my Notes are in print. As you will be aware, *some* of what you did for the *Cyclops*[7] has already been utilized for my purposes. Am not quite sure whether "the field prepared for Love" is in (i.e. in the *Notes*) already, but I think not: also *think*, but am not quite sure, it will remain out. I am glad you are dead against *Fraud* in *Ode to Naples*, for I am the same. The printer hangs fire a good deal. Moxon was very urgent to have the book out "early in December" but his urgency (as far as I have known of it) was expressed at a fatally late day. I hardly see how it can be out before early in January. It is not *my* delay in any sense or degree.

Your

W. M. Rossetti

Had Payne really the cheek to send round to reviews a notice of *Kilmansegg* for them to publish, and did the *Saturday* expose it?[8]

MS: BL.

1. Shelley's poem.
2. Swinburne suggested renaming the "hopelessly muddled" parts of Shelley's *Ode to Naples* (*SL*, 2:63-64).
3. Frederick Gard Fleay (1831-1909), schoolmaster and scholar, sent WMR several Shelley emendations.
4. See Note 8.
5. *Shelley's Heart*, published in the *Dark Blue*, 1 (March 1871), 35. John Morley edited the *Fortnightly Review*, 1867-82.
6. In response to WMR's enquiry about the gap in St. 50 of Shelley's translation of Homer's poem,

242

Swinburne supplied a translation: "He sent for sign, uplifted as he was, / Rash messenger, a piteous blast behind" (*SL*, 2:63). For WMR's decision not to quote the lines in *PWS*, see Letter 179, Note 2.

7. See Letter 157, Note 8.

8. Moxon's edition of Hood's *Miss Kilmansegg and her Precious Leg* (1869) was sent to the journals accompanied by a puff, which the *Saturday Review* printed on 4 December 1869, p. 746.

178. TO MONCURE CONWAY

56 Euston Square,
16 December [1869]

Dear Conway,

Very much obliged. I should really and greatly enjoy going to see Mrs. Lander,[1] but for these next few days am so peculiarly busy that I can't think of it. As for my sisters, they wouldn't go to a theatre to save the British Islands from disappearing off the map: and my mother, though free from such prejudices, never *does* go to any such amusements. Moxon has sworn that the last proof of Shelley shall be done by the end of this week: and though I, in view of the printer's performances, don't regard it as well possible, still I must be ready for — and in all probability immersed in — proofs on Saturday.

I shall send the card to the beautiful Miss Spartali,[2] who understands everything artistic, and will make the box a picture if she goes — which I fancy is more than likely.

There must still be 12 to 15 proofs of Shelley to be printed and revised: at the rate of progress hitherto the book would not be out till the middle of January: but *some* steam will I suppose be put on by the parties concerned. The Memoir is now in type, all but 3 or 4 final pages. If Moxon does what he said, he will be sending you advance sheets — but I know not whether he is exact in these matters.

Pray remember us kindly to Mrs. Conway.

Yours always truly,
W. M. Rossetti

MS: Ohio.

1. Jean Margaret Davenport Lander (1829-1903), English-born actress, lived in the United States from 1849. In 1869 she returned to London to appear as Queen Elizabeth in a translation of Paolo Giacometti's *Elisabetta*, which opened at the Lyceum Theatre on December 18.

2. Marie Spartali (1844-1927) married W. J. Stillman in 1871 against the wishes of her father, Michael Spartali, merchant and Greek Consul-General in London. She was a pupil of FMB, and often sat to DGR, whose style influenced hers. WMR wrote that she was "as gracious and amiable as she … [was] beautiful" (*SR*, 2:342).

179. TO ALGERNON CHARLES SWINBURNE

Somerset House,
20 December [1869]

Dear Swinburne,

I see, on looking again through my MS. Notes on Shelley (which I have just had up to give them a final revision — which proved a serious job after so many new lights etc. etc. — before printing) that I have *not* in said Notes made any mention of "the field prepared for love"[1] — though I have of various other emendations of yours. I will again ponder the point when the proof of the poem reaches me: but am not likely to put it in. I have also thought it best on the whole not to give in the Notes your very capital lines expressing Mercury's misdeed.[2] If I had given the lines, I should naturally have said they were yours: and fools have talked so much nonsense about you that I foresaw they would be saying you couldn't let even this nastiness alone, and it is the *sort* of nastiness one doesn't want to connect one's name with.

"Epode"[3] was put in in due course, and is now printed off. I see now there is another damned blunder about this. When you named "Parode," I put in that with the *figures* to correspond for the opening Parodes and concluding Epodes: then afterwards I restored Epode at the opening, but forgot to re-alter the *figures*. I have now explained this plaguy triviality in the note. It will also go into a list of Errata if possible: but there is so much hurry now about getting the book out that I am not clear that there will remain any time for reading the remaining sheets, and compiling such a list.

These Hood papers[4] are exquisite: it was a daring feat, worthy of its author.

Your Shelley sonnet[5] appears to me intensely beautiful — some of the lines as fine as they can be, as the 4th and 14th. My only demur to it is that one hears through it frequent echoes of a Galilean serpent-hiss or Jew's-harp twang, which, though perfectly appreciable in their abstract intellectual relation, and also in their conversion from the use of the enemy, do not nevertheless appear to me, I confess, the most appropriate treatment. As to details. "God's fire" I think may be the best, though I see its weak point. "In glow of things" I should retain. For my own reading, I incline to "*The* nursing earth" etc.; but would be disposed to concede "*Thy*" to the more unmistakable pointedness of the allusion.

"Cerberus"[6] sounds rather strong, but would depend on the treatment.

As to the Anti-Council I have seen nothing except two paragraphs in the *Daily News*,[7] among the summary of news forming the first leading article. The most detailed statement was that a French democrat Reggiard (I suppose Rogeard) had made a very eloquent speech, eliciting cries of "Viva la Francia Repubblicana" etc., and then the police agent declared the Congress closed, amid many protests. Today I see in the same paper that Ricciardi declares he will reopen it.[8] The affair looks *fort scabreux* certainly, and I hope someone will be brought to book for it.

Best regards to your family.

Yours,
W. M. Rossetti

MS: BL.

1. See Letter 157, Note 8.
2. See Letter 177, Note 6.
3. See Letter 177, Note 2.
4. See Letter 177, Note 8.
5. *Cor Cordium*, which Swinburne revised before its publication in *Songs before Sunrise* (see *SL*, 2:70).
6. "What should you say to a sonnet on the Most Holy Trinity, entitled 'Cerberus'?" (*SL*, 2:71).

244

7. 17 December 1869, p. 4.

8. "Signor Ricciardi and Signor Arezzana announce in the *Roma*, that as the Council was illegally dissolved, they have resolved to open it again, and will give due notice of the day of meeting" (p. 4).

180. TO JOHN CAMDEN HOTTEN

166 Albany Street,
26 December [1869]

My dear Sir,

I did write to Swinburne, and posted the letter, on Saturday — addressing to Holmwood, "To be forwarded." On Monday I received from him a letter written that morning from Dorset Street, saying he would be leaving by next train for Holmwood. Of course therefore he will not have received my letter till Monday afternoon: but that he did then receive it I see every reason to suppose.

In a matter of so much consequence to Swinburne,[1] and at your request, I with pleasure undertook to write to him: but the feeling gains ground with me that it is an affair I have no proper *locus standi* in — that in fact all I could do is to say at second hand what you can say at first hand. My disposition therefore would be to stand aloof henceforward while the persons who are really concerned in the matter ravel it out.

Very faithfully yours,
W. M. Rossetti

MS: Huntington. Extract in *HLQ*, p. 48.

1. See Letter 173.

181. TO ALGERNON CHARLES SWINBURNE

56 Euston Square,
2 January [1870]

Dear Swinburne,

I read with great gusto your last letter about Topsy's *Nolo Episcopari*[1] etc. etc.

Shelley is now done with, so far as I am concerned: I returned the last proof on Thursday morning. Moxon was panting that the book should be actually out early in December. It will not be out till early in January, and even that result has been attained by a good deal of hurry-scurry at the close, involving, I fear, some inaccuracies — though I cannot truthfully say that I have either delayed or scamped one single thing that was at my own disposal. As an example of the hurry, take this. As the printer came near the end of my Notes to volume 2, he found he had exhausted the type proper to those Notes; so he set up the remaining Notes in *other* type, sent me the proof in said last-named type which I revised accordingly, and he will, since that revision, have reset it up in the proper type, which will consequently be printed off without any revision. But anyhow the job is done, and the book will be out almost any day now, I fancy. Mind you don't procure yourself a copy, because I of course mean to send you one — to Holmwood, unless I hear to the contrary.

I shall be at once dispatching thither another small affair of mine — Essay on

Italian Courtesy-books, for the Early English Text Society. The printed copies reached me yesterday.

Any paper that spoke about unpublished Shelley poems received from "the *Shelley* family" was in error, and must have miscopied from a paragraph in the *Athenaeum*[2] embodying a statement of my own. There are two new poems[3] (short — one very musical, but neither first-rate) received from a Colonel and Mr. Catty, sons of a Mrs. Catty (still living) who, when a Miss Sophia Stacey, received them in Florence from Shelley. The poem in MS. at Oxford belongs to a Mr. Morfill[4] — do you know anything of him? It was first named to me, 2 or 3 months ago, by Mr. Appleton,[5] Editor of the *Academy*. I applied for it to Mr. Morfill, who does not refuse it, but has, as regards prompt production, hung back to an extent which will of course deprive the book of it, unless in a future edition. He terms them *vers de société: possibly* it might turn out that I have already laid hands upon them in some other form. I believe there is no reasonable doubt of their genuineness.

I have heard no more about Ricciardi's Council.

That extract from the *Guardian*[6] is indeed *impayable*, and ought to be placarded in all directions, were it not that the source it comes from is not of sufficient importance.

The antiphonal songs[7] are, I have no doubt, splendid; and the lark of pre-publishing the Christian one would be most delightful *as* a lark, though perhaps hardly worthy of the dignity of "le premier poète vivant de l'Angleterre."

About Tristram, I am really at present crassly ignorant. Will however, as soon as leisure serves, look into the Early English publications, and inform you if anything turns up. I don't *think* there is anything.

Of Tennyson's book[8] I know nothing as yet (having been too busy) save the *Northern Farmer*, hurriedly read in a copy Gabriel possesses. What a delightful "putting of the foot in it" was exhibited by the "minor periodical" in quoting, as new, a long bit of the old *Morte d'Arthur* of our infancy, beginning with those almost incredibly threadbare-worn words "The old order changes" etc.[9] The same No. of the minor periodical printed *Laon and Cynthia*.

Your affectionate
W. M. Rossetti

MS: BL.

1. Swinburne congratulated Morris on his "promotion by the reviews [of *The Earthly Paradise*] to the post of Christian laureate" (*SL*, 2:78). Peter Faulkner concludes that "the remark is perhaps due primarily to the contrast which many reviewers noted between Swinburne's exuberant celebration of pagan themes and Morris's restrained treatment of them" (*William Morris: the Critical Heritage* [1973], pp. 10-11).

2. 18 December 1869, p. 820.

3. *To Sophia* and *Time Long Past*. Sophia Stacey, the ward of Shelley's uncle, Robert Parker, married Captain J. P. Catty. In *PWS*, 2:561, WMR acknowledged Lieutenant-Colonel C. Parker Catty and Corbet Stacey Catty.

4. Probably William Richard Morfill, Ilchester lecturer in Slavonic at Oxford from 1873, who is listed in *Mathieson's Oxford Directory* as early as 1867. The poem is not identified.

5. Charles Edward Appleton (1841-79), founder of the *Academy* (1869) which he edited until his death.

6. 22 December 1869, p. 74, attacking Ricciardi's Anti-Council (*SL*, 2:77).

7. *Christmas Antiphones*, published in *Songs before Sunrise*.

8. *The Holy Grail and Other Poems* (1870 [1869]).

9. In a review of *The Holy Grail* in the *Athenaeum*, 18 December 1869, pp. 809-10. Cythna was misspelled in a note on *PWS* in "Literary Gossip," p. 820.

182. TO WILLIAM DOUGLAS O'CONNOR

56 Euston Square,
4 January [1870]

Dear Mr. O'Connor,

By all manner of means cut out that or any other portion of my introductory remarks:[1] indeed on reflection I agree with you that it would be more likely to act as a provocation and defiance than anything else, and is therefore an indiscretion.

I had a very gratifying letter from Whitman himself lately, and shall be replying directly — also some news of him from Stillman.

Poor Lady Byron![2] You pitch into her with a gusto. Really I believe the worst that ought to be said of her is that she was intensely virtuous in the way of correctness, and not of sympathy — and (perhaps) addicted to morbid broodings and baseless *idées fixes*.

I cut this short, my immediate object being the practical one embodied in the opening paragraph.

Yours very truly,
W. M. Rossetti

It has sometimes occurred to me that there was no *title* supplied to the MS. I sent you. What would seem to me about the most appropriate is — Reflections on Walt Whitman's Poems — By an Englishwoman: but you will decide.

MS: LC.

1. To Anne Gilchrist's "Woman's Estimate of Walt Whitman." O'Connor to WMR, 18 December 1869: "Your introductory remarks are very felicitous and manly, but, solely as a matter of prudence, in order that the rancor of the enemy may not be unduly provoked or challenged, I think, and Mr. Whitman thinks also, that the excision of a part of the last page is advisable" (Ohio Wesleyan).

2. See Letter 165, Note 19.

183. TO WALT WHITMAN

56 Euston Square,
9 January 1870

Dear Mr. Whitman,

I was exceedingly pleased at receiving your recent letter, and the photograph which followed it immediately afterwards. I admire the photograph very much; rather grudge its having the hat on, and so cutting one out of the *full* portraiture of your face, but have little doubt, allowing for this detail, it brings me very near your external aspect. May I be allowed to send you, as a very meagre requital, the enclosed likeness of myself.

I gave your letter, and the second copy of your portrait, to the lady[1] you refer to, and need scarcely say how truly delighted she was. She has asked me to say that you could not have devised for her a more welcome pleasure, and that she feels grateful to me for having sent to America the extracts from what she had written, since they have been a satisfaction to you. She also begs leave, with much deference, to offer a practical suggestion: — that, if you see no reason against it, the new edition might be issued in 2 volumes,[2] lettered, not volumes 1 and 2, but 1st series and 2nd series, so that they could be priced and sold separately, when so desired. She adds: "This simple expedient would, I think, overcome a serious difficulty. Those who are not able to receive aright all Mr. Whitman has written might, to their own infinite gain, have what they *can* receive, and grow by means of that food to be capable of the whole perhaps; while he would stand as unflinchingly as hitherto by what he has written. I know I am glad that your Selections were put into my hands first, so that I was lifted up by them to stand firm on higher ground than I had ever stood on before, and furnished with a golden key before approaching the rest of the poems." She also, as a hearty admirer of your original Preface, hopes that that may reappear — either whole, or such portions as have not since been used in other forms.

I know, by a letter from O'Connor, that, since you wrote, you have seen the further observations of this lady which I sent over in November. I replied to O'Connor the other day: also, still more recently, took the liberty, of posting to you a little essay of mine, written for one of our literary societies, on Italian Courtesy-books of the Middle Ages. Some of the extracts I have translated in it may, I hope, be found not without their charm and value. I wrote to Conway giving him your cordial message: probably you know that he was not long ago in Russia. Also I heard the other day from a man I am much attached to, Stillman, of his having re-encountered you in Washington. As he told you, there is a chance — not as yet *more* than a chance — that I may make my way over the Atlantic for a brief glimpse of America in the summer. If so, how great a delight it will be to me to see and know you need not, I hope, be stated in words.

Perhaps before that I shall have received here the new edition you refer to — another deep draught of satisfaction.

I could run on a great deal further on these and other topics; but should have to come to a close at last somewhere, and may perhaps as well do so now.

Yours in reverence and love,
W. M. Rossetti

MS: LC. Published: *WWC*, 1:379-81.

1. Anne Gilchrist.
2. *Leaves of Grass* 1876, sixth edition, was in two volumes, but the fifth edition of 1871 was not.

184. TO ALGERNON CHARLES SWINBURNE

56 Euston Square,
17 January [1870]

Dear Swinburne,

Though short of time for writing as I should wish, I can't help thanking you at once for the crowning your letter[1] gives me: it is one of the things one doesn't forget. I feel with you that — whatever its faults, which you too indulgently leave unnamed — the thing is something to have done; and that the man who gets his name lettered on any corner of the monument of Shelley has lived not absolutely in vain.

I know you will find me out in lots of blunders sooner or later: they will all be grist for the mill of a new edition. That is a stupid one about Wordsworth:[2] I can hardly *assert* that I ever exactly knew about the omitted phrase, and yet, now that you mention it, I find a lurking consciousness of it in my memory. Ditto as to "Both infinite as is the universe"[3] etc.: you are right, I have next to no doubt — not *no* doubt. What do you think of

Hovering in verse o'er its accustomed prey —

(*Ode to Liberty*)?[4] I am almost sure that I see the truth of it now, and made a mull in my printed note. I also would quite as soon have found the Eton lines separable from the *Serchio*:[5] but, as they are undoubtedly in the MS., part and parcel of it, had no option.

Keate:[6] I will look up about this. Your remarks satisfy me that my statement is pretty safe to be wrong, but I am as good as sure it rests on authority — Medwin's[7] most likely. Uprest:[8] I make no boggling over Up*ri*st, but think Uprest a daring and unprincipled innovation. Strange that I should have so totally forgotten the Reform pamphlet:[9] I now remember the incident as clear as if it were yesterday.

I am delighted to hear about *Hertha*: to hear itself will be still better.

Have not yet seen the R.A. Old Masters: have an overwhelming lot of work at Somerset House — say $9\frac{1}{4}$ to $5\frac{1}{2}$ daily — and can't possibly get a glimpse of a daylight exhibition.

Pierre Bonaparte[10] has clearly committed a crime for which he must be made to pay dear. I confess however I regret it is *he* of all members of the family: he has really, I believe, been worthy of respect as a consistent Republican. I believe the funeral was a *coup manqué*: the very air that day was full of revolution, if there had only been the men to take advantage of it — the troops might have fraternized — and perhaps M. Verhuell[11] would now be in London. I give this merely as my own impression.

Here is another letter of old Ricciardi, received the other day. I know it is illegible, but have not the industry to put needful decipherments on it at the moment. I really see little prospect of an English publisher,[12] and have just written to tell him so: do you see any? Have also told him I should be proud to subscribe towards covering expenses, if permissible.

A previous letter of yours is also by me, demanding more of response than I afford it. The Collect for December[13] is toothsome: though I do rather deprecate such an assault on a dead woman known to have been *spirituelle* and agreeable, and not known (to me at least) to have been anything else much amiss. That Mrs. Verhuell was unfortunate in her by-blown son seems to be the head and front of her offending. Of your alternative phrases (as you invite me to express an opinion) I would retain "Thou like a worm" etc. "Red worm" is appositely nasty in sensation: but I should stick to the simpler expression, and must especially so as "born red" occurs soon before. I don't know what else I need remark upon as "forced" etc., as queried by you: unless it is the phrase "as — thank the secret sire" etc. I can *conceive* that some less deferred course of sentence would come natural to you at some stage of revision: but if not I can't put forward any definite *objection* to the form of it at present.

Excuse haste and slovenly response.

Your

W. M. Rossetti

This moment comes a letter from old Trelawny: very gratifying, and you shall see it one day. But he calls the book hideous in aspect. Is this really the case? My own impression was much the contrary — though I don't mean there is *no* room for improvement. One thing is — Trelawny loathes any book of poems too big to be stuffed into a pocket.

MS: BL.

1. Acknowledging *PWS* (*SL*, 2:81-86).
2. WMR assigned to Shelley the motto to *Peter Bell the Third*, which was taken from the first edition of Wordsworth's *Peter Bell*.
3. Swinburne protested WMR's punctuation of the curse in *Prometheus Unbound*, Act 1. WMR revised it in *PWS* 1878.
4. St. 1. Emended in *PWS* 1878 to read "Hovering inverse o'er its accustomed prey."
5. *The Boat on the Serchio*, 11. 78-83.
6. Swinburne questioned the accuracy of WMR's statement that Dr. John Keate, the headmaster of Eton, "flogged Shelley liberally" and that Shelley in turn "plagued him without stint." WMR repeated the statement in the revised Memoir in *PWS* 1878, but in the separate issue of 1886 he conceded that it was "probably ... inaccurate" (*Memoir of Shelley* [With a New Preface], p. ii).
7. Thomas Medwin, Shelley's second cousin, published a *Life of Shelley* in 1847.
8. *The Revolt of Islam*, Can. 3, St. 21: "The uprest / Of the third sun brought hunger." WMR thought that "uprest" for uprising was coined by Shelley "on no warrant ... better than the exigency of rhyme" (*PWS*, 1:480). Swinburne objected that "uprist" was used by Spenser (actually "upryst" in *The Shepheardes Calender* [March], as Lang points out, *SL*, 2:84).
9. *An Address to the People on the Death of Princess Charlotte*, said to have been printed in 1817, but known only in a facsimile reprint of [1843?]. Swinburne reminded WMR that they had examined a copy in Monckton Milnes's library at Fryston in 1862.
10. (1815-81), son of Lucien Bonaparte. On 10 January 1870 he killed the journalist Victor Noir, was tried at the insistence of the republican press, and acquitted.
11. Napoleon III was rumored to be the son of Louis Napoleon's wife, Hortense Beauharnais, by the Dutch Admiral Verhuell.
12. For "an English version of the book on the Anticoncilio" (Bornand, p. 14).
13. Sonnet 1 of *Mentana: Second Anniversary*, published as Part 14 of *Dirae*. "Thou, like a worm" and "As, thank the secret sire" were retained.

185. TO ALGERNON CHARLES SWINBURNE

56 Euston Square,
20 February [1870]

Dear Swinburne,

Your suggestion of Trübner[1] for the Anticoncilio is, I fancy, the best that can be made: if I have to take further action in the matter, I will bear him in mind.

Did I send you the programme of the book, now some little while back sent me by Ricciardi? The strange thing is that it appears to be the work of an *enemy* to the sacred cause of atheism — though one who regards the Anticoncilio as a serious matter deserving of corresponding treatment.

Garibaldi's book[2] is, I think, advertised as out: I have not *seen* anything of it. Don't know who first called Louis Napoleon Messiah: nor *accurately* that anyone did so, though I think I did see something about it years ago — perhaps some municipal body, and as far back as 1852 or 1853. Did not see the *Times* article.[3]

"Hovering in verse." My present notion (printed in *Notes and Queries* of 12 February[4]) is that it ought to be "inverse": What do you think of that? — i.e. wheeling inwards.

"Congregator of slaves."[5] I am not clear whether you have observed my note, saying that my punctuation reproduces that of the first edition, as the "safest." My *preference* is the same as yours, though not so energetic: after what you say, I think, in any further edition, I would disregard safety, and stick to preference.

The *Athenaeum* did come it strong:[6] why I know not well. It leaves me equanimous. The only other London review I have seen is the *Examiner*:[7] very handsome on the whole.

What you say about the inferiority of Act 3 of *Prometheus* had not hitherto struck me with any *extreme* force. Now that your letter takes me by the throat on the subject, I have to admit that the general conception of what Prometheus is going to do with himself, and what constitutes the regeneration of humankind, is, in essentials, a little too much from the Leigh Huntish point of view: the Spirit of the Earth I always did regard as an *Enfant Terrible*. First 2 scenes gloriously fine. I can't say that I even now feel the objection so very strongly, for there is much transcendent work even in the remaining scenes of Act 3, and Act 4 remains to wind all up to the right pitch. Act 4, as you remember, is an afterthought. To my shame be it said, I had sometimes doubted whether, with all its supernal beauty, it was an advantage to the drama as a whole: but now that you make me reflect exactly upon where the poem would have been left at without it, I for the first time feel it to be structurally as well as severally invaluable.

Your Wordsworthian discovery[8] is no doubt a sunlike satisfaction to yourself, and may reflect a moony lumer on to Gabriel when he hears of it. For myself I am more interested to hear of the *Eve of Revolution*, and look forward to a sight of that and the other poems of the series in due time.

Dr. Dobbin[9] (whom I now find to be a Reverend) has suggested to me that *Letter to Maria Gisborne*, page 245, ought to run "which fishers found under the utmost crag": — I am not *convinced*, but think it very likely. What do you say? There is no printed *authority* for it, I am sure.

Yours always,
W. M. Rossetti

It is a curious fact that I have this evening had to answer *three* Reverends, all writing as Shelley admirers.

MS: BL.

1. Nicholas Trübner (1817-84), publisher and orientalist.
2. *Il Governo del Monaco* (1870).
3. Perhaps "French Politics," 7 February 1870, pp. 9-10. According to Swinburne the article attacked "the democratic leaders as aristocrats whose republicanism means enmity to and jealousy of the most holy Middle Class ... which has supplanted their families" (*SL*, 2:93).
4. P. 167. See also Letter 184, Note 4.
5. *Ode to Liberty*, St. 3. *PWS* reads:

> beneath sate deified
> The Sister-pest, congregator of slaves
> Into the shadow of her pinions wide.

Swinburne objected to placing the period after "wide" instead of after "slaves" (*SL*, 2:93), and WMR made the change in *PWS* 1878.
6. The anonymous attack on *PWS*, 29 January 1870, pp. 154-56, was by Robert Buchanan.
7. 5 February 1870, p. 85.
8. An ingenious but tedious parallel between Wordsworth and de Sade (*SL*, 2:94-95).
9. In *PWS*, 2:567, where Dobbin's suggestion about some lines of *The Question* is quoted, his address is given as Ballivor, Ireland. WMR silently adopted his emendation of the *Letter to Maria Gisborne* in *PWS* 1878.

186. TO JOHN CAMDEN HOTTEN

56 Euston Square,
12 April [1870]

My dear Sir,

It was out of my power to read and reflect upon your letter to Swinburne's Solicitors while I was at Somerset House; but I have now done so, and beg to return it — and to reply to the several points in your note to me.[1]

I am not inclined to take any further steps with regard to the R.A. Notes,[2] otherwise than as set forth in my letter on the subject. If Swinburne is willing to do his section, I will immediately afterwards do mine. If Swinburne is not willing, the chief reason would probably be that the business relations between you and him are for some reason or other not satisfactory; and in that case I — as being intimate with him, and without assuming any partisan attitude — fancy I should consult my own peace and quietness by standing aloof. Therefore unless and until you obtain Swinburne's co-operation I consider the Notes lapsed so far as I am concerned.

I have not seen Swinburne for months past, nor even heard from him for 3 or 4 weeks; and really don't know, except from your enclosed letter, how affairs stand between you and him. He did write me something about it a longish while back, perhaps 4 or 5 months, naming (I speak from memory) certain apparent or assumed details in which he was aggrieved by you. I replied distinctly intimating my opinion that all these matters should be thoroughly probed and verified — not prejudged; and that after verification it would behove him to act upon the ascertained facts. Since then I have heard no more about it.

As to the paragraph in your enclosed letter affecting me. I perfectly recollect the colloquy on your second floor (though I can't speak to the date): my brother, I think, was also present. I confirm in a general sense your account of the matter

252

— with this qualification. To the best of my recollection, you said that you would like to have something like a stipulation that Swinburne would continue to publish with you; and the reply was that, although no express *promise* to that effect would be given, still it might be clearly understood that, as long as he considered himself properly dealt with by you, he would, as a matter of fact, so continue.

As I had occasion to mention once before, I made some notes of this interview either at the moment or immediately afterwards, and could now speak with confidence on some points from these notes, were they in my possession. But they were handed over to Swinburne many months ago, to assist his memory in certain particulars, and have never since returned to me.

I wish it to be distinctly understood that I have taken no part against you in this matter, and have circulated or repeated no rumours. When spoken or written to about it, I have always expressed my opinion that a distinct and authentic statement of the accounts between you and Swinburne should be obtained, and that his course of action should be determined by what appears from those accounts. The last sentence in your enclosed letter seems to show that he has now seen the accounts, and is satisfied with them; a point of which otherwise I know nothing.

Very faithfully yours,
W. M. Rossetti

MS: Huntington. Extract in *HLQ*, p. 49.

1. For Hotten's letter of 12 April, see *HLQ*, p. 48.
2. Hotten had proposed a successor to WMR's and Swinburne's *Notes on the Royal Academy Exhibition, 1868.*

187. TO ALGERNON CHARLES SWINBURNE

56 Euston Square,
19 April [1870]

Dear Swinburne,

I have just been reading with exaltation, and almost with astonishment, your most splendid *Eve of Revolution*. It is the *dernier mot* of your work. Stanza succeeds stanza compelling me to say to myself, "Were this in Shelley's *Ode to Liberty* or *Ode to Naples*, one would have no option but to call it one of the finest in the poem": Can more be said by me or to you?

One thing that strikes me, in a technical point of view, is that the alexandrines are very generally without the *ordinary* emphasis of pause in the middle of the line. I take it you have done this advisedly, and I don't mean to express any doubt of its fine effect, but mention it merely as a point of execution that impresses itself on my attention.

Before a Crucifix is "very soothing" — *very* soothing: I enjoy it hugely, and reckon it indeed as also among your finest things. Its comparative simplicity of rhythm and structure are as delightful as in some other cases the contrary qualities.

Also Sublustri Luce[1] (do I read the title right?) very fine. Has this been in print, or did you read me some of it erewhile? I read it with a reminiscent sense.

These are all I have read as yet: shall go in for the others tomorrow, as now I must take up something else. As Whitman says "I do not commiserate, I congratulate you,"[2] so I can say "I do not congratulate, I tripudiate with you."

Your
W. M. Rossetti

MS: BL. Extract in *Swinburne Library*, pp. 62-63.

1. "Probably *Tenebrae*," Lang suggests (*SL*, 2:110).
2. *To One Shortly to Die.*

188. TO ALGERNON CHARLES SWINBURNE

56 Euston Square,
1 May [1870]

Dear Swinburne,

Sloth or other less condemnable motive has made me delay longer than I had thought for to express my opinion of your MS. poems. Immediately after I had written about *Eve of Revolution* etc. I read the others, and then handed over the MSS. to Scotus: have not seen him since.

The title Sublustri Luce[1] is to me a euphonious one, not *needing* alteration unless you think of something that pleases yourself better. The only objection I see to it is that to me (and to others equally unready at their Latin) the phrase is not exactly a familiar one, unmistakable in meaning. If it *entirely* corresponds to our "Twilight" — whether Evening-twilight or Dawn-twilight — I *don't particularly* see why the English word should not be substituted — nor yet why it need be.

I certainly do like the *Antiphones*;[2] and enjoy and admire the feat you have performed in the mid-line rhyming, though I don't feel *sure* but that the poem would be equally beautiful without this added difficulty and restriction in choice of expression.

Quia Multum Amavit is masterly in all ways, and one of your *great* performances in that wondrous gift you so singularly excel in — passion of rhythmical sound — which, treated as loftily as here, counts to me as an exalted form of poetic imagination. I think I a *little* grudge your frequent use of Galilean machinery: not because it is blasphemous, which is an objection natural and resignable to the professors of that creed themselves, but because it looks as if we "couldn't do without" this sphere of ideas — as if even those who profess to come out of it must really remain in it. But possibly I am putting overmuch of the zeal of sect into a poetical question: you at any rate are extremely well able to take care of yourself on the matter.

We read yesterday your article on Gabriel.[3] It is a splendid performance — truly and superabundantly rich and fine. You may be sure you have the thanks of us all for so lavish an attestation of intellectual and personal sympathy. I see there is one in *Fraser's*[4] too: also a *Responsio Shelleiana*[5] — What does that mean? I must get the No.

Your affectionate
W. M. Rossetti

MS: BL.

1. See Letter 187, Note 1.
2. *Christmas Antiphones.*
3. *"The Poems of Dante Gabriel Rossetti," Fortnightly Review*, n.s. 7 (May 1870), 551-79.
4. n.s. 1 (May 1870), 609-22, by John Skelton.
5. A poem, signed J. J. M., p. 657.

189. TO JOHN CAMDEN HOTTEN

56 Euston Square,
3 May [1870][1]

My dear Sir,

A day or two after I wrote you last Swinburne called here bringing the letter from you to his Solicitors of which you had sent me a copy, and wishing to consult me about it. I told him that I had already seen and replied to the letter, and mentioned the purport of my reply. Swinburne consequently, perceiving that the immediate practical question was disposed of, and being more inclined to read me some poems than to enter on a business discussion for its own sake, set to at reading, and I now know no more of the general state of matters between you and him than I did when I wrote before.

You ask me whether I know any cause of objection on Swinburne's part. I confess that I feel some difficulty in answering this question so explicitly as you would wish. Supposing Swinburne *had* stated to me any serious objection convincing to his own mind, this would presumably be something to your disadvantage; and, as the mention of it to me would clearly not be a "privileged communication," I might perhaps be laying Swinburne open to an action for libel. I don't say that I have any such special information to give; but that, *if* I had it, my giving it might be unbefitting at the present stage of the case.

I suppose however I may properly say thus much. For some while past Swinburne has been impressed with the idea that, while the fame of his writings is very great, and the sale of them presumably in some proportion to correspond, the profits accruing to himself have been but moderate. This no doubt is no news to you: it was the feeling which prompted Swinburne to wish to have a clear and authenticated statement of the accounts between you and himself. For months past I have heard nothing (save through you) about these accounts, or about the view which Swinburne has formed of them: and I can conscientiously say that I don't know whether he at the present moment considers that the accounts produced are complete — or, if complete, satisfactory.

I am satisfied in my own mind that what my last letter said about the original interview at your house was substantially correct as far as it goes: — that an unqualified promise to continue thenceforth publishing with you was not made by or on behalf of Swinburne; but that it was intimated that his then present intention (to be acted upon unless adequate cause should appear to the contrary) was to continue publishing with you. My opinion is that, after what was then said to the above effect, Swinburne would not be acting rightly were he to leave you through mere caprice, waywardness, or changeableness; but that, if he has any reason to allege which will stand the test of unbiased investigation (a point as to which I neither do nor at present can pronounce any opinion), he is not violating any engagement known to me by leaving you.

Wholly free as before from any partisan feeling in this matter, I remain

Very faithfully yours,
W. M. Rossetti

MS: Huntington. Extract in *HLQ*, pp. 50-51.

1. For Hotten's letter to WMR, 2 May 1870, see *HLQ*, pp. 49-50.

190. TO ALGERNON CHARLES SWINBURNE

56 Euston Square,
22 May [1870]

Dear Swinburne,

You know I am getting up a set of Poets for cheap sale,[1] including Keats (Moxon publisher). I mean to put in all the outlying poems. Do you know of any not included in Houghton's *Life*? You are so *au fait* in these matters that, if *you* don't know of such, I shall confidently believe there are none. I have by me the *one*-volume *Life* (1867), which contains — I am not sure whether the two-volume edition does so — the first *Hyperion*: also as finale "a fragment of doubtful authenticity" beginning "What sylphlike form."[2] Do you believe in this fragment? I don't remember ever seeing it till tonight. Have only read it once, and was decidedly inclined to disbelieve its earlier portion — but the speech given as spoken by Ariel looks to me *more* like Keats, and I now feel a little uncertain — though still tending strongly to disbelief.

The edition of Keats will be of little value, for Moxon, in order not to spoil the sale of his Library Edition, wants only about ⅔ of the bulk thereof reproduced in the cheap form. I see nothing for it but to miss out all the short poems, save the exceptionally fine ones. The like will be the case with the Coleridge in this series — but here much less harm done.

Yours always,
W. M. Rossetti

The *Otho* is not in the one-volume *Life*, nor any other poem of dramatic form. Surely my memory is not wrong in believing *Otho* was in the two-volume *Life*? I don't remember any other dramatic writing, but a note in the one-volume *Life* seems to imply that there are others.

MS: BL.

1. "Moxon's Popular Poets."
2. Milnes explains that the poem is "in what appears to be Keats's autograph.... If not authentic, it is a clever imitation" (*Life of Keats* [1 vol. ed., 1867], pp. 360-63). WMR (like subsequent editors) did not admit it into his edition.

191. TO ALGERNON CHARLES SWINBURNE

56 Euston Square,
23 May [1870]

Dear Swinburne,

Excuse fragmentariness or curtness in answering.

The address to Whitman[1] seems to me fine, as your work always is; also in fact appropriate — though in the case of so exceptional a man and writer, something more *exceptional* (as among your own compositions) might have seemed in keeping. In detail of execution the only points that occur to me as worth attention are these: — There are 3 instances of an adjective at end of one line connected with its substantive at beginning of next line: "strange Land," "purest Life," "holier Name." It is a peculiarity of structure which I don't dislike as having a certain peculiar zest: but I fancy, in a composition of such moderate length, if you see your way to reducing the instances below 3, it might be as well. "Lonely" and "only" are twice over given as rhymes. Similar observation.

Monotones[2] I think most amply "worth insertion." As a *practical question*, I think you might be guided yes or no by the degree of affinity which this poem bears to others *passim*: but I don't see that you should entertain the least doubt of its *worthiness*.

Bomba's[3] tartarization — sorry to say I don't know the date.

Your *Appeal to England*[4] dated 20 November 1867: I have it, but pasted into a book of extracts. The execution, I am sure, was the following morning, 21 November.

> O patria mia, vedo le mura e gli archi
> E le colonne e i simulacri e l'erme
> Torri degli avi nostri;
> Ma la gloria non vedo,
> Non vedo il lauro e il ferro ond'eran carchi
> I nostri padri antichi.[5]

The words "Sol gli uomini non vedo" don't occur (it might be still better if they did): but a good way on a stanza begins (the 3rd) "Dove sono i tuoi figli?"

I sincerely commiserate you in working imagination and invention up to time. It must be a horrible hell — which the uninventive man is mercifully spared, and which the inventive *ought to spare himself*. I would strongly in your place incline to tell Ellis[6] that the book shall only come out when it suits you, and when such pieces as you choose to insert are completed at your own discretion.

These plagues of yours make me the more grateful for the helpful amplitude of your reply concerning Keats. I possess the 1820 volume[7] — bought lately more strictly through Shelley than through Keats enthusiasm, as being the counterpart of what Shelley had with him when drowned.

A Keats compiled exactly as you propose would certainly be an artistic volume. Mine, as hitherto proposed, would not be that, and would lack visible *raison d'être* (as I just lately told Moxon). I shall further weigh conflicting claims before deciding.

What I would myself prefer to do for the forthcoming Keats, as one of a series, would be to make it *complete*: all the collected poems, and also all the outlying poems. Moxon, for trade purposes, wants to miss out ⅓ of the bulk of the collected poems; but to give the cheap book a separate claim of its own by the inclusion of *all* the outlying poems. This, though inartistic, will be an indisputable attainment in one direction, and convenience to Keats purchasers — for instance to myself: for then, by getting the Library Keats and also the cheap Keats, we shall have all his poems in a collected form, as yet non-existing.

I looked yesterday through the minor poems in the Library edition (1869) which includes some, but not nearly all, of the outlying poems. What I had marked for retention in my volume are these

Dedication to Hunt	Not on ground of merit, but for
Imitation of Spenser	bearing on Keats's biography

Nightingale	
Grecian Urn	
Autumn	
Melancholy	
Drear-nighted December	
Chapman's Homer	For merit
Picture of Leander	
On — (Think not of it)	
Belle Dame	
Eve of Saint Mark	
On a Dream	
The Day is Gone	
Last Sonnet	

To these as aforesaid would be added *all* other outlying poems, good or bad. I shall now carefully compare my selected list with yours, and see further to it. But I fancy what you propose to miss out will prove to be *less* than ⅓ of the collected bulk, and Moxon lays stress on that proportion.

Your

W. M. Rossetti

MS: BL.

1. *To Walt Whitman in America.* Published in *Songs before Sunrise* without the revisions suggested by WMR.

2. Included in *Songs before Sunrise.*

3. Ferdinand II, king of the two Sicilies, died on 22 May 1859.

4. A plea for clemency for the three Fenians who were hanged in Manchester on 23 November 1867. For details of its publication, see *SL*, 1:274.

5. Swinburne had requested WMR to copy out these lines from Leopardi's *All'Italia.*

6. Frederick Startridge Ellis (1830-1901), bookseller, scholar, Shelley enthusiast, publisher and friend of DGR and Morris. He published *Songs before Sunrise* in 1871.

7. *Lamia, Isabella, The Eve of St. Agnes and other Poems.*

192. TO ALGERNON CHARLES SWINBURNE

56 Euston Square,
5 August [1870]

Dear Swinburne,

I agree with you that your returning to Hotten under threat of legal proceedings — or even *after* said threat, supposing it to be withdrawn — is not in the category of possible solutions.

> There's that betwixt us been which men remember
> Till they forget themselves — till all's forgot[1] etc.

(What admirable lines these are!) The idea that the book[2] is not to come out at all is also not to be entertained. Therefore the only course is to publish with such publisher as you like, and let the rest take care of itself.

I would however, in your place, do my best to settle the thing on a footing of conciliation. It seems to me that the thoroughly reasonable course to adopt, in the first instance when you came to the conclusion that you could not get on with Hotten any longer, would have been to tell him as much in distinct and amicable terms, giving him a certain *term of notice* — say 6 months — to make his own reasonable arrangements, and after that to part company. If I am not mistaken, this was never done; and the consequence is that Hotten not only finds himself suddenly left in the lurch without notice, but he also may have — and I take it actually has — spent money out of pocket on advertising Songs of the Republic. I would therefore now do the nearest thing that can be done to what, in my opinion, ought to have been done from the first — i.e.:

I would instruct your lawyer to offer Hotten forthwith (and "without prejudice," as the lawyers say) £50 down as indemnity for any expense and detriment he may have suffered, requiring him to accept within (say) 3 weeks, and give a written acquittance in full; your lawyer giving him notice, along with this offer, that, whether accepted or not, you equally and irrevocably mean to publish *Songs before Sunrise* and any future books through another firm. If he accepted, I should consider you were out of a dilemma on tolerably easy terms: if he declined, he would have to do his worst, and I can't but think — with Howell's and my testimony etc. — he would fail to establish any case against you: only he would give you a horrible lot of trouble, and perhaps a long lawyer's bill.

Probably I need not tell you that I have heard *nothing* (save through yourself) of the proposal that Howell and I should arbitrate.

Supposing you to adopt the course above suggested, I would press on the publication of your book at the speediest. It is only last night that Gabriel happened to say how disastrous it is that just now — when anything of an excited political tone from you on foreign politics would ring through England and Europe — the book should be shelved.

You ask "whether I can find out whether Hotten really intends to go to law." I hardly know what I could do to this end, except call on Hotten, tell him my mind, and enquire his intentions. This I am willing to do *if you like*: but have little confidence in any satisfactory result, and would rather counsel you to stick to strictly legal communication through your Solicitor.

259

As you ask me for "*first advice*, and next help," I take no further steps till I hear from you in reply: when I do so, I shall *sollecitamente* (as the Italians say) take any practical step that may be agreed upon.

I think there would be nothing unreasonable, if more convenient to yourself, in asking Ellis to advance the £50 proposed as a sop to Hotten — to be retained out of the first incomings from *Songs before Sunrise*. I don't think I would offer Hotten *more* than £50, whatever reply he might make.

Christina and the rest of us were very greatly pleased at what you say of "Vanna's Twins," and her book[3] generally: indeed, Christina has had to *copy out the passage*, to be put among other family criticisms treasured up by motherly affection. I agree with you in a high estimate of "Vanna's Twins" — which, as it happened, I had never read till the volume was published. Perhaps the death of the babies *is* rather a shock: but we must remember the authoress's perfect conviction, or say absolute certainty, that a few minutes of pain in this world made them perfectly and incredibly happy somewhere else for ever afterwards.

I plead guilty to not remembering the line of Marlowe to which you refer in connexion with Shelley.[4]

Heartily trusting you are going on well in health,[5] I am

Yours affectionately,
W. M. Rossetti

Has Victor Hugo said anything in print about the War?[6] I presume not — his convictions being on one side, and his patriotism and its obligations on the other.

Probably you have not yet seen the cheap Byron and Longfellow to which the enclosed notices[7] pertain — indeed, I doubt whether the Longfellow is yet published. You will not suspect me of fancying that notices of so slight a sort have any particular value of any kind: but, as I happen to have a few extra copies by me, it comes natural to me to show them to you. Of course they need not be returned.

I retain Ellis's letter for the present, in case I should have to do anything making it convenient that I should refer to it.

MS: BL. Extract in *HLQ*, pp. 51-52.

1. Henry Taylor, *Philip van Artevelde*, II. vi.
2. *Songs before Sunrise*.
3. *Commonplace and Other Short Stories*.
4. Swinburne pointed out a resemblance between Shelley's *The Question* and *I walk'd along a stream, for pureness rare*, a fragment from *England's Parnassus*. Lang notes that it is not by Marlowe but by Gervase Markham (*SL*, 2:116).
5. WBS to WMR, 16 July 1870: "I heard from Letitia the other day a sad account of Algernon, and would like to hear from you what you have seen of him poor fellow, or done in the matter. Letitia said you had gone to see him and that you proposed writing to his father, which would really be the best thing to do. His powers must be impaired by these delirium tremens bouts already and if he goes on a little longer he had better die, as it is almost certain the result will be too dreadful to think of" (AP).
6. Franco-Prussian War, which began on 19 July with a declaration of war by France. From the beginning France suffered defeat, and in early September Napoleon III was taken prisoner and an insurrection in Paris proclaimed the Third Republic. The war ended early in 1871 with a peace dictated by Bismarck, which included the payment to Germany of an enormous war indemnity and the surrender of Alsace and most of Lorraine.

7. WMR to Lucy Rossetti, 11 August [1880], mentions "duplicate sheets of my prefatory notices to Moxon's Poets" (AP).

193. TO ALGERNON CHARLES SWINBURNE

56 Euston Square,
11 August [1870]

Dear Swinburne,

A few words to fill the gap. I called at Hotten's today, but he was not in. Possibly he may call on me in return, which might be the best thing: if he does not do so tomorrow or next day, I will see what further is to be done. I meant to call on him on Tuesday, but was prevented by a marriage settlement affair (Mrs. Warington Taylor's, who is going to marry again[1]) — and yesterday I was so eager after news from Paris[2] that I could not perform the duty of friendship for you.

Yesterday was "le dix Août": I almost thought so tremendous a reminiscence under circumstances so far from unlike would precipitate a real revolution. That has not come: but the beast has got the mark of the beast on him now, and I greatly doubt whether he will ever again be Emperor to much purpose. A great military success *soon* would give him a chance: whether much more than a chance even then I question. These whirling events and enormous possibilities keep one's heart fuller than one's mouth or pen can follow.

I would in your place be *very much* inclined to bring out your book[3] at the very first moment — publishing season or not.

Your encomium on my Byron and Longfellow notices has been a real pleasure to me, and almost a surprise as well to some extent. The Byron volume *does* contain everything, save some few copyright scraps. The like will be the case with some other volumes, but not all.

In haste,

Your
W. M. Rossetti

MS: BL.

1. George Warington Taylor was the business manager of Morris & Co. from 1865 until his death from consumption early in 1870. WMR recorded in his diary on 24 February 1870 that he was "executor to Taylor's will, and trustee for his Wife" (*RP*, p. 499). By June 1871 she had married Walter Wieland (Bornand, pp. 73-74).
2. See Letter 192, Note 6.
3. *Songs before Sunrise*.

194. TO ALGERNON CHARLES SWINBURNE

56 Euston Square,
21 August [1870]

Dear Swinburne,

I have as yet been prevented from calling on Hotten. To make sure of finding him in when I do call, I have now made an appointment for Wednesday next (unless countermanded by him).

Your note seems to have been written before you received the bad news (in all the papers 3 or 4 days ago) of Mazzini's arrest at Palermo, and confinement at Gaeta.[1] I say bad news: but possibly it may prove the reverse. Even I Piemontesi *can't* in Italy venture to do much material damage to Mazzini — and it may be that his arrest precipitates matters more than his exertions while at large would have done. The *probabilities* of the present Titanic struggles[2] appear to me to be these: Germany enormously consolidated, and distinctly the first power in Europe: all the Latin races (France, Italy, Spain) Republics: the Pope gone. Supreme or glorious eventualities, though I for one can't help looking upon the fearful humiliation of France with sorrow akin to a Frenchman's own.

I find the enclosed sonnets[3] decidedly fine, and so does Gabriel to whom I read them last night. Perhaps (for I feel very uncertain) "to mark thee with a name"[4] is to be preferred. "Heart and sword-hand for the whole"[5] likewise: the meaning cannot, I think, be equivocal to anyone who chooses to reflect for a moment. "The whole" is, I think, fully right for "all the world's sorrows," and its phrases in apposition: not *fully* right, but hardly to be complained of, if you mean rather "all the men who serve" etc. etc.

Things now are in such a whirl of expectation and of coming change that I don't think the immediate appearance of your poems quite so urgent *now* as it would have been 2 or 3 weeks ago. Still, the sooner the better. It seems inevitable now that, whether published soon or late, the poems will apply to a state of things much engulfed in the "unfathomable sea whose waves are years"[6] — or indeed weeks, at the present pace.

> Yours affectionately,
> W. M. Rossetti

Scott and Wordsworth ought to be out *very* soon — especially Scott. I wrote the notice of Scott a full year ago: Moxon's people lost that: and so I had lately to vamp up another notice *à contre-coeur*, and I fear not even as creditable a piece of work as its companions.

They ought to make Victor Hugo President of the French Republic — but I suppose they won't. There are those damned Orleans people too — who I fear will give no little trouble, especially under a Prussian aegis.

MS: BL.

1. He was released following the capture of Rome by Victor Emanuel's forces in September 1870.
2. See Letter 192, Note 6.
3. *Armand Barbès*.
4. Sonnet 1. "What need, O soul, to sign thee with thy name?" in *Songs before Sunrise*.
5. Sonnet 2. Thus in *Songs before Sunrise*.
6. Shelley, *Time*, l. 1.

195. TO ALGERNON CHARLES SWINBURNE

56 Euston Square,
24 August [1870]

Dear Swinburne,

This afternoon I called on Hotten, and found him conversable.

He says that certain statements and rumours got into circulation as to his having cheated you, and these reports will obtain all the greater currency if you engage with another publisher; that consequently it behoves him to look after his own interests and character; and that he must continue taking measures accordingly. I think there is some reason in this, and am happy to reflect that I at least never retailed any stories I might have heard as to your differences with him.

He is still willing that you should name (if you like) one referee, and he another, to look into the affair.

As to the nature of the legal proceedings he contemplates, he did not enter into details; and, as I thought it would scarcely be consistent with a nice sense of honour for me to sound him on this subject, for the purpose of apprizing you, I did not press it. He said that at one time he had seriously contemplated an action against you for libel, as the source of the injurious reports: but, as I understand, he has set aside this project, and contemplates some other measures. However, I think it extremely likely that, if other measures don't offer a prospect of success, he will recur to the libel scheme.

He says the document in your writing which he possesses is one which you wrote him from Lord Lytton's[1] house. After the interview at which Howell and I were present, Howell (he tells me) put into definite written form the agreement, such as he understood it to be, between you and Hotten, and sent this paper to you at Lord Lytton's: and you then forwarded to Hotten some written document upon which he relies for the support of his cause.

He says that, as you wish to leave him, he does not wish to keep you: but the separation must be effected under such conditions as not to leave any seeming slur upon him. He thinks therefore that the fair thing would be that you should now enter into communication with him, fixing some reasonable future date at which you and he are to part company, but you continuing up to that date to publish with him. I told him that in my opinion this could not well be managed so far at any rate as the *Songs before Sunrise* (already advertised as Ellis's publication) are concerned — and moreover that, on the general question, I did not consider that you would go back to him at all under any legal menace, or appearance of coercion. *His* view however evidently is that the *Songs before Sunrise*, as well as any other work of yours issued within the proposed limit of time, should be published by himself.

Barring various references to the charges which had been made against him of "overprinting" your books, not paying sums of money which he *had* paid, etc., the vexation and detriment which he had suffered from a running fire of repetitions of these charges, and the triumphant disproof of them which he had produced — the above is, I think, the gist of our conversation. I certainly think that — failing any amicable adjustment of difficulties — he is minded to take such steps as he may deem fitting and practicable for repelling any disparagement his character and position might under all the circumstances suffer from your secession.

I trust you and your lawyers will manage to find some satisfactory outlet from the whole affair — and remain

Always yours,
W. M. Rossetti

I return Ellis's letter.

MS: BL. Published (with minor omissions): *HLQ*, pp. 52-53.

1. Edward Bulwer-Lytton (1803-73), novelist and politician, whose letter to the poet praising *Poems and Ballads* was (Swinburne thanked him) "doubly acceptable to me, coming as it did on the same day with the abusive reviews of my book which appeared on Saturday" (*SL*, 1:170).

196. TO WILLIAM HOLMAN HUNT

56 Euston Square,
28 August [1870]

Dear Hunt,

It is, I believe, true that I have sometimes said you have a faculty of acquiring languages — to this extent: that you boldly undertake to say, well or ill, what you require to express, and you do so far succeed as to be understood with considerable readiness. This fact I have personally observed, and don't entertain any doubt about it. I don't — and *you* don't — think that you have in any marked degree the faculty of a *linguist* — one who grasps the principles of language in the abstract, and readily deals with the niceties of particular languages. The aptitude which you do possess is such as is more peculiarly needed by a traveller, and I persist in congratulating you upon it.

I think with you that the telling of the story in Tintoret's Miracle of St. Mark[1] is not particularly clear — i.e. I question whether *I* should ever have made it out, had it not been expounded to me in one form or another. I have sometimes looked at the picture with a view to this special question; and in doing so it has seemed to me that, strictly regarded, there is no want of perspicuity in the incidents represented, but that what makes them less telling to the mind is that the general character of the picture is so much at one with the general character of Tintoret's other pictures. There is continually so much brandishing of arms, swaying to and fro of bodies, etc. etc., that these elements of the subject, in the Miracle of St. Mark, do not tell out for so much as, in this individual case, they really mean.

I freely forgive you for having made me the medium of conveying to Scotus that small amount — or *any* amount — of chaff against myself: in fact and of course there is nothing to forgive. I rather doubt however whether you are correct in including me among theorists on art who lay down rules in a dogmatic way. To the best of my belief I have very few theories about art; and I decidedly think that an *artist* ought to have next to no theories. This I have said many times in print, in one way or another. Moreover I have myself (more especially in an article about Palgrave, reprinted in my volume) deprecated the effect which is produced on art by critics, as tending to make the artists — other than such artists as fortunately despise the critics — less individual and extreme than they naturally would be. I almost doubt whether I have more than two theories about art, worth being called theories or criteria. The 1st would be that one naturally demands Beauty in a work of art; but that even this is not an absolute *sine qua non*, as some artists (Dürer for example) have been very great with a scanty sense of Beauty, but a profound sense of Character in the objects of sight: that therefore either Beauty, or Character, or both, is indispensable. The 2nd point would be that, as Art is *Art*, good execution is also absolutely indispensable to it. To me these appear very wide and latitudinarian theories, allowing all sorts of scope to all sorts of art: indeed, not *theories* (or abstract a priori notions) in a proper sense of the term — but generalizations from the observations of works of art actually existing. And this *empirical* way of studying art — assuming that principles of art are embodied in *works* of art, and ascertaining true principle out of good work — appears to me the right way for a non-practical critic.

I barely remember the little incident at Florence which you allude to — my supposing for a moment that a certain piece of bad painting was natural scenery, and saying that deceptive painting might be bad painting. I quite accept your account of the matter, however; and really think there is next to no real difference between you and me as to the bearing of the facts. We are both agreed that that painting was a bad one: such was the very gist of my remark. But to deny that it was *deceptive* appears to be the same thing as to deny that it deceived me for a moment — which it verily did. I am somewhat short-sighted, which is the only apology I can offer for being taken in by such grossly bad work: but this bad work really did deceive me — which the work of the highest landscape-painters never did. So I must hold that this Florentine daub was deceptive, and also bad; and stick to my resultant "theory" — "that the most thoroughly deceptive painting is not the best." You, who were not deceived, certainly have a good right to think that I *ought not* to have been deceived — and, so far as involuntary infirmity of vision goes, I plead guilty at once.

4 September. Your letter enters at some length into the scrimmage you had with a nigger at a mosque. I think I must have imperfectly explained my point of view in my last. I think you were quite right to resist actual or imminent personal violence: the only time for *concession* on your part that appeared, and still perhaps appears, to me to have been fitting was at an earlier stage of the affair — when you and your friend were warned that you were not wanted there, and had better be off. That the warning was ultra-legal, and you not *bound* to obey it, I quite understand. Had the case been mine, I believe that I, being of a pacific (perhaps you will say a faint-hearted) disposition, should have been minded to comply, and thus save all further nuisance to myself and others. You chose to insist on your dues, and it is quite possible you were right. The consequence was risk to yourself, a black (or blacker than before) eye and prison to the nigger (probably at least as rational and well-meaning a man as an average crusader), and an obligation owed to you from other Christians for asserting their rights. You argue the matter with all the common sense of an Englishman. A certain teacher whom you believe in tells us, when one cheek is smitten, to turn the other

to the smiter. To a non-Christian like me this seems pretty plain: but perhaps Christians, aided by divine grace, see further into the text than I am permitted to do. As for the serpent that you shot, I think you were quite right if he was dangerous to man, and right enough if you preferred the birds to the serpent. But *why* you should do the latter is an open question: a robin redbreast is just as obnoxious to worms etc. as this serpent was to birds.

Of course, like everybody else, I can think just now of little except the war — a hellish crime, to my thinking, on the part of Napoleon, with a great part of the responsibility attaching to the French nation also — little or next to none to the Prussians. Yesterday came the news of Napoleon's surrender: so *that* serpent is neatly disposed of, as well as the one on your roof. What is to come next? My prophecy (but I don't profess to compete with Daniel, Habakkuk, Cumming,[2] or Mother Shipton[3]) is

1. A Republic in France —
2. A peace miserably humiliating to France, after a faint show, or next to no show, of defending Paris (but of this I feel very dubious, the alternative being an enormous uprising of the French people, and incalculable consequences) —
3. Germany entirely the predominant power in Europe for years and years to come, united, or quasi-united, under one government, including Austrian Germany pretty soon —
4. Austria compensating herself out of Turkey, and any amount of row in that direction —
5. All the Latin races republican — Spain and later Italy as well as France — and thus reasserting a superiority over Germany, countervailing in a different direction her military primacy. Rome included in the Italian State.

This is a pretty programme, that elates me not a little: though these horrid massacres of the last few weeks, and the overthrow and probable curtailment of France (a nation I much sympathize with, though for the nonce I am a vigorous German partizan on the question of immediate right) have made me feel more out of spirits than I can well recollect.

Great indeed would be my delight to join you in Jerusalem, as you suggest. It is however too far off for my brief holiday of 6 weeks. This will begin, I expect, towards the last days of September: I contemplate going to Spain, but — if by then France is a Republic, the war ended, and the state of society moderately secure — my Republican sympathies might tempt me to France instead. I have been by this time often in France; but, save Normandy, have made nothing deserving to be called a French tour. I shall be very glad to begin my holiday *somewhere*, having now been in London for a year and a half with hardly a day's interval, and with a good deal of literary and especially of official fagging. The work at Somerset House is really heavy now.

With our affectionate regards,

Yours always, dear Hunt,
W. M. Rossetti

How do you get on with Bishop Gobat?[4]

MS: Iowa and AP.

1. *Miracle of the Slave*, the earliest of his series of four pictures on the miracles of St. Mark.
2. John Cumming (1807-81), divine, "became most widely known by his writings on the interpretation of prophecy, holding that the 'last vial' of the Apocalypse was to be poured out from 1848 to 1867" (*DNB*).
3. Legendary Yorkshire witch and prophetess (b. 1488) who predicted the Great Fire of London, the steam engine, and the telegraph.
4. Samuel Gobat (1799-1879), Protestant bishop of Jerusalem from 1846.

197. TO WILLIAM BELL SCOTT

56 Euston Square,
12 September [1870]

Dear Scotus,

Your appeal for a little human interchange of feeling is irresistible. Swinburne is at Holmwood, and I have sent on your letter to him.

My general notion about the war is this. The declaration of war was the immediate act of Napoleon, and was a horrible and portentous crime, and as it turns out an unspeakable blunder as well. But, though one would like to do so, one cannot in candour say that Napoleon was acting in defiance of or apart from the French nation. I strongly suspect that, if he had refused to declare war, he would have been turned out for that.

The Germans were entirely right, and have been gloriously successful. They have utterly destroyed the aggression, and ought now to show something like magnanimous moderation in their triumph.

The Republican party is now uppermost in France. They were from the first honest opponents of the war: therefore the Germans ought not to find it difficult to come to some terms with them, such as to be fair to Germany, and also tolerable to France.

There are various good reasons why Germany should annex Alsace and Lorraine, and various still better reasons why they should leave those territories alone. If the Germans, not content with destroying the French army and Empire, insist on territorial conquests unbearable to French self-respect, I shall feel against them; my native sympathy with France and the Republic will predominate; and I shall wish France to thrash Germany as soundly as Germany has already — for the best of reasons — thrashed France. At the same time I perceive that it is very *unlikely* that a thrashing of the Germans should be in prospect. France therefore ought to make peace on any endurable conditions, humiliating though they may be. I trust these may not include a cession of territory: but, if they *must* do so, they must.

France should hurry on the peace, not only for its own sake, but for Republican objects. She ought to carry the social democracy further — a vast deal further — than ever hitherto: Spain and Italy ought to, and are not unlikely to, join France as Republics. These would be (as so often named) the United States of Europe, though only of the Latin race. Their political superiority of form of government, and the enthusiastic impulse connected therewith, ought to make them as good as

Germany, in a different way. Germany supreme as the military power (which she is certain to be for half a century or much more): the Latin Republics supreme as the power of thought and progress. Belgium might perhaps yet be a portion of France, and compensate for Alsace etc.

These are my ideas and sympathies — at which I know you partly laugh, determined as you are, by bias of race, to despise us of the South and West, and to believe in the German burgher, his Bismarck, and his King Wilhelm. And assuredly you have good reason now to believe in them — and I believe in them too, within their sphere.

If you have been "almost driven into a fever," I have been the same: the horrors have been too great, and the looking-forward too absorbed and incessant. But to me at least the Republic is one great thing gained, and to you it is a futility.

I certainly do think the Parisian newspapers have shown badly. They were the newspapers of Napoleonic war abroad and suppression at home, and were not quite likely to show well. Now we have a different inspiration: and, though there may be more tall talk than the event shall be found to justify, I don't think there will be much for a sympathizing man, ready to make proper allowances, to jeer at.

I should say that I consider the present condition of the Republic wholly precarious. It may at any moment turn into a Reign of Terror (which has its value too, though I would rather not see it in act) — and is even *likely* thus to turn, if war goes on much longer. This is another good reason for longing for peace.

I see nothing absurd in what Victor Hugo said:[1] but indeed I have not as yet seen any precise report of it.

.The Italians are in the Roman States. This may after all send me off to Italy, rather than either Spain or France (the latter seems to me not probable, for my holiday threatens to have come earlier than the peace, and I would not be there during the war). However, I feel considerable uncertainty still. It is something to be able to choose between three countries in the throes of Revolutionary or Republican fervour.

Kindest remembrances to Miss Boyd.

Yours always, dear Scotus,
W. M. Rossetti

MS: Princeton.

1. "The *Journal des Débats* publishes an address of Victor Hugo to the Germans ... in which he appeals to the fraternal sentiment and to the cultivation of the German people not to commit the vandalism and barbarism of attacking Paris.... [He] goes on to say: — 'The Germans have achieved the professed object of overthrowing the Empire. The Empire was the synonym of Hatred and Treason, the Republic that of Sympathy and Loyalty. What, therefore, can be the object of Germany in continuing the war? Victory would be for them only a dishonour, and Paris, if materially destroyed, would be morally affranchised'" (*Daily News*, 10 September 1870, p. 3).

56 Euston Square,
26 February [1871]

My dear Mrs. Gilchrist,

It was with great pleasure that we learned from your last letter that you are now restored to a fairly endurable state of health: may this at no distant date improve into really good health once again. You are well entitled to it, from your long sufferings and unrepining fortitude.

As yet I have seen and heard nothing of Whitman's books. Of himself however I have some news from my American friend Stillman, lately back here from his own country. He found Whitman in vigorous health and spirits: hair now quite white. I fancy his reputation is silently spreading in England to a great extent, and that the days of mere rage and abuse are pretty nearly over: for instance I see in the new *Tinsley's Magazine*, in an article on Gabriel (apparently by someone who does not know the latter)[1] a reference to Whitman treating him simply as a great poet of uncontested and incontestable claims. The wheel has got to come full circle at last, however much it may drag.

You say nothing about Shelley's *Devil's Walk*:[2] no doubt any faint hope of your being in possession of the vanished volume comes to nought.

I have always thought that, if a boy (or girl either) shows any decided tendency to any particular pursuit, it is a sin and a mistake to baulk him. I should therefore, in your place, give full scope to Herbert's[3] propensity to fine art; confident that to do so is the right plan, and that very probably his vocation is a genuine one into the bargain. His father's son may well be expected to have fine perceptions in that direction: and fine perceptions, united with strong predilection and diligence, should go far to practical success. Look at Brown's two daughters and son:[4] all more than promising artists — really good; and every reason to conjecture that, with the daughters at least, there was nothing to lead them to art had they been born into a non-artistic family: a certain moderate degree of hereditary predispostion, along with surroundings which fixed this and elicited their powers, being all that one can discern in the case.

I hardly know whether I can say anything to the purpose as to suitable training for Herbert. In Gabriel's case the tendency to drawing, and the resolve to be a painter, came very early: I suppose he was barely 6 or 7 when this was definitely regarded, all through the family, as almost a fixed and certain prospect. In childhood he did any number of designs, such as they were, without studying art in any systematic way worth speaking of. He continued to receive the ordinary schooling up to the age of 14: then, resolutely bent upon art, he finally left school, and did nothing more in the way of general education: went to a drawing academy (Cary's near Bloomsbury Square) and soon afterwards to the Royal Academy, and so progressed till he set about painting pictures for himself. I can't say that he was ever a very close student of drawing, anatomy, etc. — and his student period (save in the way of voluntary attendance from time to time at life academies and the like) must have ceased, I think, when he was about 20.

Of course, one should not try to strain into a general rule a single case like this: but my impression is that on the whole something of the same course is reasonable enough for any youth who determines that he will be a painter and nothing else, and who shows any fair amount of faculty, encouraging to those who are partly responsible for his future. If by the age of 14 or 15 Herbert shall have acquired a tolerable smattering of school-knowledge, sufficient to pick his way through Latin and French for instance, and to be capable of taking his place *in prospectu* as an educated man among men, and if his artistic ambitions hold firm, I fancy I should be prepared, in your place, to launch him vigorously on the career of an art-student — with, or if needful without, such supplementary study of other matters as the conditions allowed. And in this case I would try at once for the best art-training, which is, I believe, after all that of the Royal Academy. They seem to be now *very severe* (I know a case or two in point) in admitting probationary students there (for I dare say you are aware that every aspirant must send in drawings to the approval of the Royal Academicians before he becomes even a probationer): so Herbert would need first to go through some such preliminary training as that of South Kensington, which I imagine to be at least equal to what he would get in a private drawing academy. I think therefore your general ideas on the subject do not diverge much from mine: though perhaps, as regards the keeping up of ordinary schooling along with art-study, I should be more inclined than you to reduce it to a minimum *if* (for of course this is all-important) the determination on his part to be an artist seems likely to stand wear and tear, and to surmount some inevitable disappointments during the process of technical training. With Brown, my brother, and any other artist friends, he ought not to lack occasional advice and guidance enough to keep him in spirits, and up to the requisite standard of effort.

If there is ever any particular point you would like to ask my opinion about in this matter, pray don't — but I am sure you would not — hesitate so to honour and gratify me.

Peace seems coming at last: a sorry look-out, but better than this execrable war. Moltke[5] can't live for ever. When he is gone, the hard conditions imposed on France (and this is perhaps worse than any other point connected with them) will make it very natural, and perhaps not other than right — at least if the confiscated Alsatians and Lorrainers continue of their present mind — for France to try once more whether her ancient prowess has become a tradition, or remains a reality. If only the Republic survives — too doubtful a possibility at present — I shan't so much mind anything else. Napoleon at any rate seems to be a very dead dog, and that is something: yet I would quite as soon — to tell the truth sooner — see even Napoleon restored than any Bourbon of them all.

Yours always,

W. M. Rossetti

MS: LC.

1. Buxton Forman, "Dante Gabriel Rossetti, Poet," *Tinsley's Magazine*, 8 (March 1871), 150-60.
2. Published as an anonymous broadside in 1812. WMR reported the discovery of a copy in the Public Record Office in "Shelley in 1812-13: an Unpublished Poem, and Other Particulars," *Fortnightly Review*, n.s. 9 (January 1871), 67-85.

3. Herbert Harlakenden Gilchrist (b. 1857), her younger son. WMR informed Joseph Pennell, 9 November 1906 (LC), that he had studied under Whistler in Paris. Between 1880 and 1896 he exhibited six pictures at the R.A.

4. Lucy, Catherine, and Oliver.

5. Helmuth von Moltke (1800-1891) was appointed Prussian Chief of General Staff at the outbreak of the Franco-Prussian War.

199. TO JOAQUIN MILLER[1]

56 Euston Square,
12 April [1871]

Dear Mr. Miller,

I have just read through your sheets with very great enjoyment: there is no mistaking their quality, and no sort of doubt that you will be accepted in England as a true and fine poet — and even perhaps a popular one — when time shall have been allowed for the book to make its way. I shall most decidedly bespeak the book for reviewing it in the *Academy*.

It is really an impertinence in me to dwell upon small points which appear to me open to exception: but, as you have been pleased to consult me about the book, and as I did in reading note down a detail here and there, I will specify these: list enclosed.

If I am not mistaken, the poem *Californian* is the second of the two poems included in your previous volume. What I now see of the poem appears to me vivid, picturesque, and good: I don't agree with my brother as to its falling markedly below the standard of *Arizonian*: its interest of subject may be less.

We shall be highly pleased to see you on Saturday evening. I do expect here on that evening a gentleman and his wife — mainly to talk on a matter of business: but these details would have been got over before your arrival at 8 or 9, as you propose. I am not *certain* these people will be here, but suppose they will as I have already asked them. If you prefer another day, please fix it.

Yours very truly,
W. M. Rossetti

MS: Indianapolis.

1. Pseudonym of Cincinnatus Hiner (or Heine) Miller (1841-1913), American poet and adventurer. He had recently come to England, where he published *Pacific Poems* (1870, Privately Printed) and *Songs of the Sierras* (1871). WMR reviewed the latter in the *Academy*, 15 June 1871, pp. 301-3, calling it "a truly remarkable book ... indicating strange, outlandish, and romantic experiences." Miller became involved with Iza Hardy, novelist daughter of FMB's friend Sir Thomas Duffus Hardy. This previously undocumented adventure is the subject of two entries in MS. Diary, 18 May 1878: "In the evening we went to Lady Hardy's. Joaquin Miller there, and fervently lauded to us by Lady Hardy as having shown a noble spirit in releasing Miss Hardy from any sort of engagement to him arising out of past love-passages, and offering to return at once to America. He will now, it seems, postpone his departure for some few weeks." 24 October 1880: "We called on Lady Hardy and her daughter ... they returned 2 or 3 months ago from an extensive American tour. They are in the highest and most demonstrative spirits about the social incidents of this tour, the beauties of California, etc. It seems that Joaquin Miller presented himself at an early period of the trip; but he was distinctly warned that he could only be received on terms of ordinary friendliness, and after a time Lady Hardy (so she says) obtained positive evidence that he is now remarried. A clergyman who had married him to a woman who was just about to bear a child to him gave Lady Hardy his positive assurance of the fact."

200. TO ALGERNON CHARLES SWINBURNE

56 Euston Square,
16 April [1871]

Dear Swinburne,

The sight of your handwriting did me good. I am certain the lines "Were not the crocuses"[1] etc. are not in any one of the 3 *now current* editions by Mrs. Shelley — i.e. the big double-column single volume which contains the prose as well, the small 3-volume edition, and the medium-sized single volume. Whether they may have been in some earlier issue of these editions I can't say. The other day I went to the Museum to look up (what I think I must have mentioned to you erewhile) a tale *Sadak the Wanderer*[2] in the *Keepsake* of 1828, which has been attributed to Shelley. However I could not see it, as the Museum contains no *Keepsake* earlier than 1829. This latter volume was brought to me: and I find it (which I never knew hitherto) to contain the prose fragment by Shelley *On Love*, and the 3 short poems — *Summer and Winter, Tower of Famine*, and *Aziola*. Hence it seems to me possible that the *Recollection*,[3] with the lines you refer to, *may* also have been published in the *Keepsake* or some other annual. Warwick[4] used, I think, to be the editor of some annual or other.

Don't at all know who is the Shelley writer in the *Edinburgh*.[5] Gabriel had some valid ground for expecting a review of himself etc. in the *Quarterly*[6] (*the Quarterly*), but it proves as yet delusive.

I was greatly amused at seeing in the *Daily News*[7] that anecdote about *le nommé Dieu*, and Gabriel was crowing over it here the other day: his only regret being that possibly *you* had not seen it. But Los, it seems, had in mercy provided against that contingency.

I know the name of Dombrówski[8] as a revolutionary warrior, but not accurately otherwise. It appears he was in high esteem with Garibaldi: the Versailles people print that he was a convict, suffering for having forged some Russian notes. *Li potrebbe dare.*

Are you aware that Cincinnatus Miller, whom you fraternized with, is a poet — and really a genius in poetry, of a very marked and exceptional sort? He has a book forthcoming, *Songs of the Sierras*, full of rich capacities, and no small measure of actual achievement. He was here again last night, and is a very fine fellow. I mean to see about reviewing his book in the *Academy*.

La République is still making head in Paris against shameful odds: what will come of it all who shall say? The likeliest upshot seems a Reign of Terror — for which Thiers[9] etc. will be chiefly responsible.

Your
W. M. Rossetti

On Good Friday (not then knowing you to be out of London) I called at your place, and left the various Shelley and other books of yours I had so long been confiscating.

MS: BL.

1. *The Pine Forest of the Cascine Near Pisa*, 1. 77. Mrs. Shelley published the poem in *Posthumous Poems* (1824) and *Poetical Works* (1839, 1st ed.). In the second edition of the latter (1839) she

printed Shelley's revision into two poems, *The Invitation* and *The Recollection* (*Poetical Works of Shelley*, ed. Thomas Hutchinson, 1905, pp. 668-71). Hutchinson was the first editor to print both versions.

2. After examining the manuscript on 4 June 1872 WMR concluded that he was "quite certain it is neither the composition nor the handwriting of Shelley, and pretty certain that it is not the handwriting of Mrs. Shelley" (Bornand, p. 206). Davidson Cook in the *Times Literary Supplement*, 16 May 1936, p. 424, and K. N. Cameron, *The Young Shelley* (1950), pp. 417-18, accept the poem as Shelley's.

3. *To Jane: the Recollection.*

4. Probably Eden Warwick (pseudonym of George Jabet), editor of *The Poets' Pleasaunce* (1847).

5. *Edinburgh Review*, 133 (April 1871), 426-59; a review of *PWS* by T. S. Baynes (*Wellesley*, 1:519).

6. W. J. Courthope, "The Latest Development of Literary Poetry: Swinburne, Rossetti, Morris," *Quarterly Review*, 132 (January 1872), 59-84 (pp. 69-75 is a review of *Poems* 1870).

7. Not identified.

8. Jaroslaw Dombrowski (1838-71), who became commander-in-chief of the forces of the Commune on 9 May. He died on 23 May from wounds received the previous day.

9. Louis Adolphe Thiers (1797-1877), statesman and historian, negotiated the end of the Franco-Prussian war and persuaded the National Assembly to accept the terms of peace. Following the defeat of the Commune he became president of the Republic on 30 August.

201. TO ALGERNON CHARLES SWINBURNE

56 Euston Square,
15 June [1871]

Dear Swinburne,

I called this afternoon at Christie's, and was very glad to renew my acquaintance with so choice and capital a little Hogarth,[1] full of expression and finesse. It looks to me as if it would not fetch £50: and your letter, literally construed, would have prompted, in consequence of this impression of mine, the withdrawal of the design from the sale. However I spoke with a member of the firm, and he thinks (and of course I agree, founding on such authority) that, while one can't *count* on £50, one can't either hold it to be out of the contingencies, where there may not improbably be some one or more connoisseurs bent upon securing the lot. So I thought I should best fulfil the spirit of your commission by simply asking him to buy the work in for your family, if the other bidding falls short of £50: which he of course promised to attend to. The only inconvenience attending this arrangement, as he intimated, will be that, if the work is bought in for you, the auctioneer's commission will be payable on the price — instead of being saved, as it would be by present withdrawal. I thought however this would not be sufficient reason for withdrawing. Would you, with my best regards, explain these details to your mother — who, as I found at Christie's, had been paying some personal attention to the matter.

Excuse hurried reference to the other matters in your letter. Christina progressing, or at any rate not retrogressing: still in bed. Sorry to hear of the sickness in your house, but pleased to understand that matters are mending.

If any address is drawn up to Hugo, you know I shall be one of the first minded to sign it, and would not abstain unless on some strong grounds. I fear however some little difficulty, in the actual drawing up of such a missive, would present itself. The mere personal homage to Hugo, and protest against Belgian outrage,[2] might be a little behind time now: while Hugo has expressly disavowed not only the manifestly condemnable acts of the Commune, but their general *raison d'être* — so that to stick up for them (besides other surmountable difficulties involved therein) would not exactly fit in with Hugo. Certainly all parties could coalesce in abusing Thiers etc., if worth while. I leave these considerations with you or others: if the address is drawn up, I would certainly waive any *small* punctilio for the sake of adding my signature.

I have seen *some* of Mazzini's utterances — not that in *Roma del Popolo*.[3] No doubt right, though I have more Communal proclivity than he seemed to have.

Pall Mall review of Miller by Colvin:[4] mine (I may add) is now out in *Academy*.

Have not seen the article in *Fraser's*.[5]

Yours always
W. M. Rossetti

MS: BL.

1. "Portrait of Dr. Mead and Surgeon Misaubin — a sketch in Indian ink," item 55 in Christie's sale of 17 June 1871. It was bought in at £11.11.
2. A letter by Hugo in *L'Indépendance Belge* on 29 May protested the intention of the Belgian government to extradite the Communards who had fled to Belgium. The government retaliated by ordering Hugo to leave the country.
3. "Il Comune e l'Assemblea" on 7 June 1871 (see *SL*, 2:150).
4. *Songs of the Sierras, Pall Mall Gazette*, 2 June 1871, pp. 10-11. Sidney Colvin (1845-1927), art critic, biographer of Keats, Slade Professor of Fine Art at Cambridge; keeper of the Department of Prints and Drawings at the British Museum, 1883-1912.
5. "English Republicanism," *Fraser's Magazine*, n.s. 3 (June 1871), 751-61.

202. TO WALT WHITMAN

56 Euston Square,
9 July 1871

Dear Mr. Whitman,

I was much obliged to you for the kind thought of sending me your fine verses on the Parisian catastrophes.[1] My own sympathy (far unlike that of most Englishmen) was very strongly with the Commune — i.e. with extreme, democratic, and progressive republicanism, against a semi-republicanism which may at any moment (and *will*, if the ultras don't make the attempt too dangerous) degenerate into some form of monarchy exhibiting more or less of the accustomed cretinism.

I fancy that, unless someone sends it you from here, you may probably not see an article on your position as a poet lately published in the *Westminster Review*.[2] I therefore take the liberty of posting this article to you. I don't know who has written it: but incline to think the writer must be Edward Dowden,[3] Professor of English Literature in Trinity College, Dublin — a young man who no doubt has a good literary career before him. He is at any rate, I know, one of your most earnest admirers. Lately he delivered at the College a lecture on your poems, with much applause, I am told: and the same week someone else in Dublin delivered another like lecture. There are various highly respectful references also to your poetry in a work of some repute recently published here, *Our Living Poets*, by Forman[4] (dealing directly with *English* poets only).

274

You may perhaps be aware that the *Westminster Review* is a quarterly, founded by Jeremy Bentham, and to this day continuing to be the most advanced of the English reviews as regards liberal politics and speculation.

I trust Mr. O'Connor is well: would you please to remember me to him if opportunity offers.

Believe me with reverence and gratitude,

Your friend,
W. M. Rossetti

MS: LC. Published: *WWC*, 1:132-33.

1. *O Star of France* (*Galaxy*, June 1871; *Leaves of Grass* 1871).
2. "The Poetry of Democracy: Walt Whitman," 96 (July 1871), 33-68.
3. (1843-1913), Shakespearian scholar and biographer of Shelley, held the chair of English at Trinity College, Dublin, from 1867 until his death. Although WMR seldom met him, they were still corresponding as late as 1904. Of the forty-four Dowden letters in AP, thirty-three date from 1883-90, and concern Shelley and Whitman.
4. Henry (Harry) Buxton Forman (1842-1917), Post Office official until 1907; man of letters remembered for his editions of Shelley and Keats. Few of WMR's letters to him have been found, but the fifty-two Forman letters in AP suggest an agreeable relationship. Of their potential conflict as editors of Shelley, WMR wrote in *SR* that "no two Shelleyites could have acted in greater harmony of spirit, if not at all times of detailed opinion" (2:382). *Our Living Poets* reprinted articles that Forman contributed to *Tinsley's Magazine*.

203. TO KENINGALE ROBERT COOK[1]

56 Euston Square,
9 July [1871]

Dear Mr. Cook,

Pray excuse my not having answered you earlier: other occupations have intervened.

The probable *success* of a republican newspaper or other journal — success in the way of money, or of long continuance — is a matter as to which I have no very distinct opinion. But I think beyond a doubt such a paper would be interesting to many leading men, and would be contributed to or otherwise supported by them. Among my personal friends the following are all more or less decided republicans, and likely to respond in one form or other — Swinburne, Morris, W. B. Scott, Allingham, Hüffer,[2] Mathilde Blind, Karl Blind, Nettleship — also (artists who write little or not at all) Madox Brown and Burne Jones. My brother is not a politician, but is not absolutely without republican leanings. Colvin I rather think is a republican: and I suppose there is *something* (at any rate) republican about J. F. McLennan and Professor Dowden of Trinity College, Dublin.

As for myself, I am, always have been, and am confident of always remaining, a republican — an *ultra* republican, siding with the Paris Commune etc.: and anybody who cares to know the fact always is and shall be welcome to do so. I should certainly feel much more satisfaction in writing in a republican journal, of good literary standing, than in any other; and might probably, if invited to do so, find opportunities from time to time of writing in the projected journal —

certainly without any disguise of my real opinions. At the same time, I must admit to myself that my position as Assistant Secretary in the Inland Revenue Office would not be consistent with a direct argumentative advocacy on my part, in a public journal, of republicanism as a *de facto* government for this country: it would amount to suggesting that my paymasters should be turned adrift, and perhaps they would think that, before that consummation ensues, they might as well see whom else *they* could turn adrift. It would not suit me to jeopardize my official income, or to occupy an ambiguous position as long as I remain an official: and therefore I should abstain from engaging in writing of that class — other classes being open to me, and I to them.

There is another journalistic project that has often occurred to me as highly desirable for someone to start, if prepared to spend capital upon it in its early stages: but it is not necessarily connected with politics, so I suppose the gentleman you speak of[3] would feel no special interest in it, and I need not — for the present at least — enter into any details.

I am much obliged for the compliment you have paid me by addressing me on this matter of the proposed republican journal, and will willingly give any further information that may be asked for, if in my power.

Yours very truly,
W. M. Rossetti

I hope the extremest freedom of religious opinion would be united with republicanism in the projected paper.

MS: Berg.

1. (1845-86), clerk in the General Post Office, 1868-74; stockbroker, 1874 until his death (in partnership with H. A. Lomer from 1883); editor of the *Dublin University Magazine*, (?)-1877 (*NCBEL*). In 1869, when he called on WMR to seek his advice about publishing a volume of poems, *Purpose and Passion* (1869), the latter found him "a prepossessing young man, and evidently a man of intelligence" (*RP*, p. 406). Cook invited WMR to contribute to the *Dublin University Magazine* (see Letter 250, Note 6). In 1886 WMR invested through Cook and Lomer £640 of the £1,000 that he inherited from DGR. Shortly before his death Cook published *The Fathers of Jesus: a Study of the Lineage of the Christian Doctrine and Tradition*, which WMR reviewed in the *Revue Contemporaine*, 5 (1886), 293-96.
2. Franz Hüffer (1845-89) came to London in 1869 and soon anglicized his name to Francis Hueffer. Although in Germany he had studied philology and literature, it was as a music critic that he distinguished himself in England. He published pioneering books on Wagner in 1874 and 1881, and from 1879 was music critic of the *Times*. In 1872 he married FMB's daughter Cathy.
3. Not identified.

204. TO FORD MADOX BROWN

56 Euston Square,
20 July [1871]

Dear Brown,

Very many thanks for your friendly letter. When I last saw you I had no distinct idea when my holidays would be beginning, or how I should bestow myself during them; and the idea of getting to some English seaside, and seeing something there of such friends as you and your family, presented many attractions.

However it now turns out that I shall be released from official attendance forthwith, with a full 5 weeks before me: so I *must* as usual grill myself a little in an Italian sun. I expect to start on Saturday — or more likely Sunday — going to Ravenna through the Tyrol: am to be back not later than 31 August.

Christina is back today from Hampstead — to go very shortly to Folkestone or some such place. She is certainly a good deal more like herself now, taking meals etc. with the family. Still she is far from strong or well.

What you say about Swinburne is deplorable. Your letter reached me on Monday, and the tribulations you narrate pertain to the preceding Sunday: as I had heard nothing about Swinburne meanwhile, I am fain to hope his condition is not more catastrophic than in previous instances. I must confess I have not called to see about him (more shame to me perhaps). One consideration is that I could not hush up the fact that I am just going to Italy, and he might perhaps propose to accompany me — with what result to my comfort and peace of mind in travelling I leave you to surmise.

With warmest regards to all,

Yours ever
W. M. Rossetti

MS: AP.

205. TO WILLIAM HOLMAN HUNT

56 Euston Square,
10 September [1871]

Dear Hunt,

My long delay in answering your letter of 21 May is due partly (you will say "To laziness," which will be true, but what I mean to say is) to my having been away on my annual holiday from 22 July to 28 August. Notions of going to Spain had been with me up to the last moment: but, when that came, the attractions of my beloved Italy prevailed, and I decided to go there once more, seeing in especial Ravenna, with the tomb of Dante and the very ancient Christian mosaics — which are indeed singularly interesting, surprising in richness and preservation, and (in a certain sense) grand works in their relation to fine art. My stopping places were *Lille*, Brussels, Aix-la-Chapelle, *Bingen*, *Heidelberg*, *Innsbruck*, Verona, Padua, Bologna, *Ravenna*, *Pistoia*, Pisa, Viareggio, *Spezia*, Genoa, Turin, *Culoz*, *Tonnerre*, Paris, Folkestone. I have put a dash under the names of the places that were new to me. Innsbruck is admirably picturesque with its mountain environment; at Viareggio Shelley was burned (my cousins and Mrs. Jarves were there during my stay); Spezia is close by Shelley's last residence, Casa Magni near Lerici, which of course I went to see. In and about Paris (I only stayed 1½ days) I did not discern those wholesale devastations and wreckings which have been recorded; but of course I saw individual ruins, such as the Tuileries, Hôtel de Ville, and Ministère des Finances — this last being, as far as I observed, the block of buildings most thoroughly demolished.[1] At Folkestone I called to see my mother and sisters, who have been staying there some little while. Christina has been deplorably ill for months — not however with her chronic pulmonary malady, which fortunately has remained sufficiently quiescent. It was towards the middle of April (I think) that a severe attack of internal inflammation, with fever etc., began. For some days she was at death's door, and she had to keep her bed for I dare say a couple of months. She is still wretchedly weak and pulled down — a swelling in the throat and abscess in the gums having come on of late, when she got a little convalescent from the principal illness. I am rather afraid her health henceforward will remain permanently even worse than it had hitherto been for some years. Just of late however I hear that she has been picking up a little: she may perhaps be back from Folkestone on the 12th; or, if not, her remaining there a little longer will be to take advantage of the favourable turn which she seems just now to be taking. There is a book of nursery songs of hers[2] to come out probably in November — Arthur Hughes is illustrating it with some very charming designs, in the right spirit for such semi-childish semi-suggestive work; and I think the book ought to be a decided success. The great bulk of it was written a year or more ago: it is to appear in England and America simultaneously.

I now turn to your letter. My feeling about the painting of an open mouth showing the teeth is that it is very generally disagreeable in art — whether in a head painted from a portrait-like point of view, or in one painted as a part of an emotional composition. This feeling is my personal experience, which may or may not be reasonable, but, being mine, is of course of prime importance to *me* in estimating a work or result in art. I think however there *is* some sort of reason connected with the feeling, and it appears to me to be expressible under two propositions: 1, that the representation of anything shifting and transitory, especially in expression of which the chief vehicle is the face, is peculiarly difficult in art, and therefore is generally managed less successfully by the artist than other things; and 2, that, even supposing this difficulty to have been conquered by the artist, still, as a picture is moveless and permanent, the contemplation in a picture of something that is shifting and transitory is not so agreeable to the spectator as something of the contrary sort. Of course it may be said that this objection applies to sudden and vehement action of the limbs, as well as to a rapid movement of the face — such as a mouth open in speaking. But this rejoinder does not shut me up, for I do also demur to such action of the limbs: for instance I think Titian's Peter Martyr,[3] with one man flourishing a sword, and another running out of the canvas, much less agreeable and artistically right than a picture of less vehemence. However, I think the face — being as aforesaid the great vehicle of *expression* — a much stronger instance than the limbs. At the same time I entirely acquiesce in what you say of the monstrosity of a Raphael, in which the Baptist has a wide-open mouth, and no teeth:[4] I think this execrably wrong — being ugliness complicated with untruth and absurdity. I apprehend it would have been far better to give him teeth; and better still to make his mouth so little open that the teeth would not need to show to any extent worth mentioning.

By the way, I have just been decorous, and intended to be so — though perhaps they never made anybody *laugh*.

You refer to two water-colours of yours in the Society's Exhibition.[5] I am sorry to say I did not see them. My business being now much heavier at Somerset House, I am often kept there till 5½ or 6, and little in the habit consequently of looking in at exhibitions before returning home: and the fact of your being an exhibitor did not recur to my mind at any convenient moment. I had forgotten also that people had been trying to run these works down.[6] As to your retiring from the Society, you of course would be the best judge of the various aspects of this question. I fancy that I, were I an artist and member of any body, should do my best according to my own lights and likings, leave better and worse men to say their worst, and stick where I might be as if nothing had happened. But I never had a tendency to do anything from the point of view of *policy*, so I don't consider myself much of an adviser in such matters. I suppose you may be confident — as I am — that the works exhibited were intrinsically valuable, whatever other people may have thought or said.

Your kindly thought-of piece of basil from the cave of Adullam was prized by my mother and sisters: I presented it to poor Christina when prostrated with illness in bed.

Lucy Brown[7] asked me this morning (and of course I consented) to sit to her for Prospero, in a picture she is painting of the scene where Ferdinand and Miranda play at chess. This would be a telling reminder of the lapse of years, were such needed. She did an uncommonly good water-colour picture, exhibited this spring, of the death of Romeo. I have had of late years very little sitting for pictures — an occupation once so familiar to me. For these 15 or 16 years I think it has befallen me only once — some 5 years ago, when Wallis asked me to sit for a figure in some Italian picture.[8] I forget now the precise subject or personage.

I heartily hope, dear Hunt, that your picture[9] is going on to your satisfaction — so far as so truly conscientious and exacting a worker as you can be satisfied with anything of his own production. With love and greeting,

Always your affectionate
W. M. Rossetti

MS: AP.

1. During the second siege of Paris, which began on 2 April, buildings were destroyed by incendiary shells from the Versaillais, burned by the Communards as defensive measures, or fired as a final act of defiance.

2. *Sing-Song: A Nursery Rhyme Book* (1872). Published by Routledge in England and Roberts Brothers in the United States.

3. *Martyrdom of St. Peter Martyr*, which was destroyed in 1867 in a fire in the chapel of the Rosario of SS. Giovanni e Paolo, Venice (H. E. Wethey, *The Paintings of Titian* [1969], 1:153-55).

4. *St. John the Baptist* (Florence, Accademia).

5. *Interior of the Mosque Ar Sakara* and *The Pathless Waters* at the Old Water-Colour Society.

6. In the year of Hunt's election to the Society (1869) neither of his exhibits, *Moonlight at Salerno* and *Interior of the Cathedral at Salerno*, were well received. In 1870 the *Art Journal* dismissed *A Festa at Fiesole* with the comment that it was "so far from attaining what it intended that it provokes a laugh." After his 1871 pictures were largely ignored, Hunt did not exhibit at the Society again until 1879. (See "William Holman Hunt, Contemporary Notices of his Exhibits in Water-Colour," *Old Water-Colour Society's Club, Thirteenth Annual Volume* [1936], pp. 13-21.)

7. Emma Lucy Madox Brown (1843-94), FMB's only child by his first wife, Elizabeth Bromley, who died in 1846. WMR's mother and sister Maria undertook her education during 1855-57. She was a competent painter who exhibited at the Dudley Gallery from 1868 (*Ferdinand and Miranda Playing Chess* and *Romeo and Juliet*, both in 1871), and once at the R.A. (*The Duet*, 1870). Her abrasive personality combined with her prolonged suffering from consumption resulted in an uneasy relationship with WMR, whom she married on 31 March 1874.
8. Not identified.
9. *The Shadow of Death* (Bennett 1969, No. 45).

206. TO WALT WHITMAN

56 Euston Square,
8 October [1871]

Dear Mr. Whitman,

I was extremely obliged to you for the present of your photograph and books;[1] the volume of poems containing (what I now read for the first time in that shape) the important section of *Passage to India*, and many modifications here and there in other compositions. It happens that I have lately been compiling a volume of selections from American Poets,[2] and I *had* had to use your earlier editions for the purposes of this compilation: but I have now set those aside, and used your new edition throughout — so the kind and welcome gift came to me at a very apposite moment. I confess to a certain reluctance to lose the old title "A Voice out of the Sea"[3] of that most splendid poem (rated by most of your English admirers, I observe, as the finest of all, though I am not prepared to acquiesce in that estimate): however, in this, as all other respects where the editions differ, I have followed your new edition. Many thanks also for the separate poem subsequently received, *After All, Not to Create Only*[4] — replete with important truths. I don't well know when my American Selection will be out: my work on it is done, and the rest depends on the printer and publisher. I shall hope to beg your acceptance of a copy in due course.

I sent on the copy of your works transmitted for "The Lady,"[5] after some little delay occasioned by my being absent from England up to the end of August. She was (and I think still is) in the country: but, to judge from a letter of acknowledgement she wrote me, you have probably by this time heard from her direct. I know also that you have heard from Professor Dowden, the writer of the article in the *Westminster*.

Mr. Burroughs called here on 5 October, and is to dine with us tomorrow. I like his frank manly aspect and tone, and need not say that you were a principal subject of conversation between us. He seems very considerably impressed with the objects and matters of interest in London. I wish it might be my good fortune to see you here also some day. Rumours of your projected arrival have been rife for some while past, but, as I learn from Burroughs, the prospect is as yet not a very definite one.

Believe me
Most respectfully your friend,
W. M. Rossetti

MS: LC. Published: *WWC*, 3:376-77.

1. Fifth edition of *Leaves of Grass*, with *Passage to India* annex (1871); *Democratic Vistas* (1871).
2. *American Poems* (1872). "Dedicated with Homage and Love to Walt Whitman."
3. WMR's title in *PWW*. See Letter 128, Note 4.
4. Published in 1871 in newspapers and afterwards as a booklet, the poem also appeared in *Leaves of Grass* 1872. Since its publication in the *Two Rivulets* (1876) it has been entitled *Song of the Exposition* (Blodgett, pp. 194-96).
5. Anne Gilchrist.

207. TO DANTE GABRIEL ROSSETTI

Euston Square,
18 October [1871]

Dear Gabriel,

Buchanan had never occurred to me, but on your mentioning him it seemed to me exceedingly probable. I have now read the article[1] through again. It seems to me that in point of style etc. it might very well be Buchanan's: but still I don't feel *strengthened* in that view by the perusal. Buchanan is himself twice named — p. 334 as personating Cornelius (which seems to imply a slight more or less); p. 343 as your prototype in *Jenny*. This latter (see also the reference to Buchanan's critics attached to it) does seem very much the sort of self-assumption which Buchanan might be minded (in utter ignorance of dates etc.) to indulge in. Also p. 348, *Ballad in a Wedding*, and *Clever Tom Clinch*: I don't know whether these are Buchanan's, but they rather sound as if they might be. The phrases weird — solemn league and covenant — have a Scotch sound: but Maitland is a Scotch name rather than otherwise, so one can make little of that as suggesting Buchanan.

The observation (344) that you are not to be blamed for selecting the *subject* of *Jenny* looks rather like Buchanan, who has been censured for somewhat similar subjects: also the reference (336) to Swinburne's illness notified in *Athenaeum*. Buchanan, I know, saw that or some similar printed report: for he thereupon took the good-natured trouble (as I suppose I must have mentioned to you) of urging Dr. Chapman[2] to try to get hold of Swinburne and restore him to health — and Chapman called on me in consequence.

My opinion is that there is not at present sufficient material for pinning Buchanan as the author of that review: and at all events I have a strong belief that you will find it in the long run more to your comfort and dignity to take no public steps whatever for the scarifying of Mr. Maitland — though of course the temptation is considerable.

Your
W. M. R.

MS: AP.

1. "The Fleshly School of Poetry: Mr. D. G. Rossetti," signed Thomas Maitland, *Contemporary Review*, 18 (October 1871), 334-50; expanded in *The Fleshly School of Poetry and Other Phenomena of the Day* (1872). Buchanan eulogized DGR in dedicatory verses to *God and Man* (1881) and in *A Look Round Literature* (1887). WMR to Richard Garnett, 25 July 1903: "The lines on Buchanan ["As a critic the poet Buchanan / Thinks Pseudo much safer than Anon ... "] were at one time quite

familiar to me, but did not at all cross my memory when I was compiling the book [*RP* in which he published twenty of DGR's nonsense verses]. Even if I had thought of them, I don't think I should have put them in: Buchanan being now dead, and having in 1881 done what he could to atone" (Texas). In 1911 WMR included the lines in *Works*.

2. John Chapman (1822-94), physician, author, publisher, editor of the *Westminster Review* from 1852.

208. TO FREDERIC GEORGE STEPHENS

56 Euston Square,
19 October [1871]

Dear Steph,

Thanks for your note about O'Driscoll,[1] and the paragraph which since then I have seen in the *Athenaeum*.

About Gabriel — I really think the best thing would be that you should address him direct, by speech or letter. If I saw that any advantage would ensue from my mixing myself up in the matter, I would at your request do so — have not said *anything* as yet: but indeed I don't see that I have anything to do with it, or that a middleman is any benefit. As you know, Gabriel is a somewhat ticklish man in such matters: I am not aware that he has any *wish* to be reviewed at present, but can't say that he has any particular disinclination either.[2]

Christina continues pretty fair: not well, but not worse than she often is at times when she is not, *for her*, very bad. As to looks, she continues amiss.

Your
W. M. Rossetti

MS: Bodleian.

1. W. Justin O'Driscoll whose *Memoir* of Daniel Maclise was reviewed (probably by Stephens) in the *Athenaeum*, 30 September and 7 October 1871, pp. 435-37, 468-69. In reply to O'Driscoll's objections to the notice, the reviewer reasserted that the writer was "very fallible indeed in respect to dates" (14 October 1871, pp. 503-4).

2. Stephens reviewed *Dante's Dream at the Time of the Death of Beatrice* (Oil replica, Surtees 81 R. 2) in the *Athenaeum*, 25 November 1871, p. 694.

209. TO ALGERNON CHARLES SWINBURNE

56 Euston Square,
22 October [1871]

Dear Swinburne,

I can easily believe that you chuckled over the deliverances of the Rev. Prebendary.[1] The *Guardian* comes to this house: but you will credit me when I say that I don't invariably read it, and unfortunately the No. had gone away again before your letter apprized me that there was in it something which I should have been amused to read. But abuse of you, like charity, never faileth: so no doubt some other like occasion will arise at no very distant date.

Gabriel has been informed and believes that that article in the *Contemporary* is not written by any person bearing the name of Maitland (and for my part I know of no writer of that name), but by Robert Buchanan! Gabriel naturally takes such "criticism" in a reasonable spirit of disdain: but he is somewhat displeased with it too, and has thoughts of printing a letter[2] (he has written a little of it) to Mr.

Buchanan, not ill adapted to produce a tingling sensation on that individual's hide. However my advice to Gabriel is not to print anything: and to make *very* sure that it *is* Buchanan (though really I suppose it is) before he definitely fixes any responsibility on him. Gabriel has made one or two very good rhymes[3] also — one about

Buchanan
Who the *pseudo* prefers to the *anon*:

I am sorry I can't quote it fully — and perhaps even the above not accurately.

Thank you — Christina is anything but well: the rest of us fair enough. Her book[4] ought to be out within a fortnight or so, I think: excellently — indeed exquisitely in very many instances — illustrated by Hughes. Maria's book on Dante[5] is just out.

Yours,
W. M. Rossetti

MS: BL.

1. A speaker at the Church Congress referred to Swinburne during a discussion of the state of literature as a test of the moral condition of a country: "Swinburne insulted Him as he hung on the bitter cross" (*Guardian*, Supplement, 18 October 1871, p. 1245).
2. "The Stealthy School of Criticism," *Athenaeum*, 16 December 1871, pp. 792-94.
3. See Letter 207, Note 1, for the only lines on Buchanan published in *Works*.
4. *Sing-Song*.
5. *A Study of Dante*.

210. TO ALGERNON CHARLES SWINBURNE

56 Euston Square,
29 October [1871]

Dear Swinburne,

I have just written to Gabriel to tell him that it appears Buchanan is *not* the author of that article. Meantime Gabriel had given me these versicles[1] to send to you — which I now do. Much obliged for your friendly attention to the matter. I dare say the "essay[2] you have just begun" is rather high in flavour.

I did see about Louis Napoleon:[3] the British "interviewer" seems to have been a fool of the first water. Did also read with interest the article in the *Westminster* about Cromwell.[4]

Thanks for other details in your letters — which I don't take up singly, being in a hurry.

Your
W. M. Rossetti

MS: Folger.

1. See Letter 209, Note 3.
2. *Under the Microscope* (1872).
3. The *Bath Argus* reported that Louis Napoleon, while visiting Bath, responded with an emphatic yes when asked if he would act as a special constable should there be a republican rising in England (21 October 1871, p. 5).
4. "The Republicans of the Commonwealth," *Westminster Review*, 96 (July 1871), 106-36.

211. TO WALT WHITMAN

56 Euston Square,
31 March [1872]

My dear Mr. Whitman,

Your very interesting and valued letter of 30 January ought to have been answered before now. As you are willing to confess in it, however, to being an irregular correspondent, I gladly avail myself of so tempting an opening for saying that I am the same — and shall feel confident that my delay is pardoned.

I read with much zest the poem[1] you kindly sent me, with its deep sonata-like alternations of emotion.

It was a peculiar pleasure to me to get acquainted with Mr. Burroughs, to whom would you please remember me with great cordiality whenever the chance occurs. He may have told you — and indeed it cannot have needed telling — that you were a very principal subject of our discourse, and of my reiterated enquiries.

It interests me to see in your letter that you have a habit of taking moonlight walks out of Washington: I used to find walks of this kind highly enjoyable, and have frequently indulged in them years ago. In my youth I was living in habits of daily and brotherly intimacy with various painters (Millais, Holman Hunt, etc.); and from time to time we would all sally out, 6 or 7, say towards 11 at night, and pass the whole night, and sometimes the succeeding day as well, tramping out, and enjoying the varying effects of night, dawn, etc. — studied of course with peculiar interest, and directness of observation and purpose, by the painters: sometimes, instead of walking, we would row up the river from nightfall to day. There is a goodish deal of agreeable country round London: but, unless one lives quite out in the suburbs, it takes miles of walking to get even to the beginning of anything green or rural. I can easily imagine that to walk out of Washington at night "into Virginia or Maryland" is an experience of a very different sort, in point of grandeur and impressiveness. Though indeed, from some points of view which you of all men realize most intensely, nothing surely can be more impressive than the unmeasured size and colossal agglomeration of life in London — none the less felt through the interminable streets when all are asleep, and scarcely a passenger met athwart one's path. The interval when the streets are really deserted to this extent is but brief: I suppose from about 2¾ to 4 a.m. is the most vacant time.

What you say about the insulting and in fact ungrateful treatment which your poems continue to receive in America is deeply interesting, though painful. I suppose it is a very general if not universal experience that anything that is at once great and extremely novel encounters for some considerable time much more hostility than acceptance, and so far your experience is not surprising — rather indeed a testimonial, when properly considered, to the great intrinsic value of your writings. But certainly it does seem that in degree and duration the obduracy of Americans against your work is something abnormal and unworthy — especially considering the spirit of intense patriotic love and national insight which pervades your book through and through. That America should be so wanting (in this matter at least) in large receptiveness and quick intuition is distressing to those who love her — among whom I may humbly but truly profess myself. It seems as if she were even *less* capable than others of appreciating great work vital with the very marrow of her bones and corpuscles of her blood: perhaps this very affinity is partly the reason — but at any rate a bad and perverse reason. In this country there are of course very diverse knots of opinion, and schools of thinking and criticism, and to several of these your works are still an exasperation and an offence: but others accept and exalt you with all readiness of love and delight; and I think I may safely say that it is these which have in their holding the future of English opinion on such matters for some years to come. But I will say no more on this tack. For myself (with others) who believe in you with the certainty of full conviction, all these considerations are poor and slight: the one thing is the work itself, and the maker of the work, which has a destiny as assured and as limitless as that of any other great product of the soul or of nature.

I have not met Professor Dowden since last summer (or spring perhaps): he is seldom, I think, out of Ireland. What I saw of him I liked particularly. He seems an uncommonly young man to be a Professor — less than 30 to look at; and is in no common degree good-looking, pleasant, open, and sound-minded. There are few men, I should say, more likely to have their sympathies in literary matters sane and right — guided also by the fullest measure of lettered cultivation. Mrs. Gilchrist I dined with not many weeks ago. She seems to have fairly recovered from a very exhaustive and indeed dangerous illness that oppressed her of late (say from the early autumn of 1870 to the late summer of 1871) — only that she is not so capable as she used to be of continuous mental or bodily strain. It was a pleasure to see her surrounded by her family, the type of a true mother, guiding and nurturing all aright in her children,[2] mind and body. The eldest son bids fair to have a distinguished and prosperous career as a mining engineer: a younger son is greatly set on being a painter. One of the daughters is just about grown up, the other, I suppose, 10 or 11 years of age.

Mr. J. A. Symonds[3] I don't know personally; but, about the time when my Selection from your Poems came out, he wrote to me (2 or 3 letters) showing himself to have been for some while past one of your very ardent admirers. Tennyson I have known for years, and like much: I think him deep-hearted and high-minded, though it may be true (as has often been said, and sometimes not in a kindly spirit) that he is somewhat too self-centered, and morbidly sensitive. He hates all the *vulgarizing* aspects of fame, and some people find him present a very obtuse exterior to their advances or approaches: for myself, I can truly say my experience is the direct contrary. I think you and he would understand each other, and feel on a very friendly footing. Tennyson (as I dare say you know) is a remarkably fine manly person to look at, with a noble mould of face, and very powerful frame. He must be 6 foot 1 in height, I should suppose — but not now so erect as in his prime. If you do at any time come to England, to see Tennyson or others, I need not say what a delight it would be to me to know you personally — and several of my friends would amply share my feeling.

My volume of Selections from American Poets doesn't seem likely to be published yet awhile. It has been completed for months past: but, as it is one volume of a series, and others of the volumes are in course of printing, the printer may probably leave it over for a few months to come. I have in the briefest terms dedicated it to you (and hope you won't object). Any other dedication — at least, if to anyone on your side of the Atlantic — would be a fatuity.

Believe me honoured to be called your friend,

W. M. Rossetti

I have no doubt you will have felt sorrow as I did — though indeed sorrow is not fully the right word, nor the right emotion — at reading lately of the death of Mazzini. I, who am ¾ Italian in blood, have naturally a strong feeling on these subjects: and I regard Mazzini as the noblest of patriots, and the man to whom more than any other single person not even excepting Garibaldi, the lovers of Italian unity are beholden. It is often a pleasure to reflect that, with all the miserable oppression and depression under which she has so long been labouring, Italy has after all produced the 3 greatest public men (to my thinking such) of the last 100 years in Europe —

1. Napoleon 1, the greatest genius as a conqueror and ruler (I suppose anyone is to be allowed to admire him enormously, whether one approves him or not — and to call him a Frenchman, or anything save an Italian, is meaningless).
2. Mazzini, the greatest of ideal statesmen, patriot.
3. Garibaldi, the greatest and most flawless personal hero.

MS: LC. Published: *WWC*, 3:141-45.

1. *The Mystic Trumpeter*, published in *Kansas Magazine*, February 1872.
2. Percy Carlyle (1851-1935), Herbert, Beatrice (1854-81), Grace (b. 1859).
3. John Addington Symonds (1840-93), critic, historian of the Italian Renaissance, poet, author of *Walt Whitman, a Study* (1893). For extracts from his three letters of 1868, see *RP*, pp. 363-66.

212. TO FORD MADOX BROWN
4 April [1872]

Dear Brown,

Your letter found me here this morning.

As you word it, "Lucy being a consenting party, and supposing no legal difficulties arise," none certainly would arise on my part to your making over the *Work* picture to me on trust in security for £500 to be raised by mortgage on part (a fairly proportionate part) of the wharf[1] settled on Lucy. Of course the legal aspect of the matter would be the turning point for me, and probably for all of us. I am not very well up in my duties and liabilities as Trustee (will make a beginning tonight by reading through the deed in my possession), and am not quite clear how I should stand in case I, as Trustee, were eventually to sell *Work*; and it raised (*absit omen!*) only £300 — should I then have to make good the deficient £200 to Lucy out of my own pocket? and what would be equitable and legal concerning interest? If the former catastrophe or contingency were in prospect, it might to some extent "give me pause."[2]

I presume *you* will consult Lucy — or must it be I? Nothing here said is intended to delay you in at once consulting the lawyer if you think fit.

Your

W. M. Rossetti

MS: AP.

1. See Letter 363, Note 4.
2. "Must give us pause," *Hamlet*, III. i. 68.

213. TO FRANCES ROSSETTI

[16 Cheyne Walk],
Friday,
[Early June 1872]

Dearest Mamma,

Gabriel[1] is hippish and out of sorts to some extent, and having got me here these 2 or 3 days I see he doesn't like to lose sight of me just as yet. I dare say therefore I shall be impeded now and again from coming round as I would wish, to see you, dearest Mamma, and our dear Christina: possibly Gabriel and I might be spending a few days with Dr. Hake[2] at Roehampton pretty soon, as he has often asked us both, and I think a little fresh air would do Gabriel good, and get him more sleep than he now obtains. Look for me soon dear Mamma, but not for a certainty at any particular moment.

Your loving

W. M. R.

MS: AP.

1. DGR suffered a breakdown on 2 June. On 8 June he attempted suicide at Roehampton, and was removed to Scotland on 20 June where he remained until his return to Kelmscott on 25 September (see *PLD*). WMR to Frances Rossetti, [1 June 1872]: "Gabriel has been here, and I find he would like me to sit to him for a study of hands [possibly *Paetus and Arria*, a pencil study for a picture never executed (Surtees 230)]. Have therefore gone with him to Chelsea, and may possibly be there chiefly for some days to come" (AP).
2. Thomas Gordon Hake (1809-95), physician and poet. DGR admired his *Vates: or the Philosophy of Madness* (1840) years before their first meeting in 1869. *PLD* documents the care he and his son George gave DGR during 1872. They parted in 1877 as a result of DGR's quarrel with George, "although some genuine friendly feeling continued to subsist on both sides" (*SR*, 2:336).

214. TO MRS. CHARLTON BASTIAN[1]

56 Euston Square,
15 June [1872]

My dear Mrs. Bastian,

Family affairs of an extremely harassing kind[2] (even apart from the continued illness of my sister) make me at present both unable and unfit to mix in any society — and this may continue to be the state of things for an indefinite while to come. I would not say this if it were not strictly true. I thank you most sincerely for the great kindness which you concur with others of your family in showing me: but can under present circumstances only beg you to convey the sense of this note to your mother, whom I shall always regard as one of my earliest and most indulgent friends, and to excuse me for being unable to join your circle.

Yours very truly,
W. M. Rossetti

MS: Princeton.

1. One of the Orme daughters. Her husband, Henry Charlton Bastian (1837-1915), professor of Pathological Anatomy at University College London from 1867, "was for some years Physician at the Broadmoor Criminal Lunatic Asylum. Here he knew Dadd" (MS. Diary, 3 October 1880).
2. See Letter 213, Note 1. WBS reported to Alice Boyd on 12 June that "William's state is becoming critical he is so desponding as to the result on all the family and their affairs, Gabriel being seriously in debt and, as you know, having people depending on him" (*PLD*, p. 54). On 14 June Dr. Hake tried to reassure WMR: "It is a great happiness to think that your dear Brother is not worse, but rather better than otherwise. It is indeed an inexpressible satisfaction to learn that he has been quiet for a whole day — after passing the night peaceably. So pray take the good news to heart, and do not anticipate evil which may never arise" (AP).

215. TO WILLIAM BELL SCOTT

Tuesday Evening,
[18 June 1872]

Dear Scotus,

Gabriel now at Brown's. Marshall urges strenuously that he should as soon as possible — even as early as Thursday — avail himself of Graham's[1] offer, placing Graham's house at Gabriel's disposal for 3 weeks or so. Near Pitlochry in Perthshire, and named Urrad Castle[2] (or something of the sort). Graham understands that one or two friends would accompany Gabriel.[3] Marshall distinctly objects to my being of the party. We are therefore beating up for possible friends. Could you be one? (It would be all the nearer to Miss Boyd thereafter.) Brown would find much difficulty in going at all, and *could not* remain more than a day or two.

I write this on my own hook. Any answer should go to Brown rather than me. Different men are working in different directions towards this end of getting a suitable companion for Gabriel — so I can't say what the upshot may be, but, if you can make a serious effort of friendship, and be available in case things should so turn out, we should all be eternally grateful.

Pardon haste and brevity.

Your
W. M. Rossetti

MS: UBC. Published (with brief omission) in *PLD*, p. 59.

1. William Graham (1816-85), Liberal M.P. for Glasgow, 1865-74; friend and patron of DGR.
2. Urrard House.
3. FMB, George Hake, and DGR's servant Allan made up the party.

216. TO FORD MADOX BROWN

Monday, 6½,
[24 June 1872]

Dear Brown,

I have seen Marks.[2] He at once, without haggling, offered to take back, at the price paid by Gabriel, all such china as Gabriel purchased from himself: the rest he does not want. He says Gabriel paid him between £600 and 700 for china *and other things*. He proposes to extract from his books the prices of the various items, and then see what items remain in Gabriel's hands, and pay accordingly. He means (his own suggestion) to say nothing to anybody — especially not to Howell,[3] as I gather. The account would be ready by end of this week, or probably before.

I did not much debate the equity of the proposal, leaving all that to be considered when the account arrives. He will communicate with me (so he proposed) in the first instance.

No doubt you will let Gabriel know all this. Morris's proposal about the American[4] was of course not mentioned to Marks: but my own feeling is that that proposal should also be brought to a head meanwhile, so that the more advantageous of the two may have the preference.

Love and thanks.

W. M. R.

MS: AP. Brief extract in *PLD*, p. 62.

1. Fredeman's date, *PLD*, p. 62.
2. Murray Marks (1840-1918), art dealer, collector, benefactor of the Fitzwilliam and Victoria and Albert Museums. FMB informed WMR on 17 June that he had advised DGR to sell his blue china as a means of easing his debts: "he joyfully acquiesces, so that it would be desirable that you should go either to Murray Marks or to Howell at once and see what they could do in the matter of giving a cheque down — 700 or 800 £" (*PLD*, p. 59).
3. On 27 June Howell offered DGR "£550 or £600 cash" for the china. DGR replied on 28 June that "I wanted and want at least a sum of £700" (Cline, Letters 131-32). WMR eventually accepted a modified offer from Marks (see Letter 218).
4. Not identified.

217. TO MURRAY MARKS

56 Euston Square,
2 July [1872]

Dear Mr. Marks,

On Friday I wrote to my brother, conveying your offer of £650 for the china. As yet I have not received his reply, but hope to do so very shortly. As you are aware, the sum he himself named was £800: I am therefore not exactly prepared to say that he would close with the offer of £650, but he would beyond a doubt give it fair and full consideration. I infer from your present letter that it would be a ready-money transaction on your part, and that of course would be an added inducement to my brother to close with it. I will now write to him again, trusting to get the matter expedited.

Yours very truly,
W. M. Rossetti

MS: V & A.

218. TO WILLIAM BELL SCOTT

Somerset House,
5 July [1872]

Dear Scotus,

I have not yet had the grace to answer directly yours of 1 July: but have no doubt that you will believe not a day passes — and sometimes not an hour or two consecutively — without my being called off to write some letter, run some errand, receive some visit, offer some information, etc. etc., regarding Gabriel or his affairs, so that the pull upon my working faculties and my spirits continues not small, and I know you will be ready to make allowances.

You will be aware that the china was sold for £773.10, the drawing named *Silence*[1] going into the bargain as well, and £23.10 of the money being in the form of remission of work which Gabriel owes to Marks to that amount.[2] This morning I paid into London and Westminster Bank, 1 St. James's Square, Marks' cheque for the £750, to the joint account recently opened there in the name of Brown and of myself.

Howell is trying to dispose of the Botticelli.[3] He *had* supposed that Graham would be sure to buy it, but now finds that Graham declines, on the ground that Gabriel will soon be well (may it but prove so!) and would not like to find the picture gone from his possession.

Yesterday I saw at Brown's 2 letters from G. Hake[4] (Tuesday and Wednesday) which, along with yours to which I am now replying, make me extremely anxious that, if possible, the whiskey-dosing should be reduced — or indeed abolished, were this but possible. Brown however is by no means of quite the same opinion, and certainly it is true that Marshall countenances the present plan, though I don't think he regards it with any abstract approval. Dr. Hake suggested the other day whether it might be possible to get Gabriel to substitute (at any rate at meals) beer for whiskey. He named Bass's ale: to myself it seems that that heady Scotch ale might be more appropriate — certainly, so far as I am concerned, few things produce a more soporific effect, any number of times more so than whiskey. Brown agrees about this suggestion, and I believe will represent it when he writes to G. Hake: meanwhile I have thought it best to name the matter, sure that you will give it fitting consideration. It has not been suggested specifically to Marshall, but Brown thinks it might be first tried as an experiment, and Marshall then consulted as to continuing it.

All love, dear Scotus, from

Your

W. M. Rossetti

My mother and Maria saw Christina on Wednesday, and thought her in some degree definitely better — not of course any *great* degree. Sir W. Jenner[5] approves her remaining at present in her present Hampstead lodgings, though unable there to move off the first floor.

MS: UBC. First paragraph published in *PLD*, p. 67.

1. Surtees 214.

2. George Hake to WMR, [27 July 1872]: "I think on the whole your brother is quite satisfied about the price realized for china. He has said nothing since except to the effect that the money now in the bank relieves him from all anxiety with regard to any seizure of his property for outstanding debts. At the time he seemed to think it a fair price and when it was all settled was much relieved" (AP).

3. *Smeralda Bandinelli*, which Howell bought on behalf of DGR at Christie's in 1867 for £20 (*RP*, p. 228). It remained with DGR until "towards 1880 [when] he resold it to a friend for £315" (*FLM*, 1:264). The picture is now in the Victoria and Albert Museum, but is no longer attributed to Botticelli (Michael Levey, "Botticelli and Nineteenth Century England," *Journal of the Warburg and Courtauld Institutes*, 23 [1960], 301).

4. George Gordon Hake (1847-1903), then a student at Oxford, accompanied DGR and FMB to Scotland at the suggestion of his father. Dr. Hake to WMR, [19 June 1872]: " ... if he is determined on as the available man he is entirely at your disposal. He would be most happy I know to go with Rossetti.... George came down last night and returned this morning to be in the way at Cheyne Walk in case he should be wanted.... Of course no companion can do more than advise and persuade on material matters — such as wine, etc. I doubt if Allan could exercise control" (AP; quoted in part in *PLD*, p. 59). Later George became DGR's secretary, but difficulties between them led to their parting in January 1877. For a brief period he was a mathematics master in Lymington, after which he went to Cyprus in August 1878. MS. Diary, 20 June 1880: "Surprised by the entrance of George Hake, back from Cyprus on a 6 month leave.... Is now Chief Clerk under the Chief of Staff, with a salary of £240 p.a." 9 March 1883: "We spent the evening at Mamma's to meet George Hake — who is now filling a temporary berth connected with a Fisheries Exhibition at the Horticultural Grounds." 20 February 1904: "[Edmund] Hake informs me, and I regret to hear it, that his Brother George ... died in December in Central Africa. He had been in Africa — *South* Africa — for many years — say 1885. I presume that his wife and children (3) are still living in England: the eldest, Ursula [b. 1885], was Christina's god-daughter."

5. William Jenner (1815-98) was CGR's doctor until his retirement in 1890. He held a succession of posts at University College Hospital, attended Queen Victoria from 1861, and published conclusive papers distinguishing between typhus and typhoid fevers.

219. TO WILLIAM BELL SCOTT

Somerset House,
6 July [1872]

Dear Scotus,

Yours of the 4th received yesterday.

In consequence of what you say about Swinburne, I wrote to the latter last evening[1] explaining that, if he should be in the way of meeting Gabriel in Scotland, he ought to avoid rather than seek him. I put the thing in a form which I am satisfied Swinburne will appreciate, and not resent. So far as I know, he is as yet still in London — and, since the removal from Urrard, the chance of a meeting in Scotland is, I suppose and hope, not *very* considerable.

I note with full concurrence what you say about Mrs. Morris.

Allan is back, but I have not yet seen him.

Marshall approves the idea of Gabriel's drinking beer, as a partial substitute for spirits: he thinks however that *extract of hops* might be preferable to beer. Can such a thing be obtained at Perth, or would Gabriel drink it if forthcoming? Hops are strongly soporific, and a hop-filled pillow is in use by some people.

Dunn writes to Brown yesterday suggesting that we should now see what to do with Allan and Emma. I hardly like writing direct to Gabriel about it, for fear of agitating him, but plague you about it instead, and beg you to act as may seem to you best. Brown thinks they ought both to be paid off, with any liberal treatment that may be befitting, and I also think this the most sensible course: but no doubt they ought not to be exasperated, or they might spread many rumours abroad *on more subjects than one*, of a very unpleasant kind. Their wages are I believe £50 a year, and (besides this at present) board-wages £52 a year for the two (i.e. £1 a week) — no insignificant item amid our many expenses.

There are 2 bills come in to Dunn — Coals £32.4, and wine merchant £163.17(!!). I hardly know how to treat them, but think of paying £20 to the first bill, and £40 or 50 to the second. Of course Gabriel *ought* to decide, but here again I shrink from troubling him. Shall however (if no special obstacle) await your reply to this letter, before I do anything with these bills.

Christina still seems a shade better.

Yours in love and gratitude,
W. M. Rossetti

Have not yet seen any letter from G. Hake, so late as yours of 4 July.

MS: UBC. Extract in *PLD*, p. 68.

1. Neither WBS's nor WMR's letter has been found. Swinburne's reply (*SL*, 2:178) adds little to our understanding of his break with DGR. George Hake to WMR, 6 July 1872: "I don't think that there is any chance of meeting the Swinburne party as they would be between 30 and 40 miles from here" (AP). On 28 June DGR had moved to Graham's hunting lodge, Stobhall, near Stanley in Perthshire, "as Urrard House is to be occupied by the family" (Cline, Letter 132).

220. TO CHARLES AUGUSTUS HOWELL

56 Euston Square,
10 July [1872]

Dear Howell,

I had understood that the price you were expecting to obtain for the Botticelli was £100 or upwards. If £100 and no more can be obtained, I think it should be accepted without hesitation: £90 or 85 should I think also be accepted without further referring of the question to and fro, *if* any such delay seems likely to imperil the bargain. If less than £85 is offered, would you please consult me — or if then practicable Gabriel.

Yours truly,
W. M. Rossetti

No further news of Gabriel as yet. I hear Scott is to leave him on Friday, and Dunn is going down (probably tomorrow night) to replace Scott.

The drawing-room at Chelsea (I was there today) looks terribly denuded now that the china is gone.

MS: Texas.

221. TO WILLIAM BELL SCOTT

Somerset House,
11 July [1872]

Dear Scotus,

Yours of 9 July[1] received this morning. I am sorry to observe (and not for the first time) how far from favourable a view you take of our dear Gabriel's condition: but in fact I take the same, and regard as the too transparent palliative devices of friendship and affection those references to amelioration etc. which Brown and others sometimes give out. That in a certain space of time — say 5 or 6 months — Gabriel will be restored to soundness of mind[2] is, I fully suppose, more probable than the reverse; that any considerable progress towards that result has as yet been made I have too good ground for disbelieving.

About the time Gabriel left Cheyne Walk for Brown's house, Marshall said it would be a good thing were he then to operate (in a more permanent way than has yet been done) for the hydrocele. Other circumstances however interfered, so that nothing was done. No doubt it ought to be attended to at no very distant date.

Believe, dear Scott, in our deepest gratitude to you for your affectionate attention to Gabriel. I know you have done all that could be done. It had been proposed that Dunn should go down to relieve you: but last night Brown informed me that Dunn does not take kindly to the proposal (as indeed I can readily think, without any imputation on his well-proved friendliness), so now the idea is that Nolly[3] shall go down — this evening in all probability. But all this will be to you matter of the past by the time you receive my present letter.

I shall consult again with Brown this afternoon, and *probably* pay the coal-merchant £20, and the wine-merchant £40. Brown fully believes that there is yet *another* wine-merchant's bill in reserve, perhaps for some amount not much smaller than this dismaying one.

There might be many other details to write about, as matter of information or consideration: but I will not inflict them on you, nor on myself. I greatly fear that, as a method towards recovery, my original view was the right one — i.e. that Gabriel should be placed under treatment in an asylum of one sort or other; and I believe you did and do agree with me. Still I am most grateful for having as yet been saved from that horrible last resort; and indeed consider that it was on every ground *right* — though not perhaps conducive to recovery — to try some plan, such as is now under trial, intermediately.

Christina did seem to improve a *little* at Hampstead, but for the past 3 or 4 days no such improvement is apparent. She is likely to return to Euston Square tomorrow week, and Jenner will then consider further what can be done.

I wish you would write me whether there is any prospect of Gabriel's going to Penkill (as to which I have heard very conflicting statements) and if so when. Be under no scruple in speaking out about it — as I know that, whatever decision is come to, this will, and can alone be, compatible with the warmest and most self-sacrificing friendship towards Gabriel on the part both of Miss Boyd (to whom please remember me with corresponding warmth) and of yourself. Love also to Letitia, and believe me Always

Your friend,
W. M. Rossetti

MS: UBC. Extract in *PLD*, pp. 74-75.

1. *PLD*, pp. 71-72.

2. See also Cline, Letter 136.

3. Oliver Madox Brown (1855-74), the youngest of FMB's children. His contributions to London exhibitions (including the R.A. in 1870), and the publication of his novel *Gabriel Denver* in 1873, showed promise of fame in two arts. Dr. Hake, not Nolly, succeeded WBS as DGR's companion.

222. TO THOMAS GORDON HAKE

Sunday,
[21 July 1872]

Graham suggests these places to be enquired about.[1]

If any difficulty about servants, the gardener's wife at Stobhall might probably be willing to go if appealed to in Graham's name.

We all regret the news (received yesterday) that Gabriel may have to return to London. Pray try and avoid it (so says Brown). And ask Scott if necessary how about Penkill. Brown and I called this morning to see Marshall, but he was not in.

W. M. Rossetti

Graham says that from his local knowledge he can certify that the particular places he has indicated are *not* haunted by tourists.

MS: BL.

1. Dr. Hake informed WMR on 18 July of the necessity of leaving Stobhall "probably within a week — as some of the Willoughby family may be here" (*PLD*, p. 77). WMR consulted Graham, who provided him with newspaper advertisements of six places to let in Perthshire, but none of these was taken. On 26 July DGR and George moved to the George Hotel in Perth, and from there to a farmhouse at Trowan, Crieff, Perthshire. "Rossetti and George are coming this evening. I am *avant-courier* — Crieff is 17 miles from Perth — Trowan 3 miles from Crieff," Dr. Hake wrote to WMR on [27 July]. On the following day he reported: "This is the second place in the world in point of solitude — the desert of Sahara being the first" (AP).

223. TO WILLIAM BELL SCOTT

Somerset House,
24 July [1872]

Dear Scotus,

I am much obliged for your note of 22 July, and most deeply grateful to Miss Boyd for the invitation she has so generously sent to the 3 at Stobhall: would you express to her our sense of her great friendliness and kindness. It is one satisfaction to reflect that, if they do go to Penkill, she will find in Hake and his son two most agreeable companions for a country-house, and men whom one may be proud to get familiar with.

I need not enlarge on the fact that the invitation to Penkill came at a moment when some such solution of a difficulty[1] was greatly needed, for this you must already know, or very soon will from Stobhall itself — nor should I enter on all the details which at this moment make it to me matter of uncertainty whether or not the invitation will take actual — or at any rate immediate — effect.

Christina seems a little stronger, and so far a little better. She sits up with us in the dining-room till about 10 p.m., her ordinary bedtime of old: I myself think this too late. Sir W. Jenner has not yet called. Christina's appetite is now in no way deficient.

With warmest regards,

Your

W. M. Rossetti

The news we have of late continued receiving of Gabriel is decidedly some improvement on what it used to be up to your departure from Stobhall.

MS: UBC.

1. See Letter 222, Note 1.

224. TO WILLIAM BELL SCOTT

Somerset House,
27 July [1872]

Dear Scotus,

Thanks for yours of the 25th. I am not *entirely* surprised at Gabriel's not availing himself of Miss Boyd's extreme kindness — considering how very painful it must be to him to present himself to her under (as he supposes) a cloud of obloquy and persecution, or else (as he may understand she would consider it) in a disordered and morbid state of mind. Also that other ailment[1] to which you refer may be not without its influence in his decision: and I certainly think you are also right in suggesting that the presence at Penkill of *anyone* other than yourself and Miss Boyd would be a further dissuasive to him. We are all hoping that his mind may have begun to clear to some considerable extent before he bends his steps homewards: and possibly, at some such later stage of his stay in Scotland, he may find it more compatible with his feelings to go to Penkill, and Miss Boyd may be not less willing than now to make an exertion of friendship and kindness by receiving him.

The last news we have is that he and the Hakes were about to remove to a Hotel (I have not the paper by me so as to say *which* Hotel) at Perth, but only to stay there until some arrangement could be made for getting a lodging elsewhere. St. Andrews was the place most thought of: Graham now suggests North Berwick — a place which (as I gather) P. P. Marshall also had strongly recommended through Brown.

You seem to be "in a state of mind" against John Marshall: yet I don't see how it can be denied that he is a medical adviser of great talent and judgement. As to Nolly, while I am far from thinking that he would have been the best *conceivable* person to choose, I do none the less think that the tender of his services was by no means to be despised at that time: for really we had no idea whom else to pitch upon — a suggestion from anyone save Gabriel himself, that Dr. Hake should go down, being I apprehend not to be thought of. The telegram to which you refer as sent by me *was* in fact more Brown's production than mine: we hammered it out together. The fact is that your telegram (to which ours was a reply) was wholly reticent — I dare say for good reasons — as to *why* Nolly should not go down (viz.: in fact that Gabriel objected): and in other respects it left us in considerable uncertainty as to what remained practically to be done: for instance, Hüffer insisted and persisted in understanding it in a sense wholly different from what Brown and I did. But these are old affairs, hardly worth expounding at length now.

I am not at all surprised to hear that Gabriel wished for Howell as a companion. There are indeed grave objections to him, but on *some* grounds I think he would be one of the most likely to bring Gabriel round again, and I may add that he has proffered himself to me for any such purpose in the most unreserved and affectionate way (I have thought it best not to mention this to Gabriel). That fishy affair about Haydon[2] is already known to me — in fact he wrote to Gabriel first of all, and the letter thus written reached me, and I had replied to it, before he addressed you at all. I dare say Howell will pay *some time or other* — but certainly that is no excuse.

You acted most kindly in the matter of Mrs. Maenza.[3] It is a painful affair. If she writes again to you, before Gabriel is sufficiently restored to take the matter into his own hands, I dare say you will let me know about it, and I must see what can be done, but don't very well know what.

Christina may still be considered a little better. Sir W. Jenner saw her yesterday, for the first time since her return: confirms this view of her condition: will see her again on Monday week, and then settle whether she can go to some country-place. She thinks of Mrs. Bodichon's house in Sussex (if available) having long ago been invited thither.

With most cordial regards,

Your
W. M. Rossetti

I hope your health is re-established since your return to Penkill. I was persecuted with any amount of diarrhoea last night and this morning, and am not yet quite sure how it will turn out, but suspect the worst hours of the attack may now be over.

I have by this time done *something* in the way of paying Gabriel's bills — instalment of £25 to Foord & Dickinson,[4] of £45 to wine-merchant, of £25 to coal-merchant, Willson[5] £8.8 in full — rent paid on demand — etc. Of these bills the only one still leaving a *large* balance is the wine-merchant's: then there is a heavy account from the builder Brass,[6] which however requires some enquiry ere I can deal with it: and this, I think, is all that has yet reached me of any consequence. In accordance with your suggestion, I got Dunn to look up the present stock of wine and spirits: it is trifling. Nothing can, I suppose, be done with regard to past treatment of the wine, but only look sharp as to the future. The bill shows 2 dozen Cognac sent on 1 January 1872, and a third dozen on 19 February!!

MS: UBC. Extracts in *PLD*, pp. 78-79.

1. His hydrocele.

296

2. Probably B. R. Haydon's eldest son, Frank Scott Haydon (1822-87).

3. Giuseppe Maenza, a political refugee living in Boulogne, and his English-born wife were old friends of Gabriele Rossetti. DGR visited them several times in Boulogne, and following Maenza's death in 1870 he made the widow "something in the nature of a regular allowance to the end of her days." WBS informed WMR that DGR had sent her £10, "telling her he feared it would be the last he should be able to send; that he was so ill in Scotland" (H. R. Angeli, *Dante Gabriel Rossetti, His Friends and Enemies*, p. 26).

4. Frame makers of 90 Wardour Street (*POLD*).

5. *POLD* 1872 lists George Willson, Tobacconist, and Isaac Willson, baker, both with Chelsea addresses.

6. William Brass, 47 Old Street, E.C. and 18 Silver Street, E.C. (*POLD*).

225. TO PHILIP SPEAKMAN WEBB[1]

56 Euston Square,
4 August [1872]

Dear Webb,

You are probably aware that Gabriel, being far from well, has been in Scotland for some weeks past: recent accounts, I am happy to say, continue to be, for the most part, of a progressively improving tenor.

I am looking after his bills etc. during his absence. One of them is from Brass the Builder, of which the enclosed is a portion. I have consulted Dunn about it; and, as far as I can make out, the work to the studio was executed without estimate or contract, but may with great propriety be submitted to you (in which Brass acquiesces) prior to being finally dealt with. Would you kindly give it your consideration when convenient, and let me know whether it seems all fair and right (I don't at all mean to imply the contrary, be it understood, for I have no reason to do so).

With thanks by anticipation I am

Very truly yours,
W. M. Rossetti

MS: Texas.

1. (1831-1915), architect, designer, founding member of Morris & Co.

226. TO PHILIP SPEAKMAN WEBB

Somerset House,
10 August [1872]

Dear Webb,

I am extremely obliged for your kind attention, and shall pay the bill in due course with the comfortable sensation of not being done.

The news of Gabriel is of late *very good* — increasingly so, and in a rapid ratio. The present treatment seems to be most satisfactory, and indeed the main point seems substantially attained by this time. I am quite in favour however of his resting and recruiting for some while to come; and hope nothing will interfere with his so doing in perfect quiet. The Hakes have been most admirable friends — not to speak of dear old Brown etc. etc.

Yours always,
W. M. Rossetti

MS: Texas.

227. TO GEORGE GORDON HAKE

Dear George,

I went round to Chelsea today, and spoke to Allan.[1] He positively and repeatedly denies that he has any knowledge of any Bass's ale other than 1 dozen — and even of that, he asserts, he drank none. He says that the 2nd item in the enclosed account, whiskey for Butler, ought not to be down, because he in person paid the 3/4 for that bottle — Gabriel having given him the money beforehand. I hardly know whether or not to credit his denial about the Bass: he certainly spoke very decisively and without any show of embarrassment, and I endeavoured, in the friendliest tone, to get him to say yes if it really ought to be yes. One thing that rather disinclines me to value his testimony on *any* subject, the Bass included, is that he further insisted there had been no Edinburgh ale at Stobhall — though (as I told him more than once) you know it was there, and had yourself drunk it. You will excuse the pencilling on the bill, which I made simply to guide my eye as to what were the items discussed in your letter.

About the Cook's account, it rather appears to me that Gabriel should not pay it. Mr. Graham, having handsomely undertaken to be the host, would I fancy regard the house-service (whether supplied on a permanent or a temporary footing) as a part of his boon to Gabriel: and Gabriel, having properly given the Cook a gratuity, has I think thereby performed his *rôle*. However I would much rather that Gabriel should rather exceed than fall short in his paying for extras: perhaps your father would kindly give the casting vote on this affair of the Cook.[2]

I can't ask you to take further trouble about the disputed liquors — though of course I regard your suggestion of a hint to Haggart anent apparent overcharge as in itself apposite and politic. Shall therefore consider the whole sum as payable if nothing else transpires, and leave this 4½ dozen as one more of the many mysteries to be unravelled in the *Dies irae, dies illa*. I presume from your letter that your recollection vouches for it that *Scott* was not the consumer of the Bass — which otherwise might be partly or wholly the solution of the enigma. I trust dear old Scotus is free of diarrhoea by this time: I have not heard from him since a day or two after his arrival at Penkill.

Your father (note of 21 August) queries how it happened that a letter of mine dated 20 had reached him with unwonted celerity. I can't well account for it. Mostly (not always) my previous letters had been posted from Somerset House towards the middle of the day, or about 5 at latest: whereas this one of the 20th was posted close to Euston Square towards 8½ or 9 p.m. of the same 20th.

I don't know whether it will be deemed right to bother Gabriel about his income-tax return. Enclosed is the *second* notice that has been sent to him on that subject to Cheyne Walk. If no objection appears, it would no doubt be best that he should now return it, and post it to the official: would you do whatever is best, and let me know the result. We here can't fill it up: I for instance don't know any such details as would enable me to make the return, neither does Dunn: and I have reason to think that Gabriel would view our intervention in the matter (even were we competent thereto) with disfavour.

Excuse so arid a letter, and believe me

Always yours,
W. M. Rossetti

MS: BL.

1. Fredeman notes: "A tubercular and an alcoholic, he became an impossible burden, and shortly after the party's arrival at Stobhall, it was proposed to send him back to London" (*PLD*, p. 66). George Hake to WMR, 21 August 1872: "I enclose Haggart's [Graham's servant?] account before paying which I wish your opinion on several points. You will see 3 dozen of Edinbro' ale put down. Two of these were firstly ordered for your brother but as he did not take to them I finished them and subsequently ordered another dozen during our stay at Stobhall. The 4½ dozen of Bass for servant! are the result of an order given by your brother to Allan to procure the best beer and as much as he liked. Since however Allan was not more than 8 days with us I cannot conceive his drinking that quantity, although I can bear witness to the invariable and extreme obfuscation of his faculties during the whole time" (AP). WBS told WMR on 23 [September 1872] that he had "the greatest distrust of Emma, who is a very able woman, and of Allan who is her catspaw, and was drunk nearly all the time I was at Stobhall" (Durham).

2. See Letter 228, Note 2.

228. TO GEORGE GORDON HAKE

Somerset House,
28 August [1872]

Dear George Hake,

I snatch a moment of leisure to begin this reply to yours of the 26th: before I finish it shall no doubt have seen Dunn this evening, and may have more to say in detail.

Would you tell Gabriel that I enquired about photographing the *Silence*. Murray Marks has now sold that drawing to Heaton,[1] but has, in consequence of my enquiry, written to Heaton asking him to see about the photographing.

You say that Allan in your presence met a boy near the railway station, and paid him for a bottle of whiskey. Now this is the identical statement that had been made to me on Friday by Allan (although for brevity's sake I did not recite it in my then letter), and consequently I am the more disposed to lend some credence to his assertions on the subject generally. I fancy it must moreover be the fact that the Edinburgh ale reached Stobhall after Allan's departure: will endeavour to satisfy myself as to this by looking up letters at Euston Square, and let you know the result. If Haggart's bill had given *dates*, the whole transaction would have been clearer. If I recollect right, most of the Bass comes (in order of the items of the bill) *after* Edinburgh ale: hence one might form the inference that, if the Edinburgh ale was after Allan's departure, *a fortiori* so was most of the Bass — and then there is no way at all of accounting for the Bass that I see, save a "mistake" of Mr. Haggart's.[2]

How greatly you rejoice us, my dear George, by "fully expecting to see Gabriel quite well by the end of September"! I need perhaps hardly assure you that I have much the same confidence in your judgement (founded as it is on such minute knowledge of everything from the first) as in your kindness: and in the latter quality my confidence is, and cannot but be, unmeasured. Thanks (in large proportion) to your father and self, the improvement up till now has been more rapid and decided than I had ventured to expect; and if your present anticipation is realized, and supposing also that by hook or by crook poor Gabriel manages to continue getting some tolerable amount of natural sleep, the attack from which he has suffered will certainly have been vanquished earlier than I thought for.

29 August

Dunn left with me last evening the enclosed memorandum about Allan. Allan's answer to query 1, though not so definitely expressed as it should have been, means "*Nothing except* 1 bottle" etc.

As far as I can see, the question about getting Edinburgh ale for Gabriel must have been first started in a letter of mine dated 6 July.

Dunn seems likely to start for Trowan on or about Monday next: possibly you are already in correspondence with him about details.

I called on Marshall yesterday: he said he would write to your father about the doses of chloral and morphia etc. I see he is opposed to anything like indefinite continuance of these artificial means of sleep. He is also decidedly opposed to resumption of residence in Cheyne Walk — thinking that Gabriel, when he returns to London, ought to live in some new house altogether. Howell offers a portion of *his* house, and I don't think the offer wholly ineligible by any means, but this of the domicile is a matter which no doubt will need and receive a good deal of canvassing in its various bearings before a decision is arrived at.

Perhaps this letter may be allowed to pass as a reply to your father's of 26 August, as well as yours. With affectionate remembrances,

Yours always,
W. M. Rossetti

MS: BL. Extract in *PLD*, p. 88.

1. John Aldam Heaton (1830-97), described by WMR as "an art-loving manufacturer in Yorkshire, afterwards a decorative artist in London" (*RP*, p. 5).
2. George Hake to WMR, 4 September [1872]: "I enclose Haggart's letter which is a curiosity. I have sent him a cheque for £16.8.7 — which is £1.16.10 less than his bill and told him also to charge the cook's account to Graham" (AP).

229. TO CHARLES AUGUSTUS HOWELL

Cheyne Walk,
Thursday Night,
[13 September 1872]

Dear Howell,

I will be here all Sunday till 6 p.m. or so, and shall be glad to see you.

The news about the Botticelli[1] flurries me a little. Gabriel *may* be back almost any day now, and I should be very sorry if he found the picture gone, and no definite sign of its purchase-money. What is it sold for? The earlier it is got back, or its price (not below what Gabriel expected) got out of Pinti, the more comfortable I shall feel. I had no idea that anyone would or could walk the picture out of your house as if it were his. Would you please get this matter well settled as early as practicable. Excuse haste as I am only just back near midnight from Hake's house at Roehampton. This Botticelli affair will keep me in hot water till I see the full end of it, so do like a good fellow do the best for it. Much obliged for other matters in your note, but no time to enlarge on them.

Yours,
W. M. Rossetti

If you can't come on Sunday, please on receipt reply about the Botticelli. Who is Pinti? I have no definite idea.

MS: Texas.

1. Howell to WMR, 11 September: "As regards the Botticelli, I must inform you at once of a mistake made by Pinti respecting it. During my absence I entrusted him with it for sale and of course said nothing respecting it being Gabriel's, he is buying for the King of Italy, and having leave to do with my pictures always as he pleases, deeming this one mine, in my absence, and without consulting me, sent it off to his Majesty last Friday by passenger train" (*CAH*, p. 64). Raphael Pinti, artist, 46 Berners Street (*POLD* 1872) is undoubtedly "Raffaelli Pinti, the picture dealer" mentioned in Boyce, p. 59.

230. TO FORD MADOX BROWN

Somerset House,
25 September [1872]

Dear Brown,

I was much obliged for your letter of 21 September, though the contents of it (already partly notified to me by Gabriel) were anything but pleasant.[1] That affair remains at present in this position: — Gabriel cannot make up his mind to co-operate in prosecuting, and thus bring to ruin and degradation a person who was our playmate in childhood, nor does he want, on his own account, to have the nuisance of giving evidence in courts of justice etc. etc. He knows (having been very strenuously advised to this effect by a lawyer) that the Bank will infallibly prosecute if they obtain any evidence on which to do so: therefore Gabriel intends to give them no further clue or particulars whatever, but rather to suffer the loss of the £47.10. Would you please therefore (unless Gabriel should hereafter alter his views) sink the whole affair in the most total oblivion. I am *quite certain* the individual to whom Gabriel has referred is really the delinquent. I made enquiry at the Westminster Bank, and found all right there.

Gabriel arrived at the Euston Station yesterday morning. I can fairly say that he looks well, his manner is natural, and he said nothing odd or deficient in thorough practical sense for 2 hours or more that we remained in company. His lameness shows when he takes only a few paces — as across a room: while he was going through the streets, it was not much to be observed. He was to spend the better part of yesterday *en famille*, and at 6:30 p.m. to go off to Kelmscott — which I fully think he did, but can't *assert* it, as I was kept at Somerset House till past 6, and had to be at Cheyne Walk in the evening. George Hake was to accompany him to Kelmscott, and remain there, I dare say, a month or so.

Now that dear Gabriel's recovery has progressed to this stage is a fitting time for once again expressing to you and yours the deep gratitude which we all feel to you for the very important share which you have borne in it, and the benefits derived from your judgement and friendship. With all love,

Yours truly,
W. M. Rossetti

MS: AP.

1. FMB informed WMR of "a forgery on the Union Bank of London in Gabriel's name for Forty Seven Pounds 15/-" (AP). DGR told FMB that "the thief is this wretched Miss R[ovedino]," daughter of Signor Rovedino, described by WMR as a family friend and music master who taught Maria (DW, 3:1067; *FLM*, 2:4).

231. TO FRANCES ROSSETTI

[Kelmscott],
Thursday,
[10 October 1872]

Dear Mamma,

Just a few words. I came here all comfortable, and found Gabriel apparently just as he used to be before his attack: through the whole evening, and 2 or 3 hours today, I can discern nothing wrong or queer. He dozed in his chair an hour or more last night before bed, and I believe got fair sleep in bed as well. The house and grounds are very pleasant. I should have said Gabriel's limp is still very perceptible.

Love to Christina.

Your affectionate,
W. M. R.

MS: AP.

232. TO FORD MADOX BROWN

Manor House,
Kelmscott, Lechlade,
15 October [1872]

Dear Brown,

I ought to have written to you before now, and now ought to write at greater length than will probably be the case. You will make allowances for laziness etc. etc.

On arriving here I mentioned to Gabriel about the two drawings we set aside. He said there was no sort of objection to your taking the head of Miss Herbert with gilt background,[1] observing however at the same time that he thought something more appropriate would be discoverable. I may therefore now leave this matter in your hands.

Gabriel is just about well again now, as far as I can form an opinion: spirits good, and sleep more than tolerable. I don't find that he has any delusions, but some prejudice lingering, especially against Browning.[2] I had an opportunity the other day of speaking to him a little on a certain serious subject,[3] but found no prospect of a good result from any such talk. He utterly scouted the idea that this matter had had anything whatever to do with his recent gloomy frame of mind, and only regretted he had not at an earlier date in his convalescence come to Kelmscott.

Morris has not yet been down here since my arrival. I may stay, I dare say, 8 or 10 days yet: and Gabriel 2 months, if his expressed intention holds good. George Hake is the axis of the whole household wheel here at present, and seems well disposed to remain awhile. Today I am writing to Marshall for a new chloral prescription.

This house with its grounds was certainly a wonderfully good catch, considered apart from any collateral matters. Country round enjoyable enough, and weather not to be grumbled at, allowing for frequent variations.

Your (interrupted by cloth-laying, and people coming in)

W. M. R.

MS: AP.

1. Surtees 329. DGR contributed it, along with another unidentified drawing, to a subscription exhibition for the widow and family of the Manchester artist Henry James Holding (1833-72).
2. DGR interpreted Browning's *Fifine at the Fair* (1872), a poem about inconstancy in love and tortured memory, as an attack upon himself.
3. Jane Morris.

233. TO THOMAS GORDON HAKE

Kelmscott,
22 October [1872]

Dear Dr. Hake,

It is with much gratification that I am able at last to send you the answers from Turin and Padua,[1] which reached me today sent by my cousin.[2] The written queries which your son drew up have not returned to me: but I am in hopes that the answers are accurately to the point. Of these I send the originals, and also a translation that I have made — which, though less copious in phrase, contains, I think, whatever is needed for getting at the gist of the replies. The *printed matter* referred to in said answers has, I presume, already reached Euston Square, or will reach directly: I have already written to my mother asking her to post it on to you. My good cousin has, I am sure, taken a good deal of pains in the matter in the friendliest possible spirit: I shall without delay write to him in acknowledgement.

Here we are all comfortable, myself included: I may perhaps return to London on Friday, or close after that day. George keeps everything going, and I am convinced makes life smoother to all inhabitants of Kelmscott Manor House than they ever found it before: both the girls, were they but a few years older, would be making love to him, and he would have to make his election between Jenny and May,[3] and thereby blight the existence of the non-successful May or Jenny. May, the younger, is far the prettier — quite a beauty indeed — but perhaps the domestic virtues promise to shine forth steadier in Jenny. Morris came here on Saturday afternoon, and left this morning.

Gabriel seems to me really well on the whole: lameness visible (especially indoors) but apparently of little practical obstruction — appetite really *beyond* the mark — sleep mostly very fair, and obtained with only a very moderate use of chloral and whiskey. He *always* sleeps 2 hours or so before going to bed, and without any artificial aid. Yesterday he was put out by learning, in a letter from Dunn, the affair about the Scotch cook who stayed in the Cheyne Walk house after he was told she had left, and who pawned some of his linen etc., and he began again talking about her being introduced into the house by an insidious plan; and her making signals which set people on to getting up turmoils all round the house. This, with the addition of opprobrious terms applied to Browning, is the only instance of delusive notions I have yet seen in Gabriel: and in the cook's case something no doubt should be attributed to mere irritation and violent humour, only too natural under the circumstances. I want to close this before Gabriel comes down, so cut it short.

Yours gratefully always,
W. M. Rossetti

MS: BL.

1. Dr. Hake's youngest son Henry (1851-1930) had consulted WMR about Italian universities.
2. Teodorico Pietrocola-Rossetti.
3. Jane Alice, 'Jenny' (1861-1935); May (1862-1938). MS. Diary, 9 October 1866: "Called with Allingham on Morris.... Saw for the first time Morris's 2 daughters: the 2nd seems destined to be very beautiful." 29 October 1880: "We spent the evening at Stephens's.... Met here Morris's 2 daughters; great fullblown girls, who were but children when I saw them last; the eldest is particularly massive: in each the lower part of the face is too roomy, and this makes the younger daughter much less fine-looking than her mother, of whom otherwise she has a considerable trace."

234. TO DANTE GABRIEL ROSSETTI

56 Euston Square,
10 November [1872]

Dear Gabriel,

See preceding jottings on your very fine sonnet[1] — the "deep down" feeling of which is perfectly conveyed. You wanted me by the by to tell you what pomegranate is in Latin, and I looked it up many days ago, but forgot to tell you. It is *malum punicum,* or *malum granatum.*

We heartily sympathize with poor Graham, whose letter I return. The effect which this loss[2] may take on his health and spirits — and perhaps on his interest in external matters such as picture-collecting — has been a consideration present to my mind from the first.

The only rent I paid was in June — £25 cut down by some small deduction. No doubt it only lasted *up to* Michaelmas.

Very glad your money is being turned in so rapidly just now.

There is nothing very particular going on here. Christina certainly above the average of her condition for months past. I have been writing for the *Academy* a little notice of the book on Shelley by MacCarthy[3] just published by Hotten. He shows that Shelley published in 1811 a poem termed *A Poetical Essay on the Existing State of Things*, the profits to go to a certain political prisoner named Finnerty:[4] the poem itself has not been traced. He also reveals (what appeared, you know, in those letters of Shelley to Miss Hitchener,[5] but which I only remotely shadowed forth) that Hogg made love to Harriet, and a quarrel with Shelley ensued: also that the *Necessity of Atheism* was advertised for sale. There are many useful details in MacCarthy's book, and it gives the text of Shelley's political pamphlets.

Nolly Brown's first story[6] has been shown to Smith Williams, who is *greatly* impressed by it, and now has (I believe) the new story,[7] so far as written. There was an idea of early publication of one or other in the *Cornhill Magazine*, but this will probably be in abeyance as yet.

Love to George etc.

Your
W. M. R.

Has George got at Kelmscott an umbrella belonging to his father, which had at one time been left at this house? Some enquiry has been made about it of late, and I am puzzled to know how the facts stand. Dr. Hake expressed to me, in a note dated yesterday, the extremest gratification with your binding.[8] I had been explaining to him that I had offered the *Academy* to review his new volume, but Appleton on the whole thinks a review by Rossetti No. 2 of volume No. 2 after do. do. No. 1[9] would produce an unfavourable impression, so I have had to relinquish the idea. Dr. Hake responds in the kindest spirit.

MS: AP.

1. *Proserpina* (in Italian), *Works*, p. 252.
2. The death of his son (DW, 3:1092).
3. Denis Florence MacCarthy (1817-82), Irish poet and translator of Calderón, lived in London from 1864. His *Shelley's Early Life*, which dealt principally with the poet's visit to Dublin, was reviewed by WMR in the *Academy*, 1 December 1872, pp. 441-43.
4. Peter Finnerty (?1766-1822), Irish journalist who was imprisoned in 1811 for libeling Lord Castlereagh in the *Morning Chronicle*. N. I. White suggests that "it is quite possible that the poem was prudently withdrawn at the last minute, or even that it was never written, but was a fiction to support interest in Finnerty's case" (*Shelley*, 1:108).
5. Elizabeth Hitchener (?1782-1822), schoolmistress of liberal views which Shelley encouraged in a correspondence beginning in June 1811. She lived with Shelley and Harriet for four months in 1812, but she proved uncongenial and parted from them with bitterness. Shelley abused her to Hogg on 3 December 1812 as "the Brown Demon, as we call our late tormentor" (Jones, *Letters of Shelley*, 1:336). She later traveled to the Continent as a governess in a diplomatic family, married an Austrian officer, but soon left him to return to England to open a school. At some stage her representative deposited with H. J. Slack Shelley's letters to her and copies or drafts of her letters to Shelley, and never reclaimed them. For the subsequent history of the correspondence, see Letter 242, Note 2.
6. *Gabriel Denver*, published by Smith, Elder in 1873.
7. *The Dwale Bluth, Hebditch's Legacy, and Other Literary Remains*, ed. WMR and F. Hueffer, 1876, contains the two unfinished novels named in the title.
8. For Hake's *Parables and Tales* (1872).
9. DGR reviewed Hake's *Madeline, with Other Poems and Parables* in the *Academy*, 1 February 1871, pp. 105-7. His review of *Parables and Tales* appeared in the *Fortnightly Review*, n.s. 13 (April 1873), 537-42.

235. TO JAMES THOMSON ('B.V.')[1]

56 Euston Square,
21 April [1873]

My Dear Sir,

Here are one or two further replies, written without referring at the moment to Shelley's text. But there are still several points regarding *Adonais* and *Hellas* that I must answer about with the book before me, and all that you say concerning the *Prometheus* remains to be followed out. I expect to come to the same conclusion with yourself on most or all of these *Prometheus* matters; nor do I think that the literal verification of the time of action, etc. (conducted in such a spirit as yours) is at all out of place — the only proviso being that, whether or not Shelley proves to be wrong in these matters, the rank of the poem remains exactly where it stood before.

I am truly indebted to you in all these Shelley matters, and should feel it a great pleasure to make the personal acquaintance of so keen a critic, and (what is much better) so true a poet. Would you give me a call some evening? I am here at Euston Square almost all evenings from (say) 7½, hardly ever going out (except however to be away on 3 and 4 May). On one evening of each week I am at a different house; 16 Cheyne Walk, Chelsea: this is *Tuesday* evening from about the same hour. Cheyne Walk would be more convenient to you in point of situation: but anything I could show you about Shelley is at Euston Square — I have for instance a piece of his blackened skull, given me by Trelawny, who picked it out of the furnace, and the regard in which I hold this relic makes me understand the feelings of a Roman Catholic in parallel cases. Possibly you would be at the opposite pole of feeling in this matter. Also I am doing with much diligence another Shelley job[2] I have long contemplated — collection (with elucidatory notes, etc.) of every scrap of his poetry or prose *personal to himself* — principally letters, as far as prose is concerned.

I am a bachelor, living with the female members of my own family: all of them save one sister (the most religious of women by the by) will now be going out of town. I need hardly therefore tell you that evening dress, etc. etc. are nuisances unknown in my house. If you like a sociable pipe as well as I do, we may enjoy one together. At Cheyne Walk there is *no* member of my family, but a male friend[3] is generally there. Except tomorrow (Tuesday 22 April) and 3, 4 and 5 May, there is I think hardly a day you could name but would suit me very well. Towards the end of May I shall be leaving town.

I like the *Witch of Atlas* better than *Epipsychidion*, and in a limited sense I think it the more satisfactory poem of the two. I am far however from considering it the *greater* poem, or the one which sustains Shelley's general position as a poet at the loftier level. As regards considerations of this class, I think *Epipsychidion* hardly yields to *Prometheus*.

I have sometimes felt inclined — if you would at all like it — to forward to *Notes and Queries* the most important of your Shelley emendations:[4] of course confessing whose they are: not that I could *pledge* myself to obtaining insertion by the Editor, but I think it probable my object would partly be to express my high opinion of your capacities as a poet — which really ought not to be bottled up for the sole benefit of readers of the *National Reformer.* I would do this at leisure, if at all — being greatly occupied. Perhaps you would let me know whether you like the notion at all, and how far. Believe me,

Very truly yours,

W. M. Rossetti

MS: Bodleian (copy probably by Bertram Dobell). Published (except for fourth paragraph): *Shelley, a Poem: with Other Writings Relating to Shelley, by the Late James Thomson* (Privately Printed, 1884), pp. 98-99.

1. (1834-82), poet and advocate of secular thought, adopted the signature 'B.V.' (Bysshe Vanolis) in tribute to Shelley and Novalis. In 1872 he sent WMR his poem *Weddah and Om-el-Bonain,* which had appeared in the *National Reformer,* and WMR's untraced (as are most of his letters to Thomson) reply of 4 February began their correspondence, the bulk of which concerns the text of Shelley. In *PWS* 1878 WMR acknowledged his many suggested emendations and praised his "singular critical acumen and high poetic powers" (1:438). Thomson made the first of several visits to Euston Square on 28 April 1873 (Bornand, pp. 266-67).
2. "Cor Cordium. The Autobiographic Writings of Percy Bysshe Shelley (Letters, Poems, etc.) Collected and Annotated by William Michael Rossetti." The compilation consisted of some 2,000 pages, of which only the 9-page preface, a revised version of the *PWS* 1878 Memoir, and 252 pages of annotated extracts survive in AP. Odd sheets were acquired by T. J. Wise and are now in the Ashley Library. In his Memoir in *PWS* 1870 WMR suggested that the facts of the poet's "life, intellect, and character, might be exhibited in a very interesting manner by a proper collation and reproduction of all his known correspondence, combined with all such passages of his poetical or other works as have a distinct personal bearing" (p. xxix). The preface to "Cor Cordium" further explains: "I regard this entire mass of matter as constituting a sort of autobiography; a conscious expression of Shelley's feelings and experiences which forms, when brought into due order and relation, an unconscious autobiography.... So far as I know, this book furnishes a new plan of enticing an autobiography out of an author who never wrote one." Much of the preliminary work was completed by 21 March 1873, permission to publish the letters to Elizabeth Hitchener was given by Slack on 4 May 1873 (Bornand, pp. 250, 271), but it was not until 4 December 1878 that MS. Diary records: "This evening I got to the end of my long-pending and much-cherished work the Shelley Compilation." Moxon declined publication early in January 1879 (MS. Diary, 9 January). See Letters 298, Note 5 for further unsuccessful attempts to have it published.
3. Dunn.
4. No such communication has been found.

236. TO FREDERIC GEORGE STEPHENS

56 Euston Square,
24 May [1873]

Dear Steph,

I am off to Italy on Monday, and write in a hurry.

Charles Lucy[1] died at the age of 59. Was a married man with several children. Studied art (I think) abroad, and probably along with Brown under Baron Wappers[2] in Belgium. His name was unknown, I think, till 1847, when his Westminster Hall competition picture,[3] the Pilgrim Fathers landing in America (or else leaving England — I think the former) obtained a prize, and excited considerable notice. This was followed by the companion subject[4] (say, Pilgrim Fathers leaving England). He continued painting and exhibiting (you will dive into R.A. catalogues for this, at which you are a hero): also had a drawing-class at an Institution in Camden Town that Seddon, Brown, and others, were concerned with. Some years ago — say towards 1856 or 1857 — he made France his home, living wholly or chiefly at Fontainebleau. Had been (I believe) resettled in London these 3 or 4 years. I was told on Thursday by a man who knew him well that Lucy had a long illness, and his death had been foreseen for some while past: also that he was "killed by the Academy" — the treatment of his pictures being more or less unsatisfactory, but I don't know the details. Lucy was a small undersized man, looking more like a Scripture Reader or something of that sort than a painter: education ordinary: very unassuming, but with a certain shrewdness in conversation and manner: an honourable conscientious man, I take it: had a certain provincial intonation, belonging I presume to West of England. I remember of late years there was something wrong with his face — one eye partially closed, I think. I have met him many times on a familiar footing, but generally at long intervals, and had probably not seen him at all these last 3 years. Rather fancy Cave Thomas knew him well: also Woolner must at one time have seen him frequently, as they were together in studios in Tudor Lodge near Mornington Crescent.

Goodbye dear Steph to you and yours. Back towards earlier half of July.

Your

W. M. Rossetti

Brown and Lucy were at one time familiar, or even intimate: but for several years past there had been, I believe, an estrangement — something between Mrs. Brown and Mrs. Lucy, I believe.

MS: Bodleian.

1. (1814-73), history painter. He studied art in Paris under Delaroche, and after a period at the R.A. schools he resided for sixteen years in Barbizon. Stephens drew upon this letter in his obituary in the *Athenaeum*, 31 May 1873, p. 702.
2. Gustav Wappers (1803-74), history painter.
3. *The Departure of the Pilgrim Fathers to the Coast of America.*
4. *The Landing of the Pilgrim Fathers in America* (R.A., 1848).

237. TO FRANCES ROSSETTI

Somerset House,
9 July [1873]

Dearest Mamma,

Perhaps Madox Brown has already told you what I am about to say. You know the extreme regard in which I (as also you and all of us) have always held Lucy Brown: and while abroad I soon began to feel that she is too dear to me to allow of my ever parting from her again if I can help. It was yesterday week that I explained myself to her distinctly at Basle,[1] and she avowed that she returns my love, and would willingly accept me (spite of the serious discrepancy of age) unless her father should express distinct disapproval. We agreed to wait until I could consult him and receive his reply, which reached me yesterday, and is expressed in terms of much cordiality and affection. Lucy and I are therefore now engaged to marry: she speaks of a delay of a year or so, which to me appears more than wanted, but about this we shall see.

Dearest Mamma, I am practically quite certain that you not only acquiesce with maternal affection in this resolve, but highly approve and rejoice in it. I am pretty sure that our dearest sweetest Lucy would have been the wife of your choice for me, had you had to select one. To me she has long been the woman among women — although the difference of age, and my long habit of regarding myself as a settled bachelor, had till now diverted me from any matrimonial project in her regard. Of course as we both progress in years, the *proportional* difference in our ages is somewhat less — less now for instance than it was 5 or 8 years ago.

I told Lucy from the first that I should continue living with you and my sisters: to me any other course would be out of the question.[2] If you had heard how warmly she confirmed my resolution, you would not have any the slightest doubt that she really approves and likes this arrangement. We must enable her to use one room or other as a studio.

There will now be no *secret* about our engagement. It can be mentioned as occasion arises to all persons entitled to know of it, but, as you are aware, I am not exceedingly communicative on such subjects.

I hope you and Christina will stay out at Kelmscott your appointed time till 16 July: it would be a great pity to recede from that decision on *any* ground. Maria is pretty well: Christina's improvement as reported to me much beyond my hopes, and a subject of deep satisfaction to me. Love to her and Gabriel.

Your affectionate
W. M. R.

MS: AP.

1. On 26 May WMR and Lucy traveled to Italy in the company of the Scotts and Alice Boyd.
2. WMR to Frances Rossetti, 19 August [1873]: "Your affectionate letter was a great pleasure to me this morning. To make you as comfortable as the sorry conditions of this life permit (allowing also for my own many defects of selfishness, temper, etc.) has been the chief wish and pleasure of my life hitherto, and will certainly be not any the less at heart with me in the future" (AP).

238. TO MARIA ROSSETTI

Somerset House,
11 September [1873]

Dear Maggie,

I hope it will give you a little pleasure to receive these few words from me so early after our house loses your dear and familiar presence.[1] I said little this morning, but felt much. Few or none have more reason to think kindly of you than I have, and none, I am sure, entertains a more sincere regard and admiration for your exalted sense of duty — or I should with more accuracy say your devotional love. I know, my dear Maggie, that your longing is to die to the world, and live to Christ: to suffer, work, love, and be saved by love. There are other ideals than this, but not greater ideals — not any which raise the character higher, or make it capable of more extra-human effort. May you find (as I fully believe you will if your state of health permits you to remain) the peace which passeth all understanding, and be an example of attainment to all others, and of shortcoming only to your own noblest aspirations.

Your loving
William

MS: AP.

1. See Letter 1, Note 2.

239. TO DANTE GABRIEL ROSSETTI 12 February [1874]

Forwarded with love.[1]

McLennan subscribes £5 to the Hannay Fund.[2] Edwards[3] not yet returned so far as I know, but I will see to it shortly.

Brown still far from well: has never yet been out of the house. His right hand troubles him with gouty symptoms, also one of the feet. However, he goes on pretty *tolerably* from day to day. This evening he is to read his 1st lecture[4] at his own house to an audience of some 30 to 35 (I suppose): and on Saturday the 2nd lecture. It is on Monday that he ought to deliver the 1st at Birmingham. This he still hopes to do, but the state of his health makes it dubious, and I am sure not *desirable*. If he can't go he proposes to send Nolly instead: I think a very bungling way of meeting the difficulty, and not likely to be well received by the Lecture Committee. He would of course make the *proposal* to them in the first instance: but time is now scanty for any such negotiations.

Your
W. M. R.

My marriage is to be 31 March.

MS: AP.

1. A letter to DGR from H. Cholmondeley Pennell, 10 February 1874, asking if he could include in *The Muses of Mayfair: Selections from Vers de Société of the Nineteenth Century* (1874) "a specimen of one of your lighter poems: *A Match with the Moon* would form a very charming addition" (AP). The poem was included.

2. Hannay's death in Barcelona, where he was British consul, is recorded in WMR's diary, 15 January 1873 (Bornand, pp. 228-29). A subscription appeal (copy at Illinois which WMR sent to Allingham) explains: "The Government grants no pension, nor allowance of any kind, to Consuls dying in its service; and though Mr. Hannay was engaged up to the moment of his death in literary work ... he leaves no copyright which can be turned to account for the benefit of his seven children. Of these the three eldest are old enough to support themselves, and decline to receive assistance, while the youngest has been adopted by a relation. There remain, however, three children between the ages of six and fourteen, for whose advantage it is proposed that private subscriptions be received. The Committees of the Royal Literary Fund and Newspaper Press Fund, taking into consideration the distinguished talents and valuable services of the late Mr. Hannay, have kindly voted grants to aid the present appeal." The subscription committee included William Stirling-Maxwell, the Spanish scholar; John Oxenford, and Leslie Stephen. WMR contributed £7, DGR £20 (*FLM*, 1:351).

3. Henry Sutherland Edwards (1828-1906), writer on Russia and the Balkans, music critic, correspondent to the *Times*, was a friend of Hannay from the late 1840s, when they edited the short-lived comic journals, *Pasquin* and *Puppet-Show*.

4. "The Latest Phase of Modern Art, Style and Realism," which he was scheduled to deliver to the Birmingham and Midland Institute on 16 February (*Birmingham Daily Gazette*, 16 February 1874, p. 1). His second lecture was on "Style in Painting."

240. TO ALGERNON CHARLES SWINBURNE

Somerset House,
4 March [1874]

Dear Swinburne,

Your letter gave great pleasure to all of us. Old Brown exploded with laughter over Urizen etc.,[1] and Lucy's glee was touching. Brown is still in bed, and not nearly well: but there has been a decided improvement since Monday morning, and it looks now as if he were perhaps really on the mending hand. Thanks for your truly friendly and affectionate good wishes.

The only Blake item approaching to the Prophetic-Book standard that has been included in the Aldine volume is *Thel*:[2] all the rest are excluded. This would not have been my voluntary choice; but it was obviously the only course likely to be adopted by a Publisher — and no doubt the including of the Prophetic Books would have run up the edition to 2 or 3 volumes, instead of 1. Yesterday I received the first proofs, both of the poems and of my Prefatory Memoir. The copyright difficulty — of which I foresaw something from the first — is this. You remember that certain poems by Blake were for the first time published in Gilchrist's book — viz.: those which came from the MS. belonging to Gabriel and me,[3] and also certain others (*Auguries of Innocence, Mental Traveller*, etc.) which came from a small MS.[4] then in the hands of Mrs. Gilchrist. The poems from this small MS. are *someone's* copyright for 42 years from date of first publication (1863), just as the poems from Gabriel's and my MS. are *our* copyright. It turns out that the small book was claimed by and returned to Tatham,[5] who sold it to Harvey (bookseller), who sold it to Pickering;[6] and the latter republished these poems in or about 1865, along with the Innocence and Experience.[7] Thus Pickering is the present owner of this copyright; and he, not liking Bell,[8] nor relishing a further republication of the poems, declines to authorize reissue. This is very annoying. Bell did tell me a fortnight or so ago that he understands Dr. Wilkinson[9] is in possession of a certain Blake MS. containing perhaps these same poems, or most of them, and that Wilkinson would allow their republication from this other MS. Of this I have as yet heard no more, and fear it will prove fallacious.

I was greatly pleased to read what you say about *Bothwell*:[10] hope I may be in town when the reading comes off.

Always yours,
W. M. Rossetti

You will have seen that Wills[11] has been laying a profane hand on Chastelard: I fancy it is a *very* profane one.

Here are one or two Shelley items that come into my head: but don't be at the trouble of replying *on purpose*. (I write from memory.)

311

You may have heard Gabriel or me, some time or other, speak of an oriental poem really of fine quality published in the *National Reformer* by B. V. — B. V. proves to be James Thomson, who has sent me at intervals a large number of Notes on Shelley's text: he has few rivals in delicate and exact verbal criticism. He calls my attention to *Masque of Anarchy* (one of the stanzas descriptive of "Anarchy") —

> For he knew the palaces
> Of our kings were *nightly* his —

and he says this ought to be "*rightly.*"[12] Surely he is correct? Ought not this emendation to be made a portion of the text?

Epipsychidion (near end)

> Where secure sleep may *kill* thine innocent lights:

this always seemed to me violent and jarring, but I don't know that I had ever surmised a misprint. Thomson suggests "*veil,*"[13] and I feel almost sure he is right: or "*still*" might do, but less well.

Sensitive Plant — the "repulsive" stanza[14] towards close, missed out of most editions. First we hear of "agarics and fungi" etc. Then comes:

> Their *moss* rotted off them flake by flake,
> Till the thick stalk stuck like a murderer's stake:
> Rags of loose flesh ...
> Infecting the winds.

Thomson suggests *stunk* instead of *stuck*, as appropriate to the concluding words. This is plausible, but I incline to retain *stuck*. But now, my attention being fixed on this stanza, it seems to me that *moss* can hardly at all be right. What is the *moss* of fungi etc., that rots off them *flake by flake*, till the stalk remains bare? Surely there is no such thing in Nature. The thing that really *would* rot off flake by flake, and leave the stalk bare, is the top part, the umbrella-shaped laminated head, of the fungus: this, in a state of tattered decay, can most truly be likened to "rags of loose flesh." Now what is the true *name* of this top part of the fungus? Is there any name resembling "moss," in the look of the word as written or its sound on the ear? Could one say mops, or cups, or caps? or knops, or knobs? or mags? or hoods? or would "tops" be admissible?

MS: BL. Extract in *Blake*, pp. 5-6.

1. To his congratulations on WMR's approaching marriage Swinburne added: "To you the expression of such feelings and such wishes will not seem the less trustworthy or the less cordial that it comes from lips which must refrain from invoking the benediction of Urizen on the head of a friend whom they would rather commend to the favourable communion of Hertha" (*SL*, 2:283).

2. *Tiriel* was also included. *The Poetical Works of William Blake*, ed. with a Prefatory Memoir by WMR, 1874 ("Aldine Edition of the British Poets").

3. The Rossetti Notebook.

4. The Pickering Manuscript contains ten poems, nine of which were reprinted in WMR's edition. For details, see Letter 245. Charles Ryskamp gives a fuller and more accurate account of the

ownership of the Manuscript than that offered by WMR below (*The Pickering Manuscript, William Blake*, 1972).

5. Frederick Tatham (1805-78), portrait painter and miniaturist, was a friend, disciple, and biographer of Blake.

6. Basil Montagu Pickering (1836-78), son of the publisher William Pickering, began a business in rare books and publishing in 1858. In 1860 he issued Swinburne's first volume, *The Queen-Mother; Rosamond*.

7. *Songs of Innocence and Experience, with Other Poems*, [ed. R. H. Shepherd], [1866].

8. George Bell (1814-90) began publishing in 1840. From 1854 to 1872 he was in partnership with Frederick R. Daldy under the name of Bell & Daldy. Following the death of William Pickering in 1854, the firm acquired the rights of the Aldine Poets and other of his publications, and adapted for their title pages the Aldine symbol which Pickering had used. Bell's son Edward (b. 1844), who entered the business in 1867, was principally concerned with additions to the Aldine series. See Edward Bell, *George Bell Publisher, A Brief Memoir* (1924).

9. James Garth Wilkinson (1812-99), homeopathic doctor and Swedenborgian, was early attracted to Blake, whose *Songs of Innocence and Experience* he edited in 1839. For the manuscript he was reputed to have, see Letter 241.

10. Published in 1874.

11. William Gorman Wills (1828-91), dramatist and portrait painter, whose play *Marie Stuart* opened at the Princess's Theatre in February 1874. Swinburne's *Chastelard* was published in 1865.

12. St. 20. Swinburne agreed (*SL*, 2:287), but in *PWS* 1878 WMR contented himself with approving the suggestion in the notes (2:443).

13. Swinburne responded by quoting Shakespeare's *Troilus and Cressida*: "To bed, to bed; Sleep kill those pretty eyes" (IV. ii. 4), "so sweetly remembered and re-sounded by Shelley in his verse" (*SL*, 2:287).

14. Part 3, St. 17; "agarics and fungi" is in St. 16. WMR cited Thomson's "stunk" in his notes, and suggested "caps" for "moss" (*PWS* 1878, 2:446).

241. TO ALGERNON CHARLES SWINBURNE

Somerset House,
7 March [1874]

Dear Swinburne,

I included *Thel* not because it is the best of the Prophetic Books (of course it is far from being such), but because it is short, lyrical in tone and approximately in form, and easily accessible — being printed in Gilchrist's book. The *Visions of the Daughters of Albion* would have had to be hunted up: probably transcribed bodily from some copy in the British Museum. I don't *remember* it very exactly, but am quite prepared to think it is a finer poem than *Thel*: I *do* remember that it is one of the more startling of Blake's moral dithyrambics, and that would weight the scale against it.

Really I don't agree with you in deprecating the reprinting of *Jerusalem* etc. in ordinary book-form. Should on the contrary very much like to promote and myself possess such a reprint. But the prospective publisher is not a known emanation of the Giant Albion.

I think you are aware that I have an utter — a *prejudiced* — detestation of *extracts*, as representing a poet in any volume of his selected works. I have put into my volume such poems of Blake, inserted in *Jerusalem* etc., as are absolutely lyrical, or blank verse: not other passages, however desirable they may be in themselves, or on some grounds adapted for extraction.

It was Nolly Brown who pointed out to me that Los must be Sol: I then thought out for myself Enitharmon and Orc, but have not as yet succeeded in recasting any other names. I cannot but believe in Sol and 'Ανηριθμον: have no great confidence in Cor.

It seems Wilkinson has *not* got those rumoured Blake poems: but he has referred Bell to a lady[1] who is supposed to possess something of the kind. What will come of this matter I know not.

Bell told me the other day (irrespectively of any suggestion to the same effect contained in your letter) that the only poem to which Pickering's copyright really applies is *Long John Brown*. This is indeed a great satisfaction: for whether L. J. B. is in or out matters hardly at all. I don't however understand *why* Pickering's copyright is limited to that particular poem. My view of the matter was this: — Copyright attached to that whole series of poems for 42 years following date of first publication, 1863: Pickering, at a later date, became the legal owner of the poems, and therefore of the unexpired residue of their copyright. *Macmillan*, to whose position in this matter you refer, was never the owner of the copyright. Mrs. Gilchrist was the owner, as regards the *Life* generally: and it seems each proprietor of *poems previously unpublished* was the owner of copyright in those same poems. Hence Tatham was in 1863 owner of the copyright in the Pickering poems. I am surprised to learn that he is still the owner; but Bell's letter seems to imply as much. Tatham gave me *carte blanche* some while ago, in case he had any rights in the matter.

As to fancy emendations (Shelley) I fervently echo what you say, as to the main question. For myself, I feel the temptation, mostly resist it with firmness: in other cases, am glad to be reined in by a real authority like your own. You seem however to have rather summarily prejudged Thomson, who is by no means reckless, nor yet mechanical in his critical ideas. The line from *Troilus and Cressida* of which you remind me[2] satisfies me that "kill" may be right, and ought to be religiously respected (indeed I never had the least notion of displacing it). I don't yet think it comes in Shelley with the same fittingness that it does in Shakespeare.

Moss.[3] It strikes me that Shelley *may* have written heads — somewhat as below —

Misread by the printer as Moss. The latter word still appears to me inappropriate to an almost ultra-Shelleyan excess.

I have not read the article on Marat:[4] must try to see it. Am quite prepared to believe he was something *besides* a Death's-head-and-bloody-bones.

I have also not seen the *Tombeau de Théophile Gautier.*[5] My impression is that, at the time of its publication, I read, extracted in the *Athenaeum* or elsewhere, your poem and also Hugo's, and have no doubt I liked yours, wholly or chiefly — but must confess (the fault of a memory very different from yours as regards verse and verbal detail) that the particulars are not now present to my reminiscence.

Brown is rather improving than otherwise: still in bed.

Yours always,
W. M. Rossetti

MS: BL. Extracts in *Blake*, pp. 6-7.

1. Not identified.
2. See Letter 240, Note 13.
3. See Letter 240, Note 14.
4. *Fortnightly Review*, n.s. 15 (January 1874), 43-74.
5. A memorial volume to Gautier (Paris, 1873). Swinburne contributed six poems, including the *Memorial Verses* previously published in the *Fortnightly Review*, n.s. 13 (January 1873), 68-73. A review of the volume in the *Athenaeum*, 8 November 1873, pp. 590-91, gave extracts from Swinburne's and Hugo's poems.

242. TO FRANCES ROSSETTI

Somerset House,
5 August 1874

Dearest Mamma,

I was extremely glad to receive your letter of the 1st. It reached me on the evening of the 3rd, as Lucy and I had just been down to the house of Mr. Slack[1] in Sussex to return those Shelley letters[2] which remained so long a while in my hands. The Slacks were very much pleased with the appearance of the bound volume,[3] and got me to write something in the fly-leaf — so I gave a brief account of the place which this correspondence holds in the career of Shelley generally. They treated us with great goodwill and hospitality: it is a beautiful country all thereabouts, close to the last residence of poor old Dr. Epps. Slack, being a man of science, showed us a number of exquisite microscopical objects, and gave us a look through his telescope (for he keeps a private observatory) at Saturn and his rings, and the moon.

6 August

I am glad you have enjoyed such fine weather at Eastbourne. Here yesterday was chilly: today very fine, and not wanting in warmth. The flower of the dock has often been observed by me as very beautiful on examination.

I regret to hear about Henrietta's almost hopeless condition; also much to learn that Uncle Henry[4] is so unwell. Will see about Pillischer's[5] paper: or possibly Lucy may have returned it to him already.

Gabriel called on us on Tuesday evening. He was wanting to write to you, and took down your address. He seems quite well, and busy painting.[6] Lucy is to sit to him on Sunday for completion of the crayon portrait[7] which he began at Kelmscott. I apprehend he is resettled in London now for some indefinite while to come.

Hardman's[8] name is well known to me: I don't think I ever saw any of his painted glass that I particularly liked, but no doubt his work is up to a good average of skill.

Dearest Mamma, with Lucy's and my love to you and both sisters, believe me Always

Your affectionate
W. M. R.

In a recent *Academy*[9] there was a very brief reference (by the Editor Appleton) to Christina's *Annus Domini*. It did not amount to the expression of any opinion — prayers being outside the range of the review.

MS: AP.

1. Henry James Slack (1818-96), journalist, microscopist (president of the Royal Microscopical Society, 1878), advocate of liberal causes, editor of the *Intellectual Observer*, to which WMR contributed a review, "The Exhibition of Miniatures at South Kensington," 8 (September, October 1866), 91-100; 169-80.
    2. Shelley-Hitchener correspondence. Why the letters were deposited with Slack is not clear (see Letter 234, Note 5), since he was not a lawyer as WMR claimed in *SR*. His reply of 23 July 1869 to WMR's enquiry is obscure: "The letters have been in my possession many years, but I do not feel at liberty to use them, nor are they exactly mine, as some person still living might reclaim them. If you will have a cup of tea here on Monday at 7 I will show them to you, but it must be on condition that no reference is made to them except I see my way thereto, and that you do not mention them as in my possession without my consent. It is long since I looked at them. Most of them are quite unfit for publication, and what ought some day to be published, must be kept back now.... Some time ago a person who is entitled to be consulted about them objected to publication, and I have reasons for not repeating the request" (AP). WMR identified their owner as "a lady living in Germany, who was probably quite unaware of their existence." Although the correspondence was "of some substantial service for the purposes of my memoir, [it] has not left any overt trace in its pages: a few juvenile poems interspersed in the letters were used in my edition" (*SR*, 2:365-66). The poems were *To Mary who died in this opinion*; "She was an aged woman" (*Mother and Son* in *PWS*); "Brothers, between you and me" (*The Mexican Revolution* in *PWS*); "Bear Witness Erin!" (*To Ireland* in *PWS*).
    3. A note in the volume, now in BL, explains that it was "Presented [11 May 1907] by Rev. Charles Hargrove, to whom the letters were bequeathed in March, 1907, by Mrs. Charlotte Mary Slack, of Croydon, with a request that he would eventually bequeath them to the British Museum."
    4. Henry Francis Polydore, brother of Frances Rossetti, was "a solicitor (or mostly a solicitor's articled clerk), who preferred to anglicize his name into Polydore. This change was projected mainly as a bait for clients, but the clients never came" (*SR*, 1:7). MS. Diary, 7 January 1885: "A telegram from my Aunt Charlotte to Christina announces that my Uncle Henry died near midnight of yesterday — age 77. He was a man of narrow nature, kindly in an ordinary degree, punctiliously conscientious: in this respect I think he exceeded all other men I have known, having more of the scrupulosity of some women. A strict Catholic, devout in practice." His daughter Henrietta died of consumption in 1874. Mrs. Polydore, also called Henrietta, lived in the United States. WMR to Anne Gilchrist, 24 August [1876]: "My aunt by marriage Mrs. Polydore keeps a vast hotel at Mississippi City near New Orleans — called Barnes's Hotel, I think, but there is no Barnes. She is a somewhat curious character, with lots of business energy and power of falling on her feet in risky places. Age towards 52. Her husband is alive in England: she left him years ago as their tempers and habits disagreed, but there is no imputation on Mrs. Polydore's character. She is daughter of a Baker in Cheltenham, and has an ordinary amount of education and culture" (LC).
    5. Probably Moritz Pillischer, manufacturing optician, 88 New Bond Street (*POLD*).
    6. WMR to WBS, 27 July 1874: "[Gabriel] came up ... to London about last Thursday week, and it seems to me he is hardly likely to return to Kelmscott at all as a settled residence.... His health seems good: his spirits not exactly what I could wish them, but on the whole pretty fair" (Arizona).
    7. Surtees 454.
    8. John Hardman & Co., "medieval metal workers ... glass stainers and mural decorators," 13 King William Street (*POLD* 1874).
    9. 25 July 1874, p. 95.

243. TO WILLIAM HOLMAN HUNT

Somerset House,
12 August [1874]

Dear Hunt,

I was exceedingly pleased at receiving your note yesterday, and will tonight inform Lucy of your cordial feelings and expressions. Perhaps after such long postponements I scarcely deserved to obtain so sweet a woman as my wife: but having succeeded I shall endeavour to make her happy in proportion to the happiness she confers upon me.

I am certain that you and I, my dear Hunt, married or unmarried, will always remain true friends — true *old* friends, which makes a deal of difference indeed. Thanks for all.

Yours,
W. M. Rossetti

MS: Rylands.

244. TO DANTE GABRIEL ROSSETTI

Somerset House,
3 October [1874]

Dear Gabriel,

Lucy is still *far* from strong:[1] at times fairly well, at others much knocked up. I noticed that, when she went to Chelsea some while ago, the long cab or omnibus drives used always to fatigue her: and we both think that she is not very likely to appear on Monday. However, she might *possibly* come — and I shall come if nothing should occur to make my companionship with her at home desirable (assuming that the question can be thus left open without inconveniencing you).

What a catastrophe in poor Tadema's house![2] I called last evening (at the Epps's house in Devonshire Street) to make enquiry, and learn that the affair is not *quite* so bad as some newspapers are making out. Tadema and his wife were away in Edinburgh, and the only harm done to any person is that a servant is somewhat cut about the head. No pictures were injured, and the dining-room and studio are not so very greatly damaged. Still, the house is of course not much less than wrecked.

Your
W. M. R.

You don't mention the dinner-hour. I shall assume 7½ if I don't hear to the contrary — coming then or earlier as convenient.

MS: AP.

1. WMR to Frances Rossetti, 15 August [1874]: "We at Euston Square are ourselves in some trouble just now: Lucy had a miscarriage on Friday (yesterday) morning. Ever since the close of June or beginning of July she and I had some reason to think she was pregnant: but from motives which one woman will readily understand of another, she was reticent on the subject — hinted of it to no one save Cathy" (AP).
2. The explosion of a barge on the Regent's Canal damaged Tadema's house, which was situated in an "exposed position where the canal intersects Regent's Park" (P. C. Standing, *Sir Lawrence Alma-Tadema* [1905], p. 39). The *Athenaeum* reported that "a terrible débâcle was made of the furniture, a great deal of which had been designed by the painter" (10 October 1874, p. 489).

245. TO THE EDITOR OF THE *ACADEMY*

56 Euston Square, 5 October 1874

Mr. Pickering recently published a volume entitled *The Poems of William Blake, comprising Songs of Innocence and Experience, together with Poetical Sketches, and some Copyright Poems not in any other Edition*; and on September 5 I reviewed the volume briefly in the *Academy*.[1] Mr. Pickering, it seems, did not like the review; and he has now printed a little fly-sheet headed *William Blake and his Editors*, of which a copy reached me by post. There are in Mr. Pickering's fly-sheet two incorrect statements, which I wish to rectify — leaving its other readers to judge of any further argumentative or critical matter contained in it.

1. Mr. Pickering says that the editor of his volume, Mr. R. H. Shepherd,[2] some years ago, "had with some reason accused *the Messrs. Rossetti* of taking unwarrantable liberties with the text of Blake," as published in Mr. Gilchrist's *Life* of that artist. Now there was no reason whatever for accusing "the Messrs. Rossetti" of anything of the sort. I, being one of the two Messrs. Rossetti, had nothing at all to do with the selecting or editing of the poems of Blake in that book. (I commented one single poem, *The Mental Traveller*).

2. Mr. Pickering says that, in my review printed in the *Academy*, I have "impugned the veracity of a statement on the title-page of the new edition, to the effect that it contains some copyright poems not in any other edition." What I really did was to affirm — and I now reaffirm it — that the number of "copyright poems not in any other edition" is limited to two — viz.: the *Song by a Shepherd*, and *Song by an Old Shepherd*. It is true — and this I had already pointed out in the *Academy* — that the edition contains one other fully copyright poem, *Long John Brown and Little Mary Bell*; also nine more poems (of which Mr. Pickering now specifies the titles) taken from a MS. book by Blake lately in Mr. Pickering's possession. But these are not "copyright poems not in any other edition": for the *Long John Brown* was previously published by Mr. Pickering himself, in 1866; and the remaining nine were also thus published, and had before that, with some verbal modifications, been printed in Gilchrist's *Life of Blake*, 1863.

W. M. Rossetti

Text: *Academy*, 10 October 1874, p. 408.

1. P. 255.
2. Richard Herne Shepherd (1842-95), bibliographer and editor. In his reprint of *Songs of Innocence and Experience* (1866) he protested DGR's editorial practice as "contrary to the true principles of editing" (p. viii). Two years later, in his reprint of *Poetical Sketches*, he wrote of his "dangerous precedent ... of tampering with his author's text ... [which] destroys to a certain extent the historical value of the poems" (p. ix). He repeated the latter remarks in the volume reviewed by WMR (pp. xiii-xiv).

246. TO ALGERNON CHARLES SWINBURNE

Somerset House,
4 November [1874]

Dear Swinburne,

I read your letter about the Blake with great pleasure, and feel much indebted to you for your friendly and handsome expressions regarding my share in the volume. Sorry you are so adverse to *Tiriel* — which I for my part think fully entitled to its place in the book.

I must set right that reference to Los etc.[1] if opportunity offers. As to the textual details regarding the *Tiger*[2] etc., I can't speak unless I reinspect the original materials.

It interests me to hear of the project regarding *Joseph and his Brethren*[3] etc. As to Gabriel, I regret to say that days and weeks may possibly elapse before I see him. It might perhaps be as well for you (or Chatto[4]) to raise the question with him direct.

I write curtly, being in great trouble about Nolly Brown. I greatly fear he will not recover: indeed he was so *exceedingly* ill when I left that house this morning about 9½, that were I to find him dead on my return this afternoon, I should be not surprised, though truly distressed.

Your affectionate
W. M. Rossetti

MS: BL.

1. Swinburne pointed out that Los and Enitharmon "are *not* as you say interpreted in *Jerusalem* but in *Milton*" (*SL*, 2: 349).
2. Swinburne wrote: "delighted as I was to see the second version of the *Tiger*, I was disappointed not to see all, or the most important variations of the MS given" (*SL*, 2:349).
3. Swinburne's article on Wells, "An Unknown Poet," appeared in the *Fortnightly Review*, 23 (February 1875), 217-32; and, slightly revised, as the introduction to the 1876 reissue of *Joseph and his Brethren*.
4. Andrew Chatto (1840-1913), Hotten's successor as Swinburne's publisher. From the age of fifteen he worked for Hotten, and in 1873 purchased the business from his widow.

247. TO DANTE GABRIEL ROSSETTI

5 Fair Lawn,
Lower Merton,
15 November [1874]

Dear Gabriel,

I return the sonnet,[1] and quite agree with Watts[2] in thinking it should be published — and the *Athenaeum* seems about the most fitting medium. Brown, who read the sonnet this afternoon, concurs.

As you asked me to mention any point which might seem to me open to improvement, I name the following. Brown thinks (and I don't exactly dissent) that "mountains of work" is in some degree exceptionable, as being a well-known colloquialism. He queries whether "ranges of work" would be preferable — or "huge fields of work": to Hueffer occurs the phrase "The heights of work,[3] the floods" etc. or "Vast heights."

To me the point that seems most disputable is the final expression "We hope: does he?" "Does he (*hope*)" does not seem to be quite the essence of the question. Rather "We hope — does he possess," or "does he know," or "enjoy." I didn't however see my way to any actual verbal change consistent with the sound and run of the sentence: but Brown (agreeing with the point I raised, when I stated it to him) suggests "We hope: and he?"[4] — which I think deserves to be thought over.

We are *all* down here, and those who most need it find self-possession and courageous acceptance of the inevitable still in their power.

Your affectionate

W. M. Rossetti

The *Athenaeum* from its far larger circulation seems a better medium than the *Academy*: but I am *satisfied* the latter would very gladly accept the sonnet, were you to offer it. Perhaps the *Fortnightly* however might be next best to the *Athenaeum*.

MS: AP.

1. *Untimely Lost*, DGR's commemorative sonnet on Oliver Brown, published in the *Athenaeum*, 21 November 1874, p. 678.
2. Walter Theodore Watts (1832-1914; Watts-Dunton from 1896), solicitor and for quarter of a century influential critic of the *Athenaeum*. His gift for binding friendship (which he later extended to Swinburne) combined with his professional knowledge to make him indispensable to DGR during the last decade of his life. After DGR's death he faithfully aided WMR in settling the estate, and remained a confidant and adviser in all matters relating to DGR's reputation. His vacillation over writing DGR's life, which became a perplexing irritant to WMR, should probably be interpreted less as bungling than as canny obtuseness in a situation where it was impossible to produce a biography that would satisfy anyone.
3. Revised thus.
4. Revised thus.

248. TO ALGERNON CHARLES SWINBURNE

Somerset House,
5 January [1875]

Dear Swinburne,

I received your letter this morning. Have not yet had the opportunity of looking at the Royal Academy pamphlet:[1] but, to save time, I reply at once from Somerset House, and will see about the pamphlet this evening. I think meanwhile recollection serves the purpose.

In a general way, I should be disposed to reprint whatever you said on the ground that the works reviewed were of leading importance and interest, and to omit whatever you said on the ground that the works were futile or inefficient. This would entail, for instance, the omission of what you wrote concerning Lucy's picture of Mary Stuart[2] — (Lucy, as I think you are aware, died a year or two ago). The treatment of Millais which you now propose seems to me entirely judicious and suitable.

A quarter of an hour's pondering has not brought into my mind anything that I *quite* like as a name for your forthcoming poetical volume:[3] "National Poems" I think not far amiss — decidedly preferable to "Political." A different *sort* of name would appear to me quite equally desirable, if only you can get one to hit

the mark: as for example *Res Publica*, or *The Court of the Gentiles*: I don't
dislike, yet don't entirely like, either of these. Were a title of this class adopted, I
think it should be supplemented by one of the other class — as thus: *Res Publica,
National Poems by A. C. S.* Another (very obvious) expedient would be to say
— *A Song of Italy and other National Poems.*

Brown and the rest of us are all pretty well, thank you: Hueffer and his wife
are now staying with the Browns for awhile in Fitzroy Square, and Lucy spends
the day there, and I the evening.

I did read Milton's *Areopagitica* years ago, and admired it: this must, I fear, be
the only one of his prose writings that I have acquainted myself with. Will write
to Gabriel for Wells's address.

Here I close — but will add a word or two after looking up the Royal Academy
pamphlet. I hope your father is better.

Your

W. M. Rossetti

P.S. I have now looked through the pamphlet. I adhere to what I have before said
on the subject: but at the same time think that, were you to prefer to reprint the
work exactly as it stands, no particular objection would arise to that course.

MS: BL.

1. *Notes on the Royal Academy Exhibition, 1868.* Swinburne reprinted his portion, with deletions,
in *Essays and Studies* (1875).
2. *The Forced Abdication of Mary, Queen of Scotland.*
3. *Songs of Two Nations* (1875).

249. TO ALGERNON CHARLES SWINBURNE

Somerset House,
11 January [1875]

Dear Swinburne,

Your suggestion as to "Songs of Light and Darkness"[1] etc. has again set me
thinking, but without result. My impression is that the "Day and Night" used by
Allingham[2] should hardly be re-appropriated.

I have a dim idea that Gabriel was from a remote date aware that the book[3]
within mentioned, or some such book by Wells, existed: am practically certain
that he never *saw* anything of it, and quite sure that I never did.

It seems to me that the proposed arrangement of your *Essays and Studies* is a
very suitable one: all the better if *Jason* comes next after (or next before?)
Gabriel.[4] I am sure what you say in censure of my Shelley work[5] will be
reasonable (whether *right* or otherwise) and friendly, and believe I shan't feel the
least soreness over any syllable of it. As to my own present view of the points
your letter refers to, I regret and recede from *some* of the emendations (I think
only a few); adhere to the repunctuation in principle, and almost invariably in
detail; also to emendations of grammar, and of *thou* and *you* etc., but dare say
some instances could be pointed out which I would willingly cancel. Your
present remark as to the use (English poetry) of *thou* for earnestness and passion

is, I think, quite fair: indeed I believe it differs in no essential respect from something I have myself said or implied somewhere in the Shelley. About Fleay I must say I regret your rancour, which appears to me (so far as I know Fleay's performances) out of scale and out of measure: but it is no affair of mine.

I trust, when I hear from you next, the news concerning your father may be more decidedly favourable. For some days from next Friday I, with Brown and Lucy, am off to Newcastle and Edinburgh, at both which places Brown's lectures[6] are to be redelivered. We expect to be back by Sunday 24.

Your affectionate
W. M. Rossetti

MS: BL.

1. See Letter 248, Note 3.
2. See Letter 34, Note 2.
3. C. J. Wells, *Stories After Nature*, published anonymously in 1822.
4. "Morris's Life and Death of Jason" followed directly "The Poems of Dante Gabriel Rossetti."
5. "Notes on the Text of Shelley" in *Essays and Studies*.
6. See Letter 239, Note 4.

250. TO WALT WHITMAN

56 Euston Square,
14 April [1875]

Dear Mr. Whitman,

I am always proud to receive any scrap of your handwriting, and pleased as well: though the pleasure was a somewhat melancholy one yesterday, owing to the far from favourable account which you give of yourself. It seems a singularly perverse arrangement of nature (but *you* are not the man to complain of her) that you, with your exceptionally vigorous mould, and still hardly beginning to be an elderly man, should be subject to so lingering as well as severe an attack. Believe that you have in this country some most sincere sympathizers, to whom news of your complete recovery would be among the very best news that they could hear.

I look forward with great interest to your proposed volume of prose and verse.[1] The last thing I saw of yours was that temperate and discriminating but yet hearty (or it would not be yours) estimate of Burns. I put something about it into a literary weekly review I write in, the *Academy*.[2] This was copied into some (I daresay numerous) English papers; and one Editor wrote asking what was the American paper in which your remarks had been printed, as he wished to look them up, and reprint them in full — which has probably been done ere now. I shall now put into the *Academy* the substance of your last note, and of the article in the *New Republic*.[3] Symonds therein mentioned (at least I suppose it is the *same* Symonds) entered years ago into a correspondence with me, on the sole basis of his great admiration of your poems. Clifford[4] is regarded as a shining light among our younger men of science, very bold in his tone of thought.

I forget what the date may have been when I last wrote to you: more shame to me perhaps, as showing that it must at any rate have been a long while ago. Perhaps it may even have been before May 1873. In that month I went to Italy on a short trip with some friends, one of them being the daughter, whom I had known from childhood, of one of my oldest intimates Ford Madox Brown (a distinguished historical painter — she herself being also a painter of no small attainment). Before we came back from the trip, we had resolved that we had better part no more, and in March 1874 we married. My wife is greatly interested in you and what concerns you, and bids me not fail to say that she "admires you as much as I do." I remember that her sister,[5] then perhaps barely 17 years of age, seemed more fascinated with your poems, when my Selection of them came out towards 1868, than with any other poetical work she had ever seen. She also is an able painter — now married to Dr. Hueffer, a German learned in musical and other matters, who has of late contributed some musical articles to the *New York Tribune*. There was also a brother, Oliver Madox Brown, who showed a singular extent of genius, both as painter and as writer: a romance of his, *Gabriel Denver*, was published in 1873, and his other remaining writings will probably soon be issued. Unfortunately he died in November last of pyaemia, aged less than 20. Many a time have I heard him refer to your writings in an enthusiastic spirit.

Last month I for the first time in my life faced a public audience (in Birmingham) to deliver a lecture — on Shelley:[6] and I found myself less unfitted for the task than I had apprehended. It was a *written* lecture. There must be a great satisfaction in addressing a large audience, for one who can speak wholly or almost extempore, and who feels the magnetic personal thrill between his hearers and himself. You, I think, have on various occasions experienced this pleasure.

This afternoon I shall be seeing one of the interesting old men surviving from a past generation — Trelawny, the friend of Shelley and Byron. He has always been a wonderfully strong man, in all senses of the word: and now, well past 80, he wears no underclothing and no great-coat, bathes constantly in cold water and in the sea, prefers to dispense with stockings as he sits at home slippered — etc. He has been in all parts of the world — North and South America included: always markedly temperate — even in his youth, when the contrary habit was universally prevalent here.

I hope I have not wearied you with this talk. At all events believe me to be always

Yours with affection,
W. M. Rossetti

Have you wholly relinquished the idea of visiting Europe?

MS: LC.

1. *Leaves of Grass* 1876, 6th ed., was in 2 vols. Vol. 2, entitled *Two Rivulets*, contained poems and prose.
2. "Whitman's opinion will be regarded as far too lukewarm by the thoroughgoing enthusiasts of the ploughman-lyrist.... What he chiefly objects to is his want of ideality. This criticism should be read by those who suppose that Whitman himself is a mere blustering realist" (27 February 1875, p. 215).
3. The article in the *New Republic* contrasted the praise of Whitman by J. A. Symonds and W. K. Clifford with "the disgraceful neglect of the poet in his own country" (*Academy*, 17 April 1875, p. 398).

4. William Kingdon Clifford (1845-79), professor of Applied Mathematics at University College London, delivered a lecture at St. George's Hall, London on "The Relation between the Sciences and Modern Poetry," in which (the *New Republic* reported) he read "mostly from the pieces of Whitman ... and pronounced him the only poet whose verse, based on modern scientific spirit, is vivified throughout with what Professor Clifford terms the 'cosmic emotion'" (quoted in the *Academy*, 17 April 1875, p. 398).

5. Catherine Emily Brown (1850-1927), FMB's daughter by his second wife Emma Hill. She exhibited a portrait of Nellie Epps (Mrs. Edmund Gosse) at the Dudley Gallery in 1869. F. M. Hueffer's article on "The Younger Madox Browns" in the *Artist*, February 1897, mentions her portraits of Laura Alma-Tadema, FMB, Emma Brown, and Francis Hueffer; and several "fancy heads" (p. 51).

6. On "Shelley's Life and Writings," delivered "on March 15, at the Masonic Hall, Birmingham, to a large audience of members of the Birmingham and Midland Institute. The lecture ... was a more than usually long one" (*Academy*, 20 March 1875, p. 292). He recast it as two lectures for delivery in Newcastle on 5 and 7 January 1876 (see Letter 260); and in London on 5 and 19 December 1877 "in connexion with the Lecture-evenings projected by [Justin] McCarthy.... [On 5 December] McCarthy spoke (which gratified me) with especial reference to my impartiality regarding Shelley and the persons and powers with whom he was in conflict" (MS. Diary). The lectures were published in the *Dublin University Magazine*, n.s. 1 (February, March 1878), 138-55, 262-77. For the first lecture he was paid £5.5: "This is certainly very low, but the Editor Keningale Cook had told me from the first time that his paying power is scanty" (MS. Diary, 14 February 1878). MS. Diary, 14 September 1877: "Chatto & Windus returned the other day my Lectures on Shelley pronouncing them too long for the *Gentleman's Magazine*. This is bothering, as the sum payable would have been about £45: moreover Chatto & Windus have played fast and loose with the affair in a not very pleasant manner." He condensed the lectures into one for delivery at the South Place Institute on 24 November 1878 (at the invitation of G. W. Foote), and at Glasgow on 6 February 1881 (see Letter 312).

251. TO WILLIAM BELL SCOTT

Somerset House,
31 May [1875]

Dear Scotus,

I wrote some few days ago to Grove,[1] Editor of *Macmillan's*, proposing to write an article on your *Poems*;[2] saying also that I apprehend a regular sort of review-article on the poems individually would not be quite the sort of thing for his Magazine, so I would extend the review into a kind of sketch of English poetry of the last generation or more. Here is his reply, which you may like to see: please return it as soon as you choose. I don't quite like what he says at the end about his "right of remonstrance": for it looks like schoolmastering *me* on a subject of which perhaps I know as much as he does (and I shall of course put my name to my article), when it must be quite obvious that he does not in like manner schoolmaster all his other contributors on their respective subjects. I think I shall feel bound (on receiving the letter back from you) to say something to him on this point: but shall take care so to put the matter as not to lead to any calling-off on his part.

I am reading your volume as leisure (very scanty at present) serves, with a renewed sense of pleasure in the old poems, and admiring much in the new ones. Was glad to hear the other day that the *Pall Mall*[3] had come out handsomely: have not myself seen the article.

324

Affectionate regards at home.

Your
W. M. Rossetti

MS: Princeton.

1. George Grove (1820-1900), writer on music and first director of the Royal College of Music; editor of *Macmillan's Magazine*, 1868-83.
2. *Poems: Ballads, Studies from Nature, Sonnets*, with thirteen etchings by WBS and four by Lawrence Alma-Tadema. WBS to WMR, 24 July [1874]: "I will make a handsome book and hope the etchings will have character. Tadema who is coming here (and Laura) has offered to do some for me — one or two at any rate. I gave him a lesson on etching, devoted a Sunday to him a few months ago, and found he had no difficulties — did it as if he had done it all his life, although he never had seen a plate before" (Durham). WMR reviewed the volume in "William Bell Scott and Modern British Poetry," *Macmillan's Magazine*, 33 (March 1876), 418-29.
3. *Pall Mall Gazette*, 15 May 1875, p. 12.

252. TO ALGERNON CHARLES SWINBURNE

Somerset House,
6 August [1875]

Dear Swinburne,

Old Trelawny is extraordinarily delighted with your Essay on Shelley[1] — indeed with your book generally; vows that nobody ever did justice to or understood Shelley before you; and *ne tarit pas* in chaffing me about my being doomed to 10,000 years of purgatory etc. He has enlarged on these matters to me any number of times these 2 months, and yesterday he specially asked me to let you know, and convey his thanks for the book. I am sure, were you to call, he would be much gratified. He has now been in town (7 Pelham Crescent) since early in April or so, and might almost any day, I apprehend, be returning to the country: so, if you are minded to call, the earlier the safer.

He has written down various additional reminiscences of Shelley and Byron, and seems really disposed to reissue his book,[2] with these additions included. I looked through the volume lately, marking where the new matter might not inappositely be introduced.

Yours always,
W. M. Rossetti

MS: BL.

1. See Letter 249, Note 5.
2. *Recollections of the Last Days of Shelley and Byron* (1858); new ed. in 2 vols. as *Records of Shelley, Byron and the Author* (1878).

253. TO ALGERNON CHARLES SWINBURNE

Somerset House,
(begun) 23 August [1875]

Dear Swinburne,

Many thanks for your long letter. Trelawny was still in town on Thursday last, when I saw him, and I think would be so for 2 or 3 days yet. I am however very uncertain of seeing him again, and have therefore just sent him a note expressing your gratification.[1] That rather mysterious person his daughter (Laetitia[2]) was to arrive last Friday: Trelawny tells me she is unmarried, but a lady of my acquaintance professes to know *a* daughter of Trelawny (query the same?) who is a Mrs. Burleigh.[3] I have brought Miss Blind this year acquainted with Trelawny: he observed her name in your Shelley paper, and asked me "Who is Miss Blind?" and this led to a meeting. He and she seem to get on together extremely well.

I know you denounced the purgatorial aeons on Fleay, *nominally*: but must confess that, if he deserves them, I do too, and must take my chance accordingly. I read your Shelley Notes attentively again a few days ago, wishing to see whether all questions of *fact*, as between you and me, were stated with what I should admit to be accuracy. I thought (speaking from memory) that you were not quite correct in saying (1) that I had altered thou and you in *Cenci on some elaborate principle* — the fact being that I have only kept various thou's in immediate juxtaposition consistent, and ditto you's: (2) you speak of my having put a needlessly abstruse interpretation on *Witch of Atlas* — whereas the interpretation *you* proceed to put is practically the same as my own, and slightly the more abstruse of the two: (3) you object to my objections to *Epipsychidion*, not remarking apparently that my leading objection is the very same that you make yourself — viz.: that the allusions to matters personal to Shelley are so puzzling as to be substantially unintelligible. These are (if I remember right) the only points on which I thought your statement of *facts* not wholly accurate: the rest being diversities of *opinion*, on which you obviously have the better *right* to be right — and indeed on some of the points I no longer do differ from you.

Dear old Brown was I believe just a little nettled — as you say, on *my* account — at your disproof of what was said about Lear's 3 daughters:[4] the fact being (as he informed you) that the observation printed with my signature was really his own, but no doubt I ought to have remembered that the play says the reverse.

We were all sorry to hear of your sprain, and trust it is now well got over.

What you say of your new Greek drama[5] is the best of news: I shall be impatient to hear it when the opportunity offers. Your idea of a paper on Athens and Jerusalem, Aeschylus and Dante[6] is excellent — though I don't suppose I should entirely agree with you as to details.

Wells, I expect, had better leave his old drama[7] alone. It is only yesterday 24 August that I read your *Fortnightly* article about him, and revived my recollection (most vague for years past) of the drama, which no doubt has a *cachet* of greatness. I wanted more particularly to remember about it because I am now occupied in writing (for *Macmillan's Magazine*) an article on Scotus's poems, which I mean to make a kind of rapid résumé of the British poetry of last half-century — since death of Byron — so as to exhibit in some dim degree Scotus's relation to the poets who preceded and those who have succeeded him. Shall have to pick my steps a little when I come to speak of you, Gabriel, Christina, etc., but must do what I can. Of course the whole affair will be very summary. Article may be finished perhaps in a fortnight or so — to be *published* when other powers determine.

There is every likelihood that my (Moxon) *Lives of Poets* will be reissued in a volume, with 7 Lives added.[8] The difficulty is to know where to stop as to including or excluding, so the publishers stick to the idea Moxon's *Popular Poets*, and that will be the great criterion. Have you any idea who a Mr. Forrest[9] of Savile Club is? He has invited me to co-operate in some way in a History of English Literature, and I shall soon be looking practically into his proposal.

Affectionately yours,
W. M. Rossetti

MS: BL.

1. See Letter 252.
2. (?1842-1938), Trelawny's daughter by his third wife Augusta, whom he married in 1841 and separated from in ?1858. Sometime before Trelawny's death in 1881 she married Col. Charles Call. WMR to Roger Ingpen, 26 December 1908, described her as "a highly intelligent and pleasant lady, unfortunately of late years quite deaf" (Berkeley).
3. Maria Julia Burley (b. 1814), Trelawny's daughter by his first wife Caroline Julia Addison, whom he divorced in ?1819.
4. That they "might not improbably be surmised to have had different mothers" ("Mr. Madox Brown — *King Lear*," *Academy*, 31 July 1875, p. 126). Swinburne wrote to FMB on 1 August about WMR's "singular oversight" (*SL*, 3:50).
5. *Erechtheus* (1876).
6. See *SL*, 3:56; the paper was never written.
7. *Joseph and his Brethren*.
8. *Lives of Famous Poets* (1878) reprints with revisions the prefatory notices to sixteen volumes of "Moxon's Popular Poets." The following poets were added: Chaucer, Spenser, Shakespeare, Butler, Dryden, Gray, and Goldsmith.
9. Swinburne mentions "a Mr. Forrest, a friend of Mrs. [Bryan Waller] Procter's, who has written to solicit a contribution ... to a projected series of essays ... on English poets." Lang does not identify Forrest, but he notes that Montagu Procter "married the daughter of a Captain Forrest" (*SL*, 3:123).

254. TO ALGERNON CHARLES SWINBURNE

Somerset House,
15 October [1875]

Dear Swinburne,

I have been a long while answering your most friendly letter of 26 September: the fact being that Lucy took such excessive delight in its references to the baby that she has kept it by her all this interval, and, not having it under my hand at the moment when letter-writing had to be seen to, I have left it over hitherto. Believe me that it gave me also a certain tempered but genuine proportion of the pleasure with which it inspired Lucy. We shall of course be extremely pleased to reveal the baby to you at your convenience; and Lucy confesses to a lurking hope and ardent wish that you may yet write a verse or two to welcome the bantling, as dimly adumbrated in your letter.

16 October

The baby (named but not christened nor to be christened Olivia Frances Madox[1]) goes on very well, and Lucy also well.

Christina was away from Euston Square when your letter came, and it has slipped me as yet to speak to her, or settle the matter. Pray assure your sister that the thing shall be done in one form or other pretty soon.[2]

On Wednesday last I saw Watts, who had just seen you: he told me great things of your Greek drama.[3] Also that you were just about to return to the country, so I suppose I am right in addressing this to Holmwood.

What engages me just now is the turning into 2 lectures the one lecture on Shelley which I delivered at Birmingham last March. I am to redeliver it at Newcastle on 5 and 7 January. I am also passing proofs of Nolly Brown's writings which Tinsley Brothers are to publish.

Yours in hurry and affection,
W. M. Rossetti

MS: BL.

1. (b. 20 September; d. 1961). Like her two sisters and brother she was educated at home. Her early interest in anarchism is described in *A Girl Among the Anarchists*, written with her sister Helen and published in 1903 under the pseudonym Isabel Meredith. In 1897 she married Antonio Agresti, an Italian anarchist and writer, and settled permanently in Rome, where she worked as a tutor and interpreter. She was a close friend of the landscape painter Giovanni Costa, whose biography she wrote in 1904. She was also a friend and biographer of David Lubin, founder of the International Institute of Agriculture in Rome, and worked for the Institute from 1905 until its activities were taken over by the United Nations Food and Agricultural Organization in 1945. Swinburne greeted her birth with *A Birth Song*, published in the *Athenaeum*, 19 February 1876, pp. 263-64, and included in *Poems and Ballads*, 2d ser., 1878.
2. See Letter 256, Note 4.
3. *Erechtheus*.

255. TO JOHN PAYNE[1]

56 Euston Square,
20 October [1875]

Dear Payne,

I was much gratified (or rather *we* were) at receiving your note of yesterday. Lucy goes on very fairly indeed: and, if only the weather would permit of her getting a little out of the house, she would I think be soon perfectly restored. The small Olivia is quite well and vigorous.

I was much obliged to Mallarmé for the sumptuous present he made me some few weeks ago of his Raven,[2] illustrated by Manet. The translation appears to me truly skilful and fine: extremely faithful, and preserving more poetry than I should have thought well practicable in a prose translation from verses so much of whose effect depends upon iteration of words and sound etc. Manet's performances appear to me most outrageous affairs: artistic gift and cultivation voluntarily reducing itself to scribbling and scrabbling, and expecting us to accept it all as fine frenzy and loyalty to nature. Not that I *disbelieve* in Manet as a capable man.

21 October

I ought to have written something of this at the time to Mallarmé: don't now know his address, nor remember whether I ever had the means of knowing it — perhaps he wrote a letter which disappeared into Lucy's hands. If you are in the way of writing to him and could say a word or two of overdue civility (and I might add sincere personal liking) from me, I should be grateful. Perhaps I may write a paragraph on the work for the *Academy*.

You should see some time the splendid poem with which Swinburne has greeted the advent of our baby — sent to me yesterday — 100 lines about.

Yours always truly,
W. M. Rossetti

MS: UCLA.

1. (1842-1916), minor Pre-Raphaelite poet, whose early work DGR and Swinburne praised; prolific translator of oriental literature. In 1874 he introduced WMR and Lucy to Stéphane Mallarmé, who impressed WMR as having "solid rather than brilliant qualities of mind" (*SR*, 2:334).

2. His translation of Poe's poem, published in 1875.

256. TO ALGERNON CHARLES SWINBURNE

Somerset House,
2 November [1875]

Dear Swinburne,

You made us a most splendid present with your letter of 19 October, which Lucy, I am aware, acknowledged immediately. It is a beautiful poem,[1] cherished by us all. How many births, I wonder, have been at the instant celebrated with anything approximating to it, since the beginning of the world? I have also read your reply to Lucy, but, not having it by me now, don't attempt to take any count of it here.

In the ideas expressed in the poem there is nothing that appears to me at all "savouring of insincerity or mere poetic mechanism" — quite the contrary. I am certain Brown must admire and love the poem deeply, if he has yet read it. Lucy gave him a copy several days ago: but I am not sure that he has yet plucked up courage to read all the stanzas, these being days of poignant reminiscence to him, ending with Friday next 5 November.[2]

Resumed 4 November

We are likely to stay with Brown for some few days beginning 6 November. The revision of *Bothwell* for the stage[3] must no doubt be exasperating work — yet highly interesting too in its way.

Lucy and I (also the baby) spent last week at Bournemouth — to get up her strength, which indeed goes on very well. You know we were there close to Sir Percy Shelley. I wrote to him asking leave to see the Shelley relics etc.: he however was just then in London, and the relic-room (as he wrote in very courteous terms to inform me) shut-up — *boarded* up — as a protection during some repairs going on in an adjoining room. So we had to come away Shelleyless.

Always yours,
W. M. Rossetti

I am to redeliver (possibly I told you this before) my Shelley lecture at Newcastle on 5 and 7 January. Have made the one lecture into two.

I reopen the envelope to repair previous obliviousness, and enclose two scraps of Christina's writing, for[4]

[Incomplete]

MS: BL.

1. See Letter 254, Note 1.
2. The date in 1874 of Oliver Brown's death.
3. Mentioned several times in *SL*, first in a letter to WMR, 17 July [1874], as being in the hands of Watts-Dunton and involving John Oxenford and a Mrs. Bell, "the aspirant Mary Stuart" (2:313), but nothing came of the plan.
4. See Letter 254, Note 2.

257. TO DALZIEL BROTHERS

56 Euston Square,
18 November 1875

Dear Sirs,

A friend of mine Captain Trelawny (who accompanied Lord Byron to Greece in 1824) is proposing to bring out a new edition of a work which he published with Moxon several years ago, *Recollections of Shelley and Byron*. There are a couple of woodcuts in the book, and he wishes to add to these another representing the Burning of Shelley's corpse on the Tuscan seashore.[1] His daughter has made a water-colour sketch of the event, partly from her own observation, and partly from what her father tells her of the facts. It is too jejune a performance to be engraved exactly as it stands: but I have no doubt one of your skilled draughtsmen would soon put it into good shape, and the engraving would follow suit.

Captain Trelawny is an aged gentleman, not minded to trouble himself with the details of such a matter as this. He lives mostly at Sompting near Worthing, and is there now, but spends some months of the year — say March to July — in London, 7 Pelham Crescent, Fulham Road. He would be the responsible party for all costs arising in this matter, but I would attend to it in all other respects.

Perhaps you would name some day when I could bring the sketch round to you, and we could then arrange the details. The most convenient time for me would be some afternoon towards 4¾ or 5.

Very faithfully yours,
W. M. Rossetti

MS: Berkeley.

1. "The Burning of Shelley's Body near Via Reggio. Woodcut from a Sketch made on the spot by Miss Trelawny in 1875."

258. TO ALGERNON CHARLES SWINBURNE

Somerset House,
22 November [1875]

Dear Swinburne,

Certainly Lucy and I would have no sort of objection, but quite the contrary, to the particularization, in any printed form, of the infant to whom your beautiful poem is addressed.[1] The date of birth was 20 September: the exact name you already know, I think — Olivia Frances Madox. Garnett happened to remind me the other day that 20 September is a singularly auspicious anniversary — that of the entry of the Italian national troops into Rome in 1870.

Your article in the *Examiner*[2] gave me great pleasure — both the chaffy sarcastic portion, and the serious criticism: though I don't know the poetical works of Vacquerie. Have however long possessed *Masques et Visages*, which I picked up at a venture as possibly amusing, without having at the time any idea of the literary position of Vacquerie; and I remember that, on afterwards looking a little into it, I was surprised to observe the real calibre of the book.

I did meet Minto[3] once — more than a year ago at Scott's; found him prepossessing, but had scanty talk with him. I wish he had not, on taking possession of the *Examiner*, forthwith ousted our good friend and really capable critic Miss Blind from her post of contributor of poetical critiques. He undertook, I believe, to do most of these himself — to which of course no outsider can start the least objection: but I do think it seemed harsh — and ill-judged as well — never to give Mathilde the least further employment of any kind.

I dare say Lady Shelley is worthy of marrying into the family. Trelawny however has a dislike — I think a prejudice — against her, and ''nasty devil'' is, in his mouth, one of her most approved designations.

You speak of Marshall's[4] study of *Hamlet*. It happens that, just before your letter reached me, I had addressed Marshall, in consequence of coming across an old letter of his to me (1870) saying that he was then in possession of a certain Shelley letter: with this, it turns out, he has now parted. He, in writing back to me, tendered me the gift of a copy of the *Hamlet* book: which I now possess and mean to read, but have had no time as yet for doing so. I asked Marshall whether it had been reviewed in the *Academy* — meaning (if not, and if I found profit in perusal) to offer a review myself: he however has not replied to this query. I did not know that he had ''turned papist'' — but can recollect that he always had a weak side for Urizen, Son, and Co.

I should be *delighted* to bring you acquainted, in any form, with my Shelley lectures[5] — though I can't flatter myself that you would find much in them worthy of particular approval. Have not yet finished recasting the second lecture; but must now do so undelayingly.

You may observe the black border to my envelope. It marks another death among my wife's relatives. Her first cousin and early schoolfellow Lizzie Bromley,[6] who married an Indian ''Eurasian'' Mr. Cooper some 7 or 8 years ago (you might possibly remember her a little) died of apoplexy in a shop on 12 November (the precise anniversary of poor Nolly's burial): her corpse had to be removed to our house, and was interred last Tuesday in the plot of ground next to Nolly. This has afflicted Lucy not a little: but she goes on very fairly altogether, and the baby well.

Your affectionate,
W. M. Rossetti

What a lark, in Rennie's[7] autobiography, about Shelley's picking up *little boys*, at his first Brentford school, to hurl at other boys who teazed him!

MS: BL.

1. See Letter 254, Note 1.
2. "Auguste Vacquerie: Aujourd'hui et demain," 6 November 1875, pp. 1247-50. Vacquerie (1819-95), writer, journalist, friend of Victor Hugo, helped found the anti-imperial paper *Rappel* in 1869 and became its editor in the following year.
3. William Minto (1845-93), critic, editor of the *Examiner*, 1874-78; friend of WBS whose *AN* he edited.
4. Francis Albert Marshall (1840-89), dramatist and drama critic. According to Swinburne DGR "knew [him] as a boy" (*SL*, 3:83). *A Study of Hamlet* appeared in 1875.
5. See Letter 250, Note 6.
6. Elizabeth Clara Bromley (1843-75), daughter of Augustus Bromley (d. 1843), the brother of FMB's first wife. Augustus's widow Helen (d. 1886) kept a school at Gravesend until 1881, where she undertook Lucy's early education. WMR described Lizzie as "the chief companion" of Lucy's girlhood (*SR*, 2:426). Following her marriage to Samuel Cooper, an Anglo-Indian Opium Officer, she lived in India.
7. John Rennie (1794-1874), civil engineer, whose autobiography was published in 1875.

259. TO WALT WHITMAN

56 Euston Square,
23 December 1875

Dear Mr. Whitman,

It was a great pleasure to me to see your handwriting (letter of 19 October) — likewise to make the acquaintance of Mr. Marvin,[1] whom we all found most pleasant and sensible. The only disappointment was his short sojourn over here: for, as soon as he had called on us with your letter (which was about 1 December, I think) he went over to Paris, and then, after returning and dining with us, another day or two saw him on his way homeward across the Atlantic. I dare say he has told you (if opportunity served) something about the evening he passed with us and a few friends — *good Whitmanites* most of them. Let me see whether I can remember the names. Mr. Marvin took down to dinner our dear and admirable friend Mrs. Gilchrist (who lately lost her mother, aged more than 90, and expects to see her eldest[2] son happily married pretty soon): I found Mr. Marvin was not aware (and perhaps you are not) that Mrs. Gilchrist is the widow of a literary man of some name, Alexander Gilchrist, author of the Life of the great ideal painter-poet William Blake, and of the Life of the painter Etty: he died young of scarlet fever in 1861. Next Mr. Marvin was Joseph Knight, Editor of the *Sunday Times*, theatrical critic of the *Athenaeum*, etc.: a man of excellent critical capacity, who knows your value. Then Miss Mathilde Blind, step-daughter of the German revolutionist of 1848, a woman of singular ability and independence of mind, and a most earnest believer in the author of *Leaves of Grass*. Next, Justin McCarthy,[3] one of the foremost writers in the *Daily News*, and a novelist of much talent: he has been more than once in America — also his wife. Then my father-in-law Madox Brown the historical painter, and his wife. Lastly E. W. Gosse[4] and his bride: the former a poet of these more recent years, who has done some graceful things, and has much knowledge and good perception as a critic:

Mrs. Gosse was lately Miss Ellen Epps,[5] belonging to a family of medical homoeopathists, and is herself a painter of no ordinary talent. Her sister married a painter of European fame, Alma-Tadema, a Dutchman now naturalized in England. But perhaps I am peppering my letter with a lot of details that are not much to your purpose. Mr. Marvin informed me that your works, in their various forms, are in the Congressional Library at Washington, but not my volume of Selections, and that he would like to see the latter added to the series: so, not having a *new* copy at hand, I delivered to him my own (not yet shabby) copy of the Selections, and he will present it to the Library.

My father-in-law has, I know, ordered the publishers (Tinsley Brothers) to send you a copy of the *Literary Remains* of his son, just published: the youthful author died rather more than a year ago. I think the book will present to you evidences of uncommon faculty. You will see on the title page the names of myself and of Francis Hueffer (husband of my wife's half-sister) as editors. The Memoir however is written *principally* by the father.

I was very glad to see you attended the Edgar Poe celebration,[6] from which other men who ought to have been present were blameably (I should say) absent: and I read with great interest your printed remarks regarding Poe's genius. To me he has always been a fascinating writer — not of course that I am blind to his blemishes and perversities: the poem named *To Annie* is, I think, great — even deserving preference above *The Raven*.

I could say a good deal more: but occupations press, and I want to get this off (28 December now) without further delay. Believe how warmly I and others in this country, near or not so near to me, feel regarding you. Are you ever to come to England? and if so would you not house with us for some portion at least of your sojourn?

Yours always,
W. M. Rossetti

MS: LC.

1. Joseph B. Marvin, co-editor of the *Radical*, 1866-67, was employed by the Treasury Department in Washington, on whose behalf he was visiting London.

2. Percy.

3. Justin McCarthy (1830-1912), Irish politician, novelist, historian, and journalist, described by WMR as a "fine intellect, ardent patriot, [and] accomplished gentleman" (*SR*, 2:490). He became a leader writer on the *Daily News* in 1871.

4. Edmund William Gosse (1849-1928), poet and man of letters, was introduced to the Rossettis by WBS in 1870. WMR recalls that "he was not very often" in DGR's house: "I myself, in the earlier years of my marriage, saw him more frequently" (*SR*, 2:334). His marriage in 1875 to Dr. John Epps's niece, a pupil of Madox Brown, accounts for his acceptance by WMR and Lucy, but later relations cooled (see Letters 347, 537). One of Gosse's last articles, a centenary tribute to DGR, severely attacked WMR's later writings on his brother: "Too much was written about D. G. Rossetti, but no very serious harm was done till, in 1895, the deaths of his mother and of his illustrious sister Christina had left one brother the sole guardian of his memory. Then publications, revelations, sales of objects followed in a terrible succession.... At length, not a shilling more could be drained out of the body of the unhappy man, and public curiosity was definitely sated" (*Sunday Times*, 6 May 1928, p. 8).

5. Nellie Epps was the daughter of George Napoleon Epps, who like his half-brother John practiced homeopathic medicine. She exhibited principally at the Grosvenor Gallery.

6. In November 1875 Whitman attended the public reburial in Baltimore of Poe's remains, and the dedication of a monument to him. On 18 November he published an essay on Poe in the Washington *Star*.

260. TO LUCY ROSSETTI

Bracken Dene,[1]
6 January [1876]

Dearest Lucy,

I am much concerned to find the news of your father not yet such as we could wish: perhaps his Turkish bath will by this time have put matters on the mending hand.

Yesterday I mentioned to the Leatharts my intention of returning home by the 11 p.m. train of Friday, after lecture:[2] they were so friendly in their urgencies that I should return to their house on Friday, and only leave on Saturday morning, thus avoiding night-travelling with its discomforts, that I gave in, and have now quite concluded that that will be the upshot. It seems by this plan I ought to be at King's Cross by 5:45 on Saturday afternoon.

The Lecture passed off well yesterday. Attendance large — all parts of the hall being *moderately* full. The audience seemed very attentive and not languid, and every now and then applauded sufficiently to show the discourse did not bore them. It took exactly 1 hour and 11 minutes, just about the right time — 1.15 is considered the outermost limit of time. I felt no embarrassment or *gêne*: today my throat is decidedly rough and voice husky, but I dare say I may do well enough by tomorrow evening. Late at night a representative of the *Chronicle* newspaper called here requesting loan of MS. of first lecture, which I accorded.[3]

I am going today to Tynemouth, and must start in a few minutes: friends are to dine here this evening — I know not who, and tomorrow I am to sup at Spence Watson's.[4]

Don't get out of spirits, Lucy dear: I shall soon see you again. With all love,

Your own
W. M. R.

Kiss to kid.

MS: AP.

1. James Leathart's "severe Victorian gothic" house at Low Fell, Newcastle (*The Leathart Collection*, Laing Art Gallery, p. 3).
2. See Letter 250, Note 6.
3. A report of the lecture, delivered at the theatre of the Literary and Philosophical Society, appeared in the *Newcastle Daily Chronicle*, 6 January 1876, p. 3.
4. Robert Spence Watson (1837-1911), social and educational reformer; president of the National Liberal Federation, 1890-1902, when "he was probably the chief liberal leader outside parliament" (*DNB*); honorary secretary and later president of the Newcastle Literary and Philosophical Society. When WMR lectured to the Society in 1881 he was Watson's guest.

261. TO WALT WHITMAN

56 Euston Square,
28 February [1876]

Dear Whitman,

(If you will permit me to drop the "Mr.") — I write in some haste. Yours of 26 January[1] and 11 February received.

Ever since we in England heard that your health had received a serious shock we have had it much at heart, I assure you, to testify our love, respect, and gratitude in some tangible shape: and I could at this moment tell you of at least 3 several plans which were actively mooted, and partly started.[2] Our ideas on the subject have shifted according to the varying accounts that reached us, more especially with regard to the material comforts of your present mode of life. As to the extract which you sent me from the *West Jersey Press*, and which you vouch for as less strong than the facts, proves that some more cheerful preceding accounts were not accurate, there are some of us who would really be glad to exert ourselves to the extent of our moderate means, to prove that we are not insensible of the obligations we owe you. Professor Dowden of Dublin, and myself, have more especially been in frequent written communication on this subject, and, if I hear from you in terms to warrant my so doing, I shall call the attention of others to the subject.

Meanwhile Mrs. Gilchrist and I agreed on the 25th that we would at once ask you to oblige each of us with copies of your forthcoming books[3] to the value of £5 ($25, I believe this is) each. This morning I saw about getting the requisite letter of credit for the amount, £10, and it will no doubt be procured and transmitted to you very shortly. I could not find any suitable locality nearer than New York mentioned in the Bank documents. Mrs. Gilchrist would wish her books to be copies of the *Two Rivulets only*. I should wish for the *Two Rivulets*, and also the forthcoming edition of your poems, in whatever proportions may be most convenient, and suitable for making up the £5.

I sent the substance of the *West Jersey Press* article to the *Academy*, but regret to find the Editor not forward to publish it: if he fails, I will send it elsewhere. Will also lose no time in offering for publication the poem and prose-matter[4] which you forwarded to me — and both of which I read with great interest. I trust I may succeed in all these points.

Arthur Clive (so Dowden informed me long ago) is really Standish O'Grady,[5] an Irish barrister of good position (or good prospects, I forget which). As it happens, I have not yet seen his article. With love,

Yours,

W. M. Rossetti

Dowden has mentioned to me your "Autograph Edition,"[6] but without defining what it is, nor do I precisely know. It sounds tempting, so I hope Mrs. Gilchrist and I may come in for some specimen of it.

MS: LC.

1. With this letter Whitman sent his article "Walt Whitman's Actual American Position," which had appeared anonymously in the *West Jersey Press* on 26 January 1876. The article asserted "the

determined denial, disgust and scorn of orthodox American authors, publishers and editors'' for Whitman's poems; and described how "'Old, poor, and paralyzed,' he has, for a twelve-month past been occupying himself by preparing, largely with his own handiwork, here in Camden, a small edition of his complete works in two volumes, which he himself now sells, partly 'to keep the wolf from the door' in old age'' (*Walt Whitman's Workshop*, ed. C. J. Furness, 1928, pp. 245-46). In his letter Whitman wrote: "My theory is that *the plain truth* of the situation here is best stated. It is even worse *than* described in the article'' (*CWW*, 3:20), which WMR quoted, along with excerpts from the article, in his note in the *Athenaeum*, 11 March 1876, p. 361.

2. See Gohdes, Baum, pp. 100-101.

3. See Letter 250, Note 1.

4. The poem *The Man-of-War-Bird* (later entitled *To the Man-of-War-Bird*) was first published in the *Athenaeum*, 1 April 1876, p. 463, which paid Whitman £3.3 (Blodgett, pp. 256-57; *CWW*, 3:23). The prose, "The American War,'' appeared in the *Examiner*, 18 March 1876, pp. 317-18, but there is no record of payment. WMR to Whitman, 17 December 1877: "I feel ashamed for my colleagues the English men of the press that the Editor of the *Examiner* [William Minto] should have failed to pay you his just debt, especially after the 2 or 3 times that I raised the question with him, and he once of his own accord with me. He is a man I seldom meet: but I do meet him sometimes, and, whenever this may happen next, I shall (if opportunity allows) remind him of his obligation, and I trust he may yet attend to it'' (LC).

5. Standish James O'Grady (1846-1928) turned from law to the writing of Irish history (*The History of Ireland: Heroic Period*, 1878-80) and novels based on the history and mythology of Ireland. His article, "Walt Whitman: the Poet of Joy,'' appeared in the *Gentleman's Magazine*, n.s. 15 (December 1875), 704-16.

6. Probably the Author's or Centennial Edition, as *Leaves of Grass* 1876 was known.

262. TO THE EDITOR OF THE *DAILY NEWS*

56 Euston Square,
13 March 1876

Sir,

I have read — and read with much general concurrence and satisfaction — the letter by Mr. Robert Buchanan, published in your paper of today,[1] urging that the English admirers of Walt Whitman should show their feeling towards him by some such act as the purchase of a large number of copies of his forthcoming books. As this is a matter in which I am warmly interested, and to some extent personally concerned, I take leave to address you on the subject. It was to me that Whitman wrote those words, published in the *Athenaeum* of last Saturday, vouching for the entire truth of the statements regarding him made in the *West Jersey Press* (also partially reproduced in the *Athenaeum*). Several days ago, in conjunction with another of Whitman's English admirers (a lady[2]), I wrote to the poet commissioning for each of us a certain number of his forthcoming volumes — in fact, therefore, I have already done what Mr. Buchanan suggests; and so has the friend just mentioned, and another friend, a distinguished literary man,[3] who has been in frequent communication with me for months past, as to this or any other appropriate form in which English sympathy and regard for Whitman might take shape. In writing to the poet to bespeak the books, I asked him expressly whether he would like the same course, or any other course, to be adopted by others of his admirers in this country, and in the event of his replying affirmatively, I offered to undertake the requisite correspondence at starting. His answer may probably reach me within a fortnight or so. Let us therefore trust that, what between the steps that have been already taken, and those that will almost for certain ensue upon Mr. Buchanan's printed letter, some substantial expression will shortly be given to the feelings of a good number of English, Scotch, and Irish admirers of this powerful and moving poet. Will his own countrymen yet exhibit the fruits of a late repentance, and allow themselves to be encouraged or shamed into some measure of justice to his claims?

Your faithful servant,

William Michael Rossetti

Text: *Daily News*, 14 March 1876, p. 6.

1. P. 2. Buchanan's letter hysterically overstated Whitman's situation as one of "absolute and miserable poverty." He called upon Emerson to speak again "for the vindication of the honour of America now likely to be tarnished eternally by the murder of its only remaining Prophet." Whitman, "discarded and insulted," was compared to Christ wearing the crown of thorns and Socrates condemned to drink hemlock.
2. Anne Gilchrist.
3. Edward Dowden.

263. TO ALGERNON CHARLES SWINBURNE

Somerset House,
25 March [1876]

Dear Swinburne,

I have been much busied, or would before now have answered yours of the 17th. Will convey your message to Trelawny[1] when next I need to write to him.

Have given the baby a kiss from you: the only response she sends consists of various forms and stages of bubbling and simmering.

Much obliged for your Beaumont and Fletcher:[2] have read it with a high sense of its excellence, and Hueffer has been doing the same. I wish I knew a 200th part of what you know of the Elizabethans: you would hardly believe, but it is true, that I never tackled any one play of Beaumont, or of Fletcher, or of both.

Before your note arrived I had read your poem in the *République des Lettres*[3] — very sweet and rounded.

The Blake Exhibition at Burlington Club[4] has been as yet, I believe, in a state of semi-suspended animation, because Scotus and his accomplice don't finish off their catalogue. Yesterday however I met one of the Club secretaries, and infer that the catalogue may become available any day now. Don't well know how long the Exhibition will continue: should suppose up to end of April or so.

As for Wells's *Joseph*, I would willingly do my part, but am really too much beset with ever recurrent items of work to *volunteer* a review. The only paper to which I could readily so volunteer would be the *Academy*, and I can't doubt that Appleton assigned the book away long ago.[5]

As you make no allusion to the matter, I infer that you can hardly have been aware of what has been and now is going on concerning Whitman. Some weeks ago Whitman sent me an American newspaper, *West Jersey Press*, containing an article which sets forth in strong terms his narrow means, and the American repudiation of his writings; and he asked me to reproduce it in England. I got it into the *Athenaeum* of 11 March. Buchanan, seeing it there, wrote to *Daily*

News, 13 March, a letter full of Whitmanic enthusiasm, urging people to subscribe for his books, or otherwise aid him. I meanwhile, *before* the article appeared in *Athenaeum*, had written to Whitman sending him £10 (£5 for myself and £5 for Mrs. Gilchrist) to purchase copies of his forthcoming volumes, and had asked him whether he would like me to start the like plan among friends over here, or any other plan redounding to his advantage. On seeing Buchanan's letter in *Daily News*, I wrote to same paper, 14 March, to explain these facts, and since then both Buchanan and I, on our several hooks, have received various contributions: all that *I* receive being treated (unless Whitman hereafter decides otherwise) as purchase-money for books. I have not yet received from Whitman a reply to my letter aforenamed: when I get that I shall know more definitely what to do, and would if necessary send round circulars. The *Athenaeum*, *Examiner*, *Daily News*, *Saturday Review*, *Standard*, *Secularist*, and I dare say other papers as well, have taken some part in this Whitman movement — from one point of view or another.

Yours affectionately,

W. M. Rossetti

I have a carte-de-visite of Lucy and the baby that I mean to send you: not under my hand at the present writing.

MS: BL.

1. See *SL*, 3:154.
2. His article on them in *Encyclopaedia Britannica*, ninth edition, 1875.
3. *Nocturne*; *La République des Lettres*, 20 February 1876.
4. Reviewed by WMR in the *Academy*, 11 March 1876, p. 248. On 15 April, pp. 364-65, he reviewed the catalogue, which was "in great part compiled by Mr. W. B. Scott, and prefaced by him."
5. It was reviewed by J. A. Symonds on 22 April 1876, pp. 374-76.

264. TO MONCURE CONWAY

Somerset House,
30 March [1876]

Dear Conway,

Excuse hurry. *Athenaeum* reprint from West Jersey paper is 11 March, and contains all the more important matter: Buchanan's 1st *Daily News* letter[1] is 13 March. The *Athenaeum* is quite safe, because it is only what Whitman himself asked me to publish. Buchanan's expressions founded on it are exaggerated, and Austin[2] followed Buchanan.

Before any of this I had written to Whitman (see my letter in *Daily News* of 14 March): yesterday I received his reply, quite confirming your statement that he is not in want of any ordinary comfort of life, but he approves of my proposal to promote English purchase of his new books, and I shall take measures accordingly without delay.[3]

I don't now possess a *Daily News* of 13 or 14 March: did possess them, but my servant has without warrant used them for lighting fires. Sorry not to accommodate you.

Best regards to Mrs. Conway and yourself, and congratulations on your return.[4]

Yours always truly,

W. M. Rossetti

MS: Columbia.

1. A second letter from Buchanan appeared on 16 March 1876, p. 6: "A large number of sympathetic letters have already reached me in response to my letter ... and I have every reason to believe that substantial help will be forthcoming. Meantime I take cognisance of the letter from Mr. William Rossetti [No. 262] ... and as that gentleman is ... prepared to undertake the organization of a fund for the purchase of Whitman's works, I think all future correspondence, subscriptions, etc., should be addressed to him. For my own part I shall be glad to co-operate in any scheme for Whitman's benefit."

2. Alfred Austin objected that Buchanan's first letter "clouded a question of benevolence with untimely literary fervour," for not everyone who approved of helping Whitman was convinced of the merit of his poetry (*Daily News*, 16 March 1876, p. 6). Buchanan replied on 17 March, p. 3.

3. In his reply of 17 March Whitman declared: "My dear friend, your offers of help, & those of my other British friends, I think I fully appreciate, in the right spirit, welcome & acceptive — leaving the matter altogether in your & their hands.... Though poor now even to penury *I have not so far been deprived of any physical thing I need or wish whatever — & I feel confident I shall not, in the future*" (*CWW*, 3:29). WMR printed this letter in facsimile for distribution with a circular inviting purchase of Whitman's books through him or directly from the poet. On 18 April WMR informed Lucy that he "received this afternoon the printed set of Whitman's letter" (AP), but the circular was delayed until 20 May because of uncertainty over the price of the volumes (see Letter 265). A second circular, "of like form," was issued on 1 June (Thomas Donaldson, *Walt Whitman, the Man* [1896], p. 26). Before the first circular was sent out, Swinburne, G. H. Lewes, R. M. Milnes, and others (whose names appear in the circular) sent subscriptions to WMR, so he was able to send Whitman a first remittance of £28.4 on 19 April. Further remittances were received by the poet on 20 June (£45.9.6); 9 October (£21.18); 10 September 1877 ($23.30). Buchanan sent subscriptions independently, including £5 from Tennyson. Edward Carpenter and probably others subscribed directly to Whitman (*CWW*, 3:41, 43-44, 47, 53).

4. From Russia, which Conway had first visited in 1869.

265. TO WALT WHITMAN

56 Euston Square,
4 April [1876]

Dear Whitman,

I write in haste, and specially for the business-purpose named further on. Mrs. Gilchrist and Dowden (who happens just now to be in London) have seen your letter of 17 March, and doubtless appreciated it as I do. I have received also your postcard of 20 March, and the *Two Rivulets* which that announced.

What I want to know is the precise fact about the prices etc. of your books. The printed slip mentions only *Leaves of Grass* £1 ($5), *Two Rivulets* £1, *Memoranda During War* 6/-, and all 3 for £2: and of each of these only 100 copies printed. Is it a fact then that a *Leaves of Grass* is not anyhow obtainable at less than £1 nowadays? and that, when 100 copies are sold, no more purchasers need apply? Would you kindly tell me *precisely* about all this. Were it not that I find the uncertainty about this most embarrassing, and the presumable chance of enlisting purchasers at such high prices much diminished, I should already have drawn up my proposed circular to start the scheme. Perhaps you would prefer to *telegraph* back in fewest words: but this as you prefer.

Your poem printed in *Athenaeum* of 1 April.[1]

Some minor details when next I write.

Your affectionate
W. M. Rossetti

Please tell me also *how* you would like me to send over the various sums I have received for your books. I presume you would send the books *direct* to the purchasers: not but that I would receive and distribute them if really any object to you, but it would cause delay to all, and to me some work of a kind at which I am not particularly ready.

MS: LC.

1. See Letter 261, Note 4.

266. TO ALGERNON CHARLES SWINBURNE

Somerset House,
5 April [1876]

Dear Swinburne,

I am ashamed to say that the carte-de-visite quite slipped my memory after I had written to you last. This morning I spoke about it to Lucy: and she, with her usual boundless zeal for the baby, will I believe dispatch it to you straightway. I consider it *moderately* good.

The Blake exhibition *is* now open: may I suppose remain open till about the close of April. You can't go in by paying: but you must I presume know many members of the Burlington Club, any one of whom would give you an admission. I ceased to belong to the Club (as possibly you remember) in December 1867, when they expelled Whistler. Scott also is now no longer a member.

I continue in active communication with Whitman: who is not "miserably poor" (Buchananice), but will be extremely glad to have English book-purchasing recruits beaten up. But for an uncertainty about the range of his editions and prices, I should now be already concocting a circular: wrote to him yesterday to clear up all this, and shall then proceed without delay.

I don't know the date of the *Standard* article: did not see it. The *Secularist* of 1 April showed (without further comment) subscriptions received to the amount of £1.15.6. The leading article in the *Daily News* must (I am pretty sure) be dated 16 March. The *Secularist* exaggerated the hostility of this article to Whitman: it was in fact a moderate presentment of the pro and contra of the question, as viewed by a person outside the circle of Whitmanic enthusiasm. The writer was Justin McCarthy — a very pleasant good and able man I always find him. The *Daily News* did say that it couldn't receive Whitman subscriptions — which I regretted somewhat, but I don't know that it was meant with any particular animus.

I did see something of Whitman's about verse, rhyme, etc.:[1] perceived it to be one-sided and declamatory, but had not remembered in it any such peculiar atrocity as you denounce.

Have not communicated with O'Grady — Dowden is more serviceable for looking-up Irishmen: but will send him circulars etc. as they come out. Have not *seen* his article on Whitman.

You will find Hueffer's *Encyclopaedia Britannica* article on Boccaccio *peculiarly* good (if you agree with me): I also enjoyed his Macmillan paper[2] much. I am myself working in this *Encyclopaedia* on biographies of artists[3] now.

I lately became a subscriber to the *Secularist* (Lucy has a liking for it). Have not read it closely, but consider it up to a certain fair literary level. The things that interest me in it are the (decidedly numerous) contributions of B. V. This writer is James Thomson, author of that celebrated poem (I suppose you must have read or heard of it) *The City of Dreadful Night* — also (quite as good) *Weddah and Om-el-Bonain*, an oriental legend of passion. I remember you abused him to me once, simply on the ground that he had sent me some Shelley notes and emendations — and singularly good these are, as I who know them know. I regard him as a very remarkable genius. His verses (those I read) in the *Secularist* appear to be comparative trifles, yet with a certain *cachet* too.

I also have hitherto remained ignorant of Leconte de Lisle:[4] after what you say, I must remove from myself that stigma at the very earliest opportunity. I was sorry to hear some little while ago that Victor Hugo is blameably jealous of Leconte de Lisle, and that the (as P.[5] says) quite irrefragable fact that Lisle has made a stupendous translation of Aeschylus can never be mentioned in Hugo's presence.

Your affectionate
W. M. Rossetti

I saw in the *Examiner* a most jolly piece of chaff of yours about the Shakespeare Society[6] — read it at Brown's, but not *through*. Shall buy the No.

MS: Princeton. Published: Troxell, pp. 188-90.

1. Undoubtedly a similar statement to one in a review that Whitman himself wrote of his poem, "As a Strong Bird on Pinions Free" (Blodgett, p. 455): "He discharges himself quite altogether from the old laws of 'poetry' ... and claims to inaugurate an original modern style" (Bliss Perry, *Walt Whitman, His Life and Work* [1906], pp. 206-7).
2. Ninth edition of *Britannica*; "A Literary Friendship of the Fourteenth Century [Boccaccio and Petrarch]," *Macmillan's Magazine*, 30 (April 1876), 540-51.
3. Between 1876 and 1888 WMR contributed fifty-six signed articles (and an undetermined number of unsigned short articles), mostly on Italian artists, to the ninth edition. The majority of the articles, revised with the help of Ford Madox Hueffer, were retained in the eleventh edition.
4. Charles Leconte de Lisle (1818-94), French poet and translator of classical literature, was elected to the Academy in 1886 in succession to Hugo. His translation of Aeschylus appeared in 1872.
5. Probably John Payne, who was a friend of Leconte de Lisle.
6. "Report of the First Anniversary Meeting of the Newest Shakespeare Society," 1 April 1876, pp. 381-83.

267. TO FRANCES ROSSETTI

Somerset House,
3 August [1876]

Dearest Mamma,

I was much pleased to receive Christina's letter this morning: please tell her that I reply to *you*, knowing that you like letters, and that she likes you to get them. The news she gives me of you (and by implication herself) is not amiss; that of Maggie less satisfactory. We trust you will all be getting much benefit from the change.[1]

The same post brought me a letter (short) from Gabriel also, and I see he has been writing direct to you.[2] To me he writes in a simple frank strain, not suggesting any anxiety of any kind. Yesterday however I had a letter from George,[3] not giving a *bad* account of Gabriel in any detailed way, but leading to the inference that he again takes doses of chloral hardly smaller than those which he was taking before Jenner's visit, and George thinks this should be vigorously checked when they return to town — which apparently will be soon. I of course think so too — always allowing for the urgent necessity that sleep should by one means or another be secured.

Lucy's love to all. She is fairly well, and received this morning a letter from Isabella,[4] now at Matlock Bath. Baby well also: likewise myself — who however had on Monday, and more especially Tuesday, a sort of pain in my right foot, which may perhaps be of the same general character as what bothered me in Italy in 1873. On Tuesday afternoon I kept it in cold water for (say) ¾ hour, and since then it has been practically well — *quite* well today.

I can't pump up any *news* worth calling such: only love, which please appropriate in large measure between you 3.

Your affectionate
Wm. M. R.

MS: AP.

1. Maria had been working at All Saints Mission House, Clifton, but because of her illness had been sent for convalescence to All Saints Hospital, Eastbourne, where Mrs. Rossetti joined her towards the end of July (*FLCR*, p. 57).
2. DW, 3:1449-50. DGR and George Hake were visiting William and Georgiana Cowper-Temple at Broadlands, their eighteenth-century house (formerly the home of Temple's stepfather, Lord Palmerston), near Romsey, Hampshire.
3. George Hake to WMR, [1 August 1876]: "I thought I would send you a line as to how Gabriel is. Since we have been down here we have been taking long walks and yesterday and today DGR has been at work. I must not conceal from you that his mental condition is not improved though it is not worse: still there are the lassitude and despondency due to chloral and so fatal to work, and if this change does him no good I shall consult you on our return as to taking steps to *insist* upon his reducing chloral *absolutely and under our control*: otherwise I could not remain with him and witness this daily diminution of vital force. Do not, my dear William, think from this that his condition is even as bad as it was 3 months ago: this only means I feel we must for his own sake coerce and threaten him and that if we now neglect to do so after Jenner and Marshall have failed to impress him beyond a week then we are culpable." [14 August 1876]: "On the whole Gabriel has improved in strength and tone. From dreading to even seeing the Temples he has arrived at dining with them often and seeing their other guests to whom he shows his picture. He has also done work rapidly with somewhat less fatigue and with undiminished power during his stay. On the other hand his chloral doses have risen to the old high-chloral mark and loss of energy and weakness will assert themselves in spite of good air exercise and change: and it is the lack of these latter that I dread on our return as likely to undo the good of this place rapidly. Therefore I advised you of my serious intention to take a strong standpoint on our return and hoped for your support. The Temples are most considerate and affectionate. It is really most touching. They act towards him as to a dear relation" (AP).
4. T. Pietrocola-Rossetti's wife.

268. TO DANTE GABRIEL ROSSETTI

Somerset House,
16 September [1876]

Dear Gabriel,

I walked round to you yesterday after Somerset House. Finding Mrs. Sumner[1] was with you, and was to stay to dine, and not exactly knowing how far it is convenient that others should be dropping in on such occasions, I vanished. Should now in the ordinary course come round to you on Monday: but think, unless you write to the contrary, I will make it Tuesday instead this time — to avoid any clashing. Trust most heartily you are going on pretty well.

Poor Maggie is *very* ill: has some lymphatic malady not very far removed I fear from incipient dropsy: some active steps in the matter must be taken within these few days. If you were in the way of writing to her don't say *anything about the details*, as she is not allowed by the Doctor to hear them.

Your affectionate
W. M. R.

MS: AP.

1. Wife of Holme Sumner, the Royal Master of Hounds. She was sitting to DGR for the head of *Domizia Scaligera* (Surtees 246).

269. TO LUCY ROSSETTI

Euston Square,
16 September [1876],
8:40

Dearest Love,

I was kept today hard at work at Somerset House beyond 5½, and left without reflecting that, unless I *then* wrote and posted a letter to you, you would not receive it in the course of Sunday: which however I fear is true.

The news of Maria is bad — I can't say worse than I expected. Yesterday Dr. Fox[1] spoke to my mother, after learning Jenner's views. The latter is sure that, whatever else may be wrong (as to which he doesn't pronounce, but evidently entertains serious apprehensions) there is undoubtedly a watery deposit which *must* be got rid of, for its own sake, and to give opportunity for further scrutiny. In fact, something in the nature of dropsy. Fox is to see Maria on Monday; and on Tuesday he wishes to return with his most trusted surgeon, who will perform an operation — Fox insists, a very minor one in itself. This will relieve Maria from some pain, and enable them to come to closer quarters with the essential malady. Fox wishes to secure the surgeon Heath,[2] but is not sure of his being in town: so a little uncertainty still prevails as to what will be done within the next few days — not as to what ought to be done. Of course we are all considerably dejected about this painful state of things: that the case is a truly serious one is not at all disguised by Dr. Fox.[3]

Your first affectionate letter of yesterday reached me at 10 p.m. that evening, and your second letter at breakfast this morning. I will at once answer any practical points in them.

I don't know how your lay-figure drapery stands at present: will look tomorrow by daylight.

Don't abridge your Ventnor stay: I like you to finish out the fortnight, being pretty sure that it must be doing good to both you and Olive. The precise day for starting to Cornwall can I think very well take care of itself: I feel under no pressure either way.

Christina still coughs a good deal: she has not much in the way of *sore throat*.

You may be sure, dearest Lucy, that I *should* like to have you here to talk nonsense — or sense either, of which you are fully as capable: but at the same time I am better pleased that you should stay out the intended time, as being pleasant and beneficial to you — and I am well assured that your kind hostess enjoys your stay too.

Just at this moment I receive another letter of yours; which pains me by its confident anticipation of a letter of mine to be received by you tomorrow. *Mea culpa*.

Here the weather is sometimes very fine — yesterday a beautiful afternoon, and the trees in St. James's Park still very solid and green looking. Today however is decidedly dreary — not rightly speaking chilly.

Give dear little Olive a kiss for preferring (?) my photograph to a substitute.

I do feel sanguine about Eastern affairs.[4] It seems to me either that the European powers will combine, and reduce the Turkish power almost to a practical nullity, or that (in default of this combination) Russia will fight, and give the Turks the hiding they want. As far as this country of our own is concerned, the people won't stand the Turk at any price, nor the Tories at their own: the time has come (which always does come sooner or later) when the British householder gets tired of the people in power, and, if they don't prove very supple to his will, will turn them out, and put the other party in. And Gladstone is pledged to cut the Turk adrift.

I walked round to Gabriel's yesterday: but, finding Mrs. Sumner was there, and staying to dinner, and not being quite clear as to Gabriel's preferences in such case, I came away again without seeing him. He had been painting from Mrs. Sumner 3 successive days, so I trust he is not so greatly amiss. Have written to him proposing to go again on Monday or Tuesday as he may prefer.[5] I had a good tramp — walking all the way to Chelsea, and thence to Euston Square.

Yesterday Ward Lock & Tyler replied about the Shelley.[6] They accede to my £30: would like to get the Shelley out at once, and offer me extra time (if wanted) for the *Lives of Poets*.[7] They would make the print wider, and the volumes 3: also (by a typographical dodge) condense the printing, and bring out a cheaper edition in 2 volumes. They have sent me specimen pages, which would answer very well. All this is quite satisfactory to me.

I went on last evening with the list of extra Poets, dates etc., and pretty nearly finished the bothering part of it.

All love, dearest dear Lucy,

Wm.

344

MS: AP.

1. Wilson Fox (d. 1887), specialist in diseases of the digestive organs, frequent contributor to the *Lancet* (*Times*, 5 May 1887, p. 11). CGR and Lucy also consulted him. WMR to Lucy, 5 May 1887, announcing his death: "I fear you will not very easily get a substitute for him so trustworthy and so agreeable" (AP).

2. Christopher Heath (b. 1835), Holme Professor of Clinical Surgery, University College London.

3. WMR to Lucy, [20 September 1876]: "Yesterday morning the Doctors performed the operation with poor Maggie — who bore it excellently, and treats the actual pain of it as a veritable trifle: it lasted about 1½ hour, and a *great* quantity of water came away. It is not tapping for dropsy: but is, as I gather, the modern operation which has superseded that other rather obsolete one. I understand that Maria doesn't even yet know that I have a clear idea as to what has been done: I would not therefore speak to her in definite terms about it, and perhaps you would also maintain a similar reserve. Today she appears relieved in body and mind: passed a good night of sleep, and one may hope will be (at any rate) in less actual bodily discomfort and pain for some while to come" (AP).

4. The Eastern Question, which dominated British foreign policy throughout the century, was again under discussion with Turkey's crushing of an uprising in Bulgaria and Gladstone's pamphlet *The Bulgarian Horrors and the Question of the East* (1876). Russia attacked and defeated Turkey, 1877-78; and made territorial gains by the Treaty of San Stefano, some of which were reversed through the influence of Disraeli at the Congress of Berlin, 1878.

5. WMR to Lucy, [20 September 1876]: "Gabriel yesterday was entirely reasonable, and says his pains have left him: he was certainly not in a cheerful mood however, and was a little inclined to take things up in a spirit of querulousness and opposition. I told him you and I would like to come some day next week. To this proposal he responded with pleasure, but could not decide upon an evening — saying that Mrs. Sumner's sittings to him may probably finish with this current week, and after that he might be minded to take the earliest opportunity of getting back to Broadlands. I think however we shall manage a day next week. He has discharged his man-servant — on the ground, as he says, that the man used vile language in the kitchen, and thus annoyed the female servants. There is I suppose *something* to this, but hardly know whether it really accounts for the result" (AP).

6. *PWS* 1878.

7. See Letter 253, Note 8.

270. TO LUCY ROSSETTI

Euston Square,
Thursday, 7¾ p.m.,
[September 1876]

Dearest Lucy,

No letter of yours has as yet reached me today.

I met Watts in the street this afternoon. He had been to see Gabriel yesterday, and is impressed with his being a good deal better in health than he used to be — though Gabriel was not particularly lively. Frequent bickerings with George Hake go on — caused I think chiefly by Gabriel's own fretfulness or unreasonable expectations: but if things continue on this footing it were better to separate. I forgot yesterday to tell you about Gabriel's "mug." It seems that one evening he was overpersuaded to drink a goodish quantity of beer, in the hope of its conducing to sleep. It did not produce sleep, nor yet in the least intoxication: but he suffered in bed from heart-beat (a thing which of late bothers him a good deal), and began walking about (as he ordinarily does) to calm this. A faint feeling supervened, and he tried to rouse George from sleep, but all his efforts in shaking at him failed. The faintness continued, and he fell outside George's little sleeping-room, and struck his cheek against a water-tap which is thereabouts. The mark is of course very visible, but I dare say it will disappear one of these days.

The news of Maria today is not at all good. Yesterday she was put under chloroform, and the Doctors made the requisite examination: they say there is certainly a tumour — don't (so far as I can learn) name or consider it anything other than that. Maria is very low today — vomiting and inability to eat any solid food continue.

I have a Blake photograph this afternoon to write about for Robinson.[1] This — with the addition that Christina's cough is so far bad as to keep her in today — is I think all the direct news.

I shall rejoice to see my sweet dear Lucy on Saturday. Will see about sending tomorrow a letter receivable that morning. All love from

W. M. R.

MS: AP.

1. George T. Robinson (1828-97), architect of the Bolton Market, art critic, father of Mary Robinson.

271. TO DANTE GABRIEL ROSSETTI

Somerset House,
27 November [1876]

Dear Gabriel,

Letter written to me yesterday by Christina says: "At 9 the funeral-service[1] will commence in the Sisters' Private Chapel at the back of the Home houses. I know no way of reaching the Chapel except by ringing at No. 82 as usual. All of us who desire to go (of us relatives, I mean) are quite welcome. Any flowers brought will be available. Sister Eliza says there will be no scarves etc., and she conjectures that flys of our own will be quite convenient for going to the Cemetery: she is not aware that there will be mourning-coaches."

Christina adds that she and Mamma think it would be most advisable for you to attend the ceremony in the Chapel *only* — not in the Cemetery. I should of course go on to the latter.

If anything further turns up I will write you again, but hardly suppose there *will* be anything. My own personal course will be to have a fly at 56 Euston Square towards 8 a.m. — drive round to Brown's and take him up, as he is desirous of attending — then round to the Chapel, and thence to the Cemetery, and home to Euston Square (unless some arrangement for Torrington Square might possibly be started). Lucy would wish to attend, but is recommended not to do so, her confinement not being now very distant, and I think she will *not* attend either in Chapel or in Cemetery. If there is anything further you wish, you will of course let me know.

Your affectionate
W. M. R.

MS: AP.

1. Maria died on 24 November.

346

272. TO ALGERNON CHARLES SWINBURNE

Somerset House,
5 December [1876]

Dear Swinburne,

Your truly affectionate letter has gratified all of us most extremely. If Maria's beliefs were correct, she is certainly at this moment a Saint in heaven — she having been, of all persons I ever knew, the most naturally religious-minded and the most (perhaps the *most*) undeviating in doing exactly what she perceived or assumed to be right. If other beliefs are correct, she has lived worthily, and died in full satisfaction of soul, and she rests forever.

I don't know whether you have any idea of the particulars of her illness. It is now many years — say 10 or 12 — that her health had always been indifferent, now from one uppermost cause, and now from another (though she almost invariably *looked* robustly healthy, to a casual glance). We had not however the least idea of anything alarmingly wrong with her till about the end of July or so. It then became evident that there was some internal malady, the *symptoms* of which ever afterwards were of a dropsical character, and the medical treatment to correspond: but even the dropsy, it seems, was not all, and had it not put an early term to her life, her sufferings would probably have been very severe. As it was, she did not, after the middle of September or so, suffer very *much*, but for her last 2 months she ate (one might say) absolutely nothing, and mostly could not so much as drink the simplest thing — a sip of orange-flavoured water for instance — without immediate nausea, and in her last month she was barely alive in body, though perfectly clear, calm, and mostly quite her old self, in mind.

Thanking you for your letter — the *épanchement* of which has led me on into these details otherwise not perhaps quite in place, I am

Always yours,
W. M. Rossetti

My mother and Christina bear their loss *well* — in the truest sense of that word. There is a most loving little notice of Maria, written by dear old Scotus, in last *Examiner*.[1]

MS: BL.

1. 2 December 1876, p. 1354. WBS to WMR, 25 November 1876: "It is with the sincerest and most brotherly sympathy that I write you on the occasion of poor dear Maria's passing away. There was something between Maria's practice in life and my own, in the way of untiring industry, and continually doing something in the way of duty, that made, I used to fancy, a kind of bond between us: — and then she was always ready to come down to us in Newcastle, and make sunshine in a shady place" (AP).

273. TO THOMAS GORDON HAKE

Somerset House,
5 December [1876]

Dear Dr. Hake,

Accept my sincerest thanks for your kind letter. My mother and sister are as composed as can be expected or wished for — their religious convictions and hopes counting no doubt for much.

Always yours,
W. M. Rossetti

MS: BL.

274. TO THOMAS DIXON

56 Euston Square,
16 December [1876]

Dear Dixon,

I am sincerely thankful for your sympathetic and appreciative remarks on my dear sister Maria: they gratify not only me but my mother and Christina as well. Maria was indeed one in a hundred-thousand: intensely and in the very roots of her nature devout, *never* acting from any save the highest motive, *never* doing anything save what she saw to be right. Intellectually also she was far from commonplace: she had indeed no inventive gift, but in capacity of acquiring knowledge seriously and accurately, and imparting it explicitly, I have scarcely known her equal. Whatever the true solution of the world's mysteries may be, assuredly all has been and is well with her.

Morris wrote — I suppose towards 1 November — a long letter published in the *Daily News*,[1] about Turkish matters: Browning and Jones, I think, have not printed anything, nor do I suppose the *Athenaeum*[2] meant to imply that they had — but only that they took an active part in the recent Conference in London.

I don't know who Miss Duncan[3] of Manchester is. Were she to care to ask me anything definite about art in Paris, I would do my best to reply to the query; but, as matters stand, I hardly see how I could volunteer any observations to a stranger on so exceedingly extensive and complex a subject.

Yours always truly,
W. M. Rossetti

MS: Texas.

1. "England and the Turks," 26 October 1876, p. 2.
2. "The Eastern Question is being fought out on the Slopes of Parnassus. On one side are arranged Mr. Browning, Mr. Morris, Mr. Burne Jones, Mr. Carlyle; on the other Mr. Swinburne" (9 December 1876, p. 762). The National Conference on the Eastern Question took place at St. James's Hall on 27 November.
3. Not identified.

275. TO GEORGE GORDON HAKE

Somerset House,
12 January 1877

Dear George,

Dunn called on me this afternoon about another matter, and from him I learned with the deepest regret that you and Gabriel have parted. Regret, but not surprise. To me who know the affectionate and unwearied zeal — the brotherly devotion — with which you tended Gabriel in the most trying period of his illness, and long afterwards, this result is truly afflicting; and doubly so when I reflect on all that Gabriel and the rest of us owe to your father. I know that the mutual relations between yourself and Gabriel have for some while past been far less satisfactory than of old; and (without prejudging anything that he might have to say from his own point of view) I am sure you have had to bear, and have good-humouredly borne, a deal of unpleasant and capricious demeanour on his part. For all this please accept the apologies of myself, and I might say of all the rest of our family.

With warm regards to your father and brothers, believe me

Your affectionate and much indebted
W. M. Rossetti

My mother and sister will be both distressed and dismayed when they hear of your having left Gabriel.

MS: BL.

276. TO ALGERNON CHARLES SWINBURNE

5 Endsleigh Gardens,
28 January [1877]

Dear Swinburne,

You refer to my "conception of a paper which should be simply a literary court of appeal": and I think you understand hereby "simply a court of appeal in literary matters." I do not however contemplate that it should relate *only* to literary matters — that would, I think, be needlessly limiting its scope, and depriving it of a reasonable chance of success: I would encourage all sorts of people — for instance politicians — who find themselves misrepresented etc. in other papers, to state their own case in *this* paper — which they could as a rule do with an allowance of space (to speak of nothing else) unattainable elsewhere. If I had 2 to 5 thousand pounds to embark in a speculation — but I *have* not as many pence — I should feel much tempted to start the paper, and see what turned up with it.

The *Pall Mall Gazette* containing your note on Coleridge[1] etc. has not passed through my hands: perhaps I may yet see it some day.

I confess I do not feel with you about Russia:[2] and, whenever you have to gloat over the gallows of Gladstone, and beam upon the *bûcher* of Bright, I am afraid you would have equal cause for revelling in the racking of Rossetti (W.M.). If I can manage to say here with great *brevity* what I really mean about the matter, I will do so. Russia is, like every other country, diversely related to diverse things. In her domestic policy, I detest in Russia (as anywhere else) an autocratic despotism, and I sympathize with the revolutionist, recently sentenced to death, who proclaimed in open court that his party, having no other means of developing their views, would shoot at the Emperor as often, and kill as many governmental people, as they could, until some form of liberty were obtained. But I cannot see that this my opinion of the Russian government should make me prefer that Bulgarians and other populations should be still oppressed by Turks rather than, with their own liking, helped out of that form of oppression by Russia; nor that it should keep me in a panic about our Asiatic frontier, when my veritable opinion is that Asia contains quite sufficient room for England and Russia together. As a fact, I dislike the Russian government, do not at all dislike the Russian population, am certain that Russia will continue willy nilly in a course of material aggrandizement for very many years to come, feel no anxiety about our own relation to Russia so long as we will simply attend to *our own* affairs in a spirit of justice, righteousness, and enlightenment, and do not feel in any degree bound to be an anti-Russian by mere dint of being an Englishman. Besides, I loathe war — be it of England against Russia or Afghans or Zulus, or of any one people against any other people; and it is only some very exceptional consideration which could make me approve or sympathize with any war whatever. Every now and then certainly some such consideration does arise.

Miso-Muscovite or not, you will equally regard me as

Always yours affectionately
W. M. Rossetti

MS: BL.

1. Not identified.
2. See Letter 269, Note 4.

277. TO WALT WHITMAN

Somerset House,
15 June [1877]

Dear Whitman,

I received some little while ago your postcard of 3 May, and felt obliged to you for having sent the books to Mr. Cozens,[1] without waiting for actual receipt of the money — which, as before stated, is in my hands. The only reason why, contrary to my usual practice, I have so long delayed sending it on to you is that I have been looking out for any other stray subscriptions, promised but not yet paid, which could be sent along with Mr. Cozens's in a Bank-order — or, if more convenient, a P.O. order. On receipt of your card (other such subscriptions not making their appearance at present) I was intending to send Cozens's money at once by P.O. order; but then some little while ago now, Minto, the Editor of the *Examiner*, started in talk with me, of his own accord, the subject of the money that he owes for your article,[2] and he proposed to send it round to me at once — which of course I approved. This again made me hold over the dispatching of the P.O. order for Cozens's money, but as yet, after all, no symptom of Minto's remittance appears. One of these days Cozens's money will be properly sent off to you — accompanied, let us hope, by some other, but if not then by itself. I enter into all these tiresome details because an explanation of my delay is due to you: but I fear you will think them quite as bothering as the delay itself.

It is a goodish while ago — say 6 weeks — that I wrote to Dowden in Dublin, enquiring about those subscribers who volunteered through him (not holding any direct communication with me), and who have not yet paid. Dowden has not yet

350

replied to me: when he does so, it will behove me to look into the details of *all* the outstanding subscriptions, and get the affair finally closed.

Lately — say 3 weeks ago — I received a letter from Australia, of which I enclose some extracts, along with the printed matter which accompanied it. I replied the other day, giving the writer Mr. Adams[3] my last news of your health, and enclosing also a copy of my last circular (summer of 1876) regarding your new editions — not without some hope that some few Australians here and there may do themselves the good-service of ordering copies. Mr. Adams's wish for a copy of my "full Review" of you (as he terms it, meaning of course the introduction to the Selection from your Poems which I published in 1868) has been attended to — the Publishers sending him a copy (I hardly thought there was any remaining) of the book. The tone of his letter is agreeable to me, and I hope it will be the same to you: his name had not previously been known to me.

Please remember me to Mrs. Gilchrist — or *us*, I should rather say. My wife received lately a letter from Mrs. Gilchrist, to serve as an introduction for an American lady, Mrs. Edwards.[4] To the latter my wife sent a card for a gathering at our house of a few friends on 14 June, and we had the pleasure of seeing Mrs. Edwards and her son accordingly. I was glad to hear from her a good account of the Gilchrists generally, though she thinks Philadelphia is anything but a favourable field for the painting career of Herbert.

I have by me a note written long ago (6 January) by Foote,[5] Editor of the *Secularist*, to say that, before receiving my then last note on the subject, he had sent on to you direct the subscription-money in his hands. This, I suppose, is all right, within your cognizance.

I enclose a note written to you by C. P. O'Conor,[6] and shall without delay forward to you by post the volume of his poems. In a note addressed to me he says: "Will you kindly tell Whitman that the writer is one of his ardent admirers, and that it was a rich treat to read in your *American Poems* those of Walt Whitman's production." I never *met* Mr. O'Conor: but he has addressed me from time to time about his little volume of poems, and other such matters.

Not very long ago I received a letter from Mr. Marvin, offering a prospect, rather more definite than hitherto, of your coming to look a little about you in England, and perhaps on the European continent. I can but repeat my delight in this prospect, were it to be realized, and my wife's hope and my own that you will not, in such case, fail to give us some of your company in this house, Euston Square.

We have had a rather noticeable season here. Up to 2 June, nothing that was worthy the name even of spring: then suddenly on 3 June hot summer, which continues till now — but less decidedly these 2 days.

I am interested in hearing that the Bostonians mean to cut us out — and we deserve it for our neglectful tardy stolidity — and erect a statue to our poet Shelley.[7]

351

Believe me with all affection

Finished 22 June.

Truly yours,
W. M. Rossetti

Copy

Circular Quay,
Sydney, N.S.W.,
16 March 1877

I trust you will excuse the liberty I take in forwarding you a copy of my review on Walt Whitman — who was only really brought to our knowledge here (much less our notice) by an extract from your Review. My friend here Mr. S. Bennett,[8] Owner and Editor of the *Town and Country Journal*, and also the *Evening News* (weekly and daily respectively) is emphatically a *man* in the largest sense of the word — physically and mentally; and at once saw there was something real in Walt Whitman, from your extract. He thus hunted up a volume of his works, and asked me to review it: hence the enclosure. We had not then in all Sydney a copy of *Leaves of Grass*: but I am happy to say, now that attention has been called to him, copies of *all* his works have been ordered from home, and he will be known here more or less eventually.

I have not seen your *full* Review: and, if you can spare me a copy, I shall esteem it a great favour.

I am perhaps the principal — if not leading — rhymester here, and enclose you herewith 3 pieces.... You may possibly know me otherwise by my series of letters for years past in the *Times*, and occasional magazine-articles on the Colonies.... I myself am the head of a large business here.

R. D. Adams

MS: LC. Published (without the extract): *WWC*, 3:170-72.

1. Not identified.
2. "The American War."
3. Robert Dudley Adams (b. 1829; still living in 1908, see *Wellesley*, 2:814). His review of Whitman (see "Copy" below) is not identified.
4. Not identified.
5. George William Foote (1850-1915), secularist and republican, succeeded Charles Bradlaugh as president of the National Secular Society in 1890. He edited the *Secularist* from 1876 (with Austin Holyoake), the *Freethinker* from 1881, and *Progress: a Monthly Magazine of Advanced Thought*, 1883-87. MS. Diary, 8 January 1877: "We spent the evening at a little gathering at Miss Blind's — Mrs. [Justin] McCarthy, [James] Thomson, Foote, Henrietta Heimann, etc. The latter and Foote are now engaged ... to be married. Foote is a young man, generally prepossessing in manner and appearance." WMR to Whitman, 17 December 1877: "The deep black border of his letter marks the recent death of his wife — a Miss Heimann, daughter of old friends of ours. Within the last 2 or 3 years she has shown mental excitability of a morbid kind: she married Foote 8 or 9 months ago I suppose, and recently, say towards end of September, 'took an overdose of chloral,' or in other words committed suicide" (LC). 26 March 1878: "We attended one of Foote's readings in Langham Hall — Browning's *Hervé Riel*, Shelley's *Skylark*, Graveyard Scene in *Hamlet*, etc. He is a good elocutionist, and on the whole ranks among the best reading-declaimers that I know."
6. Charles Patrick O'Conor, Irish peasant poet, published two volumes of poems, *Wreaths of Fancy* (1870) and *Songs of a Life* (1875), and edited *Ballads and Songs of Ireland* (1870?).

7. No statue has been traced.

8. Samuel Bennett (1815-78), English-born proprietor of the Sydney *Empire* (1859-75, when it was amalgamated with the *Evening News*, which he founded in 1867) and the *Australian Town and Country Journal* (from 1870); author of *The History of Australian Discovery and Colonization* (1867).

278. TO LUCY ROSSETTI

Euston Square,
25 July [1877],
8 p.m.

Dear Lucy love,

I received your note this morning, and am glad to think that things seem pleasant around you.[1]

I don't see a prospect of getting away exactly within "a day or two," but am in some hopes it may not be very long delayed. Have therefore given directions for sending off the articles named in your list.

Yesterday Gabriel was still in his bedroom when I arrived — just 5. He came down in about an hour, and I was pleased to hear him speak in very emphatic terms of the sudden benefit he had just derived from taking a hot bath with salad oil in it: it seems his Mesmeric Lady of some months ago had told him something about this, but he had hitherto left it unattended to. He says that the pains which he had "all over" left him at once, nor did they recur in any definite way during the evening. He is minded to continue a course of these hot baths — at night etc. Watts was there, and called Olive (I repeat it because I know you will like to hear it) "a charming little girl," and Gabriel said our mother had told him Olive is "quite a beauty," and he enquired into the particulars. He has barely made a faint attempt at painting as yet.

This morning I was hardly down at the breakfast-table when Signor Milo[2] presented himself: his object, as I find, being to get a subscription from me (and from others if I can beat them up) to a raffle for that picture — by his brother, as I understood — about which he spoke to me before. I would not refuse, so handed him £1: dislike much more the pest of pestering others, but will think it over. I asked Milo (whom I really like so far as I have seen of him) to join me at breakfast. He usually never eats aught till one, nor drinks anything save water and milk: however, under considerable pressure he disposed of my eggs and ham, and of my milk, and I — not knowing whether anything else was in the house — had recourse to the toast and the milkless tea. Milo also wanted to *see* the Editor of the *Academy*, and if possible of the *Encyclopaedia Britannica* (to both of whom, you remember, I had written in his behalf): so I gave him a note to Appleton, and the address for the *Encyclopaedia*.

We had a long talk — say till past noon — and scarcely was Milo well departed when who should turn up but Isabella and Theodoric! It seems they have been about in England and Scotland since May; are now with Miss Peddic[3] at Wandsworth, who is much invalided, and they could not accept my rather urgent invitation to stay *here* as long as might suit them. They will very shortly be leaving England — Isabella to accompany Miss Peddic to some sanitary baths in Switzerland, and Theodoric to return to Florence. I need hardly tell you — but *can* tell you most truly — that they were grievously disappointed at not seeing you and the kids. They are both looking *extremely* well: Isabella however (she does not look a day older than last time) is in fact suffering from a stiff knee — not now in her feet so much.

While they were with me in came Mamma and Christina, and took off to lunch after a while Isabella and Theodoric. I could not well accompany them, my precious morning being thus gone.

Then I set to at the Poets,[4] and with deep gratitude in my heart to Urizen set the finishing strokes to it, wrote a letter to the publishers, made the whole into a parcel, and fully expect to carry the latter round to the publishers tomorrow. *Victoria, Victoria!*

Have *lots* of Shelley proofs[5] by me: did a little to one of them last night, and must make a serious attack on them this evening and tomorrow.

Good-bye to his dearest Lucy and the brood from

Fofecatus[6] Ineptus

Gabriel speaks quite affectionately of his present man-servant, and the attention the latter gives him in connexion with the bath etc.: also of the extreme tenderness of Leyland,[7] who called again on Gabriel last Sunday, and, as Gabriel says, literally clung round him and wept. Theodoric renewed very pressingly his invitation for you and me to visit him soon in Florence, and he would house the babes as well. I told him this latter would not be admissible: nor the former for the current year, but we would seriously entertain the question when circumstances allow. Their love of course has to accompany this missive in tureenfuls.

MS: AP.

1. Lucy and the children were at Gorleston on Sea, Norfolk.
2. The Marchese di Campobianco (his designation in MS. Diary, 19 April 1904), who pestered WMR at various times between 1877 and 1904 with his "many but generally airy projects" (MS. Diary, 24 March 1879), including a new system of musical notation and a book on English synonyms which he wanted WMR to revise. The latter, WMR told Lucy on 20 August 1877, "is rather a wild notion: but really I like Milo — he is refined and not conventional" (AP). T. Milo (fl. 1842) listed in Wood was probably his brother.
3. Isabella's aunt who kept a school.
4. *Lives of Famous Poets.*
5. Of *PWS* 1878.
6. WMR often signed his family letters Fofus, which he explained to Lucy on 17 January 1887: "You and I have sometimes joked about the name Fofus — whether any mortal was ever called so etc. It is curious that, in now reading the letters of Horace Walpole ... I find the word Phobus applied in much the same sense which Fofus conveys to us — obviously not very far distant from 'old fogey'" (AP). Occasionally WMR wrote Fofus in Greek, which I have translated.
7. Frederick Richard Leyland (1831-92), Liverpool shipowner, was one of DGR's principal patrons.

279. TO OSCAR WILDE

Marine House,
Gorleston, Great Yarmouth,
3 August 1877

Dear Sir,

I was much obliged to you for your letter, and the magazine which accompanied it containing your interesting little article about the grave of Keats.[1] Ought to have answered before now, but was occupied, and am just now away from home (56 Euston Square, London), but shall be back directly.

No doubt English people ought to erect a statue to Keats, and I should be glad to lend my modest co-operation to any such project. I don't however see any particular opening for it at present. Will confess also that I feel more especially interested in Shelley than in Keats: I did some while ago — when the Byron statue[2] was first projected — put into print[3] a strong suggestion that advantage might be taken of the movement so as to combine a Shelley with a Byron memorial, but it led to nothing. All three must get their statues some day, and assuredly will.

Believe me, Dear Sir,
Yours very faithfully,
W. M. Rossetti

MS: Texas.

1. "The Tomb of Keats," *Irish Monthly*, July 1877.
2. MS. Diary, 8 November 1876: "Went to see the models (at South Kensington Museum) sent in for the competition for a Byron Monument: mostly poor and none very good: the best one may, I fancy, be the work of Boehm." 26 June 1877: "Went with Lucy to the Exhibition at the Albert Hall of models for Byron Statue, and of Byron relics. Of the models, not one seems to me of any considerable promise, and the one selected decidedly the reverse." 16 September 1877: "Lucy and I lunched at Trelawny's. There met [Richard] Edgcumbe, Secretary of the Byron Monument Scheme; he says the scheme is at a nonplus at present — subscriptions having ceased, site not vouchsafed, and actual total insufficient." 23 June 1880: "Trelawny says that the Byron statue lately set up near Apsley House is not at all like Byron — has more of the type of the Burdett family; to me also it seems a very unsuccessful work, whether as likeness or in other regards." In his *History of the Byron Memorial* (1883) Edgcumbe notes that the first competition having produced nothing acceptable, the committee felt bound to select something from the second competition, even though the submissions were "little better" (p. 9). The statue by Richard Belt is just inside Hyde Park near Hyde Park Corner (Arthur Byron, *London Statues* [1981], p. 80).
3. "It is a burning shame to the English people — a reflection on their common sense, and we may say their common honesty, for cant and hypocrisy are at the bottom of it all — that fifty-one years after the death of Byron, and fifty-three years after that of Shelley, those two radiant geniuses remain without any public monumental recognition in their own country" (*Academy*, 24 April 1875, p. 423).

280. TO LUCY ROSSETTI

Euston Square,
6 August [1877],
8:40 p.m.

A short letter to my dearest Lucy, accompanying the 3 cheques — total £20.

I reached home in comfort and fair time: have not yet seen anything of your father. All here seems in good trim: of course several things to attend to — new Shelley proofs,[1] an Income-tax assessment-paper, etc. etc. My mother had called this morning, and she left a letter to me from Christina, giving an account of Gabriel up to yesterday. He seems substantially the same — Marshall still urgent for his departure to the seaside so soon as ever a suitable house can be found. I am pleased at one item — that Gabriel will gladly have my mother and Christina as his companions out of town, so they two are again deferring their own departure till Gabriel's arrangements shall be settled, when they will go with him. This obviates what I felt to be a very serious difficulty — for the prospect of a proper male friend — since the expulsion of Hake, and with every man's occupations calling on himself — was far from clear to me.

Love to you and kids: I will call on Gill[2] tomorrow morning.

Your own
W. M. R.

MS: AP.

1. Of *PWS* 1878.
2. William Gill became WMR's family doctor in 1874 on the recommendation of William Jenner. MS. Diary, 24 October 1905: "I was sorry to see in a newspaper the death of ... Gill, aged 66: I had a sincere regard and liking for him, and he I think for me." 30 October: "A Mr. Martin writes me that friendly old Gill has left me £50, 'to buy something in remembrance of me'." 14 November: "A note from Miss Newman (Executrix) saying that Gill wanted me, among other friends, to have some object which had belonged to him. She offers me Lucy's water-colour of Broadstairs, which I shall very gladly secure."

281. TO LUCY ROSSETTI

Somerset House,
7 August [1877],
4:30

Dearest Love,

I got this morning your affectionate dear little letter, and reply in much haste.

Called this morning on Gill, who will have written to you direct.

Saw your papa and Emma yesterday the moment after I had posted my letter to you. He gave me no better news of Gabriel: but on this and the other matters that he will be in the way of telling you about in person tomorrow I need not enlarge.

Saw my mother and Christina this morning — much afflicted about Gabriel: shall this evening see *him*. Shall raise question about Penkill, which perhaps has not well been thought of, but would in some respects be about the best place possible. Shall also offer to stay (from tomorrow evening) altogether at Cheyne Walk, if liked: though this would be almost a deathblow to any serious occupation of my own, and not perhaps of any distinct *real* utility to Gabriel.

All love from

Your own
W. M. R.

MS: AP.

282. TO LUCY ROSSETTI

Somerset House,
8 August [1877],
12:15

Love Lucy,

Yours of yesterday received. Thanks about Ormesby St. Michael: whereabouts is that place?

I was delayed (having been bespoken to call on a certain Britten,[1] an artist friend of Dunn) in going round yesterday to Gabriel's: and just as I was approaching the Cheyne Walk house, I met your papa and Emma driving home in a fly: they gave me a slightly improved account of Gabriel. When I saw him, I found him much inclined to wheeze and pant from any small exertion. I spoke to him as seriously and earnestly as I could (without being unkind) about the necessity for rousing himself, living a natural life like other people without hiding in holes, about diminishing and finally relinquishing chloral, and, as the immediate thing to be done, getting at once to the seaside — and I suggested Penkill. Gabriel listened with much patience to all I said, and I think he saw it to some extent to be reasonable; but he replied that he "could" not go out etc. etc., and certainly, in the course of this talk, he recurred to his old delusions about people perpetually insulting him in the street etc. — but not in an agitated tone. He could not make up his mind to take any steps regarding Penkill, and indeed said that there too he had been molested (although, as his visit there was as long ago, I think, as 1868 or 9, I greatly doubt whether, *while there*, he was under any such impression). He did not show any particular wish for me to sleep (as I proposed) for some days at Chelsea: saying reasonably enough that it would make little practical difference in what he can otherwise see of me. I had occasion to mention F[anny]: and he informed me that she left the house some few days ago in a tiff, and had not since then reappeared, nor did he know about her exactly. I didn't think it advisable to press this point much, so I know only what I here say about it. Let us hope that a proper house will soon be found for Gabriel, for certainly he badly wants some change, and that as soon as possible. Today my mother and Christina will be with him: tomorrow (I suppose) myself again:[2] must also try to see Trelawny, who has written to me. Nothing else special to announce. Dearest love to dear Lucy from

Fofus

Valentine Bromley's[3] last picture (Hidden Royalist) is to be on view tomorrow and Friday.

MS: AP.

1. William Edward Frank Britten (1848-1916), "decorative painter, mainly of Grecian figures" in the style of Leighton (whom he helped with his Victoria and Albert Museum frescoes) and Albert Moore (Wood). MS. Diary, 7 August 1877: "Called at Britten's studio, and saw his monochrome of Apollo and Marsyas, etc."
2. WMR to Lucy Rossetti, 10 August [1877]: "I saw Gabriel again yesterday: the affair of F[anny] remains as when last I wrote. Gabriel was in a melancholy mood, and nothing definite has yet been arranged about his getting out of town: I consider however that on the whole he was rather better than on Tuesday, his voice being firmer and so on. I renewed the Penkill question, and he seemed rather more inclined to it than before — and might possibly settle to do so, were it not that he fancies

357

(baselessly so far as I know) that Miss Boyd's half-sisters must probably be at Penkill. He expressed a particular inclination to see you, and was disappointed at hearing you would probably not be in London for several days yet'' (AP).

3. Valentine Walter Bromley (1848-77), historical painter and art correspondent of the *Illustrated London News*. MS. Diary, 2 May 1877: "Was startled and distressed to learn (from Robinson, whom I saw at R.A. Pressview) that Valentine Bromley died the other day of smallpox — a great blow no doubt to the Robertson family.... He was one of the finest young men I ever beheld." Bromley had recently married Ida, sister of the actor Johnston Forbes-Robertson.

283. TO LUCY ROSSETTI

Sunday, 4:30 p.m.,
[12 August 1877]

Dearest Lucy,

A few words before I run round to Gabriel's. Yesterday I found Pickering in, and handed him over Trelawny's book — with which however he can't do much until he gets the MS. material also.[1] Then I set-to at Shelley proofs,[2] and disposed of all that had reached me. Today — all day — I have had another very bothering job of minutiae — the setting my notes to Volume 2 to rights, so as to get them off to the printers: have just finished this satisfactorily.

My mother came round this afternoon: thinks Gabriel somewhat better, and finds *some* disposition on his part to go to the Marine House, Gorleston, with her and Christina: but one can't at all *reckon* on this. Then your father looked in, and has just left. He also thinks Gabriel mending in a rather encouraging degree. I shall call on your father almost directly, and with him go round to Gabriel. Marshall wants Gabriel to rise at 10, and go to bed at 10 — of late he has, within my observation, hardly sat up till 8.

Love, dearest Lu,
Fofus

I see what Hunt says is that he has had two bad fevers: now convalescent but weak. His wife also a bad fever, but recovered. The children well. The Agnews want him in England, and I suppose he will delay not very long, though he doesn't want to be hurried home.[3]

MS: AP.

1. See Letter 252, Note 2. WMR to Lucy Rossetti, 11 August [1877]: "I fear there will be a deal of bother through the necessity of dovetailing new matter into old (partly done by me a year or two ago, and partly remaining to be done as further writing progresses) — combined with Trelawny's apparent reluctance to put all the MS. material in a lump into Pickering's possession. Of course mine will be the hands to finger all the details of such work" (AP).

2. Of *PWS* 1878.

3. Hunt to WMR, 10 July 1877: "Before I had well recovered from my attack I had a letter from the Agnews urging me to come immediately. I begged a few weeks to enable me to finish my picture but the letter made me begin work too soon and I got another fever which has gone but not without leaving me very weak and very fragile as to health, my digestion refusing to do its work altogether at times. I am glad to say that my wife is getting quite right again and that both the children are very well — for whom I was much afraid at first — and that I am able to do my painting each day making good progress so that I really hope to get away in a few weeks" (Huntington).

284. TO LUCY ROSSETTI

Somerset House,
13 August [1877],
3:20 p.m.

Poor Dear,

I have received yours of yesterday, and am glad to have seen this most kind letter of your papa's. I trust he is not *quite* serious in being "not sure whether anyone wishes him to interfere," for the fact is all concerned are most grateful to him, and regard his co-operation as precious and priceless. I quite agree with him in thinking that one cook in this case would be better than twenty, or even than two: but the question is — How can the thing really practically be managed? Your father would most kindly go down with Gabriel to seaside, and start him there: but clearly he could not, at seaside or elsewhere, remain tending Gabriel for weeks or possibly months, by day and when needed by night: and short of this I fear little would be accomplished, for it is clear Gabriel would mope terribly by himself as soon as left alone at the seaside (unless indeed a total revolution in his condition were to be operated). If your father can give a friendly eye to Gabriel in the interval (let us hope a short one) before Gabriel leaves town, and can get him away, with or without actual accompanying him just as he goes out of town, I don't see what more he can well do — certainly he can't be *expected* to do even so much: from that moment some one else is needed, and my mother and Christina seem to me highly suitable — if only Gabriel will see them to be so, as at present he does. I might dilate much more on all these matters, but your own insight and feeling will supply what I omit.

Your papa and I passed all last evening with Gabriel. He was *decidedly* better (especially until a lateish period of the evening) than I had seen him the last 4 or 5 times: still I am but too sadly afraid that little real absolute progress is made as yet — or will be made unless after a fair spell of seaside or country air, with diminution or cessation of opiates and stimulants — the two things which Jenner some years ago told Gabriel would be fatal to him. Even yet nothing is fixed about house at seaside: it seems hill-country would be approved by Marshall, if more manageable than seaside.

I trust the baby's boil is disappearing: perhaps it is one of those I saw before leaving Gorleston.

Leyland was at Gabriel's in the afternoon when I arrived. Your papa tells me Leyland has lately lent Gabriel £500 at Gabriel's request — a very friendly act, without which I fear cash would be running short. Leyland is rather dispirited at being just now adjudged to pay £30,000 damages for a case of running-down at sea.[1] He told Gabriel he has had loss after loss since his mother's death. Still I suppose he can well bear them all, and more.

I will give your affectionate messages to all of my family. Glad to have a lull in Shelley[2] just now, for the *Encyclopaedia* people write me to send in by end of week the article on Dyce,[3] and I have little idea as yet whether or not I can write it without some troublesome research.

359

All love to dearest Lucy and affectionate remembrance to Emma — Gabriel was speaking warmly of her yesterday — from her

W. M. R.

MS: AP.

1. Not identified.
2. Correction of proofs of *PWS* 1878.
3. "William Dyce," *Encyclopaedia Britannica*, ninth edition, 1877.

285. TO LUCY ROSSETTI

Somerset House,
16 August [1877],
3:15 p.m.

Dear Dear,

Your affectionate letter of yesterday received with pleasure: have also seen the telegram you sent to Dunn, and the letter to Christina.

If I were to tell you all the cross-purposes, false starts, and graver tribulations, which have been besetting me ever since I set foot in Cheyne Walk house about 5½ yesterday, I should be filling several sheets. Will confine myself to the upshot —

1. Gabriel was very shaky yesterday: *much* better today, I am told, but shall see for myself this afternoon. A female nurse ordered by Marshall is now in charge of him.

2. F[anny] turned up there yesterday, much to the derangement of all rational projects for Gabriel's welfare. She was in a very obstructive mood yesterday, but I hear better today.

3. Your father is willing so far as he can to look after Gabriel prior to seaside — and would especially advocate his going at once to Fitzroy Square: would also accompany him out of town, staying a week or so, not more. We are all greatly disappointed at losing the Gorleston House: but Thursday is indeed too far off — though what may really be *done* meanwhile by way of getting out of town remains to me dubious. My voice is for going to *any* seaside place at once — ordinary lodging or hotel if nothing better offers.

Glad to hear little Ol is not greatly amiss after all. Give her a kiss from *Pa*.

I shall enclose a £10 Bank-note in this letter, and register it. My tin has been paid today. I managed to do 2 Shelley revises[1] last night (spite of all else), and made up the Dyce article for posting: couldn't show it to your papa — who, I need not say, is all kindness and promptitude in Gabriel's behalf. Also wrote yesterday to Trübner explaining Trelawny's decision,[2] and to Trelawny himself about the relation of his MS. to his printed material.

Hot here these 3 days, and very fine: would there were less anxiety to spoil the waning summer, and a Lucy to "gild its refined gold"[3] of sunshine — but this only when the seaside sojourn can properly be concluded. Love to Emma, kiss to

360

Ba[4] (not to give Olive an invidious preference over the good little man), and sincere regards to both nurses.

Your own
W. M. R.

A large brown-paper thing came for you yesterday — evidently contains mounted photographs, or something of the kind. Being so beset, I did not open it — but will if you are curious about it.

MS: AP.

1. Of *PWS* 1878.
2. Nicholas Trübner had offered to publish Trelawny's *Records of Shelley, Byron and the Author.*
3. "To gild refined gold," Shakespeare, *King John*, IV. ii. 11.
4. Gabriel Arthur Madox Rossetti (1877-1932), WMR's second child. Towards the end of 1895 he began training as an electrical engineer in the works of Jackson & Co., Salford. He was appointed manager of the Lancashire Stoker Works in 1899, and later held the post of scientific referee. In 1901 he married Dora, daughter of J. Slater Lewis, the manager of Jackson & Co.

286. TO LUCY ROSSETTI

Somerset House,
17 August [1877],
10:40 a.m.

Dearest Love,

Yours of yesterday received this morning. Let me first tell you how we stand with Gabriel.

Your father and I went round to him yester-afternoon, and found him pretty tolerable: Dunn alone there, along with the Nurse. A great effort was needed to persuade Gabriel to leave Cheyne Walk and go to Fitzroy Square, prior to starting for the seaside. At last this was managed: Gabriel dined and slept (or rather passed the night, for of sleep he got very little) at Fitzroy Square, and he expressed his willingness to go down to Herne Bay by the train of this afternoon — your father kindly accompanying him, and the Nurse — no one else at present. I for my part heartily hope this may be effected: your father however (Gabriel's stomach not being right today etc.) seems to think there would be no particular harm in postponing the start for a few days. If all goes well, they will have started before my office is over — merely relying upon the ordinary lodging or hotel accommodation.[1]

I am truly sorry you had so much bother yesterday about telegrams etc.: can't accuse *myself* of any negligence in that respect. This morning I showed to your father your letter of yesterday, enclosing Gabriel's telegram to you. Your father (and I to a minor extent) still hankers after the Marine House, Gorleston: but we think this must for the while be excluded from practical consideration, and given up altogether — or at the utmost left to take its chance hereafter, according to then existing circumstances. I told your father (say at 9:50 this morning) that I would at once telegraph to you to this effect: but he particularly asked me to leave it to *him* to do this, and he would attend to it. I trust it may have been done: if not, that will not be my fault.

It distresses me much to hear of your sleeplessness, poor dear: can't see any reason why (if so inclined) you should not procure the ordinary dose of chloral, such as Gill used to order you. I fancy that, with a little explanation to a chemist, this could readily be managed.

Thanks for this letter of your dear papa's, received last night: one more evidence of his constant kindness, spiced this time with only too well warranted exasperation. The only point I need refer to is the statement that Gabriel says my mother and Christina are converting him to Christianity. Your father had previously mentioned this same point to me: *I* know nothing about it, and can emphatically affirm that, whatever may be the wishes or suggestions of my mother and Christina in this direction, they are none the less ardently desirous of your papa's continued friendly attention to Gabriel — the very utmost of this that your papa can himself spare. My own opinion is (but it counts for nothing *practically* in this matter) that, as Gabriel has abdicated his power of reasonable self-regulation, *any*thing that would serve to make him calm or submissive in mind, and consistent in conduct, would be a benefit; that Christianity would go far towards serving this purpose; and that therefore no harm would be done were *he* to become a Christian, totally alienated though I myself am from that or other dogmatic or definite religion.

It slipped me hitherto to tell you that Marshall (having seen my mother at Cheyne Walk House last Tuesday) told her plainly that Gabriel, according to his present condition, cannot survive many months: yet there was no reason why, under proper influences such as sea air etc., he should not be himself again — a month well bestowed might make all the difference. This is, and for some while has been, my own firm persuasion: if this year witnesses one more of our *Novembers*[2] I shall not be at all surprised.

Have seen nothing of Emma's Shelley Volume 2.

All love, dearest, from

Your,
W.M.R.

MS: AP.

1. WMR to Lucy, 18 August [1877]: "On going round to Fitzroy Square yester-afternoon I found to my extreme satisfaction that Gabriel had already gone off, with your father and the nurse, to Herne Bay: and today I have a note from your father giving the address — Mrs. Joiner's, East Street, Herne Bay — 'Small house with a view to the sea up a side street — 2 sitting-rooms and 3 bedrooms and 4 beds, at £4 for first 2 weeks, and less after.' Gabriel was in favour of this house, and your father seems not dissatisfied with it'' (AP).

2. Month of the deaths of Oliver Brown, Elizabeth Cooper, and Maria Rossetti.

287. TO LUCY ROSSETTI

Somerset House,
22 August [1877],
11:30

Love Lucy,

I can easily believe that Gabriel deplores the approaching departure of your papa: for *nobody* — and certainly not my mother or Christina — could be quite so cheering and pleasant a companion to him. If possibly your papa's departure were to throw Gabriel more on his own resources, and coerce him into doing something for himself — at lowest, reading to kill time — there were some compensation in that. Let us hope for the best. No further news from Herne Bay, direct or indirect, has reached me.

No indeed, the chloral is not "quite left off": Marshall does not even sanction its being so as yet. I don't rightly know what an ordinary large dose is, but should suppose about 30 grains. Gabriel had got up to 180! Marshall reduced this to 90; and at 90 it had remained for some little while before Gabriel left London (your papa remarked to me on this as objectionable the morning they left) — and so I fear it still does remain — or at any rate it can as yet have only been lowered by some few grains.

I do continually, darling Lucy, wish for your return: pleased however to reflect that your prolonged absence is pretty sure to be doing the children good — and you too good in some respects, though she can't sleep at night, poor thing.

If Gabriel's cottage[1] would be particularly good for babies, let us look into that matter, and see what comes of it: though probably nothing.

Will send you tomorrow the article by Watts:[2] will also send £20 in Notes, obtaining said Notes in the morning from the Bank. How is good old Mrs. Seddon?[3] My affectionate regards to her.

Last evening I did 2 Shelley revises,[4] and continued the re-reading: have got on with this to not very far from end of volume 1. Found one most bestial fault of print — the printer's fault, not mine, and to the eye a slight affair, but fatal to meaning: must see whether they can't print a cancel leaf. Of course other faults also, but this *one* of most moment. Forman's volume 4,[5] it seems, is likely to be out by end of next week: that will give me still some recomparing of text etc. to do.

Cayley called here yesterday. He reminded me that tomorrow (Thursday) there is to be an eclipse of the moon, ending towards 11 p.m.: its process ought I believe, to be *visible*. Do you like to look out for it? I shall if not too lazy.

All love from

W. M. R.

MS: AP.

1. At Herne Bay.
2. Probably his review of the tenth edition of Bailey's *Festus*, *Athenaeum*, 11 August 1877, pp. 169-70.
3. Mother of Thomas and J. P. Seddon. "The ladies of the Seddon family were at all times on the most cordial terms with those of the Madox Brown household: there was perhaps no one for whom my wife had a sincerer respect and regard than Mrs. Seddon" (*SR*, 1:144).
4. Of *PWS* 1878.
5. *Poetical Works of Shelley*, 4 vols., 1876-77.

288. TO LUCY ROSSETTI

Euston Square,
24 August [1877],
9:20 p.m.

Sweet Lucy,

There might be several items of detail to mention today: but it is late, and I stick to leading facts.

Your papa's card returned — along with a letter received here this morning (I opened it to get rid of a big envelope) from Mrs. Petrici.[1]

I looked at the eclipse last night, and the moon *had* nearly turned round the corner — i.e. had left a central sky-position opposite our window for the houses to the right — the second time I looked. 1st time, 10.5: 2nd, 12.15: eclipse at 2nd time about as much over all but moon's left, as 1st time over all but her right. Very clear and beautiful; but, even when the whole moon-surface was obscured, her position and lumer were perfectly visible.

Yesterday my mother had a letter from your father, seeming to intimate that he would remain yet a day or so after she and Christina go down: today they *have* gone down. The news of Gabriel improves: he walked about 3 miles on Thursday, and gets sleep for a number of hours which anyone under ordinary circumstances would hold sufficient: still no doubt there must be vast room for improvement yet. Your papa particularly wished me to send down by Mamma, for Gabriel's recreation, some volumes of Turgenev: I sent one (*Strange Histories* etc.[2]) though sorry to trifle with a book you so especially affect. Your father has written to Dunn to get rid of the man servant and the cook: I don't see the exact reason — or rather don't *know* in detail the exact reason present to your father's mind. I suppose they will have got notice this evening.

I was round at Cheyne Walk to look up my books this afternoon. Put together those on the ground floor, and must go again for those on the first floor.

Chatto & Windus (the *firm*, for Chatto is in America) write shilly-shallying over the Shelley lectures,[3] saying they thought they were to be shortened etc.: this is not so, for I had corresponded with Chatto, and can quote his letters to show I have only done what was understood between us. If they fight shy, I shall cut it short and tell them to return MS., but would much *rather* not have to do that, and forego the money. They say the Lectures would make full 42 pages = £44.2.

All love to dear Lucy.

W. M. R.

MS: AP.

1. Helen Petrici (b. 1847), daughter of George and Katharine (née Ionides) Lascarides. WMR to J. Stanley Little, 5 August 1886: "Mrs. Petrici is an Anglo-Greek. She took to the stage some 10 years or more ago, her stage-name being Miss Edmeston, and has played all sorts of characters — Juliet, Lady Macbeth, Beatrice, Mlle de Belle-Isle, etc. etc., with considerable applause — in London, and more especially in the provinces. One of the characters in which I have myself seen her is Beatrice (*Much Ado About Nothing*): I thought her decidedly good, and in the strongest dramatic situation I liked her better than Miss Terry" (Kansas).

2. Thomas Deloney, *Strange Histories, Of Kings, Princes, Dukes* (1602).

3. See Letter 250, Note 6.

289. TO LUCY ROSSETTI

Sompting,
25 October [1877],
9 a.m.

Lucy Love,

All the early part of yesterday was remarkably beautiful: Trelawny and I towards noon sat out some while in his kitchen-garden sun-basking, smoking, and talking. The later afternoon and evening were also fine at intervals, with variation of sharp showers. Today seems set in for rain and whiteish dullness. I did yesterday a good deal of the substantial part of my Trelawnian work,[1] and did not get out of doors at all beyond what is said above: I went through all the volume, and the MS. books as already marked for insertion piecemeal. There is however enough left over for occupying I think most of the working time of today — finding places for some new documents, quotations, etc. I am made entirely comfortable here, but shall nevertheless be exceedingly glad to find myself back with you and home. I hope your cold is diminished, and especially your cough no longer troubling you — destitute as the poor thing now is of a Fofus to whom to talk about it during the night-hours, he relapsing into the stupor of somnolence without realizing the fact to himself.

Trelawny told me he was born in November 1792 (same year as Shelley): it will be worth recollecting this. He wants his epitaph to speak of him as "a man who thought independently on every subject, but never found secure holding-ground till he read Darwin's Origin of Man."[2] I fear this will be a little incompatible with Swinburnian verse;[3] but it is in itself sensible. He means to be buried (he says) in the unconsecrated part of the adjacent churchyard: though curiously enough he has *two* graves already prepared for him elsewhere — that next to Shelley,[4] and another in Kensal Green, close by an Irish lady who seems to have been in love with him and whose tomb he erected.[5] I see here this morning a photograph of his son[6] — a handsome spirited-looking young fellow. My breakfast is now (10) just over, and Trelawny down to *his* (in a separate small room) — roast apples, gingerbread, and cold water. Good night and good morning are interdicted here. I find no inclination on Trelawny's part to make Silsbee's[7] acquaintance: he seems to think Miss Clairmont[8] is plotting mischief against Byron's memory, and Silsbee is put down as a confederate.

Have not as yet any letter of yours this morning. Expect to return tomorrow as already stated.

Yours, dear Love,
Fofus

MS: AP.

1. See Letter 283, Note 1.
2. *Descent of Man* (1871).
3. Probably Swinburne's verse dedication to Trelawny of *Songs of the Springtides* (1880).
4. See Letter 293, Note 1.
5. William St. Clair has suggested that "the story may be one of Trelawny's 'bams'" (letter to the editor, 28 September 1982).
6. Trelawny had two sons by his third wife Augusta: Edgar (1839-c.1872), the elder, with whom he did not get on; and Frank (who died of consumption "when he was still a young man"), whom he adored (William St. Clair, *Trelawny the Incurable Romancer* [1977], pp. 165-66, 192-93).
7. Edward A. Silsbee (MS. Diary, 13 July 1901, records that he "has been dead these 2 or 3 years"). Richard Garnett described him as being like "Trelawny might have been if Trelawny could have been made amiable and gracious without parting with any of his native force.... A grizzled, weather-beaten veteran of fine physique, his discourse was mainly of poetry and art, on both of which he would utter deeper sayings than are often to be found in print. He was the most enthusiastic critic

of Shelley the present writer has known, but also the most acute and discriminating'' (Introd. to *Journal of Edward Ellerker Williams* [1902], p. 10). MS. Diary, 19 October 1877: "Mr. Silsbee, an American gentleman lately mentioned to me by Conway as having paid particular attention to Miss Clairmont at Florence and her Shelleyana, called on us. He seems to be a man of competent fortune, a Europeanized American, with thoughtful opinions of his own regarding both literature and art." WMR to Lucy, 22 August [1878]: "Saw Trelawny yesterday. He had a melancholy letter from old Miss Clairmont, who suffers tortures from what is called neuralgia of digestive organs, and is very hard up for money — Silsbee kind to her" (AP). MS. Diary, 26 September 1879: "Silsbee called ... talked copiously about the shabby treatment he received from Miss Paola Clairmont with regard to the Shelley relics, and about her trying to coerce him into marriage in connexion with this affair: he could have had the relics (at the last stage of the affair) for £150, the same price which Forman gave, and which he would himself willingly have given, but was then so disgusted at the shuffling and scheming that he declined." (Cf. the account of the battle for the papers in *Shelley and his Circle*, ed. K. N. Cameron, 1961, 2:910-11.) Several months earlier Paola Clairmont had offered the papers to WMR: "I replied saying that I should not wish to treat for the letters, and accompanying documents such as diaries kept by Miss Clairmont etc., at all, unless Silsbee, who is looking after them, were to assent" (MS. Diary, 5 May 1879).

8. Mary Jane (Claire) Clairmont (1798-1879), daughter of William Godwin's first wife by a former marriage, lived with Shelley and Mary until the poet's death, and afterwards settled mostly in Florence. WMR visited her there on Trelawny's behalf in June 1873 (*SR*, 2:351-54), when she made no mention of her disapproval of his treatment of her relationship with Byron in *PWS*. MS. Diary, 1 November 1877: "In the evening Silsbee called on me again. Whilst he was there, I was startled at receiving a letter from Miss Clairmont, the contents of which are seriously vexatious to me. She says that my statements regarding her, in the Memoir of Shelley published in 1870, were injurious to her interests; and she particularly wishes that in my reissue [*PWS* 1878] nothing may be said about her. I discussed this matter with Silsbee. He thinks that real injury to Miss Clairmont can scarcely have ensued from the fact that I repeated in print (and I did no more) some facts regarding her which were already printed elsewhere: and he thinks that in the long run she would be pacified by my writing to her in a conciliatory and respectful tone — which I assuredly would do. All the conversation with Silsbee was conducted by me on the assumption that my revised Memoir is already printed off.... It was only after Silsbee had left that I remembered that in fact these particular sheets have *not* been printed off: so I suppose that on the whole the publishers will consent to withdraw the statements, and I (though it damages the completeness and consistency of the biography) would of course do this rather than aggrieve Miss Clairmont." In the separately printed *Memoir* (Shelley Society Publications, 1886), WMR reintroduced the omitted details into his new preface (p. iv).

290. TO THOMAS WENTWORTH HIGGINSON[1]

56 Euston Square,
24 June 1878

My dear Sir,

My brother-in-law Dr. Hueffer (author of a recent book on the Troubadours,[2] and particularly known as a critic of music) is at present editor of the *New Quarterly Magazine*;[3] and, hearing from me yesterday of your being in London, he expressed a strong wish that he might be able to secure for his magazine some contribution from your pen. He spoke especially of anything bearing upon American military affairs, but of course he does not limit his views to that sole subject. I thought I might take it upon me to mention the matter thus to you.

The Magazine is published by Chatto & Windus, 74 Piccadilly. Hueffer's private address is 61 Blomfield Road, Paddington.

With our best regards believe me always

Very sincerely yours,
W. M. Rossetti

Col. Higginson

MS: UCLA.

1. (1823-1911), soldier who during the Civil War was colonel of the first Negro regiment; social reformer, writer, editor of the poems of Emily Dickinson.
2. *The Troubadours; A History of Provençal Life and Literature in the Middle Ages* (1878).
3. Hueffer was editor, April-October 1878 (*NCBEL*).

291. TO LUCY ROSSETTI

Somerset House,
6 August [1878],
11½

You would not, Lucy love, be "leading me about like a dog in a fair," even if you had the opportunity: but I might perhaps be "*running in and out* like" said dog at your bidding, or at little Olive's fiat, or because the little boy looked out of the corner of his eye.

Thanks about the wine.

I shall take an early opportunity of asking Ward & Co. for the Shelley money[1] — not that I think it in the least jeopardy: could also at same time bring before them definitely the question of the Shelley Compilation.[2] As to the *Academy*, I should not under present personal circumstances[3] like to put myself forward as soliciting from them even what is rightfully my own, so I propose to let August elapse (which would be nothing unprecedented) without saying anything: if not paid by end of August, I could then see about it.

I did not see the wreath. Your papa tells me that the current prices of wreaths are 7/6 and 10/6: these two, and even higher-priced ones also, being of much the same size, but by raising the price one gets rarer or costlier flowers.

I sent in my Income-tax assessment paper yesterday: the figures are not amiss — viz.:

Year to 4 April	1878	£197.15. 6
	1877	121.10. 0
	1876	166. 9.11
	3)	485.15. 5
		161.18. 5

The £161.18.5 is the sum for assessment. I fear with Tory government and Asiatic protectorate[4] etc. we shall soon see the income tax up to 7d. or 8d. in the £.

We dined yesterday with Gabriel: I walked round from Euston Square, taking Torrington Square *en route*, but my mother etc. (Charlotte is still there until Thursday next) had already started. Gabriel was very lively, and seemingly quite free from care or gloom: he looks unreasonably fat, yet in sound health. His *Fiammetta*[5] (Mrs. Stillman) is now finished, or all but: you remember the head, which we both like much — the red tint of the drapery is also very successful. I don't myself think the picture in other respects one of Gabriel's best: Fiammetta is parting the boughs of an apple-tree, and the apple-blossom scatters down —

painted certainly with much brilliancy, but I think with hardly so much grace as marks Gabriel's best work. There is a red (I suppose non-existent) bird, and various very blue butterflies. These are perhaps not to be identified in any entomological collection (not even O'Shaughnessy's[6]): but, such as they are, they seem to me to be of the Brazilian or Borneon type of insect — not the Italian. The reduced version of the Dante picture[7] is also getting on.

I learn that Gabriel wrote lately to the *Times*[8] and *Athenaeum*[9] (it must have been that very No. of *Athenaeum* which did not reach me, but in its stead a *Saturday Review*) repudiating certain crayon drawings which have been lately on sale at Attenborough's[10] in the Strand, with Gabriel's name to them: a purchaser of one called his attention to them. Gabriel says this imposture is the doing of Howell and his young woman:[11] he has no *evidence*, I think, but I suppose he is probably right. I shall get the *Athenaeum*.

Watts (no one else) was there also. He tells me that he spoke to MacColl[12] about my being disposed to contribute when opportunity offers to the *Athenaeum*, and MacColl was quite ready to fall in with such an arrangement. The fact is however that the amount of work and pay thus accruing to me could at the best be but so meagre that I lay little stress on the affair either way.

In going to Gabriel's I met Ralston.[13] He looks very thin, and certainly not well, though also not violently ill. He says he is recovered from the recent attack, but is "a poor creature at all times." It seems that Winter Jones[14] is now really leaving the Museum: Newton[15] is pretty safe (Ralston thinks) to succeed Jones, but in Newton's own department there is not anyone quite of the calibre needed for succeeding Newton, so Ralston fancies they will bring in an outsider. A German, he says, was talked of, but now apparently set aside.

Love and kisses, dearest Lucy.

Your own
W. M. R.

My mother and Christina are yet undetermined as to what seaside place to select: have made some enquiry at Walton on Naze, but that does not seem very likely to come to anything. Would like to know something about Margate. Could you perchance send them the address and any particulars of the house we were in there in 1874?

MS: AP.

1. Payment for *PWS* 1878.
2. "Cor Cordium."
3. WMR suspected that the editor of the *Academy* Charles Appleton wanted to replace him as art reviewer when on 20 April 1877 Stephens told him of a conversation with C. W. Dilke (the proprietor of the *Athenaeum*) in which Dilke reported that WMR "had arranged to discontinue writing on art in the *Academy*. Why or how Dilke supposed this I know not, as no question of the sort has ever been mooted with or entertained by me." On 26 April WMR noted a letter from Appleton written "in terms which rather suggest to me some *arrière-pensée* on his part. I replied saying that, if he is at all dissatisfied, I will at once resign all the picture-reviewing — still (if he likes) continuing to do some other work in his paper. The affair noted on 20 April looks rather suspicious to me — as if somebody or other were looking out for my berth — and I assuredly would not write for any one merely on tolerance." Nothing further on the matter is recorded until 14 June 1878: "Appleton writes me that

Comyns Carr is substituted for me as reviewer of exhibitions on the *Academy*; and he professes — I should say pretends — to base this substitution on my having asked — which I never did — to be relieved of the job. I have long thought that this would be done, but am not in the least contented with the mode of doing it. Wrote to Appleton telling him he is wrong in thinking I had asked to be relieved (it is in fact a flat untruth), and that, if this supposition really was his motive for inviting Carr, he ought to set the thing right, and countermand Carr. Of course I know Appleton will not do this: when he declines I shall act as I then see fit. But for the money consideration I would not have undertaken, and would not now continue, the picture-reviewing: but the money thence derived is of some importance to me. The *Academy* pays me about £100 a year, the major part of it for this sort of reviewing, the rate of pay for which is £3.10, while for literary notices etc. it is only £2.'' 17 June: ''Appleton replies, adhering to his arrangement with Carr, but asking me to continue writing on other subjects. His letter is moderately civil: but of course the essence of the affair is that he likes my art-criticisms little or not at all, and likes those of Carr much better, and that he bundles me out neck and crop to make room for Carr. Of course also this is not particularly soothing to my self-opinion; and I am disposed to see whether I could transfer my services, as literary or general contributor, from the *Academy* to the *Athenaeum* — which latter has from time to time appeared to offer me an opening. Probably I may address Watts on this matter. If the *Athenaeum* should prove not conveniently available, I suppose I shall go on with the *Academy* rather than lose the small incomings thence accruing, and shall pocket my *amour propre*'' (MS. Diary). WMR's review of *Thomas Moore, Prose and Verse*, ed. R. H. Shepherd, 22 June 1878, pp. 550-51, was his last contribution to the *Academy*. For his subsequent connection with the *Athenaeum*, see Note 12.

4. The protection of Asiatic Turkey from further Russian encroachments was the main emphasis of the policy of Lord Salisbury, who became foreign secretary in April 1878.

5. *A Vision of Fiammetta* (Surtees 252).

6. Arthur William Edgar O'Shaughnessy (1844-81), Pre-Raphaelite poet, was employed in the department of Zoology at the British Museum from 1863.

7. *Dante's Dream at the Time of the Death of Beatrice* (Surtees 81 R. 2).

8. 20 July 1878, p. 89.

9. DW, 4:1574-75.

10. George Attenborough, 72 Strand, pawnbroker (*POLD*).

11. Rosa Corder (1853-93), Howell's mistress, studied painting under Felix Moscheles and Frederick Sandys. She exhibited a picture at the R.A. (a portrait of her mother, 1879) and one at the Grosvenor Gallery; her portrait of E. B. Pusey is at Pusey House, Oxford. See Cline, pp. 21-22; and Wood.

12. Norman MacColl (1843-1904), Spanish scholar, was editor of the *Athenaeum*, 1871-1900. MS. Diary, 21 June 1878: ''Watts called to speak about the *Athenaeum* project. He thinks that beyond any doubt the Editor McColl would gladly have me on his staff; but, for the general class of *belles-lettres* reviews which I would undertake, there is already a great number of contributors, and Watts thinks that perhaps I should receive only one book for review in 5 or 6 weeks. The pay (as he understands, his own remuneration being special and larger) is £2.2 per article of 2 to 3 columns — the amount not being assessed with absolute precision.'' Between 14 September 1878 and 13 April 1895 WMR contributed some sixty reviews, which are identifiable from his marked file of the *Athenaeum* in the library of the Courtauld Institute.

13. William Ralston (1828-89), Russian scholar and friend of Turgenev to whom he introduced the Rossettis, was an official of the British Museum Library, 1853-75, when ill health forced him to resign. In 1863 WMR accompanied him on a visit to Bethlehem Hospital, where they observed Richard Dadd (*SR*, 1:269-70).

14. John Winter Jones (1805-81), principal librarian of the British Museum, 1866-78.

15. Charles Thomas Newton (1816-94), archaeologist and keeper of Greek and Roman Antiquities at the British Museum, 1862-85. He was considered Jones's ''natural successor, but did not wish to give up his archaeological work for administration, and the world was surprised when the comparatively unknown Keeper of Manuscripts [Edward Augustus Bond (1815-98)], a shy and reserved man, known to few outside the Museum, was given the appointment'' (A. Esdaile, *The British Museum Library* [1946], p. 132).

292. TO RICHARD GARNETT

56 Euston Square,
9 August [1878]

Dear Garnett,

I *have* read Trelawny's letter in *Athenaeum*:[1] indeed, on the one solitary occasion (towards 1 July) of my seeing him since your article was published, he showed me the earlier portion of the letter. He did not then seem at all *sore* about your article, nor did he in any way suggest that you had disparaged his seamanship. He certainly did however scout the idea that Peacock could be pitted against himself and Capt. Roberts as a nautical authority: and I am sure from the terms he used that he cannot at the time have known (or must have forgotten) that Peacock had anything to do with Cape of Good Hope steamers. I ought to be seeing Trelawny again soon, and would certainly omit no opportunity of satisfying him that you neither said nor meant anything derogatory to his seamanship.

I wish you a pleasant time at Lowestoft. I was lately with family at Charmouth, Dorsetshire close to Devonshire, and enjoyed the scenery much: Lucy and children there still for another fortnight or so. It was only some 5 minutes before my starting from Charmouth to return to London that Lucy received from her father the startling news of poor Cicely Marston's[2] death.

Yours always truly,
W. M. Rossetti

MS: Texas.

1. 3 August 1878, p. 144 (*Letters of Trelawny*, ed. H. B. Forman, 1910, pp. 261-67), Trelawny's reply to Garnett's "Shelley's Last Days" (a review of Trelawny's *Records*), *Fortnightly Review*, n.s. 23 (June 1878), 850-66. Garnett wrote "to supplement Mr. Trelawny's recollections ... and at the same time to correct some mistakes into which Mr. Trelawny has been betrayed by causes which may be regarded as incidental to an advanced period of life."
2. P. B. Marston's sister.

293. TO EMMA TAYLOR[1]

56 Euston Square,
22 August [1878]

My dear Miss Taylor,

Yesterday Mr. Trelawny alluded more than once to *my* drawing up a reply to Lady Shelley:[2] he was half bantering, but I think not *wholly* bantering. I of course know that he would do it better than I or any outsider can: but, if he would really like to see how I would put the thing, I cannot refuse to take that small trouble — and I have written enclosed what occurs to me. Would you show it to him or not, as you perceive to be more suitable.

I should naturally not wish, under any circumstances, that my *handwriting* should appear in the letter as sent to Lady Shelley: she would ever afterwards put me down as a mischief-maker and designing character.

Yours very truly,
W. M. Rossetti

MS: Yale.

1. Trelawny's so-called niece who lived with him from 1870, and after his death accompanied his body to Germany for cremation and his ashes to Rome for burial in a grave close by Shelley's. MS. Diary, 26 October 1881: "Miss Taylor called on me at Somerset House.... The matter of the cremation etc. proved to take up much more time and to cost much more than could reasonably have been anticipated.... Altogether not much less than £200.... Miss Taylor will now have a yearly income of about £300 (in equal halves from her father and from Trelawny) besides the house at Sompting.... She is under the impression that Miss Trelawny (who had a very high regard for her indeed up to August last, as I personally know) has now taken a violent antipathy to her — on account of money-matters or what else." 13 March 1884: "Mrs. Call talked a good deal to Lucy about her estrangement from Miss Taylor, arising principally ... from what she regarded as self-interested and callous demeanour of Miss Taylor towards Trelawny in the last few days of his life. From my long-standing knowledge of Miss Taylor in relation to Trelawny, I am somewhat reluctant to suppose that her conduct in that respect was such as not to admit of some explanation or defence. In another respect however it seems that Miss Taylor must have acted very improperly and absurdly: for Mrs. Call says that Miss Taylor informed her in the most explicit terms, some years ago, that I had proposed to her.... In this story there is not one word or shadow of truth. Mrs. Call says also that Miss Taylor used to misreport Lucy as an unpleasant acquaintance, whom she only tolerated because my own companionship was agreeable to Trelawny. These strange proceedings on Miss Taylor's part will make it rather difficult for Lucy and me to know what to do with her, if (as seems probable) she renews our acquaintance when she returns from India." On 6 December 1886 WMR reported to Lucy that he had sent a letter to Miss Taylor in which he "frankly stated the facts, and said that she and I had better lose sight of one another" (AP). Years later he told Roger Ingpen that he thought Miss Taylor was still living at Sompting, but advised that should he "address her, it would be best to make no mention of me" (26 December 1908; Berkeley).

2. MS. Diary, 17 August 1878: "Called on Trelawny. He lately received a long letter from Lady Shelley, consequent upon his own letter to the *Athenaeum* [see Letter 292, Note 1]. She prolongs the arguments about the personal deservings of Mary Shelley, and about the olden friendship between her and Trelawny, and his present alienation from her memory; and she says that, unless some satisfactory response comes from Trelawny, she doubts whether certain relics of him, now preserved in the Shelley Museum at Boscombe, should any longer be retained there. The general tone of the letter however is not purposely aggressive. Trelawny did not seem much inclined to make any reply: but before I left he said he would do so, briefly." 27 August: "Called on Trelawny.... He said not a syllable about my draft letter to Lady Shelley." 3 September: "Called on Trelawny. He has begun answering Lady Shelley in more detail than I had expected." WMR's draft letter is at Yale.

294. TO FREDERICK LOCKER-LAMPSON

56 Euston Square,
23 October [1878]

Dear Locker,

Shelley work is with me "never ending, still beginning."[1] I am now re-reading with great minuteness my last (3 volume) edition,[2] so as to correct any errors, and keep it up to the latest date. In this process I should consider it a great advantage if I could have your MS. of *Hellas* to compare with my text line by line. May I be privileged to borrow and use it? 3 or 4 days would probably be the whole time required. I don't remember that you have any *other* MS. of the printed poems: if you had, I would ask to borrow that also — would fetch the *Hellas* etc. away almost any day you could name.[3]

Whenever you come to our house you would see an interesting Shelley relic — a large sofa that he had in Pisa, either for his own use, or (I rather believe) bought by himself for Leigh Hunt.[4] It has long belonged to Kirkup in Florence: Trelawny lately *requisitioned* from Kirkup, and promised to give it me at his death: but he has in fact been beforehand with Fate, and has made it practically my own already.

With our best regards and wishes to you and yours.

Always yours truly,
W. M. Rossetti

MS: Huntington.

1. Dryden, *Alexander's Feast*, 1. 101.
2. *PWS* 1878. No further revision was published.
3. MS. Diary, 29 October 1878: "We called on the Lockers, and I borrowed his MS. of *Hellas*, and in the evening read it against my text line by line. There is not *much* to be learned from it, yet quite enough to make the collation useful and requisite."
4. MS. Diary, 29 October 1878: "Trelawny sends me particulars of the Shelley sofa, showing to my full satisfaction that it really is the sofa-bed which Shelley ordinarily used in Pisa — not one which he purchased for Leigh Hunt. Trelawny says that Shelley slept on this sofa in Pisa immediately before starting in the Don Juan, when he was drowned: I think therefore it must be the last couch Shelley ever slept on, which makes it extra-ordinarily interesting."

295. TO LUCY ROSSETTI

Hotel Voltaire,
[Paris],[1]
6 November [1878],
8¾ a.m.

Lucy dearest,

Yours of yesterday received. I fear I should never realize to myself what is the shape of bonnets and cloaks or be able to define it to others: besides fashionable people don't make any show to our eyes. Will however try to pay some attention to the matter today, and will mention it to your father, who seems always efficient in such matters.

All goes on well, and we shall no doubt start homewards this evening. I don't know the hour, but your papa (who is never down in the breakfast-room, be it understood, at the early moment when I write you these letters) will be aware of it.

Yesterday, except the late evening, was a particularly cheerless day — rain, cold, and dimness. Today as yet certainly the best day we have had since Sunday, but there seems every prospect of an ample allowance of rain.

Yesterday morning we all went to the Louvre, and began looking about us a *little* at the sculpture and pictures. When it was turned 11 I left to call on Gérôme:[2] your papa and mamma remaining at Louvre till lunch-time, after which they went to the École des Beaux Arts and the Musée de Cluny. I left Gérôme towards 1, walked down to the Tuileries, a somewhat considerable distance, and there saw the exhibition of old pictures got up to raise funds for a "South Kensington Museum" in Paris — a good proportion of good things. Towards 3¼ went back to Louvre, to pick up if possible your papa and mamma, but of course did not find them there. We reassembled at the Hotel towards 4½ as prearranged — dined in the Palais Royal — Dîner de Paris, *prix fixe* 3.25 francs very fair — and then went to the Théâtre du Châtelet to see a popular *féerie Les Sept Châteaux du Diable*: some of the spectacular matter, dances etc., good. This took us up to near midnight, and then, the evening being fine enough, we walked home.

Today we shall, I fancy, see little or nothing save the Exposition: the Luxembourg Gallery will however be taken in if practicable.

Gérôme is now grey — acute and pleasant, but I should hardly have recognized in him the original of that handsome photograph. Received me very courteously, and I read off to him in French Trelawny's *original* account of the Burning of Shelley. He is doing a picture of Conspirators under Napoleon I. Jacquemart[3] was sitting to him in an incredible hat and other habiliments of the time: also a statute, Anacreon holding an infant Bacchus and Cupid. Small model very promising I think.

Love and kisses from
Fofus

MS: AP.

1. MS. Diary, 1-10 November 1878: "I accompanied Brown and Emma to Paris for a few days."
2. Jean-Léon Gérôme (1824-1904), painter and sculptor, whose "care over historic and ethnographic accuracy makes him an important exponent of academic realism" (G. Norman, *Nineteenth Century Painters and Painting*). Trelawny asked WMR to acquaint the painter with the account in his *Recollections* of the cremation of Shelley for a painting of the subject. See *SR*, 2:376-77; and Gerald M. Ackerman, *The Life and Work of Jean-Léon Gérôme* (1986), p. 246.
3. Alfred-Henri-Marie Jacquemart (1824-96), sculptor.

296. TO JAMES MCNEILL WHISTLER

Somerset House,
27 January [1879]

Dear Whistler,

I received your piquant little pamphlet,[1] and read it immediately, and found in it not only plenty of point but plenty of reason. Though I have been figuring for so many years as a non-professional art-critic, I nevertheless agree to a very considerable extent in your thesis that the publishing of art-critiques by non-professionals, whom the too easy-going public allow thus to assume a dominant authority over their own minds, is noxious and deserving of protest: indeed I have myself said the same in an article which I wrote (say towards 1864) in the *Fine Arts Quarterly*,[2] and which is reprinted in my volume *Fine Art, Chiefly Contemporary*.

I had intended to acknowledge your pamphlet with thanks as soon as I received and read it, but it slipped me to do this (partly because I was laid up with gout several days about that time). I am now reminded to write through seeing in the *Academy*[3] an abusive little paragraph about the pamphlet, and apprehending that said paragraph might possibly, by you or others, be ascribed to my hand. The fact however is that I not only had nothing whatever to do with the paragraph, but that I have not for the last half-year or more written anything for the *Academy* — the Editor having substituted Comyns Carr[4] for myself as reviewer of exhibitions.

Yours always truly,
W.M. Rossetti

MS: Glasgow.

1. *Whistler v. Ruskin — Art and Art Critics*, published in December 1878, shortly after the verdict in the Whistler v. Ruskin trial, at which WMR appeared on Whistler's behalf. MS. Diary, Friday, 22

373

November 1878: "I was vexed at receiving from Rose a subpoena to give evidence on Monday in the action which Whistler brings against Ruskin for libel — I have expressed in print (long before Ruskin's utterances) a high estimate of one of the pictures which Ruskin assails [*Nocturne in Black and Gold: the Falling Rocket, Academy*, 30 October 1875, p. 462]. I wrote to Rose asking him to let me off if he can, but don't at all suppose this can be managed. Should be truly sorry to aid personally in bringing Ruskin in for damages." 23-28 November: "Absent from Somerset House 2 days for Whistler v. Ruskin." (For a transcript of WMR's evidence, see S. Weintraub, *Whistler, a Biography* [1974], pp. 205-6.) 1 December: "Wrote to Ruskin explaining that my attendance in the witness-box against him was compulsory." 3 December: "Called on Rose.... Whistler seems to be in good spirits over the result of his action: I saw a letter of his to Rose, suggesting that (as in Ruskin's case) a subscription should be got up to pay his costs, and he says (without apparently seeing the fun of the remark) that he will contribute his own mite to the fund." 8 December: "Lucy and I went to breakfast at Whistler's by invitation: first time I have seen his 'White House'."

2. Review of F. T. Palgrave, *Essays on Art, Fine Arts Quarterly Review*, n.s. 1 (October 1866), 302-11; rptd. *FACC* as "Mr. Palgrave and Unprofessional Criticisms on Art."

3. 25 January 1879, p. 85: "We have seldom come across a more silly production. Whatever may be Mr. Whistler's talents and capabilities as an artist, he seems unable to write plain English and generally ignorant of the subjects of which he treats or to which he alludes."

4. J. W. Comyns Carr (1849-1916), critic, dramatist, founder and editor of the *English Illustrated Magazine*.

297. TO THEODORE WATTS-DUNTON

56 Euston Square,
17 June [1879]

Dear Watts,

I saw yesterday that the Shepherd case[1] had gone against the *Athenaeum* — though I must confess that my expectation, from the general appearance of the case in the preceding newspapers, had been that the *Athenaeum* would conquer. I was not in any way brought into the case — not for instance required to attend at the Office of the *Athenaeum* lawyer and give any information. Is there anything that you, as a professional (legal) and literary man, think that you and I ought in reason to do? I don't myself see anything particular, but should like to have some idea of your views of the matter. Were I a *rich* man, I should like to volunteer to bear my proportional share in clearing off the liabilities (damages and costs) adjudged against the *Athenaeum*; but my circumstances render it simply impossible that I should do anything considerable in this way, and I see no advantage (as well as some personal inconvenience) in doing what would be insignificant for the purpose.

Yours always,
W. M. Rossetti

MS: BL.

1. MS. Diary, 3 February 1879: "Called on MacColl, chiefly to enquire about a matter regarding which he wrote to me about the beginning of the year — that R. H. Shepherd proposes to sue the *Athenaeum* for libel, as contained in Watts's article about his republication of Mrs. Browning's Early Poems, and my article about his Ebenezer Jones and Longfellow [15 December 1877, pp. 765-67; 14 September 1878, pp. 331-32]. This is a rather galling matter to me — who really had no wish or intention to fall foul of Shepherd, but indulged in some (probably ill-judged) chaff at the beginning of my article, simply to keep up the tone which the *Athenaeum* had previously adopted regarding his resuscitations of old literary matter. MacColl now tells me that there is every appearance of Shepherd taking the case into court: although the counsel on the *Athenaeum* side think that my article can be defended as being (so far as its depreciatory passages go) mere chaff, while Watts's article is of old

374

date, and applies to a book upon which Shepherd's name did not visibly appear. MacColl says that Shepherd is understood to persist in his action, more specially because he has learned that *I* was the writer of the latest article, and he supposes (quite erroneously) that I have some spite against him arising from his having, in his edition of Blake, spoken adversely of my edition in certain respects.'' 16 June: "The verdict has gone against the *Athenaeum*, damages £150: this of course is rather vexatious to me as a matter of feeling, and may prove in some way detrimental to my interest also: it was stupid on my part to write in irritating and fantastic terms.'' 24 June: "Watts ... offered the *Athenaeum* Editor to pay ½ of the entire expense of the trial, but the Editor replied that there is not the slightest occasion for any such offer: this relieves my mind somewhat, as it would not be in my power to make any *considerable* offer of the like kind."

298. TO ALGERNON CHARLES SWINBURNE

56 Euston Square,
22 September [1879]

Dear Swinburne,

I was glad to see your handwriting anew for several reasons, the least of which was the enclosing of the £1.1 for Keats Fund.[1]

Was much distressed to hear some while ago a bad account of your health, and heartily hope that your domestication with Watts, the steadiest and most assiduous of friends, will tend to set you up again.[2]

We are all well thank you: Lucy expecting another confinement[3] towards end of November, and the two extant kids flourishing admirably. Last Saturday was Olive's fourth birthday.

It is so long, I regret to think, since we have met that I hardly know what you do know and what you don't about my small literary doings. Early in 1878 I brought out my new and laboriously revised edition of Shelley, 3 volumes, and my *Lives of Famous Poets*, the chief (but by no means sole) material of which was those Prefatory Lives in Moxon's series of which you used to speak well in point of condensation etc.[4] Since then what has principally occupied me is the great Shelley autobiographic compilation — Letters, poems, parts of poems and essays, etc. etc., whatsoever relates to Shelley written by himself. This went to America (Harpers) in June for probable — not guaranteed — publication by them:[5] I know not why, they have never yet acknowledged its receipt, but it must certainly be in their hands. Copyright bothers would have rendered the publication of the book in England extremely dubious or risky. What I must *now* do immediately is to write two Lectures on "The Wives of Poets," which I have engaged to deliver in Birmingham in February.[6]

Yours affectionately,
W. M. Rossetti

MS: BL.

1. In 1878 Buxton Forman promoted a Civil List pension for Keats's sister Fanny, Señora Llanos, but it was refused on the grounds that she was married to a foreigner. A subscription fund was begun in June 1879, with Forman, Richard Garnett, and WMR signing the public appeal. MS. Diary, 9 September 1879, noted that "the fund is not ... a success, though certainly not so scanty as to be unworthy of Mrs. Llanos's acceptance." The subscription was closed at £300 in November 1880 when it was announced that the earlier refusal of a pension was to be reversed. (See M. Adams, *Fanny Keats* [1937], pp. 194-95.)

2. MS. Diary, 24 June 1879: "Watts gives me a melancholy account of Swinburne, who was lately in such a desperate case that Watts saw nothing for it but to take him down for a while to his house in Putney, and at last, with much ado, he got Swinburne down to Holmwood, where his mother is still living. There Swinburne now is, and has improved observably. Watts says his memory was almost entirely gone, and he has reached a particular stage of malady, due to his incurable irregularities, which Doctors pronounce to be a very advanced and in fact fatal symptom. I fear his faculties, or his life, will not hold out much longer." 22 September: "Replied to a letter from Swinburne, who is now, I find, domiciled with Watts at Putney." 21 October: "Watts ... says that Swinburne, now domiciled with him (but hardly anybody is allowed to know of this fact) is exceedingly happy and in good health — no spirits allowed, and only a moderate amount of beer and wine: his deafness is very great, and his memory for common matters remains entirely defective, and a medical man says it will never be restored: memory serves him however for such matters as reciting long snatches of verse etc."

3. See Letter 300, Note 2.

4. Swinburne reviewed the volume in the *Fortnightly Review*, n.s. 28 (December 1880), 708-21; rptd. *Miscellanies* (1886). MS. Diary, 18 October 1879: "Gabriel says that Swinburne (so he hears from Watts) has lately taken up my *Lives of Famous Poets* with much zest; and has begun writing an article about the book, or about its subject-matter, which is rapidly swelling — as usual with Swinburne — beyond the dimensions of an article into those of a volume."

5. MS. Diary, 1 March 1879: "Conway ... tells me he is now Reader for Harper's firm, and enquired about my present literary doings. I explained to him the plan of my Shelley Compilation ["Cor Cordium"], and raised the question whether it might do for Harper to publish: were this done, a great deal of bother and uncertainty about questions of copyright etc. would be at once got rid of. Conway seems not averse from the idea: will dine with me next Thursday, and look into the matter." 6 March: "Conway dined with us.... He thinks that Harper's firm might likely enough undertake it, on the system of paying so much, say 10 per cent, on copies sold: doubts whether they would pay any sum down — an arrangement for which I expressed a decided preference, in reference at any rate to the first edition. Harper's however is a firm which does not affect books of an unorthodox tendency, though they are not exactly squeamish on this point: were they to hold back from the Compilation on this account, Conway would try his own American publisher Holt. We parted on the understanding that I would write Conway a letter setting forth the nature of my book, its new matter, etc.: Conway would then write about it to Harper in favourable terms." 17 April: "Received a letter from Conway enclosing one from Harper Brothers. They wish to see my Shelley Compilation ... would pay me 10 per cent on the retail price of all copies sold, and would advance, as soon as the book is published, £100 upon the amount thus accruing. If they were not to like the book, they would negotiate with Houghton & Osgood for publishing it. I am not dissatisfied with these terms: shall feel great reluctance in parting with the copy of the Compilation, which has cost me so much pains and would be quite irreplaceable, but this seems an indispensable part of the plan." 18 April: "Wrote to Conway, assenting to Harper's proposal: with the addition that I would ask them to give me 20 copies of the book, and to pay ... my expense in postage etc." 1 October: "Harpers of New York decline to publish my Shelley Compilation on the ground that it would probably not pay, and 2 other American firms to whom they offered the book also decline. Scribners are now considering it. I don't much suppose Scribners will take it: am disposed to offer it to Harpers at terms less advantageous to myself than they had originally tendered, though even this I have little expectation now of succeeding." A final, unsuccessful proposal, for the Shelley Society to issue it, is noted on 20 May 1886: "Furnivall ... contemplates bringing out my 'Shelley Autobiography' in 2 instalments, 1887 and 1888: before it is delivered to the Printer I should have to reconsider it, and probably modify various points in it, in the light of Dowden's book, which is expected to be published next November."

6. Delivered on 16, 23 February 1880, the first lecture to a "full audience, and more than moderately favourable reception" (MS. Diary, 13-16 February). For the two lectures he was paid £25.4 (WMR to Frances Rossetti, 3 August 1879; AP). On 12 February at Euston Square he "read a portion of my 1st Lecture, and the whole of the 2nd, to an audience of some 35 friends — Hunts, Scotts, Robinsons, Formans, Locker, etc. They seemed to be very well pleased" (MS. Diary). He delivered a shortened version of the lectures at Newcastle on 31 January, 1 February 1880, and reduced them for delivery as one lecture at Wolverhampton on 21 March 1882. For the latter he was paid £12.12 (WMR to FMB, 27 February 1882; AP). The lectures were published in the *Atlantic Monthly*, 47 (January, February, March, April 1881), 55-65, 155-65, 382-91, 518-25. MS. Diary, 5 October 1880: "Conway writes me that my Lectures (slightly altered as articles) on the Wives of

Poets, which I sent in July by invitation to *Harper's Magazine*, are not accepted by that publication — why he knows not: but he has got [W. D.] Howells, the Editor of the *Atlantic Monthly*, to accept them, and at the same price, £50.''

299. TO DANTE GABRIEL ROSSETTI

56 Euston Square,
14 October [1879]

Dear Gabriel,

You may perhaps have heard that our good old friend John Tupper has finally succumbed to his maladies: he died on 29 September, leaving a widow and 2 children.[1]

Hunt has taken the initiative in seeing what can be done to set and keep these poor people going. Their means are apparently next to nothing. Mrs. Tupper has some experience in teaching, and some local connexion at Rugby: her health has been exceedingly frail for some years, but it is thought that the best thing she can do is to remain at Rugby, and do what she can in the teaching way. The son, aged 7, could it seems be placed in the subordinate school at Rugby, and receive there his first education gratis along with the sons of local tradesmen etc., and it seems likely that he would in due course be transferred to the higher Rugby School, also gratis, and there obtain all the education that he can wish for, and perhaps more than his prospects in life suggest. The other and younger child is a girl, whom her mother might manage to educate at home.

A few days ago Stephens, George Tupper, and myself, met at Hunt's, and it was decided to raise if we can a little fund,[2] to be vested in Trustees, and ultimately handed over to the *children* — only the annual proceeds of the fund (of course a mere trifle) being used meanwhile for Mrs. Tupper's benefit, and the capital not drawn upon unless to meet some special emergency. In our own circle there are apparently few people who could be counted on to contribute, and they but moderately: Tupper's medical friends promise rather better results, and perhaps the Rugby people. Gull gives his name for any purpose, and a sum not exceeding £20 or so.

A few names are wanted for heading a paper which would then be sent round: and, as Hunt particularly wishes to get some good names of people who would *not* subscribe largely, so as to encourage others to give little rather than nothing, the use of a name thus would not commit one to more than one felt disposed to do. I myself would go to the extent (I think) of £10, but this I contemplate as the outside. Will you give your name for the list?[3] An early reply would oblige — the question of the amount you would ultimately subscribe not being at present raised.

Your affectionate
W. M. R.

MS: AP.

1. MS. Diary, 1 October: "I was grieved to hear this evening, by a letter from Hunt, of the death of my good old friend John Tupper: Hunt does not give the precise particulars, but speaks more especially of the precarious position of the widow and 2 children. These latter are now at Hunt's

house, and he seems to contemplate taking charge of one of them to some considerable extent."
WMR wrote two obituaries: *Daily News*, 3 October, p. 2; *Meteor* (Rugby School Journal), 9
October, pp. 114-15.

2. MS. Diary, 16 October: "Took up a letter which I received yesterday from Hunt, enclosing
some observations on Tupper's work to form the basis of a circular, and saying that a sum of £267 has
already been subscribed in the School for Mrs. Tupper. This is a better beginning than I had
expected." 22 October: "Attended at the surgeon [A. E.] Durham's ... a meeting to consider about
the Tupper fund: only Durham and his wife, and Hunt, along with myself. It seems Mrs. Tupper has
at present 16 pupils. We took up the draft of circular I had sent to Hunt the other day (founded on
Hunt's own draft), and pretty well settled on the form it is to assume." 29 October: "Received a
letter from George Tupper, deprecating the issue of the circular as it now stands: he thinks it is too
much like an appeal for charity. I don't exactly agree, but we must see further about it." 1
November: "Hunt and his wife met me at dinner at Durham's to discuss the Tupper matter. We
unanimously decided to disregard George Tupper's objections, as being wiredrawn and impractical,
and distinctly repudiated as they are in a letter addressed by Mrs. Tupper to Mrs. Durham. We made
some slight final revisions in the circular, and I will see about getting it printed as soon as possible."
12 November: "Sent ... a conciliatory letter to George Tupper." 1 February 1882: "Today I finished
up the affair of the Tupper Subscription.... Altogether Mrs. Tupper will be enabled to buy stock to
the amount of £300, to be invested in the names of herself, Durham, and Hunt. This will only to a
small extent trench upon the other subscription which was raised for her benefit at Rugby."

3. MS. Diary, 23 November 1880: "Wrote to Gabriel suggesting that he should now pay up the £8
which he promised to the Tupper Fund — offering at the same time, if more convenient to him, to
advance the sum myself for the present."

300. TO ALGERNON CHARLES SWINBURNE

56 Euston Square,
19 November [1879]

Dear Swinburne,

The address is — E. J. Trelawny, Sompting, near Worthing. He has not come
to town at all this year.

I am certain to enjoy the sea-poems[1] much, and shall come with much delight
under favouring circumstances. It pleases me *better* however that the engagement
should not take effect immediately, as my own work (combined with looking
after Lucy and Gabriel) ties me much for the present: I am engaged to deliver in
Birmingham on 16 and 23 February 2 Lectures on "The Wives of Poets," and
the requisite reading-up for this is no trifle. I have been at it with considerable
diligence since the beginning of September, and am only *approaching* the end of
it now, and of *writing* not even a single line done as yet.

As you offer kind wishes "present and *prospective*" for my household, I
rather fancy you are not aware that what was lately a prospect is now a fact. Lucy
gave birth on 10 November to a daughter, whom we have named (not *christened*
— *absit omen*) Helen Maria Madox.[2] This small personage and Lucy are both
doing extremely well, but Lucy still in bed as yet.

The literary projects you mention are all most interesting, from one or other
point of view. I like the title Epithalassion[3] well — might almost say extremely
well: still, if you *were* to hit upon some title which, while equally terse and
suggestive, might be free from even the hint of anything far-found and *précieuse*,
I should in your place be not indisposed to give it the preference. Would not
however surrender Epithalassion without good cause shown.

I will maintain a rigorous silence — to *every*body — on the subject you name.

The American publishers won't undertake that (I think most important) Compilation that I had made of all Shelley's autobiographic writings of whatever kind.[4] *Pazienza.*

With all affection.

Your

W. M. Rossetti

Your referring to Trelawny as "the old sea-king"[5] reminds me that I found him mentioned, in a letter from a connexion of his that I saw several months ago, as "the Ancient Mariner" — a happy nickname which pleased me much.

MS: BL.

1. *Thalassius, On the Cliffs, The Garden of Cymodoce,* published in *Songs of the Springtides.*

2. d. 1969. In 1903 she married Gastone Angeli and they lived briefly in Cairo, where he was employed with the Italian Chamber of Commerce, until his ill health forced them to return to Rome, where he died in July 1904. For the next fifteen years she lived mostly with WMR, and after his death continued his vigilant promotion of the fame of the Rossetti and Brown families. Earlier she had written on DGR (*Art Journal* Easter Annual, 1902) and FMB (1901); and in 1949 published a lively biography of DGR, followed in 1954 by *Pre-Raphaelite Twilight,* an account of the Rossettis and C. A. Howell. She also continued her father's devotion to Shelley, with *Shelley and his Friends in Italy* (1911).

3. Not identified.

4. "Cor Cordium."

5. Cf. the opening line of the Dedication to Trelawny of *Songs of the Springtides*: "A sea-mew on a sea-king's wrist alighting."

301. TO ALGERNON CHARLES SWINBURNE

56 Euston Square,
31 December 1879

Dear Swinburne,

I received with thankfulness and much pleasure a copy of your study on Shakespeare[1] (I confess I think one ought to write Shakspere if his practice was always that, though heretofore I had always acted otherwise); and have read every line of it, finding it throughout highly readable, besides its various and more essential other merits. I read it indeed with hearty admiration of its general purport and treatment, and with general agreement — the agreement, that is, of one who has not so fully fathomed the points at issue as to make his opinion either way of much consequence. There are some violences which I should have preferred to see abated, but that is your affair, not mine. The observations on *King Lear* and *Othello* struck me especially, and are among the keenest and grandest things that can ever have been said on these inexhaustible themes. Must see about reading *Arden of Feversham,* which as yet I never did. I find that Gabriel agrees with you as to its Shakesperianity. I don't agree with you in exceptional liking for *Cymbeline* — rather the contrary; and must say that those words which were cited against you (as in your note) as being triple endings do appear to me to be triple endings. If not, then I hardly see what *would* be a triple ending.

But all this is mere gossip — which you will forgive as a friend though you spurn it as a critic.

379

With affectionate regards to you and Watts,

Your
W. M. Rossetti

MS: Folger.

1. *A Study of Shakespeare* (1880).

302. TO ALGERNON CHARLES SWINBURNE

56 Euston Square,
7 January [1880]

Dear Swinburne,

There is certainly a great deal in what you say about the name of Shakespeare.[1] I remember that some years ago I read in print the rights and wrongs of that controversy, the conclusion being that Shakespeare is correct — I dare say (but don't now recollect) the arguments were the same that you adduce; and ever since then I had stuck to Shakespeare (even with some hankering of my own to make it simply Shakespea*r*), until recently, seeing the arguments for Shakspere, and forgetting the others, I was "almost persuaded to be a Shaksperean"[2] — but I think I shall now revert to my former faith. Is it to be understood that those who write Shakspere pronounce Sha*ck*spere? That I should regard as a horrid and gratuitous barbarism; my own supposition being that, whatever the spelling, one equally pronounces Sh*a*kespear.

Brown, I know, did receive your book[3] in due course. Several days ago I heard him speak of intending to write you in acknowledgement: he has not been particularly well of late, and perhaps that has interfered. Scotus (I have every reason to suppose) is in his accustomed lair:[4] in relation to your book, I know nothing of him.

9 January (resumed)

It occurs to me to enquire whether Brown is certain to be aware of your present address.

Your letter seems to imply that you believe me to be a Communalist (this is the correct word, on Andrieu's[5] authority, and not Communard, which is an insult, nor of course Communist, which means something quite different) in a more positive sense than I am so. The Republic *One and Indivisible* is most assuredly my ideal — not even Federal, and still less Communalist. At the time of the Communal insurrection, I sympathized to a very large extent with the Commune, as being a protest against all the royalist and semi-royalist simmerings of the Versailles government, and as being the visible expression of that sort of republicanism which is prepared to do or die; and moreover I detested the horrid butcheries of the Versaillists when triumphant. Practically, the action (or profession) of the Parisian Communalists appears to me to have been this: "You Versaillists and other Frenchmen, determined as you appear to be to go to the devil with a king or sham-republic, shall do so if you like: for us of Paris, we are Republicans, and we mean to have a Republic in Paris, whether you have one in France or not.'' I couldn't and can't help liking that, however inconsistent it may be with correct governmental theories; and I verily believe that the deadly determination shown by the Commune has in the long run powerfully contributed to prevent the country from anti-republican backsliding. Beyond this, I don't much enter into the theory of communal government, and don't at all wish — quite the contrary — to see any such theory trammelling the march of the unitary Republic.

Yours always in liberty and fraternity, and in *quasi*-equality.

W. M. Rossetti

MS: Folger.

1. J. O. Halliwell-Phillipps had recently sent Swinburne a copy of his brochure, ''Which shall it be? New Lamps or old? Shaxpere or Shakespeare?'' privately printed in 1879 (*SL*, 4:115).
2. ''Herod the king'' (Agrippa) to St. Paul: ''Almost thou persuadest me to be a Christian'' (Acts, 26:28).
3. *A Study of Shakespeare*.
4. Penkill Castle.
5. Jules Andrieu (1837-84) was a leader of the Commune in 1871. After its fall he moved to England, where he struggled to support himself by tutoring, lecturing, and writing. He wrote the article on alchemy in the ninth edition of *Encyclopaedia Britannica*. WMR to WBS, 3 March 1876: ''Andrieu is a fine fellow, with wife, 3 children, and adopted young half-sister, to support on a half-empty pocket and incipient phthisis'' (Arizona). MS. Diary, 2 March 1884: ''Talk with Hueffer about the death ... of our estimable Communalist acquaintance Andrieu (in Jersey), and the consequent straits of his widow and family. I had already decided to send £10.''

303. TO ALGERNON CHARLES SWINBURNE

5 Endsleigh Gardens,
16 January [1880]

Dear Swinburne,

You and I seem to be not very far apart in opinion about the Commune: it is hardly a question of actual divergence, but of more or less leaning towards one side or other. I still think however that the Communal Insurrection had *something* to do with preserving a republican form of government against the almost victorious attacks of the royalists: I think that, but for the evidence, which the Commune afforded, of a furious and fighting republican party, the very strong royalist party in the *Chamber* — for that was the real *government* — with the comparatively lukewarm and indeterminate republican party there, would very likely have consummated the almost accomplished crime of re-Bourbonizing, re-Orleanizing, or re-Bonapartizing France.

About Robespierre there is something to be said on both sides. As a part-governor of the Republic, he would undoubtedly have guillotined any body of men who seceded from the republican-governmental scheme: but then he would not have been on the side of a government that was faintly, as against a population that was fiercely, republican. As a matter of fact, he did at the very end do exactly what the Commune of 1871 did — i.e., set himself in armed rebellion with the Commune of Paris against the Convention and government. This certainly was to save his own life: but I am not sure that he would have done for that object what he would have repudiated for a national object.

I have *not* yet read *Les Rois en Exil*:[1] have seen enough about it, in reviews etc., to make me often wish to read it — and I must do so one day.

About that silly, ignorant, and insolent attack on Shelley[2] — which I have not yet *seen*. I myself take next to no interest, for good or for evil, in what is said by such papers as the *Saturday Review*, *Pall Mall Gazette*, etc. — or I should rather have said the fact that a lie appears printed in the *Saturday Review* etc. (rather than in some other paper less favoured by the British Club-lounger) does not to me increase the interest of said lie. I therefore, personally speaking, should not care to demonstrate in print the Antipodism of that Shelleyan allegation from truth: but would nevertheless willingly defer to your and Watts's view, if I could see my way to managing it. *Where* is the refutation to appear? The *Saturday Review* never (as I understand) admits any such controversial matter: the *Athenaeum* and other such papers reject on principle any notice to show that some *different* paper has made a blunder. If however Watts can ensure insertion of a short statement in the *Athenaeum*, and will let me know as much, I will write what is needed.

Many a time have I said that a great desideratum in the present stage of journalism and reviewing — indeed a real necessity — is some paper which would consist wholly or chiefly of controversial matter of this kind — rectifications from authors reviewed, comments, explanations, etc. etc. I am surprised that no one with a little money or enterprise brings out such a paper: if honourably and sensibly conducted, it would receive contributions from all the best men of the day, now one and now another, and would become as entertaining and as permanently valuable as it would be convenient at the time.

Yours affectionately,
W. M. Rossetti

Please observe change of name for my house: the Euston Square murder[3] was too much for the sense of propriety of some inhabitants of this (south) side of the Square — the murder being on the north side.

MS: BL.

1. Alphonse Daudet's novel, published in 1879.
2. Not identified.
3. Of "a rather eccentric old lady," for which Hannah Dobbs was tried and acquitted in 1879. The proposal to change the name of the south side of the Square to Endsleigh Gardens had been mooted before the murder (*SR*, 1:293-94).

304. TO DANTE GABRIEL ROSSETTI

5 Endsleigh Gardens,
19 February [1880]

Dear Gabriel,

I can't remember that it was I who lent you Cottle's Coleridge.[1] At any rate I have a complete copy in my own hands, 2 volumes, and have this morning asked Lucy to post you volume 2. Lucy continues very fairly well now.

All went off agreeably at Birmingham:[2] I return thither next Monday.

We did engage that I would spend with you the succeeding Wednesday —
which I fully count on doing.

I wish you'd oblige me on that day in the following small *fad*. Frederick
Locker (who is always very civil and obliging to me) possesses Walter Scott's
MS. of *Harold the Dauntless*.[3] There are some gaps in it, which he gets filled in
(i.e. the missing lines copied in) by various poets — Tennyson, Arnold, Longfellow,
Morris, etc. He wants you to write some half-dozen lines,[4] and Christina also.
This is a funny but certainly a harmless little piece of finikin dilettantism, and if
you will humour Locker (you need not reply yes) I will bring round with me the
MS. volume, now at Somerset House.

Your

W.M.R.

MS: AP.

1. Joseph Cottle, *Early Recollections, Chiefly Relating to the late Samuel Taylor Coleridge*
(1837-39).
2. See Letter 298, Note 6.
3. Published in 1817.
4. For DGR's refusal see DW, 4:1715. WMR to Locker, 4 March 1880: ''I am sorry to say that my
brother showed more antipathy than I had expected to the proposal.... You did not wish me to press
him, and I of course did not want to bother or argue about such a matter, so I dropped it, and there it
remains. My sister, like a sensible person, wrote out her couplet the moment the book was presented
to her'' (Huntington).

305. TO DANTE GABRIEL ROSSETTI

12 Grafton Street,
Oxford Road,
Manchester,
30 June [1880]

Dear Gabriel,

One or two items. We dined yesterday with Brockbank (William Brockbank,[1]
Brock Hurst, Didsbury, Manchester), and he spoke with particular admiration
about a design of yours of the *Annunciation*[2] executed on the pulpit in Bodley's[3]
Church in Scarborough, and asked whether you possess any sketch, duplicate,
etc., of this design — which he would evidently (from his conversation) buy at
any moderate price demanded. If you think this matter worth attending to — for
its own sake or for anything it might lead to — you might as well write to
Brockbank. I told him something about your *Blessed Damozel*[4] and other works
in hand; but this did not lead to anything particular. He is a man whom you
would I think like very well.

Turner's[5] father, I am told, is just dead, and Turner is assumed to have come
into a handsome fortune, and to be not unlikely to resume picture-buying.

The enclosed is a scribble that I made from a picture in the Peel Park Museum,
Manchester, labelled ''Portrait of Chatterton by Hogarth.''[6] I have caught the
features and expression pretty well, but made the latter rather too silly: hair dark
chestnut-auburn: colour of eyes I don't *precisely* recollect, but suppose it to be
dark grey. The picture *is* I think a Hogarth — of not more than average merit. Of

course if it is really Chatterton, the work is of singular interest. The primary question would be one of date: my impression is that Hogarth died in 1762, and Chatterton later than that, and if so, the attribution seems to break down. Brown tells me (as I am in the act of writing) that the picture is one which Agnew gave to the collection, and he evidently scouts the whole affair — with what amount of reason I know not. Rowley[7] knows nothing about the picture.

On and from Friday our address will *probably* be "At Mr. M. Simpson's, Chapel-en-le-Frith, Derbyshire": not as yet certain.

Your
W. M. R.

Portrait is head-and-shoulders, less than life-size.

MS: AP.

1. Metal merchant and land surveyor (*Slater's Manchester Directory*).
2. For a pulpit in St. Martin's, Scarborough (Surtees 131).
3. George Frederick Bodley (1827-1907), ecclesiastical architect, gave Morris & Co. its first major commissions, the decoration of St. Martin's, Scarborough, and St. Michael's, Brighton.
4. See Letter 312, Note 6.
5. William A. Turner of Manchester owned several paintings by DGR, including *Proserpine, Joli Coeur* (Surtees 233, 196), and *A Vision of Fiammetta*.
6. See Letter 67, Note 2.
7. Charles Rowley (1839-1933), son of a prosperous Manchester picture-dealer and frame-maker. He worked in his father's business for twenty-five years, but much of his effort was devoted to public service, as a councillor and as the founder of educational and recreational bodies in the Ancoats district of Manchester. In *Fifty Years Work Without Wages* (1911) he gives an account of the many artists, musicians, and writers whom he involved in his projects, including Morris, Walter Crane, Bernard Shaw, Charles Hallé, and York Powell. He was a friend and supporter of FMB through whom WMR met him c. 1878. See the obituary notice in the *Manchester Guardian*, 7 September 1933, p. 4.

306. TO ALGERNON CHARLES SWINBURNE

5 Endsleigh Gardens,
15 September [1880]

Dear Swinburne,

Your Shelley emendation[1] is interesting, and of course entirely reasonable. It appears to me however hardly likely that the 2 lines were written (or intended to be written) in reverse order by Shelley. Dropping this first suggestion, I quite agree with you that Shelley's real main idea was that Anarchy on his horse presented a general total resemblance to the apocalyptic Death on his horse; yet I don't think that the line "He was pale" etc. can, as a matter of elocution or discrimination in reading the passage, be read parenthetically: I think one must read the couplet as it stands printed, and allow that Shelley's conception was more integral and more accurate than his diction.

I shall read with great interest — and I think I can say by anticipation, great satisfaction — your essay on the Dryden-Pope sequence of poetry and poets: this and whatsoever else relates to your Essay arising out of my booklet[2] possesses a special attraction to me — not uncombined with a sense that the comparison between your performance and mine will be something like that between the maelstrom and a boat which is twirled round and round within it.

Have not read Nichol's *Byron*:[3] hope to do so. Ditto the *Gentleman's Magazine*[4] if only this latter falls in my way.

Shall very much like to see you some evening. Please mention the matter to Watts, and see whether he can make an appointment: he comes within my ken so seldom now (to my regret) that I fear I shall not have an opportunity this longish while to come of settling such a point viva voce.

Did you read in Forman[5] Shelley's Essay "On the Devil, and Devils"? It amused me not a little.

Yours always,
W. M. Rossetti

MS: BL.

1. Of "He was pale even to the lips, / Like Death in the Apocalypse" (*The Masque of Anarchy*, 11. 32-33).
2. See Letter 298, Note 4.
3. Published in the "English Men of Letters" series, 1880.
4. Probably Dutton Cook, "The Eclipse of Shakespeare," 247 (September 1880), 302-14.
5. *Prose Works of Shelley*, 4 vols, 1880.

307. TO THE EDITOR OF THE *ATHENAEUM*[1]

5 Endsleigh Gardens,
9 November 1880

If you will favour me with the small space needed, I should like to set myself right in your columns with regard to a literary matter in which my name has (as it appears to me) been not fairly dealt with.

In *Macmillan's Magazine* for September there was an article written by Mr. Harry Quilter,[2] named "The New Renaissance"; and in that article was the following sentence: "We know that ... one Rossetti wrote poems and painted pictures, and the other wrote criticisms on them, and so influenced both arts."

I wrote to the editor a note for publication, asking whether this sentence "means (as, according to grammatical rules, it naturally would mean) that I wrote criticisms on the poems and pictures of my brother, Dante Rossetti, and, if so, what is the evidence which he (Mr. Quilter) adduces in proof of this?" or whether the meaning really intended was that I wrote criticisms on poems and pictures generally, other than those of my brother.

I received in reply a letter (not written by Mr. Quilter) acknowledging that "the construction is lax, and the words were not intended to bear the meaning which they do bear"; and it was added that Mr. Quilter was "very sorry" for this "oversight." I therefore had reason to expect that, when my note should come to be printed, a simple admission of inexactness would be made. But in this I was mistaken.

In *Macmillan's Magazine* for November Mr. Quilter professes to "justify" his assertion, in an answer which he expressly declares to be "final." His so-called justification consists of a reference to a passage in a book of mine published in 1867.[3] He does not quote the passage verbatim, but I will do so: "The real and only reason why I do not here republish any reviews of my brother is simply that he never has been to any moderate extent an exhibiting artist, and that consequently I never have had an opportunity of criticizing his works; except in two or three instances, when the works exhibited were of secondary importance, and the reviews were correspondingly slight." This statement is strictly true, and I here reaffirm it. The "two or three instances" in question were of the remote date 1850 to 1852.[4]

Such is the extent to which Mr. Quilter can justify, in his final answer, his assertion that I wrote criticisms on my brother's pictures. His final answer passes in total silence his original statement that I wrote criticisms on my brother's poems.

W. M. Rossetti

Text: *Athenaeum*, 13 November 1880, pp. 642-43.

1. For the context of this letter, see WMR's two letters of 10, 20 September to the editor of *Macmillan's Magazine*, George Grove, asking that his objection to Harry Quilter's article "The New Renaissance; or the Gospel of Intensity" and Quilter's response be printed in the magazine, which they were in the November number (*The Rossetti-Macmillan Letters*, ed. L. M. Packer, 1963, pp. 128-33).

2. (1851-1907), art critic, collector, amateur artist. He wrote for the *Spectator* and the *Times*, his appointment to the latter being announced in the same number of the *Athenaeum* (p. 647) in which WMR's letter appeared. MS. Diary, 24 November 1880: "Gosse ... says that Quilter, as the art-critic of the *Spectator*, was fulsome in his praise of Burne Jones and others of that class, having written the phrase (much ridiculed at the time) 'with eyes suffused with tears, we sank back on a chair' (after contemplating a picture by Jones); and his attack on the same class of artists in *Macmillan's Magazine* is understood to have been done for the express purpose of conciliating the *Times*, and so getting appointed art-critic there." 11 January 1883: "[Lowes] Dickinson ... tells me that the writer of the notice in the *Spectator* ["Rossetti at Burlington House," 6 January 1883, pp. 14-15] is Quilter: who may thus be held to have made the *amende honorable* for his uncalled-for little imputation upon Gabriel and me ... in *Macmillan's Magazine*."

3. *FACC.*

4. *Critic*, 1 July 1850, pp. 334-35 (*Ecce Ancilla Domini!*). *Spectator*, 4 January 1851, p. 20 (*Ecce Ancilla Domini!*, "slightly but beneficially retouched"; *Rossovestita*, Surtees 45). *Spectator*, 18 December 1852, p. 1212 (*Giotto Painting the Portrait of Dante* [called "Sketch for a Picture" in the review]; *Beatrice Meeting Dante at a Marriage Feast, Denies Him Her Salutation*). Later he published two brief accounts of *The Seed of David* in *Weldon's Register*, October 1861, p. 188; and *Fine Arts Quarterly Review*, 3 (October 1864), 150.

308. TO EDWARD JOHN TRELAWNY

5 Endsleigh Gardens,
12 November [1880]

Dear Mr. Trelawny,

I have here copied out the letter[1] which you sent up to me, in English; and have also turned the same letter into Italian. Am not quite sure which of the two you would think it more desirable to send off: possibly the Italian — or possibly even both, with a word to explain that the one is a translation from the other. The form of the heading and address to the letter is I presume correct.

It seems that the Rt. Hon. Sir Augustus Berkeley Paget, K.C.B.[2] is our Ambassador at Rome; Secretary of Legation, Hugh Guion MacDonell, Esq.[3]

I have heard some while ago from Mrs. Forman that her husband had with much pleasure received from you an acknowledgement of his edition of Shelley's Prose. I found the Essay "On the Devil" very amusing, and it is a great satisfaction to have at last the *Necessity of Atheism* in its original form. In the beautiful letters from Italy etc. there are many amendments of detail.

We go on well, and trust that you and Miss Trelawny[4] and Miss Taylor do the like. Quite warm today — just up to "Temperate" — moist and muddy: but we have had more than an average amount of cold this month past.

Very truly yours,
W. M. Rossetti

MS: Yale.

1. MS. Diary, 12 November 1880: "Trelawny sends me a letter embodying one addressed to the Custodian of the Protestant Cemetery in Rome [Forman, *Letters of Trelawny*, pp. 273-74], to the effect that his ashes are to be deposited in the grave which he holds next to Shelley's. He asks me to copy it out, and send it off. I copied it out, and translated it into Italian, and forwarded both papers to Trelawny, to be used as he prefers."
2. (1823-96), envoy to Victor Emanuel from 1867 and ambassador, 1876-83.
3. (1832-1904). He held the post 1878-82.
4. Laetitia.

309. TO ALGERNON CHARLES SWINBURNE

5 Endsleigh Gardens,
8 December 1880

Dear Swinburne,

Yesterday I got the *Fortnightly Review* and read with acute pleasure the observations in your article about my little book[1] — or rather I should say the article as a whole. Lucy, who insisted on my reading it aloud to her, was equally gratified. I don't know that I ever before had so many pleasant things written of me — especially as coming from such a hand.

What is my anachronism about Sir Thomas Lucy (but don't trouble yourself to reply expressly to this query)? Is it that he had not become M.P. at the date when Shakespeare could have posted up these verses?[2]

I knew a *little* about Henryson,[3] but was not aware he had done a conclusion to the *Troilus*. That final incident to which you refer is very impressively invented.

I suppose I must have sent you long ago (say in 1874) the first printed section of that elaborate and really important collation which I made of Boccaccio's *Filostrato* and Chaucer's *Troilus*, for the Chaucer Society. If by chance I was in default, I could now send you a copy: and could give Watts another if he cared. The remainder of the collation was printed within the last few months, but has not yet, I suppose, been published.

You will have heard something about a memorial for the spot where Shelley was burned.[4] I expressed my concurrence in the proposal.

Yours affectionately,
W. M. Rossetti

I don't well know which are the poets concerning whom you entirely dissent from me in opinion.[5]

MS: Folger.

1. See Letter 298, Note 4.
2. Swinburne wrote that the first line ("A parliament-member, a justice of peace") of the "doggrel affixed by tradition to the gate of Charlecote Park with the apocryphal hand of Shakespeare bears the stamp on it of forgery, in the linguistic anachronism of the title or titles therein bestowed on Sir Thomas" (*Miscellanies*, p. 10).
3. Robert Henryson, whose *Testament of Cresseid* (printed in 1593), a sequel to Chaucer's *Troilus and Criseyde*, tells of the retribution that befell Cresseid. Swinburne declared that the last meeting between Troilus and Cresseid (now a leper), "for truth and power of pathetic imagination ... may be matched against the very best work of Chaucer" (*Miscellanies*, p. 6).
4. See Letter 310, Note 4.
5. See Letter 310.

310. TO ALGERNON CHARLES SWINBURNE

5 Endsleigh Gardens,
13 December [1880]

Dear Swinburne,

I reply to your interesting letter, taking the points much as they come.

I do from time to time hear of Trelawny: indeed, have had to reply this morning to one of his brief missives. He is at Sompting, and in good trim. His neglect of acknowledging your book[1] is not strictly correct, but it is "just like him," and no doubt has no further significance.

Have not seen the *Times* upon your letter to the *Rappel*:[2] dare say it was as stupid on that subject as it is on very many others.

I confess I don't quite see why you should think that you "radically differ" from my opinion of Wordsworth and Campbell; for my Notices of these poets[3] contain eulogiums of them really not dissimilar in essence from what you now say — though there may be a discrepancy in the amount of stress and emphasis. I do most decidedly consider that Wordsworth was "one of the absolute great poets" (though indeed I would not, taken all round, place him above Byron); and I very highly admire and value Campbell's patriotic songs.

As to *Gertrude of Wyoming*, I have not the slightest doubt it has its merits, and these of no easy or unimportant kind, although in writing about it I spoke rather of its general mildness and smoothness: and *Rokeby* I, in a certain sense, sincerely like and admire — yet I think it less good than any one of Scott's other 4 leading poems.

I liked much what you have said of Dante, Chaucer, and Villon; and I think there is a great deal in your contrast between Milton and Cromwell. As to Dante, I hardly know that I am so *exclusive* a Danteite as your article speaks of; but I am free to admit that I think the height and depth of poetic totality in Dante, power and performance, do entirely outweigh the like in Milton. In fact, I think the *only* poetic figure in modern Europe that equals Dante — and he no doubt exceeds him in the general compendium of endowments — is Shakespeare.

Will look up for you and Watts the Boccaccio-Chaucer collation. It is a large-sized thing in parallel columns.

In a general way, *any* evening — except Monday evening, when I invariably go off to Gabriel's — would do for me to attend at Putney, and enjoy the reading of your new poems. Two or three days' previous notice would be apposite. I shall be out of town for some days beginning with 30 January.

The proposed Memorial on the spot where Shelley was burned[4] deserves, I think, to be considered with sympathy and favour. I decidedly think it is right to mark the *spots* connected with great men or great events. In replying to Mr. Hubbard,[5] who addressed me on this subject, I said that I presume a monument of a first-class character of high art is not contemplated in the present instance, nor likely to be obtained; and that, in default of that, I should be in favour of something of a simple and unpretentious kind. The Byron monument is no doubt a pitiful eyesore.

To my own ear "Parliament-member" had always sounded a somewhat odd phrase for Shakespeare's time — or indeed for any time: I was not aware however that this point had been raised as impugning the genuineness of the whole affair.[6] As to "Browning's wrong view of Shakespeare's nature," I fancy I should agree with you were the whole matter adequately present to my mind, but this it is not.

Very glad you think so highly of *Weddah* etc.: I have not yet read in the new volume[7] that or any other poem, but recollect the strong impression *Weddah* produced on me when first I saw it.

I did of course read in the *Athenaeum* your rendering from Aristophanes,[8] and thought it a consummate success — relying, that is, on my internal consciousness for the original.

Yours always,
W. M. Rossetti

MS: BL.

1. Probably *Songs of the Springtides*.

2. The *Times* noted Swinburne's "making merry" over Disraeli's giving the name Agrippina in *Endymion* (1880) "to an exiled monarch whom the reader is expected to admire. He suggests that Lord Beaconsfield forgot who was Nero's mother, but he himself seems to forget that Nero's grandmother was also an Agrippina and was beloved by the Romans" (2 December 1880, p. 2). For Swinburne's letter see *SL*, 4:175.

3. In *Lives of Famous Poets*.

4. No memorial was erected.

5. Theodore Stephen Hubbard was matriculated at University College, Oxford, in 1877; B.A., 1882.

6. See Letter 309, Note 2.

7. James Thomson ('B.V.'), *Vane's Story, Weddah and Om-el-Bonain and Other Poems* (1881, for 1880).

8. *Grand Chorus from Aristophanes Attempted in English After the Original Metre*, 30 October 1880, p. 568 (rptd. *Studies in Song*, 1880).

311. TO EMMA TAYLOR

5 Endsleigh Gardens,
30 December [1880]

My dear Miss Taylor,

Here is a translation:[1] no apology needed for asking me to do it.

Thank you, we have spent a sufficiently "Merry Christmas" — the 3 little ones decidedly so. Lucy is moderately well — a cold has beset her on and off for some weeks past. All best regards to you — and to Mr. Trelawny too, only that he won't have them.

Yours always truly,
W. M. Rossetti

MS: Yale.

1. Of the reply to Trelawny's request to the custodian of the English Cemetery in Rome "to put my tomb in thorough repair" (Forman, *Letters of Trelawny*, p. 274). WMR's translation of the letter, which gives details of the vault to be constructed, is also at Yale.

312. TO LUCY ROSSETTI

14 Montgomerie Crescent,
Glasgow,[1]
6 February [1881],
9½ a.m.

Dearest Lu,

I write before breakfast, and hurriedly, not to lose the moments.

Two letters of yours reached me on my arrival here, and another during the evening. I feel much for your discomforts, but would fain hope that day by day they will diminish. If no definite improvement appears, I would abandon Brighton.

I did another sonnet in the train yesterday — the introductory sonnet on *The Past*.[2]

The two letters you sent me on are one from the Cemetery custodian at Rome which Trelawny asks me to translate, and one from Theodoric asking me to interest myself to get him appointed Italian correspondent to the *Daily News* — his brother-in-law[3] having resolved to resign. Theodoric and Isabella are now in Rome, and feel better there than in Florence. Must see to these matters in due time: "somebody is always at him."

It snowed rather briskly from Melrose to Edinburgh yesterday, and the old snow carpeted the ground: but on leaving Edinburgh for Glasgow a great change was perceptible — no new snow, and next to no old. The Nichol family (I see you object to that mode of spelling the name) live at an extremity of Glasgow — with hills closing the view from the upper windows — a stone two-storied house of a hard style of architecture but replete with every convenience inside — for instance, a bath-room containing a vapour-bath as well as the ordinary bath. Professor and Mrs. Nichol received me most cordially, and made me entirely comfortable. She is partly of Spanish blood, her mother a Spaniard, her father a certain Sheriff Bell who was very well known in the Scotch literary world.[4] A fine type of face. She is a fervent admirer of Christina's poems, and asked whether I thought she might call on Christina when she happens to be in London:

I said she should call on us, and we would take her round — but all this is a mere project in the air. Nichol is a keen fine-witted man, and seems a good hater: he was near being ruined by the Glasgow Bank affair,[5] but after all got off not greatly damaged. Both he and his wife are very free in religious matters.

Nichol says that the Sunday Society for which I am to lecture is fiercely opposed by Sabbatarians, and that there may perhaps be some hostile demonstration in the lecture-room: I fancy I shall only be put on my mettle by anything of that kind.

Gabriel sends me capital news — he has sold his *Blessed Damozel* picture[6] "to very fair advantage." He speaks highly of a sonnet of mine — I suppose the *Garibaldi*,[7] which I sent him: you probably did not send.

This is a brilliant clear day: I must get a walk after lunch. Accept love as a substitute for further details.

Your own,
William M. R.

Your papa has got me a room in his lodgings.[8] You see poor O'Shaughnessy is dead!

MS: AP.

1. The home of John Nichol (1833-94), with whom WMR stayed during his visit to Glasgow to deliver a lecture on Shelley. Nichol held the chair of English Language and Literature at Glasgow, 1862-89. He was a friend of Swinburne, Kossuth, and Mazzini, a founder of the New Speculative Society, and a supporter of the North during the American Civil War, all of which readily disposed WMR towards him.

2. *Democratic Sonnets*, 2 (the final sonnet). The series is first mentioned in MS. Diary on 10 January 1881: "Gabriel thinks I should do well to write and publish a series of sonnets on the public events of my own times: and indeed I don't dislike the idea, but fear I could not do in this retrospective way what I might conceivably have done under the impulse of the facts as they occurred." On 5 February he wrote to Lucy that "Last night I drew up a list of very nearly 100 subjects for sonnets: think 100 would be the best number" (AP). Over the next couple of years he completed seventy-two sonnets, all he was to do, but they remained unpublished until 1907, when fifty of them appeared in two slim pamphlets in the "Contemporary Poetry Series" edited by Ford Madox Hueffer. See Letter 317 for his family's (and especially DGR's) discouragement of him from publishing them.

3. Dr. Steele, a physician who had been a friend of Hannay in Edinburgh (*FLM*, 2:302).

4. According to William Knight, Mrs. Nichol was "Jane Stewart Bell, eldest daughter of Henry Glassford Bell, advocate — afterwards Sheriff of Lanarkshire — by his marriage with his first wife, Sophia Stewart, only child of Captain Stewart of Shierglas, Glengarry" (*Memoir of John Nichol* [1896], p. 170). Her father (1803-74), who founded the *Edinburgh Literary Journal*, was "called 'the last of the literary sheriffs'" (*DNB*).

5. He had been a trustee for a shareholder in the City of Glasgow Bank, which crashed in 1878 (W. Knight, *Memoir of Nichol*, pp. 206-7).

6. Replica (Surtees 244 R. 1).

7. *Democratic Sonnets*, 2. For DGR's letter see DW, 4:1843-44.

8. MS. Diary, 9 February 1881: "At Manchester, staying with Brown, 147 York Street, Cheetham. We went to look at his pictures in the Townhall: the Camp of Mancenion [*The Romans Building a Fort at Mancenion*], finished since I saw it in August, and very excellent — and the Repulse [*Expulsion*] of the Danes, which is now nearly completed except the hinder group of retreating Danes: for spirit and direct force of work I think it is even the finest of the 3. Brown made a move not long ago for obtaining a higher rate of remuneration. It failed: but I find that an Alderman [Joseph] Thompson, whom I met in the Hall, is still keen to carry this point, and he showed me a letter he had written about it: he would like to get up an indemnifying subscription for Brown, if official action

fails. I mentioned this to Brown, who is not indisposed for such a solution, if postponed till the final close of his painting-work. He expects to finish the *Danes* early in March, and then return to London.''

313. TO LUCY ROSSETTI

Somerset House,
11 February [1881],
12.30

Dearest Lu,

I have this morning received 2 letters of yours — one dated Tuesday sent on to me from Manchester by your papa, and the other dated yesterday.

The details which Gabriel gives about O'Shaughnessy in the enclosed letter[1] are much the same as what I heard from him last evening. It is difficult to think that his life could not have been preserved, and a valuable life it certainly was. Gabriel understands (but it is not a matter to be mentioned to the Marston family) that O'Shaughnessy was intending to remarry — one of the Misses Salaman[2] (a musical family) whom I met at his house the only time I was there. While I was with Gabriel, a Mr. Deacon,[3] a cousin of O'Shaughnessy, came round, bringing a few articles which had belonged to the poet as reminiscences for his friends. One is for your father: the one for Gabriel (the only one that I saw) is that absurd affair of Manet's for Poe's *Raven*. There will be something for me also, but not at Gabriel's. Deacon speaks strongly to the effect that O'Shaughnessy died because he was not nursed through his illness with efficiency. Only a Doctor living somewhere near the house (Bayswater) was called in, and he did not insist on having in a nurse to give medicines etc. at proper times, nor did he take care to exclude visitors, although he said that O'Shaughnessy should be kept quiet. Hence, on the last day of his life, the Saturday, there were the Salamans and perhaps others, reading some chaffy affair, and making him talk (with congestion of the lungs), and appear amused. The volume he was about to publish will, I understand, come out, and it is hoped that after that a well-edited selection of his best things[4] might be of some advantage.

I took round my sonnets to Gabriel: read him 2 or 3, and left the whole set with him. I find his opinion is that *all* the series should be written in an exalted and poetic strain, to the exclusion of any such sarcasm and familiar touches as appear in (for instance) the sonnet on Napoleon 3.[5] In this, as a principle, I don't agree: for I think on the contrary that, with such various subject-matter suggesting such various moods of mind and modes of regard, there should be a corresponding variety in the treatment. But it may certainly be that I don't shine in the sardonic or incisive line — though I confess that I had regarded that Napoleon sonnet as one of the best. On some other grounds Gabriel's observations were decidedly encouraging: he liked the *Garibaldi* the best of those he had seen — also the *Lamartine* when I read it to him.

Leyland was the purchaser (after all) of his *Blessed Damozel* picture — £500, but price not to be bruited abroad: and he seems to be nibbling at the *Salutation of Beatrice*[6] as well. Gabriel saw him again on Wednesday, and could not see that he was in the least out of spirits — although the papers lately announced the loss of one of his ships, and of several lives in her.[7] Gabriel is getting on well with the draperies in the *Found* picture. He will be glad to see you next Monday if manageable.

I got the *Atlantic Monthly*, containing the 2nd instalment of my Lectures.[8]

Yours with all love,
William

MS: AP.

1. DW, 4:1846.
2. Daughter of the composer Charles Kensington Salaman (1814-1901).
3. Alfred Wranius Deacon (b. 1847), who edited the poet's posthumous volume, *Songs of a Worker* (1881).
4. Nothing appeared until L. C. Moulton's *Arthur O'Shaughnessy: His Life and His Works, with Selections from His Poems* (1894).
5. Published in *Democratic Sonnets*, 1, as was *Lamartine*. WMR to Lucy Rossetti, 15 February [1881]: "Gabriel was last evening in very fair trim.... We talked a good deal about the sonnets. He likes (in a broad sense) all the grave ones, except *Louis Philippe*: but will not, I see, be reconciled to those which have an infusion of the grotesque or sarcastic, though he admits some merit in some of these also. He says they are Browningism — which however is not I think the case to any serious extent. I feel that, if I do the thing at all, I must do it in my own way and not other people's way, but shall nevertheless lay to heart some of Gabriel's observations affecting details of treatment" (AP).
6. The 1880-81 version (Surtees 260).
7. Thirty-five lives were lost in the wreck of the Bohemia on 5 February (*Times*, 6, 8 February 1881, pp. 5, 10).
8. "The Wives of Poets."

314. TO ALGERNON CHARLES SWINBURNE

5 Endsleigh Gardens,
15 March 1881

Dear Swinburne,

My feelings on the Czaricide[1] are, I think, considerably more mixed and tempered than yours. I always did and shall regard tyrannicide as an ultimate (or primary) *right*, to be exercised on adequate occasion by whatever patriot is prepared to sacrifice his own life on the chance of taking a tyrant's. So far we are no doubt at one. But whether Alexander 2 deserved on the whole to have this very extreme right exercised on his person — whether his case was one which *called* for its exercise — is not equally clear to me: the most conspicuous act of his reign was the Emancipation of the Serfs; second to which comes another act which I regard as just and beneficial — the aiding of Bulgarians etc. to release themselves from Turkish oppression. However, the deed is now done, and (as Byron says) "there let it lay."[2]

What will happen with the new reign? I am rather inclined to prognosticate concessions of a somewhat considerable kind to popular demands for a constitution etc., followed by other demands and other concessions, and perhaps something not very much unlike a Russian "French Revolution." It would be a curious sensation to have a contemporary Marat, Danton, or Robespierre, actually going on, and see what one thought of them.

It slipped me on Saturday to mention to you that on 16 February old Trelawny sent me a letter containing the following passage: "If you see Swinburne, remember me kindly to him, and say age prevented my calling on him, and I want him to write a tragedy on Charles 1." This last rather abrupt suggestion receives no elucidation from anything he now writes or has heretofore said to me.

Also on Saturday I had not seen the *Athenaeum*, with Watts's fine and graceful sonnets.[3]

Yours,
W. M. Rossetti

MS: BL.

1. Alexander II was assassinated on 13 March.
2. *Childe Harold's Pilgrimage*, 4, 180: "there let him lay."
3. *Parable Sonnets*, 1 and 2 (12 March 1881, p. 364).

315. TO DANTE GABRIEL ROSSETTI

5 Endsleigh Gardens,
16 March [1881]

Dear Gabriel,

I like best Catherine's Chronicle; next, Queen Jane's Poet; and last (and this not much) The Queen's Poet-King[1] — which has I think a touch of the sentimental. Catherine's Chronicle is certainly a good title: only that it is not (even with the date added, supposing the name of James I of Scots is not also added) at all explanatory of the subject-matter: and I confess that I should still be rather disposed for The Death of the King of Scots, with date — or even The King of Scots with date — only that The King (or perhaps simply "King") of Scots was, as I said on Monday, the name of a rather recent play-version of the Fortunes of Nigel.[2]

I don't feel that under any circumstances it would be an advantage to rechristen the other poem[3] as Berold's Story.

Nothing amiss turns up as yet at home: though Lucy suffered *much* yesterday with neuralgic toothache etc., for which both Jameson[4] and Gill are in requisition. She was much pleased and obliged at your suggestion that we might at a pinch migrate to your house, but so comprehensive a flitting hardly seems to be within the range of practical likelihoods. Our housemaid died in the Fever Hospital on Monday (or Sunday?). Yesterday the more urgent operations of house-disinfection were carried out, and others will follow.

Your
W. M. R.

MS: AP.

1. Proposed titles for *The King's Tragedy*.
2. *King of Scots* by Andrew Halliday, which opened at Drury Lane on 26 September 1868.
3. *The White Ship*.
4. Probably William Edward Jameson, dental surgeon, 50 Gloucester Place, Portman Square (*POLD*).

316. TO ALGERNON CHARLES SWINBURNE

5 Endsleigh Gardens,
18 March [1881]

Dear Swinburne,

I cannot agree with you in thinking that, because Alexander 2 sanctioned atrocities in Poland,[1] therefore we should not count to his credit the armed assistance which he gave to struggling populations oppressed by Turkey. Whether the armed assistance was in itself a right thing is of course a different question: I think it was. The fact that England has been murdering Boers in Transvaal[2] would not I think furnish any reason why she should not lend armed assistance for securing the rights of Montenegro, Greece, etc.

I assure you I have not at all forgotten the righteous courage of Turkey in not giving up Kossuth[3] etc. In a despotically governed country like Turkey any such act must I suppose be rightly credited to the then *government* — the Sultan or his advisers; just as misdeeds of generals or soldiers in Poland may rightly be charged against their autocrat Alexander. Now the Sultan in the Kossuth affair was Abdul Mejid,[4] and I fear that his good deed can in no wise excuse any evil deed committed or sanctioned by the present Sultan; just as little as the misdeeds of Alexander 2 could be excused by the merits (if such there were) of Alexander 1 or Nicholas.

I don't know when I may have an opportunity of writing to Trelawny with regard to his proposal to you:[5] I replied to other portions of his letter long ago. But will do whatever turns up as manageable.

Your reference to the unspeakable (not Turk but) De Sade reminds me of an amusing detail I came upon the other day: very possibly you know of it. In the correspondence of Mirabeau (which I am now reading) from the Donjon of Vincennes[6] — very interesting it is, including some of the best love-letters I know — there occurs a most tremendous denunciation of the Marquis, who (as Mirabeau says) though condemned to death is now living at large and unmolested: Mirabeau speaks of him as a relative of his own.

Your affectionate anti-Turk and far from Pro-Russian

W. M. Rossetti

You probably know that the Philological Society is preparing an English Dictionary, and that many people send in to the Society extracts for the Dictionary from a vast number of books. I lately sent them in some 300 extracts from your *Essays and Studies*.

MS: BL.

1. During the Russian suppression of the Polish revolt in 1863.
2. In the first Boer War of 1881 when the Boers successfully regained their independence from British rule.
3. Lajos Kossuth (1802-94), Hungarian patriot, fled to Turkey in 1849. Despite demands for his delivery into the hands of the Austrians, the Turkish authorities refused. During the 1850s he lived in England, where he was a friend of Mazzini.
4. (1823-61), who succeeded his father Mahmud II in 1839.
5. That he write a tragedy on Charles I (see Letter 314).
6. *Lettres originales de Mirabeau, écrites du donjon de Vincennes*, ed. L. P. Manuel, 1792.

395

317. TO DANTE GABRIEL ROSSETTI

5 Endsleigh Gardens,
13 April [1881]

Dear Gabriel,

I thank you for your two brotherly letters;[1] although it might perhaps have been better to abstain from writing to *Lucy*, at least at the present stage of the affair. If she became anxious or urgent about the matter, a period of considerable domestic disquietude and persecution might ensue. At present however I don't perceive any symptom of this. I read your letter to her rapidly, and returned it, and am now writing at Somerset House: but I think I remember all the leading points.

I have all along been conscious that for a Government official to publish a set of *Democratic Sonnets*, exhibiting on inspection a considerable indifference to ordinary English habits of thought, and an ardent sympathy with the extremer movements in other parts of the world, is likely to excite some observation in official circles, and sure (unless the book fell absolutely stillborn) to rouse antipathy and aggression in reviews of a different tone of opinion. This I am prepared to encounter, and (I hope) to brush aside with equanimity. I think it also conceivable — by no means manifest — that if my succession to the Secretaryship were dubious (and it is so not a little) on other grounds, this affair of the sonnets would turn the balance against me.

Beyond this I do not feel any apprehension. This is a country in which political and religious opinions are free, and in this very Office men of all shades of opinion are to be found. The present government is by no means a Tory or anti-democratic one. It contains (not to speak of such men as Gladstone, Forster, and Fawcett) 3 of the most determined democrats and anti-aristocrats in the country — Bright, Chamberlain, and the avowed republican Dilke.[2] Democracy is not inconsistent with the English Monarchy: it coexists with that at the present moment to a large extent, and is certain to advance further and further. However, I am not wedded to the mere title *Democratic Sonnets*, and if I see cause (which at present I don't) I will substitute another. My liking for the title arises from its being briefly characteristic, and likely to excite interest in those who do in a general way agree with my opinions — a point I should lay much more stress upon than upon anything that might tend to propitiate opponents.

Any idea of my undertaking to write verse about the public events of my own time, and yet failing to show that I sympathize with foreign republics, and detest oppression, retrogression, and obscurantism, whether abroad or at home, must be nugatory. To set me going is to set me going on my own path.

I don't think the other persons who agree in your anxieties on this subject can count for much. I suppose Watts is the principal person, and he can have read very little of the sonnets. Perhaps Mamma and Christina also: but Mamma's great age and Christina's isolated devoteeism diminish the *practical* importance of their views.

As you evidently don't agree with the tone of the sonnets, I shall drop the idea of dedicating them to you — unless you revive the proposal; and shall abstain from reading you new items of the series, if you don't ask for them.

396

As to the affair of the *Freiheit*,[3] that appears to me to be so totally different from anything that I have written or mean to write that I cannot regard it as coming into question here.

I might have said as regards the Secretaryship that it seems about as likely as not (but impossible to say with any assurance) that that affair may have been determined *before* my book would in ordinary course make its appearance. If the book were ready first, I would certainly so far consult prudential considerations as to deliberate whether or not I would hold over the publication until the Secretaryship's question were settled: though I don't *like* even this amount of bowing down in the House of Rimmon.

There are stronger things — about execution of Charles I, merits of Robespierre, etc. — in my *Lives of Poets* than anything I have yet put into the sonnets: and nobody ever, official or reviewer so far as I know, raised any question about them. Neither is my Swinburne brochure wholly mealy-mouthed, and the *esclandre* then going on might have invited some bullying while I was a good deal lower down in the Office, but none was ever attempted.

Accept again, dear Gabriel, my thanks for your affectionate solicitude, and be assured that neither this nor anything else could ever, so far as I am concerned, "cause any kind of division between us."

With love,

Your
W. M. R.

MS: AP. Extract in L. M. Arinshtein and W. E. Fredeman, "William Michael Rossetti's 'Democratic Sonnets'," *Victorian Studies*, 14 (March 1971), 248-49.

1. One addressed to WMR, the other to Lucy (DW, 4:1864-66).
2. William Edward Forster (1818-86), John Bright, Joseph Chamberlain (1836-1914), and C. W. Dilke were ministers in Gladstone's cabinet; Henry Fawcett (1833-84) was Postmaster General without a cabinet seat.
3. *Die Freiheit* was edited in London by the German-American anarchist John Most. For publishing an article in praise of the assassination of Alexander II, Most was imprisoned for a year and a half.

318. TO ALGERNON CHARLES SWINBURNE

5 Endsleigh Gardens,
29 April [1881]

Dear Swinburne,

I was both surprised and delighted at receiving your poem:[1] a flowing and shining lilt which would be delightful to any reader, let alone a father, and might half console the latter for the paternity of twins. Lucy will not let the poem go out of her reach for the present: and, as I am writing at Somerset House, I have it not by me to particularize the stanzas I especially enjoyed — I remember however the last but one with marked predilection. Our Doctor-accoucheur[2] is half dazed at the notion of having brought five such themes for song into the world — for of course Lucy could not refuse herself the pleasure of showing him the poem when he called yesterday. Is the motto from Mrs. Gamp[3] genuine or supposititious?

You will be glad to hear that Lucy has gone on very well ever since the confinement, and will today be for the first time out of bed some short while. The twins will probably this afternoon be recorded (achristically) in the names of Mary Elizabeth Madox[4] and Michael Ford Madox.[5] They are both small — especially the girl — but Lucy thinks their profiles "chiselled" etc. In point of health the boy appears quite right, and the girl, though perhaps not robust, still not glaringly amiss. They had the disadvantage, at moment of birth, of being not only twins but also (so far as we can fix it) eight-months' children.

Are you aware that I began at end of January writing a series of sonnets on the public events and personages of my own time? I may probably call them *Democratic Sonnets*, and publish them as soon as opportune. I hope to do 100, and have already woven-off 52. Since writing the above, I remember that I have at hand here 6 printed items of the series (printed in order that I might offer them to the *Atlantic Monthly* as a foretaste): I enclose the 6, which show fairly enough the general character and scope of the series.

I have to answer (and shall do so at once) a very friendly congratulation from Watts. Shall not repeat to him all the same details which appear here, but you will probably keep him *au fait* as to Lucy etc.

Always your
W. M. Rossetti

MS: BL.

1. *Twins*, "Affectionately Inscribed to W.M.R. and L.R.," published in *Tristram of Lyonesse and Other Poems* (1882). MS. Diary, 28 April 1881: "Received from Swinburne a long lyrical effusion on the birth of our twins [22 April]: facile and taking (it seems on a first hasty perusal), but not very substantial."
2. Dr. Gill.
3. Sarah Gamp in *Martin Chuzzlewit*; the motto was not published.
4. (d. 1947). See Letter 579 on the severe arthritis which afflicted her in later years.
5. (d. 24 January 1883). He was buried in Highgate Cemetery in the grave of Lucy's mother, over which stood a Gothic cross designed by FMB. WMR added to the cross the motto "And if thou wilt, remember" from CGR's *When I am dead, my dearest*.

319. TO ALGERNON CHARLES SWINBURNE

5 Endsleigh Gardens,
6 May [1881]

Dear Swinburne,

Of course I did admire your sonnet on Carlyle and George Eliot[1] — though I hardly thought that either in the nature of the subject or in your management of it there was a very close link of connexion between these two personages — of whom to me Carlyle is beyond all comparison the superior and more interesting figure. I grieve to see you along with others denouncing Carlyle so savagely and unmeasuredly; not indeed that I doubt that the *Reminiscences*[2] (I have not read them) do supply very considerable fuel to so "fuliginous" a state of mind, but that I hold Carlyle — with or without *Reminiscences* — to be a great writer and in his totality a great man, and that I altogether refuse to reverse or even much modify my lifelong opinion of him because at his least self-possessed moment he wrote a deal of acrid stuff which (to all fair seeming) he did not intend to be shovelled out upon the public unsifted.

Shall — again of course — be delighted to hear your Ode on Athens[3] when occasion serves. I wish I had read — or *could* read, which is still more important — something of Pindar.

I agree with you in much valuing Gabriel's ballads[4] — which I regard as ranking among quite his best work: also I read with sincere pleasure Nichol's sonnets on Dobell etc.[5] — read them hurriedly, I admit, but shall not fail to recur to them.

Twins proceed in a harmless course of vegetated existence (as old Blake has it),[6] and Lucy is now so far advanced as to be out of bed some while each day — beginning Saturday last.

Your
W. M. Rossetti

MS: BL.

1. *The Deaths of Thomas Carlyle and George Eliot, Athenaeum*, 30 April 1881, p. 591; rptd. *Tristram of Lyonesse and Other Poems.*
2. Published posthumously in 1881, edited by J. A. Froude.
3. *Athens An Ode*, published in *Tristram of Lyonesse and Other Poems.*
4. *Rose Mary, The White Ship*, and *The King's Tragedy* in *Ballads and Sonnets.*
5. Two sonnets in *The Death of Themistocles and Other Poems* (1881).
6. A common idea in the Prophetic Books, especially *Jerusalem.*

320. TO DANTE GABRIEL ROSSETTI

5 Endsleigh Gardens,
18 May [1881]

Dear Gabriel,

Proofs[1] received from Miss Asher.[2] I will with the greatest pleasure attend to them, and must only ask you not to be *impatient*. I dare say I shall dispose of them pretty soon, my full intention being to give to them day by day as much time as I can properly spare from work of my own — which, as you will have gathered from what I said on Monday, is pretty thick just now. Also my evenings get considerably cut up by keeping Lucy company in her bedroom.

I will see what about red ink or some such expedient.

Your
W. M. R.

Nobody — other than Lucy — shall see the proofs, nor hear about them.

MS: AP.

1. Of *Ballads and Sonnets.*
2. DGR's housekeeper.

321. TO FORD MADOX BROWN

5 Endsleigh Gardens,
24 September [1881]

Dear Brown,

Caine[1] sent me the enclosed syllabus[2] the other day, for you to see, thinking that you would be pleased to observe the last name in his list of "Authors to be dealt with." He *and Gabriel* — wonderful to relate — are now at Fisher Place, Fisher Ghyll, Vale of St. John, near Keswick (Cumberland). They left last Monday, and would stay I suppose a month or thereabouts. Gabriel seems to enjoy the scenery and surroundings very much indeed, and to be more than usually well there. No doubt the sale of his picture[3] to Liverpool tends to keep him in good spirits.

I was sorry to see, in your last letter to Lucy, the bother about Mathilde's book.[4] It looks to me very much as if the Publisher had got frightened by somebody about the atheistic character of the book, and had determined to sell it no more. Not long ago he was similarly frightened — but here chiefly or wholly on the ground of morals — about a volume of poems by George Moore[5] which he had published, and he withdrew it from circulation. Mathilde at our house was very weak, and in that sense ill: since she left, Lucy has heard from her, but not to any very definite effect.

Swinburne and Watts dined with us on Wednesday: chiefly because Swinburne, in his whimsical way, insisted on seeing the Twins. He has just now finished his *Mary Stuart* (3rd part of his Trilogy),[6] and read us the final scene and 2 others: fine work, and perhaps hardly chargeable with over-lengthiness. The total length of this 3rd part is I understand something like full ⅔ of *Bothwell*.

Love to Emma. I trust your house,[7] as you settle down in it, seems comfortable and not other than healthy. Learned from Mathilde that it and all about it is of the extra new kind — or half finished. This is not rightly expressed: I mean, your house but just built, and some houses, roads etc., roundabout it still in course of construction, and no shops as yet. Hope all this is not seriously inconvenient.

Lucy and the tribe well. With all love,

Your

W. M. Rossetti

Did you hear of the death (say 6 weeks ago) of elder daughter of Mrs. Gilchrist?[8] caused by some mismanagement of ether in making medical experiments.

MS: AP.

1. Thomas Henry Hall Caine (1853-1931) was DGR's constant companion during the last year of his life. Caine's earliest letter to WMR in AP, dated 8 October 1878, thanks him for allowing his name to appear as a member of the Honorary Council of the Royal Institution, Liverpool, with which Caine was associated. Later in the year he addressed WMR about the dates of DGR's poems for lectures he was giving at the Institution (15, 24 November; AP). DGR did not begin corresponding with Caine until 1879. Following DGR's death and Caine's hasty publication of *Recollections of Rossetti* (1882), relations with WMR became strained. During Caine's later career as a popular novelist WMR knew him "very little save by casual correspondence" (*SR*, 2:503).
2. Of a series of Caine's lectures in which he was to discuss Nolly Brown.
3. The oil replica of *Dante's Dream*, for which the Liverpool Corporation paid £1,550.

4. Mathilde Blind, *The Prophecy of St. Oran and Other Poems* (1881).

5. MS. Diary, 19 March 1881: "George Moore, who lately published with Newman a wild book named *Pagan Poems* [1881] (certainly not deficient in poetical feeling), writes me that the volume is to be withdrawn by his publisher to appease a hostile reviewer, and he asks for my advice. I replied that, if the question is merely one of giving publicity to the withdrawal, I would say nothing about it. If the question is whether Moore should reissue his book, I would, as matters stand at present, not do so; but, if other damnatory reviews appear, the question would then be open to reconsideration." 6 May: "At George Moore's request, I had marked yesterday, in a copy of his suppressed volume, those poems which should, I think, be excluded, on grounds of morals or propriety, from any reissue; and today I left the volume at his lodgings." The volume was not reissued.

6. Published in 1881. *Chastelard* and *Bothwell* were parts one and two. MS. Diary, 21 September 1881, recorded this judgment: "Fine strongly handled work: but I think it somewhat too long and regular, and doubt the advantage of expressing Mary's execution by the statement of a spectator as to what is visible below, rather than by direct speech of Mary and others concerned."

7. MS. Diary, 9 August 1881: "Called on Brown, and found him in the thick of packing up.... He has secured at the very low rent of £28 a cottage in Cleveland Road, Crumpsall, Manchester."

8. MS. Diary, 6 November 1881, records that the circumstances surrounding her death "strongly suggest a case of suicide."

322. TO FRANCES ROSSETTI

5 Endsleigh Gardens,
23 December [1881]

Dearest Mamma,

A few words in haste. Don't know what is your latest news of Gabriel. I called there yesterday (Thursday) about 5 p.m. Saw Watts. He told me that Gabriel failed to sleep Monday and Tuesday nights, and was naturally much amiss Tuesday and Wednesday days: but on Wednesday night — neither chloral nor morphia being given him — he slept some 6 hours, and was on Thursday morning materially better in mind and spirits: the numbness seems gradually but only by slow gradations to decrease. Watts had not seen Gabriel since he returned in the afternoon: Maudsley[1] was not in. I thought — and so did Watts — that I had better not go up to Gabriel, for the quieter he is kept the better I consider. So I came away, slightly relieved in mind. Shields had been with Gabriel on Tuesday, and he looked me up on Wednesday evening — on the Tuesday Gabriel was very unsettled in mind, and did not even know who Shields was.

Your loving
William

MS: AP.

1. Henry Maudsley, described by Caine as "a young medical man ... brought into the house [Cheyne Walk] as a resident, to watch and manage the case in the intervals of Mr. Marshall's visits." He was the son of the authority on mental diseases, Henry Maudsley, who had attended DGR in 1872 (*FLM*, 1:384, 310). According to *Churchill's Medical Directory* 1881, the son was House Surgeon at University College Hospital.

323. TO FRANCES ROSSETTI

5 Endsleigh Gardens,
27 December [1881]

Dearest Mamma,

Other engagements prevent my calling today, so I send you a few words.

I saw Gabriel on Sunday and yesterday (Monday). He was calm and collected and fairly conversable — especially on Sunday: no doubt very much improved in these respects since my last preceding visit. He will not admit that the numbness of the left side is seriously diminishing: but Maudsley and others consider that it is so to some substantial extent. The morphia-injections are now resumed, and he gets a fair amount of sleep. Brown, who saw him with me yesterday, thinks Gabriel will soon be himself again. Altogether the prospects are improving.

I return 2 letters sent by Christina on Friday: also send cheque for rent. I hope Christina is now better.

Your
William

MS: AP.

324. TO DANTE GABRIEL ROSSETTI

5 Endsleigh Gardens,
16 February [1882]

Dear Gabriel,

Would you read this from Theodoric, and see what is to be done.[1] I have marked in red ink the passages claiming your practical attention. Have replied to Theodoric saying that I am sending the letter on to you — also that I will forward to him a photograph from your oil-picture of our father.[2] If you would reply to Theodoric *direct*, I should much prefer it: I always use English in writing to him.

As this affair professes to be in a hurry, I write in the same. Have no particular news to tell. Am writing a few sonnets again,[3] and shall some day send to the *Athenaeum* some "Talks with Trelawny."[4] Was rather surprised yesterday to see your telegram putting off Mamma's visit. Did you hear the rumour of Stillman's being murdered by Arnauts? promptly disproved to us, upon Lucy's going round to the Spartalis. Hope you go on pretty well — and would rather it were *very* well.

Please don't fail to return enclosed: Caine would I am sure do it if too much trouble to you.

Your
W. M. R.

MS: AP.

1. MS. Diary, 21 February 1882: "In consequence of what Theodoric wrote a few days ago regarding a statue to my father in Vasto, Mamma proposes to get photographs taken from the small bust of him which was done in Malta and to send these to Theodoric for the sculptor Celano: she would also place at his disposal, if wanted, a water-colour by Pistrucci, full-face taken about 1840. I had as good as forgotten it, but, on again seeing it now, am not so wholly dissatisfied with it as I hear we all used to be." A lifesize statue by Filippo Cifariello was finally erected in 1926 (*Times*, 10, 14 September 1926, pp. 15, 13).
2. Surtees 442.
3. See Letter 312, Note 2.
4. Extracted from WMR's Diary; 15, 29 July, 5 August 1882, pp. 78-79, 144-45, 176-77.

325. TO FORD MADOX BROWN

5 Endsleigh Gardens,
8 March [1882]

Dear Brown,

I have your letter of the 6th, and heard in a hurry the one which Lucy received from you this morning. Shall be glad to see Mathilde again, and all the more so if she arrives and continues in pretty good health. I presume she will dine with us tomorrow, and accompany Lucy, Cathy, and Rowley, to *Romeo and Juliet*.

I have seen Lord Lytton, and heard an after-dinner speech of his. Should not have said that he resembles O'Shaughnessy, but it may be that something comes out in conversation. Did he show any human intelligence regarding your pictures? It seems strange if he did not: must be "the mark of the beast"[1] — i.e., of the British aristocrat.

My mother and Christina are now with Gabriel: went down[2] on or about Thursday last. Christina has written to me once, saying that his left arm does not as yet appear better, but he is a little less immersed in gloom of conversation and manner.[3] It should be understood that he *has*, since this attack began, worked somewhat at painting. Had, before he left town, done a goodish deal to a small *Proserpine*[4] and a small *Joan of Arc*:[5] these he took down with him to Birchington, and I fancy they are now finished, or all but. And I believe he will go on with other work after certain preliminary operations shall have been completed by Dunn — with whom he lately renewed amicable business and personal relations.

We have seen two or three mutual friends these two days past. Monday, Lucy and I, with Olive and Arthur, called on Shields. He looks better in the face than he often does: showed us several of his recent cartoons — Jewish and Christian Martyrs etc.[6] — in many respects admirably fine. Also showed us a letter which the Duke of Westminster wrote him lately, speaking very highly of the last window (or last 2 windows) set up in Eaton Hall. Mrs. Shields was recently very ill with bronchitis etc., but is now sufficiently recovered to walk out under favouring conditions: she does not *look* ill, but tends on the contrary to large development of bust etc. Yesterday Mary Robinson[7] called on us: we were already aware of her being back from Florence. She seems in good trim, and will dine with us on Friday. Says Mrs. Stillman's infant[8] suffers from bronchitis, and gives some anxiety. Then in the evening Lucy and I went round to the Tademas, who are shortly to leave for a sojourn in the South of France. Tadema has 5 or 6 pictures in an advanced stage. 2 or 3 of the Roman or Greek subjects surprisingly skilful and piquant in their way. Chief subject (but not a *large* picture) Antony visiting Cleopatra in her splendid barge,[9] does not greatly please me: it is rather less advanced than some others, and is to go to Paris, not to a London exhibition. There were a good number of people present, all having an air of exaggerated prosperity: I knew comparatively few, except the Gosses and Mrs. Williams[10] — who tells me Mrs. Gilchrist is now *somewhat* recovered from the shock of her daughter's death.

Lucy well: Kids do., but for a somewhat persistent cold and discomfort of Michael. Love to Emma.

Your
W. M. Rossetti

MS: AP.

1. Revelation, 13:17.
2. WMR to DGR, 7 February [1882]: "Having received this morning your address from Caine, I write off a few words to show that I am thinking of you. To me it seems essential that you should give the bracing and inspiriting sea-air a fair trial: and I should hope that you will make up your mind to stay some moderate while at Birchington, in as much peace of mind and alacrity of body as circumstances allow you to command" (AP).
3. WMR to FMB, 27 February 1882: "I don't think you need be under any apprehension that Gabriel is 'offended,' nor yet that anyone has made mischief. Gabriel has for these several weeks been not only much depressed but not a little cross into the bargain, and I don't suppose he has written anything to anyone except to meet some occasion of the moment *of his own*: to me for instance he has only written one brief and *necessary* letter since he left London. He is still at Westcliff Bungalow, Birchington on Sea, Kent. When I heard from him (10 or 12 days ago) he himself said he was worse: but Watts, who had been with him up to a day or two preceding, told me that there was no ground for considering him worse, but rather a little better — so I don't feel exactly anxious or alarmed, although it is by this time clear that his illness of numbness etc. was not to be regarded as a trifle. I don't know when Gabriel will be back — should presume within a week or so. Caine, who pledged himself to write to me if Gabriel's health called for that, has never written — which is reassuring" (AP).
4. Surtees 233 R. 3.
5. Surtees 162 R. 3.
6. Shields began work in 1878 on the glass illustrating the *Te Deum* for the chapel of Eaton Hall, Cheshire, the seat of the first Duke of Westminster, Hugh Lupus Grosvenor (1825-99).
7. Agnes Mary Frances Robinson (1857-1944), poet and biographer, to whom WMR dedicated *RRP*. She studied Greek literature at University College London, and in 1881 published a translation of Euripides. From 1888, when she married the Orientalist James Darmesteter (1849-94), she wrote mostly in French. In 1901 she married Émile Duclaux (d. 1904), the director of the Pasteur Institute.
8. Michael.
9. *The Meeting of Antony with Cleopatra*: "His second conception of 'Cleopatra'," the first dating from 1875 (P. C. Standing, *Sir Lawrence Alma-Tadema*, pp. 57, 74).
10. Probably Mrs. W. S. Williams.

326. TO LUCY ROSSETTI

Westcliff Bungalow,
Birchington on Sea,
2 April [1882],
8.45 a.m.

Dearest Lu,

I take up the pen the moment I enter the breakfast-room before anyone else comes in. Came down yesterday in comfort to Westgate, and with Caine walked thence to Birchington. Gabriel's condition is no doubt a very melancholy one. The aspect of his face and person is I think much the same as when I saw him last: but his persistent extreme despondency, and the inertness amounting to incapacity which besets him in all ways, are most serious matters. The Doctor here, Harris,[1] spoke once to Christina indicating that he thinks the brain not right — *physically* not right: I greatly fear there may be some truth in this. *Besides* the old matters of numbness in arm etc., I find Gabriel now suffers in 3 ways — 1.

painful heat and drawing sensation in the face (it is not hot to the touch); 2. fits of vomiting; 3. eyesight so bad as to be practically gone for reading, writing, etc. *Why* all this happens is a separate question. It may be (Harris thinks it is) that he is not really physically incapable of moving the arm etc.: but, if a man goes on for months supposing himself incapable, and if he fails to move the arm when he tries, it comes practically to much the same as if he were physically incapable. Harris says emphatically that the case is not one of paralysis. In spirits I find Gabriel of course low, but not so painfully gloomy as he has been at times: he talks with perfect good sense, and listened to Christina reading a novel until he fell asleep — say 40 minutes sleep. All this was in the drawing-room.

As to chloral etc., Caine says: No chloral, no whiskey or spirits, no wine. Morphia only such small doses — almost illusory — as Marshall orders. Milk is Gabriel's beverage. The water here seems very chalky — I don't know however that it is considered unhealthy.

Gabriel did some painting when first he came down here — not any of late — and he has done that grotesque ballad,[2] and done something (I know not what) with a prose tale.[3] He never leaves the house. I asked him yesterday whether he could walk out a little today supported by Caine and by me. He says not; but might *possibly* by an exertion get into and out of a carriage for a drive. I think he fancies himself, in this as in other respects, more incapable than he is — in the absolute sense.

I grieve to say therefore that on the whole I must give a bad account of Gabriel. I see no *present* expectation of his doing anything professionally, or rallying in health and energy.

My mother and Christina are well enough. Saddened and anxious of course, but not so as to make their company different from what it habitually is. Their love to you and Olive and your father and Emma.

Here is a a newspaper paragraph of a somewhat serious kind. I suppose you know all about it, but have thought well to send it on. It comes from the *St. James's Gazette* of yesterday.[4]

Who do you think is married? Miss Trelawny. Christina saw it announced somewhere. She has married at Florence a Mr. Call, Civil Engineer.

I shall be at home tonight, I suppose, by 10.30 or so: not before.

I regretted to see in the paper the other day the death of Dora Greenwell — a poetess of some true grace and feeling known to me a little, and rather more to Christina. She was a great invalid.

Christina tells me that Scotus is confined to the house these few days, and attended by a medical man — having somehow hurt his leg. It is not a grave affair.

All love, dearest,
W. M. R.

The Bungalow is a very comfortable house, but not a sort of palace for bloated oligarchs. Its being all one floor is a particular godsend to all 3 — Gabriel, my mother, and Christina. Caine sends his best regards to you and all.

I have my quarter month's salary in my pocket. Will see about that and the Wolverhampton cheque when I am settled at home.

MS: AP.

1. James Smith Harris, medical officer for the Minster district (*Churchill's Medical Directory*). *Isle of Thanet Directory* (1883-84) lists him as surgeon, Station Road, Birchington.
2. *Jan Van Hunks*.
3. *St. Agnes of Intercession*.
4. 1 April 1882, p. 8: a report of a threat by Fenians that "at or about Easter an attempt would be made to blow up the Manchester Town Hall."

327. TO LUCY ROSSETTI

Somerset House,
3 April [1882],
11.15

Dearie Lu,

Yours of yesterday received. I did not receive any at Birchington — which is I suppose correct.

Rowley's head was partly used for the Dying Dane,[1] was it not? I hardly remember whether or not any suggestion of the likeness of the head to Nolly's was ever made to me before. I dare say there may be *something* in it.

Of course I spent the whole of yesterday at Birchington; leaving the house about 6.50, and reaching our home about 10.30 — when Matilda[2] informed me that the children had been quite well. If I were to tell you every detail of my day at Birchington, I should weary myself with a long and far from cheerful letter. Gabriel sent you (as soon as I saw him in the morning) his "warm affection," and made more than one remark showing how sincere is his regard for you. I am sorry to say it proves to be *not* quite true that Gabriel takes no wine at all; for he had taken some before I saw him in the morning, and had then vomited it up. Leyland came in from Ramsgate in the afternoon, and sat with him and me some couple of hours: very friendly.

Not long after Leyland had left, Gabriel suddenly said that he felt an oppression of breathing, and got Caine to fetch in the Dr., Harris — who shortly came, and paid a good deal of attention to Gabriel's various statements. He is a man about 40, fully equal, I should suppose, to the average of sound country Doctors. I was present all the time, and then got a longish tête-à-tête with Harris. It was a painful one. I at once asked him whether he considers the seat of disease to be the brain, and he replied Yes. He considers there is some degree of softening of the brain, consequent on the abuse of chloral, accompanied as it always was with whiskey. All the individual symptoms — loss of power in arm and leg, loss of sight, gout in toe, etc. etc. — are delusions produced by the faulty condition of the brain. The constipation — which does not I think give any great trouble now — ought to be carefully and regularly attended to, and Harris will do his best for this (he says Gabriel doesn't always take the doses prescribed); the lungs are sound, and the heart both sound and strong. The great thing, he says, would be to get Gabriel occupied: I of course agree, but there lies the difficulty. He thinks the

Birchington life too secluded, and that Gabriel would be more advantageously placed in a Sanatorium at Malvern or some such place: on my explaining however about Gabriel's horror of strangers etc. (I entered frankly into many details of past stages of the illness) Harris admitted this to be a serious obstacle. He says (and of course one knows it too well) that the natural course of softening of the brain is to weaken the mental powers progressively: at the same time he thinks it quite possible that Gabriel may again do some good intellectual work.

I need not enlarge upon the many distressing reflections arising out of these statements: they are not *necessarily* correct, but I think they are very likely to be founded in truth. I propose to see Marshall again with reference to them pretty soon.

Harris observed that Gabriel's legs are very deficient in muscle, accounting up to a certain point for his weakness (which is now most extreme indeed) in walking. When I explained how much Gabriel had shut himself up for years, he said that explained the want of muscle. I saw Gabriel's bare legs in the morning: they may be called slim, but not emaciated. The calves (or leg muscles) are no doubt flabby.

Gabriel is not so *miserable* as he has been at times: not more so than naturally arises from his present actual and supposed condition. His conversation is entirely reasonable, and he responds to whatever is stated, but of course not with his natural amount of animation.

I came home in the dark, rather cold — for the weather has taken a turn for the worse since the early afternoon of yesterday. Had a comfortable meal provided by Matilda. She, not Mathilde,[3] had accompanied Arthur to the Zoological Gardens on that afternoon.

This morning all the kiddies seem well. The twins look as if a little fresh air would benefit them: but Nurse (no doubt rightly) has not given them any as yet, and today could not certainly be selected for beginning such a process.

A letter from Mathilde reached me this morning. I don't understand that she is *very* ill now, but her state requires her to be very careful.

My mother and Christina send you and Olive much love. Arthur is pleased with the little Selection of Poems for Children[4] which Christina sent him: I brought him also a bit of chalk picked up by me on the shore (which is strewn solely with chalk-lumps when the tide is high) at Birchington, and for Coodle[5] a scrap of seaweed.

Yours, dearest, in woe as in weal,
W. M. R.

About the wine-drinking, I quite infer that it is in quantity small, and only conceded to Gabriel's importunities. Dr. Harris objects to it, and the Nurse resists up to that point where resistance becomes a serious difficulty. I have no reason to think that there is *any* spirit-drinking. Gabriel has fortunately a good deal of cash still in hand, and he speaks highly of the scrupulous care with which his money-matters are managed both by Caine and by the Nurse.

MS: AP.

1. *The Expulsion of the Danes from Manchester.*
2. A servant.
3. Blind.
4. Not identified.
5. Helen.

328. TO LUCY ROSSETTI

Somerset House,
5 April [1882],
10½

Dearest Lu,

Your note received this morning is sorrowful, and no wonder. But it is no use regretting that something which is happening or has happened does happen: one must exert oneself to meet it as best one may for others and for oneself, and stand (as Dante says) "tetragono ai colpi di ventura."[1]

The Fenian affair[2] — though it hardly seems possible to me that the statements on the subject should be merely fictitious — should not I think *seriously* trouble you. For yourself and Olive the worst that could happen would be to remain comfortably in the Crumpsall house, without going to the Townhall. For your papa and Emma — it seems in the first place highly improbable that, now the Police are aroused, the Fenians could do anything at all: but even if they did the chance of injury to anyone you are interested in, or to the pictures, is remote indeed. I can truly say that, were I on the spot — Crumpsall or Townhall — I should feel, from the personal point of view, absolutely indifferent to the whole affair.

What you say about your papa's affairs being discouraging and himself neglected pains me: of course I don't at present understand what exactly is referred to. It is too true that men of genius in the fine arts are not precisely understood by the typical "Manchester man": they must I suppose make up their minds to do without his homage.

I think the part of the Danes picture[3] where the head of the litter-borne chief comes is the very part which was not painted when I saw the work in February 1881: therefore I have not had an opportunity of realizing to myself the resemblance to Nolly.

Nurse considers the twins all right — appetite quite satisfactory. Michael is probably getting on towards having a new tooth. Weather does not yet admit of twins going out. Arthur and Helen do so, and seem quite well. Your papa will have received a little of their nonsense in the form of a letter. Arthur has begun his Copybook No. 2 (i.e., one that was already half filled in by Olive). He did not realize to himself exactly what he was intended to do with it in detail, but I think I have now set him right.

I was pleased with little Ol's letter, and will *sometime* send her another of mine. The handwriting of hers (not to speak of other points) is much less imperfect than in that missive to Mary: how was the thing done?

Yesterday I sent 1/- postage stamps for the Bradlaugh[4] Fund named in enclosed newspaper paragraph. Also paid in some money to the Bank: our little fund there now stands at £322.

After I had written to you yesterday I made up my mind to write (in first instance) to Marshall, and to lose no time about it: so on leaving Somerset House I posted him a longish letter. I explained what had come under my observation at Birchington, and what Dr. Harris had said to me: and I asked Marshall whether he agrees in the view of the case taken by Harris; also whether he would in any way object to our calling in an eminent physician to see Gabriel, and if not whether Andrew Clarke[5] seems to him a suitable man; or who else. Of course I said I would call and speak to Marshall, were he to appoint an hour. I await his reply on the main point with anxiety — but, I am happy to say, without a sense of agitation.

Watts called on me at Somerset House to know what I could say about Gabriel. He was distressed at it, having himself been rather less unhopefully inclined: he does not attach much importance to the opinion of Dr. Harris, as such. He spoke with very high approbation of my little article on Longfellow,[6] and says Swinburne shares this opinion, and seemingly MacColl. Watts himself has recently been doing something which offers well for a public and popular success — a series of sonnets on Shakespeare's plays, a sonnet to each play.[7] I urged him to publish as soon as convenient: he doesn't seem to have at present any *definite* views as to this. Swinburne, following Watts, is also doing a set of sonnets applicable to the drama — i.e., on the various Dramatists.[8]

I told you some days ago that Gill was expected to look in at the children: he did not come.

I hardly know what that Oxford examination-affair[9] will come to. It seems to me that, in order to draw up the examination-papers, I ought myself to be reading up certain books with some diligence: but no one writes to set me *au fait*, though I particularly invited some such communication from my co-examiner. I suppose the affair will adjust itself in time, but it does not satisfy me at present.

Yours, dearest, with love and kisses,
W. M. R.

MS: AP.

1. *Paradiso*, 17:24.
2. See Letter 326, Note 4.
3. *The Expulsion of the Danes from Manchester*.
4. Charles Bradlaugh (1833-91), politician and advocate of free thought, founder and proprietor of the *National Reformer*. As a freethinker Bradlaugh was prevented from taking his seat in the House of Commons, to which he was first elected in 1880. He was finally permitted to take the oath in 1885, by which time he had been re-elected four times for Northampton.
5. At this date he was president of the Medical Society of London.
6. Obituary notice, *Athenaeum*, 1 April 1882, p. 412.
7. Not identified.
8. *Sonnets on English Dramatic Poets*, published in *Tristram of Lyonesse and Other Poems*.
9. MS. Diary, 22 February 1882: "Wrote accepting the proposal lately made to me that I should act as junior examiner for a scholarship etc. in the Taylorian Institution Oxford — the subject being Italian Language and Literature. I hardly know how far I may be able to acquit myself well in this

novel function.'' The invitation came from Edward Moore (1835-1919), Dante scholar and principal of St. Edmund Hall.

329. TO LUCY ROSSETTI

56 Euston Square,
6 April [1882],
9½ p.m.

Dearest Dear — in whom I take refuge in all my troubles — This is my 3rd letter today. Nothing has happened except that I have just received a second telegram from Christina thus — it was handed in at Birchington at 8.45: "We are still waiting for Doctor — I answer your telegram to him also — Nurse reckons Gabriel somewhat revived — You and Marshall do well to come tomorrow." This shows a very melancholy state of things, which must have kept my mother and Christina in acute distress — viz.: that the Doctor did not come for hours, and was even then not arrived — May have been very bad also for Gabriel.

I have sent round Matilda to Marshall with a copy of the telegram, and a note saying I will be at the station 7.40 a.m. tomorrow, and shall expect to see him there — This is what we had fixed.

I took a look at kiddies while I was packing my bag — towards 7¾. All peacefully sleeping, except Mary, who was crying a little (for Nurse, said Matilda, who was there). Shall like to see the little dears again — but what will have happened meanwhile who shall say.

It is curious that Gabriel has just written 2 sonnets[1] (Watts showed me them) for that design of his, Youth, Manhood and Old Age consulting the Sphinx — whose secret will perhaps be very soon told to himself. They are *very fine* sonnets, especially the first: certainly it is difficult to suppose that the writer of them has anything like softening of the brain.

Your own
W. M. R.

I know how truly your dear papa will feel this impending calamity. On reflection I shall post a note to Watts along with this.

MS: AP.

1. *The Question (For a design)*, DW, 4:1952-53. The design (Surtees 241) was called *The Sphinx*.

330. TO LUCY ROSSETTI

Birchington,
7 April [1882],
2½ p.m.

Sweet Lu,

I am here, and find Gabriel alive — He is in bed, conscious, reasonable, and no apparent defect of hearing — His face has an ominous look, and his articulation is lax and imperfect in a marked degree — The eyes look strange but I don't know that his sight is worse than on Sunday: Mamma and Christina as well as can be supposed. Gabriel — I am told — was much *more* prostrate parts of yesterday even than now: I have no expectation of his mastering his illness or lingering long, but I don't see particularly but that he may live some few days.

You will appreciate the feeling with which I write this — though I feel no violent agitation.

Watts is here — came down with me by train of 9 a.m. this morning — reached here not before 1. This is the *Sunday* (for Good Friday) train. Marshall and I had misapprehended about trains — or it turned out after all Marshall could not come down *at all* today, as it would have held him from early morning till late at night, and other engagements positively prevented this. He is to be expected here tomorrow (Saturday).

I have no heart for other matters now. Received with thankfulness your letter of yesterday delivered just before I started from Endsleigh Gardens. Kids were well when I left. Arthur could enter a little into what I said to him about Gabriel.

Your

W. M. R.

MS: AP.

331. TO LUCY ROSSETTI

Birchington,
8 April [1882],
9 a.m.

Sweetest dear Lucy,

Dear Gabriel is still dying — not dead. Dr. Harris tells me this morning that he rather than otherwise expects Gabriel to last out the day: he will probably become gradually unconscious, and so yield up his life. No pretence of course is made as to precise accuracy in detail of time. I am quite convinced in my own mind that the end is not much less near than this. Gabriel is conscious, reasonable, patient, uncaptious, exceedingly weak; suffering uneasiness and discomfort but I infer not what could be called positive pain. Marshall may be expected here soon. We all bear up well — my mother *very* well, considering. A letter of yours for her arrived this morning, but I don't know as yet further about it.

As it seemed necessary to provide early for contingencies, Watts got Gabriel last evening to draw a cheque for me for £300, so that I may be able to meet out of his funds some of the expenses that will first become necessary. Harris had to witness his feeble signature, and he (Harris) then raised a question about a will. I mean to cut any such details short here, but should explain to you this much. Gabriel's intention had been to make no will, and so leave his property to go half to my mother, and half between Christina and myself. It now appeared however that he had at some time made a will leaving all to Lizzie. I raised the question whether possibly under this will, not known to be destroyed, the Siddall family might not become universal legatee. This *apparently* would not be so, but Watts couldn't say with certainty. So it was resolved that Gabriel ought to sign a revocation of any existing will, and this project of revocation (without my prompting, and only partly with my liking) grows into an intention of making a new will, which will (I understand in a general way) make Christina and me (or else my mother and me) the legatees of the bulk of the property in equal halves. Debts and liabilities are no doubt very large — as for instance Valpy's unsatisfied claim.[1] It appears to me however that in the course of years the copyrights — if nothing else remains — ought to be valuable.

Bronchial wheezing — for the pulmonar region as well as the kidneys have lately been affected — is now Gabriel's chief trouble. He eats one might say no solid food: brandy and water (all small quantities) is ordered by Harris, but Gabriel dislikes and as far as possible avoids it. He I am sure feels that he is dying: does not talk about it, and certainly shows no agitation or dread regarding it.

Yours in love
W. M. R.

I hardly know whether I told you yesterday that Watts came down with me. He is still here — and Leyland came yesterday, and will return today.

I have not received any letter of yours later than the one dated 6 April.

MS: AP.

1. See Letter 347, Note 2.

332. TO LUCY ROSSETTI

Birchington,
8 April [1882],
8.15 p.m.

Dearie Lu,

Marshall arrived here about 3, along with Dr. Harris — Marshall considers of course that Gabriel looks alarmingly ill: but, after careful examination of him, preceded and followed by consultation with Harris, he does not regard the case as desperate. He considers that the predominant feature of the illness at the *present* moment is connected with the kidney-affection: i.e., that the kidney does not deal as it ought with the urea, which consequently poisons the blood, instead of passing out of the system in the natural way: in short, there is uraemia, or blood-poisoning by urea which, if unchecked, will rapidly terminate Gabriel's life. But Marshall says it *can* be checked in a great number of cases, and he has applied himself to a special system of sodiofics, diuretics, etc., to produce this result with Gabriel. As yet we cannot speak distinctly of the result. Marshall affirms — and my eyes confirm it — that the complexion has markedly improved, which would be a natural sequel of a diminution of uraemia. Gabriel has slept or drowsed most of today, especially since Marshall's arrival: his wheezing is decidedly less bad than yesterday, and to my eyes his features less pinched. Beyond this I don't know much that I could say. Marshall does not believe in softening of the brain for Gabriel, rightly so called: sees not one of its marked symptoms manifestly present. Dr. Graves's kidney-disease — of which this malady of Gabriel's is a species — is a fatal disease, yet may allow of a man's living in moderate comfort even a score or so of years. Marshall missed his train back to London, so he spends the night here — more to our satisfaction perhaps than to his annoyance.

Shields also has come down — much unstrung: has not yet been allowed to see Gabriel.

You will have received my telegram delivered in Birchington this evening — It had appeared to me that, if there were no prospect of my being moderately well resettled in London within a few days to come, you would probably judge it best to return thither. Just at present however there appears to be that degree of uncertainty as to the probabilities affecting Gabriel and myself which would I think suggest your remaining at Crumpsall till we see our expectations rather clearer. I should be exceedingly reluctant to see your stay at Crumpsall abridged, unless this course becomes truly necessary.

Your father most likely *cannot* come, and there's an end. We all know that he would if he reasonably could.

We were all nerved up to endure what seemed the closely impending calamity. Now that a *gleam* of better hope appears, we are perhaps rather unreasonably lightened in heart. Tomorrow will probably show some clear indication in case the hope is destined to be fallacious.

I wrote today to Somerset House taking 3 weeks leave beginning on Tuesday. Thus feel free to act either way as needed.

With entire love,

Your
William

9 p.m. Marshall re-enters this (dining) room from Gabriel's, saying that an unmistakable improvement may be announced.

MS: AP.

333. TO LUCY ROSSETTI

Birchington,
9 April [1882],
8½ p.m.

Dearest Lu,

This will be a short letter — I posted another this morning, but it was written last night. Marshall left us this morning — apparently not dissatisfied with Gabriel's condition: but of course this doesn't mean *much* in the way of encouragement. My own impression through the course of today is that Gabriel is not *materially* better. His face is certainly a less bad colour, his wheezing not so bad as on Friday; he has a little increased in animation, showing more of his ordinary shortness of temper etc. However I fear he is not in any marked degree on the road to recovery. I don't so much expect an almost immediate termination of his life, and this — I must in truth and sorrow say — is the limit of my own view of the improvement. He is more melancholy and less merely passive.

Watts has caught a bad chest attack, which will I think keep him here tomorrow at least. Shields also will stay tomorrow.

Love from my mother, and sister.

Dearest Lucy, Your own
W. M. R.

A registered letter in which Nurse sent me £20 that I asked for has reached me. Please tell her so whenever you have occasion to write her: Love to dear Ol — and your papa and Emma.

MS: AP.

334. TO FRANCIS HUEFFER

Westcliff Bungalow,
Birchington-on-Sea,
10 April 1882

Dear Hueffer,

This black envelope will perhaps partly tell you its tale. My dear Gabriel died yesterday about 9½ p.m. You may imagine the state of feeling of myself and my mother and sister — not to speak of Lucy, Shields, Watts, and Caine, all of them at present in the house. The *final* form that the disease took was something in the nature of Bright's kidney-disease. Gabriel was *very* prostrate when I reached here early on Friday. Marshall saw him on Saturday — Sunday, and prescribed some active measures. There was *some* improvement, but nothing serious. So the matter continued until about 9¼ when two loud cries from Gabriel ushered in a convulsive fit: he died unconscious in a few minutes.

The funeral will be here at Birchington, apparently on Friday towards 2. Would you and Cathy see fit and find it manageable to come? Brown I fear cannot. The trains are from Victoria — to Birchington, or at some hours better Westgate, and thence 2 miles or so (by carriage or otherwise) back to Birchington.

I *particularly* wish that no public notice should be taken of Gabriel's death until the day — Friday next — when the funeral will take place, and the *Athenaeum* be published. This is for reasons more substantial than a deference to Watts's friendship.[1] You will I know oblige me by abstention from print up to the Friday, and by general reticence. Some few other friends will be invited to the funeral, but of course some refusals will ensue owing to the distance.[2]

I could not at present say more.

Your
W. M. Rossetti

MS: Princeton.

1. WMR to Hueffer, 11 April [1882]: "You might justly blame me if I did not write you these few lines — though their subject-matter may seem somewhat sordid under present circumstances. The reason for asking you yesterday not to give publicity to Gabriel's death was this. Having regard to his highly precarious condition, he signed on Friday a cheque for £300 to me, to meet impending demands and contingencies on his account. At this holiday-time the money could have been sent to me from the Union Bank so as to reach me at Birchington on Tuesday (today) but not earlier. Watts thinks it probable that the Bank if aware of Gabriel's death would not pay the money at all pending probate of will etc. and this would be a somewhat serious embarrassment. As to the Bank the upshot remains as yet unknown. But as the *Globe* of this week [11 April, p. 4] publishes Gabriel's death

414

there can be no reason for silence in other papers — and the limit (Friday next, the day of the funeral, and of the appearance of next *Athenaeum*) is now no consequence'' (Leeds; copy).

2. For a list of those who attended, see *FLM*, 1:401. Among those invited (list in AP) who did not come were Burne-Jones, WBS, Dunn, Swinburne, Marshall, Tebbs, and L. R. Valpy.

335. TO WILLIAM BELL SCOTT

Westcliff Bungalow,
Birchington-on-Sea,
10 April [1882]

Dear Scott,

Caine has shown me your telegram. It is too true that we have lost Gabriel: he died about 9½ p.m. yesterday. The immediate cause of death is said to be uraemic poisoning — or as we might say functional derangement of the kidneys, leading to a bad state of the blood. I was here Saturday and Sunday 1 and 2 April, and formed a bad opinion of his condition: then upon a telegram from Christina returned here on Good Friday, when he was fatally sinking. Up to (say) 9¼ last night he was not worse than on my arrival: then the blood-poisoning (so the Doctor says) went to the brain: Gabriel cried out twice, and immediately fell into a sort of convulsive lethargy, and to all appearance expired unconscious and unsuffering.

Down here are my mother, Christina, Caine, Watts, and Shields, with myself.

For more reasons than one we intend to have the funeral here[1] — Friday is appointed and will I believe be adhered to. Would it be consistent with your feelings and otherwise manageable to attend? If so, we shall like to see you. I shall be writing to a few other intimates to same effect.

The trains, you may be aware, are from Victoria Station: to Birchington is best, but in some instances it answers better to go to Westgate and thence back to Birchington, say 2 miles. You would look into the details for yourself. I was sorry to learn Saturday week that you have had some accident to a leg — hope this may not (of itself) be sufficient to prevent your coming.

Warm regards to Letitia and Miss Boyd.

Your old friend
W. M. Rossetti

Funeral probably towards 2 p.m.: but details hereafter.

Marshall was here Saturday afternoon to Sunday morning.

MS: Princeton.

1. See Letter 334, Note 1. WMR would also have considered DGR's horror of the family grave in Highgate Cemetery from which Lizzie had been exhumed.

336. TO WILLIAM BELL SCOTT

Westcliff Bungalow,
Birchington-on-Sea,
13 April [1882]

Dear Scott,

We are here — Lucy included — in that state of hushed sorrowfulness, tempered in every instance (I am able to say) by composure and mutual helpfulness, which you can imagine — waiting for the funeral tomorrow. In all our minds there is no doubt a real sense of relief which one does not talk of much, but which one is not at all ashamed of — namely the feeling that it really was an alternative between loss of life and gradually increasing and finally perhaps total loss of working power, perhaps even of deforce of mind — and that the loss of life is ten-thousand times the less painful and miserable branch of the alternative. He looks in death most serene and restful, and so natural as to suggest sleep more than death: I see no alteration up to this morning. On Monday I got the face and hand moulded[1] — a thing which ought not to be omitted for men of a certain degree of mark.

We are *greatly* concerned to hear of the wound in your leg. I strongly think it ought to be heedfully attended to now — even to the neglect, if so it must be, of South Kensington work:[2] nor do I suppose you ought at all to think of coming here tomorrow. Am the more obliged for your very friendly and I fear painful effort in going round to 16 Cheyne Walk.[3] I was there with Lucy on Tuesday evening, and got Dunn (who arrived meanwhile) to undertake custodianship of the house. We paid off the 2 servants, who would leave I suppose on Saturday or so.

Much as there would be to say, I hardly know what else to add just now.

Yours in old affection,

W. M. Rossetti

It is strange that Gabriel's last (I suppose *last*) writing was a brace of sonnets on that design of his — Questioning the Sphinx:[4] whom *he* has now learned the secret of. They are truly fine sonnets — I see no mental infirmity in them. Written (say) yesterday fortnight. I have seen this morning Letitia's most friendly and heart-warm letter to Christina.

MS: Princeton.

1. By D. Brucciani & Co., Galleria delle Belle Arti, 40 Great Russell Street.
2. WBS was contributing to the mural decoration at the South Kensington Museum.
3. WBS to WMR, 11 April 1882: "Yesterday on receiving the telegram, Dunn being here at its arrival, I went with him to 16 Cheyne Walk and we together put away carefully all the documents and sketches, etc. sealing up a number of drawers and receptacles, in case of anyone in your absence touching them. You may make your mind easy on the safety of everything I think" (AP).
4. See Letter 329.

337. TO FANNY CORNFORTH

Birchington-on-Sea,
14 April [1882]

Dear Madam,

Your letter of the 12th[1] only reached me this morning about 9. The coffin had been closed last evening, and the funeral takes place early this afternoon — there is nothing further to be done.

Faithfully yours,
W. M. Rossetti

MS: Delaware Art Museum. Published: Baum p. 116.

1. "Dear Sir / I would like to see your brother once more and beg of you, in the event of your granting my wish, to kindly let me know through the bearer where, and at what time, I may come. / Yours Truly / S. Schott" (AP).

338. TO THE EDITOR OF THE *ATHENAEUM*   5 Endsleigh Gardens, 26 April 1882

I beg leave to advert to a paragraph which appeared in the *Athenaeum* of April 22nd,[1] saying that I hope to organize a large exhibition of the works of my brother Dante Rossetti. This project was seriously entertained; but, as the Royal Academy have handsomely welcomed a scheme proposed from another quarter,[2] viz., the exhibition of a selection of my brother's works along with the next collection of old masters, &c., at Burlington House, I have now relinquished my own plan. I am the more anxious to say this at once, as some paragraphs published on the subject elsewhere than in the *Athenaeum*[3] were highly incorrect in themselves, and, whatever may have been professed, were wholly unauthorized by me.

W. M. Rossetti

Text: *Athenaeum*, 29 April 1882, p. 546.

1. P. 516.
2. Leyland suggested the exhibition to the R.A., and Leighton as president undertook the organization (see Letters 351, 355). Eighty-four works were shown. MS. Diary, 4 January 1883: "Went for the 3rd time to the exhibition.... An extension of space has been conceded to Gabriel's works, which are rearranged accordingly, in deference to some degree of general outcry in which Hueffer, by an article in the *Times* [rptd. *Italian and Other Studies* (1883), esp. pp. 85-86], took a leading part. The collection seems to be decidedly attractive to the public: the casual remarks which I hear in the room evidence pleasure and interest, without anything like favouring partisanship or *parti pris*. I wrote to Stephens ... expressing the opinion that Leighton personally had not endeavoured to damage Gabriel's works by mishanging." 11 January: "Went again to the R.A. Exhibition. Day so dark that pictures could hardly be seen at all, and gas not lit. Gabriel's rooms were far better filled than the others. I wrote — to send to Leighton — a few notes upon errors etc. in the Catalogue." 12 January: "I sent to Leighton ... a letter in which I referred to the complaints which have been freely made as to the hanging of Gabriel's pictures ... but added that I believe he himself acted throughout fairly and handsomely." 10 March: "Went to the closing scene at the Exhibition.... The crowd today was really considerable — approaching to a thronged day at the ordinary annual Exhibition, and 2 or 3 times (as usual) as many persons in Gabriel's rooms as in any other."
   Concurrently with the R.A. Exhibition, the Burlington Fine Arts Club showed 153 of DGR's works. MS. Diary, 13 December 1882, expressed doubts about "the policy of this move," but he agreed to lend six works. 13 January 1883: "Lucy and I attended the opening of the exhibition ... at the Burlington Club — a very interesting display, well calculated to maintain and enhance his reputation." 18 January: "I wrote some corrections, which I will send to Tebbs, for the Catalogue of the Burlington Club." 17 March: "This being announced as the day for closing the Burlington Club Exhibition ... I went round there, and found the rooms crammed — I should suppose something like 200 people in the very restricted space." Several proposals for combining the two exhibitions at the close of the Burlington show are noted in MS. Diary, but they came to nothing.
3. See Letter 339, Note 3.

417

339. TO LUCY ROSSETTI

Somerset House,
27 April [1882],
11½

Dearest Lu,

I have received your letter of yesterday. Arthur, who brought it to me in bed, was grievously disappointed to find it did not contain any direct response to his epistle of Tuesday.

Gill called yesterday about 3. He considers that the twins are going on correctly, that their state of health raises no anxiety, and that you ought decidedly not to come home on their account earlier than the time which suits yourself. They went on very fairly yesterday, and this morning Nurse tells me there has not been any further vomiting.

Am very sorry to hear of your papa's gout.

Watts called on me yesterday: was surprised to hear that a reply which he sent to your father had not reached him by the time, Tuesday morning, that I left Manchester. He told me that he and Shields had called at Agnew's. They found Agnew pledged to send to the Royal Academy a picture by Gabriel belonging to himself,[1] and he was in active communication with some Academician about the proposed Burlington House exhibition. Of course therefore Agnew could not embark upon a separate exhibition on his own account, or on mine. Watts approved (on a cursory inspection) the circular letter I had proposed to send to owners of pictures: but, taking into consideration the failure with Agnew, he questioned how far we might be successful in proceeding with our scheme; and, when I told him that your father had expressed a strong opinion that *no* exhibition (apart from some project of engraving or the like) offers a reasonable prospect of money-profits, he said that that decided his views, and he would advise to drop the scheme of an exhibition of our own. This view was on the whole my own also: so I wrote a short note to the *Athenaeum*[2] to say as much, and mean now to leave the field clear for the R.A. — not *entirely* pleased with that upshot by any means, but thinking it on the whole the right decision.

That silly and exasperating paragraph about an exhibition of our own,[3] which I attributed to Caine, *is* Caine's: Watts had ascertained this, and Caine has now written to me acknowledging it. Curious that any man should be at once so officious and so blundering. In my letter to *Athenaeum* I have used some expressions which Caine will not like (his paragraph was in the *Academy*): beyond this, I shall think no more of the affair — for no doubt he had no evil *intention*.

I hope you no longer feel that odd sensation in your hand. Have told the servants you will be back on Saturday afternoon.

I handed to Watts the letter from Gambart — and another such letter addressed to Deschamps,[4] which Deschamps sent on to me. Watts will attend to the matter.

Howell has sent for you a large photograph of his daughter[5] — whose resemblance appears to be to her mother chiefly.

I was a good deal occupied last evening in addressing the envelopes for those memorial cards. The job is not nearly finished yet. Also wrote a sonnet — Third French Republic.[6]

Shall call today on my mother — her birthday.

Yours, sweetest Lu,
W. M. R.

You see I am now back at Somerset House.

MS: AP.

1. Not identified.
2. Letter 338.
3. "We are authorized to state that the family and friends of the late Dante Rossetti are concerned and grieved at what they cannot but think the inconsiderate haste which has been displayed in certain quarters to announce forthcoming exhibitions of the painter's works. They desire it to be known, first, that all pictures painted by Rossetti, except the one belonging to the city of Liverpool, were sold under copyright restrictions which cover control of exhibition; next, that the holders of the important works positively decline to lend their pictures, except to the executor of the estate; and last, that they cannot countenance the exhibition of the lesser works to the exclusion of the greater ones on which Rossetti's fame must finally rest. They appeal to owners everywhere to help them (and prevent complications) by withholding from all applicants promises of loan at the present stage" (*Academy*, 22 April 1882, pp. 292-93). Caine explained to WMR on 26 April 1882 that the editor of the *Academy* had called upon him and "alluded to the 'indecent' haste made to announce an exhibition ... and asked if the family sanctioned such an unseemly step. I said you were strongly opposed to it and had authorized the *Times* to say so. I told him then what your brother had so frequently said as to his reservations, whereupon he asked me to write such another paragraph for them as had appeared in the *Times*. I did so, adding something, it is true." (The *Times* had merely reported that they had been "asked to state ... that neither the family nor the principal owners had been consulted when the announcement was made, and without their consent any exhibition ... would be extremely defective," 15 April 1882, p. 8.) On 29 April Caine wrote again to complain that WMR's statement would prove "more damaging far to me than mine has proved to you. You will, dear Rossetti, realize at once *how* damaging the hard phrasing of your last clause is when you reflect that as far as the Editor of the *Academy* goes, it must cast a doubt upon every innocent scrap I may in future write" (BL).
4. Charles W. Deschamps was secretary to the Parisian dealer, Paul Durand-Ruel, at his London branch, 168 New Bond Street, where from 1870 to 1875 Durand-Ruel organized exhibitions of the Society of French Artists. In 1876 Deschamps renamed the gallery after himself (D. Farr, *English Art, 1870-1940* [1978], p. 24).
5. Rosalind Blanche Catherine (b. 1877). Whistler was her godfather, but neither Mrs. Angeli nor Cline has uncovered many other facts about her. WMR's noting her resemblance to Kitty is further evidence that Violet Hunt was wrong in claiming that she was the daughter of Howell's mistress, Alice Chambers. See Cline, pp. 20, 27-29.
6. *The Third Republic* (*Democratic Sonnets*, 1).

340. TO CHARLES AUGUSTUS HOWELL

5 Endsleigh Gardens,
30 April 1882

Dear Howell,

Thanks for your friendly letter. Watts and I have had a talk about your proposal to meet us at Cheyne Walk. He thinks, and so do I, that any such step should be postponed until after the will is proved. When that is done it might very likely be to my advantage to act on your proposal. I shall particularly look out for ready money for whatever has to be sold.

I have a cast of Gabriel's head and hand. A fresh mould has to be taken from the cast before any recasts can be obtained for the use of friends. At present the moulder is seeing about having this done. When I get the new moulds, I shall have a few recasts done at my own expense for the family etc., and could besides authorize recasts to be made for those who wish to obtain them. Shall bear your wish in mind.

Thank you, Lucy and I are well — also the children more or less. As you "want to come and see them," I will — however awkward for myself and perhaps not kindly taken by you — say that I had rather not renew any visiting or family intimacy between your house and mine. Our intimacy was severed some years ago by circumstances in which I was not personally concerned, and I think we had better leave it on that footing: Mutual happiness in any business-relations which may be advantageous to both of us, without renewal of familiar visiting etc.

Thanks for the portrait of your sweet-looking little girl. Lucy was still at her father's when it came.

Madox Brown's address to write to is — Townhall, Manchester. Shields's, 7 Lodge Place, St. John's Wood, N.W. — (F. J. Shields).

Yours very truly,
W. M. Rossetti

MS: BL.

341. TO WILLIAM BELL SCOTT

5 Endsleigh Gardens,
24 May 1882

Dear Scotus,

Those casts[1] have delayed longer than I expected — why I know not. My belief is that *none* of the destined recipients has as yet received his copy.

The selecting of some object as memento should I take it be deferred till the will is proved — and this is not yet done. The convenient thing would apparently be to get together on one day all the persons named in Gabriel's will for selecting such mementoes, and they should make their selection in the order as named. But one need not be *rigid* about this.

Miss Boyd I have always regarded and regard as one of Gabriel's warmest friends: I know of many a kind act of hers towards him, and can believe in any number of others. But I don't well see how a person not named in the will can in this matter be set on the same footing as those who are named — viz.: (I speak from memory) yourself, my mother, Christina, Brown, Watts, Caine, Jones, Swinburne, myself.[2] *I* will however do what is fitting in relation to Miss Boyd, and will keep apart something for her which I will hand over.[3] Is there any *particular* thing she views with predilection? In any detail of this sort I exercise a reasonable discretion as Executor and joint-legatee.

Your affectionate
W. M. Rossetti

MS: Princeton.

1. See Letter 336, Note 1.
2. WBS added to the list the names of Valpy, Graham, and Leyland.
3. WBS to WMR, 23 May [1882]: "I want to say a word for a similar memorial to Alice Boyd. When I see you I shall inform you of an action of hers which gives her, I think, even a preference

over any of us as a kind friend to Gabriel" (Durham). On 26 August WBS replied to WMR explaining her "action" in cancelling a loan that Miss Losh had made to DGR (see *LPI*, p. 81; see also pp. 82-83).

342. TO FORD MADOX BROWN

5 Endsleigh Gardens,
7 June 1882

Dear Brown,

I have re-read your very kind and too self-abnegating letter, and will reply to its several points — tersely, but in the same spirit of affection as your own.

Lucy and I did not wish to have you and Emma with us for a week, but as long as you can conveniently stay.

I do approve of what you are doing:[1] i.e., I approve of your doing what you judge to be fit, without my being consulted beforehand or during the progress of the work, or having a voice as to the upshot.

Your continuing the work "really is desired by the parties concerned" — i.e., by Lucy and me. You mention a third, my mother. To her I have said nothing about the matter, and dare say I may not say anything. She would probably approve or be neutral, were she informed: at any rate I do not consider her preconsent to be needed.

£1.1 per half-day (I understand and wish this to mean £2.2 per day when the day's work is not greatly encroached upon) is less than I expected and like to pay. As you will not on any account alter it, I say no more. Whether you can force Lucy (contrary to my feeling) to accept £3.3 per week for board I don't well know: I shall not *assist* you in forcing her, and how loth she will be I well know.

Any advice you give me on *any* point — being advice stopping short of dictation and imperative direction — will be highly valued, seriously weighed, and very likely adopted.

Yesterday morning I wrote to Watts urging that sale of furniture etc. should be pushed on without delay. He called on me (without receiving the letter): and agreed with me, said he would at once bespeak the auctioneer, and set things going.[2]

With deep affection, dear Brown, and sincerest thanks,

Your

W. M. Rossetti

MS: AP.

1. FMB was preparing certain of the paintings and designs to be included in the sale at Christie's on 12 May 1883 of DGR's *Remaining Works*.
2. The sale was held at 16 Cheyne Walk on 5-7 July 1882 by T. G. Wharton, Martin and Co.

343. TO MONCURE CONWAY

5 Endsleigh Gardens,
9 June 1882

Dear Conway,

I really have not any idea whether the R.A. would be disposed to include in their exhibition works of the character of the two drawings by my brother that you possess:[1] I don't in fact know whether they mean to limit themselves to oil-pictures of leading importance or not. No sort of communication has been held with me on this matter, except that Leyland wrote me saying how he (without consulting me beforehand) had started the project with the R.A. and they had assented. I think your right course would be to address the R.A.

I suppose 1864 must have been the date when Gabriel *finished* that drawing from *Rosabell*. The first draft of the composition must I am sure have been quite as early as 1857 — I should say a few years earlier.

There is little I can say personally about Emerson. I jot down what occurs to me.

1. It must have been Woolner who first told me, say in 1847, that there was a pre-eminent American, Emerson, somewhat analogous to Carlyle: he gave me, or set me upon getting, the *Essays*.[2] These I read eagerly and with great admiration: and I think I can say that nothing ever exercised a more determining effect on my character than the essay "Self-Reliance." I was then very young — say barely 18 — and in that state of feeling when I was liable to be biased either (as thus) towards self-reliance or towards deference to the authority of my betters. Of all our set in those days there was none I think who so much relished Emerson as I did. Woolner was also a decided admirer — Gabriel too, and I should say Hunt, Stephens, and Hannay.

2. It was I think in 1848 that Emerson first came to England on a lecturing tour. I recollect going alone to Exeter Hall to hear his lecture (*Representative Men*) on "Napoleon."[3] Monckton Milnes (Lord Houghton) in the chair. I remember Emerson's upright figure, clear-cut physiognomy, a clear elocution (Americans generally strike English people as clear and *chiselled* in this respect), resolved self-possession. The hall must I think have been well filled — perhaps crowded. Many years afterwards — say 1870 — I was speaking about this matter to an Anglo-Greek friend of mine Dilberoglue,[4] a genial man of very superior intelligence. I found he had attended the same lecture by Emerson, or some other lecture[5] or lectures of the same series; and he had been much disappointed at (as he thought it) the *impersonal* demeanour of Emerson, his impassivity, total want of sympathetic vital relation towards his audience, etc. Dilberoglue went out of the lecture-room "chilled to the bone." No such impression was produced on myself. This is the only occasion on which I ever saw Emerson in any sort of way.

3. W. B. Scott would I think have known something of Emerson in those days, and also later.

4. In our set Emerson's first volume of *Poems*[6] (we must have read it as soon as published in England) was always admired much for its august seer-like qualities, notwithstanding some rustiness on the hinges of verse.

I would gladly say more now — or in response hereafter to any queries — but nothing further in particular occurs to my mind for the present.

Yours always,
W. M. Rossetti

MS: Columbia.

1. *The Gate of Memory* (Surtees 100), a watercolor "illustrating a scene based on W. Bell Scott's poem *Maryanne*" (originally entitled *Rosabell*); and *Head of Christ* (Surtees 109E), a watercolor study for *Mary Magdalene at the Door of Simon the Pharisee*. The former was included in the R.A. exhibition, the latter in the Burlington Club exhibition.
2. 1st ser., 1841; 2d ser., 1844.
3. "Napoleon; or, the Man of the World," published in *Representative Men* (1850).
4. Stauros Dilberoglue (1818-78), an "eminent Greek merchant in the city, and one of the Lieutenants of the City of London" (*Times*, 25 April 1878, p. 6).
5. "Plato; or, the Philosopher" (*Representative Men*).
6. Published in 1847.

344. TO FORD MADOX BROWN

Saturday,
[10 June 1882]

Dear Brown,

I am distressed at your letter, and reply as fast as possible.

I can't remember that you or anyone ever heretofore represented to me in a distinct way that you objected to sale in sale-room of the pictures worked on by you,[1] unless serious efforts for sale by private contract should first have been made. Now that I know of this objection I say at once that I will try to sell by private contract, and only if this fails will I sell in sale-room. I will take steps with Turner or Valpy,[2] Leathart, Rae,[3] Leyland, Craven,[4] or whoever you like: or if *you* prefer to take the steps I shall like it just as well or better.

I had no idea that you laid any great stress on Valpy's seeing and purchasing that magnolia-picture.[5] He *could* not see about it yesterday, having (according to his own letter) only 3 hours in London, and more than work enough at Chelsea for this brief time. To me it seems also that to raise *yesterday* any question about a picture touched since Gabriel's death would have been very dangerous — raising awkward questions whether the *Proserpine* might not also have been touched. But with any such considerations I had nothing practical to do: it was all an appointment between Valpy and Watts, and time admitted of nothing beyond a glance at what was exposed to view in Chelsea.

You say: "It seems that you and Watts yesterday settled that the pictures I am to do are to be reserved expressly for the sale next year." This is quite a mistake. Nothing of the sort was either settled or discussed. Knowing of no contrary views of yours, I *supposed* they would naturally go into said sale: now that you object I would keep them out of it if I can.

I should much regret if you were not to finish the pictures according to your previous intention: much more regret if you felt offended or aggrieved by anything I have done or am supposed to intend to do. Should gladly see you back here — and Emma when it suits her. I write abruptly and badly because in haste.

Your affectionate
W. M. Rossetti

MS: AP.

1. See Letter 342, Note 1.

2. See Letter 347, Note 2.
3. George Rae, banker and one of DGR's leading patrons.
4. Frederick W. Craven of Manchester, who owned paintings by both DGR and FMB.
5. Unfinished replica of *La Donna Della Finestra* (Surtees 255 R. 1). WMR included it in Christie's sale, where it was bought by the Birmingham Art Gallery.

345. TO FORD MADOX BROWN

5 Endsleigh Gardens,
13 June 1882

Dear Brown,

I am grieved to lose your company and co-operation[1] at so early a date: but, as you have come to the conclusion that your own interests would — or probably might — be damaged by continuing, I must submit.

As soon as your wishes were expressed to me on any particular point affecting your work, I gave immediate and explicit obedience. It only remains for me therefore to ask indulgence for not penetrating your wishes unexpressed, and to offer affectionate thanks for what you did, and what else, with quicker intuition on my part, you would have done.

The enclosed cheque will pay your and Emma's personal expenses. Please kindly inform me what else is due according to our first proposal and your written stipulations, and it shall be forthcoming without delay.

Love to Emma. Lucy's finger is still decidedly painful. Her precise arrangements for leaving town not fixed.

Yours with love,
W. M. Rossetti

MS: AP.

1. See Letter 344.

346. TO CHARLES AUGUSTUS HOWELL

5 Endsleigh Gardens,
15 June 1882

Dear Howell,

What I should like best in the matter pending between us is this: I would regard as sold to you, to be paid for promptly and at once removed by you, the following items —

Ruskin's 2 books	£ 52.10
The Bedstead	10.
The Intarsia Drawers	8.
Lion	3.10
Von Holst	5.
Lizzie's 7 Drawings (and I will give as one of the 7 one of *the better* of her works: I was too stingy on this point yesterday)	35.

424

Elizabethan Picture   10.
                                                                   £124.

Permit me to enquire whether you consider that the £10 for Bedstead includes all mattress, bedding, hangings, and other such appurtenances, or only the wooden framework. My own mind was fixed upon the framework alone, and I have an idea (vague) that the hangings are of some money-worth: if you on the contrary were thinking of the whole affair, I must see what can be done.

3 other items remain — the Smetham sofa[1] £20, "Kitty's chest" 10, and Gabriel's own sofa[2] £25 — total £55. To me all these appear to be speculative lots (if that is the right term), which might go very well, or might prove a failure. You were quite right in saying that for you to offer £55, and for me to put the things into the sale and there receive biddings up to (say) 20, and still hold you to your £55, would be one-sided, and I will add unfair. I therefore now suggest a different arrangement — viz.: you will attend the sale, and will continue bidding for these 3 items as long as other persons bid. If the biddings cease before reaching the respective sums of £20, 10, and 25, then the articles are yours according to your actual lower bid. If you run up the biddings to the 20, 10 and 25, and if other persons still bid higher, then you have fulfilled your engagement, and can continue bidding or else leave off, whichever you may choose; and for your accommodating aid in the matter I (if you will accept it) should like to pay you either (a) 10 per cent upon the lump sums thus realized, or else if not *very much more* (b) ½ of the excess prices realized beyond your stipulated biddings.

You made yesterday several important practical suggestions. At the present moment however the only one on which I want to lay stress is that about the old Venetian hangings in the chief bedroom. I decidedly think it would be very much to our advantage if you were to get some Bond Street man (as you proposed) to look at and buy these hangings. After what you said I *confide* in his offering a somewhat attractive price: and, this being assumed, I on my part pre-engage to close with his offer.

About my father — would you kindly tell me (as briefly as you like) what are the precise points wanted. I am lazy at writing down particulars on a *guess* that they may possibly be wanted.

                                                          Yours very truly,
                                                          W. M. Rossetti

MS: Rutgers.

1. Perhaps Lot 174: "A sofa ... the back artistically painted in figures and landscapes." James Smetham (1821-89), who painted several Pre-Raphaelite pictures in the 1850s, was mentally ill during the last twelve years of his life. His friendship with DGR dates from the 1860s.
2. Lot 100: "A 6 ft. couch with ... three panels at the back, 'Amor,' 'Amans,' 'Amata'; these figures and the other ornamental details were painted by Dante G. Rossetti."

347. TO LUCY ROSSETTI

5 Endsleigh Gardens,
23 June [1882],
10¼ a.m.

Dearie Lu,

I write to you before anyone else — neglecting even the executorship[1] correspondence. I must however be brief in phrase.

Watts called on me yesterday and showed me Valpy's[2] ultimatum. Watts had previously come to the conclusion, after consulting law-books, barristers, etc. that the law does not warrant me in pleading that the liability is limited to the £1575 (with supplementary items) which Gabriel owed Valpy for the returned *Dante's Dream*, but that I am liable for the £2230 (and supplementaries) which Gabriel engaged to make good in return. We had tried to get Valpy to reduce to 500 his demand of 800, giving him certain advantages: this however he declines. He will however take the *Pandora* crayon at 300 instead of the Memory crayon[3] at £200, and his demand thus abates from 800 to 700 — for which latter I remain (i.e. the estate remains) liable: he will also give me (as before offered) £300 if his Joan d'Arc and Dying Beatrice should in our sale sell for £1300 or upwards — which I am convinced they will not. I have not put this latter point quite correctly. He will pay me any sum realized beyond £1000 on these 2 pictures: but said sum shall not exceed a maximum of £300.

As no better may be, I am content with these terms: and so we conclude with Valpy.

I wrote to Murray with a view of his coming to see the MSS. at Endsleigh Gardens, and the photographs etc. at Chelsea: also propose — with Watts' concurrence expressed yesterday — to write Pollen[4] that he may have 3 or 4 of Gabriel's outstanding works to exhibit at Worcester.

After office went round to Cheyne Walk, and there saw the auctioneer Wharton. Received the concluding portion of proof of catalogue — the books etc.: an incredible mass of ignominious blunders, but I tugged through them. One blunder — which Watts showed much reluctance in assenting to my correcting — was that Gosse's first joint volume of poems[5] was catalogued as by "Blaikie and Goose." Also began wiping with duster and otherwise bringing into proper order the photographs, one by one. Made good progress with this job, and left towards 8¾ — home by rail.

On coming home rather fagged and hungry I felt inclined for a little anchovy paste or the like to my toast: the Cook's reply was that the cupboard for the paste etc. is locked — and so it is. Now *why* is this, dear? You know that to lock that cupboard deprives me not only of that sort of simple eatable, but of all my letters, however necessary it may be for me to refer to them. I have told Cook to get a Locksmith to open the cupboard: you had better however send the key up at once. I suppose any ill-temper I may have experienced on that occasion was as usual causeless and unaccountable.

The key you left with me on Wednesday evening as being the key of my black bag is certainly not that. The key you left has a somewhat ornamental handle: would it be of any use to you?

426

I expect to be again at Cheyne Walk all this afternoon — evening. From tomorrow Saturday (as you will remember) I stay away from Somerset House: shall often be at Cheyne Walk but suppose Endsleigh Gardens will be better address.

Yesterday rainy and dirty in London — trust rather better at Southend: today improved, but I doubt its continuance.

I miss you very much, and look with some dismay to weeks passing and no one to say a goodnatured (when it *is* goodnatured) word to me: but never mind, as it is quite needful you should be out of town. *Tell me at once, and frequently in future letters*, how your finger is. Kisses to dear little kids — and many more to poor Lu from her

Fofus

MS: AP.

1. Of DGR's will.
2. Leonard Rowe Valpy of the law firm of Valpy, Chaplin & Peckham, 19 Lincoln's Inn Fields; patron of DGR. When he left London to live in Bath in 1878, he returned to the artist the large replica of *Dante's Dream* with the agreement that "on re-sale ... Rossetti would make up the equivalent value in smaller pictures" (Surtees, 1:44). On 28 August 1882 WMR transferred to him five works — *Joan of Arc, Pandora, Proserpine* (Surtees 162 R. 3, 224 R. 1. A, 233 R. 3), and two crayons not identified — which left £750 owing. Valpy put into Christie's sale *Joan of Arc* (bought in at £367.10) and *Beata Beatrix* (Surtees 168 R. 6; sold at £661.10); and several crayon drawings, of which only *Aurea Catena* (Surtees 209; sold at £210) was not bought in. On 14 June 1883 WMR paid Valpy "£1598.3.3 ... made up of £751.12 sums due to him, and £846.11.3, sum for which he sold 2 works at Christie's (after adjustment of Auctioneer's percentage)" (MS. Diary).
3. *Mnemosyne* (Surtees 261).
4. John Hungerford Pollen (1820-1902), architect and painter. WMR lent three works which were offered for sale but remained unsold: No. 464, "Study of a Head for Picture, *Risen at Dawn*," £90 (Surtees 253A; sold at Christie's for £13.13); No. 465, *La Donna Della Finestra*, £180 (Surtees 255D or 255 R. 1, both of which sold at Christie's for £53.11 and £47 respectively); No. 467, "Pen and Ink Drawing," £40 (*Mrs. William Morris*, Surtees 395; sold at Christie's for £16.16).
5. *Madrigals, Songs and Sonnets* (1870) with J. A. Blaikie.

348. TO LUCY ROSSETTI

5 Endsleigh Gardens,
24 June 1882,
10 a.m.

Dearie Lu,

I finished off my work at Somerset House yesterday towards 3, and left with a sense of relief at not being compelled to attend there again while other matters claim my presence. Went round to Cheyne Walk, and found matters advancing towards the sale: some cleaning done and much comparative orderliness in studio and drawing-room. The whole centre of the studio is now occupied by a solid structure of tables covered with white cloth: all the books are to be placed hereon, in their several lots. That massive wardrobe[1] has been brought in from the passage, and a more stately piece of furniture could hardly be seen. In the drawing-room the walls are hung with pictures collected from various places, and the table is covered with ornamental items in brass, bronze, etc. Watts says that Christie[2] (not the auctioneer, but the art-dealer in whose hands Fry[3] has placed the Venus Astarte for sale, and whom Watts considers exceptionally honest) was called in yesterday to see the fireplace in drawing-room etc.: (this and some like things don't go into catalogue, for fear of "waking snakes" in the Landlord's interest). Christie would give £30 or possibly more for that fireplace, and he thought the contents of the house generally promised very well for selling-prices. But on this point I keep my mind in a state of fairly adjusted balance. Late in the evening the auctioneer called with his Catalogue made up for revise: I took it home, worked on it till past 11, posted it back to him — and copies are to be sent off, according to the list I had drawn up, early on Monday, it is promised. One will go to you. My time at Cheyne Walk was occupied in attending again to the photographs etc.: some which have no selling value (including Stephens's early drawing) I brought home.

Had written to Pollen in the afternoon offering him from 3 to 6 crayon drawings etc. for the Worcester Exhibition: but on re-reading his letter I had concluded that it is more particularly *pictures* that he wants.

Thanks for your affectionate and cheering note of 22 June. You say you paid (so I understand) the Guard "3/- a head" — which would amount to £1.4: but I suppose you mean "3d."

Please tell me what this Insurance-paper is exactly. I understand it to be *my* money — not the estate's. The policies have not reached me.

After my catalogue-job up to past 11, I took up that bundle of Howell letters: will not apply any epithet to the state in which I found them lest a charge of ill-temper should be renewed. Suffice it to say that the attempt — only partially successful — to restore them to the correct order in which by great pains I had got them when I handed them over to you took me up to a good while after midnight.

Today I propose to call on my mother — set Banking-matters right up to the present date — go on to Cheyne Walk, and work there at photographs etc. up to 7 or so — and then return home to dinner. But *may* be prevented from this last.

Your always affectionate however gouty and disagreeable

Fofus

MS: AP.

1. Probably Lot 151.
2. Not listed in *POLD*.
3. Clarence E. Fry of the photographic firm of Elliott & Fry, 55 Baker Street. In 1875 he commissioned *Astarte Syriaca* (Venus Astarte), Surtees 249, which he was shortly to sell to the Manchester City Art Gallery.

349. TO FRANCES ROSSETTI

5 Endsleigh Gardens,
6 July [1882]

Dearest Mamma,

You will I know be relieved and delighted to hear that the money which is now realized (partly paid) for the objects sold in these 2 days' sale (apart from a few things I have myself bought in), and for objects sold by private contract, is just about equivalent to the supposed total of Gabriel's debts: it (the sum realized) is £2659.13.6 to the best of my reckoning. Beyond this we have the £1100 in the Bank, the objects (books and photographs) of tomorrow's sale, the works of art to be sold next spring, and the valuable copyrights. So dear Gabriel seems to have left from the fruits of his genius and taste vastly more than enough to cover all his liabilities, the surplus being a handsome inheritance to two of those he loved best. Of course there are some *other* expenses to be met — probate duty, Auctioneer's percentage, etc. etc., but all comparatively manageable. The success of the sale startles all whom I speak with.

Your affectionate
William

Lucy bids me to tell you that the old curtains in rags in the drawing-room produced — *not* the 8/- I had estimated — but £35.14!!

MS: AP.

350. TO LUCY ROSSETTI

5 Endsleigh Gardens,
8 July 1882,
3 p.m.

Nice dear Lu,

This morning I posted you a Catalogue showing some of the principal prices etc. of yesterday: that might count in lieu of a letter, but nevertheless I will not defraud you of your ordinary dole.

The books went, I think, pretty nearly as well as the other things: for my own lot[1] very few bidders remained, yet the volumes realized more than the small total I had estimated. The Blake[2] certainly went for less than its real value: I finally put £100 upon it as reserved price. Murray, who bought it as you see for Ellis, told me after the sale that he was commissioned to go up to £130 (I think, or possibly £120): so, even if I had bidden beyond my £100, I should not have realized *much* more than was given. Ellis, I should expect, will be very unlikely to part with it at less than £250. Watts told me that Philip Marston[3] would have bought back his own books,[4] but for narrow means: so for them I bid up to £5, to present them to him, but they exceeded this and are gone. Three books seem to have been stolen — I suspect by a bloated oligarch: I was concerned — and my mother today much more so — to learn that the pretty little family Petrarch[5] was one of these: can't be helped. It would have fetched £10 to 15, I believe.

I passed the early part of today with my mother and Christina. They are both singularly delighted with that letter from Watts in the *Daily News*[6] — though you did not wholly approve it.

Heaton bought the drawing-room curtains for himself — not for Turner. I learn that he was *not* the purchaser of that lot of crewel-work etc.: so it remains mine, and we will make the best of it.

The Auctioneer's people told me that I should be doing them a favour if — busy as they are in delivering things to other purchasers — I would postpone till

Monday any steps for removing from the house articles belonging to myself. On Monday therefore I expect to see about it. *Possibly* on Tuesday or Wednesday I might succeed in getting down to Southend for a day or two.

Howell told me that there was in the Kitchen a plated teapot (not auctioned) which he would like to buy for £1. I looked at it, and said I would not sell it unless you, on being consulted, were indifferent to keeping it. The teapot is very pretty — something like this:[7] The plating has worn away — more particularly (or almost solely) at spot marked *A*, and Howell says it would cost some £3 to get it in prime condition again: still, even as it is, it would "do quite well enough for a Fofus," or I should think for a Fofus's wife, and my own inclination is rather towards keeping it. You will decide.

I have not taken any more gout-medicine since that dose you gave me yesterday morning. Today I have resumed my ordinary boot for right foot — retaining for the left foot the larger sized gout-boot. Suffer no inconvenience worth speaking of, though a certain sensation is pretty constant.

Your own with kisses,
W. M. R.

A funny incident. Yesterday one of the Clerks in Somerset House sent me round a letter addressed by "Thérèse Rubens" to "Alex. Rosetti, Revenue Office, Somerset House." It had been inadvertently opened among official letters, and was then sent to me as probably my private property. The lady lives now in Lodge Place, and I am sure from the terms of her letter she must be "a fair and frail one," seeking to renew an intimacy with a quondam lover of vague address. I have returned it to the Clerk.

MS: AP.

1. Lots 632-75 were books belonging to WMR. They brought a total of £10.1.6, which (he told Lucy on 9 July) "need not (if I came to make the minute distinction) be halved with my mother" (AP).

2. Rossetti MS. which sold for £110. For the subsequent history of the MS., see *The Notebook of William Blake*, ed. Erdman, p. 2.

3. (1850-87), the blind poet, was the son of the dramatist John Westland Marston, with whom WMR was acquainted from PRB days.

4. Presentation copies to DGR of *Song-Tide and Other Poems* (1871) and *All in All: Poems and Sonnets* (1874), "marked in pencil" by DGR (lot 560).

5. *Rivisto da Lodovico Dolce* (1553), "copy presented by John Philip Kemble to G. Polidori" (Lot 518).

6. 7 July 1882, p. 2, Watts's reply to an article on the sale (6 July, p. 5) which described the Cheyne Walk house as "that melancholy place ... [its] walls hung with repeated pictures of the same mournful face," and declared that DGR had "long ceased to be the humorous companion whom many friends remember." Watts pointed out that during DGR's last years he had seen him more often than anyone else and had often stayed at Cheyne Walk: "Therefore I can speak about the mysterious house with some authority. Our tête-à-tête conversations by the studio fire mostly lasted till two or three o'clock in the morning, and on those occasions there came from Rossetti's mouth quite as much humour, wit, fancy, and delightful whim ... as would have made the fortunes of all the wits and humorists in London."

7. A sketch follows.

351. TO FRANCES ROSSETTI

4 Devereux Terrace,
Southend,
21 July 1882

Dearest Mamma,

You will be receiving from me for perusal, addressed by Lucy, a little book named *Dante G. Rossetti, his Work and Influence*, by William Tirebuck.[1] It need not return *hither*, but can eventually be housed at Endsleigh Gardens. I saw this book advertised last week in the *Athenaeum*, and ordered it from London. The author is quite a new one to me. I read his book, and find it to be decidedly bad and overloaded in literary style — should suppose the author to be a young man who will gradually improve in this respect to some extent. As to the substance of his book: he shows a sincere and up to a certain point an intelligent admiration of Gabriel's powers, but his praise is clogged with many counter-considerations, and, even were it better expressed, could not tell for much.

I am rather surprised that *Stock*[2] should have published this book, as he is to bring out Caine's book about Gabriel now in preparation. I suppose however that Tirebuck's advent bodes no harm to Caine: and the publication of both works by one man, besides Sharp's[3] book by Macmillan, shows how much interest is taken in Gabriel.

You will I know be quite as sorry to read as I am to write that I have for these two days been again much troubled by gout: kept indoors both days, and today more especially disabled and discomforted. Possibly I may soon be better again. *Had* been very considerably better here at Southend, and must on Monday have walked little less than 5 miles, including the ancient stairs of Rochester Castle. I suppose I rather overdid the exertion of that day — although the next 2 days also passed off fairly enough. At Rochford near here is the house where Anne Boleyn was born — unoccupied, but well enough kept. We looked over it on Wednesday. Weather here varies, but tends increasingly to settled warmth and sunshine.

Lucy very fairly well, but for the finger-bother: takes most affectionate care of me, as I need not tell you. Kids full of spirits, and health too. The twins are really a fine sight now: I wish you could see them, browned (especially Michael) and fat (especially Mary). I like Southend extremely well: you were here, I think, some years back.

Leighton is now consulting me about the R.A. exhibition of Gabriel's works, and I suppose I shall be able to exercise some reasonable amount of influence over the result. Leighton himself (not other and minor R.A.s) seems to take the matter into his own hands — of which I am glad.

Love to Christina — and to Aunt Eliza if returned.

Your loving son,
W. M. Rossetti

Olive takes sea-baths here on and off, and Helen aspires to do the same. Arthur made the experiment, but was not much pleased with it.

MS: AP.

1. William Edwards Tirebuck (1854-1900), journalist and author. Hall Caine wrote a brief memoir

of him for the posthumously published *Twixt God and Mammon* (1903).

2. Elliot Stock (1838-1911) specialized in religious, antiquarian, and bibliographical books and periodicals. He seems to have taken a particular interest in the Rossetti circle, publishing books by WBS, Francis Hueffer, Marston, William Sharp, J. H. Ingram's biography of Oliver Brown (1883), and the facsimile reprint of the *Germ* with WMR's introduction.

3. William Sharp (1855-1905) published biographies, poems, and romances under his own name, and from 1894 mystical verse and prose under the name Fiona Macleod. DGR met him in 1879 through the introduction of Noel Paton. MS. Diary, 20 October 1882: "Sharp called, and will soon send Lucy successive proofs of the whole of his book about Gabriel." 30 October: "Lucy and I read together the beginning of Sharp's book (proofs).... There are several minor misapprehensions and misstatements — which Lucy points out to Sharp here and there, I never having undertaken the responsibility of doing anything of that sort. The tone is decidedly laudatory and respectful, the writing moderately good."

352. TO LUCY ROSSETTI

Somerset House,
14 August 1882,
12¼

Dearest Lu,

I have not received any letter from you this morning: am therefore fain to hope and suppose that Olive continues improving, or is perhaps by this time recovered.

Yesterday I set more or less to rights the things belonging to Gabriel which were in the black cupboard,[1] and those which were on the sofa in the smoking-room. I dusted the cupboard to some fair extent, arranged in some of its drawers and shelves (several remain quite unoccupied) a good proportion of the things, and brought out into the living-rooms some others which appear sightly and convenient. There are those two specimens of armour, now in one of the lowest shelves of the cupboard: I would like your papa to have the offer of them — perhaps you are in the way of writing to him, and would attend to this. They consist (I speak only from *general* observation) of a buff jerkin with a large quantity of chain mail attached to it, and of a considerable piecing-together of plate-armour — shoulder-piece and what not.

Late in the evening I took up that set of Gabriel's letters which I put together a few months ago, and began reading them through with a view to possible publication — marking with red pencil such parts as should not be published, whether as properly private matter or as void of general interest. I incline to think that I shall continue this work, and offer the letters to Ellis pretty soon for publication — with a short memoir.[2]

My foot got a little strained with the standing about etc. etc. in the cupboard job: today however it seems not at all the worse — I walked down to Office in comfort — but I would not venture on trying on the smaller gout-boot.

Watts has called here, and will dine with me tomorrow, and set 2 or 3 things going — surrender of lease etc. Fry's agent is at him to settle a claim of Fry's which I never rightly knew about till now — much mixed up with dormant yet extant claims from Howell. I gather that we shall have to pay Fry at the very least £50, and perhaps more like £150.[3] I again asked Watts for bills, and hope to see something of them tomorrow.

Kisses to yourself and kids from

Fofus

Can you tell me what has become of that ruler which I bought last year at Tunbridge Wells? I had none other useable, and that has disappeared.

MS: AP.

1. Described in MS. Diary, 13 August 1882 as "the old black-and-gilt cabinet which used to be our father's — bought towards 1835 — and which I bought in at Gabriel's sale."

2. After Watts agreed to undertake the memoir, *FLM* bogged down. WMR's increasing exasperation with his continuous vacillation is charted in later letters. Finally in July 1894 he told Watts that he would do it himself.

3. MS. Diary, 21 February 1883: "Today I handed to Watts a cheque for £350, which he is to pay to Fry as soon as Howell shall have given me a proper release or other document of indemnity. The £350 consists of £150 as actual payment to Fry and £200 for which Fry is to return to me 3 fine crayon drawings by Gabriel proper to the *Astarte* subject." (One of the drawings is Surtees 249C about which WMR wrote to a Mr. Howard on 18 February 1883: "I consider it as fine a head as my brother ever produced, worth more than £100 to a discerning purchaser. I am therefore quite willing to buy it at that sum" [Texas]. WMR put it into Christie's sale, where it brought £126. Surtees lists five other *Astarte* drawings which were in Christie's sale [249B, D, E, F, H] and another [G] with a WMR provenance.) 24 February: "Watts left with me 2 or 3 documents in the matter of Fry's claim, including a release from Howell in respect of the £580 which he claimed as due to himself by Gabriel. To meet a requirement of Howell's, the sum of £350 which I have paid to Fry is now apportioned thus — £240 as settlement of debt to him, and £110 as repurchase-money for the 3 crayon drawings."

353. TO LUCY ROSSETTI

Somerset House,
17 August 1882,
Noon

Dearie Lu,

Please let me know whether Olive is so far well now as to go out as usual, and otherwise resume her ordinary habits.

Before getting to bed last night I finished reading through Gabriel's letters,[1] and marking such passages etc. as should be omitted in any printing. I suppose the number of letters totally omitted (often on the mere ground of insufficient interest) would be about ¼ of the whole; and the passages omitted from letters to be published might be about ¼ of the bulk of those letters. The printable matter would make a substantial though not a very large volume. I might also last evening have finished the Mantegna article[2] but for the arrival of Shields.

He entered the room looking (as I judged by inadequate light) very pale and pulled down;[3] but I soon found that in manner, tone of thought, etc., he is quite as cheerful as usual. He tells me the facts about his condition are these. As he had gone on a long while with Andrew Clarke, and still remained far from healthy, his wife prevailed on him to see another Doctor — Hoggan, who is married to a female Dr. Hoggan[4] who attends Mrs. Shields. Hoggan examined him; and, it being understood that he had expressed a very bad opinion of the case, Shields returned to him, and asked him to be explicit. Hoggan then told Shields that he regards him as afflicted with a certain mortal disease: he named the disease to Shields, but Shields would not do so to me, to avoid leaving a painful impression.

This considerably upset Shields and his wife, and he reconsulted Clarke. Clarke gave him a careful overhauling, and told him that he does not agree with Hoggan: for, though Shields has some of the symptoms characterizing that disease, he has not all of them — and Shields says he has since then satisfied *himself* of the same fact by reading medical books about the disease, and testing thereby his own symptoms. So he regards himself as being at present as well as usual, and is working as usual, and not thinking of leaving London as a practical question, though it might in the abstract be desirable.

He looked at the *Rosa Triplex*,[5] and thought its condition (as Watts had done the previous evening) a somewhat grievous one. He considers that in various parts the surface must be absolutely bared, and new matter painted on to it.

I don't know the right answer to Leighton's query:[6] shall probably consult your papa about it.

With love,

Your
W. M. R.

I believe the Married Women's Property Bill has now actually passed into law!

MS: AP.

1. See Letter 352.
2. For *Encyclopaedia Britannica*, ninth edition.
3. MS. Diary, 15 August 1882: "Lucy having written to me — to my great concern — that Shields is in an alarming state of health, and ordered to leave off work and get away from London, I called at Shields's house to enquire. He and his wife were out.... I left a card, asking him to let me know any particulars."
4. George and Frances Elizabeth Hoggan, the former the author of papers on cancer.
5. Surtees 238; parts of the picture were repainted by Dunn.
6. See Letter 354.

354. TO FORD MADOX BROWN

5 Endsleigh Gardens,
17 August 1882

Dear Brown,

Leighton has asked me whether I know who owns a water-colour done by Gabriel in (he thinks) 1856, of the Adoration of the Magi.[1] I do not know: the subject seems to bear some relation to the Llandaff triptych. Do you happen to know anything about the matter?

I have lately paid Ellis back his £300,[2] and surrendered the Cheyne Walk house from Michaelmas by paying the £300 required for repairs, and the £100 as extra half-year's rent.[3]

Gouty foot not far from well — yet not *well*.

Shields called on me last evening, and gave a partially reassuring account of his health. Perhaps he has written to you: I have today sent the details to Lucy.

Love to Emma from

Your
W. M. Rossetti

MS: AP.

1. Surtees 105B, original design for *The Seed of David*.
2. Ellis had loaned the money to WMR when the Union Bank refused to cash the check that DGR had written two days before his death. Ellis to WMR, 14 April 1882: "To have personally known him I shall always regard as one of the very fortunate things in my life. You must allow me to place this money at your disposal without any question of interest — acting as a friend rather than the publisher" (AP). MS. Diary, 14 August 1882: "I received (delayed several days through a postal mistake) a letter from Ellis & White asking me to repay the £300."
3. MS. Diary, 22 August 1882, notes that the house was to be given up "under an arrangement ... decidedly advantageous." 29 September: "Watts tells me that Pemberton, Lord Cadogan's [George Henry Cadogan (1840-1915)] lawyer, was dismayed, on looking over 16 Cheyne Walk, to find how much there is to be done to it, and how cheap he had let me off — through Watts's diplomacy — when he accepted a bonus of £100 to cancel the lease." WMR to Lucy Rossetti, 11 July 1882, described the house a few days after the sale as "a most dismal spectacle — denuded walls, fearfully begrimed bare boards, unfurnished vacancy" (AP). MS. Diary, 26 September 1883 notes that the house had been taken by Hugh Reginald Haweis (1838-1901), "the clerical 'aesthete': I have seen him, but don't know him, and have always supposed him to be rather a humbug." WMR observed on 29 January 1884 that the house was "now greatly renovated by the present tenant Haweis. He has reddened the whole outside of it, and placed at the top a cast of John of Bologna's Mercury." Haweis was perpetual curate of St. James's, Marylebone, and the author of *Music and Morals* (1871) and *Poets in the Pulpit* (1880).

355. TO LUCY ROSSETTI

5 Endsleigh Gardens,
20 August 1882,
4¾

Lucy dearest,

I am just back from Leighton's:[1] Watts accompanied me. Leighton received us very pleasantly and frankly. I find he has not made his tour to look up Gabriel's works, but has seen several things in London, and corresponded with other owners: some of his vast work for St. Paul's[2] detained him in town. Prinsep has gone with Leighton's concurrence to Rae, to see about his works, and others in that district: Leighton, on returning from Egypt etc., which will be not later than 7 November, means to go to Leathart and others in the North. He means to admit crayon drawings etc., and consulted me as to the principle on which I think the Exhibition ought to be modelled: whether a very select one, as some advise him, or a full representation of all periods etc., as others recommend. I told Leighton I think the right plan is to get as many of the leading and best-class works as he can, and besides that to have a fair representative show of all periods and methods of Gabriel's art-work. He did not absolutely say he would adhere to this, but I think his own views correspond fairly enough with mine.[3]

His house[4] is a gorgeous specimen of oligarchical luxury: the much-talked of Oriental hall very attractive, and having as *pièces de résistance* the most splendid collection of Persian and other such tiles I ever saw — I suppose the finest in England. He wants to get G. F. Watts's portrait of Gabriel — for which it seems Leyland would *not* pay the £200 demanded by Schott:[5] he knows (without my hinting about it) all about Mrs. Schott and her affairs, and sees no reason why Schott should not be applied to. I expressed assent — Watts dissent, but not very stern. It lies with Leighton. I said nothing about the portraits of Browning and Swinburne etc.

Leighton lately did a model of a man in a yawning action (naked) for sculpture. The subject may seem odd, but it is a consummate artistic success, and I am sure if carried out will be an acknowledged masterpiece.[6]

On leaving Leighton's, I set Watts down at Mrs. Coronio's[7] (Gosse also impending for him) and came straight home myself.

This is all my news, I think — hurriedly scribbled off. Kisses to dear little kids, and warmer ones to yourself.

Fofus

Where is that sort of a beginning of an autobiography which I handed to you some few years ago? It would be the right thing to impart to Watts as material for starting him with what he is (presumably) to write about Gabriel.[8] He goes with Swinburne to Guernsey for a fortnight or so from about next Saturday.

MS: AP.

1. MS. Diary, 19 August 1882: "Received a letter from Sir Frederick Leighton suggesting whether I could call tomorrow on him, to clear up some details concerning Gabriel's works, in view of the forthcoming exhibition at the R.A."
2. His unfinished decoration of the dome of St. Paul's in collaboration with Edward Poynter.
3. MS. Diary, 20 August 1882, gives a more qualified account of Leighton's reaction to his opinion: "he seemed to agree without expressly saying so. It seems to me however that he views with some disfavour the general run of Gabriel's works produced within the last 4 or 5 years."
4. Built in 1864 by the architect George Aitchison. The Arab Hall was added in 1877.
5. The picture was No. 344 in the R.A. exhibition. It was shown again in the spring of 1883 at an exhibition arranged by Schott at "The Rossetti Gallery," 1A Old Bond Street, "the premises with which Deschamps has some connexion." WMR visited the exhibition on 22 May, and noted that it was "got up by Schott out of the works by Gabriel which remained in the hands of Mrs. Schott — some strictly her property, others no doubt not so in reality, but allowed unchallenged to pass as if they were. The collection is considerably eked out with photographs etc., but does certainly contain a fair number of thoroughly fine things. The catalogue, Watts tells me, is Howell's doing. A subscription list has been opened for engraving G. F. Watts's portrait of Gabriel" (MS. Diary, 9, 22 May 1883).
6. MS. Diary, 20 August 1882, adds: "It was done from an Italian model, who frequently thus stretched himself in the pauses of sitting, always with fine action. Owing to a mistake of Leighton's servant, the cast has got unfortunately rubbed down and its crispness gone — but it is still very sightly."
7. Aglaia, one of the five children of Alexander Ionides.
8. WMR to Lucy Rossetti, 18 August 1882, reporting on *FLM*: "We agreed with tolerable definiteness to the following. The latter-part of the book shall consist of letters to me alone, and the Memoir shall be written by Watts — partly from his own materials, and partly from what I can furnish to him. On some grounds I would of course have preferred to write the Memoir myself: but I believe *on the whole* the higher justice will be done to Gabriel by Watts's writing it. He can speak out about Gabriel's genius etc. in a tone which hardly befits a brother, and which will at any rate carry more weight with the reader. Also he wishes to *faire-valoir* the curiously exceptional mode of bringing up which affected along with Gabriel all the other members of the family, and this could hardly be done at all by me. It is certain too that Watts is not only a more picturesque but by far a more popular writer than I am, and the book will thereby run all the better chance. Of course (though we didn't raise that point) Watts would have to share in any profits: also of course I could put in any particular statement of my own that I choose" (AP).

356. TO WALTER HAMILTON[1]

5 Endsleigh Gardens,
21 August 1882

Dear Sir,

The enclosed memorandum shows the points which I regard as open to correction in your book. May I without offence add that I do not like your title-page; and I question whether any one of the men whom you eulogize as Aesthetes purifying public taste in matters of art would like it.

Very faithfully yours,
W. M. Rossetti

MS: Liverpool.

1. (1844-99), journalist and author. *The Aesthetic Movement in England* (1882) went into three editions in the year of its publication. Most of WMR's corrections (the memorandum is in Liverpool) were made in the third edition, and the design on the title page was dropped. WMR to Lucy Rossetti, 18 August 1882, described it as "A poor shreds-and-patches affair — but by no means wanting in sympathy with Gabriel etc." (AP).

357. TO THEODORE WATTS-DUNTON

5 Endsleigh Gardens,
27 September 1882

Dear Watts,

I have received a longish letter from Caine who seems to mean to stick to the insertion of *Dennis Shand* in his book:[1] he does not say so in so many words, but I can put no other construction on his reply. He seems to suppose that he has a right to do this because the poem was (so he says) *published* ere now. I don't know (nor yet suppose) it was published, nor yet that, if published, Stock acquires thereby any right to republish it. Have replied to Caine that Stock is not to republish it without consulting me, or else standing his chance of an action.[2]

Caine also says that *Dennis Shand*, and other works by Gabriel not in his 2 published volumes, are "being printed elsewhere."

Please advise me as to this (it is new to me) — and whether I can positively prohibit Stock about *Dennis Shand*.[3] If I can, and if Caine does not soon draw in his horns, I propose to write direct to Stock interdicting the publication unless or until he comes to terms satisfactory to myself.

I don't send you Caine's letter because more things than one in it are displeasing to me: and I am resolved to keep on good kindly terms with Caine if I possibly can, and therefore not to fan the embers of my dissatisfaction into flame by discussing points of detail with you or others.

Your
W. M. Rossetti

My mother has again broken down in the task of looking up Gabriel's letters.[4] We must give up the idea of combining her series with mine.

MS: BL.

1. Caine informed WMR on 20 September 1882 that his book was "now passing through the press, and I should like to send you proofs and avail myself of any practicable suggestions you may be kind enough to make.... I am compelled to say frankly that you will not enjoy my book unless you read it

from my individual standpoint. I believe I have written the exact truth in every particular, but it is the truth as it came to my mind, and I had but one informant on matters that did not come within my personal experience, and that was your brother himself'' (AP). MS. Diary, 23 September: ''Watts brought round to me the copy confided to him of the first several sheets of Caine's book. He has suggested some emendations, mainly for the sake of taste and diction. I looked through the proofs in the evening, and jotted down various errors, and some points that are contrary to my liking. On the whole I like the book well enough, but don't rate it (so far as it has yet reached me) very high, whether as literature, or as a presentation of the subject-matter. Caine has calmly printed in his text Gabriel's unpublished poem *Dennis Shand*: such a 'conveyance' of my property I do not mean to allow, and have plainly told Caine that the publisher (Stock) must either miss out the poem, or else offer me terms for the use of it, and I may or may not then consent.'' On 27 September Caine thanked WMR for his ''exhaustive and valuable notes.... Your corrections of matters of detail touching Gabriel's early life are all most important and shall certainly be made before the book goes out. In certain particulars I perceive you are right where facts of the later life are in question, but in other particulars I know you are wrong and wherever your statement of an event is unlike that given me by your brother I must perforce (other things being equal) choose his.... You say there has been a design to ignore you in all mention of friendliness to Gabriel. This is a grave mistake, and a painful one.... But I should convey a very erroneous idea of my own sense of your relations to your brother during the period in which I knew him if I tried to make it appear that you played an important part in the life drama that began *for me* in July 1881.... Of all the men of our inner circle you (though his brother) played the most inconspicuous part of all, *so far as I could see*. You came once a week, latterly twice a week, wrote frequent letters and did many acts of kindness; but of what had then to be done for Gabriel your devotion seemed only a drop of water in an ocean'' (BL).

2. MS. Diary, 27 September 1882: ''I answered with studious moderation of tone.''

3. MS. Diary, 28 September 1882: ''Watts called: knows nothing about unauthorized printing of poems by Gabriel; fully confirms my view that Caine and Stock have no sort of right to publish *Dennis Shand*. He brought me the final proofs of Caine's book, and called my attention to a passage reproducing some viva voce statements by Gabriel about Nolly Brown, sure to be much disliked (though there is really no great *harm* in them) by Lucy and Brown: and in fact Lucy was so hurt and angered when she saw them in the evening that she wrote a long letter for Caine, which on reflection she posted only to Watts, for further consideration. Unless Caine cuts out this passage, I fear — though I have no wish to lose sight of him — that, in kindness to Lucy, it will not be possible to allow him again to cross my threshold. I finished reading Caine's proofs: don't greatly like his book in any aspect, but finding nothing fresh to raise individual objection against.'' 29 September: ''I wrote to Caine representing (in the mildest of terms so far as I am personally concerned, but strongly in behoof of Lucy and Brown) the objections to what he had printed about Nolly; and late at night I posted for Lucy the letter which she had written to Caine on the same subject. She had in the afternoon seen Hueffer about it; and he had concurred in her views, and means, if the passage is not withdrawn, to speak out his mind very emphatically in reviewing Caine's book in the *Times*.'' 1 October: ''Watts has now received a telegram from Caine, showing that he yields to my requirement for omitting *Dennis Shand*, and to Lucy's requirement for omitting the report of Gabriel's talk about Nolly.'' 2 October: ''I received a letter from Stock begging permission to retain *Dennis Shand*.'' 3 October: ''Wrote to Stock saying that Gabriel decided not to publish *Dennis Shand*, and that the poem, if published, seems to have some substantial money value, say £30; that my right course would be not to publish it at all; but that, rather than put Stock to serious inconvenience, I would consider any offer of payment (even much less than £30) that he may make — and, if he does not make such, will consider the question further. This is, I think, quite as much concession as can reasonably be expected of me.'' 4 October: ''Stock replies that he regards as conclusive the objection which Gabriel entertained to publishing *Dennis Shand*, and he has asked Caine to withdraw it: so much the better. I had, before receiving Stock's letter, written in friendly terms to Caine, and am in hopes that all will now be viewed as satisfactorily disposed of.'' (Oliver Brown is discussed on pp. 186-91 of Caine's book.)

4. For *FLM*. WMR to Lucy Rossetti, 1 September 1882: ''Today, calling on my mother, I asked her (the first suggestion had come from Watts) whether she would be at all disposed to include in the same volume some of the letters addressed to *her* by Gabriel. I had thought this rather unlikely: but she at once said she would do it if in accordance with my wishes — and she will proceed to look through the letters (a good deal more numerous I should suppose than those to me), and will set aside such as she supposes I might like for the purpose'' (AP).

358. TO THEODORE WATTS-DUNTON 5 Endsleigh Gardens,
4 November 1882

Dear Watts,

I may no doubt count on seeing you one of these days: but, as I don't know *which* day, I had better lose no further time in mentioning a matter of importance to our joint project. My mother (incited thereto no further by me, but I believe by seeing some fragments of Sharp's proofs) has really taken up the examination of Gabriel's letters addressed to her; and has furnished me with 2 rather considerable bundles of them — of which I have read the first, but not as yet the second, which I understand goes up to 1876 or so. Others still remain for my mother to look through. What I have read are in many instances interesting, and in others highly pleasing for their familiar affection. The series will be a substantial and a very valuable addition to our book.

I must now see about their being properly introduced into their due sequence in the collection. All the work I have hitherto done — numbering and annotating of the letters addressed to me — will have to be topsy-turvied; the numbering for obvious reasons, and the annotating because in many instances something that I have said as elucidating a letter addressed to me will now have to be transposed so as to elucidate some *earlier* letter addressed to my mother. I think therefore it will behove you to return to me as early as convenient all the letters now in your hands, all the transcripts of them, and all my notes upon them, and I must then take up the work *de novo*. I explained to my mother the reasons why it will be fitting to get her set of letters transcribed by the same process as my set, and she acquiesces.

On 30 October Henley[1] wrote me, intimating that he hopes to get other *works* by Gabriel, as well as those 2 I showed you, engraved in the *Magazine of Art*. I have not replied, and presume I shall not be likely to take any action about the matter. Would like your advice sometime.

Have not yet read Caine's book: shall buy a copy (if on sale) this afternoon.[2] Who wrote the review in *Athenaeum*[3] — P. Marston, Gosse, or who? Sharp's book (of which I have read a large part) shows a good deal of diligence, and I think a very fair average power of criticism as applied to the works of art: it will I consider remain a work of some solidity, whatever else gets written about Gabriel. I fear however it is a little tedious. Don't hint this suspicion of mine to Sharp — though I might some day or other give some inkling of it myself to him perchance.

Lucy at Crumpsall from today till Monday: anniversary of Nolly's death.

Your
W. M. Rossetti

MS: BL.

1. William Ernest Henley (1849-1903), poet, critic, dramatist, was editor of the *Magazine of Art*, 1882-86. WMR was at first inclined to object because he doubted the adaptability of the works for engraving, but MS. Diary, 9 January 1883, notes that since Watts has advised him that he had "no legal control over such matters, I will henceforth take no part in them one way or other, but leave people who choose to engrave the works well or ill to attend to the affair for themselves."
2. MS. Diary, 8 November 1882: "I bought Caine's book, and began reading it again through: am pleased to see that one or two things which I disliked in the proofs have been cut out."

3. 4 November 1882, pp. 590-91. MS. Diary, 8 November 1882: "Watts ... informs me that [Joseph] Knight is the writer of the *Athenaeum* review."

359. TO FORD MADOX BROWN

5 Endsleigh Gardens,
9 November 1882

Dear Brown,

On Tuesday Lucy read me the passage in your letter about Stephens and Gabriel's letters:[1] I had intended to write at once a scrap for Lucy to enclose to you, but somehow it slipped me till this morning.

My *chief wish* in the matter is that you should do exactly as you like: therefore everything hereafter remains for you to settle. Subordinate to this chief wish is a feeling that I might some day like to collect and publish a number of letters from Gabriel to friends, and among them naturally those to you; and therefore that, if it suits you and Stephens that he should freely use the information accruing from the letters, without publishing *in extenso* more than a moderate proportion of them, that plan will be conformable to my views also.

Thanks for all your and Emma's loving-kindness to Arthur.

Your affectionate
W. M. Rossetti

MS: AP.

1. Stephens was intending to write a book on DGR: "an unfortunate book, or plan of a book," WMR described it in MS. Diary, 25 February 1894, "which has been haggling about from publisher to publisher any time this 11 years." The book is first mentioned in MS. Diary on 14 October 1882: "Lucy says that Stephens (who notifies in the *Athenaeum* a forthcoming book on Gabriel) wrote to her father lately, expressing himself hurt and disappointed at my not taking more interest in this project.... All I have had to do with the matter is that, when Stephens wrote to me some 2 or 3 months ago saying that he projected such a book, and asking whether I approved, I replied ... approving.... Shall write to Stephens in the hope of keeping matters straight between him and me: I should be very sorry to mortify him, even unwittingly." 21 October: "Stephens called, to explain about his proposed book regarding Gabriel. It seems that 3 successive projects on the subject have been entertained. 1, Sampson Low & Co. wanted to publish, chiefly as an illustrated book, a volume embodying Stephens's *Athenaeum* criticisms on Gabriel. This was the project about which Stephens ... wrote to me.... My suggestion that the works of Gabriel, to be engraved in this volume, should be paid for as copyright, was not acceptable to the publishers, and hence the scheme was dropped.... 2, There was some other project, which Stephens did not detail. 3, The present idea is to publish with Murray a work on a substantial scale, toward April next or so, being a critical estimate of Gabriel as an artist, and analysis of his works, with some biographical particulars." In later diary entries the Fine Art Society and George Bell are mentioned as possible publishers (18 November 1882, 14 October 1894). As late as 3 February 1899 WMR noted in MS. Diary apropos of a visit from H. C. Marillier, who was completing his *Dante Gabriel Rossetti: An Illustrated Memorial of His Art and Life* (Bell, 1899): "I showed him the various specimens about the house; and said that, as a preliminary to any further steps, I would write to Stephens, and ascertain whether or not he has finally abandoned his very old project of publishing a book of somewhat similar quality." In 1894 Stephens published a brief study: *Dante Gabriel Rossetti* (Portfolio Artistic Monographs).

360. TO THEODORE WATTS-DUNTON

5 Endsleigh Gardens,
20 December 1882

Dear Watts,

Mason[1] came this morning, and I swore to the will etc. You will have heard particulars from him. Being in a hurry, I took no notes — not even the total amount, total deduction, and net residue: nor do I now remember these with any accuracy. Please oblige me with the figures at once, and in convenient time with copies of all the documents, which are of course interesting to myself, and to my mother also.

Now here is another matter. Last evening at 6½ Burne Jones called on me.[2] He says that it is understood that letters addressed to Gabriel are in circulation, put forward by Fanny, and that Mrs. M[orris] had called on him in some disquietude. He asked whether I would co-operate in stopping any sale or diffusion of any such letters: I of course replied Yes — saying at the same time that I have no personal knowledge of any such transactions. Then Jones said that he was going round to dine by appointment with the Solicitor George Lewis[3] (88 Portland Place), his man of business, and was to consult with him about it: and he asked whether I would go thither later in the evening — I said Yes: for, as Jones is interesting himself in this matter in behalf of Mrs. M[orris], I considered that any co-operation of mine could not be put off to a later time.

I went at 9 — Jones and Lewis proposed that Comyns Carr should go round to Fanny's house as an amateur, enquire about drawings, and then about letters, and report result. I expressed an opinion that a man like Carr, highly conversant with what is said about artists etc., would not be the best person — better a total outsider such as one of Lewis's Clerks. Finally Lewis said that he would go himself, see whether any private letters are really offered for sale, and communicate with me, and I if needful should claim a right of prohibition.

The thing being much hurried, and Jones acting on his own hook with Lewis, I perhaps did not quite sufficiently take into account that *you*, and not Lewis, are the most fitting person to see about it: your being personally known to and disliked by Fanny, and therefore not capable of taking the principal direct part in the enquiry, also was in my mind. If you see it to be fitting, of course I should be highly content that you should now start the subject with Lewis in any form you like.

I myself doubt whether Fanny has any letters such as Jones speaks of. One class of letters surmised is a lot of wildly chaffy indecencies that Swinburne used to pen — strings of punning banter ringing the changes on any impropriety that he could start: certainly these ought to be rigidly suppressed. I suspect the origin of the rumour may be that Fanny once (say 1866) put together a rather noticeable collection of autographs, furnished forth by Gabriel, by myself, and others. Some or all of these she might be offering for sale — but of course they include nothing which ought to be kept unseen.

Brown still very ill — though the last news is not worse than the average, nor even so bad.[4]

> Your
> W. M. Rossetti

Among the letters addressed to Gabriel which I brought away from Cheyne Walk I found *one* letter by Swinburne of the character above described. It found its way to the fire at once. But I have not the least doubt that there had been *many* other such letters, and perhaps Gabriel did not make a point of destroying them.

MS: BL.

1. Charles Samuel Mason of the law firm of H. H. Mason & Son, 23 St. Swithin's Lane (*POLD*). Mason was Watts's brother-in-law. MS. Diary, 20 December 1882, gives the named value of the estate as "about £5200 [£5300.17.9], reduced by debts etc. to about £2700. In this valuation, £764.9 is estimated for the value of Gabriel's drawings etc. This is, I am in hopes, absurdly below the real value of them." See Letter 366, Note 2, for the amount realized at Christie's sale. The will was resworn in February 1885, when the total value was changed to £7210.1.9.
2. MS. Diary, 19 December 1882: "Jones called saying that he hears rumours to the effect that private letters addressed to Gabriel (as by Swinburne and Ruskin, and others still more confidential) are offered for sale by F[anny]." 20 December: "Jones write me that some enquiry made by Tadema seems to show that that was all a false alarm about F[anny]."
3. George Henry Lewis (1833-1911), friend of Burne-Jones, Whistler, Wilde, and Edward VII. At the time of his death he was "the most famous lawyer in England" (John Juxon, *Lewis and Lewis* [1983], p. 11).
4. During the last decade of his life FMB was frequently plagued by gout.

361. TO JOHN MARSHALL

5 Endsleigh Gardens,
9 February 1883

Dear Marshall,

It was truly kind of you to write me so full and sympathetic a letter about our severe loss. The boy[1] was a nice pretty little fellow, and I had promised myself much pleasure (though well aware how little one can *count* upon any thing of the kind) in watching from year to year the joint growth of himself and of his twin sister. To me it was a pang to part with him, and no doubt a much severer pang to Lucy. No one however could have borne herself better under such cirumstances than she has done.

These so dark days to us have been somewhat — indeed greatly — cheered by hearing better news of Brown. His illness has been truly a terrifying one; but it seems to be yielding at last, and he hopes to move to the seaside next Thursday or thereabouts. Probably you know this.

I will avail myself of this opportunity to say that I have often had a certain twinge of mind in reflecting that you attended the deathbed of my dear Gabriel on 8 and 9 April last, and gave us the consolation and advantage of your professional advice, without (as yet) a word between you and me as to my indebtedness to you on this account — which of course must be a rather considerable sum according to the professional standard. The fact is that one of our friends informed me soon afterwards that, in conversing with him, you had liberally expressed yourself willing to regard as compensation in full the sums which Gabriel had from time to time paid during his lifetime. If this is correctly stated, I also am content, with thanks to you, to leave it on that footing: but I don't like to leave the matter unmentioned from first to last. Please to reply or not as you prefer.

You may have seen that the newspapers published the amount of Gabriel's estate as some £5000. This is the gross amount — not net amount *after payment of debts*: and what hole that payment would make in the £5000 I need say nothing about. The sale of his drawings etc. remains to be effected — perhaps towards May: then, and then only, shall I know pretty well what I am to think of the estate. It seems to me that, spite of unfavourable blasts from some quarters of the compass, the freight of his genius and reputation sails onward firmer and prouder day by day: and this interests me more deeply than any aspect of the money-question.

I must not detain you any longer with these matters. Lucy proposes to add a few words.

Yours always truly,
W. M. Rossetti

MS: Exeter.

1. Michael.

362. TO ALGERNON CHARLES SWINBURNE

5 Endsleigh Gardens,
13 February 1883

Dear Swinburne,

Many and true thanks for your verses on the poor little Twin:[1] they are lovely — standing high, I think, amid your work of the like class. I am rather surprised that you run them together as stanzas 1 to 6: for to me it seems that 5 and 6 are a separate lyric. Lucy read them — as you wrote them — with tears, and adds her heartiest thanks to mine.

If all the poems in your proposed volume are to be as innocuous — and indeed to a Christian reader as edifying — as these, it seems to me that Christina will gladly accept the dedication you so kindly and delicately offer.[2] One doesn't quite *know* however, and I will at an early opportunity sound her as you suggest.

I find less progression in my mind on most subjects of speculation or opinion than in most other minds: can recollect pretty well what I was at 18, in the great year of Revolution 1848, and discern but little difference now at 53 and in 1883. It then appeared to me, and now appears to me (and indeed increasingly so) that the probabilities of personal immortality are exceedingly slender — unless indeed one believes in ghosts, and in them — perversely enough perhaps — I am less *dis*inclined to believe than many people are. By personal immortality I mean this — that Gabriel Rossetti and William Rossetti are to continue to all eternity to be Gabriel and William Rossetti, and to be conscious of so being: for anything less than this appears to me as vague a sort of immortality as pantheism (which I merge into atheism) is a vague sort of theism.

Your affectionate
W. M. Rossetti

MS: BL.

1. *A Baby's Death*. Published in *A Century of Roundels* where it consists of seven numbered lyrics.
2. The volume was dedicated to her.

363. TO THEODORE WATTS-DUNTON

5 Endsleigh Gardens,
5 April 1883

Dear Watts,

Please read the enclosed letter to Valpy,[1] and forward it at once. My Catalogue must linger no longer — the serious part of my own work upon it having been finished perhaps 4 or 5 weeks ago. I don't want to be stiff with worthy old Valpy, but decisive I must and will be. I am not inclined to brim the goblet of any Vampire.

Christie wrote me on 2 April that he sees no serious harm in that Fisheries Exhibition[2] on 12 May, and that it would be a mistake to try to make any alteration. In this view I acquiesce.

Please let me have *at once* those drawings which Fry so stupidly sent to you. They are needed for catalogue.

I have consented — as a great favour to an old friend who befriended Gabriel at the last — to include in the sale the Giotto and Dante[3] belonging to Seddon. At that I shall draw the line, and don't suppose that any other such request (supposing such to be made) would avail with me. The drawings which used to be only mounted are now framed, and very good they look.

This may — or may not — be all I have to say: it is all I remember at the moment.

Brown, having rallied a goodish deal this week past, has suddenly made up his mind to return to Manchester, and travels thither today. I trust not prematurely.

Your
W. M. Rossetti

Has anything and what been done about Brown's Wharf?[4]

I have a paper of Christie's percentages, which are somewhat lower than I supposed.

We must think seriously of a list of persons to whom our Catalogue is to be sent. Can you jot down any names? (Excuse trouble.) You might like to see this latest list of photographs.

MS: BL.

1. Letter 364.
2. International Fisheries Exhibition.
3. *Giotto Painting the Portrait of Dante*, which Thomas Seddon had bought from DGR. It was now owned by John Seddon.
4. FMB inherited from his mother shares in Ravensbourne Wharf, Deptford Creek. In 1882 he proposed to sell the shares to WMR for £250 to be paid in three installments.

364. TO LEONARD ROWE VALPY

5 Endsleigh Gardens,
5 April 1883

Dear Mr. Valpy,

The time when the sale of my brother's works must take place (12 May) is now rapidly approaching, and I must get everything in proper train for the auction,

444

including especially the Catalogue. Allow me therefore to address you on the following points, and to request a prompt reply.

1. The only works in colour belonging to you which I have undertaken to include in the sale, or which I mean to include, are the *Beata Beatrix* and the *Joan of Arc*. Both these are now in my possession, and I believe you and I are fully agreed as to how they shall be dealt with.

2. It was agreed that you might put into the sale such crayon drawings as you choose. But you have never yet told me whether you mean to act upon this agreement, or which crayon drawings you select. For the purposes of my Catalogue it is *indispensable* that I should know at once the precise title of any and every such drawing — the mode of execution (whether crayon, coloured chalks, or otherwise), and the date, actual or approximate.

3. Yesterday the person employed by the Burlington Club brought to my house the *Joan of Arc*, the *Proserpine*, and a coloured chalk drawing named (as I understand) *La Pia*.[1] With the *Proserpine* I had no concern, and I sent it away. I also told the man to take away *La Pia* — for I have never received from you any advice or request concerning it: but somehow or other the man left *La Pia* behind him. If you wish to put it into the sale, I will attend to that: if not, I shall return it to you at first opportunity. My house is blocked up with pictures, frames, etc.

4. If you mean to see about Insurance, the time will now be arriving.

5. As you informed me through Mr. Watts that you did not wish to retain that drawing (or drawings?) which was given to you under my brother's will,[2] but would prefer to have a copy of his *Ballads and Sonnets*, I on 16 March ordered a Bookseller to send you a copy of the book — which must no doubt have been done at once. The drawing should therefore return to me — and, as I propose including it in the auction-sale, should return without delay. Please see to this: and, if any the least delay takes place, I would thank you to let me know at once, for my Catalogue, whether the drawing is in pencil or what else, and its title (or subject) and actual or approximate date.

I am not sure whether or not you are now at Bath. Shall therefore send this letter to Mr. Watts, requesting him to oblige me by forwarding it to your most probable address.

With sincerest regards,

Yours always truly,
W. M. Rossetti

MS: Rutgers.

1. Surtees 207D.
2. Not identified. Valpy was one of thirteen persons named in the will who were to receive "a small drawing or other article." Mrs. Morris was to receive "the largest and best of the chalk drawings for the subjects of which she sat as are now hanging in my studio."

365. TO FORD MADOX BROWN

Somerset House,
14 April 1883

Dear Brown,

Yours of 12th received — Be sure that I am anxious to get this matter[1] adjusted: but anything like *interference* on my part only worsens matters. For instance a few words which I spoke last evening only induced Lucy to vow that Mathilde "should not come between her and her husband," and she even wrote off a letter to you to shut up the whole affair. But I got her to think better of it, and she then wrote inviting Mathilde to meet others at dinner on Wednesday,[2] and this letter I posted with my own hand — so now the next move towards amicableness lies with Mathilde — I will say no more here about the bothering and distressing affair.

Poor dear Lucy is much upset — having previously had more than enough to keep her feelings on the stretch: but probably she may yet tone down, and pretty soon. Luckily she and I are (as always I might say) on the very warmest terms of affection.

We long to hear of your prospering increasingly in health. Love to Emma.

Your affectionate
W. M. Rossetti

I might have said that Frank means to come on Wednesday, *if only Cathy will do the like*: we trust she may — but don't as yet know.

MS: AP.

1. MS. Diary, 6 April 1883: "Cathy came round, and mentioned to Lucy something which does not dispose her to make it up at once with Mathilde Blind — a coldness having arisen between them in consequence (primarily) of something said by Marshall 10 or 12 days ago. The details are irritating, and essentially insignificant, and I don't repeat them here: the distressing part of the affair is that Brown is more on Mathilde's side than on that of Lucy and Cathy, and hence he also is not in the most cordial of moods. I heartily hope the whole thing will soon be cured, but this does not seem to lie in the *immediate* future. What little I myself can do has been and shall be solely in the way of conciliation." FMB to WMR, 9 April 1883, throws some light on the squabble: "Marshall's observation to Mathilde it seems to me was made partly as a jocular compliment to her and partly that he could not imagine that Lucy and Cathy with all their children could be in a position to spare time to go with me to the seaside. And even had they been so ... he might think that in such a long illness the conversation of an old friend *not one of the family*, is the likeliest to cheer the spirits of an invalid.... Cathy's impugnable view of the matter *that either her will or her skill as a nurse was put in question* is simply childish, because no one that ever knew my two daughters could imagine either of them *wanting to me in devotion* — unless it be in the prosecution of this confounded imbroglio. One would almost imagine old-standing *dislike* at the bottom of all — and yet Emma tells me Cathy never disliked Mathilde nor do I think there was really that feeling working in Lucy either" (AP).
2. WMR to FMB, 19 April 1883: "You may like to know that Mathilde dined with us yesterday: Cathy and Frank, along with Mrs. [Lucy; W. K.] Clifford, Watts, and Ingram, to meet her. All passed over, I consider, well: Mathilde's demeanour being simple and unembarrassed, perhaps a little subdued, and that of Lucy and Cathy courteous and agreeable without *empressement*. It may be hoped that things will henceforth readjust themselves into their ordinary current — or nearly so" (AP).

446

366. TO FORD MADOX BROWN

5 Endsleigh Gardens,
24 May 1883

Dear Brown,

I drew the cheque for £100[1] yesterday, and entrusted it to Lucy, who I know has already written to you, and will see to the right disposal of the cheque. So far as my convenience goes, there is no reason why I should not pay the money as well now as hereafter, and as well to you as to Watts; although it is true that the upshot of Gabriel's sale was somewhat more meagre, for behoof of the Estate, than I had thought probable,[2] and a new and bothering demand came down upon me last Saturday. This is from Fanny, who says she holds an I.O.U. for money lent, £300.[3] After consulting Watts I believe the claim is only too well founded: I have instructed him (for I will not discuss details direct with Fanny) to require strict proof, and if we can show later payments as furnishing a set-off we shall not fail to do so.

You must be heedful not to overtire yourself: in other respects I hope and believe that you are now substantially recovered — how great a relief to all of us I need not say.

Sorry to hear of Rowley's family-trouble.[4] I had occasion to write to him 3 or 4 days ago.

Love to Emma.

Your
W. M. Rossetti

A Mr. and Mrs. Simon[5] from Crumpsall called here on Sunday — Lucy being away at Gravesend. They seem pleasant people, and hearty admirers of your work — noteably the *Crabtree*.

MS: AP.

1. Possibly related to the proposed purchase of shares in Ravensbourne Wharf (see Letter 363, Note 4).
2. MS. Diary, 8 May 1883: "I was twice at Christie's today. In the morning found that the hanging of Gabriel's works was just beginning. In the afternoon ... found the hanging advanced towards completion, and the works looking very fine; the large room and the entrance-room were about filled, and I believe some works will have to go into the side-room.... Christie expresses the opinion that — not taking into account the few leading works in Gabriel's sale — the bulk of the drawings will at the present date sell for much larger prices than they will ever again command: he refers to his experience in the Landseer and other sales effected pretty soon after the artist's death. He thinks the sale will last from 1 to 4½." 9 May: "I looked in again at Christie's, this being the 1st of the 3 days of private view: the rooms were not crowded, yet there must have been some 80 to 100 people present. The weather just now is somewhat disastrous." 10 May: "I ... looked in at Christie's: the scene was sufficiently lively, the attendance being perhaps half as much again as yesterday's." May 11 to 20: "The sale ... went moderately well taking all the lots together: but ... the result to the Estate is decidedly less than I had thought fairly probable — it amounts to about £2830, from which Auctioneer's percentage etc. remain to be deducted." The final sum was £2570.13.3, the 7½% charged by Christie's being less than WMR expected (MS. Diary, 12 June).
3. MS. Diary, 24 May 1883: "Watts ... showed me a letter he has now received from Schott, proposing that Watts should call on Schott, and look into the evidence about the I.O.U.; also saying that a further sum of £120 is in reality owing from Gabriel's estate, but not claimed by Schott, on account of a drawing of *The Loving Cup* [possibly Surtees 201 R. 2] which belonged to F[anny], and was afterwards taken up by Gabriel and sold without her receiving the proceeds. I told Watts that I think Schott should call on him, not he on Schott: this is his own view as well." 5 June: "Watts ...

has now seen the I.O.U. for £300 which F[anny] brings forward, and the letter which accompanied it: neither is dated, but it is said that the envelope which enclosed them can be produced. I shall require (and gave Watts a note to that effect) production of the envelope before the claim is further considered: so that then, by inspection of cheque-books etc., I may see what amount of money can be shown as paid to F[anny] at dates later than the I.O.U. Whether any such money can be regarded as a set-off against the I.O.U. is a separate question: Watts is evidently not sanguine on the point, as Schott professes that such money must be regarded as an acknowledgement of concurrent services and attentions — F[anny] having at all times, with but little intermission toward the date of her marriage to Schott, been calling at Gabriel's, looking after the house, attending when he wrote asking her to keep him company when otherwise solitary, etc. etc. So Watts says: though I had not myself thought that her presence in the house, for the last 4 or 5 years of Gabriel's life (or indeed since the summer of 1872) was nearly so constant as this: she was discouraged from coming, it seems, when either Watts or myself was there.''

    4. Not identified.
    5. Charles M. Simon, handkerchief manufacturer, Seymour Road, Crumpsall (*Slater's Manchester Directory*).

367. TO ALGERNON CHARLES SWINBURNE

Somerset House,
7 June 1883

Dear Swinburne,

Few things could have pleased me better to hear than your having undertaken a critical preface to the *Cenci* in a French version.[1] You will certainly do the great subject justice; and put a few other Frenchmen along with Victor Hugo in the way of understanding which, among the various richly veined pebbles dropped some 70 or so years ago into the lake of English poetry, is the one which really went nearest to the centre, and is destined to raise the most unnumbered succession of concentric circles. In one respect — supposing the translation to be excellently well done — a Frenchman will have a chance of really estimating the play higher than an Englishman can — i.e., the Frenchman will not have forced upon his attention the too frequent plagiarisms (though it clearly seems they were unconscious) from memorable passages in Shakespeare.

Well do I remember the *Fille du Policeman* and *Soeur de la Reine*:[2] should like to read them again — not alone for old memory's sake.

I am pretty sure to "like your little new book and its verses of dedication,"[3] but have not seen it yet. I hear the *Times*[4] has already (and, as I am told, for the first time during your literary history) been pleased to notice them, and with eulogium. Have also not seen the *Fortnightly* sonnets[5] — but *may* do so some day. Louis Blanc seems to me to have been a man deserving of very high public regard.

If you want to see that Marat was a noble example of the man of science and the martyr of public weal, read the Memoir of him in *Encyclopaedia Britannica*, and contrast it with the ensuing Memoir of M. Antoinette. *O Tempora O mores.* The Marat biographer is Morse Stephens:[6] is he an American? I did not remember that the immortal patriot was on the Father's side an Italian — Corsican — name really Mara: that he was partly Swiss I knew, and thus not strictly French at all.

Yours onely and indivisibly,
W. M. Rossetti

You may be aware that a new opera lately produced here with no little applause — *La Gioconda*[7] — is founded on Victor Hugo's *Angelo, Tyran de Padoue* — but it departs considerably from that story. I have seen it with enjoyment.

MS: BL.

1. *Les Cenci, Drame de Shelley. Traduction de Tola Dorian, avec préface de Algernon Charles Swinburne* (Paris, 1883).
2. Both were first published by Cecil Lang in *New Writings by Swinburne* (1964).
3. See Letter 362, Note 2.
4. 6 June 1883, p. 4.
5. *Fortnightly Review*, n.s. 33 (June 1883), 765-66, three sonnets in memory of Louis Blanc (1811-82), journalist and socialist, whom Swinburne met through Karl Blind (*SL*, 1:248).
6. Henry Morse Stephens (1857-1919), Scottish-born historian of the French Revolution; one of the principal contributors to the *DNB*. From 1894 he taught in the United States, first at Cornell University and later at the University of California.
7. It was first performed at La Scala in 1876. MS. Diary, 31 May 1883: "We joined the Hueffers in their box at Covent Garden, to see the first representation of Ponchielli's opera *La Gioconda*.... The whole has a brilliant and stirring character, and the interlude ballet of the 24 Hours is the most attractive thing of its kind, I think, that I ever saw."

368. TO THEODORE WATTS-DUNTON

5 Endsleigh Gardens,
13 June 1883

Dear Watts,

I have considered Mr. Schott's letter saying that the I.O.U.[1] was given in the early part of 1875. Of this day I have no *proof*; but I am quite content to adopt it, and shall now and henceforth assume that the I.O.U. is a valid document dated (say) 31 March 1875.

What I shall now have to do is this. I shall have to look through Gabriel's accounts to see what sums of money can be distinctly shown to have been paid to Mrs. or Mr. Schott since 31 March 1875 (that *other* and large sums of which no record exists were paid is notorious to you, me, and several others); and shall also have to take into account the works of art by or coming from Gabriel which remain in the hands of Mr. and Mrs. Schott, also the presumable value of said works — a large proportion of which works must I am certain be such as Mrs. or Mr. Schott can show no *legal* claim to — but only easy good nature on Gabriel's part in placing or leaving them in her hands, and tolerance or indifference in never reclaiming them. Having got these particulars together, I shall have to compare their total with the total of £300 — with what result I will not at present forecast; and shall then consider — with reasonable deliberation — what answer or proposal it will be legally and in right feeling proper for me to return to the claim of £300.

This is, I think, all that I can say on the subject at present. As you know, I have numerous matters to attend to: but that of looking up Gabriel's accounts etc. will be diligently and early attended to.

Yours always truly,
W. M. Rossetti

MS: BL. Extract in Baum, p. 121.

1. See Letter 366, Note 3.

369. TO THEODORE WATTS-DUNTON

5 Endsleigh Gardens,
18 June 1883

Dear Watts,

On Saturday morning I had to go to the Union Bank about Valpy's affair, and I took the opportunity (which I had been wanting for some while past) of getting thence Gabriel's last passbook, which I had seen and returned to the Bank towards the beginning of this year. The book begins in 1872, and has done me Yeoman's service in re Schott.[1]

I find in it the payments specified in the enclosed list, to Hughes and Schott (neither in these nor in any cases does "Mrs." or the like appear in the passbook) — total £1110.0.6, starting from 1 April 1875. I forget what was the exact date of Mrs. Schott's marriage — should suppose, very early in 1880: it surprises me to see the name Hughes appearing at a date later than the marriage.

In some cases — but not in any from 1880 onwards — it appears to me just conceivable that the Hughes recorded in the passbook was not Mrs. Hughes, but Arthur Hughes: this is however a mere surmise, for I don't remember having ever been aware that Gabriel had borrowed money from Arthur Hughes, and afterwards repaid it.

Now that I see this considerable sum of £1110 paid since the date proffered by the Schotts themselves as date of an I.O.U. for £300, and knowing as I do that *many* other sums of money reached Mrs. Schott's hands, and that works of art well worth (I dare say) £1000 to £1500 stuck to them, I am *very greatly reluctant* to pay the £300 — or, as a matter of absolute demand on her part, to pay anything. I know however that you have always regarded her case as strong, and mine as weak: I must therefore do the best I can, but please don't *commit* me to anything without preconcert. My present notion is to ride the high horse, and say — I utterly repudiate your claim of £300, because I can prove that since its date you were paid £1110, and you received or appropriated much besides which I might raise awkward questions about if I chose: still, I will be conciliatory as a matter of goodwill, and regard for Gabriel's memory, and will pay you *something*, as a free gift only.

For this something I would readily give £50 to £80 — or say even £100 if that seems better: more than £100 not.[2]

As I am not like Cassio a great arithmetician,[3] it is possible that I have mis-added some figures in the enclosed list: but the list will (if so) rectify itself. No doubt you will not let it out of your hands, but only a copy of it if needed. I have not kept any copy, but of course I retain the passbook.

Yours,
W. M. Rossetti

450

Perhaps one might *terrorize* a little with that portrait by Watts. My full and genuine belief is that Gabriel never *gave* it to Mrs. Schott, but only, not much liking it, transferred it from his own hands and house to hers. We might say — If we chose to raise those awkward questions aforesaid, what becomes of your pretty little subscription-list for the engraving from that portrait?[4]

MS: BL. Extract in Baum, pp. 122-23.

1. See Letter 366, Note 3.
2. MS. Diary, 31 July 1883: "Watts called at Somerset House. The Schotts put their affair into the hands of a lawyer, who happened to be [Holroyd] Chaplin, Valpy's late partner. Watts and Chaplin conferred; and it was agreed that I should pay £65, to include Schott's legal expenses, and that the Schotts should thereupon deliver to me the I.O.U. for £300, and the letter relating thereto, and should make a statutory declaration to the effect that they do not retain any other document whatever upon which a further claim could be founded.... With these terms I am perfectly satisfied, and glad to close the affair accordingly."
3. *Othello*, I. i. 19.
4. See Letter 355, Note 5.

370. TO CHRISTINA ROSSETTI

2 Saltwood Gardens,
Hythe,
18 July 1883

Dear Christina,

When I was at Birchington I talked a goodish deal to Seddon about the gravestone and windows.[1] The idea then was that I would undertake the whole affair of the gravestone; and that Seddon, along with Shields and other admirers of Gabriel, would raise funds for filling with stained glass the 2 windows of 2 lights each (whole or part thereof) which come near the grave. Shields would undertake to make the design for one light; Brown and Jones would be invited to undertake two others; for the 4th I heard nothing particular suggested. You were to be consulted as to the subjects for all 4 lights. Seddon, as I gathered, would provide for the actual supply of glass etc.

As to the gravestone my idea had from the first been to ask Brown to furnish a design generally resembling (but not identical with) the stone over Nolly's grave. Some uncertainties (not worth detailing) have arisen about this. I shall now however get the point settled. If Brown should not fall in with my views, I shall ask Seddon to see about making and carrying out a design — which would probably be of a simple but solid and very decorous kind. The Brown project might I fancy cost from £30 to £45: the Seddon project from £70 to £100.

You will perceive that the outline of this scheme is that the gravestone should be entirely the affair of myself (or of myself and family, as might be arranged *inter nos*); while the windows would be entirely the affair of admirers of Gabriel's genius (personal friends of course included) who would subscribe the needed funds.

Mamma's idea of commissioning one window (or perhaps one light in a window is rather meant) would mar the symmetry of this scheme: but I don't see that that is of the slightest consequence if Mamma prefers this course to any

451

other. It seems however that she should explain to Seddon what she intends, especially as it affects Shields with whom Seddon himself would otherwise be concerting his plans.

I don't yet know the exact day when I shall be back in London — say towards Monday or Tuesday next.

Particular thanks for the Bungalow photograph:[2] I had not got nor even seen it. Enclosed American article[3] is very laudatory and so far pleasing, but of course it shows more ignorance than knowledge of the subject.

We continue to go on nicely here. Were in Calais from Friday afternoon till Sunday afternoon — much to the enjoyment of Olive and Arthur. Lucy comes to my elbow as I am writing, and pledges me to send Mamma and you her particular love — and to say that it is only a slip on her part that she has not sent some sort of letter yet.

Yours with love,
William

Ellis has sent me £97.4 as the royalty on Gabriel's books (chiefly the *Poems* volume) for last 6 months — Very large this amount, I think.[4]

MS: AP.

1. DGR's tombstone was set up on 24 July 1884 (see Letter 378, Note 3). It was designed by FMB in the form of a Celtic cross, with bas-reliefs of (from the base up) St. Luke, the patron saint of painters; a winged ox, the saint's emblem; the spiritual marriage of Dante and Beatrice; and (occupying the center of the cross) the temptation in the Garden of Eden.

Only the two-light window commissioned by Mrs. Rossetti from Shields was erected at All Saints' Church. The second window and Gosse's suggestion of a medallion portrait for the churchyard (MS. Diary, 29 November 1883) were abandoned in favor of a bust in London (see Letter 380, Note 1). On 12 December 1882 Shields showed Mrs. Rossetti a design for one of the lights, an adaptation of DGR's *Mary Magdalene at the Door of Simon the Pharisee*, but this was objected to by the vicar of Birchington, J. P. Alcock: "he thought its treatment unedifying — and Shields, with a very bad grace, had to yield" (MS. Diary, 1 July 1884). Shields then chose DGR's *The Passover in the Holy Family* (Surtees 78), which he "completed ... in various details" (MS. Diary, 21 October 1884). For the second light he depicted Christ healing the blind man at Bethsaida (Mark, 8:22-26). MS. Diary, 21 October 1884: "Went to see at the Glass-Works of Heaton & Butler in Garrick Street, the two-light window which Shields has now executed.... On the whole I find these works satisfactory — the *Passover* better than the adaptation from Gabriel's *Magdalene*.... The colour is agreeable and solid. I don't however like either of the heads of Christ: they are over-laboured into a common sort of handsomeness and thoughtful dignity."

2. Westcliff Bungalow.

3. Probably J. H. Ward, "Rossetti in Poetry and Art," *American Church Review*, 61 (April 1883), 371-79.

4. AP (MS. Diary and statements from Ellis) provide the following details of the royalties on DGR's books up to 1886 when *Collected Works* appeared: 1st half 1882, £28.1; 2d half 1882, £68.2; 1st half 1883, £97.13; 2d half 1883, £77.14; 2d half 1884, £42.3 (137 *Ballads and Sonnets* @ 3/-, £20.11, and 144 Poems @ 3/-, £21.12). In 1882 *Ballads and Sonnets* appeared as a Tauchnitz edition, with a Memoir by Francis Hueffer, for which Hueffer and WMR received £15 each.

Dear Brown,

Most of the matters connected with Gabriel's estate having now been settled, I mean to address myself seriously to the question of putting up over his grave a not excessively costly but suitable memorial.

From the first my idea has been that I should best like to have a design from your hand, and that something nearly enough resembling the gravestone set up for Nolly would answer well. This I mentioned to Lucy, and she, only partly understanding my intention, asked and obtained (I suppose more than a year ago) your permission to duplicate Nolly's gravestone. That however was not what I at any time meant. For so extremely distinguished a man as Gabriel I should not think it appropriate merely to *copy* the memorial of anyone else — not even of so singular a youthful genius as Nolly. What I had really wished was that you would invent Gabriel's monument: and, to save you labour, and indicate a scale and general plan of memorial which would please me, I referred to Nolly's gravestone — my idea being that you would perhaps see fit to take that as the type and modify it (more or less, according to your discretion) in detail.

Would you kindly inform me whether it would suit you to do this, and perhaps you could give me some *general* idea of when the design might be ready. It must be understood that the clergyman of Birchington (Alcock)[1] has the right — and he pointedly stated this to me about the time of the funeral — to approve or disapprove any item in a monument or inscription. What *he* likes best is a Gothic cross or something of that class — which of course is far from being what *I* like best. I regard it however as certain that the clergyman would not raise, or would not maintain, any objection to a neutral form of monument, such as Nolly's.

Probably you could also inform me what was the approximate *cost* of Nolly's gravestone.

Seddon, whom I saw lately at Birchington, would be quite willing to furnish a design of his own for Gabriel's monument. I had told him long ago however that my first recourse would be to you: and I need not tell *you* that I would rather carry into execution a design of yours than of his — on every possible ground. Failing you, I would not disregard him.

I find there is a project also of some stained glass in memory of Gabriel, and I fancy you may be addressed on this subject likewise sooner or later. But that affair is not and will not be in *my* hands. My mother and Christina are now at Birchington — to stay 6 weeks or so.

I have read through Ingram's[2] book about Nolly — with considerable pleasure as to essentials, though a somewhat more potent faculty than Ingram displays in the treatment of his materials might have been wished for. The illustrations look very satisfactory.

That affair of the *Germ*[3] (Stock was to have given me £40 for re-editing it, but, failing your and Woolner's assent, it will fall through) is still pending. It may or may not fall to my lot to bore you on the subject at some future time.

Hythe suits the health and the likings of all of us. I am to return to London on Tuesday, but Lucy and the children will remain here for several weeks following. We hope Emma — to whom love — got home comfortably: Cathy had not heard from her up to last evening.

About the affair of Mrs. Schott — on learning that the date of the I.O.U. was about 31 March 1875, I looked through Gabriel's passbook, and found that since that date £1110 had been paid to her, which (not to speak of designs etc.) seems a tolerable set-off against £300. Just before leaving town I wrote Watts that I was disposed to fight rather than pay, but would give a *douceur* of some £50 to £100 rather than push matters to extremity. He has now just offered £60 — with (I suspect) very dubious prospect of acceptance.

Yours in all affection,
W. M. Rossetti

Lucy's particular love. She asks me to say that she has been intending for some while to write to you asking after your health etc., and also enquiring whether Watts has yet settled with you that matter of the Wharf — as, after his apparently being (so she says) offended with her on account of a slightly chaffy and pressing letter on her part, he seems, so far as her observation goes, to have dropped the affair again.

MS: AP.

1. John Price Alcock, B.A., Oriel College, Oxford, 1861; vicar of Birchington, 1871-88.
2. John H. Ingram (1849-1916), biographer and editor of Poe, editor of the Eminent Women series published by W. H. Allen from 1888.
3. Stock's proposal to reissue the *Germ* was first noted in MS. Diary on 29 May. On 18 June WMR dined with him "to further matters regarding the *Germ*: nothing of a marked kind was done however beyond what had been already mooted. Stock and his wife seem to be agreeable people: he has a number of fine first editions — *Faerie Queene, Paradise Lost,* A Kempis, *Pilgrim's Progress, Vicar of Wakefield,* etc. etc." 25 July: "Woolner repeats in a letter to me the refusal he had previously given to Stock as to his poems in the *Germ* — he will not have them reprinted. To all appearance this finally burkes the *Germ* project." 26 June 1893: "Stock, who again ... wanted to republish the *Germ* under my editorship, is again foiled by the refusal of Mrs. Woolner." For its republication by Stock in 1901, see Letter 542, Note 2.

372. TO THEODORE WATTS-DUNTON

5 Endsleigh Gardens,
26 July 1883

Dear Watts,

Dinneford & Co., the Chemists of 180 New Bond Street, sent in long ago, as you may remember, an account against Gabriel, chiefly (as I understand it) for chloral. They now after long lethargy write again (very civilly) renewing their claim for £52.4.6. I have no reason to doubt that Gabriel owed the money, but as the chloral is what killed him I don't want to pay the full bill if I can help. Would it be legitimate to ask what medical authority they had for supplying the chloral (Bell[1] supplying the like all the while) — or to fence with their demand in any other way? Please advise me at your convenience.[2]

Could I get back that second batch of Gabriel's letters to me which I handed to you months ago to be copied?

Yours always,
W. M. Rossetti

MS: BL.

1. "Messrs. Bell & Co., the chemists" (*FLM*, 1:343).
2. MS. Diary, 3 August 1883: "I took up the bill of the Chemist Dinneford for £52 odd, chiefly for chloral supplied to Gabriel. This is in addition to a claim of much the same amount sent in months ago by Bell, and paid. I wrote Dinneford that, before discharging his account, I should like to know what was the precise medical authority under which he supplied these terrific quantities of chloral." 7 August: "A member of Dinneford's firm called on me to talk over the matter.... He produced a prescription for chloral signed by Marshall in 1877, and entered into various details (partly familiar to me) as to the manoeuvres which were constantly adopted for making the proportion of chloral to water less than Gabriel was allowed to suppose. The firm seem to have done nothing to which serious exception can be taken, and I suppose I shall have to pay their bill."

373. TO FORD MADOX BROWN

5 Endsleigh Gardens,
30 July 1883

Dear Brown,

It gives me extreme satisfaction to find that Gabriel will have his modest monument from the hand worthiest to supply it — your own.[1] I have always contemplated the gravestone of Nolly as in general scope and quality a very proper precedent for the one to Gabriel: all I wish is that there may be so much difference between the two as to show that artistic thought and sympathy has been re-exerted for the second no less than the first, and to save me from any invidious remarks (or any personal self-reproach, which is worse) to the effect that I regarded the whole affair with so much apathy as to put up a mere duplicate of what I found ready to hand.

As to pen, brush, or palette, please suit your own views: any one or all are obviously quite *apposite*. To me a brush seems to lend itself well to bas-relief, and a pen not amiss: a palette less well. If you can conveniently give me the address of the carver of Nolly's gravestone, I shall be obliged: I always thought he had succeeded well. I am not quite sure however but that I might consider it well to commit (*if it meets your approval*) the execution of the monument more or less to Seddon's hands. He seems rather to pride himself on some of the materials which he has at command: and, if this were to entail (for more durable or more decorative material) some additional cost beyond the extremely small sum indicated in your letter, I should not have the slightest objection — rather perhaps the reverse. Christina wishes to contribute some £10 for the gravestone.

I dare say you have heard by this time from Lucy. There has been a little trouble of late about Mary (vomiting etc.), but I presume unimportant.

The affair of stained glass for Gabriel was (as represented to me by Seddon) quite irrespective of the family — i.e., it was proposed that friends and admirers should get up a subscription. However my mother, hearing of it, said she would like to provide for one window (out of two windows) of two lights, and would give £100 for it: and she went straight to Shields for a design. This is the last I know of it.

I have not seen any review of Ingram, except that one (very handsome and pleasing, but unaccountably ignoring the *painter*-work of Nolly) which you sent us in the *Liverpool Mercury*,[2] and the one in the *Athenaeum*[3] — which Lucy seems decidedly to like, and I like moderately. I don't know from what point of view the *Academy*[4] assails the book: can't myself see that there is anything *serious* to say against it.

Woolner seems quite determined against the *Germ*: so I regard the project as lapsed — though Stock seems still to hanker after it. Have heard nothing further about the Schott affair.

Yours with love,
W. M. Rossetti

I wish you well through the horrid nuisance of removal. Sympathize much therein both with you and with Emma.

MS: AP.

1. FMB to WMR, 26 July 1883: "Independently of the pleasure it will give me to do anything for you, I can assure you I feel quite proud of the idea of designing a monument for poor dear Gabriel.... I will set about this design very shortly and I dare say send it you by the first week of August. The design I made for Oliver I was much assisted in by the old tombstones I found in Merton Churchyard. Here [Manchester] I fear there is nothing of so beautiful a pattern to help me — but I will do my best. I suppose something very near the one at St. Pancras Finchley will do, with the same bronze flower holders — but the emblems altered to suit the case. A pen and either a brush or a palette I suppose indispensable" (AP).
2. 5 July 1883, p. 6.
3. 21 July 1883, pp. 69-70.
4. 21 July 1883, pp. 38-39, by J. Arthur Blaikie.

374. TO FORD MADOX BROWN

5 Endsleigh Gardens,
31 July [1883]

Dear Brown,

A letter received this morning from Christina (at Birchington) raises — or reraises — a fidgeting suggestion from my mother about a cross as part of the emblem-work for Gabriel's grave. Were it anyone other than my mother, I would settle the question by a "No": but with her, at age of 83, I must be a little more long-enduring. Shall write and endeavour to stave off the suggestion — but with a little uncertainty as to upshot. Meanwhile I have thought it only right to drop you these lines, as possibly you may see well to await some further details before you continue your friendly labours in the design. This of course as you prefer.

Your
W. M. Rossetti

I suppose there would be no artistic difficulty whatever in getting a cross into your design, without any material interference with its general idea:[1] the real obstacle being that neither you nor I *want* a cross.

Schott polished off it seems with £65: I am very well pleased to be thus quit of it.

MS: AP.

1. FMB to WMR, 1 August 1883: "It strikes me that if there is to be a cross at all it will be much better to have the monument itself in shape of one, which is so very common and *Medieval* that in Gabriel's case it would by no means excite attention. To add arbitrarily a cross — on the other hand — to a Queen-Anne headstone, where it is not usual to see one, would it seems to me, look more prepense. Something like a large Irish cross perhaps in granite might look very much in keeping" (AP).

375. TO FORD MADOX BROWN
5 Endsleigh Gardens,
14 August 1883

Dear Brown,

I am afraid you may have been thinking me rather remiss in replying to your letter of 1 August — for which I was very much obliged, showing as it does that you don't so much mind a (to me) rather irritating interference with plans which were already fairly matured.[1] My delay has arisen solely from this cause: that, as my mother wants a cross and I don't, I was strongly minded to say that she might have the cross if she liked, but then she must herself order it (of course from you and no one else); and this I did write to her, and 2 or 3 letters have been interchanged between us, but she seems to think that for her to act as I propose would be an improper interference with my rights as Executor. She therefore now insists upon leaving the matter in my hands, as if the proposal of the cross had been *non avenu*: I am thus free to act upon my own liking, but would regret to ignore hers, and so on the whole, though desperately against the grain, I reconcile myself to the idea of the cross, and of myself asking you to see about it.[2]

Much as I like your design for Nolly's tomb, and much as I should like also to have a certain affinity between the memorial of your son and that of Gabriel, I have no doubt there is some force in your view that a cross inserted into a design of that class would be less artistically satisfactory than a monument based upon the idea of a cross. I therefore beg to commit the matter *wholly* to your hands, to deal with as you see best. Of course I don't want to over-enforce — nor do you — the idea of the cross as a profession of Christianity on Gabriel's, my, or anyone's part: but you will know what to do so as to reconcile all the right requirements of the case. I would only add that there is no *hurry* about the matter — in such a sense as in any way to embarrass you in taking up and setting aside this matter of the monument according to your own convenience. Thank you *much* for all your kindness in this affair.

You will be aware that I am

[Incomplete]

MS: AP.

1. See Letter 374.

2. WMR to Lucy, 15 August 1883: "When all is said, there cannot be any *great* objection to the fact that a man who lies buried in a *churchyard* should have over his grave a memorial in keeping with other churchyard memorials of the same date: though I could well have wished it otherwise" (AP).

376. TO THEODORE WATTS-DUNTON

5 Endsleigh Gardens,
27 November 1883

Dear Watts,

It seems a longish while since I saw or heard from you: no doubt you have been well occupied meanwhile — as for instance in giving Mr. Lewis Morris[1] his due, and not other people's due. Every now and then I reflect with some surprise that the Legacy-duty people don't nag at me to pay them my debit; and speculate as to the date when I shall be doing this, paying off Dunn, Brass, and any other claimant, settling your own account — and thereupon coming to know what moderate sum of money is really at my own disposal, and to see how I might best invest it. If there is anything worth mentioning on any of these points, perhaps you would let me know at some convenient moment.

You may be aware that Brown has been designing Gabriel's gravestone in the form of an Irish Cross (I believe Stephens will be putting a paragraph about it into next *Athenaeum*[2]), and it devolves upon me to write the inscription. I should like to know whether you, as especially competent to pronounce on such a question, think the enclosed draft-inscription[3] good, bad, or indifferent: Your opinion (I dare say I may not even *consult* anyone else, save that I showed the draft yesterday to Lucy) I should very highly value; but in such a matter as this I should be ultimately guided by my own preference. These draft inscriptions I myself like to a certain extent, but am not particularly enamoured of them.

As to the 2nd inscription, what I really mean by the opening words is to suggest to the discerning agnostic that I myself would not have had a cross, but that I conceded the point to my mother's wish (she and I had a goodish deal of debate about the matter in July and August). I don't quite approve the word "*suggested* by Dante Rossetti's mother": would *proposed* or what other word be better? *Desired* would jingle unpleasantly with the ensuing *designed*. The clause "executed by the Firm of Patteson & Co., Manchester," sounds I fear a little shoppy. Unless I were *decidedly pleased* with the style of execution, I would not put in any such clause: but being so pleased I might do so. The fact is that Brown, to get his designs properly carried out, *must* keep an eye on the execution of them; and to this end his proposal is to entrust the execution to Patteson[4] (late mayor of Manchester) of whom he knows something, and who would he thinks work *con amore* and without running up an exaggerated bill.

Yours always,
W. M. Rossetti

I have to submit my inscriptions to the clergyman: might perhaps do this soon after hearing what you think of them.

MS: BL.

1. (1833-1907), poet, whose *Songs Unsung* (1883) was reviewed negatively by Watts in the *Athenaeum*, 17 November 1883, pp. 627-29.

2. 1 December 1883, p. 709.

3. The inscription on the tombstone reads in part: "Here sleeps Gabriel Charles Dante Rossetti.... This cruciform monument bespoken by Dante Rossetti's mother was designed by his lifelong friend Ford Madox Brown. Executed by J. and H. Patteson and erected by his brother William and sister Christina Rossetti." WMR to FMB, 13 December 1883: "The opening phrase 'Here sleeps' will to most persons read as merely commonplace: I intend it for the eyes of those who know the secrets of Gabriel's ill-health and hypochondria" (AP).

4. Henry Patteson, mayor of Manchester, 1879-80.

377. TO EDWARD DOWDEN

5 Endsleigh Gardens,
17 January 1884

Dear Dowden,

I received your letter with much pleasure. The Autobiographical Compilation from Shelley[1] might be sent to me by any *secure* mode of transmission whenever you like: no hurry for it on my part.

I have read and considered your list of persons who have published something in this country about Whitman.[2] There are some names in it beyond what I know of: but I dare say that I have in my time known *other* appropriate names, more than the 4 below-mentioned (which are all that for the present occur to me).

1. G. H. Lewes was I fancy the very first Englishman to put into print something about Whitman:[3] from him probably Mrs. Lewes got her cue.[4] *Leaves of Grass* came out I think in 1855, and Lewes was then Editor of a weekly review named the *Leader*, and wrote in it something discerning about Whitman. I can't *assert* that Lewes's name was signed to the article: but am sure I am not mistaken in saying it was his.

2. In or about 1876 a case came into the Courts of Law in London — Buchanan v. Taylor was I think its name: being an action for libel brought by Robert Buchanan against the Proprietor of the *Examiner* on account of certain abusive articles by Swinburne therein published.[5] Hawkins (now Judge) was Taylor's counsel; and sought to discredit Buchanan on the ground of his being an advocate of the indecent writer Whitman. Of course Hawkins did not then *write* anything on the subject: but his and other speeches, as reported by newspapers at the time, might furnish some relevant matter.

3. When my Whitman book came out (I think 1868) Charles Kent was Editor of the Evening *Sun*. He wrote in that paper a long and most enthusiastic review — about the most affectionate and overflowing tribute to Whitman's great gifts that I have ever seen in print. Kent's name was not signed to this article, but I know it to be his.

4. Mrs. Gilchrist (widow of Blake's biographer, and authoress of Memoir of Mary Lamb[6]) became amazingly enthusiastic about Whitman after reading my Selection, followed by the Complete Works which I lent her: the book seemed quite a revelation to her, and permeated her whole thought and being. She wrote

459

me at large on the subject: and I was allowed to send extracts of her letters to Whitman, and these were eventually published in an American magazine named the *Radical* — say in 1870. They were published (I think) as being written by "an Englishwoman" — but since then Mrs. Gilchrist has been several times named in print as the authoress. These letters contain some of the very best things ever said about Whitman, in my opinion. They should I consider be noticed in what you are writing: but perhaps it would be right to consult Mrs. Gilchrist first. I could do this if more convenient to you.

I must possess numbers 3 and 4, and perhaps something about 2: not (I suppose) 1. This for your information in case you want to know or see more of them.

Like yourself, I never saw Fox's article on Whitman in the *Dispatch*:[7] I may have seen somewhere some *extracts* from it. Don't know whether Lord Strangford[8] wrote on Whitman in the *Pall Mall*: yet I seem to have heard something tending that way.

My brother never wrote for publication anything about Whitman. Towards 1865-1866, when he saw Swinburne constantly, and when Swinburne (since then considerably cooled about Whitman, I suspect) admired him fervently, my brother also set a high value on Whitman — most especially the Dirge for Lincoln. Even at that time I question whether my brother read in full the most characteristic and stirring poems of Whitman: and since then I think he hardly opened his books. In this state of things his feeling towards Whitman gradually changed: and his feeling was one of impatience against professed poetry in which recognized poetic form bore so small a part. He said to me more than once that Whitman is nothing but "sublimated Tupper";[9] and seriously contended that Whitman must certainly have read Tupper's book before undertaking his own. Yet spite of all this my brother had a real deep-lying sense of Whitman's greatness of scale and powerful initiative.

Yours very truly,
W. M. Rossetti

MS: Trinity College, Dublin.

1. "Cor Cordium," which Dowden consulted in writing his *Life of Shelley*. MS. Diary, 1 August 1883: "Professor Dowden called on me at Somerset House and made an important announcement. After conferring with the Shelley family, he is authorized to undertake the long-desiderated complete Life of Shelley. He has seen Garnett, who, owing to numerous other occupations, does not intend to proceed further with his once-projected (and probably begun) Life of Shelley. Dowden called on me principally to see what could be done in regard to using the Hitchener correspondence belonging to Slack. I told him that Slack alone could authorize any use of this: but that I would gladly put Dowden in possession of all that the correspondence contains, through the medium of the copy of it which I made in my old Shelley Compilation.... I gather that Dowden is *not* in possession of any information from the Shelleys amounting to a real new light upon the affair of Shelley's separation from Harriet. I told Dowden that I knew (from the correspondence that Miss Clairmont used to send over to Trelawny) that Shelley himself made a very serious allegation on the subject, which if verified would reverse the general view of the matter; but that I did not feel warranted in giving the details."

2. Dowden was preparing an appendix on "English Critics on Walt Whitman" for R. M. Bucke's *Walt Whitman* (1884).

3. In the *London Leader* (see M. Hindus, *Walt Whitman, the Critical Heritage* [1971], pp. 94-96, where Dowden's quotation from this letter is cited as evidence of Lewes's authorship). Hindus

reprints three earlier British reviews of *Leaves of Grass* 1855, in the *Critic*, the *London Weekly Dispatch*, and the *Examiner*.

4. George Eliot used some lines from *Leaves of Grass* as an epigraph to *Daniel Deronda* (1876), Bk. 4, Chap. 29.

5. According to the *Times* the action was founded on a review (not by Swinburne) of the anonymous *Jonas Fisher: a Poem in Brown and White* (1875; *Examiner*, 27 November 1875, pp. 1336-38), which declared the poem "the work of either Mr. Robert Buchanan or the devil" (it was by the Earl of Southesk); and Swinburne's letter "The Devil's Due" (11 December 1875, p. 1388; *SL*, 3:89-93), which continued the attack. Swinburne in fact had earlier published "Epitaph on a Slanderer" (*Examiner*, 20 November 1875, p. 1304) on the assumption that Buchanan was the author of the poem, but without naming him. Buchanan was awarded damages of £150. Peter Alfred Taylor (1819-91), radical M.P. for Leicester, 1862-84, was proprietor of the *Examiner*, 1873-78. Sir Henry Hawkins, Baron Brampton (1817-1907), became a judge in 1876, and a member of the Privy Council in 1898. Whitman was referred to during Hawkins's cross-examination of Buchanan on the second day (30 June) of the three-day trial. "Mr. Hawkins ... read several selections from the writings of 'Walter Whitman,' who had been spoken of with approbation by the plaintiff, and pressed for an opinion as to their gross indecency. This the plaintiff admitted without reserve, excusing, however, Mr. Whitman on account of his youth at the time his book was published." Hawkins later suggested that "a man who could extol and praise the infamously indecent poetry of Mr. Walter Whitman had no right to condemn the fleshly school, which, however bad, was not nearly so gross and corrupt as what had been written by Whitman" (*Times*, 30 June, 1, 3, July 1876, pp. 11, 13, 11).

6. Published in 1883.

7. *London Weekly Dispatch* (see Hindus, pp. 78-79, who considers the suggestion that the review was by William Howitt, but concludes that William Johnson Fox is more likely).

8. Percy Smythe, 8th Viscount Strangford (1826-69), philologist and ethnologist, was a frequent contributor to the *Pall Mall Gazette*, in which he published an assessment of Whitman as "outrageously, purposely, and defiantly obscene," but found in him many echoes of Persian poetry (16 February 1866, p. 10).

9. A reviewer in the *Examiner* in 1857 referred to Whitman as "a wild Tupper [Martin Tupper (1810-89), the author of *Proverbial Philosophy* (1838 etc.)] of the West" (Hindus, pp. 90-93).

378. TO FORD MADOX BROWN

5 Endsleigh Gardens,
5 June 1884

Dear Brown,

Lucy has shown me your capital letter to Seddon, and I think I had better myself write in response to it. I will first briefly state my general view of the project,[1] and then refer to particular points in your letter.

The honour proposed to Gabriel — stained glass or medallion or both — is of course an insignificant affair: but, as I don't see any present likelihood of anything on a larger or more national scale, I have no feeling of antipathy to it. If it comes to effect, I should in the abstract like to see your hand in the glass. Whatever is done or not done, I should consider that I as a member of the family am entirely aloof from any practical share or influence in the matter — which is professedly and really proper to *friends and admirers* of Gabriel, not to relatives — So much for my general view.

Now as to points in your letter. 1. I think you must be correct in saying that you could not work, nor undertake to work, so as to meet the Clergyman's notions: this would therefore be a finale to any proposed co-operation of yours. 2. For the sculpture, Woolner would in my opinion do, were it not for the fatal objection that Gabriel of late years hated him. Boehm[2] saw Gabriel several times (say) towards 1870, and might be available; or G. F. Watts, who seems to be now a recognized sculptor. On the whole, were it a question between medallion and church-glass, I would sooner have the former — i.e., on the assumption that you would not be the designer of the latter. 3. Of course anything like church-glass to Gabriel *is* incongruous: yet, as he lies buried in that churchyard, it seems not unnatural that any small early memorial of him should appear in the adjacent church, and in such form as is usual in churches. 4. You speak of making Seddon's proposal known to me: but it was known to me already, and for many months past.

I don't know that I need say any more, except to thank you affectionately for the general tone and details of your letter to Seddon. I agree in the idea you express to Lucy — that it would be more politic and convenient to hold over any such outspoken letter to Seddon until the gravestone shall be safe in its place:[3] assuming that you can thus act without incommoding yourself in relation to Seddon. Not indeed that I think any amount of scorn poured forth upon the Clergyman could warrant or enable him to raise at this date any objection to the gravestone: but it might be inopportune.

Love to Emma from

Your
W. M. Rossetti

MS: AP.

1. See Letter 370, Note 1.
2. Joseph Edgar Boehm (1834-90), whose statue of Queen Victoria (1869) for Windsor Castle secured him royal patronage, was the sculptor of the statue of Carlyle on the Thames embankment at Chelsea.
3. WMR to Frances Rossetti, 26 July 1884: "The monument was set up on Thursday. I went over to Birchington [from Herne Bay] yesterday and saw it *in situ*, and am highly satisfied with it. The grass mound which used to cover the grave is now gone, and only level earth remains. Some proper arrangement should be made about this at sometime" (AP).

379. TO WALT WHITMAN

5 Endsleigh Gardens,
1 January 1885

Dear Whitman,

Some while ago I received your kind present of the 2 volumes — *Leaves of Grass* and *Specimen Days*:[1] received them, I am certain you will believe, with extreme pleasure, and with a grateful sense of your continuing to remember me across a somewhat long lapse of years. To be remembered by Walt Whitman is what any man should be proud of, and none is so more than I.

I have read the *Specimen Days* volume right through: finding various new things, and continual pleasure in renewing my acquaintance with the old ones. Am extremely pleased to find in this copy of the book something which is absent even from Mrs. Gilchrist's copy — the photographs of your mother and father. If you were blessed with an unsurpassably good mother, I can with truth say the same of myself. My mother is still with us — aged nearly 85: health and faculties sound on the whole, but naturally bowed and stricken with the weight of years.

I have also scanned with a good deal of attention (short of complete re-reading) my old and constant admiration, the *Leaves of Grass* volume. I observe that some edition (I think the Philadelphia edition is named, but my volume is not under my hand at the moment for reference) is mentioned as the only final and complete form of *Leaves of Grass*. The volume with which you favoured me is not the Philadelphia edition, but I am in hopes that it may none the less be regarded as complete.

I am glad to note in this country from time to time symptoms of the increasing appreciation of your works: especially something written by Ruskin,[2] and the Sonata from the Lincoln Dirge.[3]

Accept as heretofore the affectionate respect and regard of

Yours always,
W. M. Rossetti

MS: LC. Published: *WWC*, 1:436-37.

1. *Leaves of Grass* was probably the seventh edition of 1881-82. *Specimen Days* (1882) incorporated *Memoranda During the War*.

2. C & W contains only one reference to Whitman, an item quoted from the *Athenaeum*, 20 March 1880: "Mr. Ruskin has sent to Mr. Walt Whitman for five complete sets of *Leaves of Grass* and *Two Rivulets*. He says in a letter that the reason these books excite such hostile criticism is 'They are deadly true — in the sense of rifles — against all our deadliest sins'" (34:727).

3. Probably Charles Villiers Stanford's (1852-1924) "Elegiac Ode (Whitman)" for solo voices, chorus, and orchestra, first performed at the Norwich Music Festival in 1884.

380. TO WILLIAM BELL SCOTT

5 Endsleigh Gardens,
7 January 1885

Dear Scotus,

Thanks for your last letter. Without reflecting upon the present case, I very much agree in your general observations about coterie-management etc. I often sadly reflect that I used to urge my dear Gabriel in 1870 not to go "diplomatizing" (as I got to call it) to have his book reviewed in various papers by friends and henchmen, but to stand aside and leave it to prove its own merits; and that, if he had taken this advice and not got so jubilant a proclamation of the merits of the poems, the soreness of outsiders would perhaps never have obtained so acrid an expression as in Buchanan's attack, with all its train of morbid and miserable consequences.

I am not very clear that "a memorial of a more important character" would have been likely to appear, within any time which one can reasonably compute. One hardly sees (or rather *I* hardly see) what it would be, unless it were a bust etc. among the poets in Westminster Abbey, or else a statue somewhere or other in London: neither of these seems to me imminent. The proposed memorial will itself be a half-statue or sculpture in London.[1] Its being close to Gabriel's house (so proposed) seems to me a very approvable point; and the form which it takes of a drinking-fountain, having a utilitarian character, is likely one might hope to dispose the authorities to grant that (or some) site, which under different circumstances might possibly have been haggled over. Brown (it is true) is as a sculptor untried: but as an artist and after making every proper deduction, I am free to say that I think few of his compatriots of the day excel or rival him. Other painters — as Watts and Leighton — tried sculpture, with a result that no one laughed at.

I wrote yesterday that the present scheme was concerted between Brown and Seddon: perhaps I may as well add a few details, lest it should be supposed that Brown was precisely the prime mover. The fact then is that, ever since an early date following Gabriel's death, *Seddon* had the idea that he would supplement the monument over the grave (Christina's and my affair) and the painted glass in Birchington, (my mother's affair) by additional painted glass in Birchington, for which friends and admirers generally would be invited to subscribe. In course of time Seddon

[Incomplete]

MS: Princeton.

1. MS. Diary, 9 June 1884, records FMB's proposal to Seddon to substitute for the glass and medallion portrait of Gabriel at Birchington a bust "on the scale of the Shakespeare bust at Stratford; Brown to do the bust, and Seddon the decorative accompaniments." By 29 June FMB and Seddon had concluded that it would be "well to drop all thought of a monument of any kind to Gabriel, by subscription, in Birchington Church. Instead ... Brown suggests that a drinking-fountain should be set up in front of the Cheyne Walk house; surmounted by a bust of Gabriel in very high relief, with pen and palette, as it were looking out over the scene from his work. Bust to be bronze, by Brown; general structure to be by Seddon. Some £500 is conjectured as probably enough. Brown would wish to have a drinking-trough for dogs combined with the drinking-fountain: he truly says that the association of his monument with a boon to the thirsty dog would have been well-pleasing to Gabriel. I like this idea as a whole and suppose that it has some fair *chance* of being carried out, though I don't feel very sanguine. Sharp has been suggested by Shields to Seddon, to act as secretary — for no doubt a Committee and the like apparatus must be formed and worked. Brown rather doubted the propriety of this selection; and I finally suggested that perhaps Sharp might be working secretary, with Stephens as Honorary Secretary." On 7 July WMR drew up a list of possible committee members and subscribers. See also Letters 384, Note 2, and 425, Note 1.

381. TO ALGERNON CHARLES SWINBURNE

5 Endsleigh Gardens,
4 February 1885

Dear Swinburne,

Thank you much for sending me on that notice about the *Gil Blas*[1] etc. I don't think I ever saw a copy of the *Gil Blas*: can easily believe, from its name and nationality, that it treats themes of solemn seriousness with a levity and suggestiveness necessarily distasteful to the intransigent poet of a *Dolores* and an *Anactoria*. But to me, who have not the same character to sustain for marble majesty in erotics, it rather appears that a project for the European glorification of Hugo in which such persons as Mendès and Mme Dorian are actively concerned ought not to be so greatly *infra dig*. I yesterday took occasion to consult Hueffer about it: he told me that he has an adequate knowledge of the *Gil Blas*, which, although certainly capable of an impropriety now and again, is he thinks on a footing not inferior to

464

some leading London society-journal — say the *World*.[2] I am in the abstract rather inclined to contribute my minimum note to the Hugo paean: and, as I happen to have written 2 or 3 years ago a sonnet to Hugo, I shall probably look it up within a day or two, and, if I find an apposite 4 lines or so in it, am likely to send them on to Mendès.

The good news of your *Faliero*[3] gives me high pleasure.

Thanks for your kind message to the kids. They are all more or less well, though with colds etc. flitting about. A French nursery-governess, Mlle Cambisson, is now in charge of them this week past: as yet we like her much.

Always your affectionate
W. M. Rossetti

MS: Berg.

1. A Parisian newspaper, edited by the poet Catulle Mendès (1841-1909). WMR sent a few lines on Hugo, which appeared on 27 February 1885, p. 4, in the Hugo Anniversary Supplement.

2. A weekly newspaper founded in 1874 by Edmund Yates.

3. *Marino Faliero* (1885) of which Swinburne wrote on 2 February that he had finished three acts (*SL*, 5:97).

382. TO ANNE GILCHRIST

5 Endsleigh Gardens,
10 March 1885

My dear Mrs. Gilchrist,

It was not very long ago that I heard from Herbert, with sincerest regret, that you had been invalided during much of this winter — which unfortunately seems to have become more wintry as it merges into spring. In replying I had to inform Herbert that Lucy also has of late been suffering much. An attack of bronchial pneumonia began with her on 12 February. For the first couple of days it was alarming; but then it continued abating up to the night of 1 March, which must I fear be regarded as a relapse: certainly the long fits of coughing, troublesome expectoration, etc., have remained since then more severe. The Doctor however seems to regard the illness as following a normal and not alarming course: so we hope for the best, with lapse of time and milder weather.

Though I have begun my letter with these matters, so necessarily in the foreground for both of us, my immediate motive in writing is to show you the enclosed letter regarding Whitman.[1] It leaves a painful impression. Why is Whitman left totally alone? and as to money-means, I had rather inferred that of late these had improved to some noticeable degree, in proportion to the diminution in that dogged disfavour with which his countrymen had as yet always rewarded his great work in patriotic poetry. It may have been in November or December that Whitman kindly sent me a *Specimen Days* and a recent *Leaves of Grass*: I replied to him after some little delay, in a tone of less despondency than might now seem the right one. Dr. Bucke[2] also sent me his book soon afterwards: I read it with interest, and often with assent.

My correspondent Mr. Charles Aldrich[3] is a resident in Webster City, Iowa, who made fine collections of autographs, and presented them to the Library and some other institution in his state. He addressed me some months ago about autographs of Gabriel etc., and I sent him these and a somewhat large number of others. This is how he comes to be writing me the enclosed letter: please return it at your convenience, as I must answer it in due course.

There were some Flaxman letters etc. sold about a week ago at Sotheby's, containing some references to Blake.[4] I obtained a catalogue: would you be interested to see it?

With our warmest regards.

Yours,

W. M. Rossetti

My mourning is on account of a maternal uncle who died in January.[5]

While I am about it, I think I may as well send you also this *other* letter, from Marzials.[6] His nephew Mr. W. H. Ince is at 29 St. Stephen's Avenue, Shepherd's Bush. I replied to Mr. Ince yesterday, but could not give him *much* guidance: I took the liberty of mentioning you, as being probably willing to answer any question (should he address you any) about the Philips's Pastorals. I have not seen *that*, but the *Job* is lying at my house.[7]

I was sorry to read lately in the newspaper of the death of your connexion Mr. Thomas.[8]

MS: Duke; last page in LC.

1. A letter from Charles Aldrich to WMR, 24 February 1885, which gave an account of his recent visit to Whitman (AP). For Aldrich's letters on Whitman, see R. W. Peattie, "Whitman, Charles Aldrich and W. M. Rossetti in 1885: Background to the Whitman Subscription," *American Literature*, 58 (October 1986), 413-421.
2. Richard Maurice Bucke (1837-1902), physician, disciple and friend of Whitman, professor of Nervous and Mental Diseases at the University of Western Ontario from 1882. MS. Diary, 6 January 1885: "Finished reading Dr. Bucke's book on Whitman, and like it better than I had expected."
3. (1828-1908), newspaper editor, chief clerk of the Iowa House of Representatives from 1860, founder and curator of the Iowa State Historical Department, to which he gave his large collection of autographs. Aldrich visited Endsleigh Gardens on 14 December 1885 when WMR found him "an agreeable sensible man, of varied experience" (MS. Diary).
4. *Interesting Letters. The Collection of the Rev. Canon Hodgson*, 2 March 1885. Lots 22-94 were mostly letters of John Flaxman to William Hayley; lots 17-18 were two letters of Blake to Hayley.
5. Henry Polydore.
6. Either the poet Theophilus Marzials (b. 1850) or Frank T. Marzials, who succeeded Eric Robertson as editor of the "Great Writers" series. Ince is not identified.
7. Blake did twenty illustrations of Ambrose Philips's *Imitation of Eclogue I*, which was included in Thornton's *Pastorals of Virgil*, 3d ed., 1821 (Bentley No. 504). His *Illustrations of the Book of Job* is dated 1825 for 1826 (Bentley No. 421).
8. Sidney Gilchrist Thomas (1850-85), metallurgist and inventor of a way of using phosphoric ores in the Bessemer converter. Mrs. Gilchrist's eldest son, Percy, himself a chemist, joined his cousin in perfecting the discovery.

383. TO LUCY ROSSETTI

Somerset House,
18 May 1885,
1 p.m.

Dearie Lu,

I write in haste. I don't mean to abuse Jeaffreson's[1] book — not in the least —

indeed it is probable that *Athenaeum* would not allow me to do so. But I think it in part a harmful book (in part not) as raising and enforcing — for that is decidedly its object — every possible unpleasant question and view regarding the life of a great poet — whom as a man we ought partly to love and admire, and partly to blame with an infusion of sacred pity. This is precisely what will be done with Gabriel one day — possibly not very distant. It is clear to me now that I can only hand in my review for next *Athenaeum but one*. Probably it will quite preclude my thinking of Whitsuntide holidays out of town — this review along with the Tintoretto:[2] but we shall see.

Arthur is *sometimes* neat enough. He was washed up to dine with me yesterday. All love from

Fofus

Scott has improved:[3] so Miss Boyd (to whom I wrote for information) writes me.

Jeaffreson's book is *extremely* civil to me: always (so far as I have gone) distinguishing me from those indiscriminate adulators of Shelley who rouse his bile. And I know that I deserve no less an approval, for I *never* toned down any fault or foible of Shelley's. Garnett, along with Forman and Kegan Paul,[4] is much abused — also Lady Shelley.

MS: AP.

1. John Cordy Jeaffreson (1831-1901), novelist, archivist, biographer, contributor to the *Athenaeum* from 1858. *The Real Lord Byron: New Views of the Poet's Life* (1883), which was severely criticized, was followed in 1885 by *The Real Shelley: New Views of the Poet's Life*, reviewed by WMR in the *Athenaeum*, 30 May, 6 June 1885, pp. 687-89, 720-22. MS. Diary, 15 May 1885: "I ... began reading the book — copy in sheets. I dislike its scope and tone, but no doubt there is a good deal of prosaic masculine common-sense in it. Shall express with moderation, my real opinion." 17 May: "Was engaged all day reading Jeaffreson's Shelley, and got to near the middle of vol. 2. It is a very severe arraignment, and can hardly fail to hamper for years to come the efforts of Shelleyites to keep Shelley's character at something of the same level as his poetry.... It remains to be seen how far Dowden's book may redress the balance: so heavy is Jeaffreson's assault that I almost think Dowden will have to recast parts of his book so as to adapt them to the modified state of the controversy consequent upon Jeaffreson's book." 20 May: "Finished reading Jeaffreson's Shelley, and began writing about it: a task of some delicacy."
2. "Tintoretto" appeared in *Encyclopaedia Britannica* (1886).
3. MS. Diary, 12 May 1885: "Went round to Scott's. Miss Boyd spoke to me, and allowed me to see him for a few minutes, which may have been prolonged to 40. I found him in bed with a close cap or *capuchon* on, and looking singularly like the mask of Dante — a resemblance which I think I only now realize to myself.... He is now seemingly convalescent in a fair degree, but attenuated, exceedingly weak, and depressed in tone of mind.... As I entered the room he shed a few tears as if through mere emotionality and weakness of fibre; but at once recovered, and conversed just as well as usual, and on usual topics."
4. Charles Kegan Paul (1828-1902) took over the publishing business of Henry S. King in 1877. Author of *William Godwin, his Friends and Contemporaries* (1876), written with the help of the Shelley family; editor of Godwin's *The Genius of Christianity Unveiled* (1873), and Mary Wollstonecraft's *Letters to Imlay* (1879).

384. TO LUCY ROSSETTI

Somerset House,
19 May 1885,
4 p.m.

Dearest Luie,

This morning did not bring me a letter from you — nor from anyone.

Your papa arrived yesterday: seemed to me well, but this morning he complains of such a degree of gout in foot (*only* such) as to prefer woollen to cotton socks, and he donned a pair of mine. The *Wycliffe*[1] is a very fine work: I wish the project of its being housed in the Liverpool Gallery might take effect, and am not without some hope: it *ought* to be so. Today will I believe have brought the Art-Union project to an issue. In the evening Seddon came, bringing round the sketch of monument on which your papa had sketched a head of Gabriel (like, yet I think the space of the forehead a *little* overdone[2] — did not say so), and also a design as subsequently modified by Seddon after consultation with someone or other, with the view of raising the medallion of Gabriel higher: it was thought that in the previous instance there was an awkward look, as if Gabriel were in fact standing on the ground, his form below waist behind the fountain. Your papa thought the change now proposed a decided improvement, for the general sightliness and effect of the structure: still he considered that the medallion would thus be carried up too high for that careful inspection which it claims, and for the needful predominant importance of the bust over all the rest of the monument. So a medium course is now proposed to be adopted. I was glad to hear that the site for the fountain belongs to the Metropolitan Board — with whom Seddon anticipates no difficulty — not to any merely parochial body: also that Seddon has for himself good reason to expect that the commission for certain collegiate buildings at Aberystwyth[3] (out of which he had heretofore feared to be done) will after all come to him. He says however that at the best it will put but little money in his pocket.

Your papa wishes to see the Hueffers, W. B. Scott, Mathilde, and my mother, before leaving London: 2 of these expeditions he thought he might manage today, still dining with me at 7. He was sorry to find that Mary has been made a guy of. The silly little thing took a pair of scissors with her into bed on Saturday, and cut away her fringe of hair (for mischief's sake) in a most irregular half-and-half style: so the governess on Monday thought it needful to cut it *all* away, and certainly Mary is not a little disfigured thus. But it will now begin to grow equally, and set itself right pretty soon.

Dearest, all love from

Your own
W. M. R.

I enclose 2 things which you will please return at convenience. Shall I subscribe to the fund for helping to make you the guardian of your own kid? I would not give *much*: but if you like 5/- or so.

The prices for these pictures by Gabriel[4] — your papa is my sole informant — were in my opinion decidedly bad.

MS: AP.

1. *The Trial of Wycliffe*, cartoon of the Manchester Town Hall wall-painting. MS. Diary, 18 May 1885: "Brown arrived, bringing his *Wycliffe* picture finished. It is certainly a very fine thing in conception, distribution, and realization of the subject, and has eminent qualities of execution as well: to my eye the crowded background groups are somewhat too variegated in colour, and wanting in optical fusion. Some expectation now exists that the picture may be bought by the Walker Gallery,

Liverpool: may this prove so! Tomorrow the Art-Union people are to look at it: the immediate question being that of copyright and photogravure, but the question of purchase could also be mooted, now that [C. P.] Scott of the *Manchester Guardian* has retired from the purchasing lists.'' WMR to Lucy, 4 June: ''It is indeed afflicting that the Art-Union won't after all undertake your father's very fine picture'' (AP).

2. MS. Diary, 18 May 1885: ''For the first time I see Brown's sketch alto-relief: it is considerably like Gabriel, but not I think a very agreeable version of his face, and the size of the forehead rather overdone. Of course it is a mere suggestive sketch (pen and ink).''

3. University College of Wales (completed in 1890), which Seddon began as a hotel in 1864 but later abandoned.

4. MS. Diary, 14 May 1885: ''Went to Christie's to see the pictures by Gabriel (partly Ellis's) which are to be sold on Saturday [16th]: *Bella Mano* [Surtees 240; £865], *Donna della Finestra* [£535.10], *Venus Verticordia* [Lot 99 (sale not recorded in Surtees 173), £577.10].... Found Burton of the National Gallery viewing the *Bella Mano*: don't know whether he has any idea of bidding, but the Gallery funds are almost nil in consequence of the recent Raphael [*Altarpiece: Madonna and Child with the Baptist and S. Nicholas of Bari*] and Van Dyck [*Equestrian Portrait of Charles I*] purchases. I regret to say that the *Venus* seems to me to have had the figure wholly repainted since the picture was completed toward 1866: the present figure looks to me whiteish and out of tone, and altogether inferior to the original one. This is a bad instance of Gabriel's bad habit of reworking upon pictures.''

385. TO THEODORE WATTS-DUNTON

5 Endsleigh Gardens,
25 May 1885

Dear Watts,

Today for the first time I have found time to look into those Legacy-duty papers which you left with me a few days ago. I have verified the figures to some extent, and suppose they come near enough for all practical purposes — except the affair of Brass. He is put down for £200: but, as this has not been paid, I presume I am not entitled to deduct it. If not deducted, £3306.18.6 as the sum on which to pay duty will increase to £3506.18.6. Of course this sum remains to be *halved* — between my mother and self.

I have noted down on the enclosed slip 4 other points. I don't know that I paid Dunn the £60 ''for assistance in preparing pictures etc. for the sale'': at any rate I would rather not specify it in that form, as the pictures (rather drawings) were not supposed to be *prepared* at all. Can't we put it down as what it may fairly be called — a portion of the general sum which I paid to Dunn as Gabriel's artistic assistant?

As to query 1 you will no doubt kindly advise me. Shall I take the papers back to Somerset House, and await your appearance there?

You remember about the £70 which I paid at a venture. I computed it as £52 for myself, and £18 for my mother. But I think I understood you afterwards to say that my mother was not bound to pay anything.

I wish you would kindly tell Swinburne that today I finished reading *Marino Faliero* through. I read it as being (in essence) an attack upon Tyranny, Oligarchy of the hereditary kind, and Priestcraft — and it is certainly treated with sustained splendour of diction and work of a kind of which Swinburne alone possesses the secret. As a dramatic presentment of the actual subject, I think Act 3, especially the earlier part of it, much the ablest thing in the drama — and extremely fine indeed.

Could I but find time, I would run over to see Victor Hugo's stupendous funeral[1] — I should suppose one of the most moving and wonderful sights of the century. I thought that order as to the pauper's hearse sublime: "ridiculous" is probably the synonym supplied by the British public. The authorities must I suspect be quaking in their shoes at such an occasion for enthusiasm to rise into revolution — especially after the Communist affair of the other day.[2]

Your
W. M. Rossetti

MS: BL.

1. MS. Diary, 22 May 1885: "Death of Victor Hugo. Silence is the comment."
2. "Yesterday being the anniversary of the fall of the Paris Commune, a demonstration organized by various revolutionary societies took place in the cemetery of Père Lachaise. On a red flag being produced, the constables on duty ordered it to be given up. This was refused, and a tussle ensued. The Anarchists standing near struck the police, who thereupon drew their swords and drove back the crowd upon a heap of stones, which were used as missiles. The Republican Guards then fixed bayonets and charged the Anarchists, one of whom is said to have died from the injuries he received. Several others were dangerously wounded" (*Daily News*, 25 May 1885, p. 4).

386. TO ANNE GILCHRIST

5 Endsleigh Gardens,
27 June 1885

My dear Mrs. Gilchrist,

Excuse bother. I have occasion to write again to Aldrich (about autographs etc.). Does it occur to you as desirable or otherwise that I should inform him of the letter to President Cleveland?[1] He is *somebody* (member of State-legislature or what not), having "the Honourable" to his name: and it is conceivable that he would be pleased at learning that *his letter* brought to the fore the question of writing to President. He was very much displeased at Cleveland's election, having been on the side of his competitor: so I suppose he is not much in the way of exercising immediate political pressure etc.

Yours,
W. M. Rossetti

MS: Duke.

1. MS. Diary, 13 June 1885: "I finished writing a letter to President Cleveland [Gohdes, Baum, pp. 181-83], urging him to do something to make Whitman comfortable in his declining years. This is the result of some recent correspondence with Mrs. Gilchrist, reinforced by Lucy. I don't suppose anything will come of the effort — and indeed don't know whether Whitman would in any degree approve of it. As to this last point, I shall send the letter to Mrs. Gilchrist before it is posted, and shall leave her to settle." WMR's decision to write was also influenced by a second letter from Aldrich (2 April 1885; AP) giving a full account of Whitman's plight.

387. TO EDITH HOLMAN HUNT

5 Endsleigh Gardens,
28 June 1885

My dear Mrs. Hunt,

I am pleased in a sense to find that you and Holman have got off to Dover, for I was pained to see my dear old friend in such a sorry plight last Sunday.[1] Was

470

concerned also to leave the house without giving him a shake of the hand: I looked for him for the purpose, but did not light upon him and, having to keep in hand my 4 little pickles, could not afford to lose sight of them, and perhaps find them dispersed again.

Lucy sends you both all kindest messages and wishes. She is not well, but has I think passed this last week quite as favourably as the final days of last week. On Tuesday I mean to take her to Dr. Wilson Fox for advice: this is recommended by our Dr. Gill, in whom we have none the less much confidence.

I think Holman has had a very good idea in thinking of writing some of his Eastern reminiscences: written they must be fully as interesting as spoken, and that is saying a good deal. If he would also do his study on the Sonnets of Shakespeare, I am confident it would excite much attention. I have preserved all his Eastern (and most of his other) letters; and shall have no difficulty in laying my hands upon them, as I keep letters tied up in bundles according to years, and each bundle in alphabetical order. To save fumbling however it would be well to let me know what are the exact years to be looked out for: I think 1855-1856, and then about 1870-1872, and then again 1874-1876 or so. If you would send a line to keep me right about this, I will lose no time over the little job. As memory serves me, I have not very *many* letters, but interesting ones in some moderate number. My impression is that Stephens was the recipient of the larger number of his letters. I can understand that under present unfortunate circumstances[2] you and Holman would not apply to Stephens for the loan of any such letters. If by any chance you would like *me* to act as middleman, I would not scruple to ask Stephens to say whether he would lend them through me, yes or no: whichever he replies, that I would take as final. I presume Holman is not in want of that little Memoir of Thomas Seddon: were he so, I could lend my copy.

I am well acquainted with the extant letters addressed to my brother. They certainly do not include any letters written by Holman from the East. Gabriel must at some date have destroyed *all* the letters (with the scantiest exceptions) that he had received up to a certain comparatively recent date — say 1865 or so. To Madox Brown I will write on the subject very shortly — or Lucy will do so: she thinks he is pretty sure to have preserved the letters which he received.

With our affectionate regards, and earnest good wishes and hopes,

Yours very truly,
W. M. Rossetti

MS: Rylands.

1. MS. Diary, 21 June 1885: "I regret to find Hunt looking deplorably and alarmingly ill from one of his asthmatic attacks. He kept apart from the main company, but I found him talking to the painter Wallis about the Mosque of Amar as he saw it in 1855 etc. He kept up a steady stream of conversation on such matters, although his voice is in a poor creaky state."
2. Hunt had quarreled with Stephens over a delay in dispatching canvas and colors to him during his third visit to Palestine, 1875-78 (see *PR & PRB*, 2:387).

388. TO LUCY ROSSETTI

5 Endsleigh Gardens,
23 August 1885,
1¾

Luie dearest,

I did yesterday attend the demonstration in Hyde Park,[1] walking to the Piccadilly entrance, and thence towards the Marble Arch. It was an impressive sight. I could scarcely form a judgement of the number of persons present; but should suppose there may have been fully 20,000 at a time — and, allowing for some people going and others coming, say 35,000 on and off. Their demeanour was on the whole resolute and serious — not excited. The only 2 orators I listened to for any time were Michael Davitt,[2] and Stead[3] of the *Pall Mall Gazette* (you may or may not be aware that a series of articles on Outrages to Girls etc. which the *Pall Mall Gazette* published 6 weeks or so ago, the writer being Stead, have been exciting a frightful commotion ever since, and have thrown everything else into the shade). Davitt has an Irish physiognomy, and looks fiercely in earnest: in his speech there is no particular brogue. He spoke well and fluently, but not saying anything very *remarkable* for oratory: his theme being little as to the direct subject of the gathering, but upon the necessity of proper Land-laws etc., whereby the poverty and degradation which lead to so miserable a state of things would be remedied. Stead was naturally the hero of the day: a fine-looking man, under 40 I should think, who spoke to the point with a good deal of feeling and emphasis, mostly in generalities. I should not be surprised if he were to be returned to Parliament for 2 or 3 places, and to be a leading figure there for some years to come. I left the Park towards 6½, before — but I suppose only a *little* before — the close of the proceedings.

Morris and the Socialists were somewhere on the ground, but I failed to find them out. I bought however a copy of Morris's newspaper the *Commonweal*, and of the other Socialist paper *Justice*, and in the evening I read them. I assure you they don't mince matters.[4] The tide of Democracy is rising, and you and I, if we live a few years longer, will see a few things gone.

One effect of this agitation about protecting girls etc. will be a great increase of strength to the whole movement for emancipating Women: this is my own prophecy, for I have not seen or heard the particular point mooted elsewhere. Women (unless indeed the next parliament should prove reactionary to an at present incalculable extent) will very soon get the suffrage, and will be encouraged to take up professions, trades, etc. In fact, *Justice to Women* will be the great cry and fulcrum of advance. So be it!

I enclose a cheque for £15: am not at all surprised (as you will have noticed by my letter of yesterday) at your needing some replenishment.

The *Athenaeum* shall be posted to you at once. Don't fail to return it or bring it back.

I suppose you have not heard from your father to the effect that he has received the pen-and-ink sketch-portrait of Gabriel by himself (also of me)[5] which he wished to consult. I sent it to him last Monday by registered letter, but have not received an acknowledgement — which indeed may not have been *needed*, but, as he is generally rather precise in such matters, I begin to feel a little nervous. I shall drop him a line on the subject today.

I believe I did not tell you that on Friday Brucciani returned me my own original casts of Gabriel's head and hand, and also sent the new moulds (not casts) which he has raised from them. He and I had agreed that the moulds should come to me, so as to guard against any fresh mishap similar to that which has already happened.[6] I had not hitherto a very distinct idea of what the moulds would be like: they are very greatly larger than the casts, bulky and heavy objects. Where to bestow them was the problem. The head is too large even for the largest drawer in the wardrobe in the spareroom: but I suppose the upper part of the wardrobe, now locked up, would contain ample and convenient space. Meanwhile I found no other place so manageable as the wardrobe in *our* bedroom. There accordingly I placed the head this morning: the hand in the lowest wardrobe-drawer in the spare-room; the *casts* of head and hand (as previously) in the cabinet in the back-parlour.

The afternoon in the Park yesterday proved quite fine after all, though not brilliant. Today again is dull, and feels to me (indoors all day) chilly.

Ever, dearest, Your own

Fofus

For some days past I have been intending to post you Miss Tynan's[7] little volume of poems, but one trifle or another has put it off. As you seem now not unlikely to return to London pretty soon, I fancy it may be as well to keep the book here.

MS: AP.

1. WMR also attended the meeting on 21 August "in St. James's Hall for the Protection of Girls from Prostitution etc. (the Committee lately asked me to join, and I assented): so I got Stillman to dine with me at St. James's Restaurant, and thence we entered the Hall. There was some moving and energetic speaking: on the whole I liked Miss [Frances H.] Müller best, and next to her Mr. Wilson of Sheffield: heard also for the first time Mrs. [Catherine] Booth of the Salvation Army. The great object in my view should be to obtain a more liberal and less monkish view on all questions of sex, especially as affecting the position of women in society. Pending this consummation — which may be remotely on its way — it is no doubt most necessary to be stern, and to repress with a high hand the vile crimes against children and semi-adult girls of which so much has been said lately, owing chiefly to the initiative of the *Pall Mall Gazette*. I for the first time learned at this meeting the name of the writer of those articles, Stead: he was present on the platform but I did not clearly discriminate him from others'' (MS. Diary).
2. (1846-1906), Fenian and founder of land leagues in Ireland, England, and the United States.
3. William Thomas Stead (1849-1912), assistant editor from 1880 and editor from 1883 of the *Pall Mall Gazette*, which he made an organ of social and political protest. His articles on the brothels of London, "The Maiden Tribute of Modern Babylon," resulted in his imprisonment, but also in the raising of the age of consent to sixteen.
4. Cf. WMR to Lucy, 29 August 1891: "I looked through a *Commonweal* which came some few days ago for 'H[elen] Rossetti,' and see it has got to a stage where it really does not deserve to be upheld by any sensible person — be he or she anarchist, socialist, or what not. There is not a spark in it of good sense, good feeling, or good English: only underbred abuse, and an open advocacy of plunder. I am heartily pleased that my children should feel enthusiasm for any great cause, and would as soon that the cause should be that of socialism or anarchism as any other: but to batten on such stuff as the *Commonweal* is now made to consist of could certainly only lower their appreciation of theories, estimate of facts, and standard of feeling and taste" (AP).

5. Probably Surtees 594.

6. MS. Diary, 7 August 1885: "To my great concern and displeasure, Brucciani writes me that the moulds cannot be found: he offers to raise gratis new moulds from the casts in my hands."

7. Katharine Tynan (1861-1931), Irish poet and novelist, who had recently sent WMR her first volume, *Louise de la Vallière, and Other Poems* (1885).

389. TO WALT WHITMAN

5 Endsleigh Gardens,
28 August 1885

Dear Whitman,

You will believe that I received with pride and warm feeling the love which you sent me in a letter to Gilchrist, now published in the *Athenaeum*;[1] and that I reciprocate your love with reverential affection.

That movement for a few English people to express in a practical form the feeling which they entertain towards you has not as yet taken any extended development — nothing I believe having been done outside a few general paragraphs in journals. Gilchrist will now be taking steps in a more detailed and direct way: from him and his mother you will no doubt hear many particulars from time to time.

The sums which have as yet come into my hands as Treasurer are £22.2.6.[2] I beg to forward this amount in the within form — being

1. 3 Post-Office orders which will be made good to you upon your signing them, and presenting them at Camden — and

2. A Bank-draft which, as I am advised, you can get cashed in Camden or Philadelphia.

The draft comes from Charles Aldrich, of Webster City, Iowa, who had an interview with you some months ago, and wrote me several interesting details about it. Indeed Mr. Aldrich's letter was the immediate incentive and opportunity for Mrs. Gilchrist and the rest of us to bestir ourselves, and see who among us would honour himself by associating his name in this small way with yours.

I enclose a little list of names, and remain, like so many others who have hearts to feel and ears to hear,

Your lifelong debtor,
W. M. Rossetti

MS: Texas.

1. 22 August 1885, p. 241; also in *Daily News*, 24 August 1885, p. 2. Whitman's letter was a positive reply to queries of 21, 22 July from Mrs. Gilchrist and Herbert, about the poet's need for, and his willingness to accept, a second freewill offering from England. WMR and Mrs. Gilchrist had frequently discussed the matter during June and July, but an interview with Whitman in the Camden *Daily Post* of 3 July, in which Whitman was quoted as saying that his income was "just sufficient to keep my head above water," raised doubts about the accuracy of Aldrich's reports. (See *CWW*, 3:398-99; Gohdes, Baum, pp. 146-54.) MS. Diary, 26 June: "Wrote 2 letters about Whitman — 1, to Rowley, suggesting that any persons who wish to benefit him had better do what was done in 1876 partly through my agency — buy his books from him direct; 2, to Mrs. Gilchrist, suggesting that if any general scheme for Whitman's benefit is started, Herbert Gilchrist might perhaps act as Secretary, but I would do so if really necessary, and would subscribe £3, and would at once (if Mrs. Gilchrist advocates it) buy books to that amount." 3 July: "I made some alterations in a paragraph written out by Mrs. Gilchrist, proposed for insertion in the *Athenaeum*, and perhaps elsewhere [see Gohdes,

Baum, p. 155]; and returned it to Mrs. Gilchrist for further consideration. The object is to get up a subscription for Whitman's advantage: Herbert Gilchrist would be Secretary, and I Treasurer." 4 July: "Mrs. Gilchrist returned me the Whitman paragraph. The project may now be regarded as fairly afoot."

2. MS. Diary, 28 August 1885: "It ought to be more; but *possibly* the subscription is as yet only at its beginning." For a list of subscribers up to the middle of 1886, see Gohdes, Baum, p. 185.

390. TO JOHN SLARK[1]

5 Endsleigh Gardens,
29 September 1885

Dear Mr. Slark,

I saw in the *Pall Mall Gazette* of 25 September a statement that you are preparing a reprint of Shelley as edited by me.[2] Would you kindly let me know how the facts stand. I dare say you remember that some years ago you and I talked over some such project, and I explained some points which ought to be attended to in the interests of any reprint, for the sake of its completeness, critical accuracy, etc. The lapse of years has only tended to make some such revision the more requisite.

With best regards,

Yours very truly,
W. M. Rossetti

MS: NYP.

1. In 1882 Slark had considered publishing "Cor Cordium"; he was a member of the Shelley Society from its foundation in December 1885.
2. MS. Diary, 1 October 1885: "Slark called on me at Somerset House. As the Shelley is stereotyped, he is desirous of avoiding the great expense which would attend extensive alterations in the text. He is at present about to print a reissue of only 250 copies [200, on Van Gelder paper]: at some future time he might undertake something on a larger scale. From his commercial point of view all this seems fair enough, and I waived any question of immediate and considerable alterations. On reflection however I think I shall write to him pointing out that there are no doubt several matters of detail which require correction, and which could be corrected by some small derangement of the type — and that he would do well to send me proofs so that this may be seen to. I might probably ask some moderate sum — say £5 to £10 — for my revising-work on this scale. Slack tells me that he does not regard Forman's edition of Shelley — the 2 volume in same type as the larger edition but without any notes [1882] — as a successful venture."

391. TO WALT WHITMAN

5 Endsleigh Gardens,
4 October 1885

Dear Whitman,

I received with great gratification your postcard of 8 September acknowledging a previous missive of mine.

I now enclose a list of some further sums. These are all that have reached my hands up to date: there may *possibly* be something besides in the hands of the Gilchrists, but I have no particular reason for supposing so. I had been expecting for some weeks past to see a circular[1] in print, Herbert Gilchrist having ordered one, but have not yet seen it. When it comes, one may expect to come to closer quarters with your admirers and adherents, who are certainly neither scanty or lukewarm in this country.

I shall now without delay proceed to pay the £37.12[2] into the Post Office, so that it shall reach you in like manner with the former sum. As soon as I have actually done this, I will send you a brief letter of advice.

Some of the names on the enclosed list are unknown to me: to others I have put a brief note of explanation. The last person on the list, R.B.C., is Earl Russell:[3] he writes me, "I do not wish my *name* to be published," so I have not given details on the list itself. This youthful Earl is now 20 years of age, and is grandson of the (in England at least) celebrated Lord John Russell, who was a prime agent in passing the Parliamentary Reform-bill of 1832, was afterwards Premier more than once, and was created a Peer as Earl Russell. His son, Viscount Amberley, died while the father was still alive: the Viscount was a very liberal thinker on matters of religion etc., and published one or two books. Lord Russell writes to me as "a recent but none the less ardent admirer of Walt Whitman" — and he subscribes "with the warmest feelings of thanks and reverence for the Good Gray Poet." I am no devotee of titled people as such (would on the contrary abolish all titles if it lay with me to do so), but have thought that you might like to know these few particulars about R.B.C.

Yours with affection,
W. M. Rossetti

MS: Syracuse. Published: *WWC*, 4:209.

1. According to Miller, a facsimile was made of Whitman's letter of 1 August 1885 to Herbert Gilchrist approving a subscription (*CWW*, 3:399). This probably formed part of the circular, a copy of which has not been located.
2. The second installment.
3. John Francis Stanley Russell (1865-1931), who succeeded his grandfather in 1878 as second Earl Russell. His father, John Russell, Viscount Amberley, author of *An Analysis of Religious Belief* (2 vols., 1876), died in 1876. Lord John Russell (1792-1878) was prime minister 1846-52, and 1865-66.

392. TO FORD MADOX BROWN

5 Endsleigh Gardens,
8 November 1885

Dear Brown,

As my brief postcard showed, I shall be very glad to lend you the £100.[1] Please inform me what it is precisely that I should do next — whether send you a crossed cheque to Manchester, or what. I have no wish for interest: would indeed, of the two, rather *not* receive it.

It would be quite understood (as in your letter) that you are not to repay the first £50 until the *Chetham* is done, nor the second £50 until the *Wycliffe* is done.[2] Perhaps you could give me some *general* idea of the time when these pictures will be completed, so far as can at present be conjectured.

It is too bad — really discreditable — that the oil-picture of *Wycliffe* has not sold at Liverpool. When pearls are cast before swine, one can't persuade the swine, as such, to care about them, nor change them into some other sort of creature that *would* care.

476

You and Emma may be sure that Lucy and I thought constantly on 5 November of the ever-sad anniversary.[3]

For the Schoolboard I voted in favour of the two *female* candidates: Mrs. Westlake, who came in at the bottom of the poll, and Mrs. Hicks, Socialist, who was defeated. In London the elections went generally in favour of the party of *Economy*: I was not particularly in favour of that party, yet I don't object to its having its turn. I do mean to vote for Parliament. Here (South St. Pancras) there is simply one Liberal, Goldsmid,[4] against one Conservative. I shall vote for the Liberal, though he is not quite of my own complexion of Liberalism.

Lucy's health (I rejoice to say) may on the whole be considered good at present. Very strict precautions are however needed. I am glad that Thomas found his visit agreeable.[5]

I am just finishing my article on Shelley for *Encyclopaedia Britannica*.[6] Yesterday I learned that Ellis's successor wishes after all to continue publishing Gabriel's books: I shall in all probability gladly assent to that arrangement, and so save myself all further uncertainty and trouble on the subject.[7]

Our love to Emma.

Your
W. M. Rossetti

You may like to know (if not already aware) that Oliver is down in a book lately published under Humphry Ward's[8] Editorship, *Men of the Reign*. The notice fills a column or more: strongly laudatory, but not marked by any original feature.

MS: AP.

1. FMB to WMR, [15 November 1885]: "I find that I shall not get clear of Fitzroy Square under a considerably larger sum than I fancied — £160 it now seems I am required to give but not the whole of it at once — I can only hope that one day I shall be free" (AP).

2. Frescoes at Manchester Town Hall.

3. Of Oliver Brown's death.

4. Sir Julian Goldsmid (1838-95), M.P. for Honiton, 1866-68; Rochester, 1870-80; and St. Pancras South, 1885 until his death. He was the grandson of the financier Sir Isaac Goldsmid whom Gabriele Rossetti had known. MS. Diary, 22 October 1885: "Attended an electoral meeting at the Grafton Hall — Sir Julian Goldsmid ... explained his views on various questions, which are the views of a Liberal slightly tending toward Radicalism. I was disappointed at finding him opposed to Women's Suffrage."

5. MS. Diary, 18 October 1885: "Cave Thomas lately had to leave the Boarding-house in which he had been comfortably accommodated for some years past, and he lodges now in Fitzroy Street, without (I fear) much of comfort around him. Lucy lately asked him to look in whenever he likes for our early Sunday dinner. He did so today, and may I fancy come pretty often. A good deal of talk about his Russian experience (transporting a ton of gold to a Banker in St. Petersburg) towards the beginning of 1854."

6. Ninth edition, 1886. MS. Diary, 8 November 1885: "Finished my article on Shelley: made it up to be posted to Dowden, who consented some while ago to read it, and set me right in case I had made any statement which he knows to be inaccurate."

7. MS. Diary, 12 October 1885: "Ellis writes to me ... that his successors will not continue to publish Gabriel's books: so I have before me the rather serious trouble of finding a new publisher for the 2 volumes. Besides this, the proposed cheap stereotype of volume *Poems* lapses, and the understanding that Ellis would publish the volume of Gabriel's Family-letters prefaced by Watts's Memoir comes to nought. However there ought not to be real difficulty in such a matter, though trouble there must be." 13 October: "Wrote to Ellis saying that I cannot at the moment determine upon a new Publisher, and asking him to let me know whether his new firm will, pending my

decision, keep the sale of Gabriel's books going as usual." 23 October: "Watts dined with us, and we discussed the question of a new Publisher for Gabriel's *Poems* etc. The main points may thus be summarized. 1, He inclines to think that the most obvious and right choice would be Macmillan; but as I am somewhat reluctant to commit myself to Macmillan owing to the small advantage which Christina has ever reaped from him as Publisher, this view is in abeyance. 2, We next looked to other leading Publishers who might be eligible; and we are disposed to the alternative of Hurst and Blackett, or else Smith, Elder. Hurst and Blackett are the Publishers who are undertaking Watts's own novel [*Aylwin*, 1898] so long talked about, and he has a very good opinion of their standing in the trade, and their liberal fairness. I am therefore to give the matter a little further reflection, and then to write to Watts, and he and I will jointly call on the Publisher selected. 3, This arrangement would set aside another arrangement to which on some grounds I should be far from indisposed — viz.: to address Reeves & Turner, who publish Forman's Shelley etc., and are now likely to take over from Ellis the publishing of Morris's works. Ellis first started this suggestion to me a few days ago. The only objection to Reeves & Turner is that they are much more booksellers than publishers, being thus on the same footing as Ellis himself, and any disadvantage which attached to the past publishing scheme with Ellis would be likely to continue under Reeves & Turner." 7 November: "Ellis writes me that his successors wish after all to retain Gabriel's books: I am quite inclined that they should do so, if the contingent-arrangements prove satisfactory, and if nothing has as yet been done by Watts to commit me with other publishers." 9 November: "Watts called on me at breakfast. He says that, before receiving my note of Saturday, he had already fixed with Arthur Blackett ... that he and I would go round this afternoon to start the question of publishing with his Firm: he considers a retreat from this arrangement somewhat awkward, but still permissible. My first intention was to retreat: but, as Watts and I continued talking on the matter, especially with a view to the intended publication of the Letters-Memoir book, it became apparent to me that my most prudent course for my own interest, as well as the less awkward one, would be to see Blackett before any other step is taken. I therefore wrote briefly to Gilbert Ellis to this effect (not mentioning names); and at 4½ Watts and I presented ourselves in Blackett's Office. He seems fairly well disposed to the undertaking, saying that for the purposes of his firm individually, the Letters-Memoir book would probably be the more attractive venture of the two.... His firm has, it seems, a large interest in the Mudie business, and he himself some connexion with Mudie by marriage."

8. Thomas Humphry Ward (1845-1926), editor and journalist.

393. TO WALT WHITMAN

5 Endsleigh Gardens,
13 November 1885

Dear Whitman,

I read with great concern the statement in your note of 20 October that you are "in poorer health even than of late seasons": it would give me and others the sincerest pleasure to receive pretty soon a statement to the reverse effect.

Since I wrote last to you little sums have been accumulating in my hands: I enclose an account of them, amounting to £31.19.[1] Within the next few days I shall take the usual steps for postal remittance of this amount, and will send you the papers.

In the letter of Miss L. Agnes Jones[2] to me (more especially) there are some expressions which I think you will be pleased to read. I don't know this lady: she writes from 16 Nevern Road, Earl's Court, London. "The necessities of persons one knows, and may be bound to do all one can for, are so near and pressing that to give money to help-on the efforts of those who try to realize one's ideals is seldom possible; and, even in sign of one's gratitude to one who has partly reformed our ideals, is less so.... Yet Walt Whitman should have those: to whom it is at once instinct and natural inevitable duty not to count any cost, or weigh this claim with that; but to break the alabaster, and pour the ointment, with no thought but of *him*. Has he not? This is a long apology for sending 5/-: it seemed so poor and ungenerous to send, unless I had said what gratitude it may yet stand for. Walt Whitman knows better than most that the sense of spiritual gain can seldom find the expression it longs for; and that it may forever remain unexpressed in material terms, and yet be present and abiding. I have so often wished to thank him.''

I grieve to say that Mrs. Gilchrist has been much out of health of late, and I fear still continues so. No doubt you have details from headquarters.

Yours in reverence and affection,
W. M. Rossetti

MS: LC. Published: *WWC*, 2:330-31.

1. The third installment. MS. Diary, 4 November 1885: ''The Whitman subscription is still going on.... Two subscribers offer to pay an annual sum. The result as yet is rather below what I should have expected.''
2. Not identified.

394. TO HENRY TAYLOR[1]

5 Endsleigh Gardens,
22 December 1885

My dear Sir,

I felt very greatly gratified by your note of 20 December enclosing a subscription of £1.1 to the Shelley Society,[2] and was thinking of again raising in the Committee a question (which had been mooted already) whether we should not ask you to honour the Society by becoming its first President. This morning however I have received your second note showing that you do not wish to appear as a member of the Society.[3] This I sincerely regret: but it would be impertinent in me to intrude upon you any observations of my own on such a subject, so I shall simply refrain from in any way designating you as a member.

The small question of the cheque remains. I don't understand that you require it to be returned: so, unless I hear from you again, it will go into the funds of the Society without indication of any donor.

Thanking you, I am, with very great respect, Sir,

Yours faithfully,
W. M. Rossetti

MS: Bodleian.

1. (1800-1886), poet of *Philip van Artevelde* (1834), which held a ''great fascination'' for the Rossetti brothers in their youth (*SR*, 1:207).
2. MS. Diary, 9 December 1885: ''A few days ago Furnivall had called on me, saying that [Henry] Sweet had suggested to him that a Shelley Society ought to be formed: Furnivall consulted me as to my views, and the prospects of such a Society. Of course I should be very glad to see Shelley honoured in any such form, so I at once assented to the invitation that I should be on the Committee. We agreed that Browning ought to be President: Swinburne and Furnivall are like oil and water, but on my representation Furnivall agreed that Swinburne ought to be one of the Vice-Presidents. Furnivall thinks that the Society might be started to last 10 years, and afterward, continued or not as expedient: he particularly wants to bring out a facsimile edition of Shelley's works, to act the *Cenci*, and to receive papers from members on the various aspects of Shelley's writings and life. Today Furnivall called on me again. To the surprise of both of us, Browning, on being invited by letter to

become President, has, also by letter, declined: as I understand it (for I did not see the letter) he intimates that he no longer views Shelley's personal character with either approval or indulgence. Dowden also has declined: he professes himself overdosed with Shelley, and says that the only poets who furnish material for a Society are Shakespeare, Dante, and Goethe. Furnivall and I rather question whether, after these rebuffs, the Society could be started with a prospect of success. As I told Furnivall, the proper President, in default of Browning, and also of Tennyson who seems to be out of count, would be Swinburne, but the personal incompatibilities don't admit of that: Morris might possibly be thought of, or (as I suggested) Sir Henry Taylor — but I don't much believe either of them would assent. The present understanding is that, on receiving a certain circular which is on its way to me from Furnivall, I shall think the matter over and if deemed well write to invite Taylor — whom I don't know personally." 10 December: "Received Furnivall's circular for a Shelley Society, and jotted down the names of some persons who might be addressed." 11 December: "I see in the *Pall Mall Gazette* [p. 6] a paragraph notifying the formation of the Shelley Society giving my name among others. I had understood from Furnivall that the question of forming such a Society would be further debated, and I think the paragraph premature." 15 December: "Watts ... would not join the Shelley Society, and is satisfied that Swinburne would not join: I am however to write to Swinburne putting the invitation definitely." 16 December: "Began sending off some Shelley Society circulars — Swinburne, Tennyson, Paton, Brown, etc."

3. Taylor to WMR, 21 December 1885: "I am afraid that in sending you a subscription to the proposed Shelley Society this morning I had not considered with due care all that is set forth in the Papers sent to me on the work to be done by the Society. There is some of it in which I should not wish to join, and though I am very sorry to give you any trouble, I hope you will excuse me for asking you not to connect my name with the Society in its operations or in any list of its Members. The object of bringing the *Cenci* play on the stage is one which I should not like to promote" (AP).

395. TO LUCY ROSSETTI

5 Endsleigh Gardens,
30 December 1885,
12¼

Dearie Lu,

I have not received any letter of yours this morning, and have not much to say beyond the interview of last evening with Miss Tynan. She came punctually, and is a good deal like her photograph. The defect of her face is that her mouth is large and rather gaping: but for this she seems to be about as well-looking as the average British or Celtic female: height lowish-medium. I received her in the dining-room, from which she did not move into any other part of the house: but I brought her from the smoking-room a few things to look at, especially Lizzie's portrait of herself. There is no exceptional amount of gush about Miss Tynan's manner, but she followed with marked interest any points regarding Gabriel etc. that turned up in our conversation: your portrait by Gabriel was much observed by her. She has not very much of a brogue, but an *intonation* markedly Irish — which I found at moments even a little difficult to catch the words of: she seems an agreeable clever woman, of whom one would willingly know more. Somehow the interview closed (she leaving about 7½) without my having said a syllable about *Irish* affairs, as to which she is a proclaimed enthusiast. She expects to remain some weeks longer in London, but there is no definite prospect of our meeting again.

Ellis and Scrutton have now sent me round the 3 volumes of Gabriel's works: I shall set to at them with zest when I can.[1]

Today is a regular hard frost, with a goodish deal of ice in the streets here and there: not however a *vexatious* sort of cold, as the air is very still.

Tell me how your health goes on. I constantly think about it, dearest — and as yet the accounts have not been particularly bright.

Your own
W. M. R.

MS: AP.

1. MS. Diary, 8 December 1885: "Wrote to Ellis & Scrutton.... Their proposal is to bring out a *complete* edition (or rather they assent to this proposal made by me) — paying me 25%, no longer on the *published* price but on the *trade*-price. This would no doubt be a somewhat considerable reduction in my profits." 9 December: "Received another letter from Ellis & Scrutton. The leading proposals are — 1, to publish the Complete Works next autumn, trade-price 11/4, published price 16/-; 2, to pay me 3/- per copy sold; 3, the edition to be in stereotype." 6 January 1886: "Went on with the arrangement of Gabriel's writings for the Complete Edition.... I propose to disregard the present sequence of the poems, as distributed into the Volumes *Poems* 1881, and *Ballads and Sonnets*: any sequence of this sort, dependent partly on haphazard, appears to me decidedly contrary to the true theory of a 'Complete Works.' As to this view Watts differs from me, but Christina agrees. In the poems I make 6 divisions.... Each section would within its own limits be set in approximate order of date — many of the dates being rightly known to me, others uncertain. In theory I would specify, as near as I could, the precise date in every instance: but here there are some considerations *per contra* to which I shall defer."

396. TO WALT WHITMAN

5 Endsleigh Gardens,
5 January 1886

Dear Whitman,

I received your note of 30 November, and have been intending to write for some little while past.

You and I have both suffered a loss in the death of that admirable woman Mrs. Gilchrist — a strong warm nature, full of strong sympathetic sense and frank cordiality. I look round the circle of my acquaintance for her equal. Much might be said on such a topic: but often a little is as good as much.

The subscription has continued going on, in much the same course as previously, as you will see from the enclosed list. In the *Athenaeum* (and I believe *Academy*) of 2 January a paragraph was put in, to serve as a reminder to any well-wishers:[1] perhaps it may be expected that a few will respond, and that we may then regard our little movement as wound up. I shall always esteem it a privilege to have borne my small share in testifying the respect and gratitude to you which are due to you (I might say) from all open-minded men and women in the world — and from the shut-minded too, for the matter of that.

My wife and children are away at Ventnor (Isle of Wight), as the London winter threatened to be too much for my wife's delicate chest. I expect to join them within the next few days, staying away some 3 weeks or so. As I may be a little hurried these last remaining days, it is possible that I may not just now pay in the £33.16.6[2] shown in the enclosed list — assuming as I do that this point would not be regarded as material. However, the utmost likely delay would not be *long*.

Yours always truly,
W. M. Rossetti

I have seen 3 or 4 times Mr. Charles Aldrich, of Webster City, Iowa: he told us of his interview with you shortly before he crossed the Atlantic.[3] We liked him, and would gladly have seen more of him, but this apparently will not be, for he must now be just about to sail back from Liverpool to New York.

MS: LC. Published: *WCC*, 2:291.

1. It notes that the subscription was "from the first of a semi-private character, no urgent or conspicuous public steps being taken for giving it a wider extension. The result has corresponded, about £115 being realized as yet, and being accepted by Mr. Whitman with the same cordial frankness with which it was tendered" (p. 35; same in *Academy*, p. 9).

2. The fourth installment. He sent a fifth and last installment on 17 May 1886 (letter to Whitman; LC), which brought the subscription to £155.9.9 (Gohdes, Baum, p. 184).

3. MS. Diary, 14 December 1885: "Aldrich ... saw Whitman again lately, and found him, in various respects, in considerably better trim than when he had first seen him in February. Whitman sent a message of affection to me."

397. TO JOHN ADDINGTON SYMONDS

5 Endsleigh Gardens,
7 January 1886

My dear Sir,

I received your letter of 21 December, and read it with respectful sympathy. I have consulted Dr. Furnivall on the subject. He thinks that sooner or later a class termed Honorary Members (or the like) will be added to the Shelley Society, and that this may probably be the best mode in which to meet your views. The matter will not be forgotten at the proper time.[1]

The Society is still in rather a tentative and uncondensed stage: still one expects it to take effect, and in due course to flourish. Dr. Furnivall infuses briskness and "go" into any project of the kind — qualities in which *I* might be found a laggard.

Perhaps you will have seen in last *Athenaeum* or *Academy* a little paragraph about the Whitman Fund. That has been but a *moderate* success: yet still I would not call it, in relation to its present convenience to Whitman, and his very restricted requirements, an ill-success. At this moment the sum realized stands (so far as I am personally cognizant) at £132.17.

Please to accept my high regard, and to believe me always

Truly yours,
W. M. Rossetti

MS: Bristol.

1. Symonds to WMR, 9 January 1886: "I ... shall be gratified if some such honorary place as you hint at is found for me in the Shelley Society.... I have always thought that God did not need the Bible Society. There it is; and so, I suppose, he tolerates it as part of the human mechanism. In the same way I doubt whether Shelley or Goethe or anybody else of that magnitude requires a Society got up by Dr. Furnivall. It appears to me that these Societies ventilate living vanities far more efficiently than they can add to the eternal fame of those poets whose flag they wave in murky air" (AP).

398. TO THOMAS JAMES WISE[1]

5 Endsleigh Gardens,
10 January 1886

Dear Mr. Wise,

Perhaps I need hardly trouble you with this note. You may be aware that Forman possesses the original *Oedipus Tyrannus*.[2] He got it by a real inspiration of book-hunting genius: walked into the *Play*-bookseller's shop in the Strand, Lacey's, asked whether they had such a drama, and lo they *had* it in some old heap. The original *Margaret Nicholson* is to me, as to yourself, unknown: I possess the facsimile edition brought out by Pearson.[3]

Yours truly,
W. M. Rossetti

MS: BL.

1. Thomas James Wise (1859-1937), book collector, bibliographer, forger, was on the platform at the inaugural meeting of the Shelley Society, and became its last secretary in succession to J. S. Little. Early on he took charge of the publications of the Society, which gave him experience in preparing facsimiles which he was to call upon in his forgeries. WMR may have encountered him first in the Browning Society, but their early correspondence deals mostly with Shelley. Subsequently Wise cultivated WMR for his coveted DGR and CGR manuscripts and books, of which he acquired a substantial number.

2. Published "probably in December 1820. After only seven copies had been sold, the Society for the Prevention of Vice threatened a prosecution which the publisher averted by surrendering all remaining copies" (N. I. White, *Shelley*, 2:225).

3. Presumably the "page-for-page reprint of the first edition ... prepared by Richard Herne Shepherd, and issued *circa* 1870" (T. J. Wise, *The Ashley Library, A Catalogue* [1924], 5:49-50).

399. TO LUCY ROSSETTI

5 Endsleigh Gardens,
7 March 1886,
12½

Dear Lu,

I spent yesterday afternoon at the Hunts, amid a great and miscellaneous throng of people. Got but little connected conversation with Hunt or his wife; but gathered that the intention of going to Jerusalem, though seriously and definitely entertained, is not likely to be carried out for some weeks yet. The principal *raison d'être* of the gathering seemed to be to look at a number of Hunt's pictures, old and recent, collected together with a view to that public exhibition of his works which has lately been notified.[1] I was very glad to see some of the *old* pictures — Sylvia and Proteus, British Missionary,[2] etc. In the whole display there was much to admire and uphold, along with limited or exceptional qualities which need to be acknowledged. The pictures were displayed in the newly built studio which now forms an adjunct to Draycott Lodge.[3] I was busily occupied here from before 5 to past 7, talking to a number of people, many of whom asked with interest and particularity after you: one was Mrs. Scott who says that her husband has lately improved at Penkill, but is still restricted to the 2 rooms he occupies. The chilliness of the whole house all the time kept me anything but comfortable: it seems to me that the window-spaces are uncommonly large, and must be very unsuitable for Hunt's state of health. When I left I had to cast about for some place to dine at: chose the South Kensington Museum, the warmth of which was a great relief. I reached home before 9, and found your papa there. He had seen Mathilde and Mary Robinson off by rail, and thought their prospect on the whole favourable.

Today he has gone out to Seddon, McCarthy, Hueffer, Morris[4] — and thence will join me at Campbell's:[5] so his day will be fully occupied. I mean to call on my mother after lunch, and shall then be back a short while before starting for Campbell's. Several engagements for the next few days are pending: Shields tomorrow to dinner here. Your papa hopes to see Lord Ripon[6] Monday or Tuesday, and to return to Manchester late on Tuesday. I must try to get on today with a little necessary work — for which time is not always to be made just now.

Yours in love
W. M. R.

Hunt seemed to me less unwell than commonly of late: Mrs. Hunt looks very thin, but pretty tolerable in health. They send love.

MS: AP.

1. An exhibition of thirty-two works opened at the Fine Art Society in March.
2. *Valentine Rescuing Sylvia* and *A Converted British Family* (Bennett 1969, No. 15).
3. In Fulham, where the Hunts lived from 1882.
4. FMB quarreled with Morris and Burne-Jones in 1874 over Morris's reconstitution of Morris & Co. under his own control. MS. Diary, 25 September 1885, records that FMB recently wrote to them "to renew their old friendliness.... Jones replied to Brown in the most cordial terms, and Morris will I fancy see him on or about Sunday next, when he visits Manchester on one of his Socialistic tours." On 3 March 1886 WMR reported to Lucy on a dinner at FMB's: "Cathy's dinner was a somewhat elaborate affair: we sat down to table about 8, and the men did not leave it till 10¾ — too long for any rational creature. Morris could not come, being engaged lecturing. Mrs. Morris was there, Jones and wife, McCarthy and daughter, Mathilde Blind ... and Randall who is Hueffer's sub-editor (I suppose in the *Musical Times*). Jones, Mrs. Morris, and your father, seemed to me to get on well together; and, so far as distance apart allowed, Mrs. Jones" (AP).
5. James Dykes Campbell (1838-95), biographer of Coleridge and honorary secretary of the Browning Society.
6. George Frederick Samuel Robinson, first Marquis of Ripon (1827-1909), prominent Liberal statesman, was at this date first lord of the Admiralty during Gladstone's brief return to power.

400. TO FORD MADOX BROWN

5 Endsleigh Gardens,
2 April 1886

Dear Brown,

Thanks for your kind note and the photographs. These are I think a great improvement on their precursors. I saw this morning a little letter of yours received by Christina.

My mother is dying: I regard it as certain: whether to die today, tomorrow, or how soon afterwards, is the only uncertainty. She is not speechless nor unconscious, but still halfway towards that condition. I am in hopes that a lethargy — perhaps a rather prolonged one — will prove the close of pain and the beginning of peace. Charlotte also is extremely ill — heart not acting rightly: Christina thinks there will be little interval between my mother's death and Charlotte's — and even that the latter *might* come first of the two.

Lucy is now a *good deal* better. Her last 2 letters say so, and their tone satisfies me that the fact is really so.

Yes I "arm myself with stoicism" — and as yet it protects me to the full: I am profoundly impressed with the conviction that to an infirm and suffering woman aged nearly 86 prolonged life is a calamity, not a boon. I know myself pretty well in these matters: one of these days I shall break down, but that again may be expected to pass.

Your affectionate
W. M. Rossetti

MS: AP.

401. TO LUCY ROSSETTI

5 Endsleigh Gardens,
9 April 1886,
Noon

My dearest Dear,

My reply to your telegram yesterday told you the close of our long suspense.[1] Towards 5 a.m. the more distressing symptoms in my mother's breathing subsided, and she appeared to me to remain in one nearly uniform condition — a condition of sinking without pain or consciousness and without struggle or effort. I went out early to post my letter to you; and later on was just about to post a few other letters of Christina's and my own; had put on my great coat, and re-entered my mother's room to glance at her a moment. At the very moment when I was leaving the nurse told me I ought not to go: she had perceived some indication that the last moment was coming, and looking again I saw the approaching pallor of death in the dear face. Just then Stewart[2] knocked. I spoke to him, and he walked up, and in 2 minutes or so said that the last pulsation had ceased. It was just 25 minutes past noon. Stewart then attended Charlotte, and informed her: she took the intimation calmly, and I don't understand that she took any turn for the worse. In the afternoon I went out to get myself a few articles of mourning and a few flowers, and to engage the undertaker — Tuckey, 48 High Street, Marylebone. Christina had fixed upon him, knowing his advertisement in some church-publication.

The funeral will be on Monday — the same Highgate grave which holds my father and Lizzie. A neighbouring Clergyman Nash,[3] whose church my mother attended, wishes to show his respects by bearing some part in the rites: this I quite concur in. At present it is proposed that he should officiate at Highgate: but I think the final arrangement will be that the first part of the service will be read by him in his church Woburn Square, and the second part by the local clergyman[4] at Highgate.

Christina bears herself well — only giving way at moments. She speaks of a pain in the sole of the foot: I shall remind her of that pain you experienced immediately after Oliver's death, and advise her not wholly to neglect the matter. She alone, with myself, likely to go to Highgate. Eliza can't do that (of course not Charlotte): but perhaps Eliza could attend the service if in Woburn Square. I shall return to Somerset House on Tuesday, but not before.

To sad details let me add one that will please you. Yesterday I received that magazine with your father's *Entombment*.[5] It looks exceedingly well in tone and expression — even better I think than the larger autotype.

Your own
W. M. R.

I am now going directly to Torrington Square, but expect to dine at home towards 7. For the past 2 or 3 days I consider my throat quite *well* — no difference from its ordinary condition of the past few years.

MS: AP.

1. "My dearest mother, the pattern to me of everything that is simple, sweet, kind, and noble, died on 8 April at 25 minutes past noon" (MS. Diary, 11 April 1886; quoted in *FLCR*, p. 213). Annie Jackson was the nurse.

2. William Edward Stewart, "the regular attendant of my mother and aunts"; CGR's doctor after Jenner's retirement. He was the son of William Stewart, who attended Gabriele Rossetti during his last illness (*SR*, 2:530).

3. Joseph John Glendinning Nash, B.A., Queen's College, Cambridge, 1868; vicar of Christ Church, Woburn Square from 1879.

4. Nash also conducted the service at Highgate (*FLCR*, p. 213).

5. Published with WMR's "Ford Madox Brown: Characteristics," *Century Guild Hobby Horse*, April 1886, pp. 48-54. WMR to Lucy, 5 January 1886: "You may I think recollect a rather funny and unmeaning magazine of which a specimen No. reached me (say) 1½ years ago: it was called the *Century Guild Hobby Horse*, and was of the ultra-aesthetic kind, in a sort of travestie-combination of Blake and Jones. It is only now, I gather, that this magazine is beginning to come out regularly. Some evenings ago the Editor, Mr. [A. H.] Mackmurdo an Architect, called on me from your father, wanting to see the photograph of the *Entombment* of Christ, as he wished to get the subject autotyped.... Yesterday he returned, presented me with a copy of his magazine, explained that the autotype is to appear in the April No. of the publication, and asked me to write something, to accompany it, about the typical characteristics of your father's art. I explained to him that discredit might attach to such a transaction, owing to the family-connexion, and I mentioned Shields as a suitable writer free from such an objection: however Mackmurdo stuck to his text, and left me on the understanding that he would again write to your father (for whom he appears to entertain a particular admiration), and, if your father is in favour of my doing the article, I will assent without further ado. Of course payment in such a matter is of no consequence either way: there will or *may* however be some payment — computed on the socialistic principle that the profits of each No. of the magazine are reckoned up, and then each contributor is paid his proportional share of said profits. The No. which Mackmurdo left with me is not so merely freakish or childish a product as that old specimen No.: still I confess I doubt whether any artistic or professional advantage can accrue to your father from association with such a performance. An exclergyman who has turned painter, Selwyn Image, is the artist-in-chief and poet-in-chief of the magazine — a quarterly, exceedingly handsome in paper, type, and general get-up" (AP). WMR to W. Kineton Parkes, 22 June 1887: "The *Century Guild Hobby Horse* is certainly a very fine looking steed, and the tone of the magazine is elevated, and sympathetic with the best things. There is in it however too much (for my taste) of aesthetico-purist cliqueism, and the title of the magazine seems to me singularly absurd" (Wellesley).

402. TO FORD MADOX BROWN

5 Endsleigh Gardens,
11 April 1886

Dear Brown,

I thank you sincerely for your 2 letters, and for the kind feeling which prompted the offer that you and Emma should come up to keep me company. This, I am clear, ought not to be.[1] You will no doubt excuse my not having answered your first letter at once: along with many painful thoughts, there were many painful duties to be performed.

I am well, and quite as composed as you would think. Of Christina the same may be said. Eliza, considering her very frail condition, does well. Charlotte is in bed very ill and weak, and I think most likely dying. This is physical illness, for we don't perceive that the shock of my mother's death has aggravated her symptoms.

I should have liked to see your model at South Kensington:[2] but under present circumstances am not likely to do so, unless indeed it remains there much longer than I had expected. Gabriel's *Annunciation* was bought by the National Gallery for £840.[3]

Love to Emma and you from

Your affectionate
W. M. Rossetti

Lucy took a turn for the better several days ago, and I trust she has not materially receded since then.

MS: AP.

1. See Letter 403.
2. MS. Diary, 3 May 1886: "Went to see in South Kensington Museum the model of Brown's bust of Gabriel, with small annexed model of the drinking-fountain as a whole. The bust is an able noticeable work, and a likeness: as to likeness, I think the point most open to demur is that the nose looks rather bumpy or thickened at the tip, which was certainly not the case with Gabriel, though he had very large nostrils. I presume the bust, in South Kensington, is set at the same level which it is intended to occupy *in situ*: I suspect that, were it a foot or so higher up, it would look more commanding."
3. At the William Graham sale, Christie's, 3 April.

403. TO LUCY ROSSETTI

5 Endsleigh Gardens,
12 April 1886,
4½

Dearest Lucy,

I have just come back from the funeral, followed by an hour or two in Torrington Square. You will understand my disinclination to dwell on anything except a few external details.

I was at Torrington Square by 10.20, and took my last look at my mother. We reached the Woburn Square church at 11.10, where I saw Cathy and Frank: some half-dozen other people were present, more or less casual perhaps. The service was conducted in a way agreeable to the feelings. Then Christina, the Clergyman, and I, got into one carriage — Cathy and Frank into another which he had ordered of the undertaker: some servants etc. followed in a brougham. Eliza with her nurse returned from the church homewards, as it was thought unkind to leave Charlotte alone. The rest of us went on to Highgate, where we saw the last rites performed. Christina and I then returned to Torrington Square, setting the Clergyman down at his church.

After the early dinner Christina (Executrix) produced the will. All is left to her (and this I regard as right) except £100 to me — and there used to be the same to Gabriel. There were also a few informal memoranda, whereby certain books etc. are noted down for me; for you and Olive the items shown on enclosed slip; Christina will look out some small things to be kept by the other children. She entered into a few details from which I infer that the total sum coming to her is short of £4000.

She then — of course spontaneously — said that she had long regarded it as a sacred obligation, to be fulfilled when the conditions should permit, to compensate me for the subsistence which for many years she received from me.[1] She takes £2000 as a lump sum: it is I am sure *more* than the real total, and even a good deal more. This she intends to be mine whenever suitable: but I said, and she agrees with me, that the time for its being suitable is not in *immediate* prospect. She also intimated plainly enough that, over and above this £2000, I or our children would be her general heirs: this of course is optional and revocable, but I have no doubt it will be done. She had told me some days ago that her extant will left everything to our mother, and that consequently she must now make a new will. I told her today that I shall accept this £2000, whenever or however it reaches me, in exactly the same spirit in which it is given.

The day has been really very fine: more springlike in feeling than any preceding day, and the larger trees beginning now to come a little into bud.

I am truly sorry about Arthur's pains: one more distress to be met in the only adequate spirit. I can't discover the least reason why I should take sick leave.

They sent me 5 extra copies of that magazine containing your father's *Entombment* of Christ.[2] These are at your service: to make one of them up in a parcel is a trouble I would prefer to be spared at this moment. You will see his letter enclosed: another to the same effect — that he and Emma would come up to keep me company — had preceded. Emma's presence would tease me much: so I had to regard the entire proposal from that point of view, and yesterday I replied thanking and declining.

Yours in love
William

Do you like, or do you dislike, to have as our property Legros's portrait of me? It is one of the objects left to me. If you dislike it, I shall reconsign it to Christina. She never *liked* it, but I can see that she would be better pleased to possess it than not.

How are *you*? I have not heard with any distinctness these 2 or 3 days.

MS: AP.

1. C. 1854-76 (*FLCR*, p. 214).
2. See Letter 401, Note 5.

404. TO FREDERICK JAMES FURNIVALL 5 Endsleigh Gardens,
22 April 1886

Dear Furnivall,

You must no doubt be correct in saying "Preston[1] knows he can employ a Clerk as often as he likes." However in his conversation with me he did not *seem* to know it. Perhaps you will take a suitable opportunity of reimpressing the fact upon him.

I will send Maynard's paper[2] back to him when I know his address: don't know it at present. Shall be with my family at Ventnor up to Monday (or perhaps Tuesday) next.

I should not like to attend the *Cenci*[3] — and more especially not the dinner — so soon after my mother's death. Possibly the feeling is unreasonable: some of us are not very reasonable beings.

I have not just now time to think — who could be got to give an additional reprint?[4] As a general principle I should say that the Society should cut its cost according to its cloth, and should simply produce year by year such printed and other work as its subscriptions cover. It is founded for 10 years, and in 10 years I suppose all Shelley's books, and much besides, would be provided for out of the annual subscriptions; whereas, if we give subscribers this year much more printed matter (besides other equivalent) than their guineas are worth, there may hardly be adequate *raison d'être* for the Society for the ensuing 9 years, nor much to do with its money. But I may be wrong. Will ponder list of subscribers, and see whether I discern a likely donor of a Reprint.

I return Wise's letter. He mentions some details about my Memoir.[5] I may as well say here that Clay never sent me (what you referred to some weeks ago) a proof of the title-page. I should certainly have preferred to see it, but presume the practicable time is now past.

Yours very truly,
W. M. Rossetti

MS: BL.

1. Sydney E. Preston, the first secretary of the Shelley Society, was "a young lawyer enlisted by Dr. Furnivall; he did the work in a spirited style, but his own occupations obliged him to resign soon" (*SR*, 2:392-93).

2. MS. Diary, 12 May 1886: "Took the chair at a meeting of the Shelley Society. Henry Sweet was to have read a paper, presumably of some import ["Primitiveness of Shelley's View of Nature," *Notebook*, p. 81]: but at the last moment he proved to be too ill, and the only thing that could be thought of was a slightish paper by a Mr. [H. J.] Maynard, lying of late in my hands, on Shelley's Religion. I went home, fetched it, and read it out to a diminished audience. Invited a discussion, but failed to obtain any: the more serious Shelleyites thinking, I apprehend, that the paper was not of sufficient weight." (For an abstract of the paper, see *Notebook*, pp. 82-88.)

3. Performed under the auspices of the Society at the Grand Theatre, Islington on 7 May, with Alma Murray in the role of Beatrice Cenci. It was widely and favorably reviewed (see *Notebook*, pp. 59-80, which reprints two dozen reviews and lists more than two dozen others). *Notebook* makes no mention of a dinner.

4. "The Sub-Committee for publishing purposes (I did not belong to it) issued, in the first year or two of the Society, an amount of Shelley literature more than equivalent to the annual subscriptions of a guinea each; and we soon found ourselves burdened with a heavy debt to the printer" (*SR*, 2:391). MS. Diary, 22 February 1886: "Received the first publication of the Shelley Society — facsimile of the 1st Edition of *Adonais*."

489

5. MS. Diary, 16 March 1886: "Slark having at Furnivall's request allowed the Shelley Society to print off from his stereotype plates 250 copies of my *Memoir of Shelley*, 1878, I finished this evening the writing of a little preface to it, embodying such actual rectifications of details as have become known to me since 1878. I am well pleased that this opportunity of revising and diffusing the *Memoir* should arrive just before the appearance of Dowden's book, now shortly expected, shall lay all antecedent Shelley biographizing on the shelf." Slark also issued a trade edition of the revised *Memoir* in 1886.

405. TO LUCY ROSSETTI

Somerset House,
5 May 1886,
Noon

Dearest Luie,

I have your letters of yesterday and the day before.

The extreme fatigue which you experienced after the small exertion of going to Mill Street is distressing: but on the whole I am glad to infer that you are not exceptionally amiss — rather the reverse.

Thank you for proposing to write to your papa about the Chaucer-notice.[1] If you were not to do so, it would lie with me to do it: but confiding in your writing, I shall take no further steps at present.

No doubt Christina's position with her aged and infirm aunts is a very dull one: it will not I suppose last *very* long. Shortly before our mother's death I spoke to Christina about what her future lot in life might probably be: I proposed for instance that immediately after the funeral she should spend a little time with me (otherwise solitary) in Endsleigh Gardens. This she declined, mainly on the ground of looking after her aunts. I then raised the general question of what might be expected to ensue after the death of her aunts — and enquired whether she had any idea of settling at Birchington (a point which had at sometime or other been vaguely mooted). She does not seriously think of Birchington: but thinks it possible that she might like to reside in some country-place where religious interests would be uppermost with her: as especially in or near Rochester, where Burrows[2] (the Clergyman of Christ Church of old) is now a Canon. She thought it *possible* that she might take a house there, much more than large enough for herself, in the expectation that you and the kids, and myself, might find it a convenient sojourn from time to time. I told her plainly that the great stumbling-block would be any tendency of hers to proselytize the kids: this point was quite present to her own mind, and she said that she did not feel that her assertion of the Christian scheme need or would go beyond this limit — that she would herself openly practise her religious duties, and leave the kids to see and think what they liked of them. To this I should myself have no objection.

I wrote yesterday to Cook & Lomer, asking them to invest my surplus £62 (or some amount closely approaching that) in Spanish securities, or if they prefer in Canada 3½%; and saying I would probably call on them on Saturday, and bring round my cheque for £557.13.7, or for any larger sum which might then be cor-

[Incomplete]

490

MS: AP.

1. DGR's review of *Chaucer at the Court of Edward III* (Bennett 1965, No. 11) in the *Spectator*, 10 May 1851, p. 452, which WMR reprinted in *Collected Works*. FMB evidently hesitated because of a mildly negative comment on the color.

2. Henry Williams Burrows, B.A., 1837, St. John's College, Oxford; vicar of Christ Church, Albany Street, 1851-78; canon of Rochester Cathedral from 1881. He contributed a short preface to CGR's *Annus Domini*.

406. TO LUCY ROSSETTI

5 Endsleigh Gardens,
9 May 1886,
11¼

Dearest Lu,

You are certainly right in supposing that the Shelley Society is now a success: I think it is a very decided success in point of numbers etc. — more than 300 members. I did not like Furnivall's policy in *rushing* the affair without deliberation and feeling the way: but I must admit that the event has fully justified him. I gather that the *Cenci* performance was in most respects a marked success, but that the play was considered heavy although very fine.

From two different sources I had heard of the depreciatory remarks about Gabriel in the *Pall Mall Gazette*, and of your father's answer to them.[1] On Thursday I bought the *Pall Mall Budget* with the answer: on Friday your father sent me another copy of the answer, and one of the original paragraph. I like the answer well; and of course do not like the paragraph — though it is a painful truth that Gabriel, almost a teetotaller up to the age of 40 or upwards, did, through his habit of gulping down stiff doses of raw whiskey to qualify the chloral, betray himself into a certain sort of dram-drinking which at times culminated in a serious form, and which was, I fully believe, almost or quite as ruinous to his constitution as the chloral itself. There is one point in the paragraph which deserves (or would at an earlier date have deserved) consideration. The writer says that there is already a drinking-fountain close by. Now I had always considered that the chief *raison d'être* for a drinking-fountain form of monument, rather than some other form, lay in the fact that the authorities would be likely to grant a site for a drinking-fountain, and along with that for any associated memorial of Gabriel; whereas they might have been stiffer in relation to the memorial apart from a convenient drinking-fountain. But, if there really is (as there must surely be) a drinking-fountain close by then I fear the authorities are likely to be all the *less* inclined for that form of memorial than for some other — and apart from the supposed convenience some other form would I think be every bit as appropriate and satisfactory from our own point of view.

I trust you are getting well, dearest, through your present inconvenience, and that the flea is what Helen calls "a distinct animal" by this time.

Yesterday I was told that poor Cook[2] is still confined to bed.

Your own
W. M: R.

MS: AP.

1. A correspondent on 26 April 1886 declared the absurdity of "Rossetti and a drinking fountain! In the first place, Rossetti was far more partial to chloral, opiates, stimulants, narcotics, anything rather than cold water"; and he criticized Seddon's wild duck waterspout and the resemblance between the bust and Shakespeare's bust at Stratford (p. 4). FMB replied that "in connection with the poet of *The Sea-Limits* and *The Cloud Confines*, the bird seems rather suggestive of the long reaches of the sea, and the straight arrowy flight with the faint cry high above in the sky"; that DGR "in fact was extremely like the bust of Shakespeare. Years past, when I was painting a Shakespeare [*The Seeds and Fruits of English Poetry* (Bennett 1964, No. 12)], I found him a most valuable model"; and that for most of the more than thirty years that he had known DGR, "tobacco, tea, coffee, stimulants, were all distasteful to him. There was something almost provoking in the way he would, after a whole evening's poetry, listening, and reciting (his friends around him all smoking or partaking of coffee or toddy) pour out, at one o'clock of a winter morning, a tumbler of cold water and drink it off" (*Pall Mall Gazette*, 5 May 1886, p. 4; same in *Pall Mall Budget*, 6 May 1886, pp. 15-16).
2. Keningale Cook.

407. TO LUCY ROSSETTI

Somerset House,
10 May 1886,
11½

Dearest Lu,

Having now received back those papers of Cook & Lomer, I will make at leisure a few calculations for myself, and impart their result to you.

The Greek affair[1] may be briefly stated thus — the *facts* are undisputed.

1. In 1878 the Treaty of Berlin, dictated by all the Great Powers, required Turkey to cede certain territory to Greece. Turkey assented because she couldn't help, but *did* nothing till 1881 or 1882, when the Powers compelled her to transfer to Greece a portion (*not the whole*) of the territory defined in 1878.

2. Greece, having waited 8 years since 1878, and 4 since 1881, and seeing her neighbour and competitor Bulgaria vastly aggrandized in 1886, thinks the time has now come when Turkey should disgorge the residue of the territory, and summons Turkey to do so at risk of war.

3. The Great Powers think that a war between Greece and Turkey would perhaps lead to much larger and more dangerous complications, chiefly between Russia and Austria: so they bully Greece to abstain from claiming the very thing which they themselves assigned to her in 1878.

4. What follows is opinion, not fact. Common honesty requires that a power like England should uphold instead of bullying Greece. Were she to do so vigorously, she would have France for her ally, and to all appearance Russia. There would then be 3 Great Powers against 3, and most likely Italy and even Germany would sooner or later join England, France, and Russia, and leave Austria (the most bestial power on the Continent) in the lurch. Instead of this, England makes common cause with every other brutal bully of Europe, defrauds Greece, and bolsters up the unspeakable Turk. What comes of it we shall see.

As you think the Ventnor fine weather is now doing you good, don't *hurry* home. The London weather is also quite fine though I thought last night comparatively chill.

À toi
Guillaume

MS: AP.

1. In April 1885 Charilaos Tricoupis fell from power in Greece and was succeeded by Theodoros Delyanni, who ordered mobilization. Conflicts with Turkish troops on the border followed, and on 8 May 1886 the Great Powers blockaded Greek ports. When Delyanni was forced to resign on 11 May, Tricoupis returned to power and immediately ordered disarmament.

408. TO FREDERICK JAMES FURNIVALL

5 Endsleigh Gardens,
18 May 1886

Dear Furnivall,

Thank you for your very frank and friendly letter. Unless your words of the other evening were *reported*, I hardly know that it would be worth your while to "pluck out that [very minor][1] feather from your cap in the sight of the next assemblage of Shelleyites."[2] As you and I are now at one as to the facts, I have secured the only point I could lay stress upon. I seem to remember in a vague way that conversation in my dining-room to which you refer. What I said must have been to the effect that you had erewhile (in that talk at Holman Hunt's) heard of my "Shelley Autobiography," and had done what you could to get it published (by writing to Kegan Paul).

I am glad to infer from your letter that the Shelleys[3] saw the *Cenci*: my impression had been otherwise. When the time comes, I must reflect as to the question of consulting them or not about copyright in letters. If this were a mere act of courteous deference, I should be disposed to waive it: but a legal obligation is a stiff matter. For all these past years my *wish* would have been to bring out the book as it now stands, in all substantial respects: but I suppose that it is now inevitable to hold it over until Dowden's book comes out, and (very likely) to modify it rather considerably in accordance with such new information, new documents, etc., as his book will contain. What you say as to the eventual copyright in my book seems right enough: I was not aware that Bell[4] might with some confidence be looked to take it.

I am sorry for the pockets of my co-Committee-men if I am its next-best-off member: Buxton Forman may be the best-off for anything I know — certainly he has disbursed for Shelley-treasures sums which are quite out of *my* range. Were I at all rich, it would be a pleasure to me to give the Society a reprint — or several reprints. The case being otherwise, I have never regarded that as in my line. Should like to have some idea (which at present I have not) of what the cost is — say, of the recent *Alastor* reprint, or the *Adonais*.

It appears to me that I shall be at home *every* evening this week — and most other weeks — about 7: 6½ the better hour of the two for myself. The only thing which might be taking me up just now is the return of my wife from Ventnor.

This return *was* to have taken place yesterday, *may* take place today: if not today, then some other day, probably very near. Anyhow you and I could have a chat.

To recur to that affair of presenting reprints. I have not the least wish to appear shabby — on the contrary I dislike it. If members of the Committee think that a Chairman of do. ought to be a man who presents reprints, it is quite possible they are right. That would not make me present a reprint, as long as my finances and responsibilities dictate the contrary course; but it would make me very prompt in resigning the Chairmanship, and that without the slightest feeling of soreness. As you are aware, I was installed without seeking the post, or even knowing that I was in nomination for it.

Yours very truly,
W. M. Rossetti

I may as well send for your consideration this letter from Mr. Smart.[5] I replied to him the other day that I myself should be more inclined to leave the existing arrangement undisturbed, but that I would consult you or others about it.

I read that *Sordello* paper you sent me. Don't understand what is meant by the statement that Browning at some date rewrote *Sordello*. Can perfectly recollect that, about the time when *Sordello* was included in Browning's Collected Works, he told my brother and myself that after mature deliberation he had determined *not* to alter it, but simply to add a series of page-headings which would guide the reader. Till now I had remained — or indeed I *remain* — under the full conviction that the reprinted *Sordello* presents scarcely the least diversity from the original *Sordello*.[6]

MS: BL.

1. Square brackets in MS.
2. MS. Diary, 12 May 1886: "At an early stage of the evening Furnivall made to the meeting [Shelley Society] a statement which rather embarrassed me. He spoke of my 'Shelley Autobiography' ["Cor Cordium"] ... as a book which they are bent on publishing; and said that the idea of compiling such an autobiography had been suggested to me by himself. This is a total mistake.... I would not confute Furnivall on the spot, as that might have been unpleasant to him: but it will behove me to write to him, and remind him of the real facts."
3. Sir Percy and Lady Shelley.
4. George Bell.
5. James P. Smart, Wise's co-author in the *Bibliography of Ruskin* (1893).
6. *Sordello* (1840) was reissued in *Poetical Works*, 3d ed., 1863, "considerably altered" (W. C. DeVane, *A Browning Handbook*, p. 71).

409. TO JOHN TODHUNTER[1]

5 Endsleigh Gardens,
29 May 1886

Dear Todhunter,

I have received your note of yesterday, which has only confirmed my previous intention of writing to you to express the very great gratification which your play, and the performance of it, afforded me. I admire the play at the very least as much as the performance. Immediately after taking my seat and procuring the book I read the opening chorus, and thought it genuine and fine poetry; and perhaps I could not give you better evidence of the fact that I thought the same of the play in its entirety than by saying that as soon as I returned home I read it out *in extenso* to my wife — who fully shares my opinion of the work. I congratulate you most heartily on having done a very good thing. The iron ought to be hot for you now: and if you strike you ought to secure some arrangement for the acting of *Alcestis* Greek-wise, and of *Rienzi* as a regular stage-play. Why has *Clito*[2] been so great a hit? I don't well see why — but have not *seen* the performance.

The scheme of performance of your *Helena* was of course most interesting, and the execution to a large extent beautiful and excellent. I should incline to place the acting on the ensuing scale — of *descending* merit:

1. B. Tree[3] as Paris — fine, sometimes excellent: I thought his *vocal* dialogue with the Chorus a very effective stage-episode.
2. Chorus, taken *altogether* — Miss Kinnaird[4] a potent elocutionist — general gesture and ensemble of Chorus still leaving *something* to be desired, but the something could perhaps hardly be supplied save by a couple of generations of similar work.
3. Mrs. B. Tree[5] as Oenone, or perhaps Vezin[6] as Priam: his appeal to Zeus quite thrilling, and remainder good, though the *elocution* did not seem quite stately and abstract enough for a Greek standard.
4. Miss Murray[7] as Helena — I say the same, more strongly, of *her* elocution, and her person is not sufficiently beautiful or important, but she was always *intelligent*. Please don't give currency to any demur of mine regarding this lady, as she is the Beatrice Cenci of the Shelley Society, and as such must command my Committee-loyalty.
5. Hecuba efficient, though dry and masculine — Archer[8] a fine picturesque figure.

Excuse anything which might seem pragmatical in these remarks. Olive as well as myself enjoyed the performance greatly: and most especially the lady who (in default of my wife, whom the weather of that Thursday would have been too trying for) accompanied Olive. This was Mrs. Hollings, an accomplished, thoughtful, and most amiable lady, wife of a Doctor[9] living near us: she says that she never enjoyed any performance so much in her life before. Your artists in Greek costume will be a curious experiment — I hope a successful one.

With our best regards to Mrs. Todhunter and yourself,

Yours very truly,
W. M. Rossetti

I might have added that the *Helena music* appeared to me also good and suitable: but of that I am too little a judge.

MS: Reading.

1. (1839-1916), poet and dramatist, practiced medicine in Dublin, 1870-74, before settling in London to devote himself to literature. *Helena in Troas* (1886) was produced at Hengler's Circus, Argyll Street during May and June. His earlier books included *Alcestis* (New York, 1874; London, 1879), *The True Tragedy of Rienzi* (1881), and *A Study of Shelley* (1880). He called upon WMR on 26 February 1877 with a letter of introduction from Furnivall, and presented him with a copy of *Laurella and Other Poems* (1876) (MS. Diary).

2. A tragedy by Sydney Grundy and Wilson Barrett, which opened at the Princess's Theatre on 1 May 1886.

3. Herbert Beerbohm Tree (1853-1917), actor-manager, half-brother of Max Beerbohm, began his professional stage career in 1878.

4. Possibly Maud Kennar (*Dramatic and Musical Directory*, 1886).

5. Helen Maud Holt (1863-1937), whom Tree married in 1883.

6. Hermann Vezin (1829-1910), born in the United States, came to England in 1850. Within a decade he had established himself as an outstanding actor in comedy and tragedy.

7. Alma Murray (1854-1945), whom Browning called "the Poetic Actress without a rival" (*Notebook*, p. 105), began her career in 1870. She appeared in two of Browning's poetic dramas, *In a Balcony* (1884) and *Colombe's Birthday* (1885). In 1894 she created the part of Raina in Shaw's *Arms and the Man*. She was the "daughter of Leigh Murray [1820-70], whom I remember well as an actor many years ago: in all her early life she was half starved" (MS. Diary, 20 May 1886). She married Buxton Forman's brother Alfred. WMR noted in MS. Diary, 27 May 1886, that she "seemed ill-suited with Helena; her person unimportant, her voice not noble, and her elocution unlike what is needed for a semi-abstract Greek treatment."

8. Maggie Archer (*Dramatic and Musical Directory*, 1886).

9. Edwin Hollings, 25 Endsleigh Gardens, and 4 Gordon Street, Gordon Square (*POLD*).

410. TO ALGERNON CHARLES SWINBURNE

5 Endsleigh Gardens,
2 July 1886

Dear Swinburne,

With the greatest satisfaction did I receive your note of 16 June announcing that a copy of your new book[1] was to come to me — and in due sequel the book itself. Most of it I knew already, but not all. As your note says, you and I differ on some points: I from you, with a constant and acknowledged sense that in any such controversy it is you who have a *right* to be in the right, and to persuade others. The book is full of interesting matter, vigorously presented and dazzlingly worded: I could again and again recur to it with great pleasure. One of the articles which I already knew is the Landor, which is a fine specimen of clear-cut perception and judgement; compendiously grouped in detail: I had read it in the *Encyclopaedia Britannica*, which I regularly take in.

One thing in the volume which I find very good is the appendix on Mary Stuart: have not read Hosack's book,[2] but what you say of it seems to familiarize me with the scope of its argument, and to demonstrate that your rejoinder thereto must be right. The sentences about Buchanan and Maitland[3] are curiously apt — and amusing in proportion to

Your affectionate
W. M. Rossetti

MS: Folger.

1. *Miscellanies*.

2. John Hosack, *Mary Queen of Scots and Her Accusers* (1869; 2d ed., 1870-74).

3. George Buchanan (1506-82), scholar, historian, secretary of Regent Moray's commissioners in England, 1568-69, affirmed that the casket letters were in Queen Mary's handwriting. William Maitland (1528?-73) was entrusted with the conduct of Mary's foreign policy in 1561, and from 1570 was the leader of the Queen's party. Swinburne's summary of Hosack's argument provided another welcome chance to ridicule Robert Buchanan: "Let us suppose that a Buchanan, for example, was what Mr. Hosack has called him, 'the prince of literary prostitutes': a rascal cowardly enough to put forth in print a foul and formless mass of undigested falsehood and rancorous ribaldry, and venal

enough to traffic in the disgrace of his dishonourable name for a purpose as infamous as his act. Let us concede that a Maitland was cur enough to steal that name as a mask for the impudent malice of ingratitude" (p. 378).

411. TO FREDERICK JAMES FURNIVALL

5 Endsleigh Gardens,
12 July 1886

Dear Furnivall,

I have a very strong propensity for "cutting my coat according to my cloth": I therefore quite acquiesce in your view that we should not incur for 1886 any further expense for publications, unless it be for *Hellas*. Even as to *Hellas* — publishing *and acting* — I would not scruple to say: "If it entails expense which our funds don't meet, let us drop it absolutely for 1886, and see what turns up in 1887."[1]

I really don't know where to look for new members. I see few people: those whom I do see, and those of whom I know something without seeing them, are all, in a general way, aware of the existence and doings of the Shelley Society, and are in the way of joining "on their own hook," if disposed to join by any manner of means.

I much regret to infer, from one phrase in Wise's letter, that the accident to your son of which you lately made mention to me has continued to cause some trouble and anxiety. Heartily trust it may now be mending — or mended.

Thanks about Gladstone etc.

Yours very truly,
W. M. Rossetti

MS: BL.

1. MS. Diary, 24 October 1886: "Attended ... a meeting of the Committee of the Shelley Society. The object was to consider how far it may be practicable to carry out our announced intention of performing *Hellas* early in November: questions of time, expense, and means of performance, are all pressing for solution. My own impression was that the project would have to be postponed: but in course of discussion it was decided still to push it on, *if* the necessary arrangements for chorus etc. can be at once managed. A Committee-member named [Charles Gordon] Hall is to get this point settled. I met for the first time Forman's father-in-law Dr. [William Christian] Selle, the musician who has composed the music for *Hellas* ["16 parts for solo, duets, trios, and four-part chorus, with piano accompaniment and piano overture"; score published by Shelley Society, 1886]. He played us most of the music on the pianoforte: it seems to me bright, telling, and very tuneable ... [but] wanting in noble elevation.... I find that (contrary to my understanding hitherto) the dialogue-portion of *Hellas* is not to be acted, but only read out: Mr. [Samuel] Brandram is to be invited by Selle to do this — gratuitously. I rather regret that the play is to lack the advantage of costume: beyond that, there is certainly very little in it for which acting is more needful than reading." 7 November: "Sent to Little £1.1 towards meeting the expenses of the forthcoming performance of *Hellas*." 10 November: "First meeting of the Shelley Society for current season. We are in a horrid mess about the *Hellas* project; the Mr. Hall who undertook practical arrangements having committed us (I think most blameably) to reckless money-outlay. We shall probably be in for nearly £300, and, if we recover £80 or so of this, we may consider ourselves lucky. Our more essential operations will be crippled for a year or two to come. However, it seems we must now go through with it." Of the performance at St. James's Hall on 16 November, with Austin Podmore as the reader, WMR told Lucy on 17 November that it pleased him only "to a certain extent" (AP).

412. TO ERIC S. ROBERTSON[1]

5 Endsleigh Gardens,
6 August 1886

Dear Mr. Robertson,

It gratifies me much to learn that Knight is to write the Memoir of my brother:[2] he knew my brother familiarly and cordially, and will I think do justice to the subject. If Knight applies to me for "any hints or other aids" on any defined points, I shall assuredly be most glad to help him. I remember telling you however that my brother's family-letters are to be published as a separate book, under my editorship and preceded by a Memoir written by Watts, before the close of 1887: so I regret to say that it will not be in my power to lend Knight any letters — which otherwise I would gladly have done, supposing that he would like to have them.[3]

Yours very truly,
W. M. Rossetti

MS: Yale.

1. Editor of *Magazine of Art*, 1880-81 (*NCBEL*); editor of the "Great Writers" series of biographies. MS. Diary, 7 January 1887, notes his appointment as professor of English at the University of the Punjab, Lahore.
2. Joseph Knight, *Life of Dante Gabriel Rossetti* (1887) in "Great Writers" series. MS. Diary, 5 August 1886: "I am well pleased with this choice, and so are Lucy and Watts."
3. MS. Diary, 3 October 1886: "Sent a letter to Knight, giving a list of materials for a Memoir of Gabriel; and offering to give him the perusal of the copy-volume of Family-letters as made up for printing, my MS. monograph (begun) on Gabriel's works in art and literature [*DGRDW*], and the Preface (proof) to the *Collected Works* — also referring him to Brown in case he would covet some use of Gabriel's letters addressed to Brown. Thus I really place at Knight's disposal (for information in increasing his knowledge of the subject, though not for verbatim reproduction) all the unpublished materials that I have at command." 12 October: "Knight spent the evening with us, talking over the scheme of his Memoir of Gabriel. I lent him my copies of Caine's and Sharp's books, with various pencilled revisions of my own.... As regards Gabriel's pictorial art Knight confesses himself not at all qualified to discuss and criticize: he proposes to get the aid of Stephens on this subject, but I don't feel very confident that Stephens (whose own projects regarding Gabriel have perhaps not been absolutely dropped, though they have very long seemed to be in a state of suspended animation) will work very cordially in that groove." 2 November: "Knight called again, and read a further portion of the letters [DGR to FMB]. He showed me the passage which he has now written (founded on what he had read yesterday) regarding Gabriel's engagement etc. to Lizzie Siddal. On the whole I think there is nothing in this passage to which objection should be raised; whether as regards a reasonable reserve in using the materials proper to Brown, or as regards the spirit in which the facts are treated." 5 November: "Knight continued his inspection of Gabriel's letters addressed to Brown: I did not see him. He came upon a passage in which he himself is described by Gabriel (but without unfriendliness) as 'an old gossip': Lucy enjoyed a hearty laugh over this incident." 6 January 1887: "Began attending to a fresh little job — the Bibliography of D. G. Rossetti which a Mr. [John P.] Anderson (British Museum) is preparing, to form an appendix to the Memoir written by Knight. He has got together a large amount of items — which I shall be able to supplement to some fair extent." 5 April: "Received from Knight a large-paper copy of his Memoir of Gabriel: it makes a very good-looking book. Began re-reading it (had read it in proof at San Remo, and pointed out some errors etc.): it is agreeably done, and written in a spirit of great kindliness toward Gabriel."

413. TO THE EDITOR OF THE *PALL MALL GAZETTE*

9 September 1886

I observe in your paper of yesterday[1] a statement from "a correspondent" quoting some passages from a letter written by my old friend the late Mr. Bernhard Smith. The main object of the writer is to show that Mr. Smith was a member of the Pre-Raphaelite Brotherhood, a "P.R.B."; and, in confirmation of this statement, an inscription from a copy of Browning's poems is cited, "To Bernhard Smith, P.R.B., from Gabriel and William Rossetti, P.R.B.s." No doubt this inscription must be correctly cited. It certainly proves that my brother and I bestowed upon our friend Smith the name P.R.B.; nevertheless I must deny that he ever was, in the strict sense of the term, a member of the Pre-Raphaelite Brotherhood. The members were seven, not (as now stated) eight — namely, William Holman Hunt, John Everett Millais, Thomas Woolner, James Collinson (misnamed Collins in Mr. Smith's letter — perhaps confounded with Charles Allston Collins), Frederic George Stephens, Dante Gabriel Rossetti, and William Michael Rossetti. Collinson after a while seceded, and Walter Howell Deverell was substituted for him; though even he scarcely assumed the precise position of the original members. As to Mr. Bernhard Smith, I remember him well as one of the manliest-moulded and pleasantest of Englishmen — a sculptor and, in a minor sense, a painter; and far be it from me to say anything which could derogate from the kindly reminiscences of old. He had a share in the studio occupied by the sculptor Woolner. From this and other circumstances he was treated with great familiarity by the Pre-Raphaelites, and there was some idea that he would finally be elected into the Brotherhood, and (as the inscription in question shows) my brother and I even addressed him as if he *had* been thus elected.

Mr. Smith must have been totally mistaken in saying that the book thus inscribed was given to him in 1847. In 1847 no such affair as the Pre-Raphaelite Brotherhood existed in any sort of way; it came into being in 1848, or even 1849, and I think the acquaintance of my brother and myself with Mr. Smith can hardly have begun before 1850. Of course, too, Mr. Smith was mistaken in identifying Browning's poem about Waring with his poem entitled *The Lost Leader*. I may add (in reply to a point raised by your correspondent) that no works of art produced by Bernhard Smith in Australia ever reached either my brother or myself.

W. M. Rossetti

Text: *Pall Mall Gazette*, 10 September 1886, p. 6.

1. "The Pre-Raphaelite Brotherhood," p. 3.

414. TO THOMAS JAMES WISE

5 Endsleigh Gardens,
22 November 1886

Dear Wise,

The affair about Forman is simply this. Furnivall the other day wrote me a letter (quite reasonable on its own showing) saying that it would behove the Committee to pass a vote to the effect that the sub-committee had exceeded its powers by involving us in an expense for *Hellas* exceeding £100: and he added that, even if this vote were to lead to Buxton Forman's resignation, he thought it none the less needful. I replied in the letter which you have now seen. Furnivall answered on Saturday as follows: "All right then: but we must let HBF know (more or less) what we feel." So I judge that the idea of anything like a formal censure is abandoned.

I am the most pacific of men (as you may judge by that letter of mine to Furnivall), and it will certainly not be my fault if any one of us — Committee or Society — quarrels with any other.

Yours very truly,
W. M. Rossetti

MS: BL.

415. TO FREDERICK JAMES FURNIVALL

5 Endsleigh Gardens,
22 December 1886

Dear Furnivall,

Thanks for your card. I should hardly feel warranted in obtruding direct upon Browning the opinions of a small man about a great one: but, if you feel inclined to make yourself any sort of use of this letter, I have no objection.

I was reluctantly prevented by office-work from reaching the theatre[1] until the middle of the scene where Strafford, while fiercely upbraiding the King (whose wretched duplicity and moral cowardice are splendidly shown up by Browning throughout), finds himself in presence of the King's opponents, and immediately, with the sublime frenzy of a *preux chevalier*, kneels and affects to be seconding Charles in what he was at that very moment denouncing. I always thought *that*, in reading, a stupendous dramatic situation; and on the stage I found it to be so. Acts 3 and 4 I thought replete with interest — especially that scene where Strafford thinks he has floored his opponents, and is succeeded by Pym, who with his marble passion of patriotism proceeds to annihilate him — also (particularly effective) the preceding scene where Strafford has to give up his sword to the parliamentary official. The final Act I found splendid and extremely moving: I assure you that (as Shelley says) "mine eyes were dim with tears unshed"[2] — for as I get older I find myself more impressionable not only by the pathetic but also by the *beautiful* things in great poetry. If the theatre-goers of our present day had a heart for the great drama of the world, and not merely for the passions mirrored in a pretty face, I feel a clear conviction that *Strafford* would be a fine established stage-piece: and even the pretty face has been as well provided for as Browning's materials seemed to allow.

I could not profess to have thought the acting very good. Strafford impulsive and (as Browning makes him) sanguine upon a background of desperation, but too young and effervescing; Pym far from being rapt away from everything of self into his one mission; Charles well made up and acting intelligently. By the way I thought it a great mistake (don't exactly know whether the text requires it

500

or not) to leave him on the stage swooned away all the latter part of the last scene: as soon as he becomes incapable of taking a part in the action, his attendants or some persons ought to assist him off the stage — and I think the Headsman (though perhaps contrary to the etiquette of his office) ought to enter ominously just before the curtain drops. I thought Strafford's last passionate appeal to Pym, appeal and denunciation, sounded overcharged on the stage: ought to re-read it before expressing a clear opinion. Young Vane[3] I considered really good — a very promising actor.

This I can truly say: I did not pass a dull 5 minutes from the moment of entering to that of leaving the theatre. The play (with which I have of course been familiar from early youth, but which I had not read for I dare say 15 to 18 years past) took possession of me, and kept it throughout. It struck me that the drama would gain in *couleur locale* and sense of great issues if a little more prominence (by means of subordinate speakers) were given to the vast *religious* upheaval and conflict of the time.

Yours very truly,
W. M. Rossetti

MS: Wellesley.

1. Browning's *Strafford* was performed under the auspices of the Browning Society at the Strand Theatre on 21 December.
2. *To Mary Wollstonecraft Godwin*, l. 1.
3. E. Cyril Vane (*Dramatic and Musical Directory*, 1886).

416. TO THEODORE WATTS-DUNTON

5 Endsleigh Gardens,
14 January 1887

Dear Watts,

You may be aware that I sent Swinburne the other day a presentation-copy of my brother's *Works*. You will probably have inferred — and rightly — that the only reason why I did not at the same time send *you* a second copy is that I thought you would prefer to receive a *large-paper* copy[1] — one of those which I mentioned when we met at Eric Robertson's. These are not as yet in my hands: I presume I may get them within 3 weeks or so from now, and then I shall most likely be abroad. If by any chance you would prefer an early small-paper copy, please let me know; and it shall be substituted.

Not having at my disposal any gratis small-paper copies, I have presented very few of them — only 4. Do you think that Mrs. Morris[2] would like to receive one from me? If you do think so, I will order it without delay: but, feeling very uncertain, have as yet done nothing. Of course, all I want on this point is your personal private *opinion*.

Having occasion the other day to write to Ellis & Scrutton, I asked them how the book seems to sell. They replied yesterday — sale satisfactory, upwards of 500 copies. This I should have considered *rather* below the mark than otherwise, but they do not appear to view it so. I have always intended to raise with Ellis &

Scrutton — as soon as I should have a slight idea of how the sale of the *Works* proceeds — the question of publishing the Memoir-letters book. Does it suit your arrangements that I should now raise that question without delay? You know that *my* work upon the book was done long ago — say before spring of 1883. Since then some changes of circumstances (for instance my dear mother's death) requires that I should again go over my notes etc., making some modifications etc.: but all this would not I suppose occupy me more than 10 or 12 days when once I set-to upon it.[3]

Your

W. M. Rossetti

MS: BL.

1. MS. Diary, 6 January 1887: "Wrote to Ellis & Scrutton acquiescing in a proposal which they make for a large-paper issue of Gabriel's *Collected Works*: 25 copies, out of which I am to receive 6 gratis, as my sole remuneration from the issue." 27 March: "Ford Hueffer fetched away, for his father to whom I have presented it, one of the 6 large-paper copies of Gabriel's *Collected Works*.... The other 5 copies are disposed of thus: 1, myself; 2, Watts; 3, Forman (in recognition of his liberality to me of old with his Shelley and Keats books); 4, Wise, who has expressed a wish to *buy* the volume of me, rather than of the publishers; 5, remaining on hand." 30 April: "Sold to Wise a large-paper copy of Gabriel's *Collected Works*. The fixed price is £3.13.6, but I would only take £2.10."
2. MS. Diary records three meetings with Mrs. Morris subsequent to DGR's death. 14 June 1885 at Augusta Webster's: "I was pleased to see Mrs. Morris, whom I have not once met (I think) since Gabriel's death. Had now a rather long talk with her, telling her about the forthcoming cheap edition of Gabriel's poems [see Letter 392, Note 7] etc. etc.... [She] is not gratified at Burne-Jones's election as A.R.A.: she understands that he will henceforth contribute pretty equally between the R.A. and the Grosvenor Gallery. Mrs. Morris, though no longer young or youngish, is still very fine looking: hair thinly streaked with grey." 3 March 1886 (see Letter 399, Note 4). 30 November 1887 at Stillman's: "I talked a little to ... Mrs. Morris (who came to a kind of explanation with Lucy as to her having neglected, some considerable while ago, to return any reply to a dinner-invitation from Lucy)."
3. MS. Diary, 18 January 1887: "Watts called on me, and dined. He is in favour of *not* raising quite yet the question of getting the Letters-Memoir published through Ellis & Scrutton. I shall therefore hold over this matter until after my return from Italy, which may occur I suppose toward 1 March."

417. TO THOMAS JAMES WISE

5 Endsleigh Gardens,
23 January 1887

Dear Wise,

The more I think of it, the more I feel a little nervous about that Shelley lecture.[1] I hate not to perform what I undertake to do; and am not quite clear that to write that lecture by November would turn out practicable. Would you, in any announcement of it, kindly say that it will be delivered in November, *or at some time during the session 1887-1888*. Very *likely* it would be ready in November: but, until this alternative is notified, I feel a millstone round my neck.

On my returning from Italy — say 5 March — I shall have to do 2 articles for *Encyclopaedia Britannica*,[2] taking up probably the better part of a month. Then the Keats[3] *must* take up 3 months or more — say 4. This would come to 5 August or so. Then, if all goes well with that book of my brother's family-letters, that

502

will form my principal and close occupation for other months while it passes through the press, say 4 or 5: and I am really anxious to have it out early now. And it is 10 to 1 that some other tasks fall in meanwhile to be disposed of. But I should look with steady confidence to writing and delivering the *Prometheus* lecture before our spring session of 1888 closes.

Yours very truly,
W. M. Rossetti

MS: BL.

1. MS. Diary, 20 January 1887: "Furnivall and Wise called.... I undertook, rather reluctantly, to write a 2nd lecture on *Prometheus Unbound*, to be delivered in November [9th]."
2. Veronese and Vivarini (Antonio, Bartolommeo, Luigi), ninth edition, 1888.
3. MS. Diary, 24 July 1886: "Wrote ... to Eric Robertson, consenting to write a Memoir of Keats, to appear in a new projected series, Great Writers.... I undertake to hand in the copy by 30 September 1887 ... but subject to this consideration — That, if a biography of Gabriel, reasonably agreeable to my feelings, is not (as Robertson lately told me it was to be) included in the series pretty soon, I may call off entirely as to the Keats." 26 September: "Began reading up for the Memoir of Keats.... About a week ago I saw it announced that a Memoir of Keats by Colvin is about to appear in that other series, 'English Men of Letters.' It seems to me thus very dubious whether it would be good policy to bring out my Memoir at so early a date as had been proposed."

418. TO FREDERICK JAMES FURNIVALL

5 Endsleigh Gardens,
8 March 1887

Dear Furnivall,

It is only yesterday that I returned to London, and today I receive your friendly letter. I trust to treat the present topic[1] with frankness, and without the least asperity: in fact I feel none. Will only therefore say that I don't see in what respect my course can be regarded as at all "unfair."

At the Committee-meeting of 15 December (or else of November) you mentioned about Aveling: I then openly said that I didn't see how we could think of resisting his claim to subscribe, and that on the same grounds the Shelley Society would have turned out Shelley himself. At San Remo I received a letter from Little[2] saying that the question was about to be debated by the Committee: I replied in very strong terms to the same effect.

I do not consider that a Literary Society has anything to do with the sexual morals of actual or proposing members — most especially not a Shelley Society. A man offers £1.1 as the equivalent of certain books and lectures: he is I think (barring the most extreme cases conceivable) on the same footing as a man who buys a book at a Booksellers, or pays to attend a lecture.

If Aveling's bad habit of not paying his debts were to extend to his not paying his Shelley subscription, the result would be that he would not receive his books, and would *ipso facto* be no longer a member.

What I had hitherto understood was that Aveling had actually offered himself for membership, and had been formally rejected. You show me that the rejection was contingent upon his offering himself — not formal and actual, as he had not done this in a positive way. Still, as you afterwards told him that he would be rejected were he to offer himself, it seems to me that at the present moment the Committee have substantially rejected him. I must adhere to my resignation from the Committee — for their action appears to me to make a Shelley Society a *travestie* upon itself. If hereafter Aveling were to offer himself formally, and were admitted, and if I were then (not perhaps very likely) invited to re-enter the Committee, I should most probably assent.

Aveling may be a bad lot (I know him not at all), and the adverse majority of the Committee acted upon their own sense of right — I on mine.

Your letter to me is marked *Private*: this of mine may be used in any way you like. I would write more at length, but for being very busy: but all the amplifications would only come at last to what I have here said, so there is little or nothing lost.

Believe me to be with great regard and in the friendliest spirit

Yours very truly,
W. M. Rossetti

MS: BL.

1. MS. Diary, 21 January to 10 March 1887: "Away at San Remo most of this time." 11 March: "While I was absent a question was raised in the Committee of the Shelley Society whether, if Dr. Aveling the Socialist were to offer to subscribe to the Society, his subscription should be accepted. The only *serious* objection stated (I gather) is that the so-called Mrs. Aveling is in fact not married to him. The Committee decided that they would not accept Aveling's subscription and membership. This decision I regard as, on various grounds, absolutely monstrous and ludicrous: so I had written from San Remo that I resign my seat on the Committee. In consequence of this, the Committee reconsidered the question; and determined to admit Aveling if he applies, and retain me.... I have no personal knowledge of Aveling, nor of Mrs. Aveling (said to be Miss Marx): may *possibly* have met one or other of them some 3 years ago at Mathilde Blind's, but this is only a dubious impression." Edward Bibbins Aveling (1851-98), professor of Comparative Anatomy, London Hospital, 1875-81; author of numerous works on science, atheism, and socialism; lived with Karl Marx's daughter Eleanor (c.1855-98) from 1882-83. Aveling to WMR, 22 May 1895: "You may remember my wife and myself reading to the Shelley Society a paper on 'Shelley and Socialism.' We do not forget that you, very bravely and knowing nothing of us personally, stood up for our admission to the Society. And now, we have lit upon very evil days. For over a year I have been ill and doing and earning nothing. I have had two operations for tumor in the side. Can you help us out of an immediate and pressing trouble by advancing me £5? I can repay it by instalments if I may, as work, slowly returning and keeping pace with returning strength, comes in" (AP). A note on the MS. in WMR's hand reads: "25/5 — Sent £2."

2. James Stanley Little (1856-1940), writer on literature, art, and the politics of Empire, succeeded Sydney Preston as secretary of the Society in May 1886.

419. TO FREDERICK JAMES FURNIVALL

5 Endsleigh Gardens,
11 March 1887

Dear Furnivall,

Thanks for your amusing letter. Yesterday I received one from Little saying: "I [Little][1] am empowered to write to Dr. Aveling to say that, should he choose to become a member of the Shelley Society, he can do so." You say that the various sections of the Committee join "in authorizing you [Rossetti],[1] if you see fit, to tell Aveling that, if he wishes to join the Society, he may." I presume it is rather a matter of chaff than otherwise to propose that *I individually* should address Aveling. I have no intention of doing so, he and I being absolute strangers: and, as I infer, Little has already done so.

Yesterday I replied to Little to the following effect. If Aveling is invited by the Committee to offer himself for election, and is thereupon elected, — or if the Committee elect Aveling, and he thereupon takes up his election, — I shall consider myself (through the kindly and marked indulgence of the Committee) to be again a member of it. But, until the matter is thus settled, I am not on the Committee. To me it appears perfectly possible that Aveling, once excluded, will decline to come in; and that would create or continue for the Committee such a position (so I regard it) of anti-Shelleyism that my original reason for resigning would remain in full force. This is substantially the same that I wrote to you on the 9th.

Excuse bother and believe me

Always yours truly,
W. M. Rossetti

MS: Huntington.

1. WMR's brackets.

420. TO FREDERICK JAMES FURNIVALL

5 Endsleigh Gardens,
15 March 1887

Dear Furnivall,

Yours of yesterday received. Little also replied to me yesterday, saying that he had invited Aveling, but had received no response.

Such being the case, I defer to your view (though it is not my own) on this point of detail, and have addressed the enclosed invitation to Aveling.[1] I send it to you, being naturally reluctant that at any future time I should be supposed to have been unfair towards the Committee in my way of presenting the facts to Aveling. If you like the letter to go, please post it: if otherwise, burn it. I am not inclined to write any letter substantially different.

I don't know whether the address for Aveling which I have hit upon is the right one: I copy it out of the *Post Office Directory* for 1886.

If Aveling subscribes, and if the Committee like me to continue a member and Chairman of it, I shall accept with gratitude — and of course I recognize that under any circumstances the conduct of the Committee, in the question personal to myself, is handsome and flattering. If Aveling will *not* subscribe, the Society or its Committee will remain (in my opinion) open to the imputation of inquisitional scrutiny coupled with intolerance: qualities so anti-Shelleyan that I would rather remain outside the Committee.

There can be no reason why I should not meet the Committee on 13 April. I will do so: as I understand it, at University College, 7 p.m.

Yours always truly,
W. M. Rossetti

MS: Rutgers.

1. For Furnivall's decision not to forward the letter (which is in AP), see Letter 421. MS. Diary, 15 March records "a missive to me from Furnivall consisting of a letter addressed to Furnivall by Aveling, who enquires why he was first told that he would be excluded, and secondly that he would be admitted. Furnivall had briefly explained to Aveling." 17 March: "Aveling assents to the proposal that he should become a subscribing member ... so that storm in a teapot seems to be appeased."

421. TO FREDERICK JAMES FURNIVALL

5 Endsleigh Gardens,
16 March 1887

Dear Furnivall,

Many thanks for the enclosed and for your letter of yesterday. Your not sending on mine to Aveling indicates to me that you are now of the opinion which I expressed from the first — viz.: that, until the result of Little's authorized invitation to Aveling should be apparent, any invitation from me would be worse than superfluous: so I am fain to hope that by this time you acquit me of unfairness to the Committee.

By "inquisitional scrutiny" I didn't mean that the Committee had laboriously applied itself to finding out whether charges against Aveling are true or false: from the first I understood that they had not done this, but had acted upon knowledge or presumptions of earlier date. What I meant is that the Shelley Society and its Committee are not called upon to form any opinion upon the moral character of proposing members; and that to entertain any such question of character as preliminary to admission is an inquisitional act — and all the more when it results in exclusion.

Excuse all bothers from

Yours very truly,
W. M. Rossetti

MS: Huntington.

422. TO LUCY ROSSETTI

Somerset House,
12 May 1887,
Noon

Dearest Lu,

I went to that Shelley Music last evening.[1] Some things were agreeable, but I did not think it a clear success. Saw Mary Carmichael[2] at the piano twice — not otherwise. One of the settings — not a bad one — was by Sir Percy Shelley. He came in rather late: sat next me, and after a while I was introduced to him. There is nothing interesting in his manner or appearance, unless it be his clear blue eyes: but he seemed to me an unaffected genuine sort of man, and I was well pleased with the little I saw of him. In course of talk I learned that his wife is *not at Boscombe*: she is in London, not strong in health, and she and he are both going away shortly on a yachting excursion. Of course I said nothing tending towards your Life of his mother³ — indeed had no opportunity, even had I been inclined. You had better, I suppose, leave the thing to unravel itself between Ingram and yourself as already begun — only with the further understanding that you are not under any circumstances likely while at Bournemouth to see anything of Lady Shelley.

I saw also F. S. Ellis, who seems greatly revived in health — Mrs. Petrici — and (a distant view) Mrs. Scott. I understood from Ellis, who has lately seen Scott at Penkill, that Scott is rather busy writing his Memoirs. He seems to be as tolerable in health as can at this stage of affairs be expected. When I returned home towards 10½, I found Fairfax Murray lying in wait for me.⁴

Must I suppose go this evening to that other Shelley affair which I mentioned. It is a lecture by Stopford Brooke⁵ on *Epipsychidion*, at University Hall, to be followed by a discussion on the character of Shelley. It pertains to a Debating Society, not to the Shelley Society — but I presume it will almost take the dimensions of a Shelley Society affair.

This morning I walked round to Lyster's⁶ room, to have a little chat with him. As I opened the door I heard the voice of someone else conversing, so I walked myself off again unseen.

I hope Bournemouth weather continues good. In London yesterday was cooler than the 2 or 3 preceding days, and was damp, and today is much the same as yesterday. Tree foliage etc. has advanced vastly within the last week.

Your own
William

Since writing the above I learned that Lyster will not return to the Office after today. I went round again, and took an affectionate leave of him. He had no *wish* to retire: but I incline to think that he will find very little to regret after he has once retired.

MS: AP.

1. MS. Diary, 11 May 1887: "Attended at University College a musical soirée of the Shelley Society — various songs from Shelley set by various composers. I did not think the performance much of a success — some voices loud and out of tune. Had at last the satisfaction of being introduced (by Wise) to Sir Percy Shelley: he and I were seated side by side during the latter half of the evening. He seems an unaffected straightforward man, the antipodes of the Shelleian-poetic: bald, good blue eyes, long thin nose, thin face, ruddy complexion. I don't trace anything of his father in his face, nor yet of his mother (unless indeed there may be a certain soupçon of [Richard] Rothwell's portrait), nor of Godwin or Mary Wollstonecraft: should rather suspect the resemblance to tend more toward Sir Timothy Shelley. One of the songs was Sir Percy's setting of the *Hymn of Pan*: telling, and I thought it one of the best."

2. Mary Grant Carmichael, pianist and accompanist; composer of numerous songs, including twenty-seven rhymes from CGR's *Sing-Song* (1884), and twelve poems from R. L. Stevenson's *Child's Garden of Verse* (1888).

3. *Mrs. Shelley*, "Eminent Women Series," 1890.

4. On the following day he returned and "looked through 3 portfolios of Gabriel's drawings etc., and bought some minor specimens, which I priced at £6.10" (MS. Diary).

5. Stopford Augustus Brooke (1832-1916), divine and man of letters, seceded from the Church of England (in which he had been a popular Broad-Church preacher) in 1880 and loosely attached himself to the Unitarians. MS. Diary, 12 May 1887: "Attended, at the pressing request of Mr. [R. A.] Potts, a meeting of the Bedford Debating Society in University Hall, for a lecture by Stopford

Brooke upon *Epipsychidion*. Was forced into the chair, for which I had in no wise bargained. Brooke's lecture was really an able performance: I understand it will appear printed in the facsimile reprint of *Epipsychidion* which will shortly be issued by the Shelley Society.''

6. Alfred Chaworth Lyster, nephew and adopted son of Thomas Keightley, entered the Excise Office in 1848. WMR's friendship with him was his "one private intimacy with an official" (*SR*, 1:54). MS. Diary, 10 May 1887: "I hear that, in consequence of a new official scheme, Lyster will shortly retire from Somerset House: a very old, attached, and well-loved friend of mine, whom I shall be sorry to lose from the associations of my day-by-day life.''

423. TO THEODORE WATTS-DUNTON

5 Endsleigh Gardens,
22 May 1887

Dear Watts,

As you seemed at one moment yesterday almost to fancy that I might be finessing for the omission of your Memoir from the book of Letters, I feel impelled to say in writing — what indeed I said at once by word of mouth — that nothing could possibly be further from my intention.[1] I should regard the absence of your Memoir from that book as a most grievous loss: and a loss which nothing could compensate to me, who have been holding over the Letters for 4 years or so for the express and sole purpose of having the advantage of your Memoir to companion them. To write a Memoir myself is an alternative which on various grounds I should be most reluctant to adopt: one of the grounds being the very obvious and selfish one — that your Memoir is certain to be the better done of the two, and also considerably the more attractive to the public. I trust therefore it remains fully understood between us that, while I should like to get the Letters into the printer's hands as soon as fairly practicable, I attach still more importance to their being delivered along with your Memoir than to their being delivered early.

I have got the Gilchrist book[2] ready under my hand to be taken round tomorrow to Somerset House. It occurs to me that you have in your possession a few books of mine which when convenient to yourself, I should like to have back. I remember

1. A volume in black cloth of a set of Ballads,[3] Gabriel's property — this volume contains the Robin Hood ballads.
2. *La Légende des Siècles*.[4]
3. A volume in green roan containing (*inter alia*) Tigri's Tuscan Rispetti[5] etc.
4. A volume of Poems by Alaric Alfred Watts and his wife[6] which you borrowed from me at Somerset House, and which I have myself never had an opportunity of looking into.

Yours,
W. M. Rossetti

MS: BL.

1. MS. Diary, 21 May 1887: "Watts called and we had a long talk ... about the Memoir of Gabriel which he is writing. The publishers told him that, if the book is to be out next autumn, the Memoir ought to be delivered to them by 31 July. Watts thinks he can't get it ready by then: could get it ready for *next* publishing season, spring 1888: but would prefer that the book should appear in 1889. This is most provoking, and to my view positively unfair to me — who would have brought out the

Family-letters in 1883 but for waiting for Watts's Memoir. I reasoned with him, and hope that he parted from me on the understanding that a voluntary delay till 1889 is not the one thing needful."

2. *Anne Gilchrist, Her Life and Writings*, ed. H. H. Gilchrist, with a Prefatory Notice by WMR, 1887.

3. Not identified.

4. Victor Hugo's epic poems in three series, 1859-83.

5. *Canti Popolari Toscani*, ed. Giuseppe Tigri, 1856.

6. *Aurora: a Volume of Verses* (1875).

424. TO KATHARINE TYNAN

5 Endsleigh Gardens,
6 July 1887

My dear Miss Tynan,

This morning I received your letter, and take blame to myself for not having at an early date acknowledged with thanks the receipt of your book.[1] The simple fact is that constant occupation has as yet prevented my even beginning to read it: official occupation all day, literary occupation most of the evening, family-matters, friends in the house, a dying relative[2] etc. I *shall* read the book: and, when I do so, I confidently reckon upon finding in it the same charm of feeling and treatment as in your previous work, and mellowing ripeness of execution. What I intended was to wait until I could read the volume, and then write to you my thanks and my views.

If I owe you an apology, please accept it, like a kind-hearted Irishwoman.

Thank you, we are all reasonably well at present: my wife back from Bournemouth towards last days of May.

That vile Coercion-bill has been much in my thoughts of late. It seems destined to pass, and to be one more link in the long clanking chain of the hatred which Ireland owes to England.[3]

Yours very truly,
W. M. Rossetti

Of course I observed and mentally thanked you for the dedication to your volume. I see I have some blots on paper (as well as on conduct) to apologize for.

MS: Texas.

1. *Shamrocks* (1887), dedicated to WMR and CGR "with homage, and as a thanksgiving."

2. Charlotte Polidori, who lived until 1890.

3. The Coercion Act of 1887 went further than its predecessors in being unlimited in time, and in empowering the Lord Lieutenant of Ireland to enforce it according to his judgment of the situation. It also permitted him to substitute trial by magistrate for trial by jury in certain cases. "This Act was not restricted as every former law of the kind had been ... to meeting an emergency; it was made a standing instrument of government" (John Morley, *Life of Gladstone* [1903], 3:376).

425. TO JAMES MCNEILL WHISTLER

5 Endsleigh Gardens,
21 July 1887

Dear Whistler,

I am fully convinced of the affectionate regard in which you held Gabriel, and of your respect for his genius and memory. I and others would have been extremely well pleased to see you present at the little observance which was held last Thursday,[1] but it never occurred to me — nor *would* occur to me — that your absence was due to any other than some matter of necessity or casualty.[2]

I like the vivid character of Madox Brown's bust of Gabriel, and think the little monument as a whole looks well. The project had not entirely smooth sailing, but I am contented with its result. I need not say that I had no personal concern in the form etc. of the circulars sent out: from first to last I carefully kept myself in the background — the scheme being proper to Gabriel's friends and admirers, not to his family.

> Always truly yours,
> W. M. Rossetti

MS: Glasgow.

1. MS. Diary, 11 July 1887: "Took a cab round to Cheyne Walk, to see how the fountain-bust monument to Gabriel looks. Found it (the bust-part) covered with a white cloth; but this was removed, and I considered the work successful as a whole — the bust forcible and energetic, and the architectural ensemble dignified, according to its very moderate scale." 14 July: "The uncovering ceremony of the monument to Gabriel came off, and I thought it satisfactorily done. Spielmann made a little address to Hunt, and then Hunt uncovered the alto-relief, and read a speech of some length: I heard it not quite perfectly, but noticed several points which I thought telling and well put. Some 50 to 60 persons (I suppose) were present: many of them, including myself and Lucy etc., then inspected Gabriel's old house, courteously thrown open by Haweis to all comers. It is more showy and cheerful, and less tasteful and uncommon, than of old: in structure little or no difference. Present at the uncovering, Browning, Shields, Hughes, Mrs. Dallas-Glyn, [Alfred] Gurney, Georgiana Potter (who reintroduced herself to me, after my not having seen her for perhaps 35 years), the Stephenses, Mrs. Holman Hunt, Theodore Watts, Mrs. and Miss Webster, etc. etc. Of our own connexion — Brown and his wife, Hueffer, my aunt Eliza (with 2 servants to assist her), Lucy, the 4 children, and myself."
2. Whistler explained on [18 July 1887]: "I am so shocked to find that a lithographed letter, which with its fellows had found its way into the waste-paper basket, turns out to have been an invitation to a function from which I would not for worlds have been absent.... I am greatly mortified to know that foolish inattention to printed circulars should have lost me an occasion of doing honour to a man of your brother's rare calibre. Is it not a pity that a matter of such weight should have been heralded in such an unimportant manner! No personal note of any kind came to warn me of the event, and I never dreamed that a ceremony of this great interest was taking place within a stone's throw of my own house" (AP).

426. TO FREDERICK JAMES FURNIVALL

5 Endsleigh Gardens,
30 September 1887

Dear Furnivall,

I was extremely gratified at your letter of yesterday. Had seen the *Pall Mall Gazette*,[1] and was certainly a little surprised at the tone it adopts: not that adverse criticism is at all astonishing, but the *Pall Mall Gazette* had always hitherto been civil to my performances, and I did not and do not suppose the *Keats* to be more flimsy or more foolish than my previous doings. However I am happy to say that such matters never trouble my mind. I think I have for several years past had an accurate perception of what the demerits of my writings amount to, and what their merits. If a critic ratifies my own estimate, or praises me beyond what I perceive to be deserved, I of course am pleased: if he entertains a contrary opinion, my own remains pretty nearly as before.

As I understand it, Shaw is the writer of that critique: though I have more than once been told that notices in the *Pall Mall Gazette*, which I supposed to be by Shaw, are in fact by Oscar Wilde. Apart from seeing and hearing Shaw at the Shelley Society etc., I don't know him: but shall be equally well pleased to encounter him hereafter, and hear what he has to say — which I always find clever and telling, and the reverse of commonplace.

With thanks,

Yours truly,

W. M. Rossetti

I think it quite possible that the reviewer may be right in saying that Colvin's is the better book of the two: it is at all events a good one.

MS: BL.

1. 27 September 1887, p. 3: a review of WMR's *Life of Keats* by Oscar Wilde. Furnivall thought the reviewer "an irrational devotee of Keats, [who] got excited at some of your justly detractive phrases" (AP).

427. TO HERBERT GILCHRIST

5 Endsleigh Gardens,
8 November 1887

Dear Gilchrist,

Glad to learn you are back, and shall be highly delighted to see the Whitman portrait.[1] Could not at the moment settle my mind about a day for calling, but will not overlook it.

I have signed the petition[2] enclosed. I am not an Anarchist — but, if a man chooses to be one, I have no objection to him on that account. I presume that the 7 condemned men have fairly laid themselves open to a severe form of punishment: but to hang up 7 men in a sheaf appears to be one of those repulsive barbarisms which are below the level even of Europe as it now exists — not to speak of America.

Best regards to your sister.

Yours,

W. M. Rossetti

MS: LC.

1. Gilchrist's second portrait of the poet, painted in Camden in the summer of 1887.
2. MS. Diary, 8 November 1887: "Signed 2 petitions (duplicates) to the Governor of Illinois, to spare the lives of the 7 anarchists awaiting execution on account of a bomb-throwing outrage in Chicago." The second petition was sent by Edward Aveling. Four of the anarchists were executed on 11 November, two were given sentences of life imprisonment, and the other committed suicide in his cell (*New York Times*, 11, 12 November 1887, p. 1).

428. TO FREDERICK JAMES FURNIVALL

5 Endsleigh Gardens,
13 November 1887

Dear Furnivall,

I have 2 missives of yours, and will answer the points as far as seems requisite for the present.

Will attend to all that is said about books for 1888 and 1889 etc., when I set to at the Report.[1] That will be I suppose towards beginning of December. Will about same time ask Ellis for his statement.[2]

As to the question — Who is to leave the Committee, and who to enter it — I should like, before trying to form any opinion, to see the List of Members (of the Society) as it now stands. Don't well know where to lay my hand on this, among my own papers. Can you supply me with it, or should I address Little?

I might take this opportunity of saying that I fear Little's shaky health, and his constant moil and hurry over other matters, will pretty soon deprive our Society of his services as Secretary. What should then be done? Would not Wise be a first-rate man for the post? and would he undertake it?

Do I understand that it is a rule of our Society that a certain proportion of the Committee-members should retire periodically? and that it now falls to the lot of any 4 men to retire?

I can easily think that Revell[3] would be a good man for the Committee. Should also be in favour of Shaw. He seems to be about our best speaker if we except Brooke, and his extreme opinions are not in my eyes any disqualification.

Could you send me also a copy of our last annual Report? I should need to take its details into account, as a starting-point for the new Report. Or I could ask Little for a copy.

Yours always truly,
W. M. Rossetti

By the way, I felt much obliged to you for your kind expressions about my *Prometheus* Address, both in a post-card,[4] and the other evening viva voce. And I ought to have said that that proposed evening for a Browning Society paper[5] would, so far as I can forecast, suit me well. *Someone must remind me at the proper time*, lest I be again found in default.

As I understand it, you will *not* turn up at Aveling's lecture. I expect to do so, and may be available for taking the chair if not anyone else (to whom I would willingly yield) wants to do so.[6]

MS: BL.

1. MS. Diary, 15 October 1887: "Assented to a proposal by Furnivall that I should write the Report ... of the Shelley Society. I found this a thorny job last year, and would rather have been spared it now, but suppose it can't be helped." 3 December: "I began the Annual Report ... rather an unpleasant task, as our finances are in a muddle, owing to over-printing etc."
2. About his progress with *A Lexical Concordance to the Poetical Works of Shelley* (1892). MS. Diary, 18 June 1890: "F. S. Ellis called on me at Somerset House, and spoke about his Shelley Concordance: his expenditure upon it will ... be fully £1000: if he can recoup £500, he will count himself lucky."
3. William F. Revell, who published "Shelley's *Prometheus Unbound*: a Reading" in the *Westminster Review*, 168 (October 1907), 415-27.
4. "Oh that Shelley could have had a few disciples like you in his lifetime!" (7 November; AP).
5. WMR did not chair a Browning Society session.
6. MS. Diary, 14 December 1887: "Took the chair at a Shelley Society meeting — Dr. Aveling on Shelley and Socialism. An interesting lecture, especially in virtue of its numerous array of quotations from Shelley, developing this side of his opinions." 13 February 1889: "Shelley Society evening.... Dr. Aveling read out the 2nd and concluding part of the Lecture (written by Mrs. Aveling as well as

himself) on Shelley and Socialism.'' The first lecture was published in *Shelley Society's Papers, Part 2* (1891), pp. 180-203.

429. TO FREDERICK JAMES FURNIVALL

5 Endsleigh Gardens,
7 December 1887

Dear Furnivall,

Here is my draft Report for 1887, so far as I see my way to its composition for the present. I have followed the general form and arrangement of the Report for 1886, so far as seemed practicable. I have no doubt that you — not to speak of other Committee-men — will find several details needing to be added to it. Ellis's memorandum[1] will, I have reason to believe, reach me almost directly.

I really think that it will be desirable — or almost necessary — that I should resign the Chairmanship of the Committee immediately after the Annual Meeting.[2] Of course I have no idea of ceasing to be on the Committee, and to act on it. It seems invidious to others that one man should remain stationary as Chairman — as if he were the one person sufficiently prominent as a Shelleyite to occupy that post. Either you or Forman (H. B.) seem to me the right man to assume the Chairmanship next: or two others might be taken into consideration — Brooke and Salt.[3] My colleagues have always supported me handsomely and indulgently — and I am in hopes that I have been regarded as free from *bias* towards or against any particular person or plan of work, and so far a safe and conciliatory man for the Chairmanship. My resignation therefore would be based not on any personal feeling of any kind, but on the general consideration of what is fair and suitable to the *personnel* of the Committee.

Yours always truly,
W. M. Rossetti

N.B. I have drafted the Report on the assumption that it would not be good policy to *frighten* members by enlarging upon the details of our debt to Clay[4] etc. Don't know whether you view that point in the same light.

MS: BL.

1. See Letter 428, Note 2.
2. Furnivall to WMR, 8 December 1887: ''You must really continue to be Chairman of Committee as long as you live in London, and the Society lasts. You are the harmonizing and uniting influence among us. I and others neither trust nor like Forman: he is too much of a dealer, and has already sacrificed the Society to his precious old father-in-law. I know nothing of Shelley, and should be ridiculous as Chairman. Brooke never comes to us. Salt is too quiet. You are the man to head us, and you only'' (AP).
3. Henry Stephens Salt (1851-1939), assistant master at Eton, from which he resigned in 1884 to live a simple life in a laborer's cottage; Shelleyite, vegetarian, secretary of the Humanitarian League, 1891-1920; published books on Shelley, James Thomson ('B.V.'), Thoreau, and Richard Jefferies.
4. Richard Clay & Sons, to whom Wise contracted the printing of the Shelley facsimiles issued by the Society.

430. TO THEODORE WATTS-DUNTON

5 Endsleigh Gardens,
13 January 1888

Dear Watts,

I gather from your letter that you would not have any sort of objection to my bringing out, through Cassells or other publisher, the proposed book on Gabriel's Works in Art and Literature,[1] *prior* to our bringing out through Ellis & Elvey the pending Letters-Memoir book; but that on the contrary you would *prefer* this sequence of publication. On this assumption I shall shortly proceed to discussing terms with Cassell. I cannot say that I am satisfied with his present terms, which are considerably *below* the terms which you regard as inadequate in the case of Ellis & Elvey.

If you feel that my book on the Art and Literature would aid you in completing the Memoir, I need hardly say that I would willingly communicate my book to you, in any stage or form. These are (1) the *materials* for the book, and (2) the book itself so far as yet written — which may be some $2/5$ of the whole. No. 1 consists of the details which I have jotted down in great abundance from letters addressed to Gabriel, and from some letters written by Gabriel himself. No. 2 is my consecutive narrative embodying these details. The beginning of No. 2 is at present in the hands of Cassells, as a specimen of what the book is to be like. Naturally if I were to lend you any part of 1 or 2, I should wish to get it back pretty soon — otherwise my work would be much at a standstill.

You however express a wish to see No. 2 only when it shall be in print. This may be a longish while hence: but, when the time shall come, I could no doubt get duplicate proofs, and hand one of them over to you.

I have not yet constructed a proper title for the book. I think the heading on p. 1 is "Dante Gabriel Rossetti, a Study of his Works in Art and Literature." This expresses the nature of the book pretty well, but something briefer must be hit upon eventually.

Thanks, my cold is a good deal better now, and I am nearly as well as usual. It stuck to me for some days after you were here.

Spielmann[2] succeeded Stephens as Secretary for the Memorial to Gabriel. He is (or was) Art-Critic of the *Pall Mall Gazette*, and as such was an active upholder of Madox Brown.

Yours,
W. M. Rossetti

MS: BL.

1. *DGRDW*. MS. Diary, 5 January 1888: "Late in the evening received the proposal from Cassells about this book. They would undertake all expenses, and pay me 10% on copies sold. Must consider about this — especially in relation to my standing engagement with Watts for the Memoir-letters book." 8 January: "Wrote to Cassells to say that I will, as soon as may prove practicable, reply definitely to their proposal.... Also wrote to Watts enquiring what are his present views about the Memoir for our joint book, so that dates of publication may be suitably adjusted. I confess I should not be at all surprised if Watts were to reply that, taking into consideration certain difficulties inherent in the subject-matter, he makes up his mind not to write the Memoir at all." 2 February: "Cassells write consenting to my terms — 15% upon all copies sold — more easily managed than I quite expected."

2. Marion Harry (Alexander) Spielmann (1858-1948), writer on art (*Pall Mall Gazette*, 1883-90); editor of the *Magazine of Art*, 1887-1904.

431. TO FREDERIC GEORGE STEPHENS

5 Endsleigh Gardens,
28 January 1888

Dear Stephens,

I regret to see from your note that Inchbold is dead — was not previously aware of the fact. You I think have always known quite as much of Inchbold as I have — probably more. What I seem able to jot down is scanty and scrappy, but here it is.

I always understood Inchbold to be a Yorkshireman; and should presume him to have belonged to a family of business-men, with more or less of money in the family. Last summer I happened to see his brother, who corresponded to this impression. Inchbold's first exhibited picture was I suppose that excellent Study of a Stump[1] (say 1851) which Leathart bought, and still (I presume) owns. In 1862 Inchbold was in Venice — I and W. B. Scott met him there in the summer: at a later date he was in Spain. It may have been soon after his return from Spain — or say towards 1871 — that he was decidedly "hard up," and he haunted Brown's house in Fitzroy Square for some considerable while — I should say that a meal and a bed in that house were daily at his disposal for a period of something like half a year. Afterwards he took to the rather unusual plan of living — and I suppose painting — in an upper floor of the great Charing Cross Hotel: I never saw him in that building, but he told me that the plan suited him well. Some 10 or 12 years ago he was intimate with Coventry Patmore — staying with him at Hastings on a visit. He published a volume of Poems of a sentimental kind[2] — I found it better than I had expected: and later on I think a second volume. Inchbold had practically dropped out of my knowledge this long while past — say 15 to 18 years — and I scarcely think I saw him more than half a dozen times in that interval. The last time was in July last, when I came across him and his brother in the Manchester Jubilee Exhibition: he looked fatter than of old, more elderly, and placid as if in charity with all men — but as usual partly shy and partly demonstrative, and not easy to break the ice with.

Thanks about Scott etc.

Your
W. M. Rossetti

MS: Bodleian.

1. *A Study* (R.A., 1852), described by WMR in the *Spectator* as a "'Study' of a tree-stump and scattered autumn leaves" (19 June 1852, p. 593). In 1851 he exhibited at the R.A.: *Study from Nature — Evening* and *Sketch in November*, neither of which were noticed by WMR in his review in the *Spectator*.
2. *Annus Amoris* (1876). Stephens points out in his obituary in the *Athenaeum* that a second volume of poems was "nearly ready for printing at his death" (4 February 1888, p. 154).

432. TO THOMAS JAMES WISE

5 Endsleigh Gardens,
3 February 1888

Dear Wise,

Thanks for the *Prometheus* Lectures,[1] and for the envelopes. The latter — when they fall pat under hand — will be useful.

I hardly know whether to envy or not the possessor of a *Zastrozzi*[2] at £10. I envy his enthusiasm.

Brice's[3] letter returned. He wears his opinions rather aggressively; but, if such opinions are prevalent among our members, one ought not exactly to ignore them I think. I don't know but that it might be advisable to obtain at some time a "plebiscite" by sending out to members Circular Forms something to the following effect — "Are you in favour of limiting the operations of the Society to publications and lectures? or of extending them to theatrical and other performances?"

I am rather afraid theatrical people will be ill-disposed to us henceforth, owing to that "Outram v. Furnivall." I was extremely sorry to see the issue of that action, and really think it far from substantial justice.[4]

Parkes[5] sent me his MS. lecture (received yesterday), to be read by someone on 8 February. Really he ought not to have sent it to me. I am not a first-rate reader; and find the reading of my own lectures more than enough, from all points of view, without adding those of other men. It so happens also that a young lady[6] from the country is coming up soon, and wants to attend (she is a member I think) the Shelley lecture on 8 February: and my wife has promised her my escort — which would make it the more convenient course that I should miss the Committee-meeting, and simply accompany this lady, reaching University College at 8, and sitting with her simply as one of the audience. Parkes doesn't ask *me* to read the lecture: but possibly he means as much. Can you as Secretary provide another and fitting reader — yourself for instance? If it does so happen that I am to be reader, I must not be also Chairman, I take it.

Yours,

W. M. Rossetti

P.S. I should have explained that, as I don't consider myself, but rather the Secretary, to be the proper custodian of Parkes's lecture prior to delivery, my inclination would be to transfer it to you by any convenient mode: but I won't do this unless you let me know that it suits you.

MS: BL.

1. WMR delivered his third lecture on *Prometheus Unbound* to the Shelley Society on 11 January 1888; the lectures were printed in the *Shelley Society's Papers*, Part 1, pp. 50-72, 138-79.
2. Shelley's first book (1810).
3. Not identified.
4. In 1886 Furnivall engaged Leonard Outram as director and principal actor for a production of Browning's *Strafford* (see Letter 415). Outram promptly issued a circular, which gave the appearance of being signed by Furnivall, appealing to members of the Browning Society to contribute to a fund for the performance. Furnivall's characteristically pungent attack on Outram's circular led to a libel action in which Furnivall was adjudged to pay damages and costs amounting to £300. MS. Diary, 8 February 1888: "Furnivall was in the chair [at a Shelley Society Meeting] — not evincing any dejection consequent upon his recent severe misfortune in the action for libel." 10 February: "Wrote

to Wise offering to send a modest subscription — £1.10 or thereabouts to the fund which is being got up for indemnifying Furnivall from his recent mischance.'' The sum raised covered Furnivall's expenses. See W. S. Peterson, *Interrogating the Oracle, A History of the London Browning Society* (1969), pp. 40-48.

5. MS. Diary, 9 July 1887: "Kineton Parkes, a young man from Birmingham, very good-looking, Secretary of the Local Branch of the Shelley Society, called on us, wishing to talk over a lecture of his on Shelley's Faith.'' WMR read the lecture to the Society, and afterwards "spoke at some little length, maintaining that Shelley's opinions did not alter, so much as Parkes assumes, towards the goal of theism and Christianity'' (MS. Diary). The lecture was printed in *Shelley Society's Papers, Part 1*, pp. 204-19.

6. A Miss Burroughs (MS. Diary, 8 February 1888), but not otherwise identified.

433. TO THOMAS JAMES WISE

5 Endsleigh Gardens,
11 March 1888

Dear Wise,

Here is the subscription of Col. Call, along with part of a letter which Mrs. Call addressed some few days ago to my wife. I really don't know what she refers to about blunders regarding her father (Trelawny). If you see your way to appeasing her, and securing a continuance of her separate subscription, this might be all the better. She is, I dare say, rather easily angered, but not wholly deaf to reason.

Yours very truly,
W. M. Rossetti

MS: BL.

434. TO THOMAS JAMES WISE

5 Endsleigh Gardens,
10 May 1888

Dear Wise,

Thanks for your friendly note just received. I think Sweet's[1] paper a *very* good one, and am sorry I could not attend. Ever since Sunday afternoon I have remained indoors, but suppose I shall return to my office tomorrow. There is no pain worth so calling: but at night unmistakable sensations of gout which, if not humoured a little, might perhaps lead to a troublesome attack.

Now here is a curious matter which you as a collector might like to know of. A lady of our acquaintance called here yesterday, having 2 MSS. in her hands: she had just got them from Baroness Müller,[2] 2 Euston Square. The 2 are in one same handwriting. One is a prose story of some length, named "The Widow's Wood,'' or something of the sort. The other, which I read through, is a poem about The Pied Piper of Hamelin, written with much facility and cleverness, though not with any marked originality. A postmark in one of these MSS. seems to be 1831.

The information conveyed to me as to the authorship of these MSS. is not so precise as it might be. But I understand that they are in all probability the composition and the handwriting of the father of Robert Browning. The handwriting is certainly not that of R. B. himself, nor is the Hamelin poem at all like *his*

Hamelin poem in detailed treatment: it has rather more of the light manner of Ingoldsby,[3] but with much less direct jocularity. But certainly, if the father of R. B. wrote towards 1831 a poem about the Pied Piper, it is a literary curiosity of considerable mark.

Baroness Müller (I understand) would like to turn into money these 2 MSS., along with (so I gather) other MSS. which she possesses coming from the same quarter. The lady whom we know has now returned those 2 to the Baroness. I should perhaps add that of the Baroness herself I know nothing at all. I presume that, if you or anybody cared to look up her MSS., you would be justified in addressing her direct.

Yours very truly,
W. M. Rossetti

The Hamelin poem may be much about the same length as R. B.'s, so far as my memory of the latter serves me. I was forgetting to say that, in one or other of the 2 MSS., a note written in pencil appears, worded — "Shall I continue? R. B." — or something of that sort. Reuben, if I remember right, was the name of Robert Browning's father.

MS: BL.

1. Henry Sweet (1845-1912), phonetician, philologist, Anglo-Saxon scholar, delivered a paper to the Shelley Society on 9 May 1888 on "Shelley's Nature-Poetry" (published in *Shelley Society's Papers, Part 2*, pp. 269-324).
2. A neighbor of Robert Browning's father (also named Robert), who in 1852 sued him for breach of promise (see Maisie Ward, *Robert Browning and His World* [1967], 1:197-201). W. R. Nicoll, who published the elder Browning's poem on the Pied Piper in the *Bookman*, 42 (May 1912), 63-70, gives an account of a meeting in 1882 between the publisher Elkin Mathews and the Baroness, who "told him that she had known the poet's father very well indeed, [and] that she possessed many of his letters and manuscripts. Later on she sent a bundle of manuscripts to Mr. Mathews. He took extracts from these, retained one or two of the originals by the Baroness's permission and returned the rest to her."
3. Richard Harris Barham, *The Ingoldsby Legends* (3 ser., 1840-47).

435. TO THOMAS JAMES WISE

5 Endsleigh Gardens,
7 August 1888

Dear Wise,

I am now in possession of that *Hugh Heron* which you covet.[1] Christina has given me *all* the few copies in her possession: except the one copy which is now at your disposal, they are simply in sheets unfolded. I don't accurately know how many they amount to — say 3 or 4. For the reasons with which you are familiar I don't mean to part with any of them unless for some exceptional purpose.

On preparing to write to Slack about those Hitchener letters, I find myself somewhat withheld by the consideration that, if Slack were ever to find that a certain printed version of the letters exists, he would, putting together that printed version and my acting as intermediary for the purchase of the letters, jump to the conclusion (and you know how erroneous it would be) that I had abetted the printing scheme.[2] If I had really done so, Slack would I think have had just reason to complain: for it was a very liberal kindness on his part to allow me to transcribe the letters for the purpose (solely) of that "Cor Cordium" book, and I would not have felt in the least justified in doing — what you, as a bibliophile and outsider undertook — the putting of the letters into print in an independent form. I am thus disposed to drop the idea of writing direct to Slack about the purchase: but, if you think it would smoothe your own path, I am willing to write you a letter (giving Slack's name and address, and any other details which may appear apposite) which you can enclose in anything which *you* write to him.[3]

I have read through the printed Hitchener, and once again found it to be a very interesting section of Shelley correspondence. As I read, I noted down some points which appear to me misprinted — but I have not *verified* any of them as yet. I enclose a jotting regarding this matter: could clear up its obscurities whenever you and I have a talk, with the book before us.

Yours always truly,
W. M. Rossetti

MS: BL.

1. DGR, *Sir Hugh the Heron: A Legendary Tale in Four Parts*, printed by G. Polidori in 1843. MS. Diary, 8 August 1888: "Wise ... bought a second copy of *Sir Hugh the Heron*. He is to exchange this for some bibliographic curiosity owned by a friend, and priced at £2.10. He handed me £5.15 (same price as in the former instance) for *Hugh Heron*; but, considering the money-disadvantage which he would hereby suffer in the exchange, I declined to take more than £4."
2. MS. Diary, 7 August 1888: "Wrote to Wise, calling off a proposal which had been made a fortnight or so ago, to the effect that I should write to Slack explaining that Wise (with whom one or two others are associated) would like to buy the Shelley-Hitchener letters for a sum not exceeding £100. My objection to writing to Slack on this subject arises from the fact that Wise has — without any the least authority from Slack or from myself — printed a pretty little edition of the letters, using for this purpose his own transcripts made from the transcripts which I wrote several years ago, with a view to my book 'Cor Cordium' — Slack having authorized me to do that much. I fear that, if I were to write to Slack about the proposed purchase, and if he were hereafter to find out that this clandestine edition had already been printed, he would suspect me of being privy thereto — which I was not in any degree whatever, nor would I have been." *Letters from Shelley to Elizabeth Hitchener* carries the imprint: "1890 / London: Privately Printed / (Not for sale)." For a set of proof sheets dated 1886, and the suggestion that Wise delayed publication "until the copyright difficulties were cleared up," see *Letters of T. J. Wise to John Henry Wrenn*, ed. F. E. Ratchford, 1944, p. 79.
3. WMR wrote a letter on 10 August, but Wise did not use it. After naming Slack the letter continues: "I really don't know whether he would be at all disposed to part with them or not: but if he *is* so disposed, and as you are prepared to make a liberal offer, I can only hope you will 'go in and win'" (BL).

436. TO THOMAS JAMES WISE

5 Endsleigh Gardens,
8 September 1888

Dear Wise,

I enclose a scribble which might perhaps offer a hint as to a suitable way of presenting the case to Slack.[1] I underline one or two phrases, merely for convenience of reference thereto in this note to yourself. You see I avoid saying to Slack that the Hitchener representative might possibly contest *Slack's ownership* of the letters: I only say that he might possibly be awkward in any *copyright* question

— and then I proceed to associate this copyright question with *my* "Cor Cordium" book as well as any other book. I have introduced this reference to myself, to avoid your presenting to Slack's mind the idea that I said to you anything bringing into question Slack's own right to retain the letters, but rather to suggest that I spoke of what might possibly befall myself. Then further on you are made to speak of assuming responsibility in connexion with the *ownership* and treatment of the letters. This is intended to keep Slack's mind alive to the shakiness of his own ownership, while at the same time no direct hint of its shakiness is conveyed. In short I have tried to put the letter into a form a little diplomatic without being mendacious.

Slack is a rather eccentric sort of man — in appearance, manner, etc.: and would I think be quite apt to shut the whole case up by curt refusal or resolute silence, if his fur were rubbed the wrong way.

Today I received the enclosed printed slip from Axon[2] of Manchester. He suggests that I might "like to put this slip with other Shelley scraps." Certainly I would preserve it as an item of some interest. You also might possibly like to take some note of it for the Society's Notebook. Please return when done with.

Must write again when I have thought a little more over the affair of the meeting.[3] I suppose it must be at this house willy nilly — but will settle when I write again.

Yours very truly,
W. M. Rossetti

MS: Texas.

1. MS. Diary, 6 September 1888: "Wise called. He is still hankering after the Hitchener letters; and, as Slack does not appear to be quite so resolute against sale as had at first been thought, I undertook to consider what form of letter to Slack might be the best next move on the part of Wise."
2. William Edward Armytage Axon (1846-1913), deputy chief librarian of the Manchester Free Libraries; journalist with the *Manchester Guardian*, 1874-1905; vice-president and secretary, and from 1911 president of the Vegetarian Society. On 12 November 1891 he delivered a lecture to the Shelley Society on "Shelley's Vegetarianism" (published as a pamphlet by ?Wise, ?1891).
3. MS. Diary, 6 September 1888: "A meeting of the Shelley Society at my house, with a view to considering the debt to the Printers, and volunteering for wiping off a part of it, is in prospect, but not yet settled: a very annoying and rather harassing affair."

437. TO THOMAS JAMES WISE

5 Endsleigh Gardens,
16 September 1888

Dear Wise,

Cheque for £9.10 received.[1]

I would with great pleasure give you an opportunity, whenever suitable, of copying out that original commencement of *Jenny*.[2] As to the "unpublished poems," they remain unpublished because they are of a juvenile or otherwise defective character, such as my brother strongly objected to letting anyone see: I hardly feel that it would be fitting to authorize their being transcribed. If at any future time the existing conditions render me less strict in this regard, I will remember that you are a claimant — and you are one of the first whom I would be willing to indulge in such a matter.

Slack's letter (returned) looks to me as by no means closing up your last loophole. I think you would, from its tone, be quite justified in writing back, and proposing to call on him on whatever day best suits yourself. You will find him (according to my experience) open and cordial, and quite willing to allow other people to see things from *their* point of view, but not himself easily persuaded into the same point of view unless he chooses. He would hardly yield to mere "argufying," however sound in itself: but I think you might (without over-insistency) present the thing to his mind thus: That, after he had allowed Dowden to use the Hitchener letters so freely, and has moreover empowered me to print them all verbatim, the letters themselves are to himself merely so many documents and autographs, and as such purchasable by you at a very handsome price — and that *you* would thereby step into his shoes, and relieve him not only from all responsibility, to the possible claimant, for the documents as such, but also retrospectively for the use which has already been made of them. You might I think go so far as to offer Slack to enter into a written contract with him to the effect that you, on becoming the owner of the letters, would hold Slack harmless against all consequences, and would make equitable terms with any possible future claimant. I am quite persuaded there will be none such, and you will get off scatheless.

Always truly yours,
W. M. Rossetti

Slack must now be about 70 years old or so. He has a wife of nearly the same age, but no family.

MS: BL.

1. MS. Diary, 12 September 1888: "Wise ... looked at various MSS. etc. of Gabriel's, and made a purchase to the amount ... of £9.10. The most noticeable item is *Eden Bower*, written on several pages of notepaper, full of tentative readings, repetitions, and false starts — also, on larger paper, a much later copy of the earlier portion of the poem. I priced at £3 the whole of the *Eden Bower* MS."

2. DGR began *Jenny* "before the end of 1847.... The portion then written was short, and was merely in the nature of general reflection — not (as now) of semi-dramatic monologue" (*Works*, p. 649).

438. TO THOMAS JAMES WISE

5 Endsleigh Gardens,
16 October 1888

Dear Wise,

I have a plaguing number of letters to write, not to speak of other work: otherwise I might write rather more at large.

You have taken I think quite the right step in relation to Slack. The sooner you manage to see him the better. I do think that you (as Burns says of the Devil) "yet hae a stake."[1]

I had thought that, despite the vacuum in our purse, it was still intended to print among our Transactions such perused papers as are deemed of adequate or average value: and among these would be Hime's.[2] Your expedient however for getting that paper in print, without our making any payment, seems to me a very good one, from our Committee point of view. Whether it is compatible with our engagements (to Clay etc.) to issue texts not printed through our own agency I don't well know: you would know.

I should *imagine* the November meeting to be at least as suitable to Miss Blind as any other.[3]

Yours always,
W. M. Rossetti

MS: BL.

1. "Still hae a stake," *Address to the Deil.*
2. Probably *The Greek Materials of Shelley's Adonais* by Lieut.-Colonel H. W. L. Hime, Royal Artillery, a sixteen-page pamphlet published by Dulau & Co., 37 Soho Square in 1888.
3. She was prevented by illness from delivering a paper on "Shelley's Women" to the Shelley Society on 13 June 1888.

439. TO THOMAS JAMES WISE

5 Endsleigh Gardens,
27 October 1888

Dear Wise,

If I were to trust my own view of the crisis, I should say very decidedly — "Issue to members (at any rate to London members) a card-notice saying that the Session of the Shelley Society will begin with the *December* meeting: no paper being in readiness for the November meeting, and the one in October having miscarried owing to want of preconcerted notice." But, if my more experienced colleagues take a different view, I am of course prepared to turn up for a November meeting.[1] More than this I cannot undertake to do.

Please read the enclosed from Mrs. Simpson;[2] and please do something to calm her. I have written her this afternoon in the most conciliatory terms I could lay my pen to.

Yours always,
W. M. Rossetti

MS: BL.

1. MS. Diary does not record a meeting.
2. Jane Anne Heavisides Simpson, daughter of the poet Henry Heavisides of whom she published a memoir (1895). Wise records the pamphlet publication of a paper on *The Revolt of Islam* which she delivered to the Shelley Society in 1891 (*The Ashley Library, A Catalogue*, 5:140).

440. TO THOMAS JAMES WISE

5 Endsleigh Gardens,
4 January 1889

Dear Wise,

I must attend the meeting on the 9th. It seems to me that it might have been better to name 7, rather than 7:30, as the hour for assembling: when important matters have to be discussed, as now, the half hour prior to reading paper seems seldom sufficient. But I don't want you to make any alteration, unless you yourself should think that decidedly desirable.

I should very much like to understand distinctly the following point. My responsibility, I have been told, is this: That I, along with every other member of Committee from the starting of the Society, am liable for my proportional share of the debt which was incurred during the time I was on the Committee (in my own instance, the *whole* time of the Society).[1] Now what is the actual sum which I thus owe, reckoned proportionally? and what is the sum which each other member of Committee, past and present, owes? Your books would I suppose show this with precision, though the computation might be a little troublesome.

We are certainly in a considerable mess, and I am by no means certain whether to wind up the Society, and do our bad best about the debt — or to continue the Society, thus obtaining some funds, and incurring some further debts — would be the more prudent course, from a money-point of view. No doubt some other considerations, besides those of money, present themselves.

I enclose my monthly 5/-. Don't be at the pains of acknowledging it, now or henceforth.

Yours always truly,
W. M. Rossetti

MS: BL.

1. MS. Diary, 3 January 1889: "Tiresome news from Wise about the Shelley Society debt to the Printers — a matter which has caused me vexation and some anxiety for some while past. It is not my fault personally, for I took no part in directing the printing-operations; but the fault (as I understand) of Wise and Furnivall. The subject being distasteful, I shall say little about it in this diary." 9 January: "Shelley Society meeting. Owing to an act of conspicuous liberality on the part of F. S. Ellis, our prospect seems a little improved. Wise is to make, in conformity with a scheme suggested by himself, certain proposals to the Printer, and another meeting is to come off at my house on 23 January. On my proposal, we mean to see whether Sir Percy Shelley would be disposed to come forward with a little vigour: I am to draw up a letter to him, which will be signed by Wise."

441. TO LUCY ROSSETTI

90 Brook Green,
20 January 1889,
4½

Dearest dear Lucy,

A frightful calamity — Frank died last night — Saturday.[1]

An hour or so after I left the house he got out of bed, and had a fainting-fit. By great efforts was got back to bed: then another faint which proved fatal — towards 8½ Saturday. The heart was wrong.

I had for not more than half an hour or so finished that letter which I wrote you earlier today when Ford[2] came round and told me your father and mother were already at Brook Green and I was asked to go round. Did so. I thought on the whole the least painful thing I could do for your feelings was to send off that earlier letter exactly as it stood: this I did, adding nothing to what was *with exact truth* set forth in it.

I dread writing you in the present form or in any other to apprise you of such dreadful news: but suppose this form may do as well as another.

Your father, mother, and the 3 children,[3] are wonderfully composed and reasonable: so is poor poor Cathy, though one can see terrible affliction in her face. Your father says he means to write to you: perhaps he will do so more to the purpose than I can. He and Emma were summoned hither last night after Frank's death, but they arrived without knowing the precise fact. I have seen him — he looks calm and stately.

Of course I could say very much more about painful or sad details, but this little that I have said — the dreadful sum of all — must be sufficient for the present.

My own dearest Lucy

Your
William

MS: AP.

1. MS. Diary, 18 January 1889: "Cathy writes me that Hueffer is still in bed suffering from erysipelas: I first heard on 10 January of his being ill. Must (though considerably busied with my own affairs) go round tomorrow to see him." 19-24 January: "Frank Hueffer died on the evening of Saturday — A most troublous and grievous event not only in itself but to the prospects of all the family, myself included. I am not likely to resume this diary for some little while to come."
2. Ford Madox Hueffer (1873-1939), known as Ford Madox Ford from 1919. As later letters show, after Francis Hueffer's death WMR took a fatherly interest in him, but their relationship was never an easy one. WMR to Lucy, 1 January 1889: "Ford quite a young man now — height 5 foot 11. Says he is well enough; nor did I observe anything definitely amiss. His voice has altered: I think only what takes place with all youths of his age."
3. In addition to Ford: Oliver (1877-1931), who published novels and plays; Juliet (b. 1881), later Mrs. David Soskice, author of *Chapters from Childhood: Reminiscences of an Artist's Granddaughter* (1921).

442. TO LUCY ROSSETTI

Endsleigh Gardens,
22 January 1889,
11½ a.m.

Dearest Dear,

I feel almost worn out with writing to you (and others) on this dreadful subject:[1] but of course it must be done.

Watts talked to me here yesterday: and we agreed that I would go and see about the Cremation-office, and then go to Brook Green, and he would later on arrive there also. I had a good deal of trouble in finding out anything about the cremation — the Secretary in Argyll Street having died, and nothing being now known there. Finally I got to the right place. The Clerk doubted whether the apparatus was at all in working order: would enquire, and telegraph to Brook Green. Past 6 p.m. his telegram reached: the apparatus is *not* working, and nothing by way of cremation can be done. So without delay I started off to a neighbouring undertaker, Parsons,[2] whom Cathy had employed to her satisfaction when her servant died: I found him, and curiously enough he had some personal knowledge of Gabriel. I sent him round to Brook Green to take detailed orders from your father, and I then returned home. The funeral will be on Thursday, in the same space of ground where Nolly lies, — not in the same grave, but as near by as circumstances may allow. The Doctor, who called yesterday, recommended me to try to get the funeral not later than Thursday.

Last night my stomach was out of order: I may probably be incommoded more or less all today, and going long distances etc. might be very troublesome to me. So I telegraphed in the morning to your father — "Not quite well, but will come if you telegraph." So far as I know I am not today needed at Brook Green, nor particularly expected.

Watts, with your father's assistance, looked through drawers, documents, etc. The materials which would disclose the state of money-matters seem rather deficient as yet. The chief point traced out as yet (for it was unknown to Cathy etc.) is that the office where Frank's life was insured is the National Provident, and that he paid a premium of about £83 p.a. Considering that I pay (I think this is nearly correct) a premium of £36 for an insurance of £1000 effected when I was 44 years old, it might seem that the sum for which Frank insured, and for which he paid the much larger sum of £83 beginning from a much earlier age, ought to be something rather solid — I can't see how it could well be less that £2500 at the very least. The policy however can't at present be found, nor any indication of where it is deposited: the impression is that Frank must have borrowed money lately on the security of the policy, which latter would be deposited with the creditor — possibly the Insurance office itself. This and many other points remain to be cleared up.

I need not say poor Cathy is from every point of view *deeply* afflicted: her eyes (though I have not seen her at any time weeping profusely) looked almost extinguished on Sunday, and not very different yesterday: still she bears herself with reason and fortitude. I will confess that the stoical demeanour of the three children surprises me: if the highest ideal of life is to accept everything exactly as it comes, without emotion and without comment, they might teach a lesson to all of us.

See enclosed from Christina — which I found on returning from my miserable Sunday visit to Brook Green. Yesterday quite early I called, and saw both Christina and Charlotte: the alarm about the latter has subsided to some extent; her appearance is of course not good, but still not very different from what it has mostly been of late.

Ice-carnival. Perhaps under present unhappy circumstances I need hardly answer a query in your postcard of 17. I fancy, were I you, I should take *no* notice of the affair one way or other.

Your own — with how much affection you know —

William

Sunday and yesterday contributed to the general gloom by wretched weather — damp steaming sweltering mists, and reeking mud underfoot. Today is at least tolerably bright — probably colder too.

MS: AP.

1. Death of Francis Hueffer.
2. Not identified.

443. TO LUCY ROSSETTI

Endsleigh Gardens,
23 January 1889,
10¼ a.m.

Dearest Dear Lu,

I feel this morning particularly drear and helpless, so you must take what I write for what it is worth. Was at home all yesterday, not being well, and not receiving (what I referred to in writing to you yesterday) any summoning telegram from your father. Today I was intending to go to Brook Green immediately after breakfast: but a telegram received from Watts asks whether I shall be here at Endsleigh Gardens at noon, so I infer I had better wait here till then.

I wrote various letters yesterday — could attend to nothing else. Shall return to Somerset House on Friday.

A letter of yours (I suppose 19 January) received. It tends to relieve me from some anxiety about your cold. Have today sent the £10 cheque to Mrs. Hollings.

Dear little Helen writes — also Olive. If I can at sometime, I will reply — not now. Olive wants me to send successive volumes of Gibbon. Small as the job is, I cannot apply myself to it now. Will be borne in mind. I don't think it quite *desirable* to send this goodish edition to and fro by post: but would not on that account decline.

With this great misfortune, and the serious difference it makes in the total resources of the various branches of the family, I must I think finally relinquish the idea of treating myself to a visit to Biarritz. If you acquiesce in this as essentially the right course, we need not recur to that subject.

Your own
William

MS: AP.

444. TO LUCY ROSSETTI

5 Endsleigh Gardens,
24 January 1889,
4¾

Dearest Lu,

Another day of extreme gloom is past — the funeral is over. A moderate number of people attended, besides our own party. All went well — splendid wreaths from Wagner Society etc. But I have no heart for details.

Alexis Hüffer[1] arrived last evening. I met him at Brook Green, and was in the carriage with him and Watts to and from the funeral. I am trying to see as much of him as may be manageable these 3 or 4 days of his stay, in the hope of getting him or his brothers to do something substantial for the boys. With this object

Watts and I lunched with him today at his hotel, and on Saturday they are to dine with me.

I have told you as yet (I think) nothing about money-affairs: but they must be faced. It is only today that a little clear light is thrown on them by a letter from Frank's Bank. So far as we can make out, *nothing* remains of his private property — shares etc. There is an insurance for £2000 and the house. On the former a debt of £250: on the latter something (may perhaps be £300) remains to be paid off to clear a mortgage. This seems a terrible position for Cathy. The first immediate question is — Shall she continue living in the house? She seems inclined to do so, looking out for some lady to share expenses. Your papa advocates her going with Juliet to his house. The question still remains as to the 2 boys: that they should resume their expensive education at Folkestone[2] seems to me not possible. A family colloquy on these grave questions is taking place this afternoon, aided by the 2 Trustees Watts and Rowley. I could not join, being truly exhausted by constant flitting to and fro and grievous anxieties — and tomorrow my own work at Somerset House must be resumed. Besides I am not directly responsible, and think those who are so will be all the better for my not adding to the chaos of opinions.

My sweet Lu, I have no heart for minor matters. Am on the whole pleased that, in such a load of trouble, you made up your mind not to try Corfu at present — though no doubt the invitation had its tempting side.

Pity and love your poor harassed

William

I should have said that Alexis seems to view matters, in a general way, as an affectionate brother might be expected to do: but I have not yet succeeded in eliciting from him any clear undertaking to provide, even temporarily, for either of the boys. I learn from him that there are still 6 of the Hüffer brothers living, and 4 sisters. One principal brother, the Banker in Paris, has 2 sons of his own.

You will understand that I have not yet received any letter of yours written *after* this harrowing calamity was known to you. I feel for you, believe me, fully as much as for myself.

No further distinct news about Charlotte.

MS: AP.

1. For an account of three of the Hüffer brothers, see Arthur Mizener, *The Saddest Story, A Biography of Ford Madox Ford* (1971): Wilhelm, the "Roman Hüffer" of Letter 447, Note 1; Leopold, who died childless in 1897 leaving Ford and Oliver some £3000 each; and Hermann, professor of History at Bonn.

2. In 1881 Ford began attending a boarding-school in Folkestone. It was operated by Dr. Alfred Praetorius, who had been "a favourite pupil of ... Froebel, and had pleasingly modern ideas of education" (Mizener, pp. 9-10). Presumably Oliver followed him there a few years later. MS. Diary, 10 May 1889, records that Ford "is now attending University College School: Oliver is about to attend there also."

My dear afflicted Cathy,

I am always a poor hand at *expressing* sympathy: but I feel it, and hard indeed would be the heart which did not feel it for you at the present moment. I want now to acquit myself of what has reasonably become a debt. I shall never forget the motherly affection with which you received and treated my dear little Helen at the time when Lucy was away at San Remo and Dijon:[1] our dear Frank was equally kind. You would not at that time regard any expenses which she entailed upon you as being other than a free gift on your part. I believe I raised the question at the time: but at any rate I will now settle it to my own satisfaction by asking you to accept a sum of £30 in discharge of those expenses. A cheque for the amount is enclosed. If it relieves you for a few days from those tormenting worries which overbrim the cup of a great calamity, I shall indeed be pleased at having remembered to perform this act of simple justice.

You will have heard a good deal from Watts this afternoon — some of it very distressing to hear. I did not come round — in fact I could not well do so, for my own necessary occupations have fallen not a little into arrear: and in fact I think I should have done less good than harm by joining in discussions in which you with your father's advice, and the two Trustees, are alone qualified to express decided views. Watts and Alexis Hüffer (you will be aware) are to dine with me on Saturday: my great object in that arrangement being to see whether Alexis will not take a prompt and vigorous part in the interest of (at any rate) one or other of the boys. I will not conceal from you my opinion that Ford — if any opening whatever offers for him — ought now to regard his schooling as finished.[2] My schooling closed at the same age, 15, and I at once became one of the scanty bread-winners of my then very impoverished family. It was a hard necessity, and was felt as such: but it formed a beginning for conditions less straitened and disastrous.

I continue of course to hear from Lucy day by day: but her last-received letter was written before she knew of the terrible sorrow which has overtaken us all — including

Your always affectionate
W. M. Rossetti

My opinion is that a letter ought to be written at once to the Proprietors of the *Times*, stating briefly the position in which the death of Frank leaves his family: enquiring whether, according to the practice of the *Times*, anything is done in the interest of the survivors; and plainly saying that in such case you present yourself as a claimant. It might be well also to enquire whether they could offer any sort of suitable employment to Ford. I don't pretend to think that much good would come of such a step as this: none the less I consider that it ought to be taken. If you agree, and would like me to draft any such letter, I will attend to it at the earliest opportunity.[3]

Did the *Times* owe anything to Frank at the date of his death? Also is anything owing to him in connexion with that book (I don't know the publisher) concerning the Music of the last Half-century?[4] Sutherland Edwards spoke to me this morning, offering to do anything which might possibly be needed in revising the proofs etc. of that book. I mentioned this point to Watts, and he may have informed you of it.

If you ever want to *see* me, let me know, and I will come as soon as practicable. Short of this, I may possibly not see you for some days to come; as I must now return to Somerset House, and, when I am in attendance there, I have very little time to do anything, except just get home, work steadily all the evening, and get the requisite allowance of sleep before I rise in the morning for another day's close occupation. Then on Sundays I never go out if I can help: not exactly from selfishness, but because I really need that day for my own occupations, and especially for keeping down letter-writing etc. which had accumulated during the weekdays.

MS: Berg.

1. In 1886-87.
2. MS. Diary, 4 February 1889: "Ford Hueffer came round to me from Brown's, bringing a letter which he proposes to send to the Civil Service Commissioners, asking when the next examination for Boy Clerkships would be held; as he thinks (and I consider it a reasonable idea) of competing at such an examination." 4 March: "Ford is attending, for 3 months, a Civil Service College in Chancery Lane."
3. MS. Diary, 3 February 1889: "Wrote to Watts, as Trustee under Hueffer's will, asking (this was settled between Cathy and myself on 30 January) whether he would think well now to address the Proprietors of the *Times*, to see whether they would do anything for the advantage of the family; and I offered to Watts to draft a letter for the purpose, if he would like." 5 February: "Watts called on me at Somerset House. He has sought a personal interview with [G. E.] Buckle, Editor of the *Times*, with a view to getting some advantage from the *Times* for Cathy: was referred to [J. C.] MacDonald the Manager, and expects to speak to him directly. Rowley (who is the second Trustee under Hueffer's will) had written to Watts suggesting that a 'Hueffer Memorial Concert' might be got up by eminent musicians and vocalists — [Adelina] Patti, [Alwina] Valleria, [Alexander Campbell] Mackenzie, etc. — for the advantage of the family. Both Watts and I regard this as not a bad idea; and, as I was intending to call on Brown in the afternoon, I undertook to mention the matter to him — Watts foreseeing that he would be adverse and even angry. This view turned out to be entirely correct: for Brown was very angry, and is in fact dissatisfied with everything that is done in the direction of getting Cathy cared for by anyone but himself — such for instance as my having on 26 January told Alexis Hüffer, in a personal interview, that I consider she needs a total annual income of not less than £300, to which Frank Hueffer's brothers on the Continent should be disposed to contribute. My own strong opinion is that Brown pushes his own views in this matter a good deal too far: 1, because he himself is not well able to meet the expenses needed for Cathy and her 3 children, and 2, because Brown's own health is in such a condition as to offer no prospect of prolonged life, and, were he to die, I don't know what is to become of Cathy, her 3 children, and also Emma, except that I myself should provide for them — a condition of things very anomalous in itself, and highly irksome, or indeed next to impracticable, for me to meet.... Shall endeavour henceforth to interpose as little as possible between the conflicting views of Brown and the 2 Trustees; for I have no express right to make myself a party in these questions, and I might soon find myself involved in very painful disputes with Brown, and also with Lucy. I will here however record once for all my decided opinion that the general view of the situation taken by the Trustees, and the general course of action which they pursue or advocate, are more reasonable and more to the purpose than those of Brown."
4. *Half a Century of Music in England, 1837-1887* (1889).

446. TO PERCY WILLIAM BUNTING[1]

Somerset House,
5 February 1889

Dear Mr. Bunting,

Your telegram of yesterday reached my house some half hour before I had returned. On reading the telegram, I preferred to write a letter in reply, offering a brief explanation, rather than merely fill-in the enclosed return-telegram.

My position in this (Inland Revenue) Office imposes upon me considerable reserve in the *public* advocacy of or identification with any particular cause in politics. Up to some score of years ago the Officials in the Revenue Departments had (as you are probably aware) no parliamentary vote at all: then the exclusion was removed, but we are still under injunction from Headquarters not to take any prominent public part in politics, not to belong to Election-Committees, etc. etc. I fancy that on the whole this restriction may be right: at any rate there it is, and my position makes it binding upon me.

I am well known in this Office as a Gladstonian Home-ruler, and I greatly detest the present system of coercive and exceptional laws, entailing in their enforcement revolting and despicable brutalities: but for the reason I have given I should not be justified in joining the Committee of National Protest against Coercion.[2]

Yours very truly,
W. M. Rossetti

MS: Editor.

1. (1836-1911), editor of the *Contemporary Review* from 1882 until his death; devoted himself "from an early age ... to social reform, political liberalism, and the welfare of modern Methodism" (*DNB*).
2. See Letter 424, Note 3.

447. TO LUCY ROSSETTI

Somerset House,
6 February 1889,
Noon

Dearest Lu,

Last evening I received together 2 affectionate letters of yours: both seem to be dated 3 February.

I have not as yet done anything about the tea. Will at some time attend to your new directions regarding it.

Am pleased with what you say about Job. A hurricane of 30 hours and more seems no trifle: I trust it blew itself out at last, and did not again blow itself in.

I read that note of yours addressed to Agnes, and handed it to her, saying that I gathered from it that she and her sister had indicated to you some desire to leave; and that, if any such desire is entertained, they should speak to me, and I would make other arrangements. She replied that there is no such desire. Since then I have heard no more about the matter. Nothing has of late occurred to lead to my insisting that these 2 (or 3) servants should go: if anything does occur, I think I understand both what I had best do, and what you would like me to do.

I will endeavour to answer Olive's letter without much delay. Have *many* letters to write at this very moment.

Yesterday I went to see your papa: remained there from about 4¼ to 6½. He was alone in the studio on my arrival; but very soon afterwards Mathilde Blind came in, and remained the rest of the time. She has been back in the house since (I fancy) about 10 January. Your papa, I am glad to say, seems quite as well as usual; he insisted on accompanying me downstairs when I left, and I noticed that his gait in descending the stairs was certainly brisker than it often is. I remarked this to him, and he acquiesced. He then remarked that, while his health is now comparatively fair, his spirits are bad: which one can only too well conceive: however his long conversation with me had passed without any salient symptom of bad spirits. We naturally talked a good deal (though not by any means to the exclusion of other subjects) about Cathy's affairs. What your papa said confirmed my previous view (be it right or wrong) — that he is a little too much inclined to assume that the one thing substantially needed is that Cathy should simply resume her position as a member of his family, with her 3 children added: for instance he was ill-pleased both at my having spoken at all to Alexis Hüffer unless by express preconcert with himself, and at my having told Alexis (though in fact this was a mere answer from me to a direct and positive question put by Alexis) that I consider a total income of £300 a year to be the lowest which could be named as reasonably sufficient for Cathy and her 3 children. When I say that your papa was ill-pleased, I don't mean that he showed any want of personal kindliness to me: I took all in good part, and debated the matter as little as I could, and he and I parted on the most affectionate terms. The real fact is, I have taken no step without the previous express or tacit concurrence of *Cathy*. My desire to serve her is great, very great: but, as the 2 Trustees are the persons legally and technically qualified to act, while your papa is the nearest relative, and of course fully entitled to every prerogative belonging to him as such, I think I shall find it quite necessary to eclipse myself henceforward in the matter. I have certainly no *right* to act, except that which sympathy and affection, or which Cathy herself, may confer on me. If Cathy directly *asks* me to do anything, I will do it to the best of my ability: as long as I remain unasked, I must (I think) remain passive — not without an expectation of a catastrophe at some future day. I mean, a catastrophe would be too likely if foreign Hüffers or other well-wishers are resolutely kept at arm's length, instead of being encouraged and invited to do their best. Your father is quite of opinion that the Hüffers will *not* make any annual allowance (though possibly one of them might give a lump sum down): I am still in hopes they *will* make an allowance. You will readily believe that that matter of Alexis and the £300 was not the *only* one (concerning Cathy's affairs) which your papa dwelt upon: I have mentioned it as being the one which directly concerned myself.[1]

The Boddington picture[2] is now very nearly finished: the only bare spot of canvas being Mrs. Boddington's front arm. It comes a fine work, with a great amount of spirit and expression, and a marked avoidance of routine.

You will no doubt have received, before this letter, the one which I posted yesterday, registered, containing cheque for £40.

Dearest, your own
William

MS: AP.

1. MS. Diary, 4 March 1889, records that "the Roman Hüffer (and it may be feared his brothers also) will not do anything for Cathy personally, but only ... for the boys." WMR wrote to Lucy on 10 March about the latter proposal: "I do not entirely agree with you (nor with your father and Cathy) about that matter of the Hueffer boys. Had it rested with me to decide, I would have replied to the Roman Hüffer as follows. 'When the boys grow up, they will naturally form their own opinions on religious questions, just as their father did. If the only form in which you will assist the family is that of educating the boys in a German college of the Roman-Catholic order, I assent. At Folkestone they were in outward conformity with the English Church [this is a fact], and in Germany they may (so far as I am concerned) be in outward conformity with the Roman Church. As soon as their minds develop — say at the age of 18 or 19 — they must be consulted as to whether they choose to pursue the same course any further, and if they say no they are to act on their own decision without pressure or coercion.' This would have been my reply. One should I think take two things into account: 1, That a Roman-Catholic may be just as good a man as an 'Agnostic'; and 2, That, though it turned out natural for Franz to be more or less an Agnostic, and for some of his connexions to be the same, it does not follow necessarily that the same result will prove to be the natural one for Ford and Oliver. I say the same thing for my own children. As a matter of preference, I would prefer every one of them to be like myself, a free-thinker: but, if some or all of them examine for themselves what Christianity consists of, and finally prefer it to free-thinking, that must be their affair, not mine" (AP). For Ford's reception into the Roman Catholic Church in 1892, see Mizener, *The Saddest Story*, pp. 19-20.

2. *Boddington Group*, "a portrait of the family of Mr. Henry Boddington" (Hueffer, *Ford Madox Brown*, p. 380). WMR to Lucy Rossetti, 9 March 1889: "I called yesterday at St. Edmund's Terrace — rainy afternoon. Saw with much pleasure the *Boddington Group* finished — a very noticeable work in expression, vivacity, and ensemble — colour extremely agreeable, forcible, and taking, with some remarkable passages of realistic detail" (AP). MS. Diary, 5 February 1889, described it as "in some respects ranking among the finest things he has produced."

448. TO THOMAS JAMES WISE

5 Endsleigh Gardens,
16 February 1889

Dear Wise,

It was with some reluctance that I found myself designated as the right person to sign (along with Secretary and Treasurer) that appeal to subscribers.[1] Not having been personally responsible for the expenditure, I would rather not have assumed so prominent a position in the effort to cover it — would have preferred to see the appeal signed by *all* the present members of Committee: however, my colleagues decided otherwise, and I shall conform. I must however ask that a proof of the appeal be sent to me before any copies are finally struck off: there was really no time for pondering, during that Committee-meeting, the terms of Forman's draft. I engage not to make *fancy*-alterations on the proof, so as to run up expense.

As the lawyers have decided that the persons responsible for the debt are (in their due proportions) those who were on the Committee at the respective dates when orders were given, it would appear highly desirable that each present or past member of Committee should know what is the sum representing his personal proportion of the debt (though I am aware the legal liability does not cease at that point). I can easily perceive that to draw up an account of this kind would be a somewhat laborious task: still it ought by rights to be done.

I was out of the Committee for a short while — say 10 February to 10 April 1887:[2] and should of course expect allowance to be made for that interval, if any orders for printing were given meanwhile.

Was rather surprised to see Revell at the last Committee-meeting: I thought he had resigned. Or did he — on finding that he is *not* responsible for expenses incurred before he joined the Committee — withdraw his resignation?

Could those volumes of Trelawny's book be made of the least use as assets? You remember that Col. Call gave the Society (through me) several copies of the cheap edition. They simply lie littering a back room of mine.

Yours always truly,
W. M. Rossetti

MS: BL.

1. MS. Diary, 13 February 1889: "Shelley Society evening — Forman read out the address to members which he has at length made time to write, urging them to be liberal in subscriptions or donations: it is to be printed and issued, with 3 names to it — mine being one. Not in any respect a pleasant affair."
2. See Letter 418, Note 1.

449. TO THOMAS JAMES WISE

5 Endsleigh Gardens,
11 March 1889

Dear Wise,

I don't gather whether *you* have replied to Mr. Child's letter of 12 February.[1] If not, would you kindly let me know, as I suppose that *I* must then reply. My acknowledgement sent towards 25 February was merely a stopgap.

I see there is a misapprehension about my "being absent from England."[2] It is true that in 1887 I was absent from England from 25 January to 10 March or thereabouts: but it is not on this ground (obviously untenable) that I put forward a claim to exemption from liability incurred during a certain interval. You will probably remember that during my absence the offered membership of Dr. Aveling was rejected — chiefly on the ground (as I understood) that he had imitated Shelley in inventing a Mrs. Aveling whom he had not formally married; also, that I, on hearing of this fact, resigned my position as Committee-man, and did not resume this until some little while after I had returned to London. The period during which I was, in theory and in fact, out of the Committee, lasted (I should say) from about 10 February to 10 April 1887: your books would probably show. To me it seems quite clear that during that interval my liability ceased.

As mentioned before, I expect to be very soon off to Biarritz: *may* have started before Wednesday evening, but that is hardly likely. I remember mentioning to you once before that I don't wish my wife's mind to be kept in a state of alarm, and perhaps her health affected for the worse, by details regarding the liabilities of the Shelley Society, and of myself as a Committee-man, being brought to her attention. *Would you therefore kindly abstain from sending to me, prior to my return to London which may be towards 23 April, any account or other documents or letter regarding said liabilities.* My wife (with my full assent) opens my letters whenever she feels inclined; and, were you to address me on this point either direct to Biarritz, or by letter to a London address sent on to Biarritz, some contretemps might ensue.

For the same reason, it would be better, *after* my return to town at end of April, to send to *Somerset House* (rather than to Endsleigh Gardens) any letters etc. bearing on this untoward subject.

Excuse my pertinacity, and believe me

Always truly yours,

W. M. Rossetti

MS: BL.

1. On 25 February WMR sent on to Wise a letter from Addison Child, secretary of the Northern New York branch of the Shelley Society, in which he complained that "some months since I wrote to Mr. Wise ... in regard to the method adopted by the Shelley Society for the transmission of its publications to American subscribers, i.e. by Express, rather than by mail, and sent him the bills of charges paid on one package amounting to nearly as much as the annual subscription.... I have received no reply to my letter.... If this wanton disregard to the interests of the members of the Shelley Society continues it will not only keep away new subscribers but drive away old ones" (AP).
2. See Letter 448, Note 2.

450. TO LUCY ROSSETTI

Somerset House,
29 April [1889],
4½

It escaped me the other day to say that your father, on calling some while back upon Holman Hunt, found that he had already taken a turn for the better: he had undergone some very severe treatment from Semon[1] — red-hot needles up the nose etc. Since Friday morning the weather here continues mild and often fine.

Love,

W. M. R.

MS: AP.

1. Felix Semon, MD (Berlin, 1873), specialist in diseases of the throat (*Churchill's Medical Directory*, 1889).

451. TO ROBERT BROWNING

5 Endsleigh Gardens,
30 May 1889

Dear Browning,

Many thanks for your reply — marked by your usual promptitude and kindness. Enclosed is the Memorial.[1] Would you kindly return it to me signed, as soon as may be convenient, as I understand time is a little scanty. This is not my fault, as I was enlisted in the service on Monday only — and am not much *au fait* in the routine of such matters.

With our warm regards to you and yours, believe me

Yours very truly,
W. M. Rossetti

MS: Wellesley.

1. MS. Diary, 29 May 1889: "Am engaged now in working-up the literary contingent for signatories of the memorial soliciting a Civil List Pension for Cathy. Mrs. Cusins [wife of the pianist and conductor, W. G. Cusins], who is the mainspring of the movement, knows musical and artistic people, but not literary: so Ford spoke to me on Monday, and got me to act in this matter. I should have preferred if the whole matter could have been managed without any member of the family-connexion (such as myself) coming forward ostensibly: but, as this is said not to be practicable, I waive my feelings. Browning, Dowden, and [Walter] Besant have already replied assenting: also Leighton (to whom Lucy wrote) answers that he has already signed the memorial." 20 June 1890: "The movement ... for obtaining for Cathy a pension ... has failed — one statement made on the subject (it comes to me through Lucy) being that such pensions are not granted in relation to newspaper-writers, but I question the strict accuracy of this. Instead of the pension, a gratuity of £100 on the Queen's Bounty was tendered, and a cheque for this sum was actually produced yesterday by [A. J.] Hipkins to Brown and Cathy: Brown repelled it rather indignantly, as being only calculated to humiliate himself and Cathy. I hardly know whether in his place I should have done the same or not: prudence would suggest the contrary course, and Cathy is evidently not wholly at one with Brown on the subject."

452. TO HORACE LOGO TRAUBEL[1]

5 Endsleigh Gardens,
7 June 1889

Dear Sir,

I am obliged for your letter of 24 May, enclosing a programme of the "Whitman Testimonial," or dinner in honour of Walt Whitman which was fixed for 31 May, the 70th anniversary of his birth; and inviting me to send "some expression touching the season and the man."

I will only say that I most heartily sympathize in any demonstration of honour and love towards this great and good American — a man who, whilst specially and personally American in all his feelings, thoughts, and utterances, has, beyond almost all men in literature, gone down to the roots of the human heart, and spoken the word for all the world. I myself always have honoured and loved him, and always shall do. I consider him to be pre-eminent among the sons of men for a large human nature — broad, deep and glowing — and for the power of giving the deepest and most universal expression to the deepest and most universal feelings. With heart and with mind he embraces more than other men do, and with voice he proclaims more. This is, I think, his great and admirable excellence as writer or poet; and is quite enough for numbering Whitman among the great poetic souls of the world — whatever may be his qualifications in point of form or of diction. On this matter — were I to express my exact opinion — I could say a good deal, partly to praise and partly to demur: but it is a subordinate (though far from an unimportant) matter, and for the present I leave it alone.

Honour and love to Walt Whitman. This tribute is due from Americans, from Englishmen, and from all races of men, be they the foremost or the backward races.

William M. Rossetti

MS: LC. Published: *Camden's Compliments to Walt Whitman*, ed. Horace L. Traubel, 1889, pp. 49-50.

1. (1858-1919), friend and literary executor of Whitman; founder of the *Conservator* (Philadelphia, 1890-1919), a magazine of Marxian socialism as interpreted by a disciple of Whitman. In addition to his chief contribution to writings about Whitman, *With Walt Whitman in Camden*, he was one of the editors with R. M. Bucke and Thomas B. Harned of the ten-volume *Complete Writings of Whitman* (1902).

453. TO THOMAS JAMES WISE

Somerset House,
18 June 1889

Dear Wise,

I am much concerned to hear of your being so ill: trust that you may have improved very considerably since the date of your letter.

Scott has sent me (received this morning) the enclosed cheque for £5[1] — which is handsome. He writes me also a letter of remonstrance as to the course pursued by the Society, and in some respects I do not dissent from him. Shall send you on the letter sometime, but can't part with it just now. Have sent a brief acknowledgement of his cheque.

As to Child — If I remember right he did not in his previous letter say distinctly who it was that sent the subscription, and I, in forwarding the letter to you, pointed out this uncertainty. No blame attaches, I think, to either of us.

On Sunday I looked for a *Hugh Heron*, and did not find one. Am not *certain* about it, but now think that my very last disposable copy has been disposed of. It may have been towards September last that Forman bought of me a copy of Christina's privately printed volume,[2] and I then gave him a *Hugh Heron* (or else invert the items of sale and gift): and at the same time I gave a *Hugh Heron* to my eldest daughter, and Forman good-naturedly volunteered to have it handsomely bound for her — which has now been done. *If* I discover yet another copy, I will remember Mr. Smart's offer, which I would very willingly turn into a reality.[3]

For *Hand and Soul*[4] a Bookseller lately charged (you may remember) £6.6. I am less unconscionable, and would take £1.

It seems to me I must (through inadventure) have failed to send you as yet my monthly 5/-. Here it is.

With best wishes for your speedy recovery.

Yours always truly,
W. M. Rossetti

MS: BL.

1. WBS to WMR, 15 June 1889: "Upon my soul I send you this trifling addition to your subscription solely on your account, constrained by your so friendly note, and quite against my conscience. If any madman paid for the reprinting of Browning's exposure of his ignorance of Shelley's workmanship in prose [Browning's introduction to the forged *Letters of Shelley*, Shelley Society's Publications, 1888], the Society should not have adopted it: Why did he not go to the assembly of duffers called the Browning Society? The fact is your Society has been insane somehow or other about writing and printing about Shelley displaying all the weaknesses of infatuated worship instead of critical discrimination.... The Society has been a dead corpse from the first to the last" (AP).

2. *Verses* (1847).

3. WMR to Wise, 28 June 1889: "I *am* after all the happy owner of a *Hugh Heron*. If Mr. Smart still likes to become a purchaser at £9, I shall after that sale retain (as I found the other day by an almost casual inspection of a certain cupboard) 3 complete copies, and one extra copy of a single sheet. When these are gone, the edition will be finally and absolutely exhausted. All my copies (including what would go to Mr. Smart) are simply in unstitched sheets — no wrapper'' (BL).

4. Privately printed in 1869.

454. TO THOMAS JAMES WISE

5 Endsleigh Gardens,
19 July 1889

Dear Wise,

I have now looked up the *Hugh Heron* and the *Hand and Soul*, and have set them apart where I can at any moment lay hands upon them. Along with them is a copy of Maria's *Rivulets*[1] — deliverable to you if you like. I discovered yesterday that other copy of the *Rivulets* which I mentioned to you the other day as having disappeared unaccountably.

If I don't hear from you to the contrary, I shall understand that on some early evening or other you are likely to turn up, and fetch the papers away. I have not as yet put any sort of inscription upon any of them, but could do so if you like. If any other form of delivery proves more convenient to you, please let me know — and to me it will do equally well. I am not at present aware that I shall be away or occupied any particular evening, except this present Friday.

My monthly 5/- enclosed.

Yours always truly,
W. M. Rossetti

MS: Texas.

1. MS. Diary, 19 July 1889: "Wise bought of me a copy of Maria's little *Rivulets* [1846] for £2: this is the copy which used to belong to my Uncle Henry. I have now one extra copy remaining — no more." Cf. Wise's account in *The Ashley Library, A Catalogue* (1923): "The present copy formerly belonged to William Rossetti, from whom I purchased it in 1890. He informed me that the little book was suppressed before publication, and that the only examples preserved were the present specimen, and one given to William Bell Scott'' (4:162).

455. TO FREDERICK JAMES FURNIVALL

5 Endsleigh Gardens,
7 September 1889

Dear Furnivall,

Thanks for your note of the 1st. I can (if you like) return the extract from Mr. Shaw's letter, but meanwhile retain it.

I did not ever think of myself taking any steps by way of reprinting those letters from the *Nation*;[1] but I have been aware that Wise was plotting a reprint, and on the 5th I received the sheets of said reprint: have not yet had time to inspect them. I understood Wise to say that his reprint would not be circulated so as to acquire any character of publicity — would not for instance be issued to the Shelley Society; but would be kept quiet among a few adepts. I suspect this is the best course. I do not suppose that either Sir Percy Shelley or anyone else would take legal steps to burke the publication: but I presume he would probably be vexed, and might do the Society some bad turn or other — and we can't afford bad turns, only good ones.

My paper — which is not *very* far from completion now — takes the form of an abstract of the letters, with remarks of my own interspersed as to their character and bearings. The abstract includes (or indeed consists of) very copious quotations: in fact I quote, either in full or in a condensed form, *all* the passages which Shelleyites need to bear in mind. This I have done, not expressly as a prudent medium course between silence and publication, but because it seemed to me on the whole the most interesting thing which I could present to my audience, and it will at the same time serve practically to realize that medium course. Nobody, I suppose, can obstruct a man in delivering a lecture to a Society, containing extracts from letters published in America.

As to *printing* my paper — whether before or after I read it out to the audience — I have no particular wish either way. As soon as it gets finished I will let you know, and the point can then be settled.

Yours always truly,

W. M. Rossetti

Have you seen anything of Skipsey[2] at Stratford? Does he seem to be the square man for the square hole, or the contrary? I heartily hope, the former.

MS: BL.

1. Alfred Webb, "Harriet Shelley and Catherine Nugent," 6, 13 June 1889, pp. 464-67, 484-86. Wise issued the letters in 1889, *Harriet Shelley's Letters to Catherine Nugent*, Privately Printed.
2. Joseph Skipsey (1832-1903), collier poet, whom DGR and the Pre-Raphaelites praised and befriended. In June 1889 Skipsey and his wife were appointed custodians of Shakespeare's birthplace at Stratford, but finding the job tedious he resigned in 1891. MS. Diary, 17 May 1889: "Skipsey ... wrote me asking for any recommendations. I sent him a testimonial, and wrote to Furnivall a letter enclosing Skipsey's own papers." 18 May: "Am pleased to find that Furnivall ... wrote to Mr. [C. E.] Flower, the chief person concerned at Stratford, in favour of Skipsey."

456. TO THEODORE WATTS-DUNTON

5 Endsleigh Gardens,
4 November 1889

Dear Watts,

Your letter of yesterday has given me (I need hardly say so) extreme pleasure, mingled with the sense of abiding grief for our loss of dear Gabriel. I had hardly thought the book[1] adapted to be regarded with the quality and degree of approval which you express. Of course if you express any of it in the *Athenaeum* as well I shall be all the better pleased.

I am hardly prepared to think that *anything* would have done Gabriel much good at the pass which things had reached when he went to and stayed at Birchington: but it may be that in that instance I acquiesced too implicitly in a feeling which certainly holds me strongly at times — that of giving a thing up as past hope and irretrievable. My belief was — and mainly is — that Gabriel was not then capable of recovering bodily health; and that, even if he had recovered that in a general sense, his mind would have weakened, and at some moderate distance of time weakened most woefully: a fate in comparison with which the death-shriek and the turf at Birchington are a paradise indeed.

Yes — that Teodorico Pietrocola-Rossetti was the man you remember. His Scotch wife was most thoroughly devoted to him (her *second* husband): yet, within some 2 years or less after his death, she married a 3rd husband, some 12 years younger than herself, a Mr. Cole. He undertook, with her constant co-operation (to be secured only by a marriage), to carry on that sort of Vaudois propagandism which Teodorico had made the aim of his later life. They remain in Italy, and are I think well mated — though oddly beyond a doubt.

You will not be surprised if, now that I have got out of that volume on Gabriel, my mind recurs to the other project — the Letters-Memoir book. I wish you could give me some notion of when we may expect really to consign the whole affair to a publisher — Ellis & Elvey if they choose to act, or otherwise someone else.

I address to Lancing. A letter of mine of 3 or 4 days ago to Swinburne went to Putney, as I had supposed you were both likely to be back there at this late date in the year. Probably it was sent on to him.

Yours,
W. M. Rossetti

MS: Berg.

1. *DGRDW*; reviewed by Watts in the *Athenaeum*, 28 June 1890, pp. 823-26.

457. TO THOMAS JAMES WISE

Somerset House,
8 November 1889

Dear Wise,

I will remember the meeting for the 20th: attendance at *Committee* will I presume be 7.30 — though I generally find and think that 7.15 would not be too early. I have certainly *not* received (unless indeed it is in a packet of books which I have never yet opened) the printed card of which you speak. On reflection I fancy it *is* in that packet, and will look for it.

Glad to hear about the Hitchener Letters.

For somewhile after I last wrote about it, that proposal as to your coming to inspect some MSS. of my brother had practically slipped my memory: but these 2 or 3 days past it had recurred to me prominently, and I was intending to see about it. Am rather busy at present, but expect, within the next few days, to name an evening. There is always the "fidget" of looking up (when one is otherwise occupied) to see precisely where the MSS. are, before an evening is proposed: but it shall be done.[1]

Yours,
W. M. Rossetti

MS: BL.

1. MS. Diary, 18 December 1889: "Wise called, under a long-pending engagement, to look at

MSS. of Gabriel in my possession, being desirous of purchasing some specimens. He and I set aside a certain number: the principal things being *St. Agnes of Intercession*, and *Arme Heinrich*. I price the former (which I rate highly) at £15, and the latter at £9. The whole lot would make about £41. I allowed Wise to take them away for a little further consideration: the likelihood is that he will buy all of them, or nearly all.''

458. TO THOMAS JAMES WISE

Somerset House,
14 January 1890

Dear Wise,

Thanks for Scott's letter, herewith returned. His phrase — ''have received no acknowledgement for this sum of money, either written or printed'' — appears to me to be aimed at you only, not at me. It is a certain fact that I replied promptly, and in considerable detail upon various points, to his letter of June last sending the £5, and I have since then received some other letters from him which (if closely inspected) would, I have little doubt be found to refer to some points in that reply of mine. I think therefore that, if I were now to write to Scott asserting that I answered him, I should only be irritating him a little more: but it would seem quite right that *you* should write a polite reply, affirming in distinct terms that you did send him a proper official acknowledgement of his subscription, much about the same time when I replied as a friend to his friendly letter.

I also return Little's letter. Can easily believe that he is hard up: there may be other Shelley Committee-men who are hard up, and who nevertheless meet their legal liabilities.[1]

Yours always,
W. M. Rossetti

MS: BL.

1. WMR to Wise, 12 January 1890: ''When you last talked to me on the subject, I had understood you to say that the responsible and leading members of the Committee would be expected to pay £10 each towards making up the money due this month to Clay. Consequently I came to the meeting prepared to pay that sum. But, finding that the other members present were producing donations of much minor amount, I limited myself to £4. I don't quite understand what is the position which you personally occupy in this matter. I gather that you paid Clay £100, including a largish sum of your own private money, and that you expect to reimburse yourself pretty soon, partly out of those Committee donations, and partly out of incoming subscriptions for 1890. If however you are left in the lurch in any unfair degree, I would still manage to pay at once something beyond the £4 already produced — provided my colleagues also do not leave *me* thus in the lurch'' (BL).

459. TO THOMAS JAMES WISE

5 Endsleigh Gardens,
22 January 1890

Dear Wise,

I now address myself to your 2 letters.

It will be evident to you that, as I myself, prior to your first letter, started the proposal that I would make up my donation to £10 in case others would do the like, I can have no objection in principle to Forman's proposal. Still the details call for a little consideration.

As I understand it, you paid £100, your own private money, to Clay, and can at this moment, or very shortly hereafter, reimburse yourself out of money belonging to the Shelley Society. Therefore Clay has no further claim till 1 January 1891, and you are scatheless, and my first sentiment would be "sufficient for the day is the evil thereof."[1]

But you say that, if matters are left thus unaltered, we shall not have in 1890 funds for printing those books which ought to go to our subscribers as the equivalent of their subscriptions for 1890. Now upon this I ask my question 1 — What is the time of year at which we ought reasonably to order and to deliver those books for 1890? and is it correct to assume that, when that time comes round, we shall not in ordinary course be in possession of the necessary funds?

Then as to Forman's view that you, himself, Potts,[2] and I, ought to pay this year £10 each, while other persons, equally responsible in law, pay much less, or even nothing, I am a little disposed to jib at this. As I understand it, the *moral* responsibility rests with you and Furnivall, and perhaps with Potts as a 3rd; while the legal responsibility rests with a rather large number of persons. You certainly can confirm my statement that all orders for printing were given, not only without any active co-operation on my part, but without my being in any way consulted or apprised as to details. Therefore, before I decide to produce an extra £6 in company with only 3 other Committee-men, I should like to have a few details — thus

1. (What I have several times referred to) — a precise list of those Committee-men who are legally responsible, and the respective (approximate) sums for which they are legally responsible.

2. An account showing the various sums which have been paid by those legally responsible persons, in order to clear off the printing-debt. I fancy it would be found that I (taking into account my monthly 5/- etc.) am not in this respect behind any of my colleagues, with the sole exception of Potts and Ellis, and am ahead of most of them.

You say (or Buxton Forman said) that Alfred Forman,[3] Dobell,[4] Furnivall, Tegetmeier,[5] and Miss Blind, can't pay any such extra sums. Of Miss Blind I am sure this is true: as to the others have no real means of judging. Should have supposed that at least some of them could do something.

If it should be made to appear that I must in reason act upon *my own* proposal of paying an extra £6 in 1890, I should prefer to pay it in monthly instalments — i.e. instead of sending you 5/- a month, I would for 6 months send you £1.5.

I will retain Silsbee's postcard[6] for the present, and will some day dun him in one shape or another for the Shelley Society. I gather from his (slightly illegible) postcard that his address is "Hospital, Boston." Do you know any other?

Very many thanks about the Browning portrait:[7] I will bear in mind the stipulation as to not spoiling it.

Please remember (but only when convenient) that some items of my brother's MSS. etc. are to return to me — including pages to be cut out of a MS. book.

Sorry you have such severe work in the way of letter-writing for Shelley Society etc. Were it not also a labour of love, it would be a form of penal servitude.

Yours,
W. M. Rossetti

If at any time or in any way you find it convenient to inform any of our colleagues of the contents of this letter, I have no sort of objection.

Ought I to assume that in 1891 and ensuing years the demand upon me will be much the same as now in 1890 — some £10, more or less per year?

MS: BL.

1. "Sufficient unto the day ...," Matthew, 6:34.
2. Robert Alfred Potts, a founding member of the Shelley Society; wrote a bibliographical preface for the Society's facsimile edition of *Epipsychidion* (1887).
3. Alfred William Forman (1840-1925) published translations of the librettos of Wagner's operas, his rendering of the *Ring* being favorably received by the composer.
4. Bertram Dobell (1842-1914), bookseller, man of letters, friend of James Thomson ('B.V.').
5. William Bernhard Tegetmeier (1816-1912), naturalist, journalist, founding member of the Shelley Society.
6. MS. Diary, 22 January 1890: "Wise sends me a postcard from Silsbee, of whom he had had no news since he left London for Egypt, perhaps some 2 years ago. He is in Boston, in hospital, suffering from nervous dyspepsia which attacked him in Japan."
7. WMR was preparing his "Portraits of Robert Browning," *Magazine of Art*, 13 (1890), 181-88, 246-52, 261-67.

460. TO RICHARD GARNETT

5 Endsleigh Gardens,
23 January 1890

Dear Garnett,

Thanks for your note of 8 January about *Adonais*; also for a rightly paged copy of your *Milton* which reached me some little while ago.

As to *Adonais*, I am not pledged to any secrecy, but presume the person primarily concerned, F. S. Ellis, might not wish it to be talked about at present. He it was who wrote to me expressing an opinion that it would be a good work to bring out annotated editions of some of Shelley's medium-sized poems; and he asked whether I would undertake an *Adonais* if he would pay the cost — a very liberal and public spirited offer. I would willingly do *Adonais*, or, perhaps still *more* willingly, the *Witch of Atlas*: have today written to Ellis on this point, and, so far as I see, there is a considerable likelihood that one or other will thus be done pretty soon — I suppose *Adonais* the more probable.[1]

Yours always,
W. M. Rossetti

If I do take up the work, I should (having no previous experience of work of a precisely similar kind) require to inspect 2 or 3 books of a like class, so as to settle my ideas of what were best to be done. Perhaps you know of some book which you consider a *more* satisfactory model than others: if so, and if you would just let me know its name, you would oblige me once more.

MS: Texas.

1. MS. Diary, 25 January 1890: "Ellis ... continues to favour *Adonais* rather than the *Witch of Atlas.*" 31 January: "Ellis sends me a letter to him from the Clarendon Press, saying that they will consider the question of publishing the proposed annotated *Adonais*, and, if they assent, they will themselves undertake the expense. I am rather afraid that this would not suit me; for apparently my treatment of the poem would be subject to the approval of the Clarendon Press." 12 February: "The Delegates of the Clarendon Press write to me about *Adonais*: are willing to undertake the publication, and send me a form of agreement. I should receive 60% of the profits after reimbursement of expenses. A clause in the agreement, about submitting my MS. to sanction, stands ready cancelled: so there is every prospect of my undertaking the work." When the volume appeared in 1891, it was severely attacked for the deficiencies of its classical annotation by J. C. Collins in the *Pall Mall Gazette*, 15 April 1891, p. 3. A second edition, revised with the assistance of A. O. Prickard, fellow of New College, Oxford, was published in 1903.

461. TO THEODORE WATTS-DUNTON

5 Endsleigh Gardens,
29 April 1890

Dear Watts,

Thanks for your friendly attention in informing me of Howell's death:[1] I had not heard of it, and very likely (going about so little as I do) might not have heard of it for some while to come. I had totally lost sight of Howell since the summer of 1882: but for this circumstance, my general feeling on the subject would have been "I could have better spared a better man."

No doubt there must be, in Gabriel's letters to Howell, an appalling amount of unseemly chaff, and perhaps some very indiscreet references to individuals (one particularly[2]). I hardly know whether I should understand your letter as raising a suggestion that it would be well to see whether these letters could be recovered from Howell's legal representative.[3] His wife is dead: his daughter, I suppose, survives — aged I suppose something like 12. I don't see my way at present to any practical steps: would like a talk with you sometime or other.

There are two other matters we ought to talk about — that affair of the Letters-Memoir book, which I almost fancy you have decided to abandon (your latest proposal to me was to bring it out in the spring of 1889), but you have not *informed* me that it is abandoned; and the recovery, which was notified in my circle by Shields, of those cartoons by Gabriel which were supposed to have been lost from your house. If I remember rightly, these cartoons were Gabriel's property, consigned to you by the Morris firm when the partnership was dissolved; and they would thus be now the joint property of Christina and myself.

We have had a goodish deal of trouble lately: Lucy's chest bad from close of January; and at end of February our smallest girl Mary got a very bad dislocation of left elbow, not even yet entirely cured. We were away from London (but not any further off than Upper Norwood) most of this current April but are now resettled at home. Lucy got a good deal better at Norwood: is again less well (yet not greatly ill) since returning.

Love to Swinburne with yourself from

Yours always,
W. M. Rossetti

Thanks about the Browning portrait.

MS: BL. Extract in *Swinburne Library*, p. 129.

1. MS. Diary, 28 April 1890: "Watts writes to inform me of the death of Howell — a man whom I certainly did not esteem, but did none the less to a certain extent like." WMR quotes Prince Hal on the death of Falstaff (*1 Henry IV*, V. iv. 103).
2. A reading of DGR's letters in Cline does not suggest a candidate; if anything, the letters are discreet and dull. Perhaps the indiscreet ones were destroyed before the letters were acquired by Fairfax Murray (see Note 3, and Cline, p. 27).
3. MS. Diary, 10 June 1890: "Watts called at Somerset House.... A Miss [Alice] Chambers is Howell's Executrix.... She has come into possession of various letters addressed by Gabriel to Howell: I think, and so does Watts, that it would be desirable for me, if possible, to get a sight of these letters, and, if they seem unsuitable for strangers to deal with, then to see whether they are purchasable."

462. TO CHARLES FAIRFAX MURRAY

3 St. Edmund's Terrace,[1]
25 November 1890

Dear Murray,

Thanks for your note received this morning. I had looked at those items[2] yesterday, and my opinion was and is exactly what you express — that no line of any drawing and no letter of any writing is Gabriel's. I said so to the Clerk in the sale-room (the same to whom I spoke about it a month or so ago), and I then walked in to Mr. Hodge,[3] and said the same to him. He listened with courteous attention; said that, when the sale comes on, he will consider it his duty to announce that the authenticity of the handwriting has been strongly denied, but he hardly thinks that he ought to enter into such questions of connoisseurship as whether Gabriel did or could produce such verses and designs. In this he may be right, and I raised no objection. I did not *ask* him to tell me whence the items come, but suggested whether he would like himself to inform me: he replied that he did not at the moment recollect, but of course has by him the means of ascertaining the point.

It seems to me that the handwriting, also the designs, may very probably be Dunn's. I am perfectly familiar with Dunn's ordinary handwriting in letters etc.: the scribbled pencil-writing does not bear a marked resemblance to that, but I consider that it *may* be the same. On the further cover (inside) of the sketchbook are 3 or 4 addresses written in a very neat clerk-like hand: this is very considerably like Dunn's: I observe too (in the catalogue) that there is a letter addressed to a friend at the Lizard, Cornwall, and Dunn is a Cornishman. Do you happen to know anything of him now — or for certain whether he is alive? I doubt whether I have seen him later than year 1883: he had then fallen into very bad habits (I was sorry to learn), and I think it more than likely he is no longer alive.[4]

This evening I hear with pain that W. B. Scott is dead[5] — died on Saturday at Penkill.

Thank you we are all well here — more or less. Thus far the house seems to suit my wife's health.

Yours very truly,

W. M. Rossetti

I happened to find Morris in the saleroom. He was not aware, until I pointed it out, that anything ascribed to Gabriel was in the sale. Glancing at the verses, he laughed at the idea that Gabriel could have written them, but he paid no *attention* to the affair.

MS: Texas.

1. WMR moved to this address on 25 October 1890, Lucy believing that its higher location between Regent's Park and Primrose Hill would benefit her health. Richard Garnett had lived there until his recent appointment as Keeper of Printed Books at the British Museum necessitated his occupying premises at the Museum. FMB lived at No. 1 following his return from Manchester in 1887. WMR left Endsleigh Gardens "with regret, almost amounting to sorrow, and expecting, on various grounds, to find life less commodious at 3 St. Edmund's Terrace" (MS. Diary, 14 September 1890).

2. Lots 215-18 in a sale at Sotheby's, 26 November 1890. Three of the lots were withdrawn; lot 218, "A Folio scrapbook including 15 water-colour drawings by Dante G. Rossetti," sold for £6.10.

3. Either Edward Grose Hodge (d. 1907) or his son Tom (1860-1939), who joined the firm in the late 1870s (F. Herrmann, *Sotheby's, Portrait of an Auction House*, 1980).

4. Murray to WMR, 26 November 1890: "Dunn was alive a few days ago — I saw him walking in the Fulham Road. The last I heard of him was that he was acting as secretary to Wills the dramatist and painter — and I should think he is still connected with him" (AP).

5. Murray to WMR, 26 November 1890: "I am sorry to hear of the death of W. B. Scott.... I suppose Miss Boyd inherits much that remains of his artistic possessions — he would hardly leave them to Mrs. Scott?" (AP).

463. TO ALICE BOYD

3 St. Edmund's Terrace,
5 January 1891

My dear Miss Boyd,

I received with sympathy and affection your touching little letter of about a month ago, and should have answered earlier, but for the reluctance one feels to probe and reprobe a painful and permanent wound. Certain it is that — not to speak of you — I have lost a friend[1] hardly to be paragoned among the oldest of those I have known or still know; and of any recent or prospective friends (if friends is not too strong a term for the acquaintanceships of one's latter-day years) how futile were it to speak.

I read that article in the *Athenaeum*.[2] It treats the subject with a fair allowance of space and of detailed consideration, and the general drift of it is respectful and friendly: but I certainly found in it some very serious gaps as to matters which might and ought to have been said, and some positive slips as to points of fact. It would be a good thing if all of our dear friend's best and most permanent work, whether verse or prose, could be republished in a collected form.

Has the news yet reached you that his successor in the Chelsea house, Dr. Marshall, died the other day — of gouty bronchitis? I was told so yesterday, and was much concerned to hear it. Had known Marshall — though not with extreme intimacy — for some 35 years.

Please give my love to Letitia: I trust she goes on pretty well in health and general condition. Or possibly she is no longer at Penkill?

Our new house seems to suit the health of Lucy — who sends love to both you and Letitia — very well: her bronchial troubles have not as yet recurred there to any appreciable extent. She is troubled at present about cough-attacks of the two younger girls: but one may hope these may pass away pretty soon. London has been a monument of frost and fog these 6 weeks or so: today *much* frost (after partial considerable thaw) but at least no fog.

Yours with sincere affection,
W. M. Rossetti

I dare say you hear occasionally from Christina: she and Lucy are among your heartiest admirers and well-wishers.

MS: UBC.

1. WBS. WMR wrote to Alice Boyd shortly after his death that "there are few persons who loved our dear old friend better than I did ... and none perhaps who had a more firm belief or high appreciation of his powers of mind and solidity of character" (undated letter; UBC).
2. Obituary of WBS; 29 November 1890, p. 745.

464. TO LUCY ROSSETTI

Somerset House,
7 September 1891,
12¼

Dearest Luie,

Nothing of yours received since I wrote last.

I went round to your papa yesterday towards 3, intending to return to my own dinner at 5. He asked me however to join him and Cave Thomas at 7½, which I did. I am afraid we might have struck an outsider as a rather "fogramish" trio, but we passed a cheerful evening enough. Your papa seems for the present to be free from any *grave* inconvenience. I observed that some little more had been done to the *Bridgewater* picture[1] — chiefly the boy's barge right in front.

From your papa in the afternoon (but not from Thomas himself in the evening) I heard that poor Thomas is in rather a fix about payment for those pictures he executed for Marylebone Church.[2] The commission came to Thomas from Llewelyn Davies,[3] then (but not now) Rector of the Church. Half of the money for all or some of the pictures was paid. Thomas now writes to Davies asking that the balance may be paid: but Davies replies that he was merely one subscriber among others, and that no further responsibility attaches to himself. A serious problem appears to be — Does any real responsibility attach to *anyone*, and if so to whom, and how could it be enforced? I understood from your papa that Thomas was at first, and very naturally, a good deal put out by this trouble: yesterday however he appeared to be in as good spirits as usual, and I did not take it upon me to ask him any question.

Recently Iza Hardy[4] called on your papa. She did not seem strong, nor her eyes well, but on the whole things seemed to be progressing pretty well with her.

You may like to read the enclosed letters.

546

What seems to be the prospect as to the length of your stay at Bournemouth now?

Yours in love,
William

MS: AP.

1. *The Opening of the Bridgewater Canal* for Manchester Town Hall. MS. Diary, 10 November 1891: "Brown ... required to see Cave Thomas, in order to get him measured for a last-century wig, in which he is to sit for the figure of Boulton [? James Brindley, the engineer] in the *Bridgewater Canal* picture.... Both yesterday and today he has been painting on the picture." 11 February 1892: "Brown ... has now got on very near the end of his picture ... but finds that something considerable still remains to be done to get the general effect right." 21 February: "Brown looked in. He is now near the end of his picture ... and is sending out invitations to people to view it on the last 3 days of the current week." 23 February: "I went to see Brown's picture, now practically completed. It comes brilliant and conspicuous in colour, and has much force and variety in the very telling composition; though in some respects the execution is not quite so firm and certain as it would have been a few years ago. In its place on the walls of the Town Hall it will tell out well." 10 March: "Brown went off to Manchester today with his *Bridgewater Canal* picture." 18 March: "Brown returned from Manchester, where he has been fixing in the Town Hall his picture of the *Bridgewater Canal*. Unfortunately, in the fixing-process, some of the pigment flaked off, and he had to work at repainting. This is the first time such a mishap has occurred, and he has no settled idea as to the cause of it — perhaps some excess of medium used in the course of painting."
2. Christ Church, Cosway Street. An undated newspaper clipping in the Marylebone Public Library describes Thomas's *The Ascension* (15 ft. high by 8 ft. 6 in. wide) on the east wall above the altar. Pevsner notes *The Diffusion of Gifts*, "altar-back, 1867, in the Early Renaissance style" (*London*, 2:329).
3. John Llewelyn Davies (1826-1916), follower of F. D. Maurice, historian of the Working Men's College (1904), vicar of Christ Church, 1856-89.
4. Daughter of Thomas Duffus Hardy (1804-78), deputy keeper of the Public Record Office, and Mary Ann Hardy (d. 1891), novelist. She published some thirty novels, 1872-1920. The Hardys were long-standing friends of FMB.

465. TO THOMAS JAMES WISE

3 St. Edmund's Terrace,
13 September 1891

Dear Wise,

It is only on Friday that I finished — or rather all-but finished — a Lecture (on Leopardi) which I am to deliver in Oxford in November:[1] and I am hardly disposed to set-to at once upon another Lecture, also for November. I am willing however to do *some* Shelley Lecture, for which the January meeting would apparently be a suitable time. Have not yet succeeded in fixing my mind upon a subject: but will do so and write again.[2]

Our audiences have of late become so insignificant that I sometimes think we might as well drop the Lectures altogether: but, if colleagues don't agree as to this, I will do what I can. I quite assent to your proposal to miss out October.

I enclose my 5/- for current month.

Your
W. M. Rossetti

MS: AP.

1. On the 24th WMR gave the third annual lecture on foreign literature at the Taylor Institution,

Dowden having given the first and Pater the second; published in *Studies in European Literature, being the Taylorian Lectures, 1889-1899* (1900).

2. See Letter 466, Note 1.

466. TO THOMAS JAMES WISE

3 St. Edmund's Terrace,
4 October 1891

Dear Wise,

I know of no objection to your putting me down for the Lecture in February.

The question of the subject for the Lecture has continued present to my mind, but I have found it not very easy to decide. On the whole I am inclined to take "Shelley and Leopardi," which may be entered on the card.[1] Garnett, in his very good article on Leopardi in the *Encyclopaedia Britannica*,[2] pointed out 2 or 3 instances of a certain parallelism between the position and the writings of these 2 poets; and I, in the course of my readings for the Lecture which I lately wrote on Leopardi, had occasion to confirm what Garnett says, but in *that* Lecture I have left the question wholly untouched. I think one might develop the matter not uninterestingly in a separate Lecture — which would moreover have the advantage of starting on a track new to our Society.

Someone ought to deal with *The Centenary of Shelley*: exhibiting more particularly (so it appears to me) the progress which the ideas enunciated by Shelley have made up to the present time. Either Stopford Brooke or Salt would seem to be a good man for undertaking this — no doubt a better man than I should myself be. If you could see your way to suggesting this to either of them, I think you would be doing us good service.

My 5/- shall follow in a day or two.

Yours very truly,
W. M. Rossetti

MS: BL.

1. MS. Diary, 10 February 1892: "Shelley Society meeting. I read my paper on Shelley and Leopardi, which was received with much commendation: the audience however was exceedingly scanty, confined to the few persons who had attended the business-meeting prior to the lecture." 17 March: "Some little while ago I was requested by Mr. Hugill to redeliver at Hampden House, Somers Town, my lecture on Shelley and Leopardi — Hampden House being an institution resembling in some degree the Toynbee Hall of the East End. I did this work this evening: a very attentive, and I think interested audience, which may have amounted to 80 or thereabouts."

2. Ninth edition, 1882.

467. TO THOMAS JAMES WISE

3 St. Edmund's Terrace,
11 October 1891

Dear Wise,

Would you please reply at your convenience to the enclosed letter from Miss (I suppose *Miss*) Walker:[1] I have not written in reply.

Glad you like the Leopardi subject.[2]

I hardly know what steps (not involving undesirable expense) could be taken for getting outsiders to attend the November meeting for the Centenary discussion.

A paragraph on the subject would I *suppose* be admitted into the *Athenaeum*: if you think this desirable, I will write and forward a paragraph.[3]

Furnivall called here last Thursday and spoke to me as to proposed reperformance of the *Cenci*, and ways and means for carrying it out.[4] He and I agreed that the best step to take *first* would be to write to Lady Shelley, and see about enlisting her concurrence: I have this morning written a letter to her, and am posting it to Furnivall, for him to consider, and if approved to send on.

I believe a No. of our Shelley Transactions has been published for this year,[5] and sent out: no copy of it has as yet reached me.

5/- enclosed.

Yours,
W. M. Rossetti

MS: BL.

1. Member of the Shelley Society.
2. See Letter 466, Note 1.
3. 21 November 1891, p. 687.
4. MS. Diary, 5 November 1891: "At the request of Furnivall (more particularly) I drew up lately a circular regarding the Shelley Centenary of next year; setting forth that the Shelley Society wish to reperform the *Cenci* in honour of the occasion, but must partly rely upon extraneous support for the purpose, and inviting outsiders therefore to subscribe £1.1 for 2 tickets, thereby constituting themselves members of the Society for 1892 — also suggesting that they should come down with some further funds if eventually needed for covering expenses. They are asked moreover to come to next meeting, 11 November, of the Society, and debate any matters relating to the Centenary. I have not *much* hope from this well-meant effort, and religiously hope that the Society itself, and its Committee, will not allow themselves to be let in for any further expense, which our funds are wholly inadequate to meet. In the evening I sent off the 9 copies of the printed circular which were consigned to me — to Garnett, Swinburne, York Powell, Mrs. Call ... etc." 12 November: "Received from Salt the short letter he has written, to be printed in various newspapers, inviting subscriptions for the *Cenci* performance. He and Furnivall wish my name and address to appear on the letter: I assent, expressing however a preference for Salt's name to appear along with mine. Letters in reply, addressed to me, are to be sent on by me to Salt." 5 February 1892: "Wrote to George Moore about the proposed *Cenci* performance.... He was entrusted (as representing the Independent Theatre Society) with the responsible duty of cutting-down the play for the stage (a process admitted very generally to be indispensable), and he shortened it very considerably indeed. By the advice of myself, and also of Furnivall, he has now restored ... Scene 1 of Act 1, and he wrote asking me whether I think the drama, as it would stand after this restoration, could still be improved. I reply that ... I still have some doubt whether the whole of the Trial-scene ought to be cut out, and whether some secondary personages, especially Orsino, should be reduced to such very small dimensions as he has given them." 10 February: "The Prospects of the *Cenci* performance seem a little hazy at present.... Alma Murray declined positively to perform, and Vezin also declines — though it seems to be thought that he may perhaps yet consent. Furnivall, Todhunter, and Salt, assisted by Bernard Shaw, are to see further about it. As to the locale, the notion preferred at present is to recur to the Grand Theatre, Islington — which could not improbably be again obtained gratis, as in 1886."
5. *Shelley Society's Papers, Part 2.*

468. TO ALGERNON CHARLES SWINBURNE

3 St. Edmund's Terrace
29 November 1891

Dear Swinburne,

It is indeed an age since we have collogued: but out of sight is not always out of mind, and there are few friends or poets that I think of oftener than I do of you.

I have not yet seen *Dieu*[1] — a rhapsody over the report of which you and I have I think chaffed more than once erewhile. What you now say of it is very interesting and inciting, and I shall look out for the expected *Fortnightly*. Probably you are aware that there are two men — Yeats and Tristram Ellis[2] — following now in your vestiges, and engaged upon a large exposition and systematization of Blake's religious *arcana*, to accompany a reproduction of his Prophetic Books. They regard him as highly elaborate and self-consistent throughout — not at all frenzied or chaotic.

A writer I have studied of late is Leopardi — well known to you, I may surmise, from of old. I was asked lately to deliver at the Taylor Institution of Oxford a lecture on some Italian subject, and I selected Leopardi. My lecture was delivered last Tuesday, and did not mince matters about his atheism, pessimism, etc.: and I was really surprised at the calm complacency, and indeed high encomium, with which it was received by various academic and church dignitaries, such as Paget[3] the new Dean of Christ Church, etc. Where are the good old days of the expulsion of Shelley for the *Necessity of Atheism*, the howling over *Poems and Ballads*, etc. etc.?

Love to Watts — and to yourself all affection from this small household of the faith.

Yours,
W. M. Rossetti

MS: Berg.

1. Hugo's "great fragmentary poem" (*SL*, 6:24), intended as the completion of *La Légende des Siècles*, was published posthumously in 1891. Swinburne's article "Victor Hugo: *Dieu*" appeared in the *Fortnightly Review*, n.s. 51 (January 1892), 109-14 (rptd. *Studies in Prose and Poetry*).
2. Should be Edwin John Ellis, who with Yeats published *The Works of William Blake*, ed. with a Memoir and Interpretation, 3 vols., 1893. For two visits by Yeats and Ellis to WMR, see *Blake*, p. 9.
3. Francis Paget (1851-1911), dean of Christ Church until 1901, when he became bishop of Oxford.

469. TO HORACE LOGO TRAUBEL

3 St. Edmund's Terrace,
8 March 1892

Dear Sir,

Two or three weeks ago I received the copy kindly forwarded to me of Whitman's last edition.[1] Your letter which accompanied it, dated 20 January, only reached me the other day: it had gone down in the wreck of the steamer Eider,[2] but was recovered and sent on to me.

I need not tell you or Whitman with how much affection I regard his book, sent to me by him as from out of the jaws of the tomb. The sight of it has incited me to re-read the entire book, old poems as well as new: and I once again feel, what I have never doubted since 1855, that Whitman is one of the great spirits of the age, destined to leave his mark on this and other centuries. Would you give him my love and reverence, if manageable.

At the crisis of his recent illness I was of course anxious from day to day: Whitmanite friends in Lancashire[3] (not *personally* known to me) used to send me telegrams. If Whitman congratulates himself upon having surmounted this formidable stage of his illness, I also heartily congratulate him.

You kindly say that you "may from time to time write me concerning Whitman's condition." I should feel highly grateful to you for any such attention.

Yours very truly,
W. M. Rossetti

MS: LC.

1. *Leaves of Grass* 1891-92, the last edition issued by Whitman.
2. The Eider was stranded on the rocks of Atherfield Ledge, Isle of Wight, on 31 January 1892.
3. Members of the so-called Eagle Street College, a group which met in Bolton from 1885 to study the poet's works. It was named after the house in Eagle Street where they gathered, which belonged to an architectural assistant, James W. Wallace (1853-1926), who with a Scottish physician John Johnston (1852-1927) were the principal members of the group. Both Wallace and Johnston made pilgrimages to Camden, and published accounts of their visits. MS. Diary, 28 March 1892: "The papers notify Walt Whitman's death. I cannot regret it, as he had for so long past been reduced to the last extremity: we shall see how far his death may influence the establishment, earlier or later, of his fame. It happens that I am just now reading through *Leaves of Grass* once again.... I am just at the end of it, and still consider it a poetic document of high inspiration, in itself and in its contagion upon others."

470. TO GEORGE FREDERIC WATTS

3 St. Edmund's Terrace,
14 April 1892

Dear Mr. Watts,

I was extremely gratified at receiving your letter of 30 December, and should have replied long ago, but that the practical purport of your letter entailed some delay.

Your proposal is that at some time after resettling in London this spring you would be willing to paint a portrait of my sister Christina, to accompany other portraits forming your munificent gift to the nation.[1] This is an offer such as the most ambitious of authors would jump at: and my sister, who is one of the most modest of them, cannot refuse herself such a privilege.

Her secluded habits and shy disposition make the effort of presenting herself in your studio a rather abashing one: so I undertook to accompany her on the first occasion. Official and other occupations don't allow of my taking any or every day at my own option, and particularly just at present I could not absent myself from my Office: but I think that on and from 20 May (omitting 26) I, and my sister under my escort, could take any weekday which might be quite suitable to your own convenience.

As to the portrait of my brother lately at the Victorian Exhibition,[2] I scarcely know whether or not to agree with you in preferring to it the original likeness which Leyland owned. I think the original exceeds (as was natural under the circumstances affecting the two cases) in the look of personal presence and actuality; on the other hand I think that the duplicate exceeds in suavity of expression, and in the sort of beauty which accompanies this, and that it is not less of a definite likeness.

With thanks,

Yours very truly,
W. M. Rossetti

MS: Bodleian.

1. Some of Watts's portraits of his contemporaries were given to the National Portrait Gallery during his lifetime; others were bequeathed and came to the Gallery over a period of time under terms drawn up by his executors (*G. F. Watts, The Hall of Fame*, National Portrait Gallery [1975], pp. 6-8).

2. Watts's duplicate, painted in 1890, of his c. 1871 portrait of DGR. For an earlier WMR letter to Watts on the duplicate, see M. S. Watts, *George Frederic Watts*, 1:269-70, where two sentences from the present letter are conflated with the earlier letter.

471. TO LUCY ROSSETTI

Somerset House,
28 April 1892,
4½

Dearest Luie,

Glad you saw a rainbow yesterday, to put a little cheer into you: I see in the papers something about a recent aurora borealis. London weather has been very dismal for most of the hours since noon of yesterday — rain, wind, penetrating chill, etc. Let us hope for better things.

Please let me hear how Arthur goes on — and more especially yourself.

About Cathy, my full belief is that she has some good qualities, and some bad ones: in this she resembles myself certainly, and several other people probably. Such being the conditions of the case, it would seem to be well to make the best of her good qualities, and not lay special stress upon the bad ones. For my own personal part in the matter, I could not assume an attitude of persistent and stiff hostility to your half-sister, my father-in-law's daughter, my friend's widow, and my own half-sister-in-law.[1] "How often shall my brother offend against me, and I forgive him? Till 7 times?" "I say not unto thee till 7 times, but until 70 times 7."[2] A teaching which has still something to say for itself, in these days of Socialist and Anarchist evangels, illuminated by some *feux de joie* of dynamite.

Of course, dear, anything that you like to tell me about Cathy I am prepared — and always have been prepared — to hear. It is for you to consider whether or no.

As I was preparing last evening to look in on your father,[3] he sent round to ask whether I had heard from you. I went in to him, and spent there some 1½ hours. He was in the best of tempers and the best of spirits, and showed no symptom of any physical suffering whatever. I asked him about that abscess: he says it might almost pass for a pile — but it is not a pile, nor yet a boil, but a hard surface which might result in an abscess. The Doctor gave him some medicine to use, and as yet there is only that sensation of hardness, without definite pain.

All love from
Fofus

MS: AP.

1. MS. Diary, 3 January 1892, records strife between the Browns and the Hueffers: "All the Hueffers have for the present quitted Brown's house, and are again domiciled in Brook Green. This

was immediately consequent upon a rather unpleasant though perhaps trifling scene at our house on Christmas-day: I hardly understand whether or not the separation is likely to be permanent or prolonged, or merely casual, and just at present à *propos*. Certainly my own experience is that Brown had in many instances, and indeed systematically, been very forbearing with the two youths [Ford and Oliver], who were by no means so dutiful or deferential as they might and should have been."

2. Matthew, 18:21-22.

3. FMB had recently begun "the sketch of his last picture for Manchester Town Hall — the subject of the Bridge-fight in the Parliamentary War [*Bradshaw's Defence of Manchester*]. It seems to promise a telling composition of a popular kind — the number of figures small in proportion to the subject-matter" (MS. Diary, 15 April 1892).

472. TO THOMAS JAMES WISE

3 St. Edmund's Terrace,
8 May 1892

Dear Wise,

Today for the first time I have found a convenient opportunity for addressing Mrs. Crawshay[1] about the subscription — something else turning up which warranted my writing to her.

I don't feel very sure of appearing at Furnivall's on Wednesday. As I understand it, there is (to all appearance) no paper to be read, and only the *Cenci* matter to be discussed[2] — in which my part is but a passive one. I may here repeat my opinion — 1. That we can't act *Cenci* if the law is clearly or even disputably against us: 2. That, unless a *positive* arrangement for both Theatre and Actors shall have been made by Wednesday, we must wholly relinquish every idea of acting: 3. That we may (though I think it little use or attraction) then see about a recitation or reading: 4. That in this case we must offer to return subscriptions — and I regret to say my belief is most of the *Cenci* subscribers will call for their money back again.

The whole project has proved an unfortunate one: but we should be none the less obliged to Furnivall and the others who have taken a horrid amount of trouble over the working of it.

Yours,
W. M. Rossetti

I am very busy (double work) at Somerset House, and therefore the less inclined for engagements occupying the evening, unless there is some substantial motive for them.

MS: BL.

1. Member or prospective member of the Shelley Society.
2. MS. Diary, 13 April 1892: "Shelley Society meeting.... Numerous difficulties are besetting the project of a theatrical performance of *The Cenci*, mainly through questions concerning the Licensing of Plays: it looks to me as if the whole affair would be reduced to a sort of *caput mortuum*, hardly worth persisting in. However, Furnivall and Todhunter don't wish to drop the project." The play was not performed.

473. TO LUCY ROSSETTI

Somerset House,
20 May 1892,
12½

Dearie Lu,

Yours of yesterday received. Sorry that you have been feeling some inconvenience at that spot of the throat: quite right that you should be as heedful and quiet in all such matters as you can. Helen and Mary ought to benefit from a little overhauling from you *en tête-à-tête*.

Your father spent some while with me last evening. He exhibited every symptom of good spirits, and did not in any faintest degree allude to any jarring with the Manchester people.[1] He spoke of his new painting[2] as now well started, and appeared well contented with it. (I have seen and like the design: but have not seen any painting — am now continuing this letter at home.) Gill's medicine of which I had given him the prescription, cured his lumbago-trouble at once: but he is now again bothered a good deal with the eczema. I recurred to that old letter from George Tupper: he was disposed to bear the matter in mind, and took away the Doctor's address.

Cathy came in with your father, and for a short while Ford: they both seemed cordial, and gave no evidence of a "fantasia Hufferica."[3] I told all the party about my £500 — so, if ever it should come pat to refer to that matter, nothing would be gained by reticence.

You will be grieved to see the concluding part of the enclosed from Christina, which reached me after my return home: she means apparently that a surgical operation will in all likelihood be needed. I hope she will take chloroform or some other anaesthetic, but don't feel wholly confident that she will. It makes me uneasy — though I daresay all may pass off well, and even beneficially.

Leaving Office I had run in to the R.A. — wanting more especially to see a picture by Melton Fisher[4] — Venetian moonlight and Chinese-lantern light — of which Lord Iddesleigh[5] and some others have talked to me. It is highly remarkable, but wants charm, and something of delicacy. Perhaps the best thing in the place is the *Kiss* by Tadema. I don't care much for Leighton,[6] though one or two of his have great boldness in a certain way — nor very much for Millais,[7] nor for Orchardson's[8] *St. Helena*. There are numerous works very strong in impressionist-realistic handling: the new departure which is transforming the face of exhibitions.

I shall not, until matters become clearer, mention about Christina to the children or others. Micks,[9] back today, had heard about you from the Long family — whom I first mentioned to him.

Your own
William

MS: AP.

1. F. M. Hueffer writes of "the opprobrium with which the panel of the *Bridgewater Canal* was received on its instalment at Manchester," and the demand of "the Committee of Decoration ... that the last panel should be submitted for their sanction before its installation" (*Ford Madox Brown*, p. 394).
2. See Letter 471, Note 3.
3. See Letter 471, Note 1.

4. Samuel Melton Fisher (1860-1939), painted portraits, and subjects in Italianate settings (Wood). Graves gives *A Summer Night* as the title of the picture.

5. Walter Stafford Northcote, Earl of Iddesleigh (1845-1927), vice-chairman of the Board of Inland Revenue, 1886-92, and chairman, April-July 1892.

6. *And the sea gave up the dead which were in it* — *Revelation*, *20:13*; *At the Fountain*; *The Garden of Hesperides*; *Bacchante*; *Clytie.*

7. *Halcyon Weather*; *Blow, blow, thou winter wind*; *The little speedwell's darling blue* — Tennyson.

8. William Quiller Orchardson (1832-1910), Scottish genre and portrait painter, exhibited at the R.A. from 1863. WMR first reviewed him in 1867, when he identified "tact" as the leading characteristic of *Talbot and the Countess of Auvergne*, but questioned "placing an extremely high value upon his artistic aims and methods" (*Chronicle*, 18 May 1867, p. 182).

9. Robert Micks (1825-1902; knighted in 1892) entered the Inland Revenue in 1846. He was Receiver General for Ireland, and subsequently secretary until his retirement in 1894.

474. TO LUCY ROSSETTI

3 St. Edmund's Terrace,
22 May 1892,
11 a.m.

Dearest Lu,

I write in much sorrow and oppression of mind. That affair of Christina proves to be of the most grave and dismaying kind — I grieve to write the word, cancer. What she tells me is this. For some little while past, say 2 months, she has been conscious at times of a certain sensation in the left breast: it has never once amounted to what she would call pain: and a double lump can be felt. She spoke to Stewart, who has as yet treated the case with medicines, and she referred to cancer: he did not definitely say that such it is, but she understands him to imply it. She is now told that severe pain may shortly be expected unless an operation is performed: so on Wednesday it *is* to be performed. (I presume the breast, or some large part of it, will be removed.) The operator will be Lawson[1] — whom Christina has now already seen: she had hitherto known of him as a highly distinguished Oculist, but learns that he is also eminent in general surgery. Stewart will be present, and, to administer the anaesthetic, ether, Dr. Bailey.[2] Stewart tells her that, when the operation is over (in her own house), she will have to be attended by 2 nurses for a week — then by one nurse for a fortnight further — and that after that she may expect to resume her ordinary home-work much as usual. Of course she contemplates immediate death as a *possibility*. She looks ill, but not *extremely* ill; spoke calmly and firmly, without concealing some natural sinking of heart at what awaits her; and even branched off into ordinary talk at times. I offered to stay in her house these few days: at this she was pleased, but she did not accept the offer.[3] It happens that that very Wednesday will be a public holiday (Queen's Birthday).

The children (returning from *Henry VIII*) were with me in the cab, but I did not take them into Christina's house, nor have I said a syllable to them, even to the effect of her being more than commonly ill. Olive seems to observe that I am dispirited, but has not asked any questions.

I informed Christina that I had sent her letter on to you. She regretted that this additional harass should have been imposed on you, but of course did not *object*.

So she understands that you, and you alone, will for the present know fully how matters stand.

I will not enter here into any other subject, having no heart for any: indeed there would not be *much* to say anyhow. The children are well.

Your own
William

MS: AP.

1. George Lawson (1831-1903), surgeon-oculist to Queen Victoria from 1886.
2. George Hewlett Bailey, chloroformist at the London Dental Hospital (*Churchill's Medical Directory* 1892).
3. WMR to Lucy Rossetti, 23 May 1892: "I need not say that my spirits are not much more cheerful than when I wrote yesterday. Saw Christina this morning, who bears herself bravely indeed. I offered to stay in the house on Wednesday: she evidently preferred that I should do so, and therefore I shall be in the house while the operation is going on (but not in the *room*), some hour, not yet fixed, in the afternoon: and shall stay for the evening — possibly the night" (AP).

475. TO LUCY ROSSETTI

Somerset House,
24 May 1892,
3 p.m.

Dearest Lu,

Thanks for your affectionate letter received this morning. I saw Christina again this morning, and handed her the note which you had enclosed: she *highly appreciated* the sympathy expressed, and returned you her most affectionate love.

Tomorrow at 2½ the operation is to take place. Christina is told that, to give the ether proper effect, she should not eat soon before that is administered: so she proposes to make a full breakfast (not certainly under circumstances much conducing to appetite), and then to eat no more until she recovers consciousness. She wants me to come round only after lunch-hour in my own house: I shall remain certainly till the late evening, and seem most likely to pass the night in Torrington Square. When that shocking stage of the matter is over, let us trust that some other stage, still more shocking, will not rapidly ensue.

This affair of my passing Wednesday night at Christina's would unexplained seem so odd at home that I thought it needful yesterday to tell Olive (not Arthur) exactly thus much: That Christina is very seriously ill, and under surgical treatment, and that I mean to be with her on Wednesday. I asked her not to say anything to anybody, not even to her grandpapa: the chief reason for this is that Christina has a (to me) very natural though perhaps somewhat extreme dislike of the idea of any newspaper-paragraphs — "We regret to understand that the distinguished poetess" etc. etc.

I went round yesterday to the Dentist Carter,[1] who seems to have done me some substantial good. Pardon my mentioning this trifle at the tail of another so terrible and harassing crisis.

Your own
William

This will be my last letter, according to the prospect of your returning on Thursday.

Christina seems fully braced up to the requisite effort and endurance, and even says she is getting to feel — "The sooner now the better."[2]

MS: AP.

1. *POLD* 1892 lists Edward George Carter and Henry Charles Carter, both surgeon-dentists of 181 Edgware Road.

2. WMR stayed at Torrington Square from 1:30 p.m. on 25 May to 9:30 a.m. on 26 May. For his diary entries of 26, 28 May, and 12 June on CGR's illness, see *FLCR*. MS. Diary contains additional entries, two of which are worth quoting: 31 May: "Lucy, for the first time, saw Christina for a few minutes: thought her pulled down and languid, though her progress continues to be all that could have been hoped for, and more." 1 June: "Saw Christina: she was conversable, but says she is in a low state, with intervals of excited fancy. I suppose this may be partly due to the medicines containing opium with which she has as yet been treated: I understand a different medicine will begin tomorrow."

476. TO CHRISTINA ROSSETTI

Somerset House,
Thursday,
[26 May 1892]

Dearest Christina,

I write these few words, to be left by me for you when I call this afternoon to enquire. Of course I don't know exactly what news I shall hear in the afternoon, but am fain to hope that it will be of the same general tenor as the encouraging news I have hitherto received — indeed I *believe* it will be so.

That such a formidable matter should have passed off with as yet so little absolute suffering seems almost miraculous. You are certainly offering up your acceptable thanksgivings for such a mercy: I also offer mine in a certain way which (though partially) you would not wholly disapprove of.

I know that early last evening you made an affectionate suggestion that I could have a look at you: but this Stewart had positively forbidden, one great object now being to keep you in repose — so I abstained. When I again saw Stewart towards 10 at night I referred to the matter, and he seemed to me almost a little put out at its being so much as named. He says I should not see you for 3 days or so. I consider therefore that I ought not to start the subject at all until the afternoon of Saturday. I trust then to call, and learn whether or not it is fitting I should see you for a few minutes. Of course in one form or another we should continue getting regular news of you meanwhile.

I saw my good Aunt[1] yesterday. She was *very* clear and consecutive — herself starting *Rugby Chapel*[2] at a moment when I seemed run dry for talk. Lucy will, I still suppose, be back this evening.

Much love mingled with not a little admiration from

Your
William

MS: AP.

1. Eliza.
2. By Matthew Arnold.

477. TO GEORGE FREDERIC WATTS

3 St. Edmund's Terrace,
12 June 1892

Dear Mr. Watts,

My sister and I are greatly obliged for your kind letter of the 9th — I regret extremely to say that my sister has lately been going through the crisis of a very serious illness, and is still in bed, and will certainly be disabled for some time to come from any such exertion as that of going out and sitting for a portrait. If her condition should admit of her doing so by that time, she is to go down to the seaside within 8 or 10 days from now, and I am likely to accompany her. It would be superfluous for her to assure you how much indebted to you she felt for the more than kind and flattering proposal that you volunteered, and how reluctantly she (for the present at all events) finds herself compelled to forego its execution.[1]

Believe me
Gratefully and truly yours,
W. M. Rossetti

MS: Bodleian.

1. See Letter 470.

478. TO LUCY ROSSETTI

17 Brunswick Road,
Brighton,
23 June 1892,
8½ a.m.

Dearest Lu,

Though I wouldn't be *hounded* into writing you a fancy-letter yesterday, I set-to as soon as I am up this morning, and even before Christina and the nurse are in the room for breakfast. I reached Brighton in brilliant sunshine, and found Christina on a sofa, as well as could be looked for. She says that on Tuesday she got into the railway-carriage well enough: but *in* the carriage was extremely prostrate for the earlier part of the journey. She then rallied somewhat, and has since continued rather mending — feeling some perceptible accession of strength. Since the hour of my arrival she has not left the house: but had done so yesterday morning, going about on the Parade in a Bath chair. I hear (just now as I write) from the nurse that Christina has passed a fair night.

This house is a goodish one, clean and well kept. Miss Hughes the landlady spoke to me about Olive, recollecting her well and liking her much. "Tina," I understand, is now at St. Leonards.

Our hours are — breakfast 8½ (but Christina, it now seems to me, will have *her* breakfast in bed — it *is* so): dinner 1½: tea 4 (I missed this yesterday): supper 8. I went out, by myself, on the Pier in the afternoon — it is undergoing much reconstruction, and I looked at a very pleasant camera-obscura view of Brighton, and the sands and sea; also in the evening on the Parade. Have subscribed to a circulating library, and got the first 2 volumes of Carlyle's Correspondence edited by Norton.[1]

The sun went in towards 4 yesterday, and since then the weather is rather dim — rain this morning rather brisk. I suspect it will continue most of the day.

I don't think that Christina is in any way dissatisfied with her nurse — name Miss Bidgen. The latter is a little brisk or sharp in manner, but seems to me attentive and well-qualified: she evidently considers that patients require to be "kept up to the mark" — not allowed to sink into mere despondency and inertia: and herein she must no doubt be right. She attended Maria — but not in the final stages of her illness. Of course I see a good deal of her, as she has meals etc. along with us.

Love to all kids — especially dear little Helen. The table goes moving under me as I write, which teazes

A certain Character

Christina seems pretty well satisfied now that, to get any adequate benefit, she will need to remain in Brighton a fortnight.

MS: AP.

1. *Early Letters of Carlyle, 1814-26*, ed. C. E. Norton, 1886.

479. TO FREDERIC GEORGE STEPHENS

3 St. Edmund's Terrace,
6 July 1892

Dear Steph,

Your note of the 2nd only came into my hands yesterday, as I had been out of town for a fortnight.

I presume that the *Rosa Triplex* to which you immediately refer is the water-colour[1] (which I have seen, but don't recollect in detail beyond a certain point). I have by me a photograph from the chalk-drawing[2] (not the water-colour). In this photograph it is clear to me that the central head represents, with a moderate amount of accuracy, the face of Miss Wilding (who sat for *Sibylla Palmifera*,[3] *Sea-Spell*,[4] etc.). Gabriel *certainly* intended the 3 heads to exhibit one and the same physiognomy — as it were 3 sisters closely resembling one another, or even a single woman seen from 3 different points of view. I must therefore assume that the faces to the left and right are also meant for Miss Wilding; although the one to the (spectator's) right does not look to me much like her, but fully as much like the heads Gabriel used at times to do from May Morris (then a mere child), treating her as an adult.

I don't think there is any *meaning* whatever in *Rosa Triplex*; only that sort of art-meaning which pertains to an artistic experiment such as one sees here — the experiment of representing the same face triplicated. Also I don't remember much about how and why Gabriel did it. I may however say *in confidence* thus much. Someone who, at the date of Gabriel's death in 1882, was owner of the picture — I rather think it must have been Craven — found about that same date that the colours were changing — flesh becoming greenish or livid, etc.; and he got Dunn to execute very considerable and indeed radical restorations on the picture. Of this fact I have personal knowledge. Dunn, I thought, did his part very skilfully and successfully: but still there is a certain inevitable loss of subtlety in the features and expressions.[5]

I am afraid I can't just now pitch upon an evening when I would claim your and your wife's (to whom my affectionate regards) hospitality at dinner, nor upon a Sunday when your "little boy" could look down on me from the height of 6 foot 2, or whatever it is: for I am a waif and stray in London — just back from Brighton, where I had to go for one reason, and soon about to be spirited off, for a different reason, to some bracing place, perhaps Switzerland or Scotland — and I have many jobs to overtake in the brief interval. We want *bracing* air, because our second daughter Helen shows a rather disquieting weakness in one knee, and Doctors want her to get all the strengthening possible. Will bear your friendly suggestion in mind for a proper opportunity.

My wife has seldom been tolerably well this year: is now not so greatly amiss, but weak. We hope *your* wife is restored to sound health.

Always yours,
W. M. Rossetti

MS: Bodleian.

1. "Triple portrait of May Morris" (Surtees 238).
2. Surtees 238A (238B is an unfinished chalk drawing of the same subject). Alexa Wilding sat for DGR regularly from 1865.
3. Surtees 193.
4. Surtees 248.
5. Cf. MS. Diary, 15 August 1882: "Watts and I looked at Gabriel's water-colour *Rosa Triplex* now in my house; whither it was lately sent by the owner Craven, to see whether anything can be done by Dunn to remedy the darkening of certain portions of the flesh where malachite, I believe, was used. There certainly are some very unsightly dark patches. Dunn had lately looked at the work, and I understand he considers the only remedy to be absolute repainting of these portions."

480. TO FREDERIC GEORGE STEPHENS

3 St. Edmund's Terrace,
16 October 1892

Dear old Steph,

Thank you for your very friendly letter: it recalls old times — only too vividly and painfully recalled already by the death of our dear Woolner. For many years (as you know) he and I were like affectionate brothers: but I grieve to say that I had not so much as seen him for perhaps 12 to 15 years. I never felt alienated from him in spirit: but family circumstances, combined with my own pretty blameable habit of never going anywhere, had made us lose sight of each other. Peace and praise be with his memory. I could not get away from my Office to his funeral: my absence the previous day at Tennyson's funeral[1] was only managed by an effort.

The point is hardly worth discussion between you and me, who are not quite at one about the demerits or merits of Gladstone: but it seems to be a notorious and undisputed fact that on the Tennyson day Gladstone was not (as you put it) at

Downing Street, but at Hawarden in Cheshire, where he had been living these many days past.

Our love to your wife.

Yours,

W. M. Rossetti

MS: Bodleian.

1. He was buried in Westminster Abbey on 12 October.

481. TO THE EDITOR OF THE *ACADEMY*   16 December 1892

My attention has only now been called to two articles published in the *Academy* for December 3 and 10;[1] the first being a review by Mr. William Sharp of the *Autobiographical Notes of the late Mr. William Bell Scott*, edited by Prof. Minto, and the second being Prof. Minto's rejoinder to the review. Both these articles relate in part to my deceased brother Dante Gabriel Rossetti.

I read Mr. Scott's book soon after it came out, and felt very much inclined to say nothing about it in print; but it seems to me that I could not continue wholly silent, without appearing to shirk a duty which becomes incumbent upon me, now that the book, in its relation to my brother, is made a subject of controversy.[2] I loved and honoured Mr. Scott from the time when first I knew him, towards 1848, up to his death in 1890; yet I cannot ignore the fact that, whatever the reason on his part, some of his statements affecting my brother are, according to my view of them, unkind, unhandsome, inaccurate, and practically incorrect and misleading. The sanctity or the superstition of an olden friendship withholds me from saying a word of harshness regarding Mr. Scott. I will, however, with your permission, set down a few particulars, though these will mainly concern myself. My primary object in writing them is not to vindicate myself, who have not been assailed in any tangible way, but to suggest to the reader that, if Mr. Scott's neutral-tinted allegations concerning me are the reverse of trustworthy in detail, some of his dark-tinted allegations concerning my brother deserve to be perused with considerable suspense of judgement.

To take an illustration. Mr. Scott says (vol. ii., p. 179) that in April 1874 my brother wrote from Kelmscott, asking Scott to lend him £200 to meet a momentary need. Mr. Scott sent him a cheque for that amount, but it was immediately returned with thanks, on the ground that my brother had meanwhile received other money, and no longer needed the cheque. So far nothing appears but what does credit to the friendliness of Mr. Scott without besmirching the memory of Dante Rossetti. But Mr. Scott adds the following words: — ''He had by that time lost nearly every old friend save myself; did he now suspect that I was among his enemies, and had he done this to try me? I fear this semi-insane motive was the true one.'' Now for my own part I cannot see the least reason for supposing that this *was* the true motive; and, as I would like readers to be equally sceptical regarding Mr. Scott's inference, I proceed to show that his mode of representing some other facts is anything but correct.

Vol. i., p. 277. — Mr. Scott says that I visited him in the first year — i.e., 1848 — of his acquaintance with Dante Rossetti and his circle; "in the summer of 1848 he [myself] appeared in Newcastle," where Scott was then domiciled. This is totally incorrect. I never appeared in Newcastle, nor visited Scott, till the autumn of 1850, when I halted at Newcastle on my way back to London from Edinburgh. Then Mr. Scott proceeds to say that, when I was leaving at the close of this visit, mis-assigned by him to 1848, I introduced the subject of the magazine named the *Germ*. "He [myself] suggested that the [pre-Raphaelite] brotherhood was going to print something I might hear of." This again is totally incorrect. My visit, having really taken place in the autumn of 1850, was subsequent to the birth and death of the *Germ*, which was begun late in 1849, and ended in the early spring of 1850. I have thus demonstrated (to anyone who does not discredit my positive assertion) that in this anecdote Mr. Scott was certainly wrong as to both time and place. Moreover, I could not in 1848, even elsewhere than in Newcastle, have spoken about the project of the forthcoming *Germ*, for no such project in any way existed until 1849 was well advanced. I am not now aware that I spoke to him about the project in any place or at any time.

Vol. ii., p. 128. — Mr. Scott here makes some observations on reviews, written by personal acquaintances of my brother, upon his volume entitled *Poems*, 1870. With this matter Mr. Sharp has dealt; and I would not add any remark upon it, were it not that Mr. Scott has cited something that I said or wrote, confirming (as he considered) his own views. It is quite true that from first to last I advised my brother to care nothing about who reviewed his poems, or how they might be reviewed; I would tender the same advice to any other author, and, in reference to all my own small literary performances, I have invariably acted upon it. I must, however, dissociate myself from the tone of what Mr. Scott has said, affecting my brother, as to "working the oracle," or, as some current writers have agreed to term it, "nobbling the press."

Vol. ii., p. 172. — "William, who was made seriously ill by his brother's state" — i.e., his illness in the summer of 1872. This is a testimonial to my fraternal affection, and as such I would willingly accept it. But it is not a fact. I was not seriously ill: needed no doctor and no curative treatment, and pursued (with casual interruptions, not grounded upon ill-health) my ordinary official and other occupations.

Vol. ii., p. 174. — "His brother William had been so prostrated by anxiety, loving Gabriel much and fearing him not a little, that F. M. Brown took all business matters out of his hands." I scarcely know what is meant by saying that I feared Gabriel not a little; I feared him not at all, but I feared *for* him at that date (1872) and at other later times. It is wholly erroneous to say that Mr. Ford Madox Brown took all business matters out of my hands; but most true that he was the kindest and most thoughtful of friends and advisers both to my brother and to myself. It was I who managed my brother's money affairs in 1872, when he was disabled by illness, and for some months away in Scotland. I alone, for instance, transacted the whole matter of turning his collection of blue china into money. The fact is that, as I had at that date no banking account of my own, while Mr. Brown had an account at the London and Westminster Bank, St. James's-square, the funds accruing from the sale of the china, and perhaps some other funds proper to my brother, were placed in the bank just mentioned, in the joint names (if I remember right) of Mr. Brown and myself; certain it is that I took, from first to last, an active part in dealing with the money, so as to keep my brother's affairs properly in train until he returned from Scotland, and settled for a while at Kelmscott.

Prof. Minto writes, "I am most willing to prune [the two volumes of their mis-statements], but I must first have the mis-statements pointed out." I have here pointed out some of the mis-statements, and should be glad to see these, and others far more important, pruned away as early as opportunity may arise.

W. M. Rossetti

Text: *Academy*, 24 December 1892, pp. 591-92.

1. Pp. 499-501, 541-42.
2. MS. Diary, 4 January 1893: "Laid this Diary aside from 2 December last; partly through being busy at Somerset House, and partly through feeling very little inclined to take up any sort of voluntary work — feeling depressed and not very well. Vexed by press-scuffling over W. B. Scott's Reminiscences, and what he has said about Gabriel, a serious recurrence of Lucy's bronchial cough etc. beginning on 28 December, etc."

482. TO THOMAS JAMES WISE

Somerset House,
Room 38,
19 June 1893

Dear Wise,

I received a few days ago your letter regarding the forthcoming Shelley Exhibition[1] (the letter is not in my hands just at this moment). Your success in inducing the Corporation to take the matter up appears to me somewhat remarkable, and deserving of congratulations and thanks. If it tends to retrieve some past fiascos on the part of the Shelley Society, so much the better.

If you come to speak to me, perhaps the interview would come off here at Somerset House as well as anywhere else. My wife has been very ill, and is still very weak: during the greater part of April I greatly feared that each day would be her last. If however you do by preference call at St. Edmund's Terrace, and by any chance see my wife or any of the family, I would particularly ask you *not to refer* in any sort of way *to the debt or other mishaps of the Society*: any such matter would trouble and alarm my wife, and retard her recovery.

As to what I could lend for exhibition, I would of course reproduce those same things that I lent before. There is also the Shelley sofa. I remember there was some considerable trouble in getting it *into* the house when we entered there in 1890, and there would no doubt be the same trouble in getting it out of the house, and then back again. I would therefore prefer to leave the sofa untouched where it is. I regret to say also that it has in past years been rather knocked about by my children, and is not quite in that condition in which I should wish it to appear, were it at any time exhibited.

Yours always truly,

W. M. Rossetti

Any written reply had better be addressed to Somerset House.

MS: BL.

1. MS. Diary, 19 June 1893: "Wise writes that 11 July is fixed for the opening at the Guildhall of a Shelley Exhibition for which he has arranged with the Authorities — these latter bearing all the expense, while the Shelley Society furnishes most of the exhibits: I hardly know how he has succeeded in persuading the City people to undertake this." 30 June: "Wise called, to take possession of the Shelley items I can contribute to the forthcoming Guildhall Exhibition. He ... took away the Eton drawing by Shelley, the MS. page from *Laon and Cythna* [see Letter 147, Note 1], a photograph of Trelawny, and (volunteered by Lucy) the fragment of Shelley's skull." (For an account of the drawing and the fragment, see *SR*, 2:394-95, 375.) 19 July: "Wise called.... He says the Shelley Exhibition in the Guildhall is now a decided success: today the room was much crowded, and the Authorities mean to keep the collection on view for an extra week, to end on 29 July. As yet however no new recruits for the Shelley Society have come forward."

483. TO THOMAS JAMES WISE

Somerset House,
7 July 1893

Dear Wise,

I had better tell you while I remember it that yesterday I saw Col. Call (husband of Trelawny's daughter), and he told me that he (or she?) sent some while ago to you the subscription to Shelley Society for current year, but he has not yet received any acknowledgement. Was till lately abroad: now at 7 Pelham Crescent, Fulham Road, S.W. He raises no *complaint*, but would like it to be verified that the sum was in fact paid and received.

I don't accurately know whether or not I have a copy of *Hugh Heron* for disposal: *fancy* that I have, but can't quite as yet look into the matter. Will not forget it. I set aside some days ago a few MSS. of Gabriel's as to which I would be willing to treat with you: they still require detailed inspection before I can say anything definite. This also will be attended to.[1]

Yours,

W. M. Rossetti

MS: BL.

1. MS. Diary, 30 June 1893: "Wise ... looked by his own request at some MSS. of Gabriel's. Would give £10 for that early unpublished poem [*Algernon Stanhope*] (say 1847) which Gabriel, at the request of [Cavalier] Mortara, wrote on the death of some youth to Gabriel unknown. I hesitate to sell this juvenile though by no means ill-written performance: told Wise I would look with some care into the MSS. generally, and let him know further as to my views." 2 July: "Looked through MSS. by Gabriel, and set aside some that I would be willing to dispose of to Wise. I think on the whole the juvenile verses ... may go." 19 July: "Wise called, and bought the MSS. of Gabriel ... price £36.7."

484. TO THOMAS JAMES WISE   3 St. Edmund's Terrace,
                                                          24 July 1893

Dear Wise,

Thanks for your £36.5 for MSS.[1] — also for the Godwin volumes,[2] which I have not failed to read at once (or rather look through). Perhaps the "conjectural emendation" instinct is still strong upon me — thus: volume 2 —
p. 31, 1. 13 — I certainly think *think* ought to be *shrink*.
p. 39, 1. 5 — *Auction* seems very odd, and barely intelligible. Query? *Action*.
p. 56, 1. 4 — *Hot* town similar — I very confidently surmise *post*-town.

Will not forget about *Hugh Heron* etc. The Typewriting reached me on Friday.

All right about *Westminster Gazette* affair.[3] No symptom as yet of Catalogue of Shelley Exhibition: but I have no doubt you will oblige me when the time arrives.

Col. Call called on me on Friday, having received your offer for *Oedipus Tyrannus*. What he wished to know of me was whether you are the sort of man who want the book for yourself, as a genuine amateur in such matters, or whether, after you had acquired it, it would be likely to figure in an early book-sale, and so get hawked about as a commercial article: in the former case he was not indisposed to part with it. I assured him that said former case is *the* case, and perhaps you have already heard from him in reply.[4]

He told me that Mrs. Call is curious to see those Letters of Harriet Shelley.[5] I told him that I would place my copy at her disposal at any convenient opportunity, but it strikes me that possibly you would consider a copy of the book (supposing you have still any to spare) well bestowed upon Mrs. Call — so for the present I don't myself take any further steps in that matter.

                                                    Yours very truly,
                                                    W. M. Rossetti

Am just sending Mrs. Call a duplicate copy of a new pamphlet, *Commemorazione di P. B. Shelley in Roma*:[6] my remaining copy ought to have figured in the Guildhall, had it but reached me a few days earlier.

MS: BL.

1. See Letter 483, Note 1.
2. *Letters from Shelley to William Godwin*, 2 vols., privately printed for Wise, 1891. Two of Rossetti's conjectures proved correct: "shrink" and "p[o]st town" appear in Jones, *Letters of Shelley*, 1:323, 350.
3. In an interview in the *Westminster Gazette* Wise declared that the Shelley sofa (see Letter 294) had been brought to England by Leigh Hunt who gave it to DGR ("Shelley in the City. A Chat with Mr. Wise on the Guildhall Exhibition," 17 July 1893, pp. 1-2).
4. A note by Wise on the letter reads: "On July 30th I bought the book from Col. Call for £36. Col. Call told me that the copy had been given by Shelley to Trelawny." Wise to WMR, 1 August 1893: "Have *got Oedipus* !!!! Hurrah! — and many thanks to W. M. R. for kindly aid!" (AP).
5. See Letter 455, Note 1.
6. C. 1893 (*Catalog of Books and Manuscripts at the Keats-Shelley Memorial House in Rome* [1969], p. 149).

485. TO LUCY ROSSETTI

Somerset House,
5 October 1893,
4½

Dearest dear Lu,

I am very much grieved to say that any tolerably cheerful subject of writing (such as what the enclosed shows) is wholly overshadowed at present by your father's very serious illness. I saw him twice yesterday — 6 p.m., and 10½: he was in bed, in a deep trance-sleep produced by some very powerful opiate that Gill had been constrained to give him. Cathy told me that besides other symptoms of his illness, his mind has been quite wandering — rambling intermixture of Dijon and tombstones (Gabriel's affair I suppose). She is much depressed and concerned: was expecting Gill's reappearance at some early hour today. This morning (8¾) I with Arthur returned. Your father was still drowsing — not conscious of our presence; but he had not been wholly asleep or silent in the interval. I could scarcely form an opinion of his condition: went round to Gill. Gill says that the present illness is violent diarrhoea and colic. He does not (seemingly) particularly suspect any internal abscess or tumour; but is struck on these his last visits, by a general decline of strength in the system (last previous visit some 6 months ago). He dissuades me from inferring that there is present danger: but in all these utterances he is not very decisive or emphatic. He said he would like to have Dr. Roberts[1] in consultation today: so I at once went to Roberts (102 Harley Street) and he undertook to telegraph to Gill fixing a consultation — towards 3½ perhaps.

I am again tied to Somerset House: double work resumed yesterday, and will last till early November. In what spirits I plod through it you will imagine. I shall revisit your father's house before getting to my own, and will write to you again: but have thought it well to enter beforehand into these present details, so as not to lose time.

Have not as yet any news of you: am fain to assume that in addressing to Pallanza I am about right. Am deeply grieved to begin by such bad news: of course I think it quite *possible* that I may find this afternoon a considerable change for the better.

All love from

Wm.

MS: AP.

1. Frederick Thomas Roberts (d. 1918), professor of Clinical Medicine, University College London; assistant editor of *Quain's Dictionary of Medicine* (1894); author of *A Handbook of the Theory and Practice of Medicine* (1873; 20th ed., 1909).

486. TO LUCY ROSSETTI

3 St. Edmund's Terrace,
5 October 1893,
7¼ p.m.

Dearest Luie,

Gill and Roberts held their consultation. They agree that the stomach-trouble

566

is now subdued; but find that the blood-vessels connected with the head are congested, and that every precaution must be taken to keep your father in the utmost quiet. There is not at present any actual "lesion" in that part; and with care it *may* be avoided. Roberts also considers there are symptoms of kidney-disease: this perhaps is no more than what has been known to exist, and has been kept in check for some years past. Cathy and the rest of us remain in great apprehension as to what *may* ensue: but we are allowed to entertain a serious belief that it *may* also not ensue.

I saw your father towards 5¾: he is still in a drowse, and of course, after what the Doctors said, I did not attempt to rouse him up or make him speak to me etc.

There was no money in the house, and necessarily no power of drawing any cheque on your father's banking-account, so I left with Cathy the £20 from my monthly salary. Had already last evening drawn up a paper for paying it into my Bank, but could not this morning go to the Bank, being after Gill and Roberts — and now it is all the better that I did not pay it in.

The question of getting a nurse has been more than once raised: Cathy thinks it better not to get one for the present — as your father might be irritated (so necessary to avoid) were he to see one about. Cathy herself is the nurse — and I am sure a very attentive one.

In this great anxiety I am feeling all the more anxious because as yet no news comes from you or the girls: but I don't allow myself to draw unfavourable inferences from this.

Love from

Your own
W. M. R.

MS: AP.

487. TO LUCY ROSSETTI

Somerset House,
6 October 1893,
12¼

Dearest Lu,

I have given you dreadful news in my past letters, and must give still worse now. It is too clear that your dear father is now rapidly sinking: when I saw him this morning towards 8, he was hardly if at all conscious, and I am very much afraid that all will be over by the time I return from Somerset House. I called on Gill on my way hither: he was not surprised at this very bad news, having yesterday (with Roberts) formed an unfavourable opinion of the case: he undertook to go round to the house at the earliest moment. From Gill's I came on here (for, as I have already mentioned, I am again doing double work, which can only be kept down by constant exertion): I left word with Arthur to call for me if anything should specially need my presence. I also, after speaking to Cathy on the point, asked him to go round to apprise Shields — who it would seem knows nothing as yet.

All this is miserable to write and still more miserable for you to read. It is one more misfortune — about the greatest of all — to you and me, who were not particularly in need of any more. Fate has sometimes seemed rather determined to hunt us down: we must do our little best to resist.

I received this morning your postcard of yesterday from well-beloved Bellinzona, and it would under different circumstances have raised my spirits. As it was, I could only write — at once and very hurriedly — to Olive at that same address, explaining that there was very bad news of your father, which you, on reaching Pallanza, would find down in my successive letters. I presume you are probably by this time at Pallanza, so I now again address thither — grieved indeed to pain you so much dearest Lucy.

Cathy seems unwearying and tender in her attentions on your father: I always find her there, always attending to some point or other. The Doctors consider the illness to be of an apoplectic character, but not, when they were there yesterday, in a necessarily fatal stage. I abstained yesterday from *naming* apoplexy to spare you one shock the more.

Yours in love
W. M. R.

It pleased me a little to learn from Cathy that your father did *not* after all rise from bed and come downstairs on Sunday, to see some expected callers: he stayed in bed — which I had expressed an opinion that he should do, as the only prudent course. So he did not bring on this final attack by any over-exertion of that kind.

MS: AP.

488. TO LUCY ROSSETTI

3 St. Edmund's Terrace,
6 October 1893,
7¼ p.m.

Dearest Lucy,

The fatal anticipation expressed in my last letter has come too true — your dear father has left us for ever. He died in great peace, and assuredly no suffering, towards 4 this afternoon: Arthur was present, along with Cathy and her sons, and Maggie. I arrived towards 5¼, and looked on his beautiful features and placid countenance with its far-aloof serenity.[1]

Shields (I learn) wished to get Tadema to make a drawing of your father's face: but Tadema proves to be out of town, and the last thing I saw was that Shields returned, ready to do it himself if Cathy likes. I hardly know whether to prefer this or not. A mould by Brucciani is also to be taken: I consented to call on Brucciani for the purpose tomorrow. I offered Cathy to stay in the house tonight: she did not wish me to do so, but is resolved to pass the night herself in the same room.

You see the enclosed paragraph from the *Westminster Gazette*:[2] my attention was bespoken to it by a like announcement, foremost in the posters of that paper

— it caught my eye as I left Somerset House. I understand Ford Hueffer gave the information: and a representative of the Press Association came this evening, and learned from me a *few* details which will no doubt be in all the papers tomorrow.

What melancholy words to write — and how little what is written embodies the feeling which one has about the heart of the thing — and about you, my poor Lucy.

As to business-details etc. I don't seem to know anything yet: but shall no doubt pretty soon.

Pardon my saying that I debated whether or not to send this off in a black-edged envelope and Arthur talked it over with me: I have found him quietly kind in the whole mournful matter, and composed but genuine in feeling. We determined that on the whole the letter is better *without* the startling envelope.

Love to my dear girls — and to yourself my dearest Lu — from

Your own
William

MS: AP.

1. MS. Diary, 4 October to 20 November 1893: "Diary interrupted by press of Office-work, and also by the irreparable loss we have suffered in the death of Madox Brown on 6 October from apoplexy, supervening on a very sharp attack of diarrhoea-colic — all connected more or less with his gouty constitution. The whole illness was frightfully sudden at last, only beginning after Lucy's departure from London."
2. "We much regret to hear that Mr. Ford Madox Brown is dying. He has had a sudden apoplectic seizure and there is no hope" (6 October 1893, p. 4).

489. TO LUCY ROSSETTI

Somerset House,
17 October 1893,
5¼

Dearest Lu,

It has got rather late here, but I prefer not to leave until I write you a few lines. Nothing further received from you to be answered.

You will see Stephens's letter enclosed. I don't myself hear anything direct about actual projects of exhibition: but Ford, to whom I mentioned the matter yesterday (Cathy was not visible, having gone for the time to Brook Green), said that, if nothing is done on the Executor's part, the R.A. might be stepping in and doing it. This is I suppose merely his personal impression: but it is true that, if the precedent of the Gabriel exhibition were to be followed by the R.A., they would in first instance combine with *picture-possessors*, and only afterwards come into contact with the family. Leyland, as I understood, was the first mover in that affair. I have replied to Stephens, saying that the initiative would lie with you and Cathy — I acting as agent if wanted, but not otherwise.[1]

I also understand from Ford that Cathy did not as yet know whether or not the will is now in this country. I replied that I supposed it might likely enough be in the hands of Barraud,[2] but did not know. Cathy would value any positive information on the subject.

Yesterday the mask taken by Brucciani reached me — no other copy received as yet by anyone I assume. It is, as I foresaw it must be, different from what one could wish: I think however it is better than the mask from Gabriel.

This has been a dim, soaking, drearyish sort of day, like the beginning of a cheerless autumn-winter season. Not at all cold however: I have even had to leave off today the Inverness cape which I had been wearing these several days past.

Love from my inmost heart dear,

Your
W. M. R.

MS: AP.

1. Nothing was organized until 1896, when there were exhibitions at the New Gallery and the Grafton Gallery, Ford Hueffer providing the introductions to the exhibition catalogues (see Fredeman, p. 63).
2. Hilton Percy Barraud of the firm of Barraud, Regge and Jupp, 7 St. Mildred's Court.

490. TO LUCY ROSSETTI

Somerset House,
20 November 1893,
1½

Dearest Lu,

It would seem I have finished up my foreign paper here: must bring round some more from home.

I am much pleased to learn that Longman[1] is in favour of a fully detailed Life of your dear father, to be written by you.[2] As things have now reached this seemingly satisfactory point, I will tell you a few particulars which I thought best left in the background in the first instance. It seems that Longman is an acquaintance of Morris, and to him in the beginning he expressed his view that some such Life should be written. Morris suggested that he should apply to *me* to do it: Longman replied to Morris asking that I would enter into communication with him, and Morris sent that letter on to me. I replied to Longman naming the Executors, and saying that his only right course would be to address *you* on the subject, and if you thought fit you would yourself be quite suited for doing the work — and I mentioned your published writings. He punctually complied — writing to you without any delay after receipt of my letter.

I will of course read the beginning of your book when it reaches me, and have not the slightest intention of being "discouraging." You on the other hand would not first ask me to express my opinion, and then dislike or resent my doing that. As to my notes, I think the more satisfactory course would be to make them on separate paper when it is any matter of opinion or debate: a mere casual slip in diction etc. would be a different thing, and could be corrected on the MS.

I will look up the letters which I possess written by your father. This will be a job requiring pains and a little time, as I shall have to untie nearly every one of those thick wrapped bundles of letters with which you are familiar, and take out of each the letters that you want: these however will be readily traceable, as all

570

the letters in the bundles are (you may remember) in alphabetical order. If I find some letters of *no* consequence, I will leave them aside: my practice however has always been to leave such unpreserved, so that what I *have* preserved ought (with casual exceptions) to be of some sort of interest — though this interest may sometimes lie outside the biography of *your father*. When I have got the various letters together I will tell you, and we will then decide how they are to be sent to Italy: they would form a thickish bundle for posting — though I never had any *very active or detailed* correspondence with your father.

It is a satisfaction to hear that you have a good appetite now. Polenta is one of those things I have often looked at but never tasted: yet I know of no reason why it should not be savoury as well as nutritious.

I think you should certainly encourage Cadomo to put-up the stove: even if it were not to redound long to your benefit, it would to that of your successors.

If Longman addresses me as to terms for your book, I will fully attend to that. Am not particularly *au fait* at such matters, and would not *commit* you to anything without your own previous assent.

I reminded Arthur this morning that he ought not to fail to write to you at reasonable intervals. He undertook to repair the neglect. I always find [him] busied with something or other; yet not *so* busied but that he can and ought to write as you say.

When you see today's English papers you will see some confirmation of what I wrote yesterday about a hideous storm from the afternoon of Saturday. It is still windy and cold, but seems to have taken a sensible turn towards abatement. Snow gone this morning.

Yours in love
W. M. R.

MS: AP.

1. Charles James Longman (1852-1934), second son of William Longman, who succeeded his father in Longmans, Green, & Co. in 1877; editor of *Fraser's Magazine*, 1881-82, and its successor, *Longman's Magazine*, 1882-1905.

2. MS. Diary, 21 November 1893: "Today I received from [Lucy] ... the first instalment of a Life of her father which she has begun writing.... Longman in the first instance applied to *me* to do this work: I, for more reasons than one, was quite indisposed to undertake it, unless after due consultation between Longman and Lucy — who, along with Cathy, is Executrix to her father's will. So I recommended Longman to apply to Lucy for general information and instructions: and she, on receiving his letter, undertook herself to write the Life — a result far more pleasing to me than if I had assumed the task personally. It is to be a substantial book — some 500 pages octavo. I think Lucy has made a good beginning — trammelled partly by want, at Pallanza, of the books or documents to which she would naturally have to be referring. I am reading her MS., and making notes etc. to be communicated to her."

491. TO THOMAS JAMES WISE

Somerset House,
2 January 1894

Dear Wise,

I *am* still at Somerset House: though I believe some newspaper killed me off officially the other day — did not see the paragraph. Expect to remain here till 25 September, when I shall be 65: must then no doubt go.

Thanks for what you say about those letters of Gabriel's. I do possess "The Death of Morris":[1] but would certainly not feel justified in parting with it, even to a tempting offer such as you might perhaps make.

I don't know that one evening at Furnivall's would do less well for me than another. Whatever evening it may be, "Dilly dilly duck, come here and be killed,"[2] is the programme of music, and not an agreeable one.

Yours,
W. M. Rossetti

MS: BL.

1. "The Death of Topsy," a playlet by DGR in which he "gets rid of Morris in a murder-fantasy" (Jack Lindsay, *William Morris, His Life and Work* [1975], where it is printed in full, pp. 227-30).
2. "Dilly, dilly, dilly, dilly, come to be killed," from the nursery rhyme "Oh, what have you got for dinner, Mrs. Bond?" (I. and P. Opie, ed., *Oxford Dictionary of Nursery Rhymes* [1951], p. 91).

492. TO LUCY ROSSETTI

Somerset House,
11 January 1894,
11¾

Dearest Lu,

Nothing further has been received from Pallanza since I wrote last. I do trust you are going on favourably: also that your climate may have changed for the better. In London a considerable change set in in the course of the 8th (Monday); and now all snow and frost are gone, the streets are getting gradually cleaner, and the temperature is above an ordinary level for this time of year. I have been expecting pipes to burst in our house. This however has not as yet recurred: something remains over to be attended to from what happened towards 1 January, but it will not (I hope) be a heavy job. This is the first day (since my gout began on 20 December) that I have *walked* through the Park towards Somerset House.

Shields called on me yesterday, wishing to hear news of you, and also to get news about my gout — as to which he appeared to have heard some rather overcharged rumours. He gave me various particulars about the acquisition of the Christ and Peter for the National Gallery.[1] Said also that he would be desirous of buying for some public institution the great cartoon of Wilhelmus Conquistator:[2] had indeed just been round to No. 1 to unroll it partially, and ascertain its condition — which he considered quite sound. I understand a sum of about £100 still remains out of that subscription, and this might be offered for the Wilhelmus Conquistator. Shields believes the length of the cartoon to be some 30 feet: he regards this great size as being the essential difficulty, not knowing of *any* public building where it could (or would) be easily housed. I suggested whether the forthcoming National Gallery of British Art might perhaps offer a better chance than buildings now existing: this he thought a good suggestion. Perhaps you know something about this matter already.

Talking about congestion — or danger of congestion — of the lungs, Shields mentioned to me an experience of his, as follows. He knew some years ago a young man who had a very dangerous attack of this kind: Doctors had tried their best, unavailingly. Shields went to a very skilful Doctor in Liverpool (name I think Inman[3]) whom he already knew, and consulted him. Inman recommended to apply cotton-wool — a big piece covering the chest — steeped in olive-oil as hot as could fairly be borne. Shields carried out this plan: and in a few hours the crisis of the illness was overcome, and a good and thorough (so far as I know, permanent) recovery ensued. Perhaps you would think it well to bear this experience in mind.

> Dearest Lu,
> Your own
> William

MS: AP.

1. A subscription committee organized by Shields and F. G. Stephens commissioned FMB, a year or so before his death, to paint a duplicate of *The Trial of Wycliffe* for presentation to the National Gallery. The picture remained unfinished at his death, and the committee purchased instead *Jesus Washing Peter's Feet*, which had recently been bought in at Christie's (MS. Diary, 26 July 1892). MS. Diary, 16 February 1894, records that "a large proportion" of the money collected by the subscription had been paid to FMB during his lifetime.
2. *William the Conqueror Presenting a Charter to Marmion*, for a light in the chancel of the Church of St. Editha, Tamworth, Staffordshire (Sewter, *The Stained Glass of William Morris and his Circle*, 2:184).
3. William Inman, MD, Edinburgh, 1859 (*Churchill's Medical Directory* 1893).

493. TO CHRISTINA ROSSETTI

3 St. Edmund's Terrace,
18 April 1894

Dear Christina,

I must write you a few words: had proposed calling on you today (from this house, for I have not yet returned to Office), but other work comes on me, and I must postpone. Perhaps tomorrow.

We reached London morning of 16. Are not *ill*, and that is the best I can say of our condition.

I find (knew nothing of it hitherto) that Lucy made a will in April 1893, leaving practically all her separate property to the children — which meets my approval. There is a Trustee, Barraud a lawyer she knew (other deceased Trustee her father), and the house etc. goes to Barraud *in trust* for the children. My position thus becomes a matter of some embarrassment and speculation to myself, as I seem to have no personal right in the house — not even to live there, were Barraud to decree otherwise (not that this can be in any way expected). Business-worries thus crowd round me, to whom grief had seemed to be enough. But one must meet one's troubles.

Dear Lucy's last moments were in the early morning of 12 April. She is interred in San Remo. We would naturally have preferred interment in London: but the cost of transit would have been some £200! Her last day was less troubled by coughing etc. than some others: she was conscious to the last, and her courage never flinched for a moment.

This is all I can at present say: indeed I hardly know how I have succeeded in saying this much.

Your
W. M. R.

Be sure I think often of you, and your painful state of health.

MS: AP.

494. TO FREDERIC GEORGE STEPHENS

3 St. Edmund's Terrace,
19 April 1894

My dear old Friend,

You enter into my sorrows, and I will not enlarge upon them. They are deep indeed, and the question of how I shall succeed in looking after three daughters and a son is most alarming.

Thank you, but I could not leave this house. There is a great amount of private business — not to speak of anything else — to look after. Thank your wife for me.

The generous offer which concludes your letter affects me much. It is true I have had and shall have most formidable expenses, and I shall apparently not be in the least capable of meeting them save by selling out some of my small investments, drawing upon an insurance, or what not. Also my income will very soon diminish by ⅓ , as I retire from Somerset House (under coercion at the age of 65) in September — Still I must do what I can for myself without troubling you. £100 would go but a short way: and I will frankly say that, were I once to borrow it, I don't know when my restoring it would be possible. It must not be.

With thanks and affection,

Yours,
W. M. Rossetti

MS: Bodleian.

495. TO ALICE BOYD

3 St. Edmund's Terrace,
17 September 1894

My dear Miss Boyd,

I saw my sister Christina the other day, and opened and read to her your kind letter of the 11th. Christina, I regret to say, has been confined to bed for a month or so past, and is quite unable to write: she asked me to reply. It is too true that she is exceedingly ill — in fact she is undoubtedly dying, owing to a malady of the heart and other grave matters: I am sure she will never be out of bed again, and if her life lasts to the end of this year I shall be surprised. You will understand how much pain it gives me to say all this.

Christina would certainly like to avail herself of your most friendly offer to present to her that portrait of me which my beloved friend Scott painted many years ago. I will not conceal from you, dear Miss Boyd, that there are some things about Gabriel in that book of Scott's Reminiscences which I do not regard as either kind or friendly, or even fair: yet this does not substantially affect the feeling which I always did and always shall entertain for Scott. Christina has not read the book — knowing that it contains matter which she would not like, and with which she prefers to remain unacquainted.

Christina sends you her love and thanks — and I am sure you will accept my own expression of warm regard. I have had many sorrows lately, of which you no doubt know somewhat.

Yours very truly,
W. M. Rossetti

MS: National Library of Scotland.

496. TO THEODORE WATTS-DUNTON

3 St. Edmund's Terrace,
29 December 1894

Dear Watts,

You and Swinburne will be sorry (and yet, after such lingering stages of illness, one ought not to be sorry) that my dear good Christina died this morning — most peacefully at the last.[1]

I fancy you may contemplate writing something about her in the *Athenaeum*.[2] If so, may I remind you of her names, Christina Georgina, and the date of her birth 5 December 1830. Her illness was functional malady of the heart, with dropsy in left arm and hand: there was another matter,[3] painful to dwell upon, which I leave in the background.

If you do *not* mean to write, and would kindly tell me so, I would myself send a few details to *Athenaeum*: of course anything in the nature of critical opinion would come far better from you.

Love to Swinburne from

Yours always,
W. M. Rossetti

MS: BL.

1. For WMR's diary entries dealing with CGR's last illness, death, and burial, see *FLCR*, pp. 218-22.
2. 5 January 1895, pp. 16-18. MS. Diary, 1 January 1895: "Press-notices of Christina numerous, and (as they ought to be) very earnestly laudatory."
3. Cancer.

497. TO THEODORE WATTS-DUNTON

3 St. Edmund's Terrace,
6 January 1895

Dear Watts,

I must thank you for that splendid article in the *Athenaeum*:[1] it is a tribute, delightful to my feelings, to my admirable Christina, my dear mother, Gabriel, and indeed everyone of the clan. I notice that, since I saw the proof, you have been at the pains of introducing various modifications. The opening article in the No.[2] is (I fancy) not yours: that also is very gratifying. The Clergyman preached today a Memorial Sermon on Christina;[3] it was *all* about her, and had the character of a devotional-literary essay, with extracts: laudatory in the highest degree, and on its own lines a very fair piece of work.

Love to you and Swinburne from

W. M. Rossetti

MS: BL.

1. See Letter 496, Note 2.
2. "English Literature in 1894," 5 January 1895, p. 9.
3. J. J. G. Nash, *A Memorial Sermon Preached at Christ Church, Woburn Square, for the Late Christina Georgina Rossetti* (1895). MS. Diary, 6 January 1895: "Olive and I attended, at Christ Church, Woburn Square, a morning service planned as a memorial service for dear Christina. A large congregation, but I can't say what proportion it bore to the ordinary congregation there. The 2 hymns by Christina same as at the funeral ["This Advent moon shines cold and clear," stanzas 2-5; "Lord, grant us grace to mount by steps of grace"] — one just before the sermon, and the other immediately afterwards. Mr. Nash's sermon was entirely about Christina, with some reference to the rest of the family — *Germ*, Praeraphaelitism, etc. etc. It amounted to a devotional-literary essay on Christina, and was a very fair piece of work. Would like to get a copy of it in some form."

498. TO ALEXANDER MACMILLAN

3 St. Edmund's Terrace,
24 January 1895

Dear Macmillan,

Since the death of my dear sister Christina (29 December) I have been intending to take a suitable opportunity for writing to you about her literary interests. She has left me her Executor and universal Legatee, and the will will shortly be proved. Thus whatever rights used to belong to her in relation to books which you publish belong now to me.

I should feel obliged to you if you would let me have a detailed statement as to the publications in question, and Christina's stake in them.

You are probably aware that, besides *your* publications, there were certain publications, by the Society for Promoting Christian Knowledge, of books by my sister. One of these is named *Verses*, and has had a great sale: it consists of the lyrics interspersed amid previous volumes, mainly prose, published by that Society. The Society lately asked me whether I could add to those *Verses* other devotional poems by my sister, so as to form a new and (in that relation) complete collection. In your publications there are many and excellent devotional poems: and, before giving the matter any further consideration, I should like to understand what would be your views regarding any such project.

There is another matter. A gentleman unknown to me — J. B. Fortay,[1] 5 Abercromby Terrace, Oxford Street, Liverpool — wants to set to music 2 songs by Christina[2] — "One foot on sea" etc., and "This Advent moon shines cold" etc. I am pretty sure that Christina, in all similar cases, used to say that she had no objection, and to refer the applicant to you for a final decision. On this point also please advise me.

May I add that I have been a little surprised to observe (taking the *Athenaeum* as my guide) that you have not, since Christina's death, seen fit to readvertise her poems. There has been in the papers an immense amount of highly laudatory matter about her, and I should have supposed that a little advertising would in these past weeks have proved very remunerative. But you know your business best.[3]

With kind regards,

Yours very truly,
W. M. Rossetti

MS: BL.

1. James Butler Fortay (b. 1856), organist and composer.
2. *One Foot on Sea, and One on Shore* (*A Pageant and Other Poems*, 1881); *Advent* (*Goblin Market and Other Poems*). Neither is listed in B. N. S. Gooch and D. S. Thatcher, *Musical Settings of Early and Mid-Victorian Literature* (1979).
3. WMR to Frederick Macmillan, 27 January 1895: "I quite appreciate what you kindly say about advertisements. Have not myself any feeling that it could be contrary to delicacy for a Publisher to take early steps in the interest of himself, and of his authors or their representatives. But all is well as it now stands" (BL).

499. TO THOMAS JAMES WISE

3 St. Edmund's Terrace,
27 January 1895

Dear Wise,

Thanks for yours of the 24th. On the whole I would just as soon pay off at once the whole balance of £20.1,[1] and have no more to think about the teaze of getting Postal Orders for 5/ — so here comes the cheque.

I think I could meet you at 30 Torrington Square today (Sunday) fortnight — 10 February — towards 2¾ p.m. If this suits you, I need not trouble you for a reply: if any later Sunday suits you better, you have only to say so, and it would probably answer for me.[2]

Yours,
W. M. Rossetti

MS: BL.

1. WMR's share of the Shelley Society debt to the printers.
2. MS. Diary, 23 January 1895: "Wise looked in.... I invited him to attend one day in Torrington Square, and see whether, among the books etc. that I mean to part with, there is anything he would like to secure. This he would gladly do." 10 February: "By appointment I met Wise at Torrington Square, and showed him books etc. having family-interest or the like. He only selected a very few things, principally Maria's old Guendolen Talbot translation (several copies)." For Maria's pamphlet, see Letter 504, Note 2.

500. TO MACKENZIE BELL[1]

3 St. Edmund's Terrace,
5 February 1895

Dear Mr. Bell,

What you say about your re-reading of my sister's poems gratifies me much: I am pretty nearly at one with you about them.

My Memoir of my brother is now advanced, though not finished.[2] It necessarily contains some references to Christina, but not anything which can be called biographical notice of her. Sooner or later I may do *something* about her; but the fact that there were scarcely any *events* in her life, combined with the fact that her inner life was one of religious devoutness, makes me rather inapt for the work. Deeply as I have always reverenced her attitude of soul on religious matters, I don't in the least share her form of belief — not partaking of the Christian faith at all. Someone who knew Christina intimately, and is an earnest Christian, would be the right biographer — were such a person forthcoming.

I also happened to see that her death was not mentioned in the *Author*. Thank you for the step which you took:[3] but any such omission is to my own feelings largely a matter of indifference. Press-notices have abounded and superabounded, not only in number but in ardour of praise.

Perhaps I sent you the enclosed card[4] before: but perhaps also it only reached me after the date of my last letter to you.

Yours very truly,
W. M. Rossetti

MS: Princeton.

1. Henry Thomas Mackenzie Bell (1856-1930), poet, friend of CGR during the last years of her life, author of *Christina Rossetti: A Biographical and Critical Study* (Hurst and Blackett, 1898). He was the nephew of the Scottish judge and Solicitor-General for Scotland, Thomas Mackenzie.
2. Although WMR concluded early on that Watts would never produce the Memoir, he was held back from doing anything himself by Watts's insistence that he had not abandoned the undertaking. MS. Diary, 10 June 1890: "Watts still proposes to complete his Memoir of Gabriel, and would prefer to bring it out as part of the long-contemplated Letters-Memoir book. He is decidedly of opinion (or professes to be so) that it would be finished by close of 1891. Under present circumstances, I have no great objection to such a delay as that: if it is not then ready — and my belief is it will not be — I think I would resolutely set aside the question of Watts's Memoir, and would attend to my own concerns with the Letters." 24 April 1892: "Replied to a letter from Watts ... and took occasion to ask him how his Memoir of Gabriel now stands. In June 1890 he declared it would be ready by end of 1891: I don't suppose it *is* so, and if not would rather now close that transaction altogether." Watts's response to this is not known, but on 23 July he wrote: "Yes I am extremely anxious to see what I have written about Gabriel in print now: indeed my procrastination (as it seems) is doing me damage now I fear. I began with my introduction to Gabriel, leaving the earlier part of his life for the last, looking forward to getting much kind aid from you." WMR added the following note to the letter: "31/7/92 — Wrote to Ellis & Elvey, giving extracts from this letter — suggested that it might be well for them (rather perhaps than myself) to tell Watts that, unless his MS., or a substantial part of it, is in printer's hands by 1/1/93, we shall regard his project as lapsed, and shall do whatever we think fit apart therefrom" (AP). It was not however until after Lucy's death that he decided to write the Memoir himself. MS. Diary, 22 July 1894: "Began work on Gabriel's Family Letters. Had written to Watts some 10 days ago saying (substantially) that I now give up his proposed Memoir as a 'bad job,' and will myself do what is wanted in that way." 29 July: "Watts called by appointment. He speaks of his large assemblage of materials for the Memoir of Gabriel, but I don't gather that the Memoir itself is in a state at all approaching completion. He did not raise any distinct objection to my announced intention of proceeding with the Family-letters, and a Memoir of my own, without any co-operation from him.... Speaks of his having been unwilling, during Scott's life, to bring the Memoir to a

conclusion: he should have notified this to me at the proper time, but did not ever do so. All passed off between us on the most amicable terms." 10 April 1895: "I wrote the last sentence of my Memoir of Gabriel — which is, in dimensions and otherwise, certainly the most considerable performance of my lifetime. I began it on 4 September [1894], and thus it has occupied me 219 days, or 7 lunar months 3 weeks and 2 days."

3. See Letter 501, Note 2.

4. MS. Diary, 3 January 1895, mentions "mourning-cards (obtained from Dalziels) for dear Christina."

501. TO MACKENZIE BELL

3 St. Edmund's Terrace,
8 February 1895

Dear Mr. Bell,

Thanks for your feeling and interesting letter. Certainly I would at some time or other, gladly hear of what you speak of, a request which Christina made of you: should anything interfere, it can be left in silence.

If you saw fit, of your own accord, to write something about her for publication I am sure the writing could not be other than gratifying to me: more than this it might not befit me to say. There is an Irish lady, Miss Proctor, who knew Christina pretty well in recent years, and who wrote to me that she meant to put together some reminiscences etc.:[1] these she has offered to the Society for Promoting Christian Knowledge: I don't know the result, actual or probable. I think she would be capable of making the record an interesting one.

Much obliged about the *Author*. I should assuredly like much to read the MS.,[2] but it is quite as likely as not that I should make no alteration or suggestion upon it. There *might* be some small rectification forthcoming on some detail of fact.

Yours very truly,
W. M. Rossetti

MS: Princeton.

1. Ellen A. Proctor (1837-1909), *A Brief Memoir of Christina G. Rossetti*, with a preface by WMR, published by the SPCK in 1895, having been first offered to Macmillan. She was Irish born (*SR*, 2:540), and lived in South Africa previous to meeting CGR. WMR allowed her to live in Torrington Square for several months following CGR's death, and it was here that she wrote her Memoir. She plagued WMR with requests for the loan of money, and he was relieved when she returned to South Africa c. July 1896. She was back in England by 17 June 1900, when she called on WMR: "I trust she may not become a very frequent visitor in St. Edmund's Terrace" (MS. Diary). During her last illness in 1909 WMR called on her several times, and recorded in MS. Diary, 17 May, that she "is treating with the Rhodes Trustees with a view to her funeral; and wanted me ... to do whatever I can to facilitate matters — which I undertook. Wants to be cremated at Golders Green, with no needless expense, and without religious ceremony."

2. Of Bell's article on CGR in the *Author*, March 1895, pp. 269-70.

502. TO MACKENZIE BELL

3 St. Edmund's Terrace,
12 February 1895

Dear Bell,

I return the MS.,[1] which I regard as now free from error, and open to no sort of exception — much the reverse.

Assuredly my sister did to the last continue believing in the promises of the Gospel, as interpreted by Theologians; but her sense of its threatenings was very lively, and at the end more operative on her personal feelings. This should not have been. She remained firmly convinced that her Mother and Sister are Saints in heaven, and I endeavoured to show her that, according to her own theories, she was just as safe as they: but this — such was her humility of self-estimate — did not relieve her from troubles of soul. If there is any reality in the foundations of her creed, she now knows how greatly she was mistaken.

Yours very truly,
W. M. Rossetti

MS: Princeton. Extract in *Christina Rossetti*, p. 177.

1. See Letter 501, Note 2.

503. TO OLIVIA (MRS. RICHARD) GARNETT

3 St. Edmund's Terrace,
14 February 1895

Dear Mrs. Garnett,

Olive tells me that you have kindly asked me to dinner, to meet Mr. Mackenzie Bell. The fact is that I have for some while past entirely relinquished dining out — even when (as in your case) the severe ordeal of evening dress is remitted: I believe that the very last date when I dined out was June 1893, and that was only to accommodate my poor Lucy. So I am sure you will view me with indulgence as a harmless hypochondriac, and forgive my not coming.

I want to meet you one day at 30 Torrington Square, so that you may select some memento of Christina. Of course there are *some* things I could not make up my mind to part with: but in a general sense I would like you to fix upon what you prefer — whether furniture, drawing, book, or what not. The days which would *not* do for me for this purpose are 16 February, and 18, and 21 to 23. If you would name some other afternoon — say between 2 and 4 — I should in all likelihood be able, and much pleased, to keep the appointment.[1]

With heartiest regards to you and all yours,

Yours very truly,
W. M. Rossetti

Mackenzie Bell seems a very estimable nice man: so far as the meeting with him goes, there would be no sort of reluctance on my part.

I seem to have found the very first verses that Christina ever wrote; and the very last verses — the latter extremely good. Would these 2 MSS. be acceptable to the British Museum? If Dr. Garnett says Yes, I will present them.

MS: Texas.

1. MS. Diary, 26 February 1895: "Olive and I met Mrs. Garnett at Torrington Square, and I gave her various things as mementoes of Christina — perhaps rather more numerous than was reasonable: something like a dozen volumes, including 2 by Christina, the framed photograph *Magdalene at Door of Simon* [by DGR], a half-dozen of other photographs, and a page of MS. by Christina. Also handed to her, for the British Museum, Christina's first poem and her last [*To My Mother; Sleeping at Last*],

the printed card of former, and Gabriel's MS. sonnet *Heart's Compass.*'' 11 March: "Went to Mrs. Garnett's, and wrote inscriptions for the various books etc. which I had presented to her as mementoes of Christina.''

504. TO THOMAS JAMES WISE

3 St. Edmund's Terrace,
14 February 1895

Dear Wise,

Thanks for the £2.[1] Of course you are quite right in not taking the Talbot brochures[2] if for whatever reason they don't meet your views.

I shall not wholly forget about the *Hugh Heron*: but may as well say that, as the *wish* to sell is not at all present to me, I may very possibly never take the trouble of hunting up the volume, consigning it for rebinding, etc.

I observe Forman's remark — that I once told him I was saving for him a Talbot "of a particular variety." This matter has wholly escaped my recollection. I presume the variety is either one of those *red*-paper copies, or one of the *pink*-paper: at present writing I know of none other. If I were informed which of the two is in question, I would with more than willingness dispatch it as a present to Forman. Possibly you or he could enlighten me.

Yours always,
W. M. Rossetti

MS: BL.

1. See Letter 499, Note 2.
2. *In Morte di Guendalina Talbot*, a poem by G. P. Campana, with Maria Rossetti's translation, printed by G. Polidori, 1841. In a letter to Mackenzie Bell, 9 April 1895, WMR explained that copies in red wrappers bore a device on the title-page, the copies in pink wrappers being without the device. On 22 May he recalled that the pink-wrapper "form of the pamphlet was printed by Schulze & Co., 13 Poland Street — not by my grandfather." By 4 June he had concluded that the Schulze pamphlet "must be the *original* edition. The author ... went to Schulze: afterwards my grandfather as a matter of family-liking in relation to Maria printed an extra set" (Princeton). Wise purchased a copy in red wrappers from WMR in 1892 (*The Ashley Library, A Catalogue*, 4:161).

505. TO AMELIA (MRS. ADOLF) HEIMANN

3 St. Edmund's Terrace,
19 February 1895

My dear Mrs. Heimann,

As one of the oldest and best friends of my good Christina, you will certainly not be surprised to learn that she left with me your name as one of those (4 in all) to whom she wished some memento of her to be presented: Mrs. Moeller[1] is another.

I have just written to Mrs. Moeller, asking whether she would like to meet me one day, *after* 26 February, at 30 Torrington Square, and suggesting whether both you and she could arrange to come at the same time. If this suits you, perhaps you would kindly take any requisite steps: if however you prefer that *I* should make the selection, I will of course do so. In such case, please let me know what *sort* of thing you would like best — book, drawing, ornamental object, article of furniture, or what else.[2]

With affectionate regards,

Yours very truly,
W. M. Rossetti

MS: Iowa.

1. A daughter of the Heimanns.
2. MS. Diary, 8 March 1895: "Prepared the mementoes of Christina to be given to Mrs. Heimann and Mrs. [Felix] Moeller. For former a table in Japanese style (probably Dutch work of 18th century) which was I believe my own purchase toward 1865: it was constantly used by Christina, and more especially for her requirements during her last illness. For Mrs. Moeller, one or other of the 2 framed portraits of Henrietta Polydore (junior) by Gabriel [Surtees 415-16]; also Gabriel's early lithograph *Juliette* [see Surtees 16], and one of the leaves of his lithographed Playing-Cards [see Surtees 4], and a sample-leaf of the 2 woodcuts to *Goblin Market*."

506. TO GEORGE SCHARF

3 St. Edmund's Terrace,
2 March 1895

Dear Sir George Scharf,

From the enclosed newspaper-extract I see that the *Bookman*[1] has seen fit to say something for which I gave no sort of authority. That I "decided to present" a certain portrait to your Gallery is not an accurate statement; but it is quite true that I have for months past decided to *offer* such a portrait in case I were to learn from you that it would past doubt be accepted. I am aware of the salutary rule which excludes portraits of persons recently deceased unless there be a unanimous vote of assent by the Trustees.

In my late sister's house, 30 Torrington Square, W.C., there are 4 framed portraits of her by my brother:[2] — 1. Oil Head, small, 1848; 2. Pencil Head, small, about same date; 3. Crayon Half-figure, life-size, 1866; 4. Crayon Head and Shoulders, life-size, 1877. There are also some minor specimens,[3] unframed. All the 4 are good works of art, 3 and 4 being naturally the best; but I incline to think that 1 is the most interesting for the present purpose, and it is this which I am most minded to offer.

It shows my sister in her 18th year, advantageously (but not flattered) as regards good looks; and I almost think it must be the *first* oil-picture finished by my brother. He painted her as the Virgin in his first subject-picture, 1848-9, *The Girlhood of Mary Virgin;*[4] and it is not unlikely that he did this portrait as a preliminary essay at her face. It is however, in pose etc., totally different from the head in the Mary picture.

It happens that I intend to get this portrait, 1, engraved in a forthcoming book of mine:[5] this however need entail little if any delay in its delivery to the National Portrait Gallery in case it were accepted there.

Would you kindly inform me at your convenience whether, if I were to offer some portrait of my sister to the Gallery, I might *rely* upon its being accepted — because otherwise I would not expose myself to the chance of a rebuff. When that point gets settled, I would willingly show you (if you like) the 4 portraits here mentioned, supplemented by two (also by my brother) in this house from which I am writing, and a final decision could then be made as to which of them is the most desirable to be offered.

There is another point about which I have sometimes thought. My maternal Uncle Dr. John William Polidori[6] was Lord Byron's Travelling Physician in 1816, and was the author of a prose tale (which at first was very widely attributed to Byron) named *The Vampyre*, and of other works as well. There are various particulars about him — not exactly laudatory, I must admit — in Moore's *Life of Byron*,[7] Dowden's *Life of Shelley*, etc. He is to figure — or possibly does already figure — in the *Dictionary of National Biography*. He died long ago — in 1821. Would your Gallery at all care to have his portrait also? There is a bust of him in 30 Torrington Square, and a good oil-portrait, and a smaller oil-portrait. I regret to say that the names of the artists, though mentioned to me of old more than once, have escaped my memory.[8] The artists were not leaders in the profession: but the larger oil-picture is of more than average merit as a work of art.

Allow me to congratulate you upon your recent and excellently deserved change of designation,[9] and to remain

Yours always truly,
W. M. Rossetti

There is also by the by a portrait of my elder sister Maria Francesca (she died in 1876) — author of a book which has been very considerably successful, *A Shadow of Dante*. If that were deemed acceptable, I would reconcile myself to parting with it. It is by James Collinson, one of the 7 original P.R.B.s: he did likewise a portrait of Christina, which remains at Torrington Square, but I say nothing further about that, as the portraits done by my brother must be in all ways preferable.

MS: NPG.

1. 7 (March 1895), 167.
2. Surtees 423, 422 (on the back of which WMR inscribed: ''must be quite early say 1847''), 429, 431 or its companion piece No. 432.
3. Surtees lists six other portraits owned by WMR, Nos. 420, 424-28.
4. Surtees 40.
5. *FLM*.
6. b. 1795; *The Vampyre* was first published in the *New Monthly Magazine*, April 1819.
7. Thomas Moore, *Letters and Journals of Lord Byron, with Notices of his Life* (1830).
8. See Letter 514, Note 1.
9. Scharf had been made a KCB in recognition of his services to the National Portrait Gallery.

507. TO GEORGE SCHARF

3 St. Edmund's Terrace,
6 March 1895

Dear Sir George Scharf,

I am extremely obliged for your very considerate letter of the 4th, and only wish it contained better news as to your health.

It now appears to me that my correct course will be this — To write an official letter to you as Secretary, asking you to inform the Trustees that I am ready to present 3 works —

1. An oil-portrait of Christina by Gabriel, or else a drawing by Gabriel in tinted chalks representing Christina along with my Mother.[1]
2. An oil-portrait of Maria.
3. An oil-portrait, or else a bust, of Dr. Polidori —

also that I am ready to produce the works to the Trustees before they arrive at any decision.

I don't quite *like* doing all this, because it must be more or less mortifying to myself to risk the rebuff "Not wanted"; but I judge from your letter that in one form or another this process will have to be gone through.

I hardly think it would be much use for me to produce photographs as a preliminary. Not one of the works is bad as a work of art, and those by Gabriel are good: and as to authenticity my assertion must I suppose be the best evidence attainable.

Dr. Polidori was not a foreigner. He was a British subject, born in London of an Italian father and English mother.

If you would kindly favour me at your convenience with a reply, saying whether the course which I now propose is the best that offers, I should be much obliged, and would then proceed to act.

Yours very truly,
W. M. Rossetti

If you consider that the Trustees might probably like to admit Christina, but not the other two, please say so frankly, and I will offer Christina only.

MS: NPG.

1. Surtees 433, which the Gallery accepted in September. Although WMR did not mention this portrait in Letter 506, he recorded in MS. Diary on 2 March: "If eventually ... Scharf were to like best the crayon portrait of Christina and our mother combined, I would give that, and thus get my mother also into the Gallery: yet I should be extremely sorry to lose that work out of my own house."

508. TO SYDNEY MORSE[1]

3 St. Edmund's Terrace,
23 April 1895

Dear Mr. Morse,

I am glad that you don't see any objection to the photographing of the portrait of my Sister:[2] will take care to keep the negative to myself.

Written slip enclosed. I suppose that is about the *size* you wanted; if not, will write another. Also autograph note enclosed.

As to the choice of a Photographer, I would beg to leave this point to you. Messrs. Elliott & Fry, 55 Baker Street, are the Photographers with whom I have had most dealings of late: but I have no particular preference.

You are so good as to speak of "the chalk drawing of my Sister from the drawing-room." There were 2 such chalk drawings[3] there: one, dated 1866 (chin posed on hands) near the door, and one, 1877, near the fireplace. Both are now in *this* house of mine — just home from the Canning Town Art-exhibition.[4] I hardly know which is the better work or likeness of the two, but the 1866 one is naturally the more attractive, being in the prime of life. I am quite disinclined to part with it, but if anyone were to offer a *large* price, say £65, I would consider the matter. For the other I would take £48, as I happen to possess 2 other heads of her done by my brother at just the same time. This sum appears to me to be not beyond the fair value of the drawing as a work of art etc.[5]

Whenever you might think proper to send me a cheque for the youthful head now (as I gather) in your possession, I should of course receive it with pleasure. Don't rightly understand whether you have or have not closed with the offer, £8, which I made through Mr. Evans for that little pen-and-ink head of my mother[6] — but I rather presume not.

Yours very truly,
W. M. Rossetti

MS: Texas.

1. Solicitor of 4 Fenchurch Avenue EC (*POLD*).
2. Surtees 424, which Morse had recently bought from WMR. MS. Diary, 16 March 1895: "Met at Torrington Square Mr. Evans and Mr. Morse: the former had already purchased the MS. of *Up-hill* etc., and the latter wanted to look at drawings etc. by Gabriel. No definite offer was made by him, nor arrangement tendered; and I expressly said that, though glad to consider any suggestion that might be made, I have no *wish* to sell anything of Gabriel's." Frederick H. Evans, friend of Aubrey Beardsley for whom he secured J. M. Dent's commission for illustrations to *Le Morte Darthur*, was a bookseller in Cheapside.
3. See Letter 506, Note 2.
4. "Free Picture Exhibition," which opened on 30 March. MS. Diary, 21 January 1895: "Met by appointment in Torrington Square, a Miss [Mabelle] Pearse who is concerned in an Exhibition of Art for the working-people in Canning Town. I will lend her 8 or 9 of the portraits etc. in Christina's house." In addition to the two portraits of CGR, Nos. 243-44 in the catalogue, WMR lent: No. 237, a portrait of Frances Rossetti by DGR (see Surtees 447-51); No. 242, a portrait of G. Polidori (see Surtees 412-13); No. 238, FMB's portrait of WMR; No. 241, Shields's copy of DGR's *Mary Magdalene at the Door of Simon the Pharisee*; No. 239, Dunn's portrait of DGR, and an "amateur Head" (MS. Diary, 30 March 1895) of Margaret Polidori. Neither Surtees nor Bennett cites this exhibition.
5. Both portraits remain in the Rossetti family.
6. Nothing in Surtees fits this description.

509. TO MACKENZIE BELL

3 St. Edmund's Terrace,
10 May 1895

Dear Bell,

Those books of Christina's which I mean to sell have been removed from Torrington Square, and will be consigned to Sotheby for sale: date etc. not yet fixed. I *suppose* I shall add to them a few personal items.[1]

Those items are still in her house — also some drawings, prints, etc., and the great bulk of the furniture. Some of the furniture will be removed to my own house: another large proportion of it will be placed at the disposal of my nephew Ford Hueffer.[2] After those two removals there will not be much to be sold off — *possibly* not enough to make an auction-sale in the house worth while, but rather a simple lump-sale to some Broker.

If you would like to see the things in the house, I think a convenient course would be that you should come today week — Friday 17 May — towards 2. It happens that a friend of mine, C. Fairfax Murray, is to be there at the same time. The things that he would be most in quest of are drawings etc. by Gabriel — of which there are various remainders, many of them mere boyish affairs.[3]

Yours very truly,
W. M. Rossetti

MS: Princeton.

1. MS. Diary, 19 January 1895: "Went on sorting-out books [at Torrington Square]: I keep (I suppose) more than I set aside to be parted with. As to these latter — 1, I have authorized the servants to appropriate some.... 2, I think of asking Garnett whether he would like to look at them; as there must be some privately printed things, old-fashioned or foreign items, etc., which he might possibly find available for the Museum. 3, Some presentation-copies, or volumes with writing by Christina, might be worth selling by auction.... 4, Several other things seem of no appreciable value, mere stock for which a second-hand Bookseller would give a few shillings." 10 February: "Wise ... does not think the present volumes etc. would sell for much, and decidedly advises that a Bookseller, chiefly Sotheran, should be addressed, rather than try an auction.... Wise knows these matters well, and I am inclined to adopt his advice rather than carry out my own previous intention: I can't help thinking however that he underrates the selling-value." 18 February: "[Robert V.] Elvey called at Torrington Square, looked at books, and offered to do gratis all that is needed for preparing them for an auction-sale by Sotheby." 8 June: "Called at Sotheby's, and spoke to the partner Mr. Hodge.... After some discussion it is arranged that Christina's books are to be sold at Sotheby's before the end of July; and that the same sale may be made to include some prints, drawings, personal objects, etc.... This arrangement makes it pretty plain to me that a separate auction-sale in Christina's own house will not be needed.... Hodge was not disposed to include in his sale certain books as remainder-stock. These consist of Cayley's Homer, Petrarch [*Sonnets and Stanzas*, trans. by, 1879], and *Paradise*, mostly in sheets; and my father's Dante volume 2 [*Comento Analitico*, 1826-27], and (I think) *Spirito Antipapale* [1832] (these 2 also in sheets) and Beatrice [*La Beatrice di Dante*, 1842]: not a *large* quantity of my father's books. In my own house I have no space for all these works: so ... I can but undertake to sell them off as waste-paper, however reluctantly. I called-in Olyett, who will on Monday remove the entire stock, and pay for it per weight, whatever that may amount to. He roughly guesses it about 3 cwt., and its value 15/-." 23 July: "I wrote to Sotheby's sending a list of 44 persons to whom I should like the Catalogue to be forwarded: also posted to Stephens a small paragraph on the subject for *Athenaeum* [27 July 1895, p. 132]." 1 August: "With Helen and Mary I attended the sale at Sotheby's. The maximum I had looked for with any confidence was from £30 to 35. The upshot was ... £44.19, so I am quite satisfied.... [James] Tregaskis ... bought the great majority of the lots." Lots 737-56 were books; 757-67, miscellaneous articles including "an inlaid circular wood Box" made by G. Polidori; 768-71, framed engravings and photographs.
2. MS. Diary, 1 March 1895: "Ford and Elsie called ... offered to lend (or I might perhaps give) him some articles of furniture from Christina's house."
3. MS. Diary, 17 May 1895: "At Torrington Square met Murray and Bell: sold to each of them a few things left by Christina — more especially to Murray the crayon-portrait by Gabriel of my mother, dated 1877 or 1878 [Surtees 451] — its amount being £15."

510. TO MACMILLAN & CO.

3 St. Edmund's Terrace,
5 June 1895

Dear Sirs,

Since 24 May when I replied to your letter of 22, I have looked into the agreement which you used to have with my sister, and shall be quite prepared to bring out on the like terms the proposed supplementary volume of her Poems.[1] I suppose you will deem it proper to enter into an agreement with me for the purpose, and I therefore leave it to you to put the matter in train.

Would you think it desirable to give a portrait of Christina as frontispiece? If so, I could easily provide one in all respects satisfactory.[2]

Yours very truly,
W. M. Rossetti

MS: BL.

1. *New Poems.* MS. Diary, 16 March 1895: "Looked with some attention through that old series of MS. books in which Christina used to write down her poems as soon as brought into shape. They must I think contain *many* things which have not been published, but which might well be included in some future complete edition." 31 May: "In going on with Christina's MS. books, I find that the quantity of verse which she wrote, and left unpublished, exceeds what I had supposed. Most of it is much more than moderately good, but rather self-repeating in theme and treatment. I fancy I shall now be publishing nearly ¾ of it." 3 June: "Have now gone through the bulk of what I have here, needed for Christina's new volume: have noted down no less than 203 items. There may be a few further outlying ones here, and certainly there are a fair number at Torrington Square." 3 October: "To my great satisfaction I handed in to George Macmillan the entire copy for [*New Poems*].... The course adopted will be this: The Printers in England will print, and send me proofs, and the proofs, as revised by me, will be forwarded to the United States, where American Printers will print other sheets." 13 January 1896: "Received from Macmillan an advance-copy of [*New Poems*] ... (it is to be regularly published on 17 January)."
2. See Letter 506, Note 3.

511. TO CHARLES FAIRFAX MURRAY

3 St. Edmund's Terrace,
18 June 1895

Dear Murray,

I regret to say that nothing is known about the key proper to that screen-desk.[1] The Caretaker and her husband (a very expert man at such things) tried to trace out the proper key 2 or 3 months ago, and failed; and today the Caretaker again assured me positively that the key is not to be found in the box you speak of.

I very much hope (but don't yet know for certain) that tomorrow I shall get absolutely quit of the Torrington Square house.[2] After that I shall lose *no* time in getting off to Italy, so I could not now appoint a day for meeting you. Shall probably be back before 15 July, and we could then see further about it.

I have not sold that chalk portrait of Christina (chin on hands). The *first* price which I named to Mr. Morse was £65: before he returned any answer I bethought myself (and I adhere to this view) that £65 is really not — what I intended it to be — a *large* price, and I wrote to him again saying that I would not entertain any offer under £90, and on that I would *reflect*. He did not respond. So it remains, and in fact I have not the least wish to part with the drawing.

Christina's drawing-room contained 2 water-colours by Lizzie: Woman and Ghost in Forest,[3] and *St. Agnes' Eve* (Tennyson). I have no wish to sell either; but would take £35 (were it offered) for one or other.

I suppose I still possess the pen-and-ink of *Woeful Victory*: should have to hunt it up. Until I see what other drawings I have besides that one, I don't know whether I would dispose of it or not.

Yours,
W. M. Rossetti

MS: Texas.

1. Presumably bought by Murray from Torrington Square.
2. MS. Diary, 22 June 1895: "Mrs. Belcher [caretaker] writes me that she has now left Torrington Square, and delivered up the keys to the Landlord: a satisfaction to my mind."
3. Probably *The Haunted Tree*, mentioned in WMR's "Dante Gabriel Rossetti and Elizabeth Siddal," *Burlington Magazine*, 1 (May 1903), 277.

512. TO LIONEL HENRY CUST[1]

3 St. Edmund's Terrace,
10 August 1895

Sir,

I beg that you will be so good as to lay this letter before the Trustees of the National Portrait Gallery.

It is my wish to offer to the Trustees, for acceptance, the following work or works.[2]

1. A Portrait of my late sister Christina Georgina Rossetti, the poetess. She died on 29 December 1894, and I am aware that, in the case of a person so recently deceased, there are special regulations limiting acceptance. Nevertheless I feel emboldened to make the offer, considering especially the very high and indeed enthusiastic recognition of her position as a poetess which has been apparent in the public press since her decease (not to speak of what occurred during her lifetime). She is generally pronounced to be second only (or perhaps not second) to Mrs. Browning. I could produce scores or hundreds of extracts in confirmation, were this desired.

I offer — at the choice of the Trustees — either of the following 2 works —
(a) A head of my sister, aged 18, painted in oil by my brother Dante Gabriel Rossetti (whose own portrait[3] is already in the Gallery), in 1848. It is an approvable piece of painting, and must be the first oil-painting which he produced — i.e. the one which he *completed* earlier than any other. It has recently been reproduced in some form of photo-engraving, and will appear in a book which I am about to publish — *Dante Gabriel Rossetti — his Family-Letters, with a Memoir* (by myself). Before consigning this work (if accepted) to the Gallery, I should wish to have it photographed in the ordinary way, for my own satisfaction and use. — Or else
(b) A lifesized head of my sister, along with my mother, tinted chalks, done by D. G. Rossetti in 1877. It is one of his very best things in that medium. Has been photographed and engraved.

2. A portrait of my elder sister Maria Francesca Rossetti, authoress of *A Shadow of Dante* — a book which has gone through several editions, and is now included in Longmans' "Silver Library." She died in 1876. This is a small half-length in oil, painted by James Collinson, one of the 7 members of the "Praeraphaelite Brotherhood," towards 1850. It is a good likeness, and competently though rather stiffly painted.

3. A portrait of my maternal Uncle John William Polidori, M.D. He was in 1816 the Travelling Physician of Lord Byron, and he wrote and published a Tale

The Vampyre, which used to be very generally attributed to Byron; also other tales and poems. He is mentioned (not too advantageously) in Moore's Life of Byron, Dowden's *Life of Shelley*, and other books; and I see his name down in the list for the *Dictionary of National Biography*. He died in 1821. I could give either a bust of him or a lifesized oil head-and-shoulders portrait: the latter may be considered a good work of art. I have forgotten the names of the Sculptor and Painter.

Allow me to add that, if the Trustees should like to have the portrait of Christina Rossetti, without both or either of the others, I shall acquiesce in their decision, without feeling in any degree "hurt" or mortified.

The works are all in this house, and I could show them at any convenient time which might be appointed.[4] I expect to be out of England (in Venice) during the first half of September.[5]

Possibly the Trustees may remember that I was the donor of a portrait which has been in the Gallery for a great number of years — that of the Painter Wright of Derby.[6]

I am, Sir,
Your very obedient Servant,
William M. Rossetti

MS: NPG.

1. (1859-1929), writer on art, was employed in the Print Room of the British Museum, 1884-95, when he became director of the National Portrait Gallery in succession to George Scharf, who died on 19 April 1895.
2. See Letters 506-7.
3. By G. F. Watts.
4. MS. Diary, 23 August 1895: "Mr. Lionel Cust ... called, and looked at the 5 works, out of which I offer 3 to the Gallery. He is personally quite in favour of accepting Christina and John Polidori: would like best the crayon of Christina along with my mother, and the oil-portrait of Polidori. For Maria he is not inclined: partly I think that he considers her hardly up to the mark of celebrity, but he puts the point rather upon the mediocrity of Collinson's pictorial work.... He says there are 16 Trustees, but they don't all take an active part: the Chairman Lord de L'Isle is quite unacquainted with all matters of poetical literature, but counts as a connoisseur, especially in decorative art."
5. WMR was invited by the Sindaco of Venice to be a member of the jury at the first Venice Biennale, his fellow jurymen being Adolfo Venturi, Robert de la Sizeranne, Richard Muther, and Julius Lange.
6. Joseph Wright (1734-97). WMR to Trustees of the Gallery, 19 February 1858, gives an account of the provenance of the portrait, which he thought a self-portrait (NPG). It is not now considered a portrait of or by Wright.

513. TO THOMAS JAMES WISE

3 St. Edmund's Terrace,
24 August 1895

Dear Wise,

You and I have more than once (or more than a dozen times) talked about a *Sir Hugh the Heron*. I have just now been going through a total overhauling of all my books, consequent upon the influx of new books from Christina's house; and I find that I *do* still possess some extra copies of *Hugh Heron*. There is a packet containing (as marked by me aforetime) 3 copies and 1 surplus sheet. I have not as yet opened the packet, but assume the copies to be in average condition.

There is also 1 copy, which was Christina's. It is in a shabby state, but has the attraction of containing Gabriel's inscription to Christina — written evidently about the date of printing, 1843.

I forget what price I used to put upon *Hugh Heron*: you probably remember. I would sell for the like price any 1 of the 3 first-named copies. Have no wish to part with Christina's copy; but would sell that also for £1 additional.

I fancy you already possess a trifling little thing by Miss Hitchener called *The Fire-side Bagatelle*.[1] I have come upon an extra copy of this. If you *don't* possess one, I will *give* it you: if you do possess one, I would reserve this copy for someone else. It is considerably dust-engrained, but not seriously amiss.

Yours always truly,

W. M. Rossetti

MS: BL.

1. *The Fire-side Bagatelle: containing Enigmas on the Chief Towns of England and Wales* (1818), copies of which were given to WMR c. 1880 by "a Mr. Everest, a nephew of Miss Hitchener" (WMR to Wise, 17 October 1895; BL). For WMR's presentation inscription to Wise, see *The Ashley Library, A Catalogue* (1922), 2:187.

514. TO LIONEL HENRY CUST

3 St. Edmund's Terrace,
20 September 1895

Dear Mr. Cust,

Returning from Venice to London on 16 September, I found your letter of 13, and am most heartily pleased to see that the Trustees have accepted the two works which I had the honour and satisfaction of offering.[1]

Certainly, if I can ever hit upon the name of the painter of the likeness of Dr. Polidori, I will notify it to you. May as well mention that some months ago, among my sister's papers, I found a scrap of writing by my aunt Charlotte L. Polidori, saying that the portrait of Dr. Polidori *which she possessed* was painted by a Mr. Clover.[2] I feel tolerably confident that the portrait which she possessed is a different and less noticeable one, remaining in my possession. Of this however I am not *certain*. Is anything known of Clover and his style, and is the latter similar to that of the portrait now in your Gallery?

About Madox Brown I shall not for the present raise any further question, unless you were to give me the hint.[3] It is however a fact that his fame is rapidly widening and deepening. His name was in the mouths of my 4 Jury-colleagues in Venice (Muther, Lange, Sizeranne, and Venturi); and since my return to London I see that Sizeranne's recent much-admired book[4] opens with Brown, and Muther (English translation, p. 199) refers to him as an absolute protagonist in modern European art.[5] See also Quilter's book, *Preferences in Art*, and notice the great run upon Brown's splendid picture in the National Gallery.[6]

As to the portrait of Fawcett[7] and his wife I have been reflecting. Excuse me for saying that I would not *give* it, but were an offer made to buy it for your

590

Gallery, I would (personally speaking) think over that. I have an opinion as to the very lowest price that ought to be accepted, but need not at present define this.

But there is the further fact that I consider the portrait to be the property rather of my 4 children than of myself. It was given by Brown to my wife and me, and I suppose that in law I am now the owner; but (as a matter of good feeling) I regard it as having appertained more especially to my wife, and in that case it passed, under her will, to my children under Trusteeship. I raised this point to my eldest daughter (aged 20) the other day; and I found that she has no particular wish to part with the work, even for a goodish price. If you would like any further details, I will gladly give them — and remain

Always truly yours,
W. M. Rossetti

That portrait of Christina and my mother is in rather a dingy state as to mount etc., and I dare say you may be doing something to make its look more sightly. All the framing is my brother's concern, and ought (to my thinking) to be preserved. In a No. of the *Century Guild Hobby Horse*[8] (say towards 1886) there were some remarks by the painter F. J. Shields as to the great delicacy of these tinted-chalk drawings by my brother, and the strict precautions which ought to be taken in unframing them etc. Shields is very exactly conversant with the matter; and I am sure that, if you thought his personal counsel of any advantage, he would most gladly give it. His address is 7 Lodge Place, St. John's Wood, N.W.

MS: NPG.

1. "The Trustees held a meeting here yesterday afternoon, when the two portraits offered by you were submitted to their inspection. I am glad to say that they were unanimous in agreeing to waive their usual rule not to admit portraits of persons, who have not been deceased for ten years, in favour of your sister, Miss Christina Rossetti, on account of her high eminence as a poetess in the literary history of this country. They also agreed to accept the portrait of Polidori" (AP). WMR informed Cust on 6 August 1904 that the Polidori portrait was by F. G. Gainsford (NPG). MS. Diary, 16 September 1895, records that "few things in my life have given me more heartfelt gratification" than the acceptance of the portraits: "To get my dear old mother into the Gallery is no small thing: and how great would have been the delight of my good Grandfather, could he have forseen that his greatly beloved and lamented John would be there too." On 4 June 1896 WMR visited the Gallery in its new building in St. Martin's Place, and noted that the family portraits were "all well displayed: but the light strikes on the heads of my mother and Christina in a way that seems to me to reduce the depth and richness of effect" (MS. Diary). He suggested to Cust on 21 September 1896 that the portrait "might I fancy (if you will excuse my suggesting it) benefit by receiving light from the *opposite* corner of the frame" (NPG).
2. Joseph Clover (1779-1853), painter of historical subjects and portraits.
3. WMR offered DGR's portrait of FMB (Surtees 269) on 29 August 1895 (NPG), but Cust hesitated "as the Trustees only like to waive their rule under very special circumstances" (13 September 1895; AP). It was formally offered on 24 September 1895, and accepted on 5 December, "in view of the high eminence of Mr. Ford Madox Brown, as an artist, and also of the merit of your brother's drawing" (Cust to WMR, 6 December; AP).
4. *La Peinture Anglaise Contemporaine* (1895).
5. *History of Modern Painting* (1895), 1.
6. *Jesus Washing Peter's Feet.*
7. In 1872 FMB was commissioned by Sir Charles Dilke to paint a portrait of Henry Fawcett and his wife.
8. n.s. 5 (April 1890), 70-73; "A Note Upon Rossetti's Method of Drawing in Crayons."

515. TO THOMAS JAMES WISE

3 St. Edmund's Terrace,
23 September 1895

Dear Wise,

Thanks for yours of 19. I have really not the faintest wish to sell that *Hugh Heron* containing Gabriel's boyish inscription — so the matter can remain not further mooted.[1]

Will send you Miss Hitchener's pamphlet[2] as soon as I lay hands on it — which will not take long. Will at some time send you (as Evans suggests) one of the photographs from the early portrait of Christina.

You will kindly reply to Evans in any terms commanding themselves to your own judgement. I don't consider that I have done him the slightest wrong. Upon copies of that pamphlet[3] which I sold privately I put my own price, and he chose to pay it. Other copies remained: I put them up to auction, and had to accept whatever price was bid. Had it been more than my own price, I should have been all the better pleased, but it turned out to be less. Clearly you are right in saying that by a little management I could have served my own money-interests better in that respect; but I felt more inclined to get rid once for all of whatever I didn't myself want to keep than to hold on to the items, and keep them hanging on hand for some future contingency. In such matters I suit my own humour — which may be a silly one commercially.

All this I write without the slightest soreness against Evans — who is entitled to his own opinion, and seems a nice fellow.

Yours,
W. M. Rossetti

MS: BL.

1. See Letter 513.
2. *The Fire-side Bagatelle.*
3. Maria Rossetti's *Guendalina Talbot.*

516. TO ALGERNON CHARLES SWINBURNE

3 St. Edmund's Terrace,
3 October 1895

Dear Swinburne,

You will be aware that I am about to bring out through Macmillan a new volume of Christina's Poems. I always dedicate my books to someone: and as soon as I pondered a Dedicatee for this volume (2 or 3 days ago) I felt an earnest desire for you. Overpage you will find a copy of the dedication. Will you accept it? and, if any phrase in it strikes you unfavourably, tell me, and it shall be altered.[1]

I have been in much hurry these few days to get the affair out of hand: and this morning I handed all the copy in to Macmillan, including the dedication. You will condone this precipitation. The book has to be printed in England; and the proofs, revised by me, will go on to America, and there be reprinted — publication in both countries ensuing (it is hoped) towards Christmas. There are 300 poems as near as may be; and I am quite confident that many of them will be pronounced by you — as by me — most admirable.

Love to Watts and yourself from

W. M. Rossetti

You may have seen that I got a portrait of Christina, along with my dear loving old Mother, into the National Portrait Gallery. Christina had to be there one day, as a matter of course: but I greatly applaud myself on having thus wafted in my Mother by a side-wind.

To Algernon Charles Swinburne
the Generous Eulogist
of Christina Rossetti
who hailed his genius and prized himself
the greatest of living British Poets
my old and constant Friend
I dedicate this Book
W. M. R.

MS: BL.

1. "The" (1. 2) was altered to "A" in *New Poems*.

517. TO THOMAS JAMES WISE

3 St. Edmund's Terrace,
6 November 1895

Dear Wise,

I have looked again into that matter of the *Germ*, and am rather surprised to find that my previous statement was not correct. What I really possess is 2 complete sets; also 2 copies of No. 1; also 1 copy of No. 3. No more. One complete set I shall keep for myself.

Today I am writing to Tregaskis,[1] and offering

Complete set —— £4.10.
2 copies No. 1 ——   14.
1 copy No. 3 ——   7.

I tell him that I don't mean to take less — nor do I, whether from him or others: should be quite content to retain the lot.

If he doesn't close with my offer, I will repeat the same offer to Evans.

Yours very truly,
W. M. Rossetti

MS: BL.

1. James and Mary Lee Tregaskis, Caxton Head, 232 High Holborn, booksellers.

518. TO FREDERICK MACMILLAN

3 St. Edmund's Terrace,
3 December 1895

Dear Mr. Macmillan,

Mr. Theodore Watts — who must doubtless be known to you more or less as the leading Critic of Poetry in the *Athenaeum* — called on me yesterday about a different matter; and, hearing that the new volume of Christina's Poems may be expected (so I surmise) to be published by Christmas-time, he expressed a firm resolution to act as the reviewer of it.[1] With this view he would like to receive a copy *as soon as practicable*, so that he may be prepared to hand-in a critique without any delay after the publication. He and I agreed that I would write to you to mention this point.

I have no doubt you will concur with me as to the expediency of meeting Mr. Watts's wishes. His address (as you may know) is — The Pines, Putney Hill, S.W. — and I think it would be quite sufficient (if to you the most convenient thing) to send him the book in sheets from your house, with or without any word of message. The *portrait*, along with the sheets, would be a desirable adjunct.

Yours very truly,
W. M. Rossetti

MS: BL.

1. *Athenaeum*, 15 February 1896, pp. 207-9.

519. TO FREDERIC GEORGE STEPHENS

3 St. Edmund's Terrace,
21 December 1895

Dear Steph,

The Valentine is from Lennox Hannay[1] (but, the more I think of it, the more satisfied I am that Gabriel, before Hannay, did sit for the head to some extent), and the Sylvia, as you say, is from Miss Siddal: but the Proteus is from a man quite unlike Hannay — viz.: Aspinall.[2] I not only remember this generally as a fact, but I met the two men various times, and have a clear recollection of their looks.

Aspinall (but possibly you don't need my saying so) was a young Lawyer. He emigrated — I think to Australia — and at first made a marked success, becoming Attorney General or something of the kind. Afterwards he broke down — possibly from irregularities (but I don't know it) — and died I fancy before the age of 40. I fear he became insane, or not much short of that. He belonged in London to Hannay's set.

What you say about Gabriel's Sevenoaks landscape[3] must be correct: I seem now to remember it for myself as a fact. You seem to suggest that I should write to the *Magazine of Art*, supplementing what my book says on this subject: however I don't particularly care to do that — and my experience is that magazines etc. generally find some reason for *not* inserting what one happens to volunteer to them.

Yours,
W. M. Rossetti

MS: Bodleian.

1. James Lennox Hannay, a barrister and later a magistrate, was a cousin of James Hannay (see Bennett 1969, p. 69). The picture for which he sat was Hunt's *Valentine Rescuing Sylvia from Proteus*.
2. Butler Cole Aspinall (1830-75) emigrated to Australia in 1854. He was elected to the legislature of Victoria in 1856, and was Attorney General for several months in 1861, and Solicitor General for several months in 1870. Following a mental breakdown in 1871 he returned to England.
3. See Letter 16, Note 3.

520. TO FREDERIC GEORGE STEPHENS

3 St. Edmund's Terrace,
23 December 1895

Dear Steph,

I should of course like much to get a review from you in *Magazine of Art*, but am not disposed to moot the question with my Publishers: *possibly* they have already sent thither a copy of my book.[1] The fact is that some little while ago, having particular reason for thinking about a certain *foreign* review, I wrote to the Publishers raising this point, and also saying that, if they would send me a list of the papers etc. to which they had forwarded the book, I might perhaps, from personal knowledge, be able to make some further apposite suggestion: but they gave the matter the go-by by simply replying that they had forwarded the book to 25 reviews etc., and considered this to be all that would be serviceable. They are a little "near" in affairs of this sort. I regard the sending-out of copies as being their concern rather than mine, and would rather therefore "shut up" about it.

Lennox Hannay, as a young man, was certainly handsome in a more than usual degree. His face was that of a refined, rather conventional man of society; and I agree with you in saying that what Hunt put into the head of Valentine was not wholly discernible in that of Hannay.

About Hunt's forthcoming book[2] I have heard rumours from time to time, but have no direct knowledge. It happens that I have not seen Hunt in person since (I think) February 1894. The other day his wife wrote inviting me to call[3] — partly prompted, I fancy, by my recent book. I may do so yet, but could not take the precise day which Mrs. Hunt proposed. I rather suspect that Hunt's book will be not particularly friendly to Gabriel, and so am all the better pleased that I have had my own say in anticipation. He cannot, I take it, be annoyed by anything I have said about himself.

Your
W. M. Rossetti

MS: Bodleian.

1. MS. Diary, 2 December 1895: "Watts called. Showed me a letter from MacColl to the effect that Watts, having just now bespoken ... [*FLM*] for review in *Athenaeum*, is too late, as Stephens had bespoken it in the summer. I like the result little or not at all less well." Stephens did not, however, review the book anywhere; nor did a review appear in the *Athenaeum*.
2. *PR & PRB*, 1st ed., 1905.
3. MS. Diary does not record a visit.

521. TO THOMAS JAMES WISE
3 St. Edmund's Terrace,
1 August 1896

Dear Wise,

Thanks for your letter. I find that of the ever-memorable *Hugh Heron* I now possess only the following extras — The copy (very shabby) which in boyhood Gabriel inscribed to Christina — 2 full copies in sheets, no wrappers — 1 extra sheet as a fragment.

I don't feel any impulse towards selling any item in this small remainder, and thus, so far as I am concerned, *Hugh Heron* may be viewed as no longer a marketable commodity.

I also observed a newspaper-notice of the death of my good old friend Slack. Have not any knowledge as to the Executorship, but suppose it to be pretty sure that he has left to his widow the general bulk of his property, and probably made her Executrix as well. Were I you, I would address Mrs. Slack, and I think it more than likely that she would willingly enough treat for selling the Shelley-Hitchener letters. Not that I judge her to be otherwise than very well off.

Thank you — we are all in good health, more or less. There certainly has been some rather oppressive heat, but it seems to be fairly abated now.

Always yours,
W. M. Rossetti

MS: BL.

522. TO MACKENZIE BELL
3 St. Edmund's Terrace,
10 September 1896

Dear Bell,

You will I suppose have received by now the copy of your book, and my notes upon it. I sent them back to you yesterday by parcels-post. I read the book with interest, and frequently with agreement. You will understand that my notes do not at all aim at discussing the critical opinions which you express — for these are your affair not mine: I only address myself to questions of biographical or literary *fact*.[1]

About Dora Greenwell. She was a member of a fine old Durham family — the chief living representative of which (I *think* he is living but he must now be old) is Canon Greenwell,[2] of Durham Cathedral, a very great authority on ancient burial-mounds or "barrows." Dora was his sister; and there was another brother, Allan Greenwell,[3] an English Clergyman who joined the Church of Rome. Christina first met Dora Greenwell at the house of, or in connexion with, the Bell Scotts, then settled in Newcastle-on-Tyne. Dora and Christina met several times, and liked one another much: the acquaintance may have begun towards 1858, and continued on and off till Dora's death (which may possibly have been towards 1875): they did not meet *often*. I myself met Dora 2 or 3 times, when she was getting on towards 40: a slim dark rather tall woman, of an elegant-serious type: there was something particularly pleasing in her tone of voice and mode of elocution — a graceful sweet tripping delivery. She wrote and published a goodish deal of verse: it was quite above mere mediocrity, and had an infusion of real poetry.

Yours very truly,

W. M. Rossetti

MS: Princeton. Extract in *Christina Rossetti*, pp. 36-37.

1. MS. Diary, 2 September 1896: "Mackenzie Bell left with me the type-written copy of his book on Christina. I began reading it. Find several inaccuracies of detail. The book is of course pleasing in general tone, but as yet it seems to present nothing of a salient character in treatment." 3 September: "As I progress with Bell's book I like it somewhat better." 14 September: "Mackenzie Bell called again. He will in various respects modify his book about Christina, in accordance with the notes which I sent him. I find he had, at an early date of his undertaking, consulted Hunt and Shields, who gave him details about Christina's affairs of the heart. I take it he knows the names, but these were not mentioned between us." 27 July 1897: "Returned Mackenzie Bell's proofs, with some pencilled notes."
2. William Greenwell (1820-1918) was also librarian of the Cathedral, a noted collector of Greek coins and prehistoric bronze implements, and editor of early documents for the Surtees Society.
3. Alan Greenwell, vicar of St. James, Haydock, 1865-69 (*Crockford's Clerical Directory*).

523. TO MACKENZIE BELL

3 St. Edmund's Terrace,
6 October 1896

Dear Bell,

All right about the Dodgson photograph, and about the lines by my Father.[1] Of the latter you are welcome to give a facsimile, if this comes convenient. The handwriting is of course my Father's, which was about the best handwriting I ever saw in my life — whether in its ordinary form, or (as in this instance) done with a purpose of calligraphy.

I am glad Dr. Hare[2] has so politely entered into communication with you. I recollect him perfectly. He would know about the earliest stages of constitutional ill-health in Christina. Towards 1852 (perhaps) Christina's illness was considered to be essentially angina pectoris, and then another doctor, Crellin,[3] was called in, and he set her fairly right as regards those particular symptoms.

Christina's knowledge of Sir William Jenner began towards 1854. In 1853, when Christina with our parents went to Frome, Maria and I took lodgings in Albany Street (not the same house which we all afterwards occupied as a family-residence), over a Chemist's shop occupied by a Mr. Burcham[4] — who turned out to be also an amateur painter of still life, of considerable merit. Jenner, then a man of no professional celebrity, was I believe a sort of partner with Burcham, and thus Maria and I first met Jenner, and afterwards Christina did. She liked him, thinking his manner not unpleasantly scrutinizing, or "formidable" — a point as to which she was rather sensitive in medical concerns. I am not clear that she ever consulted him professionally until her terrible illness, exophthalmic bronchocele, beginning in 1871. He pronounced her to be "a very interesting case" — the malady being far from a common one. After that she always consulted him (until he retired from practice) at the more important crises of her illness: Dr. Stewart (who attended my mother and aunts) being also employed by Christina in the ordinary course of events.

Anything which you might mention as to this sequence of Doctors would not, I think, be calculated to ruffle any personal susceptibilities.

Yours,

W. M. Rossetti

MS: Princeton. Extract in *Christina Rossetti*, pp. 27-28.[5]

1. Lewis Carroll's photograph of CGR and her mother taken c. 1863 in the garden of Cheyne Walk, and Gabriele Rossetti's poem of c. 1834 addressed to his daughters, both of which appear in Bell's *Christina Rossetti*.
2. Charles John Hare, physician to the Westminster Ophthalmic Hospital; CGR's doctor, 1845-50.
3. *Churchill's Medical Directory* for this period lists H. Nelson Crellin and William Crellin.
4. Robert Partridge Burcham (1812-94), chemist; painter in the style of his friend W. Henry Hunt.
5. The two final sentences of Bell's extract are not in the MS.

524. TO FREDERIC GEORGE STEPHENS

3 St. Edmund's Terrace,
2 December 1896

Dear Steph,

I am sure that Woolner was the first of us who knew Patmore personally. On referring to the old P.R.B. Journal, I find that the first mention of Patmore (apart from his poems) is that Woolner was to dine with him on 23 September 1849. How Woolner first knew him I can't now recollect: possibly through some visit of his to the British Museum, or some association therein. Certainly the Ormes came into our circle *after* the Patmores: for I perfectly remember that Woolner, soon after knowing Patmore, told me that Patmore had cautioned him (before he met her) against Mrs. Orme — as being pushing, manoeuvring, or what not; but that he, as soon as he did meet Mrs. Orme, found her to be most cordial and pleasant.

It should be understood that, although Woolner was the first of us to *know* Patmore, the first to care about him were Gabriel and myself; who read towards 1846 Patmore's original volume of poems published in or about 1844, and were enthusiastic about it: and in the P.R.B. Journal there are several mentions of Patmore in this relation preceding the first reference to personal acquaintance with him.

We were grateful to your wife (and you) for kindly proposing the other day that Helen should house with you before starting for Australia. But neither I, nor Helen, when I mentioned the invitation to her, thought that it would be practicable to accept.

Best greetings to you both from the

Shortly to be expatriated
W. M. Rossetti

MS: Bodleian.

525. TO FREDERIC GEORGE STEPHENS 3 St. Edmund's Terrace,
6 December 1896

Dear Steph,

Thanks for your letter etc. I can't help thinking that what you say about Gabriel in the *Athenaeum*[1] is erroneous, and what I wrote to you correct. Have not the faintest reminiscence as to Gabriel's having "sought out" Patmore in consequence of reading his volume of 1844. He did not exactly seek out Browning or Leigh Hunt, but wrote to each of them. Did not seek out Allingham, but met him through Patmore; never in any way sought out Monckton Milnes, nor knew nor cared much about him. Am satisfied that the first P.R.B. who knew Patmore in the flesh, or who got into any personal relation with him even by correspondence, was Woolner, and that in 1849.

Have read all this Orrock correspondence,[2] and think you have fully vindicated yourself.

I knew that Martineau's picture[3] was offered to the National Gallery: it could not be other than accepted.

Yours,
W. M. Rossetti

MS: Bodleian.

1. Stephens wrote in his obituary of Patmore that DGR's reading of Patmore's *Poems*, 1844 "induced him to seek out Patmore much as, long before his days of fame began, he sought out Browning and Leigh Hunt, Allingham and Monckton-Milnes" (*Athenaeum*, 5 December 1896, pp. 797-98). See also Letter 524.
2. James Orrock (1829-1913), painter and collector, whose collection of pictures was sold at Christie's, 25-27 April 1895.
3. *The Last Day in the Old Home.*

526. TO MACMILLAN & CO. 3 St. Edmund's Terrace,
9 December 1896

Dear Sirs,

There are 2 points on which I find occasion to address you.

1. You may possibly have observed the enclosed newspaper-paragraph, or one resembling it. I had no hand in writing or inserting it. The substance of it is correct — That Mr. Bowden proposes to publish a girlish prose-story by my sister, interspersed with poems.[1] 11 of the poems have been already published by you: I enclose a list of them. As the list specifies, some of the compositions are in the *New Poems*; and possibly some of those which are noted as being "in a volume" are also in that volume of *New Poems*. Mr. Bowden is of course aware that he cannot without your consent reprint those verses which you have already published: if you are willing to give your assent, I should feel this an obligation to myself, and of course he would feel it the like to *him*self.[2]

I may add that Mr. Bowden got to know something of this early performance not through me in any way,[3] and he made me an offer which I accepted. I would not have *volunteered* in offering the tale to a Publisher, and thus I did not offer it to you: and in fact I consider that (though a niceish sort of thing in its way) it would not be deserving of figuring along with those really good things by Christina which issue from your house. It will be understood that the story is strictly a *prose*-story — the verses being only introduced as accessories to the prose.

2. It happens that one of my daughters is under medical orders to take a long sea-voyage, and I must accompany her; and we must start for Australia (Sydney) on 24 December — Steamer Nineveh. I could not be back earlier than the end of May — perhaps rather later. Meanwhile, in January, a handsome sum will be coming in to me from your Firm.[4] It would be inconvenient if the cheque for me were drawn ''to order''; so perhaps you will draw it ''to Bearer,'' or pay it in direct to my Bank — the London and Westminster, 214 High Holborn. Or, if it would suit you to let me have the cheque before I start, that would be to me the most convenient of all: but perhaps this is not compatible with your system — and the other plan would answer for me well enough.

Yours very truly,
W. M. Rossetti

MS: BL.

1. MS. Diary, 12 October 1896: ''Coulson Kernahan called — the Literary Advisor of Bowden, the Publisher who has now set up a separate business.... I assent to Bowden's publishing Christina's juvenile story called *Maude*, upon his paying me £25 or thereabouts. I will write a few prefatory words.'' *Maude, A Story for Girls* was published in an edition of 500 copies in 1897. James Bowden was a partner in Ward Lock & Co. from c. 1881 (F. A. Mumby, *Publishing and Bookselling* [1956], pp. 268-69).

2. MS. Diary, 26 May 1897: ''It appears that Macmillan has persisted in his refusal to allow Bowden the use of those poems which form a part of *Maude*. This makes Bowden's project of publication anything but a promising one; and I spontaneously offered, if he prefers to relinquish the project, to repay him the £30 which he paid me in December.''

3. Presumably through Mackenzie Bell, to whom WMR had loaned the MS.

4. MS. Diary, 30 September 1896: ''Macmillans sent in their accounts for Christina's books — a year up to 30 June. The sum which will be payable to me next January is £297, which I regard as eminently satisfactory.'' Undoubtedly a substantial part of the payment was for *New Poems*. The first royalties paid to him after CGR's death are recorded on 30 September 1895: ''Macmillans sent me an account of the sale of Christina's books, 1 July 1894 to 30 June 1895. About 2500 copies of the *Poems* volume [*New and Enlarged Edition*, 1890] were sold, and the profit to me ... is £216. I don't know that this *exceeds* what I was looking for, but it is certainly a very handsome sum.'' 14 January 1910 notes that ''the royalties from Christina are always about double what I get from Gabriel's books.''

527. TO MACKENZIE BELL

3 St. Edmund's Terrace,
30 July 1897

Dear Bell,

I return the letter of Messrs Hurst and Blackett. Don't exactly see why they should have interfered at all in such a matter, and they ''can't possibly'' know whether or not publicity ''could not possibly offend anyone.''

If you know the name of the 2 men in question,[1] you know them otherwise than through me, and do not seem to be under responsibility to me for printing the names or not. My *preference* is that they should not be printed. Had I entertained a contrary preference, it was open to myself to print the names in the notes to the *New Poems* — which I advisedly did not do.

> Yours very truly,
> W. M. Rossetti

MS: Princeton.

1. C. B. Cayley and James Collinson, whom Bell mentions casually in *Christina Rossetti*.

528. TO MACMILLAN & CO.

3 St. Edmund's Terrace,
13 August 1897

Dear Sirs,

Perhaps you remember that in 1895, when I proposed to you to bring out a fresh volume of poems by my sister Christina, since then published as *New Poems*, I also raised the question whether it might not be expedient at some future time to publish her *complete* poetical works as one uniform book. In your reply of 22 May 1895 you say: "We quite agree with you that hereafter it would be well to publish a complete edition of Miss Rossetti's poems, so far as they are in our hands, re-arranged in chronological order, and we should be very willing to undertake it. It is a great pity that it cannot be made really complete by including the verses published by the Society for the Promotion of Christian Knowledge." And again (27 May): "If they (Society) will take a payment for leave to include them only in a complete edition, we would find the money, and charge it against the expenses of the book: it would be worth while to pay £50, or even £100."

These letters of yours happened to come again under my eye the other day; and it occurs to me to enquire whether you consider that the time for taking up this question of a complete edition has now come, or is within view. I can quite imagine that your reply may be in the negative, nor have I any wish to hurry on the time unduly. I could however, if you like, begin in a leisurely way to make preparations for such an edition, even if *early* publication is not contemplated. One consideration is that I am not far from 68 years of age, and my lease of life is dwindling, and, when it terminates, no one will remain who knows much about the matter.[1]

I presume there may by this time have been an issue of the *New Poems* embodying my *latest* revisal, which involved the omission of one or two compositions.[2] If so, would you be so good as to send me a couple of copies of such last issue.

> Yours very truly,
> W. M. Rossetti

MS: BL.

1. WMR informed Macmillan on 7 September 1897 that he had "traced out with minuteness (so far as I find it possible to do so)" the dates of the poems, and that he would soon begin "the writing of Notes, Preface, etc. — and the book will then be secured against the chance of my being dead or disabled before the fitting time for its publication shall come" (BL).

2. WMR to Macmillan & Co., 31 July 1896, mentions a reprint of the volume which introduced "the few alterations which were pointed out in the original Errata-slip," and suggested that "at some future opportunity a rather more extensive change should be made in the book; as it has been pointed out to me from 2 or 3 quarters ... that some few poems, which are included in the volume, had appeared in some previous volume of Christina's" (BL). Proofs of a reissue, from which *Conference Between Christ, the Saints, and the Soul* (*Goblin Market, the Prince's Progress and Other Poems* [1875] with the title *I Will Lift Up My Eyes Unto the Hills*) and *A Christmas Carol*, "Whoso hears a chiming for Christmas at the nighest" (*Poems*) were omitted, reached WMR on 24 October (MS. Diary).

529. TO CHARLES ELIOT NORTON

3 St. Edmund's Terrace,
9 September 1897

Dear Professor Norton,

Yesterday I received your letter of 29 August, along with the typewritten letters of my Brother. I am truly most highly obliged, and have found these letters, on perusal, to be of most uncommon interest. Gabriel was in my opinion a very good letter-writer indeed — natural, thoughtful, pointed, and entertaining: certainly he did not indulge in outpouring of theory, sentiment, or description. I don't think justice was done (at least in England) to those Family-letters of his which I published at the end of 1895.

I am glad that you possess his water-colour *Before the Battle*[1] (am not quite sure that I myself ever saw that) and the *Beatrice at Marriage Feast*. In those letters with which you have now favoured me Gabriel speaks of doing a portrait of Ruskin for you: did he ever fulfil his intention? He did one portrait of Ruskin — a lifesized head in red chalk — in 1861:[2] I think it is a good likeness, a little too robust. Some years ago it belonged to a Mr. Pocock of Brighton, and I dare say still belongs to him.

I think you will find that my forthcoming book of letters etc.[3] contains a great amount of interesting matter — Gabriel's letters to Brown, Brown's diaries, my old "P.R.B. Diary," much about my Father's Dantesque writings, very numerous letters to Gabriel and myself, from Ruskin (64 of these), Christina, Browning, etc. etc. There is also the diary which my Uncle Dr. John Polidori kept in 1816, when he was Byron's Travelling Physician. The book will be quite a big one. It is likely (but by no means certain as yet) that Allen,[4] Ruskin's Publisher, will undertake it.

I hope Fortune has continued to treat you well, with regard to health as well as other matters. I (as you may be aware) had in 1894 the great sorrow of losing my wife, Madox Brown's daughter. Four children survive, and all "pregevoli" on one ground or another. The only son, aged nearly 21, is launched on his chosen career of Electrical Engineer. A Rossetti addicted to science seems an oddity: but I would much rather he did *something* in science than nothing or little of any serious account in art or literature.

Yours with thanks and true regard,
W. M. Rossetti

602

MS: Harvard.

1. Surtees 106. Norton to WMR, 29 August 1897: "*Before the Battle* still hangs in my study at Shady Hill and with it (a gift from Ruskin) Dante seeing Beatrice at the Wedding Feast. They are much more to me than mere beautiful pictures!" (AP).

2. Surtees 455. "Prov.: Crawford J. Pocock. Christie, 14 May 1891.... Presented the same year by Malcolm Maclean to Ashmolean Museum, Oxford."

3. MS. Diary, 11 November 1895: "Ever since I finished the writing of ... [*FLM*] I have been thinking of getting up a volume of 'Rossettiana' — letters, memoranda, etc., proper to various members of the family. Today I began the first practical steps to that end — looking through a first section of the family-papers which I brought away from Christina's house." 13 August 1896: "I now think that the right course will be to preserve correct order of date from the beginning to the close of the various volumes (at least 5 would I think be wanted if I draw reasonably upon my material), and to bring out at first starting 2 volumes together. Volume 1 would I take it more than exhaust the material preceding the birth of Gabriel; and volume 2 would contain a goodish deal of detail regarding his and Christina's early years. It might I suppose extend fully up to 1848, Foundation of P.R.B. The whole book might be divided into 6 sections or periods: 1, preceding Gabriel's birth 1828; 2, to 1848 as above; 3, to 1862, Lizzie's death; 4, to 1882, Gabriel's death; 5, to 1894, Christina's death; 6, beyond that date." 11 November: "To my great satisfaction, I seem now to have practically completed my 1st instalment (2 volumes I take it) of Rossettiana. I wrote a title-page, dedication, and preface. The title I now propose is 'Dante Rossetti and his Family'." 3 July 1897: "I have got on with Rossettiana rather faster than I thought for. Am in fact not very far from completing section 3.... This is all the better: for I now could, and certainly should wish to, bring out all the 3 sections in one lot — which would include, along with all the early matter about my Father etc. not highly interesting to the English public, plenty of details about the opening career of Gabriel etc., and especially the letters of Ruskin." 16 November: "[George] Allen replies to me about Rossettiana. Is not inclined to publish it as it stands, but wants it to be restricted and recast as a History of the Praeraphaelite movement. This is not a little tiresome; but perhaps something satisfactory to both of us may emerge from the impasse.... One leading point is that Allen does not want the Ruskin letters to be published by anyone except himself." 8 December: "Allen ... assents ... to begin Rossettiana [*RRP*] with Ruskin's 1st letter in 1854, and to carry it on to February 1862, including the whole of the material put together by me within those 2 dates. This is not what I should like best, but it must do." 12 February 1898: "Wrote to Allen ... that I absolutely assent to the proposal of paying me for Rossettiana a royalty of 12½% upon the published price of all copies sold; but that I think the agreement should provide for increasing this to 15 after possible sale of 1000 copies, and to 20 after do. of 2000." 19 February: "Wrote to Allen assenting to his final terms ... which involve a contingent but perhaps remote increase to a royalty of 15%." 13 December: "[*RRP*] is now out. I called at Allen's, saw the book which is truly a good-looking one, and learned that the supply for the country-trade is sent out today, and the town-trade will be attended to tomorrow. The large-paper copies will not be ready till Saturday or thereabouts." 24 December: "I learn that the large-paper [*RRP*; 250 copies] ... is in fact all sold out."

4. George Allen (1832-1907) joined Ruskin's drawing class at the Working Men's College in 1854, and soon became his engraver and general assistant. In 1871 Ruskin set him up as his publisher.

530. TO SYDNEY CARLYLE COCKERELL[1]

3 St. Edmund's Terrace,
27 November 1897

Dear Sir,

You will be agreeably surprised to learn that that picture by William Morris[2] (about which you and I were in correspondence in August last) has after all turned up in this house. This morning I happend to enter the bedroom vacated by my eldest daughter (who went off to Florence on the 18th prior to marrying), and there to my astonishment I saw the picture. Had not once set eyes on it since June or July 1882. My eldest daughter being gone, I cannot enquire of her how or

603

whence the work was found; but she was rummaging about after many things before her departure, and I learn that somewhere or other she found it. All's well that ends well.

In your letter of 11 August you assume that this picture is *my* property; and in fact I believe that it was my brother's property at the time of his death, but that he intended (though the intention was not put into writing, nor expressed to me direct) that after his decease it should return to Mr. or Mrs. Morris.[3] I therefore make no *claim* upon it whatever. You were so good as to suggest that I might be willing to take in exchange for the picture something at your disposal, such as Kelmscott Press books. I don't *expect* anything at all: but, if you like to allot to me some such thing as a goodwill gift, I see no reason for saying No. It can be *anything* — or, as you might prefer, nothing.

I now hold the painting at your disposal — possibly you could send round for it. Shall myself be off to Florence within some few days: but should not stay there long — probably back in London by 5 January.

Yours very truly,
W. M. Rossetti

MS: BL.

1. (1867-1962), secretary to Morris (whose literary executor he was) and the Kelmscott Press, 1892-98; director of the Fitzwilliam Museum, Cambridge, 1908-37; frequent visitor to St. Edmund's Terrace from this date.
2. *La Belle Iseult* (*Queen Guenevere*).
3. MS. Diary, 27 November 1897, gives Watts-Dunton as the source of this information.

531. TO SYDNEY CARLYLE COCKERELL

3 St. Edmund's Terrace,
11 January 1898

Dear Mr. Cockerell,

I am much obliged for your note of 31 December (was returning from Florence at that date), and I certainly will do what in strictness you ask — i.e., let you have the refusal of that drawing of Miss Siddal[1] in case I should ever think of parting with it. I hardly suppose I ever *shall* part with it. Should not think of doing so at present unless a very heavy price were offered — say £60: and I should yet think twice before assenting even to such a sum as that.

Best regards from

Yours very truly,
W. M. Rossetti

MS: BL.

1. Surtees 475 (see also Letter 548, Note 1).

532. TO MACKENZIE BELL

3 St. Edmund's Terrace,
24 January 1898

Dear Bell,

I send herewith autographs asked for by Dean Farrar[1] and Mr. Fagan.[2] I rather infer from your letter that they only want *signatures*, but that is no matter.

If other persons apply to you for autographs to be supplied by me, I think the simplest course, and the most convenient for both you and myself, would be that you should suggest to them to apply to me direct.

In the *Athenaeum* notice of your book,[3] 22 January, there is a phrase which I don't understand — do you? "A stronger emphasis might have been laid on the impiety of betraying to the world after death any failures of a loved friend." Is Christina herself the loved friend, or who?

Perhaps you have seen that *Literature* falls very foul of me.[4] I won't pretend to say that I like it, but luckily am rather thick-skinned in such matters. I have reflected whether there is anything in the article which ought to elicit an answer from *me*, but I hardly think there is. *You* might possibly see fit to inform *Literature* that you did not enact the part of a mouse under a kite, and that what I did was simply this: When you asked me a question (but not otherwise) I replied to it to the best of my ability, and I rigidly abstained from making any suggestions to you as to how you should treat your own book, in general drift or in detail.

Yours very truly,
W. M. Rossetti

Have you any sort of idea (I have not) *who* wrote the article in *Literature*?

MS: Princeton.

1. Frederic William Farrar (1831-1903), dean of Canterbury from 1895.
2. Not identified.
3. Pp. 109-10. Bell to WMR, 24 January 1898, suggested that the reviewer might have been "Robert Steele, Librarian of the Chemical Society, Burlington House" (copy; Princeton).
4. "Mr. Bell ... is bound hand and foot ... captive to the terrible Mr. W. M. Rossetti, that giant of mediocrity, grinding his family annals to dust in the dark.... He has hung over Mr. Bell like a kite over a mouse" (22 January 1898, pp. 66-68). MS. Diary, 22 January 1898: "As regards Christina I think that the general tone of the numerous reviews of Bell's book shows a certain re-action to her disadvantage: critics, while allowing a great deal in her favour, seem more inclined to restrict than to amplify her claims to fame. The book itself appears to be a decided selling-success: as the *Athenaeum* advertises that the 1st Edition is sold out, and a 2nd about to be issued."

533. TO MACKENZIE BELL

3 St. Edmund's Terrace,
25 January 1898

Dear Bell,

Thanks for your letter and the enclosures: I return 2 of them.

Your note to Mr. Traill[1] appears to me quite a proper one. It implies a denial of the statement that I dictated the substance of your book, and you weakly acquiesced — and that is a statement than which nothing could be more untrue. But your note is a private one, and not expressed in such trenchant and unmistakable terms of denial as might serve to counteract the printed article. If therefore you think fit to write for publication a letter such as I spoke of yesterday, I don't see that there is anything to interfere with your so doing. If you *don't* think fit, I for my part leave the matter where it stands. If *Literature* had limited itself to saying in temperate terms that I appear to be at the bottom of your biographical enterprise, and of the form which it bears, I would in equally temperate terms, have replied that such is not the fact: but, as the paper has chosen to assail me in terms the reverse of temperate, I suspect that I should be rather playing into their hands than otherwise if I were to enter into any controversy. They could always reply — "We said that you are a fool and a nuisance, and, spite of your disclaimer, we still regard you as such." Unreasonable imputations (to invent a rhyme for the nonce)

Have their day,
Which is not for ever and aye.

About "Watts [-Dunton]" etc., I can hardly suppose that Watts-Dunton meant that you were to insert "Dunton" every time that Christina called him by his then right name of Watts: I agree in the objection raised to this, and similar proceedings: but it is no affair of mine.

I have *begun* reading your published book, but have not got far with it as yet, being much engaged otherwise. My liking for the book is the same that it was before: it contains some things which I should not have said or should have said otherwise, but this also never was my affair, and I therefore adhered to my rule of leaving your book to yourself its author, and not interfering except by giving such information as was asked for.

Yours with best regards,
W. M. Rossetti

MS: Princeton.

1. Henry Duff Traill (1842-1900), author and journalist, was editor of *Literature* from its beginning in 1897 until his death.

534. TO MACKENZIE BELL

3 St. Edmund's Terrace,
28 January 1898

Dear Bell,

I certainly think (as you decide not to write to *Literature*) that it would be well to state in a Preface to a 2nd edition — in very plain and express terms — the facts (1) that I did not prompt you to write the book, nor volunteer to furnish you with materials; (2) that I did not coerce, or attempt to coerce, you in any way during the writing of the book; (3) that what I did was practically limited to answering explicitly the explicit questions which you asked, and to furnishing at your direct request, on perusal of MS. and proofs, corrections of errors and misapprehensions. I remember saying to you very downrightly, in a personal interview which we had in this house soon after you had undertaken the work, that all I did or wanted to do was to reply to such questions as you found occasion to ask — leaving it to you to use or not use my information as you might prefer, and, if you used it, to put it in your own way.

I think the Publishers went a trifle too far in advertising the book as "the Authorized Life," or something of the kind: but of this I took no notice, on the same ground which I have heretofore stated — viz.: that I did not want to interfere at all with your or their discretion, in matters as to which I was not consulted direct.

"Watts-Dunton" can be left in peace henceforth.[1] There is in your book another point of (as I think it) tedious particularity in which Watts-Dunton bore no share — viz.: that, in quoting verbatim from my jottings, you introduce such typographical eyesores as "sh[oul]d" and "wh[ich]," and a — when (for print) the right thing is a . . What can it matter to the reader of your book to know that I wrote "wh.," when it lay at my option to write "which"? But possibly you don't agree with me about this; or possibly, even if you do agree, it would not be convenient to alter these points in a new edition.

I have replied to Hurst and Blackett about Patchett Martin.[2] The matter (except that I raised no objection to what you proposed) is none of mine.

Always yours,
W. M. Rossetti

MS: Princeton.

1. See Letter 533.
2. Arthur Patchett Martin (1851-1902), Australian journalist and writer, lived in London from 1883, where he contributed regularly to the *Pall Mall Gazette*.

535. TO MACKENZIE BELL

3 St. Edmund's Terrace,
31 January 1898

Dear Bell,

I think it right to inform you of the following. Rather to my surprise I received on the 29th a letter from a Mr. Egan Mew,[1] asking me, on behalf of the Editor of *Literature*, to send to that paper from time to time news as to my literary proceedings — books in hand etc. etc.[2] I considered that this afforded me a convenient opportunity for addressing the Editor on the matter you wot of, without thereby laying myself out for a mere *réchauffé* of insolent detraction: so yesterday I wrote to the Editor, saying that I should not avail myself of his general invitation; but that, if he liked to publish my express denial of the allegation that I had dictated the substance and form of your book, I should like him to do so. I put the denial in plain express terms, and said it had better be printed in the same terms.

Of course I don't know what the Editor will do. He *may* assent to my proposal, and for that contingency it may be desirable that you should at once know how matters stand.[3]

Yours very truly,
W. M. Rossetti

MS: Princeton.

1. Author of books on china and porcelain.
2. MS. Diary, 29 January 1898: "This seems odd, after the gratuitous abuse of me in *Literature* a week ago."

3. MS. Diary, 31 January 1898: "The Editor Traill replies in rather civil terms: he *will* insert my note." *Literature*, 5 February 1898, p. 158: "Mr. Bell undertook the book of his own accord, and wrote it as he saw fit. My concern with it was limited to this — that when he asked me a question (very generally in writing), I replied according to my knowledge of the facts; and when he asked me to read his MS. and proofs, and to rectify anything which might be misstated or defective therein, I did so — not altering the MS., &c., but simply jotting down corrections, &c. for him to use or disregard as he chose. I affirm positively that I did not dictate nor attempt, nor in the least wish to dictate, anything as regards the substance or the form of Mr. Bell's book."

536. TO MACKENZIE BELL

3 St. Edmund's Terrace,
6 February 1898

Dear Bell,

I am glad that you like my note printed in *Literature*.[1] What is printed is the essential point: but my letter contained some other matter too (nothing expressive of soreness as to their abuse) which might have gone in if they had liked. I thought it only due to you to say something like this — "Mr. Bell has reason, as well as myself, to resent the unfounded allegation."

You refer to an article in the *British Weekly*. This, if I remember right, is the one signed Claudius Clear.[2] I will not go into details (indeed I don't fully remember them) beyond saying that Claudius Clear reverts to his having pointed out, 2 years ago,[3] that some things included in Christina's *New Poems* had already been published in her own volumes. He was right in 1 instance; but not right in (I believe) all the others — for these were instances set forth in my own notes to the *New Poems*, where some poems which I inserted in full had been *extracted from* in the *Verses* of the S.P.C.K.

I don't seem to have yet seen the *Bookman*,[4] which you say is hostile to me. It looks to me as if there must be a little "behind-the-scenes" in that matter. I enclose (please return it) a letter which invited me to be "interviewed" for the *Bookman*; and it is pretty clear that the interview (had it taken place) would have resulted in an adequate battering of me. I declined (in very civil terms) on the ground that I don't like to co-operate in the advertising of myself. *Hinc* [perhaps] *illae lacrimae* [5] — or *illae insolentiae*.

I am sincerely obliged to you for your American edition,[6] and glad to possess it — a very good-looking book.

A copy of the *Marzocco*[7] had already reached me, but, as you don't want your copy back, I retain it. The passage which you have marked means, in substance, as follows. "Christina in a letter expresses much satisfaction at her Italian trip and her Italian origin: yet we agree with Gosse that said origin is hardly traceable in her. Bell dissents from this. To an Italian, Christina's sentiment and poetry seem strictly English. Gosse says that Dante Gabriel was Italian, Christina English — her descriptions of scenery proper to 50 miles round London. Christina (this is the *Marzocco* man's own observation) wrote some things in Italian: they rather derogate from her repute so far as I have seen them, so formless and inept do they appear to me. One could scarcely suppose that the writer of those verses had spoken Italian from her infancy."

Of course I don't know what Italian verses by Christina the *Marzocco* writer had read: her *mature* Italian verses seem to me not in the least deserving of such scorn. His signature is "Th. Neal," and I suppose he is an Englishman.

Thanks for the enclosed letters. I read with much delight the one from Lady Mount-Temple[8] (apart from regret at seeing how invalided she is). In the list you give of the letters you don't name the one from the Bishop of Edinburgh[9] (brother I believe of Professor Dowden). I don't at all agree with him as to a general defectiveness in Christina's sonnets. They seem to me so good as barely to admit of being bettered.

Always yours,
W. M. Rossetti

I don't know who Dr. Robertson Nicoll *is*: perhaps I *ought* to know. Is he an *any*body or a nobody?

MS: Princeton.

1. See Letter 535, Note 3.
2. William Robertson Nicoll (1851-1923), editor of the theological magazine the *Expositor* from 1885; founder and editor of the *British Weekly* (1886) and the *Bookman* (1891). Nicoll began his review by observing that "The Rossettis have been far from fortunate in their biographers. Too much was written about Dante Rossetti, too much was told of his errors and his sorrows.... the chief offender was Dante Rossetti's brother ... whose very painful biography was rightly ignored in the *Athenaeum*. It is much to be regretted that Mr. Theodore Watts-Dunton, Rossetti's truest friend and best critic, did not speedily and once for all do the work which so many have attempted with less skilful and reverent hands" (13 January 1898, p. 269).
3. *British Weekly*, 23 January 1896, p. 235.
4. 13 (February 1898), 154; by Nicoll.
5. Horace, *Epistles*, I. xix. 41.
6. Published by Roberts Brothers, 1898.
7. "Christina Rossetti," *Il Marzocco* (Florence), 30 January 1898, pp. 2-3.
8. Georgiana Mount-Temple (1822-1901), wife of William Francis Mount-Temple, first baron (1811-88).
9. John Dowden (1840-1910), who became bishop in 1886.

537. TO MACKENZIE BELL

3 St. Edmund's Terrace,
9 February 1898

Dear Bell,

I return the enclosed with thanks.

Have now seen the article in the *Bookman*,[1] with very faint sensations of dislike. Dr. Nicoll says in a serious spirit that he objects on certain grounds to my dealings with Gabriel and Christina. To his so thinking and saying there can be no objection — unless it be that these considerations are hardly relevant to your book. I think I could show, so as to convince many reasonable minds, that I acted properly, and that Dr. Nicoll is therefore mistaken: but that does not diminish his right to his own opinion.

As to *Literature*, Gosse is one of the first persons who occurred to myself: but I am quite uncertain. Gosse and I used to be on very amicable terms — say towards 1872 to 1882: since then we have hardly met at all, owing chiefly no doubt to my retiring habits of life. That he disapproved of my work in relation to Christina's *New Poems* is a known fact:[2] but that he would have written about me in the tone of acrimony adopted in *Literature* is what I should not have expected. But if Gosse it is, I heartily forgive him: he and I can go our separate ways.

To feel sure that some particular person wrote an unsigned review is a very unsafe operation: 3 very strong instances, within my direct experience, are present to my mind. I dare say it may be true that whoever wrote in *Literature* wrote also in the *Saturday*.[3]

Yours very truly,
W. M. Rossetti

MS: Princeton.

1. See Letter 536, Note 4.
2. Gosse was probably the reviewer of *New Poems*, *Saturday Review*, 22 February 1896, pp. 194-97: "There is nothing ... a poet dislikes and dreads more than the raking up of the rejected attempts in verse.... Of course the temptation to any Editor who feels the attraction of the yellow dross is very considerable, if the literary remains of a deceased poet fall into his possession and can be used for his profit."
3. Review of Bell, 5 February 1898, pp. 177-78.

538. TO FRANK WILLIAM BURGESS[1]

3 St. Edmund's Terrace,
11 March 1898

Dear Mr. Burgess,

That announcement from Wise is certainly rather a startler. The first question which arises upon it is whether his Bibliography relates to D. G. Rossetti alone, or to various Rossettis. If the latter, it is *possible* that your best practical course would be to do Christina, and any others you like, leaving D. G. aside. But I only say this in a tentative sort of way; and, if you like to persevere with the whole of your original project, you will receive just the same assistance from me (when asked) as if Wise did not exist.

I had not hitherto known *any*thing about Wise's Bibliography. He and I are on very good terms, but I have not seen him since (I think) February 1895. He says that he has "a mass of important and unpublished material obtained from Rossetti himself." By Rossetti he must mean me, for he did not know my Brother. It is true that he did at times buy from me (much in the same sort of way you have done) some MSS. etc. by my Brother; but I feel safe in saying (from recollection) that this does not amount to anything like a "mass" of unpublished material — in fact I only recollect one very early MS. poem, some 80 to 100 lines or so.[2] And that would not have anything to do with a Bibliography, as I understand the word. I retain a copy of that same poem.

About *Guendalina Talbot*. I think you are under the misapprehension of supposing that the Polidori print consists of an original poem by Maria, while some other print consists of a translation of said poem. In fact, this "other print" is the earlier issue of the two, and consists of the *original poem in Italian*, with translation by Maria; and the Polidori print is the same identical thing. I have looked at my

610

list of extra copies etc., and I find that I had offered for 15/- a copy of the Polidori print marked "W. M. Rossetti from Christina 1890"; and had also offered for 8/- a copy of the other (original) print. I have looked about for that copy inscribed as above-named, and have at last found it, and I enclose it herewith.

Polidori died in December 1853, and Gabriel soon afterwards transacted the sale of his press and types. I am as good as sure that these were bought by the Tupper Firm (Printers of the *Germ*). Two members of that Firm are still in business: they used to be in Bucklersbury, E.C., and I fancy that is still their place of business. Can hardly suppose that the Polidori plant still exists.

If ever you show me anything you write in the Bibliography regarding the Polidori press, I shall have no objection to adding some few remarks of my own. I possess, among my extra copies, *many* specimens of its work — books by my Grandfather etc. Did not price them in my list of extra copies, not supposing they would have much attraction for you, but could do so if you like.

Will see pretty soon about sending on the *Germ*. As you speak about tracing through their various subsequent forms the poems contributed to the *Germ*, I may as well mention that Duckworth & Co. are about to publish *The Blessed Damozel* (*Germ* form), with a Prefatory Note by me referring to later alterations.[3] But what I have thus written is probably less precise than what would befit a Bibliography.

Your friend was far from correct in saying "You never saw a woman like Rossetti's women": at any rate Rossetti and some others were so fortunate as to see such women. *Proserpine* is an *exact portrait* of Mrs. William Morris, and *Beata Beatrix*[4] of Gabriel's own wife. Venus he painted from a handsome cook he happened to see in Portland Place. I speak here of the original oil-picture: the example in the New Gallery[5] is more or less the same face. That National Gallery Catalogue was, as you say, crammed with mistakes: I sent a list of them to the Secretary, and a new print of the Catalogue was issued some 3 weeks ago — I am surprised that you, on going just now to the Gallery, received the old blundered issue.

Yours very truly,
W. M. Rossetti

MS: Bucknell.

1. (1868-99), bookseller of Ringmer, Sussex, to whom WMR wrote some sixty letters beginning in August 1897. Several of his purchases from WMR figure in his only known catalogue (copy in Brighton Central Reference Library), the cover of which he designed. He also designed the binding of *RRP*. A sale of his remaining stock was held at Sotheby's on 6 December 1899, lots 378-487, when "the best prices were given for Rossetti items" (MS. Diary).

2. See Letter 483, Note 1.

3. Published in 1898, with art nouveau decorations by William Brown Macdougall, which WMR considered "purposeless, and at times even unsightly" (letter to Elizabeth P. Gould, 20 January 1902; Boston). He told Flora Annie Steel that he "had no concern in the bespeaking of them" (letter of 26 June 1898; Rylands).

4. Surtees 168.

5. Surtees 173 R. 2.

539. TO WILLIAM MORRIS COLLES[1]

3 St. Edmund's Terrace,
15 April 1898

Dear Mr. Colles,

You will remember some correspondence which passed between us in 1896-1897 in relation to the publication of the *Poems* of John Lucas Tupper.[2] I am now disposed to place another matter in the hands of the Authors' Syndicate.

Towards the autumn of 1895 I began compiling a book[3] — which might have been made to run to a very considerable length — out of letters, diaries, and other papers in my possession, relating to my Brother Dante Gabriel, and other members and connexions of my family. It began towards 1810, and went on (for the present) to 1862. It was ultimately found convenient that Mr. George Allen should publish one instalment of this book, 1854 to 1862, and an arrangement has been made with him for the purpose. The earlier portion of the compilation remains on my hands, and I am now less inclined to publish it as one continuous book than to bring out *some* of its material in some other form.

My compilation did not include any continuous narrative of my own. It presented the documents — or more generally *extracts* from the documents — in their original form, accompanied by copious prefatory notes etc. of mine, to explain anything that might seem in need of explanation.

The enclosed list shows the items which I think best adapted for separate publication — No. 1 is cut out, being already disposed of. I fancy that, as regards some of the items, I should find little difficulty in myself securing publication in magazines or otherwise: but this is a sort of work for which I have very little taste, and I had rather commit the whole matter to the Authors' Syndicate if willing to undertake it. Publication either in various magazines, or (for some items) in a separate form, would be equally agreeable to me. I have not yet fully made up my mind about item 8:[4] it may be that I would not publish, standing by themselves, *all* the verses etc. which I had been willing to insert in the compilation. It is also probable that I should in various instances see cause to extend the prefatory notes etc. which I had written.

I am not quite sure what is the copyright-law affecting contributions to magazines. Would you, in your reply, kindly let me know.

Of course, as soon as the matter gets fairly started, I could call upon you, and hand over any items which may be wanted.

Yours very truly,
W. M. Rossetti

MS: Texas.

1. (1855-1926), barrister of the Inner Temple, 1880; founder and managing director of the Authors' Syndicate, 1890; member of the council of the Society of Authors, 1890.
2. MS. Diary, 24 July 1896: "Holman Tupper called by appointment, and lunched with us. He is a well-grown young man, and evidently intelligent — just a *little* like his Father. His general tone of mind seems to be that which comes natural to a young Oxford student who has not particularly thought for himself. I undertook to see whether I could get published, either as a book or in a magazine, some poems by his Father which he entrusted to me a few weeks ago. Have not very sanguine hopes of succeeding." On the advice of the Society of Authors he placed the matter in the hands of the Authors' Syndicate, who arranged publication by Longmans, Green, & Co. He informed

612

the Authors' Syndicate on 15 October 1896 that he and Holman Tupper had agreed "that, before forwarding the MSS. to you, I shall again look carefully through them, and introduce, where I think it desirable, some alteration of diction, polishing of metre, etc." (Texas).

3. See Letter 529, Note 3.
4. See Letter 542, Note 1.

540. TO FLORA ANNIE STEEL[1]

3 St. Edmund's Terrace,
30 April 1898

My dear Mrs. Steel,

I have probably seen that *Astarte* [2] photograph of which you speak, but do not now expressly remember it. Can recollect that there was a large crayon-drawing of that subject — one of Gabriel's finest things; also, now in South Kensington Museum, a singularly fine and finished pen-and-ink drawing. One place where Rossetti photographs are sold is the Hanfstängel Gallery, 16 Pall Mall E.: *possibly* you might find there the photograph in question. I don't know why people in general have always disliked the *Astarte* picture, which Gabriel rated very high among his performances: or rather I *do* know — it is too severe in beauty and too far removed from prettiness.

I don't well remember about my own letters to W. B. Scott (which you mention) published in his book: Gabriel's letters there are extremely good. I (as well as Gabriel) knew "Alice" well, and liked her very much.

The observations which you make as to my treatment of Gabriel in my Memoir are highly appreciated by me: I know them to be essentially true. The ordinary run of criticism (especially of late, apropos of Bell's Life of Christina) goes quite in the contrary direction; setting me down as an over-candid simpleton, too obtuse to perceive that my dealings, with both Gabriel and Christina, damaged them grievously. But "let the galled jade wince":[3] I am quite as much interested as press-critics are in upholding, on genuine grounds, the fair fame of Gabriel and Christina, and I believe not less able to do it efficiently.

I do not feel entirely with you as to the Biography of Tennyson.[4] It is only about a month ago that I began reading the book, and I am now near the end of volume 1. The picture which it presents of Tennyson is *very* like what I knew him to be; for between about 1850 and 1870 I saw him various times, and was treated by him with a large amount of cordiality, or even intimacy. So far as I saw of him, he could hardly be praised too highly; and the grounds of praise set forth in the book seem to me correct. It is however perfectly true that the family were nervously timorous as to putting-in anything which might seem to reduce him to the ordinary stature of a man among men. This I know to be a fact: for one or two of those letters of Gabriel to Allingham[5] contained some details about Tennyson (not in the least ill-natured, not in a right sense derogatory) which were submitted to the Tennyson family; and Lady Tennyson sent back a message something to the effect that, if any of them were to appear in print, they would be pretty nearly her death-warrant.

I have not seen that book by Pennell[6] to which you refer. Doyle and Leech, and especially Hablot Browne, ought in my opinion to be very warmly praised on certain grounds, but not without a frank admission of their deficiencies. As to Browne, I think people hardly reflect sufficiently how very much he effected towards making the characters of Dickens living realities to the reader: take as examples Pecksniff, Mrs. Gamp, and Quilp.

You must be having, as I write, a horrid day at Brighton, if in proportion to our gusts of wind and swirls of rain in London. My daughter's weather in Italy has been very bad of late.

Always yours truly,
W. M. Rossetti

MS: Rylands.

1. (1847-1929), novelist; lived in India, 1868-89, where her husband, Henry William Steel, was a civil servant. Her novels, especially *On the Face of the Waters* (1896) on the Indian Mutiny, showed a sympathetic understanding of Indian life. She corresponded with WMR for almost twenty years on a variety of literary and political topics.

2. *Astarte Syriaca*, Surtees 249. None of the studies in Surtees corresponds to the two drawings mentioned in the next sentence.

3. "Let the galled jade wince, our withers are unwrung" (*Hamlet*, III. ii. 241-42).

4. Hallam Tennyson, *Alfred Lord Tennyson: a Memoir* (1897).

5. *Letters of Dante Gabriel Rossetti to William Allingham*, ed. G. B. Hill, 1897.

6. *The Illustration of Books* (1896). Richard Doyle (1824-83), John Leech (1817-64), Hablot Knight Browne, "Phiz" (1815-92). For WMR's reviews of Doyle and Leech, see "Checklist."

541. TO THOMAS BIRD MOSHER[1]

3 St. Edmund's Terrace,
29 May 1898

Dear Sir,

Mr. Bertram Dobell has forwarded to me a letter of yours, 12 May, in which you invite me to write a Preface for a re-edition of the *Germ* — also to communicate with you direct on the subject.

The project of reprinting the *Germ* has been entertained by some 4 or 5 English Publishers from time to time, beginning perhaps some 15 years ago: but in this country some copyright difficulties always existed, which naturally do not exist in the United States, and the project had to be abandoned.[2] The first projector volunteered to pay me £40 for a Preface or Introduction. He, I know, has not wholly relinquished the idea, and may possibly yet carry it out when the term of copyright ceases — which will (if I understand the matter right) be in October 1899.

As I was from the first willing to act for the proposed £40, I feel it to be due to that Publisher, before coming to any *definite* conclusion as to your offer, to reconsult him as to his present intentions. I have not yet done so, wishing to save time, but shall do it very soon. His decision would to a large extent regulate my own: but *provisionally* I can say as follows.

I would write for you a rather full Introduction (such as was contemplated for the London reprint) for £40 English; or, if you only wanted an ordinary Preface (say some 8 pages octavo), I would do it for £25. I observe that you offer the alternative of a percentage on the sales. To this also I am not entirely disinclined:

but I am necessarily in the dark as to what such a percentage might probably amount to, and it seems to me better for us both that a lump sum should be paid, and so the transaction finally closed.

You enquire of Mr. Dobell whether the original plates of the *Germ* etchings still exist. I don't know with any certainty. It appears to me just possible that all the 4 plates are in the hands of Messrs. Tupper, the Printers of the *Germ*. But more probably the plates of Collinson, Madox Brown, and Deverell, are destroyed or quite inaccessible, and the plate of Holman Hunt *may* (or may not) be in his own possession.

I shall probably hear from you further in due course, and shall by that time be able to settle my own course conclusively.

Yours very faithfully,
Wm. M. Rossetti

MS: Harvard.

1. (1852-1923), publisher of Portland, Maine. Beginning in 1891 with Meredith's *Modern Love and Other Poems*, he designed and published some eight hundred volumes, which were "not only beautiful in type and paper, but in small and inexpensive format" (*Dictionary of American Biography*).

2. See Letter 371, Note 3. WMR to W. M. Colles, 31 August 1898, mentions a proposal that Mosher and Elliot Stock "might join forces, and bring the book out as a joint speculation" (Princeton). Instead Mosher issued his reprint in 1898, using as an introduction James Ashcroft Noble's article on the *Germ*, which had appeared earlier in *Fraser's Magazine* (see Fredeman, pp. 243-44). In 1901 Stock published his facsimile edition with WMR's preface. WMR to Mosher, 5 June 1901: "It is with much satisfaction that I learn ... that you are to launch in America a portion of Mr. Stock's facsimile edition of the *Germ*" (Harvard).

542. TO WILLIAM MORRIS COLLES

3 St. Edmund's Terrace,
7 July 1898

Dear Mr. Colles,

I am much obliged for yours of yesterday. Have considered the matter, and am not at all inclined to accept £26.5 for those verses etc. by my Brother[1] — some 15 or more items if I remember right. It is not every day that a magazine has a chance of printing unpublished verse by Dante Rossetti, and Astor,[2] if anyone, can afford to pay for the opportunity. I would take double the price — £52.10, but really not anything less, for I think that even then the *Pall Mall Magazine* will have a bargain.

Will you please to remember, and to impress upon any purchaser, that those notes of mine, accompanying the verses, are not in a state fully suitable for publication. As you are aware, they were written with a view to one particular form of publication, now left in abeyance.[3] Before the verses are printed, I should have to look over the notes and recast them — perhaps to a large extent. This would not take me long, and I would do it without any further payment.

Yours always truly,
W. M. Rossetti

MS: Princeton.

1. "Some Scraps of Verse and Prose by Dante Gabriel Rossetti," *Pall Mall Magazine*, 16 (December 1898), 480-96, for which WMR received £52.10.

2. William Waldorf Astor (1848-1919) left the United States (where he had recently succeeded to the management of the family estate upon the death of his father, John Jacob Astor) in 1890 to live in England, becoming a British subject in 1899. In 1893 he purchased the *Pall Mall Gazette*, and in the same year founded the *Pall Mall Magazine*.

3. See Letter 529, Note 3.

543. TO WILLIAM MORRIS COLLES

3 St. Edmund's Terrace,
4 October 1898

Dear Mr. Colles,

Thanks for your letter of yesterday. Holman Hunt is an old friend of mine, for whom I have a hearty affection: but I don't feel quite disposed to consult him beforehand as to the publication of details in my own P. R. B. Diary[1] which, from my own point of view are not unsuited for publication. He might entertain notions which I should regard as mainly fanciful: and moreover I have been assured by more persons than one in the last 3 or 4 years (during which, as it happens, I have not seen Hunt) that his general tone of feeling and talk with regard to my Brother is not what one can call friendly.

If there is in the Diary any detail concerning Hunt which you think better out than in, I dare say I should be quite willing to cancel it. The only thing which occurs to my recollection (and in that I see no real harm) is that Hunt on one occasion caught some sparrows in a trap, painted from them into his picture, and then put a dab of oil paint on their heads.

If anything further occurs to you on the general subject, I shall be most happy to consider it.

I expect to be going pretty soon to Florence: might perhaps start from London on 3 November, and be back by 10 December. If you could give me any hint as to the fortunes thus far of my several articles (List enclosed), I should be interested to hear about them.

Yours very truly,
W. M. Rossetti

MS: Princeton.

1. Published in *PDL* along with a portion of FMB's diary and "Some Early Correspondence of Dante Gabriel Rossetti 1835-1854." The three items were among those left over from the first three parts of "Rossettiana" after George Allen made his selection for *RRP*. A fuller version of the PRB diary was given in *PDL* than had been included in "Rossettiana" (letter to Colles, 31 August 1898; Princeton). MS. Diary, 17 August 1899, notes that Hurst and Blackett offered terms for the volume which were "very fairly advantageous." This included an advance of £50 when the book was published (letter to Colles, 23 November 1899; Texas). MS. Diary, 8 November 1899: "Received from Blackett 5 or 6 alternative specimens for the binding. They look well more or less, and I shall tomorrow (when daylight shows colour properly) be able to fix upon one. Blackett writes that the book can be out almost directly." 23 January 1900: "Blackett informs me that ... [*PDL*] has not sold at all well." 28 June 1901: "I referred to the likelihood of my having to repay most of the advance which was made to me by Hurst and Blackett.... Colles however laughs at this idea of repayment, and says it is not to be thought of."

544. TO WILLIAM MORRIS COLLES

3 St. Edmund's Terrace,
29 January 1899

Dear Mr. Colles,

For clearness' sake I have put my reply to yours of the 27th into the above form. Please excuse unsightliness, and believe me

Yours very truly,
W. M. Rossetti

1. Will I sell to M. Bell for £15 the 19 letters from Christina which he holds — including originals and all rights exclusively?

Not this. The number of letters (i.e. typewritten copies of letters) held by Bell is I believe 18, not 19. For those typewritten copies, and all rights therein, I think £15 a rather low price, but would accept it.[1] I would not sell the originals at all; and so I told Bell in a personal interview towards 20 December. I also told him that, as 2 slight poems by Christina are included in the letters, I must retain the right to put these 2 poems into a Complete Edition of Christina's Poems, if such an Edition be issued at some future period; but this would not interfere with use of said poems by Bell meanwhile. To this he assented.

2. Will I sell to Bell for £100 all the letters and papers of Christina for copyright and all rights, including the originals?

Most certainly not. I should probably say No, were the offer £1000.

MS: Princeton.

1. WMR to Colles, 15 March 1899: "I return the draft agreement. I do *not* assent to the proposal that Executors, Administrators, or assigns, of Mackenzie Bell, should have the right of dealing with those letters, etc.: they would be persons of whom I do and can know nothing, and they might play ducks and drakes with the letters etc.... About 'giving Mr. Bell an option on all the material referring to Christina before disposing of it elsewhere,' I would not enter into any direct undertaking. *If* I ever wanted to dispose of such material, I should naturally think of Bell as a probable or possible customer: but beyond this I would not go" (Rylands).

545. TO CHARLES ELIOT NORTON

3 St. Edmund's Terrace,
10 April 1899

Dear Professor Norton,

Thank you much for your genial and gratifying letter of 27 March. I am sure that that book[1] does contain some interesting and even important matter: it exhibits my Brother, and more especially it exhibits — and very finely — Ruskin.

I do not much dissent from what you say about *Aylwin*.[2] Of my Brother's traits there drawn, some are true but overdone: as soon as a true one is given, it gets coupled with another which I do not perceive to be true at all. The story, in all its contours and all its details, is such a phantasmagoria that a mind nourished on realities can hardly see why it should be written. I should say however that this very fact testifies to its having real merit of a certain kind: it seems the outcome of a mind of very peculiar sort, thinking and inventing for itself, and owing little to others.

I presume that *Aylwin* is a great success in America: in England it got trumpeted to a surprising extent — and the advertisements show its 17th thousand to be now on sale.

You kindly hope "that the days go well with me." In reciprocating this good wish most heartily, I can say that I have not (since 1894, in which I lost both my wife and Christina) had much to repine at. My 4 children (the eldest daughter married in Florence) are all more or less well: and I — though a "gouty subject" — am better than might be supposed at my present age of almost 70.

With best greetings,

Yours very truly,
W. M. Rossetti

MS: Harvard.

1. *RRP*. Norton wrote: "To few persons can it be of more interest than to me, recalling vividly the memories of a delightful period of my life, when I had the good fortune of knowing your brother. His life was then at its best, and the remembrance of him, — a poetic figure, full of imagination, full too of hope and of power which justified it, with personal charm and with generous friendliness — this remembrance of him does not grow faint with the intervening years" (AP).
2. Watts-Dunton's novel published in 1898. "I have read *Aylwin* with disappointment and displeasure. The picture drawn in it of your brother seems to me curiously out of proportion, and as badly coloured as it is ill drawn. There is little truth to nature in any of the characters in the trashy book. I expected better of its author." WMR complained to Frank Burgess, 19 December 1898, that "Gipsies possess no attraction to me: they are almost the last class of people that I want to study as literary material" (Bucknell).

546. TO MACMILLAN & CO.

3 St. Edmund's Terrace,
13 July 1899

Dear Sirs,

You will probably remember that not very long after the death of my Sister Christina (December 1894), and again towards August 1897, I wrote to you suggesting that the production of a *Complete Edition* of her Poems would be a good thing. You acquiesced in the general idea; but said that the time for bringing out such an Edition had not yet come, as the existing books sell well — and far be it from me to say that this view of the matter was other than sound, as my incomings from the books have been quite to my satisfaction. However (and I fancy I informed you so at the time) I determined in August 1897 to put together the materials for a Complete Edition, with Notes, Preface, etc. — guided mainly by the consideration that I am now an old man, and that after my death there will not be anyone alive knowing much about my Sister, or about the circumstances under which her poems were produced, etc. I have now, after somewhat persistent work (as leisure permitted) for nearly 2 years, finished the task: have got all the poems into order, and done all the prefatory work etc., including a brief Memoir — which would I think be read with some satisfaction by some persons to whom Mr. Mackenzie Bell's book did not seem wholly pleasing.

My compilation includes the copyright matter (about which we corresponded before) of the Society for Promoting Christian Knowledge — also 2 small poems which appeared in the tale named *Maude*, and which are copyright to Mr. Bowden. I don't think anything *else* is outside your own copyright.

I now intend to get the whole thing bound — or perhaps secured in cases, as preferable. There will be 3 volumes of the poems, and 1 (of much larger shape) of my MS. It appears to me that, whenever the work may come to be published, 2 volumes will be quite necessary — not 3.

Perhaps you would let me know what your present views on the subject are. When the material comes back to me bound, I could hand it over to you if desirable; or otherwise could keep it in my own possession, and you would be aware that, whatever may happen to me, the whole thing is now in proper shape for publication.[1]

Yours very truly,
W. M. Rossetti

MS: BL.

1. MS. Diary, 20 April 1900: "Macmillans reply that, as the sales of Christina's current editions continue to be decidedly good, they are not in favour of launching a Complete Edition for the present."

547. TO MRS. FRANK WILLIAM BURGESS

3 St. Edmund's Terrace,
7 August 1899

My dear Mrs. Burgess,

I have received your letter of the 5th, and my MS. which stands entitled "Prefatory Memoir":[1] but this is not the thing outstanding. The Prefatory Memoir is a writing of mine (put long ago into print): I sold it to Mr. Burgess, and he paid me for it. I will return it to you at a convenient opportunity, for it is the absolute property of yourself, or of any person who is the legal representative of Mr. Burgess.

I will now restate the requisite particulars — excuse repetition.

1. There was a certain oldish looking MS. done by Blake himself:[2] it is written as if it were prose, but is in fact irregular blank verse. This you returned to me some days ago.

2. There was (I am as good as sure) another scrap of paper, also in Blake's handwriting.[3] This has not come back to me: if it has gone astray, it is of no consequence.

3. I copied out No. 1 into a form suitable for being printed — on paper of about the size of this present notepaper when opened out. In my copy it is made

to present the appearance of verse. I entitled it — "A Theogony of the Passions, by William Blake." I also wrote, same size of paper, a prefatory note regarding the poem. The whole thing — poem and note — would occupy some 12 or 14 half-sheets of paper; the back of each half-sheet being (as usual for printing-purposes) left blank. This No. 3 has not returned to me. Mr. Burgess wished to get it published; and I understood from him that he thought of associating himself with someone else, so as to meet the cost etc. of publication. It seems *possible* therefore that he may have entrusted No. 3 to that proposed associate: but (as I said before) the latter would not have any power of publishing the MS., or otherwise dealing with it, unless he makes terms with me for the purpose — for Mr. Burgess, although he had agreed with me to purchase 1, 2, and 3, for a certain sum, had not actually paid the amount.

4. (a matter which only now recurs to my memory) — I *lent* to Mr. Burgess a rather large half-sheet of drawing-paper containing a number of pencil-sketches by Blake.[4] In the centre of the half-sheet, back and front, there are 2 largish drawings — one of them represents a woman, and a man dead or in a trance. There are also several quite small figures, with names pencilled to them by Blake — names such as Love, Pity, Rage, etc. etc. I lent this No. 4 to Mr. Burgess, because he and I thought that these small figures, or some of them, might be reproduced so as to illustrate the "Theogony of the Passions." He, after a while, did not well see how such small things could be advantageously reproduced. I then suggested to him that he might get them copied in photography, *enlarged*, and from the enlarged photographs he might get suitable reproductions. He thought this a good suggestion, and so he might *possibly* have entrusted No. 4 to a Photographer, or to the proposed "associate." I should be sorry to lose No. 4: but you will understand that no money is due with regard to it: I lent it to Mr. Burgess gratis, to serve his interest in the projected publication of No. 3.

This seems to be all that I can say on the subject for the present.

Very truly yours,
W. M. Rossetti

MS: Bucknell.

1. As published in his edition of *Poetical Works of Blake*. No. 173, £7, in Burgess's catalogue (see Letter 538, Note 1); now at Texas.

2. "Four leaves bearing 'then she bore Pale desire' and 'Woe cried the muse'" (Bentley, p. 440), which WMR intended to publish in an early volume of "Rossettiana." He sold the MS. to Burgess in 1898 for £12 on the understanding that he would undertake its publication. It remained unpublished and unpaid for at Burgess's death, when WMR offered it to Mrs. Burgess for £6, but she declined it. On 30 August he put it into the hands of the Authors' Syndicate, which eventually interested Henry Newbolt in it for the *Monthly Review*, 12 (August 1903), 123-29, "*The Passions*, an Unpublished Poem by William Blake."

3. Probably "Names of Gods" (Bentley, p. 482).

4. Martin Butlin, *Paintings and Drawings of Blake*, No. 214, "Various Personifications."

548. TO SYDNEY CARLYLE COCKERELL

3 St. Edmund's Terrace,
6 September 1899

Dear Mr. Cockerell,

I consider your offer of £50 for that drawing[1] to be a highly adequate and even a liberal one: but you will excuse me for saying that I have a most particular liking myself for the drawing, and I hardly know that *any* offer which could in reason be forthcoming would tempt me to part with it.

As it happens, I could if you like sell a *different* portrait of Miss Siddal by my Brother.[2] In May last Mr. Siddal[3] (her Brother, whom I had never seen since 1862) wrote to me that he possessed such a portrait, a water-colour; and he said at the time that he had other drawings by my Brother, but these he has not as yet been able to pitch upon. I bought the water-colour for £18: a price which I consider not absolutely insufficient, but still low. I said at the same time to Mr. Siddal that, if I could dispose of the painting for a higher sum, I would hand the difference over to him. I have really no *wish* to part with the water-colour: but, if I can get anyone to pay £30, I will, in the interest of Mr. Siddal, sell it for that.

It is framed, inscribed with date 1854, exactly like Miss Siddal (it is only head and shoulders), and realizes her look with touching sweetness. It is a nice specimen, in point of art, of my Brother's work of that early date: but the colour has to some extent faded — or what I would call "bleached." I suppose it has been unduly exposed to sunlight.

If you would like to see the portrait, I could show it you. Shall be out of doors on Friday 8 September, and Monday 11, and on 12 or 13 shall be going to Matlock for some 2 or 3 weeks, as rheumatism has rather persecuted me of late.

Yours very truly,
W. M. Rossetti

MS: BL.

1. See Letter 531, Note 1.
2. Surtees 462; bought by Cockerell on 7 September for £25 (MS. Diary). MS. Diary, 9 September: "Siddal, on receiving my extra £7, has sent a valuable relic of Gabriel (in a dirty and much-neglected state unfortunately): an ink-sketch of Tennyson reading *Maud*, 27 September 1855 [Surtees 526 R. 1]. It resembles other versions of the same incident: seems the most attentively executed of them, and may I suppose be a replica done expressly for Lizzie."
3. James (1838-1912).

549. TO GEORGIANA BURNE-JONES[1]

3 St. Edmund's Terrace,
8 November 1899

My dear Lady Burne-Jones,

Certainly I should be well pleased to see the typewriting of Gabriel's letters. I am not squeamish or fussy in such matters, and have little doubt that, when you think fit to publish something, I shall think much the same — but the only satisfactory course is to see.

Helen will I fancy be back today, or else tomorrow, and I can then soon settle as to the few letters in her hands.

Gout has been my "intimate enemy" (as Gabriel well expressed it) ever since 1878, coming on at intervals: if it leaves me at peace for a couple of years or so, I consider myself lucky. Since Saturday last I am nearly well again, but not quite.

I fully feel with you about that vile Transvaal War[2] — a wicked thing for the English to do, prompted by greed and arrogance. We must necessarily beat a squad of Dutch Farmers if we choose to do it — so the best thing possibly is to beat them soon, and have a total carnage in the ratio of 10 rather than 50. But the squad isn't beaten yet, and doesn't mean to be beaten without showing their mettle. In fact — so far as I understand news true and false — the upshot is *as yet* much against us. Jingoism has for several years past been the curse of this country — and might prove its downfall (which heaven avert), were the scales of Justice held even.

Yours always truly,
W. M. Rossetti

MS: Fitzwilliam.

1. (1840-1920), who was preparing her *Memorials of Burne-Jones* (1904).
2. Boer War, 1899-1902, during which the British required nearly half a million men to reverse early Boer victories. MS. Diary, 12 October 1899: "The bestial anti-Boer war has now broken out. I have been, and in principle am, much more on the side of the Boers than of the English Government. Still I hold that the only sensible course for Kruger to adopt, in view of the overwhelming odds against him, was a policy of concession rather than defiance. He has finally chosen the latter: and now the only practical thing that remains to be wished for is that the struggle should be brought to an early and comparatively unbloody conclusion — which can only, I suppose, be a British victory and resettlement of terms. I suspect we shall detach and grab the Gold-fields."

550. TO FLORA ANNIE STEEL

3 St. Edmund's Terrace,
5 August 1900

My dear Annie Steel,

(For imitation is the sincerest flattery). I received with much pleasure — as I always do — a letter of yours after a longish interval. I trust that your "severe illness" of last autumn is quite gone. My own health continues very fair in essentials — though rheumatism, influenza, etc. etc., make unpleasant episodes now and again. There is rheumatism in my right arm now, but not by any means so troublesome as it has sometimes been.

I regard Marillier's[1] book as an extremely competent performance, and written in an agreeable spirit. Of his illustrations many are excellent, but several are too begrimed and foggy.

I see you are sympathetically interested (and with your associations this is quite natural) in the Transvaal war, whereas I detest and loathe the whole affair. I regard it as a national crime, into which we have been plunged by Cecil Rhodes,[2] Joseph Chamberlain,[3] and the jingoism of blatant and howling press-men and mobs. You must pardon my plain speaking, for "tis my nature to."[4] That our soldiers are brave fine fellows who do their work well is most true: but how any great national pride can be based upon the fact that some 250,000 trained soldiers of British breed sometimes (not always) double up some 60,000 Dutch farmers, now reduced I suppose to about 20,000, is what I am too obtuse to see. Mr. Rudyard Kipling is one of the men whom I look upon as decided nuisances. Old Kruger[5] appears to me to have been in the right throughout, so long as one views the affair as an abstract question; but, viewed as a *practical* question, he ought to have known that his country would be smashed sooner or later, and that it was his duty therefore to avoid this catastrophe by even a larger amount of concession than reason dictated.

I enter very heartily into all that you say about Madox Brown's Diary: it is a capital thing of its kind. As to a female model[6] of his whom you would have liked to shake, I should myself have liked to shake her at several conjunctures, but I never made any approach to that line of action.

Gabriel's *Helen of Troy* was not painted from Miss Herbert: the face is of somewhat the same type, but less genial though perhaps more regular. It was painted from Annie Miller — the same person (though one might scarcely guess it) who sat to Holman Hunt for *The Awakening Conscience*. The Helen head is extremely like her.

Yes that drawing of the two Lovers playing Chess[7] is by Burne-Jones: a fine thing, but with some rather baggy drapery.

I should have liked to see your Italian monkey-man, receiving the news of Umberto's[8] assassination. That assassination was a vile affair. At first I thought it might lead to widespread disturbances in Italy: but as yet there seems to be no symptom of this, and the manifesto of the new King looks rather as if he meant to start a more liberal regime — which I for one count to be highly requisite.

Always yours truly,
W. M. Rossetti

MS: Rylands.

1. Henry Currie Marillier (1865-1951), contributor to the *Pall Mall Gazette* from 1893; managing director of Morris & Company, 1905-48. WMR reviewed his *Dante Gabriel Rossetti, an Illustrated Memorial* in *Magazine of Art*, 22 (1900), 217-23.
2. (1853-1902), whose aim was to federate South Africa under British rule. He was prime minister of the Cape, 1890-96.
3. Secretary of state for the colonies in the Conservative government of Salisbury and (from July 1902) Balfour, 1895-1903.
4. "Let Bears and Lyons growl and fight, / For 'tis their Nature too," Isaac Watts, *Against Quarrelling*.
5. Stephanus Johannes Paulus Kruger (1825-1904), president of the Transvaal Republic from 1883.
6. Miss Chamberlayne (see *Diary*, ed. Surtees, p. 9 etc.).
7. Probably the "very finished pencil version ... at the Fitzwilliam Museum" for *The Backgammon Players* (M. Harrison and B. Waters, *Burne-Jones* [1973], p. 49).
8. King Humbert, assassinated on 29 July, was succeeded by his son Victor Emanuel III.

551. TO FLORA ANNIE STEEL

3 St. Edmund's Terrace,
22 August 1900

My dear Anna Steel,

The possible *future* in South Africa (at which your letter briefly glances) is no doubt a problem open to great variety of conjecture. I myself rather incline to dissent from my brother pro-Boers, who prophesy nothing but generations of animosity and race-hatred. I suspect that, after the inevitable once gets set going, the races may amalgamate pretty tolerably, and bygones become bygones, and a period of very advanced material prosperity be started. This I should like, and I partly hope for it, yet with great uncertainty.

That sjamboking Boer seems from your last account to pass among his compatriots as a *distingué* personage. I dissent, but can't help it. But, as to the suggested British parallel, I am afraid that wife-beating is a process not unknown even in "fashionable society," or some reports from the Law-courts tell the thing which is not.

I admire Chamberlain as a speaker: no one sticks up more vigorously or more ably for himself and his cause, or delivers more telling hits. His olden Radicalism I highly sympathized with — his present semi-Toryism not. His policy in the Transvaal affair I think wicked; and, even if it succeeds to the extent of confiscating the territories and the gold-fields, I shall not regard it as exactly successful — it will have cost us a frightful "butcher's bill" and tax-gatherer's bill, swamped much-needed home-reforms, and shamed us in all eyes except our own.

In part of this you of course don't agree. If in August of last year the average British Jingo had been asked — "Would you like to begin a war which, at the end of 10 months, shall not show signs of being nearly finished, and which in that space of time shall cost the nation 50,000 men (I believe that is about the figure) in killed, wounded, and prisoners, and any number of millions of money, and in which one Dutch farmer shall match himself not unequally against 5 British and Colonial soldiers? or would you rather, instead of this, accept that degree of conciliation which Kruger has already offered, and may under polite pressure increase?" — If this had been asked, I fancy the answer would have been — "I had rather come peacefully to terms with Kruger." But the Jingoes at the critical time would not have it so, Chamberlain (and as you truly say the collective British government) would not have it so — and the result is what we see.

Excuse this preachment from

Yours always,
W. M. Rossetti

MS: Rylands.

552. TO AUTHORS' SYNDICATE

3 St. Edmund's Terrace,
21 February 1901

Dear Sir,

You are quite correct in thinking that I am more bent upon getting the *Gabriele Rossetti*[1] published than upon making any money by it: in fact my real belief is that there is little or no money in the scheme, whether for the Publisher or myself or anyone else. I should therefore be *perfectly* content if you can come to terms with Mr. Sands, or with anyone, to publish the book without expense to myself. I would agree to leaving the first 200 copies sold exempt from royalty to me, and to a royalty afterwards of 10%.

If you can obtain *better* terms for me, I shall of course be pleased: I don't much expect them.

I am concerned to hear that Mr. Colles is still out of health. I trust he may soon be restored, but meanwhile have every confidence in your management of the matter.

I take this opportunity of adverting to a previous letter of yours (26 January) mentioning that Blake's Theogony of the Passions was then pending with the *Monthly Review*. As that Review is published by Murray, it occurs to me that possibly it might prove available for publishing Dr. John Polidori's Diary (relating to Lord Byron etc.).[2] I am aware that Murray had that Diary under his consideration a long while ago for some different form of publication, and declined it: the *Monthly Review* did not then exist.

Very truly yours,
W. M. Rossetti

MS: Princeton.

1. *Gabriele Rossetti, A Versified Autobiography* was published in 1901 in an edition of 1,000 numbered copies by Sands & Co., who two year later published *RP*, the last volume of "Rossettiana" for which a publisher could be found. WMR began the translation in February 1896 and finished it in September 1897 with the intention of including it in "Rossettiana." Following the publication of *RRP* and *PDL*, he consigned it to the Authors' Syndicate, to whom he wrote on 31 January 1899 agreeing to undertake their suggested revisions: "I have always had a strong feeling that that versified autobiography of my Father ... is too long, and in parts too remote from British modes of thought, to have much chance of publication as it stands. I am quite willing to cut it down, and to add to it — by way of appendix or otherwise — the Mazzini letters. I would also write such further observations of my own as might seem likely to keep the whole thing together, and make it more readable" (letter to Colles; Texas). Colles was slow to find a publisher, and on 25 January 1901 WMR raised with him the possibility "of printing a few copies — say 100 — at my own expense, for private distribution.... *Ordinary* printing and paper, neither luxurious nor mean, would suit me" (Rylands). It appears that WMR received only one royalty payment for the volume, £5.18.6, which he acknowledged on 18 July 1903 (letter to Sands & Co.; Texas).
2. Parts of the diary were originally included in "Rossettiana." MS. Diary, 25 March 1899: "Am just finishing the rearrangement of John Polidori's Diary etc., to be returned to the Authors' Syndicate. They suggested ... that I should put the Diary into some framework of remarks of my own. For this purpose not much was needed beyond cutting up my Lecture [delivered to the Shelley Society in 1892] (hitherto annexed bodily to the Diary) on the passages regarding Shelley and his party.... Don't well see after all how the Diary etc. are to get published: they would hardly come out as a volume, and would be *very* long for a magazine-article." 28 June 1901: "Colles ... says that the negotiation with *Harmsworth* [*Magazine*] for publishing Dr. Polidori's Diary seems to have failed." 2 January 1907: "Called on Lacon Watson [of Brown, Langham & Co.], and lunched with him at the Granville Club, Hanover Square.... Watson wants ... to bring out in the winter Polidori's Diary in full; my work upon it to be considerably recast, so as to be more fully explanatory and illustrative. It is also suggested that I should try to get further material out of the Hobhouse and St. Aubyn connexion — being (as I understand it) Lady Dorchester and Lord St. Levan. This suggestion I did not distinctly resist: but in point of fact I am little inclined to move in such an affair, and see not the least reason to suppose that these magnates would in any way assist." 3 July: "For a good while past I have been intending to go to the MS. Department of the British Museum, to look into the Broughton (Hobhouse) Papers, and see what there may be in them bearing upon Polidori. Today I went, and find next to nothing: one letter from Polidori to Hobhouse. It seems clear that all substantial matter connected with Byron, at whatever date, has been excluded from these Papers." 10 October: "Find ... the

finale (save index) of the Polidori proofs.'' Brown, Langham, however, deferred publication; and following the firm's bankruptcy in 1910, Colles informed WMR ''that the type for the Polidori Diary remains with the printers Clay & Co., and might possibly be released by them for £10 or so. I don't want at present to enter upon this matter, but told Colles that I might perhaps like to get Clay to print off some 20 copies at a moderate price'' (MS. Diary, 4 November). John Murray was again approached, but he refused. The volume was published by Elkin Mathews in 1911 (MS. Diary, 30 January, 3 March 1911).

553. TO THOMAS JAMES WISE

3 St. Edmund's Terrace,
14 May 1901

Dear Wise,

I received your telegram yesterday; but, having then already made up my mind that it would not quite suit me to attend, I remained obdurate — for which accept any needed apology. A bout of rheumatism or sciatica in both legs (my current experience, but not severe beyond a certain point) does not tempt an old bloke of 71 towards going out in the evening.

Although you said that in my absence you would have to postpone the meeting, I am rather in hopes that after all I was not regarded as ''the indispensable man,'' and that the business proceeded. Don't well understand what steps — which you say do not involve any further payment — can now be needed for winding up the Shelley Society. It seemed to be wound up, to all practical intents and purposes, some 6 years ago; and I was glad then to wash my hands of so expensive a friend as that Society had become. Perhaps you could give me in a few words some inkling of what is now mooted: be it understood that I agree to any and every rational proposal that my colleagues may be putting forward, and I hereby (if requisite) create you my proxy for completing formally anything which may be wanted on my part.[1]

Always yours truly,
W. M. Rossetti

MS: BL.

1. MS. Diary, 14 May 1901: ''Wise looked in in the evening — with his wife, a very handsome woman. He informs me that, at a meeting held yesterday of the defunct Shelley Society, the claims of the Printers Clay on account of certain stereotypes were considered. It was decided that the value of the stereotypes exceeds in all probability that of Clay's claim, some £114; but that the present would not be a good time for trying to realize said value, and that therefore a sum on account ought to be paid to Clay. I dare say this is correct, so I handed to Wise a cheque for my proportion, £5, of the sum on account.''

554. TO ALGERNON CHARLES SWINBURNE

3 St. Edmund's Terrace,
12 November 1901

Dear Swinburne,

I received some days ago with the liveliest pleasure your Tauchnitz Selection Edition.[1] Thanks many and warm. I suppose the selection of shorter poems is such as may be reasonably approved, though I miss many that I should like to have seen there. Also *Erechtheus* is a serious loss. But the presence of *Atalanta* compensates for much. I have been looking into it again with my enthusiasm of old; and I cannot but adhere to my expressed opinion that, taking into consideration the various points which must guide such a judgement — scale, elevation of subject-matter, poetic majesty, and splendour of execution — it is the greatest thing done in this language since *Prometheus Unbound*.

With love to Watts-Dunton,

Yours most affectionately,
W. M. Rossetti

MS: BL.

1. *Lyrical Poems*, ed. W. Sharp, 1901.

555. TO ALGERNON CHARLES SWINBURNE

3 St. Edmund's Terrace,
8 February 1902

Dear Swinburne,

I recur to the project of my giving you a visit. It appears to me that next Saturday 15 February would be as suitable a day as any other, and I propose to come at a moderately early hour — say 12 to 12½:[1] don't as yet know the accurate hours of trains. If Saturday turned out a thoroughly bad or a dismally cold day, I would miss it, and see about the following Monday or Tuesday: would not however miss the Saturday if it were *merely an unattractive* sort of day. If these suggestions meet your convenience, I need not trouble you for any answer.

When last I wrote on this subject I was expecting to give an evening to a sitting to Gilchrist,[2] and then a few days to a visit to my son at Bolton. Things turned out otherwise however: Gilchrist required 5 sittings, and my son has been away at Belfast on business, so I have not yet looked him up.

Gilchrist, I find, has a great desire to paint *your* portrait. He has done me (in my opinion) well. Perhaps you would give the matter some little consideration: we can talk it over when I come.

Love to Watts-Dunton from

Your
W. M. Rossetti

I should have explained that, since my sittings to Gilchrist terminated, I would have written to you ere now, but have been withheld by the constant succession of cold or otherwise afflictive days.

MS: BL.

1. MS. Diary, 17 February 1902: "This day was appointed for my going to see Swinburne, who had promised to read me Act 1 of his drama of Caesar Borgia [*The Duke of Gandia* (1908); only four scenes were written]. I went, and heard both this Act and his powerful and rather long lyrical outpouring called I think *The Altar of Righteousness* [*A Channel Passage and Other Poems* (1904)]. It is an assertion of the central core of Human Ethics, but is hardly less outspoken than of old in denouncing theologic faiths including dogmatic Christianity. The Caesar Borgia is of course very able, but I am not clear how far it may prove, as it progresses, very readable from the dramatic point of view. Swinburne seems in splendid health and spirits: he is not so absolutely deaf as I had feared:

did not (except in one instance and that was voluntary on my part) need that I should write what I had to express. His voice and articulation seem even more forcible than of old; his eyesight piercing — no spectacles; he never puts on a great coat; and had been on the ice today, which may be termed piercingly cold. He and I were, as always, on the most affectionate terms. He was full of talk on various subjects, mostly literary. One point this: that Rétif de la Bretonne seems to have been the first writer in *any* country who stood up (1775) for the supreme intellectual majesty of Shakespeare — dwelling not so much on his value as a poet but rather on his unequalled mental stature.... Swinburne has been engaged upon a general Essay on Dickens [*Quarterly Review*, 196 (July 1902), 20-39; rptd. *Charles Dickens* (1913)]. He read me the passages on Mrs. Gamp and on a certain Public-house 'Jack' in *Great Expectations*. I must affirm that they are irrationally overdone.... He lately picked up a copy of John Polidori's *Vampyre*, and read it. Thinks more than fairly well of it, and insists that it is much better than Byron's beginning of a Vampyre story. My own opinion was always the opposite."

2. The portrait (National Trust, Wightwick Manor) was begun on 3 December 1901 and "practically completed [on 31 January 1902] ... all concerned view and have viewed [it] with satisfaction" (MS. Diary).

556. TO SYDNEY CARLYLE COCKERELL

3 St. Edmund's Terrace,
2 March 1902

Dear Mr. Cockerell,

Since you were here I have been reflecting over that pencil head of Lizzie Siddal.[1] I see that it is certainly the most complete and portrait-like version of her head, done by my Brother, that I possess: so I should be sorry, and indeed ashamed, to part with it. I have 2 little full-length drawings of her by Gabriel —

1. Pencil (neatly executed but rather smudged) — dated "Paris — November 21/55."[2]

2. Pen and ink, good — may be 1855, or a little later.[3]

I would sell one of these, but not both. No. 1 I would price at £9, and No. 2 at £10. These sums may be (I am not certain) beyond their commercial value, but I would not care to sell either drawing for less.

Perhaps you may be coming here again, and I could then show you the drawings. If not, I should not have any real objection to sending them to you by post for inspection.

Have not forgotten that question of selling some letters by Ruskin and Gabriel. The papers are not under my hands without a little looking-out, but this will be attended to at some time.

Yours very truly,
W. M. Rossetti

MS: BL.

1. See Letter 531, Note 1.
2. Surtees 474.
3. Surtees 469. Cockerell did not acquire either drawing.

557. TO SYDNEY CARLYLE COCKERELL

3 St. Edmund's Terrace,
3 July 1902

Dear Mr. Cockerell,

I expect to make up in the course of today a parcel containing the letters etc.

specified in my list now in your hands;[1] also the letter about the *White Ship*,[2] and a *Hugh Heron*.

The letter I price at £2.5, and the *Hugh Heron* at £11. I feel ashamed of mentioning so big a price for what is really poor boyish stuff: but (if memory serves me) people have given even more than this ere now, and I must treat the affair as a matter of "prices current."

I will register the parcel.

As to books that you might possibly like to buy — I enclose a list of things[3] that I jotted down (after consulting a list which I keep for my own information) before I started for Rome. You will understand that the enclosed list merely shows certain things which I might hereafter proceed to extract from my shelves; and that, after so extracting them and fully considering what they amount to, I might or might not feel disposed to sell them. You might let me know, returning the enclosed, which of these items, if any, you would probably like to possess.

I have now marked 2 of the items as 1 and 2. At 1 I mean that I am not as yet quite sure whether I have that thing to dispose of, or whether it is a certain set of printed sheets which I lately sent off to be bound, and retained by myself. By "Family," noted under 2, I mean that, although the poems are works composed by my Father, the handwriting is that of some members of his family, including Gabriel, and also Christina.

Yours very truly,
W. M. Rossetti

That Exhibition at Bruges[4] must certainly have been highly interesting: I should like to have seen it. Have observed that newspapers lay special stress upon Memling's *Châsse de Sainte Ursule*. That is no doubt a pretty thing, and to a certain extent laudable. But surely it is a primitive and childish sort of affair — not a bit more "reasonable" than Japanese art, and utterly inferior to that in energy and *savoir-faire*.

MS: BL.

1. List of forty-four "letters etc. by Gabriel, Ruskin, and Miss Siddal" (letter to Cockerell, 27 June 1902; BL). On 5 July WMR acknowledged Cockerell's check for £34.10 (BL).
2. DGR to Frances Rossetti, [6 May 1880], DW, 4:1763-64.
3. "Extra books etc. of interest in connexion with" DGR (letter to Cockerell, 27 June 1902). For the items Cockerell wished to buy, see Letter 558.
4. Of early Flemish art, June-September 1902.

558. TO SYDNEY CARLYLE COCKERELL

3 St. Edmund's Terrace,
30 July 1902

Dear Cockerell,

I am glad to drop the "Mr.," even if you won't consent (which I should prefer) to do the like.

I am not disposed to sell any one of the extremely few copies that I still possess of *Hugh Heron*.

I enclose a list of 25 items that I am willing to sell.[1] Please at some time let me have back the list, as I keep no copy. I don't know whether you will think that some of the prices that I put down are extortionate: my own belief is that none of them goes beyond what would under the circumstances count as a reasonable average.

I would not object to send you, if you like, the whole lot by parcels-post, registered. It might however be that in some of the instances a little talk, with the object present to both of us, would come convenient. I shall be engaged on 1 and 5 August, and on 6 I may most probably be going out of town for 10 days or so, to accompany my Daughter Helen.

There was a very rough list that I sent you once before. You said from that that you would like to consider —

1. *Early Italian Poets* — I prefer not to sell it.

2. *Ballads and Sonnets*, inscribed by Gabriel to my mother, as being the first copy — I find that this is now a portion of my own personal library, not an "extra copy."[2]

3. "Various sets of proofs" — I have not put them down, thinking you might hardly want them if you saw them — could sell if wanted.

4. "*Collected Works*, volume 1, print and MS." — The MS. forms a very minor portion — I have put down 2 of the items in my present list.

5. Corrected proofs of the *Poems* privately printed, and of the *Poems* 1870, and the *Ballads and Sonnets*. These proofs, as it turns out, are what I have quite recently had bound up, to belong to my own library.

6. My volume *Lives of Famous Poets*, with a few notes by Gabriel (I see they are only 3, all relating to Keats) — Had rather not sell it.

Yours very truly,
W. M. Rossetti

MS: BL.

1. Mostly manuscripts of poems and of translations published in *Early Italian Poets*, priced at £1.5 to £1.15 per item. A c. 1854 manuscript of the beginning of *St. Agnes of Intercession* was priced at £5, the privately printed *Hand and Soul* (1869) at £5.10, and *Poems* (*Privately Printed*), 1869, at £21. MS. Diary, 19 August 1902: "Sold to Cockerell some items connected with Gabriel — £80.5: the chief thing was a copy of the privately printed poems, as nearly approaching completeness as the materials in my hands allowed. Cockerell says that he will dispose of this to an American Agent. As I don't want it to get to America under conditions that would make it probable that someone there would publish *Dennis Shand*, I stipulate that Cockerell, on coming to terms with the American Agent, shall obtain from him a guarantee that he will only sell the book to a *private* purchaser. This latter, as Cockerell truly says, will be likely to keep *Dennis Shand* to himself, as a literary curiosity, and not favour its publication."

2. WMR to Cockerell, 24 August 1902: "I would not willingly conduce to your continuing to break the 10th Commandment, so I will put a price upon that book — though, as a personal matter, I should prefer to retain it.... I propose £9 — and this is I suppose within the sum which one might be likely to obtain at Sotheby's." WMR acknowledged Cockerell's check on 27 August (BL).

559. TO SYDNEY CARLYLE COCKERELL
3 St. Edmund's Terrace,
25 September 1902

Dear Cockerell,

I acknowledge with pleasure the £26.15 for which you sent me a cheque.[1] I don't now remember distinctly about a letter to Christina containing the Blake sonnet.[2] If it passed through my hands when I was selecting the recent lot, I must, on one ground or another, have preferred to keep it. It *may* be that I gave the letter, a couple of years or so ago, to my Daughter Helen, who has got together a rather biggish collection of autographs.

Perhaps you would like to know of the following. A Mr. Maltby, Bookbinder in Oxford, wrote to me about a couple of months ago, saying that he owns a drawing by Gabriel, received by Maltby from his Father-in-law Crawley, who used to be Ruskin's Valet (I remember him well). The drawing was afterwards sent to me, and is now in this house. It is a good pen-and-ink drawing, in Gabriel's style towards 1856. Maltby calls it "Charity": but that I regard as a delusion, and I consider it to be essentially the same subject as Gabriel's water-colour called *The Bower Garden*, only with a larger number of figures.[3] Maltby wants £60 for it: which I consider to be quite enough, though perhaps not overmuch.

I told Maltby that I did not want to purchase it at that price, but offered to keep it here until Fairfax Murray could see it. Maltby (as he wrote to me on 2 September) addressed Murray, but since then I have heard nothing further about the matter. If you would like to see the drawing here, I will gladly produce it to you: but (as you will understand) I could not, in case you should wish to buy it, co-operate in your cutting Murray out, in case it should hereafter turn out that Murray becomes a bidder.

Always truly yours,
W. M. Rossetti

MS: BL.

1. WMR to Cockerell, 14 September 1902: "I have now looked through those letters written by Gabriel, and have extracted a certain number which I am willing to sell in whole or in part: have not included *any* of those minor letters which I keep to be given away as autographs. The letters extracted are 157. I have marked in pencil on each of them — always at the very *end* of the last page — the price which I think suitable. Adding up these prices, I find them to amount to £229.10. This may seem a largish figure; but I really believe that my prices are a good deal below what any Dealer etc. would require. There are only 23 instances where a price of not less than £2 is marked" (BL).
2. DGR to Frances Rossetti, 13 July [1880], which included his sonnet *William Blake* ("To Frederick Shields on his sketch of Blake's unaltered workroom and death-room"), DW, 4:1790-92.
3. Frederick Crawley's son-in-law was presumably the John Maltby (or else a connection of his) who in 1910 owned a pen and ink drawing for the watercolor *Dante's Vision of Matilda Gathering Flowers* (Surtees 72A). This drawing, which bears some resemblance to *The Bower Garden* (Surtees 112), seems to be the one described here. MS. Diary, 21 November 1902, records that Fairfax Murray called to see the drawing, but he "wouldn't buy it at any such sum as this. I gave him a very early drawing by Gabriel, 1843, from his story called *Sorrentino* [Surtees 10A]: it is of course bad. I have a second nearly similar drawing."

560. TO THOMAS JAMES WISE

3 St. Edmund's Terrace,
14 November 1902

Dear Wise,

Let me begin by thanking Mrs. Wise and you for a truly pleasant evening overnight.[1]

I don't quite like to think about our good old friend Furnivall, at his advanced age and burdened with literary researches etc., unable to "fork out" £8 odd with comfort, and having to think about instalments, and thereby (which is a minor evil) delaying a *final* settlement of those tiresome Shelley accounts. I should really not mind adding his £8 odd to my £16 odd, and so (as soon as we receive Clay's response to our Resolution of last evening) clearing off the whole affair once for all. Furnivall would then owe nothing to anybody except me: and me he might pay off at any *or no* time — for I would willingly do him this small service if he likes.

I leave the matter for the present in your hands — prepared to draw the cheque at any moment for the larger sum, if so it is settled.

Always truly yours,
W. M. Rossetti

MS: BL.

1. MS. Diary, 13 November 1902: "Wise called on me yesterday, and asked me to dine with him today, and afterwards discuss with other members of the Shelley Society Committee what should be done as to paying off the one outstanding liability — £84 odd to the Printers in respect of certain extra books, stereo-plates etc. Forman was present at the dinner: Potts, Furnivall, and Dobell, afterwards. Arrangements were made which will entail upon me one more payment, £16 odd. All passed off in a friendly pleasant way. I hardly know on what other occasion I have been out to dinner these 7 years or more — not (I should say) 4 or 5 times in all. Wise's address is 23 Downside Crescent. He lives evidently in very comfortable style with his handsome wife (who I find is a Bolton woman), but the house is not a large one."

561. TO ALGERNON CHARLES SWINBURNE

3 St. Edmund's Terrace,
15 November 1902

Dear Swinburne,

I was delighted to get your letter. I seem to remember that in the olden and golden days you used to speak of Burchard[1] as a covetable but barely possible prize, and I congratulate you much upon now possessing it.

The offer that I might hear that new scene of the Borgia tragedy[2] — or indeed anything of yours — is an offer not to be neglected. I mean to avail myself of it, but just now I could not definitely propose a day. There are 2 or 3 pending engagements which I have to fulfil; and in especial I must pretty soon be leaving London for Bolton (of all places in Philistia) where my son is settled, and where his wife, on 15 October, presented him with a son.[3] I *was* to have started for this purpose on the 13th: but, as the local Mrs. Gamp is still in the house, it turned out that I had better wait a while. When I go, my stay would last, I suppose, not more than 4 or 5 days, and I hope soon afterwards to readdress you and get a day settled.[4]

Love to Watts-Dunton.

Your
W. M. Rossetti

MS: BL.

1. *Joannis Burchardi, Capellae Pontificiae Sacrorum Rituum Magistri Diarium* (see *SL*, 6:164).
2. See Letter 555, Note 1.
3. Geoffrey William (d. 1938), educated at Cambridge; secretary of the School of Oriental Studies, University of London, 1933-38, when he was appointed first assistant registrary at Cambridge. He was considered an administrator of great promise (*Times*, 31 December 1938, p. 14).
4. MS. Diary, 27 January 1903: "Helen and I went by appointment to see Swinburne: he appears to be in the best of health and general condition. He was attentive and agreeable to Helen, and read to both of us the scene of his drama where Pope Borgia hears of the murder of his son Francesco: truly fine in a mode more like Victor Hugo than Elizabethan. He read us also part of the article on Shelley which he is writing for *Chambers's Cyclopaedia of English Literature*: some fine observations finely put."

562. TO THOMAS JAMES WISE

3 St. Edmund's Terrace,
29 January 1903

Dear Wise,

A nice friendly letter of yours has been by me this monstrous time past (date 17 November) — either unanswered or at any rate scantily answered. The reason is that I have been attending to your suggestion that you might like to get some specimens of Gabriel's MSS. To look them up required some pains and time, and my time has been very much broken in upon these weeks past. At last however things have reached a stage at which I can become articulate — so here goes.

I enclose a slight note of items and proposed prices. You have been most liberal to me with those books recently bestowed; and, if only for reciprocity's sake, I would ask you to accept from me any item or items to the value of £5. As to other things, you could consider at your leisure.

I should not be at liberty any day this week: but, if after 2 February you would like to look me up, and see the items, I would gladly attend to the affair. Please bring the enclosed round with you, as I do not keep any duplicate list. I am generally at home all day: but it would be well to fix a time a little beforehand — which I leave to you.[1]

The books which you gave me are extremely interesting: I am particularly glad to possess the Shelley Letters to Hunt,[2] and the Browning Bibliography.[3] Forman produced a copy of the Hitchener Letters. In dunning you for the Hitchener Letters I had added thereto the Clairmont Letters,[4] which do not figure in your parcel: perhaps there is not a copy available. I read my own old copy years ago, but don't now recollect whether the volume comprises any letters beyond what one can find in previous publications — Dowden etc. If not any others (Forman I think possesses some in MS.), I have no real need for the book — only a "fancy," with which a Bibliographer will sympathize.

The affair about Dodd, Mead & Co. and Gabriel's privately printed poems[5] has been rather hanging fire: but lately Dodd, Mead & Co. wrote that they would like me to make up a copy, as near completeness as the conditions permit, and to name a price for it. This I expect to see about in a few days. About my own 3 copies, I am rather afraid that I mean to keep them all: will however one day look them up, and see what they amount to precisely.

There was also an offer of mine to see what extra copies I have of the Polidori Private Press, and present you with examples. On referring to a written list that I keep I am afraid that scarcely anything remains by me: will however look properly into the suitable shelves, and see for certain how this matter stands.

Please remember me very cordially to Mrs. Wise.

Always yours truly,
W. M. Rossetti

MS: Texas.

1. MS. Diary, 23 March 1903: "Wise bought some minor MSS. of Gabriel's for about £40. Wanted to buy for £40 (after I had named £20 as an abstract price) the MS. of the *White Ship*, but I would not sell it at any figure."
2. *Letters from Shelley to Leigh Hunt*, ed. T. J. Wise, 1894 (Privately Printed).
3. T. J. Wise, *A Complete Bibliography of Browning* (1897).
4. *Letters from Shelley to Jane Clairmont*, ed. T. J. Wise, 1889 (Privately Printed).
5. Dodd, Mead were the publishers of WMR's "Bibliography of the Works of Dante Gabriel Rossetti," *Bibliographer*, 1 (December 1902), 420-30; 2 (January 1903), 34-44, in which the privately printed editions of *Poems* were first described.

563. TO JULIA ELLSWORTH FORD[1]

3 St. Edmund's Terrace,
7 February 1903

My dear Madam,

The subject of Simeon Solomon is one which I avoid speaking or writing about so far as I can. There was a most repulsive scandal about him (not an *unfounded* scandal) many years ago — say 1872: and since then I neither know nor wish to know anything definite about him. No doubt the question of what are his merits as an Artist can to some extent be dissociated from his personality; and, as you write on the subject in a reasonable spirit, I will reply in the same.

You would like to receive "any suggestions with regard to new materials, or information about any of his original oils." As to new materials, you may probably be aware that there is something about Solomon, and 3 specimens of his work, in a book published in 1899, *The English Pre-Raphaelite Painters*, by Percy H. Bate (Bell & Sons). There are also, or were, a large number of photographs from his works published by Mansell & Co., 405 Oxford Street. As to original oils, I have always thought that his best picture was the one called *Habet*[2] — Ladies in the Roman Amphitheatre giving the signal for putting a Gladiator to death: truly a remarkable and fine work, produced towards 1866. Many years afterwards, say 1893, I saw this picture again in a collection left by its (then deceased) owner in London: this owner was a Hebrew, but I forget the name — possibly Moseley.[3] Solomon also produced a number of other very able and telling paintings: but a certain morbid taint made its appearance in them, and went on increasing.

634

You say — "The time Solomon was in my Brother's Studio was the most important period of his life." I don't quite know what is here implied. True, Solomon was in my Brother's Studio every now and then, like any other visitor, between some such dates as 1863 and 1871: but, if it is supposed that he attended regularly as a student or practitioner under my Brother, this is quite a delusion. There was nothing of the sort at any time.

The first that I knew about Solomon (before my Brother knew anything) may have been in 1856 or 1857. He was then quite a youth — say 15 or 16 — and showed singular powers of invention, rapid composition, design, etc. This had attracted attention in some quarters; and I recollect that an album, stuffed full of a number of his designs, was handed about at a big gathering of men, including myself. Some of the designs were trivial enough, flashy sort of affairs; but many were exceedingly clever, and full of varied picturesque faculty. I did not about that date *meet* Solomon — not, I should suppose, earlier than 1863 or 1864.

I have no objection to your quoting (if you like) what I here say. The best thing might be to give the whole letter verbatim. If you were to miss out the first paragraph, I must stipulate that you should say in explicit terms that, although I knew something of Solomon personally between some such dates as 1863 and 1871, I have since the latter date entirely lost sight of him, and have no knowledge of his proceedings.

> Believe me, Dear Madam,
> Very faithfully yours,
> Wm. M. Rossetti

MS: Yale. Extract in J. E. Ford, *Simeon Solomon, An Appreciation* (1908), pp. 20-21.

1. (1859-1950), American writer and children's filmmaker, published a novel, plays (including several for children), and a book on G. F. Watts (1908). She visited WMR on 16 September 1903, when she showed herself "an enthusiast for Gabriel" (MS. Diary).
2. R.A., 1865.
3. Not identified.

564. TO B. F. STEVENS & BROWN[1]

3 St. Edmund's Terrace,
20 March 1903

Dear Sirs,

What is said in your letter of 18 March is of course strictly accurate. The translated *Henry the Leper* was not published by my Brother himself; though he thought well of it, and sometimes contemplated publishing it. After his death I included it in his *Collected Works*.

If the Bibliophile Society of Chicago (or is it of Boston?) wish to reprint this translation,[2] I am not sure that they require any "permission" (as your letter says) of mine. The English Publishers of the *Collected Works* are Messrs Ellis & Elvey, 29 New Bond Street. I don't well remember what arrangements they have in relation to American publication. They have I think *some* arrangements, entitling me to a percentage: but any application for permission should, as it seems to me, go to Messrs Ellis & Elvey.

I don't know what may be the particular MS. of *Henry the Leper* which was sold in London, and is now lying with the Bibliophile Society. When the *Collected Works* were in preparation (1886) *some* MS. of this translation was consigned to the Printers. Several years afterwards — say 1899 — I thought of looking it up, expecting to find it among the other copy for the *Collected Works* which had been returned to me by the Printers: but it was not there, and I can safely say that it is not anywhere in my possession. The Printers and Publishers, to whom I wrote, could not explain its disappearance. It is however *possible* that it was sent back to me in due course, and that I afterwards sold it — though I do not now remember any such transaction.[3]

I presume that this letter to you will suffice, without my replying direct to Mr. Harper.

Very truly yours,
W. M. Rossetti

MS: Huntington.

1. "American Library and Literary Agents," 4 Trafalgar Square. The firm was founded in 1866 by Benjamin Franklin Stevens (1833-1902), who left the United States in 1860 to join his brother Henry, already an established London bookseller. In 1899 he took Henry John Brown into the business.
2. Published with an introduction by William P. Trent, 2 vols., Boston Bibliophile Society, 1905. The MS., of which volume 1 is a facsimile, was acquired by William K. Bixby of St. Louis, Missouri, from Stevens & Brown.
3. Trent repeated this information in his introduction (1:vi). In some notes on the introduction, dated 4 November 1905, WMR recalled that he sold the MS. used for *Collected Works* "to T. J. Wise — may have been towards 1890" (Columbia). See also Letter 457, Note 1. Stevens & Brown confided to H. H. Harper, the treasurer of the Bibliophile Society, 20 March 1903, that when they sold the MS. to Bixby they repeated "the gossip received from the late owner to the effect that he believed it to be still unpublished" (Columbia).

565. TO MACMILLAN & CO.

3 St. Edmund's Terrace,
25 March 1903

Dear Sirs,

I received with much satisfaction your letter of the 23rd, saying that you are prepared to bring out now the complete edition of Christina Rossetti's Poems.[1] You will no doubt have borne in mind that some of the contents are at present the copyright of the Christian Knowledge Society.

Owing to the length of time which has elapsed since I put the poems together, and wrote notes etc., there must certainly be a few details which at the present date require reconsideration or revision. I am prepared to begin looking into this matter at once; but, being rather more than usually busy with other things which cannot be set aside, I could not give my *whole* time to the business. Would you kindly let me know what is the date beyond which I ought not to retain the materials undelivered to you. I could, if you prefer, deliver almost directly all the earlier portion of the poems themselves, keeping by me for some little while further the prefatory matter, notes, etc.

Yours very truly,
W. M. Rossetti

MS: BL.

1. MS. Diary, 23 March 1903: "Macmillan ... writes in reply to a letter which I had sent him yesterday, reminding him that the *Goblin Market* volume goes out of copyright in 1904."

566. TO MACMILLAN & CO.

3 St. Edmund's Terrace,
27 March 1903

Dear Sirs,

In reply to yours of yesterday, I cannot say that I "have any reason to suppose that the S.P.C.K. would grant permission to print their volume"[1] in the one which you propose to bring out. My Sister was on excellent terms with the Society, and in the very little I have had to do with them they have always been courteous and agreeable. This is as much as I can say. My impression is that any permission from them would only be granted upon terms of compensation.

I remember that, when the question of a complete edition of my Sister's poems was first started — say in 1897 or 1898 — your Firm wrote to me saying that you would be prepared to negotiate with the Society, so as to obtain authority to print those Verses: as I understood, to print them without actually cancelling the right of the Society to continue reprinting. Some sum which you would be willing to pay was suggested — I think £100.

I am quite willing to take the initiative, if you like, in addressing the Society: but perhaps, before I do so, you would give me an idea of what sort of arrangement you would at present be disposed to authorize.[2]

Very truly yours,
W. M. Rossetti

MS: BL.

1. *Verses* (1893), reprinted from CGR's devotional volumes, *Called to be Saints* (1881), *Time Flies* (1885), and *The Face of the Deep* (1892), which were also published by the Society.

2. MS. Diary, 1 May 1903: "Called on Mr. McClure of the S.P.C.K. He does not resist the idea of entering into some terms with Macmillans, but will I suspect stand up for rather hard terms. He wrote to me in the afternoon after our interview. I must now write to Macmillans, and should prefer to leave that Firm to transact direct henceforward. McClure was very civil to me, and highly laudatory of Christina, both in her work and personally." Rev. Edmund McClure (d. 1922) was secretary of the SPCK, 1875-1915.

567. TO MACMILLAN & CO.

3 St. Edmund's Terrace,
21 June 1903

Dear Sirs,

Your letter of the 19th is somewhat disappointing to me. If we can't include those poems by my Sister belonging to the S.P.C.K., I don't for my own part see any great call for a re-edition of her remaining poems — but as to this you would be the better judges. The only change which has arisen in the existing situation is that the time is closely approaching when the copyright of the *Goblin Market* volume will expire next year. This contingency could, I should imagine, be best met by issuing at once a quite cheap edition of that one volume, leaving all your other publications as they stand.

To alter my compilation of Christina's *Complete* Poems, so as to confine it to a recast of the poems which are your copyright, would entail on me a *large* amount of trouble of a rather fidgeting kind: the main reason for this being that the poems, including those of the S.P.C.K., are now all arranged in order of date, and I should now have to re-arrange the residue, cut out notes, alter numeration and references to numeration, etc. etc. Certainly I *could* do all this in process of time, and *would* do it if requisite: but I should much grudge the time and patience involved in such tedious work.

I consider that *many* of those S.P.C.K. poems are among the best things that Christina ever did; and what I want is that the public should at last see her poetic work as a whole, in one view.

Your letter implies that the only difficulty with the S.P.C.K. is that they want higher money-terms than you are disposed to accord. Rather than drop my original project, and leave Christina's poetic standing so far in the lurch, I would assent to your proposing to pay the S.P.C.K. any sum up to £100, with the understanding that the second £50 (or less) making up this amount should be deducted from royalties payable to me.[1]

Please oblige me with your views as to the points raised in this letter.

Very truly yours,
W. M. Rossetti

MS: BL.

1. MS. Diary, 3 July 1903: "Macmillans write that the S.P.C.K. accept the offer of £100 for Christina's *Verses* — I paying the second £50. So the Complete Poems can now go forward, to my no small satisfaction."

568. TO ALGERNON CHARLES SWINBURNE

3 St. Edmund's Terrace,
11 February 1904

My beloved and incomparable Friend,

(I am tempted to use adjectives which might have befitted Shelley in 1811 addressing the Brown Demon,[1] for really they express my feeling) — I was delighted to get your recent letter, showing all the verve and virus which were always yours. After such a letter, it would be almost futile to express a hope that you are now fully recovered from your late sudden and severe illness, the latest assault of Urizen — for it is clear enough that you *are* recovered. In such cases I used to say Laus Urizeno, but I suppose on this occasion it should rather be Laus Enitharmoni.[2]

I was misled into naming *Advent* as your favourite among Christina's religious poems by a passage in Mackenzie Bell's book, p. 244: "Mr. Swinburne (my authority for the statement is her brother Dante Gabriel) regards *Advent* as 'perhaps the noblest of all her poems'" — and then he speaks of its "iambic alternate 8 and 6 feet set in stanzas of 8 lines." Why Bell thus named Gabriel I don't now know: and yet I have a kind of dim idea that Gabriel did somewhere mention *Advent* to such an effect. If so, he probably used the word loosely, and meant *Passing Away*. I was well aware from of old of your extreme admiration — which I most fully share — of that wondrous outburst.

I enclose for you the little notebooks containing those rather less laudable compositions — *The Last Words of St. Telemachus*, and *The Last Words of Sir Eustace Grey*.

Of course I agree to a large extent in the views expressed by you which might have led up to a very pointed address to "Ma chère [Chri]stine." But she and I, knowing ourselves to be entirely hostile in such matters, left them largely in the background, as being the only course conducive to our mutual comfort. I will also say this much — That those ideas, however irrational I may consider them, do produce a beautiful type of character. I knew it in my mother and both my sisters — and have no doubt you have known and reverenced it too.

Really you ought to do the Jah-Jahs and Yah-Yahs:[3] it would be the most scarifying goad of the opening 20th century, and you are the one man to accomplish it perfectly. Whenever I read anything of recent days, professedly or professionally in the interest of Christianity, I see that Christianity is now quite eviscerated: all its internals, such as I knew them in boyhood and youth, are gone.

I perceive that my proceedings in relation to "a married daughter" have remained a little vague in your house. My then unmarried second daughter Helen, who saw you twice (with heart-felt contentment) in 1903, decided in the course of the autumn to marry a young Italian, Gastone Angeli, brother of a literary man in Rome of some note.[4] On 1 December Helen, with her younger sister Mary and myself, went off to Naples: and there on the 10th the wedding was performed, followed on the 13th by the departure of bride and bridegroom to Cairo — he holds an appointment in the Italian Chamber of Commerce there. We did also see in Rome my already married daughter Olivia, but this was an accessory matter: I was back in London on 18 December. I am very sorry to lose Helen — who is a bright girl, sympathetic and capable — but thus it has to be. I like what I have seen of her husband — he fought in Greece in 1897 under Ricciotti Garibaldi.[5] Did you ever see or hear anything of a book published last summer — *A Girl Among the Anarchists*, by Isabel Meredith? It is the joint performance of Olivia and Helen, and recounts (with some disguises and interchanges) their real personal experiences.

I regret to say that I don't yet know the writings of Miss Jane Barlow:[6] must look out for them — but I am much behindhand (and always was) in reading current prose fiction. I have noticed from time to time (in "the minor periodical" of your old days) very high praise of the writings of *some* Irish lady, and I fancy this may be Miss Barlow. I see from your letter that she writes in verse as well as prose.

Love to yourself and Watts-Dunton, and best regards to Mrs. Mason.[7]

> Your affectionate
> W. M. Rossetti

MS: BL.

1. Elizabeth Hitchener, to whom Shelley wrote on 16 October 1811: "I write today, because *not* to answer such a letter as your's instantly eagerly I will add gratefully were impossible.... My dearest friend, for I will call you so ..." (*Letters of Shelley*, ed. Jones, 1:149). WMR was replying to Swinburne's letter of thanks for a copy of CGR's *Poetical Works*.

2. "Enitharmon is Spiritual Beauty, the twin, consort, and inspiration of the poet Los" (S. Foster Damon, *A Blake Dictionary* [1965], p. 124).

3. "I am thinking of making public the account of a private mission to the JAH-JAH (pronounced Yah, Yah. 'Praise him in his name JAH') Islands, whose degraded inhabitants worship a three-headed, six-armed, six-legged (and so on throughout every part of the body) idol, emblematic of a God consisting of a father and a son of the same age and a tertium quid represented also as a very old pigeon" (*SL*, 6:176-77).

4. Diego Angeli, whose many books include a translation of Shakespeare into Italian.

5. (1847-1917), son of Giuseppe Garibaldi.

6. (1857-1917), poet and novelist.

7. Watts-Dunton's sister, Miranda (Mrs. Charles Mason).

569. TO MACMILLAN & CO.

3 St. Edmund's Terrace,
13 August 1904

Dear Sirs,

I have not any accurate knowledge as to how the complete edition of Christina Rossetti's *Poetical Works* has been going on. I presume however that from time to time further issues of the book have been or will be printed.

In order not to omit anything which may conduce to the accuracy of any such issues, I have lately been reading the volume through with minute attention; and I find there are some things (as indeed there were certain to be) which are not correct, and should be corrected when opportunity offers. Some of these are mere trifles — a full stop dropped out or what not; others, though open to improvement, *could* be left as they stand; but some others are real corrections of actual errors. Every now and then, subsequent or previously overlooked information has shown me that something in my Notes, Memoir, etc., is in need of revision.

I have no doubt you would bear this point in mind at any suitable time.[1]

I presume you have not any idea of bringing out any poems by my Sister in any different form from this complete edition. Yet it occurs to me to mention that I think 2 comparatively small volumes (the 2nd more especially small) could be made up as follows, and would find favour with many readers —

1. A volume containing all her *best* poems of whatever class, and these only;
2. A volume containing her poems of a narrative or quasi-narrative character.[2]

Yours very truly,
W. M. Rossetti

MS: BL.

1. MS. Diary, 16 August 1904: "Macmillans reply to my letter of the 12th March to my satisfaction. They would like to receive my emendations to Christina's Complete Poems, to be used at the next (not immediate) opportunity."

2. Proposal No. 1 was agreed upon, and *Poems of Christina Rossetti* ("Golden Treasury Series") was published in December 1904.

570. TO FORD MADOX HUEFFER

Dear Ford,

Pray think no more about that tin.[1] This stroke of the pen wipes it out, and it is a free gift. Were I otherwise minded, I might leave off signing W. M. Rossetti, and ought in conscience to sign henceforth Shylock — who was himself a most conscientious man.

Your letter has filled me with concern — but it allows me to infer that you have now turned the corner, and are on the high road to recovery. I had not known anything about your disheartening condition until 21 September, when Olive Garnett,[2] calling here, gave me some information regarding it.

You hope that I keep out of the Doctors' hands. In all essential respects I do so — my general health continuing as yet to be really very good. Have had some degree of "neuritis" in right hand and arm, treated by massage etc.: for the past month or more that is nearly well.

You also say that you have been forbidden to receive news from England. But for this, I would tell you a few family particulars, not of too cheerful a kind.[3] One is cheerful — Helen has a daughter,[4] born 15 September. I expect to be soon going to Rome with Mary — and there seems a likelihood that after that she and I will be in Algeria (or else Tunis) for some rather indefinite length of stay.

All best wishes, my dear Ford, for you and yours.

Your affectionate
W. M. Rossetti

MS: Princeton.

1. MS. Diary, 3 October 1904: "Received a letter from Ford Hueffer from Boppard. His health had been a total wreck for 2 months and more; but now he has rallied a little.... He worries over a debt of £40 to me, incurred several months ago. I always thought the money would be less a loan than a gift, and I have now replied, telling him to think no more about it."
2. Daughter of Richard Garnett; published *Petersburg Tales* (1900), and a novel, *In Russia's Night* (1918).
3. Death of Gastone Angeli on 18 July; and Mary's arthritis, about which doctors had reported that there was "not much to be done curatively whether by medicine or by regimen" (MS. Diary, 20 September).
4. Imogene Lucy Cristina Maria, who married the novelist Geoffrey Dennis in 1928.

571. TO SYDNEY CARLYLE COCKERELL

Dear Cockerell,

I have now looked you up some letters and other writings of Gabriel's — here they are. You will perceive that the former number up to 14, and the latter to 10.

I enclose also a list of proposed prices.[1] Should however (in case you purchase some of the items) be *better* pleased if you would accept as a gift 2 of the letters — whichever 2 you prefer.

Have also looked into the question of some books owned etc. by Gabriel. Have not searched among those books which form my own personal library; for, though I should certainly find there some volumes bearing his inscription etc., I foresee that, on lighting upon such an item, I should most probably not want to part with it.

But there are various volumes which I do not admit into my own bookshelves, but which I keep as extras, to be prized according to their deserts. Among these are 2, of which one might perhaps meet your liking.

1. Volume 1 of Miss Barrett's *Poems*, 1844. It bears Gabriel's inscription "Rossetti." Remained with him till his death. I then gave it to an Aunt, from whom it passed to Christina, and from her to me. I wrote in the book some while ago a note to the above effect.[2] This is the actual copy of Volume 1 (Volume 2 disappeared ages ago) which Gabriel and I used to read incessantly soon after its publication: we — especially he — as good as knew it by heart. There are some pencilings of his — noting parallel passages from other poets. This, though only an odd volume, I regard as in its way a catch, and I price it at £3.10.

2. Also an odd volume — Volume 1 of Lord Houghton's Life etc. of Keats, 1848. It was presented to Gabriel by a lady in 1859, and so inscribed by her. Contains many pencil-marks by Gabriel, and various notes of his, more or less critical, and certainly not uninteresting. It is neatly bound: the other book is shabby, but not dirty so far as I notice. I hardly know which of these 2 volumes would be regarded as the more covetable: for this also I will name £3.10.

In case (?) you should be inclined to take both of them, I safeguard myself for the present by saying that I question whether I would part with both: I would part with either of the two. They can be seen here any convenient time: next Monday and Wednesday would not be open to me.[3]

Yours very truly,
W. M. Rossetti

MS: BL.

1. Fourteen letters and ten memoranda, ranging in price from 18/- to £2.10, the total being £33.2.
2. WMR to Wise, 12 November 1905: "You once advised me to write, on fly-sheets etc. of bound volumes in my library, any short jottings as to details of family-interest etc. pertaining thereto. I thought the suggestion very sensible and not to be neglected. Began doing this job in the autumn of 1904, and, after returning from Rome last February, brought it to a conclusion" (BL).
3. WMR to Cockerell, 24 October 1904: "I received with satisfaction your cheque for £12.5. The Keats volume is at your disposal when you like" (BL). MS. Diary, 5 November 1904: "Cockerell called.... I presented to him as a gift an old relic of Gabriel — the volume 1 of Miss Barrett's *Poems* of 1844."

572. TO ELSIE (MRS. FORD MADOX) HUEFFER

3 St. Edmund's Terrace,
22 October 1904

My dear Elsie,

It relieves my mind not a little to learn that Cathy has gone off to look after Ford. Some such step was I think highly requisite, and likely to produce as good an effect as anything else could do. I am glad too that the account of him which you give is even a *little* better.

About Algeria, or Rome as a preliminary thereto, I need not for the present say any more. Whether it would be best to get Ford back to his own home is a question too delicate for me to offer an opinion upon: I will only say that, whenever that result may be manageable, it seems to be the obviously right and desirable solution.

The question whether Ford should get, or try to get, into some regular *groove* of writing, apart from pursuing a wholly speculative career of authorship, is again a ticklish one. My own opinion is — Yes. I (having always earned a *settled* income, small and then increasing) cannot but regard as very anxious and risky the position of a man with a family who has nothing beyond his talents as an Author to rely upon; for the remuneration of those talents depends, not upon their being real or even fine, but upon the capricious likings of the public. I myself should always have liked to be a literary personage, doing literary work of my own the best I could: my position did not allow of this, and what I had to be was a Government-clerk giving his spare hours to newspaper-critiques etc.

Accept my best possible wishes for you and all yours.

Your affectionate
W. M. Rossetti

N.B. I am *not* writing to Ford in reply to his postcard: shall await any further developments.

MS: Princeton.

573. TO ELSIE (MRS. FORD MADOX) HUEFFER

3 St. Edmund's Terrace,
26 October 1904

Dear Elsie,

Please excuse a very hasty note. The enclosed from Ford[1] reached me last evening, and of course does little or nothing to relieve the anxiety which I share with you. There is nothing in it to show that he had then seen his mother.

I really don't know whether it is right or *wrong* that I should reply. If I do reply, I would be sure to weigh my words, so as to avoid increasing his gloom. Would you tell me which I had better do, and I will conform.[2]

Yours affectionately,
W. M. Rossetti

MS: Princeton.

1. [24 October 1904], from Mammern: "Dear Uncle William, / Many thanks for your sympathetic letter to Elsie [No. 572, which referred to the possibility of Ford accompanying WMR and Mary to Algeria]. / Of course I would not think of burdening you with the company of an hypochondriac-lunatic — which is what I have become, I'm afraid. I get practically no better here — and have no hopes of doing so — though the Doctor here says there is nothing the matter, actually, with me except brain fag. That's more than enough, though — and I begin to think it's all up with me.... What a gloomy place this world seems to be!" (AP).
2. See Letter 574.

574. TO ELSIE (MRS. FORD MADOX) HUEFFER

3 St. Edmund's Terrace,
28 October 1904

My dear Elsie,

Consequent upon your letter of yesterday, I thought I might just as well send a few friendly words to our dear Ford — as per enclosed.[1] I enclose them to you, to dispatch or not as you see the more fitting. Possibly the safest course might be for you to transmit them to Cathy, for her to deliver or not according to the dictate of the moment.

I certainly think (replying to a point in your letter) that the *immediate cause* of Ford's gloomy self-estimate is depression, rather than serious illness. The serious illness has been there to cause the depression, and I suppose still is there — but I should very much hope both curable and abating.

Mary goes on pretty tolerably: she and I would like to be off as soon as manageable — which I fancy may be within 10 days or so, to Rome.

Yours,
W. M. Rossetti

MS: Princeton.

1. Letter 575, but it was probably not forwarded.

575. TO FORD MADOX HUEFFER

3 St. Edmund's Terrace,
28 October 1904

Dear Ford,

I received your letter of the 24th, and feel really obliged to you for writing to me under conditions so far from cheerful. But so young a man as you, with so many talents, is surely warranted in looking upon matters from the brighter side. There must be tens of thousands of people going about, "from China to Peru,"[1] or from Port Arthur to the Dogger Bank, who have had severe nervous breakdowns, and under proper treatment have recovered, and do all their work as well as ever. I cannot but assume that the treatment which you are now undergoing is judicious, and your Doctor's assurance sincere — so there is every reason to hope.

Please give my love to your mother, whose presence must be a boon and relief to you.

I say no more for the present about Algeria. Who knows but that it will after all come off — for you as for me and Mary? She goes on pretty well, but certainly is in need of something — whatever that may be — to set her up.

Much love from
W. M. R.

We of my tribe and lineage were of course all hard hit by the death of poor Gastone Angeli, whom I liked much. The baby has been Helen's consolation, and promises to continue such. The news of them both is of late quite satisfactory.

MS: Princeton.

1. Dr. Johnson, *The Vanity of Human Wishes*, 1.2.

576. TO WILLIAM HOLMAN HUNT
3 St. Edmund's Terrace,
13 December 1905

Dear Hunt,

Few recent things have given me so much pleasure as the receipt of the copy of your book[1] with your affectionate inscription. To be deemed worthy of your regard is what I count no little thing.

I am reading the book, and have got on to your return from the first eastern journey. It is greatly interesting. So far as I am personally concerned, I see nothing as yet to which I cannot yield assent, full or partial. Gabriel's motives of action are I think sometimes construed harshly when this does not necessarily ensue.

As I read I make slight jottings — not mostly as to points which might possibly be in controversy between you and me, but as to general and often slight details. If you would like, I would at the proper time write these jottings out for your consideration when a new edition is called for — which I regard as pretty safe.

What follows is quite a separate point. Just after I had last written to you a Mr. Marlow (connected with the Firm of Publishers, Brown, Langham & Co., for my forthcoming Reminiscences) called here, to see about suitable illustrations for that book. He noticed the drawing which you made in 1848 for the head of Gabriel in your *Rienzi* picture: a very good drawing it is, as you probably remember. This he would much like to use in the book. I told him that I could not authorize the use unless you consent: if you do consent, I also should be much pleased to use the drawing. Would you kindly inform me — Yes or No. Whichever it be, I shall take it as final.[2]

Affectionately yours,
W. M. Rossetti

MS: Iowa.

1. *PR & PRB* (1905). Hunt to WMR, 5 December 1905: "My dear old Friend, / Tomorrow I am told my book on Pre-Raphaelitism is to come out. / I cannot pretend that you will approve of my treatment of the subject for it is entirely in opposition to the theory for which you are specially responsible. / The fact that the world appeared to be satisfied with your story although I daily had reason to see the harm it caused me, left me disinclined to enter the list against you for this I could see was necessary if I championed my view of the truth. I know that you have not said a word opposed to your own understanding of the case and personal considerations would not have induced me to come into the arena but fresh publications were always appearing in the same tenor, so not private interest alone, but understanding of the cardinal purpose of Pre-Raphaelitism was being more and more distorted and for this I could not but feel heavily responsible. / The conviction of your own good faith assured me that you would respect the independence of an opposite witness and I could not fear that you would regard my independent course as necessarily hostile to my long standing esteem and affection for you. / Advancing age to both of us has prevented meetings between us of late years or I should explain myself by word of mouth. Now I am obliged to be content with this letter although it is a colder form for the expression of friendship, the more so in having to be written by another hand. / I am, / Yours ever devotedly / W. Holman Hunt" (AP).

WMR replied "in affectionate terms, informing him that ... [*SR*] is likely to be published next autumn, and that I might *possibly* insert into it some rejoinder to his allegations. Don't at all want to do this if it can be helped" (MS. Diary, 6 December). In January 1906 WMR paid Hunt a visit. MS. Diary, 9 January: "Mrs. Hunt writes asking me in very cordial terms to call. I must do so. Have not *seen* Hunt since (perhaps) early in 1894: but I never had any quarrel with him, and should be sorry, now that I fear he is nearly blind, to hold aloof." 19 January: "I went to lunch with the Holman

Hunts, staying some 5½ hours.... Arthur Hughes was present, and very pleased I was to see him. The Hunts received me with marked cordiality, and nothing was said on either side having any tincture of soreness. Poor old Hunt is in a very bad way as regards eyesight. He says that some while ago he went to Wiesbaden to consult a famous oculist, who incised the substance of the eyes (no chloroform but only a local anaesthetic), and only did harm thereby. Hunt also suffers a good deal from his incurable asthma, and has to expectorate from time to time: this gives him bouts of sleeplessness. Mrs. Hunt is now distinctly an old lady, but seems in sound unimpaired health.... Hunt is, as of old, an inexhaustible talker, spite of some feebleness of voice entailed by the asthma. He spoke on all sorts of subjects ... and seems fairly resigned and perfectly patient under the great affliction of quasi-blindness. This does not go to such an extent as to prevent his helping himself at table without assistance. Mrs. Hunt referred to the offer I had made a month or so ago to give Hunt if he liked, some notes on disputable points in his book. I had in fact ere now completed these notes, and had pocketed them, to be produced if at all wanted: so I now handed them over to Mrs. Hunt, to be examined at leisure.... It is truly a great satisfaction to me to have seen old Hunt once more, and with undiminished goodwill, after so long an interval. I shall try to look him up again from time to time, but, according to my habits of life, this could not be continual.''

2. It was not used.

577. TO FREDERIC GEORGE STEPHENS

3 St. Edmund's Terrace,
19 December 1905

Dear Steph,

Receive many reciprocations of your greetings. I regretted to see some days ago the news of the death of Armstead,[1] a very capable sculptor. Mary is far from right, and I am just now a little pestered — muscular rheumatism or what else in right arm and left hip. But this I take as it comes, hoping it may once again pass.

I knew of your move, and shall look your new quarters[2] up one day — not just now. Glad there is *some* improvement in the news of your wife and self, though it is less than I could wish for.

I don't well remember Whistler's portrait of Irving as Philip 2.[3] Am a hearty admirer of Whistler in those works wherein he did himself justice, which was not always.

I have nearly finished reading Hunt's book. There are things in it about you which you will not approve — and some about myself to which I do not exactly assent.[4] Just as the book was coming out, Hunt (whom I have not *seen* since 1893 or 1894) wrote me a very friendly letter, and afterwards sent me an inscribed copy of the book itself. I replied to his letter with equal friendliness: should not at all wish to enter into an angry controversy with him. There is a book of mine to come out next autumn[5] (finished 2¾ [years] ago), and I *might* possibly put into it one or two passages by way of rejoinder, yet very likely shan't.

Glad to hear about Gabriel's picture of *The Beloved* etc. In Hunt's book Gabriel is, in my opinion, not quite handsomely treated. Millais is, and Woolner pretty fairly.

Always yours,
W. M. Rossetti

MS: Bodleian.

1. Henry Hugh Armstead (1828-1905), sculptor of the external decoration of the Colonial Office, and of some of the sculpture on the Albert Memorial.

2. Stephens had recently moved from No. 10 to No. 9 Hammersmith Terrace.

3. *Arrangement in Black, No. 3: Sir Henry Irving as Philip II of Spain.*

4. Stephens to WMR, 18 December 1905: "Have you seen Holman Hunt's book on himself as the P.R.B. *solus* and sufficient? I have not, and only hope he has had the grace and self-respect to let me alone. He could not attack you" (AP). WMR told Foster Howe on 17 January 1906 that he considered the book "of solid importance for its theme, but not wholly free from faults of over-doing and self-assertion" (Kansas).

5. *SR.*

578. TO FREDERIC GEORGE STEPHENS

3 St. Edmund's Terrace,
22 December 1905

Dear Steph,

Heartiest thanks to your wife and you about Mary. She has to go day by day to a Doctor (massage-treatment of an exceptional kind) a long distance from our house, and all the substance of the day vanishes in this expedition. She could not at present get round to Hammersmith, but counts on doing so one day, and so do I.

The affair of Hunt[1] seems to me anything but clear sailing. Personally I am resolved not to have any acrimonious public discussion, though I *may* (or as likely may not) say something in print, not acrimoniously. About your own case, I will certainly — as you ask me to do so — express a candid opinion, friendly to you (as I shall remain for the brief remainder of my days) and not unfriendly to Hunt. Scattered here and there about his book, there are undeniably some slighting references to you (little if anything about any canvas mishap in Jerusalem) — as that you did not show energy in the practical work of a painter, that you have over-stated Gabriel's claims as a P.R.B., etc. There is also, but your *name* is not there given, a severe censure of a certain copy from Holbein, which (I think) was your doing at the initiative of Millais; the censure purports to come from Millais much more than from Hunt. These and the like might be regarded as mainly matter of opinion, and opinion governed by a generally unfriendly feeling: were the case mine, I should not take public notice of them.[2]

There are however 2 points which come closer to personal imputations.

1. Hunt clearly implies, though he does not absolutely affirm it as a fact, that, when his Valentine and Proteus[3] was re-exhibited, you put up someone to stating in the *Pall Mall Gazette* that, according to Hunt's own statement when the picture was painted, Valentine's sword is of the time of Charles I, and thus Hunt's pretensions to strict accuracy in accessories etc. were insidiously attacked.

2. Hunt says that, as soon as you joined the *Athenaeum*, you began a campaign against the R.A., which you afterwards dropped when Maclise showed you some civility. He cites a very blatant letter against the R.A. inserted in the *Athenaeum* soon after you joined it: does not say, nor I think *mean*, that you wrote the letter, but that it came in as part of your campaign. He also says that at a certain date, perhaps towards 1865, a book was published containing a laudatory reference to the *Claudio and Isabella*; and it was reviewed in the *Athenaeum* with depreciatory remarks on the same picture. He regards you as responsible for the depreciation.

These are the only 2 points which I *remember* as entitled to rather separate consideration.

Affectionate regards from

Your old Friend,
W. M. Rossetti

1. See Letter 577, Note 4.
2. Stephens had asked WMR on 20 December to tell him, "with that candour and affection which you always gave me during more than fifty years," whether he should reply publicly to Hunt (AP). MS. Diary, 3 January 1906: "Mrs. Stephens called, bringing back Hunt's book which I had lent to Stephens. He is much put out by statements there made to his disadvantage: and this comes at a bad time, as his heart is seriously out of order, giving rise to grave apprehensions."
3. *Valentine rescuing Sylvia from Proteus.*

579. TO FREDERIC JAMES SHIELDS

3 St. Edmund's Terrace,
19 April 1906

Dear Shields,

I have received your letter, and read it with much affection and sympathy. Was sorry to miss you from Rowley's last gathering:[1] the preceding one I was unable to attend, being then in Rome. I have heard ere now of your not being well, much to my concern. At the age which I have reached, I hardly expect anyone who approaches a like age to be exactly well. I however have little (not nothing) to complain about.

Garnett was a man whom I very much liked and valued — a model of friendly amenity combined with singular learning and much personal talent.[2] He and his daugher Olive (more especially) were among the best friends, of late years, of me and mine.

I agree very much in what you say of the present condition of fine art; though I dare say I don't agree *entirely*, being more willing than you to see partial good in works which realize a success from their own point of view, remote as it may be from that other point of view to which I more particularly adhere. Holman Hunt is with you, and in his recent book denounces impressionist and other such art in terms as fierce and unmeasured as used to be employed against Praeraphaelite art.

Probably you don't know much about my recent family-history, so I will give a few details.

Olivia and her husband Agresti are in Rome, diligent in literary and some other matters, but thinking somewhat seriously of emigrating to Arkansas (!) under a promising sort of scheme. I rather fancy they won't do it after all.

Arthur is at Bolton — Scientific Referee to the Lancashire Stoker Works — which, for a Rossetti, suggests a second! He is married, and has a little boy.

Helen in December 1903 married an agreeable young Italian, Gastone Angeli: they tried to settle in Cairo, but the condition of his health compelled their return to Italy — Rome. There he died in July 1904 — a woeful collapse of poor

Helen's married well-being. A girl was born on 15 September. Just recently, 15 April, these 2 have come to me here, and I think it more than likely that this house will be their home henceforward. I like the little girl, and am fond of Helen.

Mary, the youngest, has continued to live with me. For the last 2 years she has been much afflicted, and indeed greatly crippled, by rheumatoid arthritis — a vile malady which is still ruling her with a rod of iron. She takes it all with great pluck and fine spirits, and it darkens my home and thoughts not a little.

All affectionate regards to you from

Your old friend,
W. M. Rossetti

MS: AP.

1. MS. Diary, 30 December 1905: "I attended the year-end lunch which Rowley gives at the National Liberal Club. Met Kropotkin, Cockerell, Emery Walker, Garnett, George Milner, Oliver Hueffer: saluted Rothenstein and Crane: was introduced to T. M. Rooke, but, not quite catching his name at the moment, did not converse with him, which I should have liked to do. Saw for the first time G. K. Chesterton. Kropotkin appears hearty and in good spirits. I am glad to hear that he will not for the present go to Russia in revolution. He could obtain Police-permission to do so, but would only go when he might be free to go and come at his own option, without any such permission. I told him he ought to be made President of the (very problematic) Russian Republic: this he, as an anarchist, repudiates — would only work for public good without any sort of official post."
2. MS. Diary, 14 April 1906: "I was truly sorry to see in the newspapers the death of my excellent old friend Garnett — as genial and kindly as he was widely and brilliantly learned, with excellent natural abilities to boot. Robert Garnett also wrote to me: I propose attending the funeral (from my own house) on 16."

580. TO FREDERIC GEORGE STEPHENS

3 St. Edmund's Terrace,
8 June 1906

Dear old Steph,

I notice that your letter begins by referring to "my intended text re Holman Hunt's assertions[1] in which I and Gabriel are concerned." I fancy there may be some misapprehension as to this. Don't exactly recollect what I may heretofore have mentioned to you on the subject: but the facts are as follows. Between 1901 and 1903 I wrote a book of my Reminiscences at some length containing references to Hunt of the most friendly kind, and the book is now in print, to be published next autumn. When Hunt's book came out I thought that it might perhaps behove me to add to my work (then already passing through the press) some rejoinder to something or other in Hunt's book; but I finally made up my mind not to do so, and all that I wrote about Hunt up to 1903 will appear printed exactly as then written and without any addition. I did in January last deliver to Hunt and his wife some written observations on some of his statements; and lately I heard from him that some degree of attention (I know not how much) had been paid to those observations in case his book were to go through a 2nd edition.[2] My observations related mainly to Gabriel and myself — not in any wise to you.

As to your correspondence with Wallis.[3] My opinion is that you were fully justified, and acted very reasonably, in putting into print your refutation of

Hunt's mis-statement as to your doings in the *Athenaeum*. You have demonstrated (unless to some person who might untruthfully say that you are telling lies about dates etc.) that Hunt was entirely incorrect. It may be that in what you thus printed there are some phrases which might advantageously have been modified: but as to the essence of your statement, and the propriety of your making it, I side wholly with you.

I have read (and of course I read them at the time) the *Athenaeum* reviews of Hunt which I herewith return. They contain a great deal of extreme (maybe excessive) praise of Hunt's works, mixed with some censure. Whether I should have subscribed to all the censure, or to all the praise, is not in question: no one can conscientiously say that the articles are a tissue of abuse.

I don't of course recollect all the details about the (most highly judicious) purchase of Brown's Christ and Peter[4] for the National Gallery. Have an impression that it was I myself who first brought to Shields's notice the fact that the picture was purchasable and would be an excellent choice. You, it seems, had formed a like opinion quite independently of Shields or of me, and you made the purchase a reality.

About "monstrous and cruel inventions of Hunt against Woolner," I dare say you know a good deal more than I do. I am aware that Hunt came to a decided split with Woolner when the question was pending of Hunt's marrying Miss Edith Waugh. My feeling then was (and is) that Hunt and Miss Edith Waugh had a perfect right to attend to their own affairs for themselves, and that Woolner was more than duly officious in championing the supposed credit of the Waugh family, and of himself as connected with them. I then heard Hunt speak with some asperity about Woolner on this ground, and also as a dupe or an imposter in relation to buying and selling pictures (a point which I think Hunt exaggerated); but I don't remember hearing from Hunt anything amounting to a real calumny against Woolner. I was rather surprised to find in Hunt's book a generally mild estimate of Woolner and his works.

I have read with great attention the transcript of your letter to Wallis. No one can know much better than I do the unlimited devotion which your wife and you showed to Hunt during his almost desperate typhoid illness. About your review of Scott's Wallington series[5] — written according to Hunt without your having seen the works at Gambart's — I can only infer that Hunt tacitly admits that you must have seen the pictures *somewhere*, even though not at Gambart's: otherwise (though you may have made a mistake as to the ownership of the household-effects in the Danish subject) it would be manifestly impossible that you could have written any review of the successive paintings.

Dear Steph, I trust that you have been going on pretty well in point of health — also your wife. I have been of late rather troubled by gout, but not laid up — may now consider myself recovered. Mary is still much disabled — Helen here with her baby since the middle of April. These 3 are going almost directly to spend a few days with my son at Bolton.

Affectionately yours,
W. M. Rossetti

I don't gather that you want me to return the Wallis transcript.

MS: Bodleian.

1. See Letter 577.
2. Hunt to WMR, 17 April 1906: "It was very characteristically generous of you to give me your notes, instead of making a public descent on me for the slips in my book. I have examined all the places you commented upon and made some corrections.... I am making all ready in case a 2nd edition of my book should be called for at any time. In January 1500 out of 2000 copies had been sold and it seemed natural that the remainder might be exhausted by this time but I don't know the ways of the trade. I have been re-reading [*FLM*] ... and have been confirmed in my first impression that generally the singularly restrained determination to do no wrong either to Millais or my claims in the evolution of our P.R.B. movement is maintained. But there are passages bearing the construction to people looking for it, that your brother was really the inspirer and originator of the projected reform.... Your knowledge of your brother's great genius and naturally impressing you, made you over-estimate his influence upon a movement the beginnings of which you were not aware of. I had either to let things drift or frankly and fully to give my own arguments against the current of these. Perhaps in amateur fashion I may have insisted too often upon my points" (AP).
3. MS. Diary, 7 June 1906: "Stephens wrote to me the other day about a correspondence he has had with Henry Wallis, who considers that Stephens acted unadvisedly in printing a rejoinder to some of Holman Hunt's allegations." Stephens's rejoinder took the form of a privately printed four-page leaflet, a shorter version of which appeared in the *Times*, 16 February 1906, p. 4. MS. Diary, 22 February 1906: "Replied to a letter from Stephens, who has sent me a separate print of his letter in the *Times*. I say that he has clearly refuted Hunt's allegation as to certain action by Stephens in the *Athenaeum*; also that my full intention is to remain friends with Hunt."
4. *Jesus Washing Peter's Feet*.
5. *Athenaeum*, 18 February 1860, p. 244 (a brief note based on photographs of four designs); 13 July 1861, pp. 54-55 (a review of the eight pictures exhibited at the French Gallery).

581. TO MACMILLAN & CO.

Nayland Rock Hotel,
Margate,
29 July 1906

Dear Sirs,

I see it stated in yesterday's *Athenaeum* that the Eragny Press, Hammersmith, mean to publish Christina Rossetti's privately printed *Verses*, 1847.[1]

I don't know what right the Eragny Press suppose themselves to have in such a matter: have they any?

My impression is that, so far as that book is a privately printed book, it is my personal property, like (for instance) a pair of boots, and that no one can meddle with it. But the vast majority of that book was published by you in the *New Poems* and the *Poetical Works*, and as such I understand it to be your copyright.

Perhaps you would let me know how you view this matter. I expect to remain here at Margate up to 10 August or some such date.

Very truly yours,
W. M. Rossetti

MS: BL.

1. Published in 1906, ed. by J. D. Symon, at the price of £1.1 for 175 ordinary copies, and £5.5 for 10 copies on vellum. The Press issued thirty-one volumes between 1894 and 1914, but its founders, Lucien Pissarro (1863-1944) and his wife, Esther (d. 1951), never succeeded in making a profit (Colin Franklin, *The Private Presses* [1969], pp. 92-93, 206-7).

582. TO MACMILLAN & CO.

Nayland Rock Hotel,
Margate,
3 August 1906

Dear Sirs,

I return Messrs Pissarro's letter. If you think fit to allow them to republish those poems which are your copyright (being not far from the whole of the *Verses* booklet),[1] I should feel no objection, and would defer to your decision as to any fee to be paid.

There is however one other point, personal to myself. The *Verses* include a few pieces (perhaps less than half a dozen) which, being decidedly poor semi-childish stuff, I did not include in either of the volumes which you published.[2] These pieces therefore remain my property, as pertaining to a privately printed book. Here at Margate I cannot look up the pieces in question. As I saw reason for not publishing them, so I should prefer that no one else should publish them: yet I don't *care* about this point in any very serious degree. Perhaps, if you see no objection, your answer to Messrs Pissarro might be held over until, on returning to London, I can reinspect those unpublished items. I expect to return on 10 August or soon afterwards — not later at any rate than 17 August.

Yours very truly,
W. M. Rossetti

MS: BL.

1. See Letter 581, Note 1.
2. See Letter 583, Note 1.

583. TO MACMILLAN & CO.

3 St. Edmund's Terrace,
18 August 1906

Dear Sirs,

Having now returned to London, I have looked into that matter of compositions in the volume *Verses* which have not yet been published.

There appear to be 9 of them.[1] You would find them specified in the *Poetical Works*, p. xli etc., under the Nos. 4, 18 to 23, 25, and 26.

All these things are bad in one degree or another. I omitted them because they are bad, and for the same reason I don't want anyone else to publish them. Still I don't very much *care* about it: and, if that earlier reprint of the *Verses* was *published* (a point as to which I have no knowledge), the compositions in question have already obtained public circulation.

I presume that, if I were now to step in and say that the Eragny Press shall not publish their volume including those pieces, their project would be upset *in toto*. So, if you are contented to accept £20 or £25 (I don't mind which of the two), I shall waive any personal objection. I leave the matter wholly in your hands.[2]

Yours very truly,
W. M. Rossetti

MS: BL.

1. The number was twelve, all of which were included in Pissarro's volume.
2. MS. Diary, 19 September 1906: "Everard Meynell called on me. He wanted me to pacify Macmillans, so that they might abate a demand they are making, £25, upon a firm ... who, without any authority from either Macmillan or myself, have reprinted and mean to publish, Christina's privately printed *Verses*.... It seems from Meynell's statement that he acts mostly in the interest of a certain Symon.... I told Meynell that I could not and would not interfere: Macmillans appear to be acting reasonably, and from the first I left all details to them."

584. TO THOMAS JAMES WISE

3 St. Edmund's Terrace,
20 August 1906

Dear Wise,

Bibliography again! I thought that before "the night cometh wherein no man can work"[1] I would do my endeavour to fix for future enquirers the dates (as near as may be) of my Brother's several writings. The enclosed brochure[2] is the result, privately printed, and a copy could not be in better hands than yours.

Please present my best regards to your wife, and believe me

Always yours,
W. M. Rossetti

MS: BL.

1. "The night cometh, when no man can work," John, 9:4.
2. *Dante Gabriel Rossetti: Classified Lists of His Writings with the Dates* (100 copies printed). MS. Diary, 28 November 1905: "I took up lately a work which I find interesting though to some extent tedious. It is an attempt to fix the dates of Gabriel's published writings. For this purpose I look through MSS., indexes of books, etc. Find a large amount of material, which, on being set forth in due order, will be important to any persons studious of this matter.... It will take some time yet, though I have already been attending to it for a fortnight or more." 9 February 1906: "I have now accomplished the substantial part ... at some not inconsiderable pains.... I shall probably ask Ellis whether they would like to print the triple list. I think their assent very dubious, and, if they decline, I would get some moderate number of copies printed, for my own satisfaction, and for distribution among acquaintances."

585. TO HENRY CURRIE MARILLIER

3 St. Edmund's Terrace,
30 August 1906

Dear Marillier,

You are sure to like better than not to possess a copy of this privately-printed pamphlet[1] in which I have endeavoured to fix the dates of Gabriel's writings — so please to accept the enclosed. Experiences of your own will tell you that it was done not without some little trouble.

Fairfax Murray tells me (and I am sure he is right) that I have mis-stated one date. *Autumn Idleness* was written in autumn 1850 when Gabriel was at Knole Park, along with Holman Hunt, painting the background afterwards used for *The Bower Meadow*.

Best regards from

Yours always truly,
W. M. Rossetti

MS: PM.

1. See Letter 584, Note 2.

586. TO JOSEPH PENNELL[1]

3 St. Edmund's Terrace,
4 September 1906

Dear Mr. Pennell,

I enclose some remarks about Whistler, Howell, etc. As you will see, I have written without reserve, raising some points which count as confidential: apart from this, my remarks are at your service, for any use to which you can turn them.[2]

Pray don't hesitate to ask me anything further that may occur to you: I shall answer to the best of my ability.

Very truly yours,
W. M. Rossetti

MS: LC.

1. (1857-1926), American etcher, who lived in London from 1884, the same year in which he married Elizabeth Robins, with whom he wrote a *Life of Whistler*.
2. The Pennell Papers at LC contain nine closely written quarto sheets of notes, some of which were reproduced verbatim in the *Life*.

587. TO ROBERT SINGLETON GARNETT[1]

3 St. Edmund's Terrace,
5 September 1906

Dear Garnett,

I have received the enclosed letter from Wise (please return it at your convenience) on the 3rd; but had to ascertain from your Brother Edward your precise address in Devonshire before I could send it on to you. You see Wise offers ''say £1000'' for the 3 notebooks;[2] and I am certain he would draw the cheque at any moment. All his literary treasures have been left by will to the British Museum.[3]

Wise's offer, in due relation to the auction-sale hitherto contemplated, will certainly engage your serious attention, and it would be impertinent in me to say much about it. It would save the large percentage to the Auctioneers. I may perhaps have mentioned to you before (as I have done to others of your family, and also to Wise) that I fancy the auction-sale of the 3 notebooks, especially if in separate lots, might produce £1000 to 1200 — and I might have said even more; but it is always an uncertainty.

I have little doubt that Wise, if pressed, would go somewhat beyond the £1000: still, his offer is a very liberal one, especially as being founded on the very scanty account which I gave him of the contents and interest of the notebooks. You will understand that I did not *suggest* to him to buy them out of hand: I only put him on the qui vive as to the proposed auction-sale.

I see you are near Kingsbridge. It happens that, when Mary and I in 1903 took a steamer-trip round Great Britain, we fell in on the steamer with a Dr. Harston of Kingsbridge, and got rather intimate with him, partly on the ground that, just before that time, we had had much business-relation with a Solicitor (also Harston), a cousin of his.[4] We should have seen him here at home, but for the fact that he was bound to return to Kingsbridge at once; and he told me that, were I ever down there, he would give me some fine fishing — a thing to which I am incompetent. I wonder whether you have happened to come across him — an agreeable man towards 40 years of age.

Always truly yours,
W. M. Rossetti

MS: Texas.

1. (1866-1932) was called to the Bar in February 1893, having articled in his uncle's firm, Darley and Cumberland, solicitors. At this date he was in partnership with Constance Garnett's brother, Arthur Black (*Law List* 1906); at his death he was senior partner in Darley and Cumberland. He was an authority on Dumas, several of whose books he translated; and published two collections of essays on book-collecting. In 1917 he edited *Letters about Shelley Interchanged by Three Friends — Edward Dowden, Richard Garnett, and William Michael Rossetti.*

2. The three Shelley notebooks which Lady Shelley gave to Richard Garnett. MS. Diary, 17 May 1906: "Robert Garnett brought round the 3 notebooks of Shelley.... They contain much most interesting and important matter.... The books remain with me for the present, as I have undertaken to draw up a list of their contents, to be used in constructing the Sale-catalogue." 3 September: "Having long ago suggested to Robert Garnett that it would be as well for me to write to Wise about the 3 Shelley notebooks ... I yesterday wrote accordingly." 8 September: "Wrote to Robert Garnett, who is debating whether to accept Wise's offer.... I don't press him to close with Wise, but say that, if he does so, I think a proper sum to fix would be £1100." 18 September: "Robert Garnett having decided to put the 3 Shelley notebooks into the Sotheby sale ... I wrote to Wise to inform him." 6 December: "I attended the sale at Sotheby's of Garnett's library etc. The great lot was the 3 Shelley notebooks, which at special request were sold together. They fetched the great price of £3000, and go (as seems fully understood) to America.... This £3000 is certainly a godsend to the family." 22 June 1909: "Forman called, much pleased at having been invited to undertake an interesting Shelley job. Those 3 Shelley notebooks ... were bought by an American, [W. K.] Bixby. He intends to have their contents printed in full for the Boston Bibliophile Club [Society; 3 vols., 1911]. Forman offered not long ago to do the requisite editing on condition that the Club would afterwards allow him to reproduce the essential points in a Shelley book of his own. The Club do not close with this offer; but they ask him to transcribe and edit the MS. for some suitable pay. He consulted me as to what he might fairly and reasonably demand. I suggested £100 for transcribing, which must be a heavy job, and a further £80 for editing. He is inclined to adopt these figures, and to propose them to the Club."

3. For an account of Wise's will and the British Museum's purchase of his library, see W. Partington, *Thomas J. Wise in the Original Cloth* (1946), pp. 300-301.

4. Lionel de Courcy Eagles Harston (*Churchill's Medical Directory*); Edward French Buttermer Harston of Harston and Bennett, Solicitors (*Law List*).

588. TO JOSEPH PENNELL

3 St. Edmund's Terrace,
6 November 1906

Dear Mr. Pennell,

I gladly answer your present letter, or any other which you may find occasion for writing to me.

1. I dare say you possess some adequate newspaper-report of the Ruskin trial.[1] If not, I could lend you one, for I remember having kept one by me ever since that date.

2. I had totally forgotten about the shop near London Bridge where they gave away a Hiroshige with a pound of tea. Now that you mention it however, I do seem to have heard something of the sort from Whistler. Don't think that I myself ever saw the shop.

3. I find Queen's Road, Chelsea, still down in a recent map of London. It runs south of, and nearly parallel to, a portion of King's Road, and faces the north facade of Chelsea Hospital. I fancy (can't speak with full certainty) that the houses in Queen's Road have been much altered — or indeed wholly rebuilt — since Whistler was there in 1862-1863. They were then low (say two-storied) quite old-fashioned houses, of a cosy homely character, with small forecourts. I have a kind of idea that Whistler's house was No. 12,[2] but this is quite uncertain to me.

4. I dare say it may be true that Bracquemond[3] rather than Manet invented Japonerie. So far as I remember, I did not in those early Whistler days, hear Manet named in that connexion: but have seen him so named in print at some much later date — say within the last 10 years.

5. If the Big White Girl[4] was rejected by the R.A. in 1862, this would be before I knew Whistler personally: but, on knowing him, I should have been likely to hear of it, and it appears to me *quite possible* that I did hear, though I don't now distinctly recollect it. I believe I am right in saying that this very fine picture was rejected in the Paris Salon in some such year as 1864. The year in question was the one in which a "Salon des Refusés" was got up in Paris, and I am satisfied that I saw the picture in this last-named Salon. It was about the only thoroughly good thing there, for most of them were shamefully bad, and to have hung them in the regular Salon would have been an offence.

6. I don't remember hearing of the Duke de Montezuma[5] etc.: may very possibly have done so.

7. It was from my Brother that I heard a few details about Whistler's squabble with Legros: don't remember that the name of Fantin-Latour[6] came in in relation to it, but this *may* have been so. What I recollect is Whistler and Legros were together — in the presence, I fancy, of some third party, possibly Lewis[7] Huth. Some controversy arose between Whistler and Legros as to some question of fact. Legros said something which exasperated Whistler, and he suddenly exclaimed "Tu dis donc que je mens" — and he struck out at Legros, knocking him down. I was aware however, before this painful incident, that the brotherly friendship between Whistler and Legros had been somewhat damped. As usual, *cherchez la*

femme. Whistler (as you may very probably be aware) "kept a woman" in those years. She was an Irishwoman without education but with something rather attaching in her character and manner, a Roman Catholic, named Joanna — we all called her Jo. Her surname was not Hooligan, but something resembling it — perhaps Honrigan.[8] She sat for the *Little White Girl* [9] (which is like her), and for other figures, including I think the Big White Girl. At a certain date Whistler removed to a small house very near Cremorne Gardens,[10] and Legros took lodgings in the same house. He also just then (but not I think at all usually) "kept a woman." The ordinary result ensued — the 2 women quarrelled. I was told that one of them — and I *think* it was Legros's woman — getting into a pet, laid hold of a water-colour or canvas of the rival painter, and made water upon it — spoiling it of course. This I quite believe to be authentic. The 2 men upheld, more or less, their respective women, and hence the first beginning of a breach between them. You are no doubt correct in saying that Legros "must know a lot" about Whistler, but I am rather afraid he will persist in not imparting it.

Very truly yours,
W. M. Rossetti

MS: LC.

1. Whistler versus Ruskin.
2. 7A Queen's (now Royal Hospital) Road (S. Weintraub, *Whistler, a Biography*, p. 75).
3. Félix Bracquemond (1833-1914); "powerfully influenced by Japanese prints, he was a guiding force behind the 1860s revival of original engravings by artists" (Norman, *Nineteenth Century Painters and Painting: a Dictionary*).
4. *Symphony in White, No. 1: The White Girl.* It was rejected by the R.A. in 1862 and by the Paris Salon in 1863, when it was shown at the Salon des Refusés.
5. "Another character in the *Quartier*, of whom Whistler never tired of telling us ... an adventurer after Whistler's own heart" (Pennell, *Life of Whistler*, 1:58).
6. Henri Fantin-Latour (1836-1904), still-life and portrait painter; exhibited at the Salon, 1861-99, and at the R.A., 1862-1900. He was a close friend of Whistler, who introduced his work in England.
7. Louis.
8. Hiffernan.
9. *Symphony in White, No. 2: The Little White Girl.*
10. 7 Lindsey Row (now 101 Cheyne Walk).

589. TO MACKENZIE BELL

3 St. Edmund's Terrace,
12 January 1907

Dear Bell,

I hope you have been going on well since we parted at Margate in August last.

A matter of considerable interest to me has now arisen. You may remember my book, *Rossetti Papers*, going up to April 1870, and that I carried on the compilation of similar material up to December 1894, the date of Christina's death. More than one experiment has been made with a view to getting a publisher for these sequels of the Rossetti Papers, but as yet without any definite result.

My Reminiscences were published last October by Brown, Langham & Co., a Firm closely connected with Masters & Co.; and both these Firms are now controlled by a literary man, Lacon Watson.[1]

My Reminiscences having been a very fair success, Watson is well disposed towards anything else forthcoming from me. He is not however prepared to publish any sequel, in its present form, to the *Rossetti Papers*, but he makes a suggestion which I think a very promising one. He proposes to extract from those sequels all the letters written by or addressed to Christina, and to publish these next autumn as a volume by itself;[2] and he thinks that, as Masters & Co. have an active religious connexion, such a volume offers every prospect of success. So indeed do I.

As you see, the primary bulk of this proposed volume consists of letters ranging from 1870 to 1894, but I should add anything appropriate of earlier dates, including (if I can get authority for it) the letters printed in the *Rossetti Papers*.

Now comes the main point for you to consider. In April 1899 I sold you 18 letters written by Christina. Would you or would you not allow these 18 letters, or portions of them, to be included in the proposed volume, and if so on what terms?

I am already well engaged in putting together the material for the volume — it is copious enough. May perhaps have finished this work before April is over, and then the printing would be taken up, for publication in the autumn.

Best regards from my daughters, along with

Yours very truly,
W. M. Rossetti

To make the point clear, I may say that this question about the 18 letters is started entirely by me — not by the Publisher, who does not as yet know with any precision what I do or do not propose to put into the volume.

MS: Princeton.

1. Edmund Henry Lacon Watson (1865-1948), miscellaneous writer and journalist; war correspondent for Reuters, 1917-19.
2. *FLCR*. MS. Diary, 31 October 1907, records that Watson now wanted a less substantial book than the two-volume edition originally proposed. 14 November: "Have now done all the substantial part of the curtailment ... cutting out 200 items, more or less, and abridging some of the items that are retained."

590. TO MACKENZIE BELL

3 St. Edmund's Terrace,
12 February 1907

My dear Bell,

I am sincerely obliged for your very friendly letter. My only real feeling in this matter is that I wish to do justice to Christina by presenting an adequate view of her in her family-letters of all periods of her life; and, if those letters belonging to you[1] were omitted, the representation of her earlier years would be scanty indeed. To any money-interest of my own in the case I am indifferent enough; and indeed this could not be affected, for it is as good as certain that just as many copies of the book would be bought, whether it does or does not contain the letters in question.

Of course I see at once the force of what you say as regards the solid importance of the letters to you in a certain contingency.

Would the following arrangement be at all to your liking? If you would place those letters (I believe 18) at my disposal, I would undertake that, in the event of your bringing out a new edition of your book, you should be at liberty to use (besides of course those 18) any other 18 or 20 included in my collection. If you were to sanction this, I should have to communicate with my Publisher so as to ratify the engagement, but it seems pretty safe to say that he will concur.

If you sanction, I need not trouble you for any detail of the letters in your possession: but if otherwise I should be much obliged if you would set forth the dates of them, and the first 2 or 3 words of each, so that I may make sure of excluding them from my volume.[2]

The number of letters that I have to deal with is really large. Some I set aside as uninteresting, but am rather chary of doing this. I find a good deal to do in writing introductory explanations, like those in my Memoir of Gabriel and the *Rossetti Papers*. Have by this time got through about ¼ or ⅕ of the work.

Mary has for the past 3 or 4 months been rather *considerably* better than she was aforetime. Helen and her little girl are well: I forget whether you saw the latter at Margate. Anyhow Helen would be delighted to produce her for your inspection at any auspicious moment. Olive Agresti is I think well at present — is every now and then conscious of gout in her constitution. Her husband was lately very much knocked up with influenza and allied troubles, but I trust he may now be tolerably recovered.

We trust that you are free from any noticeable obstruction to health.

Yours always truly,
W. M. Rossetti

MS: Princeton.

1. See Letter 589.
2. WMR to Bell, 16 February 1907: "Much obliged for friendly letter. Am of course cutting out all those letters." 17 February: "While that question of the letters belonging to you was pending ... I thought the more practical course was to assume (though I knew it to be highly dubious) that I *could* use those particular letters, and to put them in their place according to order of date. Thus I wrote prefatory notes to said letters — the notes here enclosed. These have now become not serviceable to myself, but they might possibly at some future date be serviceable to you. I therefore place them at your disposal for any use you can put them to" (Princeton).

591. TO CHARLES FAIRFAX MURRAY

3 St. Edmund's Terrace,
28 March 1907

Dear Murray,

The so-called "Studies for Found" must be an item which was sold at Foster's[1] on 25 July 1894; lot 68 among 8 things which had belonged to my Wife — i.e., these 8 things came into my hands after Gabriel's death, and I gave them to her. It was called in Foster's catalogue — "Found, 2 studies in oils on one canvas, representing the composition as it stood towards 1855, 18½ inches."[2] It was catalogued as being by Gabriel, and, so far as I know or remember, it was so. This lot fetched £9.19.6.

There is not any photograph of the other *Found* [3] which is in this house: it were well that there should be one, for (as I have more than once said) this version of the subject is on the whole more telling and effective to the eye than any other whatsoever — whether done wholly by Dunn (as you consider) or chiefly by Dunn with some work by Gabriel himself (as I incline to suppose). If you would like to get this work photographed, I would give every facility. It is not now regarded as the property of my son, but rather of my daughter Helen (Mrs. Angeli), and is in her bedroom in this house.

Glad to hear that you have the Sleeve picture.[4]

I suppose you knew *something* of old Stephens.[5] One need not overstate his intellectual or other merits: but he was a very warm friend of mine, and I was affectionately attached to him, and feel his death not a little.

Yours always truly,

W. M. Rossetti

Just as I am closing this letter it occurs to me to start another point. I am now putting together a volume of Christina's letters — almost wholly letters to members of her own family — with a few added addressed to her by such members or a very few others. As you possess something of almost everything, you possibly posses some letters by or to Christina. Do you? and if so would you allow all or some of them to appear in my volume — which is to be published this next autumn?[6]

MS: Texas.

1. 54 Pall Mall.
2. Surtees 64M and 64Q. "These were framed as separate panels until recently" (A. I. Grieve, *The Art of Dante Gabriel Rossetti [1, Found; 2, The Pre-Raphaelite Modern-Life Subject]*, 1976, p. 18). Murray informed WMR on 27 March (AP) that he had purchased it at Christie's (23 March 1907, Lot 48, "Two Studies for *Found* — in one frame. On panel"; £33.12). He considered that Lizzie Siddal may have had a hand in it: "it is extremely careful and like the picture that Bancroft has [Surtees 64] only weaker, very little perhaps, but I can't imagine your brother on or at that date making such a careful copy. The calf is very good, only the head of the woman is a shade beneath his power" (letter to WMR, 9 April 1907; AP). WMR replied on 12 April that DGR "*possibly ... might* have undertaken it not exactly as a copy but rather as a new start for an original" (Texas). For the suggestion that the panel was the first version of *Found*, see Grieve, pp. 5, 18. Neither the Foster nor the Christie sale is recorded in Surtees.
3. Surtees 64 R 1.
4. Murray to WMR, 27 March 1907: "I have just purchased also the oil picture of 1869, of a lady tying a sleeve on a Knight's helmet [*My Lady Greensleeves*, Surtees 161; dated 1863]" (AP).
5. MS. Diary, 9 March 1907: "I was much grieved to receive a telegram from Mrs. Stephens saying that her husband died 'quietly' this morning — my good old P.R.B. and affectionate friend." 10 March: "Helen and I went round to Mrs. Stephens.... She is much calmer than I had been fearing: entered freely into the details of her loss.... We accompanied Mrs. Stephens into the room where his body is lying: he looks very calm, and (as he always was) markedly handsome: hair still abundant and fairly dark, and a general aspect that one would not associate with the age of nearly 80. I assented to the request that I should attend the funeral in Brompton Cemetery on the 14th: understand that [Arthur] Hughes, Wallis and Daniell (whom I knew once, but have not seen since 1860 or so) will be there. The son asked me also to write a sort of obituary notice, for the *Athenaeum* [16 March 1907, p. 329]."

6. Murray to WMR, 1 April 1907: "The letters I have of your sister's are a few addressed to the Howells, and I can't find them at this moment. Have just had a hunt amongst the bulky C. A. H. correspondence without success, but I remember that they are of small importance and mostly addressed to Mrs. Howell. One addressed to myself is with her MS. of *Seek and Find* at Cambridge, but I have one addressed to your brother in a volume that I suppose was once Fanny's [copy follows; see also Letter 592, Note 4]" (Texas).

592. TO CHARLES FAIRFAX MURRAY

3 St. Edmund's Terrace,
4 April 1907

Dear Murray,

I am perfectly satisfied that my Wife had nothing to do with the execution of that *Found* in your possession;[1] and indeed that she never did any art-work on Gabriel's behalf.

Will write to Mansell & Co. to take a negative of the *Found* in this house[2] on your behalf. You make me a present of the negative — which I accept as a spontaneous liberality on your part.

I see you had seen good old Stephens later than I did.[3] My last sight of him must have been towards June 1905 in the house of Mrs. John Marshall. Probably you know that for several years past Stephens's health was much broken down by bronchitis and heart-troubles. He was at Hastings about the autumn of last year, and came back improved, and I don't understand that any specially bad symptoms had appeared since then. He constantly sat up very late — so Mrs. Stephens has informed me. On the morning of 9 March he had not got to bed by 4 a.m., so she came down to see after him. She found him seated at his writing-table, bending over a book. Went up to him, and he was dead — may have died 2 hours earlier. He must apparently have died in a single moment through syncope or cessation of the heart's action, and therefore quite painlessly.

Though I had not seen Stephens for several months, he and I had interchanged various letters, chiefly about Hunt's book. It is sad that the last term of his life should have been embittered by what Hunt said — sometimes needlessly, and, in at least one leading instance, not correctly.

Much obliged to you about Christina's letters.[4] The Howell letters would evidently not be wanted for my purpose, and the one which you have transcribed does not seem to me, after some reflection, to claim insertion. I see that the date of it must be about April 1880, when for our Mother's 80th birthday, Christina presented to her a copy of Main's *Treasury of Sonnets*, inserting into it a MS. sonnet of her own (as referred to by you) to our Mother. Gabriel (it seems from the letter) was willing to make a design for this sonnet, to be similarly inserted. There seemed to be little material for any such design, and, instead of that, he made that well-known design for his own sonnet on "The Sonnet,"[5] and inserted it. I possess the volume.

Very truly yours,
W. M. Rossetti

MS: Texas.

1. Murray's suggestion ("Mrs. Rossetti") was Lizzie, not Lucy (see Letter 591, Note 2).
2. See Letter 591, Note 3.
3. Murray to WMR, 1 April 1907: "I also was much attached to F. G. Stephens and am very sorry to hear of his death. I met him last at the Academy Exhibition of Old Masters on the 5th January" (AP).
4. See Letter 591, Note 6.
5. Surtees 258.

593. TO THEODORE WATTS-DUNTON

3 St. Edmund's Terrace,
11 May 1907

Dear Watts-Dunton,

The idea that your wife and you would at some not distant date come round to see us is highly gratifying to me, and to my daughter Helen (Angeli) who is at present with me: Mary is now in Rome, but expected back pretty soon. Meanwhile it might be manageable — and would certainly be from all points of view *en règle* — that Helen and I should take the initiative, and be the visitors at your house. We would like to come some afternoon soon — not so early as Wednesday next 15 May — asking your wife for a cup of tea (not anything else). Helen would enjoy bringing her nice little girl, now 2½ years old: it has long been her wish that the babyolatry of Swinburne should obtain cognizance of that small person. Please give us a line in reply at any moment that suits you.[1]

Now about Charles Wells. I don't think I had any personal knowledge of the revised version of *Joseph and his Brethren*[2] that you speak of. It was certainly not among Gabriel's appurtenances at the date of his death. As Wells resided abroad, Gabriel, when he had something to transact concerning him, was in the habit of corresponding with William Smith Williams (of Charlotte Brontë fame), Wells's brother-in-law: and I think it quite *possible* that Gabriel may have sent the revised copy to Williams, for return to Wells. Williams has been dead these many years. There is a granddaughter of his known to me, Miss Dickinson (1 All Souls Place, W.), and she *might* perhaps know who is the person most fitting to be addressed as now representing the Wells-Williams connexion. If you were to write to her (mentioning my name if so inclined), I have little doubt that she would give you such information as she may possess.

Gabriel, I think, did not ever see Wells. When in 1849 he made a trip with Holman Hunt to Paris and Belgium he had an idea that he might look-up Wells in Brittany, but this came to nothing.

The successive stages of Gabriel's knowledge of Wells's writings were, *I fancy*, as follows. A great number of years ago some specimens of Wells's *Stories after Nature* (prose) were republished in a magazine with some illustrations by F. R. Pickersgill.[3] Gabriel read them with high appreciation; and then read at the British Museum the whole of the *Stories*, and also the *Joseph* drama. Soon afterwards he procured a copy of the *Joseph* for himself. I can recollect the general look of the volume, but don't possess it.

I myself (perhaps wrongfully) never took that sort of interest in the *Joseph* that Gabriel did, and I fear that I cannot say anything apposite as to the literary aspect of the matter. From someone — it must have been Smith Williams — I derived a great number of years ago a bad impression as to Wells's personality: but this may not be in your line. He was said to be a man of the typically "jesuitical" character — always intriguing in some way or fishing in troubled waters, and sowing dissensions among people he knew: with a morbid appetite for influencing and controlling people. His physiognomy was said to be fox-like, thin and sharp.

Since I began this letter I have made a little research after such documents as I can find. I enclose them — 2 letters from Williams, and 2 from Wells — all to Gabriel. Should like to receive them back as soon as done with. The 2nd letter from Wells was typewritten for my convenience, as I intended to include it in a second series of "Rossetti Papers," possibly not destined to see the light.

Always yours affectionately,
W. M. Rossetti

Wells was, whether originally or by conversion, a Roman Catholic: and I was given to understand that in Brittany he established himself in the house of a widow-lady with her son, and assumed there much the same position that a "Father Confessor" would do. He was a married man.

MS: BL. Extract in *Swinburne Library*, p. 81.

1. The visit did not take place until 6 October 1908 (MS. Diary): "By appointment I went with Olive, Helen, and Imogene, to the Watts-Duntons, and of course Swinburne. Watts-Dunton looks older than when I saw him last, but I was glad to find that his memory etc. do not seem in so shaky a state as Curle intimated to me some months ago. Mrs. Watts-Dunton, whom I see for the first time, appeared very cordial and pleasant, with a frank unaffected manner: she looks clearly under 30. Swinburne seems in capital health, and is very erect, but has a look of age. He read out to Imogene and others from an amusing old book of natural (or unnatural) history. All 3 appeared much pleased with Imogene, who behaved prettily, and strolled a little into the garden, plucking some flowers.... I got a large-paper copy of the *Duke of Gandia*, which Swinburne had intended to send to me some months ago, but it was then left *perdu* among other books. [The following sentence was later appended to the entry:] This, as it sorrowfully turns out, was my last interview with Swinburne."
2. A copy of the play made by Wells for DGR (see *SL*, 3:159).
3. Frederick Richard Pickersgill (1820-1900), historical genre painter. For an account of the magazine appearance of the stories, see *Stories After Nature*, ed. W. J. Linton, 1891, pp. xiv-xv.

594. TO EDITH HOLMAN HUNT

3 St. Edmund's Terrace,
9 August 1907

My dear Mrs. Hunt,

Allow me to thank you in writing, as I most heartily do in thought, for the thorough kindness with which you received and entertained me these 3 pleasant days[1] — I genuinely enjoyed them. I know that your kindness would have extended to my staying on a day or two longer, and only regret that I have no longer that juvenility of years, body, or mind, which qualifies one for a prolonged stay with friends, or elsewhere than in ones own home, even if a humdrum one.

I found the enclosed notice in the *Daily Chronicle* of today,[2] and thought you might perhaps like to read the point marked x.

Please give my love to my dear noble old friend, who bears his crushing affliction with such stately patience and cheerful magnanimity. As in performance when in his prime, so in endurance in the decline of life, he is a lesson to all. Would you also remember me to your Cousin, whom I was truly glad to meet.

I found all well here — allowing for Mary's standing trouble.

Always truly yours,

W. M. Rossetti

MS: Rylands.

1. MS. Diary, 5-7 August 1907: "On 6 [August] I fulfilled an engagement of some standing — that of going to spend a couple of days with the Holman Hunts at their country-place, Sonning Acre. I find it to be a very agreeable villa-cottage, wholly designed some 6 years ago by Mrs. Hunt and her daughter, and carried out by a local builder. Found dear old Hunt, spite of his not far from total blindness, and his asthma which needs about 2 hours precautionary regulation in the morning, most highly conversable: he told me an immense amount of details about the parables of Jesus, Jews, the incidents which led up to his second marriage, Woolner's picture-dealing transactions, the family history (often curious) of his father and mother etc. etc. He gave me his version of the immediate incidents of his rupture with Stephens: I may perhaps write this down at some moment of leisure — don't remember having heard about it previously. We took on 6 a long and sometimes rainy walk towards Wargrave Church; and on 7 we also had a drive skirting Bearwood Park. Mrs. Hunt kindly and attentive, and everything done to make me comfortable. A cousin of hers arrived on the same day, 6, Mrs. Kinsey or some such name: a thinking pleasant lady, who was lately Principal of the Training-College for Deaf and Dumb." 8 August: "A moderate walk with Hunt, and copious narrative as to spiritualism.... Excessively bad as Hunt's sight is, he does see some things. In our walk we passed a blackish pony standing alone on the footpath: and I mentioned to him that the pony was there, and that it wore a halter. He rejoined, 'I thought it had some harness': and in fact so it had — one or two articles of harness, of a tint only a little darker than its own body. Hunt, holding one's arm, walks ahead with perfect confidence, and at a pace at least equal to my own."

2. Not identified.

595. TO WILLIAM HOLMAN HUNT

3 St. Edmund's Terrace,
27 August 1907

Dear old Friend,

I must write you one word of congratulation. The victory of common sense and common justice has been achieved not only in accordance with your views but under your personal leadership — and perhaps under different leadership it would even now remain unachieved.[1]

You might perhaps get a laugh out of the enclosed, which I find in today's *Morning Leader*.[2] It is not a *good* specimen of S. L. H. (Hughes), who is often better at this sort of thing than anyone else I know.

Warm greetings to your wife.

Yours always,

W. M. Rossetti

MS: Iowa.

1. MS. Diary, 27 August 1907: "Wrote briefly to old Hunt to congratulate him upon the passing of the Deceased Wife's Sister bill. He has for sometime past been President of the Society working for this reform — and how the latter has been so long delayed must remain a mystery to everyone except an Englishman." The third reading of the bill was carried on 26 August by the House of Lords, 98 against 54.

2. P. 5. A satirical account of the defeat of the Bishops in the passage of the Deceased Wife's Sister bill, in the form of letters to them from sympathizers. Spencer Leigh Hughes (1859-1920), parliamentary journalist; M.P. for Stockport from 1910.

596. TO ALGERNON CHARLES SWINBURNE

3 St. Edmund's Terrace,
30 September 1908

Dear Swinburne,

Most highly obliged for your Elizabethan book,[1] and for its inscription: who could wish for a better one, to serve as an heirloom?

As it happens, I have already read the book through; for a friend of mine, Richard Curle[2] of whom you and Watts-Dunton have seen something, knowing my tastes, sent me a copy for my birthday, 25 September. I think the book full of interest, brilliancy of perception and knowledge, and lordly command of writing.

To my shame I don't know nearly so much as I ought about the Elizabethan drama. Am acquainted up to a certain point, but far from a sufficient one, with Marlowe, Webster, Heywood, Chapman and Tourneur. Have read I think some of Marston; little if anything of Dekker, Middleton, and Rowley. Marlowe was fairly familiar to me at a quite early age, and I felt the force and stress of a great deal in *Faustus*, *Edward II*, and even *Tamburlaine* and *The Jew of Malta*. Must confess that I was then apt to regard the whole afflatus of Marlowe as partaking more of barbaric rodomontade than of noble fine art before which one has to bow. I am however wiser now, partly converted by you, and by some other writers in your train. Am not sure that I should subscribe to your dictum that nothing in Spenser can be recognized as sublime. Obviously the great majority of his writing does not attain to that quality: but I fancy there are *some* passages so impressive and so gorgeously treated as to reach the mark.

It seems from your statement that Marlowe was the chief Author of Parts 2 and 3 of *Henry VI*. If so, he was the delight of my boyhood beyond all other authors whatsoever: for those parts (not to speak of Part 1) carried everything before them with me, whether Shakespeare's or anyone else's.

I wonder is it true that the Nobel prize for Literature is now tendered to you.[3] One feels ashamed of one's species (and perhaps the obloquy rests with English people more than with Swedes) to reflect that this prize comes to Algernon Swinburne only after it had come to Rudyard Kipling.

Always yours,
W. M. Rossetti

MS: Folger.

1. *The Age of Shakespeare* (1908).
2. (1883-1968), author, traveler, friend of Joseph Conrad. MS. Diary first mentions him on 27 December 1902: "A Mr. Curle, a young man to whom I sent some autographs some while ago, called by appointment: seems intelligent and agreeable." He married Cordelia Fisher, sister-in-law of Ralph Vaughan Williams.
3. The *Times* reported on 28 September that the Prize would be awarded to Swinburne, but it was not (*SL*, 6:217).

597. TO OLIVIA ROSSETTI AGRESTI

3 St. Edmund's Terrace,
13 April 1909

Dearest Olive,

Here comes the usual cheque.

Of course these few days I have been thinking of little other than Swinburne's death.[1] That his essential work was done is a sufficiently obvious fact, but one grieves much the same. I knew nothing about his illness until on the morning of the 10th, I received a note from Watts-Dunton saying that Swinburne was ill with influenza and pneumonia, and in some danger: and I saw in the newspapers a still more grave account: Watts-Dunton himself being also bed-ridden with influenza. Helen and I at once determined to go round, and we arrived at the house (Imogene with us in a motor-cab) about 2½. Swinburne had died at 10 a.m., in the presence of Mrs. Watts-Dunton — her husband being still in bed. I went up, and spoke to him for half an hour or nearly. He was then improving. Told me that Swinburne's illness had begun on 3 April, probably due to some extent to his recklessness in always going out for a walk without great coat or any such precaution.[2] He had continued getting worse and worse, spite of the care of 2 Doctors, but was always quite cheerful and strong-minded,[3] and died with great placidity. Up to the hour that I was in the house, even the Doctor did not know that the end had come. Helen and I went to look at Swinburne's body: most noble, calm, and lofty, did he appear. More of intellectual dignity could hardly be found.

Watts-Dunton had already (in anticipation of the approaching end) been in correspondence with Swinburne's sole surviving sister[4] — an invalid residing near Bonchurch, Isle of Wight. He read me the last letter received from her. She wishes the funeral to be at Bonchurch (where father, mother, etc. are buried), and with the service of the Church of England. Watts-Dunton expressed to me his dislike of such a service, but not any intention of *opposing* it; I agreed in dislike, but said at the moment that I might in any such case be disposed to submit to the wish of the family. However on reflection I quite discarded this notion, as applicable to the case of Swinburne; and on the 11th I wrote to Watts-Dunton to say as much in decisive terms. Don't as yet know how the matter will go.[5] I presume for certain that Watts-Dunton must be an executor, and perhaps the sister also.

Watts-Dunton told me — and I felt sure of it beforehand — that Swinburne was extremely fond of me — rating me as his closest and most valued friend, next to Watts-Dunton himself.

I enclose Mary's recent letter — please return it. Have sent her £100.

Nothing here calling for mention; except that we are preparing for a spring-cleaning on an extensive scale, including various repairs etc. by the Civil Service people. Yesterday Helen, vigorously seconded by Edith Dean,[6] made a clean sweep of the 2 drawing-rooms — pictures, china, etc. — and these rooms are at this moment a howling wilderness.

Love to Antonio from

Papa

MS: AP. Extract in R. W. Peattie, "Swinburne's Funeral," *Notes and Queries*, n.s. 21 (December 1974), 466-67.

1. MS. Diary, 10 April 1909: "A great grief — Swinburne died today."
2. WMR to Watts-Dunton, 20 March 1909: "I suppose Swinburne has been revelling in an Antarctic February and March, and no great-coat: while your wife and you, like rational beings, have been reduced to misery and protest" (BL).
3. MS. Diary, 10 April 1909: "he was cheerful throughout it up to the last — somewhat light-headed at times."
4. Isabel (d. 1915).
5. For Watts-Dunton's reply of 13 April, see "Swinburne's Funeral," p. 468.
6. (b. 1867), widow of the Australian poet Francis Adams, whose *Tiberius, A Drama* WMR edited in 1894. In 1896 she married the landscape painter Frank Dean (b. 1865, fl. 1885-c.1907; Wood). WMR described her as "tall and stately, and not far from being decidedly handsome, but her complexion is yellowish. She talks with liveliness and plenty of sense: spent half a year or more in a Syrian Hareem — was not an 'Odalisque' but a governess there" (letter of 24 September 1896 to Dr. A. T. Rake; Durham). She evidently separated from Dean sometime before 18 November 1909, when WMR discussed her mental condition in a letter to Richard Curle (Indiana).

598. TO THEODORE WATTS-DUNTON

3 St. Edmund's Terrace,
30 April 1909

Dear Watts-Dunton,

Thanks for your attentive letter.[1] I don't see that any *serious* harm was done in connexion with Swinburne's funeral; though my daughter, being on the spot, thought the clergyman needlessly officious, and she withdrew at one moment of the performance. It would no doubt have been quite appropriate if some capable speaker, of the same order of thinking as Swinburne himself, had come forward to deliver an address: but for my part I care little whether anything of that sort is done or not. For a great man "His works do follow him"[2] is the truest of mottoes.

The English are hideously apathetic in matters where only intellect is concerned. The funeral of a conspicuous Railway-director or a fifth-rate M.P., or let us say Donald Currie,[3] would excite more perceptible attention than that of the one great poet of the present generation. As you say, the Italians have shown much better: they have something like the *emotion* of appreciation. What seems to me the most blameable is that even our organized literary bodies, such as the English Academy and the Society of Authors, gave no sign.

I would of course like to see you and Madame when opportunity serves. Old age, inertia, distance, etc., are obstacles, but insurmountable obstacles they surely are not.[4]

Yours always,
W. M. Rossetti

MS: Leeds. Extract in R. W. Peattie, "Swinburne's Funeral," *Notes and Queries*, n.s. 21 (December 1974), 469.

1. Quoted in "Swinburne's Funeral," p. 469.

2. "Their works do follow them," Revelation, 14:13.

3. (1825-1909), founder of the Castle Steamship Company.

4. MS. Diary, 21 June 1909: "Helen and I went to see Watts-Dunton.... He appeared free from illness but at first rather depressed: this diminished considerably as our talk proceeded. The conversation turned naturally upon Swinburne in chief: his irritability with nurses, indisposition to submit to medical orders, the constant course that used to go on of his reading aloud to Watts-Dunton (Scott, Dickens, Charles Reade, etc.), his coolness of late years to Meredith's writings, his split with Whistler, etc. In this last matter, Watts-Dunton thinks that Whistler was wholly in the wrong, and, from what he says, I think so too, in a modified degree.... Speaks of Swinburne's large appetite, and fondness for some not over-healthy viands — would eat at a meal an entire pâté de foie gras."

599. TO THEODORE WATTS-DUNTON

3 St. Edmund's Terrace,
22 May 1909

Dear Watts-Dunton,

I had not heard anything about a proposed American edition of Gabriel's complete poems.[1] Had better write to the publisher Ellis on the subject: I fancy, but don't rightly know, that some arrangements were made long ago whereby some things would be permissible, and others not, to Yankees.

You will easily believe me when I say that I feel very much for you in connexion with the loss of Swinburne. I feel even for myself, but my stake was small in comparison. Apart from all other and some of them still more important considerations, the change in your daily habits, your line of mental and personal associations from week to week and year to year, is no trifle — especially at the age which you (though some years younger than myself) have reached. Fortunately there is your wife to be your solace and stay — to whom my affectionate regards.

And now Meredith is gone too.[2]

I much regret also to hear that you are still much out of health — perhaps the present burst of singular fine and hot weather will do you good. I am myself well enough: could not say that anything is wrong with me, except some degree (came on 3 or 4 months ago) of synovitis in the right knee — gouty constitution.

Of course I have read with strong interest the newspaper-details as to your undertaking to write the biography of Swinburne etc. It may do something towards reviving your energies; as the writing of Gabriel's Memoir did for me after I had lost my wife, and was compelled to look out almost daily for the death of Christina.

Always your affectionate
W. M. Rossetti

MS: BL.

1. *Complete Poetical Works of Rossetti* (Little, Brown, 1910), one of a number of editions with this title published in the United States from 1886, sometimes called "Author's Edition." For the most part they were reprints of *Collected Works*, and usually bore WMR's name as editor. WMR to Watts-Dunton, 10 June 1909: "I did write to Ellis about that American edition.... They believe there is no legal bar to the Americans doing what they like, Gabriel's poems not having ever been copyrighted there. Ellis did at times sell copies of English editions to Roberts Bros. and to Little, Brown & Co.... Ellis could prevent the sale in England of the American edition now announced" (BL).

2. MS. Diary, 18 May 1909: "Another death — George Meredith, whom I liked, without the affection that I bore to Swinburne."

600. TO MARCHESE ANTONIO DI SAN GIULIANO[1]

3 St. Edmund's Terrace,
12 September 1909

Your Excellency,

May I be excused for interrupting your more important avocations, and troubling you about a very small affair.

I have received a letter from Professor C. A. Levi,[2] Director of the Museums at Torcello and Murano, showing that he lately addressed your Excellency with a view to procuring for me some mark of distinction from the Italian Government; and I find that your Excellency, favouring this proposal much more readily than I could have expected, is ready to recommend me for the insignia of some order, provided I express my wish that it should be done. For this I feel most unfeignedly grateful to your Excellency.

Perhaps I need hardly say that Professor Levi acted entirely of his own accord. He did not give me the least hint that he thought of making such a proposal, nor had I any idea that he was likely to entertain any such project.

From the example (were there none other) of my father Gabriele Rossetti, the *esule e proscritto* in the cause of his country, I have learned throughout my long life to aim at doing my duty in my small sphere without any aim or expectation of external honours for the performance of it. Thus the proposal of a decoration comes to me not only as a great surprise, but as something extraneous to my habits of mind and incentives of conduct. I respectfully thank your Excellency, and beg that the matter may not be further proceeded with.

I have only to add that, if I wished for any such distinction, I should with gratitude and eagerness accept it from the Kingdom of Italy, which I regard as being my native country almost in equal degree with England.

> I have the honour to be
> Your Excellency's
> Most obedient humble servant
> William M. Rossetti

MS: AP (Copy).

1. (1852-1914), Italian ambassador to the Court of St. James's, 1906-9.
2. Cesare Augusto Levi, author of books on the history and architecture of Venice.

---

601. TO ELSIE (MRS. FORD MADOX) HUEFFER

Wallcot,
Sycamore Gardens,
Dymchurch,
17 September 1910

My dear Elsie,

You see we are down here, not far from you.

I feel satisfied in my own mind that Ford is not a German but an Englishman: but it is undoubtedly true that at the date of his birth his father was a German. The naturalization took place some years afterwards — say 1882 or 1883.

Olive, who is here with us and who appears to have accurate ideas on the subject, says that in any country an alien who registers his child at the consulate of his own country makes thereby the nationality of the child the same as the father's: but that, in default of this, the child belongs to the country of his birth. Though I don't *know*, I feel no doubt that Franz Hueffer did not register Ford at his own consulate.

We all feel indignant at his present move, as outlined by you.

Thank you, I am really "very well" at present. Our party here, with myself, is Olive, Helen, Imogene, and Mrs. Dean (whom perhaps you have met). We came down, partly for the general purpose of sea-air etc., but partly also because we are (from the 15th) totally turned out of our own house by some blessed (or otherwise) drainage-repairs which will take a longish while and cost me a lot of money. Mary has from the 1st September been at Cambridge, at the "Research Hospital," as a Dr. Strangeways,[1] of the University, is looking closely into her case. She makes herself comfortable there, spite of all that would make other mortals uncomfortable: relatives are not encouraged to hover about her.

Accept our affectionate regards for yourself and the girls.

Always truly yours,
W. M. Rossetti

N.B. It appears to us all that, even if Ford were to divorce you in Germany, that would make no sort of difference as to your position as his wife in England, entitled to the benefit of any legal decree here.[2]

MS: Princeton.

1. Thomas Strangeways, lecturer in Special Pathology at Cambridge.
2. Ford never succeeded in divorcing Elsie (d. 1949) or in persuading her to divorce him (see Mizener, *The Saddest Story*).

602. TO SYDNEY CARLYLE COCKERELL   3 St. Edmund's Terrace,
                                               7 December 1911

Dear Cockerell,

The new edition of Gabriel[1] is now all in print, and I can see about consigning to you the printer's "copy," as we agreed.

I have put it together, and it appears to be *practically* complete. You will find a good deal of re-arrangement and transposition of text and notes, owing to the fact that this new edition is got up on a different scheme from the old volumes. Here there are the divisions of Principal Poems, Translations, etc. etc., and, within these divisions, the poems and prose are printed (as nearly as could be managed) in the order of date in which they were written. I think the "copy" will explain itself well enough when you have looked into it a little.

I have a great dislike to making up a parcel, if only I can shirk the job. Is there anyone you could send here to fetch away the copy, make it into a parcel, and dispatch it to you? But if not I or somebody here will do it.

Possibly when you were here last you observed that I seemed listless and out of condition. Such is the fact; for, though I am not *ill*, I feel within the last 5 months or so a decided abatement of general strength and elasticity. Can't be helped, nor I suppose remedied, at the age of 82. Handwriting cranky.

I trust all goes well with you and yours, and am always

Very truly yours,

W. M. Rossetti

Scawen Blunt[2] was so good as to call here one day. I liked him much.

MS: V. Surtees.

1. *Works*, a "Revised and Enlarged Edition" of *Collected Works*, was suggested by Ellis on 11 January 1911 "in view of the early expiry (1912) of copyright on the volume of 1870" (MS. Diary). On 13 February he approached Watts-Dunton about including *Jan Van Hunks* and the two Sphinx sonnets, but he declined, saying that he intended "to use these at some time in association with something of his own. Seems rather a fanciful plan, but I suppose I shall have to submit to it" (MS. Diary, 16 February).

2. Wilfrid Scawen Blunt (1840-1922), poet, traveler, anti-imperialist, who recorded the visit in his diary: "1st October (Sunday). With [Everard] Meynell to call on old William Rossetti beyond Regent's Park. He lives with his two daughters in a villa well filled with family mementos.... He is hale and hearty, though eighty years old, with a clear, healthy complexion, somewhat bronzed and showing his Italian origin. His manner precise, with considerable dignity. He spoke of the Italian raid on Tripoli, and I was glad to find his sympathies were with the Turks. He had read my 'Secret History' [*The Secret History of the English Occupation of Egypt* (1907)], and approved all my ideas" (*My Diaries* [1919-20], 2:363-64).

603. TO RICHARD CURLE

3 St. Edmund's Terrace,
20 June 1913

Good Kind Curle,

Very much obliged for your friendly letter, and such news in it as is good. I am in a very low condition, not so much now positive illness as general derangement of the natural resources of sleep and bodily functions. Am afraid I could not for the present see you or anyone. Love to Cordelia.

Helen away with Olive and the Americans: will not be back till 8 July or so. Miss Fradeletto[1] here — a nice hearty frank girl, but of course rather adding than otherwise to my daily course of discomfort. I can do next to nothing either in reading or in smoking.

Accept the love of

W. M. Rossetti

MS: Pennsylvania.

1. Daughter of Antonio Fradeletto (1858-1930), Italian writer and politician.

604. TO CHARLES NATHAN ELLIOT[1]

15 November 1914

At the age of 85 I retain unimpaired my love for Walt Whitman, and my deep regard for his memory, and my warm admiration of his work in its broad bulk and purport — allowing for occasional demur (which I always have entertained) to some points here and there. Whitman is a towering and majestic figure in American and world-wide literature.

Wm. M. Rossetti

Text: see Note 1.

1. Compiler of *Walt Whitman as Man, Poet and Friend, Being Autograph Pages from Many Pens* (Boston, 1915), from which the text of this letter comes.

605. TO SAMUEL CLAGGETT CHEW[1]

3 St. Edmund's Terrace,
10 February 1918

When I spontaneously undertook to write that Criticism[2] I informed Swinburne, who cordially approved: but he did not see or hear any of what I wrote until he read it in the published form. He was much gratified, though there were 2 or 3 things he did not relish. Both before and after the date of the Criticism he and I were firm and affectionate friends up to the last. All good fortune to your book. Please excuse my brevity: my eyes are now very weak.

W. M. Rossetti

MS: Kansas. Published (excluding last two sentences): S. C. Chew, *Swinburne* (1929), p. 75.

1. (1888-1960), professor of English, Bryn Mawr College, from 1914.
2. *Swinburne's Poems and Ballads, A Criticism.*

606. TO OLIVIA ROSSETTI AGRESTI

3 St. Edmund's Terrace,
13 October 1918

Dearest Ol,

Your last nice letter reached me the day *before* my birthday — that dismal anniversary. All thanks. I enclose the usual £5.

What a change these few last days! It really looks as if we had won the war. A wondrous deliverance.

You will have seen the international heroine Helen some days ere this. Our warmest love to her. No distinct news here of Antonio.

Pardon so wretched a scrap from your half-seeing

Papa

MS: AP.

607. HELEN ROSSETTI ANGELI TO SYDNEY CARLYLE COCKERELL

3 St. Edmund's Terrace,
5 February 1919

Dear Mr. Cockerell,

You are one of the few old friends whom Mary and I do not wish to read first in the papers of dear Papa's death.

He died this morning at 10 o'clock — Mary and Arthur were with him — I was not — I was on my way home from Paris with all possible speed. I arrived too late.

You were one of the few persons Papa saw with pleasure these last years when a good wind blew you our way.

He will be buried on Saturday at 11:30 at Highgate (after cremation).[1]

Your affectionate friend,
Helen Rossetti Angeli

MS: V. Surtees.

1. Cockerell's diary, 6 February 1919: "Went up to London by the 4.43 to see the Rossettis, as good old William Rossetti died yesterday at the age of 89. I found the whole family gathered together. Arthur Rossetti and his wife, Mrs. Agresti, Mrs. Angeli and her bright Imogene, and Mary Rossetti.... They were not sorry to see me and we had a very good talk about the old man, his inflexible rectitude of conduct etc.'' (BL).

INDEX

I. RECIPIENTS OF LETTERS

II. SOURCES OF TEXT

MANUSCRIPT

Kansas, University of, 84, 672

Leeds, University of, 16, 22, 55, 94, 169, 191, 192, 205, 667
Library of Congress, 183, 184, 187, 190, 194, 196, 214, 247, 269, 274, 280, 284, 322, 332, 335, 339, 350, 462, 465, 478, 481, 511, 535, 550, 654, 656

National Library of Scotland, 574
National Portrait Gallery, 582, 583, 588, 590
Newcastle, University of, 127
New York Public Library, 54, 61, 69, 70, 71, 89, 90, 475

Ohio Wesleyan University, 243

Peattie, Roger W., 530
Pennsylvania State University, 671
Pierpont Morgan Library, 16, 18, 653
Princeton University, 58, 72, 97, 110, 145, 199, 267, 287, 324, 340, 414, 415, 420, 463, 578, 579, 585, 596, 597, 600, 604, 605, 606, 607, 608, 609, 615, 616, 617, 624, 641, 642, 643, 644, 657, 658, 669

Reading, University of, 494
Rutgers University, 424, 444, 505

St. John's Seminary, 172
Surtees, Mrs. Virginia, 670, 672
Syracuse University, 475

Texas, University of, 103, 105, 143, 144, 146, 147, 150, 170, 173, 292, 297, 300, 348, 355, 370, 474, 509, 519, 537, 542, 544, 580, 584, 587, 612, 633, 654, 659, 661
Trinity College, Cambridge, 125
Trinity College, Dublin, 459

Victoria and Albert Museum, 289

Wellesley College, 109, 213, 500, 534

Yale University, 195, 204, 370, 386, 390, 498, 634

PRINTED

Academy, 318, 561
Athenaeum, 385, 417

Crayon, 102

Daily News, 336

Elliot, Charles Nathan, Walt Whitman as Man, Poet and Friend, 671

Pall Mall Gazette, 498

Reader, 132

III. GENERAL INDEX

In addition to those listed on pp. x-xiii, the following abbreviations are used in the index:

ACS   Algernon Charles Swinburne

LR   Lucy Rossetti

Unless otherwise indicated, quoted matter is by WMR.

Shepherd, 374; rejects "on principle any notice to show that some *different* paper has made a blunder," 382

Atlantic Monthly, large circulation of, 139n; 376-77n, 398

Attenborough, George, 368

Austin, Alfred, 236, 338

Authors' Syndicate, xxii, xxxii, 79n, 612, 620n

Aveling, Edward Bibbins, and Shelley Society, 503-6, 533; 511n, WMR chairs Shelley Society lecture by, 512

Axon, William Edward Armytage, 520

B

Bailey, George Hewlett, 555

Bailey, Philip James, *The Angel World*, 20n; *Festus*, 23

Bancroft, Samuel, 660n

Barbès, Armand, 241

Barham, Richard Harris, *The Ingoldsby Legends*, 518

Barker, Thomas Jones, 113

Barlow, Jane, 639

Barraclough (not identified), 193

Barraud, Hilton Percy, 569, 573

Barrett, Arabel, writes WMR about portrait of E. B. Browning, 106n

Bastian, Henry Charlton, 288n

Bastian, Mrs. Henry Charlton, 287

Bate, Percy, *The English Pre-Raphaelite Painters*, 634

Bateman, Edward La Trobe, 36, 39, 44, 45n

Bath, Marchioness of, 44, 45n

Baudelaire, Charles, 240

Baynes, T. S., 273n

Beauharnais, Hortense, 250n

Beddoes, Thomas Lovell, *Death's Jest-Book*, 20n, 21; *Brides' Tragedy*, 21

Bedford Debating Society, 507

Belcher, Mrs. (caretaker), 588n

Bell & Co. (Chemists), 454

Bell, Edward, 313n, 314

Bell, George, 311, 440n, 493

Bell, Henry Glassford, 390

Bell, Henry Thomas Mackenzie, xxii, xxxii, appreciation of CGR's poems, 578; 580, 600n, applies to WMR to buy CGR MSS., 617; WMR sells, typewritten copies of 18 letters, 617, refuses to allow WMR to include 18 letters in *FLCR*, 658-59

Christina Rossetti, A Biographical and Critical Study: xxi, xxix, WMR reads MS. of, "with interest, and frequently with agreement," 596; modified in accordance with notes sent by WMR, 597n; WMR prefers CGR's "affairs of the heart" (597n) not mentioned in, 600-601; "a decided selling-success," 605n; contains things which WMR "should not have said or should have said otherwise," 606; American edition of, 608; 613, 619, 638. Reviews of: *Athenaeum*, 605; *Literature*, "falls very foul" of WMR, 605, assails WMR "in terms the reverse of temperate," 606, WMR suggests Bell should reply to, 605, WMR urges Bell answer, in new ed., 606, WMR writes to *Literature* about, 607; Gosse suggested as reviewer, 609-10; *British Weekly*, 608; *Bookman*, hostile to WMR, WMR reads, "with very faint sensations of dislike," 609; *Saturday Review*, 610

Bellars, Henry, 179n

Belt, Richard, 355n

Bendyshe, Thomas, 171

Bennett, Samuel, 352

Bentham, Jeremy, 275

Bentley, Richard, 84

Besant, Walter, 535n

Bewick, Thomas, 199

Bible, Job, xxvii, *Leaves of Grass*, "a 19th century Book of Job," 76; quoted: Acts, 380; Revelation, 403, 667; Matthew, 541, 552; John, 653

Bidgen, Miss (nurse), 559

Bird, Elfreda Elizabeth, 224

Bismarck, Otto von, 260n

Bixby, William K., 636n, 655n

Black, William, 130n

Blackett, Arthur, 478n

Blackmore, W., 130n

Blaikie, J. Arthur, 456n

Blake, William, WMR's writings on, assessed, xx-xxi; xxii, 17, English attitudes to, 133; publication of ACS's *Blake* "greatest service at present possible to," 139; Scudder plans book on, 164; Phillips's portrait of, 164; 172, facsimiles of, prepared by Hotten, 178; poems of, published by Pickering, 318; 332, exhibition of, at Burlington

682

130n, 207n, 210, 227, 234, 241, 243n, 269, 270, 271n, 275, 280n, makes over *Work* to WMR on trust, 286-87; and DGR in 1872, 288-97 *passim*, 301-2, 302-3; WMR thanks, for assisting in DGR's recovery, 302; friendship with Charles Lucy, 307, 308; 308, lectures to Birmingham and Midland Institute, 310, redelivers lectures at Newcastle and Edinburgh, 322

HEALTH: 310, 311, 315, 334, 380, 418, "very ill," 441; "illness ... a terrifying one," 442; 444, 447, 467-68, "no prospect of prolonged life," 529n; "spirits ... bad," 531; 546, 552, 554, "very serious illness," 566-68

suggests revisions to DGR's commemorative sonnet on Oliver Brown, 319-20; 321, 323, 324n, "a little nettled," 326; anniversary of Oliver Brown's death, "days of poignant reminiscence" for, 329; 332n, 332, Memoir of Oliver Brown, "written *principally* by," 333; 333n, 341, 346, 355, 356, 357, 358, his concern for DGR "precious and priceless," 359; "willing ... to look after Gabriel prior to seaside," 360; accompanies DGR to Herne Bay, 361; claims CGR and Mrs. Rossetti converting DGR to Christianity, 362; DGR deplores departure of, from Herne Bay, 362-63; 364, visits Paris with WMR, 372-73; 379n, 380, 384, 384n, 391, 392, 398n, rents cottage in Manchester, 400; 402, 405, 408, 410, 413, 414, unable to attend DGR's funeral, 414; 418, 420, difficulties with WMR over preparation of DGR's paintings and designs for "Remaining Works" sale, 421, 423-24; 432, 438n, proposes to sell shares in Ravensbourne Wharf to WMR, 444, 447; "not in the most cordial of moods," 446n; 451, designs DGR's headstone, 451, 453, 455, 456-57, 458; WMR wants hand of, in Birchington glass for DGR, 461; undertakes memorial bust of DGR, 464, 468, 487, answers press attack on memorial, 491; 468, 471, WMR loans £100, 476; 480n, 484, renews "old friendliness" with Morris and Burne-Jones, 484n; 488, 490, 498n, 510n, 514, made "a meal and a bed" available to J. W. Inchbold for

half a year, 515; and death of Francis Hueffer, 523, 524-25, 526, 528; "dissatisfied with everything" done to assist Cathy Hueffer, 529n; views of trustees of Hueffer's estate "more reasonable ... than those of Brown," 529n, 531; "repelled ... rather indignantly" £100 tendered to Cathy Hueffer on Queen's Bounty, 535n; 534, 545n, WMR dines with, 546; 547n, 552, 552-53n, "jarring with the Manchester people" over Townhall pictures, 554; 556, 562-63, death of, 568-69; mould of face taken by Brucciani, 568, 570; no immediate posthumous exhibition of, 569; will of, sought, 569; LR to write life of, 570; WMR assists LR with life of, 570-71; subscription for, 572; 573, WMR offers portrait of, to National Portrait Gallery, 590; name of, "in the mouths" of WMR's fellow jurymen at Venice Biennale, 590; 602, 615, 616n, diary of, "a capital thing," 623

WORKS: *Boddington Group*, 531; *Bradshaw's Defence of Manchester*, 553n, 554; *Chaucer at the Court of Edward III*, 490; *Chetham's Life Dream*, 476; *Crabtree Watching the Transit of Venus*, 447; *English Autumn Afternoon*, 88n; *Entombment*, autotype of, in *Century Guild Hobby Horse*, 486, 488; *The Expulsion of the Danes from Manchester*, 391n, 406, 408; Fawcett, Henry, and his Wife, portrait of, 590-91; *Jesus Washing Peter's Feet*, 31, duplicate of, 93; acquired by National Gallery, 572, 650, "great run upon ... in the National Gallery," 590; *The Last of England*, 37, 61; *Lear and Cordelia*, 61, 88n, damage to, 99n; *Looking Towards Hampstead*, 88n; *The Opening of the Bridgewater Canal*, 546, 554n; *The Pretty Baa-Lambs*, 32n, 34n; *The Romans Building a Fort at Mancenion*, 391n; DGR, bust of, 468, 487, 510; WMR, portrait of, 74, 585n; *The Seeds and Fruits of English Poetry*, 492n; *The Trial of Wycliffe*, 18n, 468, 476, duplicate of, 573n; *Waiting*, 41n; *William the Conqueror Presenting a Charter to Marmion*, 572; *Work*, 37, 74, 78, 93, 286-87

Brown, Lucy Madox (see Rossetti, Lucy)

Brown, Oliver Madox (Nolly), 93n, 210n, 269, 293, 295-96, *Gabriel Denver*, Smith Williams "*greatly* impressed" with, 305; 310, 313, WMR expects death of, 319; DGR's commemorative sonnet on, 319-20; 323, 328, 330n, 331, 333, 362n, 400n, 406, 408, 432n, 438n, anniversary of death, 439, 477; 451, 453, 455, 456, 457, 477, 485, 525

Brown, Samuel, 23

Browne, Hablot Knight, 613-14

Browning, Elizabeth Barrett, 63, WMR describes, 63, 106; 74, 87n, 93, portraits of, in *National Magazine* and *Aurora Leigh*, 105-6; 588
WORKS: *Aurora Leigh*, 63, 73, 77, article on, in *Edinburgh Weekly Review*, 82; 93, 103n, 110; *Poems* (1844), copy of, which DGR and WMR "used to read incessantly," 642; *Poems* (1850), 18-19, 21; *Poems before Congress*, 107, WMR acknowledges presentation copy of, 109; 110; *The Romaunt of the Page*, 102

Browning, Robert, Felix Moscheles's portrait of, 2n; "a most glorious fellow," 63; William Page's portrait of, "very bad," 65; presence of, in London, "most delightful," 74; 87n, 93, "*the* best of living poets," 103; 105, entrusts WMR with getting portrait of Mrs. Browning engraved, 105-6; 109, suggests subject for picture to DGR, 128; criticizes ACS's "beechnuts in spring," 136; makes CGR's acquaintance, 136; WBS condemns his "mannered method of poetizing," 137n; 145n, 150, 169-70, 172, 206, 209, WMR consults, about Shelley and Harriet, 213; 225, 236, DGR's "lingering" prejudice against, 303; 348, 389, 436, "ought to be President" of Shelley Society, 479n; refuses Presidency, "no longer views Shelley's personal character with either approval or indulgence," 479-80n; 499, attends unveiling of DGR memorial, 510n; 599, 602, 633
WORKS: *Blot in the 'Scutcheon*, 104; *Christmas Eve and Easter Day*, 24n, 25, 104; *Dramatic Lyrics*, 104; *Dramatis Personae*, 136; *Hervé Riel*, 352n; *In a Gondola*, 226n; ed., *Letters of Shelley*, xx, 206, 213-14; Lines for Felix Moscheles's *Isle's Enchantress*, 2n; *Men and Women*, 63, 104; *Paracelsus*, 104; *Pippa Passes*, 104; *Poems, a New Edition* (1849), 104; *The Ring and the Book*, 136, 201, 205, 226n; *Sordello*, 23, WBS antagonistic to, 24n, 112n; 104, 106-7, 109, 110, 494; *Strafford*, WMR attends performance of, 500-501, Leonard Outram engaged as director of, 516-17n

Browning, Robert Barrett, 93, pictures by, 93n; 136

Browning, Robert, Sr., MS. works by, 517-18

Browning, Sarianna, 93n, 214

Browning Society, 483n, 501n, 516n, WBS calls an "assembly of duffers," 536n

Brown, Langham & Co., 625-26n, 645, 657-58

Brucciani & Co., D., 416n, supplies new moulds of DGR's face and hand, 473; 568, 570

Bruce, John Collingwood, *The Bayeux Tapestry Elucidated*, 73

Bryant, William Cullen, 171

Buchanan, George, 496

Buchanan, Robert Williams, WMR's "peculiar abhorrence" of, 141; 142n 2, 156, "The Session of the Poets," 160n; 165n, review of *Leaves of Grass* by, "calculated to do more good than harm," 182; attacks WMR's *PWS*, 252n; "never occurred" to WMR he might be author of "Fleshly School," 281; concerned over ACS's illness, 281; WMR inclined to forgive, 282n; DGR believes "Fleshly School" written by, 282; WMR informed "Fleshly School" not written by, 283; and Whitman, 336-37, 337-38, 338, 340; libel action by, against *Examiner*, 459; "morbid and miserable consequences" of "Fleshly School" attack by, 463; ridiculed by ACS, 496-97n

Bucke, Richard Maurice, 465

Buckle, George Earle, 529n

Budden, W. H., 24, 26, 27, 30, 59, 76

Bunting, Percy William, 530

Burcham, Robert Partridge, 597

Burchard, Joannis, *Capellae Pontificiae Sacrorum Rituum Magistri Diarium*, 632

Burgess, Frank William, plans bibliography of Rossettis, 610; buys Rossetti MSS. and books from WMR, 610, 611; interest in G. Polidori Private Press, 610-11; book covers designed by, 611n; 618n, undertakes publication of Blake's "The Passions," 620

Burgess, Mrs. Frank W., 619

Burley, Maria Julia (née Trelawny), 327n

Burlington Club, 170, and Whistler, 174, 175, 188, 190; 340

Burne-Jones, Sir Edward, 91n, *Merlin and Nimue* (Oxford Union), 92; 100n, St. Frideswide window (Christ Church Cathedral), reviewed in *Athenaeum*, 108n; 118, "more settled in health," 124; 143n, 145n, 145, 149n, 166, 275, 348, 386n, 415n, 420, reports rumored circulation of letters addressed to DGR, 441; 451, quarrel with FMB patched up, 484n; 486n, Jane Morris "not gratified" by election of, as ARA, 502n; 623

Burne-Jones, Lady Georgiana, 201, 484n, 621

Burnet, John, *Turner and his Works*, 122n

Burns, Robert, *Address to the Deil*, quoted, 521

Burroughs, John, 176, *Notes on Walt Whitman as Poet and Person*, 176-77n, 177, 186; calls WMR's *Chronicle* article on Whitman "a grand and lofty piece of criticism," 177n; 177, 179, visits WMR, 280, 284

Burroughs, Miss, 517n

Burrows, Rev. Henry Williams, 490

Burton, Sir Frederic William, 145, 193n, 469n

Butts, Captain Frederick, 204

Byles, Marianne (Mrs. Coventry Patmore), 133n

Byron, George Gordon, 6th Baron, 228, 330, statue of, 355, 389; 365, quoted, 393; 625n, 628n

Byron, George Gordon de Luna, 207n

Byron, Lady, 228, 240, 247

C

Cadogan, George Henry, 5th Earl Cadogan, 435n

Caine, Sir Thomas Henry Hall, 400-407 *passim*, 414, 415, "officious and ... blundering," 418; 420, *Recollections*

of Rossetti, 431, WMR's objections to, 437; 439, 498n; 431-32n

Cairnes, John Elliot, 144

Call, Colonel Charles, 327n, 405, 517, 533, 564, sells copy of Shelley's *Oedipus Tyrannus* to Wise, 565

Cambisson, Mlle, 465

Cambridge Union, 171n

Cameron, Julia Margaret, "exceptional artistic value" of her photographs, 134; 176

Campana, G. P., 581n

Campbell, James, 111

Campbell, James Dykes, 484

Carlyle, Jane, 29

Carlyle, Thomas, 21, 29, 38, 52, 87n, 97, 147, denies statement attributed to him by Ruskin, 173, letter of denial to *Pall Mall Gazette* quoted, 174n; WMR disagrees with "views he takes of late years" (1867), 188; rumored view of Whitman, 196; 348n, "beyond all comparison the superior and more interesting figure" than George Eliot, 398; WMR grieved by attacks on, 398-99; 422

WORKS: *Early Letters of Carlyle, 1814-26*, 558; *Frederick the Great*, 101; *Life of John Sterling*, 23, 51n; *Occasional Discourse on the Nigger Question*, quoted, 53; 147; *Oliver Cromwell's Letters and Speeches*, 48; *Sartor Resartus*, xxx

Carmarthen, Lady, 228

Carmichael, Mary Grant, 506

Carpenter, Edward, 339n

Carr, Comyns, 369n, 373, 441

Carter, Edward George, 557n

Carter, Henry Charles, 557n

Cassell & Co., 514

Catechism, quoted, 57

Catty, Lt.-Col. C. Parker, 246

Catty, Corbet Stacey, 246

Catty, Captain J. P., 246n

Cayley, Charles Bagot, 17n, 38, 56n, 57n, 208, 363, 586n, 601n

Cayley, George John, 7

Celano (sculptor), 402n

Century Guild Hobby Horse, 486n, 488

Chamberlain (not identified), 113

Chamberlain, Joseph, 396, 622, WMR sympathizes with his "olden Radicalism ... his present semi-Toryism not," 624

Chamberlayne, Miss, 623n
Chambers, Alice, 419n, 544n
Chaplin, Holroyd, 451n
Chapman, George R., 192-93
Chapman, John, 281
Chartists, 2-3
Chatterton, Thomas, 103, 105, 383-84
Chatto, Andrew, 319, 364
Chatto & Windus, 324n, 364
Chaucer Society, 211
Chenavard, Paul, 48
Chesterton, Gilbert Keith, 649n
Chew, Samuel Claggett, 672
Child, Addison, 533, 536
Christie (art dealer), 427
Christie, James J. B., 444, 447n
Christie's, 421n, 447n
Chronicle, 172, 193
Cicero, 208
Cifariello, Filippo, 402n
Clairmont, Claire, 210n, 365, disapproves
   of WMR's account of her relationship
   with Byron, 366n; 460n, 633
Clairmont, Paola, 366n
Clarendon Press, 543n
Clarke, Andrew, 409, 433-34
Clay, Richard, 489, 513, 540n, 541, 626n
   2 & 1, 632
Cleveland, Grover, President of the United
   States, WMR writes to, about Whitman,
   470
Clifford, Lucy (Mrs. W. K.), 446n
Clifford, William Kingdon, 322
Clough, Arthur Hugh, *Bothie*, xvii-xviii, 7
Clover, Joseph, 590
Cockerell, Sir Sydney Carlyle, xxiii, xxxii,
   WMR refuses to sell, portrait of Lizzie
   by DGR, 604, 621, 628; WMR sells,
   DGR portrait of Lizzie acquired from
   James Siddall, 621; WMR offers, one
   of two DGR portraits of Lizzie, 628;
   WMR sells, DGR, Lizzie, and Ruskin
   letters, 628-29, 631, 641; WMR sells,
   copy of DGR's *Hugh Heron*, 629;
   WMR sells, Rossetti family books,
   629, 630, 641-42; WMR refuses to sell,
   additional copy of *Hugh Heron*, 629;
   WMR sells, MSS. of DGR poems and
   translations, 630; 649n, WMR gives,
   printer's copy of *Works*, 670; letter to,
   from Helen Angeli, announcing WMR's
   death, 672-73; visits Rossettis following
   WMR's death, 673n

Cohen, Ferdinand, 207n
Cole, Henry, 29, 39, 50
Colenso, John William, 136
Coleridge, Samuel Taylor, *Kubla Khan*,
   19; *Christabel*, 217
Colles, William Morris, xxii, xxxii, 612,
   625
Collier, John Payne, 39
Collins, Charles Allston, 18, 37, 48n, 65
Collinson, James, 8n, *The Child Jesus*,
   10-11; 11, 13, 14n, 499, portraits of
   Maria Rossetti and CGR by, 583; 601n,
   615
Colnaghi's, 37, 77, 135
Colvin, Sir Sidney, 274, 275, *Keats*,
   503n, 511
Commonweal, 472
Conway, Moncure, xxii, xxiv, 176n 5,
   WMR consults, about *PWW*, 176,
   179n, 185, 186, 187n, 187; 177, 183,
   184, 194, 215, 240, 248, 366n, 376-77n
   5 & 6
Cook and Lomer, 276n, 490, 492
Cook, Dutton, 385n
Cook, Keningale Robert, 275, 324n, 491
Cooper, Antony Ashley, 7th Earl of
   Shaftesbury, 148
Corder, Rosa, 369n
Cornforth, Fanny, xxxiii, 170, relations
   with WMR, 171n; 231, leaves Cheyne
   Walk "in a tiff," 357 & n; "in a very
   obstructive mood," 360; WMR refuses
   request of, to see DGR's body, 416;
   435, DGR works owned by, 436n; 441,
   holds IOU from DGR, 447, 449, 456;
   661n
Coronio, Aglaia (née Ionides), 436
Correggio, Antonio, 63
Costa, Giovanni, 328n
Cottle, Joseph, *Early Recollections,
   Chiefly Relating to the late Samuel
   Taylor Coleridge*, 382
Courthope, William John, 273n
Cowper-Temple, Georgiana, 342n 2 & 3,
   609
Cowper-Temple, William, 1st Baron
   Mount-Temple, 342n 2 & 3
Cox, Edward William, 19n, 56
Cozens, Mr., 350
Crane, Walter, 649n
Craven, Frederick W., 423
Crawley, Frederick, 631
Crawshay, Mrs., 553

691

Hamel, Ernest, *Histoire de Robespierre*, 179
Hamilton, Walter, *Aesthetic Movement in England*, WMR sends corrections for new ed. of, 437
Hamon, Louis, 47
Hampden House, 548n
Hancock, John, 6, 8, 13, 14n
Hancocks, 2n
Hannay, James, 23, 27, 28n, 33, 38, 42, 47, 50, *Eustace Conyers*, 57; 74, Subscription Fund for children of, 310; 422
Hannay, James Lennox, model for Valentine in Hunt's picture, 594, 595
Harding, James Duffield, 95n
Hardman, John, 315
Hardy, Iza, 271n, 546
Hardy, Lady Mary Ann (wife of Sir Thomas Duffus Hardy), 271n, 547n
Hardy, Sir Thomas Duffus, 271n, 547n
Hare, Charles John, 597
Hargrove, Rev. Charles, 316n
Harlan, James, 164n
Harmsworth Magazine, 625n
Harper and Brothers, 376n
Harper, H. H., 636
Harper's Monthly Magazine, 377n
Harris, James Smith, 404-12 *passim*
Harrison, Mr., 102
Harston, Edward F. B., 655
Harston, Lionel de Courcy, 655
Harvey, Francis, 134, 204, 311
Haweis, Rev. Hugh Reginald, succeeds DGR at Tudor House, 435n; opens house "to all comers" following unveiling of DGR memorial, 510n; house now "more showy and cheerful, and less tasteful and uncommon, than of old," 510n
Hawkins, Henry, Baron Brampton, 459
Haydon, Benjamin Robert, *Life of ... from his Autobiography and Journals*, 48
Haydon, Frank Scott, 296
Haydon, Samuel James Bouverie, 113
Haynes, Mr., 9
Heath, Christopher, 343
Heaton and Butler Glass-Works, 452n
Heaton, Ellen, 63
Heaton, John Aldam, 299, 429
Heimann, Adolf, 1
Heimann, Amelia (Mrs. Adolf), 2n, "one of the oldest and best friends" of CGR,

581
Heimann, Henrietta (Mrs. G. W. Foote), 352n
Henley, William Ernest, 439
Henryson, Robert, 387
Herbert, John Rogers, 6, 29, 111, 114n
Herbert, Ruth, 623
Herkomer, Sir Hubert von, xviii
Hexham Abbey, alterations to, 30
Hicks, Mrs., 477
Hiffernan, Joanna (Jo), 657
Higginson, Thomas Wentworth, 366
Hill, F., 114n
Hills, Mr., 174n
Hime, Lt.-Col. H. W. L., 522
Hinton, Richard J., article on Whitman, 193, 194
Hipkins, A. J., 535n
Hiroshige, Ando, 656
Hitchener, Elizabeth, xx, 305, 307n, 316n, WMR loans Dowden copies of Shelley's letters to, 460n; Wise's attempts to acquire Shelley's letters to, 518-20, 521, 596; *The Fire-side Bagatelle*, WMR offers Wise copy of, 590, 592; 640n
H. N. O. (reviewer in *Chronicle*), 181n
Hobhouse, John Cam, Baron Broughton, 625n
Hodge, Edward Grose, 544, 586n
Hodge, Tom, 544
Hodgson, J. Stewart, 100
Hogarth Club, xxii, formation of, 97; 100-101, 110, 111, reorganization of, 114-15; Thomas Morten "a thorn in the side of," 157
Hogarth, William, house of, at Chiswick, 94; "Portrait of Dr. Mead and Surgeon Misaubin," 274n; 383-84
Hogg, Thomas Jefferson, *Life of Shelley*, xx, conclusion of, said to be extant, 198; 200
Hoggan, Frances Elizabeth, 433
Hoggan, George, 433-34
Holding, Henry James, 303n
Hollings, Edwin, 495
Hollings, Mrs. Edwin, 495, 526
Holt, Helen Maud (Mrs. Beerbohm Tree), 495
Holt, Henry (publisher), 376n
Homer, *Iliad*, quoted by Ruskin, 49
"Homo" (unidentified poem), 33
Hood, Thomas, 243n, 244
Hook, James Clarke, 41n, 111, 117

Hookham, Thomas, 214n
Hope, Alexander James Beresford, 108n
Hope, Rev. Frederick William, 94
Horace, *Odes*, quoted, 64; *Epistles*, quoted, 608
Hosack, John, *Mary Queen of Scots and Her Accusers*, 496
Hotten, John Camden, publishes WMR's *Swinburne's Poems and Ballads, A Criticism*, xviii, 160, 162
ACS's publisher: xviii, xxii, xxix, 150 & n, 152, 157-59, 161-63, 167, 170, 171, 180, 197, consults WMR about ACS's publishing arrangements, 238-39, 245, 252-53, 255-56; WMR advises ACS how to respond to, 259-64 *passim*
commissions *PWW*, ed. WMR, xix, 177, 184, 185; 155, 165, 168, 179n 5, 180, 181, 319n
Houghton and Osgood, 376n
Howard, Mr., 433n
Howe, Foster, 647n
Howell, Charles Augustus, xxv, xxxii, secretary Cruikshank Subscription, 143-48 *passim*; and Swinburne, 170, 171, 197, 259, 263; 179, "has a very blabbing tongue," 234; 289, undertakes to sell Botticelli painting belonging to DGR, 290, 292, 300-301; proffered help to DGR "most unreserved and affectionate," 296; offers portion of his house to DGR, 300; part in forgery of drawings ascribed to DGR, 368; 379n, 418, buys objects from DGR's estate, 419, 424-25, 430; WMR "had rather not renew any visiting or family intimacy" with, 420; 428, 432, prepares catalogue of "The Rossetti Gallery," 436n; death of, WMR quotes Shakespeare on, 543; 654, 661 & n
Howell, Kate, xxxii, 171, 419n, 425, 543, 661 & n
Howell, Rosalind Blanche Catherine, 418, 420, 543
Howells, William Dean, 377n
Howitt, Anna Mary (Mrs. A. A. Watts), 36, 42, 44, 56n, 57, 62, 66, 70, 508
Howitt, Godfrey, 39, 40n
Howitt, Mary (Mrs. William), 36, 39, 57, 58n
Howitt, William, 36, 39, 45, 57, 58n, 461n
Hubbard, Richard William, 164
Hubbard, Theodore Stephen, 389

Hueffer, Catherine (Mrs. Francis), xxiii, 269, 276n, 317n, 321, 323, 403, 414, 446, 484n, 487, response to husband's death, 524, 525; financial plight of, following husband's death, 525, 527, 528, 531; Civil List Pension applied for, unsuccessfully, 535n; "has some good qualities, and some bad ones," 552; "gave no evidence of a 'fantasia Hufferica'," 554; and FMB's last illness and death, 566-71 *passim*; goes to Germany to look after Ford, 642-44
Hueffer, Elsie (Mrs. Ford Madox), xxix, 586n
Hueffer, Ford Madox, xxvii, xxix, 341n, 391n, 502n, 523, WMR takes fatherly interest in, 524n; "expensive education" of, at Folkestone, 527; 527n, attends University College School, 527n; 528, attends Civil Service College, 529n; 532n, 535n, "by no means so dutiful or deferential as ... should have been" to FMB, 553n; 554, present at FMB's death, 568; 569, 570n, WMR gives, furniture from CGR's house, 585; WMR cancels loan to, 641; health, 642-44; WMR "indignant" at move by, to divorce Elsie, 670
Hueffer, Francis (Franz Hüffer), xxv, xxvii, 275, 296, 319, 321, 323, 324n, 333, 337, 341, 366, 381n, WMR invites to DGR's funeral, 414; 417n, 432n, 438n, 446, 449n, writes Memoir of DGR for Tauchnitz ed. *Ballads and Sonnets*, 452n; 464, 468, 484, 487, 502n, 510n, death of, "frightful calamity," 523, "most troublous and grievous event ... to the prospects of all family," 524n, "serious difference it makes in the total resources of the various branches of the family," 526; WMR arranges funeral of, 524-25; 528, "Hueffer Memorial Concert" suggested, 529n; 669-70
Hueffer, Juliet (Mrs. David Soskice), xxvii, 524, 527
Hueffer, Oliver, xxvii, 524, 526, 527 & n 1 & 2, 553n, 568, 649n
Hüffer, Alexis, WMR asks, to do "something substantial" for Hueffer boys, 526, 527, 528; 529n, 531, 532n
Hüffer, Hermann, 527n, 532n
Hüffer, Leopold, 527n, 532n
Hüffer, Wilhelm, 527n, 532n

Hughes, Arthur, quoted on WMR, xxviii-
xxix; 74, 91n, 111, 450, 510n, 646n,
660n
WORKS: illustrations for Allingham's
Music Master (1855), 56; *April Love*,
65; *Eve of St. Agnes*, 65; *Two-and-half
Years Old*, 89n; illustrations for CGR's
Sing-Song, "in the right spirit," 278,
283
Hughes, Miss (landlady), 558
Hughes, Spencer Leigh, 664
Hughes, Thomas, 128
Hugill, Mr., 548n
Hugo, Victor, 167, 241, 260, ought to be
made President of the French Republic,
262; 268, 448, 449, *Gil Blas*, Hugo
Anniversary Supplement, 464-65;
"stupendous" funeral of, 470; 508,
Dieu, 550; 633n
Humbert I, King of Italy, 623
Hunt, Alfred William, 96, 100, 199
Hunt, Cyril, 192n
Hunt, Edith (Mrs. Holman Hunt), 358,
483, 484, 510n, "distinctly an old
lady," 646n; 649
Hunt, John, 210n
Hunt, Leigh, 19, 22n, 97, 209, 371, 599,
633
Hunt, Thornton, regrets WMR's resignation
from the *Spectator*, 108n; 136n, 212
Hunt, William Henry, xviii, and American
Exhibition of British Art, 88n; 111
Hunt, William Holman, xviii, xxiii, 4,
relations with WMR, 5n; and the *Germ*,
5, 13, 14; 16, nicknamed "the mad,"
18; 20, 23, 27, 33, convenes P.R.B.
meeting to discuss R.A.'s rejection of
Millais, 34, 35; 37, 38, takes riding
lessons with WMR, 44; 46-47, 48, 52,
56n, 57, 59, takes house in Claverton
Terrace, 64; Millais's works (1856)
suffer from "want of Hunt's
companionship," 65; and Seddon
subscription, 74, 77, 81n; 78, 80, 82,
and American Exhibition of British Art,
85, 89n, 95; 91n, 100, 106, proposed
subscription for, shelved, 110; 114n,
"seems stranded," 124; 130n, 133n,
marriage (1865), WMR witness at, 137;
146n, 166, death of Fanny Hunt, WMR
offers to come to Florence following,
168-69; looks "extremely" ill (1868),
192, improved, 193; 201, 204, considers

retiring from Old Water-Colour Society,
279; a "truly conscientious and
exacting" worker, 279; 284, suffered
two "bad fevers," 358; 376n, organizes
J. L. Tupper Subscription, 377; 422,
WMR visits (1885), 470-71; plans to
write Eastern reminiscences, 471; WMR
visits (1886), 483; Draycott Lodge,
"chilliness of ... very unsuitable for
Hunt's state of health," 483; 493, 499,
unveils memorial to DGR, 510n; receives
"severe treatment ... red-hot needles
up the nose," 534; 597n, 615, WMR
not inclined to consult, about publishing
references to him in "P.R.B. Journal,"
616; rumored feeling of, towards DGR,
"not what one can call friendly," 616;
WMR visits (1906), 645-46n; "as of
old, an inexhaustible talker," 646n;
relations with Woolner, 650; 654, 662,
WMR visits, at Sonning Acre (1907),
663-64; WMR congratulates, on passing
of Deceased Wife's Sister bill, 664
PR & PRB: xxix, WMR suspects, "will
be not particularly friendly to Gabriel,"
595; sends WMR copy of, with self-
justifying letter, 645; WMR prepares
list of corrections for 2d ed., 646n, 649;
DGR "not quite handsomely treated"
in, 646; treatment of F. G. Stephens
in, 646, 650; WMR "resolved not to
have any acrimonious public discussion"
about, 647, 649; sale of, 651n
WORKS: *The Afterglow in Egypt*, 68n;
The Awakening Conscience, 48n, 51n,
623; *Claudio and Isabella*, 20n, 37, 47,
647; *A Converted British Family*, 484n;
Fairlight Downs, 96n; *Festa at Fiesole*,
279n; *The Finding of the Saviour in the
Temple*, 64, 75n, 78, 108, sale of,
110-11, proposed dinner to mark
completion of, 112n; *The Hireling
Shepherd*, 28n, 30; Hunt, William,
portrait of, 59; *Interior of the Cathedral
at Salerno*, 279n; *Interior of the Mosque
Ar Sakara*, 279n; *Isabella and the Pot
of Basil*, 192; *Jerusalem, by Moonlight*,
64; *The Light of the World*, 32n, 37,
46, 51n, sketch for Keble College
version, sale of, 88n, 95; *Moonlight at
Salerno*, 279n; *New College Cloisters*,
41n; *Our English Coasts*, 37-38, 41n,
48n; *The Pathless Waters*, 279n; *The*

Landor, Walter Savage, 57n, 97, 172, 209
Landseer, Sir Edwin, xviii, 111, 447n
Lange, Julius, 589n, 590
Lawson, George, 555
Layard, Sir Austen Henry, 216
Leader, 136, 459
Lear, Edward, 35
Leathart, James, 81, 120, 124, 130n, 334
& n, 423, 435
Leconte de Lisle, Charles, 341
Leech, John, 613-14
Lees, Charles, 50
Legros, Alphonse, xviii, 165, portrait of
WMR by, 488; quarrel with Whistler,
656-57; knows much about Whistler,
but "will persist in not imparting it,"
657
Leigh, Augusta, 228
Leighton, Sir Frederic, xviii, 66, and
American Exhibition of British Art,
88n; 117-18, 165, 357n, oversees DGR
exhibition at R.A., 417n, 431, 434,
WMR discusses exhibition with, 435-
36; Leighton House, "a gorgeous
specimen of oligarchical luxury," 435;
model for sculpture by, 436; 464, 535n,
554
Leopardi, Giacomo, xxxi
Leslie, Charles Robert, 30, 34, 35n, 38,
95n
Leslie, George Dunlop, 111
Levi, Cesare Augusto, 669
Lewes, George Henry, *Goethe*, 67; 69n,
136, 200n, 201n, 339n, article on
Whitman, 459
Lewis, George Henry, 441
Lewis, John Frederick, xviii, 100
Leyland, Frederick Richard, 354, 359,
392-93, visits DGR at Birchington,
406, 412; 417n, 420n, 422, 423, 435,
551, 569
Leys, Hendrik, 224
Lies, Joseph, 51n
Linnell, John, 204
Linnell, William, 117-18
Linton, Henry, 106n
Linton, William James, 29, *Plaint of
Liberty*, 36, quoted, 53
Litany, The, quoted by J. L. Tupper, 170n
Literature, 605, 607, 609-10
Little, James Stanley, 364n, 483n, 497n,
503-6 *passim*, 512, 540
Little, William, 130n

Liverpool Academy, 27
Locker-Lampson, Frederick, 159, 376n,
383
London, "the unmeasured size and colossal
agglomeration of life in," 284
London Review, change of editors, 128
Long family (not identified), 554
Longfellow, Henry Wadsworth, 88n,
Ruskin's "painful propensity" for,
107; *Psalm of Life*, 107; 154n, *Hiawatha*,
225; 383
Longman, Charles James, 570
Losh, Miss, 222n, 421n
Losh, Sara, 221
Loudon, Jane (Mrs. John Claudius), 72
Lowell, James Russell, *Fable for Critics*,
20; *Biglow Papers*, 21, 107; 87n, reviews
ACS in *North American Review*, 149;
154n
Lubin, David, 328n
Lucy, Charles, 307-8, 320
Lucy, Sir Thomas, 387
Ludlow, John Malcolm, 128
Lush, Robert, 159
Lyster, Alfred Chaworth, 507
Lytton, Edward Lytton Bulwer-Lytton, lst
Baron Lytton, 58, 224, 263, 403
Lytton, Edward Robert Bulwer-Lytton, lst
Earl of ("Owen Meredith"), 58

M

McCallum, Andrew, 100
McCallum, Mrs. Andrew, WBS describes
as "delightful little handsome rich,"
101n
MacCarthy, Denis Florence, 305
McCarthy, Justin, WMR's letters to, not
traced, xxxii, 324n, 332, 340, 484 & n
McCarthy, Mrs. Justin, 352n
McClure, Rev. Edmund, 637n
MacColl, Norman, 368, 374-75n, 409,
595n
Macdonald, Rev. George Browne, 201
MacDonald, J. C., 529n
MacDonell, Hugh Guion, 387
Mackenzie, Alexander Campbell, 529n
Maclean, Malcolm, 603n
McLennan, John Ferguson, 53, 79n, 275,
310
Maclise, Daniel, 114n, 124n, 647
McCracken, Francis, 28n, 37, 44, 49
Macdougall, William Brown, *The Blessed*

696

Müller, Baroness, 517
Müller, Frances H., 473n
Mulready, William, 127n
Munro, Alexander, 47, 49, 52, 53n, 59, 66, 74n, sculptures by, for Oxford Museum, 77; blackballed at Hogarth Club, 100
Murray, Alma, 489n, 495, 549n
Murray, Charles Fairfax, xxiii, xxxii, 55n, 147, buys objects from Tudor House prior to sale, 426; 429, WMR finds, "lying in wait for me," 507; WMR sells, "some minor specimens" of DGR, 507n; 544n, WMR sells, "a few things left by Christina," 586n; 631, WMR gives, early drawing by DGR, 631n
Murray III, John, 240, 440n, 625, 626n
Murray, Leigh, 496n
Muther, Richard, 589n, 590

N

Napoleon I (Napoleon Bonaparte), 286
Napoleon III (Charles Louis Napoleon Bonaparte), 24, 107, 109, 168n, 181n, 182, 233, WMR calls, M. Verhuell, 249; 251, 260n, 283
Nash, Rev. Joseph John Glendinning, 485, preaches "Memorial Sermon" on CGR, 576
National Gallery, "new ... row" about, 67; funds of, "almost nil," 469n; Catalogue of, "crammed with mistakes," 611
National Portrait Gallery, xxix, 157, 164, 173, 582-84, 588-89, 590-91
Neal, Thomas, 609
Neale, John Mason, 155
Nettleship, John Trivett, 241, 275
Newbolt, Henry, 620n
Newcastle Literary and Philosophical Society, 334n 3 & 4
Newman & Co., 401n
Newman, Francis William, 144
Newman, Miss, 356n
New Quarterly Magazine, 366
Newton, Charles Thomas, 368
Nichol, Jane Stewart (Mrs. John), 390-91
Nichol, John, 385, 390, 391, 399
Nicoll, William Robertson, xxi, "an anybody or a nobody?", 609; 609n
Nightingale, Florence, 122n

Noir, Victor, 250n
Norquoy, Mrs., 23, 27, 31, 39, 48, 66
North American Review, ed. explains papers published by, "impersonal in their form," 139n
North London School of Drawing, 80
North's Monthly Magazine, 26-27
North, William, 26-27, 59
Northcote, Walter Stafford, 2d Earl of Iddesleigh, 554
Norton, Caroline Elizabeth, 67
Norton, Charles Eliot, xxii, 85n, 87n, 88n, *On the Original Paintings of Dante*, 138; 146n, 147, 160, 171, 177n, DGR's letters to, "of most uncommon interest," 602
Norton, Thomas Brinsley, 67
Nostredame, Jean de, *Les Vies des plus célèbres et anciens Poëtes Provensaux*, 110

O

Oakes, John Wright, 92n
O'Connor, William Douglas, xxii, *The Good Gray Poet*, 163, 164, 186, 191 & n; 164n, 248, 275
O'Conor, Charles Patrick, 351
O'Driscoll, W. Justin, 282
O'Grady, Standish James (Arthur Clive), 335, 340-41
Oliphant, Laurence, 83n
Oliphant, Margaret (Mrs. Laurence), 122n
Olyett, 586n
Ongaro, Francesco Dall', 152
Orchardson, Sir William Quiller, 554
Orme, Charles, 17n, 288n
Orme, Eliza (Mrs. Charles), 17, 57, 168, 287-88, 598
Orme, Emily Rosaline (Mrs. David Masson), 41n, 47
Orme, Helen, 40
Orrock, James, 599
O'Shaughnessy, Arthur, 241n, 368, death of, 391, 392; 403
Ostend, nobody has "anything but billingsgate to say of," 50
Outram, Leonard, Outram v. Furnivall, 516
Oxenford, John, 21, 310n
Oxford Union Murals, 91, "curious, and with a ruddy bloom of health and pluck about them," 92

P

Paganini, Niccolò, 1
Page, William, 65
Paget, Sir Augustus Berkeley, 387
Paget, Francis, Bishop of Oxford, 550
Palgrave, Sir Francis, 111
Palgrave, Francis Turner, *Golden Treasury*, 108n; 111, "better worth hearing than Tom Taylor," 136; denies "share in producing the withdrawal" of ACS's *Poems and Ballads*, 155, 160; 264
Pall Mall Gazette, 382
Pall Mall Magazine, 615
Paris, WMR observes "individual ruins" following second siege of, 277
Parker & Co., 78, 93n
Parker, John William, 92
Parker, Robert, 246n
Parkes, W. Kineton, 516
Parsons (undertaker), 524-25
Pater, Walter, 548n
Patmore, Coventry, contributes to *Germ*, 9, 11; 17, 21, 23, 27, 30, 33, 38, 47, *The Angel in the House*, 52, 66, 76; 74, 76, 97, 100n, 111, second marriage of, 133; 199n, 515, and P.R.B., 598-99; Rossetti brothers' enthusiasm for poetry of, 598
Patmore, Emily (Mrs. Coventry), 17n, 28n, 30, 33, 76
Patmore, Gurney, 35
Patmore, Peter George, 52
Paton, Sir Joseph Noel, 432n, 480n
Patteson & Co., J. & H., 458
Patteson, Henry, 458
Patti, Adelina, 529n
Paul, Charles Kegan, 467, 493
Paul, Saint, 118
Payne, James Bertrand, 140n, 140-41, 142n, 150n, "wipe at," in H. Morley's review of ACS's *Poems and Ballads*, "most deserved," 152; "Jewing" ACS, 155; 155-56, Woolner reports, withdrew ACS's *Poems and Ballads* "on compulsion," 156n; authorizes sale of copies of withdrawn *Poems and Ballads*, 167, 169; 198, WMR's business relations with, "satisfactory," 210; 242
Payne, John, 328
Peacock, Thomas Love, 212, 370
Pearse, Mabelle, 585n

Pearson's, 173
Peddic, Miss, 353
Pemberton (lawyer), 435n
Pennell, Henry Cholmondeley, 159, 310n
Pennell, Joseph, *Life of Whistler*, WMR assists with, 175n, 654, 656-57; 613
Percy, Thomas, *The Hermit of Warkworth*, 39
Pétion, Jérôme, and Maximilien Robespierre, *Observations sur la nécessité de la réunion des hommes de bonne foi contre les intrigans, proposées à tous les Français*, 169n, 179
Petrarch, 429
Petrici, Helen, 364, 507
Philips, Ambrose, 466
Phillips, Thomas, 164
Philological Society, *English Dictionary* prepared by, 395
Pickering, Basil Montagu, 311, 314, 318, 358
Pickersgill, Frederick Richard, 662
Pickersgill, Henry Hall, 34n
Pietrocola-Rossetti, Isabella, 277, 342, 353-54, 390, 539
Pietrocola-Rossetti, Teodorico, 44, 204n, 223, 231, 277, 303, 353-54, 390, 402, 539
Pillischer, Moritz (optician), 315
Pindar, 399
Pinti, Raphael, 301
Pissarro, Esther, 652 & n
Pissarro, Lucien, 652 & n
Pistrucci, Filippo, 3n, 402n
Pistrucci, Luigi, 3
Placee (not identified), 113
Platt, Robert, 69n
Plint, Thomas E., 102n
Pocock, Crawford J., 602
Podmore, Austin, 497n
Poe, Edgar Allan, 21, 38, 328, 333
Polidori, Charlotte, xxvi, 44, offers £100 to assist with move to Tudor House, 125; 316n, 367, 484, 485-86, 487, 490, 509n, 525, 527
Polidori, Eliza, xxvi, 44, 121, 179n, 431, 485-86, 487, 490, 510n, 557
Polidori, Gaetano, xxx, 3n, 44, 232n, 430n
Private Press: books issued by, 581n, 610-11, 634; DGR sells press and types to Tupper firm, 611
586n, 591n

700

Polidori, John William, xxi, WMR offers portrait of, to National Portrait Gallery, 583, 584, 588-89, 590, Gaetano Polidori's "greatly beloved and lamented John," 591n; 602, *The Vampyre*, ACS's high opinion of, 628n

Polidori, Margaret, 44, 121, 125, 585n

Pollen, John Hungerford, 91n, 112n

Polydore, Henrietta, 219, 316n

Polydore, Henrietta (Mrs. H. F. Polydore), WMR describes, 316n

Polydore, Henry Francis, 220n, 315, 466n, 537n

Ponchielli, Amilcare, *La Gioconda*, WMR attends performance of, at Covent Garden (1883), 449

Poole, Paul Falconer, 49

Potter, Georgiana, 510n

Potts, Robert Alfred, 507n, 541, 632n

Powell, Frederick York, 549n

Poynter, Ambrose, 29

Poynter, Sir Edward John, xviii, 436n

P.R.B. Journal, xvii, 4, 598, 602, 616

Pre-Raphaelite Brotherhood (see also WMR: Pre-Raphaelite Brotherhood), xviii, 3n, 5-8, meetings of, 11, 20, 34, 35; 27, 30, 31, 34, 37-38, 46, 499, 603n

Preston, Sydney E., 489

Prickard, A. O., 543n

Prinsep, Henry Thoby, 92, 145

Prinsep, Mrs. Henry Thoby, 92, 135n, 145

Prinsep, Valentine Cameron, 91n, "a most loveable fellow," 92; 435

Proctor, Ellen A., 579

Prout, Samuel, 95n

Purcell, John Samuel, 127

Q

Quilter, Harry, 385-86, 590

R

Rae, George, 423, 435

Rake, A. T., 667n

Ralston, William, 368

Randall, Mr., 484n

Raphael, *St. John the Baptist*, 278

Rattazzi, Urbano, 181n

Ravenna, WMR visits mosaics at, 277

Read, Thomas Buchanan, *Poems*; *Lays and Ballads*, 33

Reader, 128

Redgrave, Richard, 30, 50

Reeves and Turner, 478n

Rennie, John, 332

Rétif (Restif) de la Bretonne, Nicolas-Edme, 628n

Reveley, Henry, 206-7

Revell, William F., 512, 533

Reynolds, G. W. M., 18

Reynolds, John Hamilton, 206

Rhodes, Cecil, 622

Ricard, Gustave, 47

Ricciardi, Giuseppe Napoleone, Anti-Council organized by, 233, 235, 236, 237, 238, 241, 244, 246, 247n, 249, 250-51

Rintoul, Henrietta, xxiv, WMR's letters to, untraced, xxxii; 100n, 130n

Rintoul, Robert Stephen, xxiv, 100n, 101n

Roberts, Captain, 370

Roberts, David, 127n

Roberts, Frederick Thomas, 566, 566-67

Robertson, Charles, 114n

Robertson, Eric S., 498n, 501, 503n

Robertson, Henry Robert, 114n

Robespierre, Maximilien, 169, 237, 381, 397

Robinson, George Frederick Samuel, 1st Marquis of Ripon, 484

Robinson, George T., 346, 358n, 376n

Robinson, Mary (Mrs. James Darmesteter; later Mme Émile Duclaux), 346n, 403, 484

Roche, Antonin, 2n

Rogeard, M., 244

Ronge, Bertha, 23, 32, 50

Ronge, Johannes, 23, 32, 34n, 50

Rooke, Thomas Matthews, 649n

Roscoe, William Caldwell, 24n

Rose, James Anderson, 128, 374n

Rosetta, Frances (Mrs. Alphonse Legros), 166n

Rossetti, Arthur, xxvi, xxvii, 328n, 356, 359, 361, 367, 370, 375, 403, 404, 407, 408, 409, 411, 418, 431, 440, 452, 488, 552, 556, 566, 567, present at FMB's death, 568, "quietly kind in the whole mournful matter," 569; 571, "A Rossetti addicted to science," 602; 627, 632, 648, 651, 673 & n

Rossetti, Christina Georgina, xvii, xxi, WMR's writings on, xxi, xxii; WMR executor of, xxii-xxiii; WMR's relations with, xxv-xxvi, 2n 2 & 13; xxvii, xxviii, xxix, xxxii, 1, 3n, 11n, 17n, 23, 33, "goes on ploddingly ... with her drawing studies," 39

HEALTH: 39, 60, 124, 137, 201, 273, 277, "deplorably ill for months," 278; 279, looks continue "amiss," 282; 283, 287, 290, 292, 293, 294-95, 296, 304, 309, 344, 346, 402, operation for cancer, 554, 555-57, "contemplates immediate death as a *possibility*," 555, recovery from operation, 558-59; "undoubtedly dying," 574; WMR discusses, with M. Bell, 597-98

42, 43, 44, 45n, 46, 94 & n, 97n, 99, 106, 107, visits France with WMR, 115-16, 118; 120, WBS attributes "predetermined notions" to, 121; 127n, WMR keeps her company in Albany Street, 135; Browning calls on, 136; 144, 149n, 159, 179n, 219n, 221, 224, 243, 279, 287, 291n, 302, 309, 316, 326, 327-28, 330, 333n, 341-42, 345n, 346, 347, 347-48, 348, 349, 354, 356, 357, 358, 359, 360, 362, 363, 364, 368, 383, 390, "isolated devoteeism" of, 396; 402, looks after DGR at Birchington, 403, 404, 405, 410; 405, 407, 411-12, 414, 415, 420, 429, 431, WMR sounds out, whether she will accept dedication of ACS's *Century of Roundels*, 443; 453, contributes £10 for DGR's gravestone, 455, 459n, 464; 456, agrees with WMR's editorial principles in *Collected Works* of DGR, 481n; 484, at mother's death, "bears herself well — only giving way at moments," 485, 487; inherits £4000 from mother, 488; gives WMR £2000 "to compensate ... for the subsistence which for many years she received from" him, 488; "position with her aged and infirm aunts ... a very dull one," 490; stumbling block to WMR's family staying with, "any tendency ... to proselytize the kids," 490; 509n, 518, 525, 543, 546, "the most modest" of authors, 551; "secluded habits and shy disposition" of, 551; WMR visits, during recuperation from cancer operation at Brighton, 558-59; refuses to read WBS's *AN*, "knowing that it contains matter ... with which she prefers to remain unacquaint-

ed," 575; death of, 575; obituaries of, "very earnestly laudatory," 575n; memorial service for, 576; WMR upbraids Macmillan for not readvertising poems of, 577; WMR invites Wise to inspect books belonging to, at Torrington Square, 577; M. Bell's interest in, 578, 579, 586; WMR "inapt" as biographer of, "earnest Christian ... right biographer," 578; "mourning-cards" for, 578; her sense of "threatenings" of Gospel "very lively," 580; "her humility of self-estimate," 580; WMR invites friends of, to select mementoes at Torrington Square, 580, 581; WMR offers portrait of, to National Portrait Gallery, 582-83, 588-89, 590-91, 593; DGR's 1848 portrait of, shows her "advantageously (but not flattered) as regards good looks," 582; portrait of, by J. Collinson, 583; WMR sells portrait and MS. of, to S. Morse, 585n; WMR sells books and "a few personal items" of, at Sotheby's, 585; WMR sorts books left by, at Torrington Square, 586n; WMR gives up Torrington Square, 587; copy of DGR's *Sir Hugh the Heron* owned by, 589-90; her "affairs of the heart," names not mentioned by WMR to M. Bell, 597n, WMR prefers names "should not be printed," 600; royalties from books by, paid to WMR, 600; royalties from books by, "always about double" those from DGR's books, 600n; 602, 603n, reviews of Bell's *Christina Rossetti* show "a certain re-action to her disadvantage," 605n; 606, "*mature Italian verses*" by, not deserving of scorn, 609; sonnets by, "so good as barely to admit of being bettered," 609; 610, 613, 618, 629, 631, WMR did not discuss religion with, "the only course conducive to our mutual comfort," 639; WMR suggests Macmillan publish "2 comparatively small volumes" of, 640; 642, 668

WORKS (see also WMR, Books): *Advent*, 576n, 576, 638-39; *Annus Domini*, 316, 491n; *Commonplace and other Short Stories*, 260; *Goblin Market*, 159; *Goblin Market and Other Poems*, 122, 144, review of, in *Examiner*, 161n; 637n, 637; *I Will Lift Up My Eyes*,

702

Miller's poems, 271; 272, "not absolutely without republican leanings," 275; 276n, WMR advises, to ignore "Fleshly School" attack, 281, 283; plans "The Stealthy School of Criticism," 282-83; breakdown in 1872, WMR's reaction to, 287, 290; Marshall "distinctly objects" to WMR joining party of, in Scotland, 288; WMR arranges sale of his blue china, 288-89, 290; drawing room at Cheyne Walk "terribly denuded now that the china is gone," 292; WMR agrees with WBS in taking a "far from favourable" view of his condition, 293; WMR attends to his "dismaying" bills, 293, 296; WMR believes he should be placed in an asylum, 293; WMR sorts out his bills at Stobhall, 298, 299, 300; bank forgery in name of, 301; "natural" manner of, in September 1872, 301; WMR "can discern nothing wrong or queer" in, 302; his "lingering" prejudice against Browning, 303; WMR discusses Jane Morris with, 303; recurrence of his "delusive notions," 304; 312, 318, WMR explains, "days and weeks may possibly elapse before I see him," 319; 321, 326, 329n, 332n, 333n, WMR hesitates to interrupt when Mrs. Sumner with, 343, 344; parts from G. Hake, 348-49; 354, WMR doubts "*real* utility" of his staying at Cheyne Walk with, 356; WMR tries to caution, 357; WMR spends evening with, 359; WMR's tribulation over health of, 360; writes to *Times* and *Athenaeum* about forgeries of his drawings, 368; 376n, WMR looks after, 378; 379n, refuses to write lines in Locker's MS. of Sir W. Scott, 383n; 385, 389, opinion of WMR's *Democratic Sonnets*, 391n, 392; WMR responds to advice of, not to publish *Democratic Sonnets*, 396-97; WMR encourages, to stay at Birchington, 404n; draws check for WMR shortly before his death, 411, WMR expects "serious embarrassment" if check not honored, 414n, F. S. Ellis loans WMR £300 when check not honored, 435n; will of, 411-12; WMR anticipates "very large" debts chargeable to estate of, 412; death and funeral of, 414-15; WMR gets face and hand of,

moulded, 416, 419-20; WMR refuses Fanny Cornforth's request to view body of, 416; WMR plans exhibition of, 417, 418
ROYAL ACADEMY exhibition of: 417, 418, 421-22, WMR hopes "to exercise some reasonable amount of influence over," 431; WMR discusses, with Leighton, 435
Burlington Club exhibition of, 417n; WMR organizes selection of mementoes by friends of, 420
"REMAINING WORKS" sale: FMB prepares paintings and designs for, 421, 423-24; WMR prepares catalogue of, 444; proceeds from, "more meagre … than I had thought probable," 447
CHEYNE WALK, sale of contents: WMR plans, 421, 427; pre-sale disposal of items to Howell, 424-25, and to F. Murray, 426; WMR corrects proofs of sale catalogue, 426, 428; "success of the sale startles all whom I speak with," 429; "books went … pretty nearly as well as the other things," 429; WMR buys in black cupboard which had belonged to Gabriele Rossetti, 433n
L. Valpy's claim against estate of, 426, 444, 444-45; C. Fry's claim against estate of, 432; WMR surrenders lease of Cheyne Walk, 434; "Rossetti Gallery" exhibition, 436n; 437, Hall Caine claims WMR "played the most inconspicuous part of all" during final illness of, 438n; letters to his mother, "pleasing for their familiar affection," 439; WMR has "no legal control" over magazine engravings after pictures of, 439n; Stephens plans book on, 440; WMR swears to will of, 440-41; letters to, rumored to be in circulation, 441-42; value of estate, 442n, 442-43, 469; WMR offers to pay Marshall for attending, at Birchington, 442; posthumous reputation of, 443; Fanny Cornforth makes "bothering demand" against estate of, 447, 449-51, 454, 457
GRAVESTONE of, at Birchington: 451, 453, 455, F. Rossetti wants cross as part of, 456-57; inscription on, 458; put in place, 462n; 464

memorial window to, All Saints, Birchington, 451-52, 453, 455-56, 461-62, 464; royalties on books by, received by WMR and F. Rossetti, 452; medallion portrait of, proposed for Birchington, 452n, 461-62, 464n; memorial to, in London, 452n, 463-64, 468, correspondent in *Pall Mall Gazette* attacks memorial, 491, unveiling of memorial, 510; "manoeuvres" to dilute his chloral, 455n; WMR anxious "to know what moderate sum of money" he will inherit from estate of, 458; opinion of Whitman's poems, 460; WMR urged, "not to go 'diplomatizing'" to have *Poems* 1870 reviewed, 463; 467, "decidedly bad" prices at Christie's for pictures by, 468; his "bad habit of reworking upon pictures," 469n; 471, WMR considers new publisher for books of, 477-78n; 480, 494, and Bernhard Smith, 499; WMR pressures E. Robertson to include biography of, in "Great Writers" series, 503n; 508, 524, 538n, "sense of abiding grief" for loss of, 538; mind of, would have "weakened most woefully" had he lived longer, 539; WMR surmises "an appalling amount of unseemly chaff" in letters of, to Howell, 543; lost cartoons by, recovered, 543; forgeries of, offered at Sotheby's, 544, 545; statements about, in WBS's *AN*, "unkind, unhandsome, inaccurate," 561, 575; WMR denies he was made "seriously ill" by breakdown of, in 1872, 562; WMR "feared," "not at all," 562; 566, 570, 576, early model for Valentine in Hunt's picture, 594; and Patmore, 598, 599; "a very good letter-writer," 602; 603n, 609, 610, 611, saw "such women" as he painted, 611; 613, Hunt's "tone of feeling and talk with regard to," 616; WMR and C. E. Norton dissatisfied with portrait of, in Watts's *Aylwin*, 618; C. E. Norton recalls, 618n; 621, 622, 629, 635 & n, 638-39, 641-42, treatment of, in *PR & PRB*, 645, 646, 647, 649, 651n; 656, 661n, and Charles Wells, 662-63; proposed American edition of, 668

WORKS (Paintings and Drawings) (see also WMR, Art Criticism [Artists]):

Annunciation (design for a pulpit), 383; *Arthur's Tomb*, 63; *Astarte Syriaca*, 428, 433n, 613; *Aurea Catena*, 427n; *Beata Beatrix*, 426, 445, "an *exact portrait*" of Lizzie, 611; *Beatrice Meeting Dante at a Marriage Feast*, 41n, 63, 386n, 602; *Before the Battle*, 602; *La Bella Mano*, 469n; *La Belle Dame Sans Merci*, 68n; *The Beloved*, 139n, 646; *The Blessed Damozel*, 383, sale of, 391, 392; *The Blue Bower*, DGR "considers his best piece of painting," 138; *Borgia*, 20n; *The Bower Garden*, 631; *The Bower Meadow*, 16n, 594, 654; Brown, F. M., Portrait of, 591n; Browning, Portrait of, 63, 105, 436; *A Christmas Carol*, 83n; *Dante and Beatrice*, 49; *Dante's Dream at the Time of the Death of Beatrice*, 41n, 63, 282n, 368, 400n, 426; *Dante's Vision of Matilda Gathering Flowers*, 631n; *La Donna Della Finestra*, 424n, 427n, 469n; *Dr. Johnson at the Mitre*, 102n; *Domizia Scaligera*, 343n; *Ecce Ancilla Domini!* (*Annunciation*), 37, 386n, bought by National Gallery, 487; *The First Anniversary of the Death of Beatrice*, WMR sits for head of Dante, 45n; 46, 51n; *Found*, 53n, 57, 63, 393, studies for, 659-60, 661; 660 & n 2, 661; *Fra Pace*, 68n; *The Gate of Memory*, 423n; *Giotto Painting the Portrait of Dante*, 28n, 37, 386n, 444; *The Girlhood of Mary Virgin*, 582; *Goblin Market*, illustrations of, sample leaf of woodcuts, 582n; *The Heart of the Night*, 125n; *Helen of Troy*, 128, 623; Herbert, Ruth, Portrait of, 302; "Illustrated Scrap-book," designs in, 1; *Joan of Arc*, 128, 403, 426, 445; *Juliette* (lithograph), 582n; *Lady Lilith*, his "very completest piece of harmonious executive art," 154; Leathart, Mrs. James, Portrait of, 125n, 128; *The Loving Cup*, 447n; *Mariana in the Moated Grange*, 125n; *Mary Magdalene at the Door of Simon the Pharisee*, 176, 423n, copy of, by Shields, 452n, 585n; 580n; *Mary Magdalene Leaving the House of Feasting*, 176; *Mnemosyne*, 426; Morris, Mrs. William, Portrait of, 427n; *My Lady Greensleeves*, 660n; *The Nativity*, 63; *Paetus and Arria*, 287n; *Pandora*,

426; *Paolo and Francesca da Rimini*, 63, 124; *The Passover in the Holy Family*, 63, 452n; *La Pia*, 445; Playing-Cards (lithographs), 582n; Polidori, Charlotte, Portrait of, 48n; Polidori, Gaetano, Portrait of, 585n; Polydore, Henrietta, Portrait of, 582n; *Proserpine*, 403, 423, 427n, 445, "an *exact portrait*" of Mrs. Morris, 611; *Risen at Dawn*, 427n; *Rosa Triplex*, "grievous" condition of, 434, 559-60; "central head represents ... face of Miss Wilding," 559; Rossetti, Christina, Portraits of, 582, 584, 584-85, 587, 588, 589, 592; Rossetti, Christina, and Mrs. Gabriele Rossetti, Portrait of, 584, 588, 591 & n, 593; Self Portrait (with WMR), 472; Rossetti, Frances, Portraits of, 585, 586n; Rossetti, Gabriele, Portrait of, 402; Rossetti, Lucy, Portrait of, 315, 480; *Rossovestita*, 41n, 386n; Ruskin, Portrait of, "a little too robust," 602; *The Salutation of Beatrice*, 392; *Sea-Spell*, 559; *The Seed of David*, 69n, 74, 108, 386n, 435n; *Sibylla Palmifera*, 154, 559; Siddal, Elizabeth, Portraits of, 604, 621, 628; *Silence*, 290, 299; *Sir Launcelot's Vision of the Sanc Grael* (Oxford Union), 92; Sofa, painted by, 425; *The Sonnet*, 661; *Sorrentino*, 631n; *The Sphinx*, 410, 416; Swinburne, Portrait of, 436; Tennyson, *Poems* (1857), illustrations for, 74, 78, Tennyson's special liking for "Arthur watched by weeping queens," 99; 166; *Tennyson Reading Maud*, 621n; Thompson, Margaret, Portrait of, 41n; *Troy Town*, 130n; *Venus Verticordia*, 138, 154, 469n, 611; *A Vision of Fiammetta*, 367-68
WORKS: (Poetry and Prose) (see also WMR, Books; Literary Articles and Notes): *Algernon Stanhope*, 564n; *Arme Heinrich (Henry the Leper)*, MS. of, 540n, 636, publication of, by Boston Bibliophile Society, 635; *Autumn Idleness (House of Life)*, 231, 654; *Ave*, 217, 219n 2 & 10, 224n, 226n 3, 228-29n 2-5 & 12; *Ballads and Sonnets*, WMR corrects proofs of, 399; 445, royalties from, 452n, Tauchnitz ed. of, 452n; 477-78n, 481n, copy of, inscribed by DGR to mother, 630, corrected proofs

of, 630; *Beauty and the Bird (The Bullfinch)*, 221; *The Blessed Damozel*, 84n, 219n 3 & 4, 226n, 229n 6 & 7; "Book of Nonsense" epigram on WBS, 242, on R. Buchanan, 281-82n, 283; *The Burden of Nineveh*, 219n 5, 7, 8 & 28, 226n 1-2, 229n; *The Card Dealer*, 130n, 231; *The Choice (House of Life)*, 218, 219n, 226n; *The Cloud Confines*, 492n; *A Dark Day (House of Life)*, 230; "The Death of Topsy," 572; *Dennis Shand*, 437, 630n; *The Early Italian Poets*, 122, 144, 630, WMR sells MSS. of translations published in, to Cockerell, 630n; *Eden Bower*, WMR sells MS. of, to Wise, 521n; *For a Venetian Pastoral, by Giorgione*, 222n, 226n 9; *For Our Lady of the Rocks, by Leonardo*, 222n; *For Ruggiero and Angelica, by Ingres*, 222n; *Hand and Soul*, 101n, 222n, 226n 10; *Hand and Soul* (Privately Printed), WMR sells copy of, to Wise, 536, 537, to Cockerell, 630n; *Heart's Compass (House of Life)*, 581n; *Jan Van Hunks*, 406n, 671n; *Jenny*, 281, Wise asks permission from WMR to copy out "original commencement" of, 520; *The King's Tragedy*, 394, 399n; *A Last Confession*, 219n, 222-23, 231-32; *A Little While*, 219n; *Love-Lily*, 219n, 229n; *The Love-moon (House of Life)*, 219n; *Love's Nocturn*, 223, 226n, 229n 8, 9, 14 & 15, 229-30; *Mary's Girlhood (For a Picture)*, 222n, 230; *Mary in Summer*, 217; *A Match with the Moon*, 231, 310n; *My Father's Close*, 219n; *My Sister's Sleep*, 223; *Nuptial Sleep (Placatâ Venere)*, *(House of Life)*, 218, 221, 230; *On the Refusal of Aid Between Nations*, 223; *The Orchard Pit*, 232n; *Parted Love (House of Life)*, 231; *Penumbra*, 230; *Plighted Promise*, 219n 13 & 14; *Poems* (Privately Printed), corrected proofs of, 630; WMR sells copy of, to Cockerell, 630n, and to Dodd, Mead & Co., 633-34; *Poems* 1870, WMR corrects proofs of, 216-32, reviews of, 254, corrected proofs of, WMR offers to Cockerell, 630; *Poems* 1881, royalties on, 452, "proposed cheap stereotype of," 477n, 502n; 481n; *Proserpina* (in Italian), 305n; *The*

283; 290, 302n, 309, her "exalted sense of duty," 309; 316, final illness and death of, 342-48 *passim*, 362n; *Rivulets*, 537; 559, *In Morte di Guendalina Talbot*, 577n, 581, 592n, 610-11; 580, WMR offers portrait of, to National Portrait Gallery, 583, 584, 588; 597, 639

Rossetti, Mary, xxvi, xxvii, 328n, ACS's poem on birth of, 397; 398, 399, 400, 407, 408, 410, 418, 431, 442, 455, 468, 543, 546, 554, 586n, 639, 641, 644, 646, 647, rheumatoid arthritis rules her "with a rod of iron. She takes it all with great pluck and fine spirts," 649; 650, 655, 659, 662, 664, 666, 670, 673 & n

Rossetti, Michael, xxvii, ACS's poem on birth of, 397; 400, 404, 407, 408, 418, 431, death of, 442, ACS's poem on, 443

Rossetti, Olivia (Agresti), xxvi-xxvii, xxviii, "Anecdotage of an Interpreter," xxxiiin; 327, 328 & n, ACS's poem on birth of, 329, 330-31; 337, 340, 342, 344, 353, 360, 361, 367, 375, 403, 405, 407, 408, 414, 431, 432, 433, 452, 488, 495, 526, 531, 536, 555, 556, 558, 568, 576n, 580 & n, 591, 603-4, 614, 618, 639, 648, 659, visits ACS with WMR, 663n; 669-70, 671, 673n

ROSSETTI, WILLIAM MICHAEL
Art Criticism (General):
    assessment of, xviii, xxii, xxiii; Ruskin quoted on, xviii; G. Du Maurier quoted on, xviii; in *Critic*, 19n; British Institution Exhibition (1852), 26; French art, 47-48; English art, "possesses nothing that can be called a school or a standard," 48; on Pre-Raphaelites in *Crayon*, 54; recommended to *Crayon* by Ruskin, 55; in *Edinburgh Weekly Review*, 71, 74, 78, WBS thinks articles by, "best things in it," 83n; Oxford Union murals, 92; recommended to *Spectator* by W. C. Williams, 93n; resigns from *Spectator*, 106; dropped by *Saturday Review*, 106; R. A. Exhibition (1861), 117-18; Pre-Raphaelitism, "seems to have done its work," 117; in *Weldon's Register*, 123; in *London Review*, 124n, 128; in *Reader*, 130n; in *Fine Arts Quarterly*

Review, 131; in *Chronicle*, 173n, 176; has "very few theories about art," 264; "representation of anything shifting and transitory ... peculiarly difficult in art," 278; in *Encyclopaedia Britannica*, 341; replaced by C. Carr as reviewer in *Academy*, 368-69n; agrees with Whistler that "the publishing of art-critiques by non-professionals ... deserving of protest," 373; Japanese art, 629; willingness to see "good" in recent art, 648; Salon des Refusés (1863), 656

Art Criticism (Artists):
    Alma-Tadema, L., 403, 554; Brown, F. M., 31, 468, 487n, 510, 531, 546; Browne, H. K., 613-14; Collinson, J., 588; Doyle, R., 613-14; Fisher, S. M., 554; Hook, J. C., 111, 117; Hughes, A., 65, 278, 283; Hunt, Holman, 21, 30, 37-38, 38, 46, 48, 64, 118, 192, 483; Landseer, E., 111; Leech, J., 613-14; Legros, A., 165; Leighton, F., 436, 554; Manet, illustrations to Mallarmé trans. Poe's *Raven*, 328, 392; Memling, H., 629; Millais, J. E., 30, 38, 65, 82, 111, 554; Munro, A., 77; Orchardson, W. Q., 554; Raphael, 278-79; Redgrave, R., 50; Rossetti, D. G., 154, 367-68, 559-60, 588, 613; Scott, W. B., does "historic art ... better than any other Briton alive," 120; 129; Seddon, T., 73-74, 77; Shields, F. J., 452n; Solomon, Simeon, 99, 111, 634-35; Tintoretto, 264; Titian, 278; Turner, J. M. W., 121-22; Whistler, J. M., 111, 646; Woolner, T., 72, 77, 118

Character and Attitudes:
    xvii, xxiii, xxvi-xxix, Job "one of the great books of the world," xxvii; humor, xxvii-xxviii; encouraged his children to call him Fofus, "funny, fussy old fogey," xxvii, 354n; xxxi-xxxii, mother's influence on, 2n; father's influence on, 2n; "hope of succeeding at last," 21; "Never ... a disbeliever in ghosts," 30, 443; "scarcely ever convinced of anything either way," 60; "my humdrum style," 60; reads Swedenborg's *Heaven and Hell* "with great delight and wonder," 91; feels "more *sympathy* for the antique

in art, literature, and tone of character, than I used to," 114; 126n, apologizes for "dogmatic, pragmatic, or dictatorial tone" in letter to Howell, 148; equanimity over Ruskin's strictures, 173-74n; despairs at what tolerance and justice are "understood to mean," 174; "nothing saps character so much as the commonplaces of respectability," 194; "my usual inexpansive style," 215; sets apart "a definite portion of income annually for charitable purposes," 215; his name "one of only few and faintish reverberations (apart from family associations)," 236; "a pacific ... disposition," 265; "unfit to mix in any society" during DGR's illness in 1872, 287; WBS describes his state in 1872 as "critical he is so desponding," 288n; acknowledges "the pull upon my working faculties and my spirits" caused by DGR's breakdown, 290; admits "many defects of selfishness, temper," 309n; denigrates his critical performance in comparison to ACS, 384-85; strongly refutes statements in H. Quilter's "New Renaissance," 385-86; "To set me going is to set me going on my own path," 396; dislikes "bowing down in the House of Rimmon," 397; trusts to "stand unbent" (Dante) in face of DGR's death, 408; tactful handling of FMB, 421, 423; "determining effect" of Emerson's "Self-Reliance" on, 422; hard-headed business dealings with Howell, 424-25; "resolved to keep on good kindly terms with Caine," 437; "to ride the high horse" in dealing with Fanny Cornforth's I.O.U., 450; "I 'arm myself with stoicism'," 485; "I am the most pacific of men," 500; as gets older "more impressionable not only by the pathetic but also by the *beautiful* things in great poetry," 500; vigorously proclaims that Shelley Society has nothing to do with the "sexual morals of ... members," 503; Furnivall calls "the harmonizing and uniting influence" in Shelley Society, 513n; surmises that "the highest ideal of life is to accept everything exactly as it comes, without emotion and without comment," 525; feels "particularly drear and helpless" in face

of F. Hueffer's death, 526; F. Hueffer's funeral, "Another day of extreme gloom," 526; "poor hand at *expressing* sympathy," 528; taking job at age 15 to support family, "a hard necessity," 528; "anomalous ... and highly irksome" should he have to provide for Emma Brown and Hueffer family, 529n; tendency to give "a thing up as past hope and irretrievable," 538; misses "the good old days of the expulsion of Shelley for the *Necessity of Atheism*, the howling over *Poems and Ballads*," 550; urges forbearance in relations between LR and Cathy Hueffer, 552; "in much sorrow and oppression of mind" over CGR's cancer, 555; "blameable habit of never going anywhere," 560; "depressed and not very well," 563n; "Fate has sometimes seemed rather determined to hunt us down," 568; prospect of caring for family after LR's death "most alarming," 574; "a harmless hypochondriac," 580; critics inclined to set down as an "over-candid simpleton": "But 'let the galled jade wince'," 613; "a Government-clerk giving his spare hours to newspaper-critiques etc.," 643; English "hideously apathetic ... where only intellect is concerned," 667; refuses an Italian honor, 669; W. S. Blunt notes his "manner precise, with considerable dignity," 671n; Blunt considers he showed his "Italian origin," 671n; S. C. Cockerell notes "his inflexible rectitude of conduct," 673n

Civil Servant:
enters Excise Office, xvii, xxiii; rises through the ranks, xxiii, xxiv, 43, 215; xxv, retires from Inland Revenue, xxvi, xxviii; job in Inland Revenue never a sinecure, xxvi; position as, restrains his political expression, xxxi, 275-76, 530; doubts he will become Secretary of Inland Revenue, 396

Family, Relationship with Rossetti:
xvii, xxiii-xxiv, during DGR's breakdown in 1872, xxiv-xxv, 287, keeps family informed about DGR's state at Kelmscott, 302; xxv-xxvi, urges family to return to London, 43; resolves to continue living with family after his marriage, 309

658n; 660, 661

Fine Art, Chiefly Contemporary, 169n, 171n, 373

Gabriele Rossetti, A Versified Autobiography, xxvii, "little or no money" to be made from, 624-25; difficulties in finding publisher for, 625n

The Germ, Introd. by, 432n, 453, 615n

Keats (Moxon's Popular Poets), 256, 257-58

"Leopardi," in *Studies in European Literature, being the Taylorian Lectures, 1889-1899,* xxxi

Life of Keats, xxi, 502, attacked by O. Wilde in *Pall Mall Gazette,* 510-11

Lives of Famous Poets, 327, 344, 354, 375, 384-85, 387, 388, 397, copy of, with notes by DGR, 630

Longfellow (Moxon's Popular Poets), 260, 261

Maude, A Story for Girls by Christina Rossetti, Introd. by, 599-600, Macmillan hesitates to allow publication of poems in, 600n

Memoir of Shelley (With a New Preface), 250n, 366n, 490n

Moxon's Popular Poets, xx, 210, 327, ACS on "Prefatory Lives" in, 375

New Poems by Christina Rossetti, ed. by, 586-87, preparation of, 587n; dedicated to ACS, 592; 594, 599, royalties from, 600n; issue of, embodying WMR's "*latest* revisal," 601; 608, review of, hostile to WMR, probably by Gosse, 610n

Notes on the Royal Academy Exhibition, 1868 (with ACS), declines to undertake a 2d ser., 252; advises ACS about reprinting his portion, 320, 321

Oxford English Dictionary, supplies quotations to, 211n, 395

Poems by J. L. Tupper, 16n, 612, before publication of, WMR introduces "some alteration of diction, polishing of metre, etc.," 613n

Poems by Walt Whitman, xviii, xix-xx, xxii, 176, 177-78, dedication of, 178; 180-88 *passim,* 190-91, 194, publisher satisfied with sale of, 197; 214, 248, 285, 323, 333, 351, 459. Reviews of: *London Review,* 193, 194; *Express,* 193, 194; *Sunday Times,* 193, 194, 195; *Academia,* 193, 194; *Morning*

Star, 194; *Sun,* 195-96, 196; *Athenaeum,* 196; *Saturday Review,* 196; *Examiner,* 196

Poems of Christina Rossetti ("Golden Treasury"), proposes to Macmillan, 640

Poetical Works of Blake, with a Memoir, xxi, 311, 313-14, ACS praises, 319; 375n, MS. of "Prefatory Memoir" sold to F. Burgess, 619

Poetical Works of Christina Rossetti, xxi, proposes to Macmillan, 601; begins work on, 601n; 617, completes, 618-19; Macmillan's wish to delay publication of, 619n; Macmillan ready to publish, 636; Macmillan hesitates over inclusion of SPCK poems, 637-38; "can now go forward, to my no small satisfaction," 638n; corrects, for a reissue, 640

Poetical Works of Shelley (1870), xviii, xx, xxii, 198-203 *passim,* 205-14 *passim,* 233, 242-46 *passim,* 248-49, 251, 307n, 316n, ACS's essay on, 321. Reviews of: *Athenaeum,* 251; *Examiner,* 251

Poetical Works of Shelley (1878), 250n 3, 4 & 6, 252n 5 & 9, 307n, 313n 12 & 14, 345n, 354n, 356n, 358n, 360n, 361n, 363n, passage on C. Clairmont excised from Memoir, 366n; 368n, revision of, 371; 375, reprint of, by J. Slark, 475

A Pre-Raphaelite Collection (Catalogue of J. Leathart Collection), Prefatory Note by, 83n

Pre-Raphaelite Diaries and Letters, origins in "Rossettiana" project, 602; 616, did not sell "at all well," 616n; 625n

Rossetti Papers, xxxii, 282n, origins in "Rossettiana" project, 603n, 625n, 657; 659

Ruskin, Rossetti, Pre-Raphaelitism, 404n, origins in "Rossettiana" project, 603n; publication agreement, 603n; "a goodlooking" book, 603n; large-paper copies of, 603n; F. Burgess designs cover of, 611n; 612, 616n, 618n, 625n

Sir Walter Scott (Moxon's Popular Poets), 262

Shelley, Adonais, xxi, suggested by F. S. Ellis, 542, attacked by J. C. Collins, 543n

Some Reminiscences, 645, 647n, 649, "a

713

27, 46, praises DGR, 49; 53, 54, 55, 57 & n, health, 59; "few men I like better," 59; 63, on Hunt's *Scapegoat*, 64; "a most indefatigable man," 66; 67, 68n, on *Aurora Leigh*, 77; and Seddon Subscription, 77-78, 78-79n, 80; 87 & n, 94, "unconscionable blunderings … in his poetic apprehension," 107; 111, cuts the Hogarth Club, 115; "proposed to take a room in our Chelsea house," 124; invites WMR and DGR to dinner, 126; contributes to amateur exhibition for Lancashire relief, 127n; 143n, and Cruikshank Subscription, 145, 146n, 148; 149n, opinion of ACS's "poetic powers," 153; claims he and DGR taught WMR "whatever he knows about art," 173n; letter from, "somewhat overbearing," 174n; 174, 182n 2 & 3, WMR informs, that "attendance in the witness-box against him [at Whistler v Ruskin trial] was compulsory," 373-74n; 424, praises *Leaves of Grass*, 463; 602, 603n 1, 3 & 4, 617, 631, 656

WORKS: "Addresses on Decorative Colour," 53; *The Elements of Drawing*, 69n, 108n; *Examples of the Architecture of Venice*, 28n; *The Harbours of England*, 66; *Lectures on Architecture and Painting*, 46; 2d letter to *Times* on the Pre-Raphaelites, 22; Letters to *Times* on Holman Hunt, 49; *Modern Painters*, vols. 3 and 4, 69n, 108n; *Notes on the Construction of Sheepfolds*, 21; "Sir Joshua and Holbein," 107; *Stones of Venice*, 22n, 28n, 46, 48; *Time and Tide by Weare and Tyne*, 105n, 173-74n 3 & 4

Ruskin, John James, 46, 56n
Russell, John Francis Stanley, 2d Earl Russell, 476
Russell, John, Viscount Amberley, 476
Russell, Lord John, 1st Earl Russell, 476
Russell, William Hepburn, 83
Ruxton, Augustus A., organizer of American Exhibition of British Art, 82-99 *passim*

S

Sade, Marquis de, 177, *Justine*, 235; 252n, "the unspeakable," 395

St. Aubyn, J. H., 625n
St. Levan, John, 1st Baron St. Levan, 625n
Salaman, Charles Kensington, 393n
Salon des Refusés (1863), Whistler's *Symphony in White: White Girl*, "only thoroughly good thing there," 656
Salt, Henry S., WMR's letters to, untraced, xxxii; 513, 548, 549n
Sampson, John, ed., *Poetical Works of Blake*, xxi
Sampson Low and Co., 440n
Sands and Co., 625
Sandys, Frederick, 157, 160
San Giuliano, Marchese Antonio di, 669
Saturday Review, 191, 382
Scharf, Sir George, 83, 157
Schools of Design, 27, 29
Schott, John B., 171n, 435, 436n, 447-48n, 449, 456, 457
Schulze & Co., 581n
Scott, Charles Prestwich, 469n
Scott, David, 15, 49-50, 122, 216n
Scott, J. C. Addyes, 101n
Scott, John, 1st Earl of Eldon, 213
Scott, Letitia Margery (Mrs. William Bell), 23, 24 & n 10 & 11, 25n, 27, 29, 31, 33, 39, 48, 50, 60, 66, 67, 72, 78, 83, 91, 101, 115, 118, 124, 129, 132n, 135, 199, 260n, 293, 309n, 415, 416, 483, 507, 545n, 546
Scott, Sir Walter, *Harold the Dauntless*, MS. of, 383
Scott, William Bell, relations with WMR, xxiii, 12n; xxiv-xxv, xxvii, WMR's letters to, xxxii; xxxiiin, 15 & n 1 & 2, on Browning's *Sordello*, 24n; 44, A. Munro's medallion of, 47, 49; Carlyle on, 52; and *Crayon*, 56n, 58; 57, stays with WMR in London, 60n; on Millais's marriage, 60n; on Morris's tales in *Oxford and Cambridge Magazine*, 84n; invited to join Hogarth Club, 97; contributes to Hogarth Club exhibition, 100; proposes reorganization of Hogarth Club, 114-15; 123, 127 & n, "prince of travelling companions," 129; complains that J. W. Inchbold appropriated one of his subjects, 130n; 131-32, subscription for, at Newcastle, 136n; 156, 160, 178, loans (later presents) WMR MS. page of Shelley's *Revolt of Islam*, 199; 216n, 219, 221, 223, 225, 232, 234, 241, 242, 254,

260n, 264, 275, and DGR in 1872, 288-97; 309n, 331, 333n, 340, on Maria Rossetti, 347n; 376n, 380, 405, unable to attend DGR's funeral, 415n, 416; helps Dunn secure Cheyne Walk, 416n; 422, 432n, 467, 468, "busy writing his Memoirs," 507; 515, condemns course pursued by Shelley Society, 536; 537n, 540, WMR hears about death of, "with pain," 544; WMR "loved and honoured," 561; Watts-Dunton claims unwilling to complete Memoir of DGR during lifetime of, 578-79n; 596

WORKS (Poetry and Prose): *Albert Dürer: his Life and Works*, 201, 229n, 242; *Autobiographical Notes*, WMR refutes statements in, 561-63, WMR "vexed by press-scuffling" over, 563n; *Bede in the Nineteenth Century*, 25-26; Blake, Catalogue of Burlington Club Exhibition, 337; *Dream of Love*, 11; *Early Aspirations*, 12n; "Early German Prints of Jason and Medea" (*Notes and Queries*), 174; *Half-Hour Lectures on the History and Practice of the Fine and Ornamental Arts*, 115, 2d ed., 156; *Memoir of David Scott*, 15n, 24n; *Morning Sleep*, 11; *Poems* (1854), 27n, 53n, extracts from, in *Crayon*, 58, 62; *Poems: Ballads, Studies from Nature, Sonnets*, 156n, WMR reviews, 324, 326; Taylor, J. E., *Michael Angelo, considered as a Philosophical Poet*, review of (*Gateshead Observer*), 39; *The Year of the World*, 36, 181n

WORKS (Paintings and Designs): *Boccaccio's Visit to Dante's Daughter*, 28n; *The Border Widow*, 117; Bunyan, John, *Pilgrim's Progress*, illus. D. Scott, engraved by, 32; *The Burgher's Watch on the City Wall*, 91n; *Chorea Sancti Viti, or Steps in the Journey of Prince Legion*, designs by, 29; "Cornfield," 67; *The Daughters of Odin*, 34n; Etchings for Glasgow Art Union, 36; *Fair Rosamond Alone in the Bower*, 34n, 51n; *The Fatal Sisters Selecting the Doomed in Battle*, 28n; *A Gleaner*, 34n; *Gloaming — a Manse Garden in Berwickshire*, 131n; *The Haunted House on Allhallows Eve*, 28n, 32n, 34n; *A Messenger of the New Faith*, 122n, 129; Mural Paintings for Wallington, 72, 83,

Bernard Gilpin, 105n, *Grace Darling*, 111; *The Old English Market Town, Hexham*, 91n; Ronge, Johannes, Portrait of, 34n; Rossetti, W. M., Portrait of, A. Boyd intends to present to CGR, 575; *St. Cuthbert*, 72, DGR, FMB on, 77; Secretary of School of Design Newcastle, Portrait of, 34n; *The Trial of Sir William Wallace in Westminster Hall*, 28n; *Una and the Lion*, 110, 111; *Vicarage Garden*, 47, 49; *William Blake, Etchings from his Works*, etchings by, 132n

Scribner's Sons, Charles, 376n

Scudder, Horace Elisha, review of Gilchrist's *Blake* by, 133; 134n, plans book on Blake, 164

Sebag-Montefiore, Joseph, 1

Secularist, 340

Seddon, John Pollard, 28n, 444n, 451, 453, 455, 461, 462, part in London monument to DGR, 464, 468, 492n; expects commission at Aberystwyth, 468; 484

Seddon, Mrs. (mother of Thomas and J. P.), 363

Seddon, Thomas, Subscription Fund for, xxii, 74, 75n, 77-78, 79-80, 81; 41n, 46-47, death of, 73-74; biographical sketch of, 79-80; 84, 307, 444n, 471

Selle, William Christian, composes music for Shelley's *Hellas*, 497n; 513n

Semon, Felix, 534

Seneca, 208

Shakespeare, William, *Macbeth*, production of, at Princess's Theatre, 39; *Troilus and Cressida*, quoted, 93n, quoted by ACS, 313n, 314; *Hamlet*, "Miching Mallecho" discussed, 225-26; quoted, 287n, 614n, graveyard scene recited by G. W. Foote, 352n; *King John*, quoted, 361n; correct spelling of surname, 379, 380; *Othello*, Cassio referred to, 450; birthplace of, WMR recommends J. Skipsey as curator, 538n; 1 Henry IV, quoted, 544n; ACS on, 628n; *Merchant of Venice*, Shylock, "a most conscientious man," 641

Sharp, William, 431n, *D. G. Rossetti, A Record*, WMR and LR read proofs of, 432n, F. Rossetti looks at proofs of, 439, "a little tedious," 439, copy of, with "pencilled revisions" by WMR,

498n; 464n, 561

Shaw, George Bernard, WMR always finds talk of, "clever and telling," 511; WMR favours for Shelley Society Committee, "his extreme opinions are not … any disqualification," 512; 537, 549n

Shelley, Elizabeth, 203

Shelley, Harriet, 211, 213, Dowden has no new information on Shelley's separation from, 460n; Shelley's "very serious allegation" on separation from, 460n; letters of, to Catherine Nugent, 538n, 565

Shelley, Hellen, 201n

Shelley, Lady Jane, 199n, 201n 2, 3, & 5, 212, Trelawny calls, "nasty devil," 331; 370, argues with Trelawny about "the personal deservings of Mary Shelley," 371n; 467, 493, 506-7, 549, 655n

Shelley, Margaret, 201n

Shelley, Mary (Mrs. Percy B.), ed., *Poetical Works of P. B. Shelley* (1839), xx, 1 vol. ed. (1840, rptd. 1853), 117n, 198, 272, 3 vol. ed. (1847), 199n, 272, *Works*, 1 vol. (1847), 199n, 272; ed., *Posthumous Poems of P. B. Shelley*, 200, 272n

Shelley, Sir Percy, xx, 198, 199n, 200, 201n 3 & 5, 207, 211, 212, 329, 493, WMR meets, 506-7; 523n, 537-38

Shelley, Percy Bysshe, WMR's writings on, assessed, xviii, xx, xxi; letters of, to Elizabeth Hitchener, xx, 305, 307n, 315, 518-20, 521, 539, 596; xxii, xxx, xxxi-xxxii, "that wondrous man," 116; "that most divine man," 198; 199, 210-11, 236, 237, 238, 254, 257, 272, 275n 3 & 4, 277, 305, J. Thomson ('B.V.') on text of poems, 306-7; "piece of his blackened skull" owned by WMR, 306, 564n; 331, 351, 355, 365, WMR's Shelley work, "never ending, still beginning," 371; Trelawny gives WMR sofa owned by, 371, 563-64, 565n; 379n, "silly, ignorant, and insolent attack on," 382; proposed memorial to, 387, 389; Jeaffreson's *Real Shelley* will hamper "efforts of Shelleyites to keep Shelley's character at something of the same level as his poetry," 467n; 520, Eton drawing by, 564n; *Commemora-*

zione di P. B. Shelley in Roma, 565; 633, 638, Notebooks of, owned by R. Garnett, 654-55, WMR draws up list of contents of, for Sotheby's catalogue, 655n, sell for "great price of £3000," 655n

WORKS: *An Address to the People on the Death of Princess Charlotte*, 250n; *Adonais*, xxi, 200, 489n, 493, 542; *Alastor*, 198, 493; *Alastor, or the Spirit of Solitude, and other Poems*, 200; *Arethusa*, 242; *Aziola*, 272; "Bear Witness Erin," 316n; *The Boat on the Serchio*, 249; "Brothers, between you and me," 316n; *The Cenci*, 200, 202, 203, 205, quoted, 235; 326, 448, performance of, under auspices of Shelley Society, 479n, 480n, 489, 491, 493, Shelley Society plans second performance of, 549, 553; *Charles I*, xx, 206, 208, 209-10; *Cyclops* (Euripides), trans. by, 212, 242, 243-44; *Devil's Walk*, 269; *Epipsychidion*, 212, 306, 312, 314, 326, S. Brooke lectures on, 507; Shelley Society reprint of, 508n, 542n; *Hellas*, 306, WMR borrows MS. of, from Locker-Lampson, 371; performance of, under auspices of Shelley Society, 497, 499-500; *Hymn of Pan*, setting of, by Sir Percy Shelley, 507n; *Hymn to Mercury*, 242, 244; "If I walk in Autumn's even," 208; *The Invitation*, 273n; *Laon and Cythna*, 564n; *Letter to Maria Gisborne*, 206, 251; *Masque of Anarchy*, 312, 384; *The Necessity of Atheism*, 387, 550; *Ode to Liberty*, 208, 209, quoted, 210n; 212, 249, 252n, 253; *Ode to Naples*, 242 & n, 244, 253; *Oedipus Tyrannus or Swellfoot the Tyrant*, 206, 209, Forman acquires copy of, 483, Wise acquires copy of, 565; *On Love* (prose fragment), 272; "On the Devil, and Devils," 385, 387; *Peter Bell the Third*, 206, 250n; *The Pine Forest of the Cascine near Pisa*, 272n; *Posthumous Fragments of Margaret Nicholson*, 200, 483; *Prometheus Unbound*, 116, 208n, quoted, 235; 250n, 251, 306, 627; *Queen Mab* (*Daemon of the World*), xxxi, 191, 198, 199, 200; *The Question*, 252n, 260n; *The Recollection: To Jane*, 272; *The Revolt of Islam* (*Laon and*

720

Thornycroft, Thomas, 113

Ticknor and Fields, 92, 98

Tigri, Giuseppe, ed., *Canti Popolari Toscani*, 508

Times, "as stupid on that subject as it is on very many others," 388; 528

Tintoretto (Tintoret), *Miracle of the Slave*, 264

Tiraboschi, Girolamo, *Storia della Letteratura Italiana*, 110

Tirebuck, William Edwards, *Dante Rossetti, his Work and Influence*, 431

Titian, 65, *Martyrdom of St. Peter Martyr*, 278

Todhunter, John, *Helena in Troas*, WMR attends performance of, 494-95; 495n, 549n, 553n

Traill, Henry Duff, 605, 607

Traubel, Horace Logo, 536n

Traun, Agatha, 50

Traun, Mr., 50

Tree, Herbert Beerbohm, 495

Tregaskis, James and Mary Lee (booksellers), buys "great majority" of lots at CGR sale, 586n; WMR offers, copies of *Germ*, 593

Trelawny, Edgar, 365n

Trelawny, Edward John, xx, *Recollections of the Last Days of Shelley and Byron*, xx, 373, WMR assists with 2d ed. of, 210n, 325, 330, 358, 360, 365, "cheap edition" of, 533; xxiv, xxxii, 184n, 202n, 209, 250, 306, WMR describes, to Whitman, 323; 325, 325-26, 337, 355n, 357, WMR visits, at Sompting, 364-65; replies to R. Garnett's review of *Records of Shelley, Byron, and the Author*, 370; 370, cost of cremation, 371n; and Mary Shelley, 371n; gives WMR Shelley sofa, 371; WMR visits Gérôme on behalf of, 373; 378, 379, WMR assists, with letter to custodian of Protestant Cemetery, Rome, 386-87, 390; 388, 394, 395, 460n, 517, 565n

Trelawny, Frank, 365n

Trelawny, Laetitia (Mrs. Charles Call), 326, 330, 371n, 387, 405, 517, 549n, 564, 565

Trent, William P., 636n 2 & 3

Trevelyan, Lady Pauline, 32n, on Millais's marriage, 60n; WMR on, 72-73; 91n, 113n, 123, and Amateur Exhibition for Lancashire relief, 127

Trevelyan, Sir Walter Calverley, 6th Bart., WMR on, 73; 113n, 127, 145

Tricoupis, Charilaos, 493n

Trübner & Co., 166

Trübner, Nicholas, 250, 360

Tuckey (undertaker), 485

Tupper, Alexander, 4, 7

Tupper, Firm of, 611

Tupper, George J. F., 4, 7, 11 & n, 13, 14, 16, 34, 35n, 85n, 377, 554

Tupper, Holman, 612n

Tupper, John Lucas, xxiii, WMR's letters to, xxxii; 4, 7, 16n, relations with WMR, 16n; contributes to *Crayon*, 56n 4, 62; 106, 109n, 157, WMR sits to, for medallion, 205; death of, 377; subscription for family of, 377; *Poems*, ed. by WMR, 612

Tupper, Martin, 460

Turgenev, Ivan, 364

Turner, Joseph Mallord William, Ruskin's Turners, 49; 68n, Greenwich Sketch Book, WMR transcribes poem from, 94; 121-22, *Fallacies of Hope*, quoted, 129

Turner, William A., 383, 423, 429

Tynan, Katharine, 473, visits WMR, 480

U

Uwins, Thomas, 39

V

Vacquerie, Auguste, 331

Valleria, Alwina, 529n

Valpy, Leonard Rowe, 412, 415n, 420n, 423, 426, 444, 450

Vane, E. Cyril, 501

Venice Biennale, 589n, 590

Venturi, Adolfo, 589n, 590

Veronese, 67

Vezin, Hermann, 495, 549n

Victor Emanuel II, 181n, 182

Victor Emanuel III, 623

Victoria, Queen, 15

Von Holst, Theodore, 424

W

Walker, Emery, 649n

Walker, Miss, 548

Wallace, James W., 551n

memorial, 509-10; 646, 654, squabble with Legros, 656-57; 668n
WORKS: *At the Piano*, 111; *Symphony in White, No. 1: The White Girl*, 131n, 656, 657; *Symphony in White, No. 2: The Little White Girl*, 657; *The 25 December, 1860, the Thames*, 112n
White, David Thomas, 62n
Whitman, Walt, WMR's writings on, assessed, xviii, xix-xx; WMR's letters to, xxii, xxxii; xxiv, 126n, "a wonderful genius," 164; and Emerson, 176; and WMR, 184n; WMR's impatience with Whitmania, 184n; an "aboriginal and transcendent" genius, 191; 196, 197, 214-15, 236, 239-40, "his works are filtering here," 239; 247, 257, "days of mere rage and abuse" of, "pretty nearly over," 269; "insulting and ... ungrateful treatment" of, in America, 284-85; health, 322, 335, 478, 550-51; on Burns, 322; 1876 Subscription for, 335, 336-37, 337-40, 350-51; English writers on, 459-60; Judge Hawkins on, 461n; C. Aldrich's letter about, "leaves a painful impression," 465-66; 1885 Subscription for, 474, 475-76, 478-79, 481, 482; dinner in honor of, WMR sends belated message, 535; 550, death of, 551n; WMR's late tribute to, 671-72
WORKS: "The American War," 336n, 352n; *Camps of Green*, 180; "Democracy," 186, 187-88; *Democratic Vistas*, 281n; *Drum-Taps*, 163-64; *Leaves of Grass*, xix-xx, WBS gives WMR copy of 1st ed., 72, WMR's enthusiasm for, 72, 76-77, 1867 ed., 177, WMR considers publishing complete ed. of, 179n, 184, 1871 ed., 248, 280, 1876 ed. (impression), 248n, 322, 335, 336n, 339n, 1881-82 ed., 462-63, 465, 1891-92 ed. (impression), 550; *Memoranda During War*, 339; *The Mystic Trumpter*, 286n; *O Captain, my Captain*, 164; *O Star of France*, 274; *Out of the Cradle Endlessly Rocking (A Word Out of the Sea)*, 180, 280; *Passage to India*, 280; *The Return of the Heroes (A Carol of Harvest)*, 180; *The Sleepers (Night Poem, Sleep-Chasings)*, 180; *Song of the Exposition (After All, Not to Create Only)*, 280;

Specimen Days, 462, 465; *To One Shortly to Die*, quoted, 254; *To the Man-of-War-Bird*, 336n; *Two Rivulets*, 323n, 335, 339, 463n; "Walt Whitman's Actual American Position," 335-36n, 336, 337; *When Lilacs Last in the Dooryard Bloom'd*, 164, 180, 186, 460
Wieland, Walter, 261n
Wilde, Oscar, proposes statue to Keats, 355; negatively reviews WMR's *Life of Keats*, 511
Wilding, Alexa, 559
Wilkinson, James Garth, 311, 314
Williams ("jobbing man"), 44
Williams, Dr., 234n
Williams, Jane (Mrs. Edward; later Mrs. T. J. Hogg), 200
Williams, Mrs. William Smith, 403
Williams, William Smith, 56n, 92, 662, 663
Wills, William Gorman, 311, 545n
Willson, George (tobacconist), 297n
Willson, Isaac (baker), 297n
Wilson, John, 67, 123n
Wilson, Mr., 473n
Wilson, Mona, *Life of Blake*, xxi
Windus, B. G., 62n
Windus, William Lindsay, 100, *Burd Helen*, WMR writes to *Crayon* about, 102
Wise, Frances (Mrs. Thomas James), "a very handsome woman," 626n; 632, 634, 653
Wise, Thomas James, xxii, xxiii, WMR's letters to, xxxii; 307n, 483n
and SHELLEY SOCIETY: 483n, 489, 499-500, 502-3, 507n, "a first-rate man" for secretary of, 512; 513n, 516-17, 520, 521-23, 532-34, 536, 539-42, 547-49, 553, 563, Shelley Centenary exhibition organized by, 563-64, 565; 564, 572, 577, 626, 632
acquires Rossetti books and MSS. from WMR, 483n; 497, buys large-paper copy of DGR's *Collected Works* from WMR, 502n; buys copies of DGR's *Sir Hugh the Heron* from WMR, 518, WMR offers, then refuses to sell, additional copies of, 589-90, 592, 596; *Letters from Shelley to Elizabeth Hitchener*, prints from copies borrowed from WMR, 518-19, prints "without any the least authority," 519n, WMR